BEFORE TH
AN ANTHOLOGY OF AKKADIAN LITERATURE

BEFORE THE MUSES

AN ANTHOLOGY
OF AKKADIAN LITERATURE

Benjamin R. Foster

Third Edition

CDL Press
Bethesda, Maryland

LIBRARY OF CONGRESS CATALOGING-IN-PUBLICATION DATA

Before the muses : an anthology of Akkadian literature / Benjamin R. Foster.
– 3rd ed.
  p. cm.
Includes bibliographical references and index.
ISBN 1-883053-76-5
  1. Assyro-Babylonian literature—Translations into English. I. Foster,
Benjamin R. (Benjamin Read)

PJ3951.B44 2005
892'.1–dc22   2004065045

Cover design by Peter W. Johnson and Karen Polinger Foster: Assyrian musicians,
Nineveh, after A. H. Layard, *Discoveries Among the Ruins of Nineveh and Babylon* (1853),
389; Muses, Roman sarcophagus, after R. Ménard, *La mythologie dans l'art ancien et moderne*
(1878), figs., 224, 225.

Drawing on title page: Assyrian scribe, Til Barsib, after F. Thureau-Dangin *et al., Til-Barsib*
(1936), pl. L.

Text design by Karen Polinger Foster and Elizabeth Duncan Lyons

ISBN: 1883053-765

TABLE OF CONTENTS

CHAPTER III

THE MATURE PERIOD

(1500–1000 B.C.)

CHAPTER IV

THE LATE PERIOD

(1000–100 B.C.)

PREFACE

Before the Muses introduces modern readers to over three hundred and sixty works of Akkadian prose and poetry, including some of the world's oldest literature. Akkadian, the language of ancient Assyria and Babylonia, was written and spoken for nearly 2,500 years before the Christian era. Despite the longevity and richness of its written tradition, Akkadian is not widely appreciated today. In large part, this is for want of accessible English translations, such as this anthology is intended to provide.

As in any anthology, text selection was made according to various subjective criteria: inherent interest, intelligibility, completeness, and success in telling a story, or revealing motivation, situation, or mood. For reasons of space, the vast Akkadian scholarly literature of divination, astrology, and philology has not been sampled here; these long texts would require a separate anthology. As for the Gilgamesh Epic, the most widely known of Akkadian literary works, it is readily available in English translations.[1]

Before the Muses begins with a general introduction to the study of Akkadian literature, intended for the reader with no knowledge of the subject. The arrangement of texts into chapters is chronological: Chapter I includes texts from the end of the third millennium B.C.; Chapter II texts from the first part of the second millennium B.C.; Chapters III and IV texts from the middle of the second millennium to the Hellenistic period. Whereas texts may be easily assigned to the first two chapters on the basis of their language, those from later periods are often impossible to date precisely. Hence the decision to place a work either in the third or fourth chapters is often arbitrary.

Certain large blocs of material are grouped together, without regard to their date of composition, as follows: the mythological narrative poems in Chapter III; hymns and prayers without obvious criteria for dating them in Chapter III, alphabetically by deity addressed; proverbs and wisdom literature in Chapter III; post-Classical incantations in Chapter IV, arranged by subject matter.

---

1. Dalley, *Myths*, 39–153; Foster, *Gilgamesh*; A. George, *The Epic of Gilgamesh, A New Translation* (London, 1999).

Each selection includes a brief introduction that gives such information as the historical or cultural setting of the text, its state of preservation, a survey or outline of the contents, and interpretive proposals. The translations are provided with numbered footnotes intended for the general reader. These explain terms that the reader might not understand, give the translator's opinion as to some particularly difficult words or lines, note selected variants, and draw attention to parallels found in other texts translated in this anthology. An asterisk (*) in the translation refers to "Notes to the Text" given after the translation. These provide the specialist with a reading or restoration that might not be immediately obvious or acknowledge, where appropriate, indebtedness for understanding of a particular word or passage. The rubric "Text" after the translation gives bibliographical data on the original cuneiform manuscripts and will be of interest only to Assyriologists. The rubric "Edition" refers to publications that may include a transliteration, translation, and commentary on the text. "Translation" refers to other translations of the text that have been consulted.

The next rubric, "Literature," includes two types of material: technical publications that have been useful in preparing the translation, and studies that may be of interest to readers who wish to know more about a particular text. More technical publications are cited in short form, while publications likely to be useful to the general reader are cited in full. The same is true for the footnotes to the introductions and to the general introduction. Citation need not imply my concordance with the author's views. The work concludes with an index of cuneiform texts, intended for the specialist. While every effort has been made to include relevant publications, the ever-increasing flood of material makes completeness impossible.

Reading is a personal and culturally conditioned activity. A reader from one culture can appreciate the figurative language of another only to the extent he is willing to go beyond the familiar. The obstacles are especially great for Akkadian because, unlike other extinct literatures such as Classical Greek, Latin, or Biblical Hebrew, that belong to the cultural heritage of an English-speaking reader, Akkadian has no connection with any living cultural tradition. If this anthology of translations brings readers and Akkadian literature together once more, however tentative, groping, and unfulfilled the relationship may prove, the translator's efforts will have been successful.

ACKNOWLEDGMENTS
TO THE THIRD EDITION

The third edition of *Before the Muses* is a substantial revision and enlargement of the second edition (1996). The second edition was a limited revision and correction of the first (1993). A corrected abridgment of the first edition, including some additional pieces, appeared as *From Distant Days* (1995). This third edition has been revised throughout and enlarged by the addition of various compositions, some newly published, others long known but included here to achieve a better balance of material. I have sought to update bibliography and to include more references to general and comparative studies than hitherto. Some texts translated here have been re-edited several times by various scholars since the first edition of this work. Although not all these editions are improvements over their predecessors, I have referred to them and considered their proposals.

This work was begun in 1983 with the help of a translation grant from the National Endowment for the Humanities under the auspices of the American Oriental Society. I thank Stanley Insler of the Society and Susan Mango of the Endowment for their support and for their patience with my overly optimistic schedules. As consultants to the Endowment, W. G. Lambert and W. L. Moran read early drafts of Chapters I and II and parts of Chapter III. Lambert's numerous annotations, corrections, improved readings, and collations were decisive in the evolution of this work, more than the individual acknowledgments in the notes may suggest. His publications, translations, and studies of Akkadian literature set high standards and underlie various of the translations offered here. Moran's comments and corrections, particularly to Anzu, Atrahasis, and the Epic of Creation, were also of great value to me. W. Farber read my initial treatment of the early incantations and with his customary generosity shared with me many original readings and suggestions on these difficult texts.

My particular thanks go to the following scholars for collations to original manuscripts: J. Brinkman, I. Finkel, M. J. Geller, W. G. Lambert, P. Machinist, C. Michel, H. Neumann, M. Stol, and C. B. F. Walker. A. George contributed corrections to the first edition, kindly sent me important sources prior to their publication, and allowed me to quote them. I. Finkel allowed me free use of his unpublished copy of a literary tablet. For permission to collate tablets in the British Museum and the Louvre, I thank C. B. F. Walker and Beatrice André-Salvini.

I thank the following for suggestions, corrections, bibliographical references, and advance copies of publications: J. Cooper, E. Frahm, W. W. Hallo, C. Michel, J. Scurlock, K. Slanski, K. R. Veenhof, and N. Wasserman. I have incorporated here suggestions made by S. Dalley and J. Westenholz in reviews of the first edition.

My thanks go to Ulla Kasten and Gabriella Safran of the Yale Babylonian Collection for editorial assistance and to Karen Polinger Foster and Peter Johnson for their cover design. In addition, Karen Polinger Foster read critically various versions of the manuscript. I thank as well Daniel W. and Timothy Foster for outstanding bibliographical support. My special acknowledgment goes to the many students with whom I have puzzled over Akkadian texts and hope that they have learned from the experience as much as I have.

While all three editions utilize the publications of nearly everyone who has studied Akkadian literature, I would here single out some major sources of guidance. Modern study of Akkadian literature has first of all been made possible by the dictionary, grammar, and numerous text editions of W. von Soden. *The Chicago Assyrian Dictionary* has been an inexhaustible treasury of information and source of many new readings and suggestions used here. The bibliographical publications of R. Borger open to the reader all the widely scattered literature of Assyriology from the early nineteenth century until 1973. For orientation in the thousands of relevant publications that have appeared since then, I am indebted to the annual "Keilschriftbibliographie," currently edited by H. Neumann in the periodical *Orientalia*, and to the "Register" currently edited by M. Jursa and M. Weszeli in *Archiv für Orientforschung*. I scarcely imagine, however, that no study of importance has escaped my attention.

BRF

General Introduction

In Search of
Akkadian Literature

A. The Akkadian Language

1. SEMITIC LANGUAGES

Akkadian is a member of the Semitic family of languages.[1] Modern Semitic languages, including Arabic, Ethiopic, and Hebrew, are spoken from the Atlantic coast of Africa to the foothills of Iran, and are understood as scriptural and literary languages throughout the world.[2] Ancient Semitic languages, including Akkadian and Aramaic, were spoken mainly in the Near East, with Akkadian at home in Mesopotamia, that is, Assyria and Babylonia.

As a group, Semitic languages exhibit a distinctive morphology.[3] This is characterized by a rich inventory of verbal and nominal patterns, which may imply classes of meaning, such as recurring action. The patterns become lexically specific in combination with roots, which are groups of consonants and associated vowels. These are the primary meaning-bearing elements in Semitic languages.[4] Interaction of root and pattern opens a range of possibilities for expression corresponding to synonyms, modifiers, adverbs, and auxiliaries in English. Thus a sentence in Akkadian poetry or prose must usually be substantially reworded and expanded in length when translated into English. The variety and productivity of these roots and patterns means that Semitic languages are remarkably versatile. They have been used in an extraordinary variety of cultural contexts, from the Bronze Age to the present.

---

1. J. Huehnergard, "Languages," *The Anchor Bible Dictionary* (New York, 1992), 4:155–170; R. Hetzron, ed., *The Semitic Languages* (Padstow, 1997).
2. For discussion, G. Garbini, *Le lingue semitiche, Studi di Storia linguistica* (Naples, 1984), 15–21.
3. S. Moscati, *An Introduction to the Comparative Grammar of the Semitic Languages* (Wiesbaden, 1969); E. Ullendorff, "What Is a Semitic Language?" OrNS 27 (1958), 66–75; in T. Sebeok, ed., *Current Trends in Linguistics* 6 (The Hague, 1970), 269–273.
4. J. H. Greenberg, "The Patterning of Root Morphemes in Semitic," *Word* 6 (1950), 162–181; B. Landsberger, "Die Gestalt der semitischen Wurzel," *Atti XIX Cong. degli Orientalisti* (1935), 450–452; A. Goetze, JAOS 62 (1942), 1 note 7.

2. AKKADIAN VERNACULAR LANGUAGES

The term "Akkadian" subsumes various languages or dialects that need not all have been mutually intelligible.[1] These may be defined regionally and chronologically as follows:

Old Akkadian (2350–2000 B.C.) is attested in administrative documents, letters, inscriptions, personal names, and a few literary texts (Chapter I). Owing perhaps to the paucity of material, no significant differences have been detected between the form of the language in literary texts and that in any of the other sources for this dialect.

With the beginning of the second millennium, one distinguishes two main regional dialects of Akkadian: Assyrian, used in northern Mesopotamia, and Babylonian, used in the south. Assyrian is divided into three chronological phases. Old Assyrian (2000–1750 B.C.) is known mostly from letters and legal documents, as well as a few incantations (Chapter I). Middle Assyrian (1500–1000 B.C.) is known mostly from letters, documents, and a few inscriptions and literary texts (Chapter III). Neo-Assyrian (1000–600 B.C.) is known from royal inscriptions, letters, documents, and literary texts (Chapter IV).

Babylonian, like Assyrian, is divided into three main periods. Old Babylonian (1900–1500 B.C.) and Middle Babylonian (1500–1000 B.C.) are known from letters, documents, and inscriptions, as well as literary texts (Chapters II, III). Neo-Babylonian (1000–600 B.C.) is known from letters and documents (Chapter IV). During this period and later, Aramaic[2] gradually replaced Akkadian as the common spoken language, though as a scholarly medium Akkadian remained vigorous and productive through Hellenistic times.[3] Late Babylonian (600 B.C. to the Christian era), known from letters, documents, inscriptions, and literature, was the last phase of the Akkadian language.

---

1. E. Reiner, *A Linguistic Analysis of Akkadian* (The Hague, 1965), 20–22; "Akkadian," in T. Sebeok, ed., *Current Trends in Linguistics* 6 (The Hague, 1970), 274–303; W. von Soden, *Grundriss der akkadischen Grammatik,* AnOr 33 (1952), 1–4; "Akkadisch," in G. Levi della Vida, ed., *Linguistica Semitice: Presente e Futuro, Studi Semitici* 4 (1961), 33–57; R. Caplice, "Akkadian," *Anchor Bible Dictionary* (above, p. 1 note 1), 4:170–173; G. Buccellati, "Akkadian," in Hetzron, ed., *Semitic Languages* (above, p. 1 note 1), 69–99.

2. For remarks on the history and significance of Aramaic, see R. A. Bowman, "Arameans, Aramaic, and the Bible," JNES 7 (1948), 65–90; F. Rosenthal, "Aramaic," *Encyclopaedia Iranica* (Boston, 1987), 2:251–256; S. P. Brock, "Three Thousand Years of Aramaic Literature," *Aram* 1 (1989), 11–23. For Akkadian and Aramaic, see S. Kaufman, *The Akkadian Influences on Aramaic,* AS 19 (1974); M. J. Geller, "The Aramaic Incantation in Cuneiform Script," JEOL 35/6 (1997–2000), 127–146; N.A.B.U. 2001/101; see also p. 778 note 2.

3. Sachs, AOAT 25 (1976), 379–398; M. J. Geller, "More Graeco-Babyloniaca," ZA 73 (1983), 114–120, an Akkadian incantation with a Greek transliteration; S. Maul, "Neues zu den 'Graeco-

In this anthology, four periods of Akkadian literature have been distinguished, corresponding to the following periods of the vernacular language: the Archaic period, including Semitic languages older than Akkadian, Old Akkadian and Old Assyrian (Chapter I); the Classical period, including Old Babylonian (Chapter II); the Mature period, including Middle Babylonian and Middle Assyrian (Chapter III); and the Late period, including Neo-Assyrian, Neo-Babylonian, and Late Babylonian (Chapter IV).

3. AKKADIAN LITERARY LANGUAGES

In the Classical period of Akkadian literature, corresponding to the Old Babylonian period of the language, literary texts often were not written in the same style as were letters and documents, but in poetic and prose styles differentiated from common speech. The Babylonians believed that literature required a special idiom, using grammar, vocabulary, syntax, sound, and even spelling removed from common usage. The most refined literary style of this period is known as the "hymnic-epic dialect."[1] The origins of the Classical literary styles are complex. They show vocabulary, grammar, and usage known from Old Akkadian or, perhaps, from a somewhat later northern, regional dialect of Babylonian generalized into a literary language because of its prestige. Some Classical literary features may be neologisms or fabricated archaisms deemed appropriate for higher expression. Other features could also have been influenced by or written in imitation of literary Sumerian. The texts chosen here vary widely in the extent to which they make use of Classical literary and hymnic-epic styles; the differences will not be visible in translation.

In the Mature and Late periods of Akkadian literature, corresponding to the Middle Babylonian and Assyrian, Neo-Babylonian and Neo-Assyrian periods of the language, another literary style known as "Standard Babylonian" was used. Though influenced by the vernacular speech habits of the times and regions in which it was used, Standard Babylonian dialect tended to be consistent in its gram-

---

Babyloniaca'," ZA 81 (1991), 87 107; M. J. Geller, "The Last Wedge," ZA 87 (1997), 43–95; E. Knudsen, "On Akkadian Texts in Greek Orthography," *Studies F. Løkkegard* (Copenhagen, 1990), 147–161; "The Ashmolean Museum Incantation in Greek Orthography," AOAT 240 (1995), 135–140; M. J. Geller, "Graeco-Babyloniaca in Babylon," in Renger, ed., *Babylon*, 377–383. See also p. 778 note 3.

1. W. von Soden, "Der hymnisch-epische Dialekt des Akkadischen," ZA 40 (1932), 163–227; ZA 41 (1933), 90–183, 236; B. Groneberg, "Untersuchungen zum hymnisch-epischen Dialekt der altbabylonischen literarischen Texte," (dissertation, Münster, 1971); "Terminativ- und Lokativ-adverbialis in altbabylonischen literarischen Texte," AfO 26 (1978/79), 15–29; A. Poebel, *Studies in Akkadian Grammar*, AS 9 (1939), 71–74; Kraus, *Mensch*, 38.

matical and lexical differentiations for more than a thousand years. "Standard" here means use of a traditional poetic style and inventory of linguistic differentiations; it does not imply existence of an inherited corpus of literary texts that had to be imitated by later generations. The Standard style had a wider diffusion and longer life than the older Hymnic-Epic style, and was an accepted medium of scholarly and literary expression throughout Western Asia from the fifteenth through the fourth centuries B.C.[1]

Literary Late Babylonian was characterized by a deliberately archaizing style, as seen for example in the prayers in the names of the Neo-Babylonian monarchs (Chapter IV).

All these literary styles or dialects were Babylonian in origin, and were used in Assyria during the Mature and Late periods of Akkadian literature. Although Assyrian literature could have distinctive stylistic features (see Chapter III, Introduction), no separate Assyrian literary dialect evolved.

4. AKKADIAN WRITING AND LITERACY

Akkadian was written mostly using a stylus that made wedge-shaped impressions upon soft clay tablets.[2] This form of writing is referred to as "cuneiform," after the Latin word *cuneus* "wedge(-shaped)." It was probably invented by the Sumerians, a non-Semitic people living in southern Mesopotamia, who used it to write their own language, Sumerian, after about 3300 B.C.[3] Cuneiform writing was subsequently adapted for Akkadian and other languages, including Elamite in Iran and Hittite in Anatolia. While writing may have been invented for administrative purposes,[4] it soon acquired commemorative and expressive functions. Indeed, non-administrative texts, including incantations and word lists, figure among the earliest cuneiform documents.[5]

---

1. B. Groneberg, *Syntax, Morphologie und Stil der jungbabylonischen 'hymnischen' Literatur*, FAOS 14 (Stuttgart, 1987), 1: 1–21.

2. D. O. Edzard, "Keilschrift," RLA 5, 544–568; P. Michalowski, J. Cooper in P. T. Daniels, ed., *The World's Writing Systems* (Oxford, 1996), 33–57.

3. For the earliest development of writing, see J.-J. Glassner, *The Invention of Cuneiform Writing in Sumer*, trans. Z. Bahrani, M. Van De Mieroop (Baltimore, 2003). For later adaptations of writing, see M. W. Green, "The Construction and Implementation of the Cuneiform Writing System," *Visible Language* 15 (1981), 345–372; J. Bottéro, *Mesopotamia*, 67–86. See also the volume "Early Writing Systems" = *World Archaeology* 17/3 (1986), where more bibliography can be found.

4. H. Nissen, J. P. Damerow, R. Englund, *Archaic Bookkeeping: Early Writing and Techniques of the Economic Administration in the Ancient Near East*, trans. P. Larsen (Chicago, 1993).

5. H. Nissen, "The Archaic Texts from Uruk," *World Archaeology* 17/3 (1986), 317–334; P. Michalowski, "The Early Mesopotamian Incantation Tradition," *QuadSem* 18 (1992), 304–326.

Individual characters in this writing system were composed using one to a dozen or more wedge-shaped marks. Even in its earliest known form, the writing system was complicated, using hundreds of characters. Some signs were used for writing words, some for syllables, and most for both.[1] The same sign could be used to write different words or sounds; conversely, different signs could be used to write the same words or sounds. Individual signs could be modified or combined with others to produce units different in significance from their components taken singly. The result was that cuneiform required more effort to master than the alphabetic writing systems that were to develop centuries later. Like other complex writing systems, cuneiform was endowed by its users with a body of esoteric cultural lore all its own.[2]

The extent of literacy in ancient Mesopotamia is unknown. To read letters and documents, knowledge of two to three hundred characters was adequate,[3] but there is no way of knowing what percentage of the population possessed this basic literacy. Most modern scholars believe that few people were literate in any given period of Mesopotamian history. Perhaps businessmen, priests, administrators, rulers, and other members of the elite could read and write, even if, like their modern counterparts, they generally used professional scribes for official matters. Literacy may have been more common in some periods, such as the Classical period, than in others, such as the Late period.[4]

Access to more elaborate Akkadian literary and scholarly writings required a high level of training and skill, involving memorization of lists of characters and their significances, both practical and theoretical,[5] and study of Sumerian. Although Sumerian had probably died out as a living, spoken language during the first half of the second millennium B.C., it continued to be used as a literary and scholarly

---

1. Cooper in P. Daniels, ed., *Writing Systems* (above p. 4 note 2), 41–43.
2. J. Bottéro, *Mesopotamia*, 87–102.
3. G. Buccellati, "Comparative Graphemic Analysis of Old Babylonian and Western Akkadian," UF 11 (1979), 90–99; see in general Edzard, RLA 5, 561–562.
4. M. Larsen, "The Babylonian Lukewarm Mind: Reflections on Science, Divination and Literacy," in *Studies Reiner*, 203–225; in general, C. Wilcke, *Wer las und schrieb in Babylonien und Assyrien, Überlegungen zur Literalität im Alten Zweistromland, Sitzungsberichte der Bayerischen Akademie der Wissenschaften, Philosophisch-Historische Klasse 2000/6.*
5. A. Cavigneaux, *Die sumerisch-akkadischen Zeichenlisten, Überlieferungsprobleme* (dissertation, Munich, 1976); "Lexikalische Listen," RLA 6, 609–641; I. M. Diakonoff in *Istorija Lingvističeskih Učenij: Drevnij Mir* (Moscow, 1980), 17–37. See in general E. Reiner, ed., "La Linguistica del Vicino e Medio Oriente" in G. C. Lepschy, ed., *Storia della Linguistica* I (Bari, 1990), 85–118; T. J. H. Krispijn, "The Early Mesopotamian Lexical Lists and the Dawn of Linguistics," JEOL 32 (1991/2), 12–22; W. G. Lambert, "Babylonian Linguistics," CRRAI 42 (1995), 217–221.

language until the Hellenistic period.[1] In addition, the literate scholar had to become versed in the techniques and approaches of Mesopotamian scholarship. These had pronounced influence on the character of Akkadian literature, tending to weight it in favor of the learned and esoteric.[2]

There is some evidence for more popular forms of literature, such as love songs, fables, proverbs, and folk tales. Such texts are less common than those requiring a high degree of cultural competence to appreciate (see Chapters II and III).

B. REDISCOVERY OF AKKADIAN LITERATURE

1. LOSS AND REDISCOVERY

Akkadian has been a dead language for more than two millennia. After its disappearance in the Hellenistic period, Akkadian was forgotten until its rediscovery by European scholars in the nineteenth century. This means that the reader of Akkadian has no recourse to a living or continuous cultural tradition, but must piece together whatever evidence the tablets provide.[3]

As early as 1692, the word "cuneiform" was coined to apply to the distinctively Mesopotamian style of writing observed on stone reliefs and clay tablets brought back to Europe by travelers to the Near East.[4] But no one could read this writing or knew what language it represented. In 1842 an English adventurer named A. H.

---

1. The date of the disappearance of Sumerian as a living language is disputed. For this topic and its related ethnic questions, see J. Bottéro, "Sumériens et 'accadiens' en Mésopotamie ancienne," *Modes de contact et processus de transformation dans les sociétés anciennes, Actes du Colloque de Cortone* (Rome, 1983), 7–21; J. Cooper, "Sumerian and Akkadian in Sumer and Akkad," OrNS 42 (1973), 239–246; W. Heimpel, "Sumerische und akkadische Personennamen in Sumer und Akkad," AfO 25 (1974/7), 171–174; F. R. Kraus, *Sumerer und Akkader: Ein Problem der altmesopotamischen Geschichte,* MKNAW NR 33 No. 8 (1970). The writer has offered evidence that Sumerian was a living, spoken language in Sumer at least through the Sargonic period, OrNS 57 (1982), 297–304.

2. W. von Soden, "Leistung und Grenze sumerischer und babylonischer Wissenschaft," *Die Welt als Geschichte* 2 (1936), 411–464, 509–557; republished in *Libelli* 142, Wissenschaftliche Buchgesellschaft (Darmstadt, 1965), after p. 21; A. L. Oppenheim, "The Position of the Intellectual in Mesopotamian Society," *Daedalus* 104/2 (1975), 37–46; H. Limet, "Le Sécret et les écrits, Aspects de l'esotérisme en Mésopotamie ancienne," in *Les Rites d'initiation, Actes du Colloque de Liège et de Louvain-la-Neuve 20–21 Novembre 1984* (Louvain-la-Neuve, 1986), 243–254.

3. Various aspects of Babylonian culture survived in other languages and cultures, but not in their original languages; see S. Dalley, ed., *The Legacy of Mesopotamia* (Oxford, 1998); "Assyrian-Court Narratives in Aramaic and Egyptian: Historical Fiction," CRRAI 45 (2001), 149–161.

4. For the earliest history of cuneiform studies, see S. Pallis, *The Antiquity of Iraq* (Copenhagen, 1956), 55–65; Bottéro, *Mesopotamia,* 55–66.

Layard[1] began digging at the mound of Nineveh in Assyria, near modern Mosul, Iraq. He and his successors were rewarded with innumerable finds, among them thousands of tablets written in cuneiform script. Some of these proved to be the remains of a great library of ancient Mesopotamian literature, dating to the seventh century B.C. Interest in the contents of these documents heightened as scholars throughout Europe worked on deciphering the writing system and the texts it preserved.[2]

Akkadian was soon recognized as a Semitic language, and a flurry of publications appeared clarifying the meaning of signs, words, and whole texts. After 1850, lengthy connected texts in Akkadian could be read. Thus far, decipherment of Akkadian was primarily of interest to a small community of competitive savants. A single event brought Akkadian to the attention of the general public, and galvanized public opinion about the significance of the recovery of Akkadian literature.

This was George Smith's discovery in 1872 of an Akkadian flood story with unmistakable parallels to the biblical one, although pagan deities and a flood hero other than Noah were its *dramatis personae*.[3] That an ancient tablet from a Mesopotamian mound could yield data directly relevant to European cultural and religious tradition stunned thinkers of the time. The independence and authority of the Bible had to be reevaluated. Indeed, controversy on this subject continues to the present, mostly on the margins of serious scholarship. Following Smith's discovery, Akkadian literature was accorded special consideration for the light it seemed to shed on the Hebrew Bible and the accounts of Babylonian and Assyrian history preserved in ancient Greek and Latin authors. Early studies of Akkadian literature were replete with identifications in Akkadian texts of biblical and Classical personalities and events, most of which are now rightly abandoned and forgotten. Even today, new tablet discoveries elicit hasty biblical comparisons, many of which have to be abandoned upon reflection.[4] On the other hand, informed

1. G. Waterfield, *Layard of Nineveh* (New York, 1968); M. Larsen, *The Conquest of Assyria, Excavations in an Antique Land* (London, 1996).

2. Among the numerous accounts of the decipherment of cuneiform, the most detailed are Pallis, *Iraq* (p. 6 note 4), 94–158; C. Fossey, *Manuel d'Assyriologie* I (Paris, 1904); see also R. Borger, *Persica* 7 (1975/78), 1–216.

3. G. Smith, PSBA, December 3, 1872; B. Schmidt, "Flood Narratives of Ancient Western Asia," CANES 4:2337–2351.

4. For an essay on this topic, see J. J. Finkelstein, "Bible and Babel, A Comparative Study of the Hebrew and Babylonian Spirit," *Commentary* 26 (1958), 431–444. The main focus of biblical analogy has been the Akkadian myths and legends, as well as documents of the Neo-Babylonian period and texts from Nuzi, Mari, Ugarit, and Ebla. See J. van Seters, *Abraham in History and Tradition* (New Haven, 1975), 7–12 and B. Eichler, "Nuzi and the Bible: A Retrospective," *Studies Sachs*, 107–119.

comparison and contrasting of Mesopotamian cultural remains with those of the Hebrew Bible and Greece continue to flourish and to yield important insights.[1]

2. MAJOR SOURCES

The principal collections of Akkadian literary manuscripts are as follows:

(1) The Nineveh library recovered by Layard, Rassam, and subsequent excavators is the largest source of Akkadian literary texts.[2] Most of its tablets date to the seventh century B.C. and include scholarly editions of texts prepared for the library, assembled by order of the reigning Assyrian king, Assurbanipal. These scholarly editions preserved many texts much older than Assurbanipal's time. Originally the library may have held five to six thousand manuscripts, most of them works of scholarship dealing with magic, divination, lexicography, or ritual. Only a small number were purely literary works, that is, narrative prose and poetry of a mythological, legendary, historical, religious, or epic character.[3] Many manuscript tablets were broken into small fragments when the library was destroyed by the conquering Medes in the late seventh century B.C.

(2) An important collection of Akkadian literature has been discovered at Nimrud. This was probably the remains of a library housed in the temple of Nabu, a god of wisdom, in that city. Most of the tablets were lists of omens, as well as substantial groups of incantations and lexical lists, but hymns, prayers, and epics were found as well.[4]

---

1. W. W. Hallo, *The Book of the People* (Atlanta, 1991), with extensive bibliography; W. G. Lambert, "Old Testament Mythology in Its Ancient Near Eastern Context," *Supplements to Vetus Testamentum* 40, 124–143; C. Penglase, *Greek Myths and Mesopotamia, Parallels and Influences in the Homeric Hymns and Hesiod* (New York, 1994); M. L. West, "Ancient Near Eastern Myths in Classical Greek Thought," CANES 1:33–42; *The East Face of Helicon, West Asiatic Elements in Greek Poetry and Myth* (Oxford, 1999).

2. C. B. F. Walker, "The Kouyunjik Collection of Cuneiform Texts: Formation, Problems, and Prospects," in F. M. Fales and B. J. Hickey, eds., *Austen Henry Layard tra l'Oriente e Venezia* (Rome, 1987), 183–193; O. Pedersén, *Archives and Libraries in the Ancient Near East 1500–300 B.C.* (Bethesda, Md., 1998), 161–165; see also IV.4g.

3. Oppenheim, *Ancient Mesopotamia*, 16–17. He estimates the "tablets" (as literary units, not manuscripts) in the library as follows: omens (300), sign and lexical lists (200), bilingual devotional texts (100), conjurations (70), "literature" (30–40). Allowing for additional material, he reckons about 1500 tablets, many in multiple copies, for a total number of lines approaching 200,000. Weidner estimated the manuscript count at 5000 items, AfO 16 (1952/3), 198; see also Hallo, IEJ 12 (1962), 22. For the formation of this library, see Weidner, AfO 16 (1952/3), 197–198; S. Parpola, "Assyrian Library Records," JNES 42 (1983), 1–29; Lieberman, *Studies Moran*, 308–317.

4. Pedersén, *Archives* (above note 2), 151–152.

(3) Excavations at Assur[1] uncovered several hundred Akkadian literary tablets and fragments, some dating to the latter part of the second millennium B.C., the majority to the first millennium B.C. In many cases, these duplicate or parallel compositions are known from Assurbanipal's library. The Assur tablets are not from a single library; many seem to have been the personal property of scholars whose homes lay near the royal palace.

(4) Excavations at Sultantepe (ancient Huzirina) in Turkey have revealed about two hundred tablets and fragments dating to the late eighth and early seventh centuries B.C. and forming a single collection.[2] Like the Assurbanipal and Assur collections, this consists primarily of scholarly works, with some important literary manuscripts as well. Most of these duplicate or parallel works known from Assur and Nineveh.[3]

(5) Numerous literary and scholarly texts have been found at Uruk, mostly dating from the sixth to the fourth centuries B.C. These were found at various places in the ruins, so they do not constitute a single collection. Many of these duplicate texts already known from the collections mentioned above.[4]

(6) In 1986, discovery of a library of about 800 cuneiform tablets at Sippar was announced. This library, dating to the Neo-Babylonian and Persian periods, contained many well-preserved literary and scholarly texts, and promised to be as important as the library of Assurbanipal for the reconstruction of Akkadian literature. Many of these, too, duplicated compositions already known.[5]

(7) Akkadian literary manuscripts have been found in public buildings, such as temples, and in private houses at Babylon (III.12e), Kish (II.19d, II.25f), Larsa (II.18), Mari (II.7b, 12a, 22a, 34a, 35), Nippur (II.36),

1. W. Andrae with B. Hrouda, *Das Wiedererstandene Assur*[2] (Munich, 1977). A brief account of the publication of the tablet finds is found on pp. 315–318. See in detail O. Pedersén, *Archives and Libraries in the City of Assur* (Uppsala, 1985), more briefly in *Archives* (above p. 8 note 2), 178–180.
2. O. R. Gurney, J. J. Finkelstein, P. Hulin, STT; O. R. Gurney, "The Assyrian Tablets from Sultantepe," *Proceedings of the British Academy* 41 (1955), 21–41; Pedersén, *Archives* (above note 1), 178–180. For identification of the site, see Gordon, JCS 21 (1967), 85–88.
3. E. Reiner and M. Civil, "Another Volume of Sultantepe Tablets," JNES 26 (1967), 177–211, especially pp. 177–180.
4. Mayer, *Baghdader Mitteilungen*, Beiheft 2; Hunger, SBTU 1, 11–13; Pedersén, *Archives* (p. 8. note 2), 205–213.
5. *Iraq* 49 (1987), 248–249; Pedersén, *Archives* (p. 8. note 2), 194–197. Most of this library is said to be no longer extant, having disintegrated after excavation.

Shaduppum (Tell Harmal, II.6a), Sippar (III.14, 17; IV.17, compare II.28c), Tarbiṣu (III.23), and Ur (II.6b, 14, 15, 29; III.51a) and other sites.[1]

(8) Akkadian literature was studied and copied also outside of Mesopotamia, for example, in southwest Iran (see I.4b, III.22, IV.36b, from Susa), Anatolia (I.6, 7, from Kanesh; III.7b, 16c, 27, from Hattusha), Syria (II.36b; III.15, 16b, from Ugarit; III.37c, from Hama; III. 60, IV.21, from Emar), and Egypt (III.7a, 20, 21, from El-Amarna).[2]

From this it is plain that most knowledge of Akkadian literature is owed to collections from only a few sites, and mostly from first-millennium manuscripts that may often be late copies or reworkings of earlier texts. Important evidence is missing. The most significant lack is any large group of literary tablets from Babylon, the cultural center of Mesopotamia from the middle of the second millennium B.C. through the Persian period. A further gap is the paucity of manuscripts from the Mature period of Akkadian literature, 1500–1000 B.C., when one assumes that many of the works known from Assur and Nineveh were cast in their form now known.

3. PUBLICATION AND TRANSLATION

The journey from an ancient clay manuscript to a modern translation can be long, often entailing numerous individual contributions over many years. Ancient tablets are usually broken into many pieces that may be dispersed among different collections. Fragments of the same tablet may be published by different people years apart before recognition that the pieces join. Ancient manuscripts themselves were sometimes incomplete, for apparently Mesopotamian students began copying certain major works, then moved on to others, often without finishing the ones they had begun.[3]

Publication of cuneiform tablets is a slow and demanding task. Ideally, this begins with preparation of a precise hand-drawn facsimile of the original by someone thoroughly familiar with its contents, who reproduces as accurately as possible the intent of the original scribe and the present state of the tablet. Even within the small domain of Assyriology, few scholars have the ability and opportunity to undertake

---

1.   The archaeological background of the literary tablets from Ur has been studied by Charpin, *Clergé*.

2.   See M. Dietrich, "Babylonian Literary Texts from Western Libraries," in J. C. de Moor, W. G. E. Watson, eds., *Verse in Ancient Near Eastern Prose* (Neukirchen, 1993), 41–67; and Pedersén, *Archives* (p. 8. note 2).

3.   Reiner, *Literatur*, 157.

such epigraphic work, so publications vary widely in their reliability and completeness. Furthermore, scholarly courtesy prevailing in the discipline forbids use of a manuscript in which another scholar has previously expressed interest. The result is that for some texts treated in this anthology there are additional manuscripts or restoring fragments that could not be used here.

Anthologies of Akkadian literature in translation have appeared since the end of the nineteenth century. The reader who compares some of the renderings offered here with those found in earlier anthologies may feel uneasy or even shocked at the discrepancies he will find, especially if he follows one large text through several anthologies. This means that understanding of texts has improved, not that such wide differences in translation are still acceptable today, save for a few compositions of extraordinary difficulty. In general, anthologies more than thirty years old are out of date and cannot be profitably consulted by one unfamiliar with the original texts. With the continual discovery of new material and the publication of dictionaries and other reference works, knowledge of Akkadian is growing faster than knowledge of Greek, Latin, or Biblical Hebrew; thus the obsolescence of translations is far more rapid in Assyriology than in comparable disciplines.

The earliest anthologies in western European and American scholarship include E. Schrader's *Die Keilschriften und das alte Testament* (1872), with subsequent editions and English translations appearing in 1883, 1885, 1888, and 1903; G. Smith's *Chaldaean Genesis* (1875); H. Winckler, *Keilinschriftliches Textbuch zum alten Testament* (1892, 1903, 1909); and H. Gressmann, A. Ungnad, and H. Ranke, *Altorientalische Texte und Bilder zum alten Testament* (1905, revised 1906, 1916, 1930; English translation 1911). A scholarly edition of Mesopotamian mythological texts by P. Jensen, *Assyrisch-babylonische Mythen und Epen* (1901), was the basis for many later treatments of these texts. A French anthology was offered by C.-F. Jean, *La Littérature des Babyloniens et des Assyriens* (1924), replaced by R. Labat's chapter in *Les Religions du Proche-Orient asiatique* (1970) and J. Bottéro and S. N. Kramer, *Lorsque les dieux faisaient l'homme* (1988). English translations include E. Wilson, *Babylonian and Assyrian Literature* (1901); R. F. Harper, *Assyrian and Babylonian Literature: Selected Translations* (1904); R. W. Rogers, *Cuneiform Parallels to the Old Testament* (1912, 1926), and G. Barton's *Archaeology and the Bible* (1916).

The German and English anthologies with biblical emphasis were superseded in 1950 by a collection of translations from various ancient Near Eastern languages, *Ancient Near Eastern Texts Relating to the Old Testament* (revised 1955, 1969), edited by J. B. Pritchard. This volume made available a large body of reliable translations with comments by leading authorities. The Akkadian literary material was treated by E. A. Speiser, with updating and revision, as well as later additions, by A. K. Grayson and R. D. Biggs. Speiser's felicitous translation of Semitic idiom into good

English is enviable, and I have consulted his versions with admiration. A new German anthology, *Texte aus der Umwelt des Alten Testaments*, began publication in fascicles in 1982, with contributions by various scholars; of particular use to me were the translations by Hecker, Lambert, Müller, and von Soden. A new English anthology with biblical emphasis is W. W. Hallo, ed., *The Context of Scripture* (Leiden, 1997–2002).

Two anthologies of Akkadian in translation have appeared in Russian: *Poetry and Prose of the Ancient East* (1973), with contributions by V. Afanasieva, I. M. Diakonoff, and W. Schileiko, and a volume by Afanasieva and Diakonoff entitled *I Reveal unto You a Hidden Word* (1981), a fresh treatment of thirty-nine Akkadian literary texts with introduction and notes. Several collections have appeared in Italian, for example, G. Furlani, *Miti Babilonesi e Assiri* (1956) and G. R. Castellino, *Testi sumerici e accadici* (1977). Anthologies have appeared in Danish, Dutch, Czech, Hebrew, and other languages, but I have not systematically consulted them.

More restricted collections of translations have also appeared. Particularly noteworthy are W. G. Lambert's treatment of *Babylonian Wisdom Literature* (1960) and *Atrahasis* (1969); W. von Soden and A. Falkenstein's *Sumerische und Akkadische Hymnen und Gebete* (1953); M.-J. Seux's *Hymnes et prières aux dieux de Babylonie et d'Assyrie* (1976); S. Dalley's *Myths from Mesopotamia* (1989); and J. Westenholz's *Legends of the Kings of Akkade* (1997). I have profited greatly from all these works.

The standards of scholarly acknowledgment among translators are lower than in other areas of humanistic research. Some of the general anthologists cited above have published under their own names translations that are substantially the work of others, even to the precise wording. Since it is often impractical to determine who first established the meaning of a given line, the custom has grown of acknowledging only deviations from certain standard translations or editions, though this means that often those who have done the most work are acknowledged the least. I have cited editions and translations that I have found useful in preparing this work. In general, translations and readings taken from dictionaries are not acknowledged.

From the foregoing account of the recovery, publication, and interpretation of Akkadian literature, one will see that a literary history of Akkadian is at present impossible. Most attempts are little more than an inventory of available texts with interpretive remarks.[1] Some more specialized studies, however, have treated the dynamics, themes, and contexts of Akkadian literature.[2]

---

1. B. Meissner, *Die babyonisch-assyrische Literatur* (Wildpark-Potsdam, 1927); O. Weber, *Die Literatur der Babylonier und Assyrer, ein Überblick* (Leipzig, 1907).

2. For the general reader, the essays of Lambert, BWL, 1–20; Oppenheim, *Ancient Mesopotamia,*

C. POETRY AND PROSE

1. LINGUISTIC DIFFERENTIATION

Most of the texts in this anthology can, in modern terms, be broadly defined as literary on the basis of certain linguistic differentiations, both grammatical and lexical, that Mesopotamians considered marks of formal written expression. These linguistic features cannot for the most part be made visible in translation. Not all linguistically differentiated texts are here considered literary, but this criterion has proved helpful in making an initial selection. On the other hand, a few non-literary texts, such as letters, are included for reasons explained with each example.

The texts selected here can be divided into prose and poetry on the basis of how their language is deployed. One does not know if the Greco-Roman distinction between the two, that prose was to be read but poetry was to be sung or performed, is appropriate for Akkadian. There are good reasons to believe that some Akkadian literary works were sung or performed.[1] In any case, poetry has an apparent, if difficult to define, verse structure and meter.

2. VERSE STRUCTURE

As for verse structure,[2] individual lines of poetry generally consist of complete sentences or thoughts. Each line tends to be divided into halves, sometimes indicated, especially in later manuscripts, by a blank space in the middle of the line. Each half line tends to consist of three or four words, and the line is divided so as to allow patterning of stress units. Lines of poetry often come in pairs (distiches), which can be related to each other by sound, stress patterning, and meaning. Meaning is developed in the half line, whole line, distich, or larger unit by parallelism.[3]

228–275; Reiner, CAH[3] 3/2, 293–321, and W. Röllig, "Literatur," RLA 7, 48–66, are particularly recommended. Much information will be found in H. Hirsch and others, *Kindlers Literaturlexikon*. CANES contains excellent short essays, with bibliographies.

   1. II.1 has unusual spellings that possibly suggest some performance technique; II.5 has Sumerian liturgical indictions. See further von Soden, ZA 71 (1982), 165.

   2. Hecker, *Epik*, 101–141.

   3. Detailed discussion, with examples, by Hecker, *Epik*, 142–151. There is a vast literature on this subject, especially in the field of Biblical Hebrew. Discussion and extensive bibliography will be found in J. Kugel, *The Idea of Biblical Poetry* (New Haven, 1981); M. P. O'Connor, *Hebrew Verse Structure* (Winona Lake, Ind., 1980); E. L. Greenstein, "How Does Parallelism Mean?" in *A Sense of Text: The Art of Language in the Study of Biblical Literature, Jewish Quarterly Review Supplement* (1982), 41–70; A. Berlin, *The Dynamics of Biblical Parallelism* (Bloomington, Ind., 1985), who draws attention to the use of parallelism in prose.

3. PARALLELISM

This refers to repeated formulation of the same message such that subsequent encodings of it restate, expand, complete, contrast, render more specific, complement, or carry further the first message. The following example from Text II.1, lines 1–4, illustrates this:

> Sing of a goddess, most awe-inspiring goddess,
> Let her be praised, mistress of people,
>   greatest of the Igigi-gods.
> Sing of Ishtar, most awe-inspiring goddess,
> Let her be praised, mistress of women,
>   greatest of the Igigi-gods.

The parallelism is developed in each half line, beginning with the goddess being characterized as "most awe-inspiring." In successive lines, the name Ishtar replaces the generic term "goddess," and "people" is rendered more specific by "women," since particular needs of women are referred to later in the poem.

Here is a second example from Text III.14, Tablet I, lines 89–92:

> My slave cursed me openly in the assembly (of gentlefolk),
> My slave girl defamed me before the rabble.
> An acquaintance would see me and make himself scarce,
> My family set me down as an outsider.

In this case, parallelism is used to convey all possible instances. The first two lines include male and female, citizens and slaves, upper class and lower class—all members of society. The theme of denunciation by inferiors is developed in the second pair of lines by moving to people of equal status, then to blood relations. The lower classes slander him, his equals avoid him, his intimates renounce him. The first two lines depend on acts of speech behind his back, the second two on physical actions in his presence. More subtle aspects of the parallelism include manipulation of syntax. In the original, the subject of each sentence is set at the beginning of each successive line for extra emphasis, an uncommon pattern in Akkadian poetry. Furthermore, the subjects are ranked in successive lines from least to most intimate. Some contrasts are left to the reader to infer. For example, cursing in the first line suggests denouncing a person to the gods, while defaming in the next implies denouncing in human society. This is therefore another instance of expressing totality by use of inclusive contrasts. Note in addition that in the third line the acquaintances distance themselves from the sufferer, removing themselves from his circle, while in the fourth the family unites to exclude him from its circle, thereby distancing him.

Parallelism can be reinforced by internal rhyme of syllables, single consonants, or vowels.[1] Alliteration, with or without parallel formulations, was a favored resource of the Akkadian poet.[2] Chiasm and "word picturing" were occasionally resorted to, both to reinforce parallelism with dynamic contrast and to add a physical dimension to encoded meaning.[3] Expansion and elaboration of these and other devices and figures are characteristic of how Akkadian poetic language was artificed and manipulated.[4]

4. REPETITION

Whereas parallelism usually implies reformulation of a thought in different words, repetition implies restatement *verbatim*, or with only slight changes.[5] Extensive use of repetition in Akkadian narrative shows it to be a favored device of storytelling. Repetition lengthens narrative to allow development of details and injection of subjective elements that might otherwise burden a continuous narrative too heavily. Akkadian repetition has its modern counterpart in passages of description, judgment, exposition, and comment that interrupt the flow of narrative discourse.

Repetition was used also to achieve specific narrative effects, especially in dramatic scenes. An example is the siege of Enlil's household by the strikers in Atrahasis (II.36a), Tablet I lines 70ff. The poet emphasizes the major turns of events by continued repetition of sets of lines in staccato succession, typically with a spoken and a narrated version of the same passage (compare II.36a Tablet I lines 43–46, 57–60, 70–73, 80–83, 93–96; see also below, E.3). When negotiations between the two sides begin, the pace becomes more leisurely, with lengthier segments of text forming the units of repetition.

In another instance, Ereshkigal's plaint that she has been abandoned by her lover (III.20 C/D iv 54′–57′) is twice stated without variation, as if to stress the pathos

---

1. Hecker, *Epik*, 139–140; see also Foster, JAOS 103 (1983), 126–128. Predominance of the vowel sound /u/ in certain poetic passages could be used to convey solemnity, for example, Erra and Ishum (IV.16) Tablet I line 132, which reads: *ultu ullû aguguma ina šubtiya atbuma aškuna abūbu* "Once long ago indeed I grew angry, left my dwelling, and caused the deluge!"

2. Hecker, *Epik*, 131–140. A good instance is *naḫlaptu apluḫti pulḫātu ḫalipma*, III.17 Tablet IV line 57.

3. Hecker, *Epik*, 144; Foster, *Studies Finkelstein*, 80 note 15; JAOS 103 (1983), 127.

4. Hecker, *Epik*; Wasserman, *Style*; Vogelzang, Vanstiphout, *Poetic Language*.

5. M. Vogelzang, "Repetition as a Poetic Device in Akkadian," in Vogelzang, Vanstiphout, *Poetic Language*, 167–182; Hecker, *Epik*, 56–65, 154–160.

of the moment. In a more elaborate example, the lengthy repetitions of the first half of the Epic of Creation (III.17) convey the deliberate and ineffectual proceedings of the older generation of gods, as opposed to the rapid, non-repetitive passages in which youthful Marduk takes charge.

5. METER

Though Akkadian poetry has meter, the same metrical pattern is seldom found many lines in succession. There is uncertainty as to whether metrics were based on syllables, ideas or thought units, some type of quantitative stress, or combinations of these possibilities.[1]

6. WORDPLAY

Perhaps the most difficult aspect of Akkadian poetry for a western reader to appreciate is the importance of paranomasia or wordplay, as this can often be a primary message-bearing device. Suspect as a game in western poetic tradition, paranomasia was often used in Akkadian for serious and significant communication. Wordplay could convey an association that extended beyond the purely phonological or semantic, and was considered a useful expository tool. Wordplay could even depend on spelling rather than pronunciation.[2] In most such instances, direct translation is impossible.

7. PROSE STYLE

Akkadian prose is distinguished from poetry by its absence of short, balanced, metrical lines, although prose can seem rhythmic. Parallelism is less developed than in poetry, and may be absent altogether. Figure and ornament are sparser than in poetry and fall into more standardized patterns.[3] Sentences can be longer and more complicated than in poetry.

---

1. See W. von Soden, "Untersuchungen zur babylonischen Metrik," *ZA* 71 (1982), 161–204, *ZA* 74 (1984), 213–234, who works with accentuation scansion; differently W. G. Lambert, *Studies Moran*, 289 note 1; M. West, "Akkadian Poetry: Metre and Performance," *Iraq* 59 (1997), 175–187; for a review of the debate on this topic, see Wasserman, *Style*, 159–162.

2. See p. 5 note 2 and S. Noegel, ed., *Puns and Pundits: Word Play in the Hebrew Bible and Ancient Near Eastern Literature* (Bethesda, Md., 2000).

3. Simile is particularly common in commemorative prose, though less so in letters. See D. Marcus, "Animal Similes in Assyrian Royal Inscriptions," *OrNS* 46 (1977), 86–106 and below, p. 18 note 2. For rhetorical figures in letters, see B. Foster, "Letters and Literature: A Ghost's Entreaty," *Studies Hallo*, 98–102.

One of the most characteristic devices of ornamented prose, well attested in Akkadian commemorative inscriptions, is the use of numerous and often lengthy dependent clauses that lead up to a climactic statement conveyed by the main verb.[1] While in a broad sense this practice mirrors a basic property of Akkadian syntax, whereby the main verb comes at the end of a sentence, it offers great rhetorical possibilities for unfolding of narrative by presenting a sequence of events climaxing in a main one.

8. FORMULAE AND WORD PAIRS

Akkadian shares with many literatures a tendency to use repeatedly certain literary formulae, especially in narrative poetry, as well as fixed epithets for certain gods and cities. Furthermore, when certain words occur in a literary context, certain other words, usually synonymous or parallel in meaning, can be expected to occur also, as with English "kith," which is normally paired with "kin." More general instances, which often occur in letters as well, include pairs such as "man and woman," "right and left," "above and below," "east and west," "food and drink," used to indicate totality, all human beings, every direction, and the like. These aspects of parallel, symmetrical style are well known in other Semitic literatures such as Ugaritic and Biblical Hebrew, as well as Akkadian.[2]

Examples of formulae, pairs, and established sequences found in the texts translated here include "dreams, signs, portents" (III.44b line 48); "my (personal) god and goddess" (III.44b line 29, compare the expansion of this pair in III.44c lines 16–17); and commonly occurring contrasting or complementary pairs such as "days" and "years" (III.45b line 17); "night" and "day" (III.14 Tablet I lines 119–120). One of the most difficult word pairs to translate is the pair "heaven and earth." The Akkadian word for "earth" could also mean "netherworld," and in many instances it is impossible to be sure which was meant. In the translations, I have chosen "earth" for the second member of this pair, unless I was confident that "netherworld" was meant. See further III.51.

---

1. For this commemorative style, see, for example, II.11 and IV.2c. See also A. K. Grayson, "Assyrian Royal Inscriptions: Literary Characteristics," OAC 17 (1981), 35–47.
2. For Akkadian, the basic study is Wasserman, *Style*, 61–98. For other Near Eastern literatures, see Avishur, UF 7 (1975), 13–47; *Stylistic Studies of Word-Pairs in Biblical and Ancient Semitic Literatures*, AOAT 210 (1984); Craigie, *Semitics* 5 (1979), 48–58; Grave, OrNS 51 (1982), 171 note 51; Berlin, *Parallelism* (p. 13 note 3) 65–72 and "Parallel Word Pairs: A Linguistic Explanation," UF 15 (1983), 7–16.

9. SIMILE AND METAPHOR

Simile and metaphor lie at the heart of figurative language.[1] Similes in Akkadian[2] are easily recognized by use of "like": "He split her in two like a fish for drying" (III.17 Tablet IV line 137); "My entreaty was like the strife of a brawl" (III.14 Tablet I line 117). Their content and structure can be complex and worthy of independent study: "The citizenry of Babylon, like reeds in a thicket, had no one in charge" (IV.17 Tablet IV line 6); "Like a young man who has shed blood, who wanders alone in a swamp, whom a pursuer has overtaken, and whose heart is pounding ..." (IV.5 line 69); "Alas for Babylon, that I tended like a thriving orchard, but whose fruit I could not taste" (IV.17 Tablet IV line 42).

Metaphors[3] are also a rewarding study. Some are clichés of little literary value ("dead metaphors"). For example, "shepherd" is a cliché for king, as in III.17 Tablet VII line 148. In this case, however, the metaphor is revitalized in the same line by adding "herdsman," not a common metaphor for king. Others are more creative efforts: "The speech on their lips is a fire breaking out" (IV.4c line 6); "May his joyful songs be the prick of a thorn" (IV.4e line 29); "My friend became a malignant demon" (III.14 Tablet I line 85); "A woman is a sharp iron dagger that slashes a man's throat" (IV.20 line VI); "The writhing (armies) will writhe, two women giving birth, bathed in blood" (II.6a episode 4). Simile and metaphor are particularly common in proverbs, as for example, "A household without a master is a woman without a husband" (III.16d 1 col. iv). Combinations of simile and metaphor are found, such as, "Death, as if on a day of thirsting, slakes itself at the sight of the warrior" (III.1 v line 52′); "He is shod with the netherworld, as with [san]dals" (III.25 line 134). While both simile and metaphor are visible in translation, their import sometimes escapes the modern reader.

---

1. J. Westenholz, "Symbolic Language in Akkadian Narrative Poetry: The Metaphorical Relationship between Poetical Images and the Real World," in Vogelzang, Vanstiphout, eds., *Mesopotamian Poetic Language*, 183–206; M. Streck, *Die Bildersprache der akkadischen Epik*, AOAT 264 (1999), and Wasserman, *Style*.

2. Mayer, UFBG, 376; S. Ponchia, "Analogie, metafore e simultudini nelle iscrizioni reali assire: semantica e ideologia," OrAn 26 (1987), 223–255; G. Buccellati, "Towards a Formal Typology of Akkadian Similes," AOAT 25 (1976), 59–70; Streck, AOAT 264 (1999), 57–90.

3. Streck, AOAT 264 (1999), 97–147. Examples are discussed by Lambert in M. Minden *et al.*, eds., *Figurative Language in the Ancient Near East* (London, 1987), 25–39; see also K. P. Foster, "Ceramic Imagery in Ancient Near Eastern Literature," in P. B. Vandiver *et al.*, eds., *Materials Issues in Art and Archaeology* II, *Materials Research Society Symposium Proceedings* 185 (1991), 389–413; J. Westenholz, "Metaphorical Language in the Poetry of Love in the Ancient Near East," CRRAI 38 (1991), 381–387.

D. AUTHORS AND REDACTORS

1. AUTHORSHIP

For the majority of Akkadian literary works, the names of their authors are unknown.[1] This does not mean that they lacked authors but that the authors' names have been lost. Certain compositions show enough individuality in terms of language, art, content, and unity of purpose to suggest that they were primarily the work of one author, even if changes appeared in the text later.[2] Furthermore, some of these same texts contain passages that imply or insist that this is the case and give the reader to understand that the circumstances of authorship are crucial to evaluating the text in question. Such passages give clues for understanding Mesopotamian notions of authorship.[3]

The most important texts that refer to authorship are Erra and Ishum (IV.17), Tablet V lines 39–51; the Epic of Creation (III.17), Tablet VII lines 145–162; Atrahasis (II.39a), Tablet III col viii lines 9–16; and Agushaya (II.5), Tablet II col viii lines 15–20. Various other passages allude to authorship, referring either to divine approval of the text or to the skill used to compose it. These include the hymn to Ishtar of the Classical period (II.1) stanza xiv, The Favor of Kurigalzu (III.10b), and two compositions ascribed to Assurbanipal (IV.4c, f). Some texts name the author either in the course of the narrative (III.14) or in acrostics (III.25, 45f; IV.19).

These passages suggest the existence of a Mesopotamian literary tradition wherein the author described the genesis, divine approval, composition, authority, and traditing of his text.

Genesis. All examples imply or state divine inspiration for the text in more or less ambiguous terms. In the case of Erra and Ishum, the text was "revealed"; in the Epic of Creation, the text was proclaimed during a ceremony, and was "explained" by the author. In the Agushaya poem and the hymn to Ishtar, the author's partic-

---

1. See Hallo, IEJ 12 (1962), 13–16; Hecker, ArOr 45 (1977), 249–251; W. G. Lambert, "Ancestors, Authors, and Canonicity," JCS 11 (1957), 1–14, 112; "A Catalogue of Texts and Authors," JCS 16 (1962), 59–77; Rochberg-Halton, JCS 36 (1984), 135–137; Geller, BSOAS 53 (1990), 209–213.

2. This obviously subjective judgment is occasionally hinted at by others, e.g., Landsberger, JNES 20 (1961), 154 note 2, who refers to the "odd and confused diction of the poet" (of the Epic of Creation), and Reiner, JNES 17 (1958), 41, who refers to the "awkwardness of the scribe-poet" (of Erra and Ishum).

3. B. Foster, "On Authorship in Akkadian Literature," AIUON 51/1 (1990), 17–32; P. Michalowski, "Authorship and Textual Authority," in J. Cooper, G. Schwartz, eds., *The Study of the Ancient Near East in the Twenty-first Century, The William Foxwell Albright Centennial Conference* (Winona Lake, Ind., 1996), 183–190; J.-J. Glassner, "Être auteur avant Homère en Mésopotamie?" *Diogène* 196 (2001), 111–118.

ipation was indistinguishable from that of the god of wisdom himself, or at least the god "caused it to be." In both Atrahasis and Agushaya, ambiguity as to whether a god (first person) or the poet (third person) is speaking may be intentional.

Approval. In the cases of Erra and Ishum, the Epic of Creation, and the Ishtar hymn, a god heard and approved the texts. In Erra and Ishum, the author insists that he did not alter the text from its original inspired form. In the Epic of Creation, the poet is concerned that future generations will understand the text correctly. In Atrahasis the text is made into a command of Enlil by the artful Ea. In the Vision of the Assyrian Prince (IV.5), the scribe assures the reader that he remembered the prince's discourse accurately.

Composition is called "composing," "discoursing," "writing down," "being made." With the exception of Erra and Ishum, the precise manner of composition and the respective roles of inspirer and inspired are left unclarified.

Authority for the text is granted in the form of divine approval. Such authority is referred to in Erra and Ishum, the Epic of Creation, and implied in Atrahasis. The text can have life-giving (Ishtar Hymn) or apotropaic powers (Erra and Ishum). Its peculiar status as a "sign" of a god is found in Agushaya and Erra and Ishum. In the Epic of Creation, the text is glorified as a key for humankind to understand Marduk's reorganized universe. Erra and Ishum and the Epic of Creation are acts of mercy by a god, in the case of the former by a protagonist (Ishum), in the case of the latter by Marduk himself.

Traditing and dissemination of texts are referred to in Erra and Ishum, the Epic of Creation, Agushaya, and Atrahasis both synchronically and diachronically: "all people" are supposed to hear them, as well as succeeding generations.

Mesopotamian poetic tradition had, therefore, a notion of individual inspiration and authorship, which could be used as a literary device. Whereas modern literary tradition stresses the individual's importance as a matrix of creative impulse, Mesopotamian artistic tradition tended to stress the outside source of the inspiration that lent each work its uniqueness. Indeed, authors themselves stressed their works' inspired uniqueness by dwelling on the time or occasion of their composition. In some instances (Epic of Creation, Erra and Ishum), the poem was seen as an event of cosmic importance; the text became the climax of the events it narrated. In addition, the divine authority of the composition made it a source of blessing, security, well-being, and knowledge.

2. CREATIVITY

Already in the Archaic period, one can point to efforts at creativity and originality.[1] Whereas early Sargonic commemorative inscriptions are highly stylized and convey only simple statements of royal military victories, together with assertions of divine favor, the inscriptions of Naram-Sin have long, complicated sentences in a florid rhetorical style (see I.3).

The Classical period of Akkadian literature seems to have been a time of singular creativity, as though a vigorous literature was in formation. Atrahasis, for instance, is a poetic masterpiece. It sets forth the history and life cycle of humankind in relation to divine history, using traditional materials in a highly original manner. The nocturnal prayer of a lonely and reflective diviner (see To Gods of the Night, II.27) contains unusual passages whose lyricism was imitated in later prayers.

Perhaps most characteristic of the creativity of the Mature period of Akkadian literature (Chapter III) were large, composite compositions, which, despite their varied source material, emerged with a unity of theme and intent that made the whole greater than the sum of the parts. Examples include Ishtar Queen of Heaven (III.26) and the Shamash Hymn (III.32). The creativity of this period was marked by great experimentation with language. This included use of rare, dialectal, and scholarly words, elaborate and intricate metaphors, refinements of parallelism, and academic Sumerian loanwords. The Epic of Creation (III.17) and the Poem of the Righteous Sufferer (III.14) are good examples of this type of composition.

Experimentation with established forms produced long texts in various combinations of hymnic, confessional, narrative, scholarly, and didactic styles (for example, Kurigalzu and the Ishtar Temple [III.10a], the Marduk Prophecy [III.13], Ishtar Queen of Heaven [III.26]). The frequent combination of incantation and prayer is another example of this mature, derivative style (below, D.3). Specific political conditions occasioned a flowering of literature centering on Marduk, the Babylonian national god; see Nebuchadnezzar I (III.12); the Epic of Creation (III.17), and the Marduk Prophecy (III.13).

Creativity in the Mature period was not restricted to specific genres. Among the scores of Akkadian prayers, for example, is one that seems consciously to have taken all the clichés of the genre and molded them into an original, moving composition (Against Marduk's Anger [III.44a]).

Other instances of creativity are found in the works of beginners or brilliant youngsters whose technical competence may not be equal to their literary ambi-

---

1. See K. Hecker, "Tradition und Originalität in der altorientalischen Literatur," ArOr 45 (1977), 245–258; Hallo, IEJ 12 (1962), 18–21; Franke, *Königsinschriften*.

tions. These works may present flaws of diction, usage, and perhaps a certain untidiness (III.43b, 46b). Yet along with such blemishes, one finds a high level of feeling and originality, coupled with either the self-absorbed, amazed sensuality of newly discovered emotions, or the pedantic rhetoric of the excited novice.[1] The Faithful Lover (II.16) may be a text of this type. Perhaps such puerile eloquence is satirized in At the Cleaners (II.14).

Humor opens infinite ranges to an original and satirical thinker.[2] An early parody (I.6) of the Sargonic commemorative style (see I.3) and possibly of a lost early tradition of legends of Sargonic kings as well (see II.6, 7) is both effective and sophisticated. The spoof incantation against a bleating goat (II.25g) develops well-established magical themes and language in a ridiculous way, and was surely the product of some earthy mind wearied of magical lore. At the Cleaners (II.14) and the Gilgamesh Letter (IV.58) are likewise humorous texts. When humor shades off into satire, an elusive genre, a text such as the Dialogue of Pessimism (IV.20) results.

One must mention as well the brilliance of an individual who produces a text that is at once recognized as a masterpiece and becomes a classic. Such a person was Kabti-ilani-Marduk, author of Erra and Ishum, one of the most original and experimental Akkadian narrative texts (IV.17). This poet produced a narrative piece that, apart from its theological and spiritual profundity, can be read as a textbook of the possibilities available in Akkadian poetic tradition.

The long life span of Akkadian literary tradition did not rob it of feeling and originality. To the Late period date various royal prayers, some strongly felt and couched in sonorous prose. These combine intricacy of syntax with fine balancing of parallel rhetorical units (see IV.6–8, 10, 11).

3. INTERTEXTUALITY

Defining relationships between texts is a crucial problem in the study of any literature, including Akkadian. The texts in this anthology illustrate various types of intertextual relationships.

Two simple cases occur with Archaic period texts. The Old Akkadian letter I.5a contains phraseology, perhaps humorously intended, found in exorcisms more

---

1. Held, JCS 15 (1961), 2.
2. B. Foster, "Humor and Cuneiform Literature," JANES 6 (1974), 69–85; "Humor and Wit in the Ancient Near East," in CANES 4:2459–2469; A. George, "Ninurta-Pāqidat's Dog Bite, and Notes on Other Comic Tales," Iraq 55 (1993), 63–75; D'Agostino, Testi umoristici, 14–58 and "Some Considerations on Humour in Mesopotamia," RSO 72 (1998), 273–278.

than a millennium later.[1] Likewise, the magical phraseology of the Old Akkadian love charm (see I.4c) is echoed in the Old Babylonian love charm II.26b. It is no coincidence that both these examples involve magical language, for magical phraseology shows remarkable durability in Mesopotamian tradition.

The Classical period provides the oldest version of various compositions known from later periods in different forms. Some are magical spells, for example II.23a, of which several later versions are known. Others are narrative, for example Atrahasis (II.36), a version of which was incorporated into the Late Assyrian Gilgamesh Epic. The Mature period versions of Anzu (III.23), Etana (III.22), and the Cuthaean Legend of Naram-Sin (III.7b) were built on Classical versions of the same narratives.

Intertextual relationships between Classical and later hymnography and prayers are less amply attested, though the Literary Prayer to Marduk (III.29) is thought to have a Classical forerunner. Were the extant corpus of Classical hymnography and prayers greater, more connections might be found; the few well-preserved Classical hymns do not have extant descendants.

An unusual type of intertextuality occurs in certain composite literary texts of the Mature period (see III.26–30). These combine several independent compositions, perhaps with new material added. The results are long, complicated texts that are not sustained by a narrative thread. Intertextual tradition also combines narrative with hymnography. This is known in the Classical period (Agushaya Poem II.5) and in the Mature period (Poem of the Righteous Sufferer III.14).

Another distinctively Mesopotamian form of intertextuality is embedding of monumental and archival texts, often unaltered, in literary works.[2] Kudur-Nahhunte of Elam (III.11), for example, includes what may be actual royal letters within its poetic narrative. Other literary texts were composed outright in a pseudomonumental style (for example, the Cuthaean Legend of Naram-Sin [III.7b]). Conversely, genuine monumental texts can make literary allusions, such as the inscription of the Chaldaean king Merodach-Baladan that quotes Erra and Ishum.[3]

Borrowings between scholarly literature and belles lettres provide further examples of intertextual relationships. Belles lettres may borrow from omen series, either in specific content or general style.[4] Omens are referred to in apotropaic prayers

---

1. Thureau-Dangin, RA 23 (1926), 23–25.
2. Hallo, AS 20 (1975), 195–196.
3. J. Brinkman, *Prelude to Empire* (Philadelphia, 1984), 49 note 230.
4. J. J. Finkelstein, "Mesopotamian Historiography," PAPS 107/6 (1963), 461–472; A. K. Grayson, "Divination and the Babylonian Chronicles," CRRAI 14 (1965), 69–76; P. Michalowski, "Adapa and the Ritual Process," RO 41 (1980), 77–82.

(see, e.g., III.51a, c, d, f); the style and diction of omen apodoses can be documented in texts with prophetic or apocalyptic passages.[1] Dualities such as "favorable/unfavorable," basic to divination, appear as tropes in Akkadian literature in such forms as "good times/bad times," or "successful/unsuccessful kings."[2] Such dualities may acquire lives of their own independent of genuine historical traditions worked into literary compositions. To take another example, descriptions of suffering in laments, confessional texts, and medical incantations may draw on medical diagnostic treatises (see the Poem of the Righteous Sufferer [III.14]).

Some of the works translated here, especially incantations, devotional texts, and hymns, are excerpted from larger contexts such as rituals. It is not certain in most cases whether the incantation or hymn was composed for the ritual, or whether it existed independently and was inserted in the ritual later. Occasionally the same text can appear in different ritual contexts and with different applications. Ritual or apotropaic significance was sometimes assigned to certain narrative or literary texts after they were written or in the texts themselves (IV.17).[3]

The same passage may occur in more than one composition. For example, The Descent of Ishtar, III.19 lines 19–20 appear, in slightly different form, in the Gilgamesh Epic Tablet VI lines 97–100, as do lines 106–108 of the same text in the Gilgamesh Epic Tablet VII lines 80–84, altered and expanded. Likewise, The Descent of Ishtar lines 4–10 are found, altered and expanded, in Nergal and Ereshkigal, III.20, Late Version ii–iii. Because of the long, complex history of the Descent of Ishtar story, one may opine that it was the source of these passages, whether they are to be read as reuse of stock material or as literary allusions. In any case, literary allusion was known in Mesopotamia, as evidenced by quotation of Advice to a Prince (IV.13) in a letter, and quotation of the Cuthaean Legend of Naram-Sin by Assurbanipal in a stern warning.[4]

---

1. A. K. Grayson, "Akkadian Prophecies," JCS 18 (1964), 7–30; W. W. Hallo, "Akkadian Apocalypses," IEJ 16 (1966), 231–242; R. D. Biggs, "More Akkadian Prophecies," *Iraq* 29 (1969), 117–132; H. Hunger, S. Kaufman, "A New Akkadian Prophecy Text," JAOS 95 (1975), 371–375; A. K. Grayson, "The Babylonian Origin of Apocalyptic Literature," *Atti dell'Istituto Veneto de Scienze, Lettere et Arti* 148 (1989/90), *Classe di Scienze Morali, Lettere ed Arti*, 203–221; W. G. Lambert, *The Background of Jewish Apocalyptic* (London, 1978). See IV.62.

2. H. G. Güterbock, "Die Historische Tradition und ihre literarische Gestaltung bei Babyloniern und Hethitern bis 1200," ZA 42 (1934), 1–91; 44 (1938), 45–149; Oppenheim, OrNS 5 (1936), 203–208.

3. E. Reiner, "Plague Amulets and House Blessings," JNES 19 (1960), 148–155; W. G. Lambert, "Myth and Ritual as Conceived by the Babylonians," JSS 13 (1968), 104–112.

4. Livingstone, *Court Poetry*, 64; see, in general, A. Finet, "Allusions et reminiscences comme source d'information sur la diffusion de la littérature," CRRAI 32 (1985), 13–17; W. W. Hallo, "Proverbs Quoted in Epic," *Studies Moran*, 203–217. See also IV.9, and p. 25 note 3.

The Epic of Creation (III.17), which probably dates to the Mature period, is a particularly apt subject for intertextual study, for it draws on a variety of Akkadian and Sumerian traditions. These include narrative poems about the god Ninurta,[1] whose deeds are assigned to Marduk in the Epic of Creation. The episode of the creation of humankind is drawn from Atrahasis or a similar text; lists of divine names form a basis for the episode of the fifty names of Marduk.[2]

In its turn, the Epic of Creation exercised considerable influence on later Akkadian literature.[3] Late devotional compositions allude to or quote the epic (III.44b, 44e, 44f, 46a; IV.4d). One cannot demonstrate that in every case the epic was the source and the other text the borrowing, but there are usually circumstantial reasons for taking this to be the case. For example, Against Illness (III.44b) alludes to the epic half a dozen times in the space of ten lines. The allusions are highlighted by being concentrated in a single passage, with no further allusions to be found in the text thereafter. They refer to Marduk's power as slayer of Tiamat and his role as a vegetation and fertility deity. Prince of the Gods (III.44f) contains numerous allusions, direct and indirect, to the epic, and indeed, so far as preserved, reads like a meditation on the larger text.

Nergal the Warrior (III.46a) is a less clear case. Line 4, for example, alludes to the Six Hundred, who are said to be organized by Marduk in the epic (Tablet VI line 44); the "pitiless deluge-weapon" also recalls the epic (Tablet IV line 49); and the gods take to "secret places," as do the defeated gods in the epic. Since these are stock expressions, one could argue that they show common use of well-known material rather than borrowing. However, Sublime Nergal (III.46c) quotes the epic (Tablet I line 94) in a context making so little sense that one may conclude that this was lifted as a memorable line from the epic and misapplied in the Nergal hymn.

A lengthy hymn to Marduk offered in the name of Assurbanipal (IV.4d) is filled with allusions to the epic. The author of the hymn seems to have recognized that the author of the epic assigned to Marduk various triumphs hitherto ascribed to Ninurta, but went further than his source, assigning to Marduk even the killing of the Anzu-bird, a feat generally ascribed to Ninurta or Ningirsu (see III.23).

Peculiar intertextual problems are presented by the Names of Nabu (III.45e). This poem makes Nabu, Marduk's son, into the Marduk of the gods, just as in the epic Marduk was made into the Enlil of the gods. An explication of certain names

---

1. W. G. Lambert, "Ninurta Mythology in the Babylonian Epic of Creation," CRRAI 32 (1985), 55–60.

2. W. G. Lambert, "Götterlisten," RLA 3, 473–479.

3. E. Weissert, "Creating a Political Climate: Literary Allusions to *Enuma Eliš* in Sennacherib's Account of the Battle of Halule," CRRAI 39 (1992), 191–202.

of Nabu follows, using some of the same names assigned to Marduk in the epic. Marduk is finally equated with Qingu, the enemy he defeated in the epic. This shows that borrowed material could be used with intentions quite different from those of the source.

E. READING AKKADIAN LITERATURE

Akkadian literature offers a special challenge to the critical reader. Modern literary criticism seldom confronts fragmentary texts in incompletely understood languages, or compositions with centuries-long, complicated histories of textual development. Many of the usual topics for critical study in modern literature are not useful avenues of approach to Akkadian. Approaching these texts from a European tradition, the reader may find them in comparison lifeless, stereotyped, and without apparent form, color, or internal development. The following remarks are intended to orient the reader who wishes to approach these texts from a theoretical or critical standpoint, but who finds himself groping for landmarks on apparently featureless terrain.

1. TIME

Time, a major preoccupation of European literary tradition, is seldom a central issue in Akkadian literature. The Babylonian concept of time was linear rather than cyclical.[1] Time was concrete and calendrical, the sum total of days, months, and years.[2] Normal time and normal human lifespans were thought to have existed only since the Flood.[3] Prior to the Flood, the synchronism of biological and calen-

---

1. W. G. Lambert, "History and the Gods: A Review Article," OrNS 39 (1970), 170–177, esp. 175; differently J.-J. Glassner, *Chroniques mésopotamiennes* (Paris, 1993), 24–26. For general discussions of Mesopotamian concepts of time, see I. S. Klotchkoff, *Duhovnaja Kul'tura Vavilonii: Čelovek, Sud'ba, Vremja* (Moscow, 1983), and his "Vosprijatie vremeni v drevnej Mesopotamii," *Narody Azii i Afriki* (1980), 91–102; M. Liverani, "La valutazione qualitativa del tempo," in S. Moscati, ed., *L'Alba della Civiltà* (Torino, 1976), 3: 462–476; Archi, N.A.B.U. 1998/86; B. André-Salvini, "La conscience du temps en Mésopotamie," in F. Briquel-Chattonnet, H. Lozachmeur, eds., *Proche-Orient Ancien. Temps vécu, temps pensé, Antiquités sémitiques* 3 (1998), 29–37; D. Brown, "The Cuneiform Concepts of Celestial Space and Time," *Cambridge Archaeological Journal* 10 (2001), 103–121.

2. Klotchkoff, *Kul'tura* (note 1), 15–21; see also W. W. Hallo, "Dating the Mesopotamian Past," *Bulletin of the Society for Mesopotamian Studies* (Toronto, 1982), 7–18; "The Nabonassar Era and Other Epochs in Mesopotamian Chronology and Chronography," in *Studies Sachs*, 175–190; E. Otto, "Zeitvorstellungen und Zeitrechnung im alten Orient," *Studium Generale* 19 (1966), 743–751. This deals mostly with Egyptian matters, but offers some interesting proposals.

3. A. Malamat, "Longevity: Biblical Concepts and Some Ancient Near Eastern Parallels,"

drical time was different, in that human beings were thought to have lived impossibly long lives.[1]

Akkadian literature offers, in many instances, a subjective evaluation of periods of time.[2] The past was considered especially fit for inquiry, because humankind and human institutions were viewed as products of specific past events. Akkadian literature generally portrays the past as better than the present. Accordingly, the best hope for humankind was to re-create the past.

Intimately connected with this judgment of the past is the notion of destiny, one's past experienced as one's future. Indeed, destiny in Mesopotamian thought and literature tends to take the place of time as found in European literature.[3] Destiny was either an impersonal necessity, such as death, or it was personified as a Fate, seen as willful and capricious, hence something that could be manipulated or avoided. Especially in narrative poetry, destiny is a frequently developed theme, while the passage of time, as understood in modern literature, is used primarily for rhetorical devices.[4]

Examples of such devices include long spans of time correlated with great distance or unusually prolonged suffering, as in the Poem of the Righteous Sufferer (III.14), and short spans of time used to imply heroic achievement, as in III.6 line 23.[5] Characters do not age in Akkadian literature, though they can grow wiser, and their only acknowledgment of biological time is to contrast the rashness of youth with the measured reason of maturity (see An Old Man's Prayer, III.45b).[6]

The Mesopotamian scheme of solar and lunar time affects Akkadian literature. Certain events are peculiar to the night (dreams, visions, watching); others are characteristic of the morning (revelations, action, understanding). Night was the beginning of the day rather than the end of it. The Mesopotamian day and night

CRRAI 28 (1981), 215–224; J. Klein, "The 'Bane of Humanity': A Lifespan of One Hundred Twenty Years," *Acta Sumerologica* 12 (1990), 57–70.

1. Jacobsen, *Journal of Biblical Literature* 100 (1981), 520–521.

2. For mythological time, see Klotchkoff, *Kul'tura* (p. 26 note 1), 25; Otto, "Zeitvorstellungen" (p. 26 note 2), 750. For the past as the usual setting of Akkadian literature, at least in the Classical period, see Kraus, *Mensch*, 133–134.

3. This is the central thesis of Klotchkoff's *Kul'tura* (p. 26 note 1), which I have adopted here in its essentials.

4. F. Rochberg-Halton, "Fate and Divination in Mesopotamia," CRRAI 28 (1981), 363–371; J. N. Lawson, *The Concept of Fate in Ancient Mesopotamia of the First Millennium, Orientalia Biblica et Christiana* 7 (1994).

5. H. Tadmor, "History and Ideology in the Assyrian Royal Inscriptions," OAC 17 (1981), 14–21; *Iraq* 35 (1973), 143.

6. Klotchkoff, *Kul'tura* (p. 26 note 1), 28–30.

were divided into watches composed of "double hours," three of the night and three of the day.[1]

Babylonian thought correlated time and space, in that units of time also served as units of distance, distance being expressed in terms of the time elapsed in making normal progress from one point to another.[2]

Some authors were concerned with the relationship between narrative and event, and so experimented with narrative time. In an interesting passage in Erra and Ishum, event and discourse coexist while Erra narrates in the present certain deeds he is doing (see IV.17).

2. PLACE

The spatial background of Akkadian literature tends to be bare, almost schematic. For example, frequent reference is made to upper and lower worlds, but no further information is given as to precisely what is meant by these terms. In this anthology, the distinction is generally rendered "heaven and netherworld," though others render "heaven and earth." It is often not clear whether earth or netherworld is intended (see III.51). In the realm of human affairs, major divisions of scene are between city (civilization) and steppe (wilderness). With a few exceptions,[3] Akkadian literature presupposes an urban environment. The major Mesopotamian cities were viewed by their denizens as the source and center of civilization. Nippur, for example, according to an ancient metaphor, was the meeting place or linkage between the upper and lower worlds.[4]

Of all the aspects of the Mesopotamian city—political, economic, commercial, and cultic—literature tends to emphasize the city as cult center. Within cities, the scene of action is often vague. The street or market was generally a locus of hostility and threats, the congregating place of the rabble, and, in a persistent motif, the scene of prostitution or rape (see the incantations IV.36a, 44a, 48d; Atrahasis [II.36d] Tablet I line 275).[5] The house was the vulnerable center of family life, sometimes the setting for heights of human happiness or depths of human misery.

---

1.   S. Smith, "Babylonian Time Reckoning," *Iraq* 31 (1969), 74–81; R. K. Englund, "Administrative Timekeeping in Ancient Mesopotamia," JESHO 31 (1988), 121–185.

2.   W. al-Jadir, "The Concept of Time and Space in Ancient Mesopotamia," *Sumer* 31 (1975), 327–343; H. Limet, "La perception de l'espace dans le Proche-Orient du Ier millénaire av. J.-C.," *Transeuphratène* 8 (1994), 95–107.

3.   E. Reiner, "City Bread and Bread Baked in Ashes," *Languages and Areas: Studies Presented to George V. Bobrinskoy* (Chicago, 1967), 116–120.

4.   For the early background of this concept, see W. G. Lambert, BSOAS 1976, 430; T. Jacobsen, JNES 5 (1946), 136–137.

5.   See also Foster, *Studies Pope*, 23, 26–27.

Threats, attacks, or intrusions were most keenly felt at home and were anxiously warded off (see the diviner's prayers II.28; the Poem of the Righteous Sufferer [III.14] Tablet II line 96; the Counsels of Wisdom [III.16a] lines 66, 72–80; the Instructions of Shupe-ameli [III.16b] i line 10).

Outside the relative security of the city, the wilderness was generally seen as the hostile and dangerous abode of wild beasts and lawless men, full of real and potential threats.[1] One traversed it in fear and risk (see To Gods of the Night [II.27a]; the Instructions of Shupe-ameli [III.16b] i line 12; the Shamash Hymn [III.32] lines 135–148). Yet the Sacrificial Gazelle (III.52d) is remarkable for its lyrical portrayal of wild-animal life as symbolic of ritual purity. Texts such as the Shamash Hymn (III.32) use city and wilderness as inclusive contrasts to encompass the whole world.

Mesopotamians believed that the world was flat, disk-shaped, and surrounded by mountains and salt water beyond the edge of the land. Above the sky and below the earth was fresh water.[2] The sun's daily journey took him across the sky and then at night through "innermost heaven."[3] The physical organization of heaven and the netherworld seems to have been visualized in terrestrial terms, though the details vary from source to source. Thus the divine abodes of heaven and hell had gates, courtyards, throne rooms, dining halls, bathing chambers, and so forth. The human denizens of the netherworld lived in darkness and squalor (Descent of Ishtar to the Netherworld [III.19]; The Netherworld Vision of an Assyrian Prince [IV.5]).[4]

The world was divided into a center and four world regions, corresponding to the four cardinal points.[5] The mountains that bordered these regions were portrayed as seats of hostility and bestial human existence, as in the Hunter (III.6). Forests too were threatening in Akkadian literature (see Sargon, King of Battle [II.6a]).

1. A. Haldar, *The Notion of the Desert in Sumero-Accadian and West-Semitic Religions* (Uppsala, 1950).

2. See W. G. Lambert, "The Cosmology of Sumer and Babylon," in C. Blacker and M. Loewe, eds., *Ancient Cosmologies* (London, 1975), 42–65; W. Horowitz, *Mesopotamian Cosmic Geography* (Winona Lake, Ind., 1998).

3. W. Heimpel, "The Sun at Night and the Doors of Heaven in Babylonian Texts," JCS 38 (1986), 127–151.

4. W. G. Lambert, "The Theology of Death," CRRAI 26 (1979), 53–66; esp. 59–60.

5. J.-J. Glassner, "La division quinaire de la terre," *Akkadica* 40 (1984), 17–34; M. Liverani, *Prestige and Interest, International Relations in the Near East ca. 1600–1100 B.C.* (Padua, 1990), 33–65.

The rivers that crossed the world regions were alternately life-giving and destructive, depending on their flood crest. There is no serene reliance on a river as unfailing provider, as is usually the case with the Nile in Egyptian literature.[1]

Like the rivers, the weather was capriciously destructive or beneficial. Winds and storms are frequently terrifying in Akkadian literature, though gentle breezes could be of good omen (To Adad [III.33]; The Poem of the Righteous Sufferer [III.14] Tablet I line 6).

3. SPEECH, ACTION, CLAMOR, SILENCE

The relationship between speech and action in Akkadian narrative offers a fruitful field of inquiry to the critical reader, as it is one aspect of Akkadian literary endeavor that comes through in translation. Akkadian narrative poetry, like other ancient narrative traditions, allots more space to direct speech than to narrative, with emphasis on action rather than description. Direct speech is used to bring about or to explain action, to predict it, or to advance it. Differently from Greek drama, direct speech is seldom used to narrate action beyond the point of view of the audience, Erra and Ishum (IV.17) being a notable exception.

Direct speech is sometimes repeated as narrative. A simple instance is provided by Atrahasis (II.36a) Tablet I, lines 87–90.

> "Nusku, bar your gate,
> "Get your weapons and stand before me."
>   Nusku barred his gate,
>   Got his weapons and stood before Enlil.

Seen in the context of Atrahasis (II.36a) Tablet I lines 43–46, 57–62, 70–77, 80–84, 97–100, the pairing of speech and action in this poem serves many purposes, especially emphasis, as the narrative slows and suspense builds up.

In some examples of Akkadian narrative, speech and action are developed as major motifs. Contrasting use of the two is found in the Epic of Creation (III.17). In the first part of the poem, emphasis is on repetition of speeches within speeches, suggesting the sluggishness of the older gods. As soon as Marduk receives his charge and is off to battle, action is narrated with scarcely a repetition until the end of the poem. After the climactic battle, Marduk ushers in a new era in which his speech is effective and creative. He commands the reordering of the universe, step by step, and the gods proclaim Marduk's explanatory names in the final two tablets of the work, nearly all of which are direct speech.

---

1. T. Jacobsen in H. Frankfort, ed., *Before Philosophy* (Baltimore, 1966), 137–148.

Direct speech is normally indicated in Akkadian literature by the expression *pâ(m) epēšu(m)*, literally, "to make a mouth" (in this anthology "make ready to speak"). This may refer to formation of words or thoughts prior to giving them voice, though the expression is often translated by others "open the mouth" (to speak).[1] When this formulaic expression is absent in narrative, the omission is striking, and suggests the speaker's abruptness or excitement.[2]

As for clamor or noise, Akkadian poetic tradition seems ambivalent as to whether it was good or bad.[3] In Agushaya (II.5), clamor is portrayed in negative terms as a kind of violence that the gods wish to suppress. Noise is antithetic to speech, as in Agushaya (II.5) Tablet I vi lines 16ff., where Enki, in order to speak, has to use four different verbs to invoke silence. One may compare the Epic of Creation (III.17) Tablet I line 36, where the noise of Tiamat drowns out speech. There, as in Agushaya, noise and clamor suggest violence. On the other hand, in Atrahasis (II.36), clamor, characteristic of developing humankind, seems vital and productive, rather than evil or destructive. It is the bustle and vigorous clamor of the human race that Enlil seeks to destroy.

Silence in Akkadian poetry is eerie and frightening. Helpless and terrified, the gods fall silent in the Epic of Creation (III.17) Tablet II line 6, as in the Anzu poem (III.23), when the gods find no recourse against the monstrous bird. Akkadian is rich in words for silence, awe, and fear.[4]

4. VISUAL ASPECTS

One of the most perplexing motifs of Akkadian literature for modern readers is its emphasis on specific visual qualities, variously translated "brilliance," "fearsomeness," "awesomeness," "radiance."[5] Akkadian tradition, apparently borrowing from Sumerian, considers brilliance both visual and tactile. When a person sees

1. See Oppenheim, OrNS 16 (1947), 221 note 2. For a tabulation of Akkadian literary formulae for speaking, see F. Sonnek, "Die Einführung der direkten Rede in der epischen Texten," *ZA* 46 (1940), 225–235; Hecker, *Epik*, 174–176. A literary analysis has been undertaken by M. Vogelzang, "Patterns Introducing Direct Speech in Akkadian Literary Texts," JCS 42 (1990), 50–70.

2. Foster, *Studies Pope*, 24 note 20. For direct quotations without verbs of speaking, sometimes referred to as "virtual speech," see Gordis, *Vetus Testamentum* 31 (1981), 410–427 (biblical evidence) and Hecker, *Epik*, 45–48.

3. For the widely divergent opinions on the significance of "noise" in Mesopotamian literature, see Oppenheim, OrNS 16 (1947), 210 note 3; Pettinato, OrNS 39 (1968), 184–200, with earlier literature cited p. 173; and Michalowski, *Studies Moran*, 385–388.

4. For silence in Mesopotamian tradition, see E. Reiner, "Dead of Night," AS 16 (1965), 247–251.

5. E. Cassin, *La Splendeur divine, Introduction à l'étude de la mentalité mésopotamienne* (Paris, 1968); A. L. Oppenheim, "Akkadian *pul(u)ḫ(t)u* and *melammu*," JAOS 63 (1943), 31–34.

something divine, he shrinks back, shades his eyes, and feels physical discomfort caused by intense illumination. Correlation between this sensation and religious awe means that in Mesopotamian religious expression the numinous is endowed with blinding brilliance, associated not with heat but rather with a gem-like metallic sheen. Akkadian religious poetry is richly laden with this visual imagery, little of which emerges clearly in translation.

In addition to the numinous and physical aspects of brightness, the concept was intimately connected with notions of purity—religious, ritual, or natural.[1] Purity and brightness were interlocking concepts, and the translator has usually to choose one or the other, depending upon which range of associations he wants to suggest. Brightness of visage or complexion was a sign of happiness, good health, and hence well-being and divine favor. Anger or fear was seen as pallor or darkness, both being opposites of brightness (Atrahasis [II.36a] Tablet I line 93; The Descent of Ishtar [III.19] 29; Nergal and Ereshkigal [III.20] iii 22′).[2]

5. KNOWLEDGE

Some Akkadian literature, especially didactic pieces such as the Cuthaean Legend (III.7b), was concerned with human knowledge, how it was acquired and what was worth knowing.[3] According to some literary works, knowledge was gained more through experience and suffering than through study or mastery of an art. Indeed, experts are often portrayed in laments as baffled and helpless (Poem of the Righteous Sufferer [III.14] Tablet I line 52, Tablet II lines 6–7). They are sometimes satirized in humorous texts (The Jester [IV.25], Why Do You Curse Me? [IV.24]). Even in their own devotional expressions, scholars profess, *pro forma* at least, the uncertainties besetting many researchers (For Success in Divination [III.36a], For Help in Haruspicy [III.54a]), and the texts offer no example of a learned man resolving a dilemma. At the same time, Akkadian literature, programmatically perhaps, accorded value only to knowledge that was written down and could thus transcend the self and its narrow circles of kin and colleagues to reach across space and time to the seeker after wisdom.[4]

Literary texts show no agreement on what comprised useful knowledge. Wisdom literature stresses the social, economic, and moral value of being trustworthy, industrious, conciliatory, and self-abnegating (Words of the Wise [III.16], *passim*).

1. M.-J. Seux, "Pureté et impureté. Mésopotamie," *Supplément au Dictionnaire de la Bible* 9, 450–459; E. J. Wilson, *"Holiness" and "Purity" in Mesopotamia*, AOAT 237 (1994).
2. See also G. Dossin, *La paleur d'Enkidou* (Louvain, 1931).
3. Glassner, CANES 3:1815–1823; Foster, *Studies Pope*, 42.
4. Foster, *Studies Pope*, 22; see further p. 44 note 4.

Narrative poetry portrays superior knowledge either as direct apprehension of something remote from common experience, or as insight into questions like how and why the human race and human society came into being; whence human authority; why humans are different from gods (Atrahasis [II.36]). Some texts, such as the Old Babylonian Gilgamesh Epic, suggest that wisdom is acceptance of one's lot. They recommend security, prosperity, good name, and family over adventure.[1] Others suggest that adventure leads to knowledge, and a hero is one whose adventure expands human knowledge regardless of the cost to himself.[2]

Adapa (III.21) and Atrahasis (II.36) imply the existence of god-given knowledge beyond the knowledge attainable through human experience. Such knowledge was communicated directly by a great god, typically the god of wisdom, and its possession gave power to achieve immortality, or the next best: understanding of divine intents. Through judicious use of such knowledge, Atrahasis succeeds; for failing to grasp the full implications of his knowledge, Adapa fails. Knowledge apprehended through divine intervention is the subject of the Epic of Creation (III.17) and Erra and Ishum (IV.17). Incantations routinely attribute their wording and procedure not to the ministrant but to gods of wisdom or exorcism, thereby claiming to be a kind of divine knowledge.

6. DIVINE IMAGES

Many Akkadian literary works invoke or refer to Mesopotamian cult images, that is, statues of deities. The reader will need to understand the centrality of these images in Mesopotamian religion.[3]

Throughout the period covered by this anthology, the cult image was the most important symbol of the urban or national community. The major gods were, so far as known, represented in anthropomorphic or zoomorphic composite form. The statues dwelt in their temple homes and were fed, entertained, and presented with petitions. They held court, went in procession, decided lawsuits, and exer-

---

1. Foster, *Gilgamesh*, 75.
2. See below, Chapter II, Introduction, and p. 81 note 2.
3. A. Spycket, *Les Statues de culte dans les textes mésopotamiens des origines à la Ire dynastie de Babylone* (Paris, 1968); W. W. Hallo, "Cult Statue and Divine Image: A Preliminary Study," in W. W. Hallo et al., eds., *Scripture in Context* II (Winona Lake, Ind., 1983), 1–17; J. Renger and U. Seidl, "Kultbild," RLA 6, 307–319; M. B. Dick, "The Relationship between the Cult Image and the Deity in Mesopotamia," CRRAI 43 (1998), 111–116; A. Berlejung, *Die Theologie der Bilder. Herstellung und Einweihung von Kultbildern in Mesopotamien und die alttestamentliche Bilderpolemik, Orbis Biblicus et Orientalis* 162 (1998). Further bibliography will be found in V. Hurowitz, "The Mesopotamian God-Image, From Womb to Tomb," JAOS 123 (2003), 147–157.

cised on the divine plane all the functions one associates with temporal human rulers.[1]

Each major god had but one cult statue and was considered localized in it. Despoliation of an image or its removal from a sanctuary was more than a symbolic disaster; it signified loss of the central cultic focus of the community and opened a way for attack. The importance and centrality of this belief in Akkadian literature is apparent in Agum-kakrime and the Return of Marduk (III.9), Kudur-Nahhunte of Elam (III.11), and Nebuchadnezzar I (III.12). Some of these are concerned with the plundering of the Marduk sanctuary in Babylon by the Elamites during the eleventh century B.C., told from the point of view of the Babylonians (Nebuchadnezzar and Marduk, III.12d) or Marduk himself (Marduk Prophecy, III.13).

Erra and Ishum (IV.17) describes refurbishment of Marduk's statue. This was a time of crisis, as the author saw it, when the community was vulnerable to threats of all kinds, because Marduk had temporarily ceased carrying out his divine responsibilities. The Love Lyrics of Nanay and Muati (II.17) celebrate installation of an image; Agum-kakrime and the Return of Marduk (III.9) commemorates refurbishment of the statue of Marduk and his consort. Letters were addressed to cult images and were left before them for perusal (see Kussulu to the Moon-God [II.29] and II.30, 32).

7. DEMONIC BEINGS

Few cultures are so rich in demonic lore as the Mesopotamian. Demons pervaded Mesopotamian religious and artistic expression and formed a counterpart world both to the human race and to the gods.[2] Unlike gods or human beings, demons were classed generically and did not bear personal names. Each class of demon, such as Lamashtu (I.7a, II.21, IV.42), had its own arenas of activity. These included disease, domestic misfortune, death, anything affecting the individual (rather than the community as a whole), regardless of age, sex, or place in society. Demons could be male or female, and often came in battalions, each setting upon a separate part of the body or a particular activity, need, or power. The way was opened for them by witchcraft or by a person's own god forsaking him and failing to act. Demons were visualized as creeping through apertures into a person's house to

---

1. Oppenheim, *Ancient Mesopotamia*, 183–198.
2. See V. Haas, *Magie und Mythen in Babylonien* (Gifkendorf, 1986); "Die Dämonisierung des Fremden und des Feindes im alten Orient," RO 41 (1980), 37–49. In general see A. Farkas *et al.*, eds., *Monsters and Demons in the Ancient and Medieval Worlds, Papers Presented in Honor of Edith Porada* (Mainz, 1987) and K. van der Toorn, *Dictionary of Deities and Demons in the Bible* (Leiden, 1995).

snatch, smash, or murder. They would lie in wait in alleys or desolate spots and seize, twist, numb, or weigh their victim down in order to incapacitate his bodily or mental powers (see the incantations II.21, 22; IV.36c, 42).

Physicians and exorcists tried to ease suffering by using incantations, medical treatments, and sympathetic magic. Examples of the incantations used to such ends are found in II.20–25 and IV.34–49. Their accompanying magical and medical lore belong to the realm of Mesopotamian expository scholarship.[1] The most vivid of the incantations portray movingly the anxiety felt by the threatened person. Numerous texts seek to prevent and redress the actions of hostile demonic powers, some clearly defined, others less specific. These texts offer insights into Mesopotamian psychology and medicine.[2]

Since illness was thought to be caused by demons, it was considered symptomatic of divine disfavor. Demons peopled the Mesopotamian world in great number, and their baleful presence is felt throughout Akkadian literature.

8. PERSONAL DEITY AND GOOD FORTUNE

For most people, the great deities of the Mesopotamian urban sanctuaries seemed as remote as kings. Hence, the individual looked to a personal deity, usually referred to simply by the generic terms "god" or "goddess," who was responsible for the person's success and well-being.[3] Disaster awaited a person forsaken by his individual divine protector, for he was liable to any harm that divine, human, or demonic will could inflict upon him. Religious and penitential literature are rife with address to the personal deity, in terms sometimes pathetic, sometimes reproving, seeking to placate or shame the god or goddess into alleviating some misfortune (see To a Personal God [III.49], compare II.13). The suppliant promises in return for help to praise the deity's name and to glorify his greatness.

---

1. For discussion of Mesopotamian medical practice, see E. K. Ritter, "Magical-Expert (=*āšipu*) and Physician (=*asû*): Notes on Two Complementary Professions in Babylonian Medicine," AS 16 (1965), 299 321; R. D. Biggs, "Medicine in Ancient Mesopotamia," *History of Science* 8 (1969), 94–105; "Medezin," RLA 7, 623–629; J. Scurlock, "Physician, Exorcist, Conjurer, Magician: A Tale of Two Healing Professionals," in Abusch, ed., *Magic*, 69–79. See also p. 773 note 8.

2. J. V. Kinnier-Wilson, "An Introduction to Babylonian Psychiatry," AS 16 (1965), 289–298; M. Stol, "Psychosomatic Suffering in Ancient Mesopotamia," in Abusch, ed., *Magic*, 57–68; and p. 774 note 7. For observations on pharmacology, see H. Limet, "Croyances, superstitions et débuts de la science en Mésopotamie ancienne," *Oikumene* 5 (1986), 67–90.

3. T. Jacobsen, *The Treasures of Darkness* (New Haven, 1976), 155–160; R. DiVito, *Studies in Akkadian Personal Names, The Designation and Conception of the Personal God, Studia Pohl Series Maior* 16 (1993), 2–17.

A more intimate benefactor was a person's genius. This bestowed the qualities now referred to as talents or gifts.[1] The genius's protective counterpart was the guardian spirit, now referred to as instinct and self-preservation, which enhanced a person's capacity to avoid harm.[2] Outward signs of genius and guardianship included prosperity, high office, economic success, a large family, respect in public thoroughfares, government buildings, or assembly places of the worthy, a circle of admiring friends and colleagues, robust health, radiance of countenance (see above, E.4), and authoritative presence. Loss of such attributes implied either insufficient wardenship by one's divine protector or some external cause: black magic, a sin of omission or commission, or divine disfavor (compare the Poem of the Righteous Sufferer [III.14] Tablet I lines 43ff., 79ff.).

9. DIVINATION

Divination was the central intellectual discipline and most highly esteemed branch of Mesopotamian academic achievement during the period covered by this anthology.[3] Its status in Mesopotamian thinking was comparable to that of scholarship or science in our own. Divination comprised a body of knowledge, as well as techniques for gaining access to this knowledge, applying it, and increasing it.

Many divinatory techniques were based on systematic observation and recording of the environment. The method involved first listing observed phenomena, then pairing what was observed with prognoses in the form "If x (is observed), y (is the consequence or implication)." Observations were made of astronomical and atmospherical phenomena, as well as everyday events in the home or street, such as the scuffling of a gecko or the location of a potsherd in a ditch. They could also include characteristics and behavior of people or animals. Data gained by observation were expanded by analogic and associative reasoning. To the diviner, all the world was his purview, and divination the one universal science.[4]

Other divinatory techniques were based on eliciting phenomena useful to the diviner. Most often referred to in the texts translated here is haruspicy, divination by examining the liver and inner organs of sacrificed animals, especially sheep and

---

1. Oppenheim, *Ancient Mesopotamia*, 198–206.
2. W. von Soden, "Die Schutzgenien Lamassu und Schedu in der babylonisch-assyrischen Literatur," *Baghdader Mitteilungen* 3 (1964), 148–156; B. Groneberg, "Eine Einführungsszene in der altbabylonischen Literatur: Bemerkungen zum persönlichen Gott," CRRAI 32 (1985), 93–108, with extensive bibliography; R. Albertz, *Persönliche Frömmigkeit und offizielle Religion: religionsinterner Plurismus in Israel und Babylon* (Stuttgart, 1978).
3. See p. 772 note 2.
4. Bottéro, "Symptomes," 99–111.

goats.[1] Owing to the expense involved, sacrificial divination was for the wealthy, and the prognoses often pertained to affairs of state or matters of interest to the highly placed. Other forms of divination, such as pouring oil upon water to observe its configurations, occasionally occur in literature (see Agum-kakrime and the Return of Marduk [III.9]).[2] The prayers offered by sacrificial diviners while they waited for the gods to implant the message in the exta became a distinct genre (see the diviners' prayers II.27, III.36a, 54a). Literary texts sometimes show consultation with diviners as recourse for the perplexed or as a meritorious proceeding (Cuthaean Legend of Naram-Sin [III.7b 3]).

F. FORMATION OF AKKADIAN LITERATURE

1. CATEGORIES

Five broad categories of Akkadian literature are recognized here: celebratory, didactic, narrative, effective, and expressive. These do not necessarily correspond to ancient classifications, about which little is known. Some texts may belong to more than one category.

Celebratory refers to two main groups of texts in Akkadian, one dealing with the human sphere, the other with the divine. Texts referring to human affairs can be commemorative in origin and form. Many of these perpetuate the memory of a royal personage and some specific deed he did. Such texts tend to favor prose over poetry. They give the royal name, titulary, information pertaining to a king's parentage or ancestry, or, if that information is not given, why he is the legitimate king; an account of some deed, either in the first or third person; and a concluding statement, often with reference to some monument with which the text is associated. Texts of this type are the principal source of historical information about ancient Mesopotamia. Many of these are available elsewhere in English translation, so only a few are included here.[3]

Texts that exemplify interaction between commemorative and literary composition include the legends of Naram-Sin (II.7, III.7b). These legends may have their origin in historical tradition and inscriptions, but soon acquired legendary and exemplary qualities. For example, during his lifetime Naram-Sin was personifica-

---

1. Bottéro, "Symptomes," 111–118.
2. G. Pettinato, *Die Ölwahrsagung bei den Babyloniern, Studi Semitici* 21–22 (Rome, 1966).
3. For comprehensive collections in English, see Grayson, ARI; J. Cooper, *Sumerian and Akkadian Royal Inscriptions* (New Haven, 1986); and the publications of the Royal Inscriptions of Mesopotamia project (Toronto).

tion of the great warrior king, but after his death he was regarded in Akkadian literature as archetype of the hapless sovereign caught up in cosmic events too large for his ken or control.[1]

Other such compositions deal with the fall of the Kassite dynasty and the period of Elamite domination in Babylonia, toward the end of the second millennium B.C. (III.11). Still others may refer to a period of Babylonian national revival under Nebuchadnezzar I (see Nebuchadnezzar I [III.12]; the Marduk Prophecy [III.13] and the Epic of Creation [III.17] may belong here). The selections translated here include an actual commemorative text (Nebuchadnezzar in Elam [III.12c]) and literary pieces dealing with the same theme (The War with Elam [III.12b]).

Some apparently commemorative texts are in fact pseudonymous or fictional autobiographies. These are narratives in which a famous ruler from the remote past reflects upon certain critical events of his life. Texts of this type often end with blessings, admonitions, or pseudo-prophecies for the benefit of future generations.[2] Examples of this genre include The Cuthaean Legend of Naram-Sin (III.7b), the Shulgi Prophecy (III.8), the Marduk Prophecy (III.13), and the Birth Legend of Sargon of Akkad (IV.18).

Whereas hymns in honor of kings are a genre well known in Sumerian,[3] they are not so well attested in Akkadian, although many hymns and prayers contain blessings or a petition on behalf of the reigning sovereign (Hymn to Ishtar [II.1], Acrostic Hymn to Marduk [IV.4d]).

Texts dealing with divine deeds include hymns that glorify signs of the divine nature and, in some instances, refer to specific deeds. Though these latter passages often possess narrative character (for example, Agushaya [II.5]), hymnic texts typically begin and end with an invocation of praise, while strictly narrative texts tend to begin with an expression of time or an invocation of the subject.[4]

For the most part, the texts called here hymns or prayers[5] share formal features of both modern genres. Hymns tend to be lyrical expression of praise, together with pleas for general well-being. Prayers tend to be petitions for personal well-being. Hymns of the Classical period favor self-contained lines, in which typically

---

1. J.-J. Glassner, *La Chute d'Agadé, l'événement et sa mémoire*, Berliner Beiträge zum Vorderen Orient 5 (Berlin, 1986), 77–85.

2. H. Galter, "Probleme historischen-lehrhaften Dichtung in Mesopotamien," CRRAI 32 (1985), 71–79; T. Longman, *Fictional Akkadian Royal Autobiographies* (Winona Lake, Ind., 1991).

3. C. Wilcke, "Hymnen B," RLA 4, 539–544.

4. C. Wilcke, "Die Anfänge der akkadischen Epen," ZA 67 (1977), 153–216.

5. W. von Soden, "Hymnen A," RLA 4, 544–548; J. Klíma, "À propos des éléments profanes dans les hymnes et prières mésopotamiens," ArOr 48 (1980), 240–248.

the god being praised is the subject. By contrast, hymns of the Mature and Late periods often contain long series of dependent clauses defining the god's attributes.

Great or literary hymns and prayers (see III.25–32) can be two hundred or more lines in length. These appear in some instances to use material from different sources and periods (Ishtar Queen of Heaven [III.26], Shamash Hymn [III.32]).

Syncretic hymns form a distinctive subgroup (Syncretic Hymn to Marduk [III.44g]). These are hymns that consider separate deities as aspects of the same deity. Some hymns explain divine names in hermeneutic fashion (The Names of Nabu [III.45e], To Marduk Against Illness [III.44b]). Others honor temples (In Praise of Ezida [IV.15]) and cities (In Praise of Babylon [IV.16], In Praise of Arbela [IV.6]). Characteristic of the Mature and Late periods are hymns using acrostics in which the first and occasionally the last signs of lines convey an independent message (Compound Acrostic Prayer to Nabu [III.45d], Acrostic Hymn to Marduk [IV.4d], Acrostic Hymn to Nabu [IV.8k]).

Prayers[1] have a greater variety of forms and uses than hymns. Prayers may be part of commemorative inscriptions (for example, IV.7–11). Personal names of all periods are often prayers in miniature, such as "Shamash-Save-Me" or "Let-Me-Behold-the-Ebabbar-Temple."[2] Unlike hymns, prayers need not be metrical, though they may be drafted in a differentiated prose style similar to that of poetry. Prayers in everyday language could be written out as petitions presumably placed in front of a divine statue or read to the god by a statue of the suppliant (II.32).[3]

Prayers of diviners are well known from the Classical period on (II.27–28; III.36a, 41b, 52, 53a, etc.). These ask for a clear oracle, for assistance in interpreting it, and occasionally for professional competence and public respect. Some reflect on the silence of night, as the diviner waits to perform his extispicy (To Gods of the Night [II.27, III.41]); others celebrate in sentimental terms the birth and upbringing of the sacrificial beast (The Sacrificial Gazelle [III.52d], The Sacrificial Lamb [III.52e]). Some prayers occur in rituals as appropriate for a specific point in the proceedings (see To Girra [III.40], To Nusku [III.48]). Others were organized into collections dealing with similar themes (To a Personal God [III.49]).

Laments and complaints are less well known in Akkadian than in Sumerian. Indeed, some Akkadian laments may be based on Sumerian prototypes (Lament for a City [II.15]; see also Lament for Tammuz [IV.30]). Most Akkadian examples

---

1. W. von Soden, "Gebet II," RLA 3, 160–170.
2. J. J. Stamm, *Die Akkadische Namengebung*, MVAeG 44 (1934), 170, 85.
3. W. W. Hallo, "Individual Prayer in Sumerian: The Continuity of a Tradition," JAOS 88 (1968), 71–89; "Letters, Prayers and Letter-Prayers," *Proceedings of the Seventh World Congress of Jewish Studies, Studies in the Bible and the Ancient Near East* (Jerusalem, 1981), 17–27.

deal with suffering of an individual, sometimes in narrative form as if a priest is speaking on behalf of the sufferer (Dialogue between a Man and His God [II.13]). In others, the sufferer speaks for himself (Literary Prayer to Ishtar [III.28]).

A distinct genre known as *šu-illa*, "lifting of the hand," is called the incantation prayer because it unites prayerful appeal with the direct efficacy of a spell (III.33, 34, 35, 36b, 37b, c, etc.).[1] These compositions are addressed to a wide range of deities and often enumerate specific evils that the text is supposed to ward off, including the evil portended by such diverse events as a solar eclipse and an infestation of red ants.

Incantation prayers typically open with an invocation and praise of the divinity, often with a long series of attributive clauses. There follows a self-presentation of the speaker, wherein he may state his name and parentage. He then turns to his lament, describing first his unhappiness in general terms, then detailing his specific distress, such as estrangement from his personal deity, his fear of evil omens, social rejection, or victimization by witchcraft. He then acknowledges sins known or not, intentional or not, and pleads for forgiveness. In many such prayers, the petitioner refers to expiatory actions: seeking out the deity, making or offering a present, or following some magical or medical procedure. The speaker then turns to his prayer, asking for mercy, blessing, intercession, reconciliation, clearance of sin, rehabilitation, averting of the consequences of evil omens, good fortune, long life, and health. Incantation prayers conclude with a promise to praise the god in return for his actions; in some cases other people and gods are said to join in the thanks.

Royal prayers are best known from the second half of the first millennium, from both Babylonia and Assyria. From Assyria come, for example, the short building prayers commissioned by Sargon II for his new capital city at Dur-Sharrukin (IV.2a). Prayers in the name of Assurbanipal may reflect his scholarly interests in that they allude to literary works such as the Epic of Creation or are written in a pompous, pedantic style (see IV.4). From Babylonia come prayers in the name of Nabopolassar, Nebuchadnezzar II, Neriglissar, and Nabonidus (IV.7, 8, 10) that typically formed part of commemorative building inscriptions. These usually request durability and well-being for the structure concerned, and long life and reign for the ruler and his progeny. Other royal prayers are scattered through the vast corpus of inscriptions. Particular mention should be made of the earlier Assyrian royal prayers, for example those of Assurnasirpal to Ishtar of Nineveh and Arbela, and the bilingual psalm of Tukulti-Ninurta I (III.4, 2).

---

1. Mayer, UFBG; E. Dalglish, *Psalm Fifty-one* (Leiden, 1962), 41–51; Butler, AOAT 258 (1998), 130.

Other prayers on behalf of the king, particularly of the incantation prayer type, were incorporated into ritual series such as "The House of the Ritual Bath" (Bit Rimki) and "The House of the Ritual Enclosure" (Bit Meseri). A group of these incantation prayers to Shamash, the sun-god, is best known (III.51h–l).

While some readers may find perusal of Mesopotamian hymns and prayers tedious, there is in fact no better way to approach Mesopotamian spiritual expression.[1] Each text chosen here offers some individual point of interest or is representative of a type. The wealth of material has made selection difficult. For additional hymns and prayers in translation, the interested reader is referred to more specialized anthologies.[2]

Didactic literature seeks to convey a lesson or significant experience in order to admonish the reader and give him an opportunity to benefit from what he reads.[3] The teaching can be in the form of narrative, exhortation, or proverbial sayings (Words of the Wise [III.16]). Didactic texts usually focus on practical teaching and advice for a successful life, and were directed to all classes of society. Some offer advice to kings or rulers (Cuthaean Legend of Naram-Sin [III.7b iii], Advice to a Prince [IV.13]), others to common folk (Counsels of Wisdom [III.16a]). Didactic literature is concerned with human affairs, either in the interests of social advancement or of gaining divine favor through proper conduct. Didactic compositions tend to be short and simple, without experimentation in form or medium. Typical cachets include a sage old man offering advice to a youth (Instructions of Shupeameli [III.16b]), or the survivor of a trying experience relating what befell him for the admonition of others (Cuthaean Legend of Naram-Sin [III.7b 3]).

An important subgroup of Akkadian didactic literary texts deals with the question of divine justice.[4] Why do apparently righteous people suffer while obviously

---

1. T. Abusch, "The Form and Meaning of a Babylonian Prayer to Marduk," JAOS 103 (1983), 3.
2. Seux, *Hymnes*; von Soden, SAHG.
3. For discussion of "wisdom" in ancient Mesopotamian tradition, see Lambert, BWL, 1–2; E. A. Speiser, *Oriental and Biblical Studies* (Philadelphia, 1967), 305–312; Gordon, BiOr 17 (1960), 123; J. J. A. van Dijk, *La Sagesse suméro-accadienne, recherches sur les genres littéraires des textes sapientaux avec choix de textes* (Leiden, 1953); R. F. G. Sweet, "The Sage in Akkadian Literature: A Philological Study," in J. G. Gammie and L. G. Perdue, eds., *The Sage in Israel and the Ancient Near East* (Winona Lake, Ind., 1990), 45–65; C. Wilcke, "Göttliche und menschliche Weisheit im alten Orient," in A. Assmann, ed., *Weisheit* (Munich, 1991), 259–270.
4. W. von Soden, "Das Fragen nach der Gerechtigkeit Gottes im alten Orient," MDOG 96 (1965), 41–59; J. Bottéro, "Le Problème du Mal en Mésopotamie ancienne, *Prologue à une étude du 'Juste Souffrant'*," *Recherches et Documents du Centre Thomas More* no. 15 (1977), 1–43; Sitzler, *Vorwurf*; H. Spieckermann, "*Ludlul bēl nēmeqi* und die Frage nach der Gerechtigkeit Gottes," *Studies Borger*, 329–341.

evil ones prosper? Perhaps the most elaborate example of this type is the Poem of the Righteous Sufferer (III.14). This suggests that divine justice metes out both reward and punishment, and that rescue from seemingly undeserved suffering is itself a sign of divine power. The Theodicy (IV.19) treats the question in dialogue form; a sufferer and a friend debate with courtesy and passion, the friend taking the position that the sufferer must have sinned somehow, for none can know what the gods require. The Dialogue between a Man and His God (II.13) may belong to this genre insofar as it deals with suffering and redemption, though there is no indication that the sufferer presumes himself sinless (see also A Sufferer's Salvation [III.15]). Of course, the problem is raised in other texts such as prayers (Who Has Not Sinned? [III.49d]).

There are also proverbs, sayings, and short compositions of moral and rhetorical character that seek to entertain and educate at the same time. Most of these are Sumerian, often with an Akkadian translation. Native Akkadian proverbs are less well known today because they were not studied and copied in Babylonian and Assyrian schools, as were Sumerian proverbs. Most of the examples of native Akkadian proverbs given here are taken from letters (III.16e).

Narrative literature tells a story about gods or people. Unlike didactic texts, narratives can be of considerable length, owing especially to repetition and parallelism. Narrative tends to favor poetry over prose. The purpose of the narrative is sometimes stated, sometimes left to the reader to ascertain. If commemorative texts stress remembrance and didactic texts practical action, narrative texts are intended to deepen knowledge (see above, E.5).

Narrative texts about gods include divine exaltation (Epic of Creation [III.17]) and mythological stories such as the Descent of Ishtar to the Netherworld (III.19) and Nergal and Ereshkigal (III.20). Others tell of heroic divine deeds (Anzu [III.23], Monster Serpents [III.24]), including Creation of the World (III.18). Others show interactions of gods with people (Adapa [III.21], Etana [III.22]). Some mythological tales were transmitted as portions of rituals or incantations (Adapa Story [III.21], Against a Mote in the Eye [II.23d], Against Toothache [IV.48]). While stories of the gods are now normally read as mythological texts, it is not always clear whether they were primarily mythological in purpose or whether they were simply narrative strategies for authors in a culture that assigned little literary value to the present and empirically recognizable.

Narrative texts focused on human affairs include the legends of ancient kings (II.6, 7; III.7) and the Assyrian royal epics (III.1). The latter are lengthy, often bombastic celebrations of the valor and justice of the Assyrian kings in warfare, of which the best preserved (III.1) deals with a war against Babylonia. The Babylonian equivalent is the group of texts centering around Nebuchadnezzar I (III.12) and the Babylonian royal epics of the Mature and Late periods.[1] These are both commemorative and justificatory in character.

In *effective literature*, the text itself brings about a consequence. This is different from a petition or prayer, in which the goal of the petition is stated and a particular deity importuned to act on behalf of the petitioner. In contrast, effective literature comprises magical language (incantations or spells) that in and of their own power might cause the desired result.[2] The difference between a prayer and an incantation is often difficult to see, as many texts, especially of the Mature and Late periods, show characteristics of both.[3]

Incantations often apostrophize evil, conjuring it with threats and blandishments, or sometimes ask a deity's help against it, in the manner of a prayer. Incantations sometimes include what has been called the "cosmological motif,"[4] wherein a brief narrative traces the cosmic origins of the evil to be exorcized (Against Toothache [IV.48], Against a Mote in the Eye [II.23d, IV.33d]). This may be a means of fixing upon the evil. Incantations are often allusive and associative, such that the thought patterns may not be readily apparent to the modern reader. Sound may be as important as sense; indeed, some incantations include "abracadabra" passages that may either be gibberish or, in some cases, survivals of unidentified languages (see Against "Redness" [IV.45]).[5] The figurative language used in incantations tends to be of the simple patterns familiar today from nursery rhymes and children's songs.[6] They include, nevertheless, some of the finest poetic passages in Akkadian, for incantations were less pervaded by clichés than other genres.

Expressive literature refers to texts that seek to convey a mood or scene. Whereas narrative works tell a story, expressive texts elicit a reaction to or judgment upon a story, situation, or formal proposition. Expressive texts can be read as humorous, satirical, sad, cynical, or loving, however the reader gauges the author's intent. In this group, emotional reaction, rather than knowledge or commemoration, seems

---

1. Grayson, BHLT, 56–92. For a fragment of a Kassite royal epic, see Grayson, BHLT, 47–55.
2. E. Reiner, in *Le Monde du Sorcier* (Paris, 1966), 69–98.
3. See Mayer, UFBG, 7–13. For Sumerian, see M. E. Cohen, "The Incantation Hymn: Incantation or Hymn?" JAOS 95 (1975), 592–611.
4. J. J. A. van Dijk, "Le motif cosmique dans la pensée sumérienne," *Acta Orientalia* 28 (1964), 1–59; J. Bottéro, "Les textes cosmogoniques mineures en langue akkadienne," *Mythes*, 279–328.
5. Van Dijk, YOS 11, 3–4; CRRAI 25 (1978), 97–110; Cunningham, *'Deliver Me from Evil'*, 156–159.
6. Reiner, *Poetry*, 94–100; N. Veldhuis, "The Poetry of Magic," in Abusch, ed., *Magic*, 35–48.

the purpose. Examples include At the Cleaners (II.14), The Faithful Lover (II.16), The Gilgamesh Letter (IV.58), Why Do You Curse Me? (IV.24), The Dog's Boast (IV.22), The Dialogue of Pessimism (IV.20).

A special sub-group of expressive literature is compositions about love and love-making, both of deities and human beings (II.17–19; III.60; IV.27, 28).[1]

In addition to poetry and prose, mostly in the past and first person, dialogues and debates were a favored form in Mesopotamian literature. The preserved examples have only two parties presenting points of view (see IV.19–22).[2]

2. AKKADIAN AND SUMERIAN

In the development of Akkadian literature, the interdependence of Sumerian and Akkadian was recognized and esteemed by the Mesopotamians themselves. Some Akkadian literary works are imitations, reworkings, or translations of Sumerian prototypes (Lament for a City [II.15], Gilgamesh Tablet XII).[3] Others are based on Sumerian literary forms (Agushaya [II.5]). A rich bilingual tradition consists of numerous Sumerian texts with Akkadian translations, not always close to the Sumerian, normally in interlinear versions. Some instances, such as the bilingual Psalm of Tukulti-Ninurta (III.2) and the Seed of Kingship (III.12a), may be simultaneous composition in the two languages, such that the Akkadian is not a translation but the substrate language for the Sumerian. In others, the Sumerian is influenced by the Akkadian translation, so the distinction between source text and translation becomes blurred. Sumerian cultural tradition also influenced Akkadian literature in ways less easily definable: style, tone, subject matter. The two traditions are so closely connected that one can speak of a hybrid Sumero-Akkadian literary culture, even in the Late period.[4]

---

1. M. Nissinen, "Akkadian Rituals and Poetry of Divine Love," *Melammu Symposia* 2 (1999), 93–136.

2. G. J. Reinink, H. L. J. Vanstiphout, *Dispute Poems and Dialogues in the Ancient and Medieval Near East, Forms and Types of Literary Debates in Semitic Related Literatures*, OLA 42 (1991); "The Mesopotamian Debate Poems: A General Presentation," ASJ 12 (1990), 271–318 (see 276–278); ASJ 14 (1992), 339–367; for a general study of Akkadian debates and dialogues, see Ponchia, *Dialoghi*.

3. In general, see Hecker, *Epik*, 187–194; G. Komoróczy, "Akkadian Epic Poetry and Its Sumerian Sources," AASH 23 (1975), 41–63; W. von Soden, *Zweisprachigkeit in der geistigen Kultur Babyloniens*, Österreichische Akad. der Wissen., Phil.-hist. Klasse, Sitzungsberichte 235/1 (1960); *Sprache, Denken und Begriffsbildung im alten Orient*, Akademie der Wissenschaften und der Literatur, Mainz, *Abhandlungen der Geistes- und Sozialwissenschaftlichen Klasse* 1973 No. 6.

4. W. Hallo, "Bilingualism and the Beginnings of Translation," in M. Fox et al., ed., *Texts, Temples, and Traditions, A Tribute to Menahem Haran* (Winona Lake, Ind., 1996), 345–358; M. Civil, "Bilingual Teaching," *Studies Borger*, 1–7; S. Seminara, *La versione accadica del Lugal-e, La tecnica*

3. ORAL TRADITION

There is no concrete indication in Akkadian literary or other texts that an independent oral literature existed, though some scholars believe that oral tradition was important in the formation of Akkadian literature.[1] No "teller of tales" is mentioned in written Akkadian tradition; in fact, little in Akkadian literature compels reconstructing an oral phase or tradition behind it. There were surely popular traditions that were written down less frequently than more formal literature, if at all. Faced with a dearth of evidence, one can say little about the influence of oral tradition on Akkadian literature.[2]

4. WHAT IS AKKADIAN LITERATURE?

Like any other anthology, *Before the Muses* is a modern, personal selection from a large body of writing. Creation of such an anthology raises two important questions. First, can one properly speak of Akkadian literature as a definable group of texts, and if so, what is meant by this concept? Here no simple answer is possible. If, for example, one defines literature as writing published for the entertainment of a reading public and the support of its author, little in Akkadian could be so considered, for there is no indication of the existence of a reading public or of authors who made their living by writing. But if one deems literature to be writing of artful form, content, and expression, then there is much Akkadian literature, with nearly all the works in this book examples of it. In this sense, Akkadian may be said to have a rich and voluminous literature.[3]

babilonese della traduzione dal sumerico e le sue 'regole', Materiali per il Vocabulario Neosumerico 8 (2001), 509–557; H. Vanstiphout, "The Twin Tongues, Theory, Technique and Practice of Bilingualism in Ancient Mesopotamia," in H. Vanstiphout, ed., *All Those Nations … Cultural Encounters within the Ancient Near East, Studies Presented to Han Drijvers at the Occasion of His Sixty-fifth Birthday by Colleagues and Students* (Groningen, 1999), 141–159. For the question of translation versus interpretation, see S. Maul, "Küchensumerisch oder hohe Kunst der Exegese? Überlegen zur Betwertung akkadischer Interlinienübersetzungen von Emesal-Texten," AOAT 247 (1997), 256–267.
    1. For a survey of the problem and remarks on the social context of oral tradition in ancient Mesopotamia, see M. Liverani, "Le Tradizioni orali delle fonti scritte nell'antico oriente," in B. Bernardi *et al.*, eds., *Fonti Orali: Antropologia e Storia* (Milan, 1978), 397–406; J. Laessøe, "Literacy and Oral Tradition in Ancient Mesopotamia," *Studia Orientalia Ioanni Pedersen septuagenario … dicata* (Copenhagen, 1953), 205–218; V. K. Afanasieva, "Mündlich überlieferte Dichtung ("Oral Poetry") und schriftliche Literatur in Mesopotamien," AASH 22 (1974), 121–135; Rochberg-Halton, JCS 36 (1984), 130; and M. E. Vogelzang and H. L. J. Vanstiphout, eds., *Mesopotamian Epic Literature, Oral or Aural?* (Lewiston, N.Y., 1992), with extensive bibliography.
    2. W. Röllig, "Volksliteratur in mesopotamischer Überlieferung," CRRAI 32 (1985), 81–87; J. Black, "Babylonian Ballads," JAOS 103 (1983), 25–34.
    3. P. Michalowski, "Sailing to Babylon: Reading the Dark Side of the Moon," in Cooper,

The second question is why the works in this anthology were copied by Mesopotamian scribes, that is, what role did Akkadian literature play in its own cultural environment? In answer to this, it is important to note that many of the texts treated here may have survived not because they were transmitted over many generations as independent works of literature admired for their own sake, but because they formed part of a cluster of cultural concerns that need not, from a modern point of view, be literary in nature. For example, the Epic of Creation (III.17) is known to have been recited at the Late Babylonian New Year's festival, and the Adapa Story (III.21a) is preserved in a text dealing with dental treatment. Neither context may have been anticipated or intended by the original authors.

In the formation of a corpus of written tradition, the process of transmission itself acts as a determining factor in the survival of texts. In Mesopotamia, survival of a text normally depended upon decisions by successive generations of scholars to recopy it. Most works of the Classical period are known from only one manuscript, though Mature and Late works typically exist in several exemplars. Does this mean that there was a greater fluidity of tradition in the Classical period, whereas by the Mature and Late periods a standard corpus had been established?[1] Or is this only an indication of how few manuscripts of the Classical period have survived? Certain texts, such as Erra and Ishum, enjoyed wide popularity and distribution even though they were composed at a relatively late date, so the standard corpus remained open to inclusion of new works.

Accordingly, understanding of what Mesopotamians considered literature may be furthered by considering reasons behind scribal decisions to copy and preserve texts. One fruitful line of inquiry has been study of how texts were altered as they were recopied, what elements were added, deleted, expanded, simplified, or left intact.[2] Another avenue has been to identify universals of content, language, and form.

With respect to content, many texts were recopied that dealt with the human condition, as it was perceived or how it came to be; others were tradited that told stories about the gods. Heroic (royal) and epic (divine) elements were favored, as

Schwartz, eds., *The Study of the Ancient Near East* (p. 19 note 3), 177–193; B. Groneberg, "Towards a Definition of Literariness as Applied to Akkadian Literature," in Vogelzang, Vanstiphout, eds., *Mesopotamian Poetic Language*, 59–84; B. Pongratz-Leisten, "Öffne den Tafelbehälter und lies ...," Neue Ansätze zum Verständnis des Literaturkonzepts in Mesopotamien," WdO (1999), 69–90.

1. For the concept of a standard corpus, referred to as "canonization" in Assyriology, see p. 295 and note 2.

2. See J. Cooper, "Gilgamesh Dreams of Enkidu: The Expansion and Dilution of Narrative," *Studies Finkelstein*, 39–44; "Symmetry and Repetition in Akkadian Narrative," JAOS 97 (1977), 508–512; J. Tigay, *The Evolution of the Gilgamesh Epic* (Philadelphia, 1982); M. Vogelzang, "Kill Anzu! On a Point of Literary Evolution," CRRAI 32 (1985), 61–70.

was a setting in the remote past. Texts of a topical or historical nature were less likely to be recopied than texts which, though they might use historical events or personalities, were applicable to any period. Sometimes there were regional or local preferences; for example, the Hittites were understandably most interested in Mesopotamian texts concerned with Anatolia. As for language, poetry was favored over prose, and texts in moderately artificed language found greatest favor. Highly individual linguistic peculiarities tended to be eliminated over time. With respect to form, texts that lent themselves readily to expansion or shortening seem to have had the best chances of survival. In general, the greater a text's capacity to change in length, without losing its contours, the more likely successive generations were to preserve it. Contemporaneous political or social events may also have inspired interest in specific compositions that were seen as relevant to them.[1]

If there was no broad reading public in the modern sense, then the formation of Akkadian literature must have been in response to the tastes and requirements of a restricted group of literate people. As was noted above (see B.2), different library collections of Akkadian literary manuscripts from the Late period often include the same works. This suggests to some scholars that texts were recopied because they were part of a curriculum of scribal education that evolved during the Mature period. Students were set to copying certain works or excerpts from them as part of their training. Indeed, some scholars consider a putative educational curriculum a primary factor in the survival of Akkadian literature. The selection of works making up such a curriculum must have been guided by a combination of pedagogic, cultural, and ideological factors, and was no doubt heavily influenced by the needs and outlook of literate professional people such as diviners and other scholars. One can speculate that texts were judged in terms of their content, their broad human and professional interest, their challenging but accessible linguistic texture, and their informational and entertainment value.[2]

While curricular needs may explain the survival in multiple copies of some texts of the Mature and Late periods, it cannot explain the creative impulse that brought them into being. Akkadian literature was created by the labor, genius, and inspiration of individual writers, working in the favorable cultural environment of ancient Mesopotamian civilization.

1. E. Frahm, "Nabû-zuqup-kēnu, das Gilgameš-Epos und der Tod Sargons II.," JCS 51 (1999), 73–90.
2. Reiner, *Literatur*, 157; see further p. 294 note 1.

CHAPTER I

THE ARCHAIC PERIOD
(2300–1850 B.C.)

A. ARCHAIC LITERATURE

Tablets and fragments from Syria and Mesopotamia show that literature in Semitic languages was written down as early as the second half of the third millennium B.C., using Sumerian cuneiform. So little is known of this early literature that no name can be confidently given even to the language it was written in, though local forms of this language were used across northern Mesopotamia and Syria from the Mediterranean to the foothills of Iran. Some compositions in this oldest Semitic literature may originally have been exported from Kish, along with other forms of Mesopotamian scholarship and administrative techniques, to such urban centers as Mari on the mid-Euphrates and Ebla in northern Syria, because of the prestige and political power of Kish at the time. Akkadian might be descended from an eastern dialect of this language, spoken in the region bounded by the Tigris, Diyala, and Lower Zab rivers and the Zagros mountains.[1]

This earliest Semitic literature was written with Sumerian word signs, interspersed with occasional Semitic words or portions of words.[2] Since these most ancient texts did not survive in later versions to compare with them, they cannot at present be translated beyond connecting, with impressionistic guesses, some of the few words and expressions that seem understandable.

1. I. J. Gelb, "Ebla and the Kish Civilization," in L. Cagni, ed., *La Lingua di Ebla, Atti del Convegno Internazionale (Napoli, 21–23 aprile 1980)* (Naples, 1981), 9–73; "Mari and the Kish Civilization," in G. D. Young, ed., *Mari in Retrospect, Fifty Years of Mari and Mari Studies* (Winona Lake, Ind., 1992), 121–202; P. Steinkeller, "Early Political Development in Mesopotamia and the Origins of the Sargonic Empire," in M. Liverani, ed., *Akkad, The First World Empire, Structure, Ideology, Traditions* (Padua, 1993), 107–129; P. Fronzaroli, ed., *Literature and Literary Language at Ebla, QuadSem* 18 (1992).
2. J. S. Cooper, "Sumerian and Semitic Writing in Most Ancient Syro-Mesopotamia," CRRAI 42 (1995), 61–77.

I.1 THE VALOROUS SUN

The Archaic poem excerpted here treats of the sun, Shamash, portraying him as a heroic warrior traversing the sky, perhaps riding on a bison-like animal. From his unique vantage point he can see the soldier campaigning in a foreign land and the itinerant merchant in search of foreign goods (see III.32, line 139). Since commerce was one of Shamash's concerns, he or the merchant he protects gathers a barge load of foreign goods, which he brings to the temple of Enlil, the chief god of Sumer. The rest of the text, which cannot yet be translated coherently, may describe exploits of the sun as he crosses the mountains and seas. He confers with various gods, then retires for the night to the underwater depths where Ea reigns. His chosen city on earth is Sippar, where he governs jointly with his bison-like steed.

(i)

Imposing doorbolt of the sky,	(1)
Most exalted of the gods, whom heaven relies on,	
Shamash, the sun, who holds in his hand the life of the land,	
He is the king's right arm ...,	
The beloved of Ea the leader.	(5)

(ii)

God of joyful occasions,[1]
Shining light, fiery radiance,
Awe-inspiring splendor of the depths,
Vanguard of the Anunna-gods,
He it is who gives overpowering strength and fierce weaponry
    to young men. (10)

(iii)

Daylight, chief herald on the mountain ranges,
Herald of the (brightening) sky ...,
God of gods, imposing light, he makes his rounds,
Keeping watch over the land by day and by night,
The lands of Ea. (15)

1. Perhaps a reference to battles, though Shamash was associated with joyful celebration (III.32, line 156).

(iv)

He sustains campaigners and traveling merchants in foreign lands,
The foreign lands render up lapis and silver
    to the traveling merchant,
The cedar forest yields unworked timber, boxwood, cyprus,
    (standing tall like) splendid standards,
Fit for a nobleman to adorn his house.
He loads his barge with aromatics, oils, honey,
    the goods that merchants bring,   (20)
And incense of the gods, juniper, almond, and …-oil.

(v)

Awe-inspiring splendor lights up the bison of the sun,*
His radiance he sheds afar.
The joy of Enlil, the great courtyard,
He fills with copper, gold, silver, lapis,   (25)
The wide courtyard (of his temple).

(remainder of text mostly untranslatable)

Text: Biggs, OIP 99 326, 342; D. O. Edzard, *Archivi Reali di Ebla* 5 (Rome, 1984) 6, pl. VI–VIII,
    XLIV–XLV.
Edition: Krebernik, *QuadSem* 18 (1992), 63–149.
Literature: W. G. Lambert, JCS 41 (1989), 1–32; *QuadSem* 18 (1992), 41–62.
Notes to Text: (22) Steinkeller, *QuadSem* 18 (1992), 261–263.

I.2 STAR INCANTATION

Magic spells in Sumerian and a Semitic language, known from tablets found at Ebla in Syria, are among the earliest known.[1] For the most part, these cannot yet be translated. The rendering here, which could be disputed in nearly every word, intends only to give one possible interpretation of the contents and tenor of a spell in which a star seems to act as intermediary for a sufferer. It is not clear if the sufferer is a sick person afflicted by a demon or a woman having a difficult childbirth, in which case the star intercedes so the child is saved.

> I have bound my Demon,*   (1)
> I have bound his tongue,
> I have bound the points* of his teeth!
>
> I have bound you to a black stone,
> ...   (5)
> I have bound you to seven hoes(?) of the Mighty One,[2]
> I have bound you to the tail(?) of the Sun,
>   to the horns of the Moon.
>
> Seven youths, seven maidens are carrying(?),
> The woman ...
> Whom(?) will they(?) ...?   (10)
>
> The brickmaker will make the brick at the gate
>   of Enlil, father of the gods,[3]
> Then Star, the emissary, has brought(?) him[4]
>   to Enlil, father of the gods,
> "Let me put down my burden I bear,
> "He (the sufferer) will live life (granted him by) Enlil,
>   father of the gods."

---

1. For a survey, see Cunningham, '*Deliver Me from Evil*', 5–43; the basic philological study is M. Krebernik, *Die Beschwörungen aus Fara und Ebla, Untersuchungen zur ältesten keilschriftlichen Beschwörungsliteratur* (Hildesheim, 1984).
2. Perhaps referring to the storm god.
3. To prepare for successful childbirth?
4. The sufferer or the child to be born?

Text: Edzard, *Archivi Reali di Ebla* 5 (Rome, 1984) 1, pl. I, XLII.

Edition: Edzard, *Archivi Reali di Ebla* 5 (Rome, 1984), 17–20.

Translation: P. Fronzaroli, "Tre Scongiuri Eblaiti," VO 7 (1988), 11–23; C. Gordon, "The Ebla Exorcisms," *Eblaitica* 3 (1992), 127–137.

★Notes to Text: (i 2) I follow Gordon's proposal, *Eblaitica* 3 (1992), 129, UF 18 (1986), 129–132; otherwise, this may be a part of the body, perhaps the throat. Fronzaroli, VO 7 (1988), 13 suggests "club." (i 3) With Fronzaroli, VO 7 (1988), 14. (vi 4–7) With Fronzaroli, VO 7 (1988), 19, see also AOAT 274 (2003), 96.

B. OLD AKKADIAN LITERATURE

The earliest known Akkadian literature includes royal inscriptions of the Sargonic period (ca. 2300–2200 B.C.),[1] school exercises, and a few short magical texts, all written in Old Akkadian.[2] The Sargonic period began with Sargon's rise from court officer at Kish to ruler of a kingdom stretching east into Iran, west to the Mediterranean and north into Anatolia. This unprecedented achievement changed permanently the Mesopotamian concept of the politically possible. Sargon's accomplishment was regarded with awe, and in later periods fictional stories circulated about him. His two sons, Rimush and Manishtusu, re-established and continued his military dominion. Inscriptions of Manishtusu were copied, and even forged, in the Late period.[3]

The feats of Sargon's grandson, Naram-Sin, gave this dynasty legendary fascination for Mesopotamians. Naram-Sin turned a series of military conquests into one of history's first empires. He was the first Mesopotamian ruler to proclaim himself a god, because he had defeated a seemingly invincible coalition of enemies (I.3c, d). To Naram-Sin and his contemporaries, his victory over overwhelming odds signified divine approval of his empire and of the Sargonic way of life.[4]

Naram-Sin was succeeded by his son, Sharkalisharri, who reigned for twenty-five years but is unknown in the literary tradition. The empire was destroyed, according to some accounts, by a Zagros mountain people called the Guti, whom the Mesopotamians considered barbarous (I.5b). Some later writers were disposed to find in this a lesson of divine retribution against Naram-Sin himself.[5] A local dynasty continued to rule at Agade, but the city was of little importance by the end of the third millennium and was not referred to in literature.

---

1. For a historical survey of the Sargonic period, see A. Westenholz, "The Old Akkadian Period: History and Culture," in P. Attinger, M. Wäfler, eds., *Mesopotamien, Akkade-Zeit und Ur III-Zeit, Orbis Biblicus et Orientalis* 160/3 (1999), 17–117. Further studies and bibliography are found in M. Liverani, ed., *Akkad, The First World Empire, Structure, Ideology, Traditions* (Padua, 1993).

2. For a description of Old Akkadian and an outdated list of source material, see I. J. Gelb, *Old Akkadian Writing and Grammar*, MAD 2² (Chicago, 1961); see also A. Westenholz, "Old Akkadian School Texts, The Goals of Sargonic Scribal Education," AfO 25 (1974/77), 95–110.

3. F. al-Rawi, A. George, "Tablets from the Sippar Library III. Two Royal Counterfeits," *Iraq* 56 (1994), 135–148; I. J. Gelb, "The Date of the Cruciform Monument of Maništušu," JNES 8 (1949), 346–348 (Neo-Babylonian forgery).

4. A. Westenholz, "The Old Akkadian Empire in Contemporary Opinion," in M. T. Larsen, ed., *Power and Propaganda, Mesopotamia* 7 (Copenhagen, 1979), 107–115.

5. J. S. Cooper, *The Curse of Agade* (Baltimore, 1983), 17–18; J.-J. Glassner, *La chute d'Agadé, L'Événement et sa mémoire, Berliner Beiträge zum Vorderen Orient* 5 (Berlin, 1986).

Sargonic imperial ideology affected the evolution of Akkadian art and literature. An imperial, triumphal art[1] flourished under court patronage. Naturalistic, often monumental reliefs, stelae, and statues were distributed throughout the empire evoking the king's triumphs and the death and enslavement in store for his enemies. Artistic conceptualization and iconography were much influenced by the requirements of royal propaganda. Commemorative inscriptions celebrated the deeds of the king. The earliest examples (I.2) gave the ruler's name and titles, followed by brief, formulaic accounts of campaigns, cities taken, and casualties, and ending with dedication to a god of some commemorative object, with curses on anyone who would destroy the monument or alter its text. By the time of Naram-Sin, these texts were expanded to include direct speech, descriptive details, and admonitions about the importance of the achievements of the king.[2]

The deeds of Sargon and Naram-Sin were also the basis for later literary compositions (see II.6, 7; III.7).[3] Some of these read like reworkings of actual Sargonic commemorative texts, whereas others were freely composed. No such literary compositions are as yet known from the Sargonic period itself.[4] The grandeur and subsequent humiliation of the greatest empire known was a fit subject for reflection for Classical-period thinkers: what divine favor and rejection brought about this remarkable event, and what moral lesson could be drawn from it?[5]

Old Akkadian literature includes as well incantations, or magic spells, of which Sumerian counterparts are known from the middle of the third millennium on.[6] The two Old Akkadian incantations translated here (I.4a, c) were intended to ward off demons and to attract a woman to a man. Magical procedures were unaffected by the politics of their time and often used the vocabulary and rites of centuries before.

---

1. P. Amiet, *L'art d'Agadé au Musée du Louvre* (Paris, 1976), 9–17; J. Westenholz, "The King, the Emperor, and the Empire: Continuity and Discontinuity of Royal Representation in Text and Image," in *Melammu Symposia* 1 (2000), 99–125.

2. For a study of innovation in Sargonic inscriptions, see Franke, *Königsinschriften*.

3. J. Westenholz, *Legends*.

4. MAD 1 172, sometimes treated as a literary text, is best understood as a student excerpt copy of a genuine Naram-Sin inscription, though it was interpreted as a legend by Jacobsen, AfO 26 (1978/79), 2–3, followed by J. Westenholz, *Legends*, 223–229. For another student copy of a Sargonic royal inscription, compare MAD 1 194 (= A. Westenholz, AfO 25 [1974/77], 103 no. 14).

5. J. J. Finkelstein, "Mesopotamian Historiography," PAPS 107/6 (1963), 461–472; J. Westenholz, "Heroes of Akkad," JAOS 103 (1983), 327–336.

6. P. Michalowski, "The Early Mesopotamian Incantation Tradition," *QuadSem* 18 (1992), 304–326; Cunningham, *'Deliver Me from Evil'*, 49–64.

For some Mesopotamian dynasties of the Classic and Mature periods, such as rulers in Assur, Ekallatum, Eshnunna, and Mari, Sargon and his dynasty were honored as ancestors. For later peoples of Anatolia, such as the Hittites, the Sargonic dynasty was remembered for having invaded their homeland.[1] To later Mesopotamian peoples, the Sargonic rulers were exemplary of great achievement, which some saw as ending in dramatic catastrophe. A few light hearts parodied the tradition (I.6, II.6b). As late as the eighth century B.C., an Assyrian king who called himself Sargon took the tradition seriously as a standard to measure himself against.[2] In all cases, the basis for knowledge of this period was actual inscriptions of Sargon and his successors, examples of which are included here, and a small collection of episodes preserved in later chronicles.[3]

1. G. Beckman, "Sargon and Naram-Sin in Hatti: Reflections of Mesopotamian Antiquity among the Hittites," in D. Kuhn, H. Stahl, eds., *Die Gegenwart des Altertums, Formen und Funktionen des Altertumsbezugs in den Hochkulturen der alten Orient* (Heidelberg, 2001), 85–91.

2. M. Van De Mieroop, "Literature and Political Discourse in Ancient Mesopotamia, Sargon II of Assyria and Sargon of Agade," AOAT 267 (1999), 327–339.

3. Grayson, TCS 3, 45–49, 152–156; J.-J. Glassner, *Chroniques mésopotamiennes* (Paris, 1993), 218–220.

I.3 SARGONIC KINGS AND THEIR TIMES

(a) SARGON THE KING

Sargon (ca. 2334–2279 B.C.), founder of the Sargonic dynasty, was remembered in Mesopotamian historical tradition as the prototype of the great conqueror. Stories of his prowess and adventures were worked into legendary narratives (II.6a, III.7) and in the Late period a fictitious story of his birth and exposure as an infant was composed (IV.18). A group of genuine inscriptions of this ruler, in both Sumerian and Akkadian, celebrates his conquests and the extent of his dominion. These were studied by later Mesopotamian scholars as part of their historical heritage.[1] In this summary inscription, Sargon calls himself "king of Agade" (or, Akkad), referring to the area around the confluence of the Diyala and Tigris rivers. When he gains the support of the god Enlil, he calls himself "king of the land," that is, Mesopotamia, including both Sumer and Akkad. He states that Mari, on the mid-Euphrates, and Elam, in southwestern Iran, were obedient to him, and that he appointed his followers to governorships throughout Mesopotamia. He concludes by mentioning a project at the city Kish, the precise nature of which is not yet understood.

(§1) Sargon, king of Agade, bailiff of Ishtar, anointed priest of Anu, lord of the land, chief governor for Enlil, conquered the city Uruk and destroyed its walls. He was victorious in the campaign against Uruk, conquered the city, captured Lugalzagesi, king of Uruk, in the campaign, and brought him to the gate of Enlil in a neckstock.

(§2) Sargon, king of Agade, was victorious in the campaign against Ur and conquered the city and destroyed its walls. He conquered E-ninmar and destroyed its walls, and conquered its territory from[2] Lagash all the way to the sea. He washed his weapons in the sea. He was victorious in the campaign against Umma and conquered the city and destroyed its walls.

---

1. H. G. Güterbock, "Die historische Tradition und ihre literarische Gestaltung bei Babyloniern und Hethitern bis 1200," ZA 42 (1934), 1–91, 44 (1938), 45–149; Grayson, BHLT, 3–9, with extensive bibliographical references. See also A. K. Grayson, "Akkadian Historiography," OrNS 49 (1980), 140–194; C. Wilcke, "Zur Geschichtsbewusstsein im alten Mesopotamien," *Archäologie und Geschichtsbewusstsein* 3 (Munich, 1982), 31–52; F. R. Kraus, "Altbabylonische Quellensammlungen zur altmesopotamischen Geschichte," AfO 20 (1963), 153–155; A. Westenholz, "Assyriologists, Ancient and Modern, on Naram-Sin and Sharkalisharri," AOAT 252 (2000), 545–556.
2. Following the Sumerian, Akkadian has "and" over an erasure, apparently a mistake.

(§3) Sargon, king of the land:[1] Enlil gave him no rival! Enlil gave him the Upper Sea and the Lower Sea, all the way from the Lower Sea to the Upper Sea men of Agade hold governorships. Mari and Elam stand (in service) before Sargon, king of the land.

(§4) Sargon, king of the land, changed the two locations of Kish. He made the two occupy one city.

(§5) Whosoever shall do away with this inscription, may Shamash tear out his foundation and pluck up his offspring.

Text: Poebel, PBS 5 34 + Legrain, PBS 15 41 obv. ii 8–60; Ni 3200 obv. ii 23–25, both collated.
Edition: Frayne, RIME 2, 9–12; Kienast, FAOS 7 (1990), 170–174.
Literature: Foster, *Studies Cagni*, 309–318 (to §3). Edzard, *Studies Tadmor*, 258–263 (to §4); Franke, *Königsinschriften*, 103–111.

(b) SARGON THE VICTORIOUS

In this inscription, Sargon celebrates himself as "universal king," perhaps meaning that he had extended his dominion to include all Mesopotamia and northern Syria, and refers to his city as a center for international trade. The final section is parodied in I.6.

(§1) Sargon, king of Kish,[2] was victorious in thirty-four battles. He destroyed city walls all the way to the shore of the sea. He moored ships of Meluhha, Magan, and Dilmun at the quay of Agade.

(§2) Sargon, the king, prostrated and prayed to Dagan. He gave him the Upper Land: Mari, Yarmuti, Ebla, all the way to the cedar forest and the silver mountains.

(§3) Sargon, the king, Enlil gave him no rival! 5400 men eat every day before him.

Text: Poebel, PBS 5 34 + Legrain, PBS 15 41, obv. vi 41–47; Ni 3200, obv. vi 17–26 (both collated).
Edition: Frayne, RIME 2, 28–29; Kienast, FAOS 7 (1990), 163–167.
Literature: Franke, *Königsinschriften*, 112–115.

1. Mesopotamia is meant.
2. The title king of Kish is sometimes understood to mean "universal king" (see Maeda, *Orient* 17 [1981], 1–17; applicability to Sargonic period questioned by Westenholz, BiOr 53 [1996], 121). In Mesopotamian historical tradition, Kish was to be the first city to have a king (compare III.22).

(c) NARAM-SIN AND THE GREAT REVOLT

A defining event in the reign of Naram-Sin (ca. 2254–2218 B.C.), grandson of Sargon, was his victory, after a series of nine battles he fought in close succession, over coalitions of Mesopotamian and foreign rulers. Two focal points of resistance to him were Kish and Uruk, both of which raised up kings to rival him. In a lengthy inscription set up at Nippur, Naram-Sin commemorated his victory over these forces with a detailed narrative and long lists of killed or captured enemy leaders and soldiers. This inscription is known only from Classical period copies made by scholars at Nippur. The original may have been damaged when they studied it, and their copies, or notes for copies, are themselves badly damaged, so only excerpts from this extensive composition can be presented here. Even what remains shows that celebratory literature had developed a more elaborate style since the time of Sargon, with addition of dialogue, narrative of events taking place outside the king's immediate purview, and assertions of veracity.

The events narrated here were the inspiration for literary works from the Classical period (II.7) and thereafter, presumably based originally on inscriptions such as this one or on Archaic epic narratives that are now lost. The later tellings of the story tended to lay more emphasis on the attack than on the victory, and, by the first millennium, the enemies had become supernatural, with outlandish names (III.7b). Even in the latest version of the story, Naram-Sin was still victorious, but at great cost.

> (§1) Enlil is his god, Ilaba, mightiest of the gods, is his military strength. Naram-Sin the mighty, king of [the four quarters of the earth] (*gap*)
>
> (§2) They raised Iphur-Kish to kingship in Kish, and in Uruk likewise they raised Amar-girid to kingship. Iphur-Kish, king of Kish, raised an army and [mobilized] Kish, Cutha, Tiwa, Sippar, Kazallu, Kiritab, [Api]ak ... and Amorite highland people. He drew up between Tiwa and Urum, in the field of Sin, and awaited battle.
>
> (§3) Naram-Sin the mighty, brought up(?) his troops and held Agade. He ... to Shamash, "O Shamash, the Kishite ..." (*gap*) and he shaved their heads ... They fought a battle in the field of Sin and, by the verdict of Ishtar-Annunitum, Naram-Sin the mighty [was victorious] over the Kishite in the campaign in Tiwa. Moreover, [he took prisoner] Ili-resi the general; Ilu-muda, Ibni-Zababa, Imtalik, Puzur-Asari, captains of Kish; and Puzur-Nergal, governor of Tiwa, Ili-re'u his captain; Kullizum, captain of Eresh; Edami'u, captain of Cutha

(*gap*) Ilu-dan, governor of Borsippa; Dada, governor of Apiak, a total of 300 officers and 4,932 captive soldiers.

(§4) Then, he pursued him all the way to Kish and, beside Kish, at the gate of Ninkarrak, they fought a second battle, and, by the verdict of Ishtar-Annunitum and Anu, Naram-Sin the mighty was victorious over the Kishite in Kish and took prisoner Puzur-Numushda, governor of Kazallu; Dannum, captain of Borsippa; Pu-palim, captain of Apiak (*gap*) Iddin-[ ], governor of Cutha; Ilish-takal, governor of Sippar; Shalim-beli, governor of Kiritab; Qishum, governor of Eresh; Ita-Ilu, governor of Dilbat; Imtalik, captain of Tiwa: a total of 1000 officers and 2015 captive soldiers. Then, he filled the Euphrates with them and conquered Kish and destroyed its walls. Then he made the river flow inside it and slew 2525 men inside the city (*gap*).

(§5) [Amar-Girid], king of Uruk, raised an army and mobilized Uruk, Ur, Lagash, Umma, Adab, Shuruppak, Isin, Nippur, all the way to the Lower Sea. He drew up between Urum and Ashnak and awaited battle.

(§6) Naram-Sin the mighty heard about him and hastened from Kish against him. They fought a battle and, by verdict of Ishtar-Annunitum, [he was victorious ...] (*gap*) He (Amar-girid) kept sending messengers to the lords of the Upper Lands and the city rulers of Subartu, beseeching, "Let us be allies ..." The lords of the Upper Lands and the city rulers of Subartu, since they feared Ilaba, none of them ... followed him. Amar-girid, king of Uruk, trembled in fear, "I must march, [he having been vic]torious, so be it that he die, I live, or otherwise!" He went from Asimanum to Shishil, at Shishil he crossed the Tigris, then from Shishil to the head of the Euphrates. He crossed the Euphrates and went up to Basar, the mountain of the Amorites.

(§7) Naram-Sin the mighty heard about him and released nine captains of Agade he held against him and he hurried to Habshat. Naram-Sin the mighty, he himself went up the Euphrates to Mount Basar. They fought a seventh battle and, by the verdict of Ishtar-Annunitum and Enlil, Naram-Sin the mighty was victorious over the Urukian in the campaign in Basar, the mountain of the Amorites. Moreover, he slew... (*gap*)..., captain of Umma; Aba-Enlil, captain of Adab, a total of 9 officers and 4325(?) men in the campaign. Naram-Sin the mighty took prisoner in the campaign Amar-girid, king of Uruk; E'e the general, Enlil-galzu, city elder of Uruk (*there follows a long list of dignitaries from Uruk, Ur, Lagash, Umma, Adab, Nippur, and two Amorite leaders*). Total: 31 officers and 4980(?) captive soldiers. [Grand total: 2] kings, Grand total: 13(?) generals; Grand total: 23(?) governors; Grand total: 1210(?) officers; Grand total 80,940(?) men, as Enlil revealed, did Naram slay or take captive in the campaign.

(§8) Then Naram-Sin the mighty broke(?) their standards at the gates of his gods. I swear by [Ishtar-Annunitum and] En[lil] that this is true and no lies, this many kings, by Ishtar-Annunitum and Enlil! Naram-Sin the mighty did indeed capture them, did indeed bring them in, with the weapon of Ilaba his lord, in truth!

(§9) Naram-Sin the mighty, emissary of Ishtar his goddess, king of Agade and king [of the four world regions, executor for Ishtar-Annunitum, anointed of Anu], governor for Enlil, general for Ilaba, who reached(?) the sources of the Irnina-river, who defended Agade, who showed forth might to all kings, what no king has experienced since the creation of the human race, an attack by all four world regions together, when Naram-Sin the mighty was emissary of Ishtar, all four world regions attacked him together and confronted him. [...], emissary of Ishtar, ... was victorious over them in [...] [by] verdict of Enlil, father of the gods, with the weapon of Ilaba his lord, and restored their freedom. Then ..., he he[ard of it], he crossed and conquered Magan, in the midst of the sea, and washed his weapons in the Lower Sea.

(§10) Naram-Sin the mighty, emissary of Ishtar, when Enlil had rendered his verdict and handed over to him the leadrope of the people and gave him no rival, he dedicated to [Enlil] ... a great flagon for oil (*gap*)

(§11) Whosoever shall do away with the inscription of Naram-Sin, king of Agade, general for Ilaba, who shall put his name on Naram-Sin's great flagon for oil and shall say, "This is my great flagon for oil" or shall show it to an agent(?) or some other person and say, "Erase his name and put on my own," may Ishtar-Annunitum, Anu, Enlil, Ilaba, Sin, Shamash, [Nergal], Umu, Ninkarrak, the great gods in their totality curse him with a terrible curse. May he hold no scepter for Enlil, may he take no kingship for Ishtar, may Ninhursag and Nintu give him no male heir or descent ... May Adad and Nisaba let no furrow of his flourish, may Enki measure out only mud to his watercourses.

Text: R. Kutscher, *The Brockmon Tablets of the University of Haifa, Royal Inscriptions* (Haifa, 1989) BT 1, 110–111, 118–119; Wilcke, ZA 87 (1997), 31–32; Michalowski, JCS 32 (1980), 243, 245 N 3539 (+) Poebel, PBS 5 36 (+?) 37.

Edition: Frayne, RIME 2, 90–99, 103–108; Kienast, FAOS 7 (1990), 242–248; FAOS 8 (1994), 360–384; Wilcke, ZA 87 (1997), 11–32, with many readings and proposals adopted here.

Literature: Sommerfeld, AOAT 252 (2000), 419–436, whose over-all interpretation of the text has been adopted here; Franke, *Königsinschriften,* 159–198.

(d) NARAM-SIN AND THE GODS

In this inscription, commemorating his victory over the coalition against him, Naram-Sin claims that the citizens of his capital city, Agade, asked the great gods of the land that he be added to the pantheon as a god for his city. Naram-Sin is known from other sources to have been deified in his lifetime. In Sumer, his name was regularly thereafter written with the word "god" before it.

(§1) Naram-Sin the mighty, king of Agade, when the four quarters of the earth attacked him together, through the love Ishtar bore him, was victorious in nine campaigns in one year and captured the kings whom they raised up against him. Because he defended Agade in this crisis, his city asked of Ishtar in Eannaki,* of Enlil in Nippur, of Dagan in Tuttul, of Ninhursag in Kesh, of Enki in Eridu, of Sin in Ur, of Shamash in Sippar, of Nergal in Cutha, that he be god of their city, and built his temple in Agade.

(§2) Whosoever shall do away with this inscription, may Shamash and Ishtar and Nergal, who guard the king, and all these other gods, tear out his foundation and pluck up his seed.

Text: al-Fouadi, *Sumer* 32 (1976), plates after p. 76.
Edition: Kienast, FAOS 7 (1990), 81–83; Frayne, RIME 2, 113–114.
Translation: Hecker, TUAT II/4, 485–486; Kienast in Hallo, ed., *Context*, 2:244.
Literature: Hirsch, AfO 29/30 (1983/4), 58–61; Farber, OrNS 52 (1983), 67–72; Franke, *Königsinschriften*, 177–179.
Notes to Text: (27) Beaulieu, N.A.B.U. 2002/36.

I.4 INCANTATIONS

(a) AGAINST A DEMON

Mesopotamian magic often involved rituals or procedures where the magician acted out the desired result, reciting spells while he did so. In this spell, as in I.4c and II.22a, 25c(1), the magician says he has "seized" or incapacitated the evil.

> I have seized him — like water[1]
> I have blocked him off, like a watercourse —
> Like a dog by his neck,
> Like a whelp by his scruff.
>
> (Incantation)

Text: D. I. Owen, *Neo-Sumerian Archival Texts, Primarily from Nippur* (Winona Lake, Ind., 1984) 917.
Edition: Cunningham, *'Deliver Me from Evil'*, 85–86.
Translation: Farber, TUAT II/2, 256.

1.   As written the line seems to say "I seized him like water," scarcely the simile one expects of a firm grasp, so I assume a "double pivot" construction with the two water similes dependent on "blocked" and the two dog similes dependent on "seized." Differently Farber, "Ich fing ihn wie (mit) Wasser."

(b) AGAINST THE EVIL EYE

This ritual is an early example of magical procedure in Akkadian. The magician takes a sheep to the corners of the dwelling of a man afflicted by the evil eye or other black magic, lifts(?) the sheep in each corner of the house to absorb the evil, kills the animal outside, then stuffs its skin with pieces of some plant (for a late parody of this technique, compare The Jester [IV.25] iv). The sheep, together with bits of plants and trees, is then submerged in water. See II.22b and IV.35.

One black virgin ewe: In (each of) the corners of the house he will lift it up(?).* He will drive out the Evil Eye* and the [ ] .... In the garden he will slaughter it and flay its hide. He proceeds to fill it with pieces of ...-plant. As he fills it, he should watch. The evil man [ ] his skin. Let [him] ca[rry (it) to the river], (and) seven (pieces of) date palm, seven (pieces of) oak, and seven (pieces of...)* let him submerge.

Text: Legrain, MDP 14 90 (p. 123 and pl. 11), collated.
Edition: Legrain, MDP 14, 123–124.
Literature: Farber, ZA 71 (1981), 52, and using other suggestions communicated privately.
*Notes to Text: (3) Meaning of verb uncertain, construed here as Gt causative of *zqr*, implying some sympathetic activity. The root *zqr* is common for raising of buildings. (4) Following Farber, ZA 71 (1981), 52. (22) *zu-iš-ma-e*, word(s) of unknown meaning.

(c) LOVE CHARM

The purpose of this love charm is to enable a man to win a woman's favor by magical procedure. I propose the following divisions of the text. (a) The speaker invokes the god of wisdom and incantations, saying that the love charm, perhaps a kind of androgynous being (see II.26a), sits in the lap of the goddess of love. (b) The speaker is attracted(?) by the scent. Two young women go into a "garden" and cut off a piece of the aromatic for the speaker. This may refer to a magical procedure where some trace of the person upon whom magic is to be worked is collected to represent her. The speaker next asserts control over the woman he desires, apostrophizing her and claiming he will teach her to kiss and make love for the first time (c). In (d), through vegetation metaphors, the speaker describes his approach toward her, while she searches for him. Part (e) seems to be the imagined internal whisperings of erotic desire awakened in the woman by the love charm, while in (f) the spell has taken hold. In the final line, Ea conjures the helpless woman that she find no release from desire till her union with her would-be lover.

(a)

Ea loves the love charm,   (1)
The love charm, son of Ishtar,
It sits on [her] thighs.

(b)

I am guided by(?) the sapflow of the incense-tree.*
Two beautiful maidens were blossoming,   (5)
They[1] went down to the garden,
To the garden they went down,
They cut from the sapflow of the incense-tree.

(c)

I have seized your mouth full of saliva,[2]
I have seized your lustrous eyes,   (10)
I have seized your vagina full of wetness.[3]

---

1. Or, "you," addressing the two maidens.
2. For seizing of the mouth, see II.25c (1); for the wording, compare II.26b.
3. Literally: "urine" (see II.26b), note to a 8.

(d)

I climbed into the garden of the moon,[1]
I cut down poplar for her daylight.[2]
Seek* me among the boxwood,[3]
As the shepherd seeks the sheep,
The goat her kid,
The ewe the lamb,   (15)
The jenny her foal.

(e)

"His arms are two round bundles of fruit,*
"His lips are oil and harpsong.[4]
"A cruse of oil (is) in his hand,   (20)
"A cruse of cedar oil (is) on his shoulder,"
(So) the love charms have bespoken her,
Then driven her to ecstasy!

(f)

I have seized your mouth for love-making!
By Ishtar and Ishara[5] I conjure you: (25)
May you find no release from me
Till your neck and his neck lie close beside!*

---

1. Obscure. "Garden" might refer to his beloved's sexual parts. As Jacobsen suggests (*Studies Finkelstein*, 63), this may refer to their crescent shape. Mention of the moon-god (Sin) might refer also to his role as ruler of the nighttime. For night as the time for sexual adventure, compare "By night there's no prudent housewife, By night no man's wife makes objection" (IV.28).

2. Unclear. Perhaps this means to open her to view, or is an inclusive figure, whereby her "day and night" stand for her "all" (see General Introduction, C.8).

3. In the boxwoods male and female flowers may grow close together (Hirsch, AfO 42/3 [1995/6], 143).

4. The arms are compared in a positive sense to two long bundles of fruit on strings; fruit was commonly used to refer to sexual attractiveness (see p. 165 note 2). Oil was something pleasing and soothing (see IV.17, Tablet I line 93); the harp refers to his melodious voice (Cunningham, *'Deliver Me from Evil'*, 59).

5. Goddess of love; see p. 238 note 5.

Text: Westenholz, OrNS 46 (1977), 200.

Edition: J. and A. Westenholz, OrNS 46 (1977), 198–219.

Translation: Wilcke in B. Hrouda, ed., *Der Alte Orient, Geschichte und Kultur des alten Vorderasien* (Munich, 1991), 280–281.

Literature: Gelb, MAD 5, 7–12; von Soden, ZA 62 (1972), 273–274; W. G. Lambert in M. Minder et al., eds., *Figurative Language in the Ancient Near East* (London, 1987), 37–38, with corrections in N.A.B.U. 1989/7; *QuadSem* 18 (1992), 53–54; Cavigneaux in Abusch, ed., *Magic*, 264–270.

★Notes to Text: (4) Differently Lambert, *QuadSem* 18 (1992), 53 "superb"; I follow Wilcke, 280. Hirsch, AfO 42/3 (1995/6), 143 argues for a factitive of the same verbal root used in lines 14 and 15: "Durch den Weihrauch-Speichel bringen sie (beide) einander (sehr) nahe," but the passage seems to describe a situation rather than an action. (5) A. Westenholz, OrNS 46 (1972), 211. (13) See further Lambert, *Figurative Language*, 38; Krebernik, VO 10 (1996), 18 note 21 (zkr). (18) Gelb, *Studies Kraus*, 71–72; Civil, OrNS 56 (1987), 235. (17) I take this as a Sumerianism (gú[-da]-lá).

I.5 OLD AKKADIAN LETTERS

(a) DO NOT SIT ON A CHAIR!

This letter, included here because of its unusual flowery style, requests that someone come quickly. It uses language derived from magical formulae, presumably with humorous intent.

> Thus says Ishkun-Dagan[1] to Puzur-Ishtar: By Ishtar and Ilaba, Ashgi, and Ninhursag, by the king's life and by the queen's life you must swear it! So long as you have not seen my eyes, may you swallow neither food nor drink! Also, so long as you do not come to me, do not sit on a chair!

Text: Thureau-Dangin, RA 23 (1926), 25.
Edition: Thureau-Dangin, RA 23 (1926), 23–29; B. Kienast, K. Volk, FAOS 19 (1995), 53–55.
Translation: A. L. Oppenheim, *Letters from Mesopotamia* (Chicago, 1967), 71; P. Michalowski, *Letters from Early Mesopotamia* (Atlanta, 1993), 27.

1. Ishkun-Dagan may have been a highly placed administrator in the Lagash region about the time of Sharkalisharri (ca. 2217–2193 B.C., see Foster, JNES 37 [1978], 275; Biga, RSO 53 [1979], 204).

(b) THE PREDATORY GUTIANS

Old Akkadian letters are noteworthy for their vigorous and expressive style. The example chosen here, sent by the same writer as I.5(a), refers to Gutian bandits as a local reality. These people were credited with destruction of the city Agade in a later Sumerian poem[1] and remained a memory in Akkadian literature as barbarian marauders (see II.7b, III.3, IV.30b and p. 351 note 4).

> (1) Thus says Ishkun-Dagan to Lugal-ra: Cultivate the farmland (5) and guard the livestock! (10) Don't say, "There are Gutians, I won't cultivate the farmland." Set up watchposts(?) a half-hour's distance apart and (15) you be sure to cultivate the farmland. When they catch sight of fighting men, they should mount an attack for you and you have (20) the livestock brought into town. [If they (say)(?)], "Gutians have taken away the livestock," (25) shall I then say nothing at all? Shall I pay you the money? See here, I swear by the life of Sharkali-sharri, (30) if Gutians do take any livestock, you will have to pay yourself! When I come to town, (35) I will of course pay you the money,* will you then not guard the livestock? (40) I will require of you the regular harvest deliveries (from the farmland as well). You should keep this oath(?)* in mind.

Text: Westenholz in Volk, FAOS 19 (1995), plate 7.

Edition: Volk, FAOS 19 (1995), 89–94.

Translation: A. L. Oppenheim, *Letters from Mesopotamia* (Chicago, 1967), 71–72; Westenholz in M. Liverani, ed., *Akkad* (p.49 note 1), 157–158; P. Michalowski, *Letters from Early Mesopotamia* (Atlanta, 1993), 27–28.

Literature: Foster, N.A.B.U. 1990/46.

Notes to Text: (22) Volk's reading [*táq*!-*b*]*i-ma* seems to me dubious because the same verb is written *táq-bí* in line 10. (35) Volk's emendation of the text seems to me unjustified. (41) Reading MU.BI as a Sumerogram, resorted to at the end of the tablet to save space.

1. See p. 54 note 5.

C. OLD ASSYRIAN LITERATURE

The land of Assyria was centered around the city Assur, in origin a religious center on a promontory above the Tigris river, favorably situated to be a trade center as well.[1] From Assur, Assyrians settled in trading colonies elsewhere in the Near East, of which the best known was at Kanesh, near present-day Kayseri in Anatolia.[2] The few known examples of Old Assyrian literature were found in private houses in this merchant colony. Although Assyria had a proud, independent cultural tradition that may ultimately have descended from the Archaic Semitic culture of northern Mesopotamia, it was heavily influenced for most of its history by Babylonian culture.[3] Although the Old Assyrian selections translated here are closer in date to the Classical than to the Archaic period, they are included with the Archaic works to stress that Old Assyrian literature may have been an independent development rather than a local version of Classical Akkadian literature.

I.6 SARGON, LORD OF THE LIES

This extraordinary parody on the Mesopotamian epic tradition of the Sargonic kings antedates all known manuscripts of that tradition (see II.6, III.7). In its style and absurdity, it compares to the Sargon and Gilgamesh letters (II.6b, IV.58), the spoof incantation (II.25g), and the birds' real estate purchase (IV.26). Unlike those compositions, much of the humor here depends on elaborate wordplays and on political and ethnic jokes no longer understandable, as well as familiarity with original Sargonic inscriptions and a lost Assyrian legend about Sargon.

The narrative begins with an epic statement of territory conquered, satirizing such statements as known in actual Sargonic royal inscriptions (see I.2) and the later legends (Sargon, King of Battle, II.6, episode 7). It then turns to an elaborate conceit on setting up a stela, which depends on a wordplay on the Akkadian word for "lies" and the Sumerian word for "writing," a theme taken up again at the end, where Sargon says that what is written on a tablet must be true, and on a wordplay on Sumerian "name" and Akkadian "water." Behind these may be a play on

---

1. D. Oates, "Assur, Nineveh, and the Origins of Assyria," in *Studies in the Ancient History of Northern Iraq* (London, 1968), 19–41; W. G. Lambert, "The God Assur," *Iraq* 45 (1983), 82–86; D. Charpin, J.-M. Durand, "Assur avant l'Assyrie," MARI 8 (1997), 367–391.

2. M. T. Larsen, *The Old Assyrian City-State and Its Colonies*, Mesopotamia 4 (Copenhagen, 1976); C. Michel, *Correspondance des marchands de Kanish au début du IIe millénaire avant J.-C.* (Paris, 2001), 23–53.

3. S. Parpola, "Proto-Assyrian," in H. Waetzoldt, H. Hauptmann, eds., *Wirtschaft und Gesellschaft von Ebla*, Heidelberger Studien zum Alten Orient 2 (1988), 293–298.

Sargon's name, humorously interpreted to mean "the liar is truthful." There may also be wordplay on "throw" or "cast" and a word for "stele," hence Sargon "casts" a brick(?) into the "water" and produces a "water lie" (a wordplay on another word for "stele"), that is, a "tall tale."

Sargon then describes a disastrous and interminable repast for his army in which the food ran out. When enough food was found, Sargon's cook burned the meat. This satirizes a genuine inscription of Sargon in which claims that he fed regularly 5400 men (see I.3b), and another in which the king says he had no rival (I.3a, b, for which the Akkadian expression is "one turning the breast"), and conflates these with a legendary story about Sargon in which he was caught in darkness when he entered a great forest (II.6a episode 6), making a wordplay on "meal" and "darkness" and a further one on "turning the breast" (aside in rivalry) with turning meat on a spit before a fire. A long stay of Sargon in Anatolia is mentioned in III.7a.

Sargon next describes measures taken with various lands, each of which seems to involve some joke (compare II.6a, episode 7). Sargon concludes by expressing anxiety that the chief god of heaven will hear of his conquests, lest he be jealous (they are broad as the sky itself), and hoping for regular deliveries of adequate food from his patron in the future.

Of particular interest for the history of Akkadian literature is the connection of the episode in which Sargon runs and loses his clothes with the Epic of Gilgamesh, Tablet X, which is based on the same story. Gilgamesh ran through the wilderness, wore out his clothes, met a tavern keeper (*sabītum*, the word rendered "gazelle" here is also *sabītum*), threw objects into river, dove down in deep water to retrieve a plant, then returned home to admire the brickwork of his city (Foster, *Gilgamesh*, 66–95).

Obscure as it is, this composition bears witness to a sophisticated Assyrian literary tradition awaiting discovery.

> (1) Thus says King Sargon, King of Agade, city of great streets and squares, the mighty king who speaks with the gods, whose strength the Storm God gave him:
>
> (5) I captured territory from where the sun rises to where the sun sets. In a single day, I gave weaponry to seventy cities,[1] I captured their princes and I destroyed their cities. I swear it by Adad, lord of strength, and Ishtar, lady of battle!

---

1. Obscure, possibly a wordplay on "weapon" (*kakku*) and "cloister" (*gagû*); according to a Late period forged inscription, a Sargonic king supposedly constructed a cloister at Sippar. Since this forgery made use of a genuine Sargonic inscription, perhaps there was actually an inscription having to do with a cloister that was part of the usual repertory in early second-millennium schools but is now lost.

(13) I saw a gazelle.[1] I cast[2] a brick(?) into a river, then, while I was running,[3] my monumental inscription was formed, so I set up a falsehood for all time.[4] Then I ran after and seized the gazelle, I raised up the brick(? handiwork?) from the water.

(19) Verily I slaughter a thousand oxen, six thousand sheep every day. ... became hostile[5] to(?) my seven thousand warriors, who daily ate breast-meat before me, my three thousand runners, who ate rump-meat, my one thousand cupbearers, who ate the top cut of the lower leg, as far as it was roasted. My seven thousand warriors ate breast meat. There was not enough breast-meat for anyone behind.[6] He slaughtered his ox, the ... of his throne, and gave the breast-meat to anyone behind. My cook scorched the meat, so for his punishment he slaughtered (another) one hundred oxen and two hundred sheep and fed my servants too. I swear it by Adad and Ishtar!

(41) For seven years, a month, and fifteen days verily I sat with my troops in darkness.[7] When I came out, verily I made a package of carnelian and lapis, verily made I a distribution to the land.[8]

---

1. Wordplay on "gazelle" (*sabītu*), "tavern keeper" (*sabītu*), and "capture" (*ṣabātu*), with perhaps a further wordplay on an Old Assyrian meaning of *ṣabātu*, to initiate legal proceedings against someone. To judge from the parallel story in the Gilgamesh epic, he may have attacked the tavern keeper (Foster, *Gilgamesh*, 72–73).

2. Wordplay on "cast" (*nadû*) and a scholarly word for "stele" (*nadû*).

3. "Running" is a wordplay on an epithet of Sargon (PA.KAS4 ᵈINANNA), in which the first part is etymologized as "runner" or "courier" (LÚ.KAS4).

4. Wordplay on "commemorative inscription" (*musarû*), with "water" (*ma'u, mû*), Sumerian "write" (sar), Akkadian "lie, falsehood" (*sar*), hence "water lie" (the result of throwing the brick in the water, where the inscription was magically formed on it). Further wordplay on Old Assyrian *musarru* (*miserru*) "belt, trousers", so that the line could also be understood "As I was running, my trousers split, so I put on chain mail" (*sarû*, though this word is not otherwise attested for Old Assyrian or for centuries thereafter). The Sumerian term mu-sar meaning "inscription" occurs, however, in genuine bilingual Sargonic inscriptions, translated with Akkadian *ṭuppu* "tablet," hence the reference to a tablet at the end of this parody. As for chain mail, Classical Sargon, King of Battle mentions soldiers clad in iron (II.6a, 61'), so this may be a humorous reference to a similar passage in an Old Assyrian Sargon legend.

5. The reading of the name(?) is unclear; wordplay on "became hostile" (*igrē*, said of the dark forest in Sargon, King of Battle, II.6a, 66') and "invited for a meal" (*iqrē*).

6. "Breast-meat" alludes humorously to the use of the word "breast" in Sargonic inscriptions (see I.1b) in the expression "rival," literally "one who turns the breast," reinterpreting it to refer to cooking. "Behind" is presumably a wordplay on "after" and "rear end."

7. Wordplay on "troops" (*ummânu*) and "creditors" (*ummiānū*) and "meal" (*iklītum*) and "darkness" (*eklētum*).

8. Either Sargon distributed the left-over food or semi-precious stones at court to the land; the passage is not clear.

(47) Indeed, I smote[1] the Amanus mountains in two and, like a commemorative peg, I set up my statue between them. I made the prince of Tukrish wear animal hide.[2] I made Hutura wear animals' heads,* I covered[3] the Cypriots' heads with cloth, like women. As for the Amorites, I went through them all, cutting off their penises as well as their noses.[4] I wrapped the heads of the men of Kilaru in strapping. Once again, I released the ... of the men of Kanesh. I shaved the midline of the heads of the men of Hatti. I made a point of the Gutian togglepin of the Luhmeans.[5] I made the garments of Lulua and Hahhu sumptuous.[6] So did I touch with my hand thirteen pillars of heaven![7]

(63) Why should I speak at length of what is on a tablet?[8] May Anu himself not know how I am king, how I took the upper and lower lands. May Adad and king indeed make abundant my provisions of food![9]

1.   Wordplay on "smite" and "drive in a peg" (both senses of *maḫāṣu*, for discussion see Malul, OrAn 26 [1987], 17–35). Assyrians were familiar with public statements and commemorative inscriptions in peg form, called "nails" or "pegs." These small objects are compared, absurdly, to a triumphal relief or statue large enough to be driven between two mountain ranges. The aetiology of the Amanus range suggests another episode in the Epic of Gilgamesh, where in the struggle between Humbaba and Gilgamesh the Lebanon rift is opened up; see A. George, "The Day the Earth Divided: A Geological Aetiology in the Babylonian Gilgamesh Epic," CRRAI 34 (1987), 179–183.

2.   Normally a sign of mourning, here perhaps a disgrace, or, a joke on a social custom or the name of Tukrish.

3.   Perhaps a wordplay on Akkadian "I covered" (*aktum*) and a Sumerian word for a kind of garment (*aktum*); Streck, AOAT 264 (1999), 76 thinks a shroud is meant.

4.   Wordplay on "righteous, prosperous" (*išaru*) and "penis" (*išaru*). The word occurs with Amorites in Sargon, King of Battle, II.6(a), 15', where the speaker seems to say that the enemy have everything but righteous men (*išarūtum*), humorously reinterpreted here to mean they have become eunuchs.

5.   Obscure. Perhaps the Gutians (see III.7) were a "thorn in the side of" the Luhmeans(?), a mountain people(?).

6.   Hahhum was a caravan stop known to Assyrian merchants (Garelli, CRRAI 34 [1987], 451–456) and was said to have been conquered by Sargon (J. Westenholz, *Legends*, 250). Lullu probably refers to Lullu(bu), a mountain people northeast(?) of Assyria; the two peoples occur together in II.7b(1); see further Charpin, CRRAI 43 (1996), 104.

7.   Another obscure joke; counting the two halves of the Amanus twice, thirteen places may be mentioned in the text.

8.   Wordplay on Sumerian DUB, Akkadian *ṭuppu*. This meant "inscription" in genuine Sargonic inscriptions, and translated Sumerian "mu-sar" (literally, "written name"), but also simply "tablet." "Speak at length" (literally: "make many words") in genuine Sargonic inscriptions meant "narrate"; here the implication may be "to give multiple meanings to."

9.   Normally kings provided regular food offerings to the gods, but here Sargon, whose need for comestibles is prodigious, and whose cook is not always reliable, asks that the storm god and future kings(?) provide him with regular food supplies.

Text: Günbattı, *Archivum Anatolicum* 3 (1997), 152–155.
Edition: Günbattı, *Archivum Anatolicum* 3 (1997), 131–155; M. Van De Mieroop, "Sargon of Akkad and His Successors in Anatolia," *Studi Micenei ed Egeo-Anatolici* 42/1 (2000), 133–159.
Translation: Hecker, TUAT *Ergänzungslieferung*, 58–60.
Literature: B. Foster, "The Sargon Parody," N.A.B.U. 2002/82.
Notes to Text: (29, 42) Dercksen, NABU 2001/1. (45) Understanding *qanû* to refer to a package of reed; compare CAD Q, 87b. (52) Deriving from *bibin(n)u,* perhaps a word for the head or the skin covering it. An inscription of Naram-Sin mentions shaving the head using this word, Kienast, FAOS 7 (1990), 241; see also Stol, BiOr 57 (2000), 626.

I.7 INCANTATIONS

(a) SHE IS SINGULAR

The malevolent Lamashtu-demon specialized in interfering with birth and hurting children (see also II.21 and IV.42). This spell explains that she was cast out from heaven, so has great malice and power to harm.

> She is singular, she is uncanny,   (1)
> She is a child born late in life(?), she is a will-o'-the-wisp,
> She is a haunt, she is malicious,
> Offspring of a god, daughter of Anu.
> For her malevolent will, her base counsel,   (5)
> Anu her father dashed her down from heaven to earth,
> For her malevolent will, her inflammatory counsel.*
> Her hair is askew, her loincloth is torn away.
> She makes her way straight to the person
>   without a (protective) god.
> She can benumb the sinews of a lion,   (10)
> She can ... the sinews of a youngster or infant.

Text: Clay, BIN 4 126.
Edition: von Soden, OrNS 25 (1956), 141–148.
Literature: Farber, ZA 71 (1981), 53, collations p. 72.
Notes to Text: (7) Syntax on the basis of a suggestion by Farber.

(b) SHE IS FURIOUS

Lamashtu interferes with child birth. When a full-term baby is proceeding well, she blocks it. The premature baby she forces out in breech birth. She causes miscarriages and difficult births. For the opening lines, compare IV.42a.

<table>
<tr><td>She is furious, she is terrifying,</td><td>(1)</td></tr>
<tr><td>She is uncanny, she has an awful glamor,</td><td></td></tr>
<tr><td>She is a she-wolf, the daughter of Anu.</td><td></td></tr>
<tr><td>Her dwelling is in grass,</td><td></td></tr>
<tr><td>Her lair is in weeds.</td><td>(5)</td></tr>
<tr><td>She holds back the full-grown youth in rapid progress,</td><td></td></tr>
<tr><td>She yanks out by breech the premature child,[1]</td><td></td></tr>
<tr><td>She brains little babies,[2]</td><td></td></tr>
<tr><td>She makes the witnesses[3] swallow birth fluids.</td><td></td></tr>
<tr><td>The spell is not mine, it is a spell of Ninkilim,</td><td></td></tr>
<tr><td>   master of spells.</td><td>(10)</td></tr>
<tr><td>Ninkarrak cast it so I took it up.</td><td></td></tr>
</table>

Text: Michel, OrNS 66 (1997), 61.
Edition: Michel, OrNS 66 (1997), 58–64.
★Notes to Text: (7) Emended by Ford, N.A.B.U. 1996/6, but not accepted here.

1. Literally "hasty," sometimes understood to refer "easy" birth, but here the baby seems to be taken out prematurely (Stol, *Birth in Babylonia*, 20 with note 107, 133). "Breech" translates Akkadian "by his tail."

2. I take this expression, on the basis of parallel usage in Sumerian, to refer to miscarriage (see S. Cohen, *Enmerkar and the Lord of Aratta* (dissertation, University of Pennsylvania, [1973], 178).

3. Witnesses at birth were sometimes called upon in legal disputes over parentage (Stol, *Birth in Babylonia*, 173–176). A Classical period spell uses the motif differently: "She strangles the little ones, she makes the bigger ones swallow birth fluids" (YOS 11 20, 10–12), but there it is not clear if the "bigger ones" are larger babies or older children present, like the witnesses here. The word for "witness" is the same as "old person," so the line could mean that "young" babies are hit on the head while "old" ones are choked on fluids (merismus, see Wasserman, *Style*, 90).

(c) AGAINST DOGS

This fragment opens with magic words, a description of the feared dogs, and a rhetorical question by the exorcist as to whom he shall send for magic, purifying water. For the last motif, common in spells, compare Against a Mote in the Eye (II.16) and I.2. For other incantations against dogs, see II.25b and compare III.51d.

> *Damum-damamum!*[*][1]   (1)
> The black dog lurks on the ruin heap,
> It waits for the isolated caravan,
> It is on the look-out for the fair young man.
> Whom shall I send to the daughters of Ea,
>   seven and seven?   (5)
> Take your [pots] of carnelian,
> And your stands of chalcedony!
> Go! [   ] in the river, ... [pure] water
>
> *(gap of three lines)*
>
> Get away, fellow,
> Go back to your place![2]

Text: Veenhof, WZKM 86 (1996), 427.

Edition: Farber, JNES 49 (1990), 305–306; Veenhof, WZKM 86 (1996), 425–433.

Translation: Balkan, *Proceedings of the Twenty-second International Congress of Orientalists held in Istanbul September 15 to 22nd, 1951* (Istanbul, 1953), 20–21.

Notes to Text: (1) J. Westenholz, JAOS 119 (1999), 84–85, who suggests "moaning, bemoaning, coal-black canine."

1. Magic words (Farber, ZA 71 [1981], 70) and compare below, IV.40. They may evoke the Akkadian words for "blood" and "moaning."
2. It is not clear to whom this is addressed; I understand the dog.

CHAPTER II

THE CLASSICAL PERIOD
(1850–1500 B.C.)

The selections presented in this chapter date to the Classical or Old Babylonian period, approximately 1850–1500 B.C.[1] Toward the end of the third millennium B.C., political and economic power in southern Mesopotamia passed from Sumerians and Akkadians into the hands of Amorites, Semitic-speaking people of north-Syrian origin who entered Mesopotamia, gradually at some times, in floods at others. The various rival dynasties of Mesopotamia and north Syria during the Classical period were mostly of Amorite background. As a new ethnic element in Mesopotamia, Amorites brought with them speech habits, as well as cultural, social, and economic customs different from those previously known there. Mesopotamia, therefore, became part of a larger cultural continuum stretching along the Euphrates River and its tributaries from Aleppo to Ur and along the Tigris from Assur and Eshnunna south to the marshes at the head of the gulf. This region shared a common written language, religion, and culture that transcended numerous and important local differences.[2] Some earlier Amorite rulers in Mesopotamia, such as the kings of Isin, grafted themselves onto the older Sumerian and Akkadian political and cultural traditions of Mesopotamia, whereas later Amorite kings, such as Hammurabi of Babylon, abandoned this in favor of a common Amorite genealogical myth of origins. Likewise, the traditional Sumerian commemorative language favored by the kings of Isin, modeled on that of the Third Dynasty of Ur, gave way to vigorous and innovative expression in Akkadian, sometimes with Sumerian versions as well. In addition, a specifically literary style, archaizing and influenced by Sumerian, was cultivated. Classical Babylonian culture and language, therefore,

---

1. General historical surveys of the Old Babylonian period include A. Kuhrt, *The Ancient Near East, c. 3000–330 B.C.* (London, 1997), 1:74–117 and D. Charpin, "Histoire Politique du Proche-Orient Amorrite (2002–1595)," in P. Attinger, W. Sallaberger, M. Wäfler, eds., *Mesopotamien, Die altbabylonische Zeit, Orbis Biblicus Orientalis* 160/4 (2004), 25–480.

2. J.-M. Durand, "Unité et diversités au Proche-Orient à l'époque amorrite," CRRAI 38 (1991), 97–128; R. Whiting, CANES 2, 1231–1242; G. Buccellati, "Ebla and the Amorites," *Eblaitica* 3 (1992), 83–104; B. Lafont, "Le Proche-Orient à l'époque des rois de Mari: Un monde sans frontières?" CRRAI 44 (1997), 2: 49–55.

grew out of Sumerian, Old Akkadian, and Amorite traditions, drawing on elements of each.[1]

Political and social conditions of the Classical period were particularly important for the development of literature.[2] Mesopotamia was divided into rival kingdoms, which constantly conspired and allied against one another in competition for hegemony, control of commerce, and natural resources. The insecurity of the time left an impression on literary works, either directly, as in the Lament for a City (II.15), or more subtly, as in the Agushaya poem (II.5). Human fortune was portrayed as a chancy progress toward inevitable death. The world was not seen as inherently fair or just, for power was to the strong, whatever their moral deserts.[3] One hoped for good health, long life, an abundant family, and financial success (see II.28c). Attainment of these goals was seen as a sign of divine favor; illness, ostracism, and defeat indicated divine displeasure, perhaps because of a sin of omission or commission (see II.13). Yet divine favor need not be a matter of justice. Rather, the gods' moods, needs, competition among themselves, and individual abilities influenced human affairs, such that mortals' fortunes were caught in cross currents that they could hardly comprehend, much less control. Ideally, justice was provided by kings as representatives of the gods (II.10a).

In their own inscriptions, Classical-period kings called themselves their subjects' shepherds (II.8, 10, 11).[4] In daily life, a shepherd protected his animals, nurtured them, allowed them to pasture in safety, and, in return, could discipline them absolutely and gain a reasonable financial return. Whereas Classical-period kings used this imagery often, they expressed the profit-taking aspect of kingship only in terms of prosperity for the people.[5] Kings of the Classical period were also wont to refer

1.   W. G. Lambert, "Interchange of Ideas between Southern Mesopotamia and Syria-Palestine as Seen in Literature," CRRAI 25 (1978), 311–316; J.-M. Durand, "La Mythologème du combat entre le dieu de l'Orage et la Mer en Mésopotamie," MARI 7 (1993), 41–61.

2.   For an introduction to Old Babylonian society, see M. Stol, "Wirtschaft und Gesellschaft in Altbabylonischer Zeit," in Mesopotamien (above, p. 79 note 1), 643–975.

3.   The best general study of the Classical period, including its worldview, is F. R. Kraus, Mensch; note also the essay by H. Klengel, "Zur Rolle der Persönlichkeit in der altbabylonischen Gesellschaft," in Humanismus und Menschenbild im Orient und in der Antike (Halle, 1977), 109–117.

4.   F. R. Kraus, "Das altbabylonische Königtum," CRRAI 19 (1971), 235–261; D. Charpin, "'Le bon pasteur': idéologie et pratique de la justice royale à l'époque paléo-babylonienne," in Les Moyens d'expression du pouvoir dans les sociétés anciennes, Lettres Orientales 5 (1996), 101–114. For literature at the royal court, see G. Komoróczy, "Literatur am Königshof (2. Jahrtausend v. u. Z.)," Gesellschaft und Kultur im alten Vorderasien, Schriften zur Geschichte des alten Orients 15 (Berlin, 1982), 155–161.

5.   B. R. Foster, "Social Reform in Ancient Mesopotamia," in K. D. Irani, M. Silver, eds., Social Justice in the Ancient World (Westport, Conn., 1995), 165–177; D. Charpin, "Le Rôle économique du palais en Babylonie sous Hammurabi et ses successeurs," in L. Lévy, ed., Le Système

to their divine election, as if the gods had chosen them to lead their human flocks. When a dynasty had been established, some kings expressed their divine origins, perhaps as offspring of a "sacred marriage" (see II.18).[1] As the responsible agents for the gods, kings were supposed to govern their subjects fairly and to protect their people from outside threats.

In other Classical-period literature, however, limits to the metaphor of king as shepherd were more sharply drawn. Abuse of royal power is touched on directly in Old Babylonian Gilgamesh and satirized in the Agushaya poem (II.5). Literary heroes were often kings or those who sought the impossible. Whereas Babylonians stressed that all human undertaking, no matter how heroic, would end in the anonymity of death, they admired heroic effort. In later literature, by contrast, heroic initiative was seen as not only doomed but possibly sacrilegious, in that it ignored the limits set for mortals by their divine creators.[2]

Much Classical literature, in prose and poetry, was composed under royal patronage, celebrated kingly deeds, or asked divine blessings upon the reigning king. This points to a culture that esteemed its written language and the wealth of possibilities it offered for vivid and effective expression and admired and supported those skillful in its use. Love of language can be seen, as well, in the numerous letters of this period, some of which show a richness of expression and lavish use of figures of speech that place them somewhere between everyday speech and conscious artistic expression. The Mesopotamian practice of composing supposititious letters in the name of past kings began at this time (II.6b), just as ancient Sumerian letters of historical interest were studied, copied, and eventually translated into Akkadian. Moreover, a new, ornate Sumerian epistolary style was cultivated at some of the Amorite courts.[3]

The relationship of Sumerian to Akkadian literature in the Classical period is still largely unexplored. Mesopotamian scholars at this time saw their culture as bilingual. Sumerian and Akkadian were the only two translatable languages on the cultural level, while translation to or from other languages was the mechanical activity

palatial en orient, en Grèce et à Rome, Actes du Colloque de Strasbourg 19–22 juin 1985 (Leiden, 1987), 111–126.

1. W. W. Hallo, "The Birth of Kings," *Studies Pope*, 45–52; Å. W. Sjöberg, "Die göttliche Abstammung der sumerisch-babylonischen Herrscher," *Orientalia Suecana* 21 (1972), 87–112; J. Klein, "The Birth of a Crownprince in the Temple: A Neo-Sumerian Literary Topos," CRRAI 33 (1986), 97–106. See, however, p. 162 note 1.

2. F. R. Kraus, *Mensch*, 130–134; E. Reiner, "The Etiological Myth of the Seven Sages," OrNS 30 (1961), 1–11.

3. W. W. Hallo, "The Royal Correspondence of Larsa," AOAT 25 (1976), 209–224; "Letters, Prayers and Letter-Prayers," *Proceedings of the Seventh World Conference of Jewish Studies (Jerusalem, 1971), Studies in the Bible and the Ancient Near East* (Jerusalem, 1981), 17–27; "The Expansion of

of dragomans. Perhaps already in the Classical period a theory or school of translation between Sumerian and Akkadian had developed, which used standard equivalences from bilingual lexical texts, high semantic translation and interpretation, wordplay, and revision of both the source and the translated text to render more harmonious what seemed the best features of both. Hence, translation was not necessarily seen as subordinate to an "original text," but was an equal and opposite creative effort that might be used as a basis for revising the original and updating it.[1]

In this cultural environment, in which matching two languages was seen as a serious intellectual undertaking, each language could affect the other in phonology, morphology, syntax, vocabulary, and semantics, not to mention form, style, diction, figures of speech, and content of written works. The reader of Classicalperiod Sumerian literature may detect what he considers Akkadian influence, for example, in elaborated use of parallelism as compared to older Sumerian literature. So too, the reader of Classical-period Akkadian literature may detect what he considers to be Sumerian influence in style, expression, and choice of words. Sumerian influence may have been greater in certain types of texts, such as hymns or narrative poetry about traditional Mesopotamian deities; the Agushaya poem, for example, has Sumerian liturgical or performance indications and its obscurity may be owing to an effort of its author to make it sound like Sumerian. On the other hand, the bombastic legends of Sargonic kings (II.6, 7) have little in common with the witty elegance of the Sumerian epics about ancient kings, so their origins need not be sought in Sumerian literature. Sumerian-style royal hymns of praise were still turned out as late as the reign of Hammurabi,[2] but inspired little in the way of Akkadian imitation.[3] In sum, it would be easy to exaggerate the impact of Classical-period Sumerian literature on Classical-period Akkadian literature, and it would be easy to underestimate the reverse. A vital cultural endeavor in a few centers, such as Nippur, Sumerian literature soon ossified in most areas into a kind of arid learned accomplishment, and the influence of Akkadian upon it continued to grow.

Social and economic developments during the Classical period included the amassing of privately owned real estate,[4] money-lending (see II.29), and compe-

Cuneiform Literature," *Proceedings of the American Academy of Jewish Research* 46–47 (1979–80), 307–322; see also below, II.34a.

    1. See General Introduction (p. 44 note 4).

    2. Å. W. Sjöberg, "Ein Selbstpreis des Königs Ḫammurapi von Babylon," ZA 54 (1961), 51–70.

    3. What appears to be a royal hymn in Akkadian, in honor of Gungunum, king of Larsa, is too fragmentary for translation (TIM 9 41).

    4. For studies of this phenomenon, see D. Charpin, *Clergé; Archives Familiales et Propriété Privée en Babylonie Ancienne; Étude des Documents de "Tell Sifr"* (Geneva, 1980).

tition for agricultural labor, acquired either by contract or debt slavery.[1] Trade and commerce brought high returns for high risks.[2] Yet these do not emerge as subjects of artistic expression. Sometimes kings attempted to regulate and readjust local economies by annulling certain debts and obligations,[3] but military service and corvée were an onus on the population, as aptly portrayed in the opening lines of Atrahasis (II.36).[4]

The author of the Classical period saw his world as uncertain and competitive. He envied the imagined self-assurance of the past. Babylonians and Assyrians cultivated an interest in their past (see I.3, 6; II.6, 7) and in the origins of human society (Etana, III.22, Atrahasis, II.36).[5] In this spirit, ancient inscriptions were studied in Mesopotamian schools and both copied exactly (I.3a–c) and freely adapted as literature (II.7b).[6]

Classical-period Akkadian literature is full of human interest, lively wit, and strong emotion. The satirical (II.14), the self-knowing, the ironic are found (II.5), as well as sensuality (II.2, 17, 19), anguish (II.13, 15), longing (II.16), and tales of adventure (II.6). Subject matter includes the deeds of the gods and their significance for humankind, as in Etana (see III.22), Agushaya (II.5), Atrahasis (II.36); and deeds of men, for example, the fighting hero (II.6, 7, 9, 11), and the pretentious fool (II.14).

As in the Archaic period, incantations were considered effective against various problems such as disease and discomfort (II.23), natural pests (II.25a–e), the pangs of parenthood and infant death (II.20), the frustration of unrequited desire (II.26), and malice (II.22b). Their directness and grim vividness are the more powerful

---

1. M. Van De Mieroop, "The Archive of Balamunamhe," AfO 24 (1987), 1–29; C. Dyckhoff, "Balamunamhe von Larsa — eine altbabylonische Existenz zwischen Ökonomie, Kultus und Wissenschaft," CRRAI 43 (1996), 117–124.

2. W. F. Leemans, *The Old Babylonian Merchant: His Business and His Social Position*, SED III (Leiden, 1950); A. L. Oppenheim, "The Sea-Faring Merchants of Ur," JAOS 74 (1959), 6–17.

3. D. Charpin, "Les Prêteurs et le palais: les édits de *mîšarum* des rois de Babylone et leur traces dans les archives privées," in A. Bongenaar, ed., *Interdependency of Institutions and Private Entrepreneurs, Proceedings of the Second MOS Symposium* (Leiden, 2000), 185–211; J. Renger, "Royal Edicts of the Old Babylonian Period — Structural Background," in M. Hudson, M. Van De Mieroop, eds., *Debt and Economic Renewal in the Ancient Near East* (Bethesda, Md., 2002), 139–162.

4. M. Stol, "Old Babylonian Corvée (*tupšikkum*)," in T. van den Hout, J. de Roos, eds., *Studio Historiae Ardens, Ancient Near Eastern Studies Presented to Philo H. H. Houwink ten Cate on the Occasion of his 65th Birthday* (Amsterdam, 1995), 294–308; G. Komoróczy, "Work and Strike of the Gods," *Oikumene* 1 (1976), 9–37.

5. D. Charpin, "L'évocation du passé dans les lettres de Mari," CRRAI 43 (1996), 94–110.

6. F. R. Kraus, "Altbabylonische Quellensammlungen zur altmesopotamischen Geschichte," AfO 20 (1963), 153–155. For bibliography on Babylonian schools, see p. 297 note 1.

because of the universality of the experience they deal with. There is also a parody on the style (II.25g). The poetics of incantations are simple and immediately appealing, whereas more complex works, such as Atrahasis (II.36), show the high refinement and artistic excellence that Classical-period poets could achieve.

The Classical period was, in turn, held up in later ages as a linguistic model. Hammurabi's prose was studied in schools. Classical manuscripts were carefully copied; students attempted to reproduce Classical texts in Classical script (III.22). Classical- and Archaic-period kings were made the authors of fictitious letters of moral import (II.39). The scant and fragmentary survivals of this great period of Mesopotamian literature speak eloquently for its creativity.

A. IN PRAISE OF DEITIES

II.1 TO ISHTAR

After the opening invocation, this poem treats first the attractions of Ishtar's body, then focuses upon her features, suffused with pleasure, and her head, which is bedizened with love charms (compare Love Charm, I.4c). Mention of her eyes leads to consideration of the well-being her regard can bestow, especially, in the fifth strophe, on a woman who hopes for harmonious love. The poet thinks then of Ishtar's might and splendor—who could withstand such power? This leads to her role as queen of heaven, the morning and evening star; she reigns supreme with her spouse, the sky, and the lesser lights stand before her, partaking of her brilliance. As the gods await her command, the poet introduces the Babylonian king, Ammiditana (ca. 1683–1647 B.C.), who bears rich offerings, whose domains she ensures—may his long life be her command.

i

Sing of the goddess, most awe-inspiring goddess,   (1)
Let her be praised, mistress of people,
     greatest of the Igigi-gods.
Sing of Ishtar, most awe-inspiring goddess,
     let her be praised,
Mistress of women, greatest of the Igigi-gods.

ii

She is the joyous one, clad in loveliness,   (5)
She is adorned with allure, appeal, charm.
Ishtar is the joyous one, clad in loveliness,
She is adorned with allure, appeal, charm.

iii

In her lips she is sweetness, vitality her mouth,
While on her features laughter bursts to bloom.   (10)
She is proud of the love-charms set on her head,[1]
Fair her hues, full-ranging, and lustrous her eyes.

---

1. The love charm, sometimes a personification (see I.4c, II.26a), may here be something worn, like a necklace or headband (Westenholz, OrNS 46 [1977], 205–207); compare II.2, line 16.

iv

This goddess,* right counsel is hers,
She grasps in her hand the destinies of all that exists.
At her regard, well-being is born,   (15)
Vigor, dignity, good fortune, divine protection.

v

Whispers,* surrender, sweet shared captivation,
Harmony too she reigns over as mistress.
The girl who invokes(?) finds (in her?) a mother,
Among women(?) one mentions her, invokes her name.*   (20)

vi

Who is it that could rival her grandeur?
Her attributes are mighty, splendid, superb.
Ishtar this is, who could rival her grandeur?
Her attributes are mighty, splendid, superb.

vii

She it is who stands foremost among the gods,*   (25)
Her word is the weightiest, it prevails over theirs.
Ishtar stands foremost among the gods,
Her word is the weightiest, it prevails over theirs.

viii

She is their queen, they discuss her commands,*
All of them bow down before her: (30)
They go to her (in) her radiance,*
Women and man fear her too.

ix

In their assembly her utterance is noble, surpassing,
She is seated among them as an equal to Anu their king,
She is wise in understanding, reflection, insight.   (35)
Together they make their decisions, she and her lord.[1]

---

1. Anu is meant. "Lord" may be a term of endearment here; see p. 156 note 1.

x

There they sit together on the dais
In the temple chamber, delightful abode,
The gods stand in attendance before them,
Their ears awaiting what those mouths will command.   (40)

xi

Their favorite king, whom their hearts love most,
Ever offers in splendor his pure offerings,
Ammiditana offers in plenty before them
His personal, pure libation of cattle and fatted stags.*

xii

She has asked of Anu her spouse long life hereafter for him,   (45)
Many years of life for Ammiditana
Has Ishtar rendered to him as her gift.

xiii

By her command she gave him in submission
The four world regions at his feet,
She harnessed the whole of the inhabited world to his yoke.   (50)

xiv

What she desires, this song for her pleasure
Is indeed well suited to his mouth,
      he performed for her Ea's own word(s).[1]
When he heard this song of her praise,
      he was well pleased with him,
Saying, "Let him live long,
      may his (own) king always love him."[2]

---

1. This refers to the artfulness of the text, which pleases Ea, god of wisdom. See General Introduction D.1 and compare III.29 line 146.
2. "King" may mean the god of Ammiditana's city, Babylon (so Thureau-Dangin).

O Ishtar, grant long life enduring to Ammiditana,
the king who loves you, (long) may he live!   (55)

(Its antiphon)[1]

Text: Thureau-Dangin, RA 22 (1925), 170–171.

Edition: Thureau-Dangin, RA 22 (1925), 172–177.

Translation: von Soden, SAHG, 235–237 no. 1; Stephens, ANET[3], 383; Labat, *Religions*, 238–239; Seux, *Hymnes*, 39–42; Hecker, TUAT II/5, 721–724; Edzard, *Orbis Biblicus et Orientalis* 160/4 (2004), 510–515.

Literature: Hecker, *Epik*, 77–85.

Notes to Text: (13) Or "pure one," Hecker, TUAT II/5, 722 note 13a. (17) With von Soden, ZA 67 (1977), 279; otherwise, "mutual loves." (20) Construing *i-ni-ši* as *in(a) išši*. For *iššu* without a doubled consonant, compare *i-ši-i* in line 4. (25) I follow here von Soden's emendation to *ša!-at*, ZA 40 (1931), 195 note 4. Collation shows the copy to be exact. Hecker's proposal, *Epik*, 79 note 2, *ga!-sa!-at*, seems to me less likely because of the parallelism of the lines, which resembles that of ii. (29) Differently Hecker, *Epik,* 80 note 3: "Ihre Königin lassen sie immerwieder ihre Weisungen geben." (31) See Hecker, *Epik*, 80 note 3; Mayer, OrNS 56 (1987), 201; Wasserman, *Style*, 86 note 113. (44) Emended by CAD A/1, 336a to *as!-li*, but there seems to be no basis for this (collation by translator and also Wasserman, *Style*, 92).

---

1.   This refers to the lines in the ruled-off section. The poem may have been performed or sung antiphonally.

II.2 TO NANAY

This hymn comprises fourteen preserved strophes. The first six are in the third person, describing the goddess Nanay (here identified with the planet Venus) as a woman, proud, beautiful, and confident, whom the sky-god Anu made mistress of the world. In stanzas vi to xi, the poet changes to the second person, as if Anu were speaking, extolling the joy and prosperity she brings, especially to the reigning king, Samsuiluna of Babylon (ca. 1749–1712 B.C.). The poet then reverts to the third person, and concludes with a blessing for the king.

The structure, vocabulary, and content of this hymn are similar to those of the Hymn to Ishtar (II.1); see also II.17. For a study of the goddess Nanay, see J. Westenholz, "Nanaya: Lady of Mystery," in I. Finkel, M. J. Geller, eds., *Sumerian Gods and Their Representations* (Groningen, 1997), 57–84.

i

To the goddess, sun of her people,   (1)
To Nanay pray, and praise her rank:
For she is like the new moon to look on,
Her wondrous features full of brilliance.*

ii

Ever bursting into bloom upon her   (5)
Are abundance, self-assurance, sweetness, and charm.
She has showered down j[o]y, laughter, and loveliness:
Nanay has sung of [lo]ve.

iii

Walking ever at her side are sincerity,
[Wel]l-being, vigor, decorum,   (10)
[Fu]llness of well-being and vitality.
Her path (in the heavens) is always a propitious sign.

iv

She is b[edecked] with playfulness,
Canny mistress, she knows her powers!
She is lovable as her father could make her,   (15)

When she set forth, he himself put love charms round her neck.[1]

v

From among all goddesses great Anu
Her father raised high her head.
She is unique, proud, and cherished,
He made her lot exuberance, happiness as her ...*   (20)

vi

Laughing joyfully,* a happy speech
He made to her, causing her heart to glow,
"You shall be the mistress of all the world's inhabitants!
"The people shall look upon your light as the sun's."

vii

"O Capable, wise(?), Capable Lady,*   (25)
"Fierce Irnina, most valiant of the Igigi-gods,
"You are the highest one above them,*
"Among them your names are held highest in regard.*

viii

"Shine, let your heart be glad,
"Keep up rejoicing in the city shrines!   (30)
"May the outlying lands bring you fragrant wood,
"Approach them, that they too be filled
        with delight and abundance.

ix

"May your special pleasure, your favorite,
"The king you have designated, Samsuiluna,
        burn(?) offerings for you,
"Tribute of earth and mountain let him ever set before you,   (35)
"Let him make his dwel[ling in joy] before you.

x

"The crook of life to the h[erdsm]an,

1. See above, p. 85 note 1.

"Years of justice and truth,
"A well-founded [throne] ... well-being,
"At your command [   ]." (40)

xi

[may] he   ]
Nanay [   ] is happy.
In the [   ]
... [   ] ... she desired a hymn of praise.[1]

xii

[   ] (45)
She named [her] beloved [king]
Samsuiluna, her [   ]
She named him [   ]

xiii

She has bestowed in addition upon him
Long life enduring and wealth, (50)
To Samsuiluna, whom she loves,
She has bestowed the sun as a luminary.[2]

xiv

At her command her f[avorite] is ruler
H[igher than any] hero [in] the world,
[   ] let him rejoice whom she named (55)
[   ] in the [   ].

([Its] an[ti]phon)[3]
(fragmentary line, then text ends or breaks off)

1. Probably a reference to this text; see p. 87 note 1.
2. That is, he is a just king.
3. Refers to strophe xiv? See p. 88 note 1.

Text: Zimmern, VAS 10 215.

Edition: von Soden, ZA 44 (1938), 32–35.

Translation: von Soden, SAHG, 237–239 no. 2; Seux, *Hymnes*, 42–45; Hecker, TUAT II/5, 724–726.

Literature: Hecker, *Epik*, 86–88.

Notes to Text: (4) With CAD I/J, 43a versus AHw, 287a; Seux, *Hymnes*, 42 note 2. (20) Collation CAD N/2, 66a. (21) Wasserman, N.A.B.U. 1992/80. (25) Seux, *Hymnes*, 44 notes 20–22. (27–28) von Soden, ZA 67 (1977), 280.

II.3 TO PAPULEGARRA

The main theme of these pieces, as in other Classical-period hymns, is the relationship between a divinity's power and the success and obligations of the ruling king. Some of the imagery may be drawn from the more ancient Sumerian hymnography to Kesh,[1] a sanctuary in Sumer that was sacred to the mother-goddess. The tablet from which these passages are taken evidently held the text of three hymns, but owing to breaks it is not clear where the second began or ended, or where the third began. The god Papulegarra is little known.

(three columns of text omitted)

iv

Come, the god [   ], song of praise [   ]
[Let me sing] the splendid god, [who strikes down] enemies,
[Let me sing] splendid Papulegarra, who hunts down the enemy, (5)
[Who ...] the mighty lion, the shepherd of the people.
Who lames the arrogant ... hamstrings the hostile,
He looks in fury upon him, he pours out venom on him [   ]*
The roar of his torrent ... he pours out, venom [he ...]

(gap)

v

Spinning whirlwind, [   ] ... [   ]
Throwstick (spanning) everything [   ] the sky.   (10)
Fanged dragon spewing [deadly] foam,*
   Bronze-pointed arrow that opens the bre[ast],
Rainfall on the meadow, which increases ...,
   Yearly breeze that deposits the frost,   (15)
Saw of battle, dagger of onslaught,
   Reaper of battle, threshing flail(?)* of struggle,
Hatchet felling the forests,
   Raging fire whose onslaught is deadly,   (20)
Iron meteorite that pulverizes the ground,
   Wrecker's bar of the cella: Let me recount his praise!

1. For Kesh and its literary tradition, see Edzard, "Keš," RLA 5, 571–573. For an English translation of the Sumerian Kesh temple hymn, see Gragg, TCS 3 (1969), 155–188, with important contributions by Edzard, OrNS 43 (1974), 103–113; note also S. N. Kramer, "Keš and Its Fate: Laments, Blessings, Omens," *Gratz College Anniversary Volume* (Philadelphia, 1976), 165–175.

Swamp fire that has cracked hard ground,
    Has consumed the ... of the plain like thornbushes,*   (25)
Trampler of the crooked whose advice is dishonest:
    Papulegarra dumps them into his net!
Rampaging lion, terror(?) of the highway.

(gap)

vi

Set out* a throne that he take his (rightful) place!
[May] the king take his place whose attributes are purest,
Who knows how to rejoice(?)* in the temple on the festival day,
Let him draw out the limits, let him make ritual walkways,
Let him do what is correct for the temple of the gods,
    Let him set commemorative pegs,[1]   (20)
Let him cause a close to be built for Ishtaran,
Let him make a womb for the Mother Goddess.[2]
The Ezugal,* temple of its lady, let him build,
A recumbent bull, a high house(?) let him build.
The temple: let its head be raised high,   (25)
    Below, let its roots grasp the netherworld.
The Kesh temple: let its head be raised high,
    Below, let its roots grasp the netherworld.
Above, let its pinnacle rival heaven,
    Below, let its roots grasp the netherworld.   (30)
O Papulegarra, hunter,[3] rejoice and be glad.

Text: Pinches, JRAS *Centenary Supplement* (1924), pl. vi–ix after p. 72.
Edition: Pinches, JRAS *Centenary Supplement* (1924), 63–86.
Translation: Seux, *Hymnes*, 46–50; Hecker, TUAT II/5, 728–731.
Literature: von Soden, ZA 71 (1981), 195–197.
Notes to Text: (iv 8, v 11) von Soden, ZA 67 (1977), 280. (v 17, 25) WGL. (vi 15) von Soden, ZA 67 (1977), 280. (vi 17) WGL. (vi 23) Text: Ezuzal; see George, *House Most High*, 161.

1. That is, let him undertake construction of cult edifices.
2. This may refer to a cult object; see Jacob-Rost and Freydank, AOF 8 (1981), 325–327 with pl. XXIII–XXV (inscribed pubic triangle in bronze dedicated to Ishtar, Old Assyrian period, discussed by E. Braun-Holzinger, *Mesopotamische Weihgaben der frühdynastischen bis altbabylonischen Zeit, Heidelberger Studien zum Alten Orient* 3 [1991], 379). See also III.43d.
3. Literally: "fisherman." In the Old Babylonian period fisherman often meant marine or commando; perhaps that is meant here (see E. Salonen, BiOr 25 [1968], 160–162).

II.4 SELF-PRAISE OF ISHTAR

This small fragment is of interest as a self-predication of the warrior-goddess. It resembles the portrayal of the goddess in the Agushaya poem (see II.5). Compare also III.25 and IV.31. The change in gender in lines 12 to 13 may refer to the masculine and feminine qualities of the goddess (see III.26 iii 78).

(gap)

I rain battle down like flames in the fighting, (5)
I make heaven and earth shake(?) with my cries,
The mountains lie low when I tread on the earth,*
I, Ishtar, am queen of heaven and(?) earth.
I am the queen, ...
I cross heaven, back and forth, as I trample the earth, (10)
I destroy what remains of the inhabited world,
I devastate(?) the lands hostile to Shamash.
I am the most heroic of the gods,
    she who slays the inhabited world,
I draw back on its bridle(?), he who slays ...
The [mo]on-god begot me, I abound in terror! (15)

Text: Zimmern, VAS 10 213.

Edition: Zimmern, *Berichte über die Verhandlungen der Königlichen Sächsischen Gesellschaft der Wissenschaften zu Leipzig, Philosophisch-historische Klasse* 68 (1916), 43.

Translation: von Soden, SAHG, 239–240 no. 3.

Literature: von Soden, RA 52 (1958), 132.

Notes to Text: (7) Wasserman, *Style*, 78.

II.5 THE AGUSHAYA POEM

This poem praises the goddess Ishtar, personification of war. She always wants to fight; Ea, god of wisdom, endowed her with terrifying warlike characteristics. When her aggressiveness extends even to his own abode, Ea is angered. He convokes the gods, explains that Ishtar has become intolerable, and suggests that "discord" (Saltu) be created to contend with Ishtar. The gods are unable to produce such a creature, and suggest that Ea do it himself. This he does, apparently by taking some dirt from under his nails and mixing it with spittle.

The resulting creature is hideous, fierce, spoiling for a fight—in short, Ishtar's counterpart. Ea shouts at Saltu over the uproar she is making that her task is to humiliate a certain goddess, whom he calls Irnina; but the poet assures us that Ishtar is meant. Saltu is to rush off, barge in on Ishtar, and challenge her for no apparent reason.

Clever Ea now begins to describe Saltu's prospective opponent; the poet waxes into another lyrical description of Ishtar's prowess, putting his words into the mouth of the god of wisdom himself. Ea is carried away by his paeans to the extent that he pretends to have second thoughts, and says that, after all, Ishtar is too awful an opponent for Saltu to fight and that she had better desist. As Ea had calculated, this stings Saltu into a jealous fury and she marches off in search of Ishtar.

A large section of text is lost here. Apparently Ishtar becomes aware of the move against her, and sends out her messenger, Ninshubur, to find out about this enemy. Ninshubur finds (to his amazement) a likeness of Ishtar herself. He comes back stammering a description of Saltu's behavior, refraining from any reference to her actual appearance. Ishtar flies into a rage.

Again, the text is broken, but when it resumes, Ishtar is accusing Ea of having made this monster. She demands that he dispose of it. Ea replies that as soon as Ishtar changes her behavior, the hideous creature will disappear. He had created Saltu just to show Ishtar what she looks like. He ordains an annual holiday in which people dance madly in the streets in memory of Ishtar/Agushaya, etymologized by the poet as "The Mad Dancer in Battle."[1] Ishtar is mollified by this gesture, overlooking Ea's pointed sarcasm about how foolish these people look dancing. The poet reappears, blending his voice with that of Ea. He turns proudly to the audience and asks god and man to honor his marvelous text.

The poem is divided into ten numbered sections. These may have something to do with its performance: it was perhaps sung, recited in a special way, or even

---

1.   See further A. Vattioni, "À propos du nom propre syriaque Gusai," *Semitica* 16 (1966), 39–41.

staged dramatically. The antiphons, like the choruses in Greek tragedy, serve as an extra-narrative commentary on the action and the characters, as if speaking for the audience.

This text can be read as a lesson in violence. Wisdom (Ea) shows that valor carried to excess is brutal, indiscriminate, and stupid. True bravery knows restraint and dignity as well.

Tablet I

i

Let me praise the greatest one, the warrior among the gods,
The daughter of Ningal's might and fame let me extol!
Ishtar, the greatest one, the warrior among the gods,   (5)
The daughter of Ningal, let me tell of her might!

Her grandeur is manifest, her ways hard to fathom,   (10)
She is always in battle, cunning is her str[atagem].

(several lines lost)

ii

She dances around gods and kings in her manliness.   (1)

(First Section)

She is the preeminent of goddesses,
The praises of Ishtar let me sing!   (5)

(Its Antiphon)

She holds in her grasp all divine authority,
She bestows it wherever she wills.
Ishtar holds in her grasp the leadline of the peoples,   (10)
Her goddesses h[eed] her [command].

(several lines lost)

iii

Young men are hacked off as if for spear poles.[1]   (1)

(Second Section)

There is a certain hero, she is unique,
Ishtar is surpassing, she knows how to smite down.   (5)

(Its Antiphon)

Her celebration is the melee, staging the dance of battle:
She comes to grips with heroes, taking none by the hand,
She leads off with the most valorous.[2]   (10)
Ishtar's celebration is the melee, staging the dance of battle:
She comes to grips with heroes, taking none by the hand,
She leads off with the most valorous.

Frenzy in battle, pas[sion] in strife,   (15)
Were shown forth as [her] portion.

(twenty-six lines lost)

iv

The royal scepter, the throne, the tiara,   (1)
Are given to her, all of them are her due.
He[3] gave her bravery, fame, and might,
He surrounded her in abundance with lightning bolts flashing.   (5)
Once again he added to her uncanny frightfulness,★
He had made her wear awesome radiance, ghastliness, valor —
As for her, she felt that valor,   (10)
In her heart she schemed battle.
In the dwelling of the leader Ea, look out for her terror!

---

1. The simile may mean that the young men are lopped off like poles to be made into spears, that is, "cut down to size." Some translations prefer "Vie with each other, like spears."

2. These lines may combine terms for dancing and fighting, comparing opponents and partners, but are not clear.

3. On the basis of II.1, one expects "he" to refer to Anu, but Ea may be meant.

She is more fearsome than a bull, her clamor like its raging, (15)
In her might she set forth, turning not a hair,[1]
At her uproar Ea, the wise god, became afraid, (20)
Ea became enraged with her.

(Third Part)

"Hear [me, Great Gods! ...]
"Ishtar is wary [   ]
"[   ]." (25)

(Its Antiphon)

(several lines lost)

v

"She [   ]
"Let her be trusty [   ], let her have muscle,
"Let her raise riot, be always ready to fight. (5)

"Let her be fierce,
"Let her hair [be ext]raordinary,[2]
"More [luxu]riant than an orchard.
"Let her be strong of frame,
"Let her complain, she must be strong, (10)
"Let her gasp for breath, she shall not tire,
"Let her not hold back her cry day nor night, let her rage!"

(The gods) assembled, debated, they could not do it. (15)
They replied these words to the leader Ea,
"You are the one suited to do this thing.
"Who else could bring about what you* cannot? (20)
He heeded the words they answered him,
Ea the wise scraped out seven times
The dirt of his nails, (25)
He took spittle(?)[3] in his hand,*

---

1. Literally "Not standing in tatters," meaning obscure.
2. Exceptional hairiness was considered a sign of primitive strength.
3. Uncertain.

Ea the wise has created Saltu ("Discord").

(Fourth Section)

God Ea has straightaway set to his task,   (30)
He is making Saltu that she fight with Ishtar!

(Its antiphon)

She is powerful in her form, monstrous in her proportions,   (35)
She is artful as none could rival, she is a fighter.
Discord is her form,[1] monstrous are her proportions,   (40)
She is artful as none could rival, she is a fighter.
Her flesh is battle, the melee her hair.

vi

(several lines lost)

She is surpassing [   ]
She is fierce [   ]
She has extraordinary strength [   ]   (5)

Saltu is girded with combat for clothes,
Her clamor is born of a deluge,
She is strange, terrifying to behold!   (10)
Raging, she takes her stand in the midst of the depths,
The words that come from her mouth go round about her.

Ea the lord made ready to speak,
To her, to Saltu, whom he created, he says,   (15)
"Keep quiet, listen,
"Pay heed to what I say, hear my orders,
"What I tell you, do!   (20)
"There is a certain goddess,
"Whose greatness is surpassing, beyond all goddesses,
"Strange and cunning is her (handi)wo[rk].[2]
"[Her name] is Irnina, she is [mighty] in mail,   (25)

---

1. Or: "Saltu's form is monstrous in proportions."
2. It is not clear whether this means that she is wondrously formed or that she does wondrous deeds; the latter seems more likely.

"The supreme lady, the capable one, daughter of Ningal.
"I have created you to humiliate her: (30)
"In my cleverness I gave to your stature
    valor and might in abundance.
"Now be off, go off to her private quarters!   (35)
"You should be girded with awful splendor.
"Bring her out,★ 'You there!'
"She will rush out(?) to you, she will speak to you,
"She will demand: 'Now then, woman,
    explain your behavior!'   (40)
"But you, though she be furious, show no respect to her,
"Answer her never a word to ease her feelings.   (45)
"What advantage shall she have of you?
"You are the creature of my power!
"Speak out proudly what is on your tongue,
"And as much again before her."

(Fifth Section)

vii

… has Saltu taken her stand
While Ea, in the midst of the depths, gives her might.

(Its Antiphon)

So the Extraordinary of Form[1] dispatched Saltu,
Drove her to insults, contempt, and calumny.
Ea the wise, whose reasoning is extraordinary,   (10)
Goes on to put yet a word (right) to her feelings.
The sign of Ishtar the queen he gives her,
"It is Ishtar, indeed, she is braver than all other goddesses!"   (15)
He makes her know her grandeur,
    He well described to her that prideful self,
This lest she avoid her later.
"She is the divine princess, her commands are mighty,   (20)
"She is the mistress whose(?) way none has barred.

(gap, traces only)

---

1. Ea may be meant (Groneberg, RA 75 [1981], 111).

"... she is surpassing
"... she is unique in herself.
"She is grander than you are,
      Stir no step abroad!"[1]

viii

(gap)

"Her [fury] and anger, like the welling-up of the sea,
      will overcome you,
"Your speech will ...,
"[Inscrutable] are the ways
      of the capable mistress of the people!"   (25)
Saltu flew into a rage, her face altered horribly,
She turned, she was lordly(?),
[   ] like a fugitive,
[   ] ... truth   (30)
[   ] ...
[   ] ... did not know.

(Sixth Section)

---

1. Obscure: "Do not depart people's houses," perhaps meaning one should not go out on an impossible quest.

Tablet II

i

"Come now [   ]   (1)

"Give a command [   ]

"Prepare [   ]

"In this way(?) [ ] the signs of her strength,   (5)

"Find out all about her, learn of her haunts,

"Bring me her signs, recount to me her behavior."

The giver of orders, the tried-and-true Ninshubur,   (10)

Wise, strong, [   ]

... he[ro],

He went out to the [de]pth(?),

He went alone to [   ] to face her,   (15)

He looked twice when he s[a]w the exceedingly great one!

He fell silent, ...

He examined her form:

"She is b-bizarre in her actions,[1]   (20)

"She b-behaves unreasoningly ...,*

"In her form she is [m-mighty],

"She makes many c-cries for battle,

"She is adorned with a-awesomeness,

"I-in her onslaught she is t-terrible,*   (25)

"She is [mur]derous, bullying, vicious,

"Has the young man and the maid ...

"[   ] clamor."

So did she learn her sign.

---

1. My interpretation of the presumed speech distortion of Ninshubur, owing to his great terror, here and in the following lines, is considered "ausserordentlich" by Groneberg, RA 75 (1981), 131, who prefers to see an extraordinary succession of scribal errors, one per line, of a most unusual graphic and grammatical type.

ii

(gap)

Angrily the most capable of the gods, the all-powerful,
    took (the sign),
Proudly in her might, fiercely she drew herself up.
The warrior Ishtar, the most capable of the gods,
    the all-powerful,   (15)
Proudly in her might, fiercely she drew herself up!
In her greatness she grinds up her enemies,   (20)
She turns not back, she is the greatest among goddesses,
She is ..., like a young man!
She says a word, proudly she speaks,   (25)
"These are the signs of her might!?"

(iii, iv, v?)

(large gap)

vi?

Agu[shaya   ]   (1)
The Capable [Lady,   ]
To Ea [did say,   ]
"Why did you create [Saltu?] against me,   (5)
"Who is [ ] of mouth,
"... [   ]
"The da[ughter of Ningal] is unique,

(fragmentary lines, then gap)

vii?

"You made [her] enormity,   (1)
"Saltu has set [her] cla[mor] against me.
"Let her return to her lair!"
Ea made ready to speak and said to Agushaya,
    hero of the gods,   (5)
"As soon as you said it, then I certainly did it.

"You were driving me to it and cause delight
     at your having done with this.   (10)
"The reason Saltu was made and created is
"That people of future days might know about us.
"Let it be yearly,   (15)
"Let a whirling dance[1] be established
     among the feast days of the year.*
"Look about at all the people!
"Let them dance in the street,
"Hear their clamor!   (20)
"See for yourself the intelligent things they do,
"Learn (now) their motivation.
"As for the king who heard (from me?)
"This song, your praise, the sign of your valor,   (25)
"Hammurabi, in whose reign
"This song, this my praise of you(?), was made,[2]
"May he be granted life forever!

viii

(gap)

Let me praise Ishtar, queen of the gods,
Agushaya's might, as the Capable Lady [   ],
(As for) rapacious(?) Saltu, strange of splendor,   (15)
Whom Ea the leader created,
The signs of her might I/he[3]
Made all the people hear,
I/He have made fair her glorification.   (20)

(Tenth Section)

---

   1. The whirling dance (*gūštu*) or mock combat the people perform is a memorial to Agushaya (=Ishtar), here etymologized by the poet as "the whirling dancer." Mock combats were sometimes held in honor of Ishtar, so this may be an aetiology for the practice.

   2. A reference to the poem itself; see General Introduction, D.1.

   3. The Akkadian original is ambiguous as to whether a third or first person verb is meant. As suggested above, General Introduction D.1, this may have been left ambiguous by the poet so that one could not distinguish between his voice and that of the god of wisdom.

I/He gave her fame worthy of her.
The lioness Ishtar quieted, her heart was appeased.

(Its Antiphon)

Text: Zimmern, VAS 10 214; Scheil, RA 15 (1918), 174–182.

Edition: Groneberg, *Lob der Ištar*, 55–93.

Translation: Labat, *Religions*, 228–237; Bottéro, *Mythologie*, 204–219; Hecker, TUAT II/5, 731–740.

Literature: Foster, *Studies Finkelstein*, 79–84; Wilcke, ZA 67 (1977), 181–186; Hecker, *Epik*, 88–100.

*Notes to Text: (I iv 7) Wasserman, *Style*, 20. (I v 20) Reading *la ka-<ši>*, with Groneberg. (I v 26) Groneberg: *<ša> pí-i-šu*, but not the usual way of referring to spittle. (I vi 37/8) Dtn imperative fem. of *āru*, according to von Soden, AnOr 33/47, 106–107; perhaps meaning "make her come out for battle." (II I 21) Reading *ú-ul im-la-al-lik* (Scheil). (II i 25) *atbušša šulmat* for *tebussa šalum-mat*? (II vii 16) For reasons unclear to me, von Soden and Groneberg rejected this reading, RA 75 (1981), 133; ZA 69 (1979), 156, and emended to *gudūtu*, "offering stand." A later grammatical parallel is provided by T. Pinches, *Texts in Babylonian Wedge-writing* (London, 1882), p. 15 no. 4, 7: *araḫ ša balāṭi isinni akīti liššakin nigūtu* (see IV.16); see also Walker, AnSt 33 (1983), 148, lines 43–46. Groneberg later accepted it, *Lob der Ištar*, 93.

B. LEGENDS OF AKKADIAN KINGS

II.6 LEGENDS OF SARGON

(a) SARGON, KING OF BATTLE

Sargon of Akkad (ca. 2334–2279 B.C.) was remembered in Mesopotamian tradition as a famous conqueror. Epic poems about his exploits are known from the Classical, Mature, and Late periods (see III.7, IV.18). Sargon, King of Battle deals with an invasion of northern Syria and Anatolia. Two Classical-period manuscripts have been combined here as "A" and "B" and divided into arbitrary episodes. They are badly damaged and full of obscurities.

Episode 1 (= A obv. i)

(Sargon sets out for Anatolia, crosses the Amanus, and decides to go to Mardaman. He asks his troops if they will go on.)

[ ] until Ishtar could attain [her] desire,	(1′)
[ ] dwelt in the land, until Ishtar could attain her desire.	
[The … of] Sargon dwelt in the land,	
there were twelve [ ] with him.[1]	
Beyond the Zubi[2] … [ ]	
He brought … across the Amanus, he brought his army	
across the Amanus.	
He reached the Cedar Forest.[3]	(5′)
Bowing down among its shadows, he set down his weapons,	
He made his offerings, he prayed, he spoke in measured words,	
He made his offerings, he prayed,	
the favorite of Irnina spoke in measured words:	
"O my warriors, I will attack the land of Maldaman![4]	
Whatever you tell me, I will surely do!"	(10′)

---

1. An obscure saying about Sargon's "fifty men," (BWL, 251.10) may allude to this episode. For the topos of the king triumphing alone or with a small force, without waiting for the main mass of his troops, see Oppenheim, JNES 19 (1960), 140 and IV.2c, lines 320 and 404; M. Liverani, "Partire sul carro, per il deserto," AIUON 22 (1972), 403–415.

2. Zubi was the name of a watercourse in Mesopotamia between Sippar and Cutha (RGTC 2, 296), but it is not clear that is intended here; see further Conti, RA 82 (1988), 115–130.

3. Here, the Masius or Antitaurus mountains?

4. This place was probably near the Tigris, somewhere around the present Iraqi-Turkish border (Charpin, *Florilegium Marianum* 2 [1994], 180).

His warriors answered him, great bulls
  who had distinguished themselves against Tidnum[1]

(gap)

Episode 2 (= A obv. ii)

(Someone warns Sargon of the difficulties of his projected campaign.)

"This is no land of Amurru, where baleful folk [skulk] about,
  on the fringes of the wide pasture land surrounding it, ...
"They have what we have, except for righteous men ...   (15′)
"My lord, raise a force, form up a strong army,
"Guard the stronghold and keep yourself safe.
"Will you attack? My lord, the battle front is a league long,
  and the flank ... [   ].
"[I have seen] this terrible land, ...   (20′)

(fragmentary lines, then gap)

Episode 3 (= B 1ff.)

(Sargon is addressing his troops.)

"You have given me confidence,
"Concerning ...   (25′)
You have opened my ears.
"Courage, discipline, fighting spirit, valor,
"Have been outstanding among you since long ago,
"Bravery is all yours!
"Mind the wealth that awaits us, that I told you of,   (30′)
"[   ] stand tall, make yourselves famous and be proud!
"Approach and seize [   ] ..."

1. Tidnum was a nomadic people noted for their ferocity.

Episode 4
(Direct continuation of preceding + A rev. i 1–7)

(A speech by a commander, perhaps a champion, to the king?)

Now the commander says,
"Look to yourself, your attire, your equipment,
"You are in command, the enemy comes upon you ...   (35′)
"May your mouth set your heart on its course,
"May your heart set your legs on their course!
"Yes! This is the encounter of valiant men,
"Tomorrow Akkad will start the battle,
"The celebration of the manly will be held,   (40′)
"The writhing (ranks) will writhe back and forth,
"Two women giving birth, bathed in their own blood.[1]
"Where are comrades just watching the celebration?
"Only the ... stands aside.
"And proud the man whose mouth at dawn   (45′)
"Is game to respond to the king for the mission."
He(?) had no opponents in the king's army,
Nor, in all the ranks, did he distinguish himself
        over others for praise.
"On the morrow you will be the one
        to distinguish yourself for praise in the palace,
"Let your pageboy get your grave goods,★   (50′)
"You face the enemy's weapon, his lance.
"I have deferred to you, may the king himself proclaim you
        'my brave warrior.'
"He shall set up your statue in front of his own."

Episode 5
(Direct continuation of preceding + B rev. i 9′ff.)

The one who fell asleep caused the watchful ones to die,
The alert man saved the city for [his] lord.[2]   (55′)
He laid hands on the army and purified it,[3]

---

1. This compares the undulating ranks of fighters to two women in the last, bloody moments of childbirth.
2. With J. Westenholz, *Legends*, 66, a proverb?
3. Possibly a pre-battle ritual where the commander cleansed the army of blood guilt?

The mighty bulls, the brave warriors,
    he commanded to march.
Forty thousand, they were filled with [   ],
Those from the city[1] triply [heroic],
Those of the royal bodyguard wearing breastplates of gold,   (60′)
Those from the colony of Haššum, some in iron,
    wearing frightening helmets(?),*
While those in linen wore mountain gear.
They were quick in maneuver, outstanding in valor,
These men covered the field like stars in the sky.

Episode 6
(Direct continuation of preceding)

(Sargon begins his invasion. The terrible forest blots out the sunlight,
but heavenly beacons come out to illumine the way.
Sargon decimates the city and its surroundings.)

As Sargon made his invasion of the land of Uta-rapashtim,   (65′)
The very forest might have been his enemy,
It cast darkness over heaven, the sun grew dark!
(But) many stars* came out and were set toward the enemy.[2]
The enemy strongholds, nine of them, were founded well,
But he captured every man, ox, and sheep.   (70′)
At the same time he had [   ] Simurrum,[3]
[The trib]ute for Akkad he took away with him,
[And] the tribute of Akkad he ...
He turned the city into heaps of ruins,
He deported the population for fifty leagues
    around the palace.   (75′)

---

1. Agade?
2. This event was often referred to in Classical and later Mesopotamian historical tradition: "The omen of Sargon who underwent darkness but for whom light came out" (AfO 5 [1928/9], 215.7; RA 27 [1930], 149, B.16–17; see Riemschneider, ZA 57 [1965], 130 and Glassner, RA 79 [1985], 122–124). According to A rev. ii 6′ff., this happened when Sargon left the land of Alzi(?) and approached the forest. See also I.6, p. 73 notes 5 and 7; p. 792 note 2.
3. A campaign of Sargon against this city is commemorated in one of his year names: "The year Sargon went to Simurrum" (Kienast, FAOS 7 [1990], 49; Frayne, RIME 2, 8). For its location in northwestern Iran, see D. Frayne, "On the Location of Simurrum," *Studies Astour,* 243–269.

The [bo]nes that he did not burn, the rats gnawed.*
The war [   ] fifty cities.

(gap of about twenty lines)

Episode 7 (A, end)

(Sargon summarizes his victories and challenges anyone to equal them.)

"[I am Sargo]n,
[   ],
[No other] king will go [where I went].   (80')
"I conquered [the whole of] Alzi,[1]
"I wrecked the … that it had.
"I conquered [   ],
"[   ] fate before it.
"I conquered Amurru,   (85')
"I offered up [   ] to the god [   ].
"I conquered [the whole of] Subartu,
"I plundered …, clothing, and …
"I conquered Mutubila(?),
"I [   ] people, I [loaded …] on a raft.   (90')
"[   ]
"I conquered Carchemish(?),
"I put a halter on it [   ].
"I conquered [   ],
"I … its [   ].   (95')
"I conquered [   ],
"I cut down its [trees] and imposed mourning.
"I conquered [Nagur]zam,
"I … [   ] and set I on fire.
"After I conquered them, …"   (100')
To his [   ],
Sargon informed the army.
"So there, any king who would rival me,
"Let him go where I have gone!"   (105')

---

1. Location unknown, reading doubtful; for discussion of the places in this list, see J. Westenholz, *Legends*, 74.

Text: A = van Dijk, TIM 9 48; B = Nougayrol, RA 45 (1951), 182–183 (collated).

Edition: J. Westenholz, *Legends*, 59–93, with numerous readings and interpretations adopted here.

Literature: von Soden, OrNS 26 (1957), 319–320 (notes and collations to B); Groneberg, Hunger, JAOS 98 (1978), 522; J. Westenholz, JAOS 103 (1983), 329.

★Notes to Text: (50′) See Scurlock, N.A.B.U. 1991/3. (61′) Alternatively, read *na-ab-zu-ḫa-tim* from *buzzu'u*, "acts of rough treatment"; that is, outfitted in iron, they were prepared for the worst. (68′) Text: *kakkakkabu*, perhaps an intentional reduplication to indicate a large number, otherwise a ditto-graphy. (76′) Doubtful: Foster, RA 77 (1983), 190, rejected by J. Westenholz, *Legends*, 72–73.

(b) THE SARGON LETTER

This fictitious letter of Sargon of Akkad, studied in Classical-period schools (compare the Gilgamesh Letter IV.58), calls up Sargon's allies for a campaign against Purushhanda, a city in Anatolia (see Sargon, King of Battle, III.7a, and demands that some action be taken with an imposing list of skilled people, court staff, performers, and administrators. Perhaps they were all required to come with him.

(1) To Ilaba-andullashu, Etel-pi-Zababa, Ma[nn]um-mahirshunu, Nur-Shuruppak, (5) Gasher-Ulmash, Messag-idnum, Amurru, and Ahunim: Thus says (10) Sargon your lord: Now say "Yes!" to the warrior Shamash, Ilaba, Zababa, and Ishtar-Annunitum, to seize Purushhanda, And (15) as soon as you see my letter, [summon?] the high priest of [ ], the purifier, temple administrator, anointer, ecstatic, (20) sacristan, and acolyte; the attendant (25) who holds water for the king, sash-bearer, whisk-bearer, holder of the parasol, throne-bearer, (30) bearer of the privy purse, chief courtier, mounted envoy, messenger, recorder, (35) bowman, horseman, lion hunter, elephant warden, and the male and (40) female pensioners; the judges, elders, (45) oath bailiff, night watchman, ward overseer, timekeeper, overseer of stores, (50) overseer of food stores, warden of official gifts and funeral paraphernalia, and the opener of sealed packages and doors; the chief consort, nobleman of rank, (55) noblewoman of rank, prince, princess, governor, shepherd, (60) gamekeeper, goatherd, swineherd, master of poultry, bird hunter, (65) fisherman, warden of seafood, sea fisherman, harbor master, lock master, (70) trapper; the warden of regular foodstores, apportioner of food deliveries, chief dairymen; the blacksmith, (75) metal worker, seal cutter, silversmith, leatherworker, potter, (80) joiner, jeweler, reedworker, physician, barber, (85) gardener, felter, lineners, fuller, rug-beater, (90) builder, perfumer; the itinerant merchant, customs officers,[1] canal men, (95) boat haulers; the chief launderer(?), wringer, dyer, and lint plucker; (100) the dispenser of sweets, athlete, and master of entertainments; the groom, runner, (105) scout; the farmworker, well warden, distiller; the chief steward of the high priest's household, (110) cook, con-

---

1. See M. Dandamayev, "Customs Dues in First-millennium Babylonia," AOAT 272 (2000), 215–222

fectioner, beverage master, protocol officer, master of plate; (115) the aide, secretary, clerk, steward, provisioner, (120) tree warden, household guard; the boatman, boatwright, bargeman, (125) barge builder, basket mender, canal warden, sluice warden, immigration officer, (130) ferryman; the kennelman, collector of rents, raftsmen, master builder; (135) warden of trained animals, acrobat, lament singer, clown, jester, (140) wrestler, musician, praise poet, stuntman, singer, (145) conductor, performer, flutist, percussionist, noisemaker, (150) drummer, piper, wind player, dirge singer, wailer, (155) ..., (160) puppeteer(?), rainbowist,[1] marionette player(?); the doorman, court sweeper, (165) ..., tracker, beater, (170) stalker; the fattener, handler, pest exterminators, ...; the major domo, the queen's household, the keeper of keys, diviner, (180) dream interpreter, fan-bearers, butchers, merchant's retinue, ..., singer, chief singer, assistant chief singer, ...

Text: Gurney, UET 7 73.

Edition: Wilcke, *Archaeologie und Geschichtsbewusstsein* (Munich, 1982), 51 (= note 67), additional collations communicated privately; J. Westenholz, *Legends*, 148–169.

Literature: Hirsch, AfO 25 (1974/77), 192; Kraus, AnSt 30 (1980), 115.

1. Perhaps a performer who refracted and projected colors using glass?

II.7 LEGENDS OF NARAM-SIN

(a) THE SIEGE OF APISHAL

Naram-Sin, king of Agade (ca. 2254–2218 B.C.) appears frequently in Mesopotamian literary and scholarly tradition as the type of the "great king." This fragment of an eight-column tablet preserves part of an epic account of Naram-Sin's war with the city Apishal, the location of which is unknown.[1] The lines that remain deal with the preparations, the march, and the receipt of a conciliatory message from the king of Apishal. Naram-Sin's vizier advises him to advance, as this may be a ruse. Something makes Naram-Sin angry again. According to later Mesopotamian scholarly tradition, Naram-Sin besieged the city successfully.[2] Since most of this text is lost, fundamental elements in the plot are missing.

i

"[ ] of which I speak ...,	(1)
"When I have gone away to the strange and hostile land,	
"Let the mountain paths be opened to me,	
the hidden nooks(?) of spring water.*	
"[I will show] you going to battles, bread baked on coals,	
"[ ] drinking from waterskins."	(5)
[Naram-Sin] Agade* ...	

(breaks off)

ii

Naram-Sin went on his way,
The god of the land indeed was going with him,
Ilaba, the vanguard, before him,
Zababa, splendid of horns,* behind,   (5)
The emblems of Annunitum and Shi-laba,[3] two by two,
Right and left, horn by horn.

---

1. See Gelb, AJSL 55 (1938), 71–72; Glassner, RA 77 (1983), 10; Westenholz, *Legends*, 174.
2. J.-J. Glassner, "Naram-Sin poliorcète, les avatars d'une sentence divinatore," RA 77 (1983), 3–10.
3. Literally, "She-is-a-Lion," presumably a name for Ishtar.

(gap)

v

"Your brilliance is fire, your voice is thunder,   (1)
"You are become like a roaring lion,
"Your mouth is a serpent, your talons a storm-bird!
"Irnina marches with you,
"You have no rivals, who is like you?   (5)
"Calm yourself, let Ishtar and Ilaba be your friends!
"Pass me by[1] and I will swear an oath to you."
While the messenger was repeating this speech,
He was averted (from his purpose) and stood(?)
        while the words went forth(?),
Angry Enlil[2] was soothed(?), the king grew calm,   (10)
The fire blazing in the hero's heart was put out.
Naram-Sin made ready to speak
And said to his vizier,
"Did you hearken to the declaration of the Apishalian?
"Is what he wrote me acceptable to you?"   (15)
According to Enlil's command, the counsellor answered fully,
Saying to Naram-Sin the noble,
"My lord, you are truly a lion,
"Your enemies are foxes.
"At ... your battle cry, let them go into their burrows."   (20)

(fragmentary lines, then gap)

vi

[   ] he ... an omen,
[   ] morning and night,
[   ] a message every day,
[   ], Enlil approached the Apishal<li>an, they ...★   (5)
"Naram-Sin has sent you a message,
"What do you answer the furious king?"

---

1. That is, without attacking the city?
2. The role of Enlil is unclear; perhaps it is a metonym for the king (see p. 125).

"Shall I answer him, 'You be my god'?
"Give me your word, let me contend with him."

"I have given (it) to you, you shall be lord of Apishal.[1]
"[When you ta]ke your place on the throne,   (10)
"You shall make the land rejoice

(fragmentary lines, gap)

Text: (Güterbock)-Pinches, AfO 13 (1939/41), pl. I–II after p. 48, partial copy only; new copy by
   Finkel communicated privately.
Edition: J. Westenholz, *Legends*, 173–187.
★Notes to Text: (i 3) Reading *taprat̤ e!-ni*; the reading *ta-ab-ra-at* GIRI₁₇.ZAL (AHw, 1299b) is exclud-
   ed by new copy; note that logograms are not used elsewhere in the preserved text. (i 6) Or "the
   Akkadian"? (ii 5) WGL: *e-da-<<ša>>-am qa-ar-ni-in*; Westenholz: *e-da-<<ta>>-an*. (ii 7) WGL. (vi 4)
   ib-tu, perhaps also in v 9 and vi 13?

---

1. It is not clear who this Apishalian is, or why Enlil(?) would promise him the throne of Apishal
if he were not already king. Apishalian, at least in later periods, could refer to a person with some
bodily defect.

(b) THE GREAT REVOLT

Coalitions of Mesopotamian and foreign rulers attacked Naram-Sin (see I.3). He defeated them in a series of battles that acquired legendary, epic character in the Classical period, if not before. Classical-period versions of this story are closer to historical reality than is the Mature version (below, III.7b), which converts it into a cautionary tale. But already exaggeration of numbers has set in and Naram-Sin is dealt crushing defeats. The enemy has taken on an outlandish, supernatural character (iii 17′). Two long versions of this story are presented here as (1) and (2), incorporating the overlap of (1) in (2). A short version is presented as (3). The interrelationships among the various versions and manuscripts are difficult to understand. One scribe had a predilection for foreign places that the other did not. For example, the Mari scribe naturally inserted Mari among the list of rebellious cities. Some see fluidity of tradition in these differences, others subtle political purpose. The most probable explanation of these texts is that they were free adaptations and reworkings of copies, perfect or not, of original Naram-Sin inscriptions available for study in schools (such as I.3, above). The Old Assyrian parody (I.6) shows how far such reworking could go, but it, like other compositions, presupposes knowledge of genuine Sargonic inscriptions. If there was an Archaic-period epic tradition alongside the inscriptions that might be the source of these texts, it has not survived, and those Classical-period narratives the beginnings of which are preserved sound more like inscriptions than full-blown poetic narratives. Yet another Classical-period version of this story, similar in character to (3) below, is included with III.7b.

1. The Treachery of Kish

(i 1) [En]lil (is) his god(?),⋆ Ilaba, the warrior of the gods, [is his military strength]. Naram-Sin, the mighty king, king of Agade, king of the four quarters of the earth, emissary(?)⋆ of Ishtar and Annunitum, anointed of Anu, general for Enlil, governor for Ilaba, who guards the sources of the Irnina, Tigris, and Euphrates, who manifests the power of his weapon(?)⋆ to all kings:

(10) When the four world regions together rebelled against me, Kish, Cutha, Tiwa, Urum, Kazallu, Giritab, Apiak, Ibrat, Dilbat, Uruk, and Sippar together rebelled against me.

(16) At that time — (although) Sargon my father had defeated

Uruk, had liberated the Kishites, had shaved off their locks of servitude,[1] had broken their fetters, had taken Lugalzagesi, their oppressor, to Agade, by the verdict of Ishtar and Annunitum he defeated them in battle ...

(21) By Ishtar, Ilaba, Shullat and Hanish, Shamash and Umshu, Kish was no enemy but in brotherhood with me, yet they attacked me in a ... and wicked way![2] — at that time, Kish assembled between Tiwa and Urum, in the field of Sin, between Esabad and the temple of Gula,[3] and raised to kingship Iphur-Kish, a Kishite, son of Sumirat-Ishtar, a singer of laments. Puttimatal, king of Simurrum, (30) Ingi, king of the land of Namar, Rish-Adad, king of Apishal, Migir-Dagan, king of Mari, Hupshumkipi, king of Marhashi, Duhsusu, king of Mardaman, (35) Manum, king of Magan, Lugal-anna, king of Uruk, Ir-Enlil, king of Umma, Amar-Enlil, king of Nippur, Bubu, leader of Der, (40) Amar-gin, king of Uruk, Pashahnadgalni, leader of Lullubu (his ... was shaved, his [remaining hair] was ...), ... thirty captains, (45) 80,000 of them went to [   ] and [   ] ... they attacked me and af[ter   ] I let them go nine times ... They raised an army [for battle] and [I killed?] 50,000, ... (50) Amar-gin, king of Uruk, raised an army for battle, [I killed?] 40,000 *(gap)* Through nine levies of the men of Agade, I raised a force against them.

2. The Sparing of Agade

(ii 2′) [Gula-DINGIR, king of G]utium, [   ]-el, king of Kakmium, [   ]-ael, king of Lullu, [   ]-anda, king of Hahhu, [   ]-li-DINGIR, king of Turukku, [   ]-ha-DINGIR, leader of Kanesh, [   ]-du-DINGIR, leader of the Amorites, [   ]-me-e-DINGIR, leader of Der, [   ]-buna-DINGIR, leader of Ararru, [   ]-itluh, leader of the Kassites, [   ]-ibra, leader of Meluhha, [   ]-duna, leader of Aratta, [   ]-en, king of Marhashi, [   ]-shar, king of all Elam, [   ]-na-DINGIR, king of GIŠ.GI, *(two lines repeated by scribe)* [   ]-ge, king of the land of NINNU, [Mada]gina, king of Armanum,

---

1. This refers to a lock of hair left on the partially shorn head as a mark of servitude; it may also have meant more generally external indications of misfortune (compare III.14 Tablet IV Fragment A line m). For liberation, see p. 237 note 1.
2. The placement of this sentence between two manuscripts combined here is hypothetical.
3. Variant: "Temple of Ninkarrak."

[   ], king of Hana, ... [rose(?)] against me.

(iii 4′) My troops dug pits for [   ] leagues, but he piled up dirt [and got over]. When I heard what he had done, I went looking for him quickly, with my mighty warfare [I defeated him]. Where there is a dais of my gods Shullat and [Hanish], where I invoked the Capable Lady, Ishtar [my] m[other], and where I had provided beer in abundance that I [   ], [I defeated] Mengi, king of Nagu, with my [mighty] warfare and brought him to the port of Agade. Gula-DINGIR, king of Gutium [   ], (15′) whom I had [defeated] with my mighty warfare and had let go to his own land to [   ] — He is neither flesh nor blood, but [   ] — in the Amanus, the land of cedars, ... before a great gorge in the mountains [   ]. (20′) He seized its entrance and attacked furtively at night. He utterly defeated my troops and [trampled them], [he piled] their corpses in a confusion of burial mounds, their blood [filled] the depressions and ravines! (25′) Until sunrise, six leagues he [   ] nor did he give respite [   ]. He pursued me and [attacked me furiously], 90,000 of my troops under the command of [   ] he utterly defeated and [trampled]. (30′) I [   ] in my 360,000 troops, somebody ... [   ] and relented toward me. For the sake of Sargon [my father] [and] the deeds and suffering he had undergone [   ] they did not enter Agade [   ] nor did they [   ] (35′) to the port of Agade. [   ] Puzur-Ulmash and Rish-Zababa, [heroes of] Agade ... [   ], [   ] Rish-Zababa ... [   ] [A]gade [   ] ... [   ] x+60,000 [of my] troops

(after two fragmentary lines, breaks off)

Text: Grayson-Sollberger, Dossin, RA 70 (1976), 109–110, 113–114, 116, 118–119; Charpin, *Florilegium Marianum* 3 (1997), 11.

Edition: J. Westenholz, *Legends*, 230–257; D. Charpin, "La version mariote de 'l'insurrection générale contre Narâm-Sîn' (texte no. 1)," *Florilegium Marianum* 3 (1997), 9–17.

Literature: Jacobsen, AfO 26 (1978/9), 102–128; S. Tinney, "A New Look at Naram-Sin and the 'Great Rebellion'," JCS 47 (1995), 1–14.

Notes to Text: (i 1) Text: ID.ZU, perhaps mistake for DINGIR-*šu* (see I.3, differently J. Westenholz, *Legends*, 239–240). (i 4) *mušāpī* by etymology should be "one who makes manifest" (here, warfare?). (i 8) Text: GIŠ.ZU for GIŠ.TUKUL, or perhaps mistake for É-*sú* "his house" (though there is no parallel for such an expression).

3. The Tenth Battle

(§1) By Ishtar, Ilaba, Shullat and Hanish, Shamash, and Umshu! Nine times they rebelled against me, nine times I took them prisoner, nine times I let them go free! For the tenth time they rose against me for battle: Banana, the Harian leader(?), (and) [x+]65,000 I smote when they came out (for battle). Then did(?) Naram-Sin, [by] the weapon of Ilaba [and the scepter of Enlil] *(gap)*

(§2) [Whosoever shall do away with this inscription] *(gap)* May Ea block up(?) his watercourse ..., may no grain sprout in his furrow. May Nergal, lord of the weapon, break his weapon. May Shamash, lord of due process [   ].

Text: van Dijk, VAS 17 42.
Edition: J. Westenholz, *Legends*, 258–261.

C. Kings of Babylonia and Their Times

II.8 SIN-KASHID, KING OF URUK

A tablet found in the ruins of the palace of Sin-kashid, an Amorite ruler of Uruk (ca. 1850 B.C.), records an eloquent appeal to the king to restore certain rites in the Eanna temple so the offended goddess Nanay (see II.2) will return. This is cast as a dialogue between an unidentified speaker, perhaps a high priest of the goddess, and the goddess herself. The priest claims that the "true shepherd," Sin-kashid (whose name he etymologizes to mean "The-God-Sin-Is-Arriving [in triumph]") has, in accordance with his propitious name, "arrived" or "prevailed" (same Akkadian word) at last in Uruk and inaugurated an era of bliss. He says that the goddess predicted this when she told him he would have to look after Uruk until the coming of the true shepherd. Since the promised ruler has come "from Ur" (city of the god Sin, a further play on the royal name) and Uruk has come to life, the priests asks if the goddess will now return to her sanctuary. She evidently replies that she will once certain cultic observances have been reinstated. The petition closes by urging the king to act, making one last wordplay on his name.

Numerous inscriptions of Sin-kashid testify that he did restore Eanna, though they say nothing of any connection with Ur. Normally petitions were written in letter form, sometimes using elaborate rhetoric, but this composition begins with a proclamation. Its style may be compared to the flowery flattery of Adad-shuma-usur (see IV.57), though it could have been intended as a literary work of praise. For the oracular language, compare II.12.

> (§1) A true shepherd of propitious name, whose protective spirit abides forever, has come into the temple Eanna! Henceforth, well-being is before him, behind him is life!
>
> (§2) From the moment Nanay came to me and caused me to dwell in the court of her father, Sin, she said, "Until I provide a true shepherd and bring Uruk to life, you must grind the flour portions of Uruk. A great man will give me Uruk. They will purify(?) city and temple."
>
> (§3) Since the true shepherd has 'arrived' in this land, I said: "Dead Uruk has come to life and the true shepherd, 'he who came out hither from the city of the god Sin to [Uruk?]', has been provided. Will you ....?"

(§4) She said, "When the Urukean ... the city. And as for the true shepherd, I will not come ...." (*From the fragmentary lines that follow, it seems that the goddess wants various rites.*) My lord should hear my word, he should take what I say in hand, and he should make the goddess's desire 'arrive.'

Text: van Dijk in H. Lenzen, ed., *Abhandlungen der deutschen Orient-Gesellschaft Nr. 5, XVIII. vorläufiger Bericht über die von dem Deutschen Archälogischen Institut und der Deutschen Orient-Gesellschaft aus Mitteln der Deutschen Forschungsgemeinschaft unternommenen Ausgrabungen in Uruk Warka* (Berlin, 1960), plate 28c (Photo, 20d-f).

Edition: None.

II.9 NARAM-SIN, KING OF ESHNUNNA

This composition celebrates a military victory of Naram-Sin, a king of Esh-nunna in the late nineteenth century B.C., and his subsequent enlarging of the E-meslam, temple of the god Erra and his wife, Laz, in Cutha. Written in a highly poetic style, it tells how Naram-Sin, after a colloquy among the gods, was urged by Ishtar-Annunitum to go to Erra's temple to take up weapons, with Erra to be his comrade in battle. Naram-Sin does this, wins in his war, and commemorates his victory with artwork in bronze at the doors of the tem-ple. Laz intercedes for him with her husband, no doubt asking long life and a successful reign for Naram-Sin. Little is known of this king, save that he mod-eled himself on his great predecessor not only by using his name, but also by adopting his grand title, "universal king," and by assuming divine honors in his lifetime.[1] It seems clear that he and other rulers of Eshnunna were among those who claimed to carry on the traditions of the Sargonic empire.

Although some scholars believe that this text is about Naram-Sin, king of Agade, they must ignore its obvious formal and linguistic parallels with other Classical-period commemorative inscriptions (see, for example, II.11), which are over-whelmingly in favor of this Naram-Sin being the Old Babylonian king of that name.[2] In the Cuthaean Legend of Naram-Sin (see III.7b), Naram-Sin of Agade states that he left an inscription in the E-meslam in Cutha; perhaps the two kings were conflated there, or, like Naram-Sin of Agade, Naram-Sin of Eshnunna claimed a special personal connection with that sanctuary and its god. Compare also IV.17, Tablet I lines 1–20.

> (§1) (*fragmentary lines*) Annunitum said to Naram-[Sin], "Fear not
> … before [him]. Look for(?) what [I have …] for you, the doors have
> been opened, bring out for yourself the [   ], let your [hands] receive
> the weapon of victory." Ishtar, the Cap[able Lady, told] the king her
> wishes, "Do not leave my [ax]e and my weapon [in a corner, un-
> used], bethink you of this: [Go to] the doors of the temple of Erra,
> your protector, bring them out for yourself, go to war!"

---

1. Goetze, JCS 7 (1953), 59; Landsberger, JCS 8 (1954), 24; D. Charpin, "Le règne de Naram-Sin," *Studies Birot*, 57–61.

2. For discussion and opinion on this point, see Frayne, JAOS 102 (1982), 511–513, retracted in BiOr 48 (1991), 380 note 5; Charpin, MARI 3 (1984), 66 note 65; W. G. Lambert, JAOS 106 (1986), 793–795; J. Westenholz, *Legends*, 189 note 1; Charpin, *Histoire* (p. 79 note 1), 132.

(§2) Naram-[Sin re]ceived the weapon from his temple, saying, "May this be sharp and drink the blood of [my enemies]!"

(§3) Erra [made ready to speak] and said to Naram-Sin, his king, "Enlil ... [   ] but I will be the crusher, the protector, the flame, the fire!"

(§4) The king spoke ... "Let me hold aloft your lion-standard [in battle ...]. I will build you a temple that will bring joy to your heart. Do you reside therein, abide on the dais of royalty. I will make your close both longer and wider, I will adorn your holy dwelling with green gardens. May she praise and prosper its king, may Laz ordain his destiny before you. I will lead her, Ishtar, to her battle."

(§5) The god Erra and Naram-Sin went together, his comrade and he. His attack charged back and forth over* the land, the warrior Erra went with him. (*In the fragmentary lines that follow, Naram-Sin is victorious, establishes his reputation, and rules, like Enlil, north and south. As promised, Naram-Sin builds Erra a new temple, in which the king commissions a picture, perhaps a relief or painting, of the battle.*)

(§6) At the bolted door which gives access from the outer court, two serpents were placed, the two fixed panels were of bronze. Then the inscription of Erra and Naram-Sin was written on the serpents (about) the battle, the king's commemorative inscription was written on the serpents, (about) the good he did.[1] (*The temple is completed and furnished, then Laz asks a blessing for Naram-Sin.*)

(§7) She blessed the king before her beloved, "Do you, in whom Anu put his trust, beloved of Duranki,[2] lord of E-meslam, foremost of the [Igigi-gods], give to this king a mighty weapon and shepherd's staff, to this wise man for whom justice is joy, who built your temple, the shepherd's staff of ..." (*fragmentary lines, breaks off*)

Text: W. G. Lambert, BiOr 30 (1973), 359–360.
Edition: Westenholz, *Legends*, 189–201.
Notes to Text: (35) Gtn *nakāpu*?

1. That is, building the temple, for which Naram-Sin took sole responsibility.
2. Enlil; Erra is here compared to the hero-god Ninurta (see III.23).

II.10 HAMMURABI, KING OF BABYLON

(a) HAMMURABI, KING OF JUSTICE

King Hammurabi of Babylon (1792–1750 B.C.) commemorated his role as a pious ruler, vigorous conqueror, and giver of justice in a long inscription best known from a large diorite stela carved late in his reign. This showed the god Shamash at the top giving the prayerful king a rod and a ring, perhaps symbolizing justice. Most of the inscription consists of legal provisions, now known as the "laws of Hammurabi," but it began with an eloquent tribute to the king's character and accomplishments, now known as the "prologue," and concluded with what is now known as the "epilogue," exhortations to future people, be they rulers or people in legal difficulties, as well as curses against anyone who would disregard or tamper with Hammurabi's achievements. The terms "prologue" and "epilogue" are potentially misleading because the entire work may have been composed as a unit, drawing on well-established traditions of commemorative inscriptions, commemorative year names, collections of legal material, and hymns of praise of his reign and, in some instances, those of preceding kings.[1]

Hammurabi begins by making his accession to the throne a cosmic event in which the gods gave him specific commissions as to how to rule their subjects for them. He then surveys, in vague terms, his benefactions to various cities and sanctuaries in Babylonia and greater Mesopotamia: "the epic spirit, the true lyricism displayed in these lines was in the service of propaganda, masking, though not completely, the dreary procession of plunder, destruction, and deportation that went along with these conquests."[2] Twenty-five places in Babylonia and their gods (for two cities, Adab and Isin, no specific deity is mentioned) are listed first in carefully chosen language, corresponding to major events in Hammurabi's empire-building strategy and to major construction projects. The first seven were major Babylonian cult centers. The other nearby cities are listed geographically in a broad circle around Babylon. After describing his deeds in Babylonia, the "south" of the text, Hammurabi turns his attention to the mid-Euphrates, Mari, Tuttul (near the confluence of the Balikh and Euphrates), then to Eshnunna, Assur, and Nineveh, the "north" of the text.

1. For an introduction to scholarship on the monument, see B. André-Salvini, *Le Code de Hammurabi* (Paris, 2003). For the prologue and the epilogue, see V. A. Hurowitz, *Inu Anum ṣirum, Literary Structures in the Non-Juridical Sections of Codex Hammurabi*, OPSNKF 15 (1994).
2. A. Finet, *Le Code de Hammurapi* (Paris, 1998), 10. See in general D. Charpin, *Hammu-rabi de Babylone* (Paris, 2003).

One of Hammurabi's greatest victories, the defeat of Rim-Sin of Larsa late in his reign, is veiled as "sparing" Larsa; the same expression is used of Mari, which Hammurabi probably destroyed.[1] Although in four commemorative year names Hammurabi claims to have destroyed or defeated the city Malgium, he claims here to have treated its people well. As for Eshnunna, which Hammurabi is known to have destroyed, the city is not actually named, but he alleges the satisfaction he afforded its chief deities and refers to the resettlement of its population. As if taking his cue from the nature of each of the local deities mentioned, Hammurabi portrays himself as intelligent, productive, or warlike; these attributes may also refer obliquely to his political relationship with the various cities involved.

The prologue exists in several variant versions. The most important of these variations have been noted in the translation with †, meaning that the phrase or clause following is not found in some manuscripts. The epilogue has far fewer variants and includes a reworking and elaboration of a well-established stock and sequence of curses, the origins of which can be traced to the Archaic period (see I.3).[2] Besides the stela, numerous manuscripts of this inscription, or excerpts from it, exist from Babylonia and Assyria from the Classical through the Late periods. It was then perhaps studied in schools more as a literary monument than for its legal content, though Hammurabi enjoyed a high reputation in later periods of Mesopotamian history as an important king.[3] Some of these manuscripts introduce variants that may be mistakes rather than genuine variants of the original text; these have not been noted in the translation.

The language of this composition is replete with rare and dialectal words, difficult expressions, and the sonorous and elaborate syntax deemed appropriate for recording the deeds of a king. The ultimate source for this style and usage have not been identified, but it seems to owe less to Sumerian tradition than it does to the Archaic languages and literatures of northern Mesopotamia and Syria, although Sumerian versions or translations of Hammurabi inscriptions and Sumerian hymns

---

1. J. Sasson, "The King and I, A Mari King in Changing Perception," JAOS 118 (1998), 453–470.

2. For a brief survey of the development of curse formulae in Akkadian and Sumerian, see Michalowski and Walker, *Studies Sjoberg*, 391–394.

3. The essay of J. Laessøe, "On the Fragments of the Hammurabi Code," JCS 4 (1950), 173 –187 is out of date but contains useful observations; see also J. J. Finkelstein, "The Hammurabi Law Tablet BE XXXI 22," RA 63 (1969), 11–27; W. G. Lambert, "The Laws of Hammurabi in the First Millennium," *Studies Finet* (1989), 95–98. For references to Hammurabi in later periods, see, for example, Reiner, JAOS 105 (1985), 594 (reputed healer); von Weiher, SBTU II 50. The curse formulae were reused by a first-millennium Babylonian king in a treaty (Borger, OrNS 34 [1965], 168–169), and the reference to family ghosts in lines l 39–40 may have been the inspiration for II.38 line 14.

in honor of Hammurabi and his successor, Samsuiluna, are known.[1] Rather than in narrative, which, in this period, was preferred for events close to each other in time (see II.11), the story of Hammurabi's achievements is here conveyed with epithets, lending them a timeless quality, in this translation generally rendered in the past tense.

(Prologue)

(i 1) When exalted Anu, king of the Anunna-gods, and Enlil, lord of heaven (5) and earth, who ordains the destinies of this land, ordained to Marduk, first-born son of (10) Ea, supremacy over all peoples, (15) made him the greatest of the Igigi-gods, called Babylon[2] its exalted name, made it preeminent in the four world regions, established (20) therein for him a kingship the foundations of which are as (25) perduring as heaven and earth, then did Anu and Enlil call me, Hammurabi, (30) devout, god-fearing prince, by my name to bring happiness to the people, to show forth justice in the land, to destroy (35) the wicked and the evil-doer, to ensure that the powerful not wrong the weak, to rise (40) like the sun over the people of this land and to illumine this country![3]

(50) I am Hammurabi the shepherd, whom Enlil called by name, who heaped up (55) plenty and abundance, who completed to perfection everything required for Nippur,[4] the bond of heaven and earth, the devout (60) provider for its Ekur; the capable king who (65) restored the city Eridu, who purified (ii 1) the lustration rites of its E-abzu; who invaded the four world regions, (5) who made great the fame of Babylon, who gladdened the heart of Marduk his lord, (10) who served[5] Esagila all his days; of lineage royal, whom Sin (15)

---

1. Å. Sjöberg, "Was There a Sumerian Version of Codex Hammurabi?" *Aula Orientalis* 9 (1991), 219–225 (see also Oelsner, N.A.B.U. 1993/70); "Ein Selbstpreis des Königs Hammurabi von Babylon," ZA 54 (1961), 51–70; "Prayers for King Hammurabi of Babylon," *Ex Orbe Religionum, Studia Geo. Widengren oblata 1, Studies in the History of Religion* 21 (1972), 58–71; compare also "Two Prayers for King Samsuiluna of Babylon," JAOS 93 (1973), 544–547; J. J. A. van Dijk, "Inanna, le bon augure de Samsu'iluna," *Studies Lambert*, 119–129.

2. Variant: "Nippur," perhaps for use there.

3. Another version began, "[ ] gave to Hammurabi, son of Sin-muballit, the shepherd, his handiwork, the shepherdship of justice and bestowed upon him scepter and crown, as befits kingship." The sun was often associated with kingship (Fischer, *Iraq* 64 [2002], 132).

4. In his twenty-second year, Hammurabi built a canal system serving Nippur, Eridu, Ur, Larsa, Uruk, and Isin; this may explain the grouping and order of cities that follows.

5. Variant: "Who served in Esagila."

created, benefactor of the city Ur, humble and prayerful, (20) who brought abundance to its Ekishnugal; the king with superior understanding who heeded Shamash, the mighty one, who repaired (25) Sippar, who adorned its holy dwelling of Aya with green (gardens),[1] who decorated (30) the temple Ebabbar with paintings,[2]* so it is like a dwelling in heaven; the warrior who spared Larsa, who rebuilt its Ebabbar (35) for Shamash his ally; the lord[3] who gave new life to Uruk, who provided (40) abundant water for its people and raised high Eanna, who heaped up bounteous (45) yields for Anu and Ishtar; protector of this land, who gathered in (50) the exiled people of Isin and lavished abundance on its temple Egalmah; (55) monarch among kings, favorite brother to Zababa, who repaired the residential area of Kish, (60) who surrounded its E-meteursag with awe-inspiring splendor, who carried out to perfection the great rites of (65) Ishtar, who provided for its temple Hursagkalamma; battle net enmeshing foes, whom Erra his comrade helped to achieve (iii 1) his desire, who expanded the city Cutha and augmented (5) everything belonging to its E-meslam; rampaging wild bull goring enemies, (10) beloved of Tutu,[4] who brought joy to the city Borsippa, devout and vigilant (15) for its Ezida; god among kings,[5]* master of insight, who expanded the arable lands of (20) Dilbat, who garnered vast grain stores for the Mighty One, Urash;[6] lord fully meriting (25) scepter and diadem, whom Mama, midwife (of the gods), formed in perfection;[7] (30) who established divine services at Kesh, who provided in abundance sacred repasts (35) for Nintu; deliberative, perfect in every respect, who decreed pasture land and (40) watered ground for Lagash and Girsu, who provided (45) great food offerings for its E-

---

1. For gardens in connection with a goddess's residence, compare IV.27.

2. Meaning disputed, some translators prefer "who exalted"; see further Notes to Text (ii 29).

3. By using the term "lord" (Sumerian EN), Hammurabi may have been invoking an ancient title of the Sumerian kings of Uruk.

4. This refers to a city god of Borsippa whose name was later transferred to Marduk (see III.17 Tablet VII lines 9–14 and III.45a).

5. This epithet is disputed, some scholars preferring to emend the text (Roth, *Law Collections*, 140; but see Finet, *Code* [above, p. 126, note 2], 37); see further Notes to Text (iii 16).

6. A local deity later identified with Ninurta; for the epithet "Mighty One," compare III.22(a), 15.

7. This means that Hammurabi was worthy of being king at birth. "Midwife" is an explanatory translation for a word meaning "wise," understood as expert in child birth, like French "sage femme."

ninnu; who seized many enemies with his firm grip, the favorite of the Capable Lady, (50) who carried out the oracles of Zabala, who made Ishtar happy; (55) the holy prince whose prayer Adad acknowledged, who appeased the heart of (60) valiant Adad in the city Karkara, who provided for all time proper appointments for its E-udgalgal; (65) the king who gave new life to Adab, who provided sustenance for its E-mah; (70) hero among kings, whose onslaught was irresistible, (iv 1) the one who gave new life to the city Mashkan-shapir, who provided its E-meslam with (5) abundant water; the sage public servant who (10) plumbed the depths of wisdom; †who kept the people of Malgium secure from catastrophe, †who lavishly repaired (15) their dwellings, <who> decreed in perpetuity sacred food offerings for Ea and Damgalnunna, who made (20) his kingship glorious⋆; the foremost of kings, who, at a favorable sign from Dagan, his creator, subdued (25) the inhabited regions of the mid-Euphrates; who spared (30) the people of Mari and Tuttul; the devout prince who made (35) Tishpak's features glow with pleasure,[1] who established sacred repasts for Ninazu, †who rescued his people in time of crisis and magnanimously (40) provided them with a place to live in Babylon; (45) †shepherd of the people, whose deeds pleased Ishtar; who sustained Ishtar in the E-ulmash (50) in Agade, city of broad streets and squares; who showed forth truth, who governed folk justly; (55) who returned to the city Assur its guardian spirit; who suppressed insurgents; †the king (60) who held splendid offices for Ishtar in the E-mashmash of Nineveh; †devout and prayerful to the great gods, scion of Sumu-lael, mighty heir to Sin-muballit, (v 1) of royal lineage eternal, mighty king, sun-god (5) of Babylon who caused light to come out upon the land of Sumer and Akkad; (10) king who brought the four world regions under one rule, favored by Ishtar am I!

---

1. This refers to Hammurabi's conquest of the city Eshnunna, the name of which some scholars would insert here in the text (Kraus, WZKM 51 [1950],176; Finet, *Code*, 41).

When (15) Marduk commanded me to undertake proper governance of the people of this land, I made (20) truth and justice the
common parlance of this land, I brought happiness to the people.
(*The laws follow here*).

(Epilogue)

(xlvii 9) I am Hammurabi the perfect king, (15) I was neither heedless nor neglectful of the people of this land, whom Enlil gave to me
and whose shepherdship Marduk gave over to me.* I sought out
peaceful places for them, (20) I found the way out of numerous pressing crises, I made light come out upon them. With the mighty weaponry that Zababa and Ishtar (25) bestowed upon me, with the
superior insight that Ea ordained to be mine, with the capability that
Marduk gave over to me, I expelled enemies (30) north and south, I
extinguished warfare, I brought happiness to the people, I made all
(35) the people of the realm to lie down in green pastures, I allowed
no one to alarm them.

(40) The great gods called me and I was, indeed, the shepherd who
brought peace, whose scepter was (45) just, whose benevolent protective shadow stretched over my city. I held (50) the people of this
land, Sumer and Akkad, in my embrace. They waxed prosperous under my wardenship, I served them (55) in peace, I kept them secure
with my wisdom.

Lest the powerful (60) wrong the weak, to give just government to
the orphan and widow, I have inscribed my precious words upon my
stela and (65) set it up before the statue of me, King of Justice, in
Babylon, that city which Anu and Enlil have raised high, in its Esagila, that house whose foundations are as perduring as heaven and
earth, (70) to judge cases at law in this land, to render verdicts for this
land, to give just government to the wronged.

I am a king (80) preeminent among kings, my words are carefully
chosen, my capability unrivaled. By the command of Shamash, (85)
the great judge of heaven and earth, may my justice show forth in all
lands. By the word of (90) Marduk, my lord, may my ordinances[1]

---

1. Some scholars prefer to understand the word here translated "ordinances" as "pictures,"
referring to the relief at the top of the stele (see G. R. Driver, *The Babylonian Laws* 1 [Oxford,
1952], 1: 291; Finet, *Code*, 137).

find none who will set them aside. In Esagila, which I love, may my name be invoked favorably (xlviii 1) for all time. Let the wronged man* who (5) has a cause go before the statue of me, King of Justice, and let him read well (10) what is written and let him hear my precious words and let (15) my stela reveal to him his cause, let him see his case, let his heart be set at ease and let him say:

(20) "Lord Hammurabi, who was truly father-like to his people, subjected himself (25) to the word of Marduk, his lord, and accomplished Marduk's will north and (30) south. He gladdened the heart of Marduk his lord, ordained happiness (35) for the people for all time, and governed this land justly."

(40) He should say this and pray for me with (45) his whole heart before Marduk, my lord, and Sarpanitum, my lady.

May the protective god, the guardian spirit, and all the gods who frequent (50) Esagila, and the very structure of Esagila daily make favorable mention of me before (55) Marduk, my lord and Sarpanitum, my lady.

For all time (60) in the future, may any king who shall arise in this land observe the words (65) of justice which I inscribed on my stela, may he not change (70) the law cases of this land I judged nor the verdicts of this land I rendered. May he not repeal my ordinances.

(75) If that man has superior understanding and will govern justly this land, let him heed the words that I inscribed upon my stela. May this stela show him (80) precedent and example, the law cases of this land I judged and the verdicts of this land I rendered. May he govern the people of this land justly, (90) may he judge their law cases, may he render their verdicts, may he remove wicked and evil-doers from his land, may he bring happiness to his people.

(95) I am Hammurabi, king of justice, to whom Shamash gave truth. My words are carefully chosen, (100) my deeds unrivalled, they are lost only on the fool, for the wise (xlix 1) they stand out as praiseworthy.

If that man (5) has heeded my words that I inscribed upon my stela and has not set aside my judgments, has not revoked my words,(10) has not changed my ordinances, may Shamash (15) extend that man's scepter, even as he did for me, may he tend his people justly.

If that man has not heeded my words (20) I inscribed upon my stela, has disregarded my curses and has not feared (25) the curses of the gods and (30) has annulled the cases I judged, has revoked my words, has changed my ordinances, has erased my name inscribed here and inscribed (35) his own name or instigated another to do this to avoid the curses, that man, (40) be he king, be he lord, be he governor or be he any manner of man whatsoever, may great (45) Anu, father of the gods, who named me to reign, deprive him of royal splendor, may he break (50) his scepter, may he lay a curse upon his destiny!

May Enlil, the lord who ordains destinies, (55) whose command cannot be changed, who made my kingship great, stir up against him, in his own household, a revolt which cannot be suppressed, (60) an uprising which will lead to his ruin, may he ordain his destiny to be a reign of sighing, (65) days of want, years of famine, darkness without light, (70) blindness(?). May he, by his imposing word, command the destruction of his city, the exile of his people, the overthrow (75) of his kingship, and the extinction of his name and memory in this land!

May Ninlil, the great mother, whose word prevails in Ekur, (85) the lady who makes favorable mention of me, (90) make his case go badly before Enlil at the trial and verdict. May she (95) persuade Enlil to command the devastation of his land, the destruction of his people, and the draining away, like water, of his life!

May Ea, the great prince, whose destinies (100) take precedence over all others, sage of the gods, who knows all there is to know, (l 1) who prolonged my life, deprive him of understanding and wisdom, and (5) lead him astray. May he dam his watercourses at their source, may he let no grain, life of the people, grow (10) in his soil!

May Shamash, the great judge (15) of heaven and earth, who governs justly living creatures, the lord in whom I trust, overthrow (20) his kingship. May he misjudge his own case, may he lose his way, (25) may he trip up his forces. When he takes omens, may the prognoses be unfavorable, predicting the overthrow of his kingship and (30) the destruction of his land. May a cruel command of Shamash overtake him, may he tear him away from (35) this world of the living and make his family ghosts (40) thirst for water in the next.

May Sin, lord of the heavens, the god who created me, whose oracle* shows forth among the gods, deprive him of (45) crown and royal throne. May he lay upon him a heavy punishment, his greatest chastisement, (50) which can never quit his person. May he go through all the days, months, and years of his reign in sighs and (55) lamentation. May he show him a bitter rival for his kingship. May he ordain him a life (60) in the image of death!

May Adad, lord of abundance, (65) irrigator of heaven and earth, my ally, deprive him of rains from heaven and springtime floods (70) at their source. (75) May he destroy his land with want and starvation. May he roar furiously against his city and (80) turn his land into ruins, as if left by the deluge!

May Zababa, great warrior, firstborn son of Ekur, (85) who marches at my right hand, break his weaponry on the field of battle. May he turn day into night for him and let (90) his enemy triumph over him!

May Ishtar, mistress of battle and combat, who bares (95) my weapon, my protective spirit who loves my reign, curse his kingship in (100) her angry heart and furious rage. May she turn his good fortunes to bad, may she break his weaponry (li 1) on the field of battle and strife. May she stir up against him (5) mutiny and insubordination. May she fell his warriors, may she let the earth gorge (10) their blood, may she cast them down, one after another, into a heap (15) in the open country, may his soldiers receive no quarter! May she deliver that man into (20) his enemies' power and lead him off in fetters to the land that was at war with him!

May Nergal, (25) mighty one among the gods, whose onslaught is irresistible, who helped me attain my desire, burn up his people with his (30) terrible power, like a fire raging in a canebrake. May he let him be pounded with (35) his mighty weapon, may he smash his limbs like a clay figurine!

(40) May Nintu, exalted lady of all lands, the mother who created me, deprive him of an (45) heir and allow him no offspring. May he found no family among his people!

(50) May Ninkarrak, daughter of Anu, who speaks favorably of me in Ekur, cause (55) a horrible disease to break out on his limbs, a frightful illness, an excruciating malady which no physician (60) can diagnose nor relieve with dressings, which, like the deadly bite (of a rabid dog), cannot be cured, until he expires, bemoaning the prime of his life!

(70) May all the great gods of heaven and earth, the Anunna-gods in their totality, (75) the protective spirit of the structure of Ebabbar,

curse that man, his descendants, his land, his workers, (80) his people, and his army, with a horrible curse!

May Enlil curse him with (85) these curses by his command, which cannot be changed. May they (90) swiftly overtake him!

Text: Scheil, MDP 4 (1902), pl. 4, 14, 15; Nougayrol, RA 45 (1951), 79; Wiseman, JSS 7 (1962), 164–165.

Edition: Borger BAL², 2–9, 42–46; G. R. Driver, J. Miles, *The Babylonian Laws*, 2 vols. (Oxford, 1952, 1955).

Translation: Of the numerous translations, I have used, besides Driver and Miles, especially: Meek, ANET³, 163–165, 177–180; Borger, TUAT 1/1 (1982), 39–44, 75–80; A. Finet, *Le Code de Hammurapi* (Paris, 1998); M. Roth, *Law Collections from Mesopotamia and Asia Minor²* (Atlanta, 1997); see also Roth in Hallo, ed., *Context* 2:336–337, 351–353.

★Notes to Text: (ii 29) Preferring *mu-ṣir* as a participle of *uṣṣuru* because *ṣiārum* seems vague in comparison to the other more specific actions taken with temples in this text, and taking the relative or explicative clause to refer to the paintings because other temples are not provided with general descriptive phrases in this list. (iii 16) The emendation of Reiner, RA 64 (1970), 73 (<*šu-ba-at*>) is not accepted here for the reasons adduced by Finet, *Code*, 37 and Borger, BiOr 28 (1971), 22. Note that this emendation would require a descriptive phrase without parallel among the other temples named in the text unless the instance in ii 29 is understood differently. (iii 17) For discussion of this passage and various proposals, see Hurowitz, *Inu Anum ṣirum*, 73. (xlvii 12–15) For a discussion of this passage, see Hurowitz, *Inu Anum ṣirum*, 68–70, though his proposed emendation and rearrangement of the text have not been followed here; note that *mušarbû* is grammatically singular. (l 43) With Roth, *Law Collections*, 142.

(b) HAMMURABI, FOR WHOM DO YOU WAIT?

An inscription, in Sumerian and Akkadian, carved on a statue, opens with a series of rhetorical questions to Hammurabi, asking him what further help he needs since all the great gods have pledged their support and made him invincible. What further remains of the text shows, using descriptive phrases, as in II.10(a), that Hammurabi fulfilled his mission. Owing to a break at the beginning, one cannot tell who is speaking to Hammurabi. The tone and style of the questions may be inspired by the language of oracles and prophecies vouchsafed kings (see II.12), but its uniformity of expression and bilingualism suggest that this was an innovative literary work rather than a commemoration of oracles. As understood here, the king is exhorted by a deity, perhaps the birthgoddess, to fulfill his great destiny, then the narrator shows, by referring to the events of his reign, that Hammurabi indeed did this.

(gap)

"Enlil gave you a heroic destiny —
    as for you, for whom do you wait?   (1′)
"Sin gave you leadership —
    as for you, for whom do you wait?
"Ninurta gave you an exalted weapon —
    as for you, for whom do you wait?
"Ishtar gave you battle and strife —
    as for you, for whom do you wait?
"Shamash and Adad are watching over you —
    as for you, for whom do you wait?"   (5′)

(gap)

"… gain the victory, make of yourself a hero
    in the four world regions,
    that your name be invoked forever.
"May the numerous peoples be prayerful and supplicant to you,
"May they recount of you great (poems) of praise!
"May they sound of you exalted adulation!

(gap)

He showed forth his great power to the distant future, (10′)
Hammurabi, the great warrior king,
Who struck down his enemies, a deluge in warfare,
Who leveled the land of the foe, who extinguished warfare,
Who suppressed insurrection, who destroyed opponents,
    like figurines of clay, (15′)
Who found the way out of numerous difficult crises,

(breaks off)

Text: King, CT 21, 40–42.
Edition: Wasserman, RA 86 (1992), 3–6.
Translation: Hecker, TUAT II/5, 726–727.
Literature: N. Wasserman, "A Bilingual Report of Oracles with a Royal Hymn of Hammurabi," RA
    86 (1992), 1–18; Krispijn, *Studies Kraus*, 145–162.

(c) WILL HAMMURABI BE VICTORIOUS?

For many important decisions in Babylonian life and policy, divination was used. An inclusive set of questions was presented on the issue at hand to Shamash or Shamash and Adad, as gods of divination. In the example chosen here, Hammurabi asks whether or not a planned campaign east of the Tigris will be successful and whether or not he has chosen the best commanding officer for his forces. The next step would be examination of the liver, gall bladder, and intestines of a sacrificed sheep by a professional diviner.[1] The king did not make the inquiry himself, so was represented symbolically by a lock of hair and a piece of his garment. Inquiries such as these were collected and studied later, though without the responses. This one is taken from a manuscript of the Late period that preserved a series of such inquiries.

> To [Shamash], lord of judgment, To Adad, lord of extispicy:
>
> (§1) Whatever troops of the palace, troops of the palace gate, chariot troops, foot soldiers, élite(?) force, troops from the open country, recruits, Sutaeans,[2] or foreign auxiliaries whom Marduk commands,[3] that Hammurabi, king of Babylon. will equip, deploy, and [   ], will he drive away or capture the charioteers and soldiers? Will I defeat his forces?
>
> (§2) Should Sin-nerari, who supervises the soldiery, take command of them and lead the center? Should they campaign on the east bank of the Tigris and go to Kasaluhhu?[4] By force of conquest, by treachery, by any sort of stratagem, with the military resources available, will they capture that city, Kasaluhhu?
>
> (§3) Bringing donkey loads(?) of their shares of loot and the plunder of that city, will they return safely here and will they send back good news to the owner of this lock of hair and of this fringe of garment?

---

1.   For a study of the important role of a diviner in Classical-period Mari, see A. Finet, "La place du devin dans la société de Mari," CRRAI 14 (1996), 87–93; J.-M. Durand, "Les Devins," AEM 1/1 (1988), 3–373. For a general study of the written tradition in such inquiries, see W. G. Lambert, "Questions Addressed to the Babylonian Oracle, the *tamîtu*-Texts," in J.-G. Heintz, ed., *Oracles et Prophéties dans l'Antiquité. Actes du Colloque de Strasbourg 15–17 juin 1995* (Paris, 1997), 85–98.

2.   A warlike nomadic people; see p. 904 note 2.

3.   That is, wherever Babylon has political control.

4.   A spelling of Kazallu, a large city in northern Babylonia.

(§4) Victory or defeat? O Shamash and Adad, (this is the question for) your divinity!

Text: J. Black, D. J. Wiseman, CTN 4 63 i 1–23.

Edition: None, I have benefited from an unpublished study by T. Eby.

Literature: W. G. Lambert, "The 'Tamītu' Texts," CRRAI 14 (1965), 119–123; I. Starr, *Queries to the Sungod, Divination and Politics in Sargonid Assyria*, SAA 4 (1990); Charpin, RA 91 (1997), 187–188.

II.11 SAMSUILUNA, KING OF BABYLON

Samsuiluna (1749–1712), son and successor of Hammurabi, left inscriptions, composed in an elegant, flowing style, celebrating his military successes and construction projects. The example chosen here was drafted in several variant editions in both Sumerian and Akkadian. It is noteworthy for its *mise-en-scène* in heaven, where Enlil tells Zababa and Ishtar, the gods of the city Kish, that they should stand by Samsuiluna, his chosen emissary, and keep him safe in battle. They tell Samsuiluna of Enlil's command, so he, encouraged, defeats various enemies and rebuilds the city walls of Kish and constructs a temple for Zababa and Ishtar.

The author of this piece subtly varied its wording and syntax to avoid word-for-word repetition; for instance, he reversed the words for "enemy" and "foe" in each context he used them to avoid pairing them with the same verbs in succession. He had an ear for unusual or particularly literary expressions, such as "greatest for the gods," rather than the usual "greatest of the gods" (also in III.22a, I/A, line 4) or "shepherd who ordains destinies" (the last chosen to compare Samsuiluna with the god Enlil). This and comparable features suggest a careful, conscious, creative process, seeking to avoid clichés while staying within the expected boundaries of celebratory prose. The events referred to in this inscription are also commemorated in two year names of Samsuiluna: "the year he smote the disobedient foreign lands and defeated the army of the land of Eshnunna" (year 20), and "the year he made anew the ziggurat, the sublime dwelling of Zababa and Ishtar" (year 22).

> (§1) Enlil, whose lordship is the greatest for the gods, shepherd who ordains destinies, looked with countenance radiant with happiness upon Zababa and Ishtar, the most valorous of the Igigi-gods, and resolved with steadfast heart to make Kish, their leading sanctuary and sublime dwelling, and its fortification wall, and to raise it to unprecedented height. Enlil, the great lord, whose command cannot be transgressed, whose destiny ordained cannot be changed, gazed with joyful visage upon Zababa, his mighty eldest son, who achieves his desires, and Ishtar, his beloved daughter, whose divinity is unrivalled, and addressed them with pleasing words:
>
> (§2) "Be you, for Samsuiluna, my mighty and tireless emissary, who knows how to realize my heart's desire, his shining beacon, and let your propitious sign stand by him! Slay his enemies, his foes deliver

into his power, and let him make Kish and its fortification wall, let him raise it to unprecedented height. Let him establish you there in pleasing abode."

(§3) Zababa and Ishtar, lords perfect in every respect, the doughtiest warriors among the gods, glad and happy at the words their father Enlil said to them, turned radiantly their life-bestowing visages upon Samsuiluna, the mighty king, the valiant shepherd, their handiwork, and addressed him, rejoicing:

(§4) "O Samsuiluna, of eternal lineage divine, most fitted for kingship, Enlil has made yours the greatest of destinies! He has commanded us to act as your allies to keep you safe. We will march at your right hand, we will slay your foes, we will deliver your enemies into your power. Build Kish, our awe-inspiring sanctuary, and its fortification wall, raise it to unprecedented height!"

(§5) Samsuiluna, the capable king, who is obedient to the great gods, took great courage from the words that Zababa and Ishtar said to him and made ready his weapons to slay enemies, he launched a campaign to destroy his foes. In less than half a year he had slain Rim-Sin, suborner of Iamutbal,[1] who had been raised up to the kingship of Larsa, and he heaped up, in the territory of Kish, a burial mound over him. He slew the rebel kings, his foes, he destroyed them all. He captured Iluni, king of Eshnunna,[2] who had not been obedient to him, he paraded him in a neckstock, then executed him. He made all of Sumer and Akkad obedient, he made the four world regions to dwell under his command.

(§6) Then did Samsuiluna the mighty build Kish with his own army. He dug its moat, he surrounded it with a floodable basin,[3] he laid foundations strong as a mountain, with great masses of earth, he fashioned bricks for it, he made its fortification wall, he raised it, in one year, to unprecedented height.

---

1. A region in southern Mesopotamia, east of the Tigris; for Rim-Sin (II), see M. Stol, *Studies in Old Babylonian History* (Leiden, 1976), 44–58; Charpin, *Histoire* (p. 79 note 2), 338–339.

2. For this king, see Charpin, N.A.B.U. 1998/29.

3. This refers to a defensive strategy whereby the plain around a city could be flooded in time of war, rendering it an impassable marsh.

(§7) For this may Zababa and Ishtar command as a gift for noble Samsuiluna, their favorite brother, well-being and life as long as Moon and Sun shall abide, may that be their present to him.

Text: Stephens, YOS 9 35 (collated); Langdon in Watelin and Langdon, *Excavations at Kish* III, pl. XII; Gurney, *Studies Finkelstein*, 97, 1924–1545.
Edition: Frayne, RIME 4, 384–388.
Translation: Sollberger, Kupper, IRSA, 223–226.

II.12 ROYAL ORACLES AND PROPHECIES

A group of letters from Mari, on the Middle Euphrates, reports prophecies spoken by people in a trance-like state (a–f). Most of these have to do with current events or are general warnings to the reigning king of Mari, Zimri-Lim (early eighteenth century B.C.), to protect himself. These were usually expressed in straightforward rather than poetic or archaic style. Some messages from the gods were conveyed in written form, as if they were letters, as in (a) 7 and 8 below, from Mari, addressed to Zimri-Lim, and (b) 1 below, from Eshnunna, addressed to Ibalpiel II (early eighteenth century B.C.).[1]

(a) TO ZIMRI-LIM, KING OF MARI

1. From the God Adad

Am I not Adad, lord of Kallasu, who raised him on my lap and restored him to the throne of his father's house? After I restored him to the throne of his father's house, I restored to him a place to dwell. Now that I have restored him to the throne of his father's house, I will take a domain from his household. If he will not give it, I who am lord of throne, territory, and city will take away what I gave. If, on the contrary, he gives what I require, I will give him throne on throne, house on house, territory on territory, city on city, then I will give him this land from one end to the other.

Text: B. Lafont, RA 78 (1984), 8.
Edition: B. Lafont, RA 78 (1984), 7–18.
Translation: Durand, DEPM 3, 130–133.

1   The basic study is J.-M. Durand, "Les textes prophétiques," AEM I/1, 377–452, see also DEPM 3, 71–90; M. deJ. Ellis, "Observations on Mesopotamian Oracles and Prophetic Texts: Literary and Historiographical Considerations," JCS 41 (1989), 127–186; D. Charpin, "Prophètes et rois dans le Proche-Orient amorrite," in A. Lemaire, ed., *Prophètes et rois, Bible et Proche-Orient* (Paris, 2001), 21–53, more fully in *Florilegium Marianum* 6 (2002), 7–38; for a brief and authoritative survey, see also J.-M. Durand, "Les prophéties des textes de Mari," in J.-G. Heintz, ed., *Oracles et prophéties dans l'Antiquité, Actes du Colloque de Strasbourg 15–17 juin 1995* (Paris, 1997), 115–134.

2. From the God Adad

I gave the entire of this land to Yahdun-Lim![1] Furthermore, because of my weaponry, he had no rival. He forsook me, so the land that I had given to him I gave to Shamshi-Adad.[2] ... that I could restore you to the [throne of your father's house]. I did restore you! I gave you the weaponry with which I did battle with the Sea.[3] I anointed you with the oil of my triumph,* so no one stood against you. Hear this one word of mine: when someone in a case at law appeals to you, saying, "I have been wronged!" be ready to help, judge his case, ans[wer him jus]tly. This is what I [require] of you: when you go out on campaign, you must not [go out] without taking an omen. When I am ready to help, according to my omen, you may go out on campaign. If the contrary, you must not go out the door.

Text: Durand, Lion, MARI 7 (1993), 44.
Edition: J.-M. Durand, "Le combat entre le Dieu de l'orage et la Mer," MARI 7 (1993), 41–61.
Literature: N. Wyatt, "Arms and the King. The Earliest Allusions to the *Chaoskampf* Motif and Their Implication for the Interpretation of the Ugaritic and Biblical Traditions," AOAT 250 (1998), 833–888; A. Malamat, "Deity Revokes Kingship, Towards Intellectual Reasoning in Mari and in the Bible," CRRAI 43 (1996), 231–236 = *Mari and the Bible* (Leiden, 1998), 157–162; Charpin, *Florilegium Marianum* 7 (2002), 31.
Notes to Text: (4′) Durand, MARI 7 (1993), 53–54.

1. King of Mari (ca. 1810–1794 B.C.), grandfather(?) of Zimri-Lim.
2. King of upper Mesopotamia and northern Syria (ca. 1792–1782 B.C.), founder of a rival dynasty that displaced Yahdun-Lim's but which was, in its turn, replaced by a descendant of Yahdun-Lim, that is, Zimri-Lim.
3. Text: Temtum, a variant form of Tiamtum (in III.17 Tiamat), "Sea."

3. From the Goddess Annunitum

O Zimri-Lim! They will put you to the test with a revolt. Watch over yourself! Set in position around yourself trustworthy(?) servants whom you love, so they can watch over you. You must not go anywhere by yourself! But those men who would put you to the test, I will deliver those men into your power.

Text: Dossin, ARMT X 7.
Edition: Durand, AEM I/1 213, 441–442.
Translation: Durand, DEPM 3, 316.

4. From the Goddess Annunitum

O Zimri-Lim! Even though you have no regard for me, I will smite(?) on your behalf. I will deliver your enemies into your power
...

Text: Dossin, ARMT X 8.
Edition: Durand, AEM I/1 214, 442–443.
Translation: Durand, DEPM 3, 403–404.

5. From the God Dagan

The peace initiatives of the king of the city of Eshnunna are treachery, water flows under the straw. But I will capture him for the very net he meshes, I will destroy his city, and I will make plunder of his ancient possessions.

Text: Dossin, ARMT X 80.
Edition: Durand, AEM I/1 197, 424.
Translation: Durand, DEPM 3, 403–404.

6. From the God Dagan

O Babylon, what are you trying to do? I will assemble you for net and sword. I will deliver homes and possessions of the seven allies into the power of Zimri-Lim!

Text: Dossin, ARMT XIII 23.
Edition: Durand, AEM I/1 209, 438–439.
Translation: Durand, DEPM 3, 87.
Literature: Durand, MARI 2 (1983), 145.

7. From the Goddess Ishtar of Nineveh

Thus says Ishtar of Nineveh: I will station you at my side with my powerful weapons. Build me at Mari a house for a sleeping place. I order you as follows: when there is two hours march to your enemies, quickly kindle a fire. Then let Habdu-Malik the courier extinguish it.

Text: Durand, AEM I/1 192.
Edition: Durand, AEM I/1, 413–415.
★Notes to Text: Yuhong, N.A.B.U. 1994/38; for this goddess, see further III.4(a).

8. From the God Shamash

Thus says Shamash: I am lord of this land. Let them dispatch at once to Sippar, city where I live, a great throne for my sumptuous dwelling and your daughter whom I required of you. Now the kings who affronted [you] and who have raided you time and again have been [given] into your power. Even now funeral pyres are given [to you] in this land!

Text: Durand, AEM I/1 194.
Edition: Durand, AEM I/1, 417–419.
Translation: Durand, DEPM 3, 87–89.

(b) TO IBALPIEL II, KING OF ESHNUNNA

O King Ibalpiel, thus says Kititum: The secrets of the gods are set out before me. Because the invocation of my name is always in your speech, I shall open to you, one after another, secrets of the gods. At the advice of the gods, at the verdict of Anu, this land is given to you to rule. You shall loosen the sandals of the Upper and Lower lands,[1] you shall hoard(?) the wealth of the Upper and Lower lands. Your income shall never be insufficient, wherever in this land your hand has reached, it will re[tain your portion of] the fruits of rest from labor. I, Kititum, will defend the stability of your throne, I have provided you with a watchful[2] guardian spirit. Be attentive to me!

Text: Ellis, MARI 5 (1987), 259–260.
Edition: Ellis, MARI 5 (1987), 258–266.

1. This unparalleled expression may refer to an era of prosperity, symbolized by abundant rainfall (compare the Sumerian saying "It rained, but no sandals were untied" [that is, only a little], Alster, *Proverbs*, 3:149) or perhaps refers to peace, in that no one will have to march to war.
2. Wordplay (*naṣirtam aštanakkum*) on "secrets" (*niṣrētum*) and "set out" (*šaknā*) of the opening lines.

D. The Human Condition

II.13 DIALOGUE BETWEEN A MAN AND HIS GOD

In the lament, a man confesses his wrongs and shortcomings, pleading with his god to forgive him and to restore his health and happiness. It resembles Mature- and Late-period compositions that deal with the problem of guilt and a person's relationship to his god (see III.14, III.49d, IV.19). A further Classical-period example, too fragmentary and obscure to be included here, has been studied by W. G. Lambert, "A Babylonian Prayer to Anuna," *Studies Sjöberg*, 321–336.

i

A young man was imploring his god as a friend,*	(1)
He was constantly supplicating, he was [praying to(?)] him.	
His heart was seared, he was sickened with his burden,	
His feelings were somber from misery.	
He weakened, fell to the ground, prostrated himself.	
His burden had grown too heavy for him,	
he drew near to weep.[1]	(5)
He was moaning like a donkey foal separated	
(from its mother),	
He cried out before his god, his master.	
His mouth a wild bull, his clamor two mourners,	
[His] lips bear a lament to his lord.	

ii

He recounts the burdens he suffered to his lord,	(10)
The young man expounds the misery he is suffering:	
"My Lord, I have debated with myself, and in my feelings	
"[ ] of heart: the wrong I did I do not know!	
"Have I [ ] a vile forbidden act?	
"Brother does not de[sp]ise his brother,	
"Friend is not calumniator of his friend![2]	(15)
"The [ ] does not [ ]	

---

1. That is, in order to weep near a statue or cult symbol.
2. If the god is a friend, he will not treat the sufferer unjustly (WGL).

(large gap)

iv

(four lines lost or fragmentary)

"[From] when I was a child until I grew up,
    (the days?) have been long, when ... [   ]?   (25)
"How much you have been kind to me,
    how much I have blasphemed you, I have not forgotten.
"In[stead(?)] of good you revealed evil, O my lord,
    you made [ ] glow ...[1]
"My bad repute is grown excessive, it ... to (my) feet.
"It [rains] blows on my skull(?).
"Its [   ] turned my mouth ... to gall.   (30)

(large gap)

vii

(four lines lost)

[   ] he brought him to earth,
[   ] he has anointed him with medicinal oil,
[   ] food, and covered his blotch,★   (45)
He attended him and gladdened his heart,
He ordered the restoration of his good health to him:

viii

"Your disease is under control,★
    let your heart not be despondent!
"The years and days you were filled with misery are over.
"Were you not ordered to live,   (50)
"How could you have lasted the whole of this grievous illness?
"You have seen distress, little was held back.★
"You have borne its massive load to the end.
"I flung wide your access(?), the way is open to you,★
"The path is straight for you, mercy is granted you.   (55)
"You must never, till the end of time, forget [your] god

---

1. Possibly a reference to disease (WGL); von Soden (TUAT III/2, 138) sees here a reference to omens.

"Your creator, now that you are favored.

ix

"I am your god, your creator, your trust,
"My guardians are strong and alert on your behalf.
"The field will open [to you] its refuge.   (60)
"I will see to it that you have long life.
"So, without qualms, do you anoint the parched,
"Feed the hungry, water the thirsty,
"But he who sits there with burning e[yes],*
"Let him look upon your food, melt, flow down,
     and dis[solve].[1]   (65)
"The gate of life and well-being is open to you!
"Going away(?), drawing near, coming in, going out:
     may you be well!"

Make straight his way, open his path:
     May your servant's supplication reach your heart!

Text: Nougayrol, *Revue Biblique* 59 (1952), pl. vii and viii, collated.

Edition: W. G. Lambert, *Studies Reiner*, 187–202 (with collations).

Translation: von Soden, TUAT III/2, 135–140 (whence several readings and interpretations used here).

Literature: von Soden, OrNS 26 (1957), 315–319 (with collations); W. G. Lambert, BWL, 10–11 (= note 11); see also J. J. A. van Dijk, *La Sagesse suméro-accadienne, recherches sur les genres littéraires avec choix de textes* (Leiden, 1953), 120–121; von Soden, MDOG 96 (1965), 47–49; Bottéro, *Annuaire* 1964/5, 128–130; Sitzler, *Vorwurf*, 72–83.

Notes to Text: (1) Mayer, OrNS 64 (1995), 186 suggests "loudly." (45) von Soden, TUAT III/2, 139. (48) von Soden, TUAT III/2, 139. (52) von Soden, TUAT III/2, 139. (54) Wasserman, N.A.B.U. 1991/109. (64) von Soden, TUAT III/2, 140.

1. Perhaps a reference to an ill-wisher who will see the sufferer's good fortune and melt away magically. For the phraseology, compare III.40b.

II.14 AT THE CLEANERS

A sophomoric fop lectures a cleaner in absurd detail as to how to treat his garment. At least some of his instructions are ridiculous, for example, lines 5, 6, and 21ff. The exasperated cleaner suggests that he lose no time in taking it to the river and doing it himself.

"Come now, Cleaner, let me give you a commission:
    clean my clothes! (1)
"Don't neglect the commission I am giving you!
"Don't do what you usually would!
"You should lay flat the fringe and the border(?),
"You should stitch the front to the inside, (5)
"You should pick out the thread of the border.
"You should soak the thin part in a brew,★
"You should strain that with a strainer.
"You should open out the fringes of the ...,
"You should ... with clean water, (10)
"You should ... as if it were (fine, imported?) cloth.
"In the overnight(?) ...
"In the closed container(?) ...
"You should [   ] soap and mix in gypsum,
"You should beat(?) it on a stone, (15)
"You should stir it in a crock and [rinse(?) it],
"You may want to ... the ... and comb it,
"You should [tap it] with a cornel-tree branch,★
"You should [fluff out(?)] the flattened nap,
"[You should ...] the woven work with a pin, (20)
"You should split the seam and cool it,
"You should dry it in the cool of the evening.
"If the south wind has not dried it,
"You should put it on a rack in the east wind,
    make sure it's cool!
"Carry (this) out, I'll make you very happy fast. (25)
"You should deliver it to my home, a measure of barley
    will be poured into your lap!"

The cleaner answers him, "By Ea, lord of the washtub,[1]
    who keeps me alive,
"Lay off! Nobody but a creditor or t[ax collector]
"Would have the gall to talk the way you do,
"Nor could anyone's hands do the job! (30)
"What you ordered me I could not narrate, declaim,
    speak, or repeat.
'Come now'[2] — upstream of town, at the city's edge,
"Let me show you a place to launder,
"The big job you have on your hands
    you can set to yourself, (35)

    'Don't miss your chance, seize the day!'[3]

"Do ease if you please the countless [tangles?] of a cleaner.
"If you can't give yourself more breathing room,
"The cleaner's not yet born who will pay you any mind.
"They'll think you a ninny, so, as they say,
    you'll get all heated up,* (40)
"Then you'll have a stroke."*

Text: Gadd, UET 6/2 414.
Edition: Gadd, *Iraq* 25 (1963), 181–188.
Literature: Charpin, *Clergé*, 431–432; Livingstone, AOAT 220 (1988), 175–183; George, *Iraq* 55 (1993), 73–74; E. Reiner, "At the Fuller's," AOAT 240 (1995), 407–411; D'Agostino, *Testi Umoristici*, 139–148.
Notes to Text: (7) With Livingstone, 180–181. (18) Reading *tu-ta-a[r-ra-ak]* (WLM). (40) Reading *imeššunikkum libbakami iḫḫammaṭ*, where *-mi* = "they say," a proverbial expression? (41) With George, 73.

1. For Ea (Enki) as patron deity of cleaners, compare the Sumerian proverb "I swear by Enki your clothes won't be in the shop a long time" (Alster, *Proverbs*, 3:148), meaning, of course, that the customer should not expect them anytime soon.
2. Here the cleaner mimics the customer, as in line 1.
3. Literally: "The meal must not pass, do come in," perhaps a proverbial expression meaning "*carpe diem*."

II.15 LAMENT FOR A CITY

This fragment may preserve part of a goddess's lament for her destroyed city and lost subjects. The city lament is well known in Sumerian,[1] but unusual in Akkadian. This piece may depend on some lost Sumerian prototype.

(gap)

Whoever stood where I stand to cry out,	(1′)

Whoever stood where I stand to cry out, (1′)
To cry out like a newborn goat on her bed?
Among (all) established cities,
    my city (alone) has been smashed.★
Among (all) the established populace,
    my man (alone) has gone away.★
Among (all) the gods(?) residing there,
    I (alone) have not fled!★ (5′)
My ewe cries out in the land of the enemy,
    my lamb is bleating,
My ewe and her lamb they have taken away!
When my ewe crossed the river,★
She abandoned(?) her lamb on the bank. (10′)

(gap)

My birds [   ] ...
Those who do not understand (what they do)
    are cutting off their wings!★
Where is my house that I used to dwell in? (5′)

Text: Gadd, UET 6/2 403.
Edition: N. Wasserman, "A Forgotten Old-Babylonian Lament over a City's Destruction: UET 6/2, 403 and Its Possible Literary Content" (in Hebrew), *Eretz-Israel* 27 (2003), 127–132 (with photo).

1. See M. E. Cohen, *The Canonical Lamentations of Ancient Mesopotamia* (Potomac, Md., 1988), Vol. 1, 11–44; F. W. Dobbs-Allsopp, *Weep, O Daughter of Zion: A Study of the City-Lament Genre in the Hebrew Bible*, Biblica et Orientalia 44 (Rome, 1993), with bibliography.

Notes to Text: (3′) Reading *it!-ta-aḫ-ba-aš*, see AfO 19 (1959/60), 52, 153. (4′) I read *tebû* against *nepû* of Mayer, OrNS 56 (1987), 205, because *nepû* "take as a surety for debt" makes little sense here, and because *tebû* (Gtn) occurs in translation Akkadian as a rendering of záḫ (CT 16 44, line 91). (5′) *aḫtalqu,* affirmative subjunctive, perhaps translating a Sumerian first-person emphatic precative (GAG §185b); Wasserman drastically emends to *uḫ-ta-al-<li?>-iq*! (9′) Mayer, OrNS 56 (1987), 204. (rev. 4′) See Wasserman, *Style,* 155.

II.16 THE FAITHFUL LOVER

This poem deals with the theme of unequal love. A woman is in love with a boor who has taken up with someone else. Despite his selfishness and abuse, she remains true, and eventually wins her prize back, if only through persistence. This Mesopotamian celebration of the power of love, regardless of the merit of its object, is a compassionate forerunner, full of life and humor, to the portrayal of the woman's dilemma in the Song of Songs. One is reminded also of the second elegy of Theocritus on this topic, though there the woman looks more foolish than here.[1]

i

(He)

Good-bye,★ don't bother to answer, not so much talking!   (1)
What I have to say is said,
I haven't changed on your account any opinion that I hold.   (5)
He who sprawls next to a woman treasures up empty air!
If he doesn't look out for himself,
    he is no man worthy of the name.★

(She)

May my faithfulness stand firm before Ishtar the queen!
May my love prevail,   (10)
May she who slanders me come to shame!
Grant me to honor, seduce,
    to find my darling's favor constantly.★
I [am] always [ravishing], by Nanay's command.   (15)
Where might my rival be?

(He)

I remember better than you your old tricks,
Give up! Be off with you!
Tell your (divine) counsellor how we've sobered out of it.   (20)

---

1. A different interpretation is offered by Groneberg ("'The Faithful Lover' Reconsidered," CRRAI 47 [2001], 165–183), according to which this is a witty and eloquent contest performed at court.

(She)

I'll hang on to you, and this very day
I shall make your love harmonize with mine.
I shall keep on praying to Nanay,
I shall have your eternal good will, darling[1], freely given.   (25)

(He)

I shall keep you fenced in,
I shall bank up my clouds around you,
May (the goddess) you trust in
        take away the cuteness of your salacious talk,   (30)
Slink off, accept reality.

(gap of about twenty lines)

ii

(She)

May the queen Ishtar h[eap] oblivion on
        th(at) woman, who doesn't (really) love you.
May she, like me, [be burdened] with sleeplessness,
The whole night may she doze off [but start awake].

(He)

I despise a woman who can't seduce me,   (10)
I have no desire for her charms,
I wouldn't give her [   ].
Talking without [   ],
What does it [   ]?
I'll put a stop to those women who gossip about [me],   (15)
I'll not listen [   ]
Wherever [   ]
I have thrown away my love,
What do you keep prying into me for?

---

1. Literally: "my lord," a term of endearment. Compare II.18 line 11; IV.27 line 15 (first noted by Held, JCS 15 [1961], 5, 13–14).

(She)

The portents for me perturb me: (20)
My upper lip grows moi[st],
The lower one trem[bles]!
I shall hug him! I shall kiss him!
I shall look and look upon [him]!
I shall get what I want,
    against the wo[men who gossip about me],   (25)
And happily [return?] to [my] l[over].
When our sleep [   ]
We shall reach [   ]

(gap)

iii

(gap)

(She)

I am running, but I cannot catc[h up with him]:
She gave him away to Ishtar as a g[ift].   (5)

(He)

Just as they keep on telling you,
Y[ou] are not the one and only.
Hold off! I have taken my love away,
    [I shall] not [bring it back].
I have taken it away from your body,
I have [taken] my attractions a million leagues away.   (10)

(She)

I am pursuing your charms,
Darling, I am yearning for [your] love!
Since your smiles are [my ...],
Let them be ..., I hope [they] won't ... [   ]
I will chatter day and night [with you]!   (15)

(He)

Again, again, and a thi[rd] time I'll say it,
I will let no kind word of you [into] my mouth.
Do take your place at the window,[1]
Go on, catch up to my love!

(She)

So very tired my eyes are,   (20)
I am weary for looking out for him.
I keep thinking he will go through my neighborhood,
The day has gone by, where is [my darling?]

(gap of about fifteen lines)

iv

(She)

I ... [   ]   (1)
The one and only [   ]
Why [   ]
Come on, let me take [my place],
I shall sit and await if he is on his way to me.   (5)

(He)

I swear to you by Nanay and King Hammurabi:
I am telling you the truth about me,
Your love is nothing more to me
Than anxiety and bother.

(She)

They ... me because I still trust my lover,   (10)
The women who argue with me
        outnumber the stars of heaven.
Let them go hide! Let them contend with each other!
Right now let them go hide!
I'll stay right here, ever listening for the voice of my darling.   (15)

---

1. Perhaps a reference to looking seductively into the public street from a private house (see Groneberg, CRRAI 47 [2001], 170), meaning that she has to look for an admirer there.

(He)

My good omen, your face wasn't bad-looking before,
When I stood by you and
       you leaned your [shoulder?] against me. (20)
Call you "Miss Compatible,"* dub you "Smart Lady,"
Say the other woman is our ill omen, Ishtar be my witness!

Text: von Soden, ZA 49 (1950), 168–169.

Edition: von Soden, 49 (1950), 151–194; Held, JCS 15 (1961), 1–26; JCS 16 (1962), 37–39 (with collations); Ponchia, *Dialoghi*, 89–93, 115–119, 150–154.

Translation: Hecker, TUAT II/5, 743–747.

Literature: Groneberg, CRRAI 47 (2001), 175–182 (with numerous new interpretations and readings, some of which have been adopted here).

Notes to Text: (i 1) Differently Hecker, TUAT II/5, 743 note 1a. (i 8) Differently Groneberg, CRRAI 47 (2001), 168, but her rendering ignores the negation in the line and yields no sense in the context. (i 13, 15) WGL suggests k[a-a-a]m at the beginning of line 13 and a form of *šāmu* in the gap of 15; I follow Groneberg, CRRAI 47 (2001), 176. (iv 21) Differently Groneberg, CRRAI 47 (2001), 167, "Insolence is your name." If, indeed, there is a play on words here, I take it in the opposite sense.

E. LOVE LYRICS

II.17 NANAY AND MUATI

This poem celebrates the marriage of Nanay, goddess of love, to Muati, a god about whom little is known. The text opens with Nanay looking favorably upon Babylon and its king.[1] She is drawn to Muati and brings him to live with her there. She offers herself to him; he accepts joyfully. The poet asks the blissful groom to intercede with Nanay for the king. The poet, speaking for the king, praises Muati's newly installed image, vowing that he will complete it perfectly. The final prayer to Nanay is spoken by the poet, the king, and Muati. The king named in the unique manuscript preserving this composition is Abieshuh, king of Babylon (ca. 1711–1684 B.C.).

(obv.?)

[   ]   (1)
[   ] best, sweet [   ]
She looked upon Babylon with her favoring eyes [   ]
She blessed [it], she ordered its favor [   ]
Every day [   ] vigor (for) the king who dwells there [   ]   (5)
Nanay [   ] vigor for the king Abieshuh.
She set him in a restful abode [   ].

Attraction, attraction, just as we need [   ]
Be to us the source of joy!
She establishes handsome Muati for us, makes him dwell [   ] (10)
Love charms will rain down like dew.
[   ] form, he always takes new pleasure in her,
      thirsting for what is hers as for water.
[   ] is sweet:

(She)

[   ] "Here are my charms, arouse yourself,
      let us make love, you and I!"

---

1. So in this translation; there is no way to be certain which is the obverse and which the reverse of the tablet.

(He)

[   ] "Let me have what I want of your delights!"   (15)
[   ] whatever [   ] he will bring [   ] with her.

(four lines too broken for translation)

[   ] your love like [   ]
[   ] straightaway they [   ] together.

(rev.?)

[   ] you ... Nanay, to whom I am entrusted [   ]   (1)
[   ] of your love-making ... [   ]
[   ] O Nanay ... let us make love, you and I.
[   ] may I always stay brilliant.
[   ] well-being, may he himself be shepherd forever.   (5)
May I always do the [of] Abieshuh.
I will speak to her lover [   ],
     She will gladly fill his heart with joy!
I will speak to her lover Muati,
     She will gladly fill his heart with joy!
[O   ], your love-making is honey,
     The [ch]arm of your love is all one could want of honey.
O Muati, your love-making is honey,
     The [ch]arm of your love is all one could want of honey.
The image that you saw there is a (standing) blade,
     Never to be ...[   ]   (10)
I will make you complete, you whose form is such,
     Filled with joy [   ]
O Muati, you whose form is such,
     Filled with joy [   ]
"Let the king live forever at your (Nanaya's) command,
     "Let Abieshuh live forever [at your command]!"

Text: W. G. Lambert, MIO 12 (1966), plates after p. 48.
Edition: W. G. Lambert, MIO 12 (1966), 41–51.
Translation: Hecker, TUAT II/5, 741–743.

II.18 NANAY AND RIM-SIN

These love lyrics, partly dialogue and partly the chaffing song of the attendants outside the nuptial chamber, celebrate a springtime new year rite in which the king, here Rim-Sin, king of Larsa (ca. 1822–1763 B.C.) had intercourse with a priestess, representing the goddess Nanay (see II.2), to ensure fertility for the realm.[1] The tablet may have been a rough draft, as it was carelessly written and breaks off in the middle of a word. All indications of speakers are supplied by the translator. The motif of the goddess harboring greater feeling than her subject is found elsewhere, for example II.12a(4) and III.4a, and the unequal feeling between woman and man was the usual pattern in love poetry (for example, II.16, 19a, c, d). Emphasis on trust is found as well in IV.27. Here the goddess speaks as the chosen woman, honored for her new place in society, surrendering to his addresses, but yearning for some clearer sign of her lover's feeling. In any event, it is for her to invite the king to her bed.

(Singers)

[From his sheepskin] pregnant girls took away
　　bits of raw wool,*   (1)
[From his] ... sheep's tail she has taken a bit of combed hair.[2]*

(She)

[　], the rascal has taken power over me.*
[　], my partner in dalliance wins me over by love play.*

(Singers, to Her)

You are too joyful(?),* O my beloved, do not rely on him!   (5)
You are in too great ecstasy, do not put your trust in him!

---

1. This ritual, known as the "sacred marriage," is disputed in its nature and purpose; see J. Cooper, "Sacred Marriage and Popular Cult in Early Mesopotamia," in E. Matsushima, ed., *Official Cult and Popular Religion in the Ancient Near East* (Heidelberg, 1993), 81–96.

2. As understood here, the king dressed in shepherd's clothes made of sheepskin for the rite (compare II.19c line 21), thereby taking the part of Dumuzi. Perhaps women snatched small pieces of the sheepskin for luck, as the king passed by, and the goddess took a small piece for herself as well. In IV.27 9', the lover dries the woman's eyes with a tuft of wool.

(She to Him)

If only you would listen to one word, my beloved,
    and heed me,
(If only) you would accept my entreaties,
    to let your heart relax to me!
In the assembly, the city, and among the important people,
    you invoked my good name,   (10)
My darling,[1] you gave me special honor
At the moment you [exalted] me,
I gained great esteem in the eyes of [my] former girl friends.*

(Singers)

Yes! It is springtime,
    for which we have been praying constantly,
We have indeed been yearning to see it, for so long,
    many days, life forever.   (15)
O bringer of bliss to Rim-Sin,
    our sun-god for the new year,
He offered to her the wine
    that was sparkling in my right hand.*

(She)

Come here, let us embrace, as my heart has urged me,   (20)
Let us act as lovers do, never sleep all night,
Let both of us in bed be in the joyful mood for love-making!*
Stir together over me desire and passion,*
Feed yourself on what you need to live,
Heat up your lust on me![2]

---

1. Literally: "my lord" (see p. 156 note 1).
2. As understood here, this passage develops a unique conceit on love and cookery: preparing the ingredients, sustaining oneself, and keeping it warm, to which the man responds with a related image: his love was saved for her like grain in a storeroom, to which she may help herself.

(He to Her)

My love has been stored as provisions for you,   (25)
Take as much as you desire,
Get what is mine and my lover's,
Ask the queen, Nanay!   ·

(Singers)

She put her trust in him,
Could she not ask of him what she wanted?

(remainder of text too fragmentary for translation)

Text: Hussey-van Dijk, YOS 11 24.
Edition: None.
Translation: Hecker, TUAT II/5, 747–750, whence interpretations used here.
Notes to Text: (1) [wa]-ar-da-tim, ḫi-ib-ši. (2) Reading mu-sá-ta!-am! (3) [GA-ar]-da-mu iḫ!-ta-bu-ut (WGL). (4) Reading ṣú-ḫi!-im. (5) Deriving ta-BA-ZI from pesû. (12) sí-ma-an tu-ša-[qá]-an-ni (WGL). (13) ta-ap-pá-ti-[ja] ša pa-na e-gi-ir da-an-ni-iš. (17) WGL. (22) lu ni!? (23) Reading with tablet i-ta-ab-la-al; Hecker emends implicitly to i-ta-ap-la-as! (TUAT II/5, 749). Reading also e-li-<ja> but perhaps a third noun was intended, such as a!-li-<li>, rather than the preposition.

II.19 LOVE SONGS

Few love songs have survived in proportion to the number of titles of love
songs known. A list of love songs of the Mature period included such items
as "When my right eye winked ...," "I'll let you stay the night, boy ...," "My
darling, give me all your love," and "How good-looking she is, how radiant!"[1](1) In some, gods and goddesses were the participants, in others, human
beings. The language of love used metaphors like "fruit" and "garden" to refer
to physical attractions (hence the "gardener" or "orchardist" brought "fruit"
to a lover) and "laughter" to refer to expressions of pleasure.[2] The songs given
here are noteworthy for their warm humor, lightly sustained conceits, and
earthy directness.

(a) WHERE HAS MY LOVER GONE?

Where has my lover gone, most precious to me,	(1)
And where has he taken his charms?	
He's luscious to me as a fruit-laden tree,	
All my pleasure's in him, he's my [man].	
I've sent my lover out of town,	(5)
So now my daddy's gone.*	
I'll have to make do with my own "coo-coo,"	
For my love bird has flown away.[3]	
Some trapper must bring my stray lover home,	
So you can make sweet cooing with me,	(10)
Or, let it be the gardener-man,	
to bring me (fruit from your tree).[4]	

---

1. See Finkel, ASJ 10 (1988), 17–18; Black, JAOS 103 (1983), 28–29.
2. B. Groneberg, "Das erotisch Vokabular," AOAT 267 (1999) 181–191; see also II.1, line
10; II.2, line 7, IV.27, line 23′. General studies include R. A. Veenker, "Forbidden Fruit, Ancient
Near Eastern Sexual Metaphors," HUCA 70/71 (1999/2000), 93–159 and B. Musche, *Die Liebe
in der altorientalischen Dichtung, Studies in the History and Culture of the Ancient Near East* (Leiden,
1999).
3. Literally: "I embrace my laughter and the dove has gone away."
4. Literally: "You will embrace my laughter and the orchardman will bring to me."

I've got the coop* ready for the young man,
I'll catch the love bird (in one snap),
Then, when I "coo?"
I'll get a round "yes!" (from my trap).*   (15)

Text: Groneberg, AOAT 267 (1999), 192–193.
Edition: Groneberg, AOAT 267 (1999), 177–181.
Translation: Nissinen, *Melammu Symposia* 2 (1999), 119.
Notes to Text: (6) Reading *wa-ṣ[i]*. (12) Taking *qu-pí* as "my coop" (*quppi*). (15) Metathetic word-
    play: *alammi* :*umalla*?

(b) A LOVER'S RIDDLE

This song asks a blessing on the reigning king, Ammiditana (also blessed in
II.1), then turns to giving advice to all who will listen. It ends with a light-
hearted riddle: what do babies and lovers have in common?

The woman you love should be in your heart,   (1)
Make of her your most promising sign.
Figure it out, ask yourselves this:
What begins with a sighing wail?
Well, it's my new-born love!   (5)

Text: Groneberg, AOAT 267 (1999), 192–193.
Edition: Groneberg, AOAT 267 (1999), 177–181.

(c) COME IN, SHEPHERD!

This song, drawn from a lost larger work called "The Boy Who Loves Me,"
finds the girl Ishtar fantasizing a visit from Dumuzi the shepherd. She sees her
parents welcoming him. He has politely asked to call on her mother, though
Ishtar's thoughts are far livelier. She, as his recognized betrothed, comes in to
help serve refreshments. She imagines that she will need to mollify his comrades and sheepdogs, who are annoyed at his shirking his duties to make such
frequent visits to her. Amidst the small talk she undresses him in her mind.
While his neglected sheep languish, he lingers on, not wanting to leave. She
murmurs his name over and over, like a magic spell. But then reality intervenes.
What actually occurs is that she herself must visit Dumuzi (compare IV.61),
who gives no sign of welcoming her, while she prattles of the beauty of the
landscape to veil her emotion. In the translation, what may freely be understood as Ishtar's inner voice is in parentheses, though this does not correspond
to anything in the extant manuscript.

Come in, shepherd! (Ishtar's lover!)   (1)
(Stay the night, shepherd, Ishtar's lover!)
When you came in, my father was glad to see you,
My mother, Ningal, made a nice fuss over you,*
She offered rubbing oil from the best dish.   (5)
'When you come in, may the doorbolt welcome you.'
(Let the door fly open, all by itself!)
(You doorbolt, you piece of wood, what do you know?)
(What would you know of [my lover's] 'coming in'?)
(Yes, I'm in love, I'm in love!
        This good-looking [shepherd]'s the one!)   (10)
(He let his dogs roam, what [do they know]?)
'May I come in to visit Ningal?'
When he was paying his visit to Ningal,
        her affianced daughter came in,
Mother and daughter cut up sweet cake for him
        on the best dish.
(This fellow's a nuisance for the dogs and shepherds)   (15)
(Why should they be annoyed with him?
        He fetched and carried)
(He came and went, he fetched and carried)

(A peace-offering for the shepherds? This fellow's a nuisance!)
'Dumuzi is well, thank you' (Ishtar's lover!)
'Do take off your sandals.'   (20)
(Do take off your quilted cloak!)
(Let's eat [sweet cake] together, good-looking fellow)
(Do take off your [   ], good-looking fellow)
(No one else should bring me [   ])
(Let's eat [sweet cake] together, good-looking fellow)   (25)

(gap)

([Never mind the ...] of your lambs)
([Forget the] bleating of your sheep)
(Ignore the [   ] of the sheepfolds)
(Recite his name to me, over and over, he hates to leave)*
...   (30)
(Recite his name to me, over and over, he hates to leave!)

Ishtar went out to his sheepfold,
She made ready to speak and said to him,
"How lovely are the waters, the waters of your sheepfold,
"Your burbling waters, the waters of your paddock."   (35)

Text: Black, JAOS 103 (1983), 26–27.
Edition: J. Black, "Babylonian Ballads: A New Genre," JAOS 103 (1983), 25–34, the essentials of
   whose interpretation are followed here.
*Notes to Text: (4, 29) W. G. Lambert, RA 77 (1983), 190–191.

(d) YOUR HEARTBEAT IS MY REVEILLE

In this love song, the woman addresses her lover. Although this is not shown in the translation, she refers to herself in the plural in lines 1–13, but changes to the singular in line 14. Since this usage is otherwise attested of the goddess Ishtar,[1] one may speculate that a goddess is speaking.

> Your heartbeat is my reveille, (1)
> Up then, I want to make love with you,
> In your smooth loins, as you come awake.
> How sweet your caress,
> How voluptuous your charms, (5)
> You, whose sleeping place wafts of aromatic and fennel.
> O my loose locks, my ear lobes,
> The contour of my shoulders and the opulence of my breast,
> The spreading fingers of my hands,
> The love-beads of my waist! (10)
> Bring your left hand close, touch my sweet spot,
> Fondle my breasts!
> [O come inside], I have opened my thighs!

(gap, fragmentary lines)

Text: H. de Genouillac, PRAK II pl. 38, B 472; photo J. Westenholz, *Studies Reiner*, 418–419.
Edition: J. Westenholz, *Studies Reiner*, 415–425.

1. Foster, *Gilgamesh*, 48.

F. INCANTATIONS

II.20 BIRTH AND CHILDHOOD

The perilous journey from the womb to the world was eased by magical rites and words spoken by the midwife. See also IV.53. For pregnancy and birth, see Stol, *Birth in Babylonia*.

(a) SHE HAS NEVER GIVEN BIRTH

In this spell, Sun and Moon look with sorrow upon the agonies of the mother, transmuted into a legendary cow (see also IV.53b).

> The cow was pregnant, the cow is giving birth,   (1)
> In the paddock of Shamash, the pen of Shamkan.[1]
> When he saw her, Shamash began to cry,
> When the Pure-rited[2] One saw her, his tears were
>   flowing down.
> Why is Shamash crying,
> Why are the Pure-rited One's tears flowing down?
> "For the sake of my cow, who had never been breeched!"*
> "For the sake of my kid, who had never given birth!"*   (10)
> Whom shall I [send with an order to the
>   the daught]er(s) of Anu, seven [and seven],[3]
> [May] they [   ] their pots of [   ],
> May they bring this baby straight forth!*   (15)
> If it be male, like a wild ram,*
> If it be female, like a wild cow(?) may it come into the world.[4]

> (Incantation for a woman in labor)

Text: van Dijk, VAS 17 34.
Edition: van Dijk, OrNS 41 (1972), 343–348.
Translation: Stol, *Birth in Babylonia*, 64.

---

1. Shamkan, the cattle-god, was the son of Shamash (van Dijk, OrNS 41 [1972], 344; Cavigneaux in Abusch, ed., *Magic*, 261–264); Stol (*Birth in Babylonia*, 64) suggests that the line means the woman is in Larsa, which had an important temple of Shamash.
2. An epithet of the moon.
3. Compare II.23a, d.
4. Literally: "falls toward the ground," as Babylonian women often gave birth in a seated position.

Literature: van Dijk, OrNS 41 (1972), 339–348; Farber, ZA 71 (1981), 26; Farber, JNES 49 (1990), 308.
Notes to Text: (9) See Finkel, AfO 27 (1980), 44 note 12. (10) See AHw, 1420b. (15) Moran, RA 77 (1983). (16) Michel, Wasserman, N.A.B.U. 1997/64.

(b) THE CHILD'S ARMS ARE BOUND

This incantation asks Asalluhi, god of magic, to save a child stuck in the womb and release him to the waiting midwife. For further discussion of management of birth complications in ancient Mesopotamia, see J. Scurlock, "Baby-snatching Demons, Restless Souls and the Dangers of Childbirth: Medico-Magical Means of Dealing with Some of the Perils of Motherhood in Ancient Mesopotamia," *Incognita* 2 (1991), 137–185.

In the fluids of intercourse	(1)
Bone was formed,	
In the tissue of sinews	
Baby was formed.	
In the ocean waters, fearsome, raging,	(5)
In the distant waters of the sea,	
Where the little one's arms are bound,	
There within, where the sun's eye can bring no brightness,	(10)
Asalluhi, Enki's son, saw him.	
He loosed his tight-tied bonds,	
He set him on the way,	
He opened him the path.	(15)
"The path is [op]ened to you,	
"The way is [made straight?] for you,	
"The ... physician(?) is waiting for you,	
"She is maker of [bl]ood(?),	
"She is maker of us all."	(20)
She has spoken to the doorbolt, it is released.	
"The lock is [fre]ed,	
"The doors thrown wide,	
"Let him strike [ ],	(25)
"Bring yourself out, there's a dear!"	

Text: Hussey-van Dijk, YOS 11 16, 1–28.
Edition: van Dijk, OrNS 42 (1972), 502–507.
Translation: Scurlock, *Incognita* 2 (1991), 141.
Literature: Veldhuis in Abusch, ed., *Magic*, 39–41; Durand, MARI 7 (1993), 52.

(c) TO CALM A BABY

Babylonian parents sometimes tried magic words to calm fretting and crying babies. See also IV.54.

> Little one who dwelt in the dark chamber,[1]   (1)
> You really did come out here, you have seen the [sunlig]ht.
> Why are you crying? Why are you [fretting]?
> Why did you not cry in there?
> You have disturbed the household god,
>   the bison(-monster) is astir, (saying),[2]   (5)
> "Who disturbed me? Who startled me?"
> The little one disturbed you, the little one startled you.
> Like wine tipplers, like a barmaid's child,[3]   (10)
> Let sleep fall upon him!

(Incantation to calm a little one)

Text: Farber: ZA 71 (1981), 62 rev.
Edition: Farber, ZA 71 (1981), 60–71; *Baby-Beschwörungen*, 34–35.
Literature: Farber, *Anthropos* 85 (1990), 141–143; Stol, *Birth in Babylonia*, 212; van der Toorn in Abusch, ed., *Magic*, 139; J. Scurlock, "Ancient Mesopotamian House Gods," *Journal of Ancient Near Eastern Religions* 3 (2003), 99–106.

1. Probably, with Farber, 68, a metaphor for the womb.
2. The bison-monster may have been a protective spirit of the household; "household god" may have been god of the hearth (Scurlock, *Journal of Ancient Near Eastern Religions* 3 [2003], 99–106).
3. Perhaps a reference to the expected alcoholic intake of a child nursed by a woman of bibulous habits, and the child's resulting stupor.

II.21 AGAINST LAMASHTU

Lamashtu was one of the most dreaded figures in Mesopotamian demonology. She attacked young women and small children. The symptoms of her onslaught, according to later medical texts, could be jaundice, fever, fits of insanity, chills, paralysis, and intense thirst. She brought complications in pregnancy and delivery, as well as sudden infant death. See also I.7a, IV.42, and F. A. M. Wiggerman *apud* Stol, *Birth in Babylonia*, 217–252; W. Farber, "Lamaštu," RLA 6, 439–446, *Studies Borger*, 56–69, AOAT 247 (1997), 115–128; and K. Volk, "Kinderkrankheiten nach der Darstellung babylonisch-assyrischer Keilschrifttexte," OrNS 68 (1999), 1–30.

(a) ANU BEGOT HER

The first part of the text fixes upon the culprit by telling of her origins and mode of entry into the house. The magician then orders her out of the house to a tortured wandering in the wilderness.

Anu begot her, Ea reared her,	(1)
Enlil doomed her the face of a lioness.	
She is furious,	
She is long of hand, long(er still) of nail.	
Her forearms(?) are smeared (with blood).*	(5)
She came right in the front door,	
Slithering over the (door)post casing!	
She slithered over the (door)post casing,	
She has caught sight of the baby!	
Seven seizures has she done him in his belly!	
Pluck out your nails! Let loose your arms!	(10)
Before he gets to you, valiant Ea,	
sage of the (magician's) craft,	
The (door)post casing is big enough for you,	
the doors are open,	
Come then, be gone into the open country!	(15)
I will surely fill your mouth with sand, your face with dust,	

Your eyes with finely ground mustard seeds![1]*
I exorcise you by Ea's curse: you must be gone!   (20)

Text: Keiser, BIN 2 72.
Edition: von Soden, OrNS 23 (1954), 337–344; Veldhuis in Abusch, ed., *Magic*, 42–45.
Literature: Landsberger, JNES 17 (1958), 53 note 7, 57; Farber, ZA 71 (1981), 72; Wiggerman in
   Stol, *Birth in Babylonia*, 231–232; Edzard, *Orbis Biblicus et Orientalis* 160/4 (2002), 542–544.
Notes to Text: (2) Or: "dog's face." (3–5) Differently Wasserman, *Style*, 34. (16–19) Wasserman,
   Style, 163.

(b) SHE IS FIERCE

She is fierce, she is wicked, she is [   ],   (1)
She slinks about, she is un[canny].*
Though no physician, she bandages,
Though no midwife, she wipes off the babe.
She reckons off the month(s) of pregnant women,   (5)
She likes to block the dilation of women in labor.
She dogs the livestock's footsteps,
She spies out the country with demonic fierceness.*
She seizes the young man in the roadway,
The young woman in play,   (10)
The little one from the wet nurse's shoulder.
When the Two Gods saw her,
They made her go out through the window,
They made her slip out the (door) socket,
They tied her up to(?) a t[amarisk],   (15)
[   ] in the midst of the sea.*
   ...

(A Spell of [   ])

Text: Hussey-van Dijk, YOS 11 19.
Edition: van Dijk, YOS 11, 25–26.
Notes to Text: (2) *i!-l[a-at]*? (8) George, BSOAS 50 (1987), 360. (16) See Farber, YOS 11, 64.

1.   That is, to blind her so she cannot find her way back.

II.22 AGAINST DEMONS

Numerous incantations are directed at demons. For discussion of demons, see
General Introduction, E.7.

(a) A DEMON

In this spell the magician takes power over the demon. The tablet was found
in the royal palace at Mari in Syria.

> I have seized(?) you like a [   ],   (1)
> I have enveloped you like a mi[st].*
> I have cast you on (your) behind [   ],
> I have taken a string, I have silenced [your] lips,
> I have sprung upon you like a wolf,   (5)
> I have spewed my spittle on you like a lion.
> Let me give a command, may my command p[revail(?)]
>   over* your command,
> Let me speak, let my speech be stronger than your speech.
> As wild beasts are stronger than cattle,*
> So may my command be stronger than your command.   (10)
> As rain is stronger than the ground,
> So may my command be stronger than your command.
> You have tied your nose to your anus.
> So there! Have I not slapped you in the face?

Text: Thureau-Dangin, RA 36 (1939), 12.

Edition: Thureau-Dangin, RA 36 (1939), 10–13.

Literature: Farber, ZA 71 (1982), 53.

Notes to Text: (2) Restoration suggested by CAD K, 253; (7) e-[te-le-et]? (Farber). (9–10) Lambert,
  OrNS 55 (1986), 153; Mayer, OrNS 61 (1992), 384; Cavigneaux, ASJ 17 (1995), 91 note 52 and
  in Abusch, ed., *Magic*, 261 note 51. (11) Mayer, OrNS 61 (1992), 384; Wasserman, *Style*, 77 note
  76.

(b) AGAINST THE EVIL EYE

The evil eye, like a malignant monster, breaks into a home and wrecks nursery, storeroom, kitchen, and domestic chapel. For evil caused by gazing at a person, see A. Dundes, *The Evil Eye* (Madison, 1991); C. Maloney, ed., *The Evil Eye* (New York, 1976); M.-L. Thomsen, "The Evil Eye in Mesopotamia," JNES 51 (1992), 19–32; J. N. Ford, "Ninety-nine by the Evil Eye and One from Natural Causes: KTU2 1.96 in Its Near Eastern Context," UF 30 (1998), 201–278. See also I.4b and IV.35.

> It has broken in, it is [looking] everywhere!   (1)
> It is an enmeshing net, a closing bird snare.
> It went by the babies' doorways and caused havoc
>   among the babies,   (5)
> It went by the door of mothers in childbirth
>   and strangled their babies.
> Then it went into the jar room and smashed the seal,
> It demolished the secluded stove,   (10)
> It turned the locked(?)* house into a shambles.
> It even struck the chapel, the god of the house
>   has gone out of it.
> Slap it in the face! Make it turn around!
> Fills its eyes with salt! Fill its mouth with ashes!   (15)
> May the god of the house return.*

Text: Farber, ZA 71 (1981), 62, obv.
Edition: Farber, ZA 71 (1981), 60–68; Ford, UF 30 (1998), 205–206.
Literature: Farber, JNES 43 (1984), 70; Wasserman, N.A.B.U. 1995/70; van der Toorn in Abusch, ed., *Magic*, 141.
Notes to Text: (1) With Cavigneaux and Al-Rawi, *Studies de Meyer*, 85 note 19, though reading *it-ta-na-ap-[la-as]*; (11) van der Toorn in Abusch, ed., *Magic*, 141 note 20; (16) van der Toorn in Abusch, ed., *Magic*, 141 note 21.

II.23 AGAINST DISEASE, DISCOMFORT, UNWANTED FEELINGS

Incantations and magic rituals were as important in ancient Mesopotamian medical practice as pharmacopoeia and surgical procedure. Some incantations were used for a specific complaint, some for a variety of illnesses.

(a) VARIOUS DISEASES

This incantation is directed against an array of illnesses, the identifications of most of which are unknown.[1] This translation, which freely combines two variant versions (A, B), reflects the mood rather than the medical sense of the text.

Congestion, fever, dizziness, pox,	(1)
Falling sickness, stomach ache(?), redness,	
Boils, rash, tender sores, putrid sores,	(5)
Itch, inflammation, bloody stools, dehydration,	
Chills, discharge, and joint pain,	
Having come down from the bosom(?) of heaven,[2]	(10)
They made feverish the sheep and lambs.	
Whom shall I send with an order	
To the daughters of Anu, seven and seven,	
The ones whose juglets are of gold,	
whose pots are of pure lapis?	(15)
Let them bring their juglets of gold,	
Their pots of pure lapis,	
Let them draw pure waters of the se[a],	
Let them sprinkle, let them extinguish	(20)
Congestion, fever, dizziness, pox,	
Falling sickness, stomach ache(?), redness,	
Boils, rash, tender sores, putrid sores,	(25)

1. For a proposal that this spell refers exclusively to pox as a disease that affects both sheep and human beings, see below, "Literature." This interpretation has not been followed here, in preference to considering the spell an enumeration of various ailments.

2. A reads: "ziggurat(? Farber: closed-in place) of heaven" (corrupt?); B: "leadline" of heaven, for which von Soden suggests "Milky Way" (AHw, 1092b); C reads here "stars of heaven," and adds, "Now the earth has received them (the diseases)." For the "leadline" of heaven, see George, *Topographical Texts*, 256. See also W. Heimpel, "The Babylonian Background of the 'Milky Way'," *Studies Sjöberg*, 249–252 (later texts only).

Itch, inflammation, bloody stools, dehydration,
Chills, discharge, and joint pain

Subscription (A):

(This is a sacred incantation of Damu and Ninkarrak.
The spell is not mine,
but it is the spell that Ningirimma,
Ea, and Asalluhi cast and that I took.)

Subscription (B):

([I] exorcise you by the warrior Shamash, …, Judging God!
[Let] the (illnesses) retreat [to] your grasp.
You are [for]giving: revive him (the patient),
Let me be the one to cast the spell (that cures him).)

Text: Goetze, JCS 9 (1955), 9–10 (=A,B); widely variant parallel, Hussey-van Dijk, YOS 11 8 (C).
Edition: Goetze, JCS 9 (1955), 8–18; Kämmerer, UF 27 (1995), 140–146.
Literature: Farber, ZA 71 (1981), 54; JNES 49 (1990), 307; M. Stol, *Epilepsy in Babylonia* (Groningen, 1993), 13 note 70; T. Kämmerer, "Die erste Pockendiagnoses stammt aus Babylonien," UF 27 (1995), 129–168.
*Notes to Text: (10) Differently CAD S, 259a, which suggests "door bolts" of heaven. I follow Borger, JCS 18 (1964), 55, who sees here a corruption of *ṣerretu*; M. Stol, *Epilepsy in Babylonia* (Groningen, 1993), 13 note 70 associates this with the udder of the "Cow of Heaven."

(b) ALL DISEASES

I will cast for you the spell
    that drives away all diseases,   (1)
Which Enlilbanda[1] established, ordainer of destinies.*
Let Ea cast for you the spell of life,
Nudimmud[2] and Nammu, together with Anu.
Let Ningirimma, mistress of spells,
    cast the spell for you,   (5)
Ningirimma, mistress of spells, has cast the spell!
The sick man will rise by her spell, he will not be exhausted.
Let Ninkarrak swathe you with her gentle hands,
Let Damu make your fatigue pass from you.
As for the gall that stifles, the snatcher Lamashtu,
    dog bite, human teeth,   (10)
May Annunitum crush them with her spell,
May Adad, Shamkan, Nisaba, Shamash, and the River,
All the pure gods, be the ones to cleanse you,
Together with(?) Enlil may they cleanse you.
May Twin Son and Twin Daughter, the children of Sin,
    Shamash and Ishtar   (15)
...
... be enraged at you!
May the King of the Depths,
    the exorcist of the gods, Holy Ea
Cast for you the spell that cannot be warded off.
May he make the ... pass over, ... your travail.   (20)
I cast for you the spell that drives away all diseases.

Text: Figulla, CT 42 32.
Edition: von Soden, BiOr 18 (1961), 71–73.
Literature: Landsberger, MSL 9, 83; Farber, ZA 71 (1981), 55.
Notes to Text: (2) George.

1. Another name for Ea.
2. Another name for Ea.

(c) AGAINST AN INFANT ILLNESS

After an introduction setting forth the place of the worm in creation,[1] the magician identifies it as the cause of the child's illness and casts a spell to destroy it. See also II.21.

Anu begot heaven, heaven brought forth earth,   (1)
Earth bore stench, stench bore mud,
Mud bore fly, fly bore worm.
The worm, daughter of Gula, is clad in a traveling cloak,
She is blood-soaked,*   (5)
... the child's blood, she extinguished his eyes.
Damu cast the spell and Gula killed(?) [the worm],
... he slaughtered them ... [   ]
He (the child?) opened his mouth, took the breast,
        raised his eyes and [saw   ].

(The spell is not mine: It is the spell of Damu and Gula,
        Damu [c]ast and I took.)   (10)

Text: Hussey-van Dijk, YOS 11 5, 1–8.
Edition: Veldhuis, OLP 24 (1993), 45–46, 52.
Literature: van Dijk, YOS 11, 19; Farber, YOS 11, 61; Scurlock, AfO 48/49 (2001/2), 243–244.
Notes to Text: (5) Scurlock, AfO 48/49 (2001/2), 243.

1. For this cosmological motif, see p. 43 note 4.

(d) AGAINST A MOTE IN THE EYE

A mote or sty is magically washed out of a sufferer's eye. The sty is the result of a mote raised in the air when the gods were harvesting. This part is considered spoken in the past, a device reflected in the translation by "they say." By contrast, the effective part of the incantation uses command forms without markers of speech.

Earth, they say, earth bore mud, mud bore stalk,   (1)
Stalk bore ear, ear bore mote.
(Then) within, they say, the square field of Enlil,
    seven units in area,   (10)
Moon was reaping, Sun was gathering.
(Then it was), they say,
    that mote entered the young man's eye.   (15)
Whom shall I send with an order to the daughters of Anu,
To the daughters of Anu, seven and seven?
Let them bring to me* [pot?] of carnelian,
    vessel of chalcedony,   (20)
Let them draw up for me pure waters of the sea,
Let them drive out mote from the young man's eye!   (25)

Text: (Landsberger)-Jacobsen, JNES 14 (1955), 15.
Edition: Jacobsen and Landsberger, JNES 14 (1955), 14–21; Landsberger, JNES 17 (1958), 56–58.
Translation: Bottéro, *Annuaire* 1978/9, 93 = *Mythes*, 286; Farber, TUAT II/2, 272–273.
Literature: Farber, ZA 71 (1981), 54; Stol, *Studies Finet*, 165; Farber, JNES 49 (1990), 305; Veldhuis, OLP 24 (1993), 48–50.

Notes to Text: (20) Bottéro understands all the following to be purpose clauses, ending the question on line 25, but I have followed the Jacobsen-Landsberger interpretation; compare II.23a.

(e) AGAINST JOINT PAIN(?)

This incantation is against a condition called *maškadu*, which seems to have attacked the musculature of cattle, perhaps associated with abrupt chill after sunset.[1] "Joint pain" is simply a guess to provide a meaningful translation.

> Joint pain, [joint pain], joint pain is not *maškadu*,   (1)
> It is Shu'u.[2]
> Its lurking place is the [cattle pen?],
> Its standing place is where the sheep stand,
> It bites as a wolf bites, it springs as an Elamite dog springs,   (5)
> It enters as livestock enters, it leaves as livestock leaves.
> Go out, joint pain, before the flint knives of Gula,
>   get to you!*

Text: Hussey-van Dijk, YOS 11 14 rev. 1–6.
Edition: See van Dijk, YOS 11, 23–24.
Notes to Text: (7) Wasserman, *Style*, 11.

1. For discussion, see Herrero, RA 69 (1975), 52–53.
2. Proper name of a demon (reading Farber). The lines refer to the necessity of invoking the disease demon by its correct name for the magic to be effective (Reiner, *Studies Moran*, 424 note 18).

(f) AGAINST A DISEASE OF SHEEP AND GOATS

In heaven [above] a blaze broke out,   (1)
Congestion(?) has fallen upon all the beasts.
It has made feverish kids, lambs,   (5)
And little ones in the wet nurse's arms!
Address[1] this to my mother Ningirimma:
"Let the beasts' faces brighten!
"Let the cattle rejoice!   (10)
"Let the green plants rejoice!
"Let the roadway rejoice!"[2]
I will set for all time sun disks
On the pedestals of the great gods, with loving care.[3]   (15)

(Incantation for sheep constriction[?])

Text: Hussey-van Dijk, YOS 11 7.
Edition: van Dijk, YOS 11, 21.

1. As Farber suggested to me, the "seven and seven" (see above, II.23a, d) are called upon here.
2. This seems to be a metonym for humankind; compare II.25a, line 8.
3. This refers to placing cultic symbols on the pedestals of divine images (George, BSOAS 50 [1987], 360).

(g) AGAINST GAS PAINS

Natural atmospheric wind is, of course, beneficial (see line 3), but wind locked up in the human body is harmful. Thus the wind should come out and go to its natural habitat. See also IV.39.

Go out, wind! Go out, wind!	(1)
Go out, wind, offspring of the gods!	
Go out, wind, abundance of the peoples!	
Go out of the head, wind!	
Go out of the eye, wind!	(5)
Go out of the mouth, wind!	
Go out of the ear, wind!	
Go out of the anus, wind!	
Let the man be released,	
Let him find rest [ ],	(10)

...

Text: Gurney, OECT 11 3.
Edition: Gurney, OECT 11, 21.
Literature: Fish, *Iraq* 6 (1939), 184; Farber, ZA 71 (1981), 53 and 54 note 3; Veldhuis, OLP 24 (1993), 52–53.

(h) AGAINST STOMACH ACHE

My flesh keeps (stabbing) like a dagger,
    goring like a [bull]!
My face[1] is clouded over, like a widow's.
Like a wave, it wears away the banks,
It inflamed my intestines.
Bini-girish-kikilabi.[2]   (5)

(A spell for the insides.)

Text: Cavigneaux, Al-Rawi, *Studies de Meyer*, 83.
Edition: Cavigneaux, Al-Rawi, *Studies de Meyer*, 82–84.
★*Notes to Text*: (1) Assuming a construction with one verb and two subjects and reading GUD-*im*.
    (7) ŠÀ.MU: lexical first person, like ugu-mu?

1. Text: "His face."
2. Magic abracadabra words; see IV.45.

(i) AGAINST AROUSAL

"Arousal" may refer to onset of sexual desire or anger.[1] The speaker wishes to drive such feelings from his heart. See also II.26b (pp. 204–205).

Arousal, they say, arousal!	(1)
Arousal comes upon me like a wild bull,*	
It keeps springing at me like a dog,	
Like a lion it is fierce in coming,	(5)
Like a wolf it is full of fury.	
Stay! I will pass over you like a threshold,	
I will overreach you like a lintel,*	
I will turn back your approach like a tether,*	(10)
I will expel your fiery feeling.	

Text: van Dijk, TIM 9 72; compare Finkel, ZA 75 (1985), 184 = Gadd, UET 6/2 399.
Edition: Whiting, ZA 75 (1985), 180–181.
Literature: Farber, ZA 71 (1981), 55; Sigrist, *Studies Pope*, 86; see also II.26b i.
Notes to Text: (1) See Mayer, OrNS 64 (1995), 163. (9) See von Soden, AfO 20 (1963), 124; differently Whiting, ZA 75 (1985), 185–186. (10) With Whiting, ZA 75 (1985), 186.

1. For this correlation in Hebrew, see Waldman, *Journal of Biblical Literature* 89 (1970), 215–217; the translation "attack of rage" has been suggested by J. Westenholz, *Legends*, 100, note to 15′.

(j) AGAINST HUNGER AND THIRST

The sufferer arrests heaven, earth, and the great gods until he is nourished.

> Stars, I arrest you!   (1)
> Sky, I arrest you!
> Earth, I arrest you!
> Anu, I arrest you!
> Enlil, I arrest you!   (5)
> Until I get my food and drink.

Text: Figulla, CT 42 6, iv 1–8.
Edition: See Wasserman, *Style*, 76.

II.24 AGAINST WITCHCRAFT

Incantations against witchcraft and sorcery are better known for the Mature and Late periods than for the Classical period (see, for example, IV.49 and the excerpts from the magical series against witchcraft such as III.40a–d, 41c, 48d; IV.47, 49a-d). The complaint to Enki translated below is unique of its kind.

> On account of him, O Enki who made me—he has brought hunger, thirst upon me, he has cast chills and misery upon me—if it please you, then tell him your wish, that, by [command(?)] of Enki, who dwells in Eridu, …, I may establish the greatness of Enki. On account of him, lest he harm me.

Text: Beckman, ASJ 18 (1996), 21.
Edition: G. Beckman, B. R. Foster, "An Old Babylonian Plaint against Black Magic," ASJ 18 (1996), 19–21.

II.25 THE WORLD AROUND

(a) AGAINST A NOXIOUS HERB(?)

This incantation refers to a mythical(?) herb, perhaps a metaphor for some malaise, that has upset sun, moon, cattle, and humankind. The magician sends his envoy off to Ea, god of wisdom and magic. The envoy repeats the narrative and receives the ritual to counteract the effects of the plant.[1]

> Sun brought the herb across from the moun[tain],   (1)
> It seized the heart of Sun, who brought it across.
> It seized the heart of Moon in heaven,   (5)
> It seized the heart of ox in paddock,
> It seized the heart of sheep in fold,
> It seized the heart of young man in roadway,
> It seized the heart of maiden in play!
> Whom shall I send to the great dweller in the depths (to say),   (10)

(The text repeats itself so far as preserved, then after a break it ends with:
"I purified …")

Text: Hussey-van Dijk, YOS 11 11.
Edition: Farber, JNES 49 (1990), 308–309; Veldhuis, OLP 21 (1990), 42–43.
Literature: N. Veldhuis, "The Heart Grass and Related Matters," OLP 21 (1990), 27–44; see also
    OLP 24 (1993), 50–51; Finkel, *Studies Borger*, 82 note 15.

1. A later, expanded version of this incantation has been studied by Reiner, *Poetry*, 94–100.

(b) AGAINST DOGS

These grim descriptions of attacks by rabid dogs are remarkable for their stark power. See, in general, W. Yuhong, "Rabies and Rabid Dogs in Sumerian and Akkadian Literature," JAOS 121 (2001), 32–43.

1. Swift Dog

It is fleet of foot, powerful on the run,   (1)
Strong-legged, broad-chested.
The shadow of a wall is where it stands,
The threshold is its lurking place.
It carries its semen in its mouth,   (5)
Where it bit, it left its offspring.[1]

(Incantation to survive a dog['s bite], incantation of Ea)*

Text: van Dijk, VAS 17 8.
Edition: None.
Translation: Farber, TUAT II/2, 256.
Literature: Farber, ZA 71 (1981), 56; Sigrist, *Studies Pope*, 86; Whiting, ZA 75 (1985), 183; Gurney, OECT 11, 22; Finkel, in Abusch, ed., *Magic*, 213–223.
Notes to Text: (7) Compare Farber, ZA 71 (1981), 56 note 4.

1. That is, the dog's bite causes its "offspring" (hydrophobia) to grow in the victim, whose distended stomach could resemble pregnancy (Assante, CRRAI 47 [2001], 33 note 29).

2. Dogbite

It is long of leg,[1] it is swift to run,
It is famished for food, scarcely anything has it had to eat!
Its semen dangles from its fangs,
Where it bit, it left its offspring.[2]

(Incantation)*

Text: Böhl, BiOr 11 (1954), pl. II = LB 2001.
Edition: Whiting, ZA 75 (1985), 182–183.
Literature: von Soden, OrNS 25 (1956), 144 note 1; Farber, ZA 71 (1981), 54; Sigrist, *Studies Pope*,
    86; Gurney, OECT 11, 22; Finkel, in Abusch, ed., *Magic*, 213–223.
Notes to Text: (5) *tu-en-né-nu-ri*, see Farber, ZA 71 (1981), 54.

3. Be Born Again

The mad dog eats medicine then magically reverts to the moment of birth,
when he is once again a puppy unaffected by rabies.

Let him devour his madness like thyme!   (1)
Let his afterbirth fall,
Let him hide his face,
Let his mouth become as it was the day he was born!

Text: Böhl, BiOr 11 (1954), pl. II (LB 1001).
Edition: Böhl, BiOr 11 (1954), 82–83.
Literature: Stol, *Birth in Babylonia*, 128–129, whose interpretation is followed here.

1. Literally: "knees." "Long" (*urruk*) is similar in sound to "fleet" (*urruḫ*) (b.1 line 1), so may be considered a variant version of the same line.
2. See above, p. 100 note 1.

(c) AGAINST SNAKES

1. Lurking Serpents

In this incantation, "seize by the mouth" may mean "capture by spell"; compare I.4, line 9, where a similar expression is used. The mouth in the Mesopotamian view was the organ of independent action and effectiveness, so "control of the mouth" expresses absolute control.[1] None of these snakes can be identified, nor is it clear that they are actual species (see also below c.3).

> I seize the mouth of all snakes, even the viper,*
> > Serpent(s) that cannot be conjured: (1)
> The alabaster burrower,
> > the fish-snake with rainbow eyes,*
> The eel, the hissing snake
> > The hisser, the snake at the window.
> It came in by a crevice,
> > It went out by a drain.
> It struck the gazelle while it slept,[2]
> > It secreted itself(?) in a withered oak.*   (5)
> The snake lurks in a roof beam,
> > The serpent lurks in wool.*
> The serpent has six mouths, seven tongues,
> > Seven are the poisonous vapors(?) of its heart.*
> It is bushy of hair, horrible of feature,
> > Its eyes are frightful.
> Bubbles(?) ooze from its maw,
> > Its spittle cleaves stone.*

> > > (Incantation)

Text: van Dijk, TIM 9 65, 66.
Edition: Finkel in Abusch, ed., *Magic*, 226–229.
Literature: Farber, ZA 71 (1982), 55.
Notes to Text: ⟨1⟩ Apparently the direct object of "seize," though the grammar is difficult. (2) Geller *apud* Finkel, 225. (5) Following CAD A/1, 354; (6) With AHw, 1247b; less likely, "the bolt."

1. See further M. Marcus, "In His Lips He Held a Spell," *Source* 13/4 (1994), 9–14.
2. This may refer to a sleeping child; see IV.54b.

Variant, *šu-pa-tim*, perhaps, "reeds." (7) Following Reiner, *Literatur*, 191, where this passage is translated. (9) For "bubbles(?)," see Wasserman, *Style*, 48; Finkel, 228, reads *pu-ʿlu-uḫ-tum*ʾ. For "spittle," see Wilcke, ZA 75 (1985), 206.

2. Snakebite

A snake is here portrayed with the luminous, smooth, greenish sheen of a reed. Like a reed, the snake's head comes to a point, from which brightness radiates.

> Lush* as a reed, green like Tishpak,[1]   (1)
> His nostrils are death, his mouth burning fire,*
> His forked tongue is glaring light:
> May his glaring lights ... for me.*   (5)
>
> (Incantation to survive snakebite)

Text: van Dijk, VAS 17 4.
Edition: van Dijk, OrNS 38 (1969), 540–541.
Notes to Text: (1) Reading [u]*l-lu-ḫu* with CAD M, 153a. *elēḫu* is normally a positive attribute. (2) Wasserman, *Style*, 40. (5) Text: *li-a-PI-ti-a-am*.

1. A warrior and vegetation(?) deity, sometimes associated with a snake-like dragon; see Wiggerman in I. Finkel, M.S. Geller, eds., *Sumerian Gods and Their Representations* (Groningen, 1997), 37–39.

3. Lurking Serpent

It is very long in form,   (1)
Splendid in body.
Its nest is bits of palm,
The snake lurks in its dwelling,
The serpent lurks among reeds.   (5)
The serpent has two heads,
Seven forked tongues, seven segments(?) in its neck.
I smote the underground snake and
        the snake lying across the path(?),
The slippery(?) snake, the forest snake,
The reed(?)-snake that cannot be conjured,   (10)
The wine-dark snake that strikes at
        the one who exorcizes him!

Text: Finkel in Abusch, ed., *Magic*, 245.
Edition: Finkel in Abusch, ed., *Magic*, 224–226.

(d) AGAINST FLIES

In this text someone brushes away flies from his head and face. The swarm of flies is ordered to fly away like the rising of a plague of locusts.

> I have swatted you at the crown, (1)
> From crown to brow,
> From brow to ear, (5)
> From ear to nostril of the nose!
> I exorcise you by Ninkarrak:
> You shall rise a locust's rising (10)
> From his person(?).

Text: Hussey-van Dijk, YOS 11 6, 1–11.
Edition: Veldhuis, OLP 24 (1993), 62.
Literature: N. Veldhuis, "The Fly, the Worm, and the Chain," OLP 24 (1993), 41–63.

(e) AGAINST SCORPIONS

The speaker protects himself with magic against the dread scorpion,[1] rendering it harmless as any other trifle he might encounter along the way.

I pour (magic) over myself, I pour (magic) over my person,[2]   (1)
As if river poured over its banks.
(Be) clod of roadway, rubble of street!
(Be) cartilage of a (dead) mongoose, red patch of a garden!

(When a scorpion comes,* and he casts [this spell],
      it will not make a move.)[3]   (5)

Text: Hussey-van Dijk, YOS 11 2.
Edition: van Dijk, YOS 11, 17.
Literature: Westenholz, OrNS 46 (1977), 214–215; Mayer, OrNS 61 (1992), 378; Cooper in Vogel-zang, ed., *Poetic Language*, 47–55; Cavigneaux in Abusch, ed., *Magic*, 265–266.
Notes to Text: (5) Scurlock, BiOr 59 (2002), 469.

1. For a general discussion of scorpions, see E. Douglas Van Buren, "The Scorpion in Mesopotamian Art and Religion," AfO 12 (1937/9), 1–28.
2. In spells of the Late period, this line is understood to mean "impregnate," but this does not fit well here (see Meier, *Maqlû*, 47 lines 23–30 and Cavigneaux in Abusch, ed., *Magic*, 266–267).
3. Compare the Sumerian proverb "The dog moves, the scorpion moves, but my husband does not move at all" (Alster, *Proverbs*, 1:98).

(f) AGAINST A WATER MONSTER

This spell was to be used against a serpent-like monster that lurked in swamps.

The Tigris bore it, (1)
The Ulaya[1] raised it,
It lies under the rushes like a serpent.
Its head is like a pestle,
Its tail is like a pounding tool. (5)
Adad gave it its roar,
Nergal, the [   ] of Anu, gave it its slither.
[I] conjure you by Ishtar and Dumuzi,[2]
Not to come near me a [lea]gue and sixty cubits!

Text: Cavigneaux, *Studies Wilcke*, 62.
Edition: Cavigneaux, *Studies Wilcke*, 61–62.

1. Name for the Karun or Kerkha rivers; see p. 384 note 2. This means that the monster is both Mesopotamian and Elamite.
2. Why these two deities are invoked is unclear; in other spells they stand for closeness (see II.26b(a), line 6), while here they are supposed to assist in keeping the creature away.

(g) AGAINST A BLEATING GOAT

This bilingual parody expresses the murderous rage of a person unable to sleep because of a bleating goat. He claims that Ea, god of wisdom, also disturbed, abruptly sent off the great god Marduk (without the usual consultation), and charged him with silencing the offending animal. Marduk is commanded to insert the goat's own dung into its ears, a sort of "ear-for-an-ear" reprisal in that the goat has filled the sufferer's ears with its plaints. The sleepless one contemplates the goat's demise with relish. He hopes that the gods of livestock will not take this amiss and expresses confidence that the whole country will erupt with praise and thanksgiving at the awe-inspiring deed.

When Ea [ ],	(1)
And Enlil [ ],	
On account of what pertained to the b[easts].	
He caught sight of a goat.	
The goat is sick, it cannot [shut(?)] its mouth(?)!	(5)
The shepherd is kept awake, he cannot sleep,	
It keeps his herdsman awake,	
Who must go about, day and night, forever herding.*	
When Enki saw it,	
He called the Wise One, sent him off with weighty charge,	(10)
"A goat in pen or fold is keeping me awake at night,*	
"Go, it must not keep me awake!	
"Take its dung,	
"Stuff it into its left ear,	
"That goat, instead of falling asleep, let it drop dead!"	(15)
May Shamkan, lord of the beasts, hold nothing against me,	
Nor serve me summons for this case.	
Folk and land will sing your praises,	
Even the great gods will praise what you can do!	(20)

Text: Genouillac, PRAK II pl. 3, C1.
Edition: W. G. Lambert, *Studies Garelli,* 415–419.
Literature: Farber, ZA 71 (1981), 53.
Notes to Text: (8) With AHw, 977a. (11) Wasserman, *Style,* 24 note 81: *ú-š[a-am]-ša.*

II.26 LOVE CHARMS

(a) HORNS OF GOLD

Like the Archaic-period love charm, I.7c, this opens with a description of the love charm, which is both male and female (a). The speaker hopes that the woman of his choice will remain available (b), and that he can acquire power over her (c). He concludes by apostrophizing her (d). This translation incorporates readings and suggestions by W. G. Lambert. See also IV.50.

(a)

Love charm, love charm! (1)
His horns are of gold,
His tail is of pure lapis,
It is placed in Ishtar's heart.

(b)

I called to her, but she did not come back to me, (5)
I whistled* at her,[1] but she did not look at me.
If she is "consecrated," may her lover fall,
If she has been taken, may her accuser fall.[2]

(c)

(May this) marriageable girl, a young lady of good family,
Fall at my clamor, at my call.[3] (10)
May the dough fall from her hands,[4]
May the young man fall who is at her side.

1. This may refer to the prolonged hiss that serves throughout the Near East today as a "wolf whistle."
2. As WGL suggests, this couplet seems to refer to the speaker's proprietary attitude toward the girl's virginity. If she is pure, may any would-be lover not deflower her; if she has been deflowered, may her accuser not prove his case.
3. "Call" has a double meaning here, as it was also the term for claiming the bride at her father's house (Finkelstein, RA 61 [1967], 127–136).
4. This and the next line may refer to domestic tasks, one involving food preparation and the other child care (her younger brother?), that the beloved will be unable to perform while the charm affects her heart.

(d)

Don't lock your house against me,
Don't even look at the latchstring in your hand!
Look at me as if I were (your) tether,
Lick me over as if I were (your newborn) calf!*   (15)
Why did you wrap your head with my love,
    like a headband?
Tie it around your waist, like a belt?
Stroke your [body] with [the happly glow]
    of my fa[ce],* as if it were oil?[1]

(fragmentary lines)

Text: Hussey-van Dijk, YOS 11 87.
Literature: Westenholz, OrNS 46 (1977), 206–207; Cavigneaux, ASJ 18 (1996), 36; N.A.B.U. 1998/74.
Notes to Text: (3) Cavigneaux, ASJ 18 (1996), 36 note 10. (6) Reading *a-aḫ-zu-ši* and deriving from
    azú, *ḫezú* (etc.) "hiss." (15) Cavigneaux, ASJ 18 (1996), 36. (18) WGL; *z[i-mí]-ja*? (collated).

1.   That is, by what power does she appropriate his love and well-being to herself, leaving him
with nothing?

(b) LOOK AT ME!

These spells were intended for men and women who wished to attract or to arouse sex partners. Their explicitness can be compared with I.4c and II.19. References to speakers are supplied by the translator on the basis of grammatical forms in the original that distinguish masculine and feminine. Various Sumerian incantations in this collection have been omitted.

(a)

(She)

"With dog slaver, thirst(?), hunger(?), (1)
"Slap in the face, rolling eye,
"I have hit you on the head,
    I have driven you out of your mind!
"Set your thinking to my thinking,
"Set your reason to my reason! (5)
"I hold you fast, as Ishtar held Dumuzi,
"As liquor binds him who drinks it,
"I have bound you with my hairy "mouth,"
"With my vagina full of wetness,*
"With my mouth full of saliva, (10)
"With my vagina full of wetness,
"May no rival come to you!
"Dog is crouching, pig is crouching,
"You too keep crouching on my thighs!"

(ritual follows)

(b)

(She)

"Look at me, be joyful as a harp, (1)
"May your heart glow as with liquor,
"Keep bursting forth like the sun upon me,
"Keep renewing yourself for me like the moon,
"… may your love ever be new." (5)

(ritual follows)

(c)

(She)

"Get your legs underway, Erra-bani,[1]   (1)
"Get your middle in motion,
"Let your sinews follow after."

(He)

"Let your heart rejoice,
"Let your spirits be happy,   (5)
"I will swell large as a dog!
"Like a tether, don't let your ... escape on me!"

(Love incantation)

(d)

(He)

"Stay awake at night,   (1)
"Don't go to sleep in the day,
"You shall not sit down nights!"

(Love incantation)

(e)

(She)

"Beloved, beloved,   (1)
"You, whom Ea and Enlil installed,
"You sit on a dais like Ishtar,
"You sit in a treasure vault like Nanay.
"I close you in!"   (5)

(He)

"High priestesses love a hot spot,
"Wives despise their husbands![2]
"Cut off her stuck-up nose,

1. Personal name, whether real or proverbial is unknown.
2. This may mean that unmarried women like a good time, whereas married women are bored.
So why is this woman so standoffish? (See Scurlock, AfO 36/37 [1989/90], 110–111.)

"Set her nose under my foot!
"Just as her love was too high for me,   (10)
"So may my love grow too high for her lover."[1]

(Love incantation)

(f)

(He)

"Why are you cruel as a thorn in a thicket?"   (1)

(She)

"Why is your desire as perverse as a child's?"

(He)

"Why is your face so hostile?
"Why am I invisible, do not exist?"

(She)

"In your heart lies a dog, lurks a pig,   (5)
"You lie down with me
          and I'll pluck out your bristle,
"Get together whatever you have
          and give it to me!"

(Incantation …)

(g)

(She)

"Where is your heart going?   (1)
"Where are your eyes lo[oking]?
"Let [your heart come] to me!
"Let [your eyes look at] me!
"Look at me l[ike   ]   (5)
"Gaze at me [   ]
"You will [hunger for] me like bread,

1. She was too good to love me but let me surpass any lover of hers?

"You will [thirst for] me like beer ..."

(Love incantation)

(h)

(She)

"[Arousal], arousal!"[1]   (1)
"It ke[eps its place] in his heart.
"Let me give you cool water to drink,
"Let me give you ice and coolants.
"Like a wolf, may vigor possess you,   (5)
"Like a lion, may splendor possess you.
"Spring, O arousal of Nanay!"

(i)

(She)

"Arousal, arousal!   (1)
"He [comes upon me] like a wild bull,
"He [keeps springing at me] like a hound,
"L[ike a lion he is furious] in his onset,
"Li[ke a wolf] he goes where he lists.   (5)
"...
"I [broke the ...] of his heart,
"I will cross him like a bri[dge],
"The Tigris river is under [him].
"Spring, [O arousal] of Nanay!"   (10)

---

1. Compare II.23i. There the incantation seems to be directed against arousal, unless the last line means that she appeases him; here the same language may be used to wish arousal upon the beloved, which she will then cool off.

(j)

(She)

"Arousal, arousal!   (1)
"I will step over you like a threshold,
"I will traverse you like open gro[und],
"Spring, O [ar]ousal of Nanay!"

(Incantation using? a lump of salt)

(k)

(She)

"Big mouth, floppy ears, Iddin-Damu,[1]   (1)
"Open your mouth like a ...-fish.
"Your heart is a ...-plant.
"I lapped at your heel,
"I took the ...   (5)
"I caught your leg.
"Cuddle me like a puppy,
"M[ount] me like a dog!"

(Incantation using soap-plant)

(l)

(She)

"I have hit you on the head,   (1)
"You will squirm around me on the ground like a [   ],
"You will ... the ground like a pig,
"Until I'll have my way, like a child!"

(m)

Garlic sticks up its own stalk,   (1)
The ox raises up its own rod.[2]
As river poured over its banks,

---

1. See p. 202 note 1.
2. Wordplays on "garlic" (*šumu*) and "progeny" (*šumu*), "ox" (*alpu*) and "rod" (*palû*) (Wasserman, *Style*, 7 note 16).

I pour magic over myself,
I pour magic over my body.[1]
"I have opened my seven doors for you, Erra-bani,   (5)
"...
"Bring the constant gnawing of your heart to an end on me!"

Text: Wilcke, ZA 75 (1985), photo opposite p. 208.
Edition: Wilcke, ZA 75 (1985), 198–209.
Literature: J. Scurlock, "Was There a 'Love-Hungry' Entu-priestess Named Eṭirtum?" AfO 36/37
    (1989/90), 107–112.
*Notes to Text: (a 9) Differently W.G. Lambert in M. Minden et al., eds., Figurative Language in the
    Ancient Near East (London, 1987), 38. I follow Assante, CRRAI 47 (2001), 33 in guessing that
    "urine" could refer also to female genital outflow, for which no certain Akkadian word has been
    identified. For the complicated problems of defining ancient terms for "female fluids," see Rein-
    er, ZA 72 (1982), 132 (female "semen"); Biggs, Studies Lambert, 3 (absence of term for menses);
    Greenberg, Studies Finkelstein, 85–86.

1. See also II.25e.

G. Prayers

II.27 NOCTURNAL PRAYERS OF DIVINERS

The following two prayers are offered by a diviner to the gods of the night sky (i) or to the gods of divination, including various nocturnal creatures (ii). The first is a soliloquy by the diviner as he keeps his lonely vigil: the great gods of the daytime and humankind in general are all asleep, while he must stay awake and watch. The only other living creature he sees is a solitary wayfarer. The diviner prays that the constellations will assist in making the extispicy successful, now that the daytime gods of extispicy, especially the sun, are asleep. See also III.41.

(a) TO GODS OF THE NIGHT

The noble ones are safely guarded(?),★ doorbolts drawn,
    rings in place,[1]   ⸣   (1)
The noisy people are fallen silent, the doors are barred
    that were open.
Gods of the land, goddesses of the land,   (5)
Shamash, Sin, Adad, and Ishtar[2] are gone off to
    the lap of heaven.★
They will give no judgment, they will decide no cases.
Night draws a veil, the palace, outbuildings(?),
    and sanctuary are dark,★   (10)
The wayfarer cries out to[3] a god, even the petitioner
    (of this omen) keeps on sleeping!
The true judge,[4] father to the orphaned,
    Shamash has gone off to his bedchamber.   (15)
May the princely ones[5] of the gods of the night:
    brilliant Girra, warrior Erra,
May the "Bow," the "Yoke," Orion, the "Dragon,"

---

1. Variant (b): "Pegs and rings are set."
2. Variant (b): "Adad and Ea, Shamash and Ishtar."
3. Variant (b): "prays to."
4. Variant (b): "true father."
5. Variant (a): "'The Bow', Elamatum, Pleiades, Orion, the 'Dragon', the Great Bear, Lyra, the 'Bison'."

The Great Bear, the Lyre, the "Bison," the "Horned Serpent,"   (20)
Stand by me! In the extispicy I perform,
  in the lamb I offer, place the truth!

(b) TO SHAMASH AND GODS OF THE NIGHT

O lofty Shamash, j[udge] Shamash,   (1)
O Enki, Ninki, Ala[la, Belili],[1]
Ningizzida prefect [of the (nether)world],*
O ominous malformed creature...[   ],
O wandering nightfowls [   ],   (5)
O Moon, luminary of the [pure] sky:
In the extispicy I perform —

Text: (a) Dossin, RA 32 (1935), 182–183 (34a,b); (b) Schileico, *Izvestija Rossiskoj Akademii Istorii Material'noj Kul'tury* 3 (1924), 147. (34a only) = Horowitz, ZA 90 (2000), 197.

Edition: Dossin, RA 32 (1935), 179–187; von Soden, ZA 43 (1936), 306–308; Horowitz, ZA 90 (2000), 195–198.

Translation: von Soden, SAHG, 274 no. 20; Stephens, ANET[3] 390–391; Oppenheim, AnBi 12 (1959), 295–296; Seux, *Hymnes*, 475–480; Hecker, TUAT II/5, 718–719.

Literature: Oppenheim, AnBi 12 (1959), 289–301 (aesthetic appreciation of 34a); Hirsch, *Kindlers Literaturlexikon* I 328; von Soden, "Gebet II," RLA 3, 163–164; W. Horowitz, N. Wasserman, "Another Old Babylonian Prayer to the Gods of the Night," JCS 48 (1996), 57–60.

Notes to Text: (a 1) Livingstone, N.A.B.U. 1990/86. (a 6) Heimpel, JCS 38 (1986), 130. (a 10) Horowitz and Wasserman, ZA 90 (2000), 196. (b 3) Restoration WGL.

1.   Variant (b): "great ones."

II.28 DIURNAL PRAYERS OF DIVINERS

Extispicy, or divination by examination of the entrails of a lamb (exta), required a series of prayers and rituals, culminating in sacrifice and examination of the animal. The prayer and rituals (*ikribu*)[1] are replete with legal imagery: the procedure is a "case"; inducements are offered for a favorable decision; the outcome is a "verdict"; the principal gods concerned are Shamash, god of justice, and Adad, god of thunder. The prayers were intended to attract the god's attention, to enlist his help for a proper procedure, and to elicit, if possible, a favorable verdict for the client. Often the specific favorable features of the exta are itemized together with the more general requests of the prayer, as in The Lamb (II.35b) line 16. Where the client's name was to be given, the manuscripts refer to "so-and-so, son of so-and-so."

(a) THE CEDAR

O Shamash, I place to my mouth sacred cedar, (1)
For you I knot it in a lock of my hair,
For you I place in my lap bushy cedar.

I have washed my mouth and hands, (5)
I have wiped my mouth with bushy cedar,
I have tied sacred cedar in a lock of my hair,
For you I have heaped up bushy cedar.
Cleansed now, to the assembly of the gods[2]
    draw I near for judgment. (10)
O Shamash, lord of judgment, O Adad, lord of prayers
    and divination.
In the ritual I perform, in the extispicy I perform,
    place the truth!

O Shamash, I place incense to my mouth,
... sacred cedar, let the incense linger! (15)
Let it summon to me the great gods.

---

1. *Ikribu* is a prayer made in connection with extispicy procedure (I. Starr, *The Rituals of the Diviner*, BM 12 [1983], 45–46). I have sometimes translated the word as "ritual" (Starr, "extispicy-ritual"), and elsewhere, when it is used in a general sense as "prayer."
2. Or: "cleansed for the assembly of the gods."

In the ritual I perform, in the extispicy I perform,
    place the truth!

O Shamash, I hold up to you water of Tigris and Euphrates,
Which has carried to you cedar and juniper
    from the highlands.   (20)
Wash yourself, O valiant Shamash,
Let the great gods wash with you.
And you too, Bunene, faithful messenger,
Wash yourself in the presence of Shamash the judge.

O Shamash, to you I hold up something choice,   (25)
... sacred water for the flour.
O Shamash, lord of judgment,
    O Adad, lord of prayers and divination,
Seated on thrones of gold, dining from a tray of lapis,
Come down to me that you may dine, that you may sit
    on the throne and render judgment.
In the ritual I perform, in the extispicy
    I perform, place the truth!

O Shamash, I hold up to you a lordly tribute,
Which in the courtyard* of the gods [   ] to you.   (35)
O Shamash, lord of judgment,
    O Adad l[ord of prayers] and divination,
Seated on thrones of gold, dining from a tray of lapis,
Come down to me that you may sit
    on the throne and render judgment.
In the ritual I perform, in the extispicy I perform,
    place the truth!   (40)

O Shamash, I hold up to you seven and seven sweet loaves,
The rows of which are ranged before you.
O Shamash, lord of judgment, O Adad, lord of divination,
Seated on thrones of [gold], dining from a tray of lapis,   (45)
Come [down to me] that you may eat,
That you may sit on the throne and render judgment.

In the ritual I perform, in the extispicy I perform,
    place the truth!

O Shamash, I hold up to you the plentiful yield of the gods,
    the radiance of the grain-goddess.   (50)
O Shamash, lord of judgment, O Adad, lord of divination,
In the ritual I perform, in the extispicy I perform,
    place the truth!

O Shamash, I have laid out for you the plentiful yield
    of the gods, the radiance of the grain-goddess,
O Shamash, lord of judgment, O Adad,
    lord of prayer and divination,   (55)
In the ritual I perform, in the extispicy I perform,
    place the truth!

Take your seat, O valiant Shamash,
Let there be seated with you the great gods,
Let Anu, father of heaven, Sin, king of the tiara,   (60)
Nergal, lord of weaponry, Ishtar, lady of battle
Be seated with you.
In the ritual I perform, in the extispicy I perform,
    place the truth!

Text: Hussey-van Dijk, YOS 11 22.
Edition: Goetze, JCS 22 (1968), 25–29.
Translation: Seux, *Hymnes*, 467–470; Hecker, TUAT II/5, 719–721.
Notes to Text: (35) George.

(b) THE LAMB

[O Shamash, lo]rd of judgment,
O Adad, lord of extispicy and divination,   (1)
I [hold up] to you a sacred lamb, offspring of a ewe,
a bright-eyed(?), dappled lamb,
A sacred ...-lamb, curly of fleece,
which flopped out from the ewe's breech.*
Its fleece, which no shepherd plucked, neither right nor left,
I will pluck for you;
Its fleece of right and left side [I will set out] for you.   (5)
Invite the great gods with resin,
let cedar and resin invite (all of) you.
In the extispicy I perform, in the ritual I perform,
place the truth!
[In the matter of?] so-and-so, son of so-and-so,
in the lamb I offer, place the truth!
[I cal]l* to you, Shamash, I beseech you to cleanse me!
In the lamb I offer, place the truth!
O Shamash, you opened the bolts of heaven's gates, you
ascended (to this place) a stairway of purest lapis,
Next, you hold a scepter of lapis
at your side for judgment(?).*   (10)
The case of the great gods you judge,
the case of the wild beast you judge,
the case of humankind you judge:
Judge this day the case of so-and-so, son of so-and-so,
on the right of this lamb, on the left of this lamb,
place the truth!
Come in, O Shamash, lord of judgment;
come in, O Adad, lord of prayers and divination;
come in, O Sin, king of the tiara,
Ishtar, lady of divination,
Ishara, who dwells in the inner chamber,
Geshtinanna, recorder of the gods, herald of Anu;*
Nergal, lord of the weapon:
cause to be present the divinity in charge
of the extispicy I perform,

and in the extispicy I perform place the truth! (15)
In the handiwork of the great gods, in the tablet of the gods,
    let the "vesicle" be in place.
Let Nisaba, the scribe, write the case down.
Let the divine shepherd bring forward a sheep to the assembly
    of the great gods, so the ca[se may go we]ll(?).
Let the judges, the great gods, who sit on thrones of gold,
    who dine from trays of lapis, take their seats before you.
Let them judge the case in justice and righteousness.
Judge this day the case of so-and-so, son of so-and-so.
On the right of this lamb, on the left of this lamb,
    place the truth! (20)
I perform this extispicy for the well-being of so-and-so,
    son of so-and-so, for well-being.

Text: A = Hussey-van Dijk, YOS 11 23; B (parallel) = Nougayrol, RA 38 (1941), 87 AO 7032.
Edition: I. Starr, *The Rituals of the Diviner*, BM 12 (1983), 30–31, 37–38, 44–60 (A); 122–123 (B).
Translation: von Soden, SAHG, 275 no. 21 (B only).
Notes to Text: (3) George; cf. Foxvog, *Studies Sjöberg*, 170–171. (9) WGL. (10, 14) George.

(c) WILL UR–UTU BE ALIVE AND WELL?

This prayer, written as a letter (see II.29), is a general oracular inquiry about the well-being of Ur-Utu, a priest or professional man attached to the local temple in a village near Sippar in the Classical period. He was presumably one of the leading citizens of the community. See also II.31.

> O God, my lord Ninsianna, accept this offering, stand by me when this offering is made, place there an oracle of well-being and life for Ur-Utu, your servant! Concerning Ur-Utu, your servant, who is now standing by this offering, from April[1] 20 until April 20 of the coming year, six times sixty days, six times sixty nights, by command of a god, by command of a goddess, by command of a king, by command of a noble, by command of a commoner, by command of fate or regulation, by any command whatsoever, will Ur-Utu be alive and well? From April 20 until April 20, six times sixty days, six times sixty nights, until next year, will Ur-Utu be alive and well? In his household: his wife, his sons, his daughters, his brother, his sister, his near and distant kin, his neighbor, anyone on (his) street who likes him? In the ritual I perform ... Will Ur-Utu be alive and well? Place an oracle of well-being and life for Ur-Utu!

Text: De Meyer, *Studies Kraus*, 272.
Edition: De Meyer, *Studies Kraus*, 274–277.

---

1. Text: Nisan, the first month of the Babylonian year (spring).

H. LETTERS AND LETTER PRAYERS

Letter writing was an esteemed art during the Classical period. Whereas many letters were direct and business-like, and a few deeply personal and emotional, some were carefully composed to show the verbal abilities of their authors. Letters drafted with attention to style and rhetoric show what the correspondent considered to be literary expression and draw on the same figures and subject matter as, for example, prayers and hymns. The examples chosen here include prayers and petitions to gods in letter form. These were presumably left in a sanctuary for the god to peruse. Some of these are straightforward in style (II.31, 32), while others are lengthy and elaborate (II.29).[1]

Scribal petitions in the form of letters (II.34) were particularly calculated to demonstrate the erudition, rhetorical arts, and pressing material need of the petitioners. These mixed flattery and praise with appeal and general statements intended to be read as self-evident.

II.29 KUSSULU TO THE MOON-GOD

This bitter harangue, written on a pierced cylinder, is addressed to Nanna, the moon-god, by a certain Kussulu. He loaned money to a certain Elali without a written document, but was instead content with the debtor's four-fold oath in the precinct of the moon-god's temple at Ur, and, apparently, a symbolic gesture.[2] Perhaps Kussulu had wanted to avoid the costs of a scribe and witnesses. The debtor failed to repay. He married and raised a family, although a consequence of breaking an oath was supposed to be infertility. Kussulu had no recourse save a direct appeal to the gods concerned by the broken oath to exercise their power and thereby prove their greatness.

> (§1) O Nanna, you are king of heaven and earth, I put my trust in you. Elali, son of Girnisa, has wronged me, judge my case!
>
> (§2) Having no money, he approached me. He paid his debts with my money. He married, he had a son and daughter. He did not satisfy me, he did not repay my money in full, by his filchings(?)*, he has

1. See also F. R. Kraus, "Eine neue Probe akkadischer Literatur, Brief eines Bittstellers an eine Gottheit," JAOS 103 (1983), 205–209.

2. Gadd assumes that the oath was the climax of an unsuccessful suit by Kussulu to recover his money from Elali, but there is no mention of a suit at law, nor was there a basis for one, since no loan document had been drawn up.

wronged me. But I put my trust in Nanna!

(§3) In the orchards facing Ekishnugal[1] he swore: "May I be damned if I wrong you!" He swore at the Main Gate, under the weapon that you love, he swore inside the Main Court facing Ekishnugal, facing Ningal of the Egadi, before Ninshubur ... of the Main Court, before Alammush, before Nanna-Vanguard and Nanna-Reinforcement he swore: "May I be damned if I wrong you or your sons!" He said, "These gods be my witness."

(§4) Moreover, in the orchards facing Ekishnugal, before Nanna, before Shamash, he swore this: "May I, Elali, be damned if I wrong Kussulu! May Elali have no heir before Nanna and Shamash (if he wrongs)!"

(§5) (One says): "The false swearer (by) Nanna and Shamash shall be a leper, he shall be destitute and not have a male heir." Elali swore by Nanna and Shamash and has wronged me! May Ninshubur, master of property rights, stand (as witness), may Nanna and Shamash judge my case! Let me see the greatness of Nanna and Shamash!

Text: Gadd, UET 6/2 402.
Edition: Gadd, *Iraq* 25 (1963), 177–181; Charpin, *Clergé*, 326–329.
Translation: Hecker, TUAT II/5, 750–752.
Literature: W. L. Moran, "UET 6, 402: Persuasion in the Plain Style," JANES 22 (1993), 113–120.
Notes to Text: (13) Moran, JANES 22 (1993), 115 note 9 emends *na-aš(-)la-pa-ti-šu* of Gadd's copy to *na-aš ṭup!-pa-ti-šu*, but collation by Geller shows Gadd's copy to be accurate.

---

1   Temple of the moon-god at Ur.

II.30 UR–NANSHE TO NINSIANNA

This prayer, addressed to the goddess Ninsianna in the form of a letter, complains that she has not been looking after her protégé, Ur-Nanshe.

> Say to Ninsianna, thus says Ur-Nanshe: What have I done to you that [ ]? I cannot hold up my head for misery! For ..., I do not have enough food to eat, nor do I have decent clothes for myself, nor can I limber up my bones with oil. Misery has crept into my heart like a weed(?). I really must complain [ ]

(gap and four fragmentary lines)

Text: Thureau-Dangin, TCL 1 9 = Kraus, AbB 5 (1972), 140.
Edition: Kraus, RA 65 (1971), 27–36.

II.31 APIL–ADAD TO "GOD MY FATHER"

In this letter, addressed to his personal god, Apil-Adad complains of being neglected, and asks him to send a letter to Marduk, god of Babylon. A similar letter, written by Ur-Utu (see II.28c), too fragmentary to include here, has been edited by L. De Meyer, "Une Lettre d'Ur-Utu Galamah à une divinité," *Studies Finet*, 41–43.

> Say to god my father, thus says Apil-Adad your servant. Why have you been so neglectful of me? Who would give you one like me? Write to Marduk who loves you, let him release(?) my liability(?).[1]* Let me see your face, let me kiss your feet![2] Consider my family, old and young! For their sakes take pity on me, let your assistance reach me!

Text: Lutz, YOS 2 141 (collated).
Edition: Stol, AbB 9 (1981), 89–90; Sommerfeld, AOAT 213 (1982), 127–128.
Translation: Hecker, TUAT II/5, 752.
Literature: cited by Stol, AbB 9 (1981), 89.
Notes to Text: (11) Previous editors agree on a reading *li-ip-ṭ[ù-ur]*, but collation of the passage by the translator and by R. Marcel Sigrist did not confirm this reading.

1. This may refer to an onus assumed ritually by a cultic professional (Janssen, CRRAI 26 [1989], 77–107).
2. "Let me see your face," that is, "show yourself capable of doing something." "Let me kiss your feet," that is, "do something that I may have cause to be grateful to you."

II.32 NINURTA–QARRAD TO NINMUG

The author of this letter wants the goddess Ninmug to intercede with the god Ishum (see IV.17) on his behalf.

> Say to my lady Ninmug, thus says Ninurta-qarrad, your servant: Ishum will listen to what you say, intercede for me with Ishum for this sin that I have committed. When you have interceded for me, I, radiant with happiness, will bring Ishum an offering, and I will bring you a sheep. When I sing praises before Ishum, I will sing your praises as well.

Text: van Soldt, AbB 13 164.
Edition: van Soldt, AbB 13, 138–139.

II.33 AHUSHUNU TO THE GUARDIAN OF LIFE

This agonized letter makes a concerted effort to be literary in style. The matter at issue, perhaps a family dispute, is referred to only obliquely. The reference to the writer's erstwhile callowness or ignorance may, as Dossin suggested, refer to assistance given by the addressee toward Ahushunu's education, so the grateful pupil, despite what appear to be spelling mistakes, here seeks to demonstrate the fruits of his patron's investment; compare II.34b.

(1) Say to the Guardian of Life,[1] who favored me, thus Ahushunu. May Shamash and Ningalanna (5) keep you alive always for my sake. Apart from you I have no father, brother, king(?),* help, or ally! When I was ignorant (10) you favored me, so I owe you a lifetime's favor in return. When I have been at my last extremity, * you have favored me. So now set me on my way so that, henceforth, your name shall be (15) "Saver-of-Life."

When he heard about the matter, he moved fast. Don't proceed to the matter he will tell you about and do me no wrong! (20) Let them attack(?)* me in person(?), what would you gain? Save my life! I will be your servant. Henceforth may the (25) home fire not go out, lest they speak ill of you. I look to you, for you can favor and save life. He's a robber, so hurry! (30) We are not wanting in brotherhood. As for our cousins, they have made me lose a lot of sleep. They are spying on me at the door night and day. (35) Is there any good purpose [in] their lives? May your ill-wisher come to shame because of me![2]

Text: Dossin, *Akkadica* 6 (1978), plate 1.

Edition: Dossin, *Akkadica* 6 (1978), 2–6.

Notes to Text: (7) Reading *ša!-ar-ra-am*. (12) Reading *qa-ta-ku!-ma*. (20) *i-na eš!-me-tim-ma li-ge!?-ru-nim?*

1. For this as the name of the ark, see p. 254.
2. That is, may any person of ill-will be disappointed at how well the addressee treats his petitioner, because of the credit it will bring him.

II.34 SCRIBAL PETITIONS AND EXERCISES

Graduates of scribal schools felt entitled to comfortable and remunerative positions. In the hope of these, they sometimes drafted elaborate petitions as samples of their abilities, in the two examples translated here seeking to shame prospective patrons into supporting them.

(a) TO ZIMRI-LIM, KING OF MARI

In this lengthy petition to Zimri-Lim, evidently composed on the occasion of the birth of a royal son and heir and thereby hoping to take advantage of the king's happiness, a graduate of a scribal school, whose name is lost in a break in the tablet, tries to demonstrate his eloquence and scholarship by giving a Sumerian and Akkadian version of his appeal for employment. Opening with extravagant flattery, he refers pointedly to the king's discernment and good judgment, then turns to his own miserable lot. Portraying himself as a loyal sufferer (see II.13), he implies that the king owes him support because he remains loyal to his master. He hopes that the high scholarly level of his petition will convince the king that he can act as a capable amanuensis and observes that the land and its citizenry have prospered under Zimri-Lim's rule, except for him (see IV.57). This is an elaborate and carefully thought out piece of work, but has a pedantic creakiness that sets it well below the best prose of the period. To compare with a more elegant Sumerian petition of the same ilk, but addressed to the god of wisdom, see W. W. Hallo, "Individual Prayer in Sumerian: The Continuity of a Tradition," JAOS 88 (1968), 71–89.

> (1) Say to my lord, to the king of truth, beloved of Nunamnir, to the king whom Anu and Enlil steadfastly named for kingship from the holy womb, to whom Ea the king, the lord who ordains destinies, (5) Nudimmud, sublime prince, whose ordained destinies may not be changed, ordained for his destiny one great and favorable, and long life, and made him excel among kings, whom Ninhursag, great mother, mistress of all lands, creator of gods and humankind, made surpassing fair with her holy hands and raised for nobility, whom Dagan, great mountain, father of the great gods, monitor of the Anunna-gods, (10) omnipotent deity, creator of heaven and earth, progenitor of the gods, chose, by revealing his will, from among the populous lands and raised to kingship, into whose hand Shamash, king of heav-

en and earth, lord of Ebabbar, who renders verdicts for all heaven and earth, true god, who word is omnipotent, whose command no god can change, has set scepter and justice and given him the populous lands to rule, (15) to whom valiant Adad, greatest of the gods, first-ranked son of Anu, irrigator of heaven and earth, bestower of life upon all living creatures, has given a mighty mace as his gift and let him have no rival, whose waging of war Ishtar, mistress of heaven and earth, vanguard in battle and strife, who defends holy places, has made the most warlike ever waged and whose weaponry she has made the greatest, to that mighty king who restored this land, (20) to Enlil's warrior, shepherd of proven understanding, to him most suited for kingship, who beams forth with his radiant diadem, to the king perfect in great strength, to Zimri-Lim, valiant protector of his land, to the sublime glory of Mari, who enlarged this land, (25) to the noble and sublime prince who [   ], to the king at whose glance the wicked [tremble], through whose sublime strength enemy treachery [absco]nds, who took foes prisoner with his mighty weapon and [slew his] enemies, (30) to the well-advised, reflective king, [   ] of heart, blessed with good counsel and intelligence, to the sage king whose discourse is perfect (*fragmentary lines, then gap*)

(rev. 2′) Like a [ghost] wandering in the open country, I know no place to lay my head, like a servant without a master, I have no one to look after me. I prowl the streets like a vagabond, woe has hunched me over.[1] (5′) My abode has become an alien house, insults and poor treatment have whittled me down. Someone other than my lord hounds me without reason, so I shiver with cold in an out-of-the-way place. I go my way empty-handed, a scholarly squint has afflicted me. Yet I remain heedful to my lord. I seek no other master, is he not the only one on whom I can rely? (10′) I cannot run away, I am so weak that my legs will not carry me.

Ever since my lord has ascended to the throne of his father's house, which Dagan and Adad upheld, whose kingship and reign Adad and Enlil called forth, ever since that bygone time, my lord's pleasure has excluded me. (15′) A schoolboy from my hometown, of my lord's household, has undercut me. I am a scribal graduate, I stood ready to

---

1. For a general study of this motif, see M. Barré, "'Wandering About' as a Topos of Depression in Ancient Near Eastern Literature and the Bible," JNES 60 (2001), 17–187; for "ghost," compare II.34b.

serve my lord. I can draw up in good form my lord's commands,[1] I can remind my lord of what he has forgotten. My heart is at home in my lord's close, I was born in my lord's household, I was not rostered in from elsewhere.

(20′) My lord restored this land and upheld the scattered peoples, he has allowed homeless citizens to take up land. May my lord investigate my case and restore me as well! O my lord, may your little king-to-be intercede for me, may he rise upon me like the sun!

Text: Guichard, *Florilegium Marianum* 3 (1997), 81–82, with collations, 79–80.
Edition: D. Charpin, "Les malheurs d'un scribe, ou de l'intuilité du sumérien loin de Nippur," CRRAI 35 (1988), 7–27.
Translation: Durand, DEPM I, 103–110.

(b) A GHOST'S ENTREATY

In this letter addressed to Iltani, the queen of a small town in northern Syria during the nineteenth century B.C., a scribe complains that she raised in him false hopes and suggests that his present bad situation is discreditable to her. To achieve his ends, he structured his letter carefully. He opened with a series of metaphors to show his literary skill, then turned to a presumptive attack, depersonalized by making it sound like conventional wisdom, and using simile and parallelism typical of wisdom literature. He concluded with the language of prayer and petition. The tone and content of this piece may be compared to the indignant letters addressed to gods (II.30–31) and to the poems that complain of undeserved or uncomprehended suffering (II.13).

(1) Say to my lady, thus Yastina-abum your servant. May Shamash and Marduk let my lady (5) live forever for the sake of a ghostling, myself. I am well. No greeting from my lady ever reached me, so my heart has not quickened to life. You made me put my trust in a wild goose chase[2] in Andarig, saying, "Learn to be (10) a scribe and I'll make you of a gentleman's estate," that's what you gave me to rely

---

1. This means he can frame them properly in written form; the same verb is used by the author of Erra and Ishum (IV.17, Tablet V line 42) to refer to his role in composing the poem.
2. Literally: "in birds not caught."

on. You made me forego both fish and fowl,[1] you doomed me, the ghostling, to wander back and forth (15) among my relatives. You took no thought of that one time you let me rely on you and then tried to do something for me, (20) you felt nothing of a woman's pity. As for you, don't you know that a ghostling deserves more pity than a corpse? So now, do a good deed for a ghostling. Since I have nothing, I cannot serve in the palace. But what more should I write you? I, do I know more about these matters than you do? Don't you know that (30) a man who cannot be relied upon in his own household is of no importance in his palace,* and that he himself is contemptible, don't you know that? I write to you often enough. Just as no father gives his own son (35) the evil eye, so may my lady uphold me, the ghostling. Just as gentlemen rely on their fathers and brothers, I trust in my lady. (40) May my lady not neglect me!

Text: S. Dalley, *The Old Babylonian Tablets from Tell al Rimah* (London, 1976), 150.
Edition: S. Dalley, *The Old Babylonian Tablets from Tell al Rimah* (London, 1976), 122–123.
Literature: B. R. Foster, "Letters and Literature: A Ghost's Entreaty," *Studies Hallo*, 98–102.
Notes to Text: (31–32) Durand, in E. Lévy, ed., *Le système palatial en orient, en Grèce et à Rome, Actes du Colloque de Strasbourg 19–22 juin 1985* (Leiden, 1987), 45 note 2.

1. Literally: "water and broth."

(c) A LETTER WRITING EXERCISE

Scribes of the Classical period studied and wrote model and imaginary letters in school to prepare for composition of real letters.[1] Some of these, such as the example chosen here, have whimsical touches, in this case deliberate insults to the addressee, unexpected in a request for a favor. These perhaps brought a note of amusement to the labors of an apprentice scribe. This letter contains an unusual density of less common grammatical phenomena: unreal and real conditions, a cognate construction, independent personal pronouns. Perhaps the exercise consisted of drafting a letter with a certain number of such features present.

> (1) Say to Nabium-malik, that man of good status, whose stylus Marduk and Nabu guide aright,[2] (5) thus says Awil-Ninsianna, may Shamash and Marduk keep you well for my sake. If I had nothing I wished for, (10) I would never write to you. You were always very prodigal, but for me you had no concern, so you did not send me the five apple trees*. When did you ever send me anything (15) you promised me? I knew in my heart that to you I was not so good as one or another person to whom you gave something. You said (20) to yourself, "How will you[3] return my favor? I am the son of a gentleman, he the son of a commoner, how will he return my favor?" Any man alive returns a favor to someone who has given him one. (25) If I'm alive, I will return your favor. So get on with it! Choose and cut good hardwood trees. Send (them) to (30) Father, at our house,[4] send one to me here.

Text: Frankena, TLB 4 33.
Edition: Frankena, AbB 3 (1968), 24–25.
Notes to Text: (13) Reading ḫašḫur! (Frankena: BARAG).

1. F. R. Kraus, "Briefschreibübungen in altbabylonischen Schulunterricht," JEOL 16 (1959), 16–29. Note that in most instances, including this one, the decision as to whether or not a letter is a school exercise is intuitive.
2. A whimsical salutation for a scribe.
3. The writer of the letter is meant.
4. This may refer to the school master and "our house" the school; the hardwood may be meant for a scribe's stylus.

II.35 A DECLARATION OF WAR

Variously interpreted as a genuine or fictitious letter from a king of Aleppo of the eighteenth century B.C., this document indicts a king of Der, a city in Babylonia, for duplicity and ingratitude (compare III.1).[1] For the motif of god and king marching together to battle, compare II.11.

(1) Say to Yashub-Yahad, thus says Yarim-Lim your brother. Let Shamash investigate and make an example of you and me. I have been like a father and brother to you, (5) you have been villain and foe to me. What was the good of my rescuing the city Babylon with the weapon of Adad and Yarim-Lim and giving life to your land and to you? Were it not for Adad and Yarim-Lim, the city Der would have been winnowed away* fifteen years ago like chaff, no one could ever have found it. Would you then have been able to treat me like this? (10) Indeed, Sin-gamil, king of Diniktum,[2] repaid me time and again with hateful and perverse words. I docked 500 boats at the wharf of Diniktum and dunked[3] him and his land for a dozen years. Now you, like him, repay me time and again with hateful and perverse words. I swear to you by Adad, god of my city, and by Sin, my own god, I shall not desist until I have destroyed you and your land. (15) Now then, I shall come there in the spring and I shall install myself at your city gate. I shall show you the brutal* weapons of Adad and Yarim-Lim.

Text: Dossin, *Syria* 33 (1956), 65.
Edition: J. Sasson, "Yarim-Lim's War Declaration," *Studies Birot*, 237–253 (suggests may be literary).
Translation: Durand, DEPM 1, 394–396.
Literature: Charpin, Durand, MARI 4 (1985), 310 notes 78, 79 (believe is historical).
Notes to Text: (8) Durand, MARI 5 (1987), 667. (17) Durand, MARI 7 (1993), 53–54: "bitter."

1. Specific historical background for this letter has been argued by Charpin and Durand, MARI 4 (1985), 308–310, 319; Durand, MARI 6 (1987), 71; Villard, *Amurru* 2 (2001), 123.
2. A city near the confluence of the Diyala and Tigris rivers; for a king of Aleppo to bring an armada to such a place was no mean feat.
3. Or, "flooded," or "capsized"; Durand and others prefer "did good."

I. Mythology

Mesopotamian mythology of the Classical period is known from Sumerian and Akkadian poetic narratives in which deities play leading roles; from hymns and prayers, from allusions in incantations to divine actions, from personal names that refer to deities, and from passages in other writings, such as commemorative inscriptions.[1] Two important mythological narratives known from the Classical period, Etana (III.22) and Anzu (III.23), have been placed with the longer versions known from the Mature and Late periods.

II.36 ATRAHASIS

Atrahasis is the largest surviving Classical-period mythological narrative poem. It sets forth an interpretation of the creation of humanity, the flood, and the origins of human birth, marriage, procreation, and death, all these themes brilliantly worked out in a cohesive plot. When the story opens, Anu, Enlil, and Enki have divided the universe: Anu has taken the heavens, Enlil the earth, Enki the watery depths. Enlil imposes forced labor on a large group of the gods, who proceed to dig the courses for the Tigris and Euphrates rivers. The gods rebel against their harsh servitude, laying siege to Enlil's house. The ruling gods meet and send a representative to the rebels, ostensibly to find out why they are rebelling, but, in fact, demanding that they identify their leader. The rebels stick together, so Enlil, distressed, suggests that Anu authorize a new world order. Anu, therefore, directs that the human race be created to assume the work of the gods. Enki and the mother-goddess, variously called Nintu, Belet-ili, Mama, or Mami, accomplish this task by mixing blood of a slain ringleader of the rebels with clay. An (immortal) spirit or ghost, represented by the throb of the human pulse, will be a memorial to the slain god. Human marriage and procreation are instituted and the gods are henceforth free from labor.

The human race multiplies to the extent that Enlil is disturbed by its noise. First, he sends a plague to diminish humanity, but this fails to do so because Enki tells his favorite human being, Atrahasis, how to circumvent the plague. Next, he causes a drought, but this too fails for the same reason. Third, he causes a famine, which is evidently circumvented by Enki through the release of large

---

1. The most comprehensive presentation of Mesopotamian mythology is Bottéro, Kramer, *Mythologie.*

numbers of fish. Finally, Enlil convenes the gods and imposes an oath on them
not to reveal his next measure, a flood. Enki warns Atrahasis indirectly by talking to the wall of a reed enclosure where Atrahasis sleeps to receive divine
communication. Atrahasis builds an ark, fills it with belongings, artisans, and
animals, and survives the flood. In the aftermath of the flood, the gods discover
their dependency on the human race and so devise better ways to control the
population, including taboos on marriage and childbirth and death for all
human beings at different times and in different ways.

The story is presented here in four versions. The Old Babylonian, or Classical
version (II.36a), is based principally on an Old Babylonian manuscript of the
seventeenth century B.C. Various other Old Babylonian manuscripts have been
incorporated into the translation of this version where possible, plus some later
fragments. The original consisted of three tablets containing 1245 lines of
poetry, of which about 60 percent are preserved in whole or in part.

The Middle Babylonian version (II.36b), dating to the Mature period, is
known in two recensions, a fragmentary manuscript from Nippur (II.36b.1)
and a short Atrahasis story from Syria (II.36b.2). The Late Babylonian version
(II.36c), dating to the Late period, is often close to the Old Babylonian, but has
some significant differences, many of which appear to be misunderstandings of
an earlier text or editorial alterations. In only a few instances does the Late
Babylonian version seem poetically or linguistically superior to the Old Babylonian one. The Late Assyrian version (II.36d) was perhaps derived from a
Middle Assyrian reworking of the text, and diverges widely from the Old Babylonian. The Assyrian version, in particular, expanded some episodes, rewrote
others, and, in general, levelled out the originality of the older text into a flat,
standardized idiom full of repetition. Another version of this story is found in
Tablet XI of the Gilgamesh epic.[1] In the translations of the later versions, cross-
references are given to the Old Babylonian to assist the reader who wishes to
compare them.

For the further convenience of the reader who wishes to see the story as a
whole, key segments, as preserved in different versions, are tabulated below,
where OB means the Old Babylonian version (II.36a); MB the Middle Babylonian versions (II.36b), LB the Late Babylonian version (II.36c), and LAssyr
the Late Assyrian version (II.36d).

Prehistory and rebellion of gods	OB I, 1–180; LB I, II, 1–80; LAssyr I i
Creation of humanity	OB I, 181–247; LB II, 81–116

---

1. Foster, *Gilgamesh*, 84–91.

Institution of birth, marriage, procreation	OB I, 273–305; LAssyr I iii
Humans go to work	OB I, 328–339
Plague and rescue	OB I, 352–412; LB IV; LAssyr I iv, 1–36
Drought and rescue	OB II i, ii; LB V; LAssyr I iv, 37–62
Famine and rescue	OB II, iii, iv, v; LAssyr I v, vi
Oath and preparation for flood	OB II, vi, vii, viii
Atrahasis is warned, builds ark	OB III i, ii; MB b.1, b.2; LAssyr II iii
Flood	OB III ii, iii; LAssyr II, continuation
Aftermath	OB III iii, iv, v, vi

(a) OLD BABYLONIAN VERSION

Tablet I

(Before humankind existed, the great gods imposed forced labor on the lesser gods.)

When gods were man,[1]	(1)
They did forced labor, they bore drudgery.	
Great indeed was the drudgery of the gods,	
The forced labor was heavy, the misery too much:	
The great Anunna-gods, the seven,* were burdening	(5)
The Igigi-gods with forced labor.	
Anu their father was king,	
Their counsellor was the warrior Enlil,	
Their prefect was Ninurta,	
[And] their bailiff(?) [En]nugi.	(10)
They had taken the [ ] ... by its sides,*	
They cast lots, the gods took their shares:	
Anu went up to heaven,	
[Enlil too]k the earth for his subjects,*	

1. The line is a metaphor (Groneberg, AfO 26 [1978/9], 20), meaning "when gods were (like) men" (in that they had to work). This meaning was already argued, for different reasons, by Lambert, and borne out by a later quotation of this line in a seventh-century B.C. manuscript explicitly as "When the gods like men," (Lambert, OrNS 38 [1969], 533). This does not mean that the gods were actually human beings; rather, they had to work as humans do. A different interpretation, whereby "man" meant "boss" and "gods" was taken to be a divine name "Ilu," has been argued by Jacobsen (*Studies Finkelstein*, 117).

[The bolt], the trap[1] of the sea,   (15)
[They had gi]ven to Enki the leader.
[Those of Anu] had gone up to heaven,
[Those of Enki(?)] had descended to the depths,
[Those ...] of heaven [had nothing to do],
[They burdened] the Igigi-gods [with forced labor].   (20)
[The gods] were digging watercourses,*
[The waterways of the gods], the life of the land,
[The Igigi-gods] were digging watercourses,
[The waterways of the gods, the] life of the land.
[The Igigi-gods dug the Ti]gris river,   (25)
[And the Euphrates there]after.
[Springs they opened up from] the depths,
[Wells ...] they established.
[   ] the depth
[   ] of the land   (30)
[   ] within it
[   ] they lifted up,
[They heaped up] all the mountains.
[years] of drudgery,
[   ] the vast marsh.   (35)
They [cou]nted years of drudgery,
[and] forty years,* too much!
[   ] forced labor they bore night and day.
[They were com]plaining, denouncing,
[Mut]tering down in the ditch,   (40)
"Let us face up to our [foreman]* the prefect,
"He must take off (this) our [he]avy burden upon us!
"[The god], counsellor of the gods, the warrior,
"Come, let us remove (him) from his dwelling,
"Enlil, counsellor of the gods, the warrior,   (45)
"Come, let us remove (him) from his dwelling!"

---

1. Precise sense not clear (Falkenstein *apud* Wilcke, ZA 67 [1967], 160; Lambert's *ittadnu* is now confirmed by a later manuscript). The sea may be portrayed as a gigantic trap, holding all its fish within. In the Late Babylonian version (II.36c), the fish break out of the "trap" of the sea, according to Ea, and thus humankind is "accidentally" saved from starvation; George and Al-Rawi (*Iraq* 58 [1996], 153) suggest that the bolt "keeps the sea in check."

[Awila]¹* made ready to speak,
[And said to the] gods his brethren,
"[Let us not(?) smite]² the prefect of olden days

    (gap, the following from a later Assyrian fragment [CT 46 7])

    "[   ] let us kill [him]!   (a)
    "[   ] let us break the yoke!"
    [   ] made ready to speak,
    [And said] to the gods his brethren,
    "[Let us smite] the prefect of olden days ..."   (e)
    "The counsellor of the go[ds], the warrior,

"[The god, counsellor of the gods, the warrior],
"Come, let us remove (him) from his dwelling,
"Enlil, counsellor of the gods, the warrior,
"Come, let us remove (him) from his dwelling!   (60)
"Now then, call for battle!
"Battle let us stir up, warfare!"
The gods heard his words,
They set fire to their tools,
They put fire to their spades,   (65)
And flame to their workbaskets.
Off they went, one and all,
To the gate of the warrior Enlil's abode.
It was night, half-way through the watch,   (70)
The house was surrounded, but the god did not know.

1. One late manuscript has Alla here (see II.36c Tablet I, 42). This cannot easily be reconciled with the Old Babylonian version (see line 224). Alla was known in other Mesopotamian tradition as a "dead god," so he might have been substituted there for the original name of the rebel leader (for discussion, see M. Krebernik, "Geschlachtete Gottheiten und ihre Namen," AOAT 281 [2002], 289–298). The name Alla may, alternatively, have been etymologized by the poet as deriving from Aw-ila, which, in its turn, may have been a wordplay on the Akkadian word for "man" (*awīlu*), as pointed out by various scholars (see George and Al-Rawi, *Iraq* 58 [1996], 150; Alster, *Studies Jacobsen*, 35–40).

2. This episode seems to have undergone change across different versions, becoming increasingly violent (see II.36c, Tablet I, 43–44). An inferior late manuscript allows the reading "Let us [not] strike" (Böck and Rowe, *Aula Orientalis* 17–18 [1999–2000], 170), but a better one reads "we will smite" (or the like) (George and Al-Rawi, *Iraq* 58 [1996], 158 line 44, clear, as read, on photo). Perhaps the original logic of this episode was that the rebels wanted to "confront" (later "smite," "kill") the prefect and remove Enlil from his dwelling, but the ringleader diverted attention from the prefect, saying that Enlil could always appoint another (II.36c, 170); this interpretation is not supported by textual evidence.

It was night, half-way through the watch,
Ekur was surrounded, but Enlil did not know!
Kalkal[1] noticed it and [looked out],
He touched the bolt and looked out [   ].   (75)
Kalkal woke [Nusku],
And they listened to the clamor of [the Igigi-gods].*
Nusku woke [his] lord,
He got [him] out of bed,
"My lord, [your] house is surrounded,   (80)
"Battle has run right up [to your gate].
"Enlil, your house is surrounded,
"Battle has [ru]n right up to your gate!"[2]
Enlil had provided(?) weapons(?) for his dwelling.
Enlil made ready to speak,   (85)
And said to the courier Nusku,
"Nusku, bar your gate,
"Get your weapons and stand before me."
Nusku barred his gate,
Got his weapons and stood before Enlil.   (90)
Nusku made ready to speak,
And said to the warrior Enlil,
"My lord, your face is (gone pale as) tamarisk,[3]
"Your own offspring! Why did you fear?
"My lord, your face is (gone pale as) tamarisk,   (95)
"Your own offspring! Why did you fear?
"Send that they bring Anu down [here],
"And that they bring Enki be[fore yo]u."
He sent and they brought Anu down to him,
They brought Enki before him.   (100)
Anu, king of [hea]ven, was present,
The king of the depths, Enki, was [   ].*
With the great Anunna-gods present,
Enlil arose, the debate [was underway].
Enlil made ready to speak,   (105)

---

1. A doorkeeper god (W. G. Lambert, RLA 5, 323).
2. Note the omission of a verb of speaking, indicating excitement and abruptness.
3. Literally, "your features are tamarisk" (Borger, HKL 2, 158). For the tamarisk as symbolic of pallor born of fear, see III.19 line 29.

And said to the great [gods],
"Against me would they be [trying this]?⋆
"Shall I make battle [against my own offspring]?
"What did I see with my very own eyes?⋆
"Battle ran right up to my gate!"   (110)
Anu made ready to speak,
And said to the warrior Enlil,
"The reason why the Igigi-gods
"Surrounded(?) your gate,⋆
"Let Nusku go out, [let him learn their cause],   (115)
"[Let him take] to [your] so[ns]
"[Your great] command."
Enlil made ready to speak,
And said to the [courier Nusku],
"Nusku, open [your gate],   (120)
"Take your weapons, [go out to the group].
"In the group of [all the gods]
"Bow down, stand up, [and repeat to them] our [command]:⋆

    'Anu, [your father],
    'Your counsellor, [the warrior] Enlil,   (125)
    'Your prefect, Ninurta,
    'And your bailiff Ennugi have sent me (to say),

        "Who [is the god who was instigator of] battle?⋆
        "Who [is the god who was instigator of] hostilities?
        "Who [is it that stirred up] war,   (130)
        "[(That) battle has run up to the gate of Enlil]?"'"⋆

[Nusku took the command(?) opened] his gate,
[Took his weapons] and w[ent with the command of(?)] Enlil.
[In the group of a]ll the gods,
[He bowed down, s]tood up, set forth the c[omm]and,⋆   (135)
"Anu, your father,
"[Your counsellor, the] warrior Enlil,
"[Your prefect], Ninurta,
"And [your bailiff] Ennugi [have sent me (to say)]:

    'Who is [the god who was instigator of] battle?   (140)
    'Who is [the god who was instigator of] hostilities?
    'Who [is it that stirred up] war,

'[(That) battle has run up to the gate of Enlil]?'"

[The Igigi] answered him in [the group],
[They were defiant, the labor gang   ]*   (145)
"Every [one of us gods has declared] war,
"We formed [our group] in the [ditch].
"[Excessive] drudgery [has killed us],
"[Our] forced labor was heavy, [our misery too much]!   (150)
"And so every [one of us gods]
"Has resolved on [a battle] with Enlil."*
Nusku took [the command],
He went, he [brought back ...].
"My lord, [you sent] me to the [group of the gods],   (155)
"I went, [I bowed down, I stood up],
"I set forth [you]r great [command],
"Al[l the Igigi-gods(?), the labor gangs,
        were defiant against it(?)],*

'[Every one of us] gods has declared war,   (160)
'We [have formed our group] in the ditch.
'Excessive [drudgery] has killed us,
'Our forced labor [was heavy], the misery too much!
'[Now, every] one of us gods
'Has resolved [on a battle] with Enlil.'"   (165)

When he heard that speech,
Enlil's tears flowed down,
Enlil [became distu]rbed at what he said.
He said to the warrior Anu,
"Noble one, you should take authority off
        with you to heaven.   (170)
"Take the power you still have(?).
"With the great gods in session before you,
"Summon one god, let them make a new authority."

(for what follows, see II.36c)

(The gap in the main edition is next partly filled by an Old Babylonian fragment [CT 44
20], collations Atrahasis, pl. 11; plus the Late Babylonian version [II.36c]. In the Old
Babylonian version, Ea, rather than Anu, as in the Late Babylonian version, remonstrates,
then goes on to propose creation of human beings to do the work of the laboring gods.)

Ea made ready to speak,
And said to the gods [his brethren], (175)
"What do we denounce them for?
"Their forced labor was heavy, [their misery too much].
"Every day the earth was ...
"The outcry [was loud, we could hear their clamor].
"There is [a task to be done], (180)

(As another Old Babylonian manuscript resumes, Enki is speaking.)

"[Mami, the birth-goddess],[1] is present,
"Let the mother-goddess create a human being,* (190)[2]
"Let man assume the drudgery of god."
They summoned and asked the birth-goddess,
The midwife of the gods, wise Mami,
"Will you be the birth-goddess, creatress of humankind?
"Create a human being, let him bear the yoke, (195)
"The yoke let him bear, the task of Enlil,
"Let man assume the drudgery of god."
Nintu[3] made ready to speak,
And said to the great gods,[4]*
"It is not for me to do it, (200)
"Th(is) task is Enki's.
"He is the one who purifies everything,
"Let him give me the clay so I can do the making."
Enki made ready to speak,
And said to the great gods, (205)
"On the first, seventh, and fifteenth days of the month,*
"I will establish a purification, a bath.
"Let one god be slaughtered,
"Then let the gods be purified in it.
"Let Nintu mix clay with his flesh and blood, (210)
"Let that same god and man be thoroughly mixed
        in the clay.
"Let us hear the drumbeat for the rest of time,

1. Later versions give her already the name Belet-ili; see, however, below, line 247.
2. The standard line numbering of the Lambert-Millard edition is here to high ("190" should be about 182), but is maintained for ease of reference.
3. Nintu, Mami, Mama, and Belet-ili are all names for the birth- or mother-goddess.
4. Variant omits lines 200–205, thus making Nintu's (or Mami's) speech begin in 206.

"From the flesh of the god let a spirit remain,*   (215)
"Let it make the living know its sign,
"Lest he be forgotten, let the spirit remain."[1]
The great Anunna-gods, who administer destinies,
Answered "Yes!" in the assembly.   (220)
On the first, seventh, and fifteenth days of the month,
He established a purification, a bath.
They slaughtered Aw-ila,[2] who had the inspiration,
    in their assembly.
Nintu mixed the clay with his flesh and blood.   (225)
<That same god and man were thoroughly
    mixed in the clay.>
For the rest [of time they would hear the drumbeat],[3]
From the flesh of the god a spi[rit remained].
It would make the living know its sign,
Lest he be forgotten, [the] spirit remained.   (230)
After she had mixed that clay,*
He summoned the Anunna, the great gods.
The Igigi, the great gods, spat upon the clay.
Mami made ready to speak,   (235)
And said to the great gods,
"You ordered me the task and I have completed (it)!
"You have slaughtered the god, along with his inspiration.
"I have done away with your heavy forced labor,   (240)
"I have imposed your drudgery on man.
"You have bestowed(?) clamor upon humankind.[4]

---

1. I interpret this speech as follows: "Kill the one god (Awila) who had the "inspiration" (ṭēmu) for the rebellion, purify the executioners, but let a "spirit" (eṭemmu) remain from the slain god, this to be part of new-created man (awīlu). The pulsation of this spirit will be a perpetual reminder of the dead god." Other translations of this passage differ; for further discussion, see T. Abusch, "Ghost and God: Some Observations on a Babylonian Understanding of Human Nature," in A. I. Baumgarten, et al., ed., *Self, Soul and Body in Religious Experience, Studies in the History of Religion* 78 (Leiden, 1998), 363–383.

2. See p. 231 note 1 and III.18e line 25. Note that a later version adds "Alla, an Enlil of former time(?), they slew" (II.36c, line 104).

3. Or heartbeat. For discussion of this passage, see Kilmer, OrNS 41 (1972), 162–166.

4. That is (Pettinato, OrNS 39 [1968], 187 and 189; von Soden, OrNS 38 [1969], 425, AHw, 1128a, and ZA 68 [1978], 67), the only present given to humankind is something to complain of (rigmu). Ironically, rigmu "clamor" will be the cause for the gods' sending the flood. On the other hand, Stol suggests that rigmu means here the call to corvée work (*Birth in Babylonia*, 113 note 21).

"I have released the yoke, I have [made] restoration."[1]
They heard this speech of hers,
They ran, restored, and kissed her feet, (saying),   (245)
"Formerly [we used to call] you 'Mami',
"Now let your n[am]e be 'Mistress-of-All-the Gods'
        (Belet-kala-ili)."

(Breaks off; for the missing section, which describes the production of seven male and seven female foetuses, see Assyrian version, col. iii, 15'–37' [p. 270]. The first man and woman mature; she gives birth.)

[And the young girl ...] her breasts,[2]
[...] a beard
[... on] the cheek of the young man.
[In the garde]ns(?) and street*   (275)
Wife and husband will choose each other.*
The birth-goddesses were assembled,
And Nintu [sat rec]koning the months.
[At the] destined [time(?)], they summoned the tenth month.
The tenth month[3] arrived;   (280)
She ..., opened the womb(?).
Her face beaming and joyful,
With covered head,
She performed the midwifery.   (285)
She girded (the mother's) middle
As she pronounced a blessing.
She drew (a circle?) with meal and placed the brick,[4]
"I am the one who created, my hands have made it!

1. Freed from service, that is, returned matters to their original state before the great gods had imposed labor on the lesser gods (Charpin, AfO 34 [1987], 37–38).
2. The first pair of human beings has grown from babyhood (somewhere after line 38' of the Late Assyrian version) to adolescence (Tablet I lines 271ff.) and has matured enough to reproduce (Tablet I line 276). In 277ff. the first mother-to-be is about to give birth.
3. The Babylonians reckoned by lunar months, so pregnancy would be longer reckoned by lunar months than if reckoned by solar months.
4. The text implies that placing of a brick in the room where a woman was about to give birth was to be a common practice. For further discussion, see A. Kilmer, "The Brick of Birth," JNES 46 (1987), 211–213; Stol, *Birth in Babylonia*, 118–122.

"Let the midwife rejoice in the sacrosanct woman's house.[1]   (290)
"Where the pregnant woman gives birth,
"And the mother of the baby is separated(?),[2]*
"Let the brick be in place for nine days,
"Let Nintu, the birth-goddess,[3] be honored.   (295)
"Always call Mami their [mistres]s,
"[Always pra]ise the birth-goddess, praise Kesh.[4]*
"In [   ], when the bed is laid,
"Let wife and her husband choose each other,*   (300)
"At the time for being man and wife,
"They should heed Ishtar in the [marriage] chamber.
"For nine days let there be rejoicing,
"Let them [cal]l Ishtar Ishara.[5]
"[   ] at the destined time   (305)

(gap)

(Humankind, now reproducing, is put to work to feed the gods.)

A man [   ]
"Cleanse the dwelling(?) [   ]"
The son to [his] father [   ]   (330)
... [   ]
They sat and [   ]
He it was who was carrying [   ]
He saw and [   ]
Enlil [   ]   (335)
They took up ... [   ]*

---

1. Moran (*Biblica* 52 [1971], 58–59 with note 3) suggests that this refers to a woman who has just given birth, and so could not have intercourse for a taboo period, so line 300 would refer to the resumption of intercourse after delivery. But "sacrosanct woman" normally referred to some sort of priestess, so it is possible that certain sacrosanct women ran lying-in facilities and the birth took place there (Stol, *Birth in Babylonia*, 116).

2. The obscure verb used here may refer to separation of the child from the mother by cutting the umbilical cord or to isolating mother and child from the rest of the household (for the latter proposal, see Stol, *Birth in Babylonia*, 117, where this passage is discussed).

3. Variant: Belet-ili.

4. Sanctuary of the birth-goddess; see p. 93 note 1.

5. Lines 301ff. may refer to consummation of marriage (differently Bottéro, "Supersage") as predicted in line 276. Ishara was another name for Ishtar; see W. G. Lambert, "Išhara," RLA 5, 176–177. The nine days may refer to a wedding ceremony and attendant festivities or to a honeymoon period.

They made n[e]w hoes and shovels,*
They built the big canal banks.
For food for the peoples, for the sustenance of [the gods]

(large gap)

(Humankind reproduces continuously. Enlil is annoyed by their clamor
and sends a plague to diminish it.)

[Twel]ve hundred years [had not gone by],
[The land had grown numerous], the peoples had increased,
The [land] was bellowing [like a bull].
The god was disturbed with [their uproar],   (355)
[Enlil heard] their clamor.
[He said to] the great gods,
"The clamor of humankind [has become burdensome to me],
"I am losing sleep [to their uproar].
"[   ] let there be ague..."   (360)

(three lines lost)

(Enki advises Atrahasis how to save humanity from the plague.)

But he, [Atrahasis], his god was Enki,
[He was exceedingly wise].   (365)
He would speak [with his god],
And his god [would speak] with him!
Atrahasis [made] ready to speak,
And said to [his] lord,
"How long [   ]*   (370)
"Will they impose the disease on us [forever]?"
Enki made ready to speak,
And said to his servant,
"Summon(?) the elders*
"At the usual time in your house.[1]   (375)
"[Command]:

    'Let heralds proclaim,
    'Let them raise a loud clamor in the land:*

      "Do not reverence your (own) gods,

---

1. These lines are obscure, so the translation is hypothetical.

"Do not pray to your (own) goddesses,
"Seek the door of Namtar,[1]   (380)
"Bring a baked (loaf) before it.'"

"May the flour offering please him,
"May he be shamed by the gift and withdraw his hand."*
Atrahasis received the command,   (385)
And assembled the elders to his gate.[2]
Atrahasis made ready to speak,
And said to the elders,
"Elders ...
"[   ] ...   (390)
"[Command:]

   'Let heralds proclaim,
   'Let them raise a loud [clamor] in the land:

      "[Do not reverence] your (own) gods,
      "[Do not] pray to your (own) [goddesses],
      "[Seek] the door of [Namtar],   (395)
      "[Bring a baked (loaf) before it.'"

"May the flour offering please him,
"May he be shamed by the gift and withdraw his hand."
The elders heeded [his] words,   (400)
They built a temple for Namtar in the city.
They commanded and the [heralds] proclaimed,
They raised a loud clamor [in the land].
They did [not] reverence their (own) gods,   (405)
They did [not] pray to [their (own) goddesses],
They sought [the door] of Namtar,
They [brought] a baked (loaf) before [it].
The flour offering pleased him,
[He was shamed] by the gift and withdrew his hand.   (410)
[The ague] left them,
They resumed [their clamor?],

(two lines fragmentary)

---

1. God of plague.
2. There seems to be no way to correlate this line with the instructions in Tablet I line 375.

Tablet II

i

(Enlil sends a drought.)

Twelve hundred years had not gone by, (1)
The land had grown numerous, the peoples had increased,
The land was bellowing like a bull.
The god became disturbed by their uproar,
Enlil heard their clamor. (5)
He said to the great gods,
"The clamor of humankind has become burdensome to me,
"I am losing sleep to their uproar.
"Cut off provisions for the peoples,
"Let plant life be too scanty [fo]r their hunger. (10)
"Let Adad withdraw his rain,
"Below, let the flood not come up from the depths.⋆
"Let the wind come to parch the ground, (15)
"Let the clouds billow but discharge not a drop.
"Let the field reduce its yields,
"Let the grain-goddess close her bosom.
"Let there be no rejoicing for them, (20)
"Let [...] be gloomy,
"Let there not [   ]..."

(gap)

ii⋆

(Enki advises Atrahasis how to save humanity from the drought.)

[Enki made ready to speak],[1]
[Saying to his servant],
"[Summon(?) the elders]
"[At the usual time in your house]. (5)
"[Command:

    'Let heralds proclaim],

---

1. From the Late Babylonian version, Tablet V (see II.36c), adapted according to lines 372–375 above.

'[Let them raise a loud] cl[amor] in the land:

> "Do not reverence your (own) gods,
> "Do not pray to your (own) [goddesses],   (10)
> "Seek [the door of] Adad
> "Bring a baked (loaf) [before it].'"

"[May the flour offering] please him,
"May he be shamed [by the] gift and withdraw his hand.   (15)
"May he rain down mist in the morning,
"May he stealthily rain down dew in the night,
"That the fields just as stealthily bear ninefold."*
They built a temple for Adad in the city.   (20)
They commanded and the heralds proclaimed,
They raised a loud clamor in the land.
They did not reverence their (own) gods,
They did [not] pray to their (own) goddesses,
They [sought] the door [of Adad],   (25)
[They brought] a baked (loaf) before it.
The flour offering pleased him,
He was shamed by the gift and withdrew his hand.
He rained down mist in the morning,   (30)
And stealthily rained down dew in the night,
[The fields just as] stealthily bore ninefold.
[Their handsome features returned],
[Their former clamor resumed].[1]   (35)

(gap)

iii*

(For a fuller version of what follows, see II.36c [pp. 263–265])

(Enlil sends a famine. Atrahasis wants to communicate with Enki, but apparently knows that the god is now under oath not to speak directly with him. He sleeps by the water for an indirect communication in dreams.)

[   ] ...   (1)
[   ] of his god.
[Out] of the city he set his foot,

---

1. From the Late Babylonian version, Tablet V (see II.36c).

Every day he would weep,
Bringing dream offerings in the morning.   (5)
"My god [would speak to] me, but he is under oath,
"He will [inform] (me) in dreams.
"Enki [would speak to] me, but he is under oath,
"He will [inform] (me) in dreams."   (10)
[com]mand of his god,
[   ] seated, he wept.
He cast [the dream offering into the water],
He would sit [facing the river], weeping constantly.
W[hen the waterway] was silent,   (15)
He made libation at night,
Sleep would come double fast.[1]
He said to the [waterway] of the river,
"May the waterway take [this, may the river] bear it away,   (20)
"May my gift be set before [Enki], my [lord].
"May [Enki] see [it and think of me],
"May he [   ],
"This night [may I have a dream]."
After he had sent the message by the waterway,   (25)
He sat down [to weep] facing the river,
From the bank [   ]
To the depths [his present] went down.
Enki heard [his clamor],
He [summoned] his hairy hero-men[2] [and said],   (30)
"The man who [   ],
"Let this same one [   ],
"Go, [take him my(?)] command,
"Ask him, [tell me the news of his land]."

(gap, missing passages in II.36c, p. 264)

1. Obscure and doubtful.
2. Akkadian *laḫmu*, a kind of hairy, human-shaped creature here associated with Enki; see
Wiggermann, JEOL 27 (1981/2), 90–105 (this passage referred to on p. 96); Heimpel, AOAT 253
(1998), 129–155.

iv*

Above [   ]   (1)
The flood did not [rise] from the depths.
The womb of earth did not bear,
Plant life did not come forth.   (5)
People were not seen about,
The black fields whitened,
The broad plain was filled up with salts.
The first year they ate old grain,
The second year they exhausted their stores.   (10)
When the third year came,
Their features were [gray]* from hunger,
Their faces were crusted, like crusted malt,
Life was ebbing, little by little.*
Tall people shriveled in body,   (15)
They walked hunched in the street.
Broad-shouldered people turned slender,
Their long stance grew short.
Messengers took the command,
They went before the sea,   (20)
They stood and told him,
[Their] orders to Enki the leader

(fragmentary lines, gap)

v

(gap)

(Humanity has been saved from famine, apparently by a flood of fish.)

He[1] was filled with anger [at Enki],
"[All we] great Anunna-gods
"Resolved together [on a rule].   (15)
"Anu and Adad watched over [the upper regions],
"I watched over the lower earth.
"Where Enki went,
"He released the yoke, he made restoration.[2]

1. Enlil.
2. That is, a return to conditions before the attempt to destroy the human race; see p. 237 note 1.

"He let loose produce for the peoples,[1]   (20)
"He put [shade?] in the glare(?) of the sun."
Enlil [made] ready to speak,
He said to the vizier Nusku,
"Let them bring to me the two comrades,⋆[2]
"Let them [send] them into my presence."   (25)
They brought to him the two comrades.
The warrior [Enlil] said to them,
"[All we] great Anunna-gods
"Resolved together on a rule.
"Anu and Adad watched over the upper [regions],   (30)
"I watched over the lower earth.
"Where you (Enki) went
"[You released the yoke], you made restoration.   (1′)
"[You let loose produce for the peoples],
"[You put shade?] in the glare(?) of the sun."

(gap)

vi

(Enlil is explaining to the gods how Enki frustrated his murderous plans.)

"Adad [withheld?] his rain   (10)
"[But   ] filled the fields
"[And] the clouds(?) covered [   ].
"[You (gods) must not] feed his peoples,
"[Nor] supply provisions on which the peoples thrive."
[The god] fretted for sitting idle,   (15)
[In] the assembly of the gods, worry gnawed at him.
[Enki] fretted for sitting idle,⋆
[In] the assembly of the gods, worry gnawed at him.

---

1. I take this speech to mean that Enki loosed a flood of fish upon the land and saved the people from starvation. The trick perhaps lay in the ambiguity of the word: Enki promised to send a flood of fish, which gods understood to be a flood to overwhelm the land, but which turned out, intentionally no doubt, to be harvest for the starving human race. This may have been the result of Atrahasis' prayer to the river and Enki's instructions to the hairy hero-men. (A different interpretation is found in CAD M/2, 124a.)

2. If correctly understood, perhaps two destroyer gods are meant, Shullat and Hanish (below, Tablet II vii 50; von Soden, TUAT III/4, 634).

(four lines fragmentary)

(Enlil is speaking.)

"[All we great Anunna-gods]
"[Resolved] together [on a rule],
"Anu watched over Adad in the upper regions,★   (25)
"I watched over the lower earth.
"Where you (Enki) went
"[You] released the yoke, you made restoration.
"[You] let loose produce for the peoples,
"[You put shade?] in the glare(?) of the sun."   (30)

(gap)

vii

(gap)

"[She(?) imposed] your drudgery [on man],
"[You] have bestowed(?) clamo[r upon humankind].
"You slaughtered [the god], along with [his inspiration],
"[You] sat down and bath[ed yourselves].
"[   ] it will bring [   ]   (35)
"You resolved on [a rule   ],
"Let (humankind) return to [its] la[ir?],★
"Let us be sure to bind the leader Enki,
       who manages (all),★ by oath."
Enki made ready to speak,   (40)
And said to the gods [his brethren],
"Why would you bind me by oath [   ]?
"Am I to bring my hands against [my own peoples]?
"The flood that you are speaking of [to me],
"Who is (to do it)? I [do not know].   (45)
"Am I to produce [a flood]?
"The task of that is [Enlil's].
"Let him [   ] choose,
"Let Shullat and [Hanish] go [in front],   (50)
"Let Errakal [tear out] the mooring poles,
"Let [Ninurta] go make [the dikes] overflow.

(small gap)

viii

(large gap)

"Assemble ... [   ]
"Do not obey ... [   ]."
The gods commanded annihilation,
E[nlil] committed the evil deed against the peoples.   (35)

Tablet III

i

(gap)

(Atrahasis has had a dream from Enki, and wishes to know its meaning.)

Atrahasis made ready to speak,
And said to his lord,
"Make me know the meaning [of the dream],
"[   ] let me know,* that I may look out for its consequence."
[Enki] made ready to speak,   (15)
And said to his servant,
"You might say, 'Am I to be looking out
          while in the bedroom?'*
"Do you pay attention to the message that I speak for you:

    'Wall, listen to me!   (20)
    'Reed wall, pay attention to all my words!
    'Flee house, build boat,
    'Forsake possessions,* and save life.
    'The boat that you build,   (25)
    '[   ] be equal [   ]

(gap)

    '[Cover] her with [   ] tarpaulins,*
    'Roof her over like the depths,
    'So that the sun will not see inside her,   (30)
    'Let her be roofed over fore and aft.*
    'The gear should be very firm,
    'The pitch should be firm, make (her) strong.
    'I shall shower down upon you later

'A windfall of birds, a spate(?) of fishes.'"[1]   (35)

He opened the water clock and filled it,
He told it (the wall?) of the coming of the seven-day deluge.*
Atrahasis received the command,
He assembled the elders at his gate.
Atrahasis made ready to speak,   (40)
And said to the elders,
"My god [does not agree] with your god,
"Enki and [Enlil] are constantly angry with each other.
"They have expelled me from [the land?].
"Since I have always reverenced [Enki],   (45)
"[He told me?] this.
"I can[not] live in [   ]
"Nor can I [set my feet on] the earth of Enlil.
"[I shall dwell?] with <my> god in(?) the depths.*
"[This my god Enki] told me [   ] ..."   (50)

                    (gap of four or five lines)

                            ii

The elders [   ]   (10)
The carpenter [carried his ax],
The reed-worker [carried his stone].
[The rich man? carried] the pitch,*
The poor man [brought the materials needed].

                            (gap)

Bringing [   ]
Whatever he [had   ]   (30)
Whatever he had [   ]
Pure (animals) he sl[aughtered, cattle] ...*
Fat (animals) [he killed, sheep?] ...*
He chose [... and brought on] board.
The [birds] flying in the heavens,   (35)
The cattle(?) [and   of the cat]tle-god,

---

1. Birds and fish falling from the sky are known to be occasional consequences, though not harbingers, of severe storms (A. R. Millard, "The Sign of the Flood," *Iraq* 49 [1987], 63–69; I. Finkel, "Raining Fish," N.A.B.U. 2002/19). The precise meaning of this line is unclear.

The [creatures(?)   ] of the steppe,
[   ] he brought on board
[   ] ... the month.
[   ] he invited his people   (40)
[   ] to a feast.
[ ] his family he brought on board.
While one was eating and another was drinking,
He went in and out; he could not sit,
      he could not take his place,*   (45)
For his heart was broken, he was retching gall.
The outlook of the weather changed,
Adad began to roar in the clouds.
The god they heard, his clamor.*   (50)
He brought pitch to seal his door.
By the time he had bolted his door,
Adad was roaring in the clouds.
The winds were furious as he set forth,
He cut the mooring rope, he released the boat.   (55)

iii

(four lines lost)

[   ] the storm   (5)
[   ] were yoked
[Anzu rent] the sky with his talons,
[He   ] the land
He broke its clamor [like a pot].   (10)
[   ] the flood [came forth],
Its destructive power came upon the peoples [like a battle].
One person did [not] see another,
They could [not] recognize each other in the catastrophe.
[The deluge] bellowed like a bull,   (15)
The wind [resound]ed like a screaming eagle.*
The darkness [was dense], the sun was gone,
[The offspring became] like flies.*
[The gods became afraid of the clamor] of the deluge,   (20)
They took [refuge in heaven],
They [crou]ched [outside].
[Anu became afraid of] the clamor of the de[luge],

It was terri[fying] the gods.*
[Enki] was beside himself,   (25)
[That] his sons were carried off before him.
Nintu, the great lady,
Gnawed* her lips in agony.
The Anunna, the great gods,   (30)
Were sitting in thirst and hunger.
The goddess saw it, weeping,
The midwife of the gods, the wise Mami,
"Let the day grow dark,
"Let it turn back to gloom!   (35)
"In the assembly of the gods,
"How did I agree with them on annihilation?
"Was Enlil so strong that he forced [me] to speak?
"Like that Tiruru, did he make [my] speech confused?[1]*   (40)
"Of my own accord, from myself alone,
"To my own charge have I heard (my people's) clamor!
"[My] offspring — with no help from me —
        have become like flies.*   (45)
"And as for me, how to dwell in (this) abode of grief,
        my clamor fallen silent?*
"Shall I go up to heaven,
"I would take up my dwelling in a [well-lardered] house!*   (50)
"Where has Anu gone to, the chief decision-maker,
"Whose sons, the gods, heeded his command?
"He who irrationally brought about the flood,
"And relegated the peoples to ca[tastrophe]?"

                    (one line missing)

                          iv

                         (gap)

Nintu was wailing [   ]
"... gave birth to(?) ...*   (5)
"As dragonflies a watercourse, they have filled the sea.*
"Like rafts they lie against the river meadow(?),*

_____

1. The meaning of the reference to Tiruru is unknown.

"Like rafts capsized they lie against the bank.
"I saw and wept over them, (10)
"I have exhausted my lamentation for them."
She wept, giving vent to her feelings,
While Nintu wailed, her emotion was spent.
The gods wept with her for the land. (15)
She had her fill of woe, she was thirsty for beer.
Where she sat weeping, they too sat,
Like sheep, they filled a streambed.[1] (20)
Their lips were agonized with thirst,
They were suffering pangs of hunger.
Seven days and seven ni[ghts]
There came the deluge, the storm, [the flood]. (25)
Where it [   ]
[   ] was thrown down

(gap of about twenty-five lines)

v

(gap of twenty-nine lines)

To the [four] winds [   ] (30)
He cast [   ]
He was raining down food [   ][2]
[   ]
[The gods sniffed] the savor,
They were gathered [like flies] around the offering. (35)
[After] they had eaten the offering,
[Nin]tu arose to rail against all of them,
"Where has Anu come to, the chief decision-maker? (40)
"Has Enlil drawn nigh the incense?
"They who irrationally brought about the flood,
"And relegated the peoples to catastrophe?
"You resolved upon annihilation,
"So now (the people's) bright countenances are turned gray." (45)
Then she drew nigh the big fly (ornaments?)*
That Anu had ... [   ]*

1. The gods are hoping to find water to drink.
2. A wordplay on "rain" and "provide food" may be intended.

"Mine is [their] woe! Proclaim my destiny!
"Let him get me out of my misery, let him show me the way(?). (50)
"Let me go out ... [   ]

vi

"In [   ]   (1)
"Let [these] flies[1] be jewelry around my neck,
"That I may remember it [every?] day [and forever?]."
[The warrior Enlil] saw the vessel,   (5)
And was filled with anger at the Igigi-gods.
"All we great Anunna-gods
"Resolved together on an oath.
"Where did life(?) escape?*
"How did a man survive the catastrophe?"   (10)
Anu made ready to speak,
And said to the warrior Enlil,
"Who could do this but Enki?
"[   ] he revealed the command."   (15)
[Enki] made ready to speak,
[And said to] the great gods,
"I did it [indeed] for your sakes!
"[I am responsible] for safeguarding li[fe].
"[   ] gods [   ]   (20)
"[   ] the flood
"[   ] brought about
"[O Enlil,   ] your heart
"[   ] and relax.
"Impose your penalty [on a wrong-doer],   (25)
"[For] who is it that disregards your command?[2]
"[   ] the assembly [   ]

(gap)

"[   ] it
"[   ] put,

---

1. The episode is obscure and seems to contain a play on words; perhaps the goddess's necklace is the rainbow. For discussion, see Kilmer, *Studies Reiner*, 175–180.
2. The thrust of the argument may be that he had sworn not to tell humankind of the flood, but did not swear to annihilate life.

"[   ] ... my heart."   (40)
[Enlil] made ready to speak,
And said to Ea the leader,
"[Come], summon Nintu the birth-goddess,
"[Do you] and she take counsel together in the assembly."
[Enki] made ready to speak,   (45)
And [said to] Nintu the birth-goddess,
"[You], birth-goddess, creatress of destinies,
"[Establish death?] for all peoples!★
"[   ]
"[   ] let there be.   (50)

(one line missing?)

vii

"Now then, let there be a third (woman) among the people,   (1)
"Among the people are the woman who has borne
         and the woman who has not borne.
"Let there be (also) among the people the (she-)demon,[1]
"Let her snatch the baby from the lap of her who bore it,   (5)
"Establish high priestesses and priestesses,
"Let them be taboo, and so cut down childbirth.
"[   ] the cloistered woman,
"[   ] the sacrosanct woman,

(fragmentary lines, then large gap)

viii

(gap)

"How we brought about [the flood],
"But man survived the [catastrophe],   (10)
"You, counsellor of the [great] gods,
"At [your] command have I brought a [   ]★ to be,
"This [my] song (is) for your praise.   (15)
"May the Igigi-gods hear,
         let them extol your great deed to each other.
"I have sung of the flood to all peoples: Listen!"

---

1.   "The-One-Who-Wipes-Out" (family names).

(b) MIDDLE BABYLONIAN VERSIONS

(b.1) NIPPUR EDITION

"[   ] I will explain
"[... a flood] will seize all the peoples at once.
"[   ] before the flood comes forth,
"[Good reeds], as many as there are, should be woven(?),
    should be gathered(?) for it.★   (5)
"[   ] build a big boat.
"Let its structure be [interwoven?] of good(?) reed.
"[   ] let it be a vessel
    with the name "Guardian of Life.""[1]
"[   ] roof it over with a strong covering.
"[Into the boat that] you will make,   (10)
"[Bring aboard] wild creatures of the steppe, birds of heaven.
"Heap up [   ]

(breaks off)

1. See also II.33 (p. 220).

(b.2) AN ATRAHASIS STORY FROM SYRIA

This version of the Atrahasis story was evidently narrated by Atrahasis himself. The tablet was discovered at Ugarit, on the Syrian coast, and dates approximately to the thirteenth century B.C.

When the gods took counsel concerning the lands,   (1)
They brought about a flood in the world regions.

[   ] would listen [   ]
[   ] Ea in his heart.   (5)

"I am Atrahasis,
"I was living in the temple of Ea, my lord,
"And I knew everything.★

"I knew of the counsel of the great gods,
"I knew of their oath,
        though they would not reveal it to me.   (10)

"He repeated their words to the wall,

        'Wall, hear [   ]

                    (gap)

                    (rev.)

"[   ] the gods life [   ]   (1)
"[   ] your wife [   ]
"[   ] help and [   ]
"Life like the gods [you will] indeed [possess]."

                    (end of tablet)

(c) LATE BABYLONIAN VERSION

The Late Babylonian version given here is a conflation of manuscripts from various times and places during the first millennium B.C. The most important of these is the Sippar manuscript, dating to the late sixth century, which spread the narrative over more tablets than the Old Babylonian volume.

Tablet I

When gods were man,   (1)
The gods made the yoke, the carrying basket.
Great indeed was the drudgery of the gods,
The forced labor was heavy, the misery too much:
The great Anunna-gods, the seven,   (5)
Were burdening the Igigi-gods with forced labor.
Anu their father was king,
And their counsellor was the warrior Enlil,
Their prefect was Ninurta,
And their bailiff the god Ennugi.   (10)
They had taken the [   ] by its sides,
They cast lots, they took their shares:
Anu went up to heaven,
Enlil took the earth for his subjects,
The bolt, the trap of the sea,   (15)
They had given to Ea the leader.
Those of Anu went up to heaven,
Those of Ea went down to the depths.
Those of heaven ... had nothing to do,
Those of Enlil were burdened with forced labor.   (20)
The [gods(?)] were digging [watercourses],
The waterway of the gods, the life of the land,
The [Igigi-gods(?)] were digging [watercourses],
The waterway of the gods, the life of the land!
[   ] the Tigris,   (25)
[   ] the Euphrates

(gap)

[   ] and they were denouncing,
Muttering down in the ditch,   (40)

"Come, let us kill the prefect,
"[   ] let us break the yoke!"
Alla made ready to speak,
And said to the gods his brothers,
"We [should not kill(?] the prefect of olden days,
"Enlil will establish [another ...(?)].   (45)

(gap)

"The god, counsellor of [the gods, the warrior],
[   ],   (50)
"Enlil, counsellor of [the gods, the warrior],
"[   ].
"I will make war on Anu himself!
"[   ]"
The gods heard what he said,   (55)
[They set fire to their tools],
[They put fire to their spades],
[Flame to their] work baskets.
Off they went, making their way,
To the gate [of the warrior Enlil's abode].   (60)
It was the night watch,
Ekur was surrounded, but the god did not know,
It was the night watch,
Ekur was surrounded, but Enlil did not know!
Kalkal noticed it and looked out,   (65)
He touched the bolt and looked out.
[Kalkal woke Nusku],
They listened to the clamor [   ].
Nusku woke his lord,
[He got him out of bed],   (70)
"My lord, your house is surrounded,
"Battle has run right up to your gate,
"Enlil, your house is surrounded,
"Battle has run right up to your gate!"

(gap)

Anu, king [of heaven], was present,   (90) (OB I, 101)
The king of the dep[ths, Ea   ],

With the great [Anunna-gods present],
Enlil [arose, the debate was underway].
Enlil [made ready to speak],
And sa[id to the gods his brothers],   (95)
"Against [me would they be trying this]?
"[Shall I make] battle [   ]?
"What [did I see with my very own eyes]?
"Battle [ran right up to my gate]!"
Anu [made ready] to speak,   (100)
And said to [his brother, Enlil],
"The reason why the Igigi-gods gathered at your gate,
"Let [Nusku] go out, [let him learn their cause]."
Enlil [made ready to] speak,
And said to his courier, Nusku,   (105)
"Nusku, open [your] gate,
"Take your weapons and go out to the group,
"In the group of all the gods,
"Bow down and stand up, repeat my command:

    'Anu your father,   (110)
    'And your counsellor, the warrior Enlil,
    'Your prefect, Ninurta,
    'And your bailiff, Ennugi, have sent me (to say),

        "Who is the god who was instigator of battle?
        "Who is the god who was instigator of hostilities?   (115)
        "Who is it that stirred up war,
        "[That battle has run right up to the gate of Enlil]?"'"

Tablet II

(lines 1–30 repeat lines 100–117 of LB Tablet I)

[The Igigi-gods] answered [in the gro]up,   (OB I, 144)
They were defiant, the labor gang [   ],
"Every one of us had declared [war],
"We formed our group in the ditch.
"The drudgery has killed us,   (35)
"Our forced labor was heavy, our misery too much!
"And so every one of us gods
"Has resolved to do battle with Enlil!"
Nusku took the command,
He went back and said [to his lord],   (40)
"My lord, where you sent me,
"I betook myself, I stood up and I gave the command,
"They heard your great command.
"All the Anunna-gods, the labor gang [   ],
    'Every one of us has declared [war],   (45)
    'We formed our group in the ditch.
    'The drudgery has killed [us],
    'Our forced labor was heavy, our misery too much,
    '[And so] every one of us gods
    '[Has resolved] to do battle with Enlil!'"   (50)
When he had heard [that] speech,
Then Enlil's tears flowed down,
[The god] became disturbed at what [he] had learned,
He said to his brother [Anu],
Enlil became disturbed at what [he] had learned,   (55)
He said to his brother [Anu],
"Noble one, you should take authority off with you to heaven.
"Take the power you still have(?).
"The Anunna-gods are present before you,
"[Summon one] god and make a new order."   (60)
Anu made ready [to speak],
And said [to the gods his brothers],
"What do we denounce them for?
"Their forced labor was heavy, their misery was too much.
"Every day the earth was [piling up(?)],   (65)

"The forced labor was heavy and we could hear the clamor.
"There is a task to be done.
"Belet-ili [is present], the mother goddess,
"Let the mother goddess create humanity,
"Let man bear the drudgery of god.   (70)
"Let him bear the yoke, lordship's task,
"Let him bear the yoke, Enlil's task,
"Let man assume the drudgery of god."
They summoned the goddess, they asked,   (75)
"O midwife Belet-ili, creatress of destiny,
"You are the mother goddess, creatress of destiny.
"Make humanity, let it bear the yoke,
"The yoke let it bear, Enlil's task,
"Let man assume the drudgery of god!"   (80)
Mama made ready to speak,
And said to the gods her brothers,
"Although mine is (the power) to make things,
"Th(is) task is Enki's.
"He is the one who purifies everything,   (85)
"Let him give me the clay so I can do the making."
Ea made ready to speak
And said to the gods his brothers,
"On the first, seventh, and fifteenth days of the month,
"I will establish a purification, a bath.   (90)
"Let one god be slaughtered,
"Then let the gods be purified in it.
"Let Belet-ili mix clay,
"With his flesh and blood
"Let that same god and man   (95)
"Be thoroughly mixed together in the clay.
"For the rest of time, let it be obvious, so we can hear it.
"From the flesh of the god let a spirit remain.
"Let it make the living know its sign,
"A sign not to be forgotten, a spirit."   (100)
On the first, seventh, and fifteenth days of the month,
He instituted a purification, a bath.
They slaughtered Alla, the god who had the inspiration,
Alla, an Enlil of former time(?).

Belet-ili mixed the clay (105)
With his flesh and blood.
That same [god] and man
Were thoroughly mixed together in the clay.
For the rest of time, it was obvious so it could be heard.
From the flesh of the god a spirit remained. (110)
It would make the living know its sign,
[A sign] not to be forgotten, a spirit.
[After] she had mixed his clay,
[He summoned] the Anunnaki and all the Igigi,
[The Igigi], the great gods, (115)
Spat upon her clay.

Tablet III

Mama made ready to speak (1)
And said to the great gods

*(This tablet, corresponding to Old Babylonian Tablet I, 235–355
and the Late Assyrian version iii, is lost.)*

Tablet IV

*(This tablet, corresponding to Old Babylonian Tablet I, 356–412
and II, i and ii, is lost.)*

Tablet V

(Enlil has sent plague to reduce the human race, and this has failed. Next he caused a drought, the account of which is preserved in the Late Assyrian version, iv, and v. When this tablet begins, Ea is telling Atrahasis how to save the human race from the drought.)

Ea made ready to speak,   (1)
And said to his servant,
"The debate has been heard, the assembly convened,
"The gods resolved upon an oath.
"[Invite?] the elders at the usual time,   (5)
"Within counsel,
"Command: let heralds proclaim,
"Let them raise a loud clamor in the land:
     'Do not reverence your (own) gods,
     'Do not pray to your (own) goddess,   (10)
     'Seek the door of Adad,
     'Bring a baked loaf before it.'
"May the flour offering please him,
"May he stealthily rain down dew in the night,
"May he rain down mist in the morning,   (15)
"That a field just as stealthily bear double."
Atrahasis took the command,
He assembled the elders to his house.
Atrahasis made ready to speak
And said to the elders,   (20)
"The debate has been heard, the assembly was convened,
"The gods resolved upon an oath.
"Command: let heralds proclaim,
"Let them raise a loud clamor in the land,
     'Do not reverence your (own) gods,   (25)
     'Do not pray to your (own) goddess,
     'Seek the door of Adad,
     'Bring a baked loaf before it.'
"May the flour offering please him,
"May he stealthily rain down dew at night,   (30)
"May he rain down mist in the morning,
"That a field just as stealthily bear double."

The elders heard his words,
They built a temple for Adad in the city.
The flour offering pleased him,   (35)
He stealthily rained down dew at night,
He rained down mist in the morning,
A field just as stealthily bore double.
Their handsome features returned,
Their former clamor resumed,   (40)
The womb was open and was producing babies.
Thrice 3600 years had not gone by,
The land had become numerous, the peoples had increased,
The land was bellowing like a bull.   (45)
The gods became disturbed at their clamor,
Enlil reconvened the assembly
And said to the gods, his children,
"The clamor of humankind has become burdensome to me,
"I am losing sleep to their uproar.   (50)
"Command that Anu and Adad
    stand guard over the on high,
"That Sin and Nergal stand guard over the earth between,
"Over the bolt, the trap of the sea
"Let Ea stand guard, together with his hairy hero-men."
He commanded and Anu
    and Ea stood guard over the on high,   (55)
Sin and Nergal stood guard over the earth between,
Over the bolt, the trap of the sea,
Ea stood guard, together with his hairy hero-men.
But he, Atrahasis, a man,
Every day he would weep,   (60)
He would bring dream-offerings
    to the canebrake of the river.*
When the waterway was quiet,
He made an offering halfway through the night.
Sleep would come upon him double fast.
He would say to the waterway,   (65)
"Take this, waterway, let the river bear it away,
"May my gift be set before Ea, my lord.
"May Ea see it and think of me,

"This night may I have a dream."
After he had sent the message by the waterway,   (70)
He sat down [to weep], facing the river,
The man [fell asleep?], facing the river.
His present went down to the depths,
Ea heard his clamor.
[He summoned(?) his hairy hero-men] and said to them,   (75)
"The man who ... did(?) this,
"Be off, make haste, bring me his command,
"Ask him too and tell me the news of his land."
They crossed the wide sea,
At the wharf of the depths [   ].   (80)
They repeated Ea's command to Atrahasis,
"You, whoever you are, who weep,
"Your present has come down to the depth.
"Ea has heard your clamor,
"We are the ones he has sent to you."   (85)
"If Ea has indeed heard me,
"What [... do you bring] from [my lord]?"
They answered him forthwith,
They said to Atrahasis,
"While sleep was coming double fast,   (90)
"The waterway took it, the river brought it away,
"Your gift was set before Ea.
"Ea saw it and thought of you,
"So now we are the ones he has sent to you."
He knelt down, did obeisance before them.   (95)
The hairy hero-men [went back?] to the midst of the sea.
Ea made ready to speak and commanded,
Saying to Usmu, his courier,
"Go out to Atrahasis, tell him what I say,
        'The outlook for the land is the same as for its people.'" (100)
Usmu, Ea's courier, said to Atrahasis,
"If water forsook it, grain forsook [its fields],
"[   ]
"[   ] forsakes them.   (105)
"The land is [thrown?] on its face like a young man(?)
        [slain in battle?],

"[   ]
"The land you will pour out(?) like a ... upon ..."
On high, the bosom of heaven was sealed shut,
Below was dammed up, no water came from the depths.   (110)
The black fields turned white,
No green plants came out in the pastures, no ...
The first year they ate old grain,
The second year they exhausted their stores.
When the third year came,
Their features were distorted from hunger

(breaks off)

Tablet "VI"

(Enlil is speaking.)

"[I commanded that] Anu and Adad stand guard over
         [the upper regions],
"[That Sin and Nergal] stand guard
         over the earth in the middle,
"[That the bolt], the trap of the sea,
"[You should] stand guard over,
         together with your hairy hero-men.   (5′)
"[But you let loose] abundance for the peoples!"
[   ] the broad sea
Repeated [the message of] Enlil to Ea:
"[I commanded] that Anu and Adad watch over
         the upper regions,
"[That Sin and Nergal] watch over the earth between,   (10′)
"[That the bolt], the trap of the sea,
"[You should] stand guard over,
         together with your hairy hero-men.
"[But you let] loose abundance for the peoples!"
[Ea] made ready to speak,
And [said] to the messenger,   (15′)
"[ ] you commanded, so Anu and Adad watched over
         the upper regions,
"[Sin and Nergal] watched over the earth in the middle,
"[The bolt], the trap of the sea,
"[I] watched over, together with my hairy hero-men.
"When [   ] escaped from me,   (20′)
"[   ] a million fish, one million they bore(?).*
"I drew together [the bolt?] of the fish but it went away,
"They broke through the middle of the [trap].
"[After?] I executed the watchmen of the sea,
"I imposed [   ] upon them and punished them.   (25′)
"[After] I had punished them,

"[I repeated it] and imposed the penalty."
[The   ] took the message.
[   ] the wide sea
[Went] and repeated   (30')
[The message] of Ea to Enlil,
"[ ] you commanded, so Anu and Adad stood guard
        over the upper regions,
"[Sin and] Nergal stood guard over the earth in the middle,
"[The bolt], the trap of the sea,
"[I] watched over, together with my hairy hero-men.   (35')
"When [   ] escaped from me,
"[   ] a million fish, one million they bore(?).
"I drew together [the bolt? of] the fish, but it went away,
"They broke through the middle of the [trap].
"[After?] I had executed the watchmen of the sea,   (40')
"I laid [   ] upon them and punished them.[1]
"After I had punished them,
"[I] repeated it and imposed a penalty."

Enlil made ready to speak,
And said to the assembly of all the gods,   (45')
"Come, all of us, and take an oath to bring a flood."
Anu swore first,
Enlil swore, his son swore with him.

(breaks off)

1.   Obscure. What penalty could he lay upon them if they were already executed? Does "them"
mean humankind here?

(d) LATE ASSYRIAN VERSION

The "Late Assyrian version" given here is a conflation of different sources from Assyria and Babylonia dating to the first millennium B.C. that are very different from either the Old or Late Babylonian version. References to the Old Babylonian version are provided in the right margin.

Tablet I

i

[ ] went down	(OB I.19)
[kin]gship of the depth	
[ ] went down	(20)
[kingshi]p(?) of Ea.	
[were dig]ging the river,	
[ ] life of the land.	
[ ] the Euphrates after it	
[ ] from the deep	(25)
They set up their [ ].	
[For ten years?] they bore the drudgery	
[For twenty years] they bore the drudgery	
[For thirty years] they bore the drudgery	
[For forty years] they bore the drudgery.	(30)
[ ] ... they refused(?)*	
[ ]	
[They were complaining, denoun]cing,	
[Muttering down in the di]tch.	(OB I.40)

(fragmentary lines, then gap)

ii*

(In this version Nusku makes his visit to the rebels after the proposal to slaughter the leader has been made.)

"You [   ]   (OB I.170ff.)
"Take [   ]
"With [the great gods] in session [before you],   (5')
"With Belet-i[li the midwife] in session,
"Summon the one and kill [him]."

Anu made ready to speak, saying [to Nusku],
"Nusku, open your gate, [take] your weapons,
        [stand before them],
"Among all the great gods bow down, [stand up],   (10')
"Say to them [   ],

    'Anu [your father] has sent me,
    'Your counsellor the w[arrior Enlil],
    'Your prefect Ni[nurta and your bailiff? Annugal]:
    'Who is instigator of battle,
        [who is instigator of hostilities]?   (15')
    'Which is the god who made [the war]
    'That battle has run up to [the gate of Enlil]?'"

[When Nusku heard] this,
He to[ok] his weapons [   ].
In the assembly of the great gods [he knelt and stood up],   (20')
[He said] to the[m   ],
"[A]nu [your father has sent me],
"[Your counsellor the warrior] Enlil,
"[Your prefect Ninurta and your bailiff?] Annugal:

    '[Who is instigator of battle?
        Who is] instigator of hostilities?   (25')
    '[Which is the god who made] the war,
    '[That battle has run up to] the gate of Enlil?'"

[The great gods] made [ready to speak],
[Saying to Nusku, vizier] of Enlil,   (30')

iii

(large gap)

[   ] Ea said,   (15')
Ea, [seated before her], was prompting her,
Belet-[ili] was reciting the incantation.
After she had recited her spell,
[She s]pat in her clay.
She pinched off fourteen pieces of clay,
Seven she put on the right,   (20')
[Seven] on the left.
Between them she set the brick,
The reed cutter, to sever the umbilical cord, she had ready.⋆
She summoned the wise and accomplished
Birth goddesses, seven and seven.   (25')
Seven produced males,
[Seven] produced females.
While the birth-goddess was creating destiny,
They will crown(?) them in pairs,[1]
They will crown(?) them in pairs in her presence —   (30')
Mami was laying down the designs for the human race:

"In the house of the pregnant woman about to give birth,
"Let the brick be in place for seven days,
"That Belet-ili, the wise Mami, may be honored.
"Let the midwife rejoice in the house of the woman in labor.
"And when the pregnant woman gives birth,   (35')
"Let the mother of the baby separate(?) herself.
"A male (baby) to [   ] ...,
"[A female (baby)] ..."

(gap)

1. That is, these foetuses will one day be married, male to female. For further discussion of this obscure passage, see Stol, *Birth in Babylonia*, 114.

iv

[Twelve hundred years had not gone by]　　　　　　(OB I.352)(1)
The land had grown numerous, [the peoples had increased].
He was disturbed [at] their clamor,
[At] their uproar [sleep] could not overcome him.
Enlil convened his assembly,
And said to the gods his sons,　　　　　　　　　　　(5)
"The clamor of humankind
　　　　has indeed become burdensome for me,
"I am disturbed [at the]ir clamor,
"[At] their uproar sleep cannot overcome me.
"Command that there be ague,
"Let contagion diminish their clamor.　　　　　　　　(10)
"Let disease, head pain, ague, and malady
"Blast upon them like a whirlwind."

The[y gave the com]mand and there was ague,
Contagion diminished their clamor.
[Dis]ease, head pain, ague, and malady　　　　　　　(15)
Blasted upon them like a whirlwind.

For the destiny of the man, Atrahasis,[1]
Ea, his [god], was heedful.*
Did he not [speak] with his god?
[His god], Ea, spoke with him.　　　　　　　　　　　(20)

Atrahasis made ready to speak,
[And said to] Ea his lord,
"Lord, the peoples are groaning,
"Your [disease] is devouring the land.
"Ea, lord, the peoples are groaning,　　　　　　　　　(25)
"[The disease] from the gods is devouring the land.
"[Sin]ce you created us,
"[Will you] remove the disease, head pain, ague, and malady?"
[Ea made ready to] speak, and said to Atrahasis:
"[Command:

1. Literally: "The Broad-of-Wisdom-Man," "was heedful" is a play on the name.

"Let her]alds [proclaim],
"Let them raise a loud clamor in the land: (30)

   '[Do not reverence your (own) gods],
   'Do not pray to your (own) goddesses,
   '[...Namtar...] observe his rites,
   '[   ] the flour offering
   '[   ] before it
   '[   ] speak a blessing.'   (35)

"[He will be shamed by the] gift
   [and withdraw?] his hand."   (OB I 399)

[Enlil] convened his assembly, and said to the gods his sons,
"Do not lay contagion upon them (any longer)!*
"[The peo]ples have not dwindled,
   but have become more numerous than before!
"I have become disturbed [at] their clamor,   (40)
"[At] their uproar sleep cannot overcome me.
"Cut off provender for the peoples,
"Let plants be scanty in their stomachs.
"Above, let Adad make scarce his rain,
"Below, let (the rainfall) be dammed up, let it raise
   no flood from the depths.   (45)
"Let the fields reduce their yields,
"The grain-goddess turn aside her bosom,
"Let the black fields whiten,
"Let the broad plain produce salts,
"Let the earth's womb rebel,
"Let no plants come forth, no sheep fatten.*
"Let a malady be laid upon the peoples,   (50)
"That the womb be constricted
   and give no safe birth to a child."
They cut off provender from the peoples,
Plants were scanty in their stomachs.
Above, Adad made scarce his rain,
Below, (the rainfall) was blocked off and raised
   no flood from the depths.   (55)
The fields reduced their yields,
The grain-goddess turned aside her bosom,

The black fields whitened,
The broad plain produced salts, earth's womb rebelled,
No plants came forth, no sheep fattened.
A malady was laid upon the peoples, (60)
So that the womb was constricted
    and gave no safe birth to a child.

    (gap)

    v

The bo[lt, the bar of the sea], (1)
[Ea] stood guard over, [together with his hairy hero-men].
Above, [Adad made scarce his rain],
Below, (the rainfall) was dammed up,
    [it raised no flood from the depths].
The fields reduced [their yields], (5)
The grain goddess [turned aside her bosom],
[The black fields whitened],
[The broad plain] produced salts, [earth's womb rebelled],
[No plants] came forth, no grains [ripened].
[A malady was laid upon the peoples],
[That the womb was constricted
    and gave [no safe birth to a child].
[For one year they ate ...] (10)
[   ]
[When the second year came], they exhausted their stores,
[When the third year] came,
[The peoples' features] were distorted [from hunger].
[When the fourth year came], their [long] stance grew short, (15)
[Broad-shouldered people] turned slender.
[They walked about hunched] in the street.
[When the fifth year came], daughter saw mother [go in],
[But mother would not] open her door [to daughter].
[Daughter] watched [the scales (when) mother
    (was sold into slavery)], (20)
Mother watched [the scales (when) daughter
    (was sold into slavery)].
[When the sixth year came,
    they served up] daughter for a meal,

They served up [son for sustenance]:
[They were filled on their own children?],*
One [household] devoured another.
Their [faces] were crusted, [like dead malt].   (25)
[The peoples] were living [on the verge] of death.

[For th]e destiny of the man Atrahasis,
Ea, [his god], was heedful.
Did he not [speak] with his god?
His god Ea spoke with him.   (30)
He left the gate of his god,
He placed his bed facing the river,
But the channels were quiet.

(gap)

vi

[When the second] year [came, they exhausted their stores],   (1)
[When] the third year [came],
The peoples' [features] were distorted from [hunger].
When the fourth year [came], their [long] stance grew short,
Broad-[shouldered people] turned slender,   (5)
They walked about hunched in the street.
When the fifth year came, daughter saw mother go in,
But mother would not open her door to daughter.
Daughter watched the scales (when) mother
        (was sold into slavery),
[Mother] watched the scales (when) daughter
        (was sold into slavery).   (10)

When the sixth year came,
        they served up [daughter] for a meal,
They served up the son for sustenance:
[They] were filled [on their own children?],*
One household devoured another.
Their faces [were crusted], like dead malt.
The peoples [were living] on the verge of [death].   (15)

The command that they received [   ]

They entered and [   ]
The message of Atrahasis [   ]
"Lord, the land [   ]
"A sign [   ]   (20)

(six lines fragmentary)

"Let me go down to the d[ep]ths to dwell in your presence."
One year they ate old grain

(gap)

Tablet II

iii(?)

"Ea, lord, [I heard] you come in, (OB III i) (1)
"[I] noticed steps like [your] footsteps."

[Atrahasis] knelt, prostrated himself, stood up [ ],
He made ready [to speak] and said,
"[Lord], I heard you come in, (5)
"[I noticed] steps like your footsteps.
"[Ea, lord], I heard you come in,
"[I noticed] steps like your footsteps.
"[   ] for(?) seven years,
"Your [   ] has made the weak thirsty. (10)
"[   ] I have seen your face
"[   ] tell me your (the gods') [   ]."

[Ea] made ready to speak
[And said to] the reed hut,
"[   ] reed hut! reed hut! (15)
"[   ] pay attention to me!

*(Approximately here goes CT 46 15, another Late Assyrian recension that is different from
this one, but helps to fill the gap.)*

"[   ] let it [   ] (1')
"[   ] like a circle [   ]
"Let the [roof?] be strong fore and aft,
"[ ] caulk the [boat].
"[Mark] the appointed time of which I send word, (5')
"Enter [the boat] and shut the boat's door.
"[Bring aboard] it your barley, your goods, your possessions,
"[Your wife], your kith, your kin, and skilled crafts[men].
"[Creatures] of the steppe, all the browsing wild animals
        of the steppe,
"[I] will send to you and they will attend at your door." (10')
Atrahasis made ready to speak,
And said to Ea, [his] lord,

"Never have I built a boat [   ],
"Draw the de[sign on the gro]und,
"That I may see [the desig]n and [build] the boat."   (15')
Ea drew [the design] on the ground.
"[   ] my lord, what you commanded [   ]

(breaks off)

(Assyrian recension continues.)

[   ] he put [   ]
[He] entered and sealed up the [boat].
The wind [   ] and brought the wh[irlwind].
Adad mounted the four winds, [his] steeds: (5)
South wind, north wind, east wind, west wind.
Storm, gale, whirlwind, cloudburst,
Evil wind, ..., the winds were rising.
The south wind [   ] arose at his side,
The west wind blasted at his side,   (10)
[   ] went [   ]
[   ] the chariot of the gods [   ]
[It] rushes forward, it kills, it overruns [   ].
Ninurta went and [made] the dikes [overflow],
Errakal tore up [the mooring poles].   (15)
[Anzu rent] the sky with his talons,
[He smashed] the land like a pot, he dispersed its guidance.
[   ] the flood came forth,
Its power came [upon] the peoples [like a battle].

[   ] Anu(?) [   ] the clamor of the flood,   (20)
[   ] terrified the gods.
[Nintu   ] her sons were carried off at her own command.
[   ] her emotion was spent.

(breaks off)

Text: (a) Clay, BRM 4 1; Lambert and Millard, CT 46 1–4; Lambert, *Atrahasis* pl. 1–8; Pinches, CT 44 20. Durand *apud* Groneberg, *Studies Garelli*, 409; W. G. Lambert, *Studies Garelli*, 414 BM 22714b. Some disputed passages in the KU-Ayya manuscript were collated by the writer for this translation. (b.1) Hilprecht, BE 5 1. (b.2) Nougayrol, *Ugaritica* 5 167. (c) Lambert, *Atrahasis*, pl. 4–5, 9–10; George and Al-Rawi, *Iraq* 58 (1996), 152, 154–159, 164–167, 169, 170, 178–181; van Dijk, VAS 24 93; Böck, *Aula Orientalis* 17/18 (1999/2000), 175–177; (d) King, CT 13 31; CT 15 49; Lambert and Millard, CT 46 5–15; Lambert, *Atrahasis*, pl. 8–11; AfO 27 (1980), 72, 74; BWL, pl. 65 K 4539; JSS 5 (1960), 116; OrNS 38 (1969), 533. Tablet I i = CT 46 6 + AfO 27 (1980), 72. ii = CT 46 6 + AfO 27 (1980), 72 + *Atrahasis*, xi + Lambert, *Studies Garelli*, 414 K 21851. iii = *Atrahasis*, xii + CT 15 49. iv = CT 15 49 + OrNS 38 (1969), 533 + AfO 27 (1980), 74. v = CT 15 49. vi = CT 13 31 + CT 15 49 + OrNS 38 (1969), 533. Tablet II iii? = JSS 5 (1960), 116.

Edition: (a) Lambert-Millard, *Atrahasis*. A new edition of Tablet I was offered by von Soden, ZA 68 (1978), 50–94. (b.1) Lambert, *Atrahasis*, 126–127. (b.2) Lambert, *Atrahasis*, 131–133; Kämmerer, AOAT 251 (1998), 168–171. (c) George and Al-Rawi, *Iraq* 58 (1996), 147–190. (d) Lambert, *Atrahasis*, 116–121.

Translation: Lambert-Millard, *Atrahasis*; Bottéro, *Mythologie*, 526–601; Dalley, *Myths*, 1–38; von Soden, TUAT III/4, 612–645; George and Al-Rawi, *Iraq* 58 (1996), 147–190.

Literature: The interest aroused by this text has generated a voluminous, often polemic and contradictory literature. The essential philological contributions prior to 1970 are cited line-by-line in Borger, HKL 2, 157–159. His citations are not repeated here, except where controversy continues or to acknowledge suggestions that materially and, I think, correctly altered the Lambert-Millard reading. The work of D. Shehata, *Annotierte Bibliographie zum altbabylonischen* Atramḫasīs-*Mythos* Inūma ilū awilum, GAAL 3 (2001), cited in the notes below as Shehata, AB, with privately distributed supplement, is a highly useful line-by-line commentary on the Old Babylonian text, intending to include all philological comments since the original publication, plus selected translations and comments. It includes a large bibliography and a list of the original manuscripts; additional bibliography is provided by Wasserman, BiOr 60 (2003), 160–161. The study of C. Wilcke, "Weltundergang als Anfang, theologische, anthropologische, politisch-historische und ästhetische Ebenen der Interpretation der Sintflutgeschichte im babylonischen *Atramhasis*-Epos," in A. Jones, ed., *Weltende, Beiträge zur Kultur- und Religionswissenschaft* (Wiesbaden, 1999), 63–112, reviews in detail various key passages, with suggestions adopted here. W. L. Moran's essays on Atrahasis have been reprinted in R. S. Handel, ed., *The Most Magic Word, Catholic Biblical Quarterly Monograph Series* 35 (2002).

Notes to Text: (II.36a) (5) Lambert, JCS 32 (1980), 83–85; Kienast *apud* Pettinato, OrAn 9 (1980), 77; Matouš, ArOr 35 (1967), 6. For "sevenfold" as referring to the labor, see Wilcke, ZA 67 (1977), 157; von Soden suggests that there were only seven Igigi-gods (TUAT III/4, 618). (11) For this line, von Soden sees the gods taking a clay jar by the neck, in order to draw lots (OrNS 40 [1971], 100), but denied by Lambert, OrNS 40 (1971), 97. See also Pettinato, OrAn 9 (1980), 77; the reading *le-ti-i-ša* is provided by the Sippar ms., George and Al-Rawi, *Iraq* 58 (1996), 153, 184. (14) With Pettinato, OrAn 9 (1980), 77. For a different reading, see von Soden, ZA 68 (1978), 77. (21) For 21–26 I follow von Soden, ZA 68 (1978), 54; see further Shehata, AB, 31. (37) von Soden, ZA 68 (1978), 56 suggests 2500 years; see further Shehata, AB, 31. (41) von Soden, ZA 68 (1978), 56. (77) von Soden, ZA 68 (1978), 58. (102) The reading ⌜*ú*⌝-[*te-e*]*q-qí* proposed by Schramm *apud* Borger, HKL 2, 158, does not fit the traces (collated). (107) George and Al-Rawi, *Iraq* 58 (1996), 160. (109) The reading *i-lí* 'O Gods!' was proposed by von Soden, ZA

67 (1977), 58, possibly supported by the Sippar ms., see George and Al-Rawi, *Iraq* 58 (1996), 185. (114) Although this proposal was abandoned by von Soden, ZA 68 (1978), 79, I maintain it here; see further Shehata, AB, 44. (123) This restoration has been proposed independently by several translators and documented by Westhuizen, CRRAI 32 (1985), 89–91; compare Bottéro, in *Pour Léon Poliakov, La raisonné, mythes et sciences* (Bruxelles, 1981), 269. (128) Lambert, AfO 27 (1980), 74. (131) Lambert, AfO 27 (1980), 74. (135) See Pettinato, OrAn 9 (1979), 78; Moran, *Studies Reiner*, 249. (144) George and Al-Rawi, *Iraq* 58 (1996), 185. (152) The proposal of Westhuizen, CRRAI 32 (1985), 91–92 is excluded by collation. (159) See Shehata, AB, 53. (180 j, k) and (190) George, BiOr 49 (1992), 761. (199) For this passage, I follow many of the proposals made by Moran, BASOR 200 (1970), 48–56; see also G. Pettinato, *Das altorientalische Menschenbild und die sumerischen und akkadischen Schöpfungsmythen* (Heidelberg: 1971), 101–104; and, Bottéro, CRRAI 26 (1979), 32 and note 81 (see p. 44), also *Studies Diakonoff*, 23–32 (206) Variant: "every month" (K 17853 = AfO 27 [1980], 74). (215) Note that the reading *eṭemmu* used here is explicitly denied by von Soden, *Studies Böhl*, 350–352; see ZA 68 (1978), 65–66, 80–81. Differently Bottéro, *Studies Diakonoff*, 26–27. "From" here could mean "by means of." (231) von Soden, TUAT III/4, 624, saw a dual here, but it appears that only Nintu does the mixing. (275) von Soden, TUAT III/4, 625. (276) [*iḫ*]-*ti-ru!*, with Stol, *Birth in Babylonia*, 115. (292) Lambert's reading with ḪA, against *erû*, is supported by the Late Assyrian fragment K 17752, AfO 27 (1980), 75. Stol, *Birth in Babylonia*, 116 note 35, suggests *wurrû(m)* "cut off." (297) von Soden reads "lege hin die Matte!" in ZA 68 (1978), 68, but I follow Lambert in construing both of the epigraphically difficult readings for the last word in A and E according to the late manuscript P (= CT 46 13 rev. 11), which has *ke-e-ša*. (300) Reading *li-iḫ-ti-[ru]*; see Borger, HKL 2, 158; Moran, *Biblica* 52 (1971), 58; von Soden, TUAT III/4, 626. (336) von Soden, OLZ 1977, 29. (337) von Soden, ZA 68 (1978), 70. (370) *a-di ma-<ti>-mi* (WLM). (374) von Soden, ZA 67 (1977), 236–237 sees here a second, Hurrian, word for "elder," but this is doubtful. His proposal *i-[bi]* at the end of the line, ZA 68 (1978), 72, has not been adopted here. (377) Moran, *Biblica* 52 (1971), 54. (384) von Soden, N.A.B.U. 1991/55. (II i 14) Emending using the parallel passage II iv 2; otherwise, read "gently" for "below" (so, e.g., von Soden, MDOG 111 [1979], 32). (II ii) Lines 7–12 are from JSS 5 (1960), 123, CT 46 41; a first-millennium version; 13–35 from BRM 4 1 and *Atrahasis*, pl. 2. (II ii 19) Kraus, RA 69 (1970), 143; earlier references in Borger, HKL 2, 158; further von Soden, TUAT III/4, 630. (II iii) For discussion, see Moran, *Studies Reiner*, 251. (II iv) Moran, RA 79 (1985), 90; several readings and interpretations from Groneberg, *Studies Garelli*, 397–408. (II iv 12) George and Al-Rawi, *Iraq* 58 (1996), 190; Wilcke, N.A.B.U. 1997/120 (also III v 45). (II iv 14) Chase, JCS 39 (1987), 241–246; Propp, N.A.B.U. 1989/68; Groneberg, *Studies Garelli*, 399. (II v 24) Klein, N.A.B.U. 1990/99, though the restorations proposed there do not fit the copy; Groneberg, *Studies Garelli*, 401–408, with collations. (II vi 17) Veenhof, JEOL 24 (1975/6), 108. For a different view, Jacobsen, *Studies Finkelstein*, 114 note 11. (II vi 25) Wilcke, N.A.B.U. 1997/120. (II vii 37) von Soden, OrNS 38 (1969), 430; Moran, BASOR 200 (1970), 54 note 3; Kilmer, *Studies Finkelstein*, 132. (II vii 38) von Soden, TUAT III/4, 636. (III i 14) Borger, HKL 2, 158; von Soden, TUAT III/4, 637. (III i 17) von Soden, OrNS 38 (1969), 431. (III i 24) Hoffner, AOAT 25, 241–245 argues that *ma-ak-ku-ra* refers to "ark," that is, a large boat. This proposal does not take into account the writing *ma-ku-ra* for "ark" in v 5 of the same manuscript. Compare also CAD M/ 1, 135. I adopt his understanding of *ubut* in the preceding line; von Soden suggests *napādu* (TUAT III/4, 637). (III i 28) Durand, N.A.B.U. 1995/49. (III i 31) Shaffer, RA 75 (1981), 188; Naster, *Studies Böhl*, 295–298. (III i 37) Deller-Mayer, OrNS 53 (1984), 121, but difficult. (III ii 13) Stol,

AfO 35 (1988), 78. (III ii 32–33) Based on suggestion of WLM. (III ii 45) Charpin, N.A.B.U. 1993/123. (III ii 50) WLM; see Zamudio, *Aula Orientalis* 14 (1996), 133–136. (III iii 16) With von Soden, OrNS 38 (1969), 431. (III iii 19) Or, possibly, "sheep," von Soden, TUAT III/4, 640; I follow Wilcke, in *Weltende*, 89 for this passage. (III iii 24) von Soden, TUAT III/4, 640. (III iii 29) *ú-ka-la-la*: difficult. R-stem of *akālu*, built on a D for the two lips? (III iii 40) Moran, JCS 33 (1981), 44. (III iii 45) With WLM; von Soden, MDOG 111 (1979), 29 "über mir"; Lambert, *Atrahasis*, 95 "cut off from me." (III iii 47) *šaḫurru* may be singular here. (III iii 50) Or possibly, "enemies," (von Soden, OrNS 38 [1969], 432), though the copy favors the former. This is perhaps an ironic reference to starvation. More recently von Soden suggests *na-aq-[d]u!-ti*, TUAT III/4, 641. (III iv 5) von Soden, OrNS 38 (1969), 432 reads "two floods"; Lambert, "what?" (III iv 6) For this passage see Lambert, CRRAI 26 (1979), 57. (III iv 7/8) Note that this reading was specifically rejected by Lambert, OrNS 38 (1969), 537. (III v 46) *zubu*. Lambert and others read "flies," but the word is not written the same way and may conceal some pun; see page 252 note 1. (III v 47) The proposal of Saporetti, *Egitto e Vicino Oriente* 5 (1982), 60: *i-ba-an-ʿqaʾ-a[m]*, seems to me unlikely; differently von Soden, TUAT III/4, 642. (III vi 9) Text: *ʿpiʾ-ti-iš-tum*, otherwise unknown; emended by Lambert on the basis of Gilgamesh XI.173. (III vi 48) Lambert, CRRAI 26 (1979), 58. (III viii 14) *ga[bra]m*(?) "rendition, copy"(??), but this is doubtful. (II 36b.1 5) Emendation von Soden, OrNS 38 (1969), 432; tablet seems to have a corrupt text. (II 36b.2 8) Borger, RA 64 (1970), 189. (II.36c V 61–74) See Butler, AOAT 258 (1998), 228–229. (II.36d I i 31) For this corrupt line, see most recently Lambert, AfO 27 (1980), 72. (I ii 8′–34′) Lambert, AfO 27 (1980), 71–73; *Studies Garelli*, 412–413. (I iii 23′) The proposal of Durand, RA 73 (1979), 155 note 6, fails to take into account K 10097 (*Atrahasis*, xi); see also Jacobsen, OrNS 42 (1973), 290 note 63. (I iv 18) See K 10604 = Lambert, OrNS 38 (1969), 533. (I iv 38) K 18479=Lambert, AfO 27 (1980), 74. (I iv 49b) With Wilcke, N.A.B.U. 1997/120. (I v 23/4, vi 12) Differently Klein, N.A.B.U. 1990/98.

J. IMITATIONS OF THE CLASSICAL STYLE

Mesopotamian readers of the Mature and Late periods esteemed their Classical heritage, studied its language and writing in school, and tried to reproduce Classical manuscripts exactly. Some writers responded to an impulse to compose in the Classical style, either because they admired it or because they believed that this would lend their works greater antiquity or authority. The three examples chosen here include a literary composition affecting the Classical hymnic-epic dialect (II.37), a set piece for school study, in which the students were supposed to write out a dictation in the form of a Classical-period commemorative cone in archaizing Classical script (II.38), and a letter supposedly written by Samsuiluna, the son of Hammurabi, which was probably made up sometime in the late second millennium B.C. (II.39).

II.37 ISHTAR, HARASSER OF MEN

In this poem, the goddess Ishtar presides over the pleasures and maladies of love. The song begins by attributing to her responsibility for harmony and hostility in human relationships. Then it describes a slapstick ritual in which men and women reverse roles. The women, carrying male weaponry, harass the men with aggressive sexual advances, while the men carry domestic and feminine objects and submit to physical and verbal abuse. Jesters (see III.21) cavort in the crowd in feminine apparel, perhaps burlesquing menstruation with shouts and gestures. Part of the activity takes place near a reed enclosure, which may symbolize consummation of marriage, and which the jesters seem to travesty by preparing for a mock interment. As the occasion turns to consumption of alcohol, the text breaks off, and what remains of it thereafter is not sufficiently comprehensible for translation.

Although composed in the Classical literary dialect and copied out in Classical script, this text gives many indications, in spelling and choice of words, of being a Late imposture by an accomplished writer who wished to make the work look much older than it actually was.

i

My lady, let me tell of your divine valor,   (1)
Let the [chamber?] resound with the sound,
    may whoever is present listen!
O Ishtar, I will praise your capable* wisdom,
Let him listen, may the one present
    hear of your valor by the sound,
May the clamor call him here quickly!*   (5)

Sing for joy, O Ishtar, let them extol your great deeds,
Let them hear this song within,
It swells up, like a cresting flood,
    at the strength of your virility.
He's on the way, that one who had
    no experience of your power,*
Your footsteps will guide (him) till the end of time.   (10)

The inexpert man will learn from this,
He will seek out your doors ere
    you have laid your hand on him.
Your doings are strange, your ways unfathomable,
So many are your deeds, what god would not be like you?
Humility, ...   (15)

Leveling a home and plundering
    (its) bricks are yours, O Ishtar,
Overturning the broad seat of emotion and contentment,
Fickleness and rejection at night are yours, O Ishtar.
Discord, disturbance, uncertainty, estrangement,
Torch of strife and extinguishing conflicts[1] are yours, O Ishtar. (20)

Anger, fighting, smoulder then cooling,
Cursing, holding the tongue are yours, O Ishtar.
Falsification of truth(?), ... in the land, parlaying fair words,
Doubling tasks and dispersing stores are yours, O Ishtar.
Dignity, entreaty, good fortune, and divine protection,   (25)
Wealth, abundance, and a bed on the ground
    are yours, O Ishtar.

1. Refurbishment of II.10a, epilogue line 30? (see p. 131).

Blood relative, kinless, foreigner, underling,
Stranger, to make them brethren, is yours, O Ishtar.
[Bestowing?] success on a house and
    the woman who dwells there,
Causing an angry breach
    wherever you will are yours, O Ishtar.   (30)

Whip, bond, [ ], the command of dominance,
Partners who know …, increased income are yours, O Ishtar.
Fear, secrecy, wakefulness(?), and terror,
Preeminence, responsiveness, and wisdom are yours, O Ishtar.

Sensuality and foolish …, the best men can do,   (35)
Making a good bedroom(?) at home are yours, O Ishtar.
Raising loud battle cries, teeth chattering in fear,
Coiffing, playing with hair are yours, O Ishtar.

Misogyny, taking goddess and harlot for lover,
Making engagements, providing gifts
    are yours, O Ishtar.   (40)
Opening the loins to the lover's urge,
Twin babies, founding a family,
    then watching (it grow) are yours, O Ishtar.

Linen, moths, tender lips, the gift of a child,
Palm fronds,[1] marriage, and success in the bedroom
    are yours, O Ishtar.
Turning man to woman, girl to youth,   (45)
You made him play the tune[2]—that is yours, O Ishtar.

Gathering of women, forming a circle, luxuriant hair,
(Shouting) "how now!",[3]
    … and intimidation are yours, O Ishtar.
Weakness, strength, child-bearing, breast(?), infant,
Sleep, dreams, and satisfaction in bed(?) are yours, O Ishtar.   (50)

        (fragmentary lines, then gap)

---

   1. The palm frond is commonly associated with Ishtar, but perhaps here refers to some ceremonial use at a wedding.
   2. Literally: "You put his cheek to the flute."
   3. kiki: a cry of unknown meaning.

(ii)

Role reversed, he looks quite different!   (1)
Yes to your mockery, shiver at that "Yes!" O Ishtar!
You made men obedient with clothes
        and locks of hair, O Ishtar!
The women are feeling over a splendid young man,
        they are bold with their hair!
A man carries a salad-leaf in his hand,   (5)
A woman has a quiver like a man, she's holding a bow,
A man carries a hairpin, a mussel shell,
        kindling, and a girl's harp,
Women carry throw sticks, slingshots, and slingstones,
A man holds their gear for them, he looks quite different!

The reed enclosure is set up for him,
        they go around outside it,
        he signals with his hand.   (10)
Then a woman, dressed like a man,
        was making a bold move,
He got in her way, she points, then he ... twice.
Men carry daggers with fluttering wrappings,
As lovers they are frightening to look upon,
        they shout like flooding water:
"Go into an angle of the city wall, satisfy him, sweetie,
        preserve a souvenir of him!"[1]   (15)
One of the jesters keeps shouting, "Keep clean, long life!"
        as he buries a ...
Their backsides are peculiar, what they do is bizarre,
They hold spindles, they circle(?) you with demonic desire.
The men wear hair combs,
        their clothes are pretty as a woman's,
They wear pretty hats, and, as if renewing every month ...   (20)

---

1. Literally: "O my womb, have intercourse and save his name." The first vocative may be
obscene or disrespectful; the second sentence could mean to save his reputation or, perhaps
jocularly, that she will become pregnant and so preserve his family from extinction. For the city
wall as a trysting place, compare III.43e.

Your love charms are ready for the whole world to see,
Everyone goes by having a good time,
    pouring out quart-vessels before you,
The drinking tube(?)[1] is conveniently ready, night and day.

(fragmentary lines)

Text: Groneberg, *Lob der Ištar*, pl. I–XXVI.
Edition: Groneberg, *Lob der Ištar*, 22–54.
Literature: W. G. Lambert, AfO 46/47 (1999/2000), 274–276, with suggestions used here.
★Notes to Text: (i 3) Taking *la-wi-am* as a pseudo-archaism for *le'am*. (i 5) Taking *li-bí-a* as a pseudo-archaic precative of *nabû*. (I 9) Taking *šu* as a pseudo-archaism for *ša*.

---

1.   Mesopotamians often drank fermented beverages through tubes, perhaps to avoid dregs.

II.38 TO A PASSER–BY

This anthology piece purports to be a grave inscription addressed to anyone passing by, calling upon him to put the tomb in order. It was inscribed on six barrel-shaped cylinders, no two of which were the same, in archaizing script. This unique state of affairs is best explained by understanding the composition as a homework assignment in school. The text was dictated by the master, then copied out by the student in old-fashioned script and spelling on old-fashioned cylinders. Some students did well; others misspelled words, made signs poorly, and even wrote in the wrong direction on the cylinder. There is reason to believe that at least two of the students worked together or that one copied from the other. The language appears in many respects Classical, but later expressions, spellings, and grammar show that it was composed at a later date and made to look Classical. The peculiar choice of the plural for "spirit" in the last line may have been influenced by a similar usage in the prologue to the laws of Hammurabi (see p. 127 note 3), which was studied in Babylonian schools of the second and first millennia B.C. The cylinders were turned into the teacher, but he never gave them back to the students, so they were all found in one place by an antiquities robber about 1900.

In the future,	(1)
In times to come,	
In far-off days,	
In times hereafter,	
May he who shall see this tomb	(5)
Not do away with it,	
May he restore it.	
That man who shall see this,	
Who shall not be disrespectful,	
Who shall speak on this wise,	(10)
"I should restore this tomb,"	
May the good deed he has done	
Be requited him.	
Above, may his name be in favor,	
Below, may his spirits drink pure waters!	

Text: Thureau-Dangin, OLZ 4 (1901), 5 = Messerschmidt-Schroeder, VAS 1 54 (VA 3117); Deimel, Or 6 (1923), 62; Stephens, YOS 9 83; Messerschmidt-Schroeder, VAS 1 54 (VA 3114); Scheil RT 22 (1900), 154–155; LB 22 (unpublished exemplar in the Böhl Collection Leiden, courtesy W. van Soldt).

Edition: B. R. Foster, "Late Babylonian Schooldays: An Archaizing Cylinder," AOAT 274 (2003), 79–87.

Translation: Bottéro in G. Gnoli, J.-P. Vernant, eds., *La mort, les morts dans les sociétés anciennes* (Cambridge and Paris, 1982), 387–389.

II.39 PRIESTLY ABUSE OF OFFICE

Purporting to be a letter of Samsuiluna (see II.11) to a governor, this composition denounces corruption in the Babylonian priesthood. Internal evidence,
noted by Al-Rawi and George, suggests that it may have been written during
the reign of Nebuchadnezzar II (see III.12). Its harsh language suggests that the
king was trying to implement measures of a religious nature and was meeting
with opposition. Since texts of Hammurabi were well known, perhaps his less
well-known son and successor was chosen as the putative author of this trac-
tate. Other references to Samsuiluna are known in later literature, but these are
not well enough preserved to understand their import (see II.11).

> (§1) Say to Enlil-nadin-shumi, governor of the land ..., offspring
> of noble loins, commanding officer of every [holy place?] of Babylo-
> nia,[1] thus says Samsuiluna, king of the universe ...:
> (§2) Concerning all the holy places of Babylonia, from one end of
> the land to the other, which I have placed entirely in your hands, I
> have heard that the temple staff, governing collegium, cultic offi-
> ciants, and attendants to the gods of every holy place of the land of
> Babylonia have taken up dishonesty, commit sacrilege, have stained
> themselves with blood, and averred improprieties. Inwardly they
> profane(?) and blaspheme(?) their gods, all the while strutting about
> talking nonsense. They establish for their gods matters that the gods
> did not command.
> (§3) The great lord Marduk, king of the gods, perfect one, hero
> among his brethren, after he created gods and humankind, he or-
> dained their destinies: the purifying exorcist to cure people ..., the
> singer of laments to appease the heart of an angry god, rites for prog-
> nostication, intercession, and lamenting ... (*gap*)
> (§4) Now then, before the great gods, on account of their vice and
> sacrilege against the gods, do you destroy them, burn them, roast
> them, [throw them] into ovens,[2] see that their smoke rises up, make
> a fiery spectacle of them in raging bonfires of thorn bushes! Then ev-
> ery anointer (for divine office) should witness and learn, they should

1. Text: "Akkad," using an old term for Babylonia.
2. Burning a malefactor in an oven is attested in a Classical-period letter (Stol, AbB 9 [1981],
127 no. 197).

be afraid to speak to me, Samsuiluna, the mighty king, about the commands of Anu and Enlil!

Text: Gurney, UET 7 155, rev. v; Al-Rawi, *Iraq* 56 (1994), 136.

Edition: F. Al-Rawi, A. George, "Two Royal Counterfeits, Letter of Samsu-iluna to Enlil-nādin-šumi," *Iraq* 56 (1994), 135–139.

CHAPTER III

THE MATURE PERIOD
(1500–1000 B.C.)

The Mature period of Akkadian literature, approximately the second half of the second millennium B.C., has to be considered against a historical background very different from that of the Classical period. Following the fall of the First Babylonian dynasty to the Hittites in the sixteenth century, and the decline, somewhat earlier, of Assyrian military power, a political "dark age" set in, about which little is known.[1] Mesopotamia was ruled in the south by the Kassites, a people of non-Mesopotamian origin, and in Assyria by the Hurrians from their kingdom of Mittani, centered in the Khabur region.[2] In Anatolia, the Hittites ruled from their capital Hattusha on the central Anatolian plateau.[3]

At the beginning of the Mature period, both Babylonia and Assyria were thus ruled by non-Mesopotamian peoples who were nevertheless under considerable Mesopotamian cultural influence. The Kassites and Hurrians created new political entities whose size and interconnections permitted wide diffusion of Mesopotamian cultural tradition such that, by the end of the second millennium, Akkadian was the lingua franca of the entire Near East. Akkadian inevitably acquired an academic character, especially in regions where the language was not widely understood.

Toward the end of the Mature period, there was a resurgence of Assyrian and Babylonian national feeling. Assyria threw off Hurrian political domination and embarked on a new imperial phase. In Babylon, a native dynasty was re-established under Nebuchadnezzar I.

1. A. Kuhrt, *The Ancient Near East c. 3000–330 BC* (London, 1995), Part II, "The Great Powers," 1:185–381. The term "dark age" refers to modern historical ignorance rather than conditions in the period itself; see T. Mommsen, "Petrarch's Conception of the 'Dark Ages'," *Speculum* 17 (1942), 226–242.

2. For the Kassites, see J. Brinkman, "Kassiten," RLA 5, 464–473. For the Hurrians, extensive bibliography can be found in *Revue Hittite et Asianique* 36 (1978) and M. T. Barrelet et al., *Methodologie et critiques I: problèmes concernant les Hurrites* (Paris, 1977).

3. The standard works are A. Goetze, *Kleinasien*[2] (Munich, 1957), and O. R. Gurney, *The Hittites* (Pelican Books, 1952 and following); T. Bryce, *The Kingdom of the Hittites* (Oxford, 1998).

Throughout the Mature period, Assyria and Babylonia were political and cultural rivals, though heirs to a common tradition. Each expressed local pride and heritage in literature. Yet so much was Assyria under Babylonian cultural influence that even Assyrian nationalistic literature was written in the Babylonian literary dialect, or sometimes dialectal Sumerian (see General Introduction, A.3).[1]

Notwithstanding this influence, Assyrian hymns, prayers, and psalms (see III.2–4) can have a distinctive regional style, characterized by turgid verbosity and emphasis on the unique importance of Assyrian kingship in the universe. For example, what may be a fragment of a royal hymn in the name of Assur-bel-kala (1074–1057 B.C.) opens as follows:[2]

> To Adad, irrigator of heaven and earth,
> [Who rides] furious storms, thundering to the clamor of [   ],
> Who is possessed of vast terrors
>   [and] awe-inspiring luminosity,
> God without whom no verdicts are established
>   in heaven or netherworld,
> Light, illumination(?) of all peoples,
> For (Adad), who holds the link
>   of heaven and netherworld, his lord:
> Assur-bel-kala, whose name the god invoked
>   from the whole of Assyria,
> Leader and general for the gods [   ],

A typically Assyrian literary genre was the royal epic. The earliest preserved example deals with the exploits of Adad-nerari I (1307–1295 B.C.) against the Kassite king Nazimaruttash (1393–1298 B.C.). The text opens with the fulsome praise of the king characteristic of Assyrian literature:

> Fierce envoy of combat, favorite of the [great?] gods,
> Who winnows the enemy like a pitchfork,
>   who mashes [the ... together like a ...],
> Fierce Adad-nerari, favorite of the [great] gods,
> Who winnows the enemy like a pitchfork,
>   who mashes [the ... together like a ...],

---

1. W. von Soden, "Einige Bemerkungen zur Übernahme babylonischer Literaturwerke im neuassyrischen Grossreich," CRRAI 39 (1992), 177–180.
2. Strong, JRAS 1892, 342–343.

> Trusty herdsman of the people of this land,
>> shepherd of [the people],
> Valiant vanguard of the army, trust of [   ],
> Purifier who keeps pure the cleansing rites of the [great] gods,
> Reliable administrator of Ekur, favorite of the god [Enlil]:
> When Ishtar summoned w[arriors to battle],
> She brought down destruction upon me and [   ],
> Irnina's heart raged, [she ... for] battle.[1]

Possible models for these royal epics are poems of the Classical period about the deeds of the Sargonic kings (see II.6, 7). Similar texts were known in Assyria (see I.6). These show that Akkadian epic-style compositions existed by the early second millennium B.C., though none of them is so long as the Assyrian royal epics. The length and complexity of the Adad-nerari epic suggests that it belonged to a fully developed Assyrian royal epic tradition, even though no earlier examples have been preserved.

One can only speculate about the Assyrian attitude toward Babylonian cultural superiority. It may have varied with the personalities and interests of individual kings or court scholars. In the thirteenth century B.C., during the reign of Tukulti-Ninurta I, for example, Assyrian scholars studied Babylonian literary works brought back as booty to Assyria, at the same time cultivating their own distinctive literary style (see III.1).

With respect to Babylonian epic poetry, the only known Kassite-period epic is too fragmentary to include here.[2] An epic of a late–thirteenth-century Babylonian king, Adad-shuma-usur, is also too fragmentary to include.[3] The Kassite court was undoubtedly a center for literary activity; the Poem of the Righteous Sufferer (III.14), for example, may have been written by or about an important courtier there.

A rich assortment of texts focused on recent or contemporaneous events was produced at the court of Nebuchadnezzar I. One group of these portrays the disasters preceding his reign, when the Elamites invaded and an Elamite ruler claimed the Babylonian throne. Then the true king, Nebuchadnezzar, of impeccable antediluvian Sumerian ancestry, ascended the throne, the Elamites

---

1. Text = Schroeder, KAH II 143 = Ebeling, KAR 260; Borger, AfO 17 (1954/6), 369; Köcher, AfO 20 (1963), pl. V (VAT 9820, obv. only); VAT 10899 (unpublished), excerpts quoted by Weidner, AfO 20 (1963), 113–115. For this passage, see Wilcke, ZA 67 (1977), 187–191.
2. A. K. Grayson, BHLT, 47–55 (war with Elam?).
3. Grayson, BHLT, 56–77.

were defeated, and Marduk returned joyfully to Babylon. These narratives are less bombastic than the Assyrian epics; the lines are shorter and less weighted down with verbiage, the narrative style less ponderous. Unlike the Assyrian king, Nebuchadnezzar could have moments of self-doubt and failure. Some scholars date the Epic of Creation (III.17) to this period. It presents a decidedly Babylonian view of universal history, to the extent of excluding Enlil and his city Nippur, and so may be considered a nationalistic, political work, despite its theological emphasis. The absence of reference to Nippur, a city of first-rate importance in Kassite Babylonia, favors a post-Kassite date.

Evaluation of the literary developments of the Mature period is hampered by a paucity of manuscripts, especially from Babylonia. There is no way to be certain that all the works ascribed here to the Mature period were actually composed then, rather than in the Late or Classical periods. Criteria for dating texts include their language, subject matter, form, and personal names or other historical data within the texts, but these criteria are often debated and interpreted differently by different scholars.[1]

Akkadian literature of the Mature period shows the handiwork of authors deeply interested in words and language as objects of study. Rare words appear in literary texts, some presumably literary words, others dialectal within Akkadian, others drawn from scholarly works (see General Introduction, D.3). Allusive, intricate, and complicated expressions were esteemed (Great Hymn to Nabu [III.31], possibly dating to the Late period). Manuscripts from different repositories were studied and edited.[2] Philology flourished, both for its own sake and as a hermeneutic science that was to have a particular impact on literature.[3]

Although Sumerian had long been a dead, academic language, it was cultivated as a learned, artificial means of expression in literary works, religious observances, royal inscriptions, and devotional inscriptions on cylinder seals.[4]

---

1. The difficulties are discussed by W. von Soden, "Das Problem der zeitlichen Einordnung akkadischer Literaturwerke," MDOG 85 (1953), 14–26; W. G. Lambert, "Zum Forschungsstand der sumerisch-babylonischen Literaturgeschichte," ZDMG Suppl. III/1 (1977), 64–73.

2. For example, the colophon to a manuscript of a hymn states that it was copied from "originals from Nippur and Babylon"; see H. Hunger, AOAT 2 (1968), 30, no. 44 (KAR 15).

3. W. von Soden, "Leistung und Grenze sumerischer und babylonischer Wissenschaft," Die Welt als Geschichte 2 (1936), 411–464, 509–557, reprinted in Libelli CXLII (1965).

4. A. Falkenstein, "Zur Chronologie der sumerischen Literatur, Die nachaltbabylonische Stufe," MDOG 85 (1953), 1–13; S. N. Kramer (with T. Baqir and S. Levy), "Fragments of a Diorite Statue of Kurigalzu in the Iraq Museum," Sumer 4 (1948), 1–39; H. Limet, Les Légendes des sceaux cassites (Bruxelles, 1971), with an important review by W. G. Lambert, BiOr 32 (1975), 219–223.

Bilingual Sumerian and Akkadian texts were still composed in Assyria (III.2) and Babylonia (III.12a). Major Sumerian literary compositions were copied with Akkadian translations, the origins of which are uncertain but which perhaps originated with a school of translation at Kassite Nippur. These translations, in turn, provoked alterations to the Sumerian original so that some passages were rewritten to bring them closer to the translation.[1] Mesopotamian intellectual endeavor was still carried out, therefore, in an environment of scholarly bilingualism.

On the level of form, the Mature period sees creative combination of shorter pieces into single composite texts (see Ishtar Queen of Heaven [III.26] and General Introduction, D.2). For the modern reader, these complex works abound in literary and philological difficulties; the existence of ancient commentaries shows that they were not readily accessible to the ancients either. In addition, there is a tendency to organize disparate texts such as omens, lexicography, and magic into standardized series of tablets (see Chapter IV). One senses editors, redactors, and compilers at work along with authors.

Some Assyriologists refer to the organization of ancient Mesopotamian texts into standardized form, groups, and series as "canonization."[2] They suggest that during the Mature period texts were "canonized" by making a selection among texts inherited from the past and by discarding material not in agreement with current taste or religious and ethical concepts. Texts so selected were not radically altered from their previous forms, and new material was composed along "canonical" lines. This process is still poorly understood, and use of the term "canonization," with its scriptural overtones, can be misleading.

National feeling in Mesopotamia during the Mature period became an important influence on Akkadian literature. In Assyria, literature came to express an imperial ideology for which no clear Babylonian counterpart existed.[3]

---

1. S. Seminara, *La versione accadica del LUGAL-E: La tecnica babilonese della traduzione dal Sumerico e le sue 'regole'. Materiali per il vocabulario sumerico*, vol. 8 (Rome, 2001).

2. W. von Soden, "Zweisprachigkeit in der geistigen Kultur Babyloniens," *Sitzungsberichte der Österreichischer Akademie der Wissenschaften, Philologisch-historische Klasse* 235/1 (1960), 9–11; W. G. Lambert, "Ancestors, Authors, and Canonicity," JCS 11 (1959), 9; F. Rochberg-Halton, "Canonicity in Cuneiform Texts," JCS 36 (1984), 127–144; S. Lieberman, "Canonical Official Cuneiform Texts: Towards an Understanding of Assurbanipal's Personal Tablet Collection," *Studies Moran*, 305–336; W. W. Hallo, "The Concept of Canonicity in Cuneiform and Biblical Literature: A Comparative Appraisal," in K. Younger, Jr., W. W. Hallo, B. Batto, eds., *The Biblical Canon in Comparative Perspective* (Lewiston, N.Y., 1991), 1–19; Veldhuis, JCS 50 (1998), 79–82.

3. P. Garelli, "Les empires mésopotamiens," in M. Duverger, ed., *Le Concept d'Empire* (Paris, 1980), 25–43; "La Concept de la royauté en Assyrie," in F. M. Fales, ed., *Assyrian Royal Inscriptions, New Horizons*, OAC 17 (Rome, 1981), 1–11.

In both Assyria and Babylonia compositions of a markedly propagandistic character were addressed to the educated, influential class, seeking to sway opinion
with theological and ethnocentric terminology.[1]

The emergence of large states in Assyria and Babylonia implied palace-
centered governments with international interests, characterized by hierarchy,
attempt to control resources, and military adventurism.[2] At the same time,
some areas of Mesopotamia may have suffered a decline of population, with
settlement patterns tending toward agricultural villages dominated by fortified
enclaves. This suggests a wide gulf between a depressed producing population
and a military elite.[3] Times were often uncertain, and, outside of the elite, the
subject seemed farther from his ruler than in the Classical period. Literature
reflected to some degree these realities of Mesopotamian society. The gods,
whose order mirrored that of civilized Mesopotamian humanity, seemed
correspondingly more remote and difficult to understand than before, given to
harsh punishment of the weak and favoritism of the rich and powerful.[4]

Professionals in divination and the other sciences may have had considerable
influence among the elite. Their prayers and rituals tend to focus on the needs
and anxieties of the highly placed: generals, courtiers, administrators, the king
(see III.36b, 38a, b, 44c, 47b, 51h–l). Naturally professionals asserted the need
for their disciplines and formulated elaborate consultative procedures that
rendered them indispensable for military and political undertakings, as well as
for the day-to-day life of the powerful. These professionals adapted Akkadian
written tradition to their needs and ideology.[5] Professionals such as scholars,
priests, and singers of laments[6] were presumably responsible for training succeeding generations in literature, the techniques of Mesopotamian philology, edit-
ing of texts, historical research, cultivation of rhetoric, and allied disciplines.

---

1. A. L. Oppenheim, "The City of Assur in 714 B.C.," JNES 19 (1960), 133–147; "Neo-
Assyrian and Neo-Babylonian Empires," in H. Lasswell et al., eds., Propaganda and Communication
in World History (Honolulu, 1979), 1:111–144.

2. B. R. Foster, "The Late Bronze Age Economy: A View from the East," in R. Hägg and N.
Marinatos, eds., The Function of the Minoan Palaces, Proceedings of the Fourth International Symposium
at the Swedish Institute in Athens, 10–16 June, 1984, Skrifter utgivna av Svenska Institutet i Athen 4,
XXV (Stockholm, 1987), 11–16.

3. R. Mc. Adams, Heartland of Cities (Chicago, 1981), 168.

4. T. Jacobsen, The Treasures of Darkness (New Haven, 1976), 162–164.

5. A. L. Oppenheim, "The Position of the Intellectual in Mesopotamian Society," Daedalus,
Spring, 1975, 37–46; J. Pečírková, "Divination and Politics in the Late Assyrian Empire," ArOr 53
(1985), 155–168.

6. M. E. Cohen, The Canonical Lamentations of Ancient Mesopotamia (Potomac, Md., 1988),
1:11–44.

Whereas schools are known from the Classical period, little is known of them for the Mature or Late periods.[1]

Perhaps the most suggestive difference between Akkadian literature of the Classical and Mature periods is the place of humankind in the texts. Whereas in the Classical period man appears as an individual struggling in a difficult world, in the Mature period he is portrayed rather as a mortal lost in a vast, institutionalized cosmos. The hero is now not so much valorous as knowledgeable; the characteristic portrayal of the human plight is not so much servitude to the gods as ignorance and incomprehension of their ways. The exaltation of knowledge is among the most salient traits of maturing Akkadian literature.

1. Charpin, *Clergé*, 482–485; M. Dandamayev, *Vavilonskie Pisci* (Moscow, 1983), 27–29, 61–63; Kraus, *Mensch*, 18–27; B. Landsberger, "Scribal Concepts of Education" in C. Kraeling and R. Mc. Adams, eds., *City Invincible* (Chicago, 1960), 94–102; Å. W. Sjöberg, "The Old Babylonian Eduba," AS 20 (1975), 159–179; H. Vanstiphout, "How Did They Learn Sumerian?" JCS 31 (1979), 118–126; H. Waetzoldt, "Keilschrift und Schulen in Mesopotamien und Ebla," in L. Kriss-Rettenbeck and M. Liedtke, eds., *Erziehungs- und Unterrichtsmethoden im historischen Wandel* (Bad Heilbrunn, 1986), 36–50; "Der Schreiber als Lehrer in Mesopotamien," in J. von Hohenzollern and M. Liedtke, eds., *Magister, Lehrer, zur Geschichte und Funktion eines Berufstandes* (Bad Heilbrunn, 1989), 33–50; S. Tinney, "On the Curricular Setting of Sumerian Literature," *Iraq* 59 (1999), 159–172; N. Veldhuis, "Sumerian Proverbs in Their Curricular Context," JAOS 120 (2000), 383–399; P. Gesche, *Schulunterricht in Babylonien im ersten Jahrtausend v. Chr*, AOAT 275 (2000); E. Robson, "The Tablet House: A Scribal School in Old Babylonian Nippur," RA 95 (2001), 39–66.

A. KINGS OF ASSYRIA AND THEIR TIMES

III.1 TUKULTI-NINURTA EPIC

Tukulti-Ninurta I, a tragic and fascinating Assyrian king of the thirteenth century B.C., began his reign with significant conquests, including parts of northern Syria, Anatolia, and Babylonia. In Babylon he ruled as king for seven years. Royal agents included scholarly and literary manuscripts among the booty brought back from Babylonia. These may have stimulated literary activity in Assyria and provided writers with new themes and language.

One impressive achievement of this Assyrian renaissance is the bilingual prayer translated below, III.2, which demonstrates a capacity to compose original work in dialectal Sumerian in this period. The text treated here, the epic of Tukulti-Ninurta, is the product of a mature and learned master steeped both in Babylonian and Assyrian tradition. The text presents a distinctive, turgid splendor of language, with rare words and convoluted syntax. The idioms of treaties and diplomacy, penitential psalms and laments, heroic tales, hymnography, and commemorative inscriptions are freely used. One may speculate that the prayer and the epic came from the same hand; close to the troubled monarch was a brilliant scholar and poet whose work appealed to the king's taste.

As part of his booty, Tukulti-Ninurta brought the statue of Marduk from his temple in Babylon to Assur. The image remained in Assur for a century, to the Babylonians a maddening symbol of their political and military impotence. Furthermore, large numbers of Babylonians and Kassites were resettled in Assyria. The extent to which the king and his scholar attempted to cultivate Babylonian ways and religion at Assur is unknown. Marduk's image was treated with respect. Discontent with the influx of Babylonian ideas into Assyria may have contributed to Tukulti-Ninurta's downfall.

Having reached the natural limits of his conquests early in his reign, Tukulti-Ninurta turned his formidable energies to a massive, even frenetic building campaign. After living in the "Old Palace" at Assur, he reconstructed a palace built by his father, Shalmaneser I. Soon thereafter he cleared a large residential area and built yet another palace with walls to connect it to the fortified sector of the city. Hardly was this done when he began to build a whole new city, Kar-Tukulti-Ninurta, across the Tigris and thus isolated from the traditional capital of the land. There he seems to have shut himself up in suspicion of all around him.

The king's outrageous demands on his subjects for building enterprises opened the way for a successful conspiracy against him led by his own son. Tukulti-Ninurta was confined and murdered in his new palace.

For a portrait of this king and his times, see E. F. Weidner, "Studien zur Zeitgeschichte Tukulti-Ninurtas I.," AfO 13 (1939/41), 109–124. For English translations of his historical inscriptions and relevant passages in the Babylonian chronicles, see Grayson, ARI 1, 101–134. See also the essay on the king's personality by W. von Soden, *Herrscher im alten Orient* (Berlin, 1954), 69–74. Another account will be found by H. Klengel, "Tukulti-Ninurta I., König von Assyrien," *Das Altertum* 7 (1961), 67–77. For a study of his Babylonian campaign, see W. Mayer, "Der babylonische Feldzug Tukulti-Ninurtas I. von Assyrien," *Studi Epigrafici e Linguistici sul Vicino Oriente Antico* 5 (1988), 143–161.

i (= K 6007)

(Praises of the god Assur and of the king, Tukulti-Ninurta)

Listen to his praise, the praises of the king of [ ] lords,	(1)
I ex[tol] the [ ] of lord of the world, the Assyrian Enlil,	
Let his mighty power, his [ ] be spoken of,	
[Hear] how great his weapons were over his enemies!	
I extol and praise Assur, king of [the gods],	(5)
The great kings also [ ]	
Whom [he ...] in the campaign against Kadm[uhi],*	
And (whom) by command of the w[arrior] Shamash [he ...],	
Aside from the forty kings of [Nairi]¹	
Whom, in his reign [ ]	(10)
The triumph of his lordship [ ]	

(fragmentary lines)

i (= B obv.)

(gap)

(Introduction of the protagonist: the valiant Tukulti-Ninurta [in the broken section] and his antagonist, the treacherous Kashtiliash [as the text becomes intelligible]. The Babylonian gods become angry with Kashtiliash and forsake his sanctuaries, a sign of impending doom. After a gap in the text [A obv.], there is a fragmentary hymn to

---

1. For the incident referred to, see Grayson, ARI 1, 119.

Tukulti-Ninurta, with allusions to his birth and upbringing. In i 30' Kashtiliash is referred to again. He disdains his sworn treaty [of friendship and non-aggression?] and plots war.)

[ ] against enemies [ ]	
[ ]	
[ ] no(?) surviving [ ]	
[ ] which cannot be faced [ ]	
[ ] the wicked [ ]	(10')
[ ] and the disobedient [ ]	
[ ] … [ ]	
[the dis]obedient [ ]	
[ ] command [ ]	

(gap of nine lines)

[ ] and [ ]	(20')
[ ] to transgress [ ]	
[ ] … [ ]	
[ ] … light [ ]	
[ ] the end of the reign of [ ]	
[w]arrior of heaven and netherworld.	(25')
[ ] which he took by force [ ]	
[ ] the land that he ruled [ ]	
[ ] … [ ]	
[ ] Ishtar, the high point of the land of Akkad [ ]	
[fr]om(?) lordship the king of the Kassites	(30')
[guilt] that cannot be expunged.	

[The gods became angry at] the king of the Kassite's betrayal
      of the emblem [of Shamash],
Against the transgressor of an oath, Kashtiliash,
      the gods of heaven and netherworld [   ].
They were [angry] at the king, the land, and the people [ ],
They [were furious and with] the willful one, their shepherd.   (35')
His lordship, the lord of the world,[1]
      became disturbed, so he [forsook] Nippur,
He would not approach [   ] (his) seat at Dur-Kurigalzu.

---

1. Enlil.

Marduk abandoned his sublime sanctuary, the city [Babylon],
He cursed his favorite city Kar-[   ].
Sin left Ur, [his] holy place [   ],   (40′)
Sh[amash became angry] with Sippar and Larsa,
Ea [   ] Eridu, the house of wisdom [   ],
Ishtaran became furious w[ith Der   ],
Annunitu would not approach Agade [   ],
The lady of Uruk cast [off her   ]:   (45′)
(All) the gods were enraged [   ]
[   ] on account of the verdict [   ]

(gap)

i (= A obv.)

[   ] his ..., Assur.
[   ] the gods, lord of judgment,
[   ] he has none to calm him,
[   ] bears him   (5′)
[   ] he made light of the oath of the gods!
[   ] ... defeat,
[Who obeys] the gods' intents on the battlefield,
[   ] he made the weapons glorious.
Glorious is his heroism,
          it [   ] the dis[respectful] front and rear,   (10′)
Incendiary is his onrush,
          it burns the disobedient right and left.
His radiance is terrifying; it overwhelms all foes,
Every pious* king of the four world regions stands in awe of him.
When he bellows like thunder, mountains totter,
And when he brandishes his weapon like Ninurta,[1]
          all regions of the earth everywhere hover in panic.   (15′)
Through the destiny of Nudimmud, he is reckoned as flesh
          godly in his limbs,*[2]
By fiat of the lord of the world, he was cast sublimely
          from the womb of the gods.
It is he who is the eternal image of Enlil,

---

1. An oblique reference to the king's name.
2. Nudimmud was a name for Ea as creator, (see III.17 Tablet I line 16).

attentive to the people's voice, the counsel of the land,
Because the lord of the world appointed him to
    lead the troops, he praised him with his own lips,
Enlil exalted him as if he (Enlil) were his (Tukulti-Ninurta's)
    own father, right after his firstborn son![1]   (20′)
Precious is he in (Enlil's) family,* for where there is
    competition, he has of him protection.
No one of all kings was ever rival to him,*
No sovereign stood forth* as his battlefield opponent.
[   ] falsehood,* crime, repression, wrong-doing,
[   ] the weighty ... * the divine oath
    and went back on what he swore.   (25′)
[   ] the gods were watching his furtive deed,
[   ] though he was their follower.
[   ] the king of the Kassites made light of what he swore,
He committed a crime, an act of malice.
[Although the one] ... kept changing [   ],
    (the other's) word is sure,   (30′)
[Although the one ...], (the other) is one who pleas
    for divine mercy always.
[   ] and shall not be expunged.
[   ] ... offenses were numerous.
[   ] he turned back on a command
[   ] he spoke hostility   (35′)
[   ] put his trust in ...
[   ] he longed for battle
[   ] stratagem

(fragmentary lines, then gap)

ii (= A obv.)

(gap)

(The Assyrians capture Babylonian merchants, who were evidently spying in Assyria, and bring them before the king. He spares them out of respect for international custom. In a prayer to Shamash, god of justice, the king states that he has been faithful to the treaty, explains how it was made, reminds the god that he oversees sworn treaties, and

---

1. That is, the god Ninurta (Machinist, diss., 206–207).

calls on him for a favorable outcome in his contest with the evildoer. In A obv. 26'ff.
Tukulti-Ninurta sends a message to Kashtiliash, reminding him of the long history of
relations between their two lands, and charging him with violation of the treaty. As
suggested by Machinist, diss., 237, the letter may have ended on a conciliatory note,
offering the opportunity for reaffirmation of the oath despite the Kassite's willful viola-
tion of it.)

> Within the confines of the land of [Assyria   ] he imposed
>   an ordinance, lest any secret [of the land?] go out.
> They came [   ] very much ...
> Those who bore the in[signia?]* of the king of the Kassites,
>   merchants were captured at night(?),*   (5')
> They brought [them] before Tukulti-Ninurta,
>   lord of all peoples, bound together.*
> The king gathered(?) [them] in the place of Shamash,
>   he perpetrated no infamy,
> (But) he sustained them,
>   he did a good deed for the lord of Babylon:
> He released the merchants ..., bearers of money bags,
> He had them stand before Shamash and anointed
>   their heads with oil.[1]   (10')
> The tablets(?) of the king of the Kassites, the seal
>   impression that he had made official,[2]
> He reconfirmed(?), before Shamash he [   ], his utterance
>   he presented in measured words to the god,*
> "O Shamash, [   ] lord, I respected(?) your oath,
>   I feared your greatness.
> "He who does not [   ] transgressed before your [   ],
>   but I observed your ordinance.
> "When our fathers made a pact before your divinity,   (15')
> "They swore an oath between them
>   and invoked your greatness.
> "You are the hero, the valiant one, who from of old
>   was inexorable judge of our fathers,

---

1. A ceremony of release (Veenhof, BiOr 23 [1966], 310–311; Machinist, diss., 229–230).
2. Probably refers to official letters given by the king to the merchants as bonafide commercial agents. If the men acted as spies, this was presumably a violation of "commercial immunity," but Tukulti-Ninurta is careful to protect them as merchants, despite their questionable status.

"And you are the god who sets aright,
  who sees now our loyalty.
"Why has the king of the Kassites from of old invalidated
  your plan and your ordinance?
"He had no fear of your oath, he transgressed your
  command, he schemed an act of malice.   (20')
"He has made his crimes enormous before you,
  judge me, O Shamash!
"But he who committed no crime [against] the king
  of the Kassites, [act favorably toward him],
"By your great [   ] bestow the victory ...
  on the observer of oaths,
"[He who does not] your command,
  obliterate his people in the rout of battle!"
[The wi]se [shepherd], who knows what should be done,
  waxed wroth, [his frigh]tening brilliance
  became enraged.   (25')
He sent a message [to Kashtili]ash the wicked,
  the obstinate, the heedless,
"[Whereas] formerly you [forswore] what belonged
  to the time of our forefathers' hostilities,
"[Now] you face Shamash with false testimony about us.
"[Enlil-nera]ri, my forefather, king of all peoples, ... [   ]
"[Against? Kur]igalzu, (he) pursued the oath of the gods, [ ]   (30')
"[Adad-n]erari, my grandfather, [   ]
"[   ] Nazimaruttash [   ] in battle [   ]
"[   ] Shalmaneser, diviner of his princeship, [   ]
"[   ] the lives of their [   ] ...
"[   ] ... (35')
"[   ] ... [   ]
"[   ] among all lands he is the inexorable judge,

(fragmentary lines, then gap)

ii (= F col. "x")

(Fragment F [Lambert, AfO 18 (1957/58), 48–51 and pl. IV] the reverse(?) of an excerpt(?) tablet that preserves a section of this epic, may belong here. For placement and interpretation, I follow Machinist, diss., 15–16, 31–33, who suggests that this piece

*deals with an affront by Kashtiliash to Tukulti-Ninurta. As read here, the Babylonian
king replies insolently to Tukulti-Ninurta's letter, while preventing the Assyrian messenger from returning, a diplomatic snub. After a gap of uncertain size, Fragment D
may be placed [Machinist, diss., 11–13]. In 1–6 Kashtiliash is threatening Tukulti-
Ninurta, and, beginning in 7, Tukulti-Ninurta replies in righteous wrath.)*

[   ] the land   (5′)

[e]nemies

[   ] he sent a [mes]sage

[   ] he had decided upon a good deed,

[   ] he affirmed the compact.

[Kashtiliash said, "...] your good deed!

     Detain the messenger (here)!   (10′)

"[   ] don't let the [merchan]ts cross!

"[   ] take away!

(fragmentary lines, then gap)

ii (= D)

"[Against] your camp ... like a thunderstorm [   ]   (1)

"[   ] like a flood that spares no [   ]

"[   ] your valiant warriors like [   ]

"[   ] the mighty onslaught of the Kas[site] army

"[   ] every stratagem in the onslaught of battle [   ],   (5)

"[   ] your warriors on an [ill-fated] day [   ]!"

[The king], the wise shepherd,

     [who knows] what should be done, [   ],

[To Kashtilia]sh, the wicked, the obstinate,

     king of the Kassites [   ],

"[The ...], Kashtiliash, of your forefathers you [   ],

"[   ] in the unp[lundered?] sanctuaries,   (10)

"[   ] my [   ], to set straight [   ]

"[   ] your warriors who [   ] combat

"[   ] of my land that you plundered [   ],

"[   ] the troops that you made off with [   ],

(fragmentary lines, including a reference to Shamash)

iii (= A obv.)

(Tukulti-Ninurta exchanges letters with Kashtiliash and indicts him for his misdeeds. Tukulti-Ninurta calls upon Shamash to resolve their differences and to vindicate his adherence to the treaty by making him victorious in trial by battle. Kashtiliash is paralyzed with fear at the prospect and offers a soliloquy on his impending doom. After a gap in the text, Tukulti-Ninurta invades Babylonia and the doomed and desperate Kassite goes berserk [Fragment C].)

"And the borders of your territories [   ],
"Why did you retreat and [ ] the road from which there
    is no escape?
"And why are you turning afraid,
    and ... without engagement [   ]?
"You have plundered my whole land, [ ] pillage,   (5')
"You have made away with the armies of Assur,
    before hostilities even, you have [   ].
"The [   ] have steadily cast down in untimely death,
"Their [wives] are become widows in undue season.
"I raise aloft, therefore, the tablet of oath between us,
    and call upon the Lord of Heaven [   ]!
"You have showed forth a crime that [ ] us both to
    the battlefield,   (10')
"Saying: 'I released your father(?),* I took no revenge.'
"That you have plundered my unarmed people
    is an offense to us[1] forever!
"When we face one another in battle,
    let the judgment between us be ... [   ].
"We shall meet* that day just as a righteous man
    plunders the [   ] of a thief.
"Reconciliation cannot be made without conflict [   ],   (15')
"Nor can there be good relations without a battle,
    so long as you do not [   ].
"(And) until I expose your hair fluttering behind you[2] and
    you have [disappeared] to an untimely death,
"Until my eyes, in the battle with you, shall see ...,
    slaughter, and ...,

1. "Us" may refer to Tukulti-Ninurta and the Assyrian people.
2. That is, in flight.

"So come to me in the battle of servants (of the gods?),
      let us get to the bottom of the matter together!
"From this festival of battle may the transgressor of oath not
      away, may they cast away(?)* his corpse!"   (20')
Tukulti-Ninurta, having put his trust in his observance
      of the oath, was planning for battle,
While Kashtiliash, insofar as he had trespassed the command
      of the gods, was altered within himself,
He was appalled on account of the appeal to Shamash
      and became fearful and anxious
         about what was laid before the gods.
The mighty king's utterance constricted his body
      like a demonic presence.
So Kashtiliash deliberated with himself,
      "I did not listen to what the Assyrian (said),
      I made light of the messenger.[1]   (25')
"I did not conciliate him,
      I did not accept his favorable intention before.
"Now I understand how grievous the crimes of my land
      are become, how numerous its sins.
"Mortal punishments have smitten me down,
      death has me in its grip!
"The oath of Shamash sets upon(?) me,
      it catches me by the hem,
"You have entered in evidence against me an unalterable
      tablet with the seal impression of m[y forefather]s,   (30')
"They too have intro[duced evidence] before me,
      a [   ] whose wording cannot be changed!
"My forefathers' treaty, which was not violated, [   ]
"Thus did the just judge, the unalterable, the valiant one,
      [Shamash] establish the case against me!
"As for the plundering that my forefathers did,
      I [have made it worse]!
"For it is I, indeed,
      who have put my people into a pitiless hand,
      a grasp [from which there is no escape].   (35')

---

1. Compare F 10', where the messenger is delayed before returning to his sender, a diplomatic insult.

"Into a narrow strait with no way out
      I have gathered [my land].
"Many are my wrongdoings before Shamash,
      [great are] my misdeeds,
"Who is the god that will spare my people from [catastrophe]?
"The Assyrian is ever heedful of all the gods [   ]
"He ... the lords of our oath,
      ... of heaven and netherworld,   (40′)
"I shall not examine in the extispicy
      (the signs for) "fa[ll of the regime]."*
"The omens for well-being of my army
      are [gone] from my land,
"The signs within the [   ] are ...
"The security of my house's foundation [ ] was never firm.
"Whatever my dream(s), they are terrifying [   ]   (45′)
"Omnipotent Assur glowers at me [   ]!"
This too: "Quickly, let me cast: [   ]
"To what shall I [ ] my omen?"*
This too: "Let me know: For ba[ttle   ]
"How long [   ]?   (50′)
"... [   ]
"Let me learn the secret [   ]
"Will he overcome me and [   ]?
"Like an inferno or a cyclone [   ]?
"He has closed in on me and [   ],   (55′)
"So death [   ]!"
He was exhausted [   ]

(fragmentary lines, then gap)

iii (= C)

[   ] he entered, and the city Akka[d   ]
And like a thunderstorm against the creatures of [... he ...]
[As for] Kashtiliash, king of the Kassites,
      who had yearned [for battle],   (5′)
And whose fondest hopes were ecstatic at comb[at   ],
He jumped from his chair and [ ] his table.
He twitched, he flung away the meat, he [   ],

He discarded his royal adornment in [   ].
He could not swallow a bite [   ].   (10′)
The dining tray was not ... where he arose [   ],
The seats of his palace, which used to be firm(?) [   ].
He mounted his chariot and harangued the hor[de?   ],
He said to his army, "I fought with [   ]!"
The king of the Kassites rushed hither
    and yon like a [   ],   (15′)
He sought all over the groves [for a place to hide   ],
He went away then turned back, with [   ].
He fled as if he were quarry, like a [   ].
No fervor raised he, with the [   ],
Nor could he [   ] his victory(?) against Annunitum.   (20′)
He did not look behind him,
    [nor] over his soldiers [did he ...]
[Nor] over his own offspring, the creation of [   ]
Kashtiliash, like one in [   ]
The dust of death [   ]

iv (= C rev.)

(Despite his doom, the obstinate Kashtiliash refuses to yield, and seeks to evade Tukulti-Ninurta's advance. Kashtiliash prefers guerilla tactics to a direct confrontation. Tukulti-Ninurta challenges him to a fight, but Kashtiliash stalls, hoping for a change of fortune. An indecisive battle is fought, apparently when Kashtiliash tries to surprise the Assyrians [A rev.].)

[   ] with the point of his ar[row   ]
Which he sent off [   ]
The king of the Kassites did not trust ... [   ]
He summoned against him [   ]   (5′)
He rained down upon him [   ]
Kashtiliash went out [   ]
"Surely our lord's treaty ... [   ]
"He will not leave the innermost [   ]
"Until he catches him alive [   ]."   (10′)
They carried off the king [   ]
And the hero of his warriors [   ]
He would not submit(?) to Tukulti-Ninurta [   ]
Nor before his warriors did he [   ]

Where the weapon of Assur joins [battle   ]   (15′)
The river banks were trampled, the cities [   ]
The king overcame the city [   ]
He turned to Annunitu [   ]
He became lord of the distant city
    that [ ] had never [ ]
He reckoned the land for devas[tation   ]   (20′)
The king set to [   ]
He established for many a distant league [   ]
He dammed up the conflu[ence   ]
He repaired the paths [   ]
He overcame the city(?) [   ]   (25′)

(gap)

iv (= A rev.)

Another time he ... [   ]   (5′)
But he did not submit before Tukulti-Ninurta [ ]
Nor would he face him [in battle   ]
Another time he ... [   ]
He was drawn up in [   ]
He decided(?) [   ]   (10′)
Tukulti-Ninurta ordered [   ]
A messenger to Kashtiliash to [   ]
"How much longer is [your army] to flee?
"You keep changing your army around by command [ ]."
Saying, "For what day are you keeping
    the [weapons] of combat [ ]?   (15′)
"And which of your weapons stands by for which day?"
Saying, "I am stationed in your land, [I   ] cult center,
"I plundered all the cities you had and [ ] your people!"
Saying, "When will your usual insolence
    [provoke you] to battle?
"The fury and slaughter you wanted so much
    we will soon show!   (20′)
"Surely now you have courage,
    for the month of the spring
    flood, the water will be your ally.

"And you have pitched your camp in remote places,
    trusting in G[irra],[1]
"But in the dry season, when the peak flood ends,
    and Sirius glows,[2]
"In what remote place will you trust to save your people?
"My army is camped not many leagues from you,   (25′)
"And as for you, all your chariotry is in readiness and
    your army is massed.
"Attack me, then, like a brave man,
    fight the battle that you strive so hard to attain!
"Show your weapon, find release in the battle
    that your fondest hopes burned for!"
Kashtiliash gave the command for battle,
    but was anxious and agitated,
Saying, "Tukulti-Ninurta, your army should stand fast
    until the appointed time of Shamash arrives.   (30′)
"Do not begin your fighting
    until the right season to fight me!"
Saying, "This is the day your people's blood
    will soak the pastures and meadows,
"And, like a thunderstorm, I will make the levelling flood
    pass over your camp."
He dragged out the message-sending as a ruse
    until he could draw up his warriors,
And until he had made ready his battle plan,
    the chariotry was held back.   (35′)
Then he despatched his army,
    but Girra held it back as with a serious mutiny.
He brought his army across secret hideouts,
    blocking the crossing.
The valiant warriors of [Assur] espied
    the Kassite king's preparations,
They did not have their armor on,
    but sprang forward like lions,
Assur's unrivalled weapon met the onslaught
    of [his] ar[my?]*   (40′)

1. The heat?
2. Compare IV.2c line 100.

And Tukulti-Ninurta, the raging, pitiless storm,
    made [their blood] flow.
The warriors of Assur [struck] the king of the Kassites
    like a serpent,
A mighty attack, an irresistible onslaught [ ] upon them.
Kashtiliash turned his [face] to save himself.
The weapon of Enlil, lord of the world,
    that hems in enemies, shattered [his troops],   (45′)
The ... of battle, his allies were slaughtered like cattle,
    [his] nobles [   ]
Governors perished, warriors [   ]
[   ] the forefinger of the lord of the world.

(fragmentary lines, then gap)

v (= A rev.)

(After Kashtiliash's flight, the Assyrian troops urge their king to a decisive encounter, no matter what the cost to them. In 31′ff. the major battle is fought at last. Kashtiliash is defeated, but any account of his fate is lost in a gap in the text. According to an inscription of Tukulti-Ninurta, Kashtiliash was captured and brought to Assur: "(I) trod with my feet upon his lordly neck," see Grayson, ARI 1, 108 [No. 5].)

The k[in]g ... [   ]
His warriors ... [   ]   (10′)
"My lord, since the beginning of your reign [   ],
"Battle and hardship have been our holiday and plea[sure].
"You urge us to prepare for the melee [   ],
"With the propitious sign of your lordship
    let us proceed like men!
"In your royal reign no king has stood equal to you,   (15′)
"Your exalted power has been set over the whole world,
    the seas, and the mountains.
"With the wrath of your scepter
    you have made to submit all regions, in all quarters,
"You spread the might of your land to territories beyond count,
    you established (their) boundaries.
"Kings know your valor and live in fear of battle with you.

"They bear your frightfulness like slander and falsehood
    homing in on the source.[1]   (20')
"Now plan against the king of the Kassites,
    destroy his forces before the season!
"Rout the ranks he has set up, burn(?) his chariotry!
"For how much longer in the future
    is he to plot this evil against us?
"Plotting basely against us, he plans murder by wont.
"Daily he hopes to destroy the land of Assur,
    his threatening finger is stretched out toward it.   (25')
"He strives constantly to take control of the Assyrians' kingship.
"Let us join battle, let him live to draw breath who advances,
    let him die who turns back! (You say),
"'While I was at peace he ended our friendly relations(?),'*
    so proceed with the battle!
"[ ], when they encouraged you before on the battlefield.
"And you will gain, our Lord, by command of Shamash,
    a victorious name over the king of the Kassites!"   (30')
The lines of battle were drawn up,
    combat was joined on the battlefield.
There was a great commotion,
    the troops were quivering among them.
Assur went first,
    the conflagration of defeat burst out upon the enemy,
Enlil was whirling(?) in the midst of the foe,
    fanning the blaze,
Anu set a pitiless mace to the opponent,   (35')
Sin, the luminary, laid upon them the tension of battle.
Adad, the hero, made wind and flood
    pour down over their fighting,
Shamash, lord of judgment, blinded the eyesight
    of the army of Sumer and Akkad,
Valiant Ninurta, vanguard of the gods, smashed their weapons,
Ishtar flailed her jump rope, driving their warriors berserk!   (40')

---

1. I take this line to mean that just as lies come home to roost on the liar, so too the king's frightfulness cannot be avoided by those lesser kings; in fact, it sticks to them like some evil that they richly deserve. (For discussion of the passage, see Machinist, diss., 341–343).

Behind the gods, his allies,
>   the king at the head of the army sets to battle,
He let fly an arrow, the fierce, overwhelming,
>   crushing weapon of Assur, he felled one slain.
The warriors of Assur cried, "To battle!"
>   as they went to face death,
They gave the battle cry, "O Ishtar, spare (me)!"
>   and praise the mistress in the fray,
They are furious, raging, taking forms strange as Anzu.   (45′)
They charge forward furiously to the fray
>   without any armor,
They had stripped off their breastplates,
>   discarded their clothing,
They tied up their hair and polished(?) their ... weapons,★
The fierce, heroic men danced with sharpened weapons.
They roared at one another like struggling lions,
>   with eyes aflash(?),★   (50′)
While the fray, particles drawn in a whirlwind,
>   swirled around in combat.★
Death, as if on a day of thirsting,
>   slakes itself at the sight of the warrior.★
[   ] furiously he attacked and turned north,

(fragmentary lines, then gap)

vi (= A rev.)

(The victorious Assyrians plunder Babylonia. The first fragment mentions prisoners and treasures. In B rev. Tukulti-Ninurta plunders collections of cuneiform tablets and brings them back to Assyria. He lavishly adorns temples there and in his royal city, Kar-Tukulti-Ninurta. In the concluding lines the poet praises the king.)

[   ] the population of the cities.
[   ] his [off]spring, the offspring of [   ]
[   ] the throne, the boundary stone [   ]
[   ] daughters of princes, dwelling in [   ]
[   ] their infants, sons and daughters.   (20′)
[   ] the enclosure of which ... for leagues,

[   ] the treasure of [   ] he plundered.[1]
[   ] innumerable subjects
[he di]d seven times in excess
[   ] he took special care for their lives.   (25′)
[   ] who could pile up their [   ]?
[   ] a trustworthy house.
[so]ldiers, number of chariots,
[   ] the treasure of(?) the king of the Kassites,
[fr]om report of(?) the battle   (30′)
[   ] scepter
[   ] of the land
[   ] war vehicles

(traces, gap)

vi (= B rev.)

Treasure [   ],
Tablets of [   ],
Scribal lore [   ],
Exorcistic texts [   ],   (5′)
Prayers to appease the gods [   ],
Divination texts ... the ominous marks(?)
          of heaven and earth,
Medical texts, procedure for bandaging [   ],
The muster lists of his ancestors [   ],
Records of(?) ... slaves(?), overseers(?), and soldiers [   ]:   (10′)
Not one was left in the land of Sumer and Akkad![2]
The rich haul of the Kassite king's treasure [   ]
He filled boats with the yields for Assur [   ]
And the glory of his power was seen [   ]
[To] his victorious power the gods, lords [of   ]   (15′)

1. A late Babylonian chronicle (Chronicle P, Grayson, ARI 1, 134, 47*) states that Tukulti-Ninurta took booty from Esagila, carried off the cult statue of Marduk, installed a governor, and ruled as king in Babylon for seven years. For a booty list from this period, see Weidner, AfO 13 (1939/41), 119–123; compare Freydank, AOF 1 (1974), 55–73; Grayson, ARI 1, 132 41.

2. A clay copy of an inscription on a seal taken by Tukulti-Ninurta in Babylonia is treated by Grayson, ARI 1, 127–128, 29. For discussion of the Babylonian tablets taken to Assyria at this time, see Weidner, AfO 16 (1952/3), 199–201; 206–211.

[To] the great gods he bestowed fine [   ]
Gold and silver were [not] precious in his sight,*
He dedicated [   ] to the gods of his land.
He decorated [Ehur]sagkurkurra[1] with [   ],
[He   Ekurm]esharra,[2] dwelling of Enlil of the Assyrians,   (20')
[   ] of the city Baltil[3] with pure red gold,
[He   the san]ctuary of the Igigi-gods,
[   ] jewelry of fine [gold].
[   ] he praises his god As[sur   ],
Assur, who established him [for king]ship of his land [   ].   (25')
Adad [   ] the [   ] of his weapons,
[   ] that he rendered him [   ] greatly,
[   ] the weapons that he ... [   ]
[the oa]th that Tukulti-Ninurta [sw]ore after Shamash [   ]
Let me [   ] the designs of the gods,   (30')
[   ] let me set the [   ] of the gods in the mouth
      of the people!
[   ] to the lyre bearer let me [   ]
[   ] ... of the gods, the people who [   ]
Let me proclaim his companion [   ]
[   ] established like heaven and earth till [remotest] days.   (35')
[The gods?] of Sumer and Akkad whose ...* he praised,
[   ] whom he praised, he became lord [   ].
[   ] the oath of the gods [   ]
[   ] the snare[4] of Shamash his reign [   ]
[   ] of the oath of the gods, observer of [   ]   (40')
He established [the   of the lands of Sumer] and Akkad.
[   ] of Nabu, sage, wise, of vast u[nderstanding],
[who in the land of Sumer] and Akkad
      has no rival, who ...
[   ] the depth of his understanding [   ]
[   ] the ultimate praise, his inscription [   ]

---

1. The cella of the Assur temple in Assur (G. van Driel, *The Cult of Assur* [Assen, 1969], 34–37).

2. The Assur temple in Kar-Tukulti-Ninurta, Tukulti-Ninurta's newly built royal city south of Assur.

3. Another name for Assur, apparently, the oldest part of the city (Tadmor, OAC 17 [1981], 27; Poebel, JNES 1 [1942], 263–267; J. Lewy, *Hebrew Union College Annual* 19 [1945/6], 467–472).

4. The punishment reserved for violators of oaths; compare Etana (III.22c) Tablet II lines 16–22.

[Tu]kulti-Ninurta, the ... that he took [   ] he [   ]   (45′)
[   ] you who have no riva[l   ]

(small gap)

Text: Middle Assyrian manuscript(s) from Nineveh, A–C = Campbell Thompson, *Archaeologia* 79
(1929), pl. xlvii–lii no. 122A + *Annals of Archaeology and Anthropology, University of Liverpool* 20
(1933), pl. ci–civ no. 107; W. G. Lambert, AfO 18 (1957/8), pl. I–III. These are fragments of one
six-columned tablet. Middle Assyrian manuscript from Assur, D = Ebeling, KAR 303 +
Weidner, AfO 7 (1931/2), 280–281. E, another Middle Assyrian manuscript from Assur(?), is
published in transliteration only by Ebeling, MAOG 12/2 (1938), 42. F, a Neo-Assyrian manuscript from Nineveh (Rm 142), = W. G. Lambert, AfO 18 (1957/8), pl. IV. D and E rev. are
omitted in this translation. K 6007 = H. Winckler, *Sammlung von Keilschrifttexten* II (Leipzig,
1893/4) 76 is treated here as the opening lines of the poem, following a suggestion of W. G. Lambert.

Edition: P. Machinist, *The Epic of Tukulti-Ninurta I, A Study in Middle Assyrian Literature* (Yale University dissertation, 1978), with detailed commentary. I owe to him numerous readings and interpretations. Rather than document them all here, I refer to his treatment of the text. K 6007 is
edited by Borger, EAK 1, 73–74.

Literature: Ebeling, MAOG 12/2; W. G. Lambert, AfO 18 (1957/8), 38–51; P. Machinist, "Literature as Politics: The Tukulti-Ninurta Epic and the Bible," CBQ 38 (1976), 455–482.

★Notes to Text: (i 7) Collation Machinist. (i 13′) *šá-ah!-ṭú* (WGL). (i 16′) *mi-na-su* for *minassu*? (i 21′)
Obscure. WGL suggests *lì-me-šu* "his clan." (i 23′) *iz-zi-za-am-ma* (WGL, unpublished fragment).
(i 24′) *sarti* (WGL, *ibid.*) (i 25′) [   ] *x šá la-a-ah-tu kab-tu* (WGL, *ibid.*). (ii 5′) *š[i-kin-tí]* (WGL); *li-
la-a-at*? (WGL). (ii 6′) See Machinist, diss., 226. (ii 12′) DINGIR.MEŠ is here construed as singular,
referring to Shamash; for the usage, see Lambert, BWL, 67 and OrNS 36 (1967), 132. (iii 11′) *umma um-de-šèr-ma a-bu-uk*: obscure. (iii 14′) According to Machinist's suggestion that *ni-il-mar* is an
apocopated N-present of *amāru*, diss., 414. (iii 20′) *li-it-ta[q!-ta]*? (WGL). (iii 41′) *ni-[di kussê]*, Machinist, diss., 288. (iii 48′) For a suggestion that the following obscure word refers to an organ
examined in divination, see AHw, 884a. (v 28′) Text: *ina salimija uqetti i-si-ta-ni*: obscure. The
warrior(s) are speaking, urging Tukulti-Ninurta on to the fight. (v 48′) For suggestions about this
line, see Landsberger, WdO 1 (1950), 373 note 74; von Soden, AHw, 1003b, 1367a. (v 50′) WGL.
(v 51′) Reading [*u*] at the beginning of both 50′ and 51′. (v 52′) AHw, 1536a. (B rev. vi 17′) Lambert, AfO 18 (1957/8), 44. (B rev. vi 36′) AHw, 1345b.

III.2 PSALM TO ASSUR FOR TUKULTI-NINURTA I

The author of the Tukulti-Ninurta Epic (III.1) may also have composed this bilingual prayer in dialectal Sumerian and in Akkadian,[1] as suggested by their common style, turns of phrase, and subject matter. One imagines some imprint of the royal personality in the paranoiac tone, fondness for complex rhetoric, and in the bitter complaint, common to tyrants, that the benefits of their dominion are not appreciated. The subject of the text seems to be the hatred that the king feels on all sides, despite or perhaps because of his achievements; he seems to believe that Assur is angry and withholds support in the king's hour of need.

The text opens with an invocation of the god Assur and with a refrain. Line 7 may allude to the birth of Tukulti-Ninurta. Line 14 may refer to the exploits of Ninurta as avenger of his father Enlil (see III.23), to whom Tukulti-Ninurta is implicitly compared.

[O who has] no rival among [al]l [the gods], [The prince who sustains you makes] plentiful(?) [your offering],	(=refrain)	(1)
[O] of Enlil,	[refrain]	
[O s]on of Nunamnir,[2]	[refrain]	
[O one] created of [ ], lofty one, lord of Ekur,	[refrain]	
[ ] who is filled with [ ],	[refrain]	(5)
[ ] who was begotten by Enlil,	[refrain]	
[Pure seed?] set in a maiden, a male she bore for you.	[refrain]	
[l]ord surveyed your awesomeness,	[refrain]	
[ ] made your lordship resplendent on high,	[refrain]	
He pronounced your name foremost among all the gods, [ ] who are surpassing in your valor.	[refrain]	(10)
He pro[nounced] your name to be told of in heaven,		
...	[refrain]	
Examining your [ ], your fame is surpassing in the universe,	[refrain]	

1. This translation follows the Akkadian where possible; restorations on the basis of the Sumerian are generally not indicated. Another bilingual text with historical information has been edited by W. G. Lambert, "Tukulti-Ninurta I and the Assyrian King List," *Iraq* 38 (1976), 85–94.
2. Another name for Enlil.

[   ] ... the great gods
    [established] order in the land,   *[refrain]*
Who smo[te?] the evil gods
    insubmissive to your father,   *[refrain]*
Who [established?] his name ... with all the gods,   *[refrain]* (15)
Who [   ] with the weapon in your fury
    the irreverent(?).   *[refrain]*
Your father Enlil [established?] your kingship in
    heaven and netherworld,   *[refrain]*
You set the straight pathway for the gods,   *[refrain]*
You are holy, you [   ] justice ...   *[refrain]*
God [   ] in innermost heaven,   *[refrain]*
You ever exercise your lordship over all the gods   *[refrain]*

(fragmentary lines, then gap)

Oppressing⋆ in [your] strength in all lands,   *[refrain]*
You have instructed your country not to transgress
    the "net" and to observe the ordinances,[1]   *[refrain]* (10′)
They do not go beyond the limits you drew,
    they heed your judgment,   *[refrain]*
They heed the firm decision of your supreme godhead
    with abiding awe,   *[refrain]*
They have put their trust in your benevolent judgment,
    they have constantly sought after your divinity,   *[refrain]*
You are their broad security,
    their great good protection,   *[refrain]*
They trust in your lordship, they learn from innermost
    heaven your resolve.[2]   *[refrain]* (15′)
The lands of one accord have surrounded your city
    Assur with a noose of evil,   *[refrain]*
All [of them] have come to hate the shepherd whom
    you named, who administers your peoples,   *[refrain]*
All regions of the earth, for which you had produced
    benevolent assistance, held you in contempt,   *[refrain]*
And though you extended your protection to them,
    they rebuffed (you) [and   ] your land.   *[refrain]*

1. That is, an oath of fealty?
2. Presumably a reference to divination (Seux, *Hymnes*, 494 note 6).

The king for whom you held goodwill[1] made
    sure to disobey you,   *[refrain]* (20′)
And even those whom you treated well unsheathed
    [their] weapons (against you),   *[refrain]*
The battlefield's task is ever in full readiness
    against your city Assur,   *[refrain]*
All the onrushings of a flood are mustered against it,   *[refrain]*
Your enemies and foes are glowering at [your
    standing?] place,   *[refrain]*
They have concerted to plunder your country,
    O Assur, they ... for treachery.   *[refrain]* (25′)
The lands crave night and day for the destruction of
    your wondrous sights,   *[refrain]*
Everywhere they seek to overthrow your cities,   *[refrain]*
And they yearn to inflict a defeat upon(?) the spirits
    (of) his (ancestors?),[2]   *[refrain]*
All the evildoers await a dark day without sunshine,   *[refrain]*
Their threatening fingers[3] are stretched out to
    scatter the armies of Assur,   *[refrain]* (30′)
Vilely they plot evil against their benefactor,   *[refrain]*
They trespass the ordinance of the lord of the world,
    they muster(?) both kings and auxiliaries.   *[refrain]*
(As) you are the lord of your land, O Assur, may you
    be its mighty one, its noble champion,⋆   *[refrain]*
For the future may your supremacy be its protection,
    as it raises high its head.   *[refrain]*
O Lord, do not neglect any favor
    for your land Assyria!   (*= new refrain*) (35′)
O Assur, great lord, king of the Anunna-gods,
    the land of Assyria is yours!   *[refrain]*
O Assyrian Enlil, lord of the world,
    the land of Assyria is yours!   *[refrain]*
May Adad, hero of the gods, who inspires terror,
    come at your side,   *[refrain]*

---

1. Possibly a reference to the Babylonian king.
2. Obscure line; I take the ghosts to refer to the ancestors of the king, whose tombs might be violated by an enemy attack.
3. Compare III.1 v 25′.

May Shamash, who follows the paths of heaven and
      earth, come at your side.   *[refrain]*
Your land, Assur,
      which nooses of evil are surrounding,   *[refrain]* (40′)
(And) Tukulti-Ninurta, whom you called by
      name ... Have mercy!   *(= new refrain)*
They glower at him to find [   ]   *[refrain]*

(gap)

(It is?) your people against whom
      all the world in its entirety plots evil,   *[refrain]*
None of the lands has regard for your city.   *[refrain]*
They put their trust in their own strength,
      they have not heeded your divinity,   *[refrain]* (45′)
They treat lightly your terrible oath,
      they wipe out your guidelines,   *[refrain]*
Did they honor your great word?
      Who keeps the ordinance of your supremacy? *[refrain]*
They do not heed your lordly decision,
      nor do they seek your consideration.   *[refrain]*
They take courage on account of their own strength,
      ...   *[refrain]*
Dwelling in peaceful abode, they have [confidence?]
      in the mass of their troops.   *[refrain]* (50′)
O my trust in heaven, my judge in the netherworld,
      [... your divine supremacy]   *(= new refrain)*
O Assur, great lord, king of all the gods [   ]
      in heaven,   *[refrain]*
O Great mountain,[1] Enlil, who ordains*
      the destinies of heaven and netherworld,   *[refrain]*
You are my sweet security, my broad protection ...
      in heaven   *[refrain]*
I am he who ensures your rites,
      who keeps your ablutions pure.   *[refrain]* (55′)
My prayers are continuous before you, every[where], *[refrain]*

---

1. Epithet of Enlil.

With pure offerings and numerous sanctified food
    portions ...   *[refrain]*
I have not neglected to give you display offerings,
    I [   ] eternally(?),   *[refrain]*
I never ceased* to offer sheep and I [   ]
    "kneeling offerings."   *[refrain]*
O Lord, in ... may your tense heart be calmed ...   *[new refrain]* (60′)
O Assur, great lord, mountain of the Igigi-gods,
    [may] your inner feelings [be calmed]!   *[refrain]*
O Enlil, mighty leader of the gods, warrior, [   ]   *[refrain]*
May Shamash, your radiance, light of heaven and earth,
    calm [you]!   *[refrain]*
May Adad, voice of your divine supremacy,
    lord of all living things, calm [you]!   *[refrain]*
May Ninurta, valiant weapon-bearer, your splendid
    son, whom you love, calm [you]!   *[refrain]* (65′)
May Nusku, your beloved sublime vizier on high(?),
    calm [you]!   *[refrain]*
May Amurru, lord of the uplands, calm you!   *[refrain]*
May Mullissu, great spouse, your beloved, calm you!   *[refrain]*
May Sherua, your pure creation, goddess of dawn,
    calm you!   *[refrain]*
May Tashmetu, sublime sovereign, protective goddess
    of the land, calm you!   *[refrain]* (70′)
May the goddesses of heaven, the destinies of the entire
    netherworld, ca[lm you!]   *[refrain]*
Above, may Anu ... at your right ca[lm you!]   *[refrain]*
Below, may your lower part(?), Ea, lord of the entire
    netherworld, ca[lm you]!   *[refrain]*

(fragmentary lines, then gap)

[Pronounce] a good destiny [   ] forever,
[   ] ... the land and its people [   ]
[   ] you cause the people to dwell ..., you [   ]
[   ] may its allies(?) dwell(?) ... [   ]
[   ] ... [   ]
Let him praise your divinity to the land [   ]

> That he may deliver the sustenance of [   ]
> Let him [   ] your power!

Text: Ebeling, KAR 128 (+) 129/1, 2. I am grateful to H. Neumann for detailed information about the relationship of the fragments.

Edition: Ebeling, *Quellen* I, 62–70.

Translation: Seux, *Hymnes*, 493–497 (partial).

Notes to Text: (9′) ⌈*di*⌉-*e-šú* (collation WGL). (33′) From Sumerian (šu-gar = *gamālu*); Akkadian has "great" rather than "noble." (53′) Reading *mu-šim*! for "who ordains." (59′) Reading *ul ap-per-ku*.

III.3 HYMN TO TIGLATH-PILESER I

Tiglath-pileser I (1115–1077 B.C.), considered by one modern historian to be "an admirable oriental despot of the best kind,"[1] appears in his own inscriptions as a successful warrior king.[2] In the early years of his reign, he embarked on a series of campaigns against the Phrygians, and for about twenty years pursued a dogged war with the Arameans on the upper Euphrates. This suggests that he was not at the head of a great empire, as some historians would assert, but was rather under considerable pressure from that quarter; in fact, the wars may have been defensive.[3] Eventually the Arameans may have broken through Assyrian defenses, even occupying Nineveh. Tiglath-pileser's reign may have ended in disaster and obscurity. Much the same fate may have befallen his Babylonian contemporaries.[4]

Tiglath-pileser I enjoys greater fame today for his non-military interests. These included a taste for hunting on a grand scale, collection of exotic plants, a royal zoo, and possibly the establishment of a library of literary and scholarly tablets at Assur.[5] To judge from tablets discovered at Assur, his reign saw considerable literary and scholarly activity, including study and copying of Babylonian texts.

This poem commemorates campaigns by the king in the mountains north and west of Assyria, in lands called Qumani, Musru, and Habhu. Its style and subject matter are comparable to those of the Tukulti-Ninurta epic (III.1) and Shalmaneser in Ararat (IV.1a).

(gap)

The dweller in the [   ] plotted battle,
They prepared for w[ar], they whetted their weaponry,
The foe launched their war.
All the mountain men mustered by clans,   (10′)

---

1. Sidney Smith, *Cambridge Ancient History* (Cambridge, 1924), 2:251.

2. For English translations of the inscriptions and other relevant documents of the period, see Grayson, ARI 2, 1–45.

3. Grayson, ARI 2, 1 "Assyrian splendour shines forth in all its glory." See also Wiseman, CAH³ II/2, 457–464; I follow H. Tadmor (1970 lectures at Yale University).

4. For the Arameans at this period, see Brinkman, PHPKB, 281–285.

5. E. F. Weidner, "Die Bibliothek Tiglatpilesers I.," AfO 16 (1952/3), 197–213. For a critique of Weidner's idea, see W. G. Lambert, *Iraq* 38 (1976), 85.

Qumani[1] launched his attack,
Musrian[2] stood by him for the fray,
Their combined forces stood forth as comrades.
The Gutian[3] raged, afire with awe-inspiring splendor,
All the hordes of the mountains, the Habhi-federation,[4]
Formed a unity to help each other,   (15′)
[   ] their help [   ] before t[he]m.
They were raging like a tempest, fomenting disorder,
They were plotting [   ], seeking sedition.
Their talk of war [   ]
The Lord regally [   ] their destruction …   (20′)
[   ] Enlil,
"[   ] I have heeded(?) the god of Ekur,
"[   ] … their people,"
(So) the god made pride of the slaughter of the foe.
All the gods heard his utterance,   (25′)
Assur said, "Slaughter the enemy!"
"Destroy the foe!" came forth from [his] lips.
His heart resolved on slaughter,
His mouth com[manded] the scattering of the wicked.
In order to diminish their troops, he made war,   (30′)
He drew up battle, caused mutiny (among them).
He girded himself with awe-inspiring weapons,
He commanded his favorite to the battlefield's task,
He made proud the weaponry of Tukulti-apil-Eshara![5]   (35′)
Before him Enlil leads him into battle,
Ishtar, mistress of turmoil, aroused him to strife,
Ninurta, foremost of the gods, positioned himself at his front,
Nusku was slaughtering all enemies at his right,
Adad overwhelmed foes at his left,   (40′)

1. Qumani refers to people who lived in a mountainous region between the upper Zab and the Tigris (RGTC 5, 222–223).
2. The location of Musri is disputed; it may have been somewhere north and east of the Tigris (RGTC 5, 198–199).
3. Gutium may refer to the mountainous area around the upper reaches of the Lower Zab river; later it became a literary term for marauding mountain peoples (see I.5b, RGTC 5, 192–193).
4. Habhi may refer to an area between the upper reaches of the Upper Zab river and lakes Van and Urmia (RGTC 5, 113–114).
5. This refers to Tiglath-Pileser.

Stationed behind them, he was raining down weaponry.
Daily he set devastation upon them.
The king turned against the far-away(?)* Qumani.
He conquers every one of their sanctuaries,
Their lofty cities, all there are, he demolishes.   (45')
He tears up the grain from the fields that sustain them,
He cuts down the fruit trees, he destroys the gardens,
He made a deluge pass over their mountains.
He cast terror(?) upon them,
All enemies were frightened,   (50')
Fierce radiance covered their features,
The mountains(?) submitted fully to Assur,

(five fragmentary lines, then breaks off)

Text: Ebeling-Köcher-Rost, LKA 63.
Edition: V. Hurowitz, J. Westenholz, "LKA 63: A Heroic Poem in Honor of Tiglath-Pileser I's Muṣru-Qumanu Campaign," JCS 42 (1990), 1–49 with collations.
Notes to Text: (43') WGL: [*is*]-*saḫ*?-*ḫur*? *šarru a-na* Qu-ma-né-e *ru*?-*qu*?-*te*.

III.4 PSALMS TO ISHTAR FOR ASSURNASIRPAL I

(a) ON OCCASION OF ILLNESS

The Assyrian king Assurnasirpal I (1050–1032 B.C.) speaks here of his rise to power. He credits Ishtar of Nineveh[1] with the divine favor that led to his success, and reminds her of various compensatory achievements, including restoration of images and construction of a magnificent bed for her. In view of their past relationship, the king asks the goddess for remission of his illness. The mood and message of this text recall the righteous sufferer tradition in Meso-potamian literature (compare II.13, III.14). This and the following text demon-strate fine poetic composition during this otherwise little-known period. W. G. Lambert, AnSt 11 (1961), 157 associates this output with "a tradition of writing poetry among the priests of Ishtar of Nineveh."[2] For another work in this tradition, see below, IV.1b and for reference to Ishtar of Nineveh as the "Mistress of Poetry," see IV.4c.

i

I will tell of [   ] that befell me: (1)
To the creatress of wis[dom], the praiseworthy … [goddess],
To her, who dwells in Emashmash,
          [   ] I shall tell of myself,[3]
To the queen of the gods, into whose hands
          [all]* responsibilities are bestowed,
To the lady of Nineveh, the lofty [of the gods],   (5)
To the daughter of Sin, twin sister of Shamash
          — she exercises all kingship* —
To her, who renders verdicts, the goddess of all there is,
To the mistress of heaven and netherworld,
          who accedes to entreaties,
To her, who hears prayers, who accepts lamentations,
To the merciful goddess, who loves justice,   (10)

---

1. For the association of this goddess with healing, see G. Beckman, "Ištar of Nineveh Reconsidered," JCS 50 (1998), 1–10.
2. Lambert (AnSt 11 [1961], 157) considered (a) i–iv separate texts, of which (i) was a dedicatory inscription, but the pieces can be read, as by Brünnow, Seux, and von Soden, as a continuous discourse divided into sections by a scribe; compare III.4b.
3. Emashmash was the temple of Ishtar at Nineveh; "tell of myself" stands for Akkadian "make manifest my name."

Ishtar, whose portion it is to keep alive(?):*
I set forth* before you all the anxieties that I undergo,
May your ear turn to my weary utterance,
May your feelings take pity on my ailing speech!
Look upon me, Mistress, may your heart be pained
      as I turn to you.   (15)

ii

I am Assurnasirpal, your ailing servant,
Humble, revering your divinity, responsible, your beloved,
Who ensures your divine sustenance,
      who unfailingly supplies your food offerings,
Who looks forward to your festivals,
      who provides for your shrine,
Who provides generously the beer that you want and enjoy,   (20)
Son of Shamshi-Adad, a king who revered the great gods.
I was formed in mountains unknown to you, lady.*
I was not mindful of your dominion,
      my prayers were not continual,
The people of Assyria did not know me
      nor did they confront your divine presence.
Yet it was you, Ishtar, terrifying dragon of the gods,   (25)
That appointed me by your desire
      and wished that I should rule.
You took me from the mountains
      and named me to be shepherd of the peoples,[1]
You established for me a just scepter until the world grows old.
It was you, Ishtar, who made glorious my name!
It was you who granted me the power to save
      and requite those who were loyal.   (30)
From your mouth came (the command)
      to repair the divine (images) that were stored away,
It was I who repaired the ruined sanctuaries,
I rebuilt the damaged divine images
      and restored them to their places,
I ensured their divine allotments and sustenance forever.

---

1. According to some scholars, this is an oblique reference to an irregularity in the royal succession (Labat, *Réligions*, 250; Seux, *Hymnes*, 498).

It was I who had made a couch of boxwood,
    a well-appointed bed for your divine repose,   (35)
The interior of which I overlaid
    with the finest gold cunningly wrought,
Which I adorned with the choicest precious stones
    from the mountain(s) like a [   ].¹
I consecrated it, I filled it with splendor to behold,⋆
I made it shine like the sun's brilliance, a seemly sight.
I provided it a place in the Emashmash,
    your favorite abode,⋆ which you love.   (40)
In what way have I neglected you
    that I should draw upon myself [such hardship]?
You have blanketed me with disease, why⋆ am I at my last gasp?
[   ] … my sinews, in form a wreck.
[Panic], phobia, [   ] choke off(?) my life⋆

                    (fragmentary lines)

                         iii

Constantly [   ] I pray to your ladyship,
I sob⋆ before your divinity [   ] …
[   ] who does not fear your divinity,
    who commits abominations,   (60)
How have I incurred no sins or misdeeds (before) that I
    should draw upon myself [punishment (now)]?²
I am constantly in a state of anxiety, [I abide] in darkness,
I am cut off and shall not see [offspring],⋆
I forsook(?) my royal throne and [   ]
I do not go near the meal I am to eat, [   ]   (65)
Beer, the support of life, [is become] disgusting [to me],
I loathe the fanfare and sounding of strings, [kingship's] due,
Thus am I deprived of the joys of living! [   ]
My eyes (once) sharp-hued can perceive nothing,
I do not hold [my head] high,
    [but gaze at] the surface of the ground.   (70)

---

1. The old tablet from which the existing manuscript was copied was evidently damaged here, as well as in lines 41 and 59–70.
2. That is, perhaps, he was never blameless; what unusual behavior justifies the goddess's anger?

For how long, Mistress, have you afflicted me
   with this interminable illness?

iv

I am Assurnasirpal, in despair, who reveres you,
Who grasps your divine hem,
   who beseeches your ladyship:
Look upon me, let me pray to your divine ladyship(?),*
You who were angry, take pity on me,
   may your feelings be eased! (75)
May your ever benevolent heart
   grow pained on my account,
Drive out my illness, remove my debility!
From your mouth, Mistress,
   may the command for mitigation fall!
Have pity on your (once) favored viceroy[1]
   who never wavers,*
Banish his despair! (80)
Take his part with your beloved Assur, the [warr]ior,
   father of the gods!
I will praise your divinity forever,
I will magnify the [nob]le one
   among the gods of heaven and netherworld!

Text: Brünnow, ZA 5 (1890), 79–80; photo AfO 25 (1974/7), 40–41.

Edition: von Soden, AfO 25 (1974/7), 37–45.

Translation: Labat, *Réligions*, 250–252; Seux, *Hymnes*, 497–501. An earlier translation by von Soden appears in SAHG, 264–268 no. 14.

Literature: W. von Soden, *Herrscher im alten Orient* (Berlin, 1954), 77–78; W. G. Lambert, AfO 27 (1980), 71.

Notes to Text: (4) WGL. (6) Lambert, AfO 27 (1980), 71. (11) Tablet: *bullulu*, see von Soden, AfO 25 (1974/7), 11. (12) WGL: *a-pa?-šar*. (22) WGL. (38) Lambert, AfO 27 (1980), 72. (40) ms. accidentally repeats "favorite." (42) -[*ma*]? (44) WGL: *ú-nap-paq*. (59) WGL: *ut-ta-ḫa-as*. (63) WGL. (74) Text: NIN DINGIR.RA.KI; see Seux, *Hymnes*, 501 note 42 "ta divinité"?; von Soden, AfO 25 (1974/7), 45. (79) Differently Seux, *Hymnes*, 501 and von Soden, AfO 25 (1974/7), 44. CAD K, 39a, if I understand it correctly, applies the immutability to the suppliant, as here. The point of the line, as in 61, is that he has been consistent; why should he be punished now?

---

1. A title of the Assyrian kings expressing their subservience to Assur, the national god and deified city.

(b) ON OCCASION OF AN OFFERING

This hymn was evidently commissioned for the celebration of the reinstallation of cult objects belonging to Ishtar of Nineveh(?) by Assurnasirpal I. It opens with a song about the goddess's dominion and the special favor shown to Assurnasirpal. He asks her to bless him (i, ii). In iii is described the installation of the objects and their refitting in gold, just as the goddess wanted. In iv and v men and gods rejoice at the occasion, and in vi a blessing is asked on the king for his deed.

i

(large gap)

… who performs your rites that you lo[ve],	
[ ] … [ ]	
[ ] your face	
[ ] the [four world] regions.	
[The peo]ple of this land [ ].¹	(10)
Lo[rds] and princes bear [your]	
You turned your eyes [upon]	

ii

At your (favorable) glance, O Princess,	
The pure priest, whom you n[ominated],	
[Assur]nasirpal, pr[aiseworthy king],★	(15)
Son of Shamshi-Adad [ ],★	
The one whom among all kings you have [ ],	
By(?) your divinity [you] his prowess,	
By your ladyship you made him great,★	
By your faithful heart, you made him glorious.	(20)
You bestowed on him shepherdship of your land,	
Grant him a hearing and (time) to grow old.	
Let him always walk in your sweet protection.	

---

1. The Mesopotamians.

iii

[You] have had made for him rites for your celebration:
[In] Assur, the city of all the gods,
[In Ekur?], in the holy place, the residence of Enlil,   (25)
[In the cel]la of your joyful divinity,
He has administered the [pur]e rites.
[   ] five(?) pure [pearls?] of the seas,
[   ] the sacred [   ] that you required,
[   ] choice gold from the bowels of the earth,[1]   (30)

(two lines fragmentary)

[   ] he has administered splendidly.

iv

All lands are rejoicing
At your pure, worthy rites.   (35)
The mountains bring hither their yield.
Single out your favorite, he is always invoking you,*
The prince who reveres you, he is pure and sanctified,
He brings you the rites that you desired.   (40)
Look hither, mistress,* with your (favoring) glance,
Let your heart rejoice and be glad.

Rejoice, O Mistress of Heaven,
May Enlil, father of the gods, be happy,
May Assur rejoice in Ehursaggula,[2]   (45)
May Anu, king of heaven, be glad,
May all the gods of heaven rejoice,
May Ea rejoice in the Apsu,
May the gods of the depths beam,
May the Fates, goddesses of the land, be glad,
May all the officiants in (these) rites[3] dance,   (50)
May their hearts be glad at (this) celebration.

---

1. Literally: "choice gold of Arallu," a poetic term for the netherworld.
2. "House of the Great Mountain," part of the Assur temple in Assur.
3. I take this (with Seux, *Hymnes*, 100) to refer to the officiants at the installation ceremony, though it could mean "the other gods who are interested parties" (or the like).

May the performer of the rites rejoice [   ],
[   ] the shepherd, the viceroy [   ]
Raise high Assurnasir[pal's head],   (55)
Make glo[rious his   ]

(fragmentary lines, then breaks off)

Text: Ebeling, KAR 107, 358; Schroeder, KAH II 139.

Edition: Ebeling, *Quellen* I, 58–62; see also *Quellen* II, 76.

Translation: von Soden, SAHG, 268–269 no. 15; Seux, *Hymnes,* 98–100.

Notes to Text: (ii 15) Restoration Seux, *Hymnes,* 98 note 5. (ii 16) Variant omits. (ii 19) Reading *tu-šar-[bi-šu]* (ii 38) Seux, *Hymnes,* 99 note 17. (ii 41) Seux, *Hymnes,* 99 note 19.

III.5 PRAYERS FOR KINGS OF ASSYRIA

(a) CORONATION PRAYER

Three tablets dating sometime after the reign of Tukulti-Ninurta I preserve a new year's coronation ritual[1] of the kings of Assyria dating to the latter half of the second millennium B.C. When the text begins, the king is being hailed and carried into the Assur temple. He distributes gifts of silver and gold, which are received by the priests. The king makes an offering to Assur and various other gods. The royal diadem is then set before the altar. After a procedure with a textile that is not clear, the ritual continues with the placing of a gold ring. The priest crowns the king with a turban-like headdress, here rendered "diadem," and speaks the prayer translated below. This sums up Assyrian imperial doctrine, with its religious and territorial emphasis.

> May Assur and Ninlil, owners of your diadem,   (1)
> Let you wear the diadem on your head for a century.
> May your foot go fair in Ekur and
>   so too your hands in prayer to Assur your god.
> May your priesthood and the priesthood of your sons
>   go fair before Assur your god.
> With your just scepter, enlarge your country.   (5)
> May Assur grant you commanding, hearing,
>   and obedience, truth and peace.

Text: Ebeling, KAR 135 (+ KAR 216, 137).
Edition: Müller, MVAeG 41/3 (1937), 12–13 lines 34–40.
Translation: Seux, *Hymnes*, 112–113.

---

1. For further information on Assyrian ritual, see K. F. Müller, *Das Assyrische Ritual*, MVAeG 41/3 (1937). It is not clear whether this coronation was an annual or a once-in-a-reign ceremony; see R. Frankena, *Tākultu, De sacrale maaltijd* ... (Leiden, 1954), 63; Tadmor, JCS 12 (1958), 28 note 52; Grayson, UF 3 (1971), 319 note 50; Garelli, *Nouvelle Clio 2 bis* (Paris, 1974), 309.

(b) PRAYER AT THE GODS' REPAST

This prayer was said in honor of the Assyrian king when the gods were served a cultic repast. One manuscript names a late Assyrian king, Assur-etil-ilani (ca. 626–623 B.C.), but the prayer dates earlier than his time.

> He who made this repast, who provided food and drink to the gods, grant that he administer far and wide forever more. May he exercise the high priesthood (of Assur), kingship, and universal dominion. May he attain a ripe old age. To him who heeds these words be barley, silver, oil, wool; salt of Bariku[1] for their food, and oil for their lamps. Live, prosper, and enjoy good fortune! May the rites of the repast for the Mighty Ones in the land of Assyria be eternal. May Assur bless the one who provided this repast, Assur-etil-ilani.

Text: Ebeling, KAR 214, iv 7–27; see also Smith, III R 66, x 18–38.
Edition: Ebeling, OrNS 23 (1954), 120–121, 124–125.
Literature: R. Frankena, *Tākultu, de sacrale maaltijd* ... (Leiden, 1954), 8; Ebeling, OrNS 24 (1955), 1–15.

---

1.   An esteemed variety of imported salt. For a general study of salt in ancient Mesopotamia, see D. Potts, "On Salt and Salt Gathering in Ancient Mesopotamia," JESHO 27 (1984), 225–271.

III.6 THE HUNTER

A student's tablet from Assur preserves a short, epic-style poem about a campaign of an Assyrian king against mountain peoples, cast in a metaphor of a hunter stalking wild game. Ebeling suggested that Tiglath-Pileser I is intended, and this has been argued convincingly by Hurowitz and Westenholz, JCS 42 (1990), 46–49. The text uses various strange words and peculiar spellings, either owing to scribal errors or to an attempt to make the language look archaic.

[Who curbs] foes, trampler of his enemies,	(1)
[Who hunts] mountain donkeys,	
flushes the creatures of the steppe,	
[The Hunter]: Assur is his ally, Adad is his help,	
Ninurta, vanguard of the gods, [go]es before him.	
The Hunter plans battle against the donkeys,	(5)
He sharpens(?) his dagger to cut short their lives.	
The donkeys listened, they gamboled alert,★	
The Hunter's terror had not come down upon them.	
They were bewildered, "Who is it that stalks us?	
"Who is it, not having seen who we are,	
who tries to frighten us all?	(10)
"Our ... will cut off★ the high mountains,	
"Our dwelling place lies in the ... of the mountain.	
"Let the wind send flying the hunter's snare!★	
"May the shootings(?)★ of his bow	
not rise high enough to reach(?) (us) assembled!"	
The Hunter heard the chatter of the mountain beasts —	(15)
Their speech was anxious, their words troubled,	
"Mouth or muscles, men are what they're born!"[1] —	
To the warriors who will make the breaches(?)	
over the mountain he says,	
"Let us go and bring massacre upon the mountain beasts,	
"With our sharpened(?) weapons we will shed their blood."	(20)
He performed an extispicy for his appointed time,	

---

1. Obscure, translation doubtful. Perhaps this is a proverbial expression, "a man's a man for a' that." Lines 15–18 may be out of sequence.

He raged like a thunderstorm,
    (like the) sun he was hitching up his chariotry.
A journey of three days he marched [in one].
Even without sunshine a fiery heat was among them,
He slashed the wombs of the pregnant, blinded the babies,   (25)
He cut the throats of the strong ones among them,
Their troops saw(?) the smoke of the (burning) land.
Whatever land is disloyal to Assur will turn into a ruin.
Let me sing of the victory of Assur, the mighty,
    who goes out to c[ombat],
Who triumphs over the cohorts of the earth!   (30)
Let the first one hear and te[ll it] to the later ones!

Text: Ebeling-Köcher-Rost, LKA 62.

Edition: Ebeling, OrNS 18 (1949), 30–39.

Literature: Borger, EAK 1, 112. The date of the text is discussed by Ebeling, OrNS 18 (1949), 30; cited in AHw as a late Babylonian or Neo-Assyrian text in archaizing style (e.g., 1124); not in Grayson, ARI for this king; Hurowitz, J. Westenholz, JCS 42 (1990), 46–49.

Notes to Text: (7) *ina rēši*: perhaps "ahead," but taken here in parallelism to "listening," describing the wary unease of the herd. (11) WGL: *ina-ki-is*? (13) CAD B, 34a; CAD K, 399b. (14) AHw, 1237a.

B. LEGENDS OF FORMER KINGS

III.7 LEGENDS OF SARGONIC KINGS

(a) SARGON, KING OF BATTLE

This epic poem about Sargon of Akkad (see I.3) opens with Sargon complaining that his conquests in Anatolia are no longer subservient. One of his officers attempts to dissuade him from invading. At this point, a delegation of Mesopotamian merchants living in Anatolia (see I.6) appeals to Sargon to help them, painting a gloomy picture of their distress. They offer him rich booty in return for his campaign. Sargon's soldiers are disinclined to accept, but this is the opportunity that Sargon has been yearning for, so he launches a campaign.

The army traverses a great mountain range and a forest of thorn trees. Nur-daggal, king of Burushhanda in Anatolia, unaware of the advance, is confident that the Euphrates(?), not to mention the forest, will prove an impassable barrier, and his troops echo his confidence. No sooner has Nur-daggal spoken than Sargon bursts into the city, smites down his finest warriors, and demands his submission.

Nur-daggal's fabulous court is the scene of his humiliation. Sargon takes his seat and jeeringly parrots Nur-daggal's boasts. Nur-daggal, incredulous, confesses that some divine agency must have brought Sargon, then asks to be restored to his kingdom as a vassal. Sargon accepts and Nur-daggal offers tribute of exotic fruits never before seen in Mesopotamia. After three years in Burushhanda, Sargon departs.

Two Akkadian versions of this story are preserved (see also II.6a). (a) is known from a Middle Babylonian school tablet that was probably copied at Hattusha, the Hittite capital in Anatolia, and sent from there to El-Amarna in Egypt to train Egyptians to read and write Akkadian, the language of international diplomacy. The manuscript is heavily damaged and full of mistakes and obscurities. The interest to the Hittites no doubt lay both in the exploits of Sargon himself, reports of which were known to them,[1] and in the association with Anatolia.

---

1. H. G. Güterbock, "Sargon of Akkad Mentioned by Hattusili I of Hatti," JCS 18 (1964), 1–6; G. Beckman, "Sargon and Naram-Sin in Hatti, Reflections of Mesopotamian Antiquity among the Hittites," in D. Kuhn, H. Stahl, eds., *Die Gegenwart des Altertums, Formen und Funktionen des Altertumsbezugs in den Hochkulturen des Alten Orients* (Heidelberg, 2001), 85–91.

A small fragment (b), dating to the seventh century B.C., from Assurbanipal's library, preserves what may be an expanded or parallel version of the merchants' delegation to Sargon. The epic may have circulated in Mesopotamia in a fuller form than is known from the Hattusha-Amarna edition (as was the case with the Nergal-Ereshkigal story, III.19). A Hittite version is also known, but not translated here.

While there are points in common between Sargon, King of Battle and the Sargon epic of the Classical period (II.6a), the text of the Mature period is not a lineal descendant from the older text. The deeds of Sargon were a topic for various writers using similar historical traditions. The historicity of the events portrayed here is a matter of debate. Since there is no mention of merchants in the Classical version of Sargon's invasion of Anatolia (II.6a), this part of the tale may have been a later second-millennium interpolation. At the beginning of the second millennium, colonies of Mesopotamian merchants lived in Anatolia (see I.6 and p. 71 note 2). Recent archaeological discoveries in Anatolia, including the tentative identification of Burushhanda with Acemhöyük, point to cultural connections between Mesopotamia and Anatolia in the third millennium,[1] so evidence may turn up to provide historical background to this story.

1. Middle Babylonian Version

```
[  ] Ishtar to the bulls(?) of the city A[gade],*                    (1)
[Might]y one in battle, king of … [  ],
Sargon speaks [to his warriors],
Sargon [girds his] loins [with] his fierce weapons,
In the palace, Sargon made ready to speak,
       he gives this sp[eech to his warriors]:
"O my warriors! The land of Ka[nesh?],          ]              (5)
"[      ] thinks of war, (though) I made it submit."


[    ] brought [    ], the champion(?) of Sargon [said],
"It is a mission of [seven leagues].                           (10)
"When will we sit on chairs, rest for a while,
"[When] our arms have given out,
       and our knees exhausted from traversing the road?"
```

1. M. Van De Mieroop, "Sargon of Agade and His Successors in Anatolia," *Studi Micenei ed Egeo-Anatolici* 42 (2000), 133–159.

[The messenger from the merchants]
    made ready [to speak] and said,
"[O ... Zaba]ba, the campaigner who makes straight the way
    and spies out all the regions of the earth,
"[O ... lord of a]ll daises, who [ ] from sunrise to sunset,   (15)
"[   ] the merchants vomit up (what is in) their stomachs,
    mixed with bile, throwing up all over the [grou]nd,
"What would (even) a Kishite pluck out of Agade?[1]
"We swore (allegiance) to [Sargo]n, king of the universe,
"We have come down to him that we may meet strength,[2]
    for we are no warriors.
"Charge us the [co]sts of the journey, O king,
"Let the king be responsible for those
    who stand in battle with him.
"Let the warriors of Sargon ... gold,
    let (those great) bulls have silver to spend.[3]   (20)
"[How] shall we go about [our affairs]
    when outrages are being committed,
    where your god, Zababa, is out of action?"

The merchants assembled, they were entering the palace.
After the merchants entered,
    the warriors would not receive (them).

Sargon made ready to speak, the king of battle said,
"That fabled city, Burushhanda, I will see its ...,
"[What is] its direction? Which is its mountain?
    What is its road? Which, how should one go?"   (25)

"[The road th]at you wish to travel is a most difficult path,
    grievous to go,
"[The road to Burushha]nda that you want to go,
    the road that I worry about,
    is a mission of seven leagues."

1. That is, Sargon has never yielded to anyone? For Sargon and Kish, see I.3b.
2. Wordplay on *kiššatu* "universe" and *kiššūtu* "strength," and the city Kish, see I.3b.
3. That is, the booty will be immense.

[   ] the massive mountains,
     where the boulders are lapis, the foothills are gold,
[a]pricot tree, fig tree, boxwood, sycamore,
     evergreen(?) trees with seven cones,*
[   ] where the soldiers fought,
     the passage(?) to its summit is seven leagues long,   (30)
The brambles ... for seven leagues in all,
The trees, boxthorns, the region of thorny growth,
     the trees sixty cubits high, is seven leagues (more).

(fragmentary lines, then gap)

Nur-da[ggal] made ready to speak
     said to [his] war[riors],
"[Sargo]n does not yet come,
"Riverbank and high water will surely prevent him,
"There is the massive mountain,
     the reed thicket will surely make a forest, grove(?),
     and woods hung about with tangles."   (5′)

His warriors answered him, to Nur-daggal they said,
"Which are the kings, past or future, which king is he
     who could come here to see our lands?"

Nur-daggal had not finished speaking
     when Sargon dug into(?) his city,
     he widened the Gate of the Nobles two field-lengths!
He threw it down, he slashed through the top of its ramparts,
     he smote the most outstanding of the general's* men!
[Sar]gon set up* his throne in front of the city gate,
Sargon made ready to speak,
     [sa]ying to his warriors these words,   (10′)
"Now then! Nur-daggal, favored of Enlil,
"[Let them br]ing him in, let me see him submit!"
[With] the gem-studded crown on his head,
     and lapis footstool at his feet,
With fifty-five attendants [ ] sat before him,

Who, like him, were(?) seated on throne(s?) of gold,
    while the king sat on a throne like a god.[1]
Who is so exalted as the king?
Nur-daggal was made to sit before Sargon.
Sargon made ready to speak, saying to Nur-daggal,   (15′)
"Come, Nur-daggal, favored of Enlil, you said,

> 'Sargon will not come as far as we are!
> 'Riverbank and high water will surely prevent him.
> 'The massive mountain will surely make a reed thicket,
>   forest, it will surely produce a grove(?),
>   and a woods of tangles!'"

Nur-daggal made ready to speak, saying to Sargon,
"My lord, no doubt it was your god who showed you the way
    and brought your soldiers across,*
"Zababa, the hero of Euphrates-land!
"What lands could rival Agade? What king could rival you?   (20′)
"You have no adversary, their opponent is ...
"Your opponents are terrified and left paralyzed with fear.
"Send them back, [city], field, and lea,
    the lord (to be your) ally in charge of it."

"[We have ...] to his place and come around to it,[2]
"Its fruit let him render: apricot, fig, medlar, grape,
"[   ], pistachio, olive, pomegranate(?).
"Never need we come around to it again,
    let him render [its fruit].   (25′)
"May the city bear an obligation,
    may I fetch (from it) sweet (fruit)."

In going [the distance] and staying there,
    whoever followed Sargon?
When he withdrew from the city,
Three years [in the city] he had stayed.

(The End)

---

1. Grammatically it is not clear whether Sargon or Nur-daggal is being described here.
2. Despite the absence of a verb of speaking, Sargon seems to be speaking here.

2. Late Assyrian Version

"[   ] let your messenger bear his tribute. If ... [   ]
[   ] when he had heard the merchants' words,
          he became sick at he[art   ]
[   ] when [Sar]gon had heard the merchants' words,
          he became sick at h[eart   ]
[   ] weapons, axes, ... [   ]
[   ] on his own legs[1] he went and enter[ed   ]   (5')
[   ] Ishtar, queen of Eulmash,[2] [   ]
[   ] Ishtar, who [   ]
[Ishtar, qu]een of Eulmash, who [   ]
[   ] ... [   ]
[   ] world regions [   ]   (10')

(fragmentary line, then breaks off)

F (1) a = Schroeder, VAS 12 193 (photo MDOG 55 plates 6 and 7 after p. 42 and in Izre'el, *Amarna*, pl. XXXV, XXXVII); b = a small, illegible piece from El-Amarna published by Gordon in OrNS 16 (1947), 21 (*375) could be an excerpt from the same story or a similar one (photo Izre'el, *Amarna*, pl. XLV); c = Schroeder, KAV 138, a piece from Assur that contains a text similar, so far as preserved, to the El-Amarna edition (photo in J. Westenholz, *Legends*, 388). (2) W. G. Lambert, AfO 20 (1963), 161–162.

Edition: (1) Weidner, *Boghazköy Studien* 6 (1922), 62–75 (treats a and KAV 138), with collations; Rainey, AOAT 8 (1976), 6–11 (a and c only); see pp. 47–48 there for *375. (2) W. G. Lambert, AfO 20 (1963), 161–162; (1) Kämmerer, AOAT 251 (1998), 268–275; both re-edited by J. Westenholz, *Legends*, 102–139, with detailed commentary and many new readings and interpretations adopted here; see also S. Izre'el, *Amarna*, 66–75 (with collations, pl. XXXVI).

Translation: Albright, JSOR 7 (1923), 1–20; Dhorme, *Revue Biblique* 33 (1924), 19–32.

Literature: Borger, HKL 1, 478; Güterbock, ZA 42 (1934), 21–22 and 86–91; JCS 18 (1964), 1–6; MDOG 101 (1969), 14–26 (edition of Hittite version); M. Liverani, "Naram-Sin e i presagi difficili," in F. M. Fales, ed., *Soprannaturale e potere nel mondo antico e nelle società tradizionali* (Milan, 1985), 34–37; H. Vanstiphout, "Comparative Notes on šar tamḫari," CRRAI 34 (1998), 573–589; more recent literature cited by J. Westenholz, *Legends*, 102–139.

Notes to Text: (1) Sargon was referred to in his own inscriptions as MAŠKIM.GI₄ INANNA, "emissary of Ishtar," the Akkadian reading of which is uncertain; read here perhaps [mašk]im!? For *a-šu-ri* I follow J. Westenholz. (29) Reading 7 ṣú-um-bi-ra-šu, where *sumbir* = *snbr* "pineseed." (9') *ša* GEŠTIN *šu-pu-u eṭ-lu-tu-šu*. I take GEŠTIN to stand here for GAL.GEŠTIN, a high military rank among the Hittites, but this would be itself, even if correct in terms of this edition, a misunderstanding of the Mesopotamian original, which could scarcely have contained such a word. Perhaps the original had ANŠE "equids," a sign similar in appearance to GEŠTIN. (18') Güterbock, JCS 18 (1964), 5 note 62.

1. That is, he was so agitated that he was not borne on the royal sedan chair but rushed off to the temple on foot?
2. The Ishtar temple in Agade.

(b) THE CUTHAEAN LEGEND OF NARAM-SIN

The Cuthaean Legend of Naram-Sin is a pseudonymous[1] poetic narrative in which Naram-Sin, grandson of Sargon of Akkad, relates how a supernatural host devastated his armies and land. While the story is based on a series of battles Naram-Sin of Akkad fought against coalitions of foreign and Mesopotamian enemies (see I.3c), the events are fictionalized and presented as a divine judgment against Naram-Sin, an arrogant and impetuous king who fails to heed unfavorable omens. "Cuthaean" refers to the city Cutha, in northern Babylonia, where, according to the late version of the poem (below, 3), Naram-Sin left this account inscribed on a stela.

1. Old Babylonian Version

The Old Babylonian version of this story, on a large tablet of 300 lines or more, is included because of the close correspondence of column iii with lines 85–93 of the later version; compare II.7b(3). Column ii, in which the king dispatches a messenger, is too fragmentary for translation. The messenger episode may correspond to 63ff. of the later version. Column iv contains a lament on the destruction that was not used in the later version. A second tablet is too fragmentary for translation.

(Naram-Sin describes his moves against the enemy host.)

a′) [The first time, I sent out against it 180,000 troops],

iii

It defeated them, it lef[t no one]!   (1)
A second time I sent out against it 120,000 troops,
It defeated them, it filled the plains (with their corpses)!
A third time I sent out against it 60,000 troops,
That (host) made a greater (slaughter) than before!   (5)

---

1. A study of this genre, though outdated in details, is H. G. Güterbock, "Die historische Tradition und ihre literarische Gestaltung bei Babyloniern und Hethitern bis 1200," ZA 42 (1934), 1–91. For more recent discussion of specific aspects of the pseudo-autobiographical genre, see Finkelstein in H. D. Lasswell et al., eds., *Propaganda and Communication in World History* I: *The Symbolic Instrument in Early Times* (Honolulu, 1979), 74–83; H. Galter, "Probleme historisch-lehrhafter Dichtung in Mesopotamien," CRRAI 32 (1985), 71–79. For a detailed study of the entire genre, see Longman, *Autobiography*, this text discussed 103–117.

Having killed 360,000 troops,
      it made the greatest slaughter ever!
As for me, I was confounded, bewildered,
I was at a loss, exhausted, anxious, and reduced to naught.
I said, "What has the god[1] brought upon my reign?   (10)
"I am a king who brings no well-being to his land,
"And a shepherd who brings no well-being to his people.
"What has my reign brought me?
"How shall I place myself that
"I may bring myself out of this?*   (15)
"He has mobilized against me a mighty foe
      to lay low the plains of Akkad.
"[He has rai]sed up against me the Hari-people of Malgium,[2]

(gap)

iv

Sanctuaries [   ]
The land was [utterly] devastated [   ]
The [   ] that Adad called out over the la[nd],
It has stamped out its hubbub, scattered its reason.   (5)
It laid low cities, hamlets, and holy places,
It has levelled everything completely!
Like that deluge of water that arose,
[   ] among the ancient peoples of [the land],
It has transformed the land of [Akk]ad,   (10)
It has laid the land low,
It has so diminished* (the land) as if it had never been,
The land is [des]troyed, all of it reduced to nothing!
Because of the anger of the gods, ... [   ]
Cities are laid waste, hamlets are laid low,   (15)
The hubbub of the [land it has bro]ught low
      and stamped out.
Like a flooding channel, it has transformed the land,

---

1. Presumably Enlil; compare II.36a, Tablet I, lines 69–71.
2. A Transtigridian city and land south of the Diyala River (Groneberg, RGTC 3, 157; Kutscher, RLA 7, 300–304). For the Hari-people, compare II.7b(3), following J. Westenholz, *Legends*, 275. There may also be confusion with the later version, line 31.

[It has utterly destr]oyed Akkad(?).[1]

(gap)
(The last column consists only of fragmentary lines.)

2. Middle Babylonian Version

The Middle Babylonian version of this story was an extensive composition, to judge from the remains of the hexagonal prism from Hattusha in Anatolia that preserves portions of the text. It deals with some of the same episodes as the later version (below, 3) but contains, like the Old Babylonian one, additional episodes and a different arrangement of them. To column b' 2'–4' compare the later version, line 29; 5'–6' compare to the later version, lines 31 and 33; 7'–8' correspond to the later version, line 37. For 10'ff. compare the later version, line 94. The preserved text opens by condemning a king (Enmerkar?) who left no commemorative stela. It then describes the supernatural host. The gods decree that the host have no permanent dwelling and should not partake of civilized life. The episode preserved in column c' has no parallel in the later version.

Naram-Sin [   ]   (1)

(gap)

b'

[En]merkar(?)* did not write for me a ste[la],
[   ] he was not my brother* and did not [take] my hand,
I did not bless him before Shamash.

In the face of them, humankind entered caves,[2]   (5')
City, in the face of them, was no city,
Ground, in the face of them, was no ground.
Six were their kings, glorious allies,
Their troops were 360,000(?).
Ea, the lord, sent them against the city,

---

1. Text: *Wa-ri-x*, perhaps intending Warium, a term that some scholars suggest was an ancient name for northern Babylonia (F. R. Kraus, *Sumerer und Akkader, Ein Problem der altmesopotamischen Geschichte,* MKNAW NR 33/8 [1970], 37–39; RGTC 3, 254).
2. This line is corrupted in the later version, line 31, to read "humans with raven faces" (see below, Late Assyrian Version).

He created them from the dirt(?) of his nails(?).[1]
[He   ] ... them, and [gave them] the awesomeness of lions,   (10′)
Death, plague, mourning* ... [   ]
Hunger, want, [high] prices [   ].
The Great One sent off with them [   ].
Ea made ready to speak, saying to the gods his brethren,
"I made this host, do you pronounce its fate,   (15′)
"Lest it utterly destroy humankind.
"Let its name be spoken of for all time.
"Let them reverence the wall and the bricks of the wall,
"Let it be a god, let them worship it.[2]
"Let it not seize the city of Shamash the warrior,   (20′)
"Let it do no plundering, nor let it thrive within,
"Let it eat no food to sustain it,
"Let it smell no [ar]oma of beer,
"Let it drink water!
"Let it wander all day,
"At night, let it lie down but find [no sleep]."   (25′)

[Six] were their kings, glorious allies,
[360],000(?) were their troops.
The mountains [bore them],
[The   ] reared them [   ]
[   ] to the edge [ ] the land [   ]
[   ] plunder [   ]   (30′)
[   ] they saw [   ]

(gap)

c′

They approached Akkad, to the land of [ ]
They approached the gate of Agade [   ]
To Naram-Sin thus [they] cried,   (10′)
Saying, "We are six kings, allies, glorious, ...
"360,000(?) are our troops and with us ...,

1. Line corrupt; compare II.5, Tablet I v 25.
2. These lines may mean that the enemy is supposed to worship Naram-Sin's capital, Agade, as a god (so argued by the translator, RA 73 [1979], 179, but this has not found acceptance). Or, this passage might be a recollection of a wall built by the kings of Ur to keep Amorite invaders out of Mesopotamia, toward the end of the third millennium B.C.

"... shepherds, herdsmen, sea folk.
"They have approached you in force ..."

(Naram-Sin's response is lost.)

3. Late Assyrian Version

Known from eighth- and seventh-century manuscripts, the late version of the Cuthaean legend is about 80 percent preserved. Like the Old Babylonian version (above, 1), this text takes the form of a fictitious stela, beginning with a self-introduction of the king, turning to autobiographical narrative, and concluding with blessings on the reader who heeds its words.

The principal message of this text is that kings who carry out projects in the face of unfavorable omens are doomed to catastrophe. This renders more specific the general caution of Mesopotamian proverbs, prophecies, and oracles that deal with self-preservation of the king (see II.12), and stresses the importance of divination, especially extispicy, for important decisions.[1] This text combines the cautious, even pessimistic approach of wisdom literature with a theme more common in poetry: affirmation that one's highest duty is to transmit knowledge and experience to the future.

[Open the foundation box]* and read well the stela   (1)
[That I, Naram-Sin], son of Sargon,
[Have written for] all time.
[The Kishite(?) ruled the land],* then passed away,
[Meskiaggasher(?) ruled the land], then passed away,[2]   (5)
[Enmerkar, became r]uler of the land.[3]

---

1. For general cautions, compare, for example, this version, lines 170f. to III.16a, lines 42ff. For a literary analysis of this text from the perspective of the king's reaction to unfavorable omens, see the study of Liverani, cited below, p. 355, Literature. Grayson (AfO 27 [1980], 171) suggests that the text promotes extispicy over other means of divination such as astrology.

2. Meskiaggasher (free restoration) was the father of Enmerkar, according to Mesopotamian historical tradition, and founder of Eanna (see I.3d). Enmerkar was said to have founded nearby Uruk. The preceding dynasty ruled from Kish, hence the free restoration in line 4.

3. For discussion of this passage, see J. Westenholz, *Legends*, 301–303. It is by no means certain that Enmerkar is mentioned here or that he is the subject of lines 11–16 below. Enmerkar, a Sumerian ruler of the first dynasty of Uruk (early third millennium B.C.), was the subject of several Sumerian epic poems; for these, see H. Vanstiphout, *Epics of Sumerian Kings, The Matter of Aratta* (Atlanta, 2003). Why Naram-Sin cites Enmerkar is unclear, nor is any story now known wherein Enmerkar triumphs over an enemy host. For another allusion to Enmerkar, see below, III.20b.

[When the years] passed,
[When the days] went by,
The [gods'(?)] intentions toward [the land cha]nged.
[A host arose] and rode [against his land].   (10)
[Enmerkar(?) inquired of the] great [gods]:
[Ishtar, Ilaba?], Zababa, Annunitum,
[Shullat, Hanish, Shamash] the warrior.
[He(?) summoned] and charged [the diviners].
[Seven extispicies on seven] lambs he(?) made.   (15)
[He(?) set up ho]ly reed altars.
[The diviners spoke to him thus]:
"[   ] the 'thread' [   ]
"[   ] the 'mark' [   ]
"[   ]   (20)
"Your corpse ... [... in] the earth."
Scarcely had the great gods [spoken thus],
Enmerkar's corpse ...,
        Shamash imposed a harsh judgment on him.
The judgment on him, the decision [he made on] his ghost,
        the ghosts of [his children],
The ghosts of his family, the ghosts of his descendants —
        (the judgment of) Shamash [the warrior] —   (25)
The Lord of Above and Below, the lord of the Anunna-gods,
        lord of the ghosts (of the dead) —
Was that they would drink muddy water
        and drink no clear water (in the netherworld).
(Enmerkar), whose wisdom and weaponry captured,
        defeated, and slew that host,
Did not write upon a stela,
        so I could not spare myself (his ordeal),[1]
Nor did he publish his inscription, so I could not bless him.   (30)
Troops with bodies of "cave birds,"[2] humans with raven faces
Did the great gods create,
Their city was in the earth the gods made.*
Tiamat suckled them,

---

1. Interpretation uncertain; see J. Westenholz, *Legends*, 306–308.
2. This word could mean "partridge," but the line is corrupt (see p. 345 note 2, p. 346 note 2).

Belet-ili their mother made (them) fair.[1]   (35)
Inside the mountain(s) they grew up, became adults,
         got their stature.
Seven kings they were, allies, glorious in form,
360,000 were their troops.
Anu-banini[2] their father was king;
         their mother the queen Melili,
Their eldest brother, their vanguard, was named Memandah,   (40)
Their second brother was named Medudu,
Their third brother was named [   ]pish,
Their fourth brother was named Tartadada,
Their fifth brother was named Baldahdah,
Their sixth brother was named Ahubandih,   (45)
Their seventh brother was named Hurrakidu.
They rode against the silver mountains,
A soldier seized them, they smote their thighs
         (to spur their mounts).
At the beginning of their incursion,
         when they invaded Burushandar,[3]
The entire region of Burushandar was destroyed,   (50)
Puhlu was destroyed,
Puranshu was destroyed.[4]
"Should I go out against [   ]?

---

1. Compare Tiamat's role as creatress of monsters in the Creation Epic, III.17, and Belet-ili's role as creatress of an enemy host in the Old Babylonian fragment edited by Römer, WdO 4 (1967), 12–28.

2. This is the name of a historical personage who may have lived about the time of Naram-Sin of Agade; see D. O. Edzard, "Zwei Inschriften am Felsen von Sar-i-Pul-i-Zohab: Anubanini 1 und 2," AfO 24 (1973), 73–77. The other names are unknown and presumably imaginary; although exotic-sounding Memandah and Medudu could have fanciful Sumerian etymologies, "He added battle (to battle" and "He goes often to battle."

3. An echo of Burushhanda, a wealthy commercial city in south central Anatolia; see above, III.7a.

4. All unknown, and presumably fabulous or corrupted toponyms. I take 52ff. to be rhetorical oracular inquiries; see II.10c and I. Starr, Questions to the Sungod, Divination and Politics in Sargonid Assyria (Helsinki, 1990), xvi. These were often connected with specific military maneuvers. For further discussion of this list of places, see Landsberger, State Archives of Assyria, Bulletin 3/1 (1989), 44; J. Westenholz, Legends, 313–314.

"Is the greatness of that host
> whose camp is Shubat-Enlil ...?"[1]

Then they all [   ] inside Subartu,[2]   (55)

They destroyed the (upper?) Sealands[3]
> and invaded Gutium,[4]

They destroyed Gutium and invaded Elam,[5]

They destroyed Elam and arrived at the seacoast,

They killed the people of the crossing place,[6]
> they were thrown to [   ],

Dilmun, Magan, Meluhha,
> whatever was in the midst of the sea they killed.[7]   (60)

Seventeen kings with 90,000 troops

Came with them to support them!

I summoned a soldier and charged him,

"I [give you a lance] and a pin,

"Touch them with the lance, [prick them] with the pin.   (65)

"If [blood] comes out, they are human like us.

"If no blood comes out, then they are spirits, ill fate,

"Phantoms, evil demons, handiwork of Enlil."

The soldier brought back his report [to me],

---

1. Shubat-Enlil, modern Tell Leilan in the Habur region, was an important city at the end of the third millennium B.C. and became the capital of the empire of Shamshi-Adad in the eighteenth century B.C. Abandoned before the middle of the second millennium B.C., the place could only have been a remote historical name to an eighth-century scholar.

2. Subartu, as used here, was an obsolete name for northern Mesopotamia; see P. Michalowski, "Mental Maps and Ideology: Reflections on Subartu," in H. Weiss, ed., *The Origin of Cities in Dry-farming Syria and Mesopotamia in the Third Millennium B.C.* (Guilford, Conn., 1986), 129–156.

3. I take this to refer to the "Upper Sea," a vague term that at different times may refer to the Mediterranean, the Black Sea, or perhaps Lake Van.

4. As used here, a traditional term for the mountainous regions east and northeast of Mesopotamia; see W. W. Hallo, "Gutium," RLA 3, 708–720; Oppenheim, *Cambridge History of Iran* 2:547 note 2 and I.5b.

5. Southwest Iran.

6. May refer to peoples who may have lived where sea voyages began to the lands mentioned in line 60.

7. In the third millennium, Bahrain, Oman/Makran, and the Indus Valley respectively; perhaps by the time of this text traditional literary names for far-off lands reached by sea. See J.-J. Glassner, "Mesopotamian Textual Evidence on Magan/Makan in the Late Third Millennium B.C.," in P. M. Costa and M. Tosi, eds., *Oman Studies, Serie Orientale Roma* 63 (Rome, 1989), 181–191; D. T. Potts, ed., *Dilmun, New Studies in the Archaeology and Early History of Bahrein* (Berlin, 1983). For Meluhha, a bibliography has been assembled by S. and A. Parpola and R. Brunswig, Jr., JESHO 20 (1977), 129 note 1.

"I touched them with [the lance],   (70)
"I pricked them with [the pin], and blood came out."
I summoned the diviners and charged them,
[Seven] extispicies upon seven lambs I performed,
[I set up] holy reed altars,
I inquired of the great gods   (75)
Ishtar, Ilaba(?), Zababa, Annunitum,
Sh[ullat, Hanish],* Shamash the warrior.
The latchkey[1] of the great gods did not give me
        or my dream spirit[2] permission to go.*
Speaking to myself, thus I said,
"What lion observed divination?   (80)
"What wolf consulted a dream interpreter?
"I will go, as I like, like a brigand,
"I will cast off what belongs to the gods,
        I will hold fast (only) to myself!"[3]
When the first year had come,
I sent out 120,000 troops against them,
        not one returned alive.   (85)
When the second year arrived, I sent out 90,000 troops
        against them, not one returned alive.
When the third year arrived, I sent out 60,700 troops
        against them, not one returned alive.
I was confounded, bewildered, at a loss, anxious, in despair.
Speaking to myself, thus I said,
"What have I left for a reign?   (90)
"I am a king who brings no well-being to his land,
"A shepherd who brings no well-being to his flock.
"How shall I place myself that I may bring myself out of this?
"Fear of lions,* death, plague, convulsions,*
"Panic, ague, economic collapse, starvation,   (95)
"Want, anxiety of every kind came down with them.

1. Perhaps this refers to Shamash, god of divination (J. Westenholz, *Legends*, 317–318).
2. The dream spirit would normally give the omen, rather than receive it (Alster, *Proverbs*, 1:242).
3. Compare the Sumerian poem "The Curse of Agade," 92–99 (J. S. Cooper, *The Curse of Agade* [Baltimore, 1983], 55), in which Naram-Sin finally gives up waiting for a favorable oracle.

"Above, in [the earth?], there was a deluge,[1]
"Below, in [the netherworld?], there was [an earthquake?]."
Ea, lord of the dep[ths, made ready] to speak,
Said to the [gods his brethren],   (100)
"O great gods [   ],
"You told me [to make this host],
"And the dirt[2] [of my fingernails?] you ..."
When New Year of the fourth year arrived,
At the prayer to Ea, [sage] of the great gods,   (105)
[When I offered] the holy offerings of New Year,
I [sought] the holy instructions.
I summoned the diviners and [charged them],
Seven extispicies upon seven lambs I performed.
I set up holy reed altars,   (110)
I inquired of the great gods:
Ishtar, Ilaba(?), Zababa, Annunitum,
[Shullat and Hanish, Shamash the warrior].
The [diviners spoke to m]e [thus],
"If [   ] bears [   ]   (115)
"[   ] there is [   ]
"[   ] falls over it,
"The battleax will shed [blood],
"[   ] will be submerged [in] blood."
From their midst twelve troops flew off from me,   (120)
I went after them in haste and hurry,
I overcame those troops,
I brought those troops back.
Speaking to myself, [thus I said],
"Without divination (of liver), flesh, and entr[ails],*
      [I should not] lay [hand on them to kill?]."[3]   (125)
[I performed] an extispicy concerning them:
The latchkey of the great gods [ordered] mercy for them.[4]

---

1. Following J. Westenholz, *Legends*, 319. This compares the scourge of the host to the flood of old, both sent at the will of the gods.
2. See above, p. 347 note 1.
3. Naram-Sin has now learned to respect the outcome of divination.
4. Text possibly corrupted from an original "dream spirit" or the like (*zaqīqu*). A Sumerian incantation refers to a dream spirit being sent to Agade, possibly a reference to this episode (see Butler, AOAT 258 [1998], 321–324).

The shining Morning Star spoke from heaven thus,
"To Naram-Sin, son of Sargon:
"Cease, you shall not destroy the perditious seed!*   (130)
"In future days Enlil will raise them up for evil.
"It (the host) awaits the angry heart of Enlil,
"O city! Those troops will be killed,
"They will burn and besiege dwelling places!
"O city! They will pour out their blood!
"The earth will diminish its harvests,
        the date palms their yield.
"O city! Those troops will die!*   (135)
"City against city, house against house will turn.
"Father to father, brother to brother,
"Man to man, companion to friend,
"None will tell the truth to each other.
"People will be taught untruth,
        strange things [will they learn].   (140)
"This city is hostile, they kill,
"That hostile city (another) hostile city will capture.
"Ten quarts of barley will cost a mina of silver,[1]
"There was no strong king [to govern] in the land."
To the great gods I brought (the captives) as tribute,   (145)
I did not lay hand on them to kill.
Whoever you may be, governor, prince, or anyone else,
Whom the gods shall name to exercise kingship,
I have made a foundation box for you,
        I have written you a stela,
In Cutha in the Emeslam,   (150)
In the cella of Nergal have I left it for you.
Behold this stele,
Listen to the wording of this stela:
You should not be confounded,
        you should not be bewildered,
You should not be afraid, you should not tremble,   (155)
Your stance should be firm.

---

1. This means that barley was extremely expensive, as in time of famine.

You should do your task in your wife's embrace.[1]
Make your walls trustworthy,
Fill your moats with water.
Your coffers, your grain, your silver,
    your goods and chattels   (160)
Bring into your fortified city.
Wrap up your weapons and [lean] them in a corner,
Restrain your valor, take care of your person.
Though he raids your land, go not out against him,
Though he drives off your livestock, go not nigh him,   (165)
Though he eats the flesh of your soldiery(?),
Though he murders ... [...],
Be moderate, control yourself,
Answer them, "Yes, my lord!"
To their wickedness, repay kindness,   (170)
To kindness (add) gifts and gratifications.
Avoid them whenever you can.
Let expert scribes compose a stela for you.
You who have read my stela and so placed yourself
    to bring yourself out of [an ordeal like mine],
You who have blessed me,
    so may a future one bless you.   (175)

Text: (1) Finkelstein, JCS 11 (1957), 84–85, photo pl. III–IV. (2) Otten, KBo 19 98. (3) King, CT 13 39–41, 44; Campbell Thompson, GETh pl. 34 (K. 8582); Gurney, STT 30; OECT 11 103. Minor variants have not been noted here.
Edition: J. Westenholz, *Legends*, 263–368, with numerous readings and interpretations used here.
Translation: J. Westenholz, *Legends*, 228–231.
Literature: Walker, JCS 33 (1981), 191–194; M. Liverani, "Naram-Sin e i presagi difficili" in F. M. Fales, ed., *Soprannaturale e potere nel mondo antico e nelle società tradizionali* (Milan, 1985), 31–45; Landsberger, SAAB 3/1 (1989), 42–44; Longman, *Autobiography*, 103–117.
*Notes to Text: (OB iii 15) *pagram u ramānam šušû* (compare Late Assyrian Version 30, 93, 174, which has *pagram u pūtam šušû*). The expression means literally "cause body and face to go forth." It is generally taken to mean "save oneself"; see J. Westenholz, *Legends*, 273–274. (iii 17) [*iš*]-*ši-a*?, compare Atrahasis (II.36a) Tablet I line 58. (iv 12) "Diminished" by suggestion of WGL. (MB b' 3') WGL. (MB b' 9') Perhaps *iš-pu-ur* corrupted from *ṣu-pu-ur*? (11') *giḫlu* (WGL). (LAssyr 1) For

1. That is, he should beget an heir to the throne, lest the kingdom be weakened by uncertain succession.

this restoration, see Walker, JCS 33 (1981), 191–195. (4) The restoration of this and the succeeding lines is guesswork. (33) Text: *a-lu-šu*, meaning unclear; perhaps this is the "city" (*ālu*) apostrophized in lines 133ff. (50) AHw, 1025a (*ittaspaḫ*). (54) Or: *lul-pu-ut! lib-bu-u?* (55) *it-[taš-bu]*, WGL. (77) Restoration here (whence lines 13 and 113) courtesy von Soden. (78) For further discussion of this difficult line, see Fuchs, SAAS 8, 97; Pongratz-Leisten, SAAS 10, 9. (94) Variant adds "(at?) night"; (94 bis) Or: "famine." (125) Reading courtesy von Soden: *bi-ri še-ri ta-kal!-[ti]*. (130) For *ḫalqāte*, see Cogan and Tadmor, OrNS 46 (1977), 80 note 26, who suggest "ruinous." (135) J. Westenholz, *Legends*, 325, suggests "The city of those soldiers will die," but "city" is construed as singular in line 138, so this seems grammatically impossible.

III.8 SHULGI PROPHECY

This enigmatic text, like III.13, alludes in vague terms to future events in Babylonia, in this case through the mouth of Shulgi. Shulgi was a Sumerian king of the Third Dynasty of Ur from the end of the third millennium B.C., here considered a god and founder of the city Nippur. From the condition of the text, it is not clear whether it conveys prophecy in retrospect, referring to events that had already happened, or represents a wishful program for royal benefactions cast as an ancient prophecy. This text was paired in later scribal editions with the Marduk prophecy (III.13). References to Nippur and Babylon point to a date for its composition in the latter half of the second millennium B.C. or the first part of the first millennium B.C. The text is badly broken and written in an arcane style, so that for much of it one can only guess at its general tenor rather than translate it.

(i 1) I (am) Shulgi, beloved of Enlil and Ninlil: the noble one, Shamash, has told me, Ishtar my lady has revealed (this) to [me]. Father and mother, (personal) god [and (personal) goddess], whatever my fathers heard from the mouth of the [great] gods [   ], may Ur always s[ing], may Larsa [   ]! [When] he came down from his rooftop,[1] when from the roof of his gate [he   ], wild bulls and wild donkeys ... of my lordly city N[ippur] ... may [   ] sixfold, may [   ]. *(large gap)*

(ii 2') I was lord of the four world regions, from the rising of the sun to the setting of the sun. I founded Nippur, Bond of Heaven and Earth. When I spoke, the gods would listen to me. At my own expense, I built that wall and made it firm. Enlil ordered me, "Build ..." Enlil gave me the order, and I annihilated Baldaha.[2] Enlil ordered me, "Make war!" and I annihilated Baldaha. I ... from his family over the four world regions. Ninlil ordered me, "Put

---

1. Suitable place for prayer, especially to Shamash.
2. Meaning unknown, reference obscure. One may compare the Baldahdah of the Cuthaean Legend (III.7b 3 line 44). The "wall" referred to here may be a recollection of a wall built by the kings of Ur to resist Amorite invaders from the north and west, or it may be a tradition, not otherwise documented, that Shulgi built the walls of Nippur. A late Babylonian chronicle (J.-J. Glassner, *Chroniques mésopotamiennes* [Paris, 1993], 230) credits Shulgi with building the walls of Ur. There was also in circulation in early second-millennium schools a story about a Sumerian king called "Nanne" who never finished any project, including the walls of Nippur (Alster, *Proverbs*, 2:86).

Humba in order(?)!"[1] The [ ] of the king of Susa(?) ... *(large gap)*

(iii 3′) Babylon ... the citizens of Nippur [and?] Babylon. [The god/dess] will not stand ..., nor will (s)he give him [scepter], nor will (s)he give him reign. [A king of the] four world regions [... who?] has neglected the citizenry of Nippur [and Babylon] and rendered no righteous judgment, [ ] that prince will proceed with "Woe!" and "Alas!" All lands are given as one to the king of Babylon and Nippur. Whichever king shall arise after me, on account of(?) Balda[ha] (and) the land of Elam to the east, he will be [thrown into] complete [disorder]. The Hittites will [conquer] Babylon [ ]. *(large gap)*

(iv 1′) [ ] will be built. In the region of Babylon, the builder of that palace will come to grief, that prince will experience misery, and will have no satisfaction. So long as he is king, fighting and warfare will not cease. In that reign brother will devour his brother, people will sell their children for silver, all lands will be thrown into complete disorder. Man will forsake maid, maid will forsake man. Mother will bar her door against daughter. The possessions of Babylon will go to Subartu[2] and the land of Assyria. The king of Babylon will send out the possessions of his palace to the prince of Assur in [Baltil]. For all time Baltil[3] [ ].

(v) [ ] ... will take place, friend will slay his friend with a weapon, companion will destroy companion with a weapon, [the lands] will be totally destroyed. [The (great?) people] will become small; Nippur will be cast down. That prince's head will be held high, (because of?) the city that is established [for him?] on the bank of the Tigris and the Euphrates. By the command of E[nlil] the reign of the king of Babylon will come to an end. A certain one [ ] will arise ... he will restore Bad-Tibira, he will renew Girsu and Lagash, the [sanc]tuary of the gods will be (re)built. He will maintain [the offerings of the great gods]. He will restore the [ ] and shrines. The [sanctuar]y of Nippur [and] Isin [ ] will be (re)built, [ ] will be cast down. *(large gap)*

---

1. Elamite deity.
2. Assyria is meant; see p. 351 note 2.
3. Assur (restored from variant); see p. 316 note 2.

Text: col. i 1–17 = Borger, BiOr 28 (1971), 20; 1′–18′ = Strong, *The Babylonian & Oriental Record* 6 (1892/3), 4–5 = H. Winckler, *Sammlung von Keilschrifttexten* II (Leipzig, 1893/4) 73. cols. ii–iii = Strong-Winckler, *op. cit.* + Borger, BiOr 28 (1971), 13 (right-hand piece). col. iv = King, CT 13 49. col. v = King, CT 13 49 + Lambert, JCS 18 (1964), 26 "ii." col. vi = Lambert, JCS 18 (1964), 26 "i." Biggs in *Studies Astour*, 173–176, suggests that Wiseman and Black, CTN 4 64, 65, and 69 belong to this composition, but these are too fragmentary for translation.

Edition: Borger, BiOr 28 (1971), 14–15; earlier treatment by Güterbock, ZA 42 (1934), 83–86.

Translation: Longman, *Autobiography*, 236–237.

Literature: Longman, *Autobiography*, 142–146.

C. KINGS OF BABYLONIA AND THEIR TIMES

III.9 AGUM-KAKRIME AND THE RETURN OF MARDUK

This document, known only from mid-first millennium manuscripts, purports to be a first-person account by a certain Agum, an early Kassite king (mid-second millennium B.C.?) of how he restored the cult image of Marduk in Babylon. No one knows whether this inscription was actually composed in the time of the king named, or whether it is later and pseudonymous.

On the one hand, pseudonymity is well known in Mesopotamian literature (see III.7b). No early copies of this text are known, nor is the king known outside of this text. Another certainly pseudonymous text deals with the story of Marduk's statue (III.13).

On the other hand, without consideration of the text's genre, there is no good reason to doubt its genuineness on either linguistic or historical grounds. Even if pseudonymous, it may be based on an actual inscription. It is hard to understand why this particular king would have been chosen for a putative "author" since, unlike other pseudonymous authors in Mesopotamian tradition, he is not well known. In sum, the genuineness of the text can neither be established nor disproved.

Genuine or not, the text deals with an important event in second-millennium Babylonian history: recovery of the cult statues of Marduk and his consort, Sarpanitum, from the Hittites. The Hittites had taken the precious statues as booty from the sack of Babylon in the mid-sixteenth century. Their recovery was essential for Babylonian pride and perception of their divine favor. Compare Marduk and the Elamites (III.11c) and the Seed of Kingship (III.12a).

After an introduction praising himself, Agum explains that Marduk and the other gods had at last resolved that Marduk should return to his temple Esagila in Babylon. He does not explain how the Hittites or their allies were persuaded to relinquish the image. Agum takes omens to determine how the image is to be treated while it and its sanctuary are repaired (see also Erra and Ishum [IV.17]). The images are lavishly refurbished and the sanctuary restored with a set of magnificent doors. In addition, Agum dedicates the craftsmen who repaired the images to the temple by exempting them from taxes and service. He concludes by asking a blessing upon himself for his works. A scribal "afterword" enjoins that the text be considered privileged lore, presumably because it has to do with the fortunes of Marduk.

(i 1) [Agum]-kakrime, son of Tashshigurumash, pure offspring of (the god) Shuqamunu,[1] whom Anu and Enlil, Ea and Marduk, Sin and Shamash nominated (for kingship), the mighty man of Ishtar, the most warlike of goddesses am I!

(i 11) Intelligent and understanding king, obedient and conciliatory king, son of Tashshigurumash, descendant of Abirattash, the valorous [man] among his [brethren?], lawful heir of Agum the elder, pure offspring, royal offspring, who holds firm the leadline of humankind(?),* shepherd, lordly one am I! Shepherd of numerous humankind, warrior, shepherd who makes secure his ancestral house am I!

(i 31) King of the Kassites and the Akkadians, king of the wide land of Babylonia, he who made the numerous peoples of Eshnunna to settle down; king of Padan and Alman, king of Gutium, a stupid people, king who caused the four world regions to submit,* favorite of the great gods am I!

(i 44) When Marduk, lord of Esagila and Babylon, (and) the great gods ordered with their holy command his [ret]urn to Babylon, (and?) Marduk had set his face toward Babylon, [I prayed to?] Marduk, [   ] my prayers. I carefully planned to fetch Marduk, and toward Babylon did I set his face.* I went to the assistance of Marduk, who loves my reign.

(ii 8) I asked of King Shamash by divination(?),[2] I sent to a far-off land, to the land of the Haneans,[3] and Marduk and Sarpanitum did they conduct to me, and Marduk and Sarpanitum, who love my reign, did I return to Esagila and Babylon. In the chamber that Shamash had confirmed to me in my inquiry (by divination) did I return them. I settled various craftsmen there, metalworker, goldsmith, engraver did I [   ] ... did I [   ]. Four talents of [red gold] did I grant for the attire of Marduk and Sarpanitum; in magnificent attire, attire of red gold, did I attire Marduk and Sarpanitum. Genuine

1. Patron deity of the Kassite dynasty (see Arnaud, *Aula Orientalis* 19 [2001], 133–135).
2. Perhaps by pouring oil over water and studying the resulting pattern; see G. Pettinato, *Die Ölwahrsagung bei den Babyloniern, Studi Semitici* 21–22 (Rome, 1966). It is tempting to emend the sign to read the more common word "extispicy" rather than the unusual "oil divination."
3. Possibly here a literary term for the Hittites (Landsberger, JCS 8 [1954], 65 note 160 and 238), or to be taken literally to mean that the statue was left in Hana, a land on the Middle Euphrates, by the Hittites. For its use to mean Greeks or Macedonians, see IV.62.

lapis,[1] green chlorite(?),* chalcedony(?), ...-gems, agate,* ...-agate, Meluhha-beads, alabaster, precious *shilu*-stones, *sikillu*-stones, whatever is choice(st) in its mountains, for the sanctuary of Marduk and Sarpanitum did I grant. The surface of the attire of their great divinity did I embellish. A tiara with magnificent horns, lordly tiaras, symbolic of divinity, full of splendor, of lapis and gold did I set upon his head.* On the top of his crown a *mushsharu*-gem and choice stones did I set. The surface of his crown with chalcedony(?), *mushsharu*, chlorite(?), lapis, and agate did I embellish.

(iii 13) A dragon, an eagle, [symbolic?] of their divinity [ ], gold *(gap of thirteen lines)* did I surround and dress [ ]. The storehouse [ ] ... did I set. ... Chalcedony(?) [ ] for the second large chamber

(iii 39) ... did I add to [ ], a gold necklace, obsidian, ..., on (his?) neck did I s[et]. Jewelry [ ], jewelry [ ], eye-stones, ... beads, chlorite *(gap of four lines)* did I overlay. Upon his seat, the cedar seat, did I install him until I moved them into their magnificent godly sanctuaries.

(iv 9) [For what? the] various craftsmen used: [ ] cedar, juniper, [ ], to the holy mountain [for? its] pleasing s[cent? did] I send. Silver, *(gap of twenty lines)* ... great matching doors of cedar did I have fashioned, in the cult chamber of Marduk and Sarpanitum did I set (them) up. With long bands of bronze did I fasten them. Their doorposts with bands of refined copper did I hold fast. With serpent, hairy hero-man, bull man, lion monster, lion man, fish man, [ ], [fish] goat[2]* of lapis, yellow agate(?), carnelian, and alabaster did I inlay them. Their purification did I carry out, the sanctified doors in the sanctuary of Marduk and Sarpanitum did I set up.

(v 14) Finally, I purified Esagila throughout (with) snake charmers. After the purification of the temple throughout *(gap of seventeen lines)*... the Door of Radiance,[3] the sanctuaries of Marduk did I bring them (the gods) in, and their magnificent festivals of rejoic-

---

1. Literally: "lapis of the mountain," as opposed to artificial lapis, well known in Mesopotamia from an early date.
2. For these monsters, see the Epic of Creation (III.17), Tablet I lines 141ff. and p. 444 note 2.
3. Cella of Marduk's temple in Babylon (George, *House Most High*, 107).

ing did I perform. The Edadihegal[1] did I cause to be cared for(?).*
Their gift(?) to my lord and lady did I grant. (*gap of four lines*).

(vi 5) A chalice of gold ... [ ], a chalice of lapis, a great service(?)
of silver did I give to Marduk. Gifts of silver and gold for the gods
of Esagila did I grant. After I had appointed (what was) fine and
fair for Esagila,* for the des[tinies?] (*gap of twenty-one lines*) did I [ ].

(vi 33) Umman-[ ], together with his household, his fields, and
[his orchards]; Qishti-[ ], the exorcist, together with [his house-
hold], his fields, and his orchards; Marduk-muballit, the carpenter,
together with his household, his fields, and his orchards:

(vi 42) I,* the king, Agum, who constructed the sanctuary of
Marduk, who restored Esagila, who brought Marduk into his
dwelling (with?) gifts,* exempted those craftsmen (from service
and taxes), as well as the houses, fields, and orchards, in honor of
Marduk and Sarpanitum.

(vii 11) May King Agum's days be long, may his years be
prolonged, may his reign be awash(?)* in prosperity. May the
bosom of the vast heavens be opened for him and the clouds [ ]
rain. [ ] Marduk ... orchard [   ] forever [   ] fa[ir] fruit let it
produce for good King Agum, who constructed the sanctuaries of
Marduk, who exempted the craftsmen.

(vii 34) May Anu and Antu bless him in heaven, may Enlil and
Ninlil in Ekur ordain him a destiny of (long) life, may Ea and
Damkina, who dwell in the great depths, grant him a life of long
days! May Dingirmah, Lady of the "Great Mountains," perfect for
him pure offspring.* May Sin, the luminary of heaven, grant him
royal descent for all time! May the young (hero) Shamash, young
(hero) of heaven and netherworld, make firm the foundations of
his royal throne for all time! May Ea, lord of the deep, perfect him
in wisdom! May Marduk, who loves his reign, the lord of the deep,
perfect him with respect to his prosperity!

(viii 24) [In]sc[ription] of Agum: The one who understands
should reveal (this only) to one who understands; the one who does
[not] understand should not see (this). That would be an abomination to Shullat and Hanish, Shamash and Adad, the lords of divination.

1. Chapel in Marduk's temple in Babylon (George, *Topographical Texts*, 390).

Text: Pinches, V R 33; Campbell Thompson, GETh pl. 36 Rm 505.

Edition: Jensen, KB III/1, 134–153; P. Stein, *Die mittel- und neubabylonischen Königsinschriften bis zum Ende der Assyrerherrschaft, Jenaer Beiträge zum Vorderen Orient* 3 (2000), 150–163.

Translation: Longman, *Autobiography*, 221–224.

Literature: J. Brinkman, *Materials and Studies for Kassite History* I (Chicago, 1976), 97; Borger, HKL 1, 406; Longman, *Autobiography*, 83–88. For further discussion of the authenticity of this text, see Na'aman, *Iraq* 46 (1984), 122; Astour, JAOS 106 (1986), 327–331; Schramm, BiOr 52 (1995), 94–95; Sassmannshausen in H. Hunger, R. Pruzsinszky, eds., *Mesopotamian Dark Age Revisited, Österreichische Akademie der Wissenschaften, Denkschriften der Gesamtakademie* 32 (2004), 64.

*Notes to Text: (i 21) Reading ṣir-re-ti ni!-i-ši. (i 40) muštaškin, see Heidel, JNES 4 (1945), 252 (šukēnu); von Soden, ZA 49 (1949), 332 (šakānu); the latter seems preferable for the parallelism. (ii 1–4) See Farber, JNES 56 (1997), 229. (ii 36) Steinkeller, ZA 72 (1982), 251. (ii 38) Sollberger, *Studies Reiner*, 379–380 (iii 2) Text: "his" head, either a mistake for -šunu or intended as a distributive. (v 1) [suḫur].máš-ku₆ (WGL). (v 44) von Soden, AHw, 826b. (vi 16) Lines apparently corrupt. (vi 42) Reading a-na-<ku>. (vii 4) Obscure, perhaps referring to the craftsmen as "gifts." (vii 11) Differently Livingstone, N.A.B.U. 1990/86 ("closely guarded"). (viii 1) [zē]ra el-la! li-šak-lil-šu (WGL).

III.10 KURIGALZU, KING OF THE KASSITES

There were several Kassite kings named Kurigalzu in Babylonian history, so there can be no certainty that the two texts translated below refer to the same person.[1]

(a) KURIGALZU AND THE ISHTAR TEMPLE

This inscription, like the preceding, is known only from variant copies on clay tablets. Its authenticity is also open to question, since the lands and emoluments bestowed so generously could have been reason for a later forgery, which then could have been "rediscovered" and presented as a precedent to the ruling authority. Indeed, "The Donation of Kurigalzu" might be an appropriate nickname for this document.

> (i 1) Kurigalzu, great king, mighty king, king of the universe, favorite of Anu and Enlil, nominated (for kingship) by the lord of the gods am I! King who has no equal among all kings his ancestors, son of [Kadash]man-Harbe,[2] unrivalled king, who completed the fortifications of ..., who [fin]ished the Ekur, who [prov]ides for Ur and Uruk, who [guar]antees the rites of Eridu, who constructed the temples of Anu and Ishtar, who [guarantees] the regular offerings of the great gods,
>
> (i 16) I caused Anu, father of the great gods, to dwell in his exalted sanctuary. To Ishtar, the most great lady, who goes at my side, who maintains my army, shepherds my people, subdues those disobedient to me:
>
> (i 24) From the town Adatti, on the bank of the Euphrates, as far as the town Mangissi, bordering on the field Duranki, beloved of Enlil. From the town of my lady, Bit-Gashan-ama-kalla,* as far as the border of the city Girsu,[3] an area of 216,000 kor using a ratio per

---

1. For another, fragmentary composition about a king named Kurigalzu, see Finkel, AnSt 33 (1983), 75–80 and compare Grayson, BHLT, 47–55.

2. Brinkman, *Materials* (below, p. 366, Literature), 209.

3. Variant: Girri. Not to be confused with the well-known Girsu of Lagash; this locality is unknown otherwise.

surface unit of 30 quarts of seed barley, measured by the large cubit,[1] to Ishtar I granted.

(ii 5) 3 kor of bread, 3 kor of fine wine, 2 (large measures)[2] of date cakes, 30 quarts of imported dates, 30 quarts of fine(?) oil, 3 sheep per day did I establish as the regular offering for all time.

(ii 11) I set up boundary stones in all directions[3] and guaranteed the borders. The towns, fields, watercourses, and unirrigated land, and their rural settlements[4] did I grant to Ishtar, my lady.

(ii 16) Whosoever shall arise afterward and shall alter my deeds and change the command that I spoke, shall take out my boundary stones, shift my boundary lines, take away the towns, fields, watercourses, and non-irrigated lands, or the rural settlements in the neighborhood of Uruk, or cause (another) to take (them) away, or who shall attempt to convert them to state lands, may Ishtar, the most great lady, not go at his side in battle and combat, but inflict defeat and heavy losses upon his army and scatter his forces!

Text: Gadd, CT 36 6, 7; Keiser, BIN 2 33 (collated).
Edition: Ungnad, *Archiv für Keilschriftforschung* 1 (1923), 29–36.
Translation: Longman, *Autobiography*, 224–225.
Literature: Borger, HKL 1, 136 (considers to be genuine); J. Brinkman, *Materials and Studies for Kassite History* I (Chicago, 1976), 209: "there are at present no compelling reasons for doubting its authenticity"; see also Sommerfeld. AOAT 213 (1982), 172 note 4; Longman, *Autobiography*, 88–91.
Notes to Text: (i 29) What is combined in CT 36 6–7 as AMA is construed in BIN 2 36 as É.DINGIR, while the following traces, which I cannot decipher, have no parallel in the other manuscript.

1. The tract is measured, as was customary in this period, by expressing surface area in terms of the capacity of the dry measure of seed used to sow it, based on a schematic ratio of 30 quarts = 1 surface unit, the last expressed in linear measurements using the "large cubit." For the figures involved, see Ungnad, *Archiv für Keilschriftforschung* 1 (1923), 22. He reckons the area at about 524.88 square kilometers, or, if the sides of the tract were equal in length, a square more than twenty kilometers on a side, a princely gift.

2. Variant: 2 (ordinary) measures.

3. Literally: "above and below." This may be a reference to the "upper" and "lower" sides of the tract (long sides), but is taken here to mean "all."

4. Variant: "fields, watercourses, unirrigated land, and rural settlements of the town"(?).

(b) THE FAVOR OF KURIGALZU

This fragmentary poem opens with Kurigalzu's election to kingship by the assembled gods, then refers to his installation in Dur-Kurigalzu and Babylon. He grants a charter of privileges and exemptions to Babylon. After a gap of over a hundred lines, the text concludes with a plea, perhaps by a courtier, for royal favor and largesse, and a curse on anyone who changes the name of the petitioner in the document. The recondite style is comparable to that of the Poem of the Righteous Sufferer (III.14), and may have been typical of that cultivated at the Kassite court.

> The creator gods [   ]   (1)
> The Igigi-gods ... were assembled,
>   made the king greater than all ... .
> The great gods, one after another,
>   nominated him in the land of Karduniash,[1]
>   Dur-Kurigalzu,[2] the city [   ]
> In Babylon, seat of the Kassite king,
>   city from ancient times, founded ....
> In the temple of Shumaliya and Shuqamuna,[3]
>   the great gods, they made great his responsibilities,
>   bedizened him with awe-inspiring radiance,
>   perfected his flawless readiness for kingship.   (5)
> Kurigalzu, king of the universe, wise king,
>   who heeds mighty Shamash,
> Anu, Enlil, and Ea heed him!
> His kingship is magnificent, it has no rival,
> Weapon that overwhelms enemies, captor of his foes,
>   beloved of Marduk,
> Relentless storm, huge flood that wrecks watercraft,
>   lofty one, Anu's trust,   (10)
> Judge who finds out the truth like Shamash, who restores
>   well-being to the oppressed among all peoples,
> Grantor of a charter to the people of Babylon,
> Who exempted its people from service,

1. Kassite name for Babylonia.
2. Important Kassite city.
3. Kassite gods; see p. 361 note 1.

for the sake of Marduk, who loves his reign,
You removed from them recruiter, foreman,
    inspector, governor,
(You) who made the joyful people of Babylon lie down
    in green pastures,   (15)
[   ] of his land, who gathered in the scattered peoples [ ],
[   ] King Kurigalzu

(large gap)

I, like a (drifting) raft, have none to put confidence in me,
    like a sunken vessel, I was not deemed useful,
        the shore gave me up.
O Marduk, for the sake of Kurigalzu, your favored one,
    blot out my evil,
        shatter the consequences of my neglect!
Let me called to mind in my lord's palace, let me find favor,
    let me see relief,
Let my frustration quit me, my misery forsake me,
    let me put my evil out of my mind!
May my lord bestow upon me favor and wealth,   (5')
Grain, oil, wool, cattle, sheep and goats, arable land,
    a settlement, garden, a gift of the king, my lord,
For his servant, who made (this) praise of the king.[1]

Whosoever shall erase my name written (here) and shall write his own
name on this tablet, may the gods invoked herein curse him! [   ], may
he want for bread and water, like a wicked man who [   ] his god, [   ]
may the (whole) land learn of his case!

Text: Sommerfeld, AfO 32 (1985), 2, 4, 6–8.
Edition: Sommerfeld, AfO 32 (1985), 1–22.
Literature: W. G. Lambert in W. S. McCollough, ed., *The Seed of Wisdom, Essays in Honour of T. J. Meek* (Toronto, 1964), 8.

1.   Reference to author of text; compare Agushaya Poem (II.5) vii lines 24ff.

III.11 KUDUR–NAHHUNTE OF ELAM

Elam, or the land in the southwest corner of Iran, was a traditional enemy of Babylonia in historical times. The texts grouped in III.11 and III.12 deal with warfare and hostility between Elam and Babylonia toward the end of the second millennium B.C.

The three documents of III.11 are sometimes referred to as the "Kedor-Laomer Texts" because of the supposed affinity between the name of the Elamite king, Kudur-nahhunte, and Kedor-Laomer of Genesis 14.[1] The three tablets, which date to the Persian period (sixth to fourth centuries B.C.), refer to an Elamite invasion of Babylonia, destruction at Nippur and Babylon, and the sacking of Esagila. Although damaged and often unintelligible, these documents are included because of their connection with the texts about Nebuchadnezzar I (III.12). Their interest to a Babylonian scholar of the Achaemenid period may have lain in analogies between the Elamites and the rapacious post-Darius Persian monarchs, in addition to their historical interest as pertaining to a turning-point in Babylonian history. Although the precise time of the texts is uncertain, they may refer to events in Babylonia and Elam during the twelfth century B.C.

III.11a consists of correspondence between Kudur-nahhunte and the Babylonians. In the part preserved, the Elamite king presses his claim to the vacant throne of Babylon. This claim was based on his descent from a Kassite king through the female line. Kudur-nahhunte holds out hopes for peace and reconciliation between the two lands, traditional enemies. The Babylonians answer that his claim is unfounded; they hope for the coming of a legitimate king. They predict a defeat of Elam to occur in the hot season, such as was actually inflicted by Nebuchadnezzar I (see III.12c). For another, related letter, see van Dijk, OrNS 55 (1986), 159–170.

In (b), his claim spurned, the Elamite king invades Sumer and Babylonia, destroying holy places and incurring the wrath of the gods. Although the events took place in Nippur, the names of the destroyed sanctuaries are better known

---

1. W. F. Albright, "The Historical Background of Genesis XIV," *Journal of the Society of Oriental Research* (1926), 231–269; "A Fixed Date in Hebrew History," BASOR 88 (1942), 33–36; E. A. Speiser, *Genesis* (Anchor Bible, New York, 1964), 106–109; M. Astour, "Political and Cosmic Symbolism in Genesis 14 and in Its Babylonian Sources," in Alexander Altmann, ed., *Biblical Motifs: Origins and Transformation* (Cambridge, Mass., 1966), 65–112. For a skeptical view of the question, see L. W. King, *The Letters and Inscriptions of Hammurabi, King of Babylon ... 1* (London, 1898), l–lvi.

from Babylon, so the narrative may seek to equate the two cities for some theological purpose.[1]

In (c) destruction and warfare continue. At last Marduk is moved to anger against the invader. The text concludes with a plea for Marduk's return.

(a) KUDUR–NAHHUNTE AND THE BABYLONIANS

(obverse mostly lost, save for a ruling and the superscription
"Letter of Kudur-[nahhunte ...]")

(rev.)

(3) "[   ] the bond of heaven that [   ] to the four winds. He (Marduk) decreed for them the punishment that [   ] in Babylon, pr[aise]worthy* city. He decreed for them the property of the Babylonians, young and o[ld ....]. With their firm counsel, they established the [   ] of Kudur-nahhunte, king of Elam. Now, one who is pleasing* to them [   ] will exercise kingship in Babylon, the city of Babylonia [   ]. In Babylon, city of the king of the gods, Marduk, they have set up [his? thr]one. (10) Shall livestock and ravening wolf come to terms? Shall firm-rooted thorn and soaring raven love one another? Shall raven and venomous snake come to terms? [   ] Shall bone-gnawing dog come to terms with mongoose? Shall dragon come to terms with blood-letting bandit? (15) What king of Elam is there who provided for Esagila and ...?"

The Babylonians ... and [   ] their message: "(As for) [the wo]rds that you wrote: 'I am a king, son of a king, of [royal seed e]ternal,* [indeed] the son of a king's daughter who sat upon the royal throne.[2] [As for] Durmah-DINGIR.ME(?), son of Arad-Etusha,[3] who [carried off] plunder of [   ], (20) he sat on the royal throne ... [   ].' [As for] us, let a king come whose [lineage is] fi[rmly founded] from ancient days. He should be called lord of Babylon, ... It will be done in June and July [   ] ... the Goat (star?) ...

---

1. See further A. George, "Marduk and the Cult of the Gods of Nippur at Babylon," OrNS 66 (1997), 65–70.

2. Kudur-nahhunte evidently claimed the throne on the basis of his descent from the daughter of a Kassite king; see van Dijk, OrNS 55 (1986), 166–167.

3. The name of a usurper king; one expects here a reference to Tukulti-Ninurta I, who ruled in Babylon, but it is hard to see this in the name; for a proposal, see Astour, "Symbolism" (p. 369 note 1), 82–83 See also (c), line 9.

(which portends) one overthrowing all lands, (25) [   ] in their firm counsel [   ] ... [   ] the [king of the?] gods among the booty that they will bring out."

(traces, then breaks off)

(b) THE ELAMITE ATTACK ON NIPPUR

The obverse consists of a fragmentary poetic narrative describing the Elamite attack on the cult center at Nippur; the reverse describes the aftermath, then continues with an attack on Babylon and Borsippa. In the preserved episode, the Elamite king is afraid to loot a sanctuary and tries to force a priest to do it. The priest refuses, so the Elamite orders one of his officers to carry out the attack.

(obv.)

(several lines gone)

[	E]kur[1]	
[	] Elam	
[	] his possessions	
[	] their features	(5)

He [   ] to expose it to the sun.
[   ] he approached the great gate,
He tore out the gate of Ishtar ... and threw it aside.
Like merciless Erra he entered the grand court,
He stood in the grand court and gazed at Ekur.   (10)
He made ready to speak and cried to his followers,
To all of his warriors he sped the blasphemy on,
"Plunder Ekur, take its possessions!
"Obliterate its design, cut off its rites!"
The enemy approached Iku, the seat of Ea.[2]   (15)
He destroyed its walls [   ] before him.
[   ] Esharra,[3]
[   ] its protective spirit was frightened off.
He obliterated [Esharra], he carried off its cult objects,

---

1. Temple of Enlil at Nippur.
2. A shrine at Babylon, (George, *Topographical Texts*, 271).
3. Temple at Nippur.

He entered the Eadgigi,[1] he tore out the screen.   (20)
The enemy approached with evil intent Ennundagalla,[2]
Before him the god was clad in light,
He flashed like lightning, he shook in the dwelling!
The enemy became afraid, betook himself off.
He [   ] the priest, he said to him,   (25)
"[   ], the god was clad in light,
"He flashed like lightning, he shook in the dwelling!
"[   ] Ennundagalla, take away(?) his diadems!
"You must lead him [... from] his [dwelling]."
[The priest?] had no fear
        and was not mindful of (his own) life,   (30)
[He did not   ] Ennundagalla,
        he did not take away(?) his diadems.
[To the   ] the Elamite he spoke few words.
[To the   ] the Elamite, a vile man,
        he spoke in riddles(?).
The enemy gave reply to an officer,
"Let them bring [   ] in a surprise attack on Nippur,   (35)
"[   ] ... the great courtyard, a man, the priest!"
[   ] the officer
[   ] the priest

(fragmentary lines, then gap)

1. "House of the Counsellors," a sanctuary at Nippur (and Babylon, George, *Topographical Texts*, 279).
2. A name for part of the sanctuary of Enlil in Ekur?

(rev.)

(several lines gone)

[   ] ... the table of [   ]   (1)

When the guardian of well-being cries [   ],
The protective spirit of Esharra, [   ] was frightened away.
The Elamite hastened to evil deeds,
For the Lord devised evil for Babylon.   (5)

When the protective genius of justice stood aside,
The protective spirit of Esharra, temple of all the gods,
        was frightened away.
The Elamite enemy took away his possessions,
Enlil, who dwelt therein, became furious!

When the heavens(?) changed their appearance,   (10)
The fiery glare and ill wind obliterated their faces.
Their gods were frightened off, they went down to the depths.
Whirlwinds, ill wind engulfed the heavens.
Anu (the gods') creator had become furious!
He diminished their (celestial) appearances,
        he laid waste(?) his (own celestial) position,   (15)
With the burning of Eanna he obliterated its designs.[1]
[   ] Esharra, the netherworld trembled.

[Enlil(?)] commanded total destruction.
[The god   had] become furious:
He commanded for Sumer the smashing of En[lil]'s land:*   (20)
"Which one is Kudur-nahhunte, the evil-doer?"[2]
He called up the barbarian horde, [he level]led the land of Enlil,
He laid waste(?) [   ] at their side.

When the [   ] of Ezida
And Nabu, trustee of all [   ] hastened to [   ] ...   (25)
He set [out] downstream, toward the ocean,

---

1. Literally: "House of Heaven," temple of Anu at Uruk.
2. Apparently Enlil's speech, summoning the agent of his wrath.

Ibbi-Tutu,[1] who was on the sea, hastened to the East,
He (Nabu) crossed the sea
and occupied a dwelling not his own,
The rites of Ezida, the sure house, were deathly still.

The Elamite [enemy] sent forth his chariotry,   (30)
He headed downstream toward Borsippa,
He came down the dark way, he entered Borsippa,
The vile Elamite toppled its sanctuary.
He slew the nobles [   ] with weapons,
He [plun]dered all the temples.   (35)
He took their possessions and carried them off to Elam.
He destroyed its walls,
He filled the land [with weeping ...]

(c) MARDUK AND THE ELAMITES

(obv.)

(top half of tablet lost; two fragmentary lines)

[   ] his un[just](?) deeds [   ]
[   ] ... [   ]
[   ] ... the gods, creation of A[nu?]   (5)
[   ] ... [   ] Shamash, illuminator [ ]
[   ] lord of lords, Marduk,
in the steadfastness of his heart,
[   ] ... of everything, an improvident sovereign
[   ] he felled with weapons Dur-mah-DINGIR.ME,
son of Arad-[E]atush,
He plundered [   ] and [ ] water
over Babylon and Esagila,   (10)
He slaughtered its [ ] with his own weapon like sheep,
[   ] he burned with fire, old and young,
he [ ] with weapons,
[   ] he cut down young and old.

---

1. Identity unknown.

Tudhula son of Gazza[ ],[1] plundered
    the [... (and) ...] water over Babylon and Esagila,
[   ] his son smote his pate with his own weapon.   (15)
[   ] his lordship to the [rites] of Annunit[um   ]

(rev.)

[king of] Elam, [ ] the city Ah[ ],
    plundered the great ...,   (1)
[   ] he sent like the deluge, all the cult centers of
    Akkad and their sanctuaries he burned [with fi]re.
Kudur-nahhunte his son c[ut?] his middle and his heart
    with an iron dagger,
[   ] his enemy he took and sought out(?).
The wicked kings, criminals, [   ] captured.
The king of the gods, Marduk, became angry at them,   (5)
[   ] were ill, their breast ..., [their] plans [ ],
[   ] to the desert, all of them ... to the king our lord.
[Shazu],[2] who knows the heart of the gods,
The merciful one, Marduk, at the invocation of his name,
[... Babylon] and Esagila, let him(?) return to his place!
Let the king my lord put this [in] your [heart?],   (10)
[The doer] of evil to him [   ] his heart ...
[   ] the doer of sin must not [   ]

Text: (a) BM 35404 (collated) = Pinches, JTVI 29 (1897), 84–85. (b) BM 34062 (collated) = Pinches, JTVI 29 (1897), 86–89. (c) BM 35496 (collated) = Pinches, JTVI 29 (1897), 82–83.

Edition: (a) Jeremias, MVAeG 21 (1917), 82–94. (b) W. G. Lambert, "The Fall of the Cassite Dynasty to the Elamites, An Historical Epic," *Studies De Meyer*, 67–72 (with numerous new readings and interpretations used here). (c) Jeremias, MVAeG 21 (1917), 80–84.

Literature: Landsberger *apud* Güterbock, ZA 42 (1934), 21; van Dijk, OrNS 55 (1986), 167.

Notes to Text: (a 4) tanda[dāti], WGL. (a 7) Brinkman, PHKB, 80. Previous editors read "not pleasing," but the tablet should be read *ša eli-šú-nu ṭá-a-bi x*. (a 17) CAD D, 117a. (b rev. 20) Differently Charpin and Durand, N.A.B.U. 1994/101; further Lambert, N.A.B.U. 1995/10.

    1. Unknown. The name is written to suggest an etymology "Evil-of-Birth" son of "Slaughterer ..." Various scholars have compared the Hittite royal name Tudhaliyas.

    2. A name for Marduk, "He Who Knows the Heart," compare Creation Epic (III.17) Tablet VII lines 35ff.

III.12 NEBUCHADNEZZAR I

Nebuchadnezzar I (1124–1103 B.C.) was a successful and energetic monarch whose name became a byword in later Babylonian historical and literary tradition.[1] He ascended the throne of Babylon (or Isin?) when Babylonian fortunes were at an ebb. The Kassite dynasty had been deposed after nearly half a millennium. Assyrians and Elamites had successively invaded. The Elamite king had deported one of Nebuchadnezzar's predecessors and removed the statue of Marduk from his temple at Babylon.[2]

Nebuchadnezzar marched against the Elamites in a series of campaigns. At first turned back by an outbreak of plague among his soldiery (III.12b), he later mounted a surprise attack during the summer hot season, routed his foe, and recovered the statue of Marduk (III.12c; III.11, a23). The return of the statue occasioned a burst of patriotic literary activity.[3]

Nebuchadnezzar's dynasty, known as the Second Dynasty of Isin, was evidently fascinated by the Sumerian background of Babylonian culture. This is suggested by the following poem, which asserts the antediluvian, Sumerian origin of Nebuchadnezzar's kingship (III.12a).

(a) THE SEED OF KINGSHIP

This composition alludes to the remote descent of Nebuchadnezzar I, king of Babylon, from Enmeduranki, an antediluvian cultural figure, sage, and king of Sippar. This extraordinary claim may be interpreted in various ways.[4] As seen in III.11, an Elamite had claimed the throne on the basis of his kinship to the Kassite ruling family, so Nebuchadnezzar presses a far more ancient descent. During the Mature and Late periods, Babylonian scholars interested themselves in the remote ancestry of individuals, texts, and institutions for antiquarian, political, social, heuristic, and perhaps even patriotic reasons.[5] In particular,

---

1. For a historical survey of his reign, see Brinkman, PHPKB, 104–116.

2. J. J. M. Roberts, "Nebuchadnezzar I's Elamite Crisis in Theological Perspective," *Studies Finkelstein*, 183–187.

3. A. Boissier, "Nebukadnezzar Ier," *Revue Semitique* 2 (1894), 78, refers to "une renaissance de la littérature babylonienne." W. G. Lambert ascribes this to the emergence of Marduk at this period as supreme god of Mesopotamia, "The Reign of Nebuchadnezzar I: A Turning Point in the History of Ancient Mesopotamian Religion," in W. S. McCollough, ed., *The Seed of Wisdom, Essays in Honour of T. J. Meek* (Toronto, 1964), 3–13. See also III.17.

4. W. G. Lambert, JCS 21 (1967), 134–138; CRRAI 19 (1971), 439–440.

5. W. G. Lambert, "Ancestors, Authors, and Canonicity," JCS 11 (1957), 1–14, 112.

Nebuchadnezzar I asserts that his claim to the throne antedated that of the Kassites and that of the Amorite kings of Babylon (most of the second millennium) and could be anchored in remotest known Babylonian tradition at Sippar (the only city still important at his time that was believed to have antedated the flood). Perhaps some connection was posited between this personage and the king's lineage in order to assert a revival of native Babylonian tradition. The text was composed in both Sumerian and Akkadian, an unusual undertaking at such a late date. In all probability, the two versions were composed simultaneously, rather than one being intended as a translation of the other. The Sumerian seems heavily influenced by the non-Sumerian speech habits of its author. For another bilingual text of this type, perhaps from this same period, see Frame, RIMB 2, 31–33.

> Praise is [for him w]hose mig[ht
>   is] over the universe for eternity,   (1)
> Whose anger [is grievous but whose re]lenting is sweet,
>   glorious to praise![1]
> In his power are abandonment and repopulation,
>   he reveals to future peoples how to watch for his sign.
> Nebuc[hadnezzar], king of [Babylon],
>   who sets in order all cult centers,
>   who maintains regular offerings,
> He (Marduk) exalted his [wisdom], magnified his power,
>   made him foremost,   (5)
> He (Marduk) made great [his might],
>   he exalted his great destiny.[2]
> [Nebuchadnezzar], king of Babylon,
>   who sets [in order a]ll cult centers,
>   who maintains regular offerings,
> Scion of royalty remote (in time),
>   seed that has been watched for[3] since before the deluge,
> Descendant of Enmedura[nki], king of Sippar,

---

1. Compare Poem of the Righteous Sufferer (III.14) Tablet I lines 1ff. and Creation Epic (III.17) Tablet VII lines 153ff.

2. That is, Marduk chose Nebuchadnezzar to be the agent of his return to Babylon (so Akkadian; Sumerian slightly different in sense so far as preserved).

3. Compare line 3 above, where "watching for" is also alluded to. The poet may have had a specific omen in mind, to judge from the astrological omen(?) alluded to in III.11a.

who instituted the sacred diviner's bowl,
who held the cedar,[1]
(And) who took his place before Shamash and Adad,
the divine judges,[2]   (10)
Foremost son of [Ninurta-nadin]-shumi,
just king, faithful shepherd
who defended and upheld this land,
Superb offspring(?) of Adad and Gula, the great gods,
of Nippurian descent and lineage eternal,
Foremost attendant of Shuzianna,[3] twin sister of Anshar,
Summoned forth by Anu and Dagan,
chosen by the steadfast hearts of the great gods am I!
It came to pass that in the reign of a previous king
the signs changed: (15)
Good vanished and evil was prevailing,
The Lord became angry and waxed furious.
He commanded that the gods of the land forsake it,
its people went out of their minds,
they were incited to falsehood.
The guardian of well-being became furious
and went up to heaven,
the protective genius of justice stood aside,
[   ], the guardian of living creatures, over[threw] the people,
and they all became as if they had no god!   (20)
Malignant demons filled the land,
remorseless plague penetrated the cult centers,
The land was diminished, its counsel changed.
The vile Elamite, who did not hold precious [the gods],
whose battle was swift,
whose onslaught was quick to come,
Laid waste the habitations, ravaged the gods,
turned the sanctuaries into ruins!
Marduk, king of the gods,
who ordains the destinies of the lands, observed all —   (25)

---

1. Enmeduranki, an antediluvian king of Sippar, is here credited with being an early practitioner of divination.
2. A reference to divination, particularly hepatoscopy (Lambert, JCS 21 [1967], 133); see II.28a.
3. A healing deity known as "The Lady of Babylon."

When the Lord is angry,
>the Igigi-gods in [heaven] can[not] bear his fury,

His frightfulness is terrifying,
>no man can withstand his glowering —

The hardest ground sustained not his tread,
>oceans trembled [at] his rage,

No rocky crag withstood his footstep,
>the gods of the universe knelt before him!

All existence(?) is entrusted to his power,
>when he grew angry, who could appease him?   (30)

[   ] who learned [   ] him and sees his artfulness,
[   ] himself [   ] the capable Enlil of the gods,
[   ] the I[gigi-gods   ], solicitous prince,
[   ] who in [   ] adorned with splendor,
>enthroned in terrifying radiance,

The powerful one [   ], whose leadership excels   (35)

(gap)

(When the text resumes, the statue of Marduk returns from Elam.)

[   ] ... the arms of whomsoever the weapon touched
>turned stiff of their own accord, as if dying of cold,
>and their corpses were spread far and wide,   (1′–2′)

He (Marduk) made (it) pass over above and below,*
>right and left, front and rear, like the deluge;
>what was inside the city, outside the city,
>in the steppe, in the open country,
>he filled with deathly stillness and turned into a desert.

[?] the servant who revered him,
>who was assiduous in prayer,
>obedient, and constantly awaiting his[1] revelation,
>ceased not from praying until he (Marduk)
>would fulfill his heart's desire,   (5′–6′)

[?] "until I behold his lofty figure, dejection of heart will
>never depart from my person, even for a day,
>nor can I have full term of sleep in night's sweet lap!"

[On account of] my most distressing lamentations,

---

1. Surely Marduk's (though CAD K, 93a understands the moon's).

my ardent prayers, my entreaties,
   and the prostration that I performed in lamentation
      before him daily, his profound(?) heart(?) took pity,
And he relented to the holy city.
He made his decision and set forth from the evils of Elam,
   he took the road of jubilation,
      the path of gladness, and the way to Babylon
      (that signified his) hearing and acceptance of my prayers,
The people of the land looked upon his lofty, suitable,
   noble form, as they acclaimed his brilliance,
      all of them paying heed to him.   (15'–16')
The Lord entered and took up his comfortable abode,
The Gate of Radiance,[1] his lordly cella, beamed for joy.   (19'–20')
The heavens bore him their abundance, earth its yield,
   sea its catch, and mountains their tribute:
Their gifts beyond compare, or that tongue could tell(?),
Their massive tribute to the lord of lords!   (25'–26')
Many sheep were slaughtered, prime bulls were provided
   in abundance, food offerings were magnificent,
      incense was heaped up,
Aromatics gave off sweet fragrance,
[   ] offerings were [   ], full of gladness.   (30'–31')
[   ], there was rejoicing,
[Gods of hea]ven and netherworld exult
   as they [lo]ok upon valiant Marduk,
[   ] a song of praise of his valor,
[   ] who makes the kettle and snare drums glow(?).

(end of text)

Text: (a) W. G. Lambert, JCS 21 (1967), 134–138; CRRAI 19 (1971), 439–440; (b) K 3317 + 3319
   (+) 8319 = Pinches, IV R² 20 no. 1; (c) BM 99067, K 3444 = Meek, AJSL 35 (1918/19), 139
   (bilingual).
Edition: W. G. Lambert, JCS 21 (1967), 126–131; CRRAI 19 (1971), 434–438 (a); Frame, RIMB
   2, 23–31.
Literature: Jestin, RA 52 (1958), 193–202 (edition of Sumerian of b only); W. G. Lambert, JCS 21
   (1967), 126–127 and in W. S. McCollough, ed., *The Seed of Wisdom, Essays in Honour of T. J.
   Meek* (Toronto, 1964), 9 note 19.
*Notes to Text: (2'–3') Restored from K 5191, cited CAD A/1, 76–77.

1. See p. 362 note 3.

(b) THE WAR WITH ELAM

This fragment of a first-person narrative deals with a conflict between Babylon and Elam; the speaker may be Nebuchadnezzar I. The war was prolonged and bitter, so the avenging of their humiliation must have occasioned great joy to the Babylonians. More than half the tablet is broken away; moreover it is difficult to follow the course of events across the lacunae, so the restorations, which follow in the main Tadmor's proposals, are tentative.

(large gap)

[Shutruk-nahhunte][1] drove away(?) Zababa-shum-iddina[2]
    and ousted his royal authority,
He be[stowed royal authority upon(?)] his eldest son,
    Kudur-nahhunte.
[K.?], whose crime exceeded those of his forefathers,
    whose monstrous sin was the greatest of them all,
Plotted [wick]edness [ ] against the land of Akkad[3]
    and perpetrated villainy.
[The Babylonians? elevated] Enlil-nadin-ahi,[4]
    my predecessor,   (5')
[K.?] set to hostility,[5] vowing destruction(?).
[K.?] over[ran] all the people of Akkad like the deluge,
He turned all the sublime [hol]y places into [ruin heaps],
He made the great [lo]rd [Marduk] rise
    from his [royal] dwelling,
He carried off the [possessions]
    of Sumer and Akkad [to Elam].   (10')
He took Enlil-nadin-ahi [to Elam],
[Overthrew] his [kingship], ousted his royal authority.
[   ] not of Babylonian descent, hostile [to Marduk],

(two broken lines, then gap)

---

1. An Elamite king, ca. 1165 B.C. See M. Stolper in E. Carter and M. Stolper, *Elam, Surveys of Political History and Archaeology* (Berkeley, 1984), 39–43.
2. Penultimate king of the Kassite dynasty, ca. 1160 B.C., here replaced by the Elamite king with an Elamite prince as viceroy.
3. That is, Babylonia.
4. Final king of the Kassite dynasty, ca. 1159–1157 B.C. One can read the name also as Enlil-shuma-usur.
5. It is not clear whether the subject is the Elamites or Enlil-nadin-ahi.

(rev.)

(about three lines missing)

[... perduring ter]ror befalling him, he took to the mountains,
    [   ] ... harried the enemy.
His [sign(?)] they saw,
    and besought the decision of Mar[duk].*   (5′)
[ ], bitter, harassed, and in despair, I said to myself,
"[Unlike] my [predecessor] who flourished(?)* in Elam,
    let me die this very day!
"[   ] battle with him, let me turn not back!"
[ ] I awaited him at the 'head(?)' of the Uqnu-river[1]
    with the rest of the army,
[I did not tu]rn back, but, against the will of the gods,   (10′)
Erra, mightiest of the gods, decimated my [war]riors,[2]
The enfeebling [   ] bound(?)* my horse teams,
[   ] a demon was killing my fine steeds.*
I became afraid of death, did not advance to battle,
    but turned back.
With heavy [ ] I camped, stupefied,
    at the city Kar-Dur-Apil-Sin.   (15′)
[Then] the Elamite [advanced] and I withdrew before him.
[I lay on a] bed of misery and sighs,
    "[   ] me, that I ... before him,
    "[   ] you must not untie the ... of the doors,
    "[   ] let his enemy enter,   (20′)
    "[   ] perpetrator of wickedness,
    "[   ] the words of my lips,
    "[   ] may Enlil's heart be appeased,
    "[   ] his feelings eased."
    [   ] rebellion   (25′)
    [   ] my vow

(breaks off)

---

1. Kerkha River.
2. Probably a reference to a plague.

Text: G. Smith, III R 38 no. 2 (collated).

Edition: Tadmor, JNES 17 (1958), 137–139; Frame, RIMB 2, 19–21.

Literature: Brinkman, PHPKB, 79–80, 88–90, and 106; Hallo, IEJ 16 (1966), 238; Longman, *Autobiography*, 194–195.

Translation: Longman, *Autobiography*, 243.

Notes to Text: (rev. 5′) PPHKB, 106 note 575 (collation). (rev. 7′) Text: *uššubu*. Tadmor seems to derive from *wašābu* (form?); WGL suggests *uššubu* (*ešēbu*). (rev. 12′) WGL (compare *ubburu*). (rev. 13′) CAD K, 307b.

(c) NEBUCHADNEZZAR IN ELAM

A carved stone monument commemorating a grant of land and exemptions by Nebuchadnezzar I to one of his officers in the Elamite campaign, Sitti-Marduk, opens with a literary description of the campaign, the work of the scribe Enlil-tabni-bullit.

(1) When Nebuchadnezzar, pious and preeminent prince, of Babylonian birth, aristocrat of kings, valiant governor and viceroy of Babylon,[1] sun-god of his land, who makes his people flourish, guardian of boundaries, establisher of measuring lines(?),* righteous king who renders a just verdict, valiant male whose arms are poised for warfare, who wields a terrible bow, who fears no battle, who felled the mighty Lullubi[2] with weaponry, conqueror of the Amorites,[3] plunderer of the Kassites,[4] preeminent among kings, prince beloved of Marduk, was sent forth by Marduk, king of the gods, he raised his weapon to avenge Akkad.

(14) From Der, sanctuary of Anu, he made an incursion for a distance of thirty leagues. He undertook the campaign in July. The whole time(?), the heat glare scorched like fire,* the paths of march were burning like open flames! There was no water in the bottoms, and drinking places were cut off. The finest of the great horses gave out, the legs of the strong man faltered. On goes the preeminent king with the gods for his support, Nebuchadnezzar presses on, nor

---

1. The city name is written Eridu, an ancient place sacred to Ea/Enki in southern Sumer. The scribe wishes thereby to equate Babylon with the sacred city of the god of wisdom (see Brinkman, PHPKB, 116 note 653). Compare III.18a.

2. Here, a literary term for "mountain people" (RGTC 2, 112).

3. Here, a literary term for "(uncivilized, nomadic) West Semites," but perhaps in this context a reference to inhabitants of the Transtigridian region (as suggested by Weidner, AfO 16 [1952/3], 18 note 134).

4. Perhaps used here as a literary term for mountain peoples in the East.

has he a rival. He does not fear the difficult terrain, he stretches the daily marches!

(25) Sitti-Marduk, head of the house of Bit-Karziabku,[1] whose chariot did not lag behind the king his lord's right flank, held his chariot ready.

(28) So hastened the mighty king, and reached the bank of the Ulaya river.[2] Both kings met there and made battle. Between them a conflagration burst out, the face of the sun was darkened by their dust, whirlwinds were blowing, raging was the storm! In the storm of their battle the warrior in the chariot could not see the other at his side.

(35) Sitti-Marduk, head of the house of Bit-Karziabku, whose chariot did not lag behind the king's right flank, and who held his chariot ready, he feared no battle (but) went down to the enemy and went farthest in against the enemy of his lord. By the command of Ishtar and Adad, gods who are the lords of battle, he routed Hulteludish, king of Elam, he disappeared. Thus king Nebuchad-nezzar triumphed, seized Elam, and plundered its possessions.

(Text continues with record of the exemptions made to Sitti-Marduk's ancestral lands.)

Text: King, BBST 6 pl. 84–86.
Edition: King, BBST, 31–33; Frame, RIMB 2, 33–35.
Literature: V. Hurowitz, "Some Literary Observations on BBSt. 6," ZA 82 (1992), 39–59.
*Notes to Text: (5) Or: "heirs," see Seux, RA 64 (1970), 188; Hurowitz, ZA 82 (1992), 44; read perhaps èš-le-e? (17f.) For proposals for these damaged and difficult lines, see von Soden, RA 82 (1987), 190; Sommerfeld, Or 56 (1987), 212; George, BiOr 46 (1989), 383. (25) For the name, see Borger, AfO 23 (1970), 8.

1.   A Kassite eponymous tribal domain. Sitti-Marduk was thereby a member of the Kassite nobility.
2.   Karun or Kerkha river; see Nashef, RGTC 5, 322–323; Stève, Gasche, De Meyer, *Iranica Antiqua* 15 (1980), 104 note 71.

(d) NEBUCHADNEZZAR AND MARDUK

This epic-style poem recounts in summary fashion the events dealt with in more detail in III.12b-c.

When Nebuchadnezzar [the king] dwelt in Babylon,   (1)
He would roar like a lion, would rum[ble] like thunder,
His illustrious great men would roar like lions.
[His] prayers went up to Marduk, lord of Babylon,
"Have mercy on me, in despair and pros[trate],*   (5)
"Have mercy on my land, which weeps and mourns,
"Have mercy on my people, who wail and weep!
"How long, O lord of Babylon,
        will you dwell in the land of the enemy?
"May beautiful Babylon pass through your heart,
"Turn your face toward Esagila, which you love!"   (10)
[The lord of Babylon] heeded Nebuchadnezzar['s prayer],
[   ] befell him from heaven,
"I command you with my own lips,
"[A word of] good fortune do I send you:
"[With] my [help?] you will attack the Westland.   (15)
"Heed your instructions, [   ]
"Take me [from El]am to Babylon.
"I, [lord of Bab]ylon, will surely give you Elam,
"[I will exalt] your [kingship] everywhere."
[   ] the land of [   ] and seized [   ] of(?) his gods   (20)

(breaks off)

Text: King, CT 13 48 (collated).
Edition: Frame, RIMB 2, 18–19.
Literature: W. G. Lambert, "The Reign of Nebuchadnezzar I: A Turning Point in the History of Ancient Mesopotamian Religion," in W. S. McCollough, ed., *The Seed of Wisdom, Essays in Honour of T. J. Meek* (Toronto, 1964), 3–13.
*Notes to Text: (5) WGL: *ú-tu-[lu*], confirmed by collation.

(e) NEBUCHADNEZZAR TO THE BABYLONIANS

A fragmentary manuscript from the Late period preserves a letter, evidently addressed by Nebuchadnezzar to the Babylonians, telling them of his victory in Elam and recovery of Marduk's statue. See also II.39.

(§1) [To the citizenry of Babylon], of protected status, leaders learned and wise, [   ], men of business and commerce, great and small, [thus says Nebuchadnezzar, v]iceroy of Enlil, native of Babylon, the king, your lord, [   ] on a stele: [   ] you should know [that the great lord Marduk, who] was angry at all the holy places for a long time, took [pity] on Babylon. He gave me in his majesty the [sublime] command, [in?] the awe-inspiring sanctuary [Esagila] he ordered me to take the road of march to [the land of] Elam.

(§2) I gave reverent heed [to the command of the great lord] Marduk, assembled the army of Enlil, Shamash, and Marduk, and set forth toward [the land of] Elam. On I went, traversing distant [ways], waterless roads, night and d[ay.   At the] Ulaya River, the enemy, the vile Elamite, [blocked(?)] the watering places the troops [   ] traversed. I could give no water, nor could I relieve their fatigue.

(§3) I advanced rapidly against him, weapons [brandished] in battle. Through the might of Enlil, [Shamash, and Marduk, which] has no [equa]l, I overwhelmed(?) the king of Elam, defeating him … His army scattered, his forces dispersed, he abandoned his troops, [crossed] his watercourses, terrified [   ]. I ravaged his land. He abandoned his strongholds and disappeared.

(§4) I hastened on [   ] I beheld the [great lord] Marduk, lofty warrior of the gods, and the gods of the land [of Babylonia whom?] he commanded were present with him. I raised [   ] … and set up a wailing, I brought the great lord [Marduk] in procession and set out on the road to his homeland.

(Rest fragmentary. The king commands the restoration of Marduk and his treasures to Esagila.)

Text: van Dijk, VAS 24 87.
Edition: Frame, RIMB 2, 21–23.
Literature: George, BiOr 46 (1989), 382–383, whence several restorations used here; Hurowitz, ZA 82 (1992), 52.

(f) PRAYER IN THE NAME OF NEBUCHADNEZZAR

The following short prayer is engraved on a bronze axehead inscribed with Nebuchadnezzar's name.

> O Marduk, you can save the prayerful who frequents your shrines and make him stand (in triumph) over his enemies. Your breeze wafted upon me, I have overcome my enemies. Strengthen my weapons that I may slay my foes!

Text: Dossin, *Iranica Antiqua* 2 (1962), 158 no. 14 = pl. xxiv.
Edition: Sommerfeld, AOAT 213 (1982), 184; Frame, RIMB 2, 17.
Translation: Hecker, TUAT II/5, 781.
Literature: Borger, HKL 2, 47.

III.13 MARDUK PROPHECY

This text purports to be a speech of the god Marduk in which he relates his history prior to the time of Nebuchadnezzar I. He explains that he is wont to traverse the universe; implicitly one is not to be surprised then at his peregrinations. He dwelt for awhile among the Hittites (the image was captured by a Hittite king in 1594), and then returned to Babylonia. Unlike the Agum text (III.9), which does not explain how he was brought back from Hatti, this account may hint that Marduk was brought back by military means. Marduk then speaks of a stay in Assur (Baltil, image captured by Tukulti-Ninurta I, see III.1). He blessed Assyria during his residence there. No such blessing is in store for Elam, whose attack on Babylon in the time of Kudur-nahhunte (III.11, 12) resulted in the transport of the statue of Marduk to Elam. In fact, a terrible fate is foretold for Elam. Marduk speaks warmly of a prince who is to arise and restore the land, who will bring him home again, and through whose good offices he will be reconciled to Babylon once more. Babylon will then flourish as never before.

The Marduk Prophecy may have been composed to glorify Nebuchadnezzar I and perhaps suggest to him specific benefactions (last column). The "future" there revealed included detailed recommendations about some otherwise unknown cult centers. As Borger suggests,[1] the text may well have achieved its desired effect, for at least three manuscripts exist that are more than half a millennium later than the time of Nebuchadnezzar I.

> (i 1) O Haharnum, Hayyashum,[2] Anu, Enlil, Nudimmud, Ea, ..., Nabium, great gods who are learned in my mysteries! Now that I am ready for a journey, I will tell you my name.
>
> (i 7) I am Marduk, great lord, the most lofty one, he who inspects, who goes back and forth through the mountains, the lofty one, inspector, who smites(?)* lands, he who goes constantly back and forth in the lands from sunrise to sunset, am I!
>
> (i 13) I gave the command that I go to Hatti, I put Hatti to the test, there I set up the throne of my supreme godhead. For twenty-four years I dwelt there. I made it possible for Babylonians to send (commercial) expeditions there, and they marketed(?)* its [   ]

---

1. BiOr 28 (1971), 21.
2. Two little-known primeval deities, presumably cited here so as not to give primacy to the better-known and younger deities in the list; see also III.18b.

goods and property [in] Sippar, Nippur, [and Babylo]n.

(i 23) A king of Babylon arose [and] led [me in procession to] ... Babylon, ..., fair was the processional way of Babylon! On account of the crown of my [supreme godhead] and the image of [ ] workmanship [ ] water and [propitious] winds [ ], for three days [ ]. The crown of my supreme godhead [ ], and the image of [ ] workmanship to my body did I [ ]. I returned, [and for Babylon I said], "Bring [your tribute, ye] lands [to Babylon]!" *(gap)*

(i 3') [The king? of] Baltil was pleasing [to me], the temple of Baltil was [... to me]. His [temple]s [shone] like gems, I bestowed [ ] and abundance [upon him] ... [Month, day, and y]ear [I blessed him]. Having drawn up with him troops of Enlil, I set upon him wings like a bird and I delivered all [lands] (into his power), I blessed the land of Assur. I gave him the [tablet?] of destinies, I granted him stability. [ ] ... [I retur]ned, and for Babylon I said, "Bring your tribute, ye lands! ..."

(i 18') I am Marduk, great lord, lord of destinies and decisions am I! Who (but me) made this journey? I have returned from whence I have gone, it was I who ordered it. I went to the land of Elam, and that all the gods went, it was I who ordered it. I cut off the offerings to the temples, I caused gods of cattle and grain to go away to heaven. The goddess of fermentation sickened the land, the people's corpses choked the gates. Brother consumed brother, comrade slew his comrade with a weapon, free citizens spread out their hands (to beg of) the poor! Authority was restricted, injustice afflicted the land, rebellious kings diminished the land, lions cut off travel, dogs [went mad] and bit people. As many as they bit did not live but perished! I fulfilled my days, I fulfilled my years. I resolved to return to my city Babylon and to Ekursagila. I spoke to all the ...* It was I who ordered it, "Bring your tribute, ye lands, to Babylon! ..."

(iii 9) A king of Babylon will arise, he will renew the marvelous temple, the Ekursagila. He will create the plans of heaven and earth in Ekursagila, he will double(?)* its height. He will establish exemptions for my city Babylon. He will lead me in procession to my city Babylon and bring [me] into eternal Ekursagila. He will restore my (processional) boat, he will inlay its rudder with precious metal, he will [cover] its [com]ing with gold leaf. The boatmen who serve [it] he will bring aboard. They will be divided to [right] and left. The king will [ ] from(?) the dock(?) of Esagila *(gap, then some following fragmentary lines that deal with the restoration of another processional ship.)*

(Assur iii 7′) ... [this prince] will see the benevolence of the god. [The years of] his reign will be long.

(Assur iii 9′) He will make [Ekur]-Ekishnugal[1] shine [like] a gem, the sanctuary of Ningal, the sanctuary of Sin, to[gether] with their treasures, possessions, and properties ... *(fragmentary lines, gap)*

(Assur iv 5) ... He will provide for the city and gather in the scattered ones. Ekur-Egalmah and the other sanctuaries he will make shine like gems. Ningal, Gula, and Kurnunitum ... he will bring back to their favorite temples. This prince will cause his land to browse on the splendor of his pastures, and his days will be long ... [ ] He will make the sanctuaries shine like gems. He will bring back all their gods. He will gather in the scattered land and make firm its foundations.

(iii) The gate of heaven will be open,[2] [ ] ... will get [ ] forever. Ningirsu will prevail. The watercourses will bring fish. Field and acreage will be full of yield. The winter crop will last till the summer harvest, the summer crop till the winter. The harvest of the land will be bountiful, market prices will be favorable. Wicked deeds will be rectified, obscurities will be cleared up, wicked deeds will be brought to light. Clouds will always be visible.[3] Brother will have consideration for brother, son will revere father like a god. Mother will [ ] daughter, bride will be mar[ried] and r[evere her husband]. [There will always be] consideration among the people. The young man will [always bear] his burden(?). This prince will [ru]le [all] lands.

(iii 21) Finally, I and all the gods being reconciled with him, he will smash Elam, he will smash its cities, he will dismantle its fortresses. He will lift the great king of Der from his unsuitable position, change his desolation, [ ] his bad situation, take him by the hand, and bring him into Der and (its temple) Ekurdimgalkalamma forever.

---

1. See II.29.
2. A reference to rainfall?
3. Favorable prognosis.

(iv B′) 40 quarts of [   ], 40 quarts of [   ], 10 quarts of flour, 1 quart of [   ], 1 quart of honey, 1 quart of butterfat, 1 quart of figs(?), 1 quart of raisins, 1 quart of alabastron [oil], 1 quart of finest [   ] without alkali(?), 1 regular sheep, a fatted calf will be burned for this spirit. Month, day, and year I will bless him!

Text: Borger, BiOr 28 (1971), 5–13 (Kuyunjik); W. G. Lambert, JCS 18 (1964), 27–28 (Assur).
Edition: Borger, BiOr 28 (1971), 5–20.
Translation: Hecker, TUAT II/1, 65–68; Longman, *Autobiography*, 233–235.
Literature: Sommerfeld, AOAT 213 (1982), 188–189; Longman, *Autobiography*, 132–142.
Notes to Text: (i 9) Doubtful, see AHw, 1585b; perhaps, with Borger, "who traverses." (i 22) Hecker, TUAT II/1, 66. (ii 15′) On the basis of the parallel lines (i 15′), one expects a place; read perhaps ÈŠ *da-ra-a-ti*? Otherwise, perhaps, "goddesses." (iii 24) WLM.

D. WISDOM AND EXPERIENCE

III.14 THE POEM OF THE RIGHTEOUS SUFFERER

The Poem of the Righteous Sufferer is a poetic monologue, opening and concluding with hymns, that tells how a certain noble gentleman, once important and prosperous, for no apparent reason was driven to disgrace and disease by the god Marduk. His story is set forth as exemplary of the two sides to divine character, anger and forgiveness, and as exemplary of the unfathomable will of the gods.

The poem opens with a hymn setting forth contrasts of Marduk's nature and then proceeds to the narrative (Tablet I line 41). The speaker loses his luck and his personal defenses are lowered, exposing him to misfortune. He consults experts (line 52), to no avail. He loses favor at court (line 55) and paints a vivid picture of seven base conspirators excitedly clamoring over the advantages they plan to take of his downfall (lines 59–64). Physical disintegration sets in (lines 70ff.), followed by social ostracism. He is reviled everywhere and suffers financial setbacks (lines 99ff.). He loses his post and a long period of depression and foreboding ensues (lines 103ff.). He still hopes for deliverance (lines 119–120).

As Tablet II opens, a year has elapsed. Prayer and consultation are to no avail. One would think he was godless (Tablet II lines 12–22), but he was always scrupulous in his observances of god and sovereign. Does that matter (lines 33ff.)? Can anyone hope to understand the will of the gods? People's fortunes rise and fall — what is the lesson in that?

The speaker has no further opportunity for reflection as he comes down with a textbook of illnesses (Tablet II lines 50ff.). Pains, agony, malfunction, disability crush him. He can neither eat nor drink (Tablet II lines 86ff.). He falls bedridden (Tablet II lines 95ff.) and writhes helplessly in filth and torment. Continued consultations with experts yield nothing. He is given up for lost, his tomb is made ready, grave goods set out, his wretched obituary written (Tablet II lines 114ff.). Gloom settles over his loved ones.

As he lapses into the coma of death, the sufferer, whose name is now revealed to be Shubshi-meshre-Shakkan,[1] sees a dream visitant: a young man in fine clothes (perhaps a personification of the speaker's own self in better days?). The apparition promises him relief and dries up his sores. The ministrant speaks on

---

1.   A high official of the reign of the Kassite king Nazi-Maruttash (early thirteenth century B.C.) is known to have borne this name; he may be identical with the author of the poem (Gurney, RA 80 [1986], 190; von Soden, TUAT III/1, 111; Dalley, BiOr 52 [1995], 85).

behalf of a lady, who, as Bottéro has suggested (see p. 409, Literature), may be Sarpanitum, Marduk's wife (see Tablet IV Fragment C, lines 10'–11'). She may have interceded with her husband on behalf of the sufferer, a common motif in Mesopotamian literature (compare Against Enlil's Anger [III.38c] line 8'). In Tablet III, lines 16–18 the sufferer tries vainly to convince his skeptical family of the truth of what he saw. In a second vision, a man washes him off with water and massages him. In a third, a female figure intercedes for him in oblique terms; thereupon a scholar appears with a written text that contains the wording for his release (Tablet III, line 41). Signs are sent so the people will believe; Marduk forgives him his misdeeds. The sufferer's illnesses are thereupon cured, he begins to eat and drink, gets out of bed, and testifies to his health.

Tablet IV opens with Shubshi-meshre-Shakkan's testimony that it was Marduk who saved him. He goes through a river ordeal to prove himself guilt-less, then goes to the temple of Marduk.[1] His progress through the city echoes the note of encouragement for the human race sounded by the name of each gate and quarter and fulfills the implications of the names. In Tablet IV lines 51ff. he makes lavish thank offerings; finally, in Tablet IV Fragment C lines 3'ff., he gives a banquet for the citizenry at the site of his intended entombment. In a closing hymn, the Babylonians proclaim the wondrous healing power of Marduk to rescue humankind. So great is this healing power that it can heal even the most terrible of afflictions — those sent by Marduk himself.

The language of the poem is rich in rare words. The author was steeped in the scholarly lore of his age, including medical texts; some of the pathological terms used are otherwise attested only in diagnostic treatises. The author makes use of every poetic device in the Akkadian repertory. He is fond of wordplays (Tablet I, line 62), alliteration, rhyme, intricate parallelism, inclusion by oppo-sites (merismus, see Tablet I, lines 52–53: solicited and chance omens, meaning all omens were unfavorable; Tablet I, lines 107–108: soft moan and loud wail, meaning all sounds he made were sorrowful; Tablet I, lines 117–118, kind words and sarcastic comments, meaning all conversation, in a larger context of measured words versus impromptu speech). He builds up logical sequences, such as morning, noon, night (Tablet I, lines 51–54, compare lines 105–106), head to toe (Tablet I, lines 70–76), and degrees of intimacy, such as self, family, community, government (Tablet I, lines 79–83). He develops various elaborate over-arching symbolic frames of reference in his text, among them darkness and

---

1. For the river ordeal, see IV.14.

light, day and night.[1] He displays his humility throughout his text by various ingenious devices.[2] An ancient commentary and numerous manuscripts from different localities attest to the esteem this composition enjoyed among the educated.

The text sets forth a Mesopotamian notion of guilt and divine power. The modern term "righteous sufferer" is a misnomer when applied to this and comparable texts; at least, Shubshi-meshre-Shakkan was not so confident of his righteousness as was Job. The author of Job makes clear that Job's suffering had nothing to do with his righteousness, but was a test of faith. Here the speaker says that, so far as he knows, he has been righteous, and whatever his fault may have been (who can know?), he is sorry for it and begs forgiveness. There is none of the defiance and bitterness of Job. In short, this text sees suffering and redemption as signs of divine power, whereas Job sees them as tests of human strength. Despite these differences, the two documents belong to a common Near Eastern literary tradition.[3] Each works out its version of the problem of divinely inflicted human suffering in an original manner.

The reader is left to conclude that Marduk can redeem anyone, no matter how lost to the human race. This sounds a note of optimism that for the author outweighs his despair and agnosticism. In expatiating this theme, the poet drew freely on a vast store of knowledge to lend his text richness and broad scholarly appeal. The product is one of the finest literary monuments of Mesopotamian antiquity.

Tablet I

I will praise the lord of wisdom, solicitous god,	(1)
Furious in the night, growing calm in the day:	
Marduk! Lord of wisdom, solicitous god,	
Furious in the night, growing calm in the day:	
Whose anger, like a raging tempest, is a desolation,	(5)
But whose breeze is sweet as the breath of morn.	
In his fury not to be withstood, his rage the deluge,	
Merciful in his feelings, his emotions relenting.	

---

1. Moran, JAOS 103 (1983), 257–258; in general, see W. von Soden, "Licht und Finsternis in der sumerischen und babylonisch-assyrischen Religion," *Studium Generale* 13 (1960), 647–653.
2. Foster, "Self-Reference of an Akkadian Poet," JAOS 103 (1983), 123–130, though reservations expressed by Hirsch, AfO Beiheft 29 (2002), 14.
3. See General Introduction, p. 41 note 4.

The skies cannot sustain the weight of his hand,
His palm is gentle to rescue the moribund. (10)
Marduk! The skies cannot sustain the weight of his hand,
His palm is gentle to rescue the moribund.
He it is, in the brunt of whose anger many graves are dug,
At the same moment, he raises the fallen from annihilation.
He glowers, protective spirits take flight, (15)
He regards, the one whose god forsook him returns to him.[1]★
His severe punishment is harsh and speedy,
He stops short and quickly becomes like a mother.
He is impetuous to cherish the one he loves(?),[2]
Like a cow with a calf,
        he keeps turning around watchfully.[3] (20)
His scourge is barbed and punctures the body,
His bandages are soothing, they heal the doomed.
He speaks and makes one incur many sins,
On the day of his justice liability and guilt are dispelled.
He is the one who afflicts with demons of shaking-disease, (25)
Through his sacral spell chills and shivering are driven away.
Who dwarfs(?) the flood of Adad, the blow of Erra,
Who reconciles the wrathful god and [god]dess,
The lord divines the gods' inmost thoughts,
(But) no [god] understands his behavior! (30)
Marduk divines the gods' inmost thoughts,
No [god] understands his mind.
As heavy his hand, so compassionate his heart,
As brutal his weapons, so life-sustaining his feelings.
Without his consent, who could cure his blow? (35)
Against his will, which one could stay his hand?
I, who touched bottom like a fish,[4]
        will proclaim his anger,
He quickly granted me favor, as if he revived the dead.
I will teach the people that his kindness is nigh,

---

1. Or: "He regards, and turns toward the one whose god forsook him" (see Horowitz and Lambert, *Iraq* 64 [2002], 245).
2. A wordplay on "beloved"(?) and "wild bull" may be intended, resumed by "cow" in the following line. Variant: "love for me"(?).
3. Variant: "toward me."
4. Text: "ate mud" (perhaps like English "bit the dust").

May his favorable thought take away their [guilt?].   (40)
From the day the Lord punished me,
And the warrior Marduk became furious with me,
My own god threw me over and disappeared,
My goddess broke rank and vanished.
The benevolent angel who (walked) beside me split off,   (45)
My protecting spirit retreated, to seek out someone else.
My vigor was taken away,
  my manly appearance became gloomy,
My dignity bolted[1] and leapt for cover.
Terrifying signs beset me:
I was forced from my house, I wandered outside.   (50)
My omens were confused,
  they were contradictory every day,
(Even) with diviner and dream interpreter
  my course was undecided.
What I overheard in the street portended ill for me,
When I lay down at night, my dreams were terrifying.
The king, incarnation of the gods, sun of his peoples,   (55)
His heart hardened against me,
  turning openness to ill-will.*
Courtiers were plotting hostile action against me,
They mustered themselves to instigate base deeds:
If the first "I will make him end his life"
Says the second "I ousted (him) from his command!"   (60)
So likewise the third "I will get my hands on his post!"
"I'll come into his property!" vows the fourth[2]
As the fifth subverts the mind of fifty,*
Sixth and seventh follow on his heels![3]
The clique of seven have massed their forces,   (65)
Merciless as fiends, the likeness of demons.
So one is their body, (but seven) their mouths.
Their hearts fulminate against me, ablaze like fire.
Slander and lies they try to lend credence against me.
My eloquent mouth they checked, as with reins,   (70)

---

1. Variant: "flew off."
2. Wordplay on "come into" (*erēbu*) and "fourth" (*rebû*).
3. Literally: "like his protective spirit."

My lips, which used to discourse,
    became those of a deaf-mute.
My resounding calls died away to dumbness,
My proud head bent earthward,
My stout heart was enfeebled by terror,
My broad breast brushed aside by a stripling,   (75)
My far-reaching arms clutched each other under my clothing.
I, who walked proudly, learned slinking,
I, so grand, became servile.
To my vast family I became a loner,
As I went through the streets, I was pointed at,   (80)
I would enter the palace, eyes would squint at me,
My city was glowering at me like an enemy,
Belligerent and hostile would seem my land!
My brother became my foe,
My friend became malignant, a demon,   (85)
My comrade would denounce me savagely,
My colleague kept the taint to(?) his weapons for bloodshed,
My best friend made my life an aspersion.
My slave cursed me openly in the assembly (of gentlefolk),
My slave girl defamed me before the rabble.   (90)
An acquaintance would see me and make himself scarce,
My family set me down as an outsider.
A pit awaited anyone speaking well of me,
While he who was uttering defamation of me forged ahead.
One who relayed base things about me
    had a god for his help,   (95)
For the one who said "What a pity about him!"
    death came early,
The one of no help, his life became charmed,
I had no one to go at my side, nor saw I a champion.
They parceled my possessions among the riffraff,
The sources of my watercourses they blocked with muck,   (100)
They chased the harvest song from my fields,
They left my community deathly still,
    like that of a (ravaged) foe.
They let another assume my duties,
And appointed an outsider to my prerogatives.

By day sighing, by night lamentation,   (105)
Monthly, depression, despair the year.
I moaned like a dove all my days,
Like a singer, I wail my dirge aloud.*
My eyes endure(?) constant crying,
My cheeks scald from tears, as if eroded(?).   (110)
My face is darkened from the apprehensions of my heart,
Terror and panic have jaundiced my skin.
The wellsprings of my heart quaked in unremitting anxiety,
I was changeable(?) as a flickering fire,
Prayer was disorder, like an exploding flame,   (115)
My entreaty was like the fracas of a brawl.
My [sweet]-lipped discourse was murky, obscure,
[When] I turned a biting comment, my gambit was stifled.
"Surely in daylight good will come upon me!
"The moon will set(?),* my sun will shine!"   (120)

Tablet II

One whole year to the next! The appointed time passed.[1]   (1)
As I turned around, it was more and more terrible.
My ill luck was on the increase, I could find no good fortune.
I called to my god, he did not show his face,
I prayed to my goddess, she did not raise her head.   (5)
The diviner with his inspection
        did not get to the bottom of it,
Nor did the dream interpreter with his incense
        clear up my case,
I beseeched a dream spirit, but it did not enlighten me,
The exorcist with his ritual did not appease divine wrath.
What bizarre actions everywhere!   (10)
I looked behind: persecution, harassment!
Like one who had not made libations to his god,
Nor invoked his goddess with a food offering,
Who was not wont to prostrate, nor seen to bow down,

1. Variant: "My." The sufferer evidently projected a fixed limit to his misfortunes, perhaps by divination.

From whose mouth supplication and prayer were wanting,　　(15)
Who skipped holy days, despised festivals,
Who was neglectful, omitted the gods' rites,
Who had not taught his people reverence and worship,
Who did not invoke his god, but ate his food offering,
Who snubbed his goddess, brought (her) no flour offering,　　(20)
Like one possessed(?), who forgot his lord,
Who casually swore a solemn oath by his god:
　　I, indeed, seemed (such a one)!
I, for my part, was mindful of supplication and prayer,
Prayer to me was the natural recourse, sacrifice my rule.
The day for reverencing the gods
　　was a source of satisfaction to me,　　(25)
The goddess's procession day was my profit and return.
Praying for the king, that was my joy,
His fanfare was as if for (my own) good omen.
I instructed my land to observe the god's rites,
The goddess's name did I drill my people to esteem.　　(30)
I made my praises of the king like a god's,
And taught the populace reverence for the palace.
I wish I knew that these things were pleasing to a god!
What seems good to one's self could be an offense to a god,
What in one's own heart seems abominable
　　could be good to one's god!　　(35)
Who could learn the reasoning of the gods in heaven?
Who could grasp the intentions of the gods of the depths?
Where might human beings have learned the way of a god?
He who lived by (his) brawn died in confinement.
Suddenly one is downcast, in a trice full of cheer,　　(40)
One moment he sings in exaltation,
In a trice he groans like a professional mourner.
What the gods) intend for people changes in a twinkling:*
Starving, they become like corpses,
Full, they would rival their gods.　　(45)
In good times, they speak of scaling heaven,
When it goes badly, they complain of going down to hell.
I have ponde[red]* these things;
　　I have made no sense of them.

But as for me, in despair, a whirlwind is driving(?) me!
Debilitating disease is let loose upon me: (50)
An evil vapor has blown against me
    [from the] ends of the earth,
Head pain has surged up upon me from the breast of hell,
A malignant spectre has come forth from its hidden depth,
A relentless gho[st] came out of its dwelling place.
A she-demon came down from the mountain,   (55)
Ague set forth with the flood,
Debility broke through the ground with the plants.
[They assem]bled their host, together they came upon me:
[They struck my he]ad, they closed around my pate,
[My] features were gloomy, my eyes ran a flood,   (60)
They wrenched my muscles, made my neck limp,
They thwacked [my chest], pounded(?) my breast,
They affected my flesh, threw (me) into convulsions,
They kindled a fire in my epigastrium,
They churned up my bowels, they tw[isted] my entrails(?),   (65)
Coughing and hacking★ infected my lungs,
They incapacitated(?) my limbs, made my flesh pasty,
My lofty stature they toppled like a wall,
My robust figure they flattened like a bulrush,
I was dropped like a dried fig, I was tossed on my face.   (70)
A demon has clothed himself in my body for a garment,
Drowsiness smothers me like a net,
My eyes stare, they cannot see,
My ears prick up, they cannot hear.
Numbness has spread over my whole body,   (75)
Paralysis has fallen upon my flesh.
Stiffness has seized my arms,
Debility has fallen upon my loins,
My feet forgot how to move.
[A stroke] has overcome me, I choke like one fallen,   (80)
Signs of death★ have shrouded my face!
[If someone th]inks of me, I can't respond to the inquirer,
"[Ala]s!" they weep, I have lost consciousness.
A snare is laid on my mouth,
And a bolt bars my lips.   (85)

My way in is barred, my point of slaking blocked,
My hunger is chronic, my gullet constricted.
If it be of grain, I choke it down like stinkweed,
Beer, the sustenance of humankind, is sickening to me.
Indeed, the malady drags on! (90)
For lack of food my features are unrecognizable,
My flesh is waste, my blood has run dry,
My bones are loose, covered (only) with skin,
My tissues are inflamed, afflicted with gangrene(?).
I took to bed, confined, going out was exhaustion, (95)
My house turned into my prison.
My flesh was a shackle, my arms being useless,
My person was a fetter, my feet having given way.
My afflictions were grievous, the blow was severe!
A scourge full of barbs thrashed me, (100)
A crop lacerated me, cruel with thorns.
All day long tormentor would torment [me],
Nor at night would he let me breathe freely a moment.
From writhing, my joints were separated,
My limbs were splayed and thrust apart. (105)
I spent the night in my dung like an ox,
I wallowed in my excrement like a sheep.
The exorcist recoiled from my symptoms,
While my omens have perplexed the diviner.
The exorcist did not clarify the nature of my complaint, (110)
While the diviner put no time limit on my illness.
No god came to the rescue, nor lent me a hand,
No goddess took pity on me, nor went at my side.
My grave was open, my funerary goods ready,
Before I had died, lamentation for me was done. (115)
All my country said, "How wretched he was!"
When my ill-wisher heard, his face lit up,
When the tidings reached her, my ill-wisher,
  her mood became radiant.
The day grew dim for my whole family,
For those who knew me, their sun grew dark.* (120)

Tablet III

Heavy was his hand upon me, I could not bear it!   (1)
Dread of him was oppressive, it [me].
His fierce [pun]ishment* [   ], the deluge,
His stride was ..., it ... [   ]
[Ha]rsh, severe illness does not ... [   ] my person,   (5)
I lost sight of [aler]tness,* [   ] make my mind stray.
I gro[an] day and night alike,
Dreaming and waking [I am] equally wretched.
A remarkable young man of extraordinary physique,
Magnificent in body, clothed in new garments,   (10)
Because I was only half awake,* his features lacked form.
He was clad in splendor, robed in dread —
He came in upon me, he stood over me.
[When I saw him, my] flesh grew numb.
[   ] "The Lady(?) has sent [me],   (15)
"[   ]."
[   ] I tried to tell [my people],[1]
"[   ] sent [for me]."
They were silent and did not [speak],
They heard me [in silence and did not answer].   (20)
A second time [I saw a dream].
In the dream I saw [at night],
A remarkable purifier [   ],
Holding in his hand a tamarisk rod of purification,
"Laluralimma,[2] resident of Nippur,   (25)
"Has sent me to cleanse you."
He was carrying water, he po[ured it] over me,
He pronounced the resuscitating incantation,
        he massaged [my] bo[dy].
A third time I saw a dream.
In my dream I saw at night: (30)
A remarkable young woman of shining countenance,
Clothed like a person(?), being li[ke] a god,

---

1. These three lines may mean that when the sufferer told of his dream to his family, no one believed him. For the restoration, see line 47 below, where they need a sign to be convinced.
2. An academic Sumerian name, typical of Babylonia of the second half of the second millennium B.C. Compare Why Do You Curse Me? (IV.24).

A queen among peoples [   ],
She entered upon me and [sat down] ... [   ]
She ordered my deliverance [   ]
"Fear not!" she said, "I [will   ]   (35)
"Whatever one sees(?) of a dream [   ]."
She ordered my deliverance, "Most wre[tched] indeed is he,
"Whoever he might be, the one who saw the vision at night."[1]
In the dream (was) Ur-Nintinugga, a Babylonian(?) ...
A bearded young man wearing a tiara,   (40)
He was an exorcist, carrying a tablet,
"Marduk has sent me!"
"To Shubshi-meshre-Shakkan[2] I have brought a sw[athe],
"From his pure hands I have brought a sw[athe]."
He has entru[sted] me into the hands of my ministrant.   (45)
[In] waking hours he sent a message,
He reve[aled] his favorable sign to my people.
I was awake in my sickness, a (healing) serpent slithered by.[3]*
My illness was quickly over, [my fetters] were broken.
After my lord's heart had quiet[ed],   (50)
(And) the feelings of merciful Marduk were ap[peased],
[And he had] accepted my prayers [   ],
His sweet [relen]ting [   ],
[He ordered] my deliverance!: "He is g[reatly trie]d!"
[   ] to extol [   ]   (55)
[   ] to worship and [   ]
[   ] my guilt [   ]
[   ] my iniquity [   ]
[   ] my transgression [   ]
He made the wind bear away my offenses.   (60)

(The exact placement of the following lines is unknown.)

1. These are oblique references to the sufferer, perhaps meaning something like "whoever has seen this vision should have pity taken upon him."
2. The name of the sufferer (see p. 392 note 1). This time the object of mercy is more specific than the preceding. Note that Marduk is named here for the first time since the opening of the poem.
3. The serpent, like the serpents of Aesculapius, was sometimes associated with the goddess of healing; see D. McDonald, "The Serpent as Healer: Theriac and Ancient Near Eastern Pottery," *Source* 13/4 (1994), 21–27.

[He applied] to me his spell
    that binds [debilitating disease],[1]
[He drove] back the evil vapor to the ends of the earth,
He bore off [the head pain] to the breast of hell,   (5')
[He sent] down the malignant spectre to its hidden depth,
The relentless ghost he returned [to] its dwelling,
He overthrew the she-demon, sending if off to a mountain,
He replaced the ague in flood and sea.
He eradicated debility like a plant,   (10')
Uneasy sleep, excessive drowsiness,
He dissipated like smoke filling the sky.
The turning toward people(?) with "Woe!" and "Alas!"*
    he drove away like a cloud, earth ... [   ]
The tenacious disease in the head,
    which was [heavy] as a [mill]stone,*
He raised like dew of night, he removed it from me.   (15')
My beclouded eyes,
    which were wrapped in the shroud of death,
He drove (the cloud) a thousand leagues away,
    he brightened [my] vision.
My ears, which were stopped
    and clogged like a deaf man's,
He removed their blockage, he opened my hearing.
My nose, whose bre[athing] was choked
    by symptoms of fever,   (20')
He soothed its affliction so I could breathe [freely].
My babbling lips, which had taken on a h[ard crust?],
He wiped away their distress(?)
    and und[id] their deformation.
My mouth, which was muffled,
    so that proper speech was diffi[cult],
He scoured like copper and r[emoved] its filth.   (25')
My teeth, which were clenched
    and locked together firmly,
[He op]ened their fastening, fre[ed?] the jaws(?).*
My tongue, which was tied and [could] not converse,
[He] wiped off its coating and [its] speech became fluent(?).

---

1. See Tablet II lines 50ff.

My windpipe, which was tight and choking,
    as though on a gobbet,   (30')
He made well and let it si[ng] its songs like a flute.
My [gul]let, which was swollen so it could not take [food],
Its swelling went down and he opened its blockage.
My [   ], which [   ]
[   ] above [   ]   (35')
[which] was darkened like [   ]

(three damaged lines, then gap)

*(The following lines are known only from the ancient commentary, but must
    go in the gap here, in sequence but not necessarily seriatim.)*

a. My intestine, which was ever empty for want,
        and was coiled (tight) like basketry,
b. Accepts nourishment, holds drink.
c. My neck, which was limp and twisted at the base,
d. He shored up, a hillock,[1] he planted upright like a tree(?).
e. He made my body that of a perfect athlete.[2]
f. He pared my nails as if to drive out a "vengeance."[3]
g. He drove out their illness and made their upper parts well.
h. My knees, which were tied and b[ound] like a ... bird's
i. The shape of my bo[d]y [he made] remarkable(?)
j. He wiped off the grime, he cleansed its filth
k. My gloomy mien began to glow (=120?)*

1. The image may be of piling up around the bottom of something to make it strong (differently
CAD A/2, 1b).
2. Literally: "perfect in strength."
3. Obscure word (*naqqimtu*). The frame of reference may be witchcraft and countermeasures;
one pares the nails carefully lest "vengeance" (= black magic?) use the discarded parings to assault
the body? "Vengeance" is either male or female (as here). See also III.31 line 77.

Tablet IV[1]

(Episode A)

The Lord [ ] me,	(1′)
The Lord took hold of me,	
The Lord set me on my feet,	
The Lord revived me,	
He rescued me [from the p]it,	(5′)
He summoned me [from destruc]tion,	
[ ] he pulled me from the river of death.	
[ ] he took my hand.	
[He who] smote me,	
Marduk, he restored me!	(10′)
He smote the hand of my smiter,	
It was Marduk who made him drop his weapon.	
[He] the attack of my foe,	
It was Marduk who [ ]	

(Two fragmentary lines, then gap. Insert here, perhaps, two lines known only
from the ancient commentary.)

l.   At the place of the river ordeal,
          where people's fates are decided,
m.   I was struck on the forehead, my slave mark removed.

(Fragment B)

[   ] which in my prayers [   ]
[With] prostration and supplication [   ] to Esagila [ ]
[I who went] down to the grave
          have returned to the "Gate of [Sunrise]."[2]

---

1. The assignment of texts to this tablet remains uncertain. Various arrangements have been proposed by Lambert, BWL, 24–25; OrNS 57 (1988), 88; Borger, JCS 18 (1964), 51; von Soden, MDOG 94 (1979), 51 note 5; Vogelzang, RA 73 (1979), 180; Reiner, *Poetry*, 118. Von Soden and Reiner place Fragment A at the end rather than the beginning of the tablet (Fragment A = Lambert, BWL, 1–15; Fragment B = Lambert, BWL, 76–101; Fragment C = Lambert, BWL, 24–50).

2. This and the following are gates of the Marduk temple complex in Babylon (George, *Topographical Texts*, 90).

[In the] "Gate of Prosperity" prosperity was [given me].
[In the] "Gate of the Guardian Spirit"
    a guardian spirit [drew nigh to me].   (40′)
[In the] "Gate of Well-being" I beheld well-being.
In the "Gate of Life" I was granted life.
In the "Gate of Sunrise" I was reckoned among the living.
In the "Gate of Splendid Wonderment"
    my signs were plain to see.
In the "Gate of Release from Guilt"
    I was released from my bond.   (45′)
In the "Gate of Praise"(?) my mouth made inquiry.
In the "Gate of Release from Sighing" my sighs were released.
In the "Gate of Pure Water"
    I was sprinkled with purifying water.
In the "Gate of Conciliation" I appeared with Marduk,
In the "Gate of Joy" I kissed the foot* of Sarpanitum.   (50′)
I was assiduous in supplication and prayer before them,
I placed fragrant incense before them,
An offering, a gift, sundry donations I presented,
Many fatted oxen I slaughtered, butchered many …,
Honey-sweet beer and pure wine I repeatedly libated.   (55′)
The protecting genius, the guardian spirit,
    divine attendants of the fabric of Esagila,
I made their feelings glow with libation,
I made them exultant [with] lavish [meals].
[To the threshold, the bolt] socket, the bolt, the doors
[I offered] oil, butterfat, and choicest grain.   (60′)
[   ] the rites of the temple.

(large gap)

(insert here?)

o.   I proceeded along Kunush–kadru Street
        in a state of redemption.
p.   He who has done wrong by Esagil,
        let him learn from me.
q.   It was Marduk who put a muzzle on the mouth
        of the lion that was devouring me.

r.   Marduk took away the sling of my pursuer
      and deflected his slingstone.

(Fragment C)

[ ] golden grain [   ]   (1′)
[He?] anointed himself with sweet cedar perfume,
    upon him [ ]¹
A feast for the Babylonian(s?) [   ]
His tomb he(?) had made [was set up] for a feast!
The Babylonians saw how [Marduk] can restore to life,   (5′)
And all mouths proclaimed [his] greatness,
"Who (would have) said he would see his sun?
"Who (would have) imagined
    that he would pass through his street?
"Who but Marduk revived him as was dying?
"Besides Sarpanitum,
    which goddess bestowed his breath of life?   (10′)
"Marduk can restore to life from the grave,
"Sarpanitum knows how to rescue from annihilation.
"Wherever earth is founded, heavens are stretched wide,
"Wherever sun shines, fire blazes,
"Wherever water runs, wind blows,   (15′)
"Those whose bits of clay Aruru pinched off (to form them),
"Those endowed with life, who walk upright,
"[Tee]ming humankind, as many as they be,
    give praise to Marduk!
"[   ] those who can speak,
"[   ] may he rule all the peoples   (20′)
"[   ] shepherd of all habi[tations]
"[   ] floods from the deep
"[   ] the gods [   ]
"[   ] the extent of heaven and netherworld,
"[   ]   (25′)
"[   ] was getting darker and darker for him."*

---

1. Unlike other translators, I read these lines throughout in the third person (*elišu/bit qeberišu,*
ēpušu = Assyrianism?). This distancing is the result of attention now focusing on the Babylonians'
view of the sufferer and culminates in the Babylonians singing a hymn of praise to Marduk.

Text: (Tablet I) W. G. Lambert, BWL pl. 1–4, 74 with photos of some sources in *Iraq* 64 (2002), 239–241; Ebeling-Köcher-Rost, LKA 24; Leichty, *Studies Finkelstein*, 145; Wiseman and Black, CTN 4 201; Sippar ms. Al-Rawi and George, *Iraq* 60 (1998), 188–192; Horowitz and Lambert, *Iraq* 64 (2002), 241. (Tablet II) Lambert, BWL, pl. 4–11, 74. (Tablet III) Lambert, BWL, pl. 12–13, 74. (Tablet IV) Lambert, BWL, pl. 18. Source u = 1–15; t = 36–61, 94–116; w = 101–112; v = 107–120. See also Gurney, OECT 11 48 (not used). (Commentary) Lambert, BWL, pl. 15–17.

Edition: Lambert, BWL, 21–62, 343–345; Al-Rawi and George, *Iraq* 60 (1998), 187–201 and Horowitz and Lambert, *Iraq* 64 (2002), 237–245 (Tablet I).

Translation: Biggs, ANET³, 596–600; Labat, *Religions*, 328–341; Bottéro, *Recherches et Documents du Centre Thomas More, Document* 77/7, 11–24; von Soden, TUAT III/1, 110–135 (with readings and interpretations adopted here).

Literature: (in general) W. von Soden, "Das Fragen nach der Gerechtigkeit Gottes im alten Orient," MDOG 96 (1965), 41–59; J. Bottéro, "Le Problème du Mal en Mésopotamie ancienne, Prologue à une Étude du 'Juste Souffrant'," *Recherches et Documents du Centre Thomas More, Document* 77/7 (1977), 1–43. (To specific aspects of the poem) Foster, JAOS 103 (1983), 123–130; Moran, JAOS 103 (1983), 255–260 (with proposals for the opening of Tablet I adopted here); Groneberg, JAOS 107 (1987), 323–324 (to opening of Tablet I); Vogelzang, RA 73 (1979), 180 (basic arrangement of Tablet IV adopted here); Reiner, *Poetry*, 101–118 (translation and literary study of Tablet II, to which I owe insights); Borger, HKL 1, 266; HKL 2, 159; Albertz, AOAT 220 (1988), 25–53; Sitzler, *Vorwurf*, 84–99; H. Spieckermann, "*Ludlul bēl nēmeqi* und die Frage nach der Gerechtigkeit Gottes," *Studies Borger*, 329–341.

*Notes to Text: I owe numerous new readings, corrections, and additions to Tablet I, notably to lines 5, 12–19, 26, 35–42, 87–88, and 107–120 to Al-Rawi and George, *Iraq* 60 (1998), 187–201, where reference to earlier literature can be found. (I 18–20) Differently interpreted by Stol, *Birth in Babylonia*, 133, though his understanding is rendered unlikely by the Sippar ms. (not available to Stol), which has first-person suffixes here, with an implied male speaker. (I 63) Read from an unpublished fragment kindly communicated by George. (I 108) I follow Sippar ms. and Lambert, JSS 12 (1967), 104. (I 120) Lambert, N.A.B.U. 2003/22. (II 43) With Stol, *Studies Limet*, 179–183. (II 48) AHw, 703a. (II 66) *su-ú-lu ḫa-aḫ-ḫu* (WGL, from unpublished text); for *ḫaḫḫu*, see Adams, JRAS 1979, 4. (II 81) von Soden, TUAT III/1, 124. (II 120) For this oft-debated crux, see B. Landsberger, *Brief eines Bischofs von Esagila an König Asarhaddon*, MKNAW NR 28/VI (1965), 72 note 134 (which I follow in essentials); Cooper, JCS 27 (1975), 248–249; Moran, JAOS 103 (1983), 257 note 11; differently Lambert, 46 and 295. (III 3) Moran, JAOS 103 (1983), 259 note 18. (III 6) [*e*]-*ru-ti*, AHw, 248a. (III 11) CAD M, 200a reads *ruš-šu-qat*, seemingly without basis. I follow von Soden, TUAT III/1, 127. (III 48) von Soden, TUAT III/1, 128. (III 13′) Note that the copy shows *ina 'ù-ú-a*. (III 14′) von Soden, TUAT III/1, 129. (III 27′) Bottéro, "Juste Souffrant," 20. (k) Moran, JAOS 103 (1983), 257. (IV B 50′) Or, with CAD A/1, 9: "fell at the feet of." (IV C 26′) Moran, JAOS 103 (1983), 257 note 5.

III.15 A SUFFERER'S SALVATION

This composition, which has expressions in common with III.14, is known from a fourteenth(?)-century manuscript from Ugarit in Syria. Nougayrol has considered the possibility that the Poem of the Righteous Sufferer (III.14) and this text derive from a common ancestor of the Classical period.[1] However, both texts may simply be drawing on stock motifs. As preserved, the text does not deal with the causes of the sufferer's punishment, but portrays his privations and afflictions before glorifying Marduk, his redeemer.

(gap of about fifteen lines)

Evil [portents?] were continually set again[st me   ]   (1′)
My omens were obscure, they became like [   ]
The diviner could not reach a ruling concerning me,
The "Judge"[2] would give no sign.
The omens were confused, the oracles mixed up.   (5′)
Dream interpreters used up incense, diviners lambs,
Learned men debated the tablets (? about my case),*
They could not say when my affliction would run its course.
My family gathered round to bend over me before my time,
My next of kin stood by ready for the wake.   (10′)
My brothers were bathed in blood like men possessed,
My sisters sprinkled me with fine(?) oil from the press.
Until the Lord raised my head,
And brought me back to life from the dead,
Until Marduk raised my head,   (15′)
And brought me back to life from the dead,
I could eat scant bread,
[I took for my] drink bilge(?) and salt pools.*
[When I lay down], sleep would not overcome me,
[I would lie aw]ake my whole night through.   (20′)
My heart [   ] me, my(!) mind ...,
I was wasting away(?) from the sickness I suffered.
[I] was made most anxious [   ]

1. So Nougayrol, *Ugaritica* 5, 266–267; see also von Soden, TUAT III/1, 140–141.
2. Shamash?

My [te]ars [had to serve] as my sustenance.
[Lest] Marduk be forgotten, (25')
That Marduk be praised:
Were it not for Marduk, breath had gone from me,
Would not(?) [the mou]rner* have cried, 'Alas for him!'?
I praise, I praise, what the lord Marduk has done I praise!
[I praise, I praise], what the angry (personal) god [has done]
    I praise! (30')
[I praise, I praise], what the (personal) goddess [has done]
    I praise!
Praise, praise, do not be bashful, but praise!
[He it] is, Marduk, I entreat(?) him, I entreat(?) him,
[He it] was who smote me, then was merciful to me.
He scuttled(?) me, then moored me, (35')
He dashed me down, then grabbed me (as I fell),
He scattered me wide, then garnered me,
He thrust me away, then gathered me in,
He threw me down, then lifted me high.
He snatched me from the maw of death, (40')
He raised me up from hell.
He smashed my smiter's weapon,
He wrested the shovel from the digger of my grave.
He opened my shrouded eyes,
He made my [sp]eech intelligible, (45')
He [   ] my ears.

(breaks off)

Text: Nougayrol, *Ugaritica* 5 162 (p. 435).
Edition:. Nougayrol, *Ugaritica* 5, 265–273; M. Dietrich, "The Hymn to Marduk from Ugarit," AOAT 42 (1993), 62–67; Kämmerer, AOAT 251 (1998), 160–163.
Translation: von Soden, TUAT III/1, 140–143, whence some readings used here; Dietrich, TUAT II/6, 823–826.
Literature: von Soden, UF 1 (1969), 191; W. G. Lambert, *Ugaritica* 5, 272–273.
Notes to Text: (7') von Soden, TUAT III/1, 141. (18') Butz, JESHO 27 (1984), 309. The restoration proposed there for 19' seems to me implausible. (28') Dietrich, AOAT 42 (1993), 64.

III.16 WORDS OF THE WISE

Numerous Akkadian and Sumerian texts are known that retail conventional wisdom in the form of apodictic sayings and advice. The timelessness of the wisdom they convey makes dating of any particular collection impossible. I include as well a selection of proverbial sayings known from letters and other contexts.

(a) COUNSELS OF WISDOM

A learned man [   ]   (1?)
From [his] wisdom [   ]:
"Come, my son,
"[Pay heed to] the instruction that [I give you],
"Master the counsels [   ] ..."

Don't stop to talk with a frivolous person,*   (21)
Nor go consult with a [   ] who has nothing to do.
With good intentions you will do their thinking for them,
You will diminish your own accomplishment,
        abandon your own course,
You will play false to your own, wiser, thinking.

Hold your tongue, watch what you say.   (26)
A man's pride: the great value on your lips.
Insolence and insult should be abhorrent to you.
Speak nothing slanderous, no untrue report.
The frivolous person is of no account.

Don't go stand where there's a crowd,   (31)
Do not linger where there is a dispute.
They will bring evil upon you in the dispute,*
Then you will be made their witness,
They will bring you to bolster a case not your own.   (35)
When confronted with a dispute, avoid it, pay no heed.
If it is a dispute with you, put out the flame,
A dispute is a wide-open ambush,

a wall of sticks that smothers its opponents,[1]
It brings to mind what a man forgot and charges him.
Do no evil to the man who disputes with you, (42)
Requite with good the one who does evil to you.
Be fair to your enemy,
Let your mood be cheerful to your opponent.
Be it your ill-wisher, tre[at him generous]ly.*
Make up your mind to no evil,
Suc[h is not] acceptable [to the] gods,
Evil [ ] is abhorrent to [   ] to Marduk.

[ ] the lowly, take pity on him. (56)
Do not despise the miserable and [   ],
Do not wrinkle up your nose haughtily at them.
One's god will be angry with him for that,
It is displeasing to Shamash, he will requite him with evil.

Give food to eat, beer to drink, (61)
Present what is asked for, provide for and honor.
One's god will be happy with him for that,
It is pleasing to Shamash, he will requite him with favor.
Do good deeds and be helpful all the days of your life.

You must not make a slave girl important in your house, (66)
She must not rule your bedroom like a wife
...
Let your people have this to tell you:
"The household that a slave girl rules, she will break up."

Don't marry a prostitute, whose husbands are legion, (72)
Nor a temple harlot, who is dedicated to a deity,
Nor a courtesan, whose intimates are numerous.
She will not sustain you in your time of trouble,

---

1. Literally: "a brushwood defense that overwhelms its foes" (restored on the basis of an unpublished duplicate cited CAD A/1, 63a). "Brush" or "tinder" (*abu*) was used in similes for quick consumption by fire, as in IV.2c. A dispute is broad enough for anyone to fall into and containing and inflammable enough that both parties will be consumed in the conflagration. Hence the initial exhortation to "put out the fire" acquires special significance.

She will snigger at you
>   when you are embroiled in controversy.
She has neither respect nor obedience in her nature.
Even if she has the run of your house, get rid of her,
She has her ears attuned for another's footfall.
Variant: As to the household she enters, she will break (it) up.
The man who married her will not have a stable home life.

My son, should it be the prince's will that you serve him,   (81)
His closely guarded seal should hang (around your neck).
Open his vault and go in,
>   for there is none but you (should do so).
You may find countless treasures therein,
You must not covet any of it,
You must not set your mind on stealth.
Later the matter will be [brought out],*
And the stealth you attempted will be ex[posed].
When the prince hears, he will [   ],
His beaming countenance will [darken].
As for you, you will have an explanation [to devise] ...

>   *(gap)*

Do not backbite, speak fair words.   (127)
Do not speak of evil things,
Think of something good to say.
As for the backbiter and the speaker of evil,
They will be forced to settle their accounts with Shamash.

Do not speak lightly, guard your speech.   (131)
Do not speak your innermost thoughts, (even) when alone.
What you say on the spur of the moment
>   you will still have with you later,
So set your mind on restraining your speech.
Bless your god every day,   (135)
Sacrifice and prayer are meet with incense.
You should give freewill offerings to your god,
For this is meet for a deity.
Prayer, supplication, and genuflection:

For every grain you render,* your profit will be a talent,[1]
So you will proceed at a premium with your god.

Since you are accomplished, read this text: (142)
"Reverence begets benevolence,
"Sacrifice prolongs life,
"And prayer atones for guilt.
"He who reverences the gods is despised by [no one],
"He who favors the Anunna-gods prolongs [his days].

(fragmentary lines, then gap)

Text: W. G. Lambert, BWL, pl. 27–29; Gurney, OECT 11 50 and 88 (not used), 51.
Edition: W. G. Lambert, BWL, 96–107.
Translation: Biggs, ANET³, 595–596; von Soden, TUAT III/1, 163–168.
Notes to Text: (21) Groneberg, N.A.B.U. 1997/68 argues that *namûtu* implies boisterous shocking behavior and cross-dressing, but I maintain a more general translation here. (33) von Soden, TUAT III/1, 165. (45) von Soden, TUAT III/1, 165. (88) von Soden, TUAT III/1, 167. (140) von Soden, ZA 71 (1981), 108.

1. A large sum of money, approximately fifty pounds of silver.

(b) WISDOM OF UGARIT

1. The Instructions of Shupe-Ameli[1]

A collection of Mesopotamian wisdom, discovered in variant versions at Emar and Ugarit (quoted as "E" and "U") in Syria, deals with the necessity of making one's own way in life, trust, self-reliance, decent behavior, discretion, and other virtues. The text is often corrupt and difficult to understand, so this version contains much guesswork. A similar text, quoted here as "H," is known from Hattusha, the capital of the Hittites in Anatolia, and was provided with a Hittite translation.

i

Hear the counsel of Shupe-ameli,   (1)
   Whose wisdom Enlilbanda[2] enlarged,
The wise counsel of Shupe-ameli,
   Whose wisdom En[lilban]da gave him!
From his mouth have come forth rules for later times,
For the guidance(?) of people, for ... his son,
   has [his wisdom] come forth,   (5)
He speaks well-considered(?) exhortations.

"My son, (if) for you alone your moon has set(?),[3]⋆
"(If) the wayfarer [will forsake] his watered field,[4]   (10)
"(If) for you alone you have made yourself ready to go,
"(Then) you have only the watered field of the open country,
   who will be my replacement (for you)?
"Your going will be too easily determined by the winds,
"So carry out all your tasks with a friend.
"He who goes with a friend succeeds,   (15)
"He who goes with a troop goes in safety.
"Son, do not frequent public houses,

---

1. Though presented as a Mesopotamian sage, the name is otherwise unknown in Mesopotamian tradition.

2. Another name for Enki/Ea, god of wisdom; compare II.23b.

3. Obscure. The son may believe his time has come to leave home.

4. The father regrets that his son wants to exchange adventure for the security of home, and urges him not to go alone.

"[Excessive drinking, gluttony] bloat the body.[1]
"Son, it is not [meet] to chit-chat with menials,
"You should ... your hunger,
    you should take your pleasure in the beer.[2]   (20)
"Hold your tongue as you pass through the bustling(?)* street,
"Say nothing derogatory of people.
"A friend has nothing to say of one not his friend.[3]
"You might garner a gain.
"But the over-hasty harvest is a pitfall(?), a trick,
    and unbreakable enmity.   (25)

(fragmentary lines)

(gap)

ii

" ...   (1)
"A wayward(?) son is the bane [of his father],
"A tardy heir is a loss for [his] house.

(two lines too fragmentary for translation)

"My son, break no bread with heedless(?) men,
"You should not cause the poverty of young men
    along with old ones.[4]
"Do not speak frivolously of a god without ...
"Even if your strength be that of a king,
"Do not pit yourself against a man of (greater) strength,   (10)
"Do not (try to) jump too wide a canal:
"You will bite your tongue(?),* make yourself sick,
"[Your?] physician will examine you,
    you will have to slaughter a sheep to feed him.

---

1. Compare: "Rush to no public house feast, you will not be tied with a tether" (BWL, 256).
2. As understood here, in public places eat only what you need, keep quiet, and leave. Seminara (UF 32 [2000], 496) proposes a different understanding of the lines, which would thereby mean "Do not go, my son, with soldiers (who fight only) with words, you will plunder (only) your own food supplies and massacre (only) beer."
3. That is, not speaking to strangers is a sign of respect and not hostility? (For discussion of the line, see von Soden, UF 1 [1969], 193.)
4. Obscure.

(two lines damaged)

"Do not open your heart (too much) to a woman you care for,
"Seal [it up], however much she cuddles(?) or at[tacks you],
"Save the present[1] in your strong room,
"Do not let your wife learn what is in your purse.
"Our forebears established this of old,   (20)
"Our fathers divided income (only) with the gods.
"They drove in a peg, and, making firm a ring,
        they daubed it with clay.[2]
"Keep your seal[3] safe on (its) ring.
"Surround the (door) bolt with a ring: (so) [gu]ard your house!
"Let your seal (be the only) access to [your] capital,   (25)
"Whatever you see, leave it [there],
"When you need to, you can spend it(?)."

(five lines unintelligible)

iii

"Do [not] dig a well at the head of your [field].   (5′)
"If you dig a well at the head of your [field],
"You will have to walk all the way to get to it(?).
"There will be footmarks[4] of strangers in your field,
"...
"They will drag you away for an oath.[5]
"Do not buy [an ox? in the springtime],   (10′)
"Do not choose a girl to marry on a h[oliday].
"The ox will look good in (that) season,

1. That is, don't give a valuable gift to a woman with whom you are emotionally involved?
2. Refers to sealing a strong room with a peg and ring covered with clay and then sealed so no one can enter without breaking the seal. See Zettler, JCS 39 (1987), 211–240, with other literature cited there 197 note 1.
3. That is, the cylinder seal that is needed to reseal the storeroom.
4. Guessing from H. U has "your feet (will be?) strangers in your own field."
5. Variant: "They expelled (you) by oath." The idea may be that if the well is not at the center of the field, one has to walk farther to draw water from it, neighbors will use it without permission, and it could be the basis for contesting ownership. This would, therefore, build on the previous advice to keep assets as protected as possible.

"A girl [is wearing] b[est] clothes for the occasion."[1]

(fragmentary lines)

iii/iv

(fragmentary lines)

The son makes ready to speak, saying to his father, the sage,   (1′)
"I have heard in silence the words of my father, the king,
"(These) words would I say to you:
"We are moaning doves, birds,
"Footloose as the mighty ox, the raging wild bull,   (5′)
"We are offspring of the wild donkey

(fragmentary lines)

"The creditors are under no oath
    (for?) the holder of major capital,
"Wise men watch a truck garden in an orchard,[2]
"None (of them) eats a meal that is the work of green (fields),
"None (of them) drinks water from a dug channel,
"He looks to heaven (to slake) his thirst, he makes no [move],   (10′)
"[Heaven] floods the field crop,
    so [the owner] takes nothing … for his pains.

"O my father, you built a house, raised high the door(?),
"The storehouse is sixty cubits wide,
"What did you take (from it)?
"The loft of your house, as much as the storehouse,
    is full of grain,*   (15′)
"(But) on your day of death they will count out
    (only) nine loaves as a grave offering
    and put them by your head."

---

1. A Sumerian parallel to this adds: "Her underwear is borrowed, her clothes are borrowed, her silver (jewelry) is borrowed, her lapis (jewelry) is borrowed—(all) her clothes are borrowed, her bedding is borrowed (too)!" (see Alster, *Proverbs*, 2:425, though with a different interpretation of this passage).

2. Vegetables were often cultivated in the spaces between trees in date orchards. The saying may mean that the wisest of men are those who do not work hard to live adequately.

*(fragmentary lines in the same vein, dealing with material wealth
such as livestock, money, and textiles)*

"Many are the days for eating bread,
"Many are those for growing wan with thirst,
"Many are those we see the sun,
"(But) we dwell under a great shadow,
"We people lie asleep in a solitary chamber,*
"Ereshkigal[1] is our mother and we her children,   (15′)
"A shadow stands at the door of that solitary chamber,
"Lest the living see the dead."

This is the discourse father [and son] conversed together.

2. Akkado-Hurrian Bilingual

Deposit money for an oath,
        you can take it (back) from a god.   (1)
Respect an oath and keep yourself safe.
One who swears (falsely) is fully answerable(?) to
        the river ordeal for his life(?),
His wife will never have a son.[2]

One unconscious of guilt hastens to his god,   (10)
Without thinking, he hurriedly prays to god.
His guilt is much(?) …
He is simply unaware of it, so (that) man hastens to his god.

1. Queen of the Netherworld, ruler of the dead (see III.20).
2. Compare, however, Kussulu to the Moon-God (II.29), where this consequence did not occur.

Text: (1) (U) =Nougayrol, *Ugaritica* 5 163 (pp. 436–437); (E) = Arnaud, *Emar* 778; (H) = Weidner, KUB 4 3. U and E are unilingual Akkadian, H Akkadian-Hittite bilingual. (2) Nougayrol, in *Le Palais royale d'Ugarit* (Paris, 1955) III/2, CVI.

Edition: (1) Nougayrol, *Ugaritica* 5, 273–290 (U); Arnaud, *Emar* VI/4 377–382 (E); M. Dietrich, "Der Dialog zwischen Šupē-amēli und seinem 'Vater': Die Tradition babylonischer Weisheit-sprüche im Westen," UF 23 (1991), 33–74; "Proverb Collection of Šupē-amēli from Ugarit, Emar, and Boğazköy," AOAT 42 (1993), 52–62 (all versions); Kämmerer, AOAT 251 (1998), 176–207; S. Seminara, "Le Istruzioni di Supe-ameli, vecchio e nuovo a confronto nella "sapienza" siriana del Tardo Bronzo," UF 32 (2000), 487–529, from which various readings and proposals have been adopted here. For H, see also Laroche, *Ugaritica* 5, 779–784. (2) Nougayrol and Laroche, in *Le Palais royale d'Ugarit* (Paris, 1955), III/1, 311–324; W. G. Lambert, BWL, 116.

Literature: (1) von Soden, UF 1 (1969), 193–194.

★Notes to Text: (i 9) Lambert, N.A.B.U. 2003/22. (i 21) *epāti* = *apāti*? (ii 12) CAD S, 277b suggests "catch a cold" (because the would-be jumper is doused in the canal?), but there is unfortunately no evidence for such a meaning of *kaṣāṣu*, which refers to gnashing or baring of teeth, mutilation, or a bodily defect such as torticollis, nor is there evidence for the formation of a denominative of *kūṣu* as *★kuṣṣuṣu*. (iii/iv 15′) For *kurṣītu*, I follow Mayer, UF 21 (1989), 467–480, differently Seminara, UF 27 (1995), 467–480; for *ganūnu*, see J. Westenholz, *Studies Cagni* (2000), 1193.

(c) SUMERO–AKKADIAN WISDOM AND PROVERBS

Sumerian proverbs and wisdom were closely studied by Akkadian-speaking scholars of the second and first millennia B.C. These were often provided with Akkadian translations or equivalents. Since proverbs and epigrams were regarded as common speech, relatively few native Akkadian proverbs have come down to us. The Sumerian material may have been studied because of its antiquity and linguistic value, as well as for its content. Proverbs, as opposed to epigrams or incidental pieces of wisdom, are hard to identify with certainty, nor is it always clear where a unit of text begins or ends. Furthermore, sayings of this type are often unfathomable to those without living cultural competence. The selections that follow are mostly made from the edition by Lambert in BWL; the reader interested in the problems presented by these texts should consult his treatment, and for the Sumerian originals, where available independently, Alster's *Proverbs*. I have arbitrarily titled the various manuscripts treated here. In a few cases I have placed in italics an interpretative subtitle. This is simply a guess as to what the saying refers to, without direct authority from the texts.

1. The Assyrian Collection

This group opens with a curious prologue, in which a "blockhead" (or, possibly, an Amorite) invites his wife to switch roles with him. This is usually understood to refer to sexual activity, but could be interpreted as a school exercise in grammar.

col. i

A [b]lockhead says [to] his wife, "[Yo]u be the young man, [I] will be the girl. [When] I turn to being the young man, [let ... be] feminine, [let ...] be masculine."

col. ii

The Dumbfounded Fool

He tried to snare birds without a trap: there weren't any!   (4)

A Marriage Ditty

(He)

My face is a lion's, my figure a guardian angel's,
    my thighs(?) absolute delight!
Who will be the wife for me to adore?

(She)

My heart is discretion, my(!) inmost self is good counsel,
    my emotions are restrained,
    my lips speak delightful words!
Who will be the groom of my choice? (13)

Marrying for Money

Who is wealthy? Who is rich?
For whom shall I reserve my intimacy? (19)

That you fall in love (means) that you bear a yoke. (21)
Plan ahead, you will succeed,
Make no plan ahead, you will not succeed.

Paying for Pleasure

"Let me lie with you!" "Give god the due!"[1] (27)

The Lord helps them ...

[Gi]rd yourself, your god shall be your help. (29)
[Draw?] your sword! A god shall be your ally.

When you are down, let a friend help. (33)
You did evil to your well-wisher —
    what will you do to your enemy?

---

1. Lambert, BWL, 231, suggests that this refers to temple prostitution: pay the temple its due and then take the prostitute's services.

Wealth is not your help, but god.
(Be you) great or small, god is your help.

col. iii

The wise man is clad in finery,
    the fool is dressed in a gory rag.* (13)
May the land be destroyed over our enemies' heads,
May the tottering wall collapse on our opponents,
May the land of the foe be wholly awash.

col. iv

Shamash (=Divine Justice and Truth) will sustain
    your government, even if your king is an ignoramus. (9)
If the plow has turned up evil,
    Shamash could not be the cause(?).
People without a king are (like) sheep without a shepherd.
People without a foreman are (like) a canal without a regulator.
Workers without a supervisor
    are (like) a field without a cultivator.
A household without a master
    is (like) a woman without a husband.

Fear the Nearest?

Have a lord, have a king, (but) respect a governor. (22)

When you have seen for yourself
    the profit of reverencing god, (27)
You will praise god and bless the king.
Refuse a boy's wish, he will make a fuss(?),
Throw a sop to a puppy, he will fawn over you.

2. The Power of Government

The command of the palace is like the command of Anu,
    it cannot be repudiated. (1)
The king's command is sure as that of Shamash,
    His command cannot be rivalled nor his utterance altered.
The command of the palace is sure as that of Anu.
    Like Shamash, (the king) loves justice and hates evil.

3. Practical Wisdom

She looked at you, how far will she go with you? (13)
To go, or not to go, to god your lord?
Would you hand a clod to him who throws?

4. Domestic Wisdom

col. i

Let me drink thin beer, but let me sit in the seat of honor. (1)
Linen is laid for fleas, the meat basket(?) is woven for flies,
    the storehouse is constructed for lizards.★ (8)
The duck not eaten at the right time.[1]

Penny Wise, Pound Foolish

He saved up a lot but he slaughtered his pig.★ (17)
He saved up a lot but he used up his firewood.

col. ii

The Power of Speech

The wife of the tongue-tied talker is a slave girl. (3)
My mouth can make me the rival of men.
My mouth has made me renowned among men.

---

1. Alster, RA 72 (1978), 109, suggests that this means "strike while the iron is hot."

5. Life and Labor

col. ii

Eat no fat, void no blood.   (9)
Do no falsehood, fear of [god] will not consume you,
Speak no evil, woe will not work its way into you,
Do no evil, you will undergo no lasting [mis]fortune.
A scorpion stung a man, what did it gain?   (21)
An informer caused a man's death, [wh]at did he profit?
The scorpion [   ], informing [   ] ...
[Win]ter is malignant, summer reasonable.
As they say, is she pregnant without intercourse?   (40)
    Fat without eating?[1]
Intercourse hinders lactation.*
Let me store up, they will rob (me),   (45)
Let me squander, who will pay then?
He dug a well that had no water,
He tanned a hide that did not ...

The Unthanked Good Advisor[2]

As its(?) gods returned to its ruins,   (50)
Woe has entered the ruined house,
Where the evil man was tenant
(And) the heedful man was not to grow old.
The wise vizier, whose wisdom his master has heeded not,
And anyone valuable whom his master has forgotten,
When the need arises, he will be reinstated.

col. iii

The shadow that catches me is caught (too).   (1)
As they say, did the canebrake turn a profit on its reeds,
    the meadow on its grass?

---

1. This is noted by Mark Bryant, *Riddles Ancient and Modern* (New York, 1984), 11, as a riddle, the answer being "clouds," but I know of no textual basis for this. I take the meaning to be something like "Is there smoke without fire?"
2. Reiner, OrNS 30 (1961), 8–9. I understand the first part of the saying to refer to the consequences of not following good advice (differently Reiner).

The strong man lives by the profit of his arm,   (7)
The weak by the profit on his children.
My vagina is fine, (though) some of my folks
      consider me a has-been;   (14)
It's all fine, and I still (need to) wear a tampon.[1]
Would you slap a moving ox in the face with a pin?
My knees are always on the go, my legs are never tired,   (21)
A simpleton dogs me with adversity.
I am a riding steed, yoked to an ass,
I pull the wagon, I bear the lash!
My source of warmth is (only) the garment draped over me,   (45)
My carrying basket rests on my neck.★
I dwell in a house of brick and mortar,
      yet a lump of dirt falls on my head.   (50)
Last year I ate garlic; this year I have heartburn.

col. iv

The life of yesterday was repeated today.[2]   (5)
Like winter's chair: you decorate it and put it beside me.
Like a chair for a man whose god is Shahan:
You regret it, burn its leather, and set it on fire.[3]

When you are on the river, the water is putrid,   (19)
When you are in a garden, your dates are gall.[4]

If I instruct him, he is only what I begot,   (25)
If I polish him, he is only a blockhead.

May the furrow bear no stalk, may the seed not produce.[5]   (27)
As they say, the early grain will flourish, how can we know?   (34)
The late grain will flourish, how can we know?
Suppose I die, let me consume; suppose I live, let me store up. (42)

---

1. People consider her old, but she still menstruates (like the English vulgarism: "If she's bleeding, she's breeding").
2. "There's nothing new under the sun."
3. The chair in winter is set by the fire for warmth, the chair of a man with a communicable disease(?) is thrown into the fire (perhaps: "cast off like an old shoe"?).
4. "Things is tough all over"?
5. "Stop it before it multiplies"?

428 III. *The Mature Period*

They capsized me and I almost died,   (46)
I caught no fish and ruined my clothes.

Where the high ground comes down(?), the canal is opened,   (51)
The enemy quits not the gate of the city
        where defenses are weak.

col. v

It is as hard to change you as an old oven.   (10)

You went and plundered the enemy territory,   (14)
The enemy came and plundered your territory.

Never too late to spread out dried malt.   (23)

Would you lay out money [for] a pig's squeal?   (39)
I make the rounds for an ass's foal.   (43)

6. Prolixity

While the backside was breaking wind,
        the mouth brought forth babble(?).

7. Who Is My Keeper?

I would go to my brother, (but) my brother lives like me.   (6)
I would go to my sister, (but) my sister lives like me.

8. Wellsprings of Contentment

Long life begets a feeling of satisfaction;   (19)
Concealing a matter, sleepless anxiety;
Wealth, respect.

9. Reflections on Power

When you commit a crime (out of weakness),   (1)
The Tigris will bear (it) away.
When you commit a crime (from a position of power),*
Heaven itself will forsake you.

When you get away, you are a wild bull.   (5)
When they catch you, you fawn like a dog.

You can't jump a ditch when you're lame.

10. Every Man for Himself

When fire consumes the one in front, (2)
The one behind doesn't ask, "Where's the one in front?"

11. Fat Men and Forked Tongues

Fat is he who, when he goes in the fields,
    his pouch dangles down. (4)

The scoundrel chases after women's intimacy, (7)
The rogue has two sickles.[1]

One who has not supported a wife, (11)
One who has not supported a son,
He is a deceiver who will not support himself.*

12. Management

I am a manager: hand-picked and brawny of arm. (8)

The foreigner's ox forages, while his own lies hungry.

13. Candle under a Bushel

When oil is poured inside a stick, no one knows. (1)

Giving is for the king, giving pleasure for the cupbearer.
Giving is for the king, doing a favor for the manager.[2] (7)
Friendship is for a day, association forever.

There is quarreling among associates, (12)
Backbiting among priests.
A resident alien in another city is a slave. (16)

You need not watch a millstone.

---

1. That is, one sickle is enough for honest work.
2. The Sumerian reads: "'Give me!' is for the king, 'Be so kind!' is for the cupbearer's son, 'Do me a favor!' is for the manager" (Alster, *Proverbs*, 1:95). It is not clear whether these phrases are to be said by or to the officials in question.

14. Tempest in a Teapot

Something that has never happened from time immemorial: (5)
A young girl broke wind in her husband's embrace.

15. Blind Leading the Blind

The unskilled is the cart, the ignorant his road.   (6)

Bride, you have made a mother-in-law,   (10)
They'll do that to you too (someday).[1]

16. Favors

May kindness be requited to one who does it,   (12)
May Lumma[2] grant favor to one well spoken of.

(rev.)

As the potter looks at the rain (that might ruin his pots),   (4)
May Enlil look at the city whose fate is accursed.

The farmer is one who watches, what (else) can he do?   (9)
The day turned dark, but it did not [rain],
It rained but he did not (need) to take off his sandals.
The (very) Tigris churned at its source,
    but did not irrigate fields.

17. The Puniness of Humankind

Can strong warriors withstand a flood?   (8)
Or mighty men quiet a conflagration?

(rev.)

The will of god cannot be understood,   (7)
The way of god cannot be known:
Anything divine is [impossible] to find out.

---

1. That is, by marrying a son, she makes a mother-in-law; she is doomed, in her day, to the same fate.

2. Name of a Sumerian god, perhaps to be identified with Ningirsu (G. Marchesi, *La figura di LUM-ma nella tradizione dell'antica Mesopotamia* [dissertation, Bologna, 1998]).

18. Gain and Loss

You find something, it gets lost. (12)
You discard something, it is preserved forever.

19. The Odds

col. iii

Who will go out against mighty warriors
    who are one of purpose? (5)

Do the wish of the one present,
Slander the one not present!

20. One's Deserts

(a)

You took out a loan, but will spend it on a trifle. (5)
The mash is bitter, how can the beer be sweet?

The bucket floats on the river.[1]

Since there is no malt, let him consume, (10)
Since there is no malt, let him squander.

(b)

Flesh is flesh, blood is blood. (16)
Alien is alien, foreigner is foreigner.

21. Bestiary

The camel(?) of Anshan, the hippopotamus(?) of Parahshe, (5)
The cat of Meluhha, the elephant of the east:
These bite off a poplar tree like a leek.[2]

---

1. That is, the empty vessel merely floats on the surface, the filled one brings good?
2. Anshan: city in southwestern Iran; Parahshe: southeastern Iran; Meluhha: Indus Valley (see p. 351 note 7).

22. Bon Voyage

A young man said, "Alas!" and his boat sank. He said, "Hurrah!" and his rudder broke. He said "Alas!" and "…!" and his boat got to shore.[1]

23. A Riddle

It came in, (but) is not right,[2]
It goes out, (but) is not used up: The king's property.

24. From a Cylinder Seal

I have sought after and turned toward what pertains to god.
A man whose god chooses him shall lack for nothing.

Text: (1) W. G. Lambert, BWL, pl. 58, 59. (2) BWL, pl. 60 (K 4160+). (3) BWL, pl. 61 (K 4207). (4) BWL, pl. 60 (K 4327+). (5) BWL, pl. 61–63 (K 4347+); Wiseman and Black, CTN 4 202 iii. (6) BWL, pl. 60 (K 5688). (7) BWL, pl. 60 (K 7654). (8) BWL, pl. 64 (K 7674+). (9) BWL, pl. 63 (K 8216). (10) BWL, pl. 64 (K 8315). (11) BWL, pl. 64 (K 8338). (12) BWL, pl. 65 (K 15227+). (13) BWL, pl. 65 (Sm 6). (14) BWL, pl. 65 (BM 98743). (15) BWL, pl. 67–68 (VAT 10810). (16) BWL, pl. 66 (BM 38283). (17) BWL, pl. 66 (BM 38486). (18) BWL, pl. 67 (BM 38539). (19) BWL, pl. 69 (BM 38596). (20) BWL, pl. 70 (BM 56607). (21) BWL, pl. 71 (N.3395). (22) VAS 24 113. (23) BWL, 275; CAD E, 259. (24) Gordon, *Iraq* 6 (1939), p. v 31 (photo).

Edition: (1) W. G. Lambert, BWL, 225–233. (2) BWL, 233–234. (3) BWL, 234–235. (4) BWL, 235–238; Alster, *Proverbs*, 1:111, 156, 157. (5) BWL, 239–250. (6) BWL, 251; Alster, *Proverbs*, 1:118. (7) BWL, 251. (8) BWL, 252–253. (9) BWL, 253–254. (10) BWL, 254–255; Alster, *Proverbs*, 1:111. (11) BWL, 255; Alster, *Proverbs*, 1:32, 81. (12) BWL, 257–258; Alster, *Proverbs*, 1:91. (13) BWL, 258–259; Alster, *Proverbs*, 1:24, 83, 95. (14) BWL, 260; Alster, *Proverbs*, 1:9. (15) BWL, 260–262. (16) BWL, 262–264; Alster, *Proverbs*, 1:105, 216, 217. (17) BWL, 264–266. (18) BWL, 266–267. (19) BWL, 267–269. (20) BWL, 270–271. (21) BWL, 272–273; Alster, *Proverbs*, 1:289. (22) BWL, 274; Alster, *Proverbs*, 1:110. (23) BWL, 275. (24) W. G. Lambert, BiOr 32 (1975), 223.

Literature: See, in general, Römer, TUAT III/1, 23–46. (4) Alster, RA 72 (1978), 103–112. (21) Collation, CAD M/1, 278a; Civil, JCS 50 (1998), 11; see also Steinkeller, RA 74 (1980), 9.

Notes to Text: (1 iii 13) For restoration of Sumerian, see CAD E, 314. (4 i 18); Alster, RA 72 (1978),

---

1. Unfortunately the meaning of the last exclamation, essential for the "punch line," is unknown. It is most likely an expression of hope. In the first case the man was overly pessimistic, in the second overly optimistic, and in the third he tempered his expectations and so was not disappointed.

2. Either "not just" or perhaps in the sense "won't do."

108–109; Alster, *Proverbs*, 2:412. (4 i 17) See Gordon, *Drevnij Mir* (=*Studies Struve*) (Moscow, 1962), 243 and note 86; I follow CAD L, 101; Alster, RA 72 (1978), 109. (5 ii 44) CAD E, 165a. (5 iii 46) For the second part of the saying, see Civil, JAOS 88 (1968), 10 (ba-ab-ri-ri). (9 3) Translation a guess based on *ḫbt* i/i "prevail" (or the like), admittedly a rare poetic word(?), see Kraus, RA 69 (1975), 33. (11 13) Following the interpretation of E. Gordon, *Sumerian Proverbs* (Philadelphia, 1959), 121 note 3. The Akkadian text may be corrupt.

(d) PROVERBS FROM LETTERS

1. The Hasty Bitch

The bitch in her haste gave birth to blind whelps.

2. Making an Example

When fire consumes a rush, its companions will pay attention.

3a. A Dog's Thanks

When the potter's dog enters the kiln,
    it (still) will bark at the potter.

3b. An Adulteress's Word

In court what the (accused) adulteress says carries more weight
    than the words of her husband.[1]

4. Brains over Brawn

The man who seized the lion's tail sank in the river.
He who seized the fox's tail escaped.

5. Servitude

Man is the shadow of god, and slave the shadow of man.

6. No Hiding Place

Where can the fox go to escape the sun?

7. The Valorous Ant

When an ant is struck, does it not fight back
    and bite the hand of the man that strikes it?

---

1. Apparently adultery could be proven in court only if the husband caught the wife *in flagrante delicto*, as suggested by Roth, JESHO 31 (1988), 195. The different interpretation of Livingstone, AOAT 220 (1988), 185–186, seems to me unconvincing.

8. Silenced Protest

He who has been struck on the back, his mouth may still speak.
He who has been struck on the mouth, how shall he speak from it?

9. The Dangerous Fool

The ignoramus worries the [jud]ge,
 the inept makes the powerful nervous.

Text: (1) Dossin, ARMT 1 5, 11–13. (2) Dossin, ARMT 10 150, 9–11. (3) Harper, ABL 403, obv. 4–7, 13–15. (4) Harper, ABL 555, rev. 3–6. (5) Harper, ABL 652, rev. 9–13. (6) R. Campbell Thompson, *The Prisms of Esarhaddon and Assurbanipal Found at Nineveh*, 1927–8 (London, 1931), p. 24 line 25. (7) C. Bezold, E. A. W. Budge, *The Tell el-Amarna Tablets in the British Museum* (London, 1892), 61, 16–19 (EA 252). (8) Harper, ABL 1285, rev. 11–13; photo Parpola, *Studies Reiner*, 266–267. (9) Harper, ABL 37, rev. 3–6.

Edition: (1) Dossin, ARM 1 5, 11–13. (2) Dossin, ARM 10 150, 9–11. (3) W. G. Lambert, BWL, 281. (4) BWL, 281. (5) BWL, 281–282. (6) BWL, 282. (7) BWL, 282. (8) Parpola, *Studies Reiner*, 257–278. (9) Parpola, LAS 12.

Literature: (1) Moran, *Eretz-Israel* 14 (1978), 32–37; *Harvard Studies in Classical Philology* 82 (1978), 17–19; Alster, WO 10 (1979), 1–5; Avishur, WO 12 (1981), 37–38; Durand, DEPM 2:116. (2) A. Marzal, *Gleanings from the Wisdom of Mari* (Rome, 1976), 23–27; Durand, DEPM 3:293. (3) W. G. Lambert, BWL, 281. (4) Alster, JCS 41 (1989), 187–193. (5) W. G. Lambert, BWL, 281–282. (6) W. G. Lambert, BWL, 282.

Translation: (7) W. L. Moran, *The Amarna Letters* (Baltimore, 1992), 305.

E. MYTHOLOGICAL POETRY

III.17 EPIC OF CREATION

The Epic of Creation celebrates the exaltation of the Babylonian god Marduk
to supreme deity of the Mesopotamian pantheon after he had saved the gods
from attack by Tiamat, the ocean. The poem ascribes to Marduk reorganization
of the universe, with Babylon at the center of it, and inspiration for the creation
of humankind in order to sustain the gods. It offers an explanation of various
names it assigns to Marduk. This poem should not be considered "the" Mesopotamian creation story; rather, it is the individual work of a poet who viewed
Babylon as the center of the universe, and Marduk, god of Babylon, as head of
the pantheon. This message was not lost on contemporary readers, for, in some
Assyrian versions of the poem, Assur was substituted for Marduk.[1] Therefore
this poem can be read as a document of Babylonian nationalism. It may be a
product of Babylonian nationalistic revival at the time of Nebuchadnezzar I
(see III.12), though there is no firm evidence for its date of composition. To
judge from its language and content, the poem dates to the latter part of the
second millennium B.C.[2]

Some modern scholars have used this text as a Babylonian explanation for the
necessity of absolute rule. According to them, it portrays an evolution of political authority from an assembly of equals working out policy to an absolute
monarch proclaiming policy. In their view, the text can be read as a metaphor
for the evolution of Mesopotamian political institutions from a reconstructed
local assembly of elders to absolute kingship claiming divine sanction on a
regional or international scale. The catalyst for this change is portrayed as an
outside threat calling for a resolute war leader. The leader demanded, as his
terms for leadership, absolute obedience, even when the threat of war was
removed.[3]

1. W. G. Lambert, "The Assyrian Recension of *Enūma Eliš*," CRRAI 39 (1992), 77–79.

2. W. G. Lambert, "Studies in Marduk," BSOAS 47 (1984), 4–6 (time of Nebuchadnezzar I);
W. Sommerfeld, *Der Aufstieg Marduks*, AOAT 213 (1982), 174–181 (Kassite period); T. Abusch, in
K. van der Toorn, ed., *Dictionary of Deities and Demons in the Bible* (Leiden, 1995), 1017–1019; see
also p. 376 note 3.

3. T. Jacobsen, "Primitive Democracy in Ancient Mesopotamia," JNES 2 (1943), 159–172;
similar ideas were developed independently by I. M. Diakonoff, *Obščestvennyj i gosurdarstvennyj stroj
drevnego Dvureč'ja: Šumer* (Moscow, 1956), 120 note 1. Information on assemblies found in other
literary contexts, such as omens, does not support such a hypothesis, although it can suggest the
possibility of opposition between assembly and king; see Oppenheim, OrNS 5 (1936), 224–228.

As the poet portrays this, the gods willingly surrender their power in return for perpetual safety and maintenance. For the latter purpose humankind is created. The rebellious human spirit, as seen in Atrahasis (II.36), has no place in this poem, where the highest good for man is to discover and understand his place in the divinely ordered universe.

The poem is a work of great complexity and abounds with conceptual and philological problems. There are still many obscure passages and words. A predilection for certain types of words and constructions, together with the over-arching scheme of the poem, suggests the work of a single author. Though naturally there are variants in the manuscript tradition, there is no reason to suppose that the fundamental content of the work has been altered by successive generations, as has sometimes been suggested, just as there is no reason to elevate this composition to a greater authority than it deserves. It was esteemed highly in the first half of the first millennium B.C., as witnessed by the numerous copies that have turned up in both Assyria and Babylonia, by the preparation of an ancient commentary to the names of Marduk (Tablet VII), and by the ritual use of the composition in the Babylonian New Year's festival as stated in late sources.[1] It was quoted or referred to in other texts about Marduk; see General Introduction, D.3.

The least accessible part of the text for the modern reader will be the passage dealing with the names of Marduk, as it exemplifies techniques of Mesopotamian explanatory philology. The names are explained or translated, where their etymology seemed transparent, and then expounded in other ways through assigning further significance to elements within the name. For some names an ancient commentary is preserved; this is excerpted below in the notes to each name. There is no proof that the commentary reflects the original author's intent in every instance, but it stands as an example of how a learned Mesopotamian reader approached this document.

The poem begins and ends with concepts of naming. The poet evidently considers naming both an act of creation and an explanation of something already brought into being. For the poet, the name, properly understood, discloses the significance of the created thing. Semantic and phonological analysis of names could lead to understanding of the things named. Names, for this

---

1. A. Heidel, *The Babylonian Genesis*[2] (Chicago, 1951), 16–17; W. G. Lambert, TUAT III/4, 568–569; an older, considerably overstated view, is S. Pallis, *The Babylonian Akîtu Festival, Det Kgl. Danske Videnskabernes Selskab., Historisk-filologiske Meddelelser* XII/1 (1926), 297. For general discussion of this ritual, see B. Pongratz-Leisten, *Ina šulmi irub. Die Kulttopographische und ideologische Programmatik der akītu-Prozession in Babylonien und Assyrien im 1. Jahrtausend v. Chr.* (Mainz, 1994); M. E. Cohen, *The Cultic Calendars of the Ancient Near East* (Bethesda, 1993), 400–453.

poet, are a text to be read by the informed, and bear the same intimate and revealing relationship to what they signify as this text does to the events it narrates. In a remarkable passage at the end, the poet presents his text as the capstone of creation in that it was bearer of creation's significance to human-kind.

The poetry of the Epic of Creation shows command of a wide range of tradi-tional poetic techniques and profound learning. A contrast between speech and action is drawn in the first four tablets, in that speech, characteristic of the old order of the gods, can run to considerable length and repetition. A hint of circularity is provided by the concentrically arranged rehearsals of the narra-tive; by the climax of Tablet III, speech occurs within speech within speech within speech. This device is favored in traditional tale-telling as a narrative frame and as a demonstration of virtuosity, but it is seldom developed to such an extent in Akkadian literature (though compare the Anzu poem, III.23, on which the Epic of Creation may have been modeled). By contrast, the speech and action characteristic of the new order of the gods under Marduk are narrated rapidly, with a minimum of repetition. The last part of the poem is one continuing speech, explaining and celebrating Marduk's fifty names.

Tablet I

(Before anything was, mother ocean [Tiamat] and fresh water(?) [Apsu] mingled to produce the first of a series of pairs of gods. The descendants, with their boisterous behavior, stir Tiamat and Apsu. Although Tiamat bears it in good part, Apsu wishes to kill the offspring. The father is urged on by his counsellor. Apsu's intentions are foiled by Ea, who kills him and restrains his counsellor. He founds his home in Apsu, the watery domain represented by the slain primeval father, and dwells there with his wife.)

When on high no name was given to heaven,   (1)
Nor below was the netherworld* called by name,
Primeval Apsu was their progenitor,
And matrix-Tiamat[1] was she who bore them all,
They were mingling their waters together,   (5)
No canebrake was intertwined nor thicket matted close.[2]*
When no gods at all had been brought forth,
Nor called by names, none destinies ordained,
Then were the gods formed within the(se two).
Lahmu and Lahamu[3] were brought forth,
      were called by name.   (10)
When they had waxed great, had grown up tall,
Anshar and Kishar[4] were formed, greater than they,
They grew lengthy of days, added years to years.
Anu their firstborn was like his forebears,
Anshar made Anu, his offspring, (his) equal.[5]   (15)

---

1. Tiamat is the name of the ocean; Apsu is generally taken to refer to fresh water. The word rendered here "matrix" (after Jacobsen) is *mummu*, meaning "wisdom" or "skill," according to W. G. Lambert, JSS 14 (1969), 250; hence "creator" or "craftsman" (CAD M/2, 197). *Mummu* can mean also "noise"; see Michalowski, *Studies Moran*, 386.

2. That is, nothing divided or covered the waters.

3. For Lahmu and Lahamu, see W. G. Lambert, "The Pair Lahmu-Lahamu in Cosmology," OrNS 54 (1985), 189–202.

4. Anshar and Kishar are the totality of heaven and earth, understood as a circle or horizon. Anshar was later used by Assyrian scholars as a way of referring to Assur, thus giving him primacy over Marduk; see p. 817 note 1.

5. Or: "Anu, his offspring, was equal to Anshar."

Then Anu begot his own equal, Nudimmud,[1]
Nudimmud was he who dominated(?) his forebears:
Profound in wisdom, acute of sense, he was massively strong,
Much mightier than his grandfather Anshar,
No rival had he among the gods his brethren.   (20)
The divine brethren banded together,
Confusing Tiamat as they moved about in their stir,
Roiling the vitals of Tiamat,
By their uproar distressing the interior of the Heavenly Abode.[2]
Apsu could not reduce their clamor,   (25)
But Tiamat was silent before them.
Their actions were noisome to her,
Their behavior was offensive, (but) she was indulgent.
Thereupon Apsu, begetter of the great gods,
Summoned Mummu[3] his vizier, saying to him,   (30)
"Mummu, vizier who contents me,
"Come, let us go to Tiamat."
They went, took their places facing Tiamat,
They took counsel concerning the gods their offspring.
Apsu made ready to speak,   (35)
Saying to her, Tiamat, in a loud voice,
"Their behavior is noisome to me!
"By day I have no rest, at night I do not sleep!
"I wish to put an end to their behavior, to do away with it!
"Let silence reign that we may sleep."   (40)
When Tiamat heard this,
She grew angry and cried out to her spouse,
She cried out bitterly, outraged that she stood alone,
(For) he had urged evil upon her,[4]
"What? Shall we put an end to what we created?   (45)

1. Another name for Ea, god of wisdom.
2. Andurunna, a cosmic locality; see also p. 776 note 2.
3. The same word, *mummu*, translated above as "matrix," here the personal name of Apsu's advisor; see p. 439 note 1.
4. Or: "She suppressed the evil thought."

"Their behavior may be most noisome,
    but we should bear it in good part."
It was Mummu who answered, counselling Apsu,
Like a dissenting vizier's was the counsel of his Mummu,
"Put an end here and now, father, to their troublesome ways!
"By day you should have rest, at night you should sleep."   (50)
Apsu was delighted with him, he beamed,
On account of the evils
    he plotted against the gods his children.
He embraced Mummu, around his neck,
He sat on his knees so he could kiss him.[1]
Whatever they plotted between them,   (55)
Was repeated to the gods their offspring.
The gods heard it as they stirred about,
They were stunned, they sat down in silence.
Surpassing in wisdom, ingenious, resourceful,
Ea was aware of all, discerned their stratagem.   (60)
He fashioned it, he established it, a master plan,
He made it artful, his superb magic spell.
He recited it and brought (him) to rest in the waters,[2]
He put him in deep slumber, he was fast asleep,
He made Apsu sleep, he was drenched with slumber,   (65)
Mummu the advisor was drowsy with languor.
He untied his sash, he stripped off his tiara,
He took away his aura, he himself put it on.
He tied up Apsu, he killed him,
Mummu he bound, he locked him securely.   (70)
He founded his dwelling upon Apsu,
He secured Mummu, held (him) firm by a leadrope.
After Ea had captured and vanquished his foes,
Had won the victory over his opponents,
In his chamber, in profound quiet, he rested.   (75)
He called it "Apsu," They Recognize Sanctuaries.[3]

---

1. As interpreted here, Apsu bends down to kiss Mummu in his joy; Bottéro, "Création," 33, suggests that Mummu is sitting on Apsu's knees; so also Lambert, TUAT III/4, 571.

2. Variant: "on the waters," perhaps meaning that the spell was laid on the waters themselves.

3. An Akkadian hermeneutic explanation of the Sumerian name (Durand, N.A.B.U. 1994/100); compare Tablet V line 129.

He established therein his chamber,
Ea and Damkina his wife dwelt there in splendor.

(Birth and childhood of the hero Marduk, who is born with full strength. He is given the four winds by his grandfather.)

In the cella of destinies, the abode of designs,
The most capable, the sage of the gods,
    the Lord[1] was begotten, (80)
In the midst of Apsu Marduk was formed,
In the midst of holy Apsu was Marduk formed!
Ea his father begot him,
Damkina his mother was confined with him.
He suckled at the breasts of goddesses, (85)
The attendant who raised him endowed him well with glories.
His body was magnificent, fiery his glance,
He was a hero at birth,
    he was a mighty one from the beginning!
When Anu his grandfather saw him,
He was happy, he beamed, his heart was filled with joy. (90)
He perfected him, so that his divinity was strange,
He was much greater, he surpassed them in every way.
His members were fashioned with cunning
    beyond comprehension,
Impossible to conceive, too difficult to visualize:
Fourfold his vision, fourfold his hearing, (95)
When he moved his lips a fire broke out.
Formidable[2] his fourfold perception,
And his eyes, in like number, saw in every direction.
He was tallest of the gods, surpassing in form,
His limbs enormous, he was surpassing at birth. (100)
"The son Utu, the son Utu,[3]
"The son, the sun, the sunlight of the gods!"

---

1. Or: Bel.

2. "Formidable" is an attempt to render a pun in the original between *rabû* "great" and *erbu* "four."

3. A series of interlingual puns on son and sun, only one level of which can be rendered in English. The cuneiform signs used to write the name Marduk, AMAR.UD, are here construed as *māru* "son" and Utu "sun."

He wore (on his body) the auras of ten gods,
       had (them) wrapped around his head(?) too,
Fifty glories[1] were heaped upon him.
Anu formed and produced the four winds,   (105)
He put them in his hand, "Let my son play!"[2]
He fashioned dust, he made a storm bear it up,
He caused a wave and it roiled Tiamat,
Tiamat was roiled, churning day and night,
The gods, finding no rest, bore the brunt of each wind.⋆   (110)

    (Tiamat is stirred to action by the angry gods.)

They plotted evil in their hearts,
They said to Tiamat their mother,
"When he killed Apsu your husband,
"You did nothing to save him but sat by, silent.
"Now he has made four terrible winds,   (115)
"They are roiling your vitals so we cannot sleep.
"You had no care for Apsu your husband,
"As for Mummu, who was captured, you remained aloof,
"Now,⋆ you churn back and forth, confused.
"As for us, who cannot lie down to rest,
       you do not love us!   (120)
"Think of our burden, our eyes are pinched,⋆
"Lift this unremitting yoke, let us sleep!
"Battle has begun, give them what they deserve,⋆
"[Ma]ke a [tempest], turn them into nothingness."
When Tiamat [heard] these words, they pleased her,   (125)
"[As y]ou have counselled, we will make a tempest,[3]
"[We will   ] the gods within it,
"(For) they have been adopting [wicked ways]
       against the gods [thei]r parents."

---

    1. Marduk has fifty names in this text. In a Late period god-list, Marduk was assigned the number 50. Perhaps this was done so that Marduk could replace Enlil (also number 50) as head of the pantheon; see W. G. Lambert, BSOAS 47 (1984), 3 and below, p. 484 note 3.
    2. Or: "My son, let them whirl."
    3. Or: "monsters," but this would leave the reference in line 127 unclear.

[They clo]sed ranks and drew up at Tiamat's side,
Angry, scheming, never lying down night and day,   (130)
[Ma]king warfare, rumbling, raging,
Convening in assembly, that they might start hostilities.
Mother Hubur,[1] who can form everything,
Added countless invincible weapons,
     gave birth to monster serpents,
Pointed of fang, with merciless incisors(?),   (135)
She filled their bodies with venom for blood.
Fierce dragons she clad with glories,
Causing them to bear auras like gods, (saying)
"Whoever sees them shall collapse from weakness!
"Wherever their bodies make onslaught,
     they shall not turn back!"   (140)
She deployed serpents, dragons, and hairy hero-men,
Lion monsters, lion men, scorpion men,
Mighty demons, fish men, bull men,
Bearing unsparing arms, fearing no battle.[2]
Her commands were absolute, no one opposed them,   (145)
Eleven indeed on this wise she crea[ted].[3]
From among the gods her offspring,
     who composed her assembly,

1. Another epithet of Mummu-Tiamat, as a proper name suggesting a creative force (so Speiser, JAOS 68 [1948], 12), more commonly (as in IV.17 line 17) a name of the netherworld river, construed here as "Mother Noise" by Michalowski, *Studies Moran*, 385 (see General Introduction E.3); see also Conti, RA 82 (1988), 128.

2. For the appearance and names of the demons in this list, see W. G. Lambert, "The History of the muš-ḫuš in Ancient Mesopotamia," *Les Cahiers du CEPOA, Actes du Colloque de Cartigny 1981* (Geneva, 1985), 87–94; A. Green, "A Note on the 'Scorpion-Man' and Pazuzu," *Iraq* 47 (1985), 75–82; "A Note on Assyrian 'Goat-Fish', 'Fish-man' and 'Fish-woman'," *Iraq* 48 (1986), 25–30; "Neo-Assyrian Apotropaic Figures," *Iraq* 45 (1983), 87–96; R. S. Ellis, "'Lion-Men' in Assyria," *Studies Finkelstein*, 67–78; F. Wiggermann, "Exit Talim! Studies in Babylonian Demonology I," *JEOL* 27 (1981/2), 90–105. For discussion of the list as a whole, see W. G. Lambert, CRRAI 32 (1985), 56–57; F. Wiggermann, *Babylonian Prophylactic Figurines: The Ritual Texts* (Amsterdam, 1986), 268–323.

3. This number was reached by adding the "monster serpents" of 134, the "fierce dragons" of 137, and the nine creatures of 141–143. As shown by W. G. Lambert, CRRAI 32 (1985), 56–57, this is an expansion of a traditional list of eight in order to incorporate the heroic deeds of Ninurta into Marduk's *res gestae*.

She raised up Qingu[1] from among them,
>   it was he she made greatest!
Leadership of the army, command of the assembly,
Arming, contact, advance of the melee,   (150)
Supreme command in warfare,
(All) she entrusted to him, made him sit on the dais.
"I cast your spell.
>   I make you the greatest in the assembly of the gods,
"Kingship of all the gods I put in your power.
"You are the greatest, my husband, you are illustrious,   (155)
"Your command shall always be greatest,
>   over all the Anunna-gods."
She gave him the tablet of destinies,[2]
>   had him hold it to his chest, (saying)
"As for you, your command shall not be changed,
>   your utterance shall endure.
"Now that Qingu is the highest and has taken [supremacy],
"And has [ordained] destinies for his divine children,   (160)
"Whatever you (gods) say shall cause fire to [subside],
"Your concentrated venom shall make the mighty one yield."[3]

---

1. A male deity about whom little otherwise is known. Jacobsen, SANE 2/3, 16 has proposed to derive his name from the Sumerian word for "work," and hence, he infers, Qingu's blood used to create man gave him his working capacity.

2. The tablet of destinies, though not a clearly defined concept in Mesopotamian tradition (see W. G. Lambert, OrNS 39 [1970], 174–175), gave its possessor the power to give especially powerful commands. In the Anzu story (III.23), on which this episode is based, the tablet gave the power to control divine spheres of responsibility and thus universal authority. For discussion, see Lawson, *Fate*, 19–25.

3. Contrast Tablet I line 96. "Fire" and "might(y one)" are both references to warfare; Tiamat's magic is intended to make Qingu and his army invincible.

Tablet II

(Tiamat's preparations are known to Ea, who, in apparent despair, goes to Anshar, king of the gods. The relevant passages of Tablet I are repeated verbatim. Anshar is horror-stricken; he blames Ea for what has occurred. Since Ea started the trouble, he must find a solution to it. This accords well with Ea's plans for his son.)

Tiamat assembled her creatures,	(1)
Drew up for battle against the gods her brood.	
Thereafter Tiamat, more than(?) Apsu,	
was become an evildoer.[1]	
She informed Ea that she was ready for battle.	
When Ea heard this,	(5)
He was struck dumb with horror and sat stock still.	
After he had thought and his distress had calmed,	
He made straight his way to Anshar his grandfather.	
He came in before his grandfather, Anshar,	
All that Tiamat plotted he recounted to him,	(10)
"My father, Tiamat our mother has grown angry with us,	
"She has convened an assembly, furious with rage.	
"All the gods rallied around her,	
"Even those you created are going over to her side,	
"They are massing around her, ready at Tiamat's side.	(15)
"Angry, scheming, never lying down night and day,	
"Making warfare, rumbling, raging,	
"Convening in assembly, that they might start hostilities.	
"Mother Hubur, who can form everything,	
"Added countless invincible weapons,	
gave birth to monster serpents,	(20)
"Pointed of fang, with merciless incisors(?),	
"She filled their bodies with venom for blood.	
"Fierce dragons she clad with glories,	
"Causing them to bear auras like gods, (saying)	

'Whoever sees them shall collapse from weakness!	(25)
'Wherever their bodies make onslaught,	
they shall not turn back!'	

---

1. With Bottéro, "Création," 36. One could also understand "on account of Apsu" or "against Apsu" (in that case now the domain of Ea).

"She deployed serpents, dragons, and hairy hero-men,
"Lion monsters, lion men, scorpion men,
"Mighty demons, fish men, bull men,
"Bearing unsparing arms, fearing no battle.   (30)
"Her commands were absolute, no one opposed them,
"Eleven indeed on this wise she created.
"From among the gods her offspring,
          who composed her assembly,
"She raised up Qingu from among them,
          it was he she made greatest!
"Leadership of the army, command of the assembly,   (35)
"Arming, contact, advance of the melee,
"Supreme command in warfare,
"(All) she entrusted to him, made him sit on the dais.

          'I cast your spell. I make you the greatest
               in the assembly of the gods,
          'Kingship of all the gods I put in your power.   (40)
          'You are the greatest, my husband, you are illustrious.
          'Your command shall always be greatest,
               over all the Anunna-gods.'

"She gave him the tablet of destinies,
          had him hold it to his chest, (saying)

          'As for you, your command shall not be changed,
               your utterance shall endure.
          'Now that Qingu is the highest
               and has taken [supremacy],   (45)
          'And has [ordained] destinies for his divine children,
          'Whatever you (gods) say shall cause fire to [subside],
          'Your concentrated venom
               shall make the mighty one yield.'"

(Anshar flies into a passion at Ea, blaming him for what has transpired. Ea defends himself by pointing out the necessity of Apsu's murder. Anshar thereupon orders Ea to subdue Tiamat. Ea is unable to do so, so Anshar sends out Anu, who is likewise unable. This situation was no doubt anticipated by Ea, who is waiting to produce his favorite son from the wings. This provides the opportunity for Marduk to take his place and to make his great demand.)

[When Anshar heard] the speech, the affair was confused,
He cried out "Woe!"; he bit his lip,   (50)
His spirits were angry, his mind was uneasy,
His cries to Ea his offspring grew choked,
"My son, you yourself were instigator of battle!
"Do you bear the consequences of your own handiwork!
"You went forth and killed Apsu,   (55)
"So Tiamat, whom you have enraged,
          where is one who can face her?"
The sage counsellor, wise prince,
Producer of wisdom, divine Nudimmud,
Answered [his] father Anshar gently,
With soothing words, calming speech,   (60)
"My father, inscrutable, ordainer of destinies,
"Who has power to create and destroy,
"O Anshar, inscrutable, ordainer of destinies,
"Who has power to create and destroy,
"I will declare my thoughts to you, relent for a moment,   (65)
"Recall in your heart that I made a good plan.
"Before I undertook to kill Apsu,
"Who had foreseen what is happening now?
"Ere I was the one who moved quickly to snuff out his life,
"I indeed, for it was I who destroyed him,
          [wh]at was occurring?"   (70)
When Anshar heard this, it pleased him,
He calmed down, saying to Ea,
"Your deeds are worthy of a god,
"You can(?) [   ] a fierce, irresistible stroke,
"Ea, your deeds are worthy of a god,   (75)
"You can(?) [   ] a fierce, irresistible stroke,
"Go then to Tiamat, sub[due] her onslaught,
"May her anger [be pacified] by [your] magic spell."
When he heard the command [of his father] A[nshar],
He set off, making straight his way,   (80)
Ea went to seek out Tiamat's stratagem.
He stopped, horror-stricken, then turned back.
He came before Anshar the sovereign,
He beseeched him with entreaties, saying,

"[My father], Tiamat has carried her actions beyond me,   (85)

"I sought out her course, but [my] spell cannot counter it.

"Her strength is enormous, she is utterly terrifying,

"She is reinforced with a host, none can go out against her.

"Her challenge was not reduced,
   it was so loud(?) against me,

"I became afraid at her clamor, I turned back.   (90)

"My father, do not despair, send another to her,

"A woman's force may be very great,
   but it cannot match a man's.

"Do you scatter her ranks, thwart her intentions,

"Before she lays her hands on all of us."

Anshar was shouting, in a passion,   (95)

To Anu his son he said these words,

"Stalwart son, valiant warrior,

"Whose strength is enormous, whose onslaught is irresistible,

"Hurry, take a stand before Tiamat,

"Soothe her feelings, let her heart be eased.   (100)

"If she will not listen to what you say,

"Say something by way of entreaty to her,
   so that she be pacified."

When he heard what his father Anshar said,

He set off, [made str]aight his way,

Anu went to seek out Tiamat's stratagem.   (105)

He stopped, horror-stricken, then turned back.

He came before [Ansha]r, [his father who begot him],

He beseeched him with entreaties, s[aying],

"My father, Tiamat has carried her actions beyond me,

"I sought out her course, but my s[pell cannot counter it].   (110)

"Her strength is enormous, she is utterly terrifying,

"She is reinforced with a host,
   none can [go out against] her.

"Her challenge was not reduced, it was so loud(?) against me,

"I became afraid at her clamor, I turned back.

"My father, do not despair, send another to her,   (115)

"A woman's strength may be very great,
    but it cannot match a man's.
"Do you scatter her ranks, thwart her intentions,
"Before she lays her hands on all of us."
Anshar fell silent, gazing at the ground,
Nodding toward Ea, he shook his head.   (120)
The Igigi-gods and Anunna-gods were all assembled,
With lips closed tight, they sat in silence.
Would no god go out [at his] command?*
Against Tiamat would none go as [he] ordered?
Then Anshar, father of the great gods,   (125)
His heart was angry, he would not summon anyone!*

(Ea summons Marduk privately and informs him that his hour is now come. He enjoins him to present himself respectfully before his great-grandfather as a volunteer in time of crisis. Ea does not explicitly advise Marduk what price to set on his services, as the poet makes that come from the heart of Marduk himself. Marduk is warmly received by the elder gods and his offer to be champion is willingly accepted. Now Marduk offers his terms: if he is to save all the gods, he is to become their supreme, unquestioned leader, always.)

The mighty firstborn, champion of his father,
Hastener to battle, the warrior Marduk
Did Ea summon to his secret place,
Told him his secret words,[1]   (130)
"O Marduk, think, heed your father,
"You are my son who can relieve his heart!
"Draw nigh, approach Anshar,
"Make ready to speak. He was angry(?),
    seeing you he will be calm."
The Lord was delighted at his father's words,   (135)
He drew near and waited upon Anshar.
When Anshar saw him, his heart was filled with joyful feelings,
He kissed his lips, he banished his gloom.
"My father, let not your lips be silent but speak,
"Let me go, let me accomplish your heart's desire.   (140)
"[O Anshar], let not your lips be silent but speak,

---

1. Uncertain. While this could be a reference to magic words (CAD K, 36a; AHw, 420a ["wish"]), it could as well refer to Marduk's demand, lines 156–163.

"Let me go, let me accomplish your heart's desire!
"What man is it who has sent forth his battle against you?
"Why,* Tiamat, a woman,
      comes out against you to arms!
"[My father], creator, rejoice and be glad,   (145)
"Soon you will trample the neck of Tiamat.
"[Anshar], creator, rejoice and be glad,
"Soon you will trample [the neck] of Tiamat!"
"[Go], son, knower of all wisdom,
"Bring Tiamat to rest with your sacral spell.   (150)
"Make straight, quickly, with the storm chariot,
"Let it not veer from its [course], turn (it) back!"
The Lord was delighted at his grandfather's words,
His heart was overjoyed as he said to his grandfather,
"Lord of the gods, of the destiny of the great gods,   (155)
"If indeed I am to champion you,
"Subdue Tiamat and save your lives,
"Convene the assembly, nominate me for supreme destiny!
"Take your places in the Assembly Place of the Gods,[1]
      all of you, in joyful mood.
"When I speak, let me ordain destinies instead of you.   (160)
"Let nothing that I shall bring about be altered,
"Nor what I say be revoked or changed."

---

1. Ubshu-ukkenna, a cosmic locality, called "abode of counsel" in IV.42d line 28.

Tablet III

(Anshar convokes the gods for this purpose, commissioning his vizier, Kakka, to wait upon Lahmu and Lahamu to tell them the story of Tiamat's threat and Marduk's offer. Lahmu and Lahamu are terrified. They and the other gods convene, eat and drink liberally, and, in the festive mood of a reunion, they surrender their authority to Marduk.)

Anshar made ready to speak,   (1)
Saying to Kakka his vizier these words,
"Kakka, vizier who contents me,
"Let it be you that I send off toward Lahmu and Lahamu.
"You know how [to find a way], you can make a fine speech.   (5)
"Send over to my presence the gods my ancestors,
"Let them bring all the gods before me.
"Let them converse, sit down at a feast,
"On produce of the field let them feed, imbibe of the vine.
"Let them ordain destiny for Marduk, their champion.   (10)
"Be off, Kakka, wait upon them,
"All that I tell you, repeat to them:

'It is Anshar your son who has ordered me to come,
'He has bade me speak in full the command of his heart,
'To wit:

"Tiamat our mother has grown angry with us,   (15)
"She has convened an assembly, furious with rage.
"All the gods rallied around her,
"Even those you created are going over to her side.
"They are massing around her, ready at Tiamat's side.
"Angry, scheming, never lying down night and day,   (20)
"Making warfare, rumbling, raging,
"Convening in assembly, that they might start hostilities.
"Mother Hubur, who can form everything,
"Added countless invincible weapons,
      gave birth to monster serpents,
"Pointed of fang, with merciless incisors(?),   (25)
"She filled their bodies with venom for blood.
"Fierce dragons she clad with glories,
"Causing them to bear auras like gods, (saying)

'Whoever sees them shall collapse from weakness!
'Wherever their bodies make onslaught,
    they shall not turn back!' (30)
"She deployed serpents, dragons, and hairy hero-men,
"Lion monsters, lion men, scorpion men,
"Mighty demons, fish men, bull men,
"Bearing unsparing arms, fearing no battle.
"Her commands were absolute, no one opposed them. (35)
"Eleven indeed on this wise she created.
"From among the gods her offspring,
    who composed her assembly,
"She raised up Qingu from among them,
    it was he she made greatest!
"Leadership of the army, command of the assembly,
"Arming, contact, advance of the melee, (40)
"Supreme command in warfare:
"All she entrusted to him, made him sit on the dais.

    'I cast your spell, I make you the greatest
        in the assembly of the gods,
    'Kingship of all the gods I put in your power.
    'You are greatest, my husband, you are illustrious, (45)
    'Your command shall always be greatest,
        over all the Anunna-gods.'

"She gave him the tablet of destinies,
    had him hold it to his chest, (saying)

    'As for you, your command will not be changed,
        your utterance will endure.
    'Now that Qingu is the highest and
        has taken over [supremacy],
    'And has [ordained] destinies for his divine children, (50)
    'Whatever you (gods) say shall cause fire to [subside],
    'Your concentrated venom
        shall make the mighty one yield.'
"I sent Anu, he could not confront her,
"Nudimmud was afraid and turned back.
"Marduk came forward, the sage of the gods, your son, (55)
"He has resolved to go against Tiamat.

"When he spoke, he said to me,

    'If indeed I am to champion you,
    'Subdue Tiamat and save your lives,
    'Convene the assembly,
        nominate me for supreme destiny!   (60)
    'Take your places in the Assembly Place of the Gods,
        all of you, in joyful mood,
    'When I speak, let me ordain destinies instead of you.
    'Let nothing that I shall bring about be altered,
    'Nor what I say be revoked or changed.'

"Come quickly to me,
    straightaway ordain him your destinies,   (65)
"Let him go and confront your powerful enemy."

Kakka went and made straight his way
Toward Lahmu and Lahamu the gods his ancestors.
He prostrated, kissed the ground before them.
He stood up straight and said to them,   (70)
"It is Anshar your son who has ordered me to come,
"He has bade me speak in full the command of his heart:

    'Tiamat our mother has grown angry with us,
    'She has convened an assembly, furious with rage.
    'All the gods rallied around her,   (75)
    'Even those you created are going over to her side.
    'They are massing around her, ready at Tiamat's side.
    'Angry, scheming, never lying down night and day,
    'Making warfare, rumbling, raging,
    'Convening in assembly, that they might start hostilities.   (80)
    'Mother Hubur, who can form everything,
    'Added countless invincible weapons,
        gave birth to monster serpents,
    'Pointed of fang, with merciless incisors(?),
    'She filled their bodies with venom for blood.
    'Fierce dragons she clad with glories,   (85)
    'Causing them to bear auras like gods, (saying)

        "Whoever sees them shall collapse from weakness!
        "Wherever their bodies make onslaught
            they shall not turn back!"

'She deployed serpents, dragons, and hairy hero-men,
'Lion monsters, lion men, scorpion men,   (90)
'Mighty demons, fish men, bull men,
'Bearing unsparing arms, fearing no battle.
'Her commands were absolute, no one opposed them.
'Eleven indeed on this wise she created.
'From among the gods her offspring
       who composed her assembly,   (95)
'She raised up Qingu from among them,
       it was he she made greatest!
'Leadership of the army, command of the assembly,
'Arming, contact, advance of the melee,
'Supreme command in warfare:
'(All) she entrusted to him, made him sit on the dais.   (100)

    "I cast your spell and make you the greatest
       in the assembly of the gods,
    "Kingship of all the gods I put in your power.
    "You shall be the greatest, you are my only spouse,
    "Your name shall always be greatest,
       over all the Anunna-gods."

'She gave him the tablet of destinies,
       had him hold it to his chest, (saying)   (105)

    "As for you, your command shall not be changed,
       your utterance shall endure."
    "Now that Qingu is the highest
       and has taken over [supremacy],
    "And has [ordained] destinies for his divine children,
    "Whatever you (gods) say shall cause fire to [subside],
    "Your concentrated venom shall make
       the mighty one yield."   (110)

'I sent Anu, he could not confront her,
'Nudimmud was afraid and turned back.
'Marduk came forward, the sage of the gods, your son,
'He has resolved to go against Tiamat.
'When he spoke, he said to me,   (115)

    "If indeed I am to champion you,
    "Subdue Tiamat and save your lives,

"Convene the assembly,
>   nominate me for supreme destiny!
"In the Assembly Place of the Gods take your places,
>   all of you, in joyful mood.
"When I speak, let me ordain destinies instead of you.   (120)
"Let nothing that I shall bring about be altered,
"Nor what I say be revoked or changed."

'Come quickly to me,
>   straightaway ordain him your destinies,
'Let him go and confront your powerful enemy.'"

When Lahmu and Lahamu heard, they cried aloud,   (125)
All of the Igigi-gods wailed bitterly,
"What (is our) hostility,[1] that she has taken a[ct]ion (against) us?
"We scarcely know what Tiamat might do!"
They swarmed together and came.
All the great gods, ordainers of [destinies],   (130)
Came before Anshar and were filled with [joy].
One kissed the other in the assembly [   ],
They conversed, sat down at a feast,
On produce of the field they fed, imbibed of the vine,
With sweet liquor they made their gullets run,   (135)
They felt good from drinking the beer.
Most carefree, their spirits rose,
To Marduk their champion they ordained destiny.

---

1. Or, "Why be opposed?" Lambert, TUAT III/4, 583: "What was wrong?"

Tablet IV

(Marduk takes the throne and is hailed by all the gods in a coronation ceremony. Proof is administered of his supremacy. He is hailed as king, is given the trappings of royalty, chooses his weapons, and sets forth on his quest.)

They set out for him a princely dais, (1)
He took his place before his fathers for sovereignty.
"You are the most important among the great gods,
"Your destiny is unrivalled, your command is supreme.
"O Marduk, you are the most important
    among the great gods, (5)
"Your destiny is unrivalled, your command is supreme!
"Henceforth your command cannot be changed,
"To raise high, to bring low, this shall be your power.
"Your command shall be steadfast,
    your word shall not be misleading.
"Not one of the gods shall go beyond the limits you set. (10)
"Support is wanted for the gods' sanctuaries,
"Wherever their shrines will be, your own shall be established.
"O Marduk, you are our champion,
"We bestow upon you kingship of all and everything.
"Take your place in the assembly, your word shall be supreme. (15)
"May your weapon never strike wide but dispatch your foes.
"O Lord, spare his life who trusts in you,
"But the god who has taken up evil, snuff out his life!"
They set up among them a certain constellation,
To Marduk their firstborn said they (these words), (20)
"Your destiny, O Lord, shall be foremost of the gods',
"Command destruction or creation, they shall take place.
"At your word the constellation shall be destroyed,
"Command again, the constellation shall be intact."
He commanded and at his word
    the constellation was destroyed, (25)
He commanded again and the constellation was created anew.
When the gods his fathers saw what he had commanded,
Joyfully they hailed, "Marduk is king!"
They bestowed in full measure scepter, throne, and staff,

They gave him unopposable weaponry
      that vanquishes enemies.   (30)
"Go, cut off the life of Tiamat,
"Let the winds bear her blood away as glad tidings!"
The gods, his fathers, ordained the Lord's destiny,
On the path to success and authority
      did they set him marching.
He made the bow, appointed it his weapon,   (35)
He mounted the arrow, set it on the string.
He took up the mace, held it in his right hand,
Bow and quiver he slung on his arm.
Thunderbolts he set before his face,
With raging fire he covered his body.   (40)
Then he made a net to enclose Tiamat within,
He deployed the four winds that none of her might escape:
South Wind, North Wind, East Wind, West Wind,
Gift of his grandfather Anu;[1] he fastened the net at his side.
He made ill wind, whirlwind, cyclone,   (45)
Four-ways wind, seven-ways wind, destructive wind,
      irresistible wind:
He released the winds that he had made, the seven of them,
Mounting in readiness behind him to roil inside Tiamat.
Then the Lord raised the Deluge, his great weapon.
He mounted the terrible chariot,[2]
      the unopposable Storm Demon,   (50)
He hitched to it the four-steed team, he tied them at his side:[3]
"Slaughterer," "Merciless," "Overwhelmer," "Soaring."
Their lips are curled back, their teeth bear venom,
They know not fatigue, they are trained to trample down.
He stationed at his right gruesome battle and strife,   (55)

---

1. The gift refers to the four winds (see Tablet I lines 105–106), not the net. The original has an elaborate poetic structure that cannot be reproduced clearly in translation. "At his side" could also mean "on his arm" (Landsberger, JCS 21 [1967], 150 note 62).

2. Literally: "the storm chariot …, the terrible one." A late bilingual fragment may preserve part of a hymn(?) to Marduk's chariot; see W. G. Lambert, "The Chariot of Marduk," *Studies Böhl*, 275–280.

3. Apparently the ends of the reins, normally held by an attendant, are here strapped to him, to keep both hands free for fighting. Balancing in a chariot with weapons in both hands and guiding a four-steed team by the belt is, of course, a heroic feat of the first order.

At his left the fray that overthrows all formations.
He was garbed in a ghastly armored garment,[1]
On his head he was covered with terrifying auras.
The Lord made straight and pursued his way,
Toward raging Tiamat he set his face. (60)
He was holding a spell ready upon his lips,
A plant, antidote to venom, he was grasping in his hand.
At that moment the gods were stirring, stirring about him,
The gods his fathers were stirring about him,
        the gods stirring about him.

(Marduk approaches for battle while the gods hover fearfully near him. Qingu is terrified. Tiamat intimates that Marduk's support is disloyal. Ignoring Qingu, he challenges her to single combat and indicts her for the contemplated murder of her own children. Stung to a fury, Tiamat herself advances for battle. Marduk kills her, destroys her forces, takes the tablet of destinies, and puts it on himself.)

The Lord drew near, to see the battle[2] of Tiamat, (65)
He was looking for the stratagem of Qingu her spouse.
As he[3] looked, his tactic turned to confusion,
His reason was overthrown, his actions panicky,
And as for the gods his allies, who went at his side,
When they saw the valiant vanguard, their sight failed them. (70)
Tiamat cast her spell pointblank,
Falsehood, lies she held ready on her lips.★
"... lord, the gods rise against you,
"They assembled [where] they are,
        (but) are they on your side?"[4]
The Lord [raised] the Deluge, his great weapon, (75)
To Tiamat, who acted conciliatory,[5] sent he (this word),

---

1. This line is a remarkable example of alliteration, a device esteemed by this poet: *naḫlapti apluḫti pulḫāti ḫalipma.*
2. Wordplay on "middle" or "inside" and "battle."
3. Presumably Qingu is meant.
4. Uncertain. Tiamat evidently tells Marduk that the gods he is championing are actually disloyal to him. For a discussion of the battle between Marduk and Tiamat, see Jacobsen, JAOS 88 (1968), 104–108; Jacobsen interprets these lines quite differently, *The Treasures of Darkness* (New Haven, 1976), 177.
5. Or: "who was furious" (so CAD K 109a etc.; I follow Bottéro, "Creation," 46).

"Why outwardly do you assume a friendly attitude,[1]
"While your heart is plotting to open attack?
"Children cried out, they oppress their parents,
"But you, their own mother, spurned all natural feeling.[2]   (80)
"You named Qingu to be spouse for you,
"Though he had no right to be, you set him up for chief god.
"You attempted wicked deeds against Anshar,
        sovereign of the gods,
"And you have perpetrated your evil against the gods my fathers.
"Though main force is drawn up,
        though these your weapons are in array,   (85)
"Come within range, let us duel, you and I!"
When Tiamat heard this,
She was beside herself, she turned into a maniac.
Tiamat shrieked loud, in a passion,
Her frame shook all over, down to the ground.   (90)
She was reciting an incantation, casting her spell,
While the gods of battle were whetting their blades.
Tiamat and Marduk, sage of the gods, drew close for battle,
They locked in single combat, joining for the fray.
The Lord spread out his net, encircled her,   (95)
The ill wind he had held behind him he released in her face.
Tiamat opened her mouth to swallow,
He thrust in the ill wind so she could not close her lips.
The raging winds bloated her belly,
Her insides were stopped up, she gaped her mouth wide.   (100)
He shot off the arrow, it broke open her belly,
It cut to her innards, it pierced the heart.
He subdued her and snuffed out her life,
He flung down her carcass, he took his stand upon it.
After the vanguard had slain Tiamat,   (105)
He scattered her forces, he dispersed her host.
As for the gods her allies, who had come to her aid,

1. Or: "Why are you aggressive and overbearing?" (Lambert, JSS 27 [1982], 283).
2. The precise significance of Marduk's remarks is not clear. While he may refer to Tiamat's natural goodwill toward her children (Tablet I lines 28, 46), it seems more likely that he refers to her insinuation that he had best beware the loyalty of those he championed. Line 79 may mean that children are normally trying to their parents, so her intended infanticide is unnatural. For "crying out" of children, compare II.20c, IV.54.

They trembled, terrified, they ran in all directions,
They tried to make a way out(?) to save their[1] lives,
There was no escaping the grasp that held (them)! (110)
He drew them in and smashed their weapons.
They were cast in the net and sat in a heap,
They were heaped up in the corners, full of woe,
They were bearing his punishment, to prison confined.
As for the eleven creatures, the ones adorned with glories, (115)
And the demonic horde(?),
     which went in attendance at her side,
He put on leadropes, he bound their arms.
He trampled them under, together with their belligerence.
As for Qingu, who was trying to be great among them,
He captured him and reckoned him among the doomed gods. (120)
He took away from him the tablet of destinies,
     which he had no right to,
He sealed it with a seal and affixed it to his chest.

(Splitting Tiamat's corpse in half, Marduk uses one piece to create the heavens. Her blood is borne off by the wind as evidence of her death. Marduk makes Esharra, an abode in heaven, as a counterpart to Apsu.)

Having captured his enemies and triumphed,
Having shown the mighty(?)* foe subservient(?),[2]
Having fully achieved Anshar's victory over his enemies, (125)
Valiant Marduk having attained what Nudimmud desired,
He made firm his hold over the captured gods,
Then turned back to Tiamat whom he had captured.
The Lord trampled upon the frame of Tiamat,
With his merciless mace he crushed her skull. (130)
He cut open the arteries of her blood,
He let the North Wind bear (it) away as glad tidings.
When his fathers saw, they rejoiced and were glad,
They brought him gifts and presents.
The Lord calmed down, he began inspecting her carcass, (135)

1. Text has "his life."
2. This may refer to a triumphal parade.

That he might divide(?) the monstrous lump
    and fashion artful things.
He split her in two, like a fish for drying,
Half of her he set up and made as a cover, heaven.[1]
He stretched out the hide* and assigned watchmen,
And ordered them not to let her waters escape.   (140)
He crossed heaven, he inspected (its) firmament,[2]
He made a counterpart to Apsu, the dwelling of Nudimmud.
The Lord measured the construction of Apsu,
He founded the Great Sanctuary, the likeness of Esharra.[3]
(In) the Great Sanctuary, (in) Esharra,
    which he built, (and in) heaven,   (145)
He made Ea, Enlil, and Anu dwell in their holy places.

1. That is, he made the sky to hold back the waters.

2. For discussion of this line, see Moran, *Eretz Israel* 14 (1978), 35. Marduk models his new heaven after Apsu, the domain of Ea. "Firmament" is a free rendering of *ašrātu*, a difficult word; Lambert suggests it might mean something like "covering" (AfO 23 [1975], 43 and Tablet V line 121); more recently "Himmelsteile" (TUAT III/4, 583).

3. Esharra means "House of the Universe," the abode of Enlil. See Tablet IV line 145, V line 120, VI line 66 and Moran, AnBi 12 (1959), 264 note 2. For discussion of this passage and its cosmological implications, see W. G. Lambert in C. Blacker and M. Loewe, eds., *Ancient Cosmologies* (London, 1975), 55–58; Livingstone, *Explanatory Works*, 79–81; Horowitz, *Cosmic Geography*, 112–114.

Tablet V

(Marduk organizes the stars and planets and marks off years. He establishes his own planet, called Neberu, as a marker for all the others in their motion. He regulates the moon, sun, weather, and subterranean waters. He links the various parts of the cosmos.)

He made the position(s) for the great gods,   (1)
He established (in) constellations the stars, their likenesses.[1]
He marked the year, described (its) boundaries,[2]
He set up twelve months of three stars each.[3]
After he had patterned the days of the year,   (5)
He fixed the position of Neberu
    to mark the (stars') relationships.[4]
Lest any make an error or go astray,
He established the position(s) of Enlil and Ea in relation to it.[5]
He opened up gates on both (sides of her) ribs,★
He made strong bolts to left and right.   (10)
In her liver he established the heights.
He made the moon appear, entrusted (to him) the night.
He assigned to him the crown jewel of nighttime
    to mark the day (of the month),
Every month, without ceasing,
    he exalted him with a crown.★
"At the beginning of the month, waxing over the land,   (15)
"You shine with horns to mark six days,
"At the seventh day, the disk as [ha]lf.
"At the fifteenth day, you shall be in opposition,

1. These lines and the following, especially 24, parallel a passage from the astrological omen series Enuma Anu Enlil, where the same proceedings are assigned to Anu, Enlil, and Ea. See Weidner, AfO 17 (1954/6), 89; Landsberger and Kinnier Wilson, JNES 20 (1961), 172; Rochberg-Halton, AfO *Beiheft* 22 (1988), 270–271; Horowitz, *Cosmic Geography*, 114–117. For translations of similar texts, see below, III.18.

2. That is, laid out the ecliptic?

3. Babylonian astrolabes assign three stars to each month; here Marduk is portrayed as creating this pattern; see Horowitz, *Cosmic Geography*, 115.

4. For Neberu, see J. Koch, "Der Mardukstern Nēberu," WdO 22 (1991) 48–72. Koch argues that the planet Mercury best fits the astronomical data, though Neberu, in another tradition, could also have referred to Jupiter or the central area in the sky where Jupiter was to be found. As pointed out to me by I. Zbikowska, Jupiter is more likely to serve as a marker than is Mercury, which is often difficult to see.

5. "It" refers to Neberu. Variant substitutes Anu for Ea.

at the midpoint of each [month].[1]
"When the sun f[ac]es you from the horizon of heaven,
"Wane at the same pace and form in reverse.   (20)
"At the day of di[sappeara]nce, approach the sun's course,
"On the [   ] of the thirtieth day, you shall be in conjunction
          with the sun a second time.
"I d[efined?] the celestial signs, proceed on their path,
"[   ] approach each other and render (oracular) judgment.
"The sun shall [   ] ..., killing, oppression   (25)
"[   ] me."
W[hen he   ]
The val[iant   ]
The sun [   ]
In [   ]   (30)
"Let [   ]
[   ]
"Let there arise no [   ]
"Let there be [   ]
"In [   ]   (35)
"Da[ily   ]."
After [he had   ]
[He made the night   ]
He made the day [   ]
The year [was equal] (in days and nights).[2]   (40)
At New Year [   ]
(Another) year [   ]
"Let [   ]
"The doorbolt of sunrise [ ]."
After he had as[signed   ],   (45)
[And fixed] the watches of night and day,
[   ] the foam of Tiamat,
Marduk created [   ]
He compacted (the foam) into c[louds]
          and made (them) billow.
To raise the wind, to cause rainfall,   (50)

---

1. For discussion, see Vanstiphout, JCS 33 (1981), 196–198; Livingstone, *Explanatory Works*, 39–40; Horowitz, *Cosmic Geography*, 117.
2. For restoration and suggested meaning, see Horowitz, *Cosmic Geography*, 117.

To make mists steam, to pile up her spittle (as snow?),
He assigned to himself, put under his control.
He set down her head and piled di[rt]¹ upon it,
He opened underground springs, a flood was let flow(?).*
From her eyes he undammed the Euphr[ates] and Tigris,   (55)
He stopped up her nostrils, he left ...
He heaped up high-peaked mo[unt]ains from(?) her dugs.
He drilled through her waterholes to carry off the catchwater.
He coiled up her tail and tied it as(?) "The Great Bond."²
[   ] Apsu beneath, at his feet.   (60)
He set her crotch as the brace of heaven,
Spreading [half of] her as a cover, he established the earth.
[After] he had completed his task inside Tiamat,
[He spre]ad his net, let all (within) escape,
He formed(?) the ... [   ] of heaven and netherworld,   (65)
[Tightening] their organization and ...

*(Marduk distributes trophies, parades his defeated enemies,
and is celebrated as a returning hero.)*

After he had designed his prerogatives
        and devised his responsibilities,
He put on leadropes,³* entrusted (those) to Ea.
[The tablet] of destinies, which he took from Qingu
        and brought away,
As the foremost gift he took away, he presented (it) to Anu. (70)
The [   ] of battle, which he had fastened on
        and set on his head,⁴
[   ] he led before his fathers.
[And as for] the eleven creatures that Tiamat created ...
He smashed their [wea]pons, he tied them to his feet.

---

1. Compare Tablet VII line 71; Horowitz, *Cosmic Geography*, 118.
2. That is, the link that holds heaven and the world below together; Horowitz, *Cosmic Geography*, 120.
3. See p. 177 note 2.
4. Compare perhaps Tablet I line 103 and IV lines 38ff.

He made images [of them] and set them up
    at the [Gate of] Apsu:[1]   (75)
"Lest ever after they be forgotten, let this be the sign."
When [the gods] saw, they rejoiced and were glad,
Lahmu, Lahamu, and all his fathers.
Anshar [embra]ced him,
    proclaimed (his) salutation (to be) "king."
[A]nu, Enlil, and Ea gave him gifts,   (80)
[   ] Damkina his mother made cries of joy over him,
She(?) made his face glow with (cries of) "Good …!"[2]
To Usmu,[3] who brought (Damkina's) gift at the glad tidings,
[He en]trusted the ministry of Apsu
    and care of the sanctuaries.
All the Igigi-gods together prostrated before him,   (85)
[And] the Anunna-gods, all there are,
    were doing him homage,
The whole of them joined together to pay him reverence,
[Before him] they stood, they prostrated, "This is the king!"

        (Marduk cleans himself and dons his insignia.
The gods swear allegiance to him; he undertakes to maintain them.)

[After] his fathers had celebrated him in due measure,
[   ] covered with the dust of battle.   (90)
[   ] …
With cedar [oil] and [   ] he anoi[nted] his body,
He clothed himself in [his] princely [gar]ment,
The kingly aura, the awe-inspiring tiara,
He picked up the mace, he held it in his right hand,   (95)
[   ] he held in his left hand.
[   ]
[   ] he made firm at his feet.
He set over [   ]
The staff of success and authority [he hung] at his side.   (100)

---

1. Gate of Marduk's temple in Babylon (George, *Topographical Texts*, 301). This passage may be an aetiology for some reliefs or statuary there known to the poet.

2. This is evidently a congratulatory exclamation, with a play on Damkina and *dumqu* ("good").

3. Advisor or messenger god to Ea, a Janus-like figure with a double head; see R. M. Boehmer and W. G. Lambert, "Isimu," RLA 5, 178–181.

After he [had put on] the aura of [his kingship],
His netted sack, the Apsu [   ] awesomeness.
He was seated like [   ]
In [his] throne room [   ]
In his cella [   ]   (105)
The gods, all there are, [   ]
Lahmu and Lahamu [   ]
Made ready to speak and [said to] the Igigi-gods,
"Formerly [Mar]duk was 'our beloved son',
"Now he is your king, pay heed to his command."   (110)
Next all of them spoke and said,
"'Lugaldimmerankia' is his name, trust in him!"
When they had given kingship over to Marduk,
They said to him expressions of goodwill and obedience,
"Henceforth you shall be provider for our sanctuaries,   (115)
"Whatever you shall command, we will do."

(Marduk creates Babylon as the terrestrial counterpart to Esharra, abode of the gods in heaven. The gods are to repose there during their earthly sojourns.)

Marduk made ready to speak and said
(These) words to the gods his fathers,
"Above Apsu, the azure dwelling,
"As a counterpart to Esharra, which I built for you,   (120)
"Below the firmament, whose grounding I made firm,
"A house I shall build, let it be the abode of my pleasure.[1]
"Within it I shall establish its holy place,
"I shall appoint my (holy) chambers,
        I shall establish my kingship.
"When you go up from Apsu to assembly,   (125)
"Let your stopping places be here, before your assembly.[2]*
"When you come down from heaven to [assembly],

---

   1. For discussion of this passage, see Livingstone, *Explanatory Works*, 80–81; W. G. Lambert, "Himmel," RLA 4, 411–412; George, *Topographical Texts*, 296; Horowitz, *Cosmic Geography*, 120–122. Babylon and the temple of Marduk, Esagila, are at the center of the universe, above Apsu (water below the earth) and below heaven (water held back by the firmament).
   2. That is, when the gods or their cult images travel to Babylon, they can find accommodation in specific chambers of Marduk's temple.

"Let your stopping places be there to receive all of you.
"I shall call [its] name [Babylon],
        Houses of the Great Gods,[1]
"We shall all hold fe[stival]s with[in] it."   (130)
When the gods his fathers heard what he commanded,
They ... [   ]
"Over all things that your hands have created,
"Who has [authority, save for you]?
"Over the earth that you have created,   (135)
"Who has [authority, save for] you?*
"Babylon, to which you have given name,
"Make our [stopping place] there forever.
"Let them[2] bring us our daily portions,
"[   ] our [   ].   (140)
"Whosoever shall [   ] our task that we [   ],
"In his place [   ] his toil [   ]."
[Marduk] rejoiced [   ]
The gods [   ] ... them.
... [   ] them li[ght].   (145)
He opened [   ] ... [   ]

(two fragmentary lines)

The gods prostrated before him, saying,
To Lugaldimmeran[ki]a, their lord, they [said],   (150)
"Formerly [we called you] 'The Lord, [our beloved] son',
"Now 'Our King' ... [shall be your name],
"He whose [sacral] sp[ell] saved [our lives],
"[au]ra, ma[ce], and ne[t],
"[Ea?   ev]ery [sk]ill.   (155)
"Let him make the plans, we ... [   ]."

---

1. Hermeneutic etymology of the name Babylon (George, *Topographical Texts*, 253–255).
2. Who "they" refers to is disputed. It may refer to the defeated gods (Landsberger and Kinnier Wilson, JNES 20 [1961], 178–179); it may be impersonal, or it may refer proleptically to the Babylonians.

Tablet VI

(The rebellious gods are offered a general pardon if they will produce their leader. They produce Qingu, claiming that he started the war. He is sacrificed, and his blood is used to make a human being; compare Atrahasis [II.36] Tablet I lines 224ff.)

When [Mar]duk heard the speech of the gods,	(1)
He was resolving to make artful things:	
He would tell his idea[1] to Ea,	
What he thought of in his heart he proposes,	
"I shall compact blood, I shall cause bones to be,	(5)
"I shall make stand a human being, let 'Man' be its name.	
"I shall create humankind,	
"They shall bear the gods' burden that those may rest.[2]	
"I shall artfully double the ways of the gods:	
"Let them be honored as one but divided in twain."[3]	(10)
Ea answered him, saying these words,	
He told him a plan to let the gods rest,[4]	
"Let one, their brother, be given to me,	
"Let him be destroyed so that people can be fashioned.	
"Let the great gods convene in assembly,	(15)
"Let the guilty one be given up that they may abide."	
Marduk convened the great gods in assembly,	
He spoke to them magnanimously as he gave the command,	
The gods heeded his utterance,	
As the king spoke to the Anunna-gods (these) words,	(20)
"Let your first reply be the truth!	
"Do you speak with me truthful words!	
"Who was it that made war,	
"Suborned Tiamat and drew up for battle?	
"Let him be given over to me, the one who made war,	(25)

1. Literally: "his utterance," but to judge from the context, the utterance is so far purely internal.
2. From the necessity of providing for themselves; see Atrahasis (II.36 Tablet I lines 240–243).
3. A reference to two main divisions of the Mesopotamian pantheon, Anunna-gods and Igigi-gods, or to the supernal and infernal deities (compare Tablet VI lines 39ff.).
4. The text assigns Marduk primacy in the creation of humans by giving him the "idea," since Mesopotamian tradition, established centuries before this text was written, agreed that Ea/Enki had been the actual creator, along with the Mother Goddess.

"I shall make him bear his punishment, you shall be released."
The Igigi, the great gods answered him,
To Lugaldimmerankia, counsellor of all the gods, their lord,
"It was Qingu who made war,
"Suborned Tiamat and drew up for battle."   (30)
They bound and held him before Ea,
They imposed the punishment on him and shed his blood.
From his blood he made humankind,
He imposed the burden of the gods and exempted the gods.
After Ea the wise had made humankind,   (35)
They imposed the burden of the gods on them!
That deed is beyond comprehension,
By the artifices of Marduk did Nudimmud create!

(Marduk divides the gods of heaven and netherworld.
The gods build Esagila, Marduk's temple in Babylon.)

Marduk the king divided the gods,
The Anunna-gods, all of them, above and below,   (40)
He assigned to Anu for duty at his command.
He set three hundred in heaven for (their) duty,
A like number he designated for the ways of the netherworld:
He made six hundred dwell in heaven and netherworld.
After he had given all the commands,   (45)
And had divided the shares of the Anunna-gods
        of heaven and netherworld,
The Anunna-gods made ready to speak,
To Marduk their lord they said,
"Now, Lord, you who have liberated us,
"What courtesy may we do you?   (50)
"We will make a shrine, whose name will be a byword,
"Your chamber that shall be our stopping place,
        we shall find rest therein.
"We shall lay out the shrine, let us set up its emplacement,
"When we come[1] (to visit you), we shall find rest therein."
When Marduk heard this,   (55)
His features glowed brightly, like the day,

---

1. Or: "When we achieve (the task)."

"Then make Babylon the task that you requested,
"Let its brickwork be formed, build high the shrine."
The Anunna-gods set to with hoes,
One (full) year they made its bricks.   (60)
When the second year came,
They raised the head of Esagila,[1] the counterpart to Apsu,
They built the upper ziggurat of Apsu,[2]
For Anu-Enlil-Ea[3] they founded his ... and dwelling.
He took his seat in sublimity before them,   (65)
Its pinnacles were facing toward the base of Esharra.[4]
After they had done the work of Esagila,
All the Anunna-gods devised their own shrines.

> *(The gods come to the new temple for a celebration.*
> *After a feast they take their places to ordain destinies.)*

The three hundred Igigi-gods of heaven
        and the six hundred of Apsu all convened.[5]
The Lord, on the Exalted Dais,
        which they built as his dwelling,   (70)
Seated the gods his fathers for a banquet,
"This is Babylon, your place of dwelling.
"Take your pleasure there, seat yourselves in its delights!"*
The great gods sat down,
They set out cups, they sat down at the feast.   (75)
After they had taken their enjoyment inside it,
And in awe-inspiring Esagila had conducted the offering,
All the orders and designs had been made permanent,
All the gods had divided the stations of heaven and netherworld,

---

1. Wordplay on the name of Marduk's temple ("House whose Head Is High").

2. Esagila is therefore a counterpart or replica of the abode of Ea (Apsu) and the abode of Enlil (Esharra). For discussion of this passage, see George, *Topographical Texts*, 296, 299 ('upper ziggurat' the one visible to humanity in Babylon).

3. The three divine names together may here be taken as a syncretism for Marduk; compare Tablet VII lines 136, 140, and below, p. 475 note 2. For discussion of this passage, see Moran, AnBi 12 (1959), 262.

4. The significance of this line is obscure; variant: "He was looking at." See Horowitz, *Cosmic Geography*, 124.

5. This is an unresolved contradiction with lines 39–44 above, so was presumably drawn from a different source; for discussion, see George, *Topographical Texts*, 368.

The fifty great gods took their thrones,   (80)
The seven gods of destinies were confirmed forever
    for rendering judgment.

(Marduk's bow becomes a constellation.)

The Lord took the bow, his weapon, and set it before them,
The gods his fathers looked upon the net he had made.
They saw how artfully the bow was fashioned,
His fathers were praising what he had brought to pass.   (85)
Anu raised (it), speaking to the assembly of the gods,
He kissed the bow, "This be my daughter!"
He named the bow, these are its names:
'Longwood' shall be the first,
    'May It Be on Target' shall be the second."
The third name, 'Bow Star', he made visible in heaven,   (90)
He established its position
    with respect to the gods his brethren.[1]

(Marduk is made supreme god. Anshar gives him a second name, Asalluhi.
Anshar explains Marduk's role among gods and men with respect to this second name.)

After Anu had ordained the destinies of the bow,
He set out the royal throne
    that stood highest among the gods,
Anu had him sit there, in the assembly of the gods.
Then the great gods convened,   (95)
They made Marduk's destiny highest, they prostrated themselves.
They laid upon themselves a curse (if they broke the oath),
With water and oil they swore, they touched their throats.[2]
They granted him exercise of kingship over the gods,
They established him forever
    for lordship of heaven and netherworld.   (100)
Anshar gave him an additional name, Asalluhi,
"When he speaks, we will all do obeisance,
"At his command the gods shall pay heed.

---

1. Aetiology for an unidentified star; mentioned as a "god of the night" in II.27a.
2. A symbolic slashing gesture meaning that they may die if they break the oath.

"His word shall be supreme above and below,

"The son, our champion, shall be the highest.   (105)

"His lordship shall be supreme, he shall have no rival,

"He shall be the shepherd of the people of this land,
    his creatures.

"They shall tell of his ways, without forgetting, in the future.

"He shall establish for his fathers great food offerings,

"He shall provide for them,
    he shall take care of their sanctuaries.   (110)

"He shall cause incense burners to be savored,
    he shall make their chambers rejoice.

"He shall do the same on earth as
    what he brought to pass in heaven,

"He shall appoint the people of this land to serve him.

"Let the subject peoples be mindful
    that their gods should be invoked,

"At his command let them heed their goddess(es).   (115)

"Let their gods, their goddesses be brought food offerings,

"Let (these) not be forgotten, let them sustain their gods.

"Let their holy places be apparent(?),★
    let them build their sanctuaries.[1]

"Let the people of this land be divided as to gods,

"(But) by whatever name we call him, let him be our god.[2]   (120)

(Beginning of the explanation of Marduk's fifty names. Names 1–9 are those borne by Marduk prior to this point in the narrative. Each of them is correlated with crucial points in the narrative as follows: (1) his birth, (2–3) his creation of the human race to provide for the gods, (4) his terrible anger but his willingness to spare the rebellious gods, (5) his proclamation by the gods as supreme among them, (6) his organization of the cosmos, (7) his saving the gods from danger, (8) his sparing the gods who fought on the side of Tiamat, but his killing of Tiamat and Qingu, and (9) his enabling the gods to proceed with the rest of what is narrated.)

"Let us pronounce his fifty names,
    "That his ways shall be (thereby) manifest, his deeds likewise(?):★

---

1. As interpreted here, the holy places show forth their own qualities of holiness so that humankind builds shrines there, but the meaning of the line is doubtful.

2. That is, Marduk is to be the one god of all the gods, no matter how many gods humankind may serve.

(1) MARDUK!

"Who, from his birth, was named by his forefather Anu,

"Establisher of pasture and watering place,
     who enriches (their) stables,

"Who by his Deluge weapon subdued the stealthy ones,   (125)

"Who saved the gods his forefathers from danger.

"He is indeed the Son, the Sun,[1]
     the most radiant of the gods,

"They shall walk in his brilliant light forever.

"On the people whom he made,
     creatures with the breath of life,

"He imposed the gods' burden, that those be released.   (130)

"Creation, destruction, absolution, punishment:

"Each shall be at his command, these shall gaze upon him.

"(2) MARUKKA shall he be,
     the god who created them (humankind),

"Who granted (thereby) the Anunna-gods contentment,
     who let the Igigi-gods rest.

"(3) MARUTUKKU shall be the trust of his land,
     city, and people,   (135)

"The people shall heed him forever.

"(4) MERSHAKUSHU, angry but deliberative,
     furious but relenting,[2]

"Deep is his heart, all encompassing his feelings.

"(5) LUGALDIMMERANKIA is his name
     that we all pronounced,

"Whose commands we exalted above those
     of the gods his fathers.   (140)

"He shall be Lord of All the Gods
     of Heaven and Netherworld,[3]

The king at whose revelations
     the gods above and below stand in dread.

"(6) NARI-LUGALDIMMERANKIA

---

1. See above, Tablet I lines 101f. and p. 442 note 3. For the name Marduk, see Sommerfeld, AOAT 213 (1982), 7–12.

2. The text construes MER = "angry," SHAKUSHU = "be appeased, calm." This contrast is developed more fully in the hymn to Marduk that opens the Poem of the Righteous Sufferer; see III.14 Tablet I lines 1–36; III.12a lines 1–3.

3. See Tablet V line 112, translation of Sumerian name.

is the name we invoked, instructor of all the gods,[1]
"Who founded for us dwellings out of danger
    in heaven and netherworld,
"And who divided the stations
    for the Igigi- and Anunna-gods. (145)
"At his name the gods shall tremble and quake in (their) dwellings.
"(7) ASALLUHI is that name of his which Anu,[2]
    his father, pronounced.
"He is the light of the gods, the mighty leader,
"Who, according to his name,
    is protective spirit of god and land,
"And who in mighty single combat
    saved our dwellings from harm.[3] (150)
"Asalluhi they named secondly (8) NAMTILA,
    god who maintains life,[4]
"Who, according to his nature, repaired the shattered gods,
"The lord who revived the moribund gods by his sacral spell,[5]
"Let us praise the destroyer of the wayward foes!
"Asalluhi, whose name was called thirdly (9) NAMRU, (155)
"The pure god[6] who purifies our ways."
Anshar, Lahmu, and Lahamu named three each of his names,
They said to the gods their sons,
"We have named three each of his names,
"Do you, as we have, invoke his names." (160)
Joyfully the gods heeded their command,
As they took counsel in the Assembly Place of the Gods,
"The valiant son, our champion,
"Our provider, we will exalt his name!"
They sat down in their assembly to name (his) destinies, (165)
In all their rites they invoked of him a name.

1. Interpretation of Sumerian name.
2. One expects Anshar on the basis of Tablet VI lines 101 and 159. The substitution may have been intentional if the poet was trying to include the triad Anu-Enlil-Ea (see Tablet VII lines 136, 140; Tablet VI line 64).
3. Etymologizing elements in the name.
4. Interpretation of Sumerian name. It is unclear whether or not DINGIR should be construed as part of the proper name; variant has Namtilaku.
5. That is, saved the gods whom Tiamat would have killed (see p. 477 note 4).
6. Interpretation of NAMRU as Akkadian *namru* "shining," hence "pure" (see General Introduction, E.4).

Tablet VII

(This section deals with Marduk's three Asaru-names [10–12], his five Tutu-names [13–17], his six Shazu-names [18–23], his four Enbilulu-names [24–27], his two Sirsir-names [28–29]. Some of these reflect Marduk's role as a vegetation deity.)

"(10) ASARI, bestower of cultivation, who established surveys,   (1)

"Creator of grain and fibrous plants,
    who causes vegetation to sprout,[1]

"(11) ASARALIM, who is honored in the house of counsel,
    whose counsel excels,

"Whom the gods heed, without fear,[2]

"(12) ASARALIMNUNNA, the honored one,
    light of the father who begot [him],   (5)

"Who implements the decrees of Anu, Enlil, Ea,
    (who is) Ninshiku.

"He is their provider who assigns their portions,

"Whose tiara increases abundance for the land.[3]

"(13) TUTU is [he] who effected their restoration,

"He shall purify their shrines that they may be at rest,   (10)

"He shall devise the spell that the gods may be calm.

"Should they rise in anger, they shall turn [back].

"He shall be supreme in the assembly of the gods his [fathers],

"No one among the gods shall [make himself equal] to him.[4]

"Tutu is (14) ZIUKKENNA, life of [his] masses,   (15)

"Who established the holy heavens for the gods,

"Who took control of where they went, assigned their stations,

---

1. Commentary: RI = "bestower," RU = "bestow," SAR = "cultivation," A = "border," RA = "establish," RU = "creation," SAR = "grain" and "herbs," SAR read MA as "cause to sprout," and SAR = "vegetation."

2. Or: "and feel fear before him" (Lambert, TUAT III/4, 557, with different text). Commentary: SA = "house," SA = "counsel," ALIM = "honored," SA = "excelling," SA = "counsel," DINGIR = "god," SA = "heed," SA = "fear," SA = "learn" (i.e., "has not learned to fear").

3. Or: "Who increases abundance of the field for the land." Commentary to this name broken.

4. Commentary: TU = "effect," TU = "restore," DA (implied phonetic complement to TU) = "he," TU = "purify," DU (rhyming sound) = "shrine," DA = "he," [DA] = "should," DU_6.DU(?) = "relieve," TU = "devise," TU = "spell," DINGIR = "god," TI (like TU) = "be at rest," TU = "be angry," DA = "should," TU = "rise," TU+DU = "turn back," DA = "should," DA = "lofty," elative "supreme," TA = "in, from among," TU = "assembly," DINGIR = "[god, father]."

"He shall not be forgotten by teeming humankind,
        [let them hold fast to] his [deeds].¹
"Tutu they called thirdly (15) ZIKU, who maintains purity,
"God of the fair breeze,²
        lord who hears and accedes (to prayers),   (20)
"Producer of riches and wealth, who establishes abundance,
"Who turned all our want to plenty,
"Whose fair breeze we caught whiff of in our great danger,
"Let them ever speak of his exaltation, let them sing his praises!³
"Tutu let teeming humankind magnify fourthly
        as (16) AGAKU,   (25)
"Lord of the sacral spell, reviver of the moribund,
"Who had mercy on the vanquished gods,
"Who removed the yoke imposed on the gods, his enemies,
"Who, to free them, created humankind,
"The merciful, whose power is to revive,   (30)
"Word of him shall endure, not to be forgotten,
"In the mouth of the people of this land,
        whom his hands have created.*⁴
"Tutu, fifthly, is (17) TUKU,
        his sacral spell shall ever be on their lips,
"Who with his sacral spell uprooted all the evil ones.
"(18) SHAZU, who knows the heart⁵ of the gods,
        who was examining the inside,   (35)
"Lest he allow evildoers to escape from him,

---

1. "Life of his masses" = translation of Sumerian name; "establish" = play on Sumerian ukkenna ("in the assembly") and Akkadian *ukinnu* "which he establishes." Commentary: ZI = "[go = way?]," ZI = "[hold?]," ZU (=ZI+U) "[determine]," NA = "sta[tion]," TA = "must not," TU/ZI = (forget?), TA = "by, from among," UKKIN = "tee[ming humankind]," TU = "deeds," DU = "hold."
2. Literally: "Propitious wind," "(holy) spirit."
3. Commentary: DU = "create, name," ZI = "maintain," KU = "pure, purity," DINGIR = "god," TU = "wind," DU (rhymes with TU) = "fair," DINGIR = "lord," ZI = "listen, agree, produce," KU = "riches, abundance," ZI = "establish." Commentary breaks off here.
4. "Sacral spell" (translation of Sumerian) means primarily an incantation to revive the ill, a special concern of Marduk's, but here refers as well to the protective spell used against Tiamat, as in Tablet V line 61. The "revival" includes saving the gods from Tiamat, sparing the rebellious gods who were doomed to death, and the creation of humankind. How the other explanations were construed in the commentary is unknown.
5. Translation of Sumerian name. The following clause may be read either as a general statement or as a reference to Tablet IV lines 65f., 110ff.

"Who established the assembly of the gods,
  who contented them,
"Who subdued the unsubmissive,
  their (the gods') broad [pro]tection,
"Who administers justice, uproots twisted testimony,
"In whose place falsehood and truth are distinguished.[1]   (40)
"Shazu they shall praise secondly as (19) ZISI,
  who silenced(?) those who rose (against him),
"Who banished paralyzing fear from the body
  of the gods his fathers,[2]
"Shazu is, thirdly, (20) SUHRIM,
  who uprooted all enemies with the weapon,
"Who thwarted their plots, turned them into nothingness,
"Who snuffed out all wicked ones,
  as many as came against him.[3]   (45)
"The gods shall ever be joyful in the assembly!
"Shazu is, fourthly, (21) SUHGURIM,
  who ensured obedience for the gods his fathers,
"Who uprooted the enemy, destroyed their offspring,
"Who thwarted their maneuvers, excepting none of them.
"His name shall be invoked and spoken in the land!"[4]   (50)
"Shazu later generations shall tradite fifthly as (22) ZAHRIM,
"Who destroyed all adversaries, all the disobedient,
"Who brought all the fugitive gods into their sanctuaries.
"This his name shall be the truth!"[5]
"To Shazu, moreover, they shall render all honor sixthly as
  (23) ZAHGURIM,   (55)

---

1. Commentary preserved for lines 37–40, construing [ZI] (like ZU) = "[establish]," [ŠA = "assem]bly" (semantic extension from 'within' to 'corporate body' easily made in Akkadian); DINGIR = "god," [ŠA] = "[goo]d," ŠA ="heart," Z[I = "sub]due, one who assents," ZU = "[pro]tect, broad, falsehood," ZI = "true, di[sti]nguish, [pl]ace."

2. Commentary lost. The first element ZI = "rise up, banish," SI = "silence, paralyzing fear," SI (like SU) for "body" (so Böhl, AfO 11 [1936/7], 204); "silences the attacker" (translation uncertain, AHw, 1177b) is evidently a translation of ZI.SI; a wordplay may underlie it.

3. Translation uncertain. Commentary not preserved. SUḪ = "uproot, thwart, turn back, extinguish(?)," RIM = "all" (etc.).

4. Presumed explanations similar to preceding. Note the progression of each name's sphere of recognition: "place" (18), "body of the gods" (19), "assembly" (20), and "land" (21), the first name as locus for action, the others loci for praise.

5. Presumed explanations similar to the preceding.

"He it is who destroyed all foes in battle.[1]
"(24) ENBILULU, lord who made them flourish, is he,
"The mighty one who named them, who instituted offerings,
"Who established grazing and watering places for the land,
"Who opened channels, apportioned abundant waters.[2]   (60)
"Enbilulu they shall [invoke] secondly as (25) EPADUN,
        lord of open country and flood(?),*
"Irrigator of heaven and earth, former of furrows,
        who formed the sacred(?) plowland in the steppe,
"Who regulated dike and ditch,
        who delimited the plowed land.[3]
"Enbilulu they shall praise thirdly
        as (26) ENBILULU-GUGAL,
        irrigator of the watercourses of the gods,
"Lord of abundance, plenty, high yields,   (65)
"Producer of wealth, enricher of all the inhabited world,
"Bestower of grain,* who causes barley to appear.
"Enbilulu is (27) HEGAL,
        who heaps up abundance[4] for the ...* peoples,
"Who rains prosperity over the wide earth,
        who makes vegetation flourish.
"(28) SIRSIR,
        who heaped up the mountain(s) above Tiamat,   (70)
"Who ravaged the corpse of Tiamat with [his] weapon,
"Ruler of the land, their faithful shepherd,
"To whom have been granted* the cultivated field,
        the subsistence field, the furrow,[5]
"Who crossed vast Tiamat back and forth in his wrath,
"Passing back and forth, as a bridge,
        at the place of single combat.[6]   (75)

1. Presumed explanations similar to the preceding.
2. Commentary lost. The first epithet is intended as a translation of the Sumerian name.
3. Commentary lost.
4. Epithet = translation of Sumerian name; other explanations not preserved.
5. Or: "Whose hair is the cultivated field, whose tiara is the plowed land."
6. This passage may contain mythological material about a little-known deity, Sirsir, that is here worked into the Marduk story by association and syncretism. Sirsir, made into a name of Marduk, evidently figured in a tradition in which he slew the ocean in single combat. For discussion, see Landsberger, WO 1 (1950), 362–366.

"Sirsir they named secondly (29) MALAH, let it remain so,
"Tiamat is his vessel and he the boatman.[1]

(The remaining names are treated singly or in groups, beginning with the defeat of Tiamat and ascending to proclamation of Marduk as lord of the universe. Whereas his earlier names referred to his innate nature, his later ones commemorate his roles, accomplishments, and their outcome. Names 30–50 ascend in scope from earth to heaven.)

"(30) GIL, who stores up grain in massive mounds,
"Who brings forth barley and flocks,
        grantor of the land's seed.[2]
"(31) GILIMMA, who established the bond of the gods,
        creator of enduring things,   (80)
"The bridle(?)* that curbed them,
        provider of good things,[3]
"(32) AGILIMMA, the lofty one, remover of the diadem,
        who controls the sn[ow],
"Creator of the earth above the waters,
        establisher of the heights.[4]
"(33) ZULUM, who assigned fields,
        measured off tracts(?) for the gods,
"Grantor of portions and food offerings,
        tender of sanctuaries.[5]   (85)
"(34) MUMMU, creator of heaven and netherworld,
        who guides those astray(?),
"Divine purifier of heaven and netherworld,[6] is, secondly,
        (35) ZULUMMU,

1. Malah = Akkado-Sumerian word for "boatman."
2. Commentary lost.
3. The sign GIL(IM) is two crossed reeds, here explained as a (celestial) linkage and restraint. "Good things" and "enduring things" could also mean "excellence" and "truth."
4. Commentary: IL = "lofty," MA = "remove," GIL = "diadem" (could "diadem" refer to the royal pretensions of the enemy?); GIL = "guide," (hence "provide"), "snow," MA = "create," IM = "cloud(?)," read in the commentary erroneously or with a different text as "ea[rth]," DINGIR = "hi[gh?]," MU = "waters" (bilingual pun), GI = "end[ure]." Horowitz, *Cosmic Geography*, 129 suggests that removing the diadem refers to the melting of snow on the mountain peaks.
5. Commentary: ZU = "[know]" (transitively as "designate"), UL = "[fields]," ZU = "[measure off]," UL = "[forms]" (here: "tracts"); further explanations not preserved.
6. Explanations broken in commentary; "creator" = translation of Sumerian.

"To whom no other among the gods was equal in strength.[1]

"(35) GISHNUMUNAB, creator of all people,[2]
    who made the world regions,

"Destroyer of the gods of Tiamat,
    who made humankind from parts of them.[3]   (90)

"(36) LUGALABDUBUR,
    the king who thwarted the maneuvers of Tiamat,
    uprooted [her] weapons,

"Whose support was firm in front and rear.[4]

"(37) PAGALGUENNA, foremost of all lords,
    whose strength was supreme,

"Who was greatest of the gods his brethren, lord of them all.[5]

"(38) LUGALDURMAH, king of the juncture of the gods,
    lord of the great bond,   (95)

"Who was greatest in the abode of kingship,
    most exalted among the gods.[6]

"(39) ARANUNNA, counsellor of Ea,
    fairest(?) of the gods [his] fathers,

"Whose noble ways no god whatever could equal.[7]

"(40) DUMUDUKU, whose pure dwelling is
    renewed in holy hill,

"Son of holy hill, without whom the lord of holy hill
    makes no decision.[8]   (100)

"(41) LUGALSHUANNA, king whose strength

---

1. Commentary lost.
2. Commentary lost. NUMUN means "seed" or "semen," see Böhl, AfO 11 (1936/7), 206.
3. That is, "from something of them" = "their substance" or the like.
4. Commentary: [LUGAL = "king"], B[IR? = "thwart"], DU = "ac[tions]" = "maneuvers," AB = "Tiamat" (by extension from AB.BA "ocean"), BU = "root out," DU = "weapon," LU = "[who]," (commentary breaks off; [DUBUR = "foundation"]).
5. Preserved explanations are [DINGIR] = "god," [PA] = "brethren(?)," [GAL] = "great, hero," [GU] = "totality."
6. "King" and "lord" = translations of Sumerian. Commentary: LUGAL = "king, lord," DUR = "bond," DINGIR = "god," LU = "who," DUR = "in, dwelling," LUGAL = "king(ship)," MAH = "great(est)," DUR = "among," DINGIR = "god," MAH = "most," "exalted."
7. Commentary: A.RA = "counsel(lor)," NUN = "Ea," RU = "creator," DINGIR = "god," A = "father," RA = "who," A.RA = "way," N[UN] = "[pr]ince," NU = "no," RU = "[equal]," (breaks off).
8. "Holy Hill," throne dais in Marduk's temple in Babylon (George, *Topographical Texts*, 287–291). Commentary lost. Dumu-Duku means "Son of Holy Hill" and Lugal-Duku "King of Holy Hill" (the latter refers to Ea).

was outstanding among the gods,

"Lord, strength of Anu, who became supreme
    at(?) the nomination(?) of Anshar.[1]

"(42) IRUGGA, who ravaged all of them amidst Tiamat,

"Who gathered all wisdom to himself,
    profound in perception.[2]

"(43) IRQINGU, ravager of Qingu, ... of battle,[3]   (105)

"Who took charge of all commands, established lordship.[4]

"(44) KINMA, leader of all the gods, grantor of counsel,

"At whose name the gods quake for fear like a whirlwind.[5]

"(45) ESIZKUR shall dwell aloft in the house of prayer,[6]

"The gods shall bring in their presents before him,   (110)

"Until he receives (all?) their due.

"None besides him can create artful things,

"The four people of this land are his creatures,[7]*

"No god but he knows how long they will live.

"(46) GIBIL, who maintained the ... of the weapon,   (115)

"Who because of the battle with Tiamat
    can create artful things,

"Profound of wisdom, ingenious in perception,

"Whose heart is so deep that none of the gods
    can comprehend it.[8]

"(47) ADDU shall be his name, the whole sky he shall cover,

"His beneficent roar shall thunder over the earth,   (120)

---

1. Commentary lost; perhaps LUGAL = "king," LU = "who," AN = "among," (etc.), ŠU = "strength(?)."

2. IR = "ravage," GU = "all," [IR] = "amidst(?)," [GU] = "all," [GI = "wisdom"], [UR = "gath]er," [GI = "perception, profound"].

3. Variant: "like an enemy"; Bottéro, "en plein combat." The passage remains uncertain.

4. Commentary lost; IR = "ravage."

5. Or perhaps "quake (as in a) whirlwind." Commentary lost.

6. "House of Prayer" = translation of Sumerian name. Commentary partially preserved, e.g., IL = "high," RA = "in," E = "house," SIZKUR = "prayer," RA = "dwell," DINGIR = "god," (rest fragmentary).

7. That is, the people of the four points of the compass? For different renderings of this line, see Dalley, BiOr (1995), 86.

8. Commentary: GI = "[be permanent]" (factitively "establish"), ... [LU = "who"], RA = "[in]", IR = "[battle]," MA = "T[iamat]" (from mû, Akkadian word for water?), RU = "c[reate, do something artful]," GI = "p[rofound], wi[sdom]," RU = "[do]," GI = "p[erception]," I[R = "heart, remote]," RA = "[whose, not]," [IR? = "comprehend"] (breaks off). For line 115, Bottéro, 59 suggests "l'issue de la guerre."

"As he rumbles, he shall reduce the burden of the clouds,
    below, for the people, he shall grant sustenance.[1]
"(48) ASHARU, who, according to his name,
    mustered the gods of destinies,
"He has taken all peoples in his charge.[2]
"(49) NEBERU shall hold the passage of heaven and earth,
"So they shall not cross above and below
    without heeding him,   (125)
"Neberu is his star that he made visible in the skies.
"It shall hold the point of turning around,
    they shall look upon him,
"Saying,

    'He who crossed back and forth,
        without resting, in the midst of Tiamat,
    'Neberu ("Crossing") shall be his name,
        who holds the position in its midst.'

"He shall maintain the motions of the stars of heaven,   (130)
"He shall herd all the gods like sheep.
"He shall keep Tiamat subdued,
    he shall keep her life cut short,
"In the future of humankind, with the passing of time,
"She shall always be far off, she shall be distant forever."[3]
Because he created the firmament
    and fashioned the netherworld,   (135)

1. Commentary mostly lost.
2. Commentary mostly lost. "Muster" in the Akkadian is a word homophonous with the name.
3. Or: "May he be without hindrance, may he endure until distant days" (Lambert, TUAT III/4, 601, using different text). The text etymologizes *neberu* as *nēberu* "crossing, passage." Commentary: DINGIR = "star," RA = "which, in," DINGIR = "heaven," E = "visible, splendid," RA = "shall, hold," KUN.SAG.GA = "front-back," DINGIR = "front," RU = "back," RU = "look upon," MA = "saying, son," RA = "which, in," IR = "inside," MA = "ocean" (see above, p. 482 note 8), BU = "cross," RA = "not," BI = "resting, his name" (from Sumerian mu-bi "its name"), RA = "shall," NEBERU = Neberu; RA = "hold," IR = "within," RA = "which," DINGIR = "star, heaven," RA = "go, be permanent," IR = "like," RI = "sheep, shepherd" (from Akkadian *rē'û*, shepherd?), DINGIR = "god," IR = "heart," ŠA = "heart, all (of them)," IR = "subdue," MA = "ocean, ..." ŠI = "li[fe]," RIM = "be sh[ort]" (life).

Father Enlil has pronounced
    his name (50) 'Lord of the World'.[1]
The Igigi-gods pronounced all the names.
When Ea heard (them), he was joyful of heart.
He said, "He whose name his fathers have glorified,
"His name, like mine, shall be 'Ea'.[2]   (140)
"He shall provide the procedures for all my offices,
"He shall take charge of all my commands."
The great gods called his fifty names
"The Fifty," they made his position supreme.[3]

(Composition and purpose of this text, its approval by Marduk.)

They must be grasped: the "first one"[4] should reveal (them),★ (145)
The wise and knowledgeable should ponder (them) together,
The master should repeat, and make the pupil understand.
The "shepherd," the "herdsman" should pay attention,[5]
He must not neglect the Enlil of the gods, Marduk,
So his land may prosper and he himself be safe.   (150)
His word is truth, what he says is not changed,
Not one god can annul his utterance.
If he frowns, he will not relent,
If he is angry, no god can face his rage.
His heart is deep, his feelings all encompassing,   (155)
He before whom crime and sin must appear for judgment.
The revelation (of the names) that the "first one"
    discoursed before him (Marduk),
He wrote down and preserved for the future to hear,
The [wo]rd of Marduk who created the Igigi-gods,

---

1. The commentary glosses "places" as "heaven"; RU = "create, fashion." For "lord of the world" (that is, "lands"), the commentary has MA = "name," A = "father." "Lord of the Lands" = "Enlil," meaning that Enlil has given Marduk his own name (as Ea does in the succeeding lines). The commentary continues through line 139 as if 137–139 were part of the explanation of "Lord of the World," or at least could be used for such an explanation.
2. Marduk is now made god of wisdom and magic.
3. Marduk is here assigned the number fifty. In Mesopotamian scribal practice, the number 50 was used to write the name of Enlil, so herewith Marduk has replaced Enlil as supreme deity; see p. 443 note 1.
4. See General Introduction, D.1.
5. Kings and other rulers; see p. 18.

[His/Its   ] let them [   ], his name let them invoke.   (160)
Let them sound abroad* the song of Marduk,
How he defeated Tiamat and took kingship.

Text: W. G. Lambert and S. Parker, *Enuma Eliš, The Babylonian Epic of Creation* (Oxford, 1966). I
have used this standard text where possible and have indicated only a few variants. Tablet II is
based on al-Rawi and George, *Iraq* 52 (1990), 150, 152. Additional fragments have been listed by
Borger, HKL 2, 151–152; see also Vanstiphout, N.A.B.U. 1987/70 and W. G. Lambert,
N.A.B.U. 1987/100. An additional manuscript of Tablet VI was published by Al-Rawi and
Black, JCS 46 (1994), 136–139.

Edition: R. Labat, *Le Poème babylonien de la création* (Paris, 1935). Tablet II is edited by al-Rawi and
George, *Iraq* 52 (1990), 149–157; Tablet V by Landsberger and Kinnier Wilson, JNES 20 (1961),
154–179. I have benefited from detailed comments by Moran on an earlier version of this translation.

Translation: A. Heidel, *The Babylonian Genesis*² (Chicago, 1951); Speiser and Grayson, ANET³, 60–
72, 501–503; Labat, *Religions*, 36–70; Dalley, *Myths*, 228–277. I am particularly indebted to the
treatment by J. Bottéro, *Mythologie*, 602–679. The translation has been extensively revised in accordance with Lambert's 1994 German translation, TUAT III/4, from which I have drawn many
new readings and interpretations of key passages. In some cases a different text is implied; these
are given in notes pending publication of the sources.

Literature: In general, see Borger, HKL 1, 259–260; HKL 2, 151–152; J. Bottéro, *Annuaire* 1975/6,
70–126; D. O. Edzard, "Schöpfung," WdM, 121–124; T. Jacobsen, *The Treasures of Darkness*
(New Haven, 1976), Chapter 6; "The Battle between Marduk and Tiamat," JAOS 88 (1968),
104–108; A. Kragerud, "The Concept of Creation in Enuma Elish," in *Ex Orbe Religionum, Studia Geo. Widengren, Pars Prior* (Leiden, 1972), 39–49; R. Labat, "Les origines et la formation de la
Terre, dans le poème babylonien de la création," AnBi 12 (1959), 205–215; W. G. Lambert, "A
New Look at the Babylonian Background of Genesis," *The Journal of Theological Studies* NS 16
(1965), 287–300; Horowitz, *Cosmic Geography*, 108–129. For the names of Marduk, the following two studies have been used, but will prove a challenge to the non-specialist reader: F. M. Th.
de L. Böhl, "Die fünfzig Namen des Marduk," AfO 11 (1936/7), 191–217; J. Bottéro, "Les Noms
de Marduk," *Studies Finkelstein*, 5–28.

*Notes to Text: (I 1–8) The proposal of West, *Iraq* 59 (1997), 187, against all manuscripts, is uncon-
vincing. (I 2) Hutter, RA 79 (1985), 187–188. (I 6) Held, AOAT 25 (1968), 233–237; for the
syntax of this and the first ten lines, Wilcke, ZA 67 (1977), 163–170; Moran, N.A.B.U. 1988/21;
Buccellati, *Studies Moran*, 125–128. (I 110) Translation uncertain; see Streck, OrNS 64 (1995), 50
and note 68. (I 119, 121, 123) Lambert, TUAT III/4, 572. (II 126) al-Rawi and George, *Iraq* 52
(1990), 157. (II 144) George (unpublished fragment). (IV 72) Borger, RA 72 (1980), 95–96. (IV
125) With AHw, 976a; see CAD M/2, 304. (IV 139) Reading *mašku*. CAD M/1, 342a suggests
parku "dividing line." (V 9) See Heimpel, JCS 38 (1986), 134. (V 14) Lambert, TUAT III/4, 588.
(V 54) Emending: *a-<gu>-ú*. The text of the second half of the line is obscure; see AHw, 1207b.
(V 68) George, *Topographical Texts*, 257. (V 126) George, *Topographical Texts*, 256. (V 136) After
Bottéro, *Mythologie*, 637. (VI 73) Reading *wṣb* with WLM, Lambert, TUAT III/4, 594. Some
read *šebû* "have a sufficiency of"; compare CAD N/1, 124a; Bottéro, *Mythologie*, 641. (VI 118)
Unclear, for suggestions see CAD M/1, 419b and CAD A/2, 204b; AHw, 634b. (VI 122) CAD

A/1, 298a ("likewise"), Bottéro, *Mythologie*, 644. (VII 61) Translation uncertain; see CAD A/2, 518. (VII 67) So AHw, 1294b, but the parallel in Tablet VII 79 suggests that *šú* "sheep" could be meant here. (VII 68) Word of uncertain meaning, see AHw, 987b. (VII 73) Translation uncertain; compare Lambert, TUAT III/4, 599; CAD M/2, 24e; AHw, 1192a and Bottéro, *Mythologie*, 649. (VII 81) CAD L, 113a; others suggest "trap," "ring," "yoke," or the like. (VII 113f.) Differently Jacobsen, OIP 98 (1990), 103; Dalley, BiOr 52 (1995), 86; von Soden, GAG, 24★★. (VII 145–162) Wilcke, ZA 67 (1977), 171–174. (VII 161) Collation by Lambert, CAD M/1, 367b, *[l]ì-šas-s[u-m]a*; von Soden, OLZ 91 (1996), 286: *ši-sis-s[u-ma]* "ist sein Ruf."

III.18 MYTHS OF ORIGINS

Stories of origins and creation give different versions of how the universe, the world, and the human race came into existence.[1] In Marduk's Creation (III.18a), Marduk is portrayed as a creator deity and his temple, Esagila, as the first result of creation. Several accounts exist for how the human race was created (see II.36, III.17, III.18a, c). In II.36 and III.18c, the human race is created using the blood of a slain god or gods. In addition, stories of origins or creation were sometimes included in magic spells and rituals, focusing on the cosmological background for the subject of the composition (II.23d, IV.48). The Myth of the Plow (III.18b) portrays successive generations of gods engaged in parricide and incest.

The creation narratives translated here are badly preserved and full of linguistic perplexities, to the extent that they are scarcely in a condition for fruitful comparative study.[2] The accounts incorporated in spells and rituals are not creation stories in general so much as accounts of how specific phenomena came to be.

(a) MARDUK, CREATOR OF THE WORLD

This creation story, like III.17, opens in a world without recognizable features. The primeval cities had not been built and everything was sea. The first place created is Babylon (written Eridu, which the Mesopotamians considered the first city), thus making Babylon's sanctuary, Esagila, the first creation. Next certain gods are created who pronounce the name of Babylon. Marduk makes the earth by piling dirt on a raft in the primeval waters, then populates the new landscape with human beings to serve the gods, and wild animals. He creates the twin rivers. He next provides other basic elements of Mesopotamian environment: reeds, domesticated animals, orchards, and exotic or game beasts. He dries out a place in the reed marshes, the manufacture of bricks begins, and from this houses and cities are constructed. At this point the text breaks off.

The principal manuscript is clumsily written with numerous mistakes. Some scholars have rearranged the material in what would seem a more logical order, but in this translation the original order of the lines is maintained.

---

1. See Bottéro, *Mythologie*, 470–679.
2. For a careful discussion, though out of date in many details, see Heidel, *Babylonian Genesis*, 82–140.

No holy house, no house for the gods
     had been built in a pure place,   (1)
No reed had come forth, no tree had been created,
No brick had been laid, no brickmold had been created,
No house had been built, no city had been created,
No city had been built, no settlement had been founded,   (5)
Nippur had not been built, Ekur had not been created,
Uruk had not been built, Eanna had not been created,
The depths had not been built, Eridu had not been created,
No holy house, no house of the gods,
     no dwelling for them[1] had been created,
All the world was sea, the spring in the midst of the sea
     was only a channel.   (10)
Then was Eridu[2] built, Esagila was created,
Esagila, which Lugalduku[3] established in the depths!
Then was Babylon built, Esagila completed,
The Anunna-gods — Marduk made them all as one —   (15)
Named it sublimely "Holy City, Pleasurable Dwelling."
Marduk tied together a raft on the face of the waters,
He created dirt and heaped it on the raft.
In order to settle the gods in a comfortable dwelling,
He created humankind,   (20)
Aruru created the seed of humankind with him.
He created the wild animals,
     the living creatures of the open country.
He created and put in place the Tigris and Euphrates rivers,
He pronounced their names with favor.
He created the dry rush, the pulpy reed,
     the marsh, the reed thicket,   (25)
     the stand of reeds, the vegetation of the open country
— The world was marsh and canebrake! —
The cow and her calf, the bull,
The ewe and her lamb, the sheep of the fold,
The orchards and forests,

1. Akkadian: "his/its dwelling."

2. Eridu was a theological way of writing Babylon (George, *Topographical Texts*, 19, 252); compare III.12(c).

3. A name for Ea, perhaps here transferred to Marduk, see III.17 Tablet VII, line 100 and note.

The wild ram, the mountain sheep,
>   stood each in its appointed place therein.*   (30)

The lord Marduk heaped up fill at the edge of the sea,

He made a dry place (in the) marsh.

He provided it with [   ],

[He m]ade [   ], he made trees,

He created [   ] in that place.   (35)

[He laid bricks], he created the brickmold.

[He built houses], he created cities,

[He built cities], he founded settlements,

[He built Nippur], he created Ekur.

[He built Uruk], he created Eanna   (40)

(breaks off)

Text: King, CT 13 35–37; Zimmern, ZA 28 (1914), 100–101; Langdon, OECT 6, pl. XVII Rm 97.
Edition: King, STC 1: 130–139.
Translation: Heidel, *Babylonian Genesis*, 61–63; Bottéro, *Mythologie*, 497–502; Hecker, TUAT III/4, 608–611.
Literature: Bottéro, *Mythes*, 302–312, with detailed discussion and philological commentary; Bottéro places line 31 after line 18 and line 29 between 27 and 28; Horowitz, *Mesopotamian Cosmology*, 129–132.
Notes to Text: (9) Differently Bottéro, *Mythes*, 498: "de nulle Demeure sainte ... L'emplacement n'avait été préparé," whereas Heidel, *Babylonian Genesis*, 62, suggests "its dwelling" (referring to Eridu). (30) Interpretation on basis of Sumerian; see Civil, JNES 31 (1972), 386. von Soden, StOr 46, 330 amends the Akkadian to *ina! libbi-šu*; *<aš>-ru-<uš>-šu* might fit the Sumerian better.

(b) THE MYTH OF THE PLOW

In this myth, children of gods kill one or both parents and marry either parents or siblings. It centers on a mythical(?) city Dunnu, translated here as "Fortress" (a place of that name is also mentioned in IV.30b line 9). The date of this composition is unknown. Grammatical features suggest the Late period, though it may have been composed at an earlier date. The emphasis on where the deceased rulers were buried, for example, is found in a Mature period king list that was evidently meant to be a continuation of the Sumerian King List of the Archaic period.[1] For the reader's convenience, the names of the actors are translated where possible.

1.   J.-J. Glassner, *Chroniques mésopotamiennes* (Paris, 1993), 142–145.

[Plow(?)] in the beginning [married Earth],   (1)
[   ] lordship
"We shall break the soil of the land with the plow."
With the thrust of their plow they created Sea,
[The furro]ws bore Beasts of their own accord.   (5)
They both built the primeval city Fortress.
Plow(?) kept the lordship of Fortress for himself alone.
[Earth] cast her eye on Beasts, her son,
"Come, let me make love to you," she said to him.
Beasts married Earth, his mother,   (10)
And he killed Plow(?), his [father],
And he laid [him] to rest in Fortress, which he loved.
Then Beasts took the lordship of his father.
He married Sea, his older sister.
Flocks, son of Beasts, came there,   (15)
And he killed Beasts
And he laid him to rest in his father's tomb in Fortress.
He married Sea his mother.
Then Sea killed Earth, her mother,
In the month of December, on the sixteenth day,
      he took lordship and kingship.   (20)
[   ], son of Flocks, married River, his own sister,
And he killed [Flocks], his father, and Sea, his mother,
And he laid them to rest, as if napping, in the tomb.
In the month [January?], on the first day,
      he seized kingship and lordship for himself.
[Shepherd?], son of Flocks, [married] Pasture-and-Poplar,
      his sister,   (25)
He made the [green plants] of the earth luxuriant,
He provided sheepfold [   ]
[   ] fathers [   ]
He pro[vided] for the needs of the gods.
He killed [   ] and River, his mother.   (30)
And he caused them to dwell [in the tomb].
[In the month February?, on the — day],
      he took lordship and kingship for himself.

[Haharnum?], son of [Shepherd?],
>   married] Lady-of-the-Open-Country, his sister.

He [killed Shepherd? and Pasture-and-Poplar, his mother,   (35)
[And] he caused them to dwell [in the tomb].
[In the month March?],
>   on the sixteenth (or: twenty-ninth) day,
>   [he took] kingship and lordship.

[Hayyashum?], son of Haharnum [   ],
Married [   ], his own sister.
[At new year] he took his father's lordship,
He [did not] kill him ...

(fragmentary lines, breaks off)

Text: Millard, CT 46 43.
Edition: T. Jacobsen, "The Harab Myth," SANE 2/3 (1984).
Translation: W. G. Lambert, P. Walcot, "A New Babylonian Theogony and Hesiod," *Kadmos* 4 (1965), 64–72; Bottéro, *Mythologie*, 472–478; Dalley, *Myths*, 278–281.

(c) CREATION OF HUMANKIND

This bilingual account of the origins of the human race explains that it was created to serve the gods and to improve their domains. In the final lines, the destiny of the human race is explained as labor, celebrating the gods' rites and festivals, and the attainment of scholarly wisdom. The last is symbolized by the goddess Nisaba: just as grain stands over a fertile field, so the stylus stands over the ready tablet. The Sumerian and Akkadian versions often diverge; this translation combines elements of both.

When heaven had been separated from earth,
>   in a pair established,[1]   (1)

When the mother goddesses had appeared,
When the earth had been founded, the earth built up,
When they established the plans for heaven and earth,

1. The translation of the opening line is disputed.

And, to regulate watercourses and irrigation canals,   (5)
Had established the Tigris and Euphrates channels,
Anu, Enlil, Ninmah,[1] and Ea, the great gods,
And the Anunna gods, the great gods,
Took their places on their sublime daises,
They conferred among themselves.   (10)
Since they had established the plans for heaven and earth,
Had laid out watercourses and irrigation canals,
And established the Tigris and Euphrates channels,
<Enlil said to them>:
"What should we do next?   (15)
"What should we make now?
"O Anunna-gods, great gods,
"What should we do next?
"What should we make now?"
The great gods who were present,   (20)
And the Anunna-gods, ordainers of destinies,
Both replied to Enlil,
"In Uzumua,[2] the linking-place of heaven with earth,
"Let us slaughter Alla-gods,[3]
"Let us create humankind from their blood.   (25)
"Their labor shall be labor for the gods:
"To maintain the boundary ditch for all time,
"To set pickaxe and workbasket in their hands,
"To make the great dwelling of the gods,
"Worthy to be their sublime sanctuary,   (30)
"To add field to field!
"To maintain the boundary ditch for all time,
"To regulate irrigation works for you(?),
"To water the four abodes (of the earth),
"To make the plant life flourish,   (35)
"[   ] rainfall [   ]."

---

1. Text: Shamash, emended according to line 16′ below.

2. This was a place in Nippur where, according to a Sumerian creation tradition (discussed by Jacobsen, JNES 5 [1946], 134–137; for a recent translation of the whole text, see G. Farber in Hallo, ed., *Context* 1: 511–513), people grew out of the soil, later attributed to Babylon (George, *Topographical Texts*, 259, 443).

3. See II.36a, line 224. There only one god is killed but here perhaps two, one for male and one for female.

"For maintaining the boundary ditch,
"For heaping up piles of harvested grain

(gap)

"For making the fields of the Anunna-gods yield in plenty,   (1')
"For making great the prosperity of the land,
"For celebrating the gods' festivals as they should,
"For libating cool water,
"For making the great house of the gods worthy
        to be their sublime dwelling,   (5')
"You shall call their names Ullegarra and Annagarra."[1]
To increase cattle, sheep, wild beasts, fish, and birds,
For prosperity in the land,
Enul and Ninul[2] affirming, using their holy words,
And Aruru, worthy to be mistress of them all,   (10')
Laid down the master plans themselves:
Skilled upon skilled, unskilled upon unskilled,
Making many of them spring out of the earth, like grain,
A pattern unalterable as the stars of heaven!
To celebrate the gods' festivals, day and night,
        as they should,   (15')
Anu, Enlil, Enki, and Ninmah, the great gods,
Laid down the master plans themselves!
Where humankind was created,
There also was Nisaba[3] cherished!*

Text: Ebeling, KAR 4; Bezold, PSBA 10 (1887–88), plate after p. 418; Meek, RA 17 (1920), 189; (also Weidner, AJSL 38 [1921], 209); G. Pettinato, *Das altorientalische Menschenbild und die sumerischen und akkadischen Schöpfungsmythen* (Heidelberg, 1971), pl. 1.
Edition: Pettinato, op. cit., 74–85.
Translation: Heidel, *Babylonian Genesis*, 68–71; Bottéro, *Mythologie*, 502–508; Hecker, TUAT III/4, 606–608.
Notes to Text: (19') With Hecker, TUAT III/4, 608.

1. These names may mean something like "establishing abundance / prosperity," but may also contain the Akkadian words for "no" and "yes" (compare III.26 lines 56–57).
2. "Lord" / "Lady of Abundance."
3. Goddess of grain and scribal lore.

(d) PROVIDING FOR THE GODS

This short passage was incorporated during the Late period into a ritual for repairing or reconstructing a temple. Obscure, corrupt, and cryptographically written, this composition could date to the Mature period.

> When Anu, Enlil, and Ea undertook[1] heaven and earth,   (1)
> They artfully provided for the gods.
> They made a pleasurable dwelling for them in this land,
> The gods moved into their dwelling,
>   the original house of the gods.[2]
> ... a share of the food deliveries to the king,*   (5)
> They established food offerings for the share of the gods.
> The gods loved their dwelling,
> [Thus] the gods [established] their dominion ...
>   in the land of the original people.

Text: Borger, BiOr 30 (1973), 180.
Edition: Borger, BiOr 30 (1973), 182.
Translation: Bottéro, *Mythologie*, 491–493.
Literature: Bottéro, *Mythes*, 299–301.
Notes to Text: (5) CAD N/1, 273a.

(e) CREATION OF SUN AND MOON

These brief accounts of the creation of the moon to illumine the night sky and to mark the beginning of the day and month, began a great work on astrological omens called "When Anu (and) Enlil" (after these opening lines). The reference to "signs" in line 3 probably refers to omens, though it could also have a more general significance for the moon as a guide. The Sumerian version was perhaps a late concoction from an Akkadian original. These narratives could date as well to the Late period.[3]

1. Text may be corrupt, understood to mean "plan" or "have the idea for" (Borger, Bottéro).
2. This refers to Esagila, temple of Marduk at Babylon; compare III.17, Tablet VI, 73–74; III.18a, line 12.
3. Borger (BiOr 30 [1973], 163) suggests a date towards the end of the Mature period.

(Sumerian)

When Anu, Enlil, and Enki, [the great gods],
 in their infallible wisdom,   (1)
Had, in the plans for heaven and earth,
 laid down the crescent-shaped vessel of the Moon,
Had established it as a sign for heaven and earth,
That crescent-shaped vessel shed light in heaven,
The stars came out, to be visible in heaven.   (5)

(Akkadian)

When Anu, Enlil, and Ea, the great gods, in their wisdom,
Had laid down the plans for heaven and earth,
Had confided to the hands of the great gods to bring forth
 the day, to start the month for humankind to see,
They beheld the Sun in the portal of his rising,
The stars came out faithfully in heaven.*

Text: C. Virolleaud, *L'Astrologie Chaldéenne, Text Cunéiforme, Sin I* (Paris, 1908), plate 1; King, STC II, pl. XLIX.
Edition: King, STC 1, 124–126.
Translation: Heidel, *Babylonian Genesis*, 73–74; Bottéro, *Mythologie*, 493–494.
Literature: Bottéro, *Mythes*, 316–317.
Notes to Text: (5) With Heidel, *Babylonian Genesis*, 73; Bottéro, *Mythes*, 317 note 28.

(f) CREATION OF THE KING

A damaged tablet of the Late period preserves portions of a creation story modeled on the story of the creation of the human race as described in Atrahasis (II.36) and modified in the Epic of Creation (III.17). To this a new element has been added, the creation of a king after the creation of the first human being. This was no doubt intended to elevate the status of royalty to a cosmic level, whereas in the Etana story (III.22 [LV] Tablet I, lines 19–23) a king is chosen only after cities have been built. The pairing of kingship and right counsel in this composition may be compared to the same motif already in Etana ([OV] Tablet I, line 13, though the relevant line does not appear in the later version of Etana. The latter part of this story appears also in an Assyrian royal prayer

known from a Late-period manuscript in hon'or of Assurbanipal (IV.4a),
though which text was the basis for the other is unknown. The Assurbanipal
prayer has here been used to restore the missing lines at the end.

(gap)

[Their faces] were [aver]ted.
Belet-ili [their] mistress [became frightened] at their silence,
Said to Ea the exorcist (these) words,
"The forced labor of the gods became p[ainful] upon them   (5')
"... [   ]
"[Their faces] are averted, hostility has arisen.
"Let us make an image of clay,
        let us impose [the forced labor upon it],
"Let us relieve their weariness for all time."
Ea made ready to speak and said to Belet-ili,   (10')
"You are Belet-ili, mistress of the great gods

(two lines lost)

Belet-ili pinched off its clay,
[   ] she made artful things.[1]   (15')
[   ] she purified and mixed the clay with it.
[   ] she adorned [with excellence] its body,
[   ] its entire figure.
She put on [   ]
[She put on ...], she put on ...   (20')
[She put on ...], she put on [ea]rs,
She put [   ] on [its] body.
[   ] Enlil, warrior of the great gods,
[   ] when he saw it, [his face] glowed with pleasure.
[   ] in the assembly of the gods he saw to [its features],   (25')
[   ], he [perfected] its body.
[   ] Enlil, warrior of the great gods,
He established its name as ["human being"],
He commanded that the forced labor of the gods
        be imposed on it.
Ea made ready to speak, said to Belet-ili,   (30')

---

1. Epic of Creation (III.17) Tablet VI, line 2.

"You are Belet-ili, mistress of the great gods,
"You are the one who made the human-man.
"Make a king, a counsellor-man,
"Adorn his whole body with excellence.
"See to his features, make fair his body."   (35′)
Belet-ili fashioned the king, the counsellor-man,
They gave the king warfare on behalf of the [great] gods.
Anu gave his crown, Enlil ga[ve his throne],
Nergal gave his weapon, Ninurta gave [his splendor],   (40′)
Belet-ili gave [his] fea[tures],[1]
Nusku commissioned a (wise) counsellor and
            he stood in attendance upon him.
He who shall speak [lies and falsehood] to the king,
Be [he important, he shall die violently],
[Be he rich, he will become poor].   (45′)
[He who shall harbor evil against the king in his heart],
[Erra will call him to account in a plague].
[He who shall think disrespectful thoughts of the king,
            a whirlwind shall crush him,
            his accumulated goods shall be a puff of wind].
[The gods of heaven and netherworld assembled],
[They blessed the king, the counsellor-man],   (50′)
[They delivered the weapon of combat
            and battle into his hand],
[They gave him the people of this land,
            that he serve as their shepherd].

Text: van Dijk, VAS 24 92.
Edition: Mayer, OrNS 56 (1987), 55–68.
Translation: Livingstone in Hallo, ed., *Context*, 1:476–477.
Literature: H.-P. Müller, "Eine neue babylonische Menschenschöpfungserzählung im Licht keil-
    schriftlicher und biblischer Parallelen," OrNS 58 (1989), 61–85; Livingstone, *Court Poetry*, xxiii–
    xxiv.

1. For the style of this passage, compare III.44g, III.47c.

III.19 DESCENT OF ISHTAR TO THE NETHERWORLD

In this poem, Ishtar decides to visit the netherworld and demands to be admitted. Her sister, Ereshkigal, queen of the netherworld, is suspicious and jealous, and instructs her gatekeepers to remove all of Ishtar's clothing as she enters. As she enters the netherworld naked, her sister sets upon her sixty disease demons and she dies. Sexual reproduction vanishes from the world; the gods need a way to bring Ishtar back to life. Ea, god of wisdom, sends a male prostitute to the netherworld, who so pleases Ereshkigal by adroit flattery that she grants him any wish. He asks for the body of Ishtar, as instructed by Ea. The enraged queen gives up the body, but dooms the prostitute to a squalid earthly existence. Ereshkigal orders the death god to bring someone else in Ishtar's stead and at the same time to get revenge on Ishtar. The death god finds Ishtar's lover, Tammuz, removes all signs of mourning for Ishtar's death from him, and gives him a ring and a flute to play on. The next part of the story is omitted in the Akkadian text, perhaps presumed as understood. When Ishtar returns from the netherworld to find her lover dallying with harlots and not in mourning, in a fit of jealous passion she offers him to the netherworld in her stead. In lines 131ff. the text switches abruptly to Tammuz's sister Belili, who, when she hears the wailing for her dead brother, institutes a ceremony for the dead.

   This composition, known from two manuscripts from Assurbanipal's library, and an earlier, variant version from Assur, may have emerged from a Sumerian original. The present text is shorter than the Sumerian version of the same story, with large pieces omitted. The final episode of the text is so elliptical as to be incomprehensible to the modern reader. To him, the Akkadian text will seem poorly conceived in comparison to its Sumerian forerunner. In any event, the story is not without drama and narrative art.

   For the Sumerian background of this composition, see S. N. Kramer, *The Sacred Marriage Rite* (Bloomington, 1969), 107–133; full translation in Bottéro, *Mythologie*, 276–300. For a retelling of the Sumerian poem, see D. Wolkstein and S. N. Kramer, *Inanna, Queen of Heaven and Earth: Her Stories and Hymns from Sumer* (New York, 1983), 52–73. A fragmentary Akkadian text of related interest has been edited by W. G. Lambert, "A New Babylonian Descent to the Netherworld," *Studies Moran*, 289–300.

To the netherworld, land of n[o return],[1]   (1)
Ishtar, daughter of Sin, [set] her mind.
Indeed, the daughter of Sin did set [her] mind
To the gloomy house, the seat of the ne[therworld],
To the house that none leaves who enters,   (5)
To the road whose journey has no return,
To the house whose entrants are bereft of light,
Where dust is their sustenance and clay their food.
They see no light but dwell in darkness,
They are clothed like birds in wings for garments,   (10)
And dust has gathered on the door and bolt.
When Ishtar reached the gate of the netherworld,
She said (these) words to the gatekeeper,
"Gatekeeper! Open your gate for me!
"Open your gate for me that I may enter!   (15)
"If you will not open the gate that I may enter,
"I will break down the door, I will smash the bolt,
"I will break down the frame, I will topple the doors.[2]
"I will raise up the dead to devour the living,
"The dead shall outnumber[3] the living!"   (20)
The gatekeeper made ready to speak,
Saying to the great one,[4] Ishtar,
"Stay, my lady, do not cast it down.[5]
"Let me go announce your name to the queen E[resh]kigal."
The gatekeeper went in and said to Ereshkigal,   (25)
"Here is your sister Ishtar at [your gate],
"She who holds the great play-rope,[6]
        who roils up the deep before Ea the [king?]."
When Ereshkigal heard this,
Her face went pale as a cut-down tamarisk,
Her lips went dark as the lip of a vat.*   (30)
"What made her resolve on me?

1. Translation of Sumerian word for netherworld. See also III.20b iii.
2. A adds: "I will smash the 'balance' and tear off the knob."
3. Variant: "I will make the dead outnumber ..."
4. Variant: "the lady."
5. Or: "Do not leave it."
6. Some sort of toy, symbol of the warlike Ishtar (Landsberger, WZKM 56 [1960], 121–124; Dalley, *Myths*, 130).

What has aroused bad feelings in her against me?*
"Here now, shall I drink water
     with the (netherworld) Anunna-gods,
"Shall I eat clay for bread, shall I drink dirty water for beer?
"Shall I weep for the young men
     who have left [their] helpmeets?
"Shall I then weep for the young women
     who are wrenched from lovers' loins?   (35)
"Shall I weep for the helpless infant
     who was taken before its time?[1]
"Go, gatekeeper, open [your] gate to her,
"Treat her according to the age-old rules."
Off went the gatekeeper and opened [the] gate to her,
"Enter, my lady, that Cutha[2] rejoice over you,   (40)
"That the palace of the netherworld be glad at your presence."
He brought her in the first gate,
     he loosed and removed the great tiara of her head.
"Why, gatekeeper, did you remove the great tiara of my head?"
"Enter, my lady.
     Thus the rules of the mistress of the netherworld."
He brought her in the second gate,
     he loosed and removed the earrings of her ears.   (45)
"Why, gatekeeper, did you remove the earrings of my ears?"
"Enter, my lady.
     Thus the rules of the mistress of the netherworld."
He brought her in the third gate,
     he loosed and removed the beads of her neck.
"Why, gatekeeper, did you remove the beads of my neck?"
"Enter, my lady.
     Thus the rules of the mistress of the netherworld."   (50)
He brought her in the fourth gate,
     he loosed and removed the garment pins of her breast.
"Why, gatekeeper, did you remove
     the garment pins of my breast?"

---

1.   That is, if Ishtar succeeds in her plan, Ereshkigal will join the dead, instead of being their queen? Bottéro, *Mythologie*, suggests that lines 32–36 are Ishtar's thoughts, as imagined by Ereshkigal (p. 320).
2.   Cult center of Nergal, god of the netherworld.

"Enter, my lady.
>Thus the rules of the mistress of the netherworld."
He brought her in the fifth gate,
>he loosed and removed the girdle of birth stones
>of her waist.
"Why, gatekeeper, did you remove the girdle of birth stones
>of my waist?"   (55)
"Enter, my lady.
>Thus the rules of the mistress of the netherworld."
He brought her in the sixth gate,
>he loosed and removed her bracelets and anklets.
"Why, gatekeeper, did you remove my bracelets and anklets?"
"Enter, my lady.
>Thus the rules of the mistress of the netherworld."
He brought her in the seventh gate,
>he loosed and removed the loincloth of her body.   (60)
"Why, gatekeeper,
>did you remove the loincloth of my body?"
"Enter, my lady.
>Thus the rules of the mistress of the netherworld."
As soon as Ishtar had entered the netherworld,
Ereshkigal saw her and trembled with fury at her.
Ishtar, without thinking, sat(?) (in the place of honor)[1]
>above her.⋆   (65)
Ereshkigal made ready to speak, and said
To Namtar her vizier these words,
"Go, Namtar, [take her from] my presence!
"Let loose against her sixty di[seases   ] Ishtar,
"Eye disease [against] her [eyes],   (70)
"Side disease a[gainst] her [sides],
"Foot disease a[gainst] her [feet],
"Heart disease a[gainst her heart],
"Head disease [against her head],
"I [let them loose?] against all of her!"   (75)
After the lady Ishtar [went down] to the netherworld,
The bull would not mount the cow,
>[the ass would not impregnate the jenny],

---

1. What Ishtar does is uncertain. Some translators understand "attacked her" or the like.

The [young man would not impregnate] the girl
    in the thoroughfare,
The young man slept in [his bedroom?],
The g[irl s]lept [by herself].   (80)
Papsukkal, vizier of the great gods, was downcast
    and his features [were gloomy].
He was dressed in mourning and [left] his hair unkempt.
Off went he in despair before Sin his father, weeping,
Before Ea the king[1] [his] tears flowed down.
"Ishtar has gone down to the netherworld,
    she has not come up.   (85)
"As soon as Ishtar went down to the netherworld,
"The bull will not mount the cow,
    the ass will not impregnate the jenny,
"The young man will not impregnate the girl
    in the thoroughfare,
"The young man has slept in his [bedroom?],
"The girl has slept by herself."   (90)
Ea, in his wise heart, conceived (what was) called for,[2]
He created Asushunamir, an impersonator.[3]
"Go, Asushunamir, make your way to the netherworld,
"Let the seven gates of the netherworld be opened before you.
"Let Ereshkigal see you and feel well-disposed toward you.   (95)
"When she calms and her feelings are well-disposed,
"Have her swear the oath of the great gods,[4]
"Look up and set your mind on the waterskin,

    'Oh, my lady, let them give me the waterskin,
        that I may drink water from it.'"[5]

---

1. A omits "king."

2. A: w[ord?]. The Akkadian word (*zikru*) is of disputed meaning in the sense used here. It may imply something commanded or required for a specific situation; Reiner, "stratagem," Bottéro, "idée." There is a wordplay on the word for "man" (*zikaru*).

3. Male prostitutes or transvestites were devotees of Ishtar. It is not clear how such a person could avoid being held by the netherworld. Perhaps a male in female costume "partook of both worlds" or could pass anywhere as an itinerant entertainer. The name means "He is resplendent as he comes forth." In A the name is Asnamir. For discussion, see M. Nissinen, *Homoeroticism in the Biblical World*, trans. K. Stierna (Minneapolis, 1998), 32–37.

4. A adds a line here, too broken to read, which refers to a "midwife" and "creatress."

5. A section may have been omitted here by the scribe, consisting of the narrative recapitulation of lines 93–99.

When Ereshkigal heard this,   (100)
She smote her thigh, she bit her finger.
"You asked of me[1] the unaskable!
"Come, Asushunamir, I will curse you a great curse,
"Let me ordain you a fate never to be forgotten.[2]
"May bread of the public plowing be your food,[3]*
"May the public sewer pipe be your drinking place.   (105)
"The shadow of a wall be your station,
"The threshold be your dwelling.
"May drunk and sober slap your cheek!"
Ereshkigal made ready to speak,
Saying these words to Namtar her vizier,   (110)
"Go, Namtar, knock at the Egalgina,[4]
"Decorate the thresholds with cowrie shells.
"Bring out and seat the (netherworld) Anunna-gods
            on thrones of gold,
"Sprinkle Ishtar with water of life
            and take her from(?) my presence."
Namtar went and knocked at the Egalgina,   (115)
He decorated the thresholds with cowrie shells,
He brought out and seated the (netherworld) Anunna-gods
            on thrones of gold,
He sprinkled Ishtar with water of life and brought her away.[5]
He brought her out the first gate
            and returned to her the loincloth of her body,
He brought her out the second gate
            and returned to her bracelets and anklets,   (120)
He brought her out the third gate
            and returned to her the girdle of birth stones of her waist,
He brought her out the fourth gate
            and returned to her the garment pins of her breast,

1. A adds Asnamir.
2. This clause in A only.
3. Line 104 may refer to commercial homosexual activity, discussion by Maul, *Xenia* 32 (1992), 162–163; Biggs, N.A.B.U. 1993/74 suggests emending to "garbage dump."
4. As construed in the Nineveh version, evidently a palace in the netherworld. A has DI.LI.GI.NA.
5. A adds three broken lines: (a) "Go, Namtar [ ] (the god) [ ]/ (b) "[I]f she does not pay [you] her ransom, bring her back." / (c) Namtar [ ] her [   ]. Compare below, line 126.

He brought her out the fifth gate
    and returned to her the beads of her neck,
He brought her out the sixth gate
    and returned to her the earrings of her ears,
He brought her out the seventh gate
    and returned to her the great tiara of [her h]ead.   (125)
"If she does not pay you her ransom, bring [her] back here.
"Tammuz, her childhood lover,
"Bathe in a bath of pure water and a[noint with] fine oil,
"Dress him in a red garment,
    let him strike up a lapis flute [… a carnelian ring?],
"Let prostitutes turn [his] mood." [1]   (130)
[The lady] Belili was put[ting right?] her jewelry,
[ ] eyestones with which she filled her l[ap?].
When she heard the wailing for her brother,
    Belili smote the jewelry of her body,
The eyestones that filled the Wild Cow's face(?).*
"Do not rob me of my only brother!   (135)
"On the day Tammuz (says) "Hurrah!"*
    the lapis flute and carnelian ring (say) "Hurrah!"
"With him (say) "Hurrah!" the wailing men and wailing women,
"Let the dead come up and smell the incense." [2]

Text: (N)ineveh: King, CT 15 45–48; CT 34 18; (A)ssur: Ebeling, KAR 1 (+) KAR 288, collated Borger, HKL 2, 55; (C) = Ebeling-Köcher-Rost, LKA 62, rev. 10–20. Some variants, such as in formulae of direct speech, are not noted here, nor is text C.

Edition: Borger, BAL 2, 86–91.

Translation: Speiser, ANET³, 106–109; Reiner, *Poetry,* 29–49, including Text C; Bottéro, *Mythologie,* 318–324; Dalley, *Myths,* 155–162, in Hallo, ed., *Context,* 1:382–384.

Literature: Borger, HKL 1, 96, 227; G. Buccellati, "The Descent of Inanna as a Ritual Journey to Kutha?" *Syro-Mesopotamian Studies* 4/3 (1982), 3–7; A. Kilmer, "How Was Queen Ereshkigal Tricked? A New Interpretation of the Descent of Ishtar," UF 3 (1971), 299–309; Reiner, *Poetry,* 29–49 (literary analysis of the whole poem); Bottéro, *Annuaire* 1971/2, 79–97; *Mythologie,* 325–330.

1.   I assume here a gap in the narrative, including a narrative recapitulation of 127–130, Ishtar's catching sight of him, and Tammuz's removal to the netherworld by Namtar.

2.   The meaning may be that when Tammuz emerges with a joyful shout from the netherworld, the dead will rise too. One has here, apparently, an aetiology for some cult festival. For further information, see Notes to Text to line 136.

★*Notes to Text*: (30) See Streck, AOAT 264 (1999), 70–72.(31) *uš-tam-ṭa-an-ni* (WGL); *uš-per-da-an-ni* (CAD K, 13b, Borger, etc.). (65) *uš-bi*. See, e.g., CAD E, 85a; CAD Š/3, 171b; AHw, 1256b; Groneberg, RA 75 (1981), 124. The meaning of the word is unknown. (104) Differently Reiner, *Languages and Areas: Studies Presented to George V. Bobrinskoy on the Occasion of His Academic Retirement* (Chicago, 1967), 116–117; *Poetry*, 44–45. (134) von Soden, ZA 58 (1967), 194. (136) Differently other translations, e.g., CAD E, 122a; Reiner, *Poetry*, 47, which have "On the day Tammuz comes up to me, with him will come up …" I follow a suggestion of Lambert's, who sees in *el-le-an-ni* a word for a shout or cry (for references, including its use in the Tammuz cult, see CAD E, 101b); as a verb form the word is grammatically difficult to explain.

III.20 NERGAL AND ERESHKIGAL

The poem of Nergal and Ereshkigal relates how Nergal, also called Erra, became king of the netherworld. The story hinges on the isolation and sexual frustration of the queen of the netherworld, Ereshkigal. This aspect of the tale is related with warmth, even humor. The narrative turns on a play on words between "death" and "husband." The plague god, Nergal, who is condemned to death for slighting the goddess of the netherworld, Ereshkigal, becomes her husband instead.

Whereas the outline of the story is fairly well known (see below), considerable portions of text are still missing. A short Middle Babylonian version (A+B) is known from a manuscript discovered at El-Amarna in Egypt. This text is not only badly damaged but was written by someone not familiar with Akkadian, so contains numerous aberrant spellings and obscure words.

A large eighth-century manuscript (C) from Sultantepe contributes the most to our understanding, but this too was heavily damaged and contains many obscurities. A Neo-Babylonian manuscript from Uruk (D), treated here with C, restores a few episodes and lines. C and D clearly belong to the same tradition, and A+B to a different one. Because of the complicated interrelationships of these versions, an interpretive outline by numbered episodes is provided below.

1. (= A+B 1–6, C i 5′–15′). The celestial gods give a banquet and send a messenger to Ereshkigal, queen of the netherworld, inviting her to send up a messenger to receive her share. In C i 16′–37′ the messenger of Anu, Kakka, descends to the netherworld, greets Ereshkigal, and relates the message. In C i 38′–50′ Ereshkigal and Kakka exchange civilities.

2. (= A+B 7, C i 51′–56′). Ereshkigal sends off Namtar, her messenger, up to heaven to get her food portion.

3. (= A+B 8–12). Namtar comes into the celestial court to collect the food. All the gods show him respect (A+B: stand up; C: kneel) in deference to his mistress—all except one, Nergal. The incident itself is not well preserved. One may hypothesize that Namtar did not accept the food under these conditions and returned to the netherworld empty-handed. Ereshkigal, in mortification, refuses to sit on her throne and exercise judgment over the netherworld. The gods are thrown into consternation. In C ii 1′–11′, Ea is remonstrating with Nergal, demanding to know why he showed no respect despite his cues that Nergal pretended not to see. Nergal's reply, C ii 18′–20′, is lost in a break.

He evidently announces his intention to go the netherworld, either as an act of defiance or to set things right again; in the earlier version he is being summoned for execution.

4. (= C ii 21′–35′). Ea resolves to take advantage of this for some purpose that is lost in a break. Perhaps he had decided that Nergal should be king. In any case, he gives instructions as to how to avoid execution at the hands of the angry goddess. He commissions Nergal to make a throne out of various kinds of wood that are painted to imitate precious materials Since in some periods a chair was part of expensive interments, his carrying the chair may have been seen as a rite of death, though in reality it prepares him to assume kingship of the netherworld, standing for his throne of kingship.[1]

5. (= C ii 36′–48′). Ea enjoins Nergal not to accept any of the norms of hospitality in the netherworld, and not to become aroused when he sees Ereshkigal strip for her bath.

6. (= C ii end - C iii 8′). Nergal descends to the netherworld. This part of the text uses the same language as the Descent of Ishtar (III.19) and is quotation of a stock motif.

7. (= C iii 9′–22′). The gatekeeper, in reply to Nergal's call, goes to his mistress and informs her that there is a visitor whose identity he does not know. Namtar volunteers to go identify the visitor. To his astonishment, he recognizes the very god who showed no respect when he came for the food.

8. (= C iii 23′–29′). Namtar tells Ereshkigal the story of her slight in heaven once again.

9. (= C iii 30′–36′). Ereshkigal orders Namtar to take her place as ruler of the netherworld, but not to attempt any heroics or usurpation; she will go up herself to get her food. Given the state of the text, the logic of her rejoinder is not readily apparent. One expects this exchange to have been the climax of Episode 3 above, and its presence here may be owing to a repetitive expansion of the text. Perhaps she imagines leaving the netherworld and taking the visitor's place in heaven.

10. (= C iii 37′–60′). Nergal is admitted to the netherworld, announces to Ereshkigal that the supernal deities have sent him to ask her to resume her offices, and declines all offers of hospitality. When she strips for her bath, he remains unmoved.

---

1. For chairs as burial goods, see J. Cooper, *Sumerian and Akkadian Royal Inscriptions* (New Haven, 1986), 71.

11. (= C iv 4′–20′). After a gap in the text, Ereshkigal is found stripping again for her bath. This time, however, Nergal is aroused; they embrace and become passionate lovers. After six days of lovemaking, Nergal arises early and urges Ereshkigal not to be concerned. She drifts back to sleep.

12. (= C iv 21′–32′). Nergal is released from the netherworld by tricking the gatekeeper, and reascends to heaven. The gods are astonished. Certain that a hue and cry will be raised, Ea disguises Nergal by deforming him.

13. (= C iv 33′–45′). Ereshkigal rises in a leisurely way, enjoys a bath, and calls that the rooms be freshened and breakfast served.

14. (= C iv 46′–59′). Namtar breaks the news to her that her lover has absconded. Sobbing, she laments bitterly that she wants him back. Namtar, touched, vows to go up to heaven, find him, and bring him back.

15. (= C v a–30′). Ereshkigal dispatches Namtar with a double plea. She asks pity first of all, for she has never had a lover, and, as queen of the dead, has never enjoyed the pleasures of childhood. She wants her lover back. Then her plea turns to threat: she will raise up the dead to devour the living. Namtar ascends to heaven with her message.

16. (= C v 31′–41′). Namtar examines the gods, all of whom, it seems, are careful to receive him respectfully this time. He sees no one unusual except the deformed Nergal, whom he fails to recognize. He returns empty-handed. Ereshkigal, however, sees through the ruse and sends him back to fetch down the deformed god.

17. (= C v 42′–54′). Namtar returns to heaven but is still unable to find Nergal, this time perhaps because he has resumed his normal shape?

18. (= C vi 1′–42′). After a gap in the text, Nergal is being told by Ea(?) that he can take over dominion of the netherworld if he proceeds as instructed. He is to take the throne he made. At each gate an item of clothing(?) is removed, so he enters Ereshkigal's court naked. While the dead entered the netherworld naked, here his nakedness may have sensuous impact, especially since he enters without forewarning. He yanks Ereshkigal from her throne and they become passionate lovers again, this time for seven full days and nights.

19. (= C vi 42′–49′). Anu sends Kakka to announce that Nergal is king of the netherworld forever.

Comparison of the two versions of the story is instructive for understanding the formation and expansion of Akkadian literary works (see also Reiner, *Poetry*, 55–56). A+B foreshortens episodes 4–16 such that the initial snub is treated as the cause of Ereshkigal's sending up Namtar to bring back the offending god that she may execute him. In A+B Ea arms Nergal with seven plagues that he stations by each of the seven gates to the netherworld. They hold the gates open while he makes a rush for Ereshkigal, yanks her from her throne, and makes ready to decapitate her. She submits and proposes marriage. They reign happily thereafter as king and queen.

One need not conclude that C is an expansion of A+B. Rather, A+B is perhaps a drastic shortening of some earlier version now lost, while C is perhaps an expansion of a different earlier version, also lost.[1] One may suggest that the expansion and revision of the story developed its motif of sexuality, and in fact makes this the cause of Nergal's triumph, rather than his derring-do, as in A+B. This expansion worked in liberal quotations from the same material used in the Descent of Ishtar, though in each instance with an interesting reversal of their application. Furthermore, the exchanges of messengers are expanded to nearly the fullest potential of repetition of speech and action (see General Introduction, C.4 and E.3). Although in both versions the triumph of Nergal was engineered by Ea, who presumably had reasons of his own for wishing Nergal to be king in the netherworld, C omits the plagues given Nergal in A+B as his weapon, and uses his nakedness and the throne to gain his end. In short, this is the same story, but told differently in different sources.

(a) MIDDLE BABYLONIAN VERSION

(A+B)

When the gods prepared a banquet,	(1)
They sent a messenger	
To their sister, Ereshkigal,	
"We cannot come down to you,	
"Nor can you come up to us.	(5)
"Send here that they may take your food portion."	
Ereshkigal sent Namtar her messenger.	
Up went N[amtar] to high heaven,	
[Namtar] came in and the gods [stood up],	
... [ ] they greeted(?) Namtar,*	(10)
The messenger of their great [sister].	

1. For further discussion, see M. E. Vogelzang, "Some Aspects of Oral and Written Tradition in Akkadian," in M. E. Vogelzang and H. L. J. Vanstiphout, eds., *Mesopotamian Epic Literature, Oral or Aural?* (Lewiston, N.Y., 1992), 265–278; Pettinato, *Nergal ed Ereškigal*, 48–57.

[The gods] set out (the food) ...* he saw him, Nergal,
The exalted gods ... [   ] him.
[the] fo[od fo]r his mistress,
[   ] was weeping and sobbing   (15)

(fragmentary lines, then gap)

Ea [   ] ...
He we[nt   ] returned(?),
"Go [their great] sister,   (25)
"Wh[ere is the one who] did not stand [in the
        presence of] my [mes]senger?
"Send him to here me that I may kill him."
Namtar came to speak to the gods,
They summoned him and the gods spoke with him,
"Look at us, one by one, for the god who did not stand
        in your presence,   (30)
"Take him before your mistress."
Namtar looked at them one by one, the last god was bald.[1]
"[The god who did not stand in my presence] is not here."
Namtar [   ] goes to [give] his report:
"[My lady, I looked at them] one by one,   (35)
"[   ] the last god was bald,
"[The god who did not stand in my presence] was not there."
[   ]
[   ] her [mess]enger
[   ] months.   (40)
Ea, pre-eminent lord, [   ]
He placed a chair in [Nergal]'s hands,*
"Take (this) to Ereshkigal."
[Nergal] began to weep before Ea his father,
"When she sees me, she will not let me live!"   (45)
"Do not fe[ar],
"I will give you seven and seven wa[tchers]* to go with you,
"[Id..., ..., ..., Mutabriqu[2]],

---

1. Perhaps Ea has persuaded Nergal to take off his divine headgear so he cannot be recognized. In the Late Version he is altered physically, but in the original story he may simply have been bare-headed.
2. "Lightning Flash."

"Sharabda, [Rabisu,[1] Tirid, Idibtu[2]],
"Ben[nu,[3] Sidanu,[4] Miqit,[5] Beluri],
"Umma, [Libu,[6] shall go] with you."   (50)
[Nergal went and, as he stood at the g]ateway
        of Ereshkigal, he was calling,
"G[atekeeper, gatekeeper, open] your gate,*
"Free the lock that I may enter,
"I am sent to the presence of your mistress Ereshkigal."
Off went the gatekeeper and said to Namtar,
"A certain god is standing at the gateway,   (55)
"Go and examine him that he may come in."
Out went Namtar, when he saw him, he r[an(?)], very happy,*
        and said [to his mis]tress,
"My lady, [it is the god who] month[s] a[go] disappeared
"And did not stand [in my pre]sence."
"Bring him in, [le]t him come here that I may kill [him]."   (60)
Out went Namtar, [saying], "Enter, [my] lord,
"Into your sister's house. Re[cei]ve your portion."
[... said] Nergal, "May [her] he[art] be happy with me [   ]." (65)

(gap)

He stationed Id[ ] at the first, [   ] at the second,
[   ] at the third, Mutabriqu at the fourth,
[Sha]rabda at the fifth, Rabisu at the sixth,
Tirid at the seventh, Idibtu at the eighth,   (70)
Bennu at the ninth, Sidanu at the tenth,
Miqit at the eleventh, Beluri at the twelfth,
Umma at the thirteenth, Libu at the fourteenth gate ...
He cut down Hurbashu[7] (and) Namtar in the courtyard,
He ordered his troops,   (75)
"Let the gates stand open! Now I will run by you!"

1. "Lurker."
2. "Wind."
3. "Epilepsy."
4. "Vertigo."
5. Often used as a word for epilepsy; see M. Stol, *Epilepsy in Babylonia* (Gronigen, 1993), 9–14.
6. A disease symptomized by spots on the skin and high fever.
7. "Chill of fear," taken here to be the name of a courtyard attendant, but the meaning of this line is uncertain and disputed.

In the palace he seized Ereshkigal by her hair,
He bent her down from the throne to the ground
    to cut off her head.
"Don't kill me, my brother! Let me say a word to you!"   (80)
When Nergal heard her, his grip relaxed.
She was weeping and sobbing,
"You be my husband, I will be your wife!
"Let me make you hold dominion
    over the vast netherworld,
"Let me set the tablet of wisdom in your hand,
"You be lord, I be lady!"
When Nergal heard this that she said, he seized her
    and kissed her, wiping away her tears,   (85)
"What (else) have you wished for from me
    for these months (past) till now?"[1]*

(end of tablet)

(b) LATE VERSION

(C, D)

i

[Anu made ready to speak],   (5′)
[Saying to Kakka his messenger],
"[Let me send you, Kakka, to the Land of No Return],
"[To the house of Ereshkigal, who dwells in the netherworld],
"[Saying],

    '[You are not able to come up],
    '[Not (once) in a year can you come up before us].   (10′)
    '[We cannot go down],
    '[Nor (once) in a month can we descend before you].
    '[Let your messenger come here],
    '[Let him remove food from the table,[2]
        let him receive your serving].

1. She has wished for his death (*mūtum*) but gets him as her husband (*mutum*).
2. Or: "Uncover the tray (he carries up there)"; in the Gilgamesh Epic a man carrying food a long distance uses a "table" or "tray" (Foster, *Gilgamesh*, 15).

'[Whatever I give him, let him bring safely to] you.'"   (15')

[Kakka descended the long staircase] of heaven.
[When] he reac[hed the gate of Ereshkigal he said],
"[Gatekeeper], o[pen] the gate [to me]."
"[Enter, Kakka], may the gate ble[ss you]."
He brought [the god K]akka in [the first gate],   (20')
He brought [the god] Kakka [in the second] gate,
He brought [the god] Kakka [in the third] gate,
He brought the god Kakka in the fourth gate,
He brou[ght] the god Kakka in the fifth gate,
He br[ough]t the god Kakka in the sixth gate,   (25')
He br[ough]t the god Kakka in the seventh gate.
He entered her b[roa]d courtyard,
He knelt and k[issed] the ground before her.
He straightened, stood, and said to her,
"Anu [your] father has sent [me],   (30')
"Saying,

> 'You are not able to come up,
> 'Not (once) in a year can you come up before us.
> 'We cannot go down,
> 'Nor (once) in a month can we descend before you.
> 'Let your messenger come here,   (35')
> 'Let him remove food from the table,
>   let him receive your serving,
> 'Whatever I give him, let him bring safely to you.'"

Ereshkigal made ready to speak,
        saying to K[akka] (these) words,
"Messenger of Anu our father, who has come to us,
"(I hope) all is well with Anu, Enlil, and Ea, the great gods?   (40')
"(I hope) all is well with Nammu and Nanshe,[1]
        the pure gods?
"(I hope) all is well with the husband of
        the Mistress of Heaven?
"(I hope) all is well with Nin[urta, mightiest] in the land?"

---

1. As Gurney suggests (AnSt 10 [1960], 111 note 16), the "Nash" of the text may be a form of Nanshe, a Sumerian goddess. Nammu was a Sumerian mother goddess.

Kakka made ready to speak,
      saying to Ereshkigal these words,
"All is well with Anu, Enlil, and Ea, the great gods,   (45')
"All is well with [Namm]u and Nanshe, the pure (gods),
"All is wel[l with the husband of the M]istress of Heaven,
"All is we[ll] with Ni[nurt]a, the mightiest in the land."
[K]akka made ready to speak,
      saying to Ereshkigal these words,
"[   ] may all be well with you."   (50')
[Ereshkigal] made ready to speak, saying to Namtar,
      her messenger, these words,
"Nam[tar], my [messenger], let me send yo[u to] heaven
      to Anu our father.
"Namtar, go up the long [staircase of heaven],
"Take food from the table, [receive my serving].
"Whatever Anu will give [you,
      you must bring safely to me]."   (55')
[Namtar went up the long staircase of heaven]

(gap)

ii

[Ea made ready to speak, saying to Nergal these words],
"[   ]   (1')
"[When Ereshkigal's messenger a]rrived i[n heaven   ]
"[   ] the path [   ]
"[The gods] all k[nelt before] him,
"[The great god]s, lords of destin[ies],   (5')
"[For he] bore the authority, the authority [of the gods],
"[The gods] who dwell in the netherworld.
"Why were you not [kneeling] before him?
"[   ] I kept winking at you,
"But you were [affe]cting not to be aware.   (10')
"[You were not ...],
      y[our] e[yes] were looking at the ground."

(gap)

[Nergal made ready to speak, saying to Ea these words],
"Let me proceed [   ]

"[   ] what you said.

"[   ] ... I will twine it double." (20')

When Ea heard this, he said to himself,

"[Let me bring it] about that I send ..."[1]

Ea made ready to speak, saying to Nergal these words:

"Wayfarer, do you wish to go on your mission

with (just) a ... thorn(?) in your hand?

"Go down to the forest of sissoo-trees(?), (25')

"Cut down sissoo(?), whitewood(?), cedar(?),

"Cut off a[romatic] and evergreen(?) branches."

[He went down to the forest of sissoo-trees?],[2]

[He cut down sissoo(?), whitewood(?),[3] and c]edar(?)

He cut off aromatic and evergreen(?) branches, (30')

He made [...], a throne of Ea, the leader.[4]

[In imitation of] silver he colored with gypsum(?),

In imitation of lapis he colored with faience,

In imitation of gold he made multicolored

with cobalt(?) and potash(?).*

The work was complete, the throne done. (35')

Then he (Ea) summoned him to give his instructions,

"Wayfarer, if you wish to go,

"[Take to] heart whatever instructions I [give you].[5]

"When you arrive there,

"When they bring you a chair,

"Do not proceed to sit upon it. (40')

"When the baker brings you bread, do not proceed to eat.

"When the butcher brings you meat, do not proceed to eat.

"When the brewer brings you beer, do not proceed to drink.

"When someone brings water for your footbath,

do not proceed to wash your [feet].

"When she goes in to bathe, (45')

"And puts on her [   ] garment,

"She will let you see her body ...

---

1. Uncertain. Ea evidently wishes to ensure that Nergal will survive the journey to the netherworld.

2. D adds: "He lifted the axe in his hands, he [dr]ew the sword from his belt."

3. C: "Apple."

4. C: "[   ] and Ningizzida."

5. Variant omits.

"You must not [become arous]ed as man and woman."
Nergal [   ]

(gap)

[To the netherworld, Land of No Return],
[Nergal set his mind ...]
[To the gloomy house, seat of the netherworld],
[To the house that none leaves who enters],

iii

[To the road whose journey] has no return,   (1′)
[To the house whose entrants] are bereft of light,
[Where dust is their sustenance and] clay their food.
[They are clothed like bi]rds in wings for garments,
[They see no light] but dwell in darkness,   (5′)
[   ] moaning,
[they moan] like [do]ves.
[   ] ...
[The gatekeeper made ready to speak],
        saying to Nergal these words,
"I shall take back report [concerning the wayfarer standing]
        at the gate."   (10′)
[The gatekeeper went in to Ereshkiga]l to say (these) words,
"[Mistress, a certai]n [wayfarer] has com[e to us],
"[Wh]o will [identify?] him?"

(gap)

(Namtar is speaking.)

"[let me] identify him.
"[I will look at] him outside the gate,
"I shall take back report [   ] to my mistress."[1]
Namtar went and looked at Erra
        [through the si]de* of the gate,   (20′)
Namtar's face went pale as a cut-down tamarisk,
His lips went dark as the lip of a vat.[2]

---

1. Text: "Lord."
2. See Descent of Ishtar (III.19) lines 29f. with note to text.

Namtar went to [his] mis[tress] to say (these) words,
"Mistress, that time you sent me [to Anu] your father,
"When I entered the court of [Anu],   (25')
"[All the gods] knelt humbly [before me],
"[The gods of the land] knelt humbly ...
"The god who kept on st[anding] in my presence[1]
"Is now come down to the Land of No Return."
[Ereshkigal made ready to speak, saying]
        to [Namtar, her messenger, (these) words],   (30')
"Namtar, you must not strive for divine supremacy,
        nor let your spirit imagine deeds of valor.
"Go up and take your seat on the throne, the royal dais,
"Do you render the judgments of the vast netherworld.
"Let me go up to the heaven of Anu my father
        that I may eat the food of Anu my father,
"And drink the beer of Anu my father.   (35')
"Go, Namtar, bring that god into my presence."
Namtar went and brought in the god Erra.
When he entered the first gate, Pituh,
When he entered the second gate, Enkishar,
When he entered the third gate, Endashurimma,   (40')
When he entered the fourth gate, Nerulla,
When he entered the fifth gate, Nerubanda,
When he entered the sixth gate, Endukuga,
When he entered the seventh gate, Ennugigi,
He entered her spacious court,   (45')
He knelt and kissed the ground before her,
He straightened, stood, and said to her,
"Anu your father sent me to your presence,

        'Do you (be the one to) sit on this throne
        'And render the judgments of the great gods,
        'The great gods who dwell in the netherworld.'"   (50')

As soon as he came, they brought him a chair,
He did not proceed to sit upon it.
The baker brought him bread,
        he did not proceed to eat his bread,

---

1. 28'–29' and 35'ff. from D iii 2'ff. and 5'ff.

The butcher brought him meat,
>he did not proceed to eat his meat,

The cupbearer[1] brought him beer,
>he did not proceed to drink his beer,   (55′)

They brought him water for his footbath,
>but he did not proceed to wash his feet.

Finally she went in to the bathing chamber,

She put on her [   ] garment,

She let him see [her body],

[He was not ar]oused as man for woman   (60′)

(gap)

iv

(gap)

Nergal ... [   ]

She [went] in to the ba[th]ing chamber,   (5′)

[She put on   ] garment,

[She let him see her body].

He [became aroused as man for woman],

They embraced [one another],

Pa[ssionately they went] to bed.   (10′)

One day, a second day they lay,
>[Queen Ereshkigal and Erra],

A third day, a fourth day [they lay,
>Queen Ereshkigal and Erra],

[A fifth day], a sixth day [they lay,
>Queen Ereshkigal and Erra].

[When the seventh] day [came],

Nergal was [   ] for not being present [in heaven],   (15′)

He ... after him [   ]

"Release me, sister, [   ]

"[Do not] make a fuss [at my going   ],

"I must go from(?) the Land of No Return ..."

As for her, her [   ] turned dark.   (20′)

[Nergal went strai]ght to [   ]

[To   ] the gatekeeper (he said these words),

---

1. So D; C presumably had "brewer" on the basis of ii 43′ above.

"[Ereshkigal] your [mis]tress [has sent me, saying],

 '[I would send you to the heaven] of Anu [our father].'

"Let me out that [I may deliver] the message."   (25′)
Nergal went [up the long staircase of heaven].
[When he reached] the gate of Anu, En[lil, and Ea],
Anu, Enlil, and [Ea saw him],
"The son of Ishtar [has come up to us]!
"[Ereshkigal] will look for [him to take him back].   (30′)
"[Let] Ea his father [sprinkle him] with spring water
  that he be bald,[1]
"Have a tic, be la[me, ... let him sit among all the gods]."
Ereshkigal [   ]
[Went into] the bath chamber [ ]
... [   ]   (35′)
[   ] her body
... [   ]
She called out [   ]
"[Bring a] cha[ir   ]
"S[prinkle] the rooms with [ ] water,   (40′)
"Sprin[kle] the rooms with [ ] water,
"[... the] two daughters of [ ] and Enmeshar,
"Sprinkle them with [water of] ...
"The messenger of Anu our father who came to us,
"Let him eat our bread, let him drink our beer."   (45′)
Namtar made ready to speak,
Saying to Ereshkigal, his mistress, (these) words,
"[The messenger] of Anu your father, who came to us,
"Made off before daybreak."
[Eresh]kigal let out an anguished wail,   (50′)
She fell [fr]om her chair to the ground,
[She got] up [from] the ground, her eyes raining tears,
Her tears ran down the sides of her nose,
"Erra, my voluptuous lover!
"I had not had my fill of his charms, but he left me! (55′)
"Erra, my voluptuous lover!
"I had not had my fill of his charms, but he left me!"

---

1. Or, possibly, "stunted."

Namtar made ready to speak, saying to Ereshkigal,
"Send me [to Anu] your [father], let me seize that god,
"Let me fetch him to you!"   (60')

v

[Ereshkigal made ready to speak],
    saying to Namtar (these) words,
"[to] Anu, Enlil, and Ea and say as follows,   (1')

   'Since I was a young girl,
   'I have not known the play of maidens,
   'Nor have I known the frolic of little girls.
   '[That god whom] you sent, he has had intercourse
       with me, so let him lie with me.   (5')
   'Send me [that go]d that he be my husband
      and spend the night with me.
   'Am I defiled, impure?
   'Can I not render judgments for the great gods,
      the great gods who reside in the netherworld?*
   'If [you do not] send t[hat] god,
   'Accor[ding to the authority of the lower regi]ons
      and the great netherworld,   (10')
   'I shall raise up the dead to devour the living,
   'I shall make the dead outnumber the living!'"

Up went Namtar the long staircase of heaven.
When he reached the gate of Anu, Enlil, and Ea,
[An]u, Enlil, and Ea saw him,   (15')
"[Wh]y are you come, Namtar?"
"Your [daught]er sent me,
"Saying,

   'Since I was a young girl,
   'I have not known the play of maidens,
   'Nor have I known the frolic of little girls.   (20')
   'That god whom you sent,
       he has had intercourse with me,
       so let him lie with me.
   'Send me that god that he be my husband
      and spend the night with me.

'Am I defiled, impure?
'Can I not render judgments for the great gods,
      the great gods who reside in the netherworld?
'If you do [not] send that god,   (25′)
<'According to the authority of the lower regions
      and the great netherworld,>
'I shall raise up the [dead to devour] the living,
'I shall make the dead [outnum]ber the living.'"

Ea made ready to speak, [saying to Namtar] (these) words,
"Na[mtar, come into] the cour[t of Anu],
"[   ]."   (30′)
When he came into [the court of An]u,
All the gods kne[lt humbly   ],
[The god]s of the land k[nelt   ].
[He went straight to the] first one, but did not see that god,
He went straight [to a second, a thi]rd,
      but did not see that god.   (35′)
Namtar went to speak to his mistress,
"My lady, [in the heaven of] Anu, your father,
      where you sent me,
"My lady, [there was a certain god, b]ald, with a tic, lame,
    [ ], sitting among all the gods."
"Go, seize that god, f[etch] (him) t[o m]e!
"Ea his father has spri[nkled him] with spring water,   (40′)
"So he is bald, has a tic, is lame,
    [is sitting] among all the gods."
Up went Namtar the long staircase of heaven.
When he re[ached] the gate of Anu, Enlil, and Ea,
Anu, Enlil, and Ea saw him,
"Why are you come, Namtar?"
"Your daughter sent [me],   (45′)
"Saying, 'Seize that god, fetch him to m[e].'"
"Namtar, come into the court of Anu,
"Look for him ... and t[ake him]."
He went straight to the first, but did not see [that god],
He went straight to a [second, a thi]rd,
      [but did not see that god],   (50′)

He went straight to [a fourth, a fifth,
    but did not see that god].
[   ] made ready to speak, saying to Ea [   ],
"[Na]mtar the messenger, who has come to [us],
"[Let him dr]ink water, bathe, anoi[nt his body] ..."

(gap)

vi

"Let him not wrest away [ ].	(1′)
"Erra, I shall make you go [ ] upon him [ ]	
"I shall kill you ... [ ].	
"Namtar, [ ] to [ ] your task.	
"Erra [ ]	(5′)

"All the authority of the great netherworld
    shall [I grant to you?].
"When you go from here,
"[You] shall c[arry] the throne there.[1]
"[You shall car]ry [   ]
"[You shall carr]y [   ]   (10′)
"You shall [carr]y [   ]
"You shall [carr]y [   ]
"You sh[all c]arry [   ]
"[   ]
"[   ] your chest."   (15′)
[Nergal] took the word of [Ea] to heart,
He [   ] and readied his bow.
[Down went Ne]rgal the long stair[case of he]aven(?).
When he re[ache]d the gate of Eresh[kigal],
"Gatekeeper, op[en] the gate [to me]!"   (20′)
The gatekeeper hung up his [ ] at the gate,
    and would not allow him to ...
The second one of the g[ate] hung up his [ ],
    and would not allow him to ...
The third one [of the gate hung up his ...],
    and would not allow him to ...

---

1. See above, I ii 24′–35′.

The fourth one [of the gate hung up his ...],
    and would not allow him to ...
The fif[th one of the gate hung up his ...],
    and would not allow him to ...   (25')
[The sixth one of the gate hung up] his [...],
    [and would not allow him to ...].
[The seventh one of the gate hung up his ...],
    [and would not allow him to ...].
He en[ter]ed her broad court,
Approached her and burst out laughing.
He seized her by her coiffure,   (30')
He [pulled] her from [the throne],
He seized her by her locks,
[   ] his arousal(?).
They embraced one another,
Passionately they went to bed.   (35')
One day, a second day they lay,
    Queen Eresh[kigal and Er]ra,
A third day they lay, Queen Ereshkigal and Erra,
A fourth day they lay, Queen Ereshkigal and Erra,
A fifth day they lay, Queen Ereshkigal and Erra,
[A sixth day they lay, Queen Ereshkigal and Erra],   (40')
[A seventh day they lay, Queen Ereshkigal and Erra].
[Anu made ready to speak], saying
[To Kakka his messenger] these words,
"[Kakka, I sh]all send you [to the Land of No Return],
"[To the house of Ereshkiga]l, who dwells in
    the netherworld,   (45')
"[Saying,

    'That god] whom I sent to you,
    '[Let him dwell with you] forever.
    '[   ] upper regions,
    '[   ] lower regions,

        (breaks off about twelve lines from the end)

Text: A = C. Bezold, E. W. Budge, *The Tell el-Amarna Tablets in the British Museum* (London, 1892), 82 (+) B = Schroeder, VAS 12 195, see Izre'el, *Amarna Scholarly Tablets*, pl. xxiii–xxx; C = Gurney, STT 28, 113–114; D = Hunger, SBTU I 1.

Edition: J. Knudtzon, *Die El-Amarna Tafeln*, VAB 2 (Leipzig, 1915) 357 (A+B); Gurney, AnSt 10 (1960), 105–131 (C); Hunger, SBTU I, 17–19 (D); S. Izre'el in A. F. Rainey, ed., *Kinattūtu ša darāti, Raphael Kutscher Memorial Volume* (Tel Aviv, 1993), 58–67 (with new readings for A+B); C. Saporetti, *Nergal ed Ereškigal, una storia d'amore e di morte* (Pisa, 1995, not accessible to me); (A+B) re-edited by Izre'el, *Amarna Scholarly Tablets*, 51–61 (with collations); Kämmerer, AOAT 251 (1998), 168–171 (A+B); all sources re-edited with commentary by G. Pettinato, *Nergal ed Ereškigal, il poema assiro-babilonese degli inferi, Atti della Accademia Nazionale dei Lincei* 379 (2000), Classe di Scienze Morali, Storiche e Filologiche, Memorie serie IX vol. XIII/1.

Translation: Speiser-Grayson, ANET[3], 103–104, 507–512; Labat, *Religions*, 98–113; Bottéro, *Mythologie*, 437–464; Dalley, *Myths*, 163–181; Müller, TUAT III/4, 766–780.

Literature: Bottéro, *Annuaire* 1971/2, 97–110; Oppenheim, OrNS 19 (1950), 152; von Weiher, AOAT 11 (1971), 48–54; Reiner, *Poetry*, 50–60; Borger, HKL 1, 239–240; HKL 2, 132; M. Hutter, *Altorientalische Darstellungen der Umwelt. Literar- und religionsgeschichtliche Überlegungen zu "Nergal und Ereškigal,"* Orbis Biblicus et Orientalis 63 (Freiburg, 1985), with translation and literary analysis; C. Saporetti, "Appunti sul poemetto 'Nergal ed Ereškigal'," *Orientis Antiqui Miscellanea* 1 (1994), 25–38 (with presentation of texts "in score'); S. Chiodi, "Nergal, un dio 'doppio'," *Rivista di Studi Fenici* 26 (1998), 3–20; R. Harris, "Gender and Sexuality in the Myth of Nergal and Ereshkigal," in R. Harris, *Gender and Aging in Mesopotamia* (Norman, Ok., 2000), 129–146; N. Walls, *Desire, Discord and Death, Approaches to Ancient Near Eastern Myth* (Atlanta, 2001), 127–182.

*Notes to Text: (A+B 9–10) Pettinato's proposal, *Nergal ed Ereškigal*, 67, that Nergal did not greet Namtar, is not accepted here because the offense was not rising, as stated in lines 26 and 33. His restoration *ú-pa-r[a-am]* at the beginning of line 10 relies on interpretation of a unique Old Assyrian occurrence, so it is not accepted here. (A+B 12) Reading *ik-ru-ú-ru* "set up" (Pettinato's *šumātišu* "la sua reazione" lacks basis). (A+B 43) Izre'el, *Kutscher Memorial Volume*, 64. (A+B 57) Izre'el, *Amarna Scholarly Tablets*, 59.(A+B 86) I build on a suggestion of Jacobsen in *The Encyclopedia of Religion* (New York, 1987), 9:462 ("It was but love you wanted of me from months long ago till now"). Others take *adu kinanna* to be a scribal notation meaning something like "up to this point," "so far" (referring to dictation?); see Moran, *Catholic Biblical Quarterly* 49 (1987), 115. (C, D ii 34′) K. Foster, *Aegean Faience of the Bronze Age* (New Haven, 1979), 21; P. R. S. Moorey, *Materials and Manufacture in Ancient Mesopotamia* (Oxford, 1985), 133–135. (C, D iii 20′) Reading *ṣ[e-li]*. (C, D v 7′–8′) With Edzard, ZA 79 (1989), 126–127.

III.21 THE ADAPA STORY

(a) ADAPA AND THE SOUTH WIND

The story of Adapa reveals the goodwill and malice of the gods toward men. Adapa was the most perfect of mortals, a favorite of Ea's, whose cult he administered with wonderful assiduity. So great was his magical power that when the south wind[1] capsized his boat on an otherwise calm day, he cursed it and incapacitated it. When the absence of the wind was noticed in heaven, Adapa was summoned before Anu to give an account of himself. Ea admonished him to ingratiate himself with the vegetation deities standing at the door of the celestial palace. This he was to do by dressing himself in mourning for their seasonal absence from the land. These gods, amused, would put in a good word for him, and this is what occurred. Ea enjoined Adapa from accepting food or drink in heaven, though he may avail himself of the other offices of hospitality. Anu, after the intercession of the gods at the door, was so impressed that Ea would single out a man for his favor, that he offered him the hospitality fit for a visiting god. When Adapa declined the food and drink, which would have made him a god and released him from Ea's service, Anu was vastly amused by Ea's cleverness and his sage's stupidity, and so sent the swindled mortal back home.

The lessons of this simple text are numerous. Surely one is that if a man so perfect could not obtain immortality, despite his close relationship to a great god, who else could expect to? Even the apparent goodwill of the gods is limited; they will not gratefully manumit men from their service no matter how well performed.

Much has been written about this bitter little tale, including biblical comparisons, and many different constructions have been put on it.[2] Later Mesopotamian scholars incorporated the story into incantations as a means of identifying and localizing the magical powers of Adapa for medicinal ends. Some Assyriologists see in this text an aetiology for the origins of magic, though others will read here a somber Mesopotamian statement on the lot of humankind.

---

1. The south wind was considered especially powerful. According to a Sumerian proverb: "The south wind knocks over the man it hits" (Alster, *Proverbs*, 1:114).

2. For bibliography and discussion, see the works by Izre'el and Picchioni cited below, p. 530, "Literature."

A and A'

(about six lines lost)

Un[derstanding   ]   (1)
His utterance could command, like the utterance [of Anu],⋆
He made him perfect in wisdom,
  revealing (to him) the designs of the land.
To him he granted wisdom,
  eternal life he did not grant him.
In those days, in those years, this sage, the citizen of Eridu,   (5)
Ea made him (his) vicegerent among men.⋆
This sage whose pronouncement no one gainsaid,
Able one, exceedingly wise, he was (servant)
  of the Anunna-gods,
Pure, clean of hands, anointed one
  who was solicitous after divine rites,
He performed the baker's office with the baker,   (10)
He performed the baker's office with the bakers of Eridu,
Every day he (himself) made the food and drink
  for Eridu('s cult).[1]
He prepared the table with his own clean hands,
Nor without him was the table cleared.
He steered the boat,
  he made the daily fish catch for Eridu('s cult).   (15)
At that time Adapa, citizen of Eridu,
At the drawing of the [bo]lt of Ea from its socket(?),⋆
Would each day see to the bar himself.
[At] the sacred quay, the quay of "Heavenly Splendor,"⋆
  he boarded the sailboat.
[Without? a st]eering oar his boat could drift on course,   (20)
[Without? a pu]nting pole he could pilot his boat.[2]
[Into the … ocean, into the] wide sea

---

1. That is, he was so concerned with correct ritual observance that he assumed personally even menial temple duties, such as the baking of sacrificial loaves. An original interpretation of these lines has been offered by Talon, BiOr 40 (1983), 686–687, whereby Ea is the sage who does the baking and so forth, not Adapa, but this is unconvincing.

2. I take these to be signs of magical powers, rather than poor seamanship, differently Talon, BiOr 40 (1984), 687; Izre'el, *Adapa*, 14.

(fragmentary lines, then breaks off)

Fragment B[1]

He ma[de ready to speak, saying to the south wind],   (1)
"O south wind! [   ]
"I have done enough(?), let me [   ]
"[   ], O south wind, [the wi]nds, your brothers,
    as m[any as there be],
"I will fracture your w[in]g!"   (5)
As soon as he said it,
The south wind's wing was fractured.
The s[outh wind] not having blown
    for seven days toward the land,
Anu called to his courier Ilabrat,
"Why has the south wind not blown
    for seven days toward the land?"   (10)
His courier Ilabrat answered him,
"My Lord, Adapa, son of Ea,
    has fractured the south wind's wing."
When Anu heard this,
He cried, "(Heaven) help (us)!" He rose from his chair,
"Se[nd word and let] them bring him here."   (15)
Ea, who knows the ways of heaven, touched him,
[   ] made him wear his hair unkempt,[2]
[Had him put on] mourning weeds,
Gave him instructions,
"[Adapa], you are to go [before Anu] the king,   (20)
"[You are to go up to heaven].
"When y[ou go up] to h[eav]en,
"[And draw near to Anu's door],
"[Tammuz and Gizzi]da will be standing at Anu's door.
"When they see you, they will ask you,   (25)

      'Fel[low], for whom are you like this?
      'A[da]pa, why are you in mourning weeds?'

---

1. Fragment C is, for the most part, parallel to B, with minor variants, but because of its condition I omit it here.
2. A sign of mourning.

'Two gods are disappeared from our land,
'That is why I am decked out so.'

'Who are the two gods
          who have disappeared from the land?'   (30)

'They are Tammuz and Gizzida.'

"They will look at each other and laugh and laugh,
"They will say a favorable word to Anu,
"They will help you see Anu's benevolent side.
"When you come before Anu,   (35)
"If they proffer you food of death, do not eat!*
"If they proffer you water of death, do not drink!
"If they proffer you a garment, put it on.
"If they proffer you oil, anoint yourself.
"Do not neglect the instructions I give you,   (40)
"Hold fast to the words that I have spoken."
Anu's messenger reached him,

     'Adapa fractured the wing of the south wind,
     'Send him to me!'

He brought him along the [ro]ad to heaven,   (45)
He went up to heaven.
When he went up to heaven,
And drew near Anu's door,
Tammuz and Gizzida were standing at Anu's door.
When they saw Adapa, they cried, "(Heaven) help (us)!   (50)
"Fellow, for whom are you like this?
"Adapa, why are you dressed in mourning?"

"Two gods have disappeared from the land,
"So I am dressed in mourning."

"Who are the two gods
          who have disappeared from the land?"   (55)

"Tammuz and Gizzida."

They looked at each other and laughed and laughed.
When Adapa made his approach to Anu the king,
Anu saw him and cried,
"Come now, Adapa, why did you fracture
          the wing of the south wind?"   (60)

Adapa answered Anu,
"My lord, I was fishing in the depths of the sea,
"For my master's temple.
"At sea, it was like a mirror,
"Then the south wind blew upon me and capsized me.　　　　(65)
"I spent the rest of the day in (my) lord's house.[1]*
"In my fury, I cursed the [win]d."
There spoke up beside [him Tammuz] and Gizzida,
Saying a favorable word about him to Anu.
His heart grew calm, he became quiet.　　　　(70)
"Why did Ea disclose to a human being
"Something bad of heaven and earth,[2]
"And give him such a stout heart?*
"Since he has so treated him,
"What, for our part, shall we do for him?　　　　(75)
"Bring him food of life, let him eat."
They brought him food of life, he did not eat.
They brought him water of life, he did not drink.
They brought him a garment, he put it on.
They brought him oil, he anointed himself.　　　　(80)
Anu stared and burst out laughing at him,
"Come now, Adapa, why did you not eat or drink?
"Won't you live? Alas for the wretched peoples!"*
"Ea my lord told me,

　　　'You must not eat, you must not drink.'"

"Take him and [ret]urn him to earth."　　　　(85)

(breaks off)

(another version of this episode)

Fragment D

[He ordered bread of life for him, he did not eat],　　　　(1)
He ordered [water of life] for him, he did not drink.
He ordered [oil] for him, he anointed himself,
He ordered a [gar]ment for him, he put it on.

1.　That is, in the depths, the abode of Ea.
2.　That is, allowed him sufficient harmful magical power to disable the wind.

Anu laughed uproariously at what Ea had done, (5)
"Who else, of all the gods of heaven and netherworld,
    could d[o] something like this?
"Who else could make his command outweigh Anu's?"[1]
Adapa [surveyed] from the horizon to the heights of heaven,
He saw the awesomeness of [   ].
[At that ti]me Anu imposed on Adapa an observance, (10)
[   ] ... Ea released him.
[An]u ordained that he be distinguished
    for his leadership for all time.[2]

*(follows fragments of an incantation invoking Adapa's powers
against diseases caused by the south wind.)*

Text: A = Clay, BRM 4 3 = Picchioni, *Poemetto*, Fig. 1 = Izre'el, *Adapa*, pl. 1, 2; A′ = Schramm, OrNS 43 (1974), 162 = Izre'el, *Adapa*, p. 2; B = Schroeder, VAS 12 194 = Picchioni, *Poemetto*, Figs. 2, 3 = Izre'el, *Adapa*, pl. 3–6; C (K 8743) = Langdon, PBS 10/1 3 = Picchioni, *Poemetto*, Fig. 4= Izre'el, *Adapa*, pl. 8; D (K 8214) = Strong, PSBA 16 (1894), 274–275 = Furlani, *Rendiconti della Accademia Nazionale dei Lincei, Classe di Scienze Morali* 5 (1929), 132 = Picchioni, *Poemetto*, Fig. 5 = Izre'el, *Adapa*, pl. 8.

Edition: S. A. Picchioni, *Il Poemetto di Adapa* (Budapest, 1981); T. Kämmerer, AOAT 251 (1998), 254–259; S. Izre'el, *Adapa and the South Wind, Language Has the Power of Life and Death* (Winona Lake, Ind., 2001), from which I have adopted various readings.

Translation: Speiser, ANET[3], 101–103; Dalley, *Myths,* 182–187; Hecker, TUAT *Ergänzungslieferung,* 51–55.

Literature: See Picchioni, *Poemetto*, with bibliography, 14–23; P. Michalowski, "Adapa and the Ritual Process," RO 41 (1980), 77–82; M. Liverani, "Adapa ospite degli dei," *Religioni e Civiltà* (Bari, 1982), 293–319; H.-P. Mueller, "Mythus als Gattung archaischen Erzählens und die Geschichte von Adapa," AfO 29/30 (1983/4), 75–89; M. Dietrich, AOAT 42 (1993), 42–48 and S. Izre'el, in M. E. Vogelzang and H. L. J. Vanstiphout, eds., *Mesopotamian Epic Literature, Oral or Aural?* (Lewiston, N.Y., 1992), 173–188, have discussed B in detail.

★Notes to Text: (6) Translation uncertain; see Picchioni, *Poemetto*, 127, with collation by Lambert; Izre'el, *Adapa*, 12. (17) For the various proposals for this difficult line, see Picchioni, *Poemetto*, 119. I follow Lambert's suggestion, quoted there: [giš]-*ru* ᵈÉ-a. Note the new proposal of CAD M, 118a: [MAŠ.S]UD = "When [the w]ise Ea lies in his bed." This is epigraphically difficult. See further Izre'el, *Adapa*, 13–14, who suggests "Ea lying, lingering in bed." (19) For the problem with this name, see Picchioni, *Poemetto*, 130, whose reading I adopt. (B 36–39) With Edzard, OrNS 71 (2002), 415–416. (B 66) Izre'el, *Adapa*, 27. (B 73) Compare Poem of the Righteous Sufferer (III.14), Tablet I, line 73; differently Streck, AOAT 264 (1999), 124: "tiefes Wissen." (B 83) Izre'el, *Adapa*, 32.

1. That is, by thwarting Anu's good intentions to give Adapa eternal life.
2. That is, he could not live forever, but would be famous forever.

(b) ADAPA AND ENMERKAR

This composition deals with the sage Adapa and Enmerkar, an early Sumerian king well known from Sumerian epic poems.[1] Sages and famous kings of the past were paired in other Mesopotamian texts,[2] while Enmerkar is also referred to in the Cuthaean Legend of Naram-Sin (III.7b(3)). Little of this text can be understood, owing to the broken condition of the manuscripts. The composition opens with Adapa apparently lamenting someone's death. Although the gods hear his lament, they do nothing to help him. Enmerkar, king of Uruk, becomes interested in the matter. An ancient tomb, deep in the earth, is excavated. They break into it but cannot see at first. Adapa does something rash, at which point the text breaks off. When the text becomes coherent again, Adapa engages the services of a smith to refit(?) the coffin they had broken into.

The moral of the story may have lain in Adapa's desire to see someone long dead. When he attains his wish, he is horrified at the sight, so makes sure to reseal the tomb forever. This text should perhaps take its place among those Mesopotamian compositions concerned with death and immortal life.

```
[                              ]                    (1)
He sets his [                  ]
Adap[a                         ]
... [                          ]
He wailed to the lord, to [    ]                    (5)
[When ... ] heard [his] w[ail],
[He said] this [              ],
"[         that] he has seized,
"This clamor [          ] how good."
At the speech of [    ] he wailed,                  (10)
And the great gods [   ] his second 'hand',[3]
[                ] to him.
His second 'hand' [              ]
[    reached] the [gate?] of Anu, Enlil, [and Ea],
[          ] the [ ] of the great lord Marduk.      (15)
Adapa [                              ]
```

1. See p. 348 note 3.
2. Hallo, JCS 23 (1970), 62.
3. Unclear.

Enmerkar [exercised] king[ship] in Uruk.
When [he had   ] all the land of Akkad,
[He   ] his reign until the gods [   ].
Adapa [went down] nine cubits in the depths,   (20)
Enmerkar [   ] for the sake of [   ] of Adapa.
They lifted [   ] before [   ],
Enmerkar [   ] in order not to [   ].
An ancient corpse from remotest times [   ].
He made a terrible clamor in the palace(?) [   ].   (25)
They went down nine cubits [in the depths],
[Nine] cubits of earth they went down [   ].
He destroyed the door of the tomb
    [with]out(?) seeing the [corp]se.
Adapa [said to Enmerkar   ],

(two lines lost)

Adapa did not answer, but [   ]   (32)

(rev.)

They buried [   ] minas of copper inside [   ],
The blacksmith who [ ] and(?) set up(?) [the do]or above,
[   ] and who fastened its latch(?) to the frame(?),
As [   ] Adapa was passing through the street,
He saw the blacksmith and said to him,   (5)
"[and?] is your latch(?) securely on the frame(?)?"

(fragmentary lines, then breaks off)

Text: W. G. Lambert, AfO 17 (1954/6), 321; Lambert *apud* Picchioni, *Poemetto*, Fig. 6, 7; Campbell
    Thompson, GETh pl. 14 (K 9220); Hunger, SBTU I 4.
Edition: Picchioni, *Poemetto*, 102–109.
Literature: J.-J. Glassner, *Chroniques mésopotamiennes* (Paris, 1993), 231.

III.22 ETANA

The legend of Etana enjoyed particular popularity in Mesopotamian tradition. The manuscripts date to the Classical and Mature periods, and there is a diverse group of fragmentary manuscripts from Assurbanipal's library. These three principal versions are translated separately below as OV, MV, and LV respectively.

What now remains of the story may be outlined as follows. The gods build a city for the human race, the lesser gods doing the work, the greater gods making the plans. When the city is completed and surrounded with defenses, a king is needed. Ishtar looks over all the cult cities in the realm for a suitable candidate. This turns out to be Etana. Kingship is created, with Enlil's approval, and Etana is made the first king. Etana builds a temple for Adad, and a poplar tree grows there. A serpent takes up residence in the roots of the tree, an eagle in its crown. The two creatures swear an oath of friendship to each other. They produce their young and share the task of feeding them. As his children grow up, the eagle conspires to devour the serpent's children. One of his own children attempts vainly to dissuade him, a reversal of the usual wisdom motif whereby an elder advises a youngster. The eagle devours his friend's children. When the serpent returns and discovers his children gone, he calls upon Shamash, lord of the oath, to witness the eagle's perfidy. Shamash hears his plaint and arranges for a wild ox to die. He enjoins the serpent to hide in the belly of the cadaver to seize the eagle when he comes to feed. He can then pluck his feathers and throw him into a pit to die of hunger and thirst. The ruse is successful, despite the warnings of the eagle's youngster, for the greedy eagle plunges into the carcass to feed and is captured by the vengeful serpent. The eagle's pleas for mercy are rejected, first by the serpent and second by Shamash. He is left to languish in a pit. Shamash is moved by his continued pleas, but, since the eagle violated an oath, the god cannot rescue him himself. He decides upon an agent, whom he advises the eagle to expect.

Meantime, Etana, the king, has been praying to Shamash for an heir. All of his efforts to produce one have proved unsuccessful, so his last hope is to find a certain plant of birth. Shamash tells Etana of the eagle's plight, and advises him to save the eagle in return for the bird's assistance in finding the plant of birth. Etana sets forth and approaches the pit.

The Old and Middle versions explain how Etana got the eagle out of the pit, but this episode appears to be omitted from the Late version. In the Late version, the eagle first looks for the plant of birth in a remote mountain, but cannot find it. The eagle then tells Etana that they must go to Ishtar, goddess of procreation, to obtain it. Etana holds onto the eagle and they fly toward heaven. As they mount higher and higher, Etana's courage fails him, so they return to earth without the plant. After a gap in the text, Etana is telling the eagle of a dream (multiple dreams in the Middle version), in which he goes up to heaven, passes through its portals, enters a building, and sees a goddess seated on aggressive lions. The eagle encourages him to try another ascent to heaven. This time they reach it, pass through the portals, and enter the building. At this point the text breaks off. A small fragment (III/C) suggests that Etana did somehow get the plant and took it home to his wife.

The table below summarizes the episodes as preserved in the different versions.

	OV	MV	LV
Creation of the world, institution of kingship	I/A		I/A
Serpent and eagle next in tree near temple Etana builds			II, 1–34
Serpent and eagle swear oath of friendship, produce young, and hunt together	I/C	I/A	
Eagle eats serpent's young, serpent curses eagle	I/C		II, 35–71
Eagle is trapped and thrown into pit	I/D	I/B	II, 72–130
Etana prays for plant of birth, Shamash sends him to eagle		I/C	II, 131–150
Etana and eagle converse		I/D	III/A, 1–19
Etana rescues eagle	I/E	I/E	
Eagle tries to find plant			III/A, 20–22
First trip to heaven			III/A, 23–52
Etana's dream(s)		I/G	III/B, 100–113
Second trip to heaven			III/B, 114–144
Etana returns home			III/C

The earlier versions have interesting variations that show how both the motivation and details of the story were reinterpreted in the millennium that lies between the earliest and the latest versions. Note for example LV's expansion of the episode of the dialogue between Etana and the eagle in the pit, and how the eagle's impulsive offer of any favor in OV is made in LV into a demand by Etana. Compare also the expansion of the hunting episode in LV. In OV only the serpent is portrayed as hunting, and the eagle feeds on his success, whereas in the later version the force of analogy expands the whole passage and robs it

of some of the contrast the earlier shows between the behavior of the two creatures. Such comparisons illustrate the levelling-off and expansion so characteristic of the development of Akkadian literature.

(a) OLD BABYLONIAN VERSION (OV)

I/A

The great Anunna-gods, ordainers of destiny,	(1)
Sat taking counsel with respect to the land.★	
Those creators of the world regions,	
establishers of all physical form,	
Those sublime for the people, the Igigi-gods,	
Ordained the festival(?)[1] for the people.	(5)
Among all the teeming peoples they[2] had established no king,	
Then no headdress had been assembled, nor crown,	
Nor yet scepter had been set with lapis,	
No throne daises at all had been constructed,	
Full seven gates were bolted against the hero.[3]	(10)
Scepter, crown, headdress, and staff	
Were set before Anu in heaven.	
There was no right counsel for their(?) people:	
(Then) [ ] came down from heaven.[4]	

(fragmentary lines, then gap)
(After a gap, the serpent and eagle are making friends.)

---

1. Langdon, Speiser, and other translators have taken this to refer to a "fixed time," that is, mortality, but there is no philological basis for such an interpretation. If the Akkadian word used here really means "festival," the older version would still refer not to death but rather to a holiday. The line remains obscure; perhaps "lineage" or "genealogy" is meant. Or, perhaps it means that religious observance was established first, then kingship was provided (Haul, *Etana-Epos*, 7); compare III.18c, 3'.

2. Presumably the gods are meant.

3. This line expresses the absence of opportunity for the superior mortal (W. G. Lambert, JCS 32 [1980], 81–85). In the later version, the line is interpreted differently to imply that the lesser gods shut the gates at night, a task that was to be the king's.

4. Usually restored "[king]ship," though Wilcke (ZA 67 [1977], 157), suggests that Ishtar is coming down from heaven in search of a king (see LV Tablet I line 20).

I/C

"May the path vanish from him, may he not find the way,   (1)
"May the mountain hold back its pass from him,
"May the oncoming weapon make straight for him!"
(This was) the oath they swore to each other.
Both conceived, both bore.   (5)
In the shade of the poplar the serpent gave birth,
The eagle gave birth above it.[1]
When the serpent hunted down a wild ox or a wild sheep,
The eagle ate, his children ate.
When the serpent hunted down a panther or a tiger(?),   (10)
The eagle ate, [his] children ate.
After his children had grown big and [flourished],

...

The eagle [plotted evil] in his heart.
"My children [have grown big and flourished],   (15)
"They are gone forth to seek [their own food?],
"To seek ...
"I shall eat the serpent's children,
"I will go up to [heaven],
"I will dwell [there and come down to the top of the tree]   (20)
"Who is there that [   ]?"
The [littlest] fledgling, [exceedingly wise],
[Said] to the ea[gle, his father],
"My father, [do not   ]

(gap)

At dawn [the serpent went out to hunt?],
At nightfall [he returned?].   (30)
The serpent approached [his nest?],
The meat [he was carrying   ],
The serpent cast down before [his nest].
He looked, [his children] were gone!
[The eagle had gouged] the ground [below] with his talons,
[Above, its cloud of dust darkened] the sky.   (35)
[The serpent] set to weeping, sick (at heart),

---

1. Wordplay on "above" (ṣēru) and "serpent" (ṣēru).

[Before Shamash?] his tea[rs] were flowing down,
"I put my trust in you, O warrior Shamash!
"I was the one who gave good will(?) to the eagle,   (40)
"I respected and honored you!
"I harbored no evil against my friend!
"As for him, his nest is safe, but [my] nest is scattered,
"The serpent's nest is turned into a moan of grief.
"His fledglings are safe, my children are gone!
"He came down and ate up my brood,   (45)
"You know, O Shamash, the evil he did!
"Your net is the wi[de] meadow,
"Your trap [is the distant heaven]:
"May the eagle not [escape] from your net,
"Th(at) perpetrator of ev[il and ab]omination,   (50)
"Who harbored e[vi]l against his friend!"

(After a gap, the serpent imprisons the eagle in a pit.)

I/D

The serpent [made ready to speak, saying to the eagle],
"Were I [to set you free   ]
"Your punishment [would come upon me   ]."
He ... [   ]
He plucked out (his feathers) [and cast him into a pit],
A place of dea[th by starvation and thirst].
The eagle ... [   ]   (10')
  ... [   ]
Daily [the eagle entreated Shamash, saying],
"O Shamash, ta[ke] my hand [   ]
"[   ] me!"
Shamash m[ade] ready to speak, [saying to the eagle],   (15')
"[   ] wicked deeds(?),
"[You have committed] an abomination of the g[ods ...]

I/E

He took him by the hand in (his) se[venth month (in the pit)],   (1')

In the eighth month he brought him over (the edge) of his pit.[1]
As the eagle took food like a ravening lion,
He gained strength.★
The eagle made ready to speak and said to Etana,   (5′)
"My friend! Let us be friends, you and I!
"Ask of me whatever you desire and I shall give it to you."
Etana made ready to speak and said to the eagle,
"My eyes …, open up what is hidden."

(breaks off)

(b) MIDDLE ASSYRIAN VERSION (MV)

I/A

(The oath of friendship is sworn and betrayed.)

"May [the oath of Shamash] overcome him,   (1)
"[May the mesh of Shamash's oath] ensnare him,
"[May the mountains] turn their [passes] away from him,
"May the oncoming [weapo]n make straight for him,★
"May Shamash single him out for the slaughterer,★   (5)
"May Shamash deliver the offender to the executioner,
"May he station a malignant demon over him!"

At the top of the tree the eagle gave birth,
At the root of the poplar the serpent gave birth.
In the shade of that poplar,   (10)
Eagle and serpent became friends with each other.
They swore the oath together and became comrades.
They told each other their innermost desires.

The serpent would go out to hunt,   (★15)
Wild sheep(?) and aurochs(?) of the steppe(?)★
        the serpent would hunt down.

---

1. Numerical parallelism, meaning that the eagle has been a long time in the pit, not that it took a month to get him out. The lines could also mean that Shamash held the eagle's hand for seven full months and brought him out in the eighth (Haul, *Etana-Epos*, 130).

The eagle would eat, turn away, his children would eat.
[Bu]ck, gazelle of the steppe the serpent would hunt down,   (*20)
[The ea]gle would eat, turn away, his children would eat.

[Beasts of?] the steppe, animals of the earth,
      the serpent would hunt down,
[The eagle] would eat, turn away, his children would eat.
[After the] eagle's [children]
[Had grown big] and flourished,   (*25)
Had acquired [   ] ... [   ],
[The eagle set his thoughts]
[Upon eating his friend's young].

(gap)

I/B

(The eagle is trapped by the serpent and denounced.)

They were hungry ... [   ],   (1)
They gathered [   ]
The littlest fledgling, exceedingly [wise],
[Said these words] to the eagle, his father,
"Do not go down!
      No doubt [the serpent is lurking in the wild ox]!   (5)
"The netherworld will h[old you fast]!
"[It is] the [serpent's] counterplot,[1]
"[His] wings are stretched out [to seize you],
"The netherworld [will hold you fast]!"

[The eagle] did not ag[ree   ]   (10)
Nor did he [listen to his sons' words].
He went down and [lit on the wild ox],
With ... [the birds?]

A first time [inspecting in front and behind it],
The eagle lo[oked at the meat].   (*15)

---

1. Kinnier Wilson suggests that the little one has seen the serpent's traces going to the wild ox, but not his "return" (here: "counterplot"). The passage is uncertain.

A second time [inspecting in front and behind it],
The eagle loo[ked at the meat].
A third time [inspecting in front and behind it],
The eagle lo[oked at the meat].   (*20)
He plunged(?) into the inna[rds of the wild ox],
In search of the juiciest meat,
[He was working forward] into the belly of the w[ild ox].
[As he entered] into its vitals,
The serpent seized him [by his wings]!   (*25)

He brought him out and [   ]
"[You were] the intruder [   ]!
"Before Shamash [   ]
"May the king of the g[ods ...] be great!
"[May the] judge of [my] case [   ]   (*30)
"[   ] who binds fast [   ]
"You are the one, eagle, [   ]
"You flew down [   ]

(gap)

I/C

(Etana prays to Shamash for an heir.)

"[   ], open what is hidden."
"Take away (my) disgrace,* give me an heir!"

Etana [l]ay down* to see (a dream),
He had a dream [in] bed at night.   (*5)
"... go on the road, cross the highlands.
"As you traverse the [mou]ntains,
"[Loo]k for a pit, approach near to it.   (*10)
"An eagle is cast inside it,
"He will give you the plant of birth."

I/D

The eagle looked at him ...,
He said [   ] to Etana,
"You are Etana, king of the wild beasts,

"You are Etana, [   ] among(?) birds.   (*10)
"Bring [me] up from [thi]s [pi]t,
"Give me [   ] your hand,
"... [   ]
"I will si[ng] your [pra]ises for all time."

Etana [said] to the eagle (these) wor[ds],   (*15)
"(If) I save your life, [   ]
"(If) I br[ing you up fr]om the pit,
"[From th]at moment we [must be ...]."

(gap)

I/E

"[   ] to me ... [   ]   (1)
"From sunrise till [   ]
"From his rising, where [   ]
"... [   ]
"I will give you the [plant] of life."   (5)

When Etana h[eard] this,
He filled the front of the pit with [   ].[1]
Next(?) he threw in ... [   ].
He kept throwing in [   ] in front of(?) him,[2]
The eagle ... from the pit.   (10)
As for him, he flapped [his wings].
[A first time and a second time ... the eagle ...] in(?) the pit,
As for him, he flapped [his] w[ings   ]
[A third time] and a fourth time ... [the eagle ... in? the pi]t,   (15)
As for him, he flapped [his wings   ]
[A fifth and a sixth time   ] ...

(fragmentary lines, then gap)

---

1.   Ebeling (AfO 14 [1941], 307) restores *pu[qulta]* "thorn bushes"; Kinnier Wilson restores *bu[rāšu]* "juniper."

2.   As understood here, Etana keeps tossing bushes into the pit for the eagle to scramble up on. The second dream in the MA version I/G *15 is perhaps based on this. Kinnier Wilson has Etana constructing a ladder of juniper-wood (63 and 74–75).

I/G

(Etana relates dreams to the eagle, who interprets them as propitious.)

"[   ] above
"[   ] at my feet."

[The eagle made Etana] understand [the dream],
[   ] seated before him,   (*5)
"[   ] your [dream] is propitious,
"[   ] burden[1] is brought,
"They will give [   ]
"You have done [   ] of the people
"You will seize ... in your hand,   (*10)
"The sacred bond[2] [   ] above
"[   ] at your feet."

Etana said to him, to the eagle,
"My friend, [I saw] a second dream,   (*15)
"[   ] reeds [   ] in the house,
"In all [   ], the whole land,
"They heaped up loads (of them) in piles.
"[   ] enemies, they were wicked serpents,   (*20)
"[   ] were coming before me,
"[   ] they were kneeling before me."

[The eagle made Etana] understand [the dream].
[   ] seated before him,
"[   ] your [dream] is propitious,

(gap)

---

1. Here and in the next dream "weight" (*biltu*) and "tribute" (*biltu*) are used with a play on the words. Etana's ascent is no doubt referred to, his weight being borne by the eagle. In the second dream there is a wordplay on *biltu* "weight" and *elpetu* "reed," but the whole passage is too fragmentary to be understood.
2. A cosmic feature, being the linkage of heaven and earth.

I/H

[Etana said to him, to the eagle],
"[The lan]d is a hi[ll],
"[And the se]a has turned into a brook(?).

He bore [him] up a [thi]rd league,
[The eagle said to] him, [to E]tana,   (5)
"[Look], my friend, how the land [is now],
"[Examine] the sea, [look for] its features."

[Etana] said to [him, to] the eagle,
"[The land] is set out (as if) for an orchard,
"[And the sea] has turned into an irrigation ditch."

(fragmentary lines, then gap)

(c) LATE VERSION (LV)

Tablet I

I/A

They planned the city [   ],[1]   (1)
[The gods? laid its foundations],
[They planned the city? Kish?],
[The Anunna-gods?] laid its foundations.
The Igigi-gods founded its brickwork* [   ]   (*5)
"Let [a man]* be their (the people's) shepherd,
"Let Etana be their master builder ...
The great Anunna-gods, or[dainers of destinies],[2]
[Sa]t taking their counsel [concerning the land],
The creators of the four world regions,
        [establishers of all physical form],   (10)
By(?) command of all of them the Igigi-gods
        [ordained the festi]val f[or the people],
No [king] had they established [over the teeming peoples].
At that time [no headdress had been assembled, nor crown],
Nor yet scepter [had been set] with lapis,   (15)
No throne daises(?)[3] whatsoever [had been constructed].
The seven gods barred the [gates] against the multitude,
Against the inhabited world they barred [the gates ...],
The Igigi-gods surrounded the city [with ramparts?].[4]
Ishtar [came down from heaven? to seek] a shepherd,   (20)
And sought for a king [everywhere].
Innina [came down from heaven? to seek] a shepherd,
And sought for a king e[verywhere].
Enlil examined the dais of(?) Etana,
The man whom Ishtar st[eadfastly   ]   (25)
"She has constantly sought ...

---

1. This passage has been discussed by Sauren, CRRAI 19 (1971), 460–461; Haul, *Etana-Epos*, 7–8.
2. Old Babylonian version begins here, suggesting that the first seven lines of the Late version were added as a prologue.
3. Text: "world regions," presumably a mistake; compare OV I/A 9.
4. See above, p. 535 note 3.

"[Let] king[ship] be established in the land,
    let the heart of Kish [be joyful]."
Kingship, the radiant crown, throne, [   ]
He(?) brought and [   ]
The gods of the land[s   ]

(gap)

His wife [said] to him, [to Etana],
"[   ] made me have a dream.
"Like Etana ... [   ]   (60)
"Like you ... [   ]
"Etana the king [   ]
"His ghost to [   ]

(gap)

Tablet II

[   ] that he called [   ]   (1)
[   ] he had built a tower(?) [   ]
[   ] shrine for Adad, his god [   ]
In the shade of that shrine a po[plar] was growing [   ],
In its crown an eagle settled,   (5)
A serpent ... at its root.
Daily they wa[tched the wild beasts].*
[The eagl]e made ready to speak, [saying to the serpent],
"[Co]me, [let us make] friend[ship],
"Let us be comrades, [you] and I."
[The serpent] made ready to speak, [saying to the eagle],   (10)
"[Shamash] is the one who [   ] friendship.
"[If you are wicked, you will do a deed abhorrent] to him,
"[You will commit] an abomination of the gods,
    [a forbidden act].
"Come then, let us set forth [and go up a high mountain],
"Let us swear [an oath] by the netherworld."   (15)
Before Shamash the warrior they swo[re] the oath,
"Whoever [transgresses] the limits of Shamash [   ],

"May Shamash [deliver him] as an offender
        into the hands of the executioner,
"Whoever [transgresses] the limits of Shamash,
"May the [mountains] remove
        [their pas]ses far away from him,   (20)
"May the oncoming weapon [make straight for him],
"May the trap and curse of Shamash overthrow him
        [and hunt him down]!"
After they had sworn the oath by the netherworld,
They set forth, going up the high mountains,
Each day by turns watching for [the wild beasts].   (25)
The eagle would hunt down wild oxen and asses,
The serpent would eat, turn away, then his children would eat.
The serpent would hunt down buck and gazelle,
The eagle would eat, turn away, then [his] children would eat.
The eagle would hunt down wild sheep and aurochs,   (30)
The serpent would eat, turn away, then his children would eat.
The serpent would hunt down b[easts of the field,
        crea]tures of the earth,*
[The eagle would eat, turn aw]ay, then his children would eat.
... [   ] the food,
The eagle's children grew big and flourished.   (35)
After the eagle's children were grown big and were flourishing,
The eagle's heart indeed plotted evil,
Evil his heart plotted indeed!
He set his thoughts upon eating his friend's young!
The eagle made ready to speak, saying to [his children],   (40)
"I will eat the serpent's children,
"The serpent [   ]
"I will go up and d[well] in heaven,
"I will come down to the crown of the tree and eat fruit."
The littlest fledgling, exceedingly wise,
        [said] these words to the eagle, his father,   (45)
"Do not eat, my father!
        The net of Shamash will hu[nt you] down,
"The mesh and oath of Shamash
        will overthrow you and hunt you down.
"Whoever transgresses the limits of Shamash,

Shamash [will deliver] him as an offender
    into the hands of the [executioner]!"
He did not heed them nor listen to [his sons' words],   (50)
He went down and ate the serpent's [children].
In the evening of the same day(?),*
The serpent ca[me], bearing his burden,
At the entrance to his nest [he cast down the meat].
[He loo]ked around, his nest was gone!
He looked down, [his children were] not [   ]!   (55)
[The eagle had gouged] the ground with his talon,
The cloud of dust from the nest [darkened] the sky.
The serpent collapsed, weeping before Shamash,
[Before] Shamash [the warrior his tears ran down],   (60)
"I trusted in you, [O warrior Shamash],
"I [was the one who gave provisions?] to the eagle,
"Now my nest [   ]!
"My nest is gone, [while his] ne[st is safe],
"My young are destroyed, [while his young are] sa[fe].   (65)
"He came down and ate [my children]!
"[You know], O Shamash, the evil he has done me,
"Truly, O Shamash, your net is the [wide] earth,
"Your trap is the [distant] heaven.
"[The eagle] must not es[cape] from your net,   (70)
"Th(at) malignant Anzu,
    who harbored evil [against his friend]!"
[When he had heard] the serpent's lament,
Shamash made ready to speak, [and said] to [him],
"Go (your) way and cros[s the mountains],
"[I?] have captured for you a wi[ld ox].   (75)
"Open its insides, [rend its belly],
"Set an ambush [in its belly],
"[Every kind of] bird of heaven
    [will come down to eat the meat].
"The eagle [will come down] with them [to eat the meat].
"[As] he will not know [the evil in store for him],   (80)
"He will sea[rch for] the juiciest meat [   ],
    he will walk about outside(?),
"He will work his way* into the covering of the intestines.

"When he comes inside, seize him by his wing,
"Cut off his wings, his pinions, and tail feathers,
"Pluck him and cast him into a bottomless(?) pit,   (85)
"Let him die there of hunger and thirst."
As Shamash the warrior commanded,
The serpent went and crossed the mountain.
Then did the serpent reach the wild ox,
He opened its insides, he rent its belly.   (90)
He set an ambush in its belly.
Every kind of bird of heaven came down to eat the meat.
Did the [ea]gle know the evil in store for him?
He would not eat the meat [with] the other birds!
[The eagle] made ready to speak, saying to his children,   (95)
"[Co]me, let us go down
        and we too eat the meat of this wild ox."
The little [fled]gling, exceedingly wise,
        said [these] words to the eagle [his father],
"Do not go down, father,
        no doubt the serpent is lurking inside the wild ox."
The eagle said to himself,
"Are the birds [afraid]?
        How is it they eat the meat [in peace]?"   (100)
He did not listen to them,
        he did not listen to his sons' words,
He went down and perched on the wild ox.
The eagle looked at the meat,
        searching in front and behind it.   (105)
A second time he looked at the meat,
        searching in front and behind it,
He walked around outside(?),
        he worked his way into the covering of the intestines.
When he came inside, the serpent seized him by his wings,
"You intruded into my precious nest,
        you intruded into my precious nest!*   (110)
The eagle made ready to speak, saying to the serpent,
"Have mercy on me!
        I will make you such a gift as a king's ransom!"[1]

---

1. Literally: "I will give you a wedding present."

The serpent made ready to speak, saying to the eagle,
"If I release you, how shall I answer to Shamash on high?
"Your punishment would turn upon me, (115)
"Me, the one to lay punishment upon you!"
He cut off his wings, pinions, and tail feathers,
[He pluc]ked him and ca[st him into] a p[it],
That he should die [there] of hunger [and thirst].
[As for him, the eagle], ... [   ] (120)
He kept on beseeching Shamash day after day,
"Am I to die in a pit?
Who would know how your punishment
          was imposed upon me?[1]
"Save my life, me, the eagle!
"Let me cause your name to be heard for all time." (125)
Shamash made ready to speak and said to the eagle,
"You are wicked and have done a deed abhorrent to me,
"You committed an abomination of the gods, a forbidden act.
"Were you (not) under oath? I will not come near you.
"There, there! A man I will send you will help you." (130)
Etana kept on beseeching Shamash day after day,
"O Shamash, you have dined from my fattest sheep!
"O Netherworld, you have drunk of the blood
          of my (sacrificed) lambs!
"I have honored the gods and revered the spirits,
"Dream interpreters have used up my incense,
"Gods have used up my lambs in slaughter. (135)
"O lord, give the command!
"Grant me the plant of birth!
"Reveal to me the plant of birth!
"Relieve me of my disgrace,[2] grant me an heir!" (140)
Shamash made ready to speak and sa[id] to Etana,
"Go (your) way, cross the mountain,
"Find a pit, [look insi]de,
"An eagle is cast within it.
"He will reveal to you the plant [of birth]." (145)

---

1. That is, there is no exemplary value in his solitary death; compare the passage in the penitential hymn III.29 lines 66–69.
2. Or: "burden." See p. 542 note 1.

According to the command of the warrior Shamash,
Etana went (his) way, [he crossed the mountains].
He found the pit, he looked inside,
[The eagle was cast] with[in it].
There he was for him to bring up!   (150)

Tablet III

III/A

The eagle made ready to speak, [saying to Shamash his lord],   (1)
"[My lord,   ],
"[him] the speech of birds,
"[So that whatever he will say, I will understand],
"[So that whatever I will say, he will understand].   (5)
"I am [a bird and he is a human being]."
According to the command of Shamash the warr[ior],
[Etana could understand] the speech of birds.
[The eagle made ready to speak, saying to (E)tana],
"[Tell, O tell me why you are come]!"   (10)
[Etana made ready to speak], saying to the [ea]gle,
"[Friend, give me] the plant of birth!
"[Reveal to me] the plant of birth!
"[Relieve me of my disgrace], give me an [he]ir!
"I left behind [   ] the plant of birth!   (15)
"It comes out [where the birds] fly forth,
"Take me there and [   ] me!"
"I alone can [   ] the mountains,
"I will bring you [the plant of birth]."
He went and [   ] the mountains alone,   (20)
The eagle hunted [   ],
[The plant of birth] was not there.
"Come, my friend, [   ],
"[The plant of birth is] with the lady, [   ] Ishtar.
"[We must go] to Ishtar, the lady [   ].   (25)
"Put [your arms] against my sides,
"Put [your hands] against my wing feathers."
He put [his arms] against his sides,

He [put his hands] against his wing feathers.
[When he had borne him aloft] one league,   (30)
"Look, my friend, how the land [is now]!"
"The land's [circumference?] has become one fifth of (its size?).[1]
"The vast sea has become like a paddock."
[When he had borne him aloft] a second league,
"Look, my friend, how the land [is now]!"   (35)
"The land has become a garden plot [   ],
"And the vast sea the size of a trough."
[When he had borne him aloft] a third [league],
"Look, my friend, how the land [is now]!"
"I looked, but could not see the land!   (40)
"Nor were [my eyes] enough to (find) the vast sea!
"My friend, I won't go up to heaven!
"Set me down, let me go off to my city!"
One league he dropped him down(?),
Then the eagle plunged and caught him in his wings.   (45)
A second league he dropped him down(?),
Then the eagle plunged and caught him in his wings.
A third league he dropped him down(?),
Then the eagle plunged and caught him in his wings.
Within three cubits of the earth [he dropped him down].*   (50)
The eagle plunged, and ca[ught him in his wings].
The eagle [   ] Etana's [   ].

(gap)

III/B

(Etana tells the eagle of a dream he had.)[2]

E[tana made ready to speak and said to the eagle],   (100)
"[My] fr[iend], that god let me have a dream.
"[We] passed through the gates of Anu, Enlil, [and] Ea.[3]
"We did obeisance [together], yo[u] and I.
"We passed through the gates of Sin, Shamash, Adad, and Ishtar,

---

1. Very uncertain; some translators suggest that the clamor of earth is very faint here.
2. Note that in the Middle Assyrian version Etana has several, shorter dreams.
3. The major portals of heaven.

"[We did obeisance together], yo[u] and I.   (105)
"I saw a house, I opened [its] seal,[1]
"I pushed the door open and went inside.
"A remarkable [young woman] was seated therein.
"Wearing a tiara, beautiful of [fe]ature.
"A throne was set out, [worthy of?] divinity,   (110)
"Under the throne lions were [c]rou[ching].
"As I went in, the lions [sprang at me?].
"I awoke with a start and shuddered* [   ]."
The eagle [said] to him, to Etana,
"My friend, the [dream] is obvious,   (115)
"Come, let me take you up to heaven [of Anu].
"Put [your chest] against my chest,
"Put [your hands] against my wing feathers,
"Put [your arms] against my sides."
He put [his chest] against his chest,   (120)
He put [his] hands against his wing feathers,
He put [his] hands against his sides,
Great indeed was the burden upon him.
When he bore [him] aloft one league,
The eagle said to him, to Etana,   (125)
"Look, my friend, how the land is now!
"Examine the sea, lo[ok for] its boundaries."
"The land stretches(?) to the mountains,
"The sea has become a stream(?)."
When he had borne [him] aloft a second league,   (130)
The eagle said to him, to Etana,
"Look, my friend, how the land is now!"
"The land is [   ]."
When he had borne him aloft a third league,
The eagle said to him, to Etana,   (135)
"Look, my friend, how the land i[s now]!"
"The sea has become a gardener's ditch."
After they had ascended to the heaven of A[nu],
They passed through the gates of Anu, Enlil, and Ea.
The eagle and E[tana] did obei[sance to]gether.   (140)
[They passed] through the gates of S[in, Adad, and Ishtar],

---

1. See p. 418 note 2.

[The eagle] and Etan[a did obeisance together].
He saw [a house, he opened its seal],
[He pushed the door open and went inside].

(breaks off)

(Presumably, the goddess on the throne, Ishtar, gives Etana the plant of birth. As the goddess who took a special interest in kingship [Tablet I, line 20], she would, no doubt, favor the dynastic principle.)

III/C

(A small fragment may describe Etana's return home with the plant of birth.)

[   ] to his house,   (1′)
He reached his city and his house.
[His wife made ready to speak] and said to Etana,
"[   ] the plant of birth?"
"[   ] the ground,   (5′)
"[   ] I [did not(?)] see where it came out."[1]
She ... [   ] to cook it

(breaks off)

(According to Mesopotamian historical tradition, Etana had a son, Balih, who succeeded him to the throne.)

Text: Old Babylonian (OV I) = Clay, BRM 4 2; (OV II) = Scheil, RA 24 (1927), 106. Middle Assyrian (MA) = Ebeling-Köcher-Rost, LKA 14; Ebeling, KAR 170, 335; VAT 10291 (collation Haul, *Etana-Epos*, pl. XIII–XIV), 10137, 10529 = Kinnier Wilson, *Etana*, pl. 7–10. Late Assyrian (LV) Tablet I = Kinnier Wilson, *Etana*, pl. 11–12; Tablet II = Kinnier Wilson, *Etana*, pl. 13–19 (composite text); Tablet III = Kinnier Wilson, *Etana*, pl. 11, 12, 20–25 (collation Haul, *Etana-Epos*, pl. XIII–XIV). Copies of K 2606, K 2527+, K 1547, K 8563, K 3651+ in Haul, *Etana-Epos*, pl. III–XII. The "Pittsfield" tablet (Haul's manuscript Ep) collated from photo. III/C = Kinnier Wilson, *Etana*, pl. 12.

Edition: J. V. Kinnier Wilson, *The Legend of Etana* (London, 1985); M. Haul, *Das Etana-Epos, Ein Mythos des Himmelfahrt des Königs von Kiš*, GAAL 1 (2000); J. Novotny, *The Standard Babylonian Etana Epic*, SAACT 2 (2001), with additional collations communicated privately.

1. See above, Tablet III, lines 15–16. Perhaps this means that Etana deceived his wife as to where he got the plant. Or, perhaps, in a missing episode, Ishtar told the eagle and Etana where to find the plant, but, as with Gilgamesh and the plant of eternal rejuvenation (Foster, *Gilgamesh*, 94), it was somewhere Etana could never return for more, so this was the only use of it.

Translation: Speiser, ANET³, 114–118; Labat, *Religions*, 294–305; Dalley, *Myths*, 189–202 and in Hallo, ed., *Context*, 1:453–457; Hecker, TUAT *Ergänzungslieferung*, 34–51.

Literature: Haul, *Etana-Epos*, 231–246; G. Selz, "Die Etana-Erzählung, Ursprung und Tradition einer der ältesten epischen Texte in einer semitischen Sprache," ASJ 20 (1998), 135–179; for a literary study of Old Babylonian Etana, see S. Izre'el, "Linguistics and Poetics in Old Babylonian Literature: Mimation and Meter in Etana," JANES 27 (2000), 57–68.

★Notes to Text: Haul, *Etana-Epos*, offers a detailed commentary, with many original proposals adopted here. I have generally followed the arrangement of text argued by Haul and Novotny. I have made a selection from among the various conflicting collations and readings of broken signs and passages in recent publications without the benefit of personal collation of the manuscripts. (OV I/A 2) For the difficulties with this line, see Wilcke, ZA 67 (1977), 157. Is the *ša* distributive and paralleled in line 13? (OV I/E 3–4) Differently Streck, AOAT 264 (1999), 82. (MV I/A 4) *mul-ta[k-š]i-du* (WGL); for this obscure word, see CAD K, 283a. Kinnier Wilson reads *mul-ᵣtarᵢ-pi-du*. (MV I/A 5) Kinnier Wilson, *Etana*, 72. (MA I/A ★16) Text corrupt, reading from LV II.30. (MV I/C ★3) Moran, *Studies Tadmor*, 328–329. (MV I/C ★4) Borger, HKL 2, 171. (LV I/A ★5) CAD N/1, 349b. (LV I/A 6) Novotny. (LV II 7) Kinnier Wilson, *Etana*, 88. (LV II 32) Kinnier Wilson, *Etana*, 129. (LV II 52) Streck, OrNS 64 (1995), 59 note 108 suggests that *qer-bet u₄-me* means the approach of the following day. (LV II 82) von Soden, WZKM 55 (1959), 61; CAD M/1, 349b; Streck, ZA 84 (1994), 170. (LV II 110) von Soden, WZKM 55 (1959), 61; Kinnier Wilson, *Etana*, 132; Edzard, ZA 76 (1986), 137; Haul, *Etana-Epos*, 222. (LV III A 50) von Soden, ZA 45 (1939), 77–78; Horowitz, OrNS 59 (1990), 512–513. (LV IIIB 113) von Soden, WZKM 55 (1959), 61.

III.23 ANZU

This poem tells how the god Ninurta proved his valor and was acclaimed by the other gods as their deliverer. When the universe was still only partly organized, the Tigris and Euphrates rivers existed but no one worshipped the gods in separate sanctuaries yet, nor was there water for irrigation and rainfall. An eagle-like bird, Anzu, lived in a mountain to the north of the land. Enlil, chief of the gods, asks about Anzu. Ea explains that he was the product of the flood waters. Perhaps hoping to undermine Enlil's authority as the chief god of Sumer,[1] Ea suggests that Enlil make Anzu the guardian of his cella and bed-chamber.

The gods are given their responsibilities. The bird looks enviously upon Enlil's exercise of kingship and covets it for himself. While Enlil is in his bath, Anzu snatches and flies off with the tablet in which is the power to control all destinies,[2] leaving Enlil and the other gods in disarray. The gods convene and seek a champion to recover the tablet and destroy the monster. Adad, god of rainstorms, is called but declines; Girra, god of fire, likewise. Shara, son of Ishtar, is no more eager than they. Throughout this portion of the story, as in the Creation Epic (III.17), suspense and a feeling of helplessness are conveyed by the verbatim repetitions of speech and action, mostly the former. Thrice turned down, the gods are at a loss (Tablet I line 157).

Ea, god of wisdom, offers a plan that is gladly acceded to. Mami, the mother goddess, is named by a new name, Belet-ili "Mistress of the Gods," because her son, Ninurta, is to be champion of the gods. Mami, now Belet-ili, accepts this honor and orders her dutiful son to avenge his father's dishonor, thereby to allow the gods to reassert their authorities.

Ninurta marches off on his mission (Tablet II line 28) and confronts his opponent. Since Anzu has the tablet of destinies, he has efficacious incantations against any attack, so Ninurta's onslaught is stopped. Anzu orders the oncoming arrows to return to their original elements. Ninurta sends Sharur back to Ea to explain this impasse (Tablet II lines 86ff.). Ea sends him back with advice: cut off his wing feathers. When Anzu sees them fluttering about, he will order them to return to him. At that moment the arrow, which also has feathers on it, will find its mark. Again, lengthy repetitions are used to heighten suspense and delay resolution of the action.

---

1. See II. 36, where Enki (Ea) regularly thwarts Enlil's plans, and S. N. Kramer, "Enki and His Inferiority Complex," OrNS 39 (1970), 103–110.

2. See p. 445 note 2.

In Tablet III Ea's suggestion is carried out. Ninurta succeeds in killing Anzu and regaining the tablet that controls destinies. The gods rejoice, but their festivity turns to consternation when the conquering hero does not return to yield the tablet back to Enlil. A messenger is sent to invite Ninurta's return. It appears, however, that Ninurta is not eager to return the tablet. At this point the text is damaged. When it resumes, Ninurta has returned and the gods are praising him as the most important among them. Various names of Ninurta are celebrated in a passage similar to Tablet VII of the Creation Epic (III.17).

The Anzu story is presented here in two versions. What survives of an Old Babylonian (Classical period) version corresponds to Tablets II and III of the later one. The later version is known from various Middle and Late Assyrian and Neo-Babylonian manuscripts (Mature and Late periods) that preserve most of Tablets I and II, as well as substantial parts of III. The Middle Assyrian fragments are treated here with the later version.

Of interest is substitution of Ninurta in the later version for Ningirsu in the Old Babylonian version; evidently the two were then considered equivalent. The basic story was borrowed and adapted by the author of the Creation Epic (III.17), who made major changes in it. For example, in the Creation Epic Marduk demands highest authority among the gods before the battle, as a plan already thought out by Ea before his son volunteers. Here Ninurta's supremacy is forced upon the gods by the mutinous hero after his victory.

Readers are advised to begin with the later version and then to return to the Old Babylonian.

(a) OLD BABYLONIAN VERSION

"Tablet II"

He snatched away supremacy,
     divine authority was overthrown,   (1)
Their father and counsellor Enlil was speechless.
Panic spread,[1] deathly stillness reigned,
He threw all the Igigi-gods into confusion.
The cella was stripped of its divine splendor.   (5)
The gods of the land convened, one after another, for a plan.
Anu made ready to speak,
Saying to the gods his children,

---

1. Literally: "was poured out."

"O gods, who will slay Anzu?
"He will make his the greatest name among them all."⋆   (10)
They called the Irrigator, Anu's son.[1]
        Plan made(?),⋆ he said to him,
"[   ] your battle, blitz Anzu with your weapons.
"[Your name shall be greatest] among the great gods,
"You shall ha[ve] no equal [among the gods your brethren].
"[Show yourself mighty] before the gods,
        your name shall be 'M[ighty One]'."   (15)
[The Irrigator said to Anu his father these words],
"[My father, who would assault an inaccessible mountain]?
"[Who of your] children can defeat [An]zu?
"[He has taken control of the tablet of destinies],
        he has snatched away [supremacy] from (the) god.
"[He has soared off to his moun]tain,
        he has lifted high his head,   (20)
"His command [has become] like that of divine Duranki.[2]
"[If he commands, the one he curses] will turn into clay."
At his [words] the gods were despondent,
[He turned away], he refused to go.
They called [Girr]u, firstborn of Annunitum.   (25)
[Pl]an made(?), he said to him,
("... your battle, blitz Anzu with your weapons,[3]   (a)
("Your name shall be greatest among the great gods,
("You shall have no equal among the gods your brethren.
("Show yourself mighty before the gods,
        your name shall be 'M[ighty One]'."
(Girru said to Anu his father these words,   (e)
("My father, who would assault an inaccessible mountain?
("Who of your children can defeat Anzu?
("He has taken control of the tablet of destinies,
        he has snatched away supremacy from (the) god.
("He has soared off to his mountain, he has lifted high his head.   (i)
("His command has become like that of divine Duranki.

1. Adad.
2. Enlil.
3. Lines a–m are not in the manuscript but were presumably indicated with ditto marks or omitted by the scribe to save effort.

("[If he commands, the one he curses] will turn into clay."
(At his words the gods were despondent,
(Girru turned away, he refused to go.)
They called Shara, firstborn of Ishta[r   ],   (27)
Plan made(?), he said to him,
("... your battle, blitz Anzu with your weapons!   (a)
("Your name shall be greatest among the great gods,
("You shall have no equal among the gods your brethren.
("Show yourself mighty before the gods,
      your name shall be 'M[ighty One]'."
(Shara said to Anu his father these words,   (e)
("My father, who would assault an inaccessible mountain?
("Who of your children can defeat Anzu?
("He has taken control of the tablet of destinies,
      he has snatched away supremacy from (the) god.
("He has soared off to his mountain,
      he has lifted high his head.   (i)
("His command has become like that of divine Duranki.
("[If he commands, the one he curses] will turn into clay."
(At his words the gods were despondent,
(He turned away, he refused to go.)
Being spent, the gods [left off making] proposal(s).
The Igigi-gods were (still) assembled,
      [frowning?] and in a turmoil.   (30)
The lord of wisdom, who dwells in the depths,
      [Ea], the clever one,
Said [to Anu] his [father] the words in his mind,
"Let me give a com[mand],
      for then I will appoint Anzu's [conqueror]."
When the god[s of the land] heard [this] speech of his,
[Restored,* they did hom]age to him.   (35)
[He summoned] Belet-ili, mistress of divine plans,
      he proclaimed her supremacy in the assembly,
"[Give us] the mighty one, your superb beloved,
"Broad of chest, who leads the seven combats,
"N[ing]irsu, the mighty one, your su[per]b beloved,
"Broad of chest, who leads the seven combats."   (40)

When she heard this speech of his,
>   she of surpassing greatness, Belet-ili, assented,
At her utterance the gods of the land rejoiced,
>   and, restored, they did homage to him.
In the assembly of the gods she summoned
And commissioned her son, her heart's beloved, saying to him,
"Before Anu and Dagan, the valorous ones(?),   (45)
"They have discussed in the assembly
>   what has h[appened] to their authority.
"The [Igi]gi-gods, I gave birth to all of them!
"[I bore] the assembly of the gods, I am Mami.
"I appointed [supremacy] to my brother,
>   and to Anu the kingship of heaven.
"The kingship that I appointed [is overthrown]!   (50)
"[He has snatched away supremacy],
>   he has spurned your father![1]
"[Blitz the way],* choose (your) moment,[2]
"Make light come out for [the gods I made],
"Launch your [fullest] attack,
"Let [your seven ill winds] go up* to the mountain.   (55)
"Conquer [soaring] Anzu,
"[   ] ... press hard upon his abode.
"[Let fear] weigh heavily upon [him],*
"[Let him tr]emble [   ]

> *(three fragmentary lines)*

"[Draw the bow, let the arrows] carry [poi]son,
"Let the curse of your battle cry cast [gloom] upon him,
"Let him suffer darkness, let him become confused,
>   his vision fail,   (65)
"Let him not evade you,
>   (but) let his wings fall in the confrontation,
"Let your face change into a fiend's,
>   send forth a mist so he cannot distinguish your features,
"May the ever-bl[az]ing one not blaze on high,

---

1. Addressed to Ningirsu.
2. The line may mean that the hero is to stop Anzu's forward progress and put an end to his usurpation.

the bright day turn to gloom for him!
"Cut short his life, conquer Anzu!
"Let the winds bear off his wing feathers as glad tidings*   (70)
"To Ekur, to your father,
"Let the winds bear off his wing feathers as glad tidings."*
The warrior heeded his mother's word,*
The valiant one of battle became mighty,
          [he made his way] toward [his] mountain.
She who harnessed seven [   ]   (75)
[The seven whirlwinds] who make [the dust dance],
[   ] who harnessed seven ill winds,*
[   ] his battle
[   ] ...
[   ] Anzu's mountain the god appeared.   (80)

"Tablet III"

Anzu [saw him] and shook at(?) him (in fury),*   (1)
He raged like a demon,
          his terrifying radiance enveloped the moun[tain],
[Anzu roared like a lion], carried away(?) with rage,
[In the fury] of his heart he shrieked at the hero,
"[I am] he [who carried off] all authority,   (5)
"[You who] have come [for battle with me,
          account] for yourself!"
Ningirsu answered Anzu, [to the words] he spoke,
"[I am the son of Dura]nki, upholder of Duranki,
          ordainer of destinies,
"[   ] I am come, your crusher.
"[   ] whirlwind [   ] armor."   (10)
[When he heard this], within the mountain
          he let forth in fury his shriek,*
[Armor's surface was] bathed in blood,
[   ] battle roared
[The ..., son of] Mami, hope of Anu and Dagan,
          beloved of the Leader,[1]

---

1. Ninshiku (=Ea).

[He shot a shaft] at him. It did not approach Anzu,   (15)
[For he cried out again]st it,
      "Shaft that has come, go b]ack [to your thicket],
"[   ] shaft that has come, go b[ack to your reedbed]!"[1]

     (Gap of about forty lines. Ea is speaking.)

"Hurry to overwhelm [   ],*
"[you must not] spare Anzu's life!*
"[Let kingship return] to Ekur,
      let authority return to the father who begot you,
"Let [your?] daises [be built],   (70)
"Establish y[our] holy places [in the] fo[ur world regions]."
[When the Lord heard the] command of his fathers,
[The valiant one of bat]tle became mighty,
      and returned to [the mountain].
[   ] the four winds [ ] for battle,
[   ] the earth heaved, ... [   ]   (75)
[The su]n became dark, the heavens turned gloomy,
      [his vision] fa[iled],*

[An]zu [let fall] his wings in the confrontation
      with the tempest.

     (tablet ends, continuation lost)

(b) LATE VERSION

Tablet I

Son of the king of the inhabited world, splendid one,
      beloved of [Ma]mi,   (1)
The mighty one will I ever sing, divine firstborn of [En]lil,
Ninurta, the splendid one, beloved of Mami,
The mighty one will I ever praise, divine firstborn of Enlil.
Born (in) Ekur, leader of the Anu[nna-gods], Eninnu's[2] hope, (5)

---

1. Magic words to ward off the arrow; see Later Version, Tablet II lines 63–65.
2. Temple of Ningirsu at Lagash.

Who [wa]ters pen, garden, town, street, and city,*
Wave of battles, dancer (in combat),[1] sash of valor,
Whose tireless onset raging fiends dread,
Hear the praise of the mighty one's power!
It is he who in his fierceness bound
      and fettered the stone creatures,[2]*   (10)
Overcoming soaring Anzu with his weapon,
Slaying the bull man in the midst of the sea.[3]
Doughty, valorous, murderous with his weapon,
Mighty one, fleet of foot, always leader in fight and fray!
Before that, no dais had been built among the Igigi-gods,   (15)
It was the Igigi-gods who knelt in their supremacy.[4]
Tigris and [Euph]rates rivers had been fashioned,
But the [springs] were not bearing [their?] waters to the land.
The very seas [   ]
Clouds were ... from the horizon [   ]   (20)
Then were the [Igigi-gods] convened from all parts,
To Enlil, their father, wa[rrior of the gods?],
Did his children bring [the news],
"Hee[d? you well] the propitious word!
"On Sharshar Mountain[5] ... [   ]   (25)
"In its fork the Anu[nna-gods   ]
"It[6] bore Anzu [   ]
"[His] beak a saw[7] [   ]
"[Go] out and [   ]

(four fragmentary lines)

At [his] clamor [   ]   (35)
The south wind [   ]

---

1. Compare II.5, I iii 6–14.
2. An allusion to a Sumerian poem called "Ninurta and the Stones," for which see J. J. A. van Dijk, *LUGAL UD ME-LÁM-bi NIR-GÁL* (Leiden, 1983), and Cooper, AnOr 52 (1978), 121.
3. Cooper, AnOr 52 (1978), 148–149; for the bull man, see Green, *Iraq* 48 (1986), 26 with pl. VIIC.
4. WGL: "though supreme gods." I take this obscure line to mean that the Igigi-gods worshipped but were not yet worshipped by anyone themselves.
5. Jebel Bishri(?); see Erra and Ishum (IV.17) Tablet IV lines 139, 141.
6. Antecedent unclear. Perhaps the flood is meant; see line 50 below.
7. Akkadian *šaššāru*, a wordplay on the name of the mountain in line 25 above (W. G. Lambert, JCS 41 [1989], 17).

The massive [   ]
The voluminous [flooding crest   ]
The whirlwinds [   ]
They met and [   ]   (40)
The four winds [   ]
When the fat[her of the gods] saw him [   ]
He took what [they] said of him [to his heart],
He inspected Anzu closely [   ]
Debated with [himself   ]   (45)
"Who bore [   ]?
"Why this [   ]?"
[Ea] answered the query of his heart,
The Leader [said] to En[lil these words],
"No doubt the waters of the fl[ood   ]   (50)
"The pure waters of the gods of the deep [   ]
"The [wide] earth conceived him,
"He is the one [born] in the rocks of the mountain,
"It is Anzu you have seen [   ]
"Let him serve you ce[aselessly],   (55)
"Let him always block the way to the cella [seat]."

(gap)

The god con[sented to the word] he spoke to him,
He took up holy places [   ]
And gave to all the [gods] their responsibilities.   (60)
He would reinstitute the decree (each morning?)
        and Anzu would hold [   ],
Enlil entrusted him with the entrance to the cella,
        which he had wrought.
He was wont to bathe in pure waters before him.
His eyes looked upon the trappings of supremacy,   (65)
On his lordly crown, his divine apparel,
On the tablet of destinies in his hands
        Anzu was wont to gaze.
He was wont to gaze, indeed, at the father of the gods,
        divine Duranki,
He resolved in his heart to make off with supremacy.

Anzu was wont to gaze on the father of the gods,
  divine Duranki,   (70)
He resolved in his heart to make off with supremacy!
"I myself will take the gods' tablet of destinies,
"Then I will gather to myself the responsibilities of all the gods,
"I will have the throne for myself,
  I will take power over authority,
"I will be commander of each and every Igigi-god."   (75)
His heart plotted the assault,
At the entrance to the cella, where he was wont to gaze,
  he bided (his) time.
When Enlil was bathing in the pure waters,
Undressed(?),* his crown set on the throne,
He took control of the tablet of destinies,   (80)
He took supremacy, [authority] was overthrown!
Anzu soared off and [made his way] to his mountain,
Awful silence spread, deathly sti[llness] reigned.
Their father and counsellor Enlil was speechless.
The cella was stripped of its divine splendor.   (85)
The gods of the land converged,
  one after another, for a pl[an].
Anu made ready to speak,
Saying to the gods his children,
"Which one would slay Anzu?
"He shall make for himself the greatest name
  in every habitation."   (90)
They summoned the Irrigator, Anu's son,
Plan made(?), he said to him,
They summoned Adad, the irrigator, Anu's son,
Plan [ma]de(?), he said to him,
"O mighty one, Adad, victorious Adad,
  let your battle not waver,   (95)
"Blitz Anzu with your weapon.
"Let your [name] be greatest among all the great gods,
"You shall have no equal [among] the gods your brethren.
"Let there be daises to be built,   (100)
"Establish your holy places in the four [world regions],
"Let your [holy places] come into Ekur.

"[Show yourself] mighty before the gods,
      for your name shall be 'Mighty One'."
[Adad] answered the command,
[To] Anu his father he said these words,   (105)
["My father], who would assault an inaccessible [moun]tain?
"[Which] of the gods your children can overcome Anzu?
"He took control of the [tablet of destinies],
"He took away [supremacy], authority is overthrown.
"[Anzu] soared off and made his way to his mountain,   (110)
"His [utterance] has become like that of divine Duranki.
"[If he commands, the one he cur]ses will turn into clay."
The gods were despondent [at his utteranc]e.
[He turned away, he refused to go].
[They called Girra, firstborn of Annunitum],   (115)
[Plan made(?), he said to him],
"[O mighty one, Girra, victorious Girra,
      let your battle not waver].
"[Blitz Anzu with your weapon],
"[Let your name be greatest among all the great gods],
"[You shall have no equal among the gods your brethren].   (120)
"[Let there be daises to be built],
"[Establish your holy places in the four world regions],
"[Let your holy places come into Ekur].
"[Show yourself mighty before the gods,
      for your name shall be 'Mighty One'."
[Girra answered the command],   (125)
[To Anu his father he said these words],
"[My father, who would assault an inaccessible mountain]?
"[Which of the gods your children can overcome Anzu]?
"[He took control of the tablet of destinies],
"[He took away supremacy, authority is overthrown].   (130)
"[Anzu soared off and ma]de [his way to his mountain],
"[His utterance] has become like that of divine Duranki.
"[If he commands, the one he curses] will turn into clay."
The gods were despondent [at his utter]ance.
[He turned away], he refused to go.   (135)
They [called Shara], firstborn of Ishtar,
[Pl]an [made](?), he said to him,

"[O mi]ghty one, [Shara], victorious Shara,
        let your battle not waver.
"[Bli]tz Anzu with your weapon.
"Let yo[ur name] be greatest among all the great gods,   (140)
"You shall have no equal among the gods your brethren.
"Let there be daises to be built,
"Establish your holy places in the four world regions,
"Let your holy places come into Ekur.
"Show yourself mighty before the gods,
        for your name shall be 'Mighty One'."   (145)
Shara answered the command,
To Anu his father he said these words,
"My father, who would assault an inaccessible mountain?
"Which of the gods your children can overcome Anzu?
"He took control of the tablet of destinies,   (150)
"He took away supremacy, authority is overthrown.
"Anzu flew off and [made his w]ay to his mountain.
"His utterance has become like that of divine Duranki.
"If he commands, the one he curses will turn into clay."
The gods were despondent at his utterance.   (155)
He turned away, he refused to go.
The gods were spent and left off making proposals,
The Igigi-gods, (still) in session,
        were frowning(?) and in a turmoil.
The lord of wisdom, who dwells in the depths,
        the clever one,
Was devising an idea in his cunning mind.   (160)
Ea devised wisdom(?) in his heart,
What he thought of in his mind he explained to Anu,
"Let me give a command and so find the god,
"For then I will appoint Anzu's conqueror in the assembly,
"Let me be the one to find the god,   (165)
"For then I will appoint Anzu's conqueror in the assembly."
When the Igigi-gods [he]ard this speech of his,
The Igigi-gods, restored, did homage to him.
The Leader made ready to speak,
[Saying t]o Anu and Dagan these words,   (170)

"Let them summon to me the mistress of the gods,
     sister of the [great] gods,
"The resourceful one, coun[sellor] of the gods [her] brethren.
"Let them proclaim her surpassing greatness in the as[sembly],
"Let all the gods honor [her] in their assembly.
"[Then I will explain to her] the idea of my heart."   (175)
They summoned thither the mistress of the gods,
     the sister [of the great gods],
The resourceful one, counsellor of the gods [her brethren].
They proclaimed her surpassing greatness [in the assembly],
The gods honored her in their assembly.
Ea [explained the idea] from his cunning mind,   (180)
"Formerly w[e called you]* 'Mami',
"Now let 'Mistress of All the Gods' [be your name].
"Give (us) the mighty one, [your] superb [beloved],
"The broad-chested one who is ever leader in fight or fray.
"Give (us) Ninurta, your superb beloved,   (185)
"The broad-chested one who is ever leader in fight or fray.
"[He shall be   ] lord in the assembly of the gods,
"He shall be proud in the [   ]
"In all [   ]
"A holy place [   ]   (190)
"Lord [   ]
"A fes[tival   ]
"In [   ]."
[When she heard this speech of his],
[She of surpassing greatness,
     the most exalted mistress of the gods, assented].   (195)
[When she spoke, the Igigi-gods rejoiced],
[Restored, they did homage to her].
[She summoned her son in the assembly of the gods].
Commissioning her heart's beloved, saying to him,
"Be[fore Anu and Dagan   ]   (200)
"[They have discussed in the assembly]
     what has happened [to authority].
"[I bore] all the Igigi-gods,
"I made every [single one of them],
"I made all the A[nunna-gods].

"[To my brother I ...] supremacy,   (205)
"[I assigned] kingsh[ip of heaven] to Anu.
"Anzu has thrown into confusion [the kingship I appointed],
"The tablet of destinies, ... Anzu ... has taken control,
"He has snatched from Enlil, he has spurned your father.
"He has snatched away authority,
        [he has turned it over to himself].   (210)

Tablet II

"Blitz the way, choose (your) moment,★   (1)
"Make light come out for the gods I made.
"Launch your fullest attack,
"Let your ill winds go against him!
"Conquer soaring Anzu,   (5)
"Flood the earth where he was made,
        bring chaos upon his dwelling.★
"Let (your) armor clash against him,
"Let your fierce battle keep raging against him,★
"May whirlwinds totally block him.★
"Draw the bow, let the arrows be poison to him,   (10)
"Let your features turn into a fiend's,
"Send forth a mist so he cannot distinguish your face.
"Let your brilliant glow move against him,[1]
"Let your radiance be glorious,
        you should have an awe-inspiring sheen,
"Let the sun not shine upon him,[2]   (15)
"Let the bright day turn to gloom for him.
"Kill him, conquer Anzu!
"Let the winds bear off his wing feathers as glad tidings,
"To the temple Ekur, to your father Enlil.
"Flood and bring mayhem to the mountain meadows,   (20)
"Kill wicked Anzu!
"Let [king]ship (re-)enter Ekur,
"Let authority return [to the] fa[ther] who begot you.

1. Variant: "on high"(?) or: "against us."
2. Variant: "on high."

"Let there be daises to be built,
"Establish your holy places [in the f]our [world regions],   (25)
"[Let your shrine] come into Ekur.
"Show yourself mighty before the gods,
      for your name shall be 'Mighty One'."
The warrior heeded his mother's word,
Seething with fury,
      he made his way toward his mountain.
My lord hitched up the seven battles,   (30)
The warrior hitched up the seven ill winds,
The seven whirlwinds that make the dust swirl.
He launched a terrifying assault, made war,
The winds were ready at his side for battle.
Anzu and Ninurta met on the mountainside.   (35)
When Anzu saw him, he shook with fury at him,
He ground his teeth like a cyclone,
      he enveloped the mountain with his horrible glow.
He was roaring like a lion, seized with passion.
In his rage he cried to the w[arrior],
"I have carried off all possible authority,   (40)
"So I control the responsibilities all the gods must do.
"Who are you who have to come fight with me?
      Account for yourself!"
He advanced upon him, saying to him,
The warrior Ninurta [answered] Anzu,
"I [am Ninurta, the son of] divine Duranki,   (45)
"Upholder of the vast netherworld, of Ea, king of destinies!
"I am come to fight with you, your crusher!"*
When Anzu heard what he said,
He let loose his piercing shriek within the mountain.
It grew dark, the face of the mountain was enveloped,   (50)
The sun, light of the gods, became dark.
Adad roared in great (thunderclaps),*
      the sign of Anzu was his clamor.
In the midst of the melee, the conflict,
      battle was joined, the deluge onset,*
Battle array was on the move, bathed in blood,*
Clouds of death rained down, arrows flashed as lightning,   (55)

Battle ran on,* thundering between them.
The Mighty One, the splendid firstborn of Mami,
Hope of Anu and Dagan, beloved of the Leader,
Mounted the bow with a shaft,
From the handhold of the bow he sent against him an arrow.   (60)
The shaft did not approach Anzu but returned!
Anzu cried out against it,
"Shaft that has come, go back to your thicket,
"Frame of the bow to your forests,
"Bowstring to the sheep's sinews,
     feather to the birds: go back!"   (65)
Because he held the tablet of destinies of the gods in his hand,
The bowstring brought forth arrows,
     but they did not approach his body.*
Battle die[d do]wn, attack was held back,
The fighting stopped,
     within the mountain they did not conquer Anzu.
He summoned Sharur[1]* and commissioned him,   (70)
"Tell Ea the Leader what you saw happen,
"Say this:

   'Lord, Ninurta had surrounded Anzu,
   'Ninurta was enveloped with the dust of battle.
   'He readied the bow, mounted the shaft,[2]   (75)
   'He readied the bow, shot the shaft toward him.
   'It did not approach Anzu but returned.
   'Anzu cried out against it,

     "Shaft that has come, go back to your thicket,
     "Frame of the bow to your forests,   (80)
     "Bowstring to the sheep's sinews,
       feathers to the birds: go back!"

   'Because he was holding the tablet of destinies
     of the gods in his hand,
   'The bowstring brought forth arrows,
     but they did not approach his body.
   'Battle die[d d]own, attack was held back,

1. Usually a deified weapon of Ninurta/Ningirsu, here a separate deity.
2. Variant omits here and at line 89.

'The fighting stopped,
'Within the mountain they did not conquer Anzu.'" (85)

Sharur did obeisance, received the command,
Bore the battle message to Ea the Leader,
He repeated to Ea all the lord told him,
"O lord, he says this,

'Ninurta had surrounded Anzu,
'Ninurta was enveloped with the dust of battle.
'He readied the bow, shot the shaft toward him, (90)
'The shaft did not approach Anzu but returned.
'Anzu cried out against it,

"Shaft that has come, go back to your thicket,
"Frame of the bow to your forests, (95)
"[Bowstr]ing to the sheep's [sinews],
feathers to the birds: go back!"

'[Because he was h]olding the [tablet of destini]es
of the gods in his ha[nd],
'[The bowstring brought forth arrows,
but they did not approach his body].
'[Battle died down, attack was held back],
'[The fighting stopped], (100)
'[Within the mountain they did not conquer Anzu].'"

When [the Lea]der heard the words of his son,
He [called Sharur] and commissioned him,
"[Heed for your lord, what I say,*
"What I shall tell you, heed for him.

'Do not tire in battle, strive for victory, (105)
'Tire him out that he let his wings fall
to the brunt of the storm,
'Take, O lord, your darts toward the bottom,
'Cut off his pinions and hurl them, right and left,
'Once he sees his feathers,
they will take away his (magic) words.
"My wings!" to the wings he will cry; fear him not.[1]* (110)

1. Or: "fear him still."

'Ready your bow, let the lightning shafts fly from it,*
'Let pinions and wing feathers
      dance about like butterflies.*
'Kill him, conquer Anzu!
'Let the winds bear off his wing feathers as glad tidings   (115)
'To the temple Ekur, to your father Enlil.
'Flood and bring mayhem to the mountain meadows,
'Kill wicked Anzu!
'Let kingship (re-)enter Ekur,
'Let authority return [to the father] who begot you.   (120)
'Let there be daises to be built,
'Establish your holy places in the four world regions,
'[Let] your holy places come into Ekur.
'Show yourself mighty be[fore the gods],
      for your name shall be 'Mighty One'.'"

[Sharur did ob]eis[ance] and received the command,   (125)
Bo[re] off the battle message [to] his [lord],
Every[thing] Ea to[ld him he repea]ted to him,

'Do not ti[re] in battle, strive for victory,
'Tire him out that he let his wings fall
      [to the brunt of] the storm.
'Take, O lord, your darts toward the bottom,   (130)
'Cut off his pinions and hurl them, right and left.
'Once he sees his feathers,
      they will take away his (magic) words.
"My wings!" to the wings he will cry; [fear him] not.
'Ready your bow, let the [lightning] shafts fly from it.   (135)
'Let pinions and wings dance about like butterflies.
'Kill him, conquer Anzu!
'Let the winds bear off his wing feathers as glad tidings
'To the temple Ekur, to your father Enlil.
'Flood and bring [mayhem] to the mountain meadows,   (140)
'Kill wicked Anzu!
'Let kingship (re-)enter [Ekur],
'Let authority [return] to the father who begot you.
'Let there be [dais]es to be built,
'[Estab]lish your holy places in the four world regions,   (145)
'[Let] your holy places [come into] Ekur.

'Show yourself mighty before [the gods],
    for your name shall be 'Mighty One'.'

The lord heeded the words of Ea the Leader,
Seething with fury,
    he made his way toward his mountain.
The lord hitched up the seven battles,   (150)
[The warrior hitched up] the seven ill winds,
[The seven] whirlwinds [that make the dust swirl].
He launched a [terrifying] assault, made war,
[The winds were ready at his side] for his battle.

Tablet III[1]

(two fragmentary lines)

Armor ...
Constantly striking one another ... [ ]
The blazing of the fiery glare [   ]   (5)
[ ] to the four winds, the storm [   ]
The weapons he struck and struck, in horrible protection,⋆
Both were bathed in the sweat of battle.
Then Anzu grew tired,
    at the onslaught of the storm he dropped his wings,
The lord took his darts toward the bottom,   (10)
He cut off his pinions, hurled them right and left.
When Anzu saw his wings, they took away his (magic) words.
When he cried "My wings!" to the wings,
    the arrow flew against him,
The shaft passed through the ... of his heart,
He made his dart pass through pinion and wing,
The shaft pierced through his heart and lungs.   (15)
He flooded, brought mayhem to the mountain meadows,
He flooded the vast earth in his fury,
He flooded the midst of the mountains,
He killed wicked Anzu!   (20)

---

1. What follows is largely from R, based on the work of Saggs.

The warrior Ninurta took control
    of the tablet of the gods' destinies.
The wind bore Anzu's wing feathers
As a sign of his glad tidings.
Dagan rejoiced when he saw his sign,
He summoned all the gods, saying to them in joy,   (25)
"The Mighty One has outroared Anzu in his mountain,
"He has regained control of Anu and Dagan's weapons.
"Go to him, that he come to us,
"Let him rejoice, let him dance, let him celebrate,
"Let him stand with the gods his brethren,
    that he may hear the secret lore,   (30)
"[   ] the secret lore of the gods,
"Let [ ] grant him responsibilities ...
    with the gods his brethren."
[Ea?] made ready to speak,
Saying [to] Dagan (these) words,
"... he took the skin,   (35)
"When he killed wicked Anzu in the mountains,
"The warrior Ninurta regained control of the tablet
    of the gods' destinies.
"Send to him, let him come to you,
"Let him place the tablet of destinies in your lap."
Enlil made ready to speak,   (40)
Saying to Nusku his courier (these) words,
"Nusku, go outside,
"Bring Birdu[1] before me!"
He brought Birdu into Enlil's presence.
Enlil made ready to speak,   (45)
Saying to Birdu (these) words,
"Birdu, I am sending you ...

        (gap)

Ninurta [made] ready to speak,
[Saying these words] to Birdu,
"O Birdu, why did you come at such a furious pace to ...?"   (5′)
Birdu m[ade ready] to speak,

1. A god; see E. Ebeling, "Birdu," RLA 2, 31.

[Saying these words] to Ninurta his lord,
"My lord, [   ] to you,
"Your father Enlil sent me,
"Saying,

> 'The gods heard [   ]   (10′)
> 'That [you killed] wicked Anzu in the mountain.
> 'They were joyful and glad, but [   ].
> 'Before you [   ] ...
> 'Go to him [   ] ...
> 'Let him rejoi[ce   ] ...   (15′)

(three fragmentary lines)

Ninurta [made ready to speak, saying to Birdu],
"Why [surrender] the trap[pings of kingship]?   (20′)
"[My utterance has become] like that of the ki[ng of the gods].
"I will not re[turn] the tablet of destinies."

(fragmentary lines, then breaks off)
(A god is speaking to Ninurta.)

"Let [   ] not be built,
"[   ] Anzu in Ekur.
"[   ] the sign of the warrior,   (115)
"Let him look upon wicked Anzu
      [in] the greatness of his might,
"O warrior, you could slay mountains in your might,
"You defeated Anzu, you could slay his might,
"You could slay the might of soaring Anzu!
"Because you were valiant and killed mountains,   (120)
"You have made all enemies submit before your father, Enlil,
"O Ninurta, because you were valiant and slew mountains,
"You have made all enemies submit before your father, Enlil!
"You have gained lordship, each and every divine authority,
"For(?) whom besides you
      is the divine authority of the mountain?   (125)
"Greatness has been given you
      at the daises of the gods of destinies,
"They called your lustrations 'Nisaba',
"They called your name in the furrow 'Ningirsu'.

"They assigned to you full shepherdship of the people,

"As king, they gave (you) your name
   'Guardian of the Throne'.   (130)

"In Elam they gave (you) the name Hurabtil,

"In Susa they speak of you as Inshushinak.[1]

"In E-Ibbi-Anu[2] they gave you the name
   'Master of Secret Lore',

"[ ] among the gods your brethren

"[ ] your father,   (135)

"They gave you your name '[Pabilsag]' in Egalmah,

"They [called] your name '[ ]' in Ur,

"[ ] you ... Duranki,   (140)

"[In Der] they speak of you as 'Ishtaran',

"[In] 'Zababa,'

"[ ] they call as his name.

"Your valor [ ] Enlil over all the gods,

"[ ] to make surpassing your divinity,   (145)

"[ ] I praise you.

"In NI.SUR [they gave (you)] your name 'Lugalbanda',

"[Your name] 'Lugalmarade' they gave you in Egishkalamma,

"[In] Esikilla they gave (you) [your name]
   'Warrior Tishpak',

"In Bube in the E-nimmanku [ ],   (150)

"In Kullab they called (you) by your name '[Pis]angunuk',⋆

"[ ] Belet-ili your mother,

"[ ] lord of the boundary,

"[ ] Panigarra,

"They called ... [   ]   (155)

"[ ] 'Papsukkal, the vanguard'.

"O ... lord, your names are surpassingly great among the gods,

"Lord of understanding, capable and dreaded one,

"[ ] Ea the Leader, your father,

"[ ] battle and conflict,   (160)

"He [ ] you '[ ] of their lands'.

    (fragmentary lines, then breaks off)

---

 1. Elam and Susa are in southwestern Iran (see III.11); the other cities and cult centers listed thereafter are Mesopotamian, so far as known.

 2. Temple at Dilbat, a town in Babylonia (Moran, AfO 34 [1987], 29).

Text: (a) = Scheil, RA 35 (1938), 20–21 = Vogelzang, BSD, 92–95, collated by the translator. These two tablets appear to be Middle or Neo-Babylonian copies that attempt to preserve faithfully an Old Babylonian text. Vogelzang reached similar conclusions independently. (b) Tablet I = Hallo, JCS 31 (1979), 106–115 (A) collated by George, BSOAS 42 (1992), 146; King, CT 15 39–40 + W. G. Lambert, CT 46 39 (G); W. G. Lambert, CT 46 36 (C), 37 (B), 40 (+) AfO 27 (1980), 81 (Sm 2195) (D); Saggs, AfO 33 (1986), 6–9 (R). Unfortunately there is no consistent line numbering for this tablet; I have used a continuous count based on R and BSD. Tablet II = 1–46 = Ebeling-Köcher-Rost, LKA 1 (E); 1–64 = Gurney, STT 21 (F); 26–41 = Gurney, STT 22 (H); 27–43 = W. G. Lambert, CT 46 38 (G); 41–90 = Gurney, STT 19 (I); 53–138 = Ebeling-Köcher-Rost, LKA 1 (E); 59–64 = K 18740 = W. G. Lambert, AfO 27 (1980), 82; 65–81 = W. G. Lambert, CT 46 41 (J); 82–88 = Gurney, STT 21 (I); 89–92 = K 19368 = W. G. Lambert, AfO 27 (1980), 82; 101–129 = Gurney, STT 21 (I); 131–142 = W. G. Lambert, CT 46 38 (G); 140–150 = Gurney, STT 21 (I); 141–150 = Ebeling-Köcher-Rost, LKA 1 (E); Saggs, AfO 33 (1986), 9, 20. Tablet III = i 1′–18′ = W. G. Lambert, CT 46 42 (K); ii 1′–25′ = W. G. Lambert, CT 46 42 ii (K) + AfO 27 (1980), 82; Saggs, AfO 33 (1986), 20, 26. A small Old Babylonian school excerpt published by K. Van Lerberghe, *Northern Akkad Project Reports* 6 (1991), 74, and identified by Cavigneaux, N.A.B.U. 2000/19, adds nothing but shows that the text was studied in Classical-period schools.

Edition: (a) Vogelzang, BSD, 96–118. (b) Moran, JCS 31 (1979), 65–102 (I); Saggs, AfO 33 (1986), 7, 8, 10; Vogelzang, BSD, 27–47 (I); Vogelzang, BSD, 48–67; Saggs, AfO 33 (1986), 10–19, 21 (II); Vogelzang, BSD, 68–72; Saggs, AfO 33 (1986), 21–25, 27, 28 (III); A. Annus, *The Standard Babylonian Epic of Anzu*, SAACT 3 (2001).

Translation: (both versions) Grayson-Speiser, ANET³, 111–113, 514–517; Labat, *Religions*, 80–92; Bottéro, *Mythologie*, 390–418; Dalley, *Myths,* 203–227.

Literature: B. Hruška, *Der Mythenadler Anzu in Literatur und Vorstellung der alten Mesopotamier* (Budapest, 1975); F. M. Wiggermann, "On Bin Šar Dadmē, the 'Anzu-Myth'," in *Studies Kraus*, 418–425; Vogelzang, BSD; Moran, AfO 34 (1987), 24–29.

★*Notes to Text*: (OB II 10) Wiggermann, *Studies Kraus*, 41. (OB II 11) Moran, JCS 31 (1979), 97, also AHw, 1386b. Other translators understand "the commander" (or the like), and make that the subject, but this is grammatically difficult. (OB II 35) Moran, JCS 31 (1979), 100; see p. 237 note 1. (OB II 52) Reading [bi-riq] from source F, though the reading bi-šim (WGL) can also be considered. (OB II 55) Vogelzang, BSD, 116–117. (OB II 58) AHw, 943b. (OB II 70) CAD B, 347a vs AHw, 885b. (OB II 72) Possible dittography, or, as taken here, a "pivot" construction (aba). (OB II 73) Moran, JCS 31 (1979), 67–68. (OB II 77) ⌜im-ḫul⌝-li, collated CAD I/J, 116b. (OB III 1) [i-mu-ur/mur-šu-ma] An-zu-um i-ru-ba-aš-šu (collation). (OB III 11) For proposals to this line, see Moran, JCS 31 (1979), 93 note 45; Wiggermann, *Studies Kraus*, 419; AHw, 369a. My collation favors šam★-ra★-x-x, here read šam-ra-t[am-m]a by suggestion of W. Mayer. (OB III 67) ri-ḫi-iṣ dú-ul-li-iḫ (see CAD D, 45b). (OB III 68) AHw, 1221b, tablet has [t]a-ši-it. (OB III 76) Wiggermann, *Studies Kraus*, 419. (LV I 6) George, BSOAS 54 (1991), 145. (LV I 10) šiknāt abni (WGL) (LV I 79) Moran, JCS 31 (1979), 96. (LV I 181) Restoration WGL. NI is possible for the broken sign (collated), but the trace does not closely resemble the NI in the line above. (LV II 1) See to OB II 52. (LV II 6) AHw, 1035a; Moran, AfO 34 (1987), 24 (also to line 7). (LV II 8) Differently CAD N/1, 258b; see also AHw, 932b; Moran, AfO 34 (1987), 24. (LV II 9) George, BSOAS 54 (1991), 146. (LV II 47) Differently Annus, *Anzu*, 24. (LV II 52) Differently AHw, 1355b. (LV II 53) WLM: ina birīt qabli tuqmāte … aṣ-ṣ[er-ma]. (LV II 54) George, BSOAS 54

(1991), 146. (LV II 56) George, *Nabu* 1991/19. (LV II 67) Saggs, AfO 33 (1986), 15. (LV II 70) Reading from Saggs. (LV II 103) George, BSOAS 54 (1991), 146. (LV II 110) Moran, AfO 34 (1987), 27. (LV II 111) It is unclear whether line 75, which should be repeated here, is a doublet there, or whether it has been accidentally omitted here. (LV II 112) CAD K, 564a, but see Wiggermann, *Studies Kraus*, 421. (LV III 7) Moran, AfO 34 (1987), 27–28. (LV III 151) George, BSOAS 54 (1991), 146; Beaulieu, N.A.B.U. 1993/22.

III.24 MONSTER SERPENTS

(a) THE SERPENT

A huge serpent has grown up in the ocean. The mother goddess is summoned and is asked who is the most valiant of her offspring. She names Nergal, perhaps referred to as "the Vanguard" in lines 17ff. The rest of the text may have told of Nergal's successful defeat of this monster and his exaltation among the gods. Most of the story is lost, owing to breaks in the tablet. There are obvious parallels with Anzu (III.23), as well as The Lion-Serpent (III.24b), and the Epic of Creation (III.17).

i

(lost except for a few signs)

ii

"[   ] there is no ... [   ]   (5)
"It was lying in the water, and I [   ]."

[   ] made ready to speak,
And said to [   ] his [   ] these words,
"Bring hither A[ruru], let [Arur]u [come here],
"Listen to me, Aruru, pay [attention to me].   (10)
"O ... Aruru, you are now 'Mis[tress of the Gods]',*
"Among the sixty-six sons and brothers [of yours],*
"To which one did you grant strength?
"To which one did you give the fullest [ ]?"
"I granted strength to Nergal,   (15)
"To Nergal did I give the fullest [ ]."
"Bring hither the Vanguard, ... [ ] the Vanguard,
"I myself will tell the Vanguard about it ...
"Listen to me, O Vanguard, O Vanguard ... [ ]
"O Vanguard, listen carefully to what I have to say.*   (20)

"In the ocean a dra[gon]-snake was created,
"Its ba[ck]* reached sixty leagues,
"Its he[ad] is thirty leagues high.
"Its blink(?)* is half a league,

"Its [feet?] can go twenty leagues at a step.   (25)
"It ate the fish, creatures of [the sea],
"It ate the birds, creatures of [the sky],
"[It ate] the donkeys, creatures of [the steppe],
"[It ate] the people of this land. [Go help?] the people."
The Vanguard, tamer of serpents, heeded the [   ],   (30)
[Nergal] made ready to speak,
[And said to   ] these words,

(five fragmentary lines, then breaks off)

Text: Ebeling, KAR 6.
Edition: Ebeling, OLZ 1916, 106–108.
Translation: A. Heidel, *The Babylonian Genesis*[2] (Chicago, 1951), 143 (partial).
★*Notes to Text*: (11) Restoration doubtful: *at-ti e-nin-na* [d]*Be-[let-ili]*. (12) WGL. (20) *si-qir* [*šap-ti-ja*] (WGL). (22) von Soden, AnOr 27 (1948), 107. (24) "Outer rim of the eye" (or the like)? See CAD L, 192a.

(b) THE LION-SERPENT

This is another telling of what appears to be much the same story as the preceding. Various gods refuse to fight a huge monster that is decimating the land. One does so at last in return for kingship and slays it with an arrow. The text as copied for Assurbanipal's library seems to the modern reader abbreviated or incomplete; note the absence of indication of speakers on the obverse and the abrupt ending.

Aside from its parallels with III.24a, the basic plot of this text recalls that of the Creation Epic (III.17) and Anzu (III.23).

> The cities have fallen into ruins, the people [   ],   (1)
> The people have diminished, [   ].
> No one [   ] to their lamentations,
> No one p[ities] their cries of woe.
> Who [produced] the serpent?   (5)
> The sea [produced] the serpent!
> Enlil has drawn [the image of the serpent] in heaven:[1]
> Its length was fifty leagues, [its height] was one league,
> Its mouth was six cubits, [its tongue?] twelve cubits,
> Its ear flaps(?) twelve cubits.   (10)
> At sixty cubits [it snatches?] birds,
> It draws nine cubits water [   ],
> If it raises its tail, it [   ].
> All the gods of heaven [   ],
> The gods knelt before [Sin] in heaven,   (15)
> And [seized] the hem[2] of Sin in has[te],
> "Who will go [to kill] the Lion-serpent?
> "[Who] will sa[ve] the vast land,
> "And exercise kingship [in the land]?
> "Go, Tishpak, ki[ll the Lion-serpent],   (20)
> "Sa[ve] the vast land [   ]
> "And exercise kingship [in the land]."
> "You sent me, lord of the offspring of the river [   ],

---

1. This line may be an aetiology for a constellation (see Beaulieu, JCS 51 [1999], 94). Although some scholars suggest that this mean that Enlil caused the serpent to attack the land, this is hard to see in "draw" and the text states that the sea was its creator.
2. A gesture of entreaty.

"I do not know [the ways?] of the Lion-serpent,
"[   ] before [   ]."   (25)
[   ] the people [   ]

(fragmentary lines, then gap)

[Ea?] made ready to speak, saying to [Tishpak]   (1′)
"Fling up a cloud, [   ] a storm,
"[Grasp] the cylinder seal at your throat,[1] before you,
"Shoot (an arrow), ki[ll] the Lion-serpent."
He flung up a cloud, [   ] a whirlwind,   (5′)
[He grasped] the cylinder seal at his throat before himself,
He shot (an arrow) [and killed] the Lion-serpent.
Three years, three months, one day and night,
The b[lood of the Lion-serpent [   ].

(end of tablet)

Text: King, CT 13 33–34 (Rm 282).
Edition: King, STC 1, 116–121.
Translation: A. Heidel, *The Babylonian Genesis*[2] (Chicago, 1951), 141–143; Bottéro, *Mythologie*, 464–469.
Literature: Jacobsen, *Oriental Institute Communications* 13 (1932), 53–54; W. G. Lambert, CRRAI 38 (1985), 55–56; Wiggerman, in O. Haex, et al., ed., *To the Euphrates and Beyond, Archaeological Studies in Honour of Maurits N. van Loon* (Rotterdam, 1989), 117–133, with proposals adopted here; T. J. Lewis, "CT 13 33–34 and Ezekiel 32: Lion-Dragon Myths," JAOS 116 (1996), 28–47.

1. Cylinder seals were often worn around the neck on a cord (see Collon, CRRAI 45 [1998], 15–30).

F. Great Hymns and Prayers

III.25 GULA HYMN OF BULLUTSA-RABI

This hymn extols in alternating stanzas Gula, goddess of healing, and her spouse, using different names (see also III.42a). The text is unusual because of the author's "signature" in the concluding lines. It is a work of great learning; rare and dialectal words abound. The hymn makes numerous allusions to mythology and may quote directly other compositions. It was popular in learned circles and was quoted in an ancient commentary. It is attested also in an ancient list of famous authors of the past and their putative literary works.

The frame of the composition is a third-person prayer by Bullutsa-rabi. He introduces the goddess in the first stanza and concludes the whole composition with a prayer that she intercede for him. The goddess speaks her own praises, a well-attested mode in Akkadian.[1] She discourses upon her astral character, her elevation to a position of authority, her interest in agriculture, her unalterable word, her healing abilities, her control of destinies, her sexual attractiveness, her upbringing and education, marriage, and scholarship.

The poet thereby proceeds from her general attributes of divinity, her role, function, and physical attributes to her major "rites of passage" and concludes with praise of her medical learning. Perhaps this aspect of her persona was of particular appeal to the poet, who says he is sick and in need of her ministrations. By contrast, her spouse, Ninurta, is consistently portrayed as a fierce and terrible warrior, without developing a theme. Gula's personality is more complex; she has more names than her husband. Despite the dual structure of the hymn, the goddess is clearly the author's primary interest.

i

The goddess is the most capable of all deities who sit on daises,   (1)
"I am noble, I am lordly, I am splendid and sublime.
"My station is on high, I am a woman of dignity.
"I excel among goddesses,
"Great is my star in heaven, my name in the netherworld.   (5)

---

1. Von Soden (RA 52 [1958], 132) suggests possible cultic significance for first-person texts of this type; this genre seems to be restricted to goddesses. Whatever the literary background, the goddess's self-predication seems to lend her praises extra authority. Compare the self-praise of Ishtar II.4 and III.43f and E. Reiner, "A Sumero-Akkadian Hymn of Nanâ," JNES 33 (1974), 221–236.

"Fair it is to hold me in mind, (it is) good health and life.
"People discourse of me (in) sickness (and in) health,
"My great name is Nintinugga.[1]

ii

"My spouse is the warrior, son of Enlil, the mighty,
"Valorous one, trampler of the foe,   (10)
"Who crushes the enemy,
        (but) who makes the righteous stand,
"Who fulfilled Enlil's wishes, whose strength is sublime,
"The strong lord who slew Anzu,
"[   ] the responsibility of (Enlil's) supremacy.[2]
"[   ] to whom Ninlil listens,   (15)
"Ninurta, the merciful offspring of heaven,
"Pure progeny, heir of Esharra.[3]

iii

"I was sought out, for E[nli]l chose me among goddesses,
"He looked up [   ], he fell in love with me.
"He wed me [for the ...] his supremacy,   (20)
"He allotted the management of Esharra [   ] into my hands.
"He added [   ] procedures,
"He [   ] me,
"He made fair my name [   ] among goddesses.
"He called [me   ] Nin-[   ], I have no rival.   (25)

iv

"[(My spouse is)] the great master of portions,
"Pure light of heaven, the one who calls for the work song,
"Resettler of devastated agricultural lands,
"Pursuer, wild bull with head held high,
"Who seized ..., who split stones[4] and begot grains,   (30)

---

1. Sumerian healing deity, "Lady Who Revives the Dead" (see in general H. Hirsch, "Den Toten zu Beleben," AfO 22 [1968/9], 39–58).
2. Allusion to the Anzu poem, see III.23.
3. A temple of Enlil in Nippur, hence the author is saying "son of Enlil."
4. Allusion to the Sumerian poem "Ninurta and the Stones," for which see J. J. A. van Dijk, LUGAL-UD ME-LÁM-bi NIR-GÁL (Leiden, 1983), 37–44, with this passage alluded to 42 note 139.

"Heaper up of grain piles,
      who performed the great festival for Enlil,
"Who makes teeming humankind live in abundance,
      who resettles abandoned mounds,
"Stately, tall of form, pure shining son of Anu,
"Mightiest of the gods, great Ningirsu.

v

"Opener of the furrow, director of daybreak,   (35)
"Who drives out the (plow) ox, mistress of (its) track,
"Beloved of the stars that are the signs for plowing,
"Who silos fodder for the oxen,
"Who grants good work to the plowman,
"Mistress of basket, seed grain, plow, plowfield, share,
      and field hand(?),   (40)
"Who stretches out the measuring cord, cubits,
      and measuring rod,
"Who carries a stylus as she works, doing the accounts,
"Mother Nanshe,[1] mistress of the field boundary am I.

vi

"My towering husband is an honored noble of heaven,
"Clad in awesomeness and divine splendor,   (45)
"Who makes heaven and netherworld quake,
      lofty one among the Igigi-gods,
"Who charges through canebrakes, who dances in battle,
"Who examines the heights of heaven,
      who investigates the bottom of the netherworld,
"Who implements wise counsel, master of decisions,
"Who gathers to himself wisdom, of profound intelligence,   (50)
"Reared by the depths, splendid one, offspring of Mami,
"Rider of all the winds, lord of battle and warfare,
"Great storm, brilliant of feature, lord of lords, Ninazu.[2]

---

1. A goddess at home in the Lagash region, not usually equated with Gula, but perhaps through Ningirsu (Lagashite god) = Ninurta (see Anzu [III.23]); see also line 34.
2. "Lord Physician," a Sumerian deity (usually a brother of Ninurta).

vii

"I am sublime in heaven, I am queen in the netherworld,

"Among the gods I have no peer,   (55)

"Among goddesses I have no equal.

"I am mistress of the depths, Ea's place,

"Lofty and great are my responsibilities.

"The limits I (set) cannot be changed,

"(My) command cannot be altered.   (60)

"My name is great, I am sublime,

"I tower in my stance, I am enormous in form.

"I grant portions to all the gods.

"I am daughter, I am bride, I am spouse,

  I, indeed, manage the household,   (65)

"Wife of the foremost one, Pabilsag,[1]

"Ninkarrak,[2] mistress of counsel, am I.

viii

"The lofty one, favorite of the gods, Anu's son,

"He is the foremost one, surpassing all lords.

"The Igigi-gods consult with him,

  the shining breastplate(?)* of heaven.   (70)

"Great is fear of him among the gods,

  every one of them is in awe of his name,

"They await his command.

"He is the foremost one, towering hero, noble,

  virile one, bastion,

"He is firm of foot in heaven, powerful in the depths,

"Great in the netherworld, sublime in Ekur,   (75)

"Cherished son of Enlil,[3]

"Pure offspring of Nin<lil>,

"Double of Anu, the warrior Ninurta.

---

1. Sumerian deity, husband of Nininsina, a healing goddess.
2. Healing goddess.
3. Variant omits Enlil.

ix

"I am the physician, I can save life,
"I carry every herb, I banish illness.   (80)
"I gird on the sack with life-giving incantations,
"I carry the texts that make (one) well.
"I give health to humankind.
"(My) clean dressing salves the wound,
"(My) soft bandage relieves the pain.   (85)
"At my examination, the moribund revives,
"At a word from me, the feeble one arises.
"I am merciful, [I am] kindly [   ]
"The mighty man [   ]
"I am she who gives [   ]   (90)
"Ninigiziba[ra¹   am I].

x

"My beloved is the young man ... [   ]
"The mighty one, endowed with strength [   ]
"Overpowering lord whose vigor cannot be equalled,
"Towering, with stately physique,
        standing ready to charge mountains,   (95)
"Lovely, adorned with allure, and gorgeous all over,
"Who dances in the pride of young manhood,
        adorned with joy,
"First fruits of the harvest song, whose look is abundance,
"Fierce, irresistible, overcoming foes,
"Crusher of stones,² Zababa.³   (100)

xi

"I am a warrior, skilled through experience,*
"I am the spouse of the mighty one, light of the gods.
"I make decisions, I give commands,
"In Esharra (my) way is sublime,
"In Ekur, dwelling of the gods, (my) dwelling is on high.   (105)

1. Sumerian epithet, "Lady looked upon with confidence."
2. See p. 584 note 4.
3. A warrior god sometimes equated with Ninurta; see, for example, Anzu (III.23) Tablet III line 142.

"I have mercy on the weak, I enrich the destitute,
"I bestow life on the one who reveres me.
"I make straight the path of the one who seeks after my ways,
"I am the great one, daughter of Anu, mother Ba'u,[1]
      life of the people.

xii

"My beloved is the warrior, foremost one, king of kings,   (110)
"Furious one, slayer who tangles (in) battle,
"Launcher of the deluge,
"Who loves [   ] and bride.
"Being merciful, he heeds prayers,
"He turns the wicked and enemies into clay.   (115)
"He burns the roots of all disobedient like reeds,
"Ninurta, foremost of the vanguard, mighty son of Enlil.

xiii

"I am fairest voiced among goddesses,
"I am the most beautiful among queens,
"I am the most attractive among young women,   (120)
"I am the most seemly among fine ladies.
"I have been given to his divinity,
"I am led to the foremost one, lord of the gods.
"My face is attractive,
"I am seductive to the mighty one,
      son of the lord of the gods.   (125)
"I have come into his pure place,
"Into awe-inspiring Eshumesha,[2]
"Into (its) Ekashbar, house of decisions, place of commands,
"I am Ungalnibru,[3] the pure princess.

xiv

"Lofty one, lord who is the very greatest in heaven,   (130)
"Terror of whom makes all lands quake(?),[4]

---

1. Sumerian goddess, wife of Ningirsu (see p. 585 note 1).
2. Temple of Ninurta and spouse at Nippur.
3. Sumerian epithet, "Queen of Nippur."
4. See p. 584 note 4.

"Fear of whom envelops the mountain[s],
"He wears the heavens on his head, like a tiara,
"He is shod with the netherworld, as with [san]dals,
"He holds in his grasp commands that no [god kn]ows of,   (135)
"At his glance ... [   ]
"Swift [   ], multiplying prosperity,
"[   ], trampler, lofty Uta'ulu.[1]

xv

"Antu bore me, cherished me steadfastly,
"She taught me fair counsel, adorned me with charm,   (140)
"She gave me to the fullest the joys of young girls.
"Anu my father named me according to his own name,⋆
"He made me excel among my brothers.
"Ea in the depths gave me in full of his wisdom,
"He gave me the tablet stylus from his own hand,   (145)
"He entrusted to me the physician's craft, a secret of the gods,
"Enlil chose me as bride for the mighty one, his son.
"I am Gula, mistress of heaven and netherworld.

xvi

"Foremost one, slayer, mountain, overwhelmer of the sea,
"Irresistible storm, battle deluge,   (150)
"Instigator of discord, declarer of war,
"Who brings opponents to submission, mastering the foe,
"Mighty one who relies on his own strength,
"Savage, pitiless, who musters the ill wind,
      who grants victory,
"Esharra's trust, sublime son, who takes his own high rank,   (155)
"Avenger of the father who begot him,
"Pure god, deserving of kingship,
"My fair spouse, Lugalbanda.[2]

---

1. Another name for Ninurta; compare the hymn to Ninurta III.47b, line 4.
2. Legendary Sumerian king of Uruk, who, like Ninurta, contested with Anzu. For the equation of Lugalbanda and Ninurta, compare Anzu (III.23) Tablet III line 147.

xvii

"...

"My allure is compelling ... [   ]   (160)

"I am adorned with ... [   ]

"My [   ] are ...

"My [   ] are piping,

"I wear(?) a ...

"When I go in procession, charm falls like the dew,   (165)

"When I come in there is splendor,

"In my bed ...

"There is no one like me,

"I am Ninsun,[1] the merciful goddess.

xviii

"My beloved is the favorite among goddesses,   (170)

"He wears on his head a tiara with superb horns,

"He wields sharp weapons,

"He leads about fierce storm demons,

"Conqueror of all mountains,

"Who overthrew hard stones, as many as there were,[2]   (175)

"He forced to submit those who were insubmissive to Enlil,

"Strongest of the strong, slayer of slayers, Lugalbanda.

xix

"I am merciful, I hear (prayer) from afar off,

"I fetch up the dead from the netherworld,

"I am girded with the leather bag,

    I ... the scalpel and knife.   (180)

"I examine the weary, I watch over the sick,

    I open(?) the sore,

"I am mistress of life.

"I am physician, I am diviner, I am exorcist,

"I, who am expert in calculations,

    no one has explained (to me) a single wedge,[3]

---

1. "Wild Cow," mother of Gilgamesh.
2. See p. 584 note 4.
3. This may refer to calculation of propitious times or the time suffering could be expected to last; compare Poem of the Righteous Sufferer (III.14) Tablet II line 1.

"I ... every one of them.   (185)

"There is life in my [   ],

"I am Ninlil, the merciful [goddess]."★

xx

[   ] bo[th] gods [   ],

Have mercy on the servant who fears your divinity [   ]!

Heed what he says, stand by him when he prays,   (190)

Accept his entreaty, listen to his words,

Take your seats (of judgment) and administer his case,

Set right his confusion, illumine his darkness.

Let him strip his mourning weeds,

     let him put on (normal) clothes.

That servant, meek and lowly,   (195)

May his life be prolonged at the unalterable command

     of your great divinity.

O Gula, great lady, whose help is Ninurta,

Intercede for him with the mighty one,

     your splendid spouse,

That he bring forth recovery for Bullutsa-rabi,

That he may kneel before you daily.   (200)

Text: W. G. Lambert, OrNS 36 (1967), pl. VIII–XXIII.

Edition: W. G. Lambert, OrNS 36 (1967), 105–132, to which this translation is greatly indebted.

Translation: Hecker, TUAT II/5, 759–764 (partial).

★*Notes to Text*: (70) CAD N/1, 149a, "pectoral," though see Lambert, OrNS 36 (1967), 131 *ad loc.*
(101) CAD L, 154a suggests that this line is a faulty adaptation of the Epic of Creation Tablet I line 59; however, the same expression occurs in KAR 321.10′: *ṭu-ub-ba et-pe-šu i-le-'a-a*, so one need not seek a parallel in the Epic of Creation. (142) Not clear. The first-person referent *-anni* occurs eight times in nine successive lines; an etymological play may lie there (W. G. Lambert, OrNS 36 [1967], 132). (187) Butler, AOAT 258 (1998), 372.

III.26 ISHTAR QUEEN OF HEAVEN

As W. G. Lambert has shown, this hymn is a conflation and reworking of various texts about Ishtar. The basic components were three or four hymns of varying styles and subject matter sewn together with a penitential psalm.

One of these hymns, portions of which are found in i 1–26, iii 39–92, and iv 16–53, is characterized by learned etymological speculations, archaizing grammatical forms, and repeated use of certain words (e.g., the word rendered below as "cherish"). The psalm portion speaks of a sufferer in the third person who is understood to be the speaker, and who unfolds his sad fate in the style usual for the genre (compare II.13, III.14, 15, 28 etc.). A hymn with refrain, a well-known Sumerian style (see III.2, III.38c) but rare in Akkadian, is preserved in iii 1–38.

Column iv 1–15 preserves a hymn in honor of Nippur and the sanctuary there called Ebardurgarra, considered to be Ishtar's. Column iv 54–87 is a hymn dealing with Ishtar's festivity and relaxation in her favorite abode; this could originally have been an independent composition. The end of the text may contain either a further blessing on the Ebardurgarra or a blessing on the author or ruling king.

The text is therefore a celebration of the goddess, her residence, cult, and aspects. She is honored as a celestial phenomenon, compared to the moon and sun. One section deals with her names (compare III.17, III.45e).

This composition is typical of one kind of creativity in the Mature period. Novelty was not always an end in itself in the Mesopotamian creative process. Successful adaptation and reuse of earlier material was esteemed highly. While this composition may seem like an extreme case of creative reuse, resembling a pastiche, it offers a unity of purpose that makes its varying styles seem symphonic rather than disconcerting. The very choice of materials suggests that the compiler was a person of unusual talents. Perhaps one or more segments of the composition were original with the compiler, though this is impossible to tell.

(first part of text, consisting of praises for Ishtar,
too fragmentary for translation)

ii

There was a man, he made no provision for the Capable Lady,
I was th(at) [man] who did not speak to Ishtar!

She [thun]dered at him like a storm,
     she grew full of anger at him,
[She ...] his dignity, she drove off his protective spirit.[1]
His [god forsook him], his goddess threw him over.   (10)
[   ] family, kept away and did not come near.
His lofty stature he bent to a crook,
He leaned his head beside his feet.
His city avoided him, his people were afraid of him,
He was always walking, hunched over,
     in the outskirts of his city,   (15)
Nor did hair and beard(?) remain.*
He had not sought her sanctuary,
     indeed, he did not wait upon her!
One of furious strength, her established envoy,
The Owl demon, who peers into bedrooms,
Leaned malignantly through the window, heard that man.   (20)
She cast a chill of fear upon him, so he fell silent ...
She set the Dusk demon to spy on him,
She drove him out of his mind [   ]
[   ] terrified him [   ]
He knew [no] dignity, (his) [sought] another,   (25)
He kept walking about [na]ked [   ].
Her [merciless ...] were clustered around.
[Mother?], infant, spouse, [father?],
[   ] chamber, abode of [   ]
[   ] her chamber, her storehouse [   ]   (30)

(fragmentary lines, then breaks off)

iii

(hymn with refrain, names of Ishtar)

No one but she can   (1)
[Hold the lead]line[2] of heaven
No one but she can
[ ] mountains and seas [   ]
No one but she can   (5)

1. For this motif, compare the Poem of the Righteous Sufferer (III.14) Tablet I lines 42–46.
2. For the leadline of heaven, compare II.23a, line 10, with note.

Grant kingship, lordship [   ]
No one but she can
[   ] the inhabited world [   ]
No one but she can
... the staff of [   ]   (10)
No one but she can
[Sur]round the main street of [   ] with excellence.
No one but she can
Make fairest all that exists [   ]
No one but she can   (15)
Make the voice [of the people?] heard.
No one but she can
Complete their pure governance [   ]
No one but she can
Become enraged, relent, have mercy [   ]   (20)
No one but she can
Punish, take pity, forgive, [   ]
No one but she can
[   ] where there is anger.
No one but she can   (25)
[Lead by the han]d out of danger.
No one but she can
Bring back the one who reveres her from the grave.
No one but she can
Revive the dead, restore [   ]   (30)
No one but she can
Grant long life to him who heeds her.
No one but she can
Do without ... [   ]
No one but she can!   (35)
Ishtar is mistress of the [   ] designs of land and peoples,
She has made everything perfect,
Completed the rites and gathered to herself everything.
Which god brought forth her sign?

(eleven lines fragmentary)

[   ], her names are [sur]passing:

Anu, Enlil, and Ea made her important,
        the Igigi-gods cherished her.
Her very first name, her great appellation
That her father Anu, whom she adores, named her of old,
Is Ninanna "Queen of Heaven" (= An),   (55)
Mistress of the inhabited world, who loves the peoples,
        companion to the sun,
Fierce in terror, Minu-anni,[1]
Exalted (in) the awesome strength of a young bull, Minu-ulla.
Her second great appellation,
By which her begetter, divine Duranki,[2] made her great,   (60)
Is Ne'anna, "She whose Strength is Sublime,"
[   ] of humankind, goddess who is the strength of Anshar,
[   ] of Anu, she bears terror,
[   ] of heaven, impetuous, goddess of pity.
[For a third] did Ninshiku, the warrior Ea,   (65)
[In his art]ful wisdom distinguish her as a name:
Zannaru "The Capable One,"
[Mistress? of] the four world regions, cherished of Dagan,
[A]nunu,[3] creatress of subject peoples,
[Who can tu]rn man to woman and woman to man.[4]   (70)
... Namrasit, "Brightly Rising God,"[5]
        father of [her] favorite brother,[6]
[   ] for a fourth [name] did cherish her,
[   ] totality [   ]
[bo]nd of the peoples, life of [the land],
[   ] light of humankind,   (75)
[   ] she glows awesomely, she overwhelms [   ],
[   ] discord, ter[rifying aura]
[   ] she is a woman, she is a man [   ].

    1. This and the byname in the next line are of unknown meaning (literally: "Why Yes?" or "Why No?").
    2. A name for Enlil; compare, for example, Anzu (III.23), Old Babylonian Version, Tablet II line 21, and below, iv 1.
    3. A byname; see W. G. Lambert, *Studies Sjöberg*, 323–325.
    4. A reference to sexual deviation, one of Ishtar's domains; see p. 904 note 3.
    5. Sin, the moon.
    6. Possibly a reference to Ishtar's pairing with the moon in the evening sky, as opposed to her pairing with the sun in the morning sky (56); on the other hand, WGL suggests that Tammuz is meant.

(thirteen fragmentary lines)

iv

(Ishtar and Nippur)

[Nippu]r, bond of heaven and earth,[1]
    li[nkage] of the four world regions,   (1)
Growing on the [fla]nk of an unapproachable mountain,
[The city Ni]ppur, surrounded by splendor,
    having coming forth within it,
Enlil built (it) for himself to live in.
[He ap]proached her
    and bestowed it upon her for her queenship,   (5)
He ordained her Ebardurgarra[2] as its sanctuary,
"Let the house be a shrine just like his dwelling!"[3]
The [ ] of supremacy lies within it,
High indeed is its head, it is the double of Ekur.
Brilliant is its light, covering the whole inhabited world, (10)
Its radiance is found in the heart of the mountain.
It adores(?) her and looks after her,
Its inside is always filled with gladness,
Ebardurgarra adores(?) the mistress.
The four world regions of one accord bring it their yield. (15)
She ordains destiny foremost with Enlil,
She sets out regulations for the great gods, as Anu does.
Daily the gods assemble around her,
    the great gods for counsel,
The great Igigi-gods hurry, one after another,
To fix their portions, to receive their com[mands].   (20)
All the goddesses of the peoples kneel down before her,
They supplicate her together, they kneel at her feet.
She examines their sanctuaries, she inspects their chambers,
She fixes the portions of the gods of holy places.
She is the very greatest, the most important of goddesses, (25)

---

1. Translation of Duranki; see above, p. 595 note 2.
2. Sanctuary of Ishtar at Nippur (George, *Topographical Texts*, 454).
  3. Lambert (*Studies Kraus*, 216) suggests that this is an Akkadian etymological explanation of the Sumerian name.

Mighty daughter of the luminary of the night sky,
    the heart's delight of Enlil,
Cherished goddess, princess of her brothers.[1]

Living handiwork of Dagan, female double of Anu,
Beloved of Ea, who is master of wisdom,
Cherished of the Mother Goddess, the omnipotent, princess,   (30)
She is princess, cherished, goddess, and mistress,
Spouse, mistress, beloved, ...,[2]*
Bride of the "Fierce Lion,"[3] mistress of Eridu,
The Ishtar of Anu, who dwells in the sanctuary Eanna,[4]
She is the most lofty one, supreme, sublime, and queen.   (35)
Sweet are songs of her praise, great her cherishing,
The Queen of Nippur is sublime and queen,
Sweet are songs of her praise, magnificent her cherishing,
Who is cherished like the goddess,
    Queen of Nippur, their deity?
The Seven Gods have proclaimed her seven names.*   (40)

May this song be pleasing to you, O Ishtar,
May it never cease before you, may it abide at your command.
Where there is lamentation, may there be a dirge for you,
Where there is happiness, may there be cherishing of you.
In the chamber of your rites may they hail you,   (45)
Where your rituals are performed, may they address you,
In the chambers of the monthly festival, rejoicing and festivity.
Listen, O Mistress, may your mood be joyous,
May your heart gladly demand festivi[ty],
May the day bring you gladness, the night repose,   (50)
May Inimanizida[5] bring you [   ]
May the goddesses of beer [   ]

(about ten lines lost or fragmentary)

1. Sun and moon (both male); see iii 56, 71.
2. The parallelism calls for an epithet like "Divine Mother of Eridu."
3. Reference uncertain.
4. Wordplays on the proper names Ishtar, Anu, and Eanna.
5. "His-Word-is-True," messenger of Ninurta.

Take your seat in the immensities, O Ishtar,
May Anu, Enlil, and Ea be seated with you.
In a [   ], sweet drink in a lapis [   ]   (65)
Let them drink wine, "Drink, drink wine!"
[   ] ...
May your features beam and [   ]
May your hearts be glad and be full of rejoicing!
Rejoice, O Ishtar, may [   ] be joyous,   (70)
Be at ease, O Daughter of Sin, [   ]
They have given you the destiny of divine Duranki,
    your begetter,
Be at ease in Ebardurgarra,
    take up residence in your [dwel]ling.
When you decree destinies with Anu, Enlil, and Ea,
Make the destiny of Duranki surpassing [   ]   (75)
[Command] the well-being of Uruk,[1]
[Command] a favorable lot for Akkad,
May Larsa [raise high its head?] to heaven,
May [   ] shine,
May Badtibira [   ] repose,   (80)
As for the Ekur of Badtibira [   ]
May Kish [   ]
May Hursagkalamma be(?) a sanctuary(?) [   ]
May Ur be renewed [   ]
May Edilmunna [   ]   (85)

(seven fragmentary lines)

The invocation of its name [   ] forever.

Text: W. G. Lambert, *Studies Kraus*, 182–191.
Edition: W. G. Lambert, *Studies Kraus*, 173–218.
Translation: Seux, *Hymnes*, 93–98.
★*Notes to Text*: (ii 16) Very doubtful; emending text to *zi-iq-na!-su*. (iv 32) Perhaps DINGIR. AMA.NUN.ME(?), WGL: Amazilla. (iv 40) Following CAD I/J, 321–322 against AHw, 411a; see Lambert, *Studies Kraus*, 217.

1. The proper names that follow are cities and sanctuaries in Sumer and Babylonia.

III.27 GREAT PRAYER TO ISHTAR

This composition is of particular interest for its literary history, as one can discern definite stages in the evolution of its text. An older version, dating to the latter part of the second millennium, is known from a learner's tablet from Hattusha, the capital of the Hittites in Anatolia, while the later one is known from a Neo-Babylonian manuscript from Mesopotamia. There is also a Hittite translation from a lost Akkadian original that was apparently superior to the Akkadian version now preserved from Hattusha.

Comparison of the two versions will show that the prototype text was enlarged, although the structure and organization of the original were not greatly affected. Ideas and patterns already in the text were expanded and elaborated. Some of the variants between the early and later versions given here are the results of mistakes in the earlier manuscript, as shown by the Hittite version, which agrees in some instances with the later version against the older one.

Comparison of the two versions provides an excellent case study in how a Mesopotamian literary text could evolve or expand and still remain true in its essentials to the intentions of the original author.

(a) OLDER VERSION (from Hattusha)

I implore you, lady of ladies, goddess [of goddesses],   (1)
Ishtar, lady of all the inhabited world,
     who governs the four world regions,
Innana, noble one, greatest of the Igigi-gods,
You are exalted, you are queen, exalted in your name,
You are the luminary of heaven, daughter of Sin, Capable Lady, (5)
Who brandishes weapons and sets up [   ],
Fierce one, the most capable of the Igigi-gods,
Most valiant among [the gods] her brethren,
Who gathers to herself all rites, who takes nobility for her own.
O Mistress, splendid is your greatness,
     exalted over all the gods,   (10)
Planet for the war cry, who can make harmonious brothers
     set at one another,
Who can make the wives of kings afraid(?),*

Strong mistress of the winds(?), who gores mountains,
[Gus]hea[1] of combat, clothed in chilling fear,
You render final judgment and decision,
      the command for heaven and netherworld,   (15)
Chapels, sanctuaries, altars, [and daises are attentive] to you.
Where is not your name, where are not your daises?
Where are not your rites,
      where are your designs not put into effect?
[   ] have exalted you,
      they have made your authority the greatest,
[They exalt you] among all the gods,
      they have made your position highest of all.   (20)
At mention of your name,
      the [gods] totter, the great gods tremble,
The countries extol [your awe-inspiring name],
      you are the great one, the exalted [one].
[All   ] living creatures, humankind praise [your valor],
[Have mercy, O mis]tress of heaven and earth,
      shepherd of the human [race],
[Have mercy, O mis]tress of holy Ayakku,[2]
      the pure [treasury],   (25)
[Have mercy, O mistress] whose feet weary not,
      [whose legs are strong to ru]n,
[Have mercy], O mistress of combat [and of every melee],
[O splendid lioness] of the Igigi-gods,
      who makes [furious gods submissive],
[   ] ... [   ]
[   ]   (30)
G[reat is your valor], O [vali]ant mistress,
[   ] who goes to the fight.
Fiery glow [that blazes against the enemy, that wr]eaks
      destruction on [the fierce],
[who] masses the multitude,
[   ] which [no one] can learn,   (35)
[   ] ... the evil one perishes,
[   ] joy

1. Byname of Ishtar; compare the Agushaya Poem (II.5) Tablet II vii 16.
2. Eanna, temple of Ishtar at Uruk; see I.3d, note to line 27.

[   ] may your heart be calmed,
[Furious] wild bull, [may your feelings be] eased,
May your benevolent eyes rest [upon me],   (40)
[   ] ... me,
[May my angry god and goddess be reconci]led with me,
    my entreaty [   ].
How long, my mistress,
    will imbeciles [and weaklings surpass me]?

(possibly one or two lines missing)

[   ] night and day [   ]
Look steadfastly upon me!
Your sweet [wind] wafted upon me
[With] my eyes, I will see your light,   (5′)
[   ], preserve me!

(b) LATER VERSION

I implore you, lady of ladies, goddess of goddesses,   (1)
Ishtar, queen of all the inhabited world,
    who governs the peoples,
Irnini, you are noble, the greatest of the Igigi-gods,
You are powerful, you are queen, exalted is your name.[1]
You are the luminary of heaven and earth,
    the valiant daughter of Sin,   (5)
Who brandishes weapons, who prepares for battle,
Who gathers to herself all rites, who dons the lordly tiara.
O Mistress, splendid is your greatness,
    exalted over all the gods.
Planet for the war cry,
    who can make harmonious brothers set at one another,
Who can always grant a comrade,   (10)
Strong(?) one, mistress of the tilt, who gores mountains,
Gushea, whose mail is combat, clothed in chilling fear.
You render final judgment and decision,
    the command for heaven and netherworld,

1. Or: "are your names."

Chapels, sanctuaries, altars, and daises are attentive to you.
Where is not your name, where are not your rites?   (15)
Where are your designs not put into effect,
        where are your daises not set up?
Where are you not great, where are you not exalted?
Anu, Enlil, and Ea have lifted you high,
        they have made your authority greatest among the gods,
They have given you the highest rank among all the Igigi-gods,
        they have made your (heavenly) station highest of all.
At the thought of your name, heaven and netherworld quake,   (20)
The gods totter, the Anunna-gods tremble.
Humankind extols your awe-inspiring name,
You are the great one, the exalted one.
All the people of this land, living creatures,
        humankind, praise your valor.
You are the one who renders verdicts for subject peoples
        in truth and justice,   (25)
You look upon the oppressed and abused
        and always set them right.
Have mercy, mistress of heaven and earth,
        shepherdess of the human race!
Have mercy, mistress of holy Eanna, the pure treasury!
Have mercy, mistress whose feet weary not,
        whose legs are strong to run!
Have mercy, mistress of combat and of every melee!   (30)

O splendid lioness of the Igigi-gods,
        who renders furious gods submissive,
Most capable of all sovereigns, who grasps the leadline of kings,
Who opens the veils of all young women,
You rise up, bring yourself down,★
        great is your valor, O valiant Ishtar,
Shining torch of heaven and earth,
        brilliance of all inhabited lands,   (35)
Furious in irresistible onslaught, hero to the fight,
Fiery glow that blazes against the enemy,
        who wreaks destruction on the fierce,

Dancing one, Ishtar, who masses the multitude,
Goddess of men, Ishtar of women,
     whose intentions no one can learn,
Wherever you look the dead comes to life, the sick arises,   (40)
The unjustly treated prospers at the sight of you.
I myself call upon you, your exhausted,
     desperate, most stricken servant,
Look upon me, mistress, accept my entreaty!
Look steadfastly upon me, hear my prayer!
Speak a word of mercy for me, let your feelings be eased.   (45)
Have mercy on my wretched person,
     which is full of confusion and perturbation!
Have mercy on my most stricken heart,
     which is full of tears and sighing!
Have mercy on my wretched omens,
     confused and perturbed!
Have mercy on my anguished household,
     which moans for grief!
Have mercy on my feelings,
     which abide in tears and sighing!   (50)
Irninitum, raging lion, may your heart be calmed.
Furious wild bull, may your feelings be eased.
May your benevolent eyes rest upon me,
Look upon me with your beaming features!
Drive off the evil witchcraft from my person,
     let me see your shining light!   (55)
How long, my mistress, will my opponents glower at me,
And with lies and falsehood plot evil against me?
My harassers and ill-wishers are raging against me,
How long, my mistress,
     will imbeciles and weaklings surpass me?
The feeble has gone on ahead, I have lagged behind,   (60)
The weak has grown strong, I have grown weak.
I churn like a wave that an adverse wind masses,
My heart soars and flutters like a bird of heaven.
I moan like a dove, night and day,
I am ..., I cry bitterly.   (65)

My feelings are most stricken
    from crying "Woe!" and "Alas!"
I, O my god, O my goddess, what have I done?
I am dealt with as if I did not revere my god and my goddess.
Disease, headpains, decline, and ruin beset me,
Constraints, averted faces, and anger beset me,   (70)
Wrath, rage and fury of gods and men.
I have experienced, O my mistress, days of darkness,
    months of gloom, years of grief,
I have experienced, O my mistress,
    a judgment of upset and turmoil.
Death and misery have a hold on me,
My chapel is deathly still, my sanctuary is deathly still,   (75)
A ghastly stillness has fallen upon my household,
    my courtyard, and my fields,
My god's face is turned some other place,
My relations are scattered, my fold dispersed.
I am attending you, my mistress, waiting for you,
I implore you, absolve my debt!   (80)
Absolve my crime, misdeed, sin, and wrong-doing!
Forget my sin, accept my plea,
Loose my fetters, set me free!
Make straight my path, let me pass through the street,
    proud and radiant among the living.
Speak, that from your speaking the angry god be reconciled,   (85)
That the goddess who became furious relent!
May my dark and smoky hearth burn clear,
May my snuffed-out torch burst to flames,
May my scattered relations regroup themselves,
May my paddock enlarge, my fold expand,   (90)
Accept my supplication, hear my prayer!
Look steadfastly upon me, ...
How long, my mistress,
    will you be angry and your face averted?
How long, my mistress,
    will you be enraged and your feelings in a fury?
Turn toward me your cast-down head,
    resolve on a favorable word!   (95)

Like water, the standing pool(?)* of a canal,
    may your feelings come to ease.
Let me trample down like dirt those who rage against me!
Make submissive those furious against me
    and flatten them under my feet!
May my prayers and entreaties sit well with you,
May your magnificent forbearance be with me,   (100)
That those who see me in the street
    may magnify your name,
And that I too may proclaim your divinity
    and valor to the people of this land,
"Ishtar is preeminent, Ishtar is queen,
"The lady is preeminent, the lady is queen,
"Irnini, the valiant daughter of Sin, has no rival."   (105)

(The later version ends with a subscript calling it an "Incantation of Raising of the Hand" [in prayer, see General Introduction, F.1] and follows with four lines of instructions for a ritual, in the course of which the text is recited three times. The ritual and recitation are to deal with frustration or the like.)

Text: (a) Ehelolf, KUB 37 36, 37; (b) King, STC II, pl. LXXV–LXXXIV; duplicate cited JCS 21 (1967), 262.

Edition: (b) Ebeling, AGH, 130–136; (a) Güterbock-Reiner, JCS 21 (1967), 257–262, with parallel lines from (b) and a translation of the Hittite version.

Translation: von Soden, SAHG, 328–333 no. 61; Stephens, ANET[3], 383–385; Labat, *Religions*, 253–257; Seux, *Hymnes*, 186–194.

Literature: Güterbock-Reiner, essential for comparing the two versions in Akkadian, and the basis for the interpretation presented here.

Notes to Text: (a 12) WGL. (b 34) WGL. (b 96) Seux, *Hymnes*, 193 note 65.

III.28 LITERARY PRAYER TO ISHTAR

This relates the speech of a sufferer, variously in the first or third person, who falls ill and is given up for lost because of the goddess' withdrawal of favor (compare also III.14). The only wickedness the speaker can think of is evil things he did and said during his physical and mental disintegration (compare IV.19), so he does not know what caused initial disgrace. The final hymn of praise, perhaps originally a separate composition, is addressed to a group of women, and stresses the merciful and protective nature of Ishtar, hoping thereby to bring these qualities to bear on the supplicant. This "great prayer," like the others in its style, appears to be a composite of various sources, but all the same the product of an erudite and ardent poet.

(The first sixty or more lines of the text are lost or badly damaged. From them, one gleans that the text opened with a hymn of praise to Ishtar, mentioning her loud cry, her power, her shearing-off of mountains, her command of the four winds, her strong arms, and wide stance. Around line 47 the speaker refers to the circumstances that brought him low: he is surrounded, restrained, and various parts of his body are afflicted.)

[   ] the utterance of my mouth is stopped short,
[   ] my hearing is blocked,   (65)
[O Ishtar], bespeak, drive out the demon that binds me!
I have been remiss, I have sinned, I have made light (of my
       obligations), I have committed iniquity:
All of them are my sins and [my] iniquities!
I have done I know not what wrong,
       I have transgressed your commands,
[I] have been false to my vow to you,
       I have not observed your due.   (70)

I trample my misdeeds on the ground [   ]
[   ] ..., my iniquities are ...
Ishtar can rescue from danger,
When fear is revealed to her, she knows how to save.
Who among the gods can measure up to you?   (75)
None has ever been seen for answering prayers like you!
She braces the one who reveres her while he prays,
She [entrusts him?] to a protective spirit.

She is not slow to resuscitate [   ],
Anger is closely followed by reconciliation [   ].   (80)

Since you forgot your servant [   ],
He has no father [   ]
Confusion covers him [   ]
A fearless tormentor [   ]
A chill has seized him [   ]   (85)
Paralysis consigns him ... [   ]
His shanks are sluggish, [his knees] are crumpling,
His neck is bent [   ]
He has trouble keeping his balance [   ]
Like a tottering wall [   ]   (90)

You have been gracious to him, you will open [   ]
His life [   ]
His arms [   ]
He was moaning like a dove [   ]

(five lines lost or fragmentary)

May he not be crushed [   ]
May your breeze waft upon him [   ]   (100)

... his neck ...
He who defeated an opponent must have heeded his goddess,
His prayer was surely set before his god.

(eight lines fragmentary, then gap)

At your command [   ]
Your splendor that you [   ]
His throat quivers [   ]
His songs of joy are bitter [   ]
Awash in tears, he weeps [bitterly].   (145)
His mourners cal[led in] his family,*
For a bitter lamentation over him did [his] kin assemble.
By day he lacerates himself(?), at night he sobs,
Pity and pleading have withdrawn from him.
He is seared(?), cast aside, completely boxed in.   (150)

By an ill wind from(?) a god he [   ] out of his mind,
His feet are weak, [his] hands shake,
His chest is bruised, his tongue [   ].
He has grown short of breath, his arms fall limp,
His temperament is grim, his vigor gone,   (155)
He has suffered hearing loss(?),
       nor does he comprehend* [   ],
He has lost his mind, he forgets himself.
How has he neglected you that you ... his ...?
In mourning weeds and unkempt hair
       he ... [   ] your name,
Take his hand lest he be bruited as a curiosity(?) ...[1]   (160)

Fortify his path, fi[rm up] his foundations,
Strengthen the weak one,* let the [   ] be dissolved,
Rescue him from the maw of annihilation lest he [   ].
The dream interpreters must not exhaust [   ].[2]
And the diviner must not [   ] the ... [   ]   (165)
So run to his aid [   ]
May he not linger so, [   ] his life!
May he go no [fur]ther without you,
He must get to the bottom of his trouble and [   ],
He ... [   ]   (170)

Companion and friend [   ] him alone,
He let himself become enraged [   ]
He let himelf go berserk [   ]
"Of course my lips spoke blas[phemy],
"I uttered profanities, [I said] improper words.   (175)
"My flesh heaved, ... [   ]
"My eyes rolled up(?) like [   ]."
After he made [   ],

1. Literally: "be asked about," that is, become a public spectacle where everyone asks, "What is the matter with him?"

2. That is, save him lest the experts he retains to find the reason for his troubles use up his resources without helping him. This refurbishes the topos of the bafflement of experts (compare Poem of the Righteous Sufferer [III.14] Tablet I line 52, Tablet II lines 7–9; A Sufferer's Salvation [III.15] line 6'); differently Seux (*Hymnes*, 198 note 50).

A comfortable bed [   ]¹

(gap of about eighteen lines)

[   ] let him turn around,
[   ] let me support,
[Stop the] pall[bearers] at your cry,²
Open wide [the sealed tomb].   (200)

[   ] make glow in the east
[   ] with my own ...,
[   ] walking around, he has cut short the bruit of curiosity,³
May the whole world [   ] ...
[   ] who calls on the mistress of the Anunna-gods.   (205)
[   ] relieve my suffering,
[   ] my [   ], that I may praise you,
[   ] like the father who begot me,
[Like the mother who bo]re me, take pity on me!
[   ] can relieve [   ]   (210)

The [   ] of the [daugh]ter of Sin is sweet to praise,
[   ] she releases the captive.
She reveals light to the [one in pri]son,
[To the   ] her mercy is close at hand,
[   ] swift her relenting.   (215)
Bow down⁴ to her, [   ] of the gods,
Pray before her, [   ]
[From the rising of the] sun to the setting of the sun,
Continue to bless her [   ].
[Wherever   ] daises are established.   (220)
[Wherever   ] their "mountain" is invoked,
[   ] she alone is lofty,
[   ] she alone is mighty,
[   ] heroism,

---

1. Perhaps a reference to his presumed final illness: a bed of final rest.
2. Literally: "basket [ ]." I understand the fragmentary reference to "basket" here to mean the people carrying his funerary goods to the tomb. His redemption comes at the very moment his funeral procession is moving through the streets; compare III.15, line 43'.
3. See above, line 160.
4. Feminine plural, addressed to women adorants?

[   ] leadership,   (225)
[ ] mercy and forgiveness.
Praise [Ishtar, who shows] kindness to their people,
Acquire a protective spirit [   ].
Receive herewith of me your offering [   ],
[ ] gifts, sacrifices.   (230)

[ ] extol and keep her in your thoughts,
Enlil [granted her power] to rescue and save,
Shalash[1] ordained her [power to   ] and forgive,
Her hands [are clean], her arms washed,
Support her [   ], provide for her,   (235)
Prayer and abjuration are yours, Ishtar!
[   ] your mercy!

Text: W. G. Lambert, AfO 19 (1959/60), pl. VIII–XI.
Edition: W. G. Lambert, AfO 19 (1959/60), 50–55.
Translation: Seux, *Hymnes*, 194–199.
Literature: von Soden, ZA 61 (1971), 48–49.
★*Notes to Text*: (146) von Soden, ZA 61 (1971), 49. (156) *adima*, perhaps a learned pseudo-correction, intended for a stative of *idû*? (162) AHw, 1474a, but doubtful.

1. Wife of Adad and Dagan, for whom apparently Enlil is here substituted. Lines 211 to 237 may have been adapted from a hymn referring to Adad or Dagan, appended to the preceding psalm-like passage.

III.29 LITERARY PRAYER TO MARDUK

Marduk is both fierce and gentle. He is angry with a person, so let him now be merciful to that person (compare III.14). Blandishments and excuses are offered: a live servant is better than a dead one; a mortal cannot know right from wrong as the gods understand them. The servant is truly repentant and has been sorely tried. Now is an opportunity to proclaim the god's wondrous power to the whole world, but only if the sufferer is spared to spread his story. How else will the god's cult be maintained? At the end, the text returns to the theme of anger and appeasement, with a final appeal for mercy. Language and content set this text apart in Mesopotamian literature as the work of a master. A fragment, said to be Old Babylonian in date,[1] suggests that this composition, like III.26 and III.28, is a composite of various earlier texts.

> O furious lord, let [your heart] be c[almed], (1)
> Be eased in your feelings for [ ],
> O furious Marduk, let [your heart] be calmed,
> Be eased in your feelings for [ ]!
> Your look is a serpent, the crushing power [of a flood], (5)
> The onslaught of a conflagration, where is your equ[al]?
> O Marduk, whose look is a serpent,
>   the crushing power of a fl[ood],
> The onslaught of a conflagration, where is your equal?
> [ ] in your fury, you can h[elp],
> [Gentle your pity], like a father's your mercy,[2] (10)
> [O Marduk, in your fury, you] can help,
> [Gentle your pity, like a father's] your mercy.
> You know how to pardon in the very jaws of criminality*
> To waive the punishment in even grievous cases.
> O Marduk, you know how to pardon
>   in the very jaws of criminality, (15)
> To waive the punishment in even grievous cases!
> Your heart is merciful, your feelings [ ],
> [You can?] show [favor?] in guilt and wrong-doing.
> O Marduk, [your] heart is merciful, your feelings [ ],

---

1. Examination of the original was not conclusive. The piece could be Middle Babylonian or even, like the "Old Babylonian" Anzu, a late manuscript affecting Old Babylonian script.
2. Old Babylonian version: "like a merciful father."

[You can?] show [favor?] in guilt and wrong-doing!   (20)
O lord, you are [of] understanding,
Who holds deep counsel [   ], wise.
O Marduk, you are [.   of] understanding,
Who holds deep counsel [   ], wise!
O receiver of prayers, who accepts entreaties,   (25)
Guardian of life, solicitous god,
O Marduk, receiver of prayers, who accepts entreaties,
Guardian of life, solicitous god!
O hearer of blessings, who bestow[s li]fe,
To whom swift relenting is natural,   (30)
O Marduk, hearer of blessings, w[ho bestows life],
To whom swift relenting is natural,
What reason could any god besides you [   ],
[Rem]itting punishment, granting [favors   ]?
[O Marduk], what reason could any god besides you [   ],   (35)
[Rem]it punishment, grant [favors   ]?
Who is most fierce ... [   ]?
[Wh]o among the gods [can turn you back]?
O Marduk, who is most fierce [   ]?
Who among the gods can turn [you back]?   (40)
O Lord, you are ra[ging] in your fury,
Amidst the seas of the far-off [   ]
O Marduk, [you are raging in your fury],
Amidst [the seas of the far-off   ],
Every day the tide [   ]   (45)
The flood has raised [   ]
The (sufferer) bound in helplessness ... [   ],
He re[   ]ed to himself,
He arose [   ],
He leaned against [   ],   (50)
He cannot [stand   ].
They take hold of his feet [   ] ...
You are the lord, [   ] his life!
He has turned into clay, [   ] ...
You are Marduk, [   ] his life!   (55)
He has turned into clay, [   ] ...
O lord, look upon your exhausted servant,

Let your breeze waft, release him quickly,
Let your heavy punishment be eased,
Loosen his bonds, let him breathe forthwith!   (60)
[Break] his manacle, undo his bonds,
[In ev]il(?)* have regard for him, be solicitous for him,
Let him not be murdered [in] your [fury], spare his life!
O Marduk, [   ] have regard for him, be solicitous for him,
Let him not be murdered [in] your fu[ry], spare his life!   (65)
Do not destroy the servant who is your handiwork,
What is the profit in one who has turned [into] cl[ay]?
It is a liv[ing] servant who reveres his master,
What benefit is dead dust* to a god?
[He has from of ol]d* counsel and solicitude,   (70)
[He is always ...   ] to remit guilt
[   ]
In his fury [   ]
He did not know [   ]
The servant [   ] his lord.

(lines 76–103 lost or fragmentary)

Who is he that [   ], not s[inned]?
Who is he so watchful that has incurred no sin?   (105)
Which is he so circumspect
        that has committed no wrong-doing?*
People do not know their invisible [fault]s,
A god reveals what is fair and what is [fo]ul.
Sins are overcome by one who has a god,
He who has no god has much guilt.   (110)
When you, his god, are at his side,
His words were well chosen and his speech controlled.

(lines 113–124 lost or fragmentary)

Illness, head pains, [debil]ity(?), sleeplessness,   (125)
They have relentlessly imposed upon him
        emaciation, exhaustion.
Nagging anxiety, nervousness, panic, terror,
Are let loose upon him and banish his zest for living.
He has reviewed his ills, he is weeping to you,

His feelings are afire, he burns for you,   (130)
He is given over to tears, he rains them down like a mist,
He sobs and makes much weeping,
    [like] a woman who cannot give birth.
Like a hired wailer he makes bitter his cries,
He speaks of his sleeplessness in his lamentation,
"What has my lord ... and devised against his servant?   (135)
"Let me bring his acknowledgment* that he did not know!
"Many are my guilty deeds, I have sinned in every way!
"My lord, I have indeed transgressed,
    let me escape from distress,
"Many are my guilty deeds, I have sinned in every way,
"O Marduk, I have transgressed,
    let me escape from distress!"   (140)
He bears a curse, he has donned heavy punishment.
They took him, gloomy of face,
    remanding him to the place of judgment.
His arms are bound at the court[1] of your punishment,
While he tries to explain to you all he intended.
They are addressing you in prayers,   (145)
Let the text of Ea[2] appease your heart,
Let his right wording hold you back on high,
Let sighs and pity speak to you for mercy.
Look upon the wretchedness dealt him!
Let your heart be calmed, have mercy on him,   (150)
Take his hand, absolve his guilt,
Banish from him head pain and sleeplessness.
Your servant is cast into the maw of annihilation,*
Lift your punishment, save him from the morass.
[Break] his manacle, undo his hands,   (155)
Make [his face] beam,
    entrust him to the god who created him.
Revive your servant [that he may pra]ise your valor,
Let him pro[claim] your greatness
    [to] the whole inhabited world.

1. Literally: "gate." Legal proceedings and trials were often held at the city gate.
2. A reference to Ea's role as author of incantations, and a statement that the present text was a product of sublime wisdom; compare II.1 line 52.

Accept his present, take his offering(?).*
Let him walk before you on firm ground of well-being,   (160)
Let him come to shower upon your dais a plenteous yield.
Ensure his perpetual upkeep of your house,
Let him bathe your door fastenings in oil, as if with water,
Let him lavish finest oil on your thresholds.
Let him burn cedar resin for you,   (165)
Delightful fruits, abundant grain,

(gap)

May your [ben]evolent eyes rest up[on him],
May he himself [   ] in your heart for benevolence.
Lay no wrong-doing [to his] charge,
Do not make him bear his guilt,
    do not make him bear (his) sin,
Raise his head, ... [   ],   (175)
May his protective spirit be greater than be[fore].*
May his king[1] [   ] the words he speaks.
At your command may he [   ]
May he fulfill his vow [   ].
The road and path [   ],   (180)
May he who sees him in the street [praise] your divinity,
May they say one to the other,
    "Indeed, the Lord c[an revive the dea]d!"
May he who sees him in the street pr[aise] your divinity,
May they say one to the other,
    "Indeed, Marduk ca[n revi]ve the dead!"
And as for the servant whom [   ] you spared,   (185)
[May he procl]aim your greatness to all peoples.
May he praise the one who revealed to him light
    while he was dying [   ],
May he continue to bless you [   ].
As your servant [   ] at [night]time,
To all peoples [in the day he made to] be heard.[2]   (190)

(fragmentary lines, gap)

---

1. Presumably the sufferer's personal god is here meant; for "king" in this sense, see II.1 lione 54.
2. If this restoration is correct, one may compare Erra and Ishum (IV.17) Tablet V line 43.

Have m[ercy] on him, pity for your servant!   (206)

Text: W. G. Lambert, AfO 19 (1959/60), pl. XII–XVI; Pinches, CT 44 21; Matouš, LTBA I 68 obv. 1–4 (ref. WGL).

Edition: W. G. Lambert, AfO 19 (1959/60), 55–60.

Translation: von Soden, SAHG, 270–272 no. 18 (lines 125ff.); Seux, *Hymnes*, 172–181; Hecker, TUAT II/5, 754–758.

Literature: Sommerfeld, AOAT 213 (1982), 129–134.

Notes to Text: (13) Oshima, N.A.B.U. 2001/15. (62) von Soden, ZA 67 (1974), 283. (69) Seux, *Hymnes*, 175 note 28. (70) Restoration from Old Babylonian version: [*i-ba-aš-ši iš-t*]*u ul-la*. (106) Unpublished duplicate quoted CAD N/1, 3b. (136) Hecker: "auch wenn dessen Mund vorbrachte ..." (153) See Oshima, N.A.B.U. 2001/15: "open grave." (159) Emendation AHw, 367a (IGI!.SÁ-*e*); otherwise *pedû* "release, exempt." (176) von Soden, ZA 67 (1974), 283.

III.30 GREAT HYMN TO MARDUK

Like the other great hymns (see General Introduction, F.1), this is a masterpiece of intricate thought and expression. Too much of the text is lost to see
its over-all structure, but the preserved portions deal with the mercy of
Marduk and the wisdom of walking in his ways.

O lord, sage of the Igigi-gods, I praise your name,   (1)
Sweet is the thought of you, impetuous, willful one(?),
O Marduk, among the Igigi-gods I praise your name,
Sweet is the thought of you, impetuous, willful one.
Who guides the rivers inside the highlands,   (5)
Who opens the well springs inside the mountains,
Who releases the bounteous flood to the entire inhabited world,
Who makes abundant* the ... of the broad earth with grain,
[Who makes the] dew [fall] from the bosom of heaven,
[   ] the breezes, the sprinklings over the lea land,[1]   (10)
[Who ...] bountiful yields to the grain fields,
[   ] abundance, plenty, yields, increase.
[Who allots] to the Igigi-gods great food offerings,
[   ] all daises,
[a]nointing of the door fastenings.[2]   (15)
[w]ine, a meal of food portions
      and free-will offerings,
[   ] the Anunna-gods, the whole creation of
   "The Lord of Heaven and Netherworld,"[3]
[   ] your benevolences reached,
[al]l of them were fed.
[   ] your benevolences reached,   (20)

(lines 21–27 fragmentary)

[   ] pasture [   ]
[   ] he provides grass
[   ] and princes, speak well of him!   (30)
[   ] the merciful, solicitous god.

---

1. Compare Epic of Creation (III.17) Tablet V lines 49–51, 54; Tablet VII lines 1–4, 57–69.
2. Compare Literary Prayer to Marduk (III.29) line 163; Prayer to Anu (III.34) line 14.
3. Ea (Lambert, AfO 19 [1959/60], 62 note 17).

There is [none] among all the Igigi-gods
　　who can boast before you,
You have [no] rival above or below.
Whatever the gods of all the inhabited world may have done,
　　they cannot be like you, lord!
[   ] of the depths of knowledge, where is your equal?　　　(35)
Anu, who dwells in heaven, made you greatest,
Nunamnir,[1] father of the gods, pronounced your name.
Ea in the depths bestowed upon you wisdom,
Ninmenna,[2] the creatress, clo[thed?] you with awesomeness,
Your head is raised high in [your] splendid temple,　　　(40)
Damgalnunna[3] made your genius terrible,
Your dread, O lord, is fearful to the gods.
Like the surge of battle, you swell massively … the sea,
You incinerate the enemy like a raging conflagration.
Your rage is a dragon, you tie up evil ones,　　　(45)
You catch up with troublemakers, instigators,
　　and malcontents,
Passing (unscathed) through corruption,
　　you bring swift misfortune upon the enemy.
You select the few that are good,
　　you make good the many (that are not),*
You cause the just to prosper, you leave the wicked wanting.
May the establisher of gifts, the warden of life,　　　(50)
Nabu, beloved of Shazu,[4] hear what was in
　　their hearts and [learn?] about their behavior.
The just man and obedient ones are unlimited waters [   ],
Rationed sips are the corrupt, contentious, disobedient, [   ].
[   ] those obedient to him … [   ],
He who spreads deceit, instigates […,
　　Marduk] is furious(?) with him.*　　　(55)
[He who spreads de]ceit, who utters [   ],
Who gives intelligence to those who were not given [   ],

---

1. A name for Enlil.
2. A name for the mother goddess.
3. Wife of Ea, mother of Marduk.
4. Literally: "Who knows the heart," presumably Marduk. See the Epic of Creation (III.17) Tablet VII lines 35–40.

You make short their days and [   ],
You turn [their   ] into ruin heaps.
[   ] whose intentions change,   (60)
[They   ] and commit a crime,
The humble, the reverent, the prayerful follows the god,
[   ], the arrogant, the irreverent,
They plot hostilities like [   ],
His god does not g[o at his side
        but] lets him be overcome by corruption.   (65)
Marduk, god of the peoples [   ], who absolves everything,
The god of redemption, [   ], solicitous prince,
When he has given judgment, the lord [·] and appeases,
Marduk appeases [   ] for benevolence.
He accepts prayers [   ] night,   (70)
He raises the head of him
        whom he [   ] in the fury of his heart.
Marduk, [   ] your servant,
        the sage¹ whom you [   ], have mercy on him!
Take away, O lord, his guilt, absolve his misdeed.
His own mouth has confessed the sin he committed [   ],
Lift him from the mighty torrents [   ]   (75)
Marduk, you rage where [   ] was destroyed,
He has turned and flown into a fury at [   ]

> *(fragmentary, then large gap)*
> *(Several fragments of text remain.)²*

[... O Mar]duk, precious life of the people,   (1′)
[   ] their [   ], he foregoes their punishment.
[He   ] the reverent, he makes the pious prosper,
He is benevolent to the obedient,
        he makes the upright prosper.

One is ever mindful of you, they are glad now,
        when your name is pronounced,   (5′)
They are in awe of your words, like the roar of thunder.

---

1. Text: "Adapa." For this personage, see III.21.
2. English translation of the other pieces are found in Lambert, AfO 19 (1959/60), 64–65 (also CAD N/1, 132a, restoration of iii middle 7 from unpublished duplicate).

From among those afire with purpose,
You save the ones who worship Marduk,
    you open up to them unending yield and flow(?).[1]
To the traffic of the ferry landing, where the way is crowded,
You make a quick path for the king of the world,
    unequalled and irresistible.[2]   (10′)
You guard property, you cle[ar] profit.
You grant (receipt of) offerings forever,
    you are always, in all respects, at your task.
You set up the weak, you give the wretched room,
You bear up the powerless, you shepherd the meek.
O Marduk, you extend your benevolence over the fallen,   (15′)
The weakling takes his stand under your protection,
    you pronounce recovery for him.

(breaks off)

Text: W. G. Lambert, AfO 19 (1959/60), pl. XVII–XXIII; additional joins to ms. B include K 16922 and Sm 1732, not used here.
Edition: W. G. Lambert, AfO 19 (1959/60), 61–66.
Translation: von Soden, SAHG, 253–254 no. 7 (10′ff.); Seux, Hymnes, 70–75.
*Notes to Text: (8) Seux, Hymnes, 71 note 7. (48) Reading la me-na as la mīna "innumerable." (55) WGL.

1. The sense may be that Marduk favors, of all firebrands, the ones eager in his service, and makes them prosper. "Flow," if correctly understood, may refer metonymically to prosperity as an abundance of water.

2. That is, in the hurly-burly of everyday life, Marduk speeds the king's progress. With a similar metaphor, Ishtar of Arbela assures Esarhaddon in an oracle, "I will bring you over the river in good order"; see IV.3.

III.31 GREAT HYMN TO NABU

This hymn is dedicated to Nabu, god of scribal lore. Its recondite language suggests a late date. Despite its fragmentary condition, it clearly belongs to the Babylonian tradition of great hymns (General Introduction, F.1). Like III.28 and III.29, it takes the form of a narrative about a penitent's wretched condition and expresses his hopes for absolution. It contains original ideas and involved imagery, much of which is still imperfectly understood.

[O lord,   ], cresting like a wave [   ],
[   ], your absolution [   ],   (10)
[O Nabu,   ], cresting like a wave [   ],
[   ], your absolution [   ].
[O lord, who ... the anxio]us like a [   ],
[   ] he has turned [   ],
[O Nabu, who ... the anxio]us like a [   ],   (15)
[   ] he has turned [   ].
[   ] your [an]ger, your raging* yoke,
[You ... ab]undance, you release the yield,
[O Nabu, ...] your anger, your raging yoke,
[You ... ab]undance, you release the yield.   (20)
[O lord, ...] in your [   ], fire in your pitilessness,
[   ] of the gods, you inspect Anshar,
[O Nabu, ...] in your [   ], fire in your pitilessness,
[   ] of the gods, you inspect Anshar.
[O lord,   ] is your [   ], your glower is a (dark) cloud,   (25)
[   ] you support the just.
[O Nabu, ... is your ...], your glare is a (dark) cloud,
[you] support the [just].
[O lord, ...] your [   ] is an earthquake,
[   ] they hold,   (30)
[O Nabu, ... your ...] is an earthquake,
[   ] they hold.
[O lord, ... of heaven],
[   ] ... family, ... profit,
[O Nabu,   ] ... of heaven,   (35)
[   ] ... family, ... profit.
O excellent [lord], be calm at once!

May your [feat]ures(?) relax, have pity!
O excellent [Na]bu, be calm at once!
May your [features?] relax, have pity!   (40)
O erudite l[ord], sage in …,
Wise one, master of the literate arts,
O erudite Nabu, sage in …,
Wise one, master of the literate arts,
O furious lord, you are angry with your servant,   (45)
Want and misery have beset him,
O furious Nabu, you are angry with your servant,
Want and misery have beset him!
He is cast into the midst of the billow,
        the flood cl[oses] over him,
The shore is far from him, dry land remote from him.   (50)
He languished in a mesh of machination,
        impossible to cut through,
He sprawled in a morass, held fast by the mire.
Take his hand, let not your servant go under,
Lift his punishment, raise him from the morass,
O Nabu, take his hand, let not your servant go under,   (55)
Lift his punishment, raise him from the morass.
He bellows in ter[ror],
        like a bull being slaughtered with a butcher's knife,
He is cast into the maw of something mighty,
        overpowering … [   ]

                      (gap)

"I am fallen, let me be borne up, let me [   ],
"In order to expel the 'vengeance'[1] (from me),
        let me make straight for [   ].
"Like a vagrant(?), let me go about out[side].
"Indeed(?), why should a one-handed man(?)
        stand ahead of me?[2]
"[   ] brings suffering and misery (upon me).   (80)
"You are the lord, you called [my] n[ame in the womb?],
"At your command the midwife [   ].

---

1. See Poem of the Righteous Sufferer (III.14), p. 405 note 3.
2. For this motif, compare III.27(b), 59–61.

"You are Nabu, you called [my name in the womb?],
"At your command, the midwife [   ].
"From my father's 'It's my child!'[1] [   ],   (85)
"The 'It's my child!' of his ancestors [   ]
"[   ] not [   ]."
He staggers(?) [   ]
"My father ... (his personal) god painfully [   ]
"He unceasingly heeded (his personal) goddess."   (90)
Omnipotent lord, (let) iniquity (be) era[sed],
O Swift-to-forgive, (let) foul crime (be) for[given],
Omni[potent Nabu, (let) ini]quity (be) era[sed],
O Swift-[to-forgive, (let) fo]ul [crime] (be) forgi[ven].

(two lines lost)

[   ] overlook [his] misdeed,
[   ] negligence, banish [his] s[in].
[Without] your consent, O lord,
          there can be no [forgiveness],
[Un]less by you, my iniquity and crime
          [will not be absolved],   (100)
[Without] your consent, O Nabu,
          there can be no [forgiveness],
[Un]less by you, my iniquity and crime
          [will not be absolved].
Your servant [has done wron]g,
          and you continue to turn away from him in anger,
In your [ ] you cast down [   ].
[   ] ..., the burrowing beetle, a hostile deity [   ]   (105)

*(The next eight fragmentary lines continue with a description of various
plagues undergone by the sufferer.)*

The horror of headlice was grievous upon him,
The symptoms of ...-disease(?) he showed on [his] face(?).   (115)
"How long, a whole year, must I keep on waiting?
"Let me praise the lord, your fury is anger,
"[   ] your awesomeness to heaven [for]ever,

---

1. Text: "by father's 'Indeed'(?). I take this to be the initial acknowledgment of paternity after
birth of the child.

"[Let me praise Nabu], your fury is anger,

"[   ] your awesomeness to heaven forever.   (120)

"My [family]* is (well) supplied with beer,
      is (well) supplied with flour,

"The land set aside for my ancestor's [   ]
      is (worth) a talent of silver.[1]

[   ] associates, constantly, may the night be at an end(?).

[   ] let them dispatch that I may be set right for all time.

    (lines 125–172 lost or too fragmentary for translation)

Loose his fetters, break [his] chains!

A wall is created against the severity of the wintry blast,

For the whole land a breeze makes the summer heat
      easier to bear.[2]   (175)

The morn of my help, the first fruits of the tree,
      ... bitter ...

What has (seemed) always unpalatable
      he will sweeten like honey.

The (early) dates on the tree are bitter as stinkwort,

But later the good ones are sweet and the sprout [   ].[3]   (180)

The grain in its budding was affected by smut [   ],

(But) when it matured it [gave full] yield.

The putrid flux of the body's channels, something abhorrent to
      the gods,[4] is universal(?) among(?) people.

Where it was dark it is bright, the raging one (is) for[giving].

The obedient, dutiful son makes a special bles[sing]
      for his father,   (185)

The disobedient, undutiful son curses [him] who be[got him].

You discipline your servant,
      (now) give him a vent to breathe through,

---

1. This and the preceding line may refer to his lavish maintenance of his ancestor cult.

2. While these lines refer to the relief brought upon the sufferer by Nabu's forgiveness, it is not clear precisely how they are to be understood. Is Nabu's help the wall and the breeze?

3. This and the following couplet may refer to a period of misery followed by a period of good, "darkest before dawn"; compare also IV.19 260–263.

4. I take this to mean that people are by nature impure and disgusting to the gods, so, like the dutiful and ungrateful sons of line 185, humans and gods are by nature poles apart. The "putrid flux" normally refers to urinary disease (CAD M/2, 46) or gonorrhea (Adamson, JRAS 1979, 5), but here may refer to semen.

Incline your face to him, turn your head toward him,
O Nabu, you discipline your servant,
        (now) give him a vent to breathe through,
Incline your face to him, turn your head toward him.   (190)
Produce a substitute[1] for him, let him [find] self-preservation.
At your command [   ] good [   ]

                        (gap)

[let] him build his storehouse,
[   ] let him build his sanctuary.
[   ] let his body be released,
[   ] let his[2] vision be clear.
[May your radiant features] turn toward him,   (205)
[Your servant, ... comp]assion, have pity on him,
[O Nabu], may your radiant features turn toward him,
Your servant, ... compassion, have pity on him!
May the [   ] fields be restored,
May the [   ] revenues be his forever.   (210)
May his sanctuary be in order in village and marshland.
May his mood brighten [in the] four world [regions].
[Ta]ke his hand that he may ever glorify your divinity,
Let him proclaim your greatness [to all] the world,
[O Nabu, t]ake his hand, let him ever glorify your divinity,   (215)
Let him proclaim your greatness [to all] the world!
[Accep]t his abasement, immobility, and entreaty,
[   ] his petition, may his prayer come true.
May all the [Igi]gi-gods take his part,
May the [hai]ry hero-man[3] ... speak in his favor.   (220)
[O lord, among] the gods your greatness is surpassing,
[The people] have sung your praises for all time,
[O Nabu, among the gods] your greatness is surpassing,
[The people] have sung your [pra]ises for all time!

            (six or seven lines missing till end)

---

1. That is, someone to die in his stead.
2. Text: "their," possibly, but not likely, referring to eyes.
3. For these beneficent monsters, see p. 243 note 2. These are not to be confused with the primeval gods Lahmu and Lahamu (see p. 439 note 3).

Text: Brünnow, ZA 4 (1889), 252–258 (= K 2361+3193+Sm 389). Additional pieces, with col-
   lations of the earlier copies, published in transliteration by von Soden, ZA 61 (1971), 50–60.
Edition: von Soden, ZA 61 (1971), 44–71, to which this translation is greatly indebted.
Translation: Seux, *Hymnes*, 181–185; earlier treatment by von Soden, SAHG, 263–264 no. 13.
Notes to Text: (17) So text; perhaps there is an implied comparison with a weapon. (121) [*kim*]*tija*.

III.32 SHAMASH HYMN

This hymn to the sun-god, Shamash, was frequently copied and studied by Mesopotamian scholars of the Late period.[1] The text begins with Shamash as the all-seeing sun (1–20), whose energies and responsibilities lead him over the entire world every day (21–52). His importance in divination is alluded to (53f.), as well as his role in oaths, treaties, and contracts (55f.). His ability to illumine the darkest places leads to a celebration of his role in investigation, trial, and verdict (56–64). Mention of his concern for travelers and the homeless (65–74) is followed by a fragmentary passage dealing with his interceding mercy (75–82?) and his inexorable retribution against the wicked (83?–102). An interesting passage (103–121), perhaps another independent composition inserted here, delves into his role as supervisor of honest business transactions.[2] Shamash can see through the cleverest fast-talk and the most stringent false denial (122–127). He is the principal divine communicant with the perplexed, the lost, meek, venturesome, and the most wretched human beings beyond the pales of civilization (128–148). This leads to a reflection upon his relationship to the human race as a whole; he grants knowledge, and receives joyous cultic observances in return, including beer at wharfside in honor of his interest in commerce and shipping (149–162). In a climactic paean, the hymnist marvels at the sun's universal dominion, extending to the unseen corners and depths of the cosmos (163–175). He considers the alternately harsh and tender qualities of the god (176–185?). The text is fragmentary at the end, but may conclude with reference to a ceremony and a plea for the god's goodwill.

The language of the hymn suggests that it, like the other great hymns (General Introduction, F.1), is not of a piece, but is a second-millennium compilation using some older materials and reworking imagery known elsewhere.

> Illuminator of all, the whole of heaven,   (1)
> Who makes light the d[arkness for humankind]
>   above and below,
> Shamash, illuminator of all, the whole of heaven,

---

1. W. G. Lambert, BWL, 121–123.
2. Remarks on this topic are offered by J. Nakata, "Mesopotamian Merchants and Their Ethos," JANES 3 (1970/71), 90–100.

Who makes light the dark[ness for humankind
    a]bove and below,[1]
Your radiance [spre]ads out like a net [over the world],   (5)
You brighten the g[loo]m of the distant mountains.
Gods and netherworld gods rejoiced when you appeared,
All the Igigi-gods rejoice in you.
Your beams are ever-mastering secrets,
At the brightness of your light,
        humankind's footprints become vis[ible].   (10)
Your dazzle is always seeking out [   ],
The four world regions [you set alight] like fire.
You open[2] wide the gate of all [sanctuaries],
You [   ] the food offerings of the Igigi-gods.
O Shamash, humankind kneels to your rising,   (15)
All countries [   ]
Illuminator of darkness, opener of heaven's bosom,
Hastener[3] of the morning breeze★ (for?) the grain field,
        life of the land,
Your splendor envelops the distant mountains,
Your glare has filled all the lands.   (20)
Leaning over the mountains, you inspect the earth,
You balance the disk of the world in the midst of heaven
        (for) the circle of the lands.
You make the people of all lands your charge,
All those king Ea, the counsellor,
        has created are entrusted to you.
You shepherd all living creatures together,   (25)
You are their herdsman, above and below.
You cross regularly through the heavens,
Every day you traverse the vast earth.
High seas, mountains, earth, and sky,

---

1. Either "in every direction," or a reference to Shamash's position in both heaven and netherworld, as in line 31.

2. Text: "You opened ..." (so also 7, 20 and others), as if focusing on the most recent sunrise (see Hirsch, AfO 40/41 [1993/1994], 49).

3. Or, "who heats," in which case the meaning would be that the rising sun heats the breezes of morn from their night coolness.

You traverse them regularly, every day, like a ...¹ (30)
In the lower regions
        you take charge of the netherworld gods,
        the demons, the (netherworld) Anunna-gods,
In the upper regions you administer all the inhabited world.
Shepherd of the lower regions,
        herdsman of the upper regions,
You, Shamash, are regulator of the light for all.
You cross time and again the vast expanse of the seas, (35)
[Whose] depths not even the Igigi-gods know.
[O Sham]ash, your radiance has gone down to the deep,
[The hairy hero-m]an of the ocean can see your light.
[O Shamash], you tighten like a noose,
        you shroud like a mist,
Your [bro]ad protection is cast over the lands. (40)
Though you darken each day, your face is not eclipsed,★
For by night you traverse★ [the below?].²
To far-off regions unknown and for uncoun[ted] leagues
You have persevered, O Shamash,
        what you went by day you returned by night.
Among all the Igigi-gods there is none who does such
        wearisome toil but you, (45)
Nor among the sum total of the gods
        one who does so much as you!
At your rising the gods of the land assembled,
Your fierce glare covered the land.
Of all the lands of different tongues,
[You] know their intentions, you see their footprints. (50)
All humankind kneels before you,
[O Sha]mash, everyone★ longs for your light,
[From] the diviner's bowl to the knots of cedar,³
[You are] the most reflective of dream interpreters,
        explicators of night visions.★

---

1. Word broken, perhaps "cultivated field" or the like, in which case the sun is like a conscientious farmer going over his domain.

2. The meaning may be that even though the sun sets, his brightness remains undimmed as he passes the other side of heaven, so he is not to be considered in unfavorable eclipse.

3. For cedars in the diviner's ritual, see above, II.28a lines 7–8 (tied in the hair and piled up), and II.28b line 6. Perhaps totality is implied, "from alpha to omega."

[The parties to] contracts[1] kneel before you,   (55)
[Be]fore you both wicked and just kneel down.
[No one] goes down to the depths without you.[2]
You clear up the case of the wicked and criminal,
[   ]
He pours out sleep [   ]   (60)
You send back (to court?) the rogue surrounded
        by [false witnesses],
You rescue from the brink of hell
        the [innocent] one tied up in a lawsuit,[3]
What you pronounced in just verdict, O Shamash, [   ],
Your utterances are manifest, they cannot be changed,
        [you show] no favoritism.★
You give support to the traveler whose j[ourney] is trying,   (65)
To the seafarer in dread of the waves you lend [aid],
You are wont to g[uide] the roamer(?) on unexplored routes,
You always guide [on the ro]ad any
        who turn toward [Shamash].
You rescued from the flashflood
        the [mer]chant bearing his purse,[4]
You bring up★ the one gone down to the deep,
        you set wings upon him.   (70)
You reveal havens to refugees and runaways.★
You show the exile roads he did not know.★
[You set free] the one in a hid[den dungeon],
You save the displaced cast in prison.★
[You reconcile promptly] the god
        [who is angry] with someone,★   (75)
Upon seeing ... [   ]
You stand by(?) the si[ck man   ]
You investigate the cause [   ]

---

1. Sworn documents, such as treaties and contracts, were Shamash's area of concern (see above, III.1).

2. Reiner, *Poetry*, 72 suggests that this refers to a water ordeal; compare III.14 Tablet IV, IV.13.

3. Lines 61–62 may refer to the comfortable(?), scot-free evildoer being packed off for legal action, while the just man is rescued from the machinations of the law. For different views, compare W. G. Lambert, BWL, 129 and Seux, *Hymnes*, 56.

4. The bag used by commercial agents to carry their means and, by extension, "capital."

You bear [   ]
From the Land of No Return you [   ]   (80)
The angry(?) goddesses [   ]
You are exalted [   ]
O Shamash, with [your] battle net [you   ]
From your meshes no [can escape   ].
He who, in taking an oath [   ],   (85)
For the one who does not fear [   ],
Your wi[de] net is spread   [   ].
The man who co[vets] his neighbor's wife,
He will make to [   ] before his appointed day.
A snare is set for him, the wicked man will [   ],   (90)
Your weapon makes straight for him,
        there [will be no]ne to save him.
[His] own father will not be present at his trial,
Nor will his own brothers reply to the judge's queries.
He is caught unawares in a metal trap!
You blunt the horns of a scheming villain,   (95)
The perpetrator of a cunning deal is undermined.*
You show the roguish judge the (inside of) a jail,
He who takes the fee but does not carry through,
        you make him bear the punishment.
The one who receives no fee
        but takes up the case of the weak,
Is pleasing to Shamash, he will make long his life.   (100)
The careful judge who gives just verdicts,
Controls the government, lives like a prince.
What return is there for the investor in dishonest dealings?
His profits are illusory, and he loses his capital.
He who invests in long-range enterprises(?),
        who returns (even?) one shekel to the ... [   ],   (105)
Is pleasing to Shamash, he will make long his life.
He who [commits] fra[ud as he holds the ba]lances,
Who switches weights,[1] who lowers the [   ],
(His) profits are illusory, and he lo[ses the capital].

---

1. That is, buys with a heavy standard and pays back with a light one, taking advantage of varying local standards of weight.

The one who is honest in holding the balance,
[   ] plenty of [   ],   (110)
Whatever (he weighs) will be given to him in plenty [   ].
He who commits fra[ud] as he holds the dry measure,
Who pays loans by the smaller standard,
        demands repayment by the extra standard,
Before his time, the people's curse will take effect on him,
Before his due, he will be called to account,*
        he will bear the consequence(?).   (115)
No heir will (there be) to take over his property,
Nor will (there be) kin to succeed to his estate.
The honest merchant who pays loans
        by the [ex]tra(?) standard,
        thereby to make extra virtue,
Is pleasing to Shamash, he will grant him extra life,
He will make (his) family numerous,
        he will acquire wealth,   (120)
[His] seed will be perpetual
        as the waters of a perpetual spring.
For the man who does virtuous deeds,
        who knows not fraud,
The man who always says what he really means,*
        there will be [   ],
The seed of evildoers wi[ll not be perpetual].
The nay-sayers' speeches are before you,   (125)
You quickly analyze what they say.
You hear and examine them,
        you see through the trumped-up lawsuit.
Each and every one is entrusted to your hands,
You make their omens the right ones for them,
        you resolve what perplexes.
You heed, O Shamash, prayer, supplication, and blessing,   (130)
Obeisance, kneeling, whispered prayer, and prostration.
The feeble one calls you as much as his speech allows him,[1]
The meek, the weak, the oppressed, the submissive,
Daily, ever, and always come before you.
He whose family is far off, whose city is distant,   (135)

---

1. Literally: "according to the hollow of his mouth."

The shepherd [in] the afflictions of the wilderness,
The herdsman in trouble, the keeper of sheep
     among the enemy, come before you.
O Shamash, there comes before you the caravan
     in anxious progress,
The travelling merchant, the agent carrying capital.
O Shamash, there comes before you
     the fisherman with his net, (140)
The hunter, the archer, the driver of the game,
The fowler among his snares comes before you,
The skulking thief who hates the daylight,
The bandit on the wilderness paths come before you,
The wandering dead, the vagrant spirit come before you, (145)
O Shamash, you have listened to them all.
You did not hold back(?) those who came before you,
     you heeded them,*
For my sake, O Shamash, do not despise them!
You grant wisdom, O Shamash, to humankind,
You grant those seeking you your raging, fierce light. (150)
[You make] their omens [the rig]ht ones for them,
     you preside over sacrifices.
You probe their future in every way.
You grant wisdom to the limits of the inhabited world.
The heavens are too puny to be the glass of your gazing,
The world is too puny to be (your) seer's bowl. (155)
On the twentieth of the month
     you rejoice with mirth and joy,[1]
You dine, you drink fine brew,
     the tavernkeep's beer at wharfside.[2]
They pour barkeep's beer for you, you accept it.
You are the one who saved them,
     surrounded by mighty waves,
You accept from them in return their fine, clear libations. (160)
You drink their sweet beer and brew,
You are the one who makes them achieve
     the goals they strive for.

1. In Mesopotamian menology, the twentieth of the month was Shamash's day.
2. Refers to Shamash's protection of travelers and commercial venturers (see lines 65ff.).

You release the ranks[1] of those who kneel to you,
You accept prayers from those who are wont to pray to you.
They revere you, they extol your name,   (165)
They(?) praise your greatness(?) forever.
Imposters, those whose tongues urge sedition,[2]
Who, like clouds, have neither face nor ap[pro]ach(?),
Those who go all over the wide earth,
Those who tread the lofty[3] mountains,   (170)
The hairy hero-men [of the oce]an, filled with fearsomeness,
The yield of the ocean, which goes all over the deep,
The catch of the rivers, (are?) what pass,
         O Shamash, before you.
Which are the mountains that are not arrayed in your beams?
Which are the corners of the earth that are not warmed
         by the brightness of your rising?   (175)
Brightener of gloom, illuminator of shadow,
Penetrator of darkness, illuminator of the wide world,
Who makes daylight shine, who sends down the heatglare
         of midday to the earth,
Who makes the wide world glow like flame,
Who can shorten the days and lengthen the nights,   (180)
[Who can cau]se cold, frost, ice, (and) snow,
[Who shuts ... the ga]te,* the bolt of heaven,
         opens wide the doors of the inhabited world,
[Who is master of] socket and pin, latchkey, and bolt,[4]
[Who ...] is relentless, (but) bestows life,
[Who ...] the captive in a fight to the death.   (185)
[rea]son, counsel, deliberation, advice,
[   ] ... of morning(?) to the wi[despread] people
[   ] scepter, throne, rule, [   ]
[   ] strength, [   ]

                    (gap of three lines)

1. Refurbishment (or conflation? so CAD K, 120a) of "release sins" and "break ranks." If intentional, this could mean that the submissive are spared the discipline reserved for the others.
   2. Variant: "fra[ud]."
   3. Variant: "pure."
   4. The terms for parts of a door are of disputed meaning (Leichty, JCS 39 [1987], 190–196; J. Westenholz, *Legends*, 316–317, where this line is discussed; Scurlock, OrNS 57 [1988], 421–433).

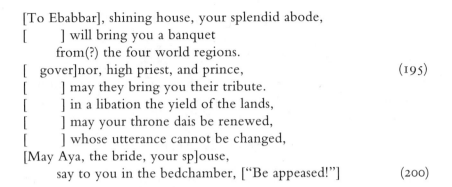

[To Ebabbar], shining house, your splendid abode,
[   ] will bring you a banquet
    from(?) the four world regions.
[gover]nor, high priest, and prince,   (195)
[   ] may they bring you their tribute.
[   ] in a libation the yield of the lands,
[   ] may your throne dais be renewed,
[   ] whose utterance cannot be changed,
[May Aya, the bride, your sp]ouse,
    say to you in the bedchamber, ["Be appeased!"]   (200)

Text: W. G. Lambert, BWL, pl. 33–36, 73 (see list on p. 125; additional fragments cited CAD A/1, 53b, A/2, 153a, N/1, 218a); George and Al-Rawi, *Iraq* 60 (1998), 202–203.

Edition: Lambert, BWL, 121–138, 318–323, 346.

Translation: von Soden, SAHG, 240–247 no. 4; Stephens, ANET³, 387–389; Labat, *Religions*, 267–274; Seux, *Hymnes*, 51–63; Reiner, *Poetry*, 68–84.

Literature: G. R. Castellino, "The Šamaš Hymn: A Note on Its Structure," AOAT 25 (1976), 71–74; H. Hirsch, "Die Vergangenheit im Šamaš-Hymnus (BWL 121ff.)," AfO 40/41 (1993/1994), 46–51; Hurowitz, SAAB 12 (1998), 45 note 17.

*Notes to Text: (18) Seux, *Hymnes*, 53; Lambert, BWL, 318–319 (41–42) Reading with CAD A/1, 107b ⸢*ta*⸣-*ta-šu-uš* ... *pa-nu-ka*; for *tu-šaḫ-bat* see von Soden, ZA 67 (1977), 281. (52) Or, *mitḫurtu* could be parallel to *šunna lišānu* of 49, rather than "totality" or the like. See Lambert, BWL, 128; Seux, *Hymnes*, 55 with note 30. (54) *mu-ši -mi* and restoration uncertain; WGL suggests *šummû*. (64) *ul t[u-ub-bal]*, von Soden, ZA 67 (1977), 281. (70) Restored from Rm IV 177, unpublished duplicate quoted CAD A/1, 53b. (71) Lambert, JSS 27 (1982), 285 (unpublished duplicate). (72) von Soden, ZA 67 (1977), 281. (74) Restored from BM 35077, unpublished duplicate quoted CAD A/2, 153a. (75) Seux, *Hymnes*, 56 note 47. (96) For opinions on this line, see Seux, *Hymnes*, 57 note 54; AHw, 1221b. (115) Literally: "asked about," see Lambert, BWL, 321; reading here *iššal*; see also Seux, *Hymnes*, 58 notes 61, 62; Moran, *Studies Tadmor*, 329–330. (123) Seux, *Hymnes*, 59 note 64. (147) For a suggestion to this line, see CAD K, 97a (*ta-šal ta-ti*). (182) [KÁ].GAL, see von Soden, ZA 67 (1977), 281.

G. Devotional and Ritual Poetry

III.33 TO ADAD

Adad was the god of thunderstorms. The three texts translated below have been chosen to illustrate different aspects of the god's nature as seen in devotional literature.

(a) AGAINST THUNDER

This prayer is addressed to the thunderstorm in the hope of averting portended evil. It ascribes to Adad certain feats of Ninurta, such as slaying of the Anzu-bird (III.23). A fragmentary Middle Babylonian manuscript from Hattusha in Anatolia, with variants and lines not attested in the later manuscripts, attests to the antiquity of this prayer. Two copies are known edited for Sargon II of Assyria.

> O most great and perfect one, heir of divine Duran[ki].[1]*   (1)
> Storm unabating, who keeps up str[ife and combat],
> O Adad, great and perfect one, [heir of divine Duranki],
> Storm unabating, who keeps up str[ife and] combat,
> Founder of the clouds, master of the deluge,   (5)
> Who strikes with his[2] lightning bolts,
>   [who blitzes] Anzu with his lightning bolts!
> O overwhelming, perfect one, furious and fierce,
> Unrelenting and a wh[irlwind],
> O Adad, overwhelming, perfect one, furious and fierce,
> Unrelenting and a whir[lwind],   (10)
> Who overturns raging (enemies), lord of strength,
> Fetter that restrains the haughty,
> [Fur]ious, stately, awe-inspiring sovereign of the heavens,
> Heir of Esharra, who is the perfect one
>   among his brothers, hero,
> The one who makes lightning flash,
>   who carries [torches?] and flame,   (15)
> Who destroys mountains, peaks, and boulders!

---

1. "Divine Duranki" is a way of referring to Enlil, commonly used in the Anzu poem (III.23).
2. Variant omits.

[Who for]ms* clouds in the midst of heaven,
[Who brings dow]n* the scorching heat,
    who rains down abundance!
[O Adad, who fo]rms clouds in the midst of heaven,
[Who brings down the scorching he]at,
    who rains down abundance,   (20)
The one at whose clamor[1]
    people are struck dumb with terror,
The meadows [quiver], the steppe heaves!
O Adad, at whose clamor
    people are struck dumb with terror,
The meadows [quake], the steppe heaves,
May you, who hears the secrets of Anu, perfect one,
    mighty one among [his brethren?],   (25)
Most awe-inspiring of the great gods, lord of combat,
Accept my prayer, hear my entreaty!
May (each) day bring me well-being, month joy,
    and year its prosperity.
[   ] ... my fault,
Take away my sin, accept my entreaty!   (30)
I have sought after you, I have turned to your divine power,[2]
Grant to me that my words be heard!
Let me proclaim your greatness, let me sound your praises!

Text: Ebeling-Köcher-Rost, LKA 53; King, BMS 20, 8–20 (+) BMS 49, obv. 21 (= 1), rev. 22–33 (= 11ff.); "Konstantinopel 517" = Ebeling, AGH, 96–98 (transliteration only); Weidner, KUB 4 26a (variants in general not noted here).
Edition: Ebeling, AGH, 96–99.
Translation: Seux, Hymnes, 305–307.
Literature: Mayer, UFBG, Adad 1a.
Notes to Text: (1) Mayer, UFBG, 378. (17) Seux, Hymnes, 306 note 13. (18) Seux, Hymnes, 306 note 14.

1. Later versions add "of his mouth."
2. Variants add here a prayer in the name of Sargon II, king of Assyria, to avert the evil portended by an eclipse, the standard phraseology of which is as follows: "on account of the evil portended by the eclipse of ___ on the month ___ on the day ___, on account of the evil portended by signs and evil, unfavorable omens, either in my palace or in my country."

(b) AGAINST LIGHTNING

This is a prayer against the effects of lightning. The first part of the text is lost or damaged, but the surviving fragments complement well the preceding.

(gap)

O lord of [lightning, whose she]en illumines [the gloom],
Might[y   ] whose [command] cannot be altered,
Irriga[tor of heaven and earth], who rains down [abundance],   (5)

(fragmentary lines)

Who [destroys the wic]ked, storm unrelenting,
I cal[l upon you, lord], in the midst of [holy] heaven,   (12)
I, [your servant], come before you,
    I seek you out and [kneel be]fore you,

(fragmentary lines)

[O Adad, fire] has come down and [fallen] upon my city,   (16)
[At] your [command fire] has come down [from] heaven.
(If) the brickwork of the temple [or the palace],
    or the foundation of the city wall have collapsed,
[Or, ... during] a rainstorm or hail, lightning and fire
[Have consumed my] city god o[r any ot]her [god?],   (20)
O Adad, great lord, I [call upon] you, I invoke you,
[Stand?] by me, I invoke you!
[I come before you this d]ay, receive my lamentations,
    accept my ple[as]!
Let the [evil] portended by your utterance not come near me,
    [approach me, draw] nigh me, nor reach me,
Let me proclaim your greatness,
    let me so[und your praises] to the numerous peoples!   (25)

Text: King, BMS 21, 1–23 + K 6612 (pl. 76).
Edition: Ebeling, AGH, 98–101.
Translation: Seux, *Hymnes*, 307–309.
Literature: Mayer, UFBG, Adad 4.

(c) IN GRATITUDE FOR RAIN

This is a grateful paean to the beneficent rainstorm.

O Adad, [thun]derer, splendid, mighty god,   (1)
[ter]ror, doughty warrior,
[Who forms?] clouds, who curtains daylight,
… everything,
Who wields lightning, master of the deluge,   (5)
Who administers heaven, mountains, seas,
Your [na]mes are [good],* your invocation is heard abroad.
At [your] clamor the mountains rejoice,
The meadows are joyous, the fields are happy,
[The people] are exuberant,
          they sound praises of your valor!   (10)
You relieve dr[yn]ess by night and day,
You make abundant greenery, you reconcile the angry.
Maintain your kindnesses [to] me, your servant,
Ordain mercy for me, let me sound your praises,
Let me extol your good [names] to the numerous peoples!   (15)

Text: King, BMS 21, 76–90.
Edition: Ebeling, AGH, 104–105.
Translation: Seux, Hymnes, 311–312.
Literature: Mayer, UFBG, Adad 2.
Notes to Text: (7) Seux, Hymnes, 312 note 6.

III.34 TO ANU

Anu, god of the sky, was head of the pantheon, and to human beings a remote, inaccessible figure. This bilingual prayer to Anu was used in royal lustration rituals (see III.51h) and is one of the rare devotional compositions addressed to him.

O most great lord, whose lu[strations are pure in heaven],★   (1)
O Anu, greatest lord, [whose] purifications [are pure in heaven],
God[1] of heaven, lord [of heaven],★
Anu, god of heaven, [lord of heaven],
Who releases the day, [crowned] lord, lord of signs,   (5)
Anu, who releases the day, c[rowned] lord, lord of signs,
Dispeller of evil, wicked, and terrifying dreams,
    evil signs and portents,
May my wickedness, [sin, and grave mis]deed
Be absolved with your [life-giving] incantation,
And all that I have committed or neglected
    against my (personal) god
    [and my (personal) goddess] be absolved.[2]   (10)
May the angry hearts of my (personal) god
    and [my (personal) goddess] be re[conciled to me],
May your furious heart b[e calmed],
And [your] feelings be eased, have mercy!
Let me endow [your] temple richly,
    and anoint your door bolt [with oil],
Let me sou[nd] my lord's praises,   (15)
Let me ever exalt the greatness of your great divinity!

Text: King, BMS 6, 1–16; Campbell Thompson, CT 51 211; Ebeling-Köcher-Rost, LKA 50.
Edition: Ebeling, AGH, 34–36.
Translation: Seux, *Hymnes*, 270–271.
Literature: Mayer, UFBG, Anu 1.
★*Notes to Text*: (1) Seux, *Hymnes*, 270 note 3, though CT 51 211 omits *ina*. (3) Seux, *Hymnes*, 270 note 6.

1. Variant: "Lord."
2. Variant: "O averter of wickedness, sin, and grave misdeed, may the afflictions that have be[set me] and that continue to harass and hamper me ..."

III.35 TO DUMUZI

Tammuz/Dumuzi is celebrated in various Sumerian religious poems as the shepherd who wooed and married the youthful Inanna/Ishtar and subsequently met a violent death.[1] He was also known as a netherworld deity, and is here referred to as a son of Ea (Nudimmud, line 2). The following incantation prayer to Dumuzi exists in two versions, of which this is the earlier. It was at some time inserted in a medical ritual. This appeals to Dumuzi in his aspects as shepherd and lover of Ishtar. See also II.19c and IV.30.

O lord Dumuzi, awe-inspiring shepherd of Anu,   (1)
Lover of Ishtar the queen, eldest son of Nudimmud,
O mighty one, leader without rival,
Who eats pure loaves baked in embers,
Who is clad in a cloak and carries a staff,   (5)
Who drinks water from a ... waterskin,
Creator of everything, lord of the [sheep]fold,
You are the lofty prince, the noble one!
Drive away from me the "evil gazer," the worker of evil,
[Who] has fixated upon me
    and is trying to cut short my life.   (10)
Herewith I bring you my life!
I hand him over to an evil spirit,[2] a merciless demon,
Let him be cut off from me, grant me life!
Tear out the "evil gazer" who is present in my body,
Let me sound your praises
    until the end point of these (my) days.   (15)

Text: Köcher, BAM 339, 33′–42′.
Edition: Farber, *Ištar und Dumuzi*, 190–192, lines 33–42.
Translation: Farber, *Ištar und Dumuzi*, 191–193; Seux, *Hymnes*, 440–441.
Literature: Mayer, UFBG, Dumuzi 1b.

1. T. Jacobsen, "Towards the Image of Tammuz," *History of Religions* 1 (1961), 189–213 = HSS 21 (1970), 73–101, but compare II.19c.
2. Later version substitutes "Humba," a name of uncertain significance; compare III.16d (16). This problem is discussed by Farber, *Ištar und Dumuzi*, 148 and 173.

III.36 TO EA

As god of wisdom, knowledge, and skill, Ea was a particular favorite among diviners and exorcists; indeed, magic was one of his special concerns. For the nature of this divinity, see J. Bottéro, "Intelligence and the Technical Function of Power: Enki/Ea," in *Mesopotamia* (1987), 232–250; S. N. Kramer and J. Maier, *Myths of Enki, The Crafty God* (Oxford, 1989). A more technical study will be found in H. D. Galter, *Der Gott Ea/Enki in der akkadischen Überlieferung* (dissertation, Graz, 1981).

(a) FOR SUCCESS IN DIVINATION

Excerpted from an exorcistic work, this bilingual prayer expresses the exorcist's hope for success and professional high repute.

O Ea, king of the depths, finder of [good counsel],★ (1)
I am the exorcist your servant.
Come to my right hand, hasten to my left,
Set your sacral spell for mine,
Set your sacral utterance for mine, (5)
Make my sacral word effective,
Make what I say successful.
Command that my procedures be pure,
Let me succeed wherever I shall go.
Let the person I treat become well. (10)
Let favorable comments precede me,
Let favorable gestures follow me.
Be my protective genius,
Be my good fortune!
May Marduk, the god who brings (me) success, (15)
[Bring]★ success wherever my going.
Let the patient's (personal) god speak of your greatness,
Let this man sound your praises,
I too, the exorcist, let me sound your praises!

Text: Campbell Thompson, CT 16 7, 8, 260–297.
Edition: Campbell Thompson, *Devils* I, 26–29.
Translation: Seux, *Hymnes*, 239–240.
★*Notes to Text*: (1) Seux, *Hymnes*, 239 note 2. (16) Seux, *Hymnes*, 240 note 11.

(b) PROTECTOR OF THE KING

This prayer is extracted from a ritual for royal lustration, for which see III.51h.

O wise king, perceptive creator, (1)
Lofty prince, ornament of the Eabsu,[1]
Enlilbanda,[2] artful, venerated one,
Hero of Eridu, sage of the Igigi,
Lord of the E[engur]ra,[3] protection of the Eunir,[4] (5)
Bringer of the high waters (that cause) abundance,
     who makes the rivers joyful,
In oceans and in reed thickets you make plenteous prosperity,
In the meadows you create the livelihood of the peoples.
Anu and Enlil rejoice because of you,
The Anunna-gods bless you in their holy places, (10)
The peoples of the land extol your weighty command,
You give counsel to the great gods.
O Ea, the moribund need not die,
     thanks to your life-giving spell.
Raise up my head, call (my) name!
At your command, may my words be heard, (15)
At your utterance, may I achieve good fortune.
Grant me life, let me live a long time.
May what I say be pleasing to god and goddess,[5]
May god and king do what I order.
May mouth and tongue say good words for me,
May [   ] not [   ], (20)
May nothing evil, nothing harmful reach me,
Nor any actions of sorcerer or sorceress.
O Ea, thanks to your life-giving spell,
     may everything evil, everything harmful retreat,

1. Temple of Enki/Ea in Eridu.
2. "Little Enlil," an epithet of Ea; see also II.23b.
3. Byname for temple of Enki/Ea in Eridu.
4. Ziggurat of temple of Enki/Ea in Eridu.
5. Variant: "king."

May the spell of Eridu undo the preparations of
    sorcerer and sorceress,
May Marduk, prince of the gods,
    undo their evil preparations.[1]   (25)
May my limbs be pure, my members healthy for me.
May the heavens rejoice because of you,
May the depths rejoice because of you,
May the great gods nobly(?) acclaim you,[2]
May the Igigi-gods speak favorably of you!   (30)

Text: Ebeling, KAR 59, obv. 29–36, rev. 1–22; King, BMS 10, 1–5 (same text, but addressed to
    Marduk); Loretz-Mayer, AOAT 34 33, 34; Finkelstein, STT 67; von Weiher, SBTU II 55;
    Wiseman and Black, CTN 4 167; compare III 78.
Edition: Mayer, UFBG, 442–449.
Translation: von Soden, SAHG, 295–296 no. 40; Seux, *Hymnes*, 275–277.
Literature: Mayer, UFBG, Ea 1a.

1. Variant: "magic knots."
2. Variant: "[sa]tisfy [your he]art" and "may the gods of the universe bless you."

III.37 TO EA, SHAMASH, AND MARDUK

Ea, god of wisdom, Shamash, god of justice, and Marduk, son of Ea, were a group frequently invoked in magical prayers and rituals. Marduk is sometimes referred to with a byname, Asalluhi, as in (b), though Asalluhi was originally a separate god and sometimes said to be Marduk's son. Their functions in such contexts are not normally differentiated, save that, in a general way, Ea provides the spell, Marduk the effective execution of it, and Shamash the powers of purification. In this respect the last line of (b) is unusual.

(a) AGAINST CONGENITAL GUILT

O Ea, Shamash, and Marduk, what is my guilt?	(1)
An abomination has confronted me, evil has me in its power.	
My father begot me, my mother bore me,	
They laid their plans and like a snake I [ ],[1]	
From the dark within I came forth and saw you, O Shamash!	(5)
An ill wind has brought down my branches,★	
A mighty tempest has bent low my crown.	
My pinions were shorn like a bird's,	
I moulted my plumage, I could not fly.	
Paralysis has seized my arms,	(10)
Debility has befallen my knees.	
I moan like a dove night and day.	
I am feverish and weep bitterly,	
Tears are coursing from my eyes.	
O Shamash, abatement is within your reach:	(15)
Dispel, drive off the guilt of my mother and father.[2]	
Go away, curse (upon me)!	

---

1. This line may express parents' hopes and ambitions for their child. As Lambert points out, p. 294, the "snake" is an image for the child passing through the birth canal from the womb (the "dark within" of line 5; compare IV.53c). The sense of the whole passage seems to be that the first thing this sufferer did was to behold the sun, so his life began auspiciously. Furthermore, the sun should know all about him, since he was born as he is now. This speaker is evidently wrestling with the problem of personal guilt.

2. The text seems to impute the sufferer's trouble to his parents (compare III.45c line 5), who made him the mere human that he is; for a different interpretation, that the speaker has wronged his parents and is therefore being punished, see Seux, *Hymnes*, 171 note 22.

Drive it away, O Ea, king of the depths,
      [and A]salluhi, lord of exorcism!
May my guilt be 3600 leagues far distant,
May the river accept (it) from me
      and take (it) down within.   (20)
O Ea, Shamash, and Marduk, come to my help!
Let me be clean in your presence,
      let me be pure before you.

Text: Myhrman, PBS I/I 14, 1–23; W. G. Lambert, JNES 33 (1974), 308 (Rm 414, 21–22).
Edition: W. G. Lambert, JNES 33 (1974), 274–275, lines 1–22.
Translation: von Soden, SAHG, 338–339 no. 65; Seux, *Hymnes*, 199–201; Hecker, TUAT II/5, 776–
   777.
Notes to Text: (6) Seux, *Hymnes*, 200 note 7.

(b) AGAINST ANY EVIL

This prayer could be used against the consequence of any unfavorable omen.

O Ea, Shamash, and Asalluhi, great gods,   (1)
You are the ones who judge cases for the land,
Ordainers of destinies, the ones who draw up designs,
Apportioners of lots for heaven and earth!
In your power is decreeing of destinies
      and drawing up of designs,   (5)
The destiny of life is yours to ordain,
The design of life is yours to draw up,
The ruling for life is yours to render.
Your spell is life, your utterance well-being, your speech is life.
You are the ones to pass judgment on the land,   (10)
Who tread the vast netherworld,
      who tread the distant heavens, as far as the heavens extend.
O opponents of evil, upholders of good,
Who obliterate evil signs and portents,
      terrifying, evil, foul dreams,
Who cut the wicked skein,
      who dissolve portended evil,
Wherever there are signs and portents,

as many as there are,   (15)
I, so-and-so, son of so-and-so,
Whose (personal) god is so-and-so,
Whose (personal) goddess is so-and-so,
Against whom evil signs keep occurring,
I am afraid, frightened, and terrified!   (20)
Let me escape the evil
          (portended by) an eclipse of the moon,
The evil (portended by) an eclipse of the sun,
The evil (portended by) the stars (and) the stars of Ea,
          Anu, and Enlil,
The evil (portended by) the planets
          that approach the path of the stars,

          (long list of portents follows)[1]

[Lest I perish, be injured], or be turned ov[er to] a demon,
[Let a good] wind [blow] and this evil not,
[Let] the [south] wind [blow] but this evil not,
[Let] the [no]rth wind [blow] but this evil not,   (5')
[Let] the east wind [blow] but this evil not,
Let the west wind blow but this evil not!
At your sublime command, which cannot be altered,
And your firm assent, which cannot be changed,
Let me live in well-being!   (10')
O Ea, Shamash, and Asalluhi,
          let me sound at this very time
          praises of your great divinity,
O Shamash, make great the exorcism that Marduk,
          sage of the gods, performs.[2]

Text: Ebeling-Köcher-Rost, LKA 109; Langdon, OECT 6 pl. XXII K 2784 + King, BMS 62;
    Caplice, OrNS 40 (1971), pl. IX, 54C, pl. X, 54D; Laessøe, *Bit Rimki*, pl. III no. X Sm 290 (slightly
    variant); Gadd, CT 41 24.
Edition: Caplice, OrNS 40 (1971), 157–158, no. 54, lines 1–20: Ebeling, RA 48 (1954), 8–11; Maul,
    Zukunftsbewältigung, 465–483.
Translation: von Soden, SAHG, 339–340 no. 66; Seux, *Hymnes*, 349–351.
Literature: Mayer, UFBG, Ea, Šamaš, Marduk/Asalluhi 1a.

1. For this list, see Maul, *Zukunftsbewältigung*, 469–475, 480–482.
2. Variant omits this line.

(c) TO PURIFY A CULT IMAGE

This prayer, part of a ritual for purifying a statue of a deity, was reapplied in a ninth-century manuscript from Syria to deal with snakebite. Its general entreaty is similar to the preceding. See p. 775 note 5 and III.51l.

O Ea, Shamash, and Asalluhi, great gods,   (1)
Who judge cases for heaven and earth,
      ordainers of destinies,
Who render rulings, who expand holy places,
Who found sanctuaries, who establish designs,
Who draw up designs, who apportion lots,   (5)
Who care for sanctuaries,
Who make lustrations purifying,
Who created the ritual of purification,[1]
In your power is to ordain destinies, to draw up designs!
The destiny of life is yours to ordain,   (10)
The design of life is yours to draw up,
The ruling of life is yours to render.
You sur[vey] completely sanctuary of god and goddess,
You, O great gods, administer rulings for heaven
      and earth, depths and seas,[2]
Your command is life, your utterance well-being,
      your speech is life.   (15)
You tread the remoteness of heaven,
You drive away evil, establish good,
You dispel evil signs and portents; foul, terrifying dreams,
You cut the wicked skein!
I am the chief purifier (who knows?) the sacred spells of Eridu. (20)
I have cast pure water, I have purified the ground for you.
I have set up pure chairs for you to sit on.
I have bestowed upon you pure red garments.
I have set up for you the pure (cultic) apparatus.
I have libated for you a pure libation.   (25)
I have set up for you a bowl of light beer,

---

1. Variant omits next four lines.
2. Variant omits next six lines.

I have libated wine and fine beer for you.
Because the power to execute the rites of the g[reat] gods
    and to perform lustration rites rests with you,
Stand by me at this time,
Ordain majestically a destiny for this statue
    that stands before you, (30)
That his mouth may eat, that his ears may hear.
Let this god become pure as heaven,
    clean as the netherworld,
Let him shine like innermost heaven!
Let all evil speech stand aside.[1]

Text: Laessøe, *Iraq* 18 (1956), p. XIV (after p. 60); Al-Rawi and George, *Iraq* 57 (1995), 226-227; Maul, *Zukunftsbewältigung*, 541 Sm 1414; see also "Edition."
Edition: Maul, *Zukunftsbewältigung*, 300–303; C. Walker, M. Dick, *The Induction of the Cult Image in Ancient Mesopotamia, The Mesopotamian Mīs Pî Ritual*, SACT 1 (2001), 131-135.
Translation: Seux, *Hymnes*, 352-354; Al-Rawi and George, *Iraq* 57 (1995), 225-228.
Literature: Mayer, UFBG, Ea, Šamaš, Marduk/Asalluhi 1b.

(d) AGAINST A GHOST

This prayer uses a figurine of the ghost afflicting the patient as part of its magical procedure. The figurine is equipped for a journey and dispatched to the netherworld. With the departure of the figurine, the ghost was expected to quit the patient.

[O administrator of all the] numerous [peoples],
    light of the earth, Shamash the judge, (1)
O mighty [lord Ea], Eridu's [tru]st,
O sage of the universe, wise Marduk, [lo]rd of Eengurra,[2]
O Ea, Shamash, and Marduk, run to my aid,
Let me prosper with your assent! (5)
O Shamash,[3] a terrifying ghost has attached itself
    to my back for many days,

1. Variant adds: "I, so-and-so, son of [so-and-so], your servant, am afraid, frightened, and terrified, on account of the evil of a snake."
2. Byname for the temple of Enki/Ea at Eridu.
3. Variant: "O figurine."

and does not release its hold,
It harasses me all day, terrifies me all night,
Always at hand to hound me,
    making my hair stand on end,
Pressing my forehead, making me dizzy,
Parching my mouth, paralyzing my flesh,
    drying out my whole body.[1]   (10)
Be it a ghost of my kith or kin,
Be it a ghost of someone killed in battle,
Be it a wandering ghost, this is it, this is its figurine!
O Shamash, I have worked on it before you:
I have portrayed on it clothes to wear,
    sandals for its feet,[2]   (15)
A belt for its waist, a waterskin for it to drink from, and flour,
I have given it provision for a journey.
Let it go to the setting sun,
Let it be entrusted to Bidu,[3]
    the great gatekeeper of the netherworld,
May Pituh, great gatekeeper of the netherworld,
    keep it under close guard,[4]   (20)
May he hold fast the bolt (of) their lock(?).
O Shamash, at your sublime command,
    which cannot be changed,[5]
At the command of the sage of the gods, Marduk,
Drive it from my body, cut it off [from] my [bo]dy,
    remove it from my body!
Be it conjured by your life!
    Be it conjured by the life of Ea and [As]alluhi!   (25)
Be it conjured [by the life
    of the gre]at [gods of heaven and netherworld]!][6]
May it not approach me, may it not draw near me!
[May it not reach me], may it not catch up with me!

1. Variant omits.
2. Variant: "great Shamash."
3. Literally: "He opened" (W. G. Lambert in T. Abusch, ed., *Riches Hidden in Secret Places, Ancient Near Eastern Studies in Memory of Thorkild Jacobsen* [Winona Lake, Ind., 2002], 209).
4. Variant omits this line.
5. Variant adds here a prayer to avert the evil portended by an eclipse; see p. 637 note 2.
6. Variant omits.

May it cross river, go beyond mountain,
[May it be 3600 l]eagues distant from my person! (30)
May it mount to the sky like smoke,
[Like an] uprooted [tamar]isk, may it not return where it was!¹
May (this) tamarisk purify [me],
[May] (this) [... plant re]lease me!*
May the netherworld receive (it) of me, (35)
May it give me its awe-inspiring sheen,
        may it remove my sickness!
[O Ea, Shamash], and Marduk, run to my aid!
Remove the [sic]kness of my body,
        that the one who sees me may sound your praises,
Eradicate the disease of my body!
I turn to you, grant me life! (40)

Text: King, BMS 53; Ebeling, KAR 267, rev. 1–24.
Edition: J. Scurlock, "KAR 267 // BMS 53: A Ghostly Light on bīt rimki?" JAOS 108 (1988), 203–209.
Translation: von Soden, SAHG, 340–342 no. 67; Seux, *Hymnes*, 416–418.
**Notes to Text*: (34) von Soden, ZA 43 (1936), 269; AHw, 198a.

---

1. This formula is encountered elsewhere; compare III.51a lines 7–9, III.51i lines 101–104, III.51o lines 35–36, IV.51b line 14.

III.38 TO ENLIL

As chief god of the Sumerian pantheon, Enlil continued in Assyro-Babylonian tradition as one of the great gods. His domain was the earth, though he is often portrayed in Akkadian literature as inimical to humankind, angry, harsh, and malevolent.

(a) SPOKEN BY A PERSON IN AUTHORITY

[He who has ga]thered to himself all,
    king of heaven and netherworld, swift god,* (1)
Wise one who knows the people's portents,
Who surveys (all) qua[rters],
Noble sovereign, whose [command] cannot be changed,
Whose utterance cannot be altered, [ ] ... (5)
The command of whose lips no god can set aside,
Greatest lord, mountain of the Igigi-gods,
Sovereign of the Anunna-gods, solicitous noble one,
Enlil, greatest lord, mountain of the Igigi-gods,
Sovereign of the Anunna-gods, solicitous noble one, (10)
Ever-renewing one, whose command cannot be altered,
The command of whose lips no god can set aside,
Lord of lords, king of kings,[1]
    father who begot the great gods,
Lord of destinies and designs, last resort for judgment,
You are the leader of heaven and netherworld,
    lord of the lands! (15)
At your command humankind is born,
You nominate king and governor.
Of all the stars of heaven,
... it is your name I have invoked,
I have been attentive to you. (20)
Ordain a favorable [destiny] for me,
[Grant me]* your great prosperity.
[Set upon me] your great vitality,
[May god?],* king, lord, prince es[teem me],
[Ma]y the one who sees me extol [your] greatness. (25)

1. Variant: "king of the world."

May the people's mouths speak praise of me.
Set [as]sent, obedience, and peace upon my lips.
[By] your eternal assent, which cannot be changed,
Let my (personal) god stand at my right,
Let my (personal) goddess stand at my left,   (30)
Let the god who keeps (me) in well-being
    always be at my side,
Let courtier and official speak a favorable word for me.
Look upon me, lord, accept my supplication!
Reconcile with me the hearts of my angry, furious,
    wrathful (personal) god and my (personal) goddess,
    who are angry, furious, and wrathful with me,
As well as the heart of your great divinity!   (35)
Each day, as long as I live,
Let me proclaim your greatness,
    let me sou[nd] your praises!

Text: Ebeling, KAR 68; KAR 25, iii 21–33; see also III.38b.
Edition: Ebeling, AGH, 20–23.
Translation: Seux, *Hymnes*, 271–273.
Literature: Mayer, UFBG, Enlil 1b.
Notes to Text: (1) Mayer, OrNS 46 (1977), 388. (22) CAD Ḫ, 168b. (24) Seux, *Hymnes*, 273 note 19.

(b) PROTECTOR OF THE KING

This prayer, to be spoken during a royal lustration ritual (see III.51h), is partly a duplicate of the preceding, but then turns specifically to the needs of one in authority.

O greatest lord, mountain of the Igi[gi]-gods,	(1)
Sovereign of the Anunna-gods, solicitous prince,	
O [En]lil, greatest lord, mountain of the Igigi-gods,	
[So]vereign of the Anunna-gods, solicitous prince,	
Ever-renewing one, whose command cannot be altered,	(5)
The command of whose lips no god can set aside,	
Lord of lords, king of kings, father who begot the great gods,	
Lord of destinies and designs,	
leader of heaven and netherworld,	
Lord of the lands,	
Last resort in judgment, whose command cannot be altered,	(10)
Who ordains destinies for all the gods,	
At your command humankind is born,[1]	
You nominate king and governor.	
Because creation of god and man is in your power,	
And because you can make the weak equal to the strong,	(15)
From among all the stars of heaven,	
My lord, I put my trust in you, extol you,	
And I have been attentive to you.	
Ordain for me a destiny of (long) life,	
Command a good name for me.	(20)
Dissolve evil and establish justice,	
Take away [po]verty and give me prosperity,[2]	
Set upon me your great vitality.	
May [god] and king esteem me,	
May noble and prince do what I command,[3]★	(25)
May the one who sees me act in awe of me,	
May my word be heeded in the assembly,	

---

1. Variant adds a prayer to avert the evil portended by an eclipse; see p. 637 note 2.
2. Variant for 21/22: "take away evil and give favor."
3. Variant: "what befits me."

May the protective spirit of command, hearing,
    and acceptance go with me every day!
May my (personal) god exalt you,
    may my (personal) goddess seek you!*   (30)
And as for me, your servant, may I live in well-being,[1]
Let me proclaim your greatness,
    let me sound your praises!

Text: Myhrman, PBS 1/1 17; King, BMS 19; compare Ebeling, KAR 25, iii 21–33, KAR 68, obv.
10–19 (above, III.38a), with numerous variants not noted here.
Edition: Ebeling, AGH, 20–22.
Translation: von Soden, SAHG, 296–297 no. 41; Seux, *Hymnes*, 274–275.
Literature: Mayer, UFBG, Enlil 1a; Lawson, *Fate*, 57–58.
Notes to Text: (25) Walker, AfO 24 (1973), 124–125. (30) Mayer, OrNS 46 (1977), 389.

---

1. Variant omits these two lines and ends here with an incomplete one:
        At your sublime command, which cannot be altered,
        And your eternal assent, which cannot be changed …

(c) AGAINST ENLIL'S ANGER

This bilingual Sumero-Akkadian psalm is an example of a type intended to appease angry gods, a well-known genre in Sumerian called "heart-appeasing laments."[1] It invokes Enlil by various epithets, seeking to bring about his reconciliation with his people and to restore order in the land. The preserved portion opens with an address to the god, hoping to stir his attention. The consequences of his withdrawal of favor are mentioned. There follows a lament over the destruction of the land; then the psalm ends with a plea for reconciliation. Compare III.49c.

> How long, O lord, how long? Help me!   (1)
> How long, ...? Help me!
> How long, [O lord of the world]? Help me!
> How long, [O lord of the sure command]? Help me!
> How long, [O Mullil,[2] father of the land]? Help me!   (5)
> How long, O shep[herd] of the people of this land? Help me!
> How long, [O keeper of your own counsel]? Help me!
> How long, [O wild bull who lets his herd stray]? Help me!
> How long, [O sleeper of feigned sleep]? Help me!
> How long, O lord of Nippur? Help me!   (10)
> How long, O lord, how long will a mighty foe
>   have had full control of your land?
> [How long, O lord, will an enemy] destroy your land?
> [   ] has scattered the people of your land to a distant [la]nd,
> [   ] has left the cult centers moaning,
> [   ] has scattered [   ]   (15)

(gap)

> [May Asalluhi-Marduk, lord of Babylon],[3]
>   (join) my prayer,
> [May his wife, Panunan]ki-Sarpanitu,
>   (join) my supplication.

---

1. E. Dalglish, *Psalm Fifty-one* (Leiden, 1962), 21–35; Maul, HBKl.
2. Sumerian dialectal form for Enlil.
3. The hyphenated names that follow are Sumerian names or epithets of gods followed by Akkadian names or epithets of the same gods.

[May your trusty messenger?, Muz]ebbasa'a-Nabu,
    (join) my prayer,
[May the daughter-in-law?], eldest child of Urash,
    (join) my supplication.
May the righteous princess, Gashanguteshsiga-Tashmetu,
    join my prayer, (5')
May the great princess, the lady Nanay,
    (join) my supplication.
May your father Enki, who begot you,
    (your mother) Ninki, (join) my prayer,
May your beloved wife, the great mistress Ninlil,
    (join) my supplication.
May your trusty messenger, the commander Nusku,
    (join) my prayer:
May they say to you, "[Look steadfastly upon him]!" (10')
May they say to you, "[Incline your head toward him]!"
May they say to you, "[Let your heart be calmed]!"
May they say to you, "[Let your feelings be soothed]!"
[As if my real mother, let your heart be reconciled],
[As if my real mother, my real father,
    let your heart be reconciled]! (15')

Text: Maul, HBKl, pl. 6–7.
Edition: Maul, HBKl, 90–96 no. 3.
Translation: Seux, *Hymnes*, 147–149.

III.39 TO FAMILY GHOSTS

While Mesopotamians believed in the finality of death and a dreary eternity in a dusty, cheerless netherworld (see III.19 lines 7–11, III.20 iii 2′–5′), they accepted as well the possibilities of traffic with spirits of the dead. Survivors of the deceased were responsible for providing food and water for the spirit in the netherworld. Spirits of the dead not properly interred or cared for might exercise a baneful influence. There is evidence at various periods for a household ancestral cult as well.[1] This is alluded to in the Great Hymn to Nabu (III.31), lines 121–122. For spells against ghosts, see also IV.44b, c.

> O ghosts of my family, progenitors in the grave(?),* (1)
> My father, my grandfather, my mother,
>   my grandmother, my brother, my sister,
> My family, kith and kin,
>   as many as are asleep in the netherworld,
> I have made my funerary offering,
> I have libated water to you, I have cherished you, (5)
> I have glorified you, I have ho[no]red you.
> Stand this day before Shamash and Gilgamesh,[2]
> Judge my case, render my verdict!
> Hand over to Namtar, messenger of the netherworld,
> The evil(s) present in my body, flesh, and sinews! (10)
> May Ningizzida, prefect of the vast netherworld,
>   guard them well,
> May Bidu, great gatekeeper of the netherworld,
>   [cover?] their faces.
> Seize (them)[3] and send (them) down
>   to the Land of No Return!
> May I, your servant, live in well-being,
> Let me be purified* [in] your name from witchcraft, (15)

---

1. See J. Bottéro, "La Mythologie de la mort," CRRAI 26 (1979), 25–52 = *Mésopotamie*, 323–346; "Les Morts et l'au-delà dans les rituels en akkadien contre l'action des 'revenants'," ZA 73 (1983), 153–203; M. Bayliss, "The Cult of Dead Kin in Assyria and Babylonia," Iraq 35 (1973), 115–125; J. Cooper, "The Fate of Mankind: Death and Afterlife in Ancient Mesopotamia," in H. Obayashi, ed., *Death and Afterlife, Perspectives of World Religions* (New York, 1991), 20–33.
2. Here a netherworld deity.
3. Text: "it," though preceding line has objects of verb in plural.

Let me libate cool water in your drinking pipe,[1]
Revive me, let me sound your praises!

Text: Ebeling, KAR 227, rev. iii 8–24; Ebeling-Köcher-Rost, LKA 89, rev. right, 3–7.
Edition: Ebeling, TuL, 131–132.
Translation: Seux, *Hymnes*, 431–432.
Literature: Mayer, UFBG, *eṭemmū kimtija* 1.

Notes to Text: (1) Reading von Soden, ZA 43 (1944), 266; translation uncertain. Seux suggests "builders of tombs(?)"; variant has "Anunna-gods." (15) Seux, *Hymnes*, 432 note 9, following Mullo Weir, reads "let me invoke your name," but this does not accord well with LKU 89, rev. 16, where [*i*]*na* MU-*ku-nu* supports Ebeling's reading.

1. Conduit for water to the netherworld where the dead could receive fresh water, if offered to them by the living.

III.40 TO GIRRA

Girra, the fire god, was invoked in rituals against black magic or to ward off the evil portended by nightmares. In magic rituals fire was used to consume a figurine or other representation of the witch believed to be afflicting the patient. The selections translated below illustrate different appeals to the fire god's power. Many such prayers are found in two large magical works entitled "Burning" (*Maqlû*) and "Incineration" (*Šurpu*) (see, for example, IV.47, 49 and Introduction to Chapter IV, p. 775 notes 7 and 8); see also Maul *Zukunftsbewältigung*, 144–145. For a general study, see J. Bottéro, "Le feu dans les textes mésopotamiens," in *Le feu dans le Proche-Orient Antique, Actes du Colloque de Strasbourg (9 et 10 juin 1972)*, (Leiden, 1973), especially 24–26, and Michalowski, *Studies Hallo*, 156–157. For Sumerian spells to the fire-god, see G. Conti, "A proposito di Gibil, dio del fuoco," *Studies Cagni*, 125–134.

(a) ILLUMINATOR

O blazing Girra, firstborn of Anu,   (1)
You are the one to render judgment
    (on what is) spoken and secret,
You illumine darkness,
You set straight confusion and perturbation.
You make decisions for the great gods,   (5)
Without you, no god reaches a verdict,
You are the giver of instruction and direction.
You straightaway restrain the evildoer,
You straightaway overcome the wicked enemy.
I, so-and-so, son of his (personal) god,
    whose (personal) god is so-and-so,
    whose (personal) goddess is so-and-so,   (10)
Have been afflicted by sorcery, I stand before you,
Being cursed before god and king, I ... before you,
Being [ob]noxious to whoever s[ees me],
    I kneel at your feet.
O Girra, most great one, pure god,
Now, before your great divinity,   (15)
I have made for your power two bronze figurines
    of my sorcerer and of my sorceress,

I have made crossed marks(?) upon them,
>   before you, I have given them over to you.
Let them be the ones to die, let me live,
Let them be the ones to be taken astray, let me go straight,
Let them be the ones to come to an end,
>   let me be productive,   (20)
Let them be the ones to be weak, let me be strong![1]
O stately Girra, eminent one of the gods,
Overcome them,
>   you who overcome the evil and the enemy,
>   that I be not oppressed,
That I, your servant, live in well-being
>   and serve you.
You are my god, you are my lord,   (25)
You are my judge, you are my help,
You are my champion!

Text: Tallqvist, *Maqlû* II 69–90; Ebeling, KAR 235, obv. 8–20; Gurney, STT 140, obv. + Finkelstein, STT 79, 76–84, 81, obv. 96–102.
Edition: Meier, *Maqlû*, 15–16 lines 76–102.
Translation: von Soden, SAHG, 347–348 no. 73; Seux, *Hymnes,* 384–385.
Literature: Meier, AfO 21 (1966), 73; Mayer, UFBG, Gira 2; Abusch in Abusch, ed., *Magic,* 93.

(b) MELTER

O stately Girra, firstborn of Anu,   (1)
Pure offspring of sublime Shalash,[2]
Stately, ever-renewing, eternal requirement(?)[3] of the gods,
Giver of food portions to the Igigi-gods,
Who imparts brilliance to the Anunna, the great gods,   (5)
Raging Girra, who burns up canebrakes,[4]*
Brave Girra, who destroys trees and rocks,

---

1. Possibly (Seux, *Hymnes,* 385 note 12) a reference to progeny.
2. Normally the wife of Adad or Dagan, but here assigned to Anu; compare above, p. 610 note 1.
3. Uncertain. See p. 502 note 2.
4. Variant: "enemies."

Who burns up evil ones, the tribe of sorcerer and sorceress,
Who destroys malefactors,
    the tribe of sorcerer and sorceress,
Stand by me this day in my case,   (10)
Overcome the seditious, corrupter(?), the evil one!
Just as these figurines dissolve, melt, drip away,
Let my sorcerer and sorceress dissolve, melt, drip away.

Text: Tallqvist, *Maqlû* II 124–135; Ebeling, KAR 235, rev. 6–12.
Edition: Meier, *Maqlû*, 18 lines 135–147.
Translation: von Soden, SAHG, 349 no. 75; Seux, *Hymnes,* 387.
Literature: Mayer, UFBG, Gira 5.
Notes to Text: (6) Meier, AfO 21 (1966), 73; Seux, *Hymnes*, 387 note 4.

(c) JUDGE

O Girra, mighty one, terrifying storm,   (1)
You govern gods and sovereigns,
You judge the case of the oppressed man and woman.
Stand by me in my case, and, like the warrior Shamash,
Judge my case, render my verdict!   (5)
Burn up my sorcerer and my sorceress,
Consume my enemies,
    devour those who are wicked to me,
Let your furious storm overcome them!

Text: Tallqvist, *Maqlû* II 114–121; Ebeling, KAR 235, rev. 1–4.
Edition: Meier, *Maqlû*, 17–18, lines 126–133.
Translation: von Soden, SAHG, 348 no. 74; Seux, *Hymnes*, 386–387.
Literature: Mayer, UFBG, Gira 4.

(d) REFINER

O Girra, sage, exalted in the land,   (1)
Valorous one, son of Apsu, exalted in the land,
O Girra, with your pure flame★
You provide light to the House of Shadows,
You ordain the destiny★ of whatever is called by name.   (5)
You are the one who mixes copper and tin,
You are the one who refines gold and silver.
You are the companion of the fermentation goddess,
You are the one who, at night, turns back the evildoer.
May the limbs of (this) man,
     son of his (personal) god, be purified!   (10)
May he be pure as the heavens,
May he be pure as the netherworld!
May he shine like innermost heaven,
[May] the evil [tongue stand] aside.★

Text: Pinches, IV R² 14 no. 2 = Haupt, ASKT 9, rev. 6–29 (bilingual, translation follows Akkadian);
    Gurney, OECT 11 40.
Edition: Reiner, *Šurpu*, 53 lines 6–29.
Translation: Seux, *Hymnes*, 251–252.
★*Notes to Text*: (3) Sumerian adds "clear." (5) Sumerian: "you put a branding mark on." (14) Sumerian
    only.

III.41 TO GODS OF THE NIGHT

(a) AGAINST PESTILENCE

This prayer was used in a ritual against pestilence.

> The steppe is deathly still, doors are barred,
>> [gates are sh]ut,★   (1)
> Bolts are set, the go[ds of the night][1] are hushed,
> (But) the gr[eat?]★ gates of heaven are open.
> O great gods of the night, whose p[ath?] is discernible,
> Come in, O gods of the night, gre[at] stars,   (5)
> Yoke-star, Sipazianna,[2] Shulpae,[3] [   ],
> Chariot,[4] Jupiter, Kidney, Mouse,[5] Field,[6]
> Come in, gods of the night, goddesses [of the night ...],
> Of south and north, of east and west.
> Come, Ninsianna,[7] great lady, and the many ... stars,   (10)
> That he who is mindful of you may attain his desire,
> That so-and-so, who is mindful of you,
>> may attain [his desire].★
> From of old there has been acceptance [   ],
> Vitality, obedience, and revival <are yours (to grant)>,★
> Yours is to dissolve bondage, anger, fury, and scheming.   (15)
> Accept the speech of him★ who has invoked you,
>> dignify [his] speech,
> Accept the speech of [so-and-so],
>> who has invoked you, dignify his speech!

(obscure lines, then gap)

Text: K 3507 = Langdon, OECT 6 pl. XII = Sidersky, JRAS 1929, 786 (collated).
Edition: Ebeling, TuL, 163–164.
Translation: Seux, Hymnes, 243–245.

1. So the parallel from Hattusha, though this is hard to reconcile with line 4.
2. Orion?
3. Procyon?
4. Great Bear.
5. Centaurus?
6. Pegasus?
7. Venus.

Literature: Meier, ZA 45 (1939), 197 (parallel from Hattusha in Anatolia); Oppenheim, AnBi 12 (1959), 291; Mayer, UFBG, *ilū mušīti* 2c.
*Notes to Text: (1) Seux, *Hymnes*, 243 note 3. (3) Seux, *Hymnes*, 244 note 6. (12) Langdon's copy conflates the first half of tablet line 18 with the second half of tablet line 19; see Sidersky's copy. (14) *ittikunu* was apparently omitted by the scribe. (16) Seux, *Hymnes*, 245 note 26. First preserved sign is šá, not a.

(b) AGAINST CULTIC IMPURITY

This prayer was used in a ritual designed to protect a person from the evil incurred from an improperly performed cultic rite. For other prayers of this type, see von Soden, SAHG, 343 no. 69; Seux, *Hymnes*, 248–250 (a) = Caplice, OrNS 39 (1970), 128–129; Maul, *Zukunftsbewältigung*, 429, lines 9–23.

> Stand by me, O gods of the night, (1)
> Heed what I say, O gods, lords of silence!
> O Anu, Enlil, Ea, great gods,
> O Ninshiku, exceedingly wise!
> I call upon you, Ishtar, mistress of silence, (5)
> I call upon you, Night, bride of Anu, laden with splendor!
> O Yoke-star, stand at my right,
>   O Yoke-star, stand at my left!
> God sends you as a messenger to man, man to god,
> It is I who sends you to the god who eats my bread,
>   who drinks my water, the one who receives my offering.

Text: Ebeling, KAR 38, rev. 18–27; Caplice, OrNS 39 (1970), pl. II K 8863; Hunger, SBTU I 11, rev. 4–8; Wiseman and Black, CTN 4 134, side B 7–14.
Edition: Caplice, OrNS 39 (1970), 127, 130, no. 38 lines 18–27; Maul, *Zukunftsbewältigung*, 426, 430, lines 56–65.
Translation: Seux, *Hymnes*, 250 (b).
Literature: Mayer, UFBG, *ilū mušīti* 3b.

(c) AGAINST WITCHCRAFT

I call upon you, O gods of the night,   (1)
Along with you I call upon night, the veiled bride,
I call upon the evening, midnight, and dawn watch.
Because a sorceress has bewitched me,
(And) a deceitful woman has denounced me,   (5)
They have driven away from me
        my (personal) god and my (personal) goddess,
I have become obnoxious to whoever sees me,
I am burdened with sleeplessness, day and night.
They keep filling my mouth with skeins(?),[1]
They have deprived my mouth of food,   (10)
They have diminished my drinking water.
My joyful song is a dirge, my happiness sorrow.
Stand by me, O great gods, hear my complaint,
Judge my case, learn of my proceeding!
I have made a figurine of my sorcerer and of my sorceress,   (15)
He and she who contrive against me,
I have set (them) before you, I plead my case.
Because she has done evil and has attempted villainy,
May she be the one to die, let me live!
May her sorcery, spells, and black magic be dissolved,   (20)
May the full-crowned tamarisk absolve, purify me,
May the palm that withstands all winds absolve me,
May the ...-plant, full of pulp(?),[2] cleanse me,
May the pine cone, full of seeds, absolve me.
Before you I have become pure as the grass,   (25)
I have become clean and pure as soap plant.
Her spell, that of the wicked sorceress,
Her speech is turned back to her mouth,
        she is tongue-tied.

---

1. Variant: "silence" (Meier, *Maqlû*, 66). According to CAD Q, 304b, "silence" is an erroneous variant; according to AHw, 925b, 927b, "skeins" is erroneous. Tying thread on the mouth as a metaphor for blocking speech and effectiveness is known in other magical contexts though not filling the mouth with thread. Line 12 is in favor of "thread." For a magical procedure that involves stopping up a mouth with wool, see Falkenstein, ZA 45 (1939), 26.

2. Literally: "Earth." The symbolism of the trees may include tallness, strength, inner resources, and promise of productivity for the future, all attributes that might desert a man under an evil spell.

May the gods of the night strike her
    on account of her sorcery,
May the three watches of the night
    dissolve her wicked spells!   (30)
May her mouth be tallow, her tongue be salt,
May she who said the evil word against me
    melt like tallow,
May she who worked sorcery be dissolved like salt,
May her magic knots be untied,
    her contrivances be destroyed,
May all her words fill the wilderness,   (35)
At the command spoken by the gods of the night!

Text: Tallqvist, *Maqlû* I 1–36; Finkelstein, STT 78, 1–36.
Edition: Meier, *Maqlû*, 7–8 lines 1–36.
Translation: Seux, *Hymnes*, 375–377; Farber, TUAT II/2, 262–263.
Literature: Meier, AfO 21 (1966), 70–71; Mayer, UFBG, *ilū mušiti* 1; Abusch, *Witchcraft*, 85–147.

III.42 TO GULA

Gula was goddess of healing and the physician's arts. For additional hymns to Gula, see C. J. Mullo-Weir, "Four Hymns to Gula," JRAS 1929, 1–18, and above, III.25; for spells invoking her healing power, see Butler, AOAT 258 (1998), 349–377.

(a) HEALER

This song invokes her by various names and extols her life-giving powers.

> [Let me sing of y]our [pr]aises,
> > let me extol your [sovereign]ty, (1)
> Let me exalt your [divin]ity, let me glori[fy your val]or.
> [O Gula], let me sing of your praises,
> > let me extol your sovereignty,
> Let me exalt your [divin]ity, let me glorify [your] valor.
> Let me proclaim [your] name to the people of this land,
> > however many they be, (5)
> You keep (people's) bod[ies] healthy in all world regions
> > you have allowed to fete you.
> O Gula, great physician, there is no equal to you,
> > great is [your] responsibility!
> Let me glorify your sovereignty,
> > let me exalt your na[me] in all holy places,
> You dwell in Ekur, in Esharra go [your pa]ths.[1]
> [   ] your [   ] among the gods you are warrior,
> > who among the gods can [   ] your sovereignty? (10)
> You are the one [   ] who, with the great gods,
> > ordains destinies.
> You stand out [   ] ..., O lady,
> > the mention of your name is un[ ],
> Who [   ] dogs,[2] who gives health to god and man,
> > they call on you as "Mistress of Health."

---

1. This may refer to a temple in Assur or Nippur.
2. The dog was associated with the goddess of healing.

You give [ ] to the great lords,
    they call on you in all of Baltil,[1]
You govern human beings [on] earth,
    you exalt [your] na[me] to the great gods.   (15)
You judge cases and ordain destinies
    [in response to?] prayers,
You hold [sov]ereignty of heaven,
    you give instructions to the Igigi-gods.
Which destiny among the gods' [   ]
    have you not ordained?
You prolong the days of the [ki]ng(?) [   ],
    you let him see light,
[   ], as he grows old, his eyes will see much,   (20)

(three lines fragmentary)

He who was plunged [into dis]as[ter],
    you saved him from distress,
You gave subsis[tence to the poor].   (25)
O merciful [   ], may your heart be cal[med],
O [   ] ..., may your feelings be ap[peased]!
May the mori[bund] revive [at] your sublime [command],
At your firm as[sent],
    the moaning world regions shout for joy,
They summon you as "queen of (all) world regions" [   ],   (30)
Your names are important [   ], O spouse of Uta'ulu,[2]
[Me]me,[3] who establishes festivals
    for the lords who lo[ve you].
[   ] of the Anunna-gods, [your] responsibilities* are lofty.
[Allu]ring [goddess], who grants heirs(?),*
    who makes abundant [   ],
Beloved [   ], crea[tr]ess,
    mistress of the lords of [heaven],   (35)
[   ], preeminent spouse whose sovereignty has no rival,

---

1. Assur; see p. 316 note 2.
2. Name for Ninurta.
3. Like Ba'u in line 40, here another name for Gula. Lines 32ff. may explain Meme hermeneutically or may extol this aspect of the goddess. The fragment K 232, not included here, lists numerous other names of Gula; see Mullo-Weir, JRAS 1929, 9–18 and compare above, III.25.

You are greatest [among …] the gods,
>   who is as capable as [you]?
You pull up the bo[dy] of the [fallen   ],
[You make splen]did the [   ] of heaven and netherworld,
>   O mer[ciful la]dy,
O [Ba]u, let praise of you [   ] on people's lips,   (40)
Let them [gl]orify [your] sovereignty [in] all lands,
[In all world reg]ions* you are the greatest, [   ].
[Grant?] health, strength, [   ], a fortunate course,
[   ] of body [   ]
[   ], let me glorify your greatness!   (45)

Text: Ebeling-Köcher-Rost, LKA 17.
Edition: Ebeling, OrNS 23 (1954), 346–349.
Translation: Seux, *Hymnes*, 103–106.
Notes to Text: (33) Compare K 232 line 17 = Mullo-Weir, JRAS 1929, 11. (34) Seux, *Hymnes*, 106 notes 33, 34. (42) Seux, *Hymnes*, 106 note 40.

(b) INTERCESSOR

O Gula, most great lady, merciful mother,
    who dwells in the great heavens, (1)
I call upon you, my lady, stand by me and hear me!
I seek you out, I turn to you, I seize your hem[1]
    as if it were that of my (personal) god
    and my (personal) goddess.
Because judging the case, rendering the verdict,
Because reviving and granting well-being
    are yours (to grant), (5)
Because you know how to save, spare, and rescue,
O Gula, most great lady, merciful mother,
I turn to you, from among all the stars of heaven,
O my lady, I turn to you, I am heedful of you.
Accept of me my flour offering, receive my plea, (10)
Let me send you to my angry (personal) god,
    my angry (personal) goddess,
To the god of my city who is in a rage and furious with me.
On account of omens and dreams
    that are continually besetting me,
I am afraid and always anxious.
O Gula, most great lady,
    with the utterance of your sublime command,
    which is greatest in Enlil's Ekur, (15)
And with your firm assent, which cannot be changed,
May my angry (personal) god return to me,
    may my angry (personal) goddess relent to me,
May the god of my city who is in a rage and furious with me,
Who is angry, calm down;
    he who was vexed, may he be soothed!
O Gula, most great lady, who intercedes for the weak, (20)
Intercede for me with Marduk, king of the gods,[2]
    the merciful lord; say a favorable word.

---

1. Gesture of entreaty; see further Finet, *Annales du Centre d'Études des Religions* 3 (1969), 101–130 and III.43b line 25; p. 675 note 1.
2. Variant omits.

May your broad protection and imp[osing] forgiveness
>   be wi[th] me,
[Grant me] favor and life,
Let me proclaim your greatness,
>   [let me] sound your praises!

Text: King, BMS 6, 71–94, BMS 37, 7′–13′; Loretz-Mayer, AOAT 34 18; Ebeling, KAR 341; Finkelstein, STT 59, rev. 1–23. King, BMS 7, 9′–33′; Loretz-Mayer, AOAT 34 19; Scheil, SFS 6(?) are texts of the same hymn addressed to Belet-ili. Variant manuscripts insert additional prayers not included here.

Edition: Mayer, UFBG, 450–454.

Translation: Mullo-Weir, JRAS 1929, 1–4; von Soden, SAHG, 327–328 no. 60; Seux, *Hymnes*, 337–339.

Literature: Mayer, UFBG, Gula 1a.

III.43 TO ISHTAR

Ishtar, one of the most complex figures in Mesopotamian religion, is early attested as a goddess of warfare and as the morning- and evening-star (see II.1, III.26, III.43b). Partly through syncretism with the Sumerian goddess Inanna, she became as well a goddess of fertility, reproduction, and love (see III.43d). She is often portrayed as harsh, capricious, and vindictive (III.28); fearless and joyful in the battle fray (II.4, 5); urgent, ardent, and alluring as a lover (II.1, IV.55). She was also associated with prostitution, sexual impersonation, self-mutilation, and homosexuality (p. 502 note 3, p. 904 note 3, IV.55). Penitential and devotional literature tends to stress her valor and queenly tenderness. For further discussion and documentation of Ishtar, see C. Wilcke, "Inanna/Ištar," RLA 5, 74–87; R. Harris, "Inanna-Ishtar as Paradox and a Coincidence of Opposites," *History of Religions* 30 (1991), 261–278; G. Selz, "Five Divine Ladies," *NIN* 1 (2000), 29–62; T. Abusch, "Ishtar," *NIN* 1 (2000), 23–27.

(a) AGAINST SORCERY

O pure Ishtar, lofty one of the Igigi-gods, (1)
Who makes battle, who brings about combat,
Most stately and perfect of goddesses,
At your command, O Ishtar, humankind is governed.
The sick man who sees your face revives, (5)
His bondage is released, he gets up instantly.
At your command, O Ishtar, the blind man sees the light,
The unhealthy one who sees your face becomes healthy.
I, who am very sick, I kneel, I stand before you,
I turn to you to judge my case, O torch of the gods, (10)
I have seen your face, may my bonds be released.
Do not delay,* I am confused and anxious.
I live[1] like one bastinadoed.
I did what you said to do, O Ishtar!
A sorcerer or a sorceress (15)
Whom you know, but I do not know,
With magic rites of malice and assassination,
Which they have worked in your presence,

1. Literally: "My life has become like one ..."; variant "my family."

Have laid figurines of me in a grave,
Have come to assassinate me!   (20)
They have worked in secret against me,
    I work against them openly!
By your sublime command, which cannot be altered,
    And your firm assent, which cannot be changed,
May whatever I say come true.
Let life come forth to me from your pure utterance,
(May) you (be the one to say) "What a pity about him!"
    O you who are the (supreme) goddess among the gods.   (25)

Text: Ebeling, KAR 92, rev. 9–33; Ebeling-Köcher-Rost, LKA 144, rev. 3–17; Farber, *Ištar und Dumuzi* pl. 20 BM 54650, obv. ii 1–25; pl. 22 Rm 247, rev.
Edition: Farber, *Ištar und Dumuzi*, 238–240, lines 3′–29′.
Translation: von Soden, SAHG, 337–338 no. 64; Seux, *Hymnes*, 457–458.
Literature: Mayer, UFBG, Ištar 24.
Notes to Text: (12) Seux, *Hymnes*, 458 note 6.

(b) THE GREATNESS OF ISHTAR

This devotional composition contains unusual and obscure expressions, such as suggest an effort at originality. It stresses the astral character of the goddess and her control of destinies.

O warrior Ishtar, most cherished of goddesses,   (1)
Torch of heaven and earth,
    splendor of the four world regions,
Innini, firstborn of Sin, offspring of Ningal,
Twin sister of the bearded, magnificent warrior, Shamash,
O Ishtar, you are (supreme like) Anu, you rule the heavens,   (5)
[With] Enlil the counsellor you order the inhabited world.
O Mother-Matrix,[1] bringer into being of rites and lustrations,
At(?) the revelation of Ea, you hold the bonds in the depths,[2]
Wheresoever floor plans are laid, brickwork built,*

1. Akkadian *mummu*; see above, p. 439 note 1.
2. Line not clear; precise sense of "bonds" uncertain.

Like the sun, you take charge of
     whoever has the power of speech. (10)
Who is your equal even among the Igigi-gods,
Who is your rival even among the Anunna-gods?
You are the one who, in the womb* of humankind,
     establishes poverty and wealth,
You reverse destiny so the unlucky may have good fortune.
I sought among gods, prayers were given to you,
     I turned to goddesses, for you was entreaty. (15)
Before you is a protective spirit,
     behind you is a guardian spirit,
At your right is justice, at your left good fortune.
Obedience, acceptance, and peace
     are established in your presence,
Round about you are set life and well-being.
How sweet to pray to you, how near at hand your listening, (20)
Your look is hearing, your speech light!
Have mercy upon me, O Ishtar, order my prosperity,
Look upon me steadfastly, accept my entreaty!
I have followed your guidance, let there be wealth (for me),
I have seized your litter,[1] let there be satisfaction (for me). (25)
I have borne your yoke, grant release!
I have waited upon you, let peace come directly,
I have gazed upon your radiance,
     let there be hearing and acceptance,
I have sought out your brilliance, may my face beam,
I have turned to your dominion,
     may there be life and well-being (for me). (30)
May I acquire the protective spirit that is before you,
May I acquire the guardian spirit that goes behind you,
May I add (to mine) the wealth at your right,
May I attain the good fortune at your left.
Order that my speech be heeded, (35)
That the word I shall say be agreed to, as I say it.
Guide me each day in good health and happiness,

---

1. The image is of the goddess being carried through the streets in a sedan chair. The petitioner has rushed forward to grasp a part of it in entreaty. Perhaps this is a refurbishment of the expression "seize the hem," more common in devotional literature (see III.42b line 3, IV.2b iv line 18).

Prolong my days, grant life.
Let me live in well-being, let me glorify [your] divinity,
Let me attain whatever I desire.   (40)
May heaven rejoice because of you,
        the depths rejoice because of you,
May the gods of the universe bless you,
May the great gods please you.

Text: King, BMS 5, 11–19 + K 7243+; BMS 8, 1–19 [(+) BMS 48]; BMS 1, 29–35; Ebeling, KAR
    250 obv.; Loretz-Mayer, AOAT 34 14; Mayer, OrNS 59 (1990), 488 BM 57532.
Edition: Geers-von Soden, ZA 42 (1934), 220–225; Ebeling, AGH, 60–63; Sperling, WO 12 (1981),
    8–20.
Translation: von Soden, SAHG, 333–336 no. 62; Seux, *Hymnes,* 321–323.
Literature: Mayer, UFBG, Ištar 1.
Notes to Text: (9) Mayer, OrNS 46 (1977), 389. (13) Veenhof, RA 79 (1985), 94–95, confirmed by
    BM 57532; see also Mayer, OrNS 66 (1997), 168.

(c) AGAINST IMPOTENCE

Like the preceding, this prayer dwells on the astral character of Ishtar and asks
her help in a magical procedure.

O luminary of heaven, capable Ishtar,   (1)
Mistress of the gods, whose "yes" (means) "yes,"
Princely one among the gods, whose command is supreme,
Mistress of heaven and netherworld, ruler of all settlements,
Ishtar, (at?) your invocation(?) all lords are kneeling,   (5)
I, so-and-so, son of so-and-so, kneel before you.
I, against whom sorcery has been done,
        figurines of whom have been laid in the ground,
May my body be pure as lapis,
May [my] features be bright as alabaster,
Like pure silver, red gold, may I never tarnish,   (10)
May (these seven) plants[1] drive away the magic against me!

1. Seven plants are listed here, the modern names of which are unknown.

Text: Ebeling, KAR 236, obv. 25-rev. 7; KAR 243, rev.! 1–4; Ebeling-Köcher-Rost, LKA 99b, d I
10–19; Gurney, STT 280, iii 7–17; Biggs, *ŠÀ.ZI.GA*, pl. 3 K 11076.
Edition: Biggs, *ŠÀ.ZI.GA*, 28.
Translation: Seux, *Hymnes*, 400–401.
Literature: Mayer, UFBG, Ištar 27.

(d) A GIFT TO ISHTAR

You are Ishtar, whose lover is Dumuzi,   (1)
The valorous daughter of Sin, who traverses pasture lands,
You are she who loves rustic shelters,[1]
    who loves all humankind.
I have given your great gift:
A lapis vulva, a star of gold, as befits your divinity.[2]   (5)
Intercede for me with Dumuzi your lover,
May Dumuzi your lover take away my tribulation.

Text: Farber, *Ištar und Dumuzi* pl. 10 K 2001+ (114–120); pl. 16, BM 76976, rev. i 3–9; Ebeling,
KAR 57 rev. i 1–16 + Ebeling-Köcher-Rost, LKA 70.
Edition: Farber, *Ištar und Dumuzi*, 146–149, lines 114–120.
Translation: Seux, *Hymnes*, 440.
Literature: Mayer, UFBG, Ištar 19.

1. Protection for shepherds, for whom Dumuzi was patron deity.
2. Compare above, Hymn to Papulegarra (II.3), p. 94 note 2.

(e) ISHTAR WILL NOT TIRE

A damaged manuscript from Nippur preserves part of a Mature or Late period hymn to Ishtar that a subscript ascribes to the time of Hammurabi (Classical period, see II.5). Each line is followed by a refrain: "The city's built on pleasure!" Refrains are unusual in Akkadian poetry, and may be a sign of Sumerian influence; compare III.2 and III.38c. For the explicit language of love, compare II.18, 19, 26; IV. 27, 28, 50, 56.

(seven fragmentary lines)

One comes up to her ...	*(refrain)*	
"Come here, give me what I want ..."	*(refrain)*	
Then another comes up to her,	*(refrain)*	(10)
"Come here, let me touch your vulva."	*(refrain)*	
"Since I'm ready to give you all what you want,	*(refrain)*	
"Get all the young men of your city together,	*(refrain)*	
"Let's go to the shade of the wall!"	*(refrain)*	
Seven for her midriff, seven for her loins,	*(refrain)*	(15)
Sixty then sixty satisfy themselves in turn		
upon her nakedness.	*(refrain)*	
The young men have tired, Ishtar will not tire.	*(refrain)*	
"Put it to my lovely vulva, fellows!"	*(refrain)*	
As the girl demanded,	*(refrain)*	
The young men heeded, gave her what she asked for.	*(refrain)*	(20)

(Hymn of praise to Ishtar)

Texts: von Soden, OrNS 60 (1991), pl. CVI (photo HS 1879).

Edition: von Soden, OrNS 60 (1991), 339–342.

Literature: V. Hurowitz, "An Old Babylonian Bawdy Ballad," in Z. Zevit, S. Gitin, M. Sokoloff, eds., *Solving Riddles and Untying Knots, Biblical, Epigraphic, and Semitic Studies in Honor of Jonas C. Greenfield* (Winona Lake, Ind., 1995), 543–558.

(f) SELF-PRAISE OF ISHTAR

These excerpts from a lengthy but badly damaged self-predication of Ishtar
may be compared to the earlier fragment II.4. The passages chosen here
illustrate Ishtar's prowess in battle, concern for the king, and her love of
opposites and reversal (compare also IV.17 Tablet IV line 56).

> Hurrah for me, hurrah for me,
> > the foremost one who [has no] rival, (1)
> [I am] Ishtar, who sets kings to fighting,
> > who causes c[onfusion],
> [I am she who] gives the brevet, who casts down [   ],
> [   ] bow, quiver, and combat.
> Anu is my father, Shamash [my] twin, (5)
> At my appearance my glow is like the sun's.
> All the great gods stand in attendance upon me,
> The Igigi-gods p[ress] their lips to the ground.
> I hold the staff of the gods,
> > [I] grasp the leadline[1] of heaven in my hands,
> [I am she who ca]uses confusion, sets enemies to fighting! (10)

★ ★ ★

> I watch over the king in his combat,
> [I] cre[ate] goodwill where there is discord,
> [I] cau[se] discord where there is goodwill.
> [I am she who] le[vels] the lands by strife,
> I am the charging wild ox that gores. (15)
> [I am she wh]o slays the king's enemies!

Text: Ebeling, KAR 331+306.
Edition: C. Frank, *Kultlieder aus der Ischtar-Tamūz-Kreis* (Leipzig, 1939), 36–42.

---

1. For this concept, see p. 177 note 2.

III.44 TO MARDUK

Marduk, god of Babylon, emerged as preeminent in the Babylonian pantheon during the second half of the second millennium B.C. (see p. 376 note 3). Although his original role as a vegetation deity and warden of spring waters is alluded to in devotional literature, he is often appealed to as father, warrior, and ruler. Some hymns to Marduk, such as b, e, and f below, may allude to the Epic of Creation (III.17) or use the same phraseology. For further discussion and documentation of Marduk, see W. Sommerfeld, "Marduk," RLA 7, 360–374.

(a) AGAINST MARDUK'S ANGER

This unilingual prayer, related to the bilingual prayers (see III.34) and "heart-appeasing" laments (see III.38c), is one of the finest of its type. An agnostic theme, taken up at length in the Poem of the Righteous Sufferer (III.14) and penitential psalms (see III.55), is balanced with expressions of goodwill (lines 12f.) and resignation (lines 14f.). The unanswered cries of the penitent provide a dramatic opening address, at once a reminder of the penitent's past observance and a description of his physical and emotional distress. His becoming an old man through Marduk's punishment (line 6) suggests that youth is a metaphor for his happy condition prior to Marduk's punishment, rather than his actual youth. This figure is carried through by the conclusion, whereby the suppliant becomes, if forgiven, a child of his god again (compare III.45b). Although there is scarcely a line in this poem that does not have parallels elsewhere, the harmony and effectiveness of the whole are striking and set this composition apart as a masterpiece.

> O warrior Marduk, whose anger is the deluge,   (1)
> Whose relenting is that of a merciful father,
> I am left anxious by speech unheeded,
> My hopes are deceived by outcry unanswered,
> Such as has sapped my courage,   (5)
> And hunched me over like an aged man.
> O great lord Marduk, merciful lord!
> Men, by whatever name,
> What can they understand of their own sin?*

Who has not been negligent,
>which one has committed no sin? (10)
Who can understand a god's behavior?
I would fain be obedient and incur no sin,
Yes, I would frequent the haunts of life!
Men are commanded by the gods to act under curse,
Divine affliction is for humankind to bear. (15)
I am surely responsible for some neglect of you,
I have surely trespassed the limits set by the god.
Forget what I did in my youth, whatever it was,
Let your heart not well up against me!
Absolve my guilt, remit my punishment,
Clear me of confusion, free me of uncertainty, (20)
Let no guilt of my father, my grandfather, my mother,
>my grandmother, my brother, my sister,
>my family, kith or kin
Approach my own self, but let it be gone!
If my god has commanded (it) for me,
>purify me as with medicaments.★
Commend me into the hands of my (personal) god
>and my (personal) goddess for well-being and life,
Let me stand before you always in prayer,
>supplication, and entreaty, (25)
Let the fruitful peoples of a well-ordered land praise you.
Absolve my guilt, remit my guilt!
O warrior Marduk, absolve my guilt, remit my guilt!
O great lady Erua-Sarpanitum, absolve my guilt,
O Nabu of the good name, absolve my guilt, (30)
O great lady Tashmetu, absolve my guilt,
O warrior Nergal, absolve my guilt,
O gods who dwell <in> Anu's <heaven>,★
>absolve my guilt!
The monstrous guilt that I have built up from my youth,
Scatter it hence,[1] absolve it sevenfold. (35)
Like my real father and my real mother,
Let your heart be reconciled to me.
O warrior Marduk, let me sound your praises!

---

1. Variant: "and disperse it."

Text: King, BMS 11; Ebeling-Köcher-Rost, LKA 61; Loretz-Mayer, AOAT 34, 35–39; additional
    manuscripts cited by Borger, HKL 2, 124.
Edition: Ebeling, AGH, 72–75.
Translation: von Soden, SAHG, 298–300 no. 43; Seux, *Hymnes*, 169–172.
Literature: von Soden, *Iraq* 31 (1969), 83; Mayer, UFBG, Marduk 4.
Notes to Text: (9) Mayer, OrNS 46 (1977), 387. (23) Mayer, OrNS 46 (1977), 388. (33) WGL.

(b) AGAINST ILLNESS

This exorcistic prayer is one of the longest and most elaborate of its type. Its
apparent allusions to the Epic of Creation (III.17) suggest a first-millennium
date for its composition. See General Introduction, D.3.

O Marduk, lord of the world, ra[ging], terrifying,   (1)
Stately, ever-renewing, perfe[ct, ca]pable,
Lofty, magnificent, whose [com]mand cannot be altered,
Capable one, profound of understanding,
        [no]ble one(?), sa[ge ...]!
O Marduk,[1] eminent, surpassing,
        whose [pos]ition is on hi[gh],   (5)
Mighty, powerful, eminent van[guard],
"Deluge weapon,"[2] [hopeless] to combat,
        [whose onslaught] is furious!
O Dumuduku,[3] most perfect [of ..., or]dainer of [des]tinies,
Son of Lugal-du[ku   ] of the great gods!
O planet Marduk,[4] lord [   ] prosperity![5]   (10)
O Marduk, lord of abundance and prosper[ity,
        w]ho rains down luxuriance,[6]

1. Variant adds: "lord."
2. Compare Epic of Creation (III.17) Tablet IV line 49, 75; Tablet VI line 125. As Lambert has indicated to me, "flood" (*amaru*) plus "weapon" (TUKUL) is a play on Marduk, etymologized as (A)mar(u)tuku(l).
3. Compare Epic of Creation (III.17) Tablet VII line 99. Marduk is here etymologized as "son of the holy hill" (a dais, see George, *Topographical Texts*, 287–291).
4. According to Seux, *Hymnes*, 444 note 7, an allusion to Epic of Creation (III.17) Tablet VII line 126.
5. Compare Epic of Creation (III.17) Tablet VII line 65.
6. Compare Epic of Creation (III.17) Tablet VII line 69.

Lord of underground springs, mountains, and seas,
    who overlooks the mountains,
Who opens wells and waterholes, who guides watercourses,[1]
Overseer of grain-god and sheep-god, creator of ear and fiber,
    who makes abundant green plants,[2]
You create food for god and goddess,
    you are creator of the cropland for them.   (15)
O dragon of the Anunna-gods, monitor of the Igigi-gods,
Wise son of Enanki,[3] creator of all humankind,
You are the lord,
    you are like "father" and "mother" in people's speech,
You are the one who, like the sun, illumines their darkness.
Each day you give justice to the oppressed and abused,   (20)
You administer the destitute, the widow,
    the wretched and anxious.
[You] are what they listen for,
    [the shepherd who leads them],
[At] your weighty [command],⋆
    the numerous lands and peoples prosper.
You are merciful, lord,
    you rescue the weak⋆ from danger and hardship,
[You look upon the] exhausted and des[perate],
    the one whom his god punished,⋆   (25)
You are comrade of [   ] ..., you release the captive,
[You t]ake the hand and raise the injured from his bed,
You make the [cap]tive in darkness and prison,
    the [hos]tage, see light.
[I] your [servant], so-and-so, son of so-and-so,
    whose (personal) god is so-and-so,
    whose (personal) god[dess] is so-and-so,
Bathed, clean of hands,
    [I have set up] for you pure utensils,[4]   (30)
I have spread out a [clean] red cloth beneath your feet,⋆
Hearken to my prayer, ac[cept] my [en]treaty.

---

1. Compare Epic of Creation (III.17) Tablet VII line 60.
2. Compare Epic of Creation (III.17) Tablet VII lines 2, 69, 79.
3. "Lord of Heaven and Netherworld" = Enki/Ea.
4. Variant adds: "I have made you a pure (offering)."

You know the illness from which I suffer, I do not.
It flattens me like a net, shr[ouds me like a me]sh.
Torment, head pain, and fatigue, inflammation,
     an[xiety? and ... have ...] my limbs, (35)
Foul disease, oath and curse, make my flesh cr[ee]p.
They have made my frame feverish,
     I am clothed in them as if with a garment.
Symbols(?) and images of me are interred.[1]
They have collected dust from under my feet,
     they have taken my measure,
     they have taken away my vitality.
I am infected and beset by people's wicked machinations, (40)
The fury of my (personal) god and goddess[2]
     and humankind are against me.
My dreams are terrifying, awful, evil,
My signs and omens are confused
     and have no clear interpretation.
O my lord, stand by me this day, hear what I say,
     judge my case, render my verdict!
Banish the disease that is set upon me,
     drive the head pain from my person!
May my (personal) god and goddess
     and humankind be reconciled with me.[3] (45)
At your command may no evil approach me
     from machinations of sorcerer or sorceress,
May no spell, enchantment, sorcery,
     nor wicked machination of humankind approach me,
May no evil portent from dreams, signs,
     or portents celestial or terrestrial approach me,
May no evil portents for city or land affect me personally,
May I be safe in your presence from evil thought
     and speech of humankind, (50)

---

1. This refers to a magical procedure whereby an image of the person to be bewitched is ritually interred, presumably to bring about the death of the person represented. "Symbols" (is/lqu) may refer to objects intended to represent the person who is the target of the spell (Nougayrol apud Seux, Hymnes, 446 note 38).
2. Variant omits.
3. Variant adds: "May they have pity on me."

May the amulet set around my neck
  keep all evil away from me,
May it drive away curse against me
  or utterance portending evil,[1]
May my light shine like alabaster, may I have no gloom,[2]
May my life be as precious as lapis in your sight,
  let there be mercy for me.
May my (personal) god and goddess be reconciled with me,
  as with gold,   (55)
May people speak well of me,
May I keep away my troubles
  as if with (imperishable?) wood,[3]
May no wicked, foul curse against me
  come near or approach me,
May my descent and progeny prosper in my sight,[4]
May the (medicinal) plants and salves you cherish
  drive out my faults,   (60)
May they let no divine fury or anger come nigh me,
May they release (me from) affliction(?), crime, or sin,
May prayer and invocation of the great gods
  release an oath or curse (against me),
May I progress proudly at your command,
  order that I live (long)!
May I be as pure as heaven from enchantment against me, (65)
May I be clean as the netherworld from foul sorcery.
May I shine like innermost heaven,
  may the wicked devices against me be dispelled,
May the tamarisk purify me, may the ...-plant release me,
  may the palm bough dispel my sin,
May the water stoup of Asalluhi bestow favor upon me,
May the censer and torch of Girra and Kusu[5] cleanse me. (70)
At the command of Ea, king of the depths,
  father of the gods, Ninshiku,

---

1. That is, directed malice and random malice.
2. Variant: "curse or gloom."
3. Text: "sissoo wood," an exotic wood used for fine woodwork.
4. That is, may he attain old age and see his descendants happy.
5. A divinity often mentioned in connection with purification rituals (Seux, *Hymnes*, 448 note 62; Bauer, *Altorientalische Notizen* 19 [1982], 4–7; Michalowski, *Studies Hallo*, 158–159).

May your heart be calmed at my prayer![1]
O Asalluhi, exorcist of the great gods, sage of the Igigi-gods,
I shall heed Ea's command,
    and queen Damkina will guide me to the right.*
May I, your servant, so-and-so, son of so-and-so,
    live in well-being,   (75)
May I exalt your divinity and sound [your] praises,
May my (personal) god exalt [your] valor,
May my (personal) goddess speak of your greatness.
(May I too, the exorcist, your servant, sound your praises!)[2]

Text: King, BMS 12, 17–94; Loretz-Mayer, AOAT 34 40–46; Mayer, OrNS 59 (1990), 487 K 20155.
Edition: Ebeling, AGH, 76–83; von Soden, *Iraq* 31 (1969), 84–89 (partial).
Translation: von Soden, SAHG, 302–306 no. 46; Seux, *Hymnes*, 443–449.
Literature: Mayer, UFBG, Marduk 5; Abusch, *Witchcraft*, 45–75.
Notes to Text: (23–25) Restored from unpublished duplicate (courtesy WGL). (31) Mayer, OrNS
   46 (1977), 391. (74) Seux, *Hymnes*, 449 note 66.

(c) PROTECTOR OF THE KING

This prayer was used in royal lustration rituals.

O mighty, resplendent, noble one of Eridu,   (1)
Lofty prince, firstborn of Nudimmud,
Raging Marduk, who rejoices Eengurra,[3]
Lord of Esagila, Babylon's trust,
Who loves Ezida,[4] who safeguards the living,   (5)
Foremost one of Emahtila,[5] renewer of life,
Protection of the land, bestower of benevolence upon
    the numerous peoples,
(Protective) dragon of all daises,

---

1. Variant: "may my prayer be the right one that your heart ..."
2. Lines 1–78 are to be spoken by the sufferer; the exorcist adds his lines at the end as the attending professional.
3. Byname for temple of Ea (= Nudimmud) at Eridu or part of Marduk's temple in Babylon.
4. Temple of Nabu at Borsippa, city of Nabu.
5. Cella of Nabu in Ezida.

Sweet is your name on the lips of people everywhere!
O Marduk, great lord, merciful god,[1]   (10)
Let me live in well-being at your steadfast[2] command,
      that I may glorify your divinity.
Let me attain whatever I desire!
Set truth on my lips,
Set good words in my heart,
May courtier and functionary speak well of me.   (15)
May my (personal) god stand at my right,
May my (personal) goddess stand at my left,
May my guardian deity always be at my side.
Grant me hearing and acceptance of what I say,
May the word I say be accepted even as I say it.   (20)
O Marduk, great lord,
      grant me life and command that I may live it,
Let me proceed, radiant, before you, to my heart's desire,
May Enlil be happy because of you,
      may Ea rejoice because of you,
May the gods of the universe bless you,
May the great gods please you.[3]

Text: Ebeling, KAR 59, obv. 1–25; KAR 23, i 1–17, KAR 25, i 29–38; Finkelstein, STT 55, 1–24; King, BMS 9 obv.; BMS 54; Lutz, PBS 1/2 108; Loretz-Mayer, AOAT 34 26–30; von Weiher, SBTU III 78 rev.
Edition: Meier, AfO 14 (1941/4), 140–143; Ebeling, AGH, 64–67.
Translation: von Soden, SAHG, 297–298 no. 42; Seux, *Hymnes*, 290–292.
Literature: Mayer, UFBG, Marduk 2.

1.   Variant omits.
2.   Variant "sublime," "eminent."
3.   Variants add a prayer, in one instance for Shamash-shum-ukin, king of Babylonia, against the evil portended by an eclipse (see p. 637 note 2); other variants have rearrangements of the text not noted here.

(d) REVIVER OF THE SICK

O Marduk, great lord, merciful god,   (1)
Who grasps the hand of the fallen,
[Who releases] the bound, revives the moribund,
[For wro]ng-doing known or not known,
[Which] I committed [through carelessness],
    negligence, or malfeasance,[1]   (5)
[Which] against your great divinity,
    [as against] one's own father,
I committed [through carelessness],
    negligence, or malfeasance,
[I bring] my life before your great divinity.
May the [soo]thing [water] be accepted by you,
May your [angry] heart be calmed.   (10)
May your [swee]t forgiveness,
Your great [absol]ution,
[Your] migh[ty] indulgence [be mine],
Let me sound the praises of your great divinity!

Text: Ebeling, KAR 23, i 19–31; KAR 25, ii 1.
Edition: Ebeling, AGH, 12–13.
Translation: von Soden, SAHG, 300–301 no. 44; Seux, Hymnes, 292–293.
Literature: Mayer, UFBG, Marduk 18.

(e) LORD OF THE UNIVERSE

This hymn may allude to the Epic of Creation (III.17, see III.44b).

O most great one, prince of the gods, mighty Marduk,   (1)
Counsellor, beloved of Ea,
    whose utterance cannot be changed,
To whose stately utterance the great Igigi-gods pay heed,
Before whom the Anunna-gods are ever kneeling,

---

1. Variant adds: "[I] feared and was frightened."

Lord of living creatures, merciful one, who increases grain,　　(5)
Giver(?) of food offerings to the gods,
　　maintainer of holy places,[1]*
Who governs underground springs and watercourses,
　　who opens wells,[2]
Lord of the gods, king of heaven and netherworld,
　　who heaps up prosperity,
God without whom no people's destiny
　　is ordained in the depths,
You look upon all the inhabited world,
　　you quickly wipe out the hostile,　　(10)
You strike blind(?) the narrow and shifty-eyed,*
You destroy quickly the talk of gossipers,*
You harshly force the stiffest neck to bow.*
What god in heaven or netherworld
　　can come forth against you?
You are higher than all the gods!　　(15)
Your counsel is supreme among the gods,
You are superior to Ea, the father who begot you,

(fragmentary lines, then breaks off)

Text: K 3505b = Hehn, BA 5, 385; Scheil, SFS 7.
Edition: Ebeling, AGH, 92–95.
Translation: von Soden, SAHG, 310–312 no. 48; Seux, *Hymnes*, 289–290.
Literature: Mayer, UFBG, Marduk 1.
Notes to Text: (6) Seux, *Hymnes*, 289 note 3; CAD K, 512b. (11) CAD M/2, 245a, with collation.
(12) CAD L, 211b, with collation. (13) CAD K, 147a, with collation.

1. Compare Epic of Creation (III.17) Tablet VI line 109.
2. Compare Epic of Creation (III.17) Tablet VII line 60.

(f) PRINCE OF THE GODS

This fragmentary hymn, like the preceding, may allude to the Epic of Creation (III.17, see III.44b).

[Valorous] prince, son of Ea, l[ofty] hero,   (1)
[Forem]ost one of a[ll] heaven and netherworld,
         ordainer of destinies,
[Lord] Mard[uk?], … w[ho is surpassing] of form,[1]
[   ] form of Tutu,[2]
[Sarpanitum], great queen, bride of Shazu,[3]   (5)
Lo[rd En]lil,[4] prince surpassing of perception.[5]
Battle formation and warfare are in the hand of
         the sage of the gods, Marduk,
He at whose warfare the heavens quake,
At whose cry the depths are roiled,
At whose blade edge the gods retreat.   (10)
There was none came forth against his furious onslaught.[6]
Awe-inspiring lord,
         none like whom has arisen among the gods,[7]
Stately is his progress through the shining firmament,
Heavy his responsibilities in Ekur,[8] the cherished dwelling.
In the ill wind[9] his weapons are flashing,
Tortuous mountains are destroyed by his flame,[10]   (15)
The surging(?) ocean[11] tosses up its waves.

1. Restoration doubtful; compare Epic of Creation (III.17) Tablet I lines 92–93.
2. One of the fifty names of Marduk; see Epic of Creation (III.17) Tablet VII lines 9, 15, 19, 25, 33.
3. One of the fifty names of Marduk; see Epic of Creation (III.17) Tablet VII lines 35, 41, 43, 47, 51, 55.
4. That is, Marduk as supreme god; compare Epic of Creation (III.17) Tablet VII line 149.
5. Compare Epic of Creation (III.17) Tablet I lines 95–98.
6. Lines 8–11 may refer to Marduk's vanquishing Tiamat and her forces.
7. Perhaps a reference to Epic of Creation (III.17) Tablet I line 91.
8. Enlil's temple in Ekur; compare line 6.
9. One of Marduk's weapons; see Epic of Creation (III.17) Tablet IV lines 45, 96, 98.
10. Epic of Creation (III.17) Tablet IV line 40.
11. Reference to Tiamat?

His name is "Heir to Esharra,"[1]
> he is called "Warrior of the Gods."

He is lord of all the gods of the inhabited world,
> from the farthest depth.

They clustered against heaven before his furious bow,[2] (20)

Those who slumbered in the high sanctuary
> cowered and shook.

[   ] all the Anunna-gods,

[   ] the Igigi-gods.

> *(breaks off)*

Text: King, STC I 205.
Edition: Ebeling, AGH, 94–95.
Translation: Seux, *Hymnes*, 76–78.
Literature: Mayer, UFBG, Marduk x = p. 399 "unsicher."

1. Compare Epic of Creation (III.17) Tablet IV line 145. This name was also given to Ninurta; see further p. 462 note 3 and p. 711 note 2.
2. Compare Epic of Creation (III.17) Tablet IV line 35, Tablet VI lines 82–91.

(g) SYNCRETIC HYMN TO MARDUK

This text suggests henotheistic tendencies in that it represents the other gods as aspects of Marduk. A parallel is provided by the text known as the "Marduk Theology," for translations and discussion of which see T. J. Meek, *Hebrew Origins* (New York, 1960), 197–198; W. G. Lambert, *Unity and Diversity*, 197–198; see also the bilingual hymn to Nanay (p. 583 note 1).

(gap)

Sin is your divinity, Anu your sovereignty,
Dagan is your lordship, Enlil your kingship,
Adad is your might, wise Ea your perception,   (5)
Nabu, holder of the tablet stylus, is your skill.
Your leadership (in battle) is Ninurta, your might Nergal,
Your counsel is Nus[ku], your superb [minister],
Your judgeship is radiant Shamash, who arouses [no] dispute,
Your eminent name is Marduk, sage of the gods.   (10)
Your hurtling arrow is a piti[less li]on,
O eminent lord, who tramples down all foes,
    who wards off attack,
Your escort is the Pleiades,
    O judge just and true of gods and goddesses.
Your greatness is the Igigi-gods,
    your primacy(?) is the warrior Irnini,
Your[1] basin is the depths,
    your incense stand is Anu's heaven,   (15)
Your ... is the vast netherworld, ...
The one who in the temple has ... offerings,
The widow with roasted grain,
    the rich man with sheep call upon you.
Come hither to the food and drink
    from those who revere you,   (20)
By your unalterable utterance absolve their misdeeds,
Let me proclaim your greatness,
    let me sound your praises!

---

1. Text uses the plural pronoun, perhaps referring to Marduk as the sum total of all the gods, whereas previously only individual aspects were referred to.

Text: Ebeling, KAR 25, ii 3–24.
Edition: Ebeling, AGH, 14–15.
Translation: von Soden, SAHG, 301–302 no. 45; Labat, *Religions*, 73–74; Seux, *Hymnes,* 129–131.
Literature: von Weiher, AOAT 11 (1971), 66–67.

(h) FOREMOST OF THE GODS

O Marduk, great lord,
     foremost one of heaven and netherworld, (1)
Sage of the universe, who knows everything,
Merciful god, who accepts prayers,
Who receives entreaties,
Who watches over the life of humankind,
Who grasps heaven and netherworld,
Wise king who loves to revive, (5)
Lord of freshwater depths and the seas,
     who puts a stop to(?) combat,
Bringer of abundance,
     who makes abundant grain
     for the numerous peoples!
O Marduk, great lord, lofty one of the gods, without rival,
Proud(?) god, glorious with the tiara of supreme divinity,
You are the light of the corners (of the earth),
     the shepherd of humankind! (10)
Without you, heaven and netherworld are defective,
Without you, Sin, luminary of heaven,
     does not rise on high as a sign for the people,
Without you, Shamash judges no case,
Without you, no verdict is decided and rendered for the land,
Without you, no god whatsoever keeps in good order
     the sanctuary of god or goddess, (15)
Without you, the wise gods hold no festivals,
Without you, Shamash the judge does not set in the sheep
     the right coil (of the intestines),
     the correct (state of) the lungs,[1]

---

1. References to divination; see General Introduction, E.9 and Chapter IV, Introduction.

Without you, the diviner does not do
    his manipulations correctly,
Without you, the exorcist does not
    bring his hand to the sick man,
Without you, the conjurer, ecstatic, snake charmer[1]
    do not pass through the st[reet],   (20)
Without you, one escapes neither strait nor hardship,
Without you, the destitute and widow are not cared for.
The destitute and widow call upon you, O lord,
You give a husband(?) to those who have no child,*
It is you, O [lor]d, who has pi[ty] on them.   (25)
The strong, the common man,
    the rich man call upon you daily ...,
All lands call, "Marduk!"

(Prayer concludes with a personal supplication, a long list of ills, and ends with a plea for purification plus the usual offer to sing the god's praises together with those of his spouse, Sarpanitum.)

Text: Ebeling, KAR 26, obv. 11-rev. 6; here in excerpt only; Mayer, OrNS 68 (1999), pl. 28 Rm 2171.
Edition: Ebeling, ZDMG 69 (1915), 96–101; Mayer, OrNS 68 (1999), 145-163.
Translation: von Soden, SAHG, 306–310 no. 47; Seux, *Hymnes*, 449–453.
Literature: Abusch, *Witchcraft*, 45–75; Mayer, UFBG, Marduk 24.
*Notes to Text: (24) see Mayer, OrNS 68 (1999), 161.

---

1. Snake charmers were used for purification rites; see III.9 v 14 and N. L. Corkill, "Snake Specialists in Iraq," *Iraq* 6 (1939), 45–52.

III.45 TO NABU

Nabu, son of Marduk and Sarpanitum, was in later Assyro-Babylonian tradition the god of the scribal arts. His principal cult center was at Borsippa, near Babylon, and was called the Ezida (see IV.15).

For other prayers to Nabu, see W. G. Lambert, RA 53 (1959), 134–138; "Nabu Hymns on Cylinders," in B. Hruška and G. Komoróczy, eds., *Festschrift Lubor Matouš* (Budapest, 1978), 2: 75–111; Seux, *Hymnes*, 299–300. For a general study of this deity, see F. Pomponio, *Nabu, Il culto e la figura di un dio del pantheon babilonese ed assiro, Studi Semitici* 51 (Rome, 1978).

(a) FOR PROTECTION FROM BLACK MAGIC

O foremost prince, firstborn of Tutu,[1] (1)
Proven leader, offspring of Panunanki,[2]
Nabu, who bears the gods' tablet of destinies,[3]
    monitor of Esagila,
Lord of Ezida, protection of Borsippa,
Beloved of Nudimmud,[4] bestower of life, (5)
Foremost one of Shuanna,[5] guardian of life,
Protection of the inhabited world, rescuer of humankind,
    lord of sanctuaries,
Invocation of you is an especially sweet protection
    on the lips of the people!
O son of the great prince Marduk, at your steadfast word,
At your eminent word,
    at the command of your great divinity, (10)
I, so-and-so, son of so-and-so, your sick, very sick servant,
Who have been seized and hounded by the power of a ghost,
    black magic, and something accursed,
Let me live in well-being, may I attain whatever I plan,
Put truth on my lips,
Set a good word in my heart! (15)

1. Name for Marduk, see Epic of Creation (III.17) Tablet VII lines 9, 15, 19, 25, 33.
2. Sarpanitum, wife of Marduk.
3. For tablet of destinies, see p. 445 note 2.
4. Ea; variant has Panunanki.
5. Babylon.

May courtier and functionary speak well of me,
May my (personal) god stand at my right,
May my (personal) goddess stand at my left,
May a good guardian deity and a good protective spirit
    be [clo]se by me,
Grant me hearing and acceptance [of what I say],   (20)
May my speech be of good purport.
O son of great prince [Marduk], gr[ant me li]fe!*
Let me proceed in all confidence before you,
May Shazu[1] be h[appy because of you,
    may Nudimmud] rejoice because of you,
May the gods of heaven and netherworld bless you,   (25)
May heaven [and netherworld ...] exalt you,
[May the] great [gods please you],
May Tashm[etu, your beloved spouse,
    speak well of me] in E[zida],
      House of Bestowing Life[2] of the great gods.*

Text: King, BMS 22, obv. 1–29; Loretz-Mayer, AOAT 34 54–57; Ebeling-Köcher-Rost, LKA 56.
Edition: Mayer, UFBG, 473–475.
Translation: von Soden, SAHG, 312–313 no. 49; Seux, Hymnes, 297–299.
Literature: Mayer, UFBG, Nabu 3; Lawson, Fate, 55–57.
*Notes to Text: (22) Seux, Hymnes, 298 note 18; Mayer, UFBG, 474. (28) Mayer, OrNS 66 (1997),
   174.

1. Name for Marduk, see Epic of Creation (III.17) Tablet VII lines 35, 41, 43, 47, 51, 55.
2. An explanatory etymology of the name of the temple.

(b) AN OLD MAN'S PRAYER

This prayer appeals to Nabu as intercessor with his father Marduk, asking his help in averting divine displeasure. The speaker notes, perhaps with nostalgia, that Nabu counts off the years (lines 3, 17). Perhaps, as with III.44a, the speaker's old age is a metaphor for his being bowed down by suffering, but a more literal reading has been preferred in this instance.

O [Nab]u, eldest (son), rightful heir,   (1)
[Holder] of the tablet stylus, of profound intelligence,
[Who ... the days], who examines the years,
[Who safeguards] life, who requites good,
[Foremost one] of the gods, of eminent name!   (5)
The father who begot him does not change his command,
Tutu does not change the utterance of Nabu his son,
His word is supreme among the gods his peers.
You turn the face of a god toward the victim of his anger,
You reconcile with him the goddess* who is hostile,   (10)
You absolve the wrong-doing of the [   ].
[I], so-and-so, son of so-and-so,
        the servant who reveres you,
In my youth I prayed ...*
Now that I am old, my hands make petition to all the gods,
I am breathless [from] prostration!   (15)
[Before] humankind I am like a whirlwind![1]
My days have elapsed, my years have come to an end.
I have seen no favor, I have had no mercy.
O rightful [heir], mighty Nabu,
[I] pray(?) to you, show me[2] the light,   (20)
Let me proclaim your [grea]tness,
        let me sound your praises!

Text: Finkelstein, STT 55, 28–48; Ebeling, KAR 25, i 1–19; Loretz-Mayer, AOAT 34 73.
Edition: Mayer, UFBG, 469–472.
Translation: Seux, *Hymnes*, 301–302.

1. I take the line as hyperbole, referring, perhaps humorously, to the speaker's continuous prostrations, rather than as a metaphor for his poor physical condition. For different views, see Seux, *Hymnes*, 302 note 15; Mayer, UFBG, 471.
2. Variant: "Let me see."

Literature: Mayer, UFBG, Nabu 1.

Notes to Text: (10) Text: "destiny," see Mayer, UFBG, 472. (13) Differently CAD M/2, 37a, but there seems to be no basis for the reading proposed there; see Mayer, UFBG, 472.

(c) DISCOURAGEMENT

This sad prayer reflects on the joy of premature happiness and the bitterness of premature sorrow. All has gone by too quickly, and the suppliant begs that his life be made worth living.

(gap)

O Nabu, lest I sin, O son of the Lord, [lest] I offend,
[On account of the heed]less deeds of my ancestors
    and kinfolk, who heedlessly neglected
    [the rites of Tashmetu],[1]★   (5)
I have longed [for] Ezida, the high ground,
    the house in which we put our trust,
I have longed for Ezida, the threshold of delight, ...
[Even as] an infant(?), I have longed for the collegium,
    to take my place in (its) house of learning,
My strength was the precious offerings
    of the temple of Nabu.★
I was ever mindful of its beauties,
    it was the fire of Ezida that stoked my heart.   (10)
I gained wealth, I attained what I wanted ahead of my time.
(Now) old age has me bedridden prematurely,
I am wasted by suffering, as if I were not fearing your divinity.
I weep, for I have not seen the beauty of my life.
I have become the smallest of the small,
    I have become the lowest of the low,   (15)
My (begging) hands are outstretched
    (even) to the poverty-stricken who frequent my door,
I have entreated slaves and slave girls,
    whom I used to buy in commerce,[2]

---

1. Wife of Nabu; see IV.27; for the motif of blaming ancestors, see III.37a, line 16.
2. Literally: "by the scales."

When I moved against an enemy,
      a sorceress splashed water on my back.*
I am cut off from my community,
      enemies of (my) family glower at me,
Anguish, sickness are upon me,
      I am stricken with weakness,   (20)
I keep crying out to estranged gods,
      raising my hands (in prayer) in heed of my goddess.
I have gone everywhere for a mother,
      she has shrunk from me and is clawing at me.*
Death has tantalized me like a precious stone.
I constantly go up to the roof to jump off,
      but my life is too precious, it turns me back.
I try to encourage myself,
      what is there for me to encourage?   (25)
I try to keep control of my thoughts,
      but what is there for me to control?
O Nabu, where is your forgiveness,
      O son of the [lo]rd, where are your oracles?
Where is your favorable breeze
      that wafts over your weakling (subjects)?
O lord, how long will there be darkness
      in my time of trouble?*
The sun lights up for the land, (but) for me [   ].   (30)
Prosperity rains down on the people,
      (but) for me rains down [ ] and gall.
My life is spent, O account-keeper of the u[niverse],
      where shall I go?
I have reached death's door, O Nabu,
      why have you forsaken me?
Do not forsake me, my lord,
      for the [com]pany of my numerous ill-wishers,
To the hands ... of my sorceress do not forsake me,
      O god called by the good name![1]   (35)
I am a weakling who fears you,
      do not shame me in public!

---

1.   This refers to a byname of Nabu, Muzebbasa'a, which means "called by a good name," as in III.38c, line 3′.

I am a guardian of truth,
>   do not destroy the truth [I have] guarded!
May the lonely one not die
>   who has called up to you, O lord!
O Nabu, take the hand of the fallen one
>   who attends your divinity,
Spare the life of the weakling
>   whom ill-wishers hemmed in,   (40)
Whom baleful witches have splashed with conjured water.
Let the dead man revive [by your] breeze,
Let his squandered life become gain!

Text: Finkelstein, STT 65.
Edition: Livingstone, *Court Poetry*, 30–32.
Literature: W. G. Lambert, RA 53 (1959), 129–131; Deller, OrNS 34 (1965), 458–461.
★Notes to Text: (5, 9, 18, 22) von Soden, WdO 22 (1991), 191. (29) Reading *ma-ru-<uš>-ti-ya*.

(d) COMPOUND ACROSTIC PRAYER TO NABU

This fragmentary prayer, in four- or five-line strophes, forms an acrostic at the beginning and end of each line, though its meaning is not clear. The tight restriction of form and meter make for artificiality of expression.

i

I understand the deed [   ]
I hamstring(?) myself, I make my heart cry out in mourning,
My inmost self wails a dirge like [   ] (5)

ii

No [head] can be raised (proudly) among the gods
      without your approval.
You strengthen the weak and lowly,
One who is girt about with sickness and disease waits on you,
May your favorable breeze blow upon me
      and grant me release!

iii

I call upon you, O Nabu, be gracious to me, O brave one. (10)
I abased myself among the multitude, I always held my peace.*
I became like one possessed, I ... I know not what.
I kept calling out to the gods, but all was silence!

iv

The lowly who trusts in you will have his fill of abundance,
You strengthen the foundations of the righteous
      and make firm his support, (15)
You grant me good fortune, you banish sin,
You can turn a rock wall into clay.

(rest fragmentary)

Text: K 8204 (collated) = Strong, PSBA 17 (1895), 137–138.
Edition: Strong, PSBA 17 (1895), 139–140.
Literature: Ebeling, "Alliteration," RLA 1, 71.
Notes to Text: (11) CAD Q, 75b.

(e) THE NAMES OF NABU

Like the prayer to Nabu by Nabu-ushebshi (f), this hymn assigns to Nabu many of the attributes ascribed in other compositions to Marduk. The text uses phraseology known from the Epic of Creation (III.17) and may date to the seventh century B.C. See also IV.8k and General Introduction, D.3.

[Let me ever sp]eak of your grandeur,
    O Nabu, glorious king,   (1)
[Let me] exalt your greatness,
    O monarch of the gods, stately leader,
[L]et me proclaim your lordship, O sage of the depths,
    firstborn of the gods,[1] bearer of king[ship],
Hear ever of the valor [of the leader] of the gods, Marduk.[2]
Let me praise the names of the king(?), [heir?] of Esagila,
    torch of the gods,   (5)
Which other [c]reator of the whole inhabited world,
    of all regions, should I be speaking of?
Your command is the strongest(?)* in the universe
    and sublime, (for) you are Nabu!
O Dimmerankia,[3] "divine lord, king of heaven
    and netherworld" they cal[led]* your name.
Your first name is Shazu,[4]
    "who knows the hearts of the gods,"
    "who shall not examine [his] enemy,"[5]
Your second name is Urrunzu,[6] whose name [   ],   (10)
Your third name is Asari,[7] "clasher at arms(?),

---

1. Or, perhaps, "the god" (= Marduk).

2. Nabu may be referred to here as "Marduk of the gods."

3. Compare Marduk's name, Lugaldimmerankia, of Epic of Creation (III.17) Tablet VI line 139. Perhaps one should restore "lord" (EN) at the beginning of the name so as to account for the "lord" of the explanation.

4. One of the names of Marduk in Epic of Creation (III.17) Tablet VII lines 35, 41, 43, 47, 51, 55.

5. A misquotation of Epic of Creation (III.17) Tablet VII line 35. This should read "who examines the inside." Here the line may mean something like "no enemies appear before him" (because he is so mighty).

6. Approximately, "the one of the moon," an attribute peculiar to Nabu (Ebeling, WdO 1, 477; Seux, *Hymnes*, 135 note 16).

7. Name of Marduk, Epic of Creation (III.17) Tablet VII line 1.

who provides incense offerings,"[1]
Your fourth name is
    "Bearer of the Tablet of Divine Destinies[2]
    (of) all the su[preme] Igigi-gods,"
Your fifth name is "Hana,"[3]
    <who grasps> the circumference of heaven
    and netherworld, who establishes [   ],
Your sixth name is
    "Incorruptible Judge, Who Enforces [Justice],"[4]
Your seventh name is "The Seven,"[5]
    valiant hero, who scans [the mountains],   (15)
Your eighth [name] is "Sirsirra,"[6]
    offspring of Qingu,[7] who [   ].
O lord, you grew high from the depths
    and are warrior [in the land], (for) you are Nabu!

Text: Ebeling-Köcher-Rost, LKA 16.
Edition: Ebeling, WdO 1, 476–479.
Translation: Seux, *Hymnes*, 134–136; Hecker, TUAT II/5, 770–772.
Literature: Pomponio, *Nabu* (see III.45a), 170–173.
Notes to Text: (7) Seux, *Hymnes*, 135 note 11. (8) Seux, *Hymnes*, 135 note 13.

1. For a different interpretation, see Seux, *Hymnes*, 135 note 20: "who makes evil-doer go up in smoke."
2. For the tablet of destinies, see p. 445 note 2.
3. According to Seux, *Hymnes*, 136 note 22, to be understood as Hayya (written Ḫa-NI), spouse of the grain-goddess. The grain-goddess was also a patron deity of scribal lore. One may see here also an allusion to Marduk's sojourn in Hana, for which see III.13.
4. See Epic of Creation (III.17) Tablet VII line 39 (noted by Seux, *Hymnes*, 136 note 25).
5. For the Seven, see Erra and Ishum (IV.17), Tablet I.
6. See Epic of Creation (III.17) Tablet VII lines 70–77, a mythological episode there assigned to Marduk.
7. Since Qingu was an enemy of Marduk and was executed in the Epic of Creation, Marduk took over his name and it is here given to Nabu. See Lambert, *Atrahasis*, 153; A. Livingstone, *Explanatory Works*, 234; Pomponio, *Nabu*, 173–174.

(f) ACROSTIC PRAYERS OF NABU–USHEBSHI

These prayers to Marduk and Nabu form compound acrostics at the beginning and end of each line. The beginning signs of both prayers spell "Nabu-ushebshi the exorcist." In prayer (i) the end signs of the lines spell "the servant who proclaims your lordship"; in prayer (ii) "the supplicant servant who reveres you." Nabu-ushebshi was presumably the author of both prayers. He may have lived about the middle of the eighth century B.C. The author displays both cleverness and a penchant for rare vocables.

(i) To Marduk

Sun to his forefathers, exalted leader Asari,[1]   (1)
Skilled, acute grantor of longevity of days,
Yours is to keep alive and in well-being!
Mortals magnify your worthy name,
Afflicted and lowly are attentive to you.   (5)
[You hear] their prayers, you grant offspring.
The peoples of the land m[aintain]⋆ daily their song of praise,
Living creatures ex[tol] your sweet appellation.
May there be protection for Nabu-ushebshi,
        the [sup]pliant [s]erv[ant],
May he have the destiny of humankind: progeny and descent,   (10)
May his descendants last for all time before you!

*(Eleven lines not set in paragraphs,⋆ the beginning and end of each
line may be read in two directions.)*[2]

(ii) To Nabu

O lofty hero, Asari's son,   (1)
Who called (into being) all that is, [who h]ears prayers,
Radiant of feature, coun[s]ellor of h[is] forefathers,
Monarch without equal, heir to Nudimmud,[3]
Archetype of the Igigi-gods, lord of w[isdom],
        who [gathers to himself] all learning,   (5)

---

1. Name for Marduk; see Epic of Creation (III.17) Tablet VII line 1.
2. Scribal indication, meaning that the text is an acrostic.
3. Ea, god of wisdom, grandfather of Nabu.

The lore(?)¹ of heaven and netherworld is forever
　　[in your hand].
O merciful* Nabu, you can ordain a favorable destiny,
Quicken [Nabu-ush]ebshi, your thrall,
[May he reach] a fullness of lifespan, a ripe old age,
[May all that is] sound the praises of your valor!　　　　　(10)

Text: W. G. Lambert, JAOS 88 (1968), 131.
Edition: W. G. Lambert, JAOS 88 (1968), 130–132.
Translation: Seux, *Hymnes*, 264–266.
Literature: R. F. G. Sweet, "A Pair of Double Crostics in Akkadian," OrNS 38 (1969), 459–460.
Notes to Text: (i 7) Seux, *Hymnes*, 265 note 7. (i 12) AHw, 1514b. Not clear, but perhaps refers to indentations or paragraphing, hence "not continuous text?" (ii 7) Sweet, OrNS 38 (1969), 460 note 3.

1.　The word used here (*šipkat*) is not clear, but may mean something like "things piled up."

III.46 TO NERGAL

Nergal, a major netherworld deity with his sanctuary at Cutha in northern
Babylonia, is portrayed as a pitiless, destructive warrior. This hymn may refer
to the Epic of Creation (III.17); see General Introduction, D.3. Nergal is
often associated with battle, plague, and violence. For further information, see
E. von Weiher, *Der babylonische Gott Nergal*, AOAT 11 (1971). For other hymns
to Nergal, see Seux, *Hymnes*, 312–314 = Hecker, TUAT II/5, 773–775.

(a) NERGAL THE WARRIOR

O warrior, splendid one, offspring of Nun[amnir],[1]   (1)
Let me sound your [praises?],★ O lordly one,
    arrayed in awesomeness.
O bearer of pointed horns,[2] clad with frightening sheen,
    firstborn son of Kutumshar,[3]
Monitor of the lower world, overseer of the Six Hundred,[4]
    let me always praise your greatness!
You are supreme in strength, overwhelming all disobedient,
    forcing the …★ to submit.   (5)
O tireless mighty one, who gladdens Enlil's heart,
Mighty of arms, broad of chest,
    perfect one without rival among all the gods,
Who grasps the pitiless deluge-weapon,
    who massacres(?)★ the enemy,
Lion clad in splendor,
    at the flaring-up of whose fierce brilliance
The gods of the inhabited world took to secret places,
    evildoer and wicked have found their way into crevices.   (10)
[   ] has adorned you [   ] … with awesomeness,
Nudimmud[5] has bestowed [upon you] irresistible weaponry,
[   ] has [   ] your [   ] among the gods your brethren.

---

1. Name for Enlil.
2. Nergal is sometimes referred to as a bull; in general, horns were a Mesopotamian symbol of
divinity.
3. Name for Ninlil, Enlil's wife.
4. Gods of the netherworld; compare Epic of Creation (III.17) Tablet VI line 44 and General
Introduction, D.3.
5. Another name for Ea, god of wisdom.

(breaks off)

Text: K 9880, Rm 290 (collated) = Böllenrücher, *Nergal* no. 8 (p. 50), transliteration only.
Edition: Böllenrücher, *Nergal,* 50–52.
Translation: Seux, *Hymnes,* 84–85.
Notes to Text: (2) Z[À.MÍ.MEŠ-k]a? (5) K 9880 has MUŠ.ŠID, not clear. Rm 290 inserts *pa-ni-šú* after
   ma-gi-ri. (8) *etem/nu,* meaning unknown.

(b) THE TERRORS OF NERGAL

This hymnic fragment is known from a manuscript of the Achaemenid period.
The scribe was fond of visual effects in that the first writing of certain key
words is logographic and the second syllabic.[1] Note also that the third line of
the first four distiches has the god's name in initial rhythmic position. The
disjointed expression and unusual style suggest a late date for the composition
of this text, perhaps by someone familiar with, but not well-versed in, traditional Akkadian hymnic style. Compare IV.12.

Warrior among his brothers, princely god,*	(1)
Lord surpassing all the Igigi-gods,	
Nergal, princely god,	
Lord surpassing all the Igigi-gods,	
He has fastened on a vestment of divine splendor	
and awesomeness,	(5)
The god who is furious in joy(?) (and) fe[arsomeness],[2]	
Nergal has fastened on a vestment of divine splendor	
and awesomeness,	
The god who is furious in joy(?) (and) fea[rsomeness]!	
His cheekbones gleam like the glint* of a gem,	
His cheeks flash like a lightning bolt.	(10)
Nergal's cheekbones gleam like the glint of a gem,	

1. Nougayrol (RA 41 [1947], 38) suggests that the text was written respectively for an expert,
then for apprentices, but this is not convincing. Perhaps the second writing is simply an
explanation of the first (though often elementary), in the spirit of other texts that explain names
and attributes (see, for example, III.17, 26, 45e).
2. This may mean that Nergal is terrible even in a good frame of mind or that he is happiest
when in a fury.

His cheeks flash like a lightning bolt!
His weapon is mighty, his onslaught irresistible,
Like a tempest (and) overwhelming flood, he has no equal,
Nergal's weapon is mighty, his onslaught irresistible,   (15)
Like a tempest (and) overwhelming flood, he has no equal!
Impetuous warrior, lord,
            proven one of the gods,[1] untrammeled,
Valorous heir of Belet-ili, who brings satisfaction to Enlil,
Valorous courier, fleet of foot,*
Inspector of everything, beautiful heir,* untrammeled,   (20)
Ninlil gave him a full quiver,
She has placed a splendid bow in his hands.

(manuscript ends)

Text: Nougayrol, RA 41 (1947), 40.
Edition: Ebeling, AGH, 118.
Translation: Seux, *Hymnes,* 88–90.
Notes to Text: (1) For a different reading, see Seux, *Hymnes,* 88 with note 3: "Héros de ses frères
les dieux, (leur) souverain." (9) <*ni*>-*ip-ḫu* with Seux, *Hymnes,* 89 note 7. (19) *birbirki,* called for
by the meter, may be a reduplicated form for emphatic effect, not a dittography. (20) *bānu aplu
šammar,* perhaps a refurbishment of *bāni apli* "creator of an heir."

(c) SUBLIME NERGAL

This hymn is known from a small fragment said to have come from Uruk. The
allusion to the Epic of Creation (III.17) in line 7 suggests a late date of composition; the manuscript itself dates to late in the first millennium.

[O Nergal], warrior of the gods,
            who possesses the lofty strength of Anu,   (1)
[Lion] with gaping maw,* marauding lion monster,
            who takes his place nobly in the height of heaven,
[Who hol]ds lordship, whose features ever glow in heaven,
[Who bears] bow, shaft, and quiver,
            who grasps glaive, fearing no battle,

1. Or: "proven god."

[Van]guard whose strength is sublime,
    mounted on a steed, deluge irresistible,   (5)
Stately [offspring] of Anu, fair in horns,
    worthy of a lordly vestment,
[Adorned] in splendid array, masterful, deeply courageous,
Impossible to perceive, difficult to understand.[1]
[O Nergal, warrior]* of the gods, long of arms,
    whose divine splendor is sublime in heaven,
[Star] ever shining, sublime of features,   (10)
[Who] holds [lord]ship [   ],
    who wields a knife, who knows fighting,
[Vict]orious [   ], who flashes wickedly in strife,
[Who   ] weapon and staff, whose sleep is a feint,
[Who] has no rival [in me]lee or battle.
[   ] of Uruk,
    who slaughters evil demons,   (15)
[   ] who annihilates the foe,
    who uproots the enemy,
[who le]vels the hostile land,
[who holds the hand] of the fallen

(breaks off)

Text: Böhl, BiOr 6 (1949), pl. vi, vii.
Edition: Böhl, BiOr 6 (1949), 165–170, updated in *Opera Minora* (Groningen, 1953), 207–216, 496–497.
Translation: Seux, *Hymnes,* 85–88.
*Notes to Text: (2) [Pirig]-kaduha, see Seux, *Hymnes*, 86 note 3. (9) Seux, *Hymnes*, 87 note 11.

1. The same expression occurs in the Epic of Creation (III.17) Tablet I line 94. Seux (*Hymnes,* 87 note 10) suggests that this is a direct allusion to the passage; see General Introduction, D.3.

III.47 TO NINURTA

Ninurta was a warrior and vegetation deity, son of Enlil, husband of Gula (see III.25). He appears as the avenging hero of the Anzu poem (above, III.23).

(a) PRESCRIPTIVE HYMN TO NINURTA

This fragment, known from a Middle Assyrian bilingual tablet, is the remains of a text similar to the Shamash hymn (III.32) in content. The second part describes a ceremony of the citizens of Nippur and of the Mesopotamians in general.

(gap)

Grievous is the guilt of him who has intercourse
    with (another) man's wife.   (4)
He who says frivolous words, the backbiter,
Who points the finger of malice toward his equal,   (10)
Who impugns the unspeakable to (his) brother,
Who oppresses the poor,
Who gives the weak over to the strong,
Who [   ] a fellow citizen with calumny,   (16)
Pilferer(?) who [   ] from his neighbor's field,

(gap)

(Songs) are sung to you with tympani, drum,
    and [... har]p.   (3)
Fatted cattle, [fatted sheep] are slaughtered for you
    as the king's offering,
Young men of strength compete with each other in wrestling
    and athletic games [in your honor].
The citizens of Nippur, clan by clan,
    [keep the occasion] in abundance,   (9)
The people of this land sing your songs of praise.
When [you] set your face toward that place,
When [you] enter the sanctuary gate as a shower of rain,   (15)
When y[ou] pass through the square of the sanctuary gate
    as it is full of rejoicing,

When you enter Eshumesha,[1] the house that stretches
>to heaven and netherworld,
When [you] behold your beloved [   ]   (21)

(breaks off)

Text: W. G. Lambert, BWL pl. 32 (VAT 10610) = Ebeling, KAR 119.
Edition: W. G. Lambert, BWL, 118–120.

(b) PROTECTOR OF THE KING

This text was incorporated into the royal lustration ritual "House of the Ritual Bath," for which see III.51h.

O mighty heir, firstborn son of Enlil,   (1)
Most great one, perfect one, offspring of Esharra,[2]
Who is clad in terror, arouses chilling fear,
Uta'ulu,[3] whose battle is irresistible,
Whose (celestial) station is outstanding among the great gods,   (5)
Your head is raised high in the Ekur, splendid house,
Enlil your father has given you
(His) power of command over all the gods,
>you hold it in your hand.[4]
You judge the case(s) of humankind,
You do justice to the wronged, the powerless,
>the destitute girl,   (10)
You grasp the weak by the hand, you exalt[5] the helpless,
You bring back the person
>who is being sent down to the netherworld,
You absolve the guilt of the guilty.

1. Temple of Ninurta at Nippur.
2. Name of the temple of Enlil in Nippur; hence Ninurta is the son of Enlil.
3. Name for Ninurta, personification of a storm.
4. Or, perhaps, "(which) is held in your hand."
5. Variant: "make esteemed."

You promptly reconcile the man
    whose (personal) god or goddess[1] is angry with him.
O Ninurta, foremost of the gods, you are the warrior.   (15)
I, so-and-so, son of so-and-so,
    whose (personal) god is so-and-so,
I have prepared an offering for you, given you flour,
I have given you sweet-smelling incense,[2]
I have libated to you sweet beer (made from) grain.
May the gods of Enlil[3] stand with you,   (20)
May the gods of Ekur stand with you.[4]
Look steadfastly upon me and hear what I say,
Accept my entreaty, receive (my) prayer!
May what I say content you,
Be reconciled with me,* who reveres you.   (25)
I have seen your face, may I prosper.
You are regardful, regard me steadfastly.
Absolve my guilt, dissolve my wrong-doing,
Dismiss my crime, undo my sin.
May my (personal) god and my (personal) goddess
    esteem me and speak favorably (of me),   (30)
Let me proclaim your greatness, let me sound your praises!

Text: King, BMS 2, 11–41; BMS 3, 10–16; Loretz-Mayer, AOAT 34 3–7; Mayer, OrNS 59 (1990), 486 K 16934; Ebeling-Köcher-Rost, LKA 41.
Edition: Ebeling, AGH, 24–27.
Translation: von Soden, SAHG, 314–316 no. 51; Seux, *Hymnes,* 314–316.
Literature: Mayer, UFBG, Ninurta 1.
Notes to Text: (25) Seux, *Hymnes,* 315 note 12.

1. Variant omits.
2. Variant omits this line.
3. Group of astral deities in the celestial path of Enlil.
4. Variant adds here prayer against the evil portended by an eclipse; see p. 637 note 2.

(c) SYNCRETIC HYMN TO NINURTA

This henotheistic hymn syncretizes various gods, male and female, with organs of
Ninurta; compare III.44g.

(gap)

[   ] of the great gods has exalted [you],
O Ninurta, warrior, you [   ]
You [   ], who gather to yourself their powers,   (5)
You take their responsibilities, you [   ].
Kingship of lords is [entrusted]* to your hands.
O lord, your anger is a [   ] deluge,
O warrior of the gods, you are lofty [   ].
O lord, your face is Shamash, your locks [Nisaba],   (10)
Your eyes, O lord, are Enlil and [Ninlil],
Your eyeballs are Gula and Belet-il[i],
Your eyelids, O lord, are the twins Sin [and Shamash],
Your eyebrows are the corona of the sun that [   ],
Your mouth's shape, O lord, is the evening star,   (15)
Anu and Antu are your lips, your speech [is Nusku(?)],
Your discoursing tongue(?) is Pabilsag, who [   ] on high,
The roof of your mouth, O lord,
      is the circumference of heaven and earth, abode of [   ],
Your teeth are the Seven, who slay evildoers,
Your cheeks, O lord, are the rising of bri[lliant] stars,   (20)
Your ears are Ea and Damkina, sages of wisdom [   ],
Your head is Adad, who [makes] heaven and earth
      [resound] like a smithy,
Your brow is Shala, beloved [sp]ouse
      who contents [Adad's heart],
Your neck is Marduk, judge of heaven [and netherworld],
      the deluge [   ],
Your throat is Sarpanitum,
      creat[ress of peo]ple,* who [   ],   (25)
Your chest is Shullat, who examines [   ],
Your upper back[1] is Hanish, who establishes p[lenty,
      who r]ains down* abundance,

---

1. Variant adds "O lord."

Your right side[1] is Uta'ulu, who [   ],
Your left side[2] is Ninpanigarra [   ],
Your fingers are [   ],   (30)
Your [   ] are Dagan [   ],
Your navel, O lord, is [   ],
Your [   ] is Zababa [   ]

(fragmentary lines, then breaks off)

Text: Ebeling, KAR 102+328; Gurney, STT 118 rev.

Edition: Ebeling, *Quellen* 1, 47–49.

Translation: von Soden, SAHG, 258–259 no. 101; Labat, *Religions,* 93; Seux, *Hymnes,* 131–133.

Literature: H. Lewy, ArOr 18 (1950), 355–356 (dates to Middle Assyrian period or earlier); T. J. Meek, *Hebrew Origins* (New York, 1960), 198.

Notes to Text: (7) Seux, *Hymnes,* 131 note 5. (25) Seux, *Hymnes,* 133 note 25. (27) Seux, *Hymnes,* 133 note 27.

1. Variant adds "O lord." For Uta'ulu, see p. 711 note 3.
2. Variant adds "O lord."

(d) NINURTA AS SIRIUS

In this prayer a diviner calls upon the Sirius star for aid in the divination he is to perform.

O greatest Ninurta, warrior god,
      vanguard of the Anunna-gods,
      commander of the Igigi-gods, (1)
Judge of the universe, who oversees (its) equilibrium,
      who makes bright darkness and illumines gloom,
Who renders verdicts for teeming humankind!
O my splendid lord, who satisfies the needs of the land,
      at whose [   ] fell head pain takes to corners(?),
The critically ill recovers, (5)
Merciful one, who spares life, reviver of the d[ea]d,
Who grasps truth and justice and destroys [   ],
[Un]swerving arrow[1] that [kills] all enemies,
Great storm, who grasps the leadline
      [of heaven and netherworld],
Judge of verdicts, diviner of oracle[s   ], (10)
Conflagration that incinerates and burns up the wick[ed   ],
Whose celestial name is "Straight Dart,"
      whose [   ] is the greatest among the Igigi-gods,
Among all the gods your divinity is singular.
When the stars come out,
      your features shine [like] the sun,
You survey the entire inhabited world,
      [ ] of your light [ ], (15)
To set [right] the distressed
      and sleepless(?) of humankind [   ],
You are the [   ] of the one who has no one to trust in,
You rescue the kidnapped and abandoned [   ],
You summon him back to life from hell [   ].
On the one who, in the thick of battle,
      seems destined to die and calls your name, (20)
On him you have mercy, O lord,
      you rescue him from disaster.

---

1. "Arrow" is a name for Sirius, Sumerian kak-si-sá "Straight Dart."

And as for me, the reverent diviner, your servant,
I was anxious by day, I was essaying a bad case,
The verdict is extremely trying and difficult to discover,
I am far from getting to the bottom of it.   (25)
In the daylight(?) I came(?),* in the night I await you.
I take my place before you to discover the outcome,
          to make the right verdict.
I have my hands raised (in prayer);
          stand by me and [in] the pure heavens hear what I say.
Absolve (any) fault, efface (any) mistake,
          may my handiwork be blessed by you.[1]
May my presents soothe your heart,
          do not disdain to stand by me!   (30)
[Ren]der a verdict, accept my entreaty, and hear my prayer.
In all I have planned give a verdict.
Let me say what is needful for your firm assent.
As for me, may I live a long life in your service.
O greatest Ninurta, O pure [god], attend this sacrifice.   (35)
In what I say and pray, in whatsoever I do,
In the inquiry I ask your blessing on, let there be truth!

          (Prayer to Sirius when it is in position at sunrise)

Text: K 128 = Burrows, JRAS 1924 *Centenary Supplement*, pl. II-III.
Edition: Burrows, JRAS 1924 *Centenary Supplement*, 33–36.
Translation: von Soden, SAHG, 275–277 no. 22; Seux, *Hymnes,* 480–482.
Notes to Text: (26) Differently CAD A/1, 423b "O Shamash!" This would equate Ninurta with
     Shamash. For the reading *akušamma,* see Deller-Mayer, OrNS 58 (1989), 275. Note, however, in
     favor of *ašāšu* that the diviner has had a worrisome day (*urri dalpākma,* but see Mayer, OrNS 46
     [1977], 392) and awaits the intervention of Sirius with hopeful trepidation.

---

1.   A request to overlook any mistakes in procedure and to consider only the offerings and the
divinatory medium.

III.48 TO NUSKU

Nusku, courier of the gods, is invoked in prayers as a protective, beneficent deity.

(a) GUARDIAN OF THE NIGHT

O Nusku, king of the nighttime, illuminator of darkness, (1)
You stand forth in the night, you examine the people.
Without you, no meal is prepared in Ekur.[1]
The protector-demon, the watcher-demon,
    the lion-headed demon, the oppressor-demon,
    the *gallu*-demon, the lurker-demon, the wicked deity,
The phantom, the male ghost, the female ghost
    that lean in hidden corners, (5)
By means of your divine light,
    drive out the malignant demon,
    expel the phantom, overcome the wicked one,
The lion-demon who goes about at night,
    the touch of whom is death.
I look upon you, I turn toward your divinity,
Set above me a watcher of well-being and life,
Station at my head a protective guardian
    and a god who safeguards, (10)
Let them be looking out for me all night until daybreak.
O Nusku, perfect one, lord of wisdom,
Let me proclaim your greatness before Shamash every day!

Text: Ebeling, KAR 58, obv. 39–50; Figulla-Walker, CT 51 149, rev. 1'–3'; von Weiher, SBTU II 9, obv. 8–17, 10, obv. 7–16; Butler, AOAT 258 (1998), pl. 17 K 7664+ i 40'–48'; pl. 18 K 9000 14'-16'; pl. 20 K 11706+, obv. 1'–13'; one line in LKA 132 obv. 19'.
Edition: Mayer, UFBG, 485–486; Butler, AOAT 258 (1998), 339–347, with improved readings adopted here.
Translation: von Soden, SAHG, 351–352 no. 78; Seux, *Hymnes*, 254–255.
Literature: Mayer, UFBG, Nusku 4.

1. Variant adds here a line: "Without you, no judgment or verdict is rendered." For Nusku and Enlil in his temple Ekur, compare II.36a, Tablet I, lines 76ff.

(b) COURIER OF DREAMS

O Nusku, sublime vizier, who wal[ks abroad at night],   (1)
[   ] of the gods of the (four) world regions,
    lord of sublime powers, ...,
Whose battle cry humankind hears from afar,
I, so-and-so, son of so-and-so, entreat you,
    inform me [ab]out my case!
[With res]pect to [my] case, provide [merc]y(?) (for me),   (5)
Do not go [to] another case.
May the evening watch, the midnight watch,
    the morning watch,
May night bring me (a dream), let me sound your praises.
O [An]zagar, Anzagar,[1] who brings (dreams) to humankind,
Messenger of prince Marduk,   (10)
O Nightfall, awesomeness of the nighttime,
O three watches of the night, who are wakeful,
    watchful, alert, and non-sleeping,
Since you are wakeful, watchful,
    alert, and non-sleeping,
You will grant a verdict to wakeful and sleeping,   (15)
You will fulfill your responsibility,
    you will look out all night until the morning watch.
May night bring me (a dream),★
Let me sound your praises!

Text: Ebeling, KAR 58, rev. 1–17.

Edition: Ebeling, AGH, 40–41; Butler, AOAT 258 (1998), 344–348, with improved readings adopted here.

Translation: von Soden, SAHG, 350–351 no. 77; Seux, *Hymnes*, 320–321.

Literature: Mayer, UFBG, Nusku 5.

★*Notes to Text*: (8, 17) with Butler, AOAT 258 (1998), 348.

1. Dream-god.

(c) FORFENDER OF NIGHTMARES

O Nusku, you are companion to the sun,	(1)
You are the judge, judge (my) case!	
This dream that was brought to me in the evening,	
midnight, or morning watch,	
That you understand but I do not,	
If it is propitious,	
may the good (it portends) not pass me by,	(5)
If it is evil, may the evil (it portends) not overtake me,	
It is not for me!	
Just as this pulled-up reed cannot return to its place,	
And (as) this hem cut from my garment,	
Being cut from it, cannot return to my garment,	(10)
So may the evil (portended by) this dream,	
Which was brought to me in the evening,	
midnight, or morning watch,	
Not overtake me, it is not for me!	

Text: Butler, AOAT 258 (1998), pl. 3 K 3333+ obv.; pl. 11 79-7-8,77 rev.
Edition: Butler, AOAT 258 (1998), 313–319.
Translation: Seux, *Hymnes*, 373.
Literature: Mayer, UFBG, Nusku 12.

(d) PROTECTOR AGAINST SORCERY

O Nusku, most great one, offspring of Anu,   (1)
Image of (your) father, firstborn of Enlil,
Raised in the depths, creation of Enanki,[1]
I have raised a torch, I have made you glow.
A sorcerer has bewitched me,
    bewitched me with the sorcery
    he worked against me,   (5)
A sorceress has bewitched me,
    bewitched me with the sorcery
    she has worked against me,
A male witch has bewitched me,
    bewitched me with the witchcraft
    he has worked against me,
A female witch has bewitched me,
    bewitched me with the witchcraft
    she has worked against me,
A worker of spells has bewitched me,
    bewitched me with the spells
    she has worked against me!
Those who have made figurines that are figurines of me,
    who have made a likeness of my features,   (10)
Who have taken of my spittle,
    who have plucked out (a lock) of my hair,
Who have cut off a piece of my clothing,
    have collected dust where my feet have passed,
May Girra, the warrior, dissipate their spells!

Text: Tallqvist, *Maqlû* I 122–134; Finkelstein, STT 78, 122–134; Wiseman and Black, CTN 4 90, i 1′–5′.
Edition: Meier, *Maqlû*, 11–12 lines 122–134; see also AfO 21 (1960), 72.
Literature: Mayer, UFBG, Nusku 10.

1. "Lord of heaven and netherworld," a name for Ea. Variant reads Ninmen[na].

III.49 TO A PERSONAL GOD

Belief in personal gods, supposed to act as protectors and intercessors for the individual, is widely expressed in Assyro-Babylonian literature. Pleas to them express a range of feelings such as guilt, frustration, sorrow, even anger and reproof. The selections translated below sample the variety of this class of prayers, a treatment of which will be found in W. G. Lambert's study, "DINGIR.ŠÀ.DIB.BA Incantations," JNES 33 (1974), 267–322. For a study of the personal god, mostly based on evidence from the Classical period, see R. Albertz, *Persönliche Frommigkeit und offizielle Religion: religionsinterner Plurismus in Israel und Babylon* (Stuttgart: 1978), and above, General Introduction (E.8).

(a) GOD OF MY FAMILY

O my god, my lord, who created my name,[1]   (1)
Guardian of my life, producer of my progeny,
O angry god, may your heart be calmed,
O angry goddess, be reconciled with me.
Who knows where you dwell, O my god?   (5)
Never have I seen your pure standing place
    (or sleeping) chamber.[2]
I am constantly in great distress: O my god, where are you?
You who have been angry with me, turn toward me,
Turn your face to the pure godly meal of fat and oil,
That your lips receive goodness. Command that I thrive,   (10)
Command (long) life with your pure utterance.
Bring me away from evil that, through you, I be saved.
Ordain for me a destiny of (long) life,
Prolong my days, grant me (long) life!

Text: Myhrman, PBS 1/1 14, 41–54; W. G. Lambert, JNES 33 (1974), 307, 309; Ebeling-Köcher-Rost, LKA 26, 27 (collated Lambert, 317).
Edition: W. G. Lambert, JNES 33 (1974), 276–277, lines 40–53.
Translation: von Soden, SAHG, 353 no. 79; Seux, *Hymnes*, 204–205.

1. Variant places lines 1–4 at end, thus beginning with line 5.
2. Variant adds: "sublime."

(b) FURIOUS GOD

My god, I did not know (how) [har]sh
     your punishment would be!   (1)
I have sworn lightly a solemn oath by your name,
I have disregarded your rites, I went too far,
I have skirted(?)* your duty in difficulty,
I have trespassed far beyond your limits.   (5)
I certainly did not know, much [   ].
My crimes being (so) numerous, I do not know all I did.
O my god, clear, forego, dispel your ire,
Disregard my iniquities, accept my entreaties,
Transmute my sins into good deeds.   (10)
Your hand is harsh, I have seen your punishment.
Let him who does not revere his god and goddess
     learn from my example.
O my god, be reconciled, O my goddess, relent!
Turn hither your faces to the entreaty of my prayer.
May your angry hearts be calmed,[1]   (15)
May your feelings be soothed, permit me reconciliation,
Let me ever sing your praises, not to be forgotten,
     to the numerous peoples.

Text: Myhrman, PBS 1/1 14, 24–40; W. G. Lambert, JNES 33 (1974), 306, 308, 318; J. J. A. Van Dijk, W. Mayer, *Texte aus dem Rēš-Heiligtum in Uruk-Warka, Baghdader Mitteilungen Beiheft 2* (Berlin, 1980) 15.
Edition: W. G. Lambert, JNES 33 (1974), 274–277 lines 23–39.
Translation: von Soden, SAHG, 352 no. 79; Seux, *Hymnes*, 203–204 Hecker, TUAT II/5, 777.
Notes to Text: (4) Guess based on context; see CAD Š/2, 259 vs. AHw, 1208 (*šeʾēru*).

1. Variant adds: "May the hostile goddess be reconciled with me."

(c) THE PITEOUS SUFFERER

This bilingual lament portrays the suffering of a man who believes himself
forsaken by his god. Compare Dialogue Between a Man and His God (II.13).

(gap)

[In agony of] heart, in terrible weeping,   (1′)
He abides in grief.
With bitter plaint, agony of heart,
Terrible weeping, terrible grief,
He moans like a dove, in crushing distress, night and day.   (5′)
He lows[1] like a cow to his merciful god,
He keeps setting forth his bitter grief,
He abases himself before his god in supplication.
He weeps and knows no restraint in sobbing:
"Shall I speak of what I did?
    What I did is unspeakable!   (10′)
"Shall I repeat[2] what I said?
    What I said should not be repeated!
"O my god, shall I speak of what I did?
    What I did is unspeakable!
"O my lord, shall I speak to someone (of it)?
    It is unspeakable!
"Shall I repeat what I said?
    What I said should not be repeated!
"I am deaf, I am blindfolded, I cannot see.   (15′)
"You have gone beyond what you intended,[3]
"Let your sweet breeze wa[ft upon me].
"I am caught up like reeds in the wind.
"My god, [absolve] my sin,
"My god, look steadfastly upon me from your abode,[4]   (20′)
"Take pity on me, may your angry heart be calmed,

  1. Variant: "cries out."
  2. Variant: "speak of."
  3. Literally: "commanded." I take this to mean that the punishment has exceeded the limits
imagined by the sufferer to have been imposed upon it by the god.
  4. Variant: "wherever," omits last two lines.

"[May your heart, like a real mother's, like a real father's],
    be [restored],
[Like a real mother's, like a real father's, may it be restored]."

Text: Maul, HBKl, pl. 31–35 (with numerous variants not noted here).
Edition: Maul, HBKl, 216–228 no. 40–42.
Translation: Seux, *Hymnes*, 143–145.

(d) WHO HAS NOT SINNED?

Be it [offen]se, crime, iniquity, sin,   (1)
[I] have offended against my god,
    I have sinned against my goddess.
I have (indeed) perpetrated [all] my crimes,
    all my sins, all my iniquities.
[I] gave my word, then changed (it),
    I was trusted but did not deliver.
I did [un]seemly deeds, I said something harmful.   (5)
I repeated [what should not be spoken of],
    harmful (speech) was on my lips.
[I was ig]norant, I went too far!
Absolve, my god ... [   ]
Let my [iniquities] be dissolved,
    [transmute] my sins into good deeds.
You decide [   ]   (10)
Save safe and sound the one who sinned [   ]!
Who is there who is guilty of no sin against his god?
Which is he who kept a commandment forever?
All human beings there are harbor sin.
I, your servant, have committed every sin,   (15)
I stood before you, (but) I ... falsehood,
I uttered lies, I indulged crimes,
I spoke harmful words, you know what they are.
I committed an abomination
    against the god who created me,
I acted sacrilegiously, I kept on doing evil.   (20)
I envied your vast possessions,

I yearned for your precious silver,
I lifted my own hand to touch what should not be touched.
I entered the temple without being pure,
I committed one terrible outrage after another against you,   (25)
I went beyond your limits of what was offensive to you,
I cursed your divinity in the rage of my heart.
I have persisted in every sort of crime,
I kept on going as I liked and incurred iniquity.
It is enough, O my god, let your heart be calmed!
May the goddess who grew angry be pacified completely.   (30)
Dissolve the ire you harbored in your heart,
May your inmost self, which I swore by,
        be reconciled with me.
Though my crimes be numerous, clear my debt,
Though my iniquities be seven(-fold),
        let your heart be calmed.
Though my [si]ns be numerous,
        show great mercy and cleanse [me].   (35)
[O my god], I am exhausted, grasp my hand,
[from the gr]ound and hold up [my] head,
[   ] save my life!

(thirteen lines fragmentary)

Let the day be joyful [for] the shepherd of the people,
[Let me si]ng of you, let me p[r]aise your divinity,
Let me sound your praises [to] the numerous [peoples]!

Text: Ebeling, KAR 39 "rev.?" 18–27; KAR 45 "rev." + KAR 39 "obv."; W. G. Lambert, JNES 33 (1974), 314–315, with collations, p. 322.

Edition: W. G. Lambert, JNES 33 (1974), 280–285, lines 121–175.

Translation: von Soden, SAHG, 272–273 no. 19 (partial); Seux, *Hymnes*, 206–208; Hecker, TUAT II/5, 779.

III.50 TO THE RIVER

The cleansing river was often invoked in rituals to dispose of evil that had fallen upon a person, through witchcraft and through everyday occurrences. Many versions of this prayer, long and short, are found, with numerous variants. This translation conflates the address of some manuscripts with the petition of another.

O River, creator of all things,   (1)
When the great gods dug your bed,
They set well-being along your banks,
Ea, king of the depths, built his dwelling within you.
They gave you an irresistible flood,   (5)
Ea and Marduk gave you flamboyance and anger,
    splendor and awe.[1]
You judge the cases of all peoples.
O great River, sublime River, your waters run straight,
Receive from me the evil of sorcery,
Let your channel receive all my sins!   (10)
You run straight, O River,
Take this down to your depths, O River!
May that evil not come near me nor my house,
May it gain no hold on me, may it not overcome me!
May I live on in well-being, that I may sing your praises.   (15)

Text: King, STC 1, 200–201; Ebeling, KAR 254, 294; Caplice, OrNS 34 (1965), pl. 18 no. 11; OrNS 39 (1970), pl. 6; Nougayrol, RA 65 (1971), 164.

Edition: King, STC 1, 128–129; Caplice, OrNS 34 (1965), 130–131; OrNS 36 (1967), 290, 293; OrNS 39 (1970), 135, 138; Nougayrol, RA 65 (1971), 163, 165.

Translation: Heidel, *Babylonian Genesis*, 74–75; Seux, *Hymnes*, 366–368; Bottéro, *Mythologie*, 486–487.

Literature: W. G. Lambert, RA 53 (1959), 135; Bottéro, *Mythes*, 288–291 (with citation of further, shorter parallels); Maul, *Zukunftsbewältigung*, 86–89, 147, 275, 290, 447, 492.

1. Variant: "He has given you noontime heat and anger, splendor and awe. At your word, Ea and Marduk gave (you) the noontime heat." Another variant: "Ea and Asalluhi gave you wisdom" (a reference to magic powers).

III.51 TO SHAMASH

Shamash, the sun, was the god of justice and fair dealing. He was often invoked in prayers against evil magic and in the prayers of diviners, as investigation and perception of the truth were his special responsibility. Compare also III.32.

The cosmology of the hymns to the sun can seem contradictory and confusing to the modern reader, especially in connection with the word pair *šamê u erṣetum* (usually translated "heaven and earth," see General Introduction, C.8). The second word in the pair can mean "earth" or "netherworld," and it is often diffi-cult to decide which is meant. For example, in III.51a, the opening lines refer to "heaven and —, above and be[low, lord of the dead, gui]de of the living" (assuming the restoration is correct, see Caplice, OrNS 39 [1970], 140). The contrasts above/below and dead/living, presumably inverted for poetic reasons, imply that "below" and *erṣetum* refer to the netherworld. However, the relation-ship could be understood as symmetrical and tripartite (heaven : earth // neth-erworld : earth), in which case *erṣetum* should refer to the earth. In III.51h the sun "administers dead and living ..., scrutinizes all there is," implying, like the preceding, that the sun had access to the netherworld, even if the dead them-selves were bereft of light (see III.19, lines 7ff.). The next line calls the sun "light of heaven and —, splendor of the world." This could be tripartite, and so be read as heaven : netherworld : world, or it could be bipartite, with the last word parallel to the middle one, heaven : earth // world. A further example, in III.51n, calls the sun "king of heaven and —," with parallel "Anu and Enlil convene no assembly in heaven, Nor would they take counsel concerning the land." This implies bipartite division, heaven : earth // gods : land. The solution to this difficult conceptual problem may be that in poetry a contrast can be drawn between heaven and that which is below it, earth and netherworld being considered as a unit in opposition to heaven. Further development within an individual poem can separate earth from netherworld, or define that larger unit more closely, as in III.51h, where the sun is judge of heaven and —, then "light of the gods, light of living things." For these reasons, the pair *šamê u erṣetum* might best be translated with an awkward paraphrase such as "heaven and world-below," but out of deference to tradition and the need for intelligibility, "heaven and earth" has been retained, except where it seemed clear that the netherworld was meant.

(a) AGAINST IMPENDING EVIL

O Shamash, king of heaven and earth,
    judge above and be[low,
    lord of the dead, gui]de of the living,   (1)
You are preserver of life, the great leader of humankind,
You are [averter of sp]ells, signs, and portents,
    whatever they may be,
You are the one to cut off evil, celestial or terrestrial.
Because of the evil of sorcer[y, witchcraft, magic],
    and machinations that have seized me
    and are not dissolved,
Because of the evil of unfavorable signs and portents
    that are present in my house,
    that have stymied me,[1]
Each day I am afraid, anxious, terrified.   (5)
Now, may the evil of this sorcery that has been put upon me,
    the evil of the signs and portents
    that are present in my house,
    not approach me or my house,
    nor bes[et me, n]or affect me.
May that evil cross river, may it go beyond mountain,
May that sorcery be 3600 leagues distant from my person.
May it mount to the sky like smoke,
    like an uprooted tamarisk, may it not return where it was.
May the river receive the[se evils] from me,
    may the river redeem me.   (10)
Let me live in well-being and proclaim your greatness,
Let me sound your [pra]ises to the numerous peoples!

Text: Caplice, OrNS 39 (1970), pl. vi K 2773+; OrNS 36 (1967), pl. lix K 8932; Ebeling-Köcher-
    Rost, LKA 111, obv. 7 – rev. 3; Gadd, UET 6/2 405.
Edition: Caplice, OrNS 39 (1970), 134–135, 137–138, no. 40, lines 8–17; see Maul, *Zukunftsbewälti-*
    gung, 330, 446–447, lines 8–17; 505–506.
Translation: Seux, *Hymnes*, 356–357.
Literature: Mayer, UFBG, Šamaš 24.

1.   Variant same to here, then goes on with another prayer against the evil portended by a stray
cat (compare III.51d).

(b) AGAINST A KNOWN SORCERER

O Shamash, judge of heaven and earth,
   judge of upper and lower regions,
Who administers the people of this land,
   who releases the prisoner,
   who revives the moribund,
O Shamash, these images[1] are of my enemy,
   of my persecutor, of my opponent,
Who has worked against me witchcraft,
   subversion, sickness, disease, assassination, injustice,
   suppression, every sort of evil and machination.
O Shamash, in the presence of your great divinity,
   may their own persons retain the assassination and witchcraft
   they are attempting!

Text: Caplice, OrNS 39 (1970), pl. vi K 2773+; Maul, *Zukunftsbewältigung*, 550 K 11625.
Edition: Caplice, OrNS 39 (1970), 136, 139 no. 40 lines 35–40; Maul, *Zukunftsbewältigung*, 446–447,
   451, lines 34–39.
Literature: Mayer, UFBG, Šamaš 8.

(c) AGAINST SNAKES

O Shamash, king of heaven and earth,   (1)
Lord of truth and justice,
Lord of the Anunna-gods, lord of the spirits of the dead,★
Whose assent no god can change,
Whose command cannot be reversed,   (5)
O Shamash, in your hands is revival of the dead,
   loosing of the bound.
O Shamash, I, your servant, so-and-so, son of so-and-so,
Whose (personal) god is Marduk,
   whose (personal) goddess is Sarpanitum,
I come before you,★ I have seized the hem of your garment.[2]

   1. Refers to a set of six figurines, male and female, inscribed with names and subsequently
buried in a magic ritual (compare III.51f).
   2. Gesture of entreaty; see p. 671 note 1.

On account of the evil omen of a snake
    I saw come right into my house for (its) prey,   (10)
I am afraid, anxious, frightened.
Deliver me from this evil!
Let me proclaim your greatness, let me sing your praises,
Let those who see me sound of your praises forever!

Text: Schollmeyer, *Šamaš* p. 139, VAT 5; Maul, *Zukunftsbewältigung*, 542.
Edition: Maul, *Zukunftsbewältigung*, 296–297.
Translation: von Soden, SAHG, 320–321, no. 55; Seux, *Hymnes*, 364–365.
Literature: Mayer, UFBG, Šamaš 25.
*Notes to Text: (3) Maul, *Zukunftsbewältigung*, 296 note 8. (9) Copy not clear, but this is what is
    expected; see also Seux, *Hymnes*, 365 note 4.

(d) AGAINST DOGS

O Shamash, king of heaven and earth,
    judge of above and below,   (1)
Light of the gods, guide of humankind,
Who judges the cases of the great gods,
I turn to you, I seek you out.
Command among the gods life (for me),   (5)
May the gods who are with you speak favorably of me.
On account of this dog that has urinated on me,
I am afraid, anxious, frightened.
Deliver me from the evil of this dog,
Let me sound your praises!   (10)

Text: Ebeling, KAR 64, obv. 24–33; KAR 221, 8–12; Gurney, STT 64, 11–17; Caplice, OrNS 36
    (1967), pl. 1 DT 169; Maul, *Zukunftsbewältigung*, 543 BM 50659.
Edition: Caplice, OrNS 36 (1967), 2–3, 5–6 no. 12 lines 24–33; Maul, *Zukunftsbewältigung*, 316–317,
    321.
Translation: Caplice, SANE 1/1, 21; Seux, *Hymnes*, 363–364.
Literature: Mayer, UFBG, Šamaš 9.

(e) AGAINST GHOSTS

O Shamash, noblest of the Anunna-gods,
    most lordly among the Igigi-gods,
      sublime leader, guide,   (1)
Judge of heaven and earth, not changing in his command,
O Shamash, who controls darkness,
    who provides light for the people,
O Shamash, when you set, the peoples' light is darkened,
O Shamash, when you rise, the four quarters brighten.   (5)
The destitute, widow, waif, female companion,
At your rising, all humanity is warmed.
Beasts, living creatures, animals of the steppe,
Bring(?) you(?) their life(?), their wealth(?).*
You judge the case of the oppressed man and woman,
    you administer their verdicts.   (10)
I, so-and-so, son of so-and-so, exhausted, kneeling,
Who am bound by the anger of a god or goddess,
A ghost, a lurking demon, a spirit, a "wind" spirit,
    goose pimples, dizziness, paralysis(?), vertigo,
Joint pain, irrational behavior, have exacted a toll
    of me and each day have left me (more) stunned.
O Shamash, you are the judge, I bring you my life,   (15)
I kneel for a verdict on the disease
    that has me in its grasp.
Judge my case, give a verdict for me,
Do not go [   ] to another case.
After you have administered case and verdict,
And my constraint is loosed
    and flown away from my [body],*   (20)
I will always trust in you.
May the gods bless(?) you,*
May the heavens rejoice on account of you,
May the earth rejoice on account of you.

Text: Köcher, BAM 4 323, obv. 19–35; Gray, SRT, pl. XII K 2132.
Edition: Ebeling, *Quellen* I, 43–45.
Translation: von Soden, SAHG, 323–324, no. 57; Seux, *Hymnes*, 426–427.

Literature: Mayer, UFBG, Šamaš 73.
★*Notes to Text*: (9) CAD M/2, 41a; AHw, 629a, 698a. (20) Seux, *Hymnes*, 427 notes 24, 25. (22) Seux, *Hymnes*, 427 note 26.

(f) AGAINST A CURSE

O Shamash, king of heaven and earth,
    who administers above and below, (1)
O Shamash, it is in your power to revive the moribund,
    to release the bound.
Incorruptible judge, administrator of the peoples,
Sublime offspring of the lord Brightly Rising God,[1]
Mighty son, splendid one, light of the world, (5)
You are Shamash, creator of all there is of heaven and earth.
O Shamash, because of a curse that,
    many days ago,
Has attached itself to my back and cannot be removed,
Expense, loss, and poor health have beset me,
It has reduced my household, livestock, everything. (10)
It fills me with a relentless distress of disease,
Anxiety and weight loss have beset me,[2]
And so I am afflicted with insomnia day and night,
With digestive troubles and poor health
    I am bringing myself to an end.
I go on, downcast in misery, (15)
I enfeeble myself with hardship and misery.
When I was young I was an ignoramus,
    I did not understand the crime I committed!
Even as a youngster I had sinned,
I transgressed the boundaries of my (personal) god.
O lord, stand by me, hear my prayer! (20)
O Shamash, stand by me, hear me!

Because of a curse of disease
    that besets me and hounds me,

1. Namrasit, a name of Sin, the moon-god.
2. Variant omits.

Or a curse of my father
　　or a curse of my mother,
Or a curse of seven generations
　　of my father's house,
Or a curse of my family or relatives,   (25)
Or a curse of my kith or kin,
Or a curse of a dead or living person,
Or a curse of descendants new born or yet to be,
Or a curse that I swore or did not swear,
Or that I swore by father or mother,   (30)
Or that I swore by brother or sister,
Or that I swore by friend or comrade,
Or that I swore by watercourse or well,
Or that I swore by weapon or spindle,
Or that I swore falsely by the life of my (personal) god,   (35)
Or that I sw[ore] by human, beast,
　　or anything whatsoever of wilderness or city,
O Shamash, great lord, command that the curse
　　of disease that has a hold on me [be dissolved],
[May] Ea [dissolve] the substitution[1] for me
　　which has been made,
May Marduk dis[perse] the stand-ins for me
　　which have been produced.

(Text continues with list of demons
and describes fashioning of a magic figurine.)

Text: Gray, SRT, pl. IV, K 5022+S 787+833+303+949 (= Craig, ABRT 2, 3–5); K 8457+8926+2387
　　+6300 (all collated), see Gray, SRT, pl. XX.
Edition: Schollmeyer, *Šamaš*, 96–99, no. 18.
Translation: von Soden, SAHG, 321–323 no. 56; Seux, *Hymnes*, 403–405.
Literature: Mayer, UFBG, Šamaš 78.

1.　That is, figurines or other representations of a person fashioned to work black magic against
him (compare III.51b).

(g) GOLDEN TIARA OF THE HEAVENS

O great lord who occupies an awe-inspiring dais
    in the pure heavens,   (1)
Golden tiara of the heavens, fittest for kingship,
O Shamash, shepherd of the people, noble god,
Who scrutinizes the land, leader of the people,
Who guides the escapee to the right path,   (5)
O Shamash, judge of heaven and earth,
Who directs the Igi[gi]-gods,
Who grants incense offerings to the great gods,
I, Assurbanipal, son of his (personal) god,
Call upon you in the pure heavens,   (10)
[And] I seek (you) out in your radiant dwelling.
I invoke your name at the great gods' table,
I libate [   ] before you.
Learn(?) my [   ]* and direct me.
[Whatever I have done],
    from my youth [until] my adulthood,   (15)
May it not affect me!
May it be 3600 leagues [distant] from my person!
[I], Assurbanipal, your servant,
[Whoever seeks out] the ways of your great divinity,
Cleanse me bright [as] your daylight!   (20)
[Let] me li[ve] in well-being,
Let me proclaim your greatness [with my] mouth,
Let me sound [your pr]aises!

Text: Ebeling, KAR 55.

Edition: Ebeling, AGH, 52–53.

Translation: von Soden, SAHG, 317–318 no. 53; Seux, *Hymnes*, 286–287; Hecker, TUAT II/5, 772–773.

Literature: Mayer, UFBG, Šamaš 2.

Notes to Text: (14) Or: "pronounce my name" (Hecker).

(h) PROTECTOR OF THE KING (1)

This prayer was used in the ritual series "House of the Ritual Bath." This was a royal lustration procedure that took place in various bathing chambers of a bathhouse, during which an officiant pronounced some prayers and the king others. Although many of the officiant's were in Sumerian, the king was expected to recite only Akkadian prayers. Each stage was accompanied by elaborate rituals. The basic procedure involved washing off evil from the king and transferring it magically to those believed to be the source of it. In this instance a figurine is splashed with the dirty wash water. One cycle of this series was devoted to Shamash, from which this and the following prayers have been excerpted. For more information on the ritual bath, see Laessøe, *Bît Rimki*, 9–19, 99–102, W. G. Lambert, BiOr 14 (1977), 227, W. Farber, CRRAI 39 (1997), 41–46, and p. 775 note 6.

(said by the king)

O Shamash, king of heaven and earth,
    lord of truth and justice, (1)
You are purifier of god and man.
O Shamash, I take my place before you in the reed booth
    of the house of the ritual b[ath],[1]
O Shamash, I do not know who has a hold over me,*
    assuming a woman, here is a figurine (to represent) her.
O Shamash! Since it is made of pure barley,[2]
    which creates humankind, (5)
The figurine is like a (human) shape,
    the head is like a (human) head,
The shape of the body is like the shape of a (human) body.
O Shamash! This is the figurine of the witch
    (who is doing the) sorcery, who has harassed me,
    who is making the attempt against me,
Who has said to a sorceress, "Bewitch!"
    who has said to a harasser "Harass!"
    who has incited another, (10)

1. Variant: "so-and-so, son of so-and-so, be[fore you]."
2. The figurine is made of a grain paste.

Who has made me eat (bewitched) bread,
>   who has made me drink (bewitched) beer,
Who has made me wash in (bewitched) water,
>   who has made me anoint with (bewitched) oil,
Who has made me eat (bewitched) food:
Because of whatever she made me eat,
>   because of whatever she made me drink,
Because of whatever she made me wash with,
>   because of whatever she made me anoint with,
>   or dispatched against me,   (15)
Because she pronounced my name with evil intent,
>   interred symbols of me,
Made figurines of me and took my measurements,
Collected dust grains from my footprints,
>   took up my spittle,
Plucked out a lock of hair, cut off a piece of my clothing,
>   snooped for something bad about me,
Because she has made accusations against me, hampered me,
>   seized me, polluted me,   (20)
Has made me full of stiffness and debility,
Has seized my heart,
>   has turned the heart <of my god> against me,*
Has twisted my muscles, weakened my strength,
Has overthrown my arms, hobbled my feet,
Has set upon me discord, ill temper, misery, anxiety, panic,   (25)
Terror, cursing, fear, worry, loss of sleep,
>   speechlessness, depression,
Misery,[1] dissatisfaction, illness,
Has cast "dog tongue"[2] between us,
O Shamash, this is she, here is her figurine!
Even though she is not here, her figurine is here!   (30)
I wash the water off upon her,
>   whatever is known to me of her or not known,
I pollute her with it, let her receive it from me.
She has worked against me furtively,
>   but I wash myself off on her openly* before you.

---

1. Variant omits.
2. Meaning unknown, perhaps expression for "bad blood."

Through the greatness of Ea and the procedures of Asalluhi,   (35)
Through the command of Marduk and Sarpanitum,
Through the command of Nabu and Tashmetu,[1]
I wash myself off upon her, I bathe myself off upon her.
Just as the water is cleared from my body
  and goes upon her and her form,
So do I cast off upon her wrong and bondage!
May all evil in my person, flesh, and sinews   (40)
Be cleared like the water from my body
  and go against her and against her form!
O Shamash, her own wicked intents and actions
  turn against her and her form.
On account of the evil of signs
  and [bad, unfavorable] portents
   which are [present] in my palace [and in my land],[2]
O Shamash, may my sorceress fall but I rise,
May she be hamstrung but I proceed,   (45)
May she be polluted but I become pure,
May she die but I live!
O Shamash, let me proceed straight on my way,
  according to your judgment.
O Shamash, since I did not work against her
  — it was she who worked against me —
O Shamash, since I did not harass her
  — it was she who harassed me —   (50)
I have washed myself off upon her,
  I have bathed myself in water upon her,
I have polluted her, may she receive it from me!
Just as the water is cleared from my body
  and goes to this (figurine),
May all evil in my person, my flesh, my sinews
Be cleared from my body and leave my body.   (55)

Text: Laessøe, *Bît Rimki*, pl. I no. 1–3; pl. II, no. 4; Lutz, PBS 1/2, 129; Finkelstein, STT 76, 77.
Edition: Laessøe, *Bît Rimki*, 37–47.
Translation: Seux, *Hymnes*, 388–392.
Literature: Mayer, UFBG, Šamaš 41.

1. Variant omits.
2. Variant omits.

Notes to Text: (4) W. G. Lambert, BiOr 14 (1977), 229; Borger, AfO 18 (1957), 139. (22) Reiner, JNES 17 (1958), 207. (34) Variant obscure.

(i) PROTECTOR OF THE KING (2)

Bilingual incantation prayer from a royal lustration ritual, see III.51h.

(To be spoken by the exorcist)

O Shamash, when you come forth from the great mountain,   (1)
When you come forth from the great mountain,
 the mountain of the deep,
When you come forth from the holy hill
 where destinies are ordained,
When you [come forth] from the back of heaven
 to the junction point of heaven and earth,
The great gods attend upon you for judgment,   (5)
The Anunna-gods attend upon you to render verdicts.
Humankind, including (all) peoples, await your command,
Livestock, wildlife, all four-footed creatures,
Fix their eyes upon your great light.
O Shamash, you are greatest of sages,
 your own (best) counsellor,   (10)
O Shamash, you are greatest of leaders,
 judge of heaven and earth.
Whatever is (secret) in the heart is spoken out [before you?],
All people's passing thoughts speak (as if aloud) to you.[1]
You strike down instantly the party in the wrong,   (15)
You single out truth and justice.
The oppressed and maltreated,
The one trapped inadvertently in an oath,
The one who encountered the unforeseen,
The one in the grip of contagion,
The one held hostage by a fiend,   (20)
The one beset by a malignant phantom,

---

1. *ziqīqu*, a disembodied spirit that can express a person's motivation or will, here apparently referring to unspoken thoughts.

The one smothered in his bed by a malignant apparition,
The one flung down by a malignant shade,
The one slain by a huge spectre,
The one whose limbs a malignant god twisted,   (25)
The one whose hair a malignant lurking demon stood on end,
The one taken by Lamashtu,
The one flung down by a paralyzing demon,
The one made feverish by a snatching demon,
The one wedded by a female ghost,   (30)
The young man frustrated by a female ghost,
The one thwarted by a bad sign,
The one bound by a curse,
The one despised by a mouth of malice,
The one cursed by a tongue of malice,   (35)
The one glowered at balefully by an eye of malice,
The one bound by witchcraft,
The target of machination,
Shamash, you have the power to revive (all of) them.
You resolve conflicting testimony as if it were one.   (40)
I (the exorcist) am the messenger of Ea,
He sent me to revive th(is) troubled man,
I repeat to [you] Ea's commission,
"Ren[der] a verdict for the king, son of his god,
"Ban[ish] the foul sickness from his body,   (45)
"[Pour out] pure water, clean water, clear water upon him.
"When [he bathes] the image of his substitute
        in the bath water,
"When the water [flows] from its body,
"May the malignant phantom, malignant apparition,
        malignant shade, malignant spectre, malignant god,
        malignant lurking demon,
"Lamashtu, paralyzing demon, snatching demon,   (50)
"Male ghost, female ghost,
"Contagion, fiend, foul sickness,[1]
"(All) flow like water from the body of the king,
        son of his (personal) god, and [quit?] his person!"

---

1. Variant adds: "bad signs, curse, mouth of malice, tongue of malice, lips of malice, enchantment, witchcraft, magic, machination" (Borger, JCS 21 [1967], 6 "Einschub C").

O Shamash, whose mightily (given) command
    cannot be ch[anged],
This day let his wrong be dissolved.   (55)
May the tongue of malice be deflected,
May the king's god proclaim your greatness!
May the king [sound] your praises,
And I too, the exorcist, your servant,
    will render you homage.

(to be spoken by the king)

O Shamash, judge of heaven and earth,
    lord of above and below,
Light of the gods, guide of humankind,★
Who sets free the captive, who revives the moribund,[1]
Who averts evil (consequences) of signs and portents,
    who eliminates illness,
Who dispels darkness and brings illumination,   (90)
I, so-and-so, son of so-and-so, your servant,
    turn to you, seek you.
Stand in judgment upon my case this day,
Illumine my darkness, clear up my confusion,
    set right my uncertainties!
Save me from bad signs and portents, from magic circles,   (95)
    or any human agency that may block my progress,
Release my bond, give me life, for I am afraid, anxious,
    terrified of the evil (consequences of) bad signs
    and portents that are present in my house.
Avert from me the evil (consequences) of the signs
    and portents, lest I die or come to harm.   (100)

May this evil not approach me,
    may it not draw near me,
May it not reach me, may it not catch up with me,[2]

---

1. Variant: "fallen."
2. Variant may have ended here; for the longer version, I follow Seux (*Hymnes*, 358 note 6);
see also Maul, *Zukunftsbewältigung*, 139 (lines 130–131); differently Borger (JCS 21 [1967], 10); see
III 37d lines 27–32.

May it cross river, may it go beyond mountain,
May it be 3600 leagues distant from my person,
May it mount to the sky like smoke,
Like an uprooted tamarisk, may it not return where it was![1]
[Let me proclaim your greatness], let me sound your praises!   (105)

Text: Ebeling-Köcher-Rost, LKA 75; Gray, SRT, pl. XII Sm 166+; XIII (K 4922) + Borger, JCS
21 (1967), 16 (K 4977+), K 4830+; XV (K 4654+), K 3462, K 5069+; XVI (K 5069+), K 3138+;
XVII (K 4986+) + Borger, JCS 21 (1967), K 4998, K 4610+, K 5135+; Haupt, ASKT 7; Pinches,
V R 50–51 + Borger, JCS 21 (1967), 16 (K 5196); see further Borger, ZA 61 (1971), 84–88 and
Maul, *Zukunftsbewältigung*, 138–139.
Edition: Borger, JCS 21 (1967), 2–7, 9–10 (lines 1–59, 86–101); see also Maul, *Zukunftsbewältigung*,
138–139.
Translation: Seux, *Hymnes*, 357–358 (= 86–101).
Literature: Mayer, UFBG, Šamaš 42 (= portion to be spoken by king).
★Notes to Text: (88) With Maul, *Zukunftsbewältigung*, 151.

(j) PROTECTOR OF THE KING (3)

From a royal lustration ritual (see III.51h), this prayer stresses the centrality of the
sun for the gods and creatures of the universe, especially the Mesopotamians.

(bilingual, to be spoken by the exorcist)

O great lord, when you come forth from the pure heavens,   (1)
O warrior Shamash, young hero,
    when you come forth from the pure heavens,
When you raise the latch pin
    from the lock of the pure heavens,[2]
When you free the bolt of the pure heavens,
When you open the great door of the pure heavens,   (5)
When you cross the sublime boo[ths] of the pure heavens,
Anu and Enlil greet you with joy,
[Ea] and Belet-ili stand happily in attendance upon you,
[Asalluhi] stands in attendance upon you each day
    to calm your feelings,

---

1. Variant has additional lines (=III.37d 33–34, III 510 37 etc.).
2. Or: "from the transverse door bar" (see Scurlock, OrNS 57 [1988], 432).

The great [gods of the] sanctuaries of all lands
    pay close heed to you,   (10)
[The Anunna-gods?] of the high daises of heaven and earth
    stand in attendance upon you.
[You ordain their destinies], you render verdicts for them,
[You look upon the beasts of the] steppe
    [who live on grain and water].
You make the [the people of this] land have [truth and justice],
You set right [the oppressed and maltreated],   (15)
You look on [the numerous gods and men].
[O Shamash, sublime judge,   ] night and day,
You [absolve] sin, you remove wr[ong-doing].
Freeing the captive and reviving the sick are in your power.
A man's (personal) god stands in attendance upon you
    for his devotee's sake.   (20)
The lord sent me, the great lord (Ea) sent me,
Stand by, learn what he said, render his verdict!
As for you, when you come,
    you set right the people of this land.
Establish for him (the king) protective splendor,
    let his illness be set right.   (25)
Th(is) man, son of his (personal) god, has sinned
    and has been punished,
His members are painfully diseased, he lies painfully in disease.
O Shamash, heed my prayer!
Eat his food (offering), accept his sacrifice,
    set his (personal) god at his side.
At your order, may his offense be dissolved,
    his wrong-doing removed,   (30)
May he be released from his bondage,
    may he revive from his illness,
Let this king live!
As long as he lives, let him proclaim your greatness,
Let the king sound your praises!
And I, the exorcist, your servant,
    let me sound your praises!   (35)

Text: Pinches, IV R² 17, obv. 1-rev. 6; Gray, SRT, pl. XIII Bu 91–5–9, 180; BM 99077+99257
   (Sumerian only) (all collated).
Edition: Langdon, OECT 6, 45–48.
Translation: Seux, *Hymnes*, 226–229.

(k) PROTECTOR OF THE KING (4)

From a royal lustration ritual, see III.51h.

(to be spoken by the king)

I call upon you, Shamash, in the pure heavens,	(1)
Take your seat in the shade of cedar,	
Let your feet be set on a platform* of juniper.	
The lands rejoice over you,	
the humming (world) exults over you,	
All peoples behold your brilliant light!	(5)
Your net embraces all lands,	
O Shamash, you are the one	
who understands their arrangements.	
O destroyer of the wicked,	
implementer of preventive rituals	
(Against) bad signs and portents, terrifying nightmares,	
O cutter of the magic knot	
that can destroy people and land,	(10)
I have drawn before you the worker(s) of witchcraft,	
magic, and sorcery,	
I have made figurines of them in pure flour.	
Those who worked magic against me, plotted treachery,	
Their hearts are perverted and full of malice.	
Stand by me, Shamash, light of the great gods,	(15)
Let me be the one to prevail	
over the one working magic against me,	
Let my (personal) god, who created me, sta[nd] by my side.	
My mouth is washed, my hands are set right,	
Set me right, lord, light of the universe, Shamash the judge!	
May the day, month, year, [seventh], fifteenth,	
[twentieth], and thirtieth day undo their plots.	(20)

May [   ] dissolve the sorcery.*
[Accept my entreaty], dissolve my bondage,
[Let me, your servant], sound [your praises]!

Text: Pinches, IV R² 17, rev. 8–30.
Edition: Langdon, OECT 6, 48–49.
Translation: von Soden, SAHG, 324–325 no. 58; Seux, *Hymnes*, 392–394.
Literature: Mayer, UFBG, Šamaš 43.
Notes to Text: (3) Seux, *Hymnes*, 393 note 3. (20–21) Mayer, OrNS 46 (1977), 390.

(l) PROTECTOR OF THE KING (5)

O most great one, perfect son of the Brightly Rising God,[1]   (1)
Perpetually renewing light, beacon of the people,
    discloser of light,[2]
O Shamash, who administers dead and living,
    who scrutinizes all there is,
O Shamash, light of heaven[3] and earth,
    splendor of the world,
O lord of Sippar, protection of the Ebabbar,[4]   (5)
Twin of Marduk, Babylon's trust,
The peoples heed your light,[5]
The Igigi-gods await your command,[6]
The numerous people of this land[7] praise your valor.
You provide a comrade for the lonely man,   (10)
You give an heir to the impotent,
You open wide the fast doorbolts of heaven,
You provide light for the one who cannot see.
You can read the cased tablet that has not been opened,
You inscribe omens in sheep, you provide a verdict.[8]   (15)

1. Namrasit, a name of Sin, the moon-god.
2. That is, to those bereft of light, such as the sick.
3. Variant: "of the gods."
4. Temple of Shamash at Sippar.
5. Variant omits.
6. Variant: "heed."
7. Variant: "god and king, the people of this land."
8. Variant omits.

O judge of the gods, lord of the Igigi-gods,
O Shamash, you are master of the land's destiny,[1]
Ordain my destiny, make my course a propitious one!
May my signs be favorable,
May my dreams be propitious,
Make the dream I had[2] a propitious one for me,   (20)
Let me proceed in favor and acquire a comrade.[3]
May there be good fortune in my days,
Grant me a good repute!
May my speech be acceptable in public,[4]
May I pass my days in pleasure and joy,   (25)
May truth stand at my right,
May justice stand at my left,
May a safeguarding god go ever at my side,
May a watcher of well-being never cease to be behind me.
May Bunene, the courier,
    speak to you a favorable word (of me),   (30)
May Aya, your beloved wife, say, "Peace upon you!"[5]
O Shamash, you are foremost of the gods, have pity![6]
May the heavens rejoice because of you,
    may the earth rejoice because of you,
May the gods of the universe bless you,
May the great gods content your heart.[7]

Text: King, BMS 6, 97–130; Loretz-Mayer, AOAT 34 23; Myhrman, PBS 1/1 12; Langdon, OECT 6 pl. XXX, K 2854+K 17249 (not used); Gurney, STT 60+ 233 (see Gurney, AfO 28 [1981/2], 93), 61, 122; von Weiher, SBTU II 18; abbreviated version King, BMS 10, 7–25.
Edition: Mayer, UFBG, 503–510.
Translation: von Soden, SAHG, 318–320 no. 54; Seux, *Hymnes*, 283–286.
Literature: Mayer, UFBG, Šamaš 1; Lawson, *Fate*, 60–61; Butler, AOAT 258 (1998), 93, 308.

1. Variants list specific prognostications here (e.g., rodents) or rearrange lines.
2. Variant: "will have."
3. Variant: "comrades" = protective spirit(s)?
4. Literally: "in the street"; variant adds, "May god and king es[te]em me, May nobleman and prince do what I say."
5. Variant omits.
6. Variant adds: "May a god content your heart ..."
7. Variant replaces this and preceding with "May Anu, Enlil, and Ea grant [   ]."

(m) ABSOLVER

O Shamash, you are supreme judge of the great gods,   (1)
Whether, as I walked through a street,
    an accursed man touched me,
Or, when I crossed a square, I stepped in a puddle of wash water,
Or, I walked over nail pairings, shavings from an armpit,
A worn-out shoe, a broken belt, a leather sack
    (holding things) for black magic, a leper's scales,   (5)
(Any)thing unlucky for humankind,
Let it be released for me, let it be dissolved for me!
O Shamash, if in your view I have been neglectful this day,
If I sinned or erred or committed a crime,
Let it be released for me, let it be dissolved for me!   (10)
Through all my misdeeds, all my sins, all my crimes,
May the one who does not revere his (personal) god or his
    (personal) goddess learn from my example,
One who was neglectful of his (personal) god
    or of his (personal) goddess,
    who sinned, erred, committed a crime.
I gave my word then changed (it),
    I was trusted but did not deliver,
I did unseemly deeds, harmful speech was in my mouth,   (15)
I repeated what should not have been told.
I am an ox who does not recognize his forage,
I am the water of a watercourse that knows not where it runs.
The misdeeds and crimes of humankind
    outnumber the hairs of their heads!
My misdeeds, sins, and crimes that are heaped up like chaff,
    I have trampled them,   (20)
Let them be released for me, let them be dissolved for me!

(fragmentary lines)

Text: K 3059+ = Reiner, JNES 15 (1956), 142–143 (transliteration only); Ebeling, KAR 295 "1.
  Seite"; Finkelstein, STT 75, 26′–41′.
Edition: Reiner, JNES 15 (1956), 142–143, lines 40′–58′.
Translation: Seux, *Hymnes*, 409–410.
Literature: Compare also IV.51b, extracted from the same group.

(n) THE SUPREMACY OF SHAMASH

This text glorifies Shamash as the central creative power of the universe. Sin the moon-god, great as he may be, must take a secondary position.

i (= a 'rev.', b 'rev.' 1–17)

Without Shamash, king of heaven and earth,
    jud[ge] of the upper and lower regions,   (1)
Who renders verdicts, the young king Shamash,
Anu and Enlil would convoke no assembly in heaven,
Nor would they take counsel concerning the land.
They would produce no harvest in summer,
    nor in [win]ter dew, fog, and ice.   (5)
Pasturage, waterholes, grass, ear, or green plants,
[Vege]tation, subsistence for the beasts of the lands,
Without Shamash none would be granted!

Sin, chief god of heaven, great son of Enlil,
Sin, principal(?)* light of heaven and earth,   (10)
Who goes out before[1] the gods his brethren,
    prince whose command is [un]alterable,
The radiant god, splendid, noble [   ],
[Who determines] how many days (make) a month, a year,

(gap)
(fragmentary lines)

The gods convene when Sin appears,
Kings, bringing their pure offerings, prostrate themselves,
Whether to settle lands or to abandon them,
Whether to make them hostile to one another
    or war on one another:
They heed[2] Sin, the very luminary.   (10')
Without Sin and Shamash,
No other god in heaven will give an affirmative reply.[3]

---

1. Reference to precedence of Sin, perhaps referring to the appearance of the moon at night before the stars.
2. Reference to use of menologies or hemerologies for decision-making?
3. Reference to divination.

Without Shamash, Sin does not ...[1] in heaven,
Scepter, crown, throne, staff(?), where would they be?
They are not granted to king or his land without Shamash!   (15')
Without Shamash, king of heaven and earth,

(large gap = col. ii, iii)

iv (= a 'obv.', b 'obv.')

(Without Shamash ...)
Shakkan, the son(?) whom you love,   (1')
The pure herdsman, the leader for Anu,
Who carries the staff of office before his body,
Lord of headpiece, garment, and cloak,
Who carries a sublime staff, who is clad in a robe,   (5')
Who covers the nakedness[2]★ of the world,
No garment of rank★ nor royal attire,
No splendid crown, symbol of lordship,
Brings he, whatsoever, to king or to his land,
Without Shamash, none is granted.   (10')
Without Shamash, king of heaven and earth,
Latarak,[3] king of the steppe,
Who is supreme among the beasts,
Who overcomes cattle, sheep, wild beasts, and men,
Could not bring on his punishment,   (15')
Nor without Shamash [ ] would ...★
The wild creatures fall into no pit ...

(a breaks off, b ends excerpt)

Text: (a) Ebeling, KAR 19 (archaizing script); (b) Ehelolf, KBo 1 12 (excerpt tablet).
Edition: Ebeling, OrNS 23 (1954), 209–216.
Translation: Seux, Hymnes, 66–70, whose ordering of the text I follow.
★Notes to Text: (i 10) Beginning of line problematic. von Soden, AHw, 989b derives rīšu from rī'āšum; though rēšu "head" (for rēštu?) might be preferable on the basis of the parallelism. (iv 6') CAD B, 352a reads būl ṣēri "who clothes the beasts of the steppe." (iv 7') Seux, Hymnes, 69 note 34. (iv 16') b adds "Shakkan" here, perhaps a misunderstanding of ANŠE?

1. Verb broken, but the passage is evidently intended to subordinate the moon to the sun.
2. That is, wool and leather provide clothing for the human race.
3. Disease demon.

(o) HEALER

The following address to Shamash is part of an elaborate ritual against a variety of afflictions, including impotence, death of a spouse, and black magic of all types. It describes the sun's importance to the gods and the human race, especially the Mesopotamians.

> [O Sham]ash, pure lord, who administers heaven and earth,
> O Shamash the judge, (1)
> [O Shamash, l]ight of above and below,
> who brings about renewal,
> [   ] Shamash, pure lord, who administers heaven and earth,
> divine jud[ge],
> [O Shamash], light of above and below,
> who brings about renewal,
> O magnificent [or]b, who knows all and whose [   ] is final, (5)
> [O Shamash, c]reator of all there is,
> who makes all omens appropriate and understandable,
> [Who defines] time spans,
> who illumines all world regions and mountains,
> [O Shamash], yours is power to revive the dead,
> to release the captive,
> [O Shamash], the human race cannot continue without you,
> [Nor without you] can the decisions of heaven
> and netherworld be made. (10)
> [Without you] the gods of the universe smell no incense,
> [Without you] the (netherworld) Anunna-gods accept
> no funerary offering,
> [Without you] no case is judged in the land,
> no decision is made in the land,
> [Without you] the dream interpreter
> performs no rite for the king,
> [Without you the exorcist] cannot he[lp] the sick man, (15)
> [Without you Anu gives] no scepter, diadem,
> or st[aff?]* to the king.
> [Beloved of En]lil, leader of huma[nkind],*
> [Faithful shepherd] of the people of this land,

(one line lost)

[O Shamash, w]ithout you the [sick man cannot surviv]e,   (20)
[O Shamash, y]ou are the shepherd
    of all [numerous] humankind!
[I, so-and-so, son] of so-and-so, call upon you,
    exhausted, des[perate, sleepless].
[... affliction] has beset me, I knee[l before you].
[Lo]ss, des[truction], and ev[il against my spouse],
[And] my wives, my sons and daughters [have fastened]
    upon me and relentlessly cru[sh me].   (25)
[O Shamash],* yours is power to save, spare, and res[cue],
As you are generous, [spa]re life!
As you are wont to look with [radiant] features,
    let [the lord of lords]* so look upon me!
O lord, let me see [your light],
    let me warm myself in the [warmth] of your [rays].*
Let me praise your divinity [to] gods and goddesses,   (30)
L[et me proclaim] your [val]or [to all] the human race.
[Let me si]ng [your glorification,
    let me] sound your praises,
[And let] the ... [your servant], exalt your valor!*
[O Shamash, as you are foremost of the gods], have pity!
[Make my evil go] beyond mountain and cross river,*
    drive it 3600 leagues distant from my person.   (35)
[May it mount to the sky] like sm[oke],
    like an uprooted tamarisk, may it not return where it was.
May the tamarisk cleanse me, [may the ...-plant] release me,
May the <earth>* give me its splendor,
    may it take away [my aff]liction.
May the south wind blow toward me,
    but the evil [   ] not blow,
May the north wind blow toward me,
    but the evil [   ] not blow,   (40)
May the east wind blow toward me,
    but the evil [   ] not blow,
May the west wind blow toward me,
    but the evil [   ] not blow!
According to your august command,
    which cannot be ch[anged],

And your eternal assent, which cannot be altered,
May I, so-and-so, son of so-and-so, live in well-being,   (45)
Let me praise your greatness, [let me sound] your [praises]!

Text: Campbell Thompson, AMT 71–72/1, obv. 27 – rev. 24.
Edition: Ebeling, ZA 51 (1955), 170–179 obv. lines 27–44, rev. lines 1–24; most of the restorations used here are from him.
Translation: Seux, *Hymnes*, 454–457.
Notes to Text: (16) Seux, *Hymnes*, 455 note 11. (17) Ebeling, ZA 51 (1955), 172, 177. (26) Seux, *Hymnes*, 456. (28) Text: EN.E[N.MEŠ]: "the lords(?)." (29, 33) Mayer, OrNS 46 (1977), 392. (34) Text uncertain here, though the expressions are well known; see III.37d. (38) Seux, *Hymnes*, 457 note 32.

(p) AGAINST THE CONSEQUENCES OF A NIGHTMARE

You have burst into light, Shamash,   (1)
    from the Mountain of Cedars,[1]
The gods rejoice on account of you,
    humankind is glad on account of you.
The diviner brings you cedar, the widow a flour offering,
The poor woman oil, the rich man a lamb from his wealth.[2]
I bring you a clod of earth, product of the depths.   (5)
You, clod, product of the depths,
Part of me is pinched off in you,
Part of you is pinched off in me.
I am mixed with you,
You are mixed with me.
Just as you, clod, dissolve, dissipate, and disappear
    when you are thrown into water,   (10)
So may the evil [portended by the dream] I had last night,
Which I had about a god, which I had about a king,
    which I had about a noble,
    which I had about a prince,

1. Although the cedar mountain was often understood to be in the west (see I.3b), here it must refer to the east, perhaps the Zagros (for bibliography, see Butler, AOAT 258 [1998], 308).
2. The flour and oil were cheap, the cedar and lamp expensive (merismus, see George and Al-Rawi, *Iraq* 58 [1996], 174).

which I had about a dead man,
which I had about a living man,
In which I went to the right or turned to the left,
May it, like you, fall into water to dissolve,
dissipate, and disappear!
Sheep of a storm, slaughtered with a knife of air,[1]   (15)
The dead eat and drink, but (this dream) was nothing but air!
Just as the tip of the foot cannot come near the heel,
May the evil (portended) by the dream I had during the night
not approach me or come near me!

Text: Oppenheim, Dreams, pl. II, K 3333 = Butler, AOAT 258 (1998), pl. 3, 4; Gray, SRT, pl. III
K 3286 obv.; Ebeling, KAR 252, rev. i 20–36.
Edition: Butler, AOAT 258 (1998), 274–276, 298, with improvements adopted here.
Translation: Oppenheim, Dreams, 301; Seux, Hymnes, 369–371.

(q) HOMECOMING

This little bilingual prayer, designated to be used at sunset, portrays the sun
coming home to his abode, Ebabbar, at the end of the day. His gates hail him,
his steward escorts him inside, his wife meets him happily, and he has his
evening meal.

O Shamash, when you enter innermost heaven,   (1)
May the pure bolt of heaven greet you,
May the door of heaven salute you.
May Justice, your beloved vizier, bring you straight in.[2]
Show your splendor to the Ebabbar, your lordly dwelling.   (5)
May Aya, your beloved wife, meet you happily,
May she make you relax,
May your godly meal be set before you.
O youthful warrior Shamash, let them ever praise you.[3]

1. From a variant version of this spell (see Butler, AOAT 258 [1998], 279, line 52; 299); text
here has "slaughter." The idea may be that the nightmare was like an imaginary sheep produced
by disordered atmosphere and could be eliminated in the same fantastic way it appeared.
2. Wordplay in the original, justice and straightness having the same root.
3. Sumerian adds: "with one voice."

O lord of Ebabbar, go straight on your path, (10)
Make straight your way, go the true course to your dwelling.
O Shamash, you are judge of the land,
      administrator of its verdicts.

Text: Bertin, RA 1 (1886), 157–161; Abel-Winckler, *Keilschrifttexte zum Gebrauch bei Vorlesungen* (Berlin, 1890), 59–60.
Edition: Langdon, OECT 6, 11–12, 101.
Translation: Falkenstein, SAHG, 221 no. 42; Seux, *Hymnes*, 215–216.
Literature: Heimpel, JCS 38 (1986), 129–130.

III.52 TO SHAMASH AND ADAD

The following group of diviner's prayers are addressed to the principal deities of divination. They form part of a procedure in which ritual acts and prayers are interspersed. They are translated here as prose, though they are arranged in poetic form in the original manuscripts.

(a) THE CLEANSING WATER

O Shamash, lord of judgment, O Adad, lord of divination, cleanse yourselves! O Shamash, lord of judgment, O Adad, lord of divination, [here are brought you] pure water of the Amanus, sprigs from the mounts of apples(?) and cedar, fruit of cedar, cypress, alum, juniper, reed, and incense from the abode of [Irnina?]. The "pure mountains," the "children of Anu,"[1] are set up for you and fully purified, their [   ] are provided. Stand by me, O Shamash and Adad! In whatever I ask your blessing on, in what I [say] or pray, in whatsoever I do, in the inquiry I ask your blessing on, let there be truth!

Text: Zimmern, BBR, pl. LXII no. 75, 5–10.
Edition: Zimmern, BBR, 190–191.
Translation: Seux, *Hymnes,* 471–472.

(b) LIGHTING THE INCENSE

O Shamash, lord of judgment, O Adad, lord of divination, I burn for you pure cedar incense, branches, sprigs, sweet sap, bunches of pure cedar, beloved of the great gods. I burn bushy cedar as befits your great divinity. May the cedar linger, may it invite the great gods to render a verdict for me. Take your places and render a verdict! O Shamash and Adad, stand by me! In what I say or pray, in whatsoever I do, in the inquiry I ask your blessing on, let there be truth!

---

1. Types of offerings.

Text: Zimmern, BBR, pl. LXIII no. 75, 56–61; pl. LXIV no. 78, 56–61.
Edition: Zimmern, BBR, 192–193.
Translation: von Soden, SAHG, 278 no. 23a; Labat, *Religions*, 278; Seux, *Hymnes*, 472–473.

(c) PLACING THE FLOUR OFFERING

[O Shamash, lord of judgment], O Adad, lord of divination, accept (this)![1] O Shamash and Adad, who dwell in the pure heavens, O Shamash and Adad, may your great divinity accept (this)! O Shamash and [Ad]ad, accept this, accept the meal of all the great gods! O Anu, Enlil, Ea, Sin, Shamash, Belet-seri, Ninurta, accept this! In what I say and pray, in whatsoever I do, in the inquiry I ask your blessing on, let there be truth!

Text: Zimmern, BBR, pl. LXIV no. 78, rev. 69–74.
Edition: Zimmern, BBR, 194–195.
Translation: von Soden, SAHG, 279 no. 23c; Seux, *Hymnes*, 470–471.

(d) THE SACRIFICIAL GAZELLE

This prayer is notable for its lyrical portrayal of the growth of a young gazelle in the wilderness. It forms part of a group of diviner's prayers arranged for the offering of specific animals.

O Shamash, lord of judgment, O Adad, lord of divination, I bring and ask your blessing upon a pure fawn, offspring of a gazelle, whose eyes are bright-hued, whose features are radiant(?), a pure, tawny sacrificial animal, offspring of a gazelle, whose mother bore him in the steppe, and the steppe set its kind protection over him. The steppe raised him like a father, and the pasture like a mother. When the warrior Adad saw him, he would rain abundance(?) upon him in the earth's close: grass grew up, he would rejoice in (its) fullness, the ... of the livestock would sprout luxuriantly. He would eat grass in the steppe; never would he want for water to drink at pure pools. He would feed on the ...-

1. Refers to flour the diviner is placing on the incense stand.

plants and then return (to his haunts). He who never knew a herdsman [   ] in the steppe, from whom the lamb was kept away, I ask your blessing (upon him as my offering). O Shamash and Adad, stand by me! In what I say and pray, [in whatsoever I d]o, in the inquiry I ask your blessing on, let there b[e] truth!

Text: Craig, ABRT I, 60–62, obv. 12–22 (see 2, x).
Edition: Zimmern, BBR, 214–217 (with collations).
Translation: von Soden, SAHG, 278 no. 23b; Labat, *Religions*, 277–278; Seux, *Hymnes*, 473–474.

(e) THE SACRIFICIAL LAMB

[O Shamash, lord of judgment, O Ada]d, lord of divination, I bring and ask your blessing upon (this) yearling [lamb] that no ram has mounted, into which [no] beast's seed has fallen. It ate grass on the plains, it always drank water from pure pools, the male lamb was kept away from it. I ask your blessing upon (this) lamb, I set in this lamb's mouth pure cedar in bunches, sprigs, and sweet sap. O Shamash and Adad, stand by me in this lamb (offering). In what I say and pray, in whatsoever I do, in the inquiry I ask your blessing on, let there be truth!

Text: Craig, ABRT I, 61–62 obv. 10–17.
Edition: Zimmern, BBR, 216–217.
Translation: Labat, *Religions*, 277; Seux, *Hymnes*, 474–475.

III.53 TO SHAMASH AND MARDUK

This prayer formed part of a ritual to reconcile estranged couples and to reunite lost or separated people.

> O ever-renewing Shamash, perpetual light of the gods,   (1)
> O Marduk, ordainer of destinies,
> Who can make short times long,
> Who can gather in scattered people,
> You are the ones who can bring together people
>   who are far apart,
>   can bring together the fugitive, the absconded.   (5)
> O Shamash and Marduk, you are the ones
>   who grant togetherness to young man and woman,
>   who provide the solitary young man with a companion,
> O Shamash and Marduk, you are the ones to bring back safely
>   [to] their [city] the one whose city is distant,
>   whose [journey] is afar off, who have been led into
>   captivity or imprisoned,
> With you, O Shamash and Marduk, is to bring
>   an abandoned wife back to her husband.
> I, your servant, owing to the anger of my (personal) god or
>   my (personal) goddess, go about alone,
> My years have gone by me in numbness and woe.   (10)
> Stand by me now! With your sublime command,
>   which cannot be changed, your firm "yes,"
>   which cannot be transgressed,
> Grant us togetherness, the ones led into captivity, kidnapped,
>   abandoned, forgotten, or far away,
>   who were once close!
> Obliterate the unhappiness from our hearts,
> Make our lives longer, grant us years of life into the future.
> [Let me] sound your praises to the numerous people.   (15)

Text: Ebeling, RA 49 (1955), 142–145 A-186; von Weiher, SBTU III 79; Maul, *Zukunftsbewältigung*, 549 K 6362, 550 Sm 824, 551 BM 72232.
Edition: Maul, *Zukunftsbewältigung*, 409–414.

III.54 TO SIN

(a) FOR HELP IN HARUSPICY

This prayer to the moon-god is one of many for the use of diviners preparing at night to examine the livers and entrails of animals to be slaughtered for divinatory purposes. It glorifies the beauty and majesty of the moon, seeking his help in the rite to follow.

O Sin, shining, radiant god, luminary of [heaven],
    firstborn son of Enlil, [foremost one] of Ekur,   (1)
You reign as king of the uni[verse],
    you s[et] your throne [in] the [shining] heavens,
You set out a superb linen,
    you [don] the resplendent tiara of lordship
    whose waxing never fails!
O noble Sin, whose light goes be[fore] the people,
    resplendent prince
Whose command is never cha[nged],
    whose intents no god can know!   (5)
O Sin, at your appearance the gods convene,
    all sovereigns do obeisance,
O luminary Sin, [   ], you come out amidst shining
    carnelian and lapis.
At sight of Sin, the stars are jubilant, the night rejoices.
Sin takes his place in the center of the shi[ning] heaven,
    Sin, the cherished eldest son, belo[ved] offspring.
Solicitous prince, eldest son of Enlil, foremost [ ],   (10)
Luminary of the skies, lord of all lands
    whose [head?] is h[igh?] in Ekur,
Whose word is assented to in Eridu [   ],
You founded Ur on a [ ] dais*
    [and raised its] head(?) [on high],
O Sin, luminary of heaven,
    protection of [the inhabited world?], shining god [   ],
Foremost one, Sin, you [open] the gates of heaven
    when you appear.   (15)
At your appearance, the peoples rejoice,

all the people of this land [are joyful],★
The peoples pray to you,
    all humankind convenes before you.
Sheep, goats, and cattle, creatures of the steppe
    all convene before [you].
Sin has come forth, lord of crescent and halo,
    who administers pasture and drink[ing place],★
Stand by me, Sin, in the midst★ of shining heaven,
    may the [great] gods stand by.   (20)
May the divine judges stand by with you,
    the ... [   ] stand by,
May Alammush your vizier inform you,
    bring the case before you,
May he set the diviner's qu[ery] before you.
    O Sin, shining god, [stand by me] in this offering!
In what I say or pray, in whatsoever I do, in the inquiry
    I ask your blessing on, let there be truth!

Text: K 3794 + Ki 1904–10–9,157 = Perry, *Sin*, pl. I K 3794 (17ff. =1–13 of this translation) +
  Langdon, RA 12 (1915), 190 (= 13–24 of this translation); K 2792+7973+9242+10011+13785 =
  Perry, *Sin*, pl. II (ii 13ff. = 1–16 of this translation), all mss. collated.
Edition: Perry, *Sin*, 23–24 + Langdon, RA 12 (1915), 191–192.
Translation: Seux, *Hymnes,* 478–480.
★*Notes to Text*: (13) *pa-rak*-[*ki*]. The AR.KI copied by Langdon at the top of his plate is not clear on
  the tablet; perhaps ⌜*ri-ši*⌝. (16) Seux, *Hymnes*, 479 note 20. (19) Seux, *Hymnes*, 479 note 23. (20)
  Seux, *Hymnes*, 479 note 24.

(b) ILLUMINATOR OF DARKNESS

O Sin, luminous and splendid one, foremost of the gods,   (1)
O perpetually renewing Sin, illuminator of darkness,
Provider of illumination to the teeming peoples,
Your brilliance is released to the people of this land,
Your rising illumines the p[ure?] heavens,   (5)
Your torch[1] is magnificent, your ra[diance?] is like fire.
The vast earth is filled with your luminosity,
The people proud(ly) vie to see you.[2]
O Anu of the heavens, whose counsel no one can learn,
Your rising is superb as [your] offspring, the sun.   (10)
The great gods kneel before you,
        the verdict(s) of the world are placed before you.[3]
The great gods inquire of you and you give advice,[4]
They sit in assembly, they debate at your feet.   (15)
O Sin, splendid one of the Ekur, they inquire of you
        and you give (reply) to the gods' inquiry.
Your day of disappearance is your day of splendor,[5]
        a secret of the great gods.
The thirtieth day is your festival,
        day of your divinity's splendor.
O Brightly Rising One,[6] strength without rival,
        whose intent no one can learn,[7]
I make for you a pure night offering,
        I libate for you the finest sweet beer.[8]   (20)
I take my place on my knees, as I seek you(r attention),
Grant me a favorable and just oracle.
My (personal) god and <my> (personal) goddess,
        who have been angry with me for many days,
May they be reconciled with me in truth and justice.

1. Variant: "rising."
2. Variant adds: ... "they constantly heed your divinity."
3. Variant inserts prayer to avert the evil portended by an eclipse; see p. 637 note 2.
4. Variant adds seven different lines, mostly fragmentary.
5. That is, prior to reappearing as the new moon.
6. Namrasit, a name for Sin.
7. Variant adds here a royal name, with "your servant."
8. Variant adds: "With the holy ... I invoke your name and call upon you, my lord, in the pure heavens ..."

May my path be propitious, my way straight. (25)
If he commissioned Anzagar, god of dreams,
Let him absolve my wrong in a dream.
Let me be well, let my wrong-doing be cleansed,*
Let me sound your praises forever!

Text: King, BMS 1, 1–27; Loretz-Mayer, AOAT 34 1; Finkelstein, STT 56, 19–37; Ebeling-Köcher-Rost, LKA 39; Langdon, PSBA 40 (1918), pl. VII; Scheil, SFS 18; additional mss. cited by Mayer, UFBG, 490 and Butler, AOAT 258 (1998), 380. Minor variants and rearrangements of the text in the mss. are not noted here.

Edition: Mayer, UFBG, 490–494; Butler, AOAT 258 (1998), 379–389, 391–392, with improvements adopted here.

Translation: Stephens, ANET³, 386; von Soden, SAHG, 316–317 no. 52; Labat, *Religions,* 284–285; Seux, *Hymnes,* 278–280.

Literature: Mayer, UFBG, Sin 1; Sperl, BSOAS 57 (1994), 221–225.

Notes to Text: (28) Butler, AOAT 258 (1998), 394–395.

III.55 TO SIN AND SHAMASH

A royal prayer to be said upon commencing an enterprise.

O Sin and Shamash, gods both,   (1)
Sin of the night, Shamash of all the day,
You <pronounce> the verdicts of heaven and earth.
You look each day upon the dimensions of day,
        month, and year.
O Sin and Shamash, it is you who ordain the destiny of the lands, (5)
You are the remote gods
Who daily control(?)* the speech of the people.
Without you no regular offering is set out
        among the Igigi-gods,
You light all the Anunna-gods like the day.*
You prepare(?) their food portions,
        you take care of their chapels.   (10)
The lands rejoice at your appearance,
They watch for you carefully,[1] [n]ight [and day].*
It is you who stands by to dissolve the unfavorable signs
        of heaven and earth.
I, your servant, who watch for you,
Who daily gaze upon your faces,   (15)
Who am attentive to your appearance,
Make my unfavorable signs pass away from me,
Set for my person propitious and favorable omens,
Order for me that my reign be long-lasting
        and watch over (it) together!
Grant me your radiant beacons,   (20)
Let me constantly bless you, night and day,
And let me proclaim your greatness to the heights!

Text: Lutz, PBS 1/2 106, rev. 3–25.
Edition: Ebeling, ArOr 17 (1949), 179–181.
Translation: von Soden, SAHG, 342–343 no. 68; Seux, *Hymnes,* 490–491.
Literature: Mayer, UFBG, Sin und Šamaš 1.
Notes to Text: (7) Seux, *Hymnes,* 459 note 5; CAD Ḫ, 119b; AHw, 343a. (12) von Soden, SAHG, 490.

    1. Perhaps a reference to lunar observation, for example, time of appearance and disappearance.

III.56 TO ANY GOD

According to its subscription, this bilingual address, consisting of a prayer, confession, lament, and concluding supplication, could be used for any deity.

May (my) lord's angry heart be reconciled, (1)
May the god I do not know be reconciled,
May the goddess I do not know be reconciled,
May the god, whoever he is, be reconciled,
May the goddess, whoever she is, be reconciled, (5)
May my (personal) god's heart be reconciled,
May my (personal) goddess's heart be reconciled,
May (my) god and (my) goddess be reconciled (with me)!
May the god who [has turned away]* from me
    [in anger be re]conciled,
May the goddess [who has turned away from me in anger
    be reconciled], (10)
[I do not know] what wrong [I have done],
[   ] the wrong [   ].
[My god did not call my name]* with favor,
[My goddess did not call my name] with favor,
[My god did not] pronounce my name [with favor], (15)
[My goddess did not pronounce my name with favor].
I could not eat for myself the bread I found,[1]
I could not drink for myself the water I found.
I have perpetrated un[wittingly] an abomination to my god,
I have unwittingly violated a taboo of my goddess. (20)
O (my) lord, many are my wrongs, great my sins,
O my god, many are my wrongs, great my sins,
O my goddess, many are my wrongs, great my sins,
O god, whoever you are, many are my wrongs, great my sins,
O goddess, whoever you are, many are my wrongs,
    great my sins! (25)
I do not know what wrong I have done,
I do not know what sin I have committed,
I do not know what abomination I have perpetrated,

---

1. That is, he offered it all to his gods in vain (Maul, HBKl, 245).

I do not know what taboo I have violated!
A lord has glowered at me in the anger of his heart,   (30)
A god has made me face the fury of his heart,⋆
A goddess has become enraged at me
      and turned me into a sick man,
A god, whoever he is, has excoriated me,
A goddess, whoever she is, has laid misery upon me!
I keep on searching, but nobody will help me,   (35)
When I wept, they would not draw near,
When I would make a complaint, no one would listen,
I am miserable, blindfolded, I cannot see!
Turn toward me, merciful god, as I implore you.[1]
I do homage to you, my goddess,
      as I keep groveling before you,   (40)
O god, whoever you are,
      [turn toward me, I implore you],
O goddess, [whoever you are,
      turn toward me, I implore you],
O lord, tur[n toward me, I implore you],
O goddess, lo[ok upon me, I implore you],
O god, [whoever you are, turn toward me,
      I implore you],   (45)
O goddess, whoever [you are, turn toward me,
      I implore you]!
How long, O my god, [until your furious heart is calmed]?
How long, O my goddess,
      [until your estranged heart is reconciled]?
How long, O god, whosoever you are,
      until y[our angry heart is calmed]?
How long, O goddess, whosoever you are,
      until your estranged heart is reconciled?   (50)
Humans are slow-witted and know nothing,
No matter how many names they go by, what do they know?
They do not know at all if they are doing good or evil!
O (my) lord, do not cast off your servant,
He is mired in a morass, help him!   (55)

---

1. Here and in the next three lines Akkadian has "I keep turning toward my merciful god."

Turn the sin that I perpetrated into virtue,[1]
Let the wind bear away the wrong I committed!
Many are my crimes, strip them off like a garment,
O my god, though my wrongs be seven times seven,
    absolve my wrongs,
O my goddess, though my wrongs be seven times seven,
    absolve my wrongs,   (60)
O god, whosoever you are,
    though my wrongs be seven times seven,
    absolve my wrongs,
O goddess, whosoever you are,
    though my wrongs be seven times seven,
    absolve my wrongs,
Absolve my wrongs, let me sound your praises!
As if you were my real mother, let your heart be reconciled,
As if you were my real mother, my real father,
    let your heart be reconciled!   (65)

Text: Pinches, IV R² 10 (see also Maul, HBKl, pl. 38).
Edition: Maul, HBKl, 236–246.
Translation: Stephens, ANET³, 391–392; Falkenstein, SAHG, 225–228 no. 45; Seux, *Hymnes,* 139–143.
Literature: Y. Rosengarten, *Trois aspects de la pensée religieuse sumérienne* (Paris, 1971), 133–163.
★*Notes to Text*: (9) Seux, *Hymnes,* 140 note 8. (13) Falkenstein, SAHG, 226. (31) Differently Seux, *Hymnes,* 141 note 20.

---

1. Sumerian in this and the following lines has preterites, "he turned ..."

III.57 PRAYER FOR LAYING
THE FOUNDATION OF A TEMPLE

O Enmesharra,[1] lord of the netherworld,
    prince of the infernal regions,   (1)
Lord of (this)* place and of the land of no return,
    mountain of the Anunna-gods,
Who pronounces the verdicts of the netherworld,
    great bond of Andurunna,[2]
O great lord, without whom Ningirsu regulates
    no dikes or canals, nor forms furrows,
Champion who mastered the netherworld by his strength,   (5)
Who made heavy its fetter,
    grasping the circuit of the netherworld,
Grantor of scepter and staff(?) to Anu and Enlil,
May, at your command, the foundation of this place
    endure before you,
May this brickwork be as lasting as your lordly abode
    in the netherworld!
May Anu, Enlil, and Ea take up lasting residence there.   (10)
And I too, so-and-so, the prince, your servant,
May I always be called by a good name
    in your divine presence.
May th(is) abode of the great gods be eternal(?),
May all my land dwell in peaceful abode.

Text: Craig, ABRT 2 13, 1–16 (+, see Borger, ZA 61 [1971], 72–74).

Edition: Borger, ZA 61 (1971), 72–80, lines 42–57.

Translation: von Soden, SAHG, 345–346 no. 71; Seux, *Hymnes*, 492–493.

Notes to Text: (2) So Seux, *Hymnes*, 492 note 6 (compare line 8); otherwise, perhaps a euphemism for the netherworld.

---

   1. Ancestor of Anu and Enlil (George, *Topographical Texts*, 277).

   2. A cosmic locality, here evidently meaning where heaven and netherworld are linked. Compare p. 440 note 2.

III.58 LITIGANT'S PRAYER

This little bilingual prayer, written in Akkadian on one side of the tablet and in Sumerian on the other, forms part of a family archive of legal and business documents from Kassite Babylonia (ca. 1500–1200 B.C.). It may reflect the anxieties of a person embroiled in a lawsuit or other difficulties. Some idea of the troubles this family faced may be gleaned from Text 96 in the archive, a list of transactions including several outrages or abuses. First, a plow is taken away on the day cultivation was supposed to begin, second, some equipment, including a wagon, was stolen or misappropriated, and third, the remaining wagons were purloined and someone was incapacitated from work or detained at threshing time. Although there is no reason to assume that the texts are related to each other, these are the sorts of problems that the supplcant had on his mind.

> Shamash, my ... has sealed it, (1)
> Nabu, master of my truthfulness, has sealed it,
> May my harasser disappear!
> May my ill-wisher be plucked out!
> I put my trust in my god, (5)
> Let Nabu judge(?) my case(?),
> Let me see a favorable (outcome)
> through the command of Nabu!

Text: F. Peiser, *Urkunden aus der Zeit der dritten babylonischen Dynastie* ... (Berlin, 1905), 92.
Edition: Peiser, *Urkunden*, 4.

H. Miscellaneous Expressive Compositions

III.59 THE MONKEY MAN

In this spoof legal document drawn up on a clay model of a simian or human foot, a woman adopts a monkey rescued from the river (in the manner of Sargon of Akkad, see IV.18), proclaiming a frightful penalty for any "monkey business" with her adopted son. For monkeys in Mesopotamia, see S. Dunham, "The Monkey in the Middle," ZA 75 (1985), 234–264. Compare IV.26.

> Ms. Anhuti-remeni,[1] slave woman of Ms. Kursibtu,[2] the palace woman of Assur-iddin,[3] who lifted Naru-eriba,[4] the monkey-man, out of the river, has raised him. He is her son. Whosoever shall bring a lawsuit or complaint concerning him, he shall give up six sons and let him go free. In accordance with the command of the gods, they must not monkey with this monkey. February 1, eponym year of Adad-resh-ishi.[5]
> Witness: Sin, Shamash, Ishtar, Gula.

Text: Wilhelm, *Jahrbuch des Museums für Kunst und Gewerbe Hamburg* NF 4 (1985), 23.

Edition: S. Franke, G. Wilhelm, "Eine mittelassyrische Fiktive Urkunde zur Wahrung des Anspruchs auf ein Findelkind," *Jahrbuch des Museums für Kunst und Gewerbe Hamburg* NF 4 (1985), 19-26 (with photos of object).

1. The name may mean something like "My-exhaustion-is-merciful-to-me," presumably a joke, but obscure.

2. The name means "Butterfly."

3. The name means "Assur-has-given," and should be the name of a king, but no such king is known. This too may be a joke.

4. The name means "The-river-god-has-provided-a-replacement-child."

5. In Assyria, years were named after high officials, referred to as "eponyms." This date would fall in the eleventh century B.C.

III.60 THE BALLAD OF FORMER HEROES

This Akkadian drinking song, known in widely variant versions from both Syria and Mesopotamia, was originally a Sumerian text about ancient rulers studied in schools and provided with an Akkadian translation during the Classical period. It enumerates great heroes of the past who have vanished, then recommends intoxication as preferable to despair.

Plans are made by Enki, (1)
Lots are drawn by the gods' will.
From former days only empty air remains:
Whenever has aught been heard from any who went before?
These kings were superior to those, and others to them. (5)
Your 'eternal abode' is above their homes,[1]
It is far away as heaven, whose hand can reach it?
Like the depths of the earth, no one knows anything of it.
The whole of a life is but the twinkling of an eye,
The life of humankind is surely not forever. (10)
Where is king Alulu, who reigned for 36,000 years?[2]
Where is king Etana, who went up to heaven?[3]
Where is Gilgamesh, who sought life like Ziusudra?[4]
Where is Huwawa, who was seized and
    knocked to the ground(?)?
Where is Enkidu, who [showed] forth strength in the land? (15)
Where is Bazi? Where is Zizi?[5]
Where are the great kings from former days till now?
They will not be begotten (again),
    they will not be born (again),

1. That is, you will someday be buried above where people once lived, a reference to the progressive growth of ancient city mounds, or tells, in Mesopotamia.
2. Antediluvian king of Eridu, credited with a reign of 28,800 years in Sumerian historical tradition.
3. See III.22.
4. Gilgamesh and his friend Enkidu, as well as the monster Huwawa, appear in the group of Sumerian poems about the exploits of Gilgamesh, king of Uruk. These were later reworked into a lengthy Akkadian narrative poem (see Foster, *Gilgamesh*). Ziusudra was the Sumerian flood hero.
5. Two kings of Mari.

How far did a life without glamor transcend death?
Fellow, I will teach you truly who your god is,   (20)
Cast down unhappiness in triumph,
    forget the silence (of death)!
Let one day of happiness make up for 36,000 years of
    the silence (of death)!
Let the beer-goddess rejoice over you
    as if you were her own child!
That is the destiny of humankind.

Text: Arnaud, *Emar* 767; Nougayrol, *Ugaritica* 5 164–166 (pp. 438–440); Alster and Jeyes, ASJ 8 (1986), 10–11; Pinches, CT 44 18 ii'; see Alster, OLP 21 (1990), 6–7.
Edition: Wilcke in J. von Ungern-Sternberg, H. Reinau, eds., *Colloquium Rauricum* 1, *Vergangenheit in mündlicher Überlieferung* (Stuttgart, 1988), after p. 138; Alster OLP 21 (1990), 5–25; Dietrich, UF 24 (1992), 9–29; Kämmerer, AOAT 251 (1998), 208–213.
Translation: W. G. Lambert, "Some New Babylonian Wisdom Literature," in J. Day *et al.*, eds., *Wisdom in Ancient Israel, Essays in Honour of J. A. Emerton* (Cambridge, U.K., 1995), 37–42; J. Klein, "'The Ballad about Early Rulers' in Eastern and Western Traditions," CRRAI 42 (1992), 9–29.
Literature: Alster, N.A.B.U. 1999/88(D).

CHAPTER IV

THE LATE PERIOD
(1000–100 B.C.)

The Late period of Assyro-Babylonian literature is characterized both by preservation and standardization of Mesopotamian written tradition and by production of vital new works. It is often difficult to decide whether a text was composed in the Late or Mature period.[1] Scholars agree that many important and original works, such as Erra and Ishum, were composed during the Late period, even if they disagree over what other works to date to this period.

As part of the standardization of Assyro-Babylonian written tradition in the Late period, related texts were compiled into "series." Within a series, the title of which was normally the first half-line of text (incipit), the tablets were numbered in sequence. Numbered tablets therefore correspond to chapters of modern works.[2] Colophons at the ends of tablets in a series provided information such as the number of tablets in the series; the name, title, parentage, and family name of the copiest; the date the manuscript was copied; a statement about the collation of the text (for example, copied from an older manuscript, compiled from manuscripts from different cities); an injunction to safeguard the manuscript.[3]

The largest and most important group of these tablet series consists of scholarly works, which are essential components of the Mesopotamian literary heritage. Scholarship had, of course, specialties, such as divination, astrology, magic, and exorcism, Sumerian cult laments and medicine, each with its own often substantial written sources and specific techniques and approaches.

All branches of scholarship depended on literacy, and the basic evidence for literacy includes lexical texts, or lists of names, words, and phrases from Sumerian, Akkadian, and occasionally other ancient Mesopotamian languages, studied and memorized as part of education. Lists are attested in standardized forms

---

1. W. von Soden, "Das Problem der zeitlichen Einordnung akkadischer Literaturwerke," MDOG 85 (1953), 14–26; E. Reiner, "First-Millennium Babylonian Literature," CAH[3] 3/2, 293–321.
2. W. W. Hallo, "New Viewpoints on Cuneiform Literature," IEJ 12 (1962), 23–24.
3. H. Hunger, *Babylonische und assyrische Kolophone*, AOAT 2 (1968); E. Leichty, "The Colophon," *Studies Oppenheim*, 147–154; L. Pearce, "Statements of Purpose: Why the Scribes Wrote," *Studies Hallo*, 185–193.

as early as the mid-third millennium B.C. Many appear to be pedagogically oriented. One important group of lexical texts is arranged graphically, that is, by cuneiform signs, simple and compound. Another group is arranged semantically, for example, words for animals, stones, wooden objects, fish, pottery, and other things. Lists can include divine and personal names, stars, planets, and temples, as well as Sumerian legal formulae that could have been encountered in contracts and legal documents as late as the mid-second millennium B.C. Lists of foreign, rare, and dialectal Akkadian words occur, as well as lists that assign numbers to cuneiform signs as if for cryptographic purposes.[1]

Texts on divination make up the bulk of Assyro-Babylonian scholarly writings. Divination, in its many forms, was both the most highly esteemed intellectual endeavor in Mesopotamian civilization and the one for which Babylonia was famed in the Mediterranean world. Divination was related to Mesopotamian historical tradition because it sometimes preserved prognoses of certain significant events of the past, such as the death of kings under unusual circumstances. Divination was concerned not so much with the cause of an event, that being a matter of divine will, as it was with what might presage an event. The scientific labor of divination required collection of portents and consequences in encyclopedic form. This allowed a diviner to identify portents from the past similar to those before him, and to know consequences of those portents in the past. Knowledge of portents could lead to control of events, because a diviner could then take corrective or preventive measures to save a person from harm or ensure him good fortune. Some of the omens collected in the series were actual occurrences; others were evidently reasoned analogically or hermeneutically according to principles not always apparent to a modern reader.[2]

Collection of omens into series resulted in several large compilations including different types of information. Certain collections had individual significance, whereas others contained omens affecting the community at large.[3] Tak-

1. A. Cavigneaux, "Lexikalische Listen," RLA 6, 609–641; D. O. Edzard, "Sumerisch-akkadische Listenwissenschaft und andere Aspekte altmesopotamischer Rationalität," in K. Groy, ed., Rationalitätstypen (Freiburg, 1999), 246–267; see also p. 5 note 5.

2. J. Bottéro, "Symptomes, signes, écritures," in J. P. Vernant, ed., Divination et Rationalité (Paris, 1974), 70–193; more briefly, "Divination and the Scientific Spirit," Mesopotamia, 125–137; La Divination en Mésopotamie Ancienne (Paris, 1966); U. Jeyes, "Divination and Science in Ancient Mesopotamia," JEOL 32 (1991/2), 23–41; "The Art of Extispicy in Ancient Mesopotamia, An Outline," Assyriological Miscellanea 1 (1980), 13–32; A. L. Oppenheim, Ancient Mesopotamia, Portrait of a Dead Civilization (Chicago, 1977), 206–227; B. Böck, "Babylonische Divination und Magie," in Renger, ed., Babylon, 409–425. For a concise survey, see S. Maul, "Omina und Orakel," RLA 10, 45–88.

3. F. Rochberg, Babylonian Horoscopes, Transactions of the American Philosophical Society 88/1 (1998).

ing of omens for events of public significance (for example, construction of a monumental building, beginning a military campaign, installing a high official in office) is attested by the third millennium B.C. and continued until the end of cuneiform tradition (see, for example, III.7b and III.51n, lines 7′–10′).

Some omens were deductive: based on observation and assessment of events. These might include the behavior of animals and birds,[1] sounds overheard in the street,[2] dreams,[3] or monstrous births.[4] Other omens were deliberately induced by following certain procedures and then studying and recording the consequences. These procedures included extispicy, sacrificing a sheep and studying its entrails, liver, and gall bladder under controlled conditions,[5] pouring oil on water and studying its appearance,[6] or burning incense and watching the smoke rise.[7] Diviners were among the most esteemed literate professionals in Mesopotamia. They appear in literature as consultants (III.14 Tablet II, lines 6–9). Many of the prayers translated in Chapters II and III were to be spoken by diviners and exorcists; some of them refer directly to personal concerns such as reputation and professional competence (II.27, 28; III.36a, 52, 53a).

Medical series also included omens.[8] Some deal with physical symptoms, others with events observed by the exorcist or physician on his way to the

---

1. Bottéro, *Symptomes*, 105–106; J.-M. Durand, "La divination par les oiseaux," MARI 8 (1997), 273–282; Maul, RLA 7, 82–83.

2. A. L. Oppenheim, "Sumerian: inim.gar, Akkadian: *egirrû* = Greek kledon," AfO 17 (1954/6), 49–55; Bottéro, *Symptomes* (p. 772 note 2), 98–99.

3. A. L. Oppenheim, *The Interpretation of Dreams in the Ancient Near East, with a Translation of the Assyrian Dream-Book, Transactions of the American Philosophical Society* NS 46/3 (1956), 179–373. A brief account is found in G. von Grunebaum *et al.*, eds., *The Dream and Human Societies* (Berkeley, 1966), 341–350 and a general study by S. Butler, *Mesopotamian Concepts of Dreams and Dream Rituals*, ASOAT 258 (1998); W. Sommerfeld, "Traumdeutung als Wissenschaft und Therapie im Alten Orient," in A. Karenberg, C. Leitz, eds., *Heilkunde und Hochkultur* I (Münster, 2000), 201–219; A. Zgoll, "Die Welt im Schlaf sehen — Inkubation von Träumen im antiken Mesopotamien," WdO 32 (2002), 74–101; Maul, RLA 7, 68–69.

4. E. Leichty, *The Omen Series šumma izbu*, TCS 4 (1970); Maul, RLA 7, 62–64.

5. Bottéro, *Symptomes* (p. 772 note 2), 179–181; U. Jeyes, *Old Babylonian Extispicy Omen Texts in the British Museum* (Leiden, 1989); I. Starr, *The Ritual of the Diviner*, BM 12 (1983), "Chapters 1 and 2 of the *bārûtu*," SAAB 6 (1992), 45–53.

6. G. Pettinato, *Die Ölwahrsagung bei den Babyloniern*, Studi Semitici 21–22 (Rome, 1966); Maul, RLA 7, 83–84.

7. G. Pettinato, "Libanomanzia presso i Babilonesi," RSO 41 (1966), 303–327; R. D. Biggs, "À propos des textes de libanomancie," RA 63 (1969), 73–74; E. Leichty, "Smoke Omens," Studies Finkelstein, 143–144; I. Finkel, "A New Piece of Libanomancy," AfO 29/30 (1983/4), 50–55; Maul, RLA 7, 84–85.

8. R. D. Biggs, "Medicine in Ancient Mesopotamia," *History of Science* 8 (1961), 94–105; "Medizin," RLA 7, 623–629; H. Avalos, *Illness and Health Care in the Ancient Near East, Harvard Semitic Museum Monographs* 54 (1995). See also General Introduction, p. 35 note 1.

patient's bedside.[1] Others are physiognomatic omens that assess various human physical and behavioral characteristics as favorable or unfavorable.[2]

Extensive astrological omen collections, made in the Late period, tend to presage events affecting the king, the government, or the community. So great was the esteem astrology enjoyed in the Late period that the astrological series "When Anu and Enlil" (seven thousand or more astrological omens) was said to have been written by the antediluvian sage Adapa.[3]

The most extensive omen series is the terrestrial group entitled "If a City Is Situated on a Height." This series of over one hundred tablets deals with settlements and houses, atmospheric phenomena, birds, animals, reptiles, insects, plants, trees, and other aspects of the everyday Mesopotamian environment.[4] Even when large series were standardized, empirical collection of ominous data continued throughout the Late period.[5]

Divination and ritual were closely connected. Divination implies the ability to read and predict divine will, ritual, to avert presaged evil or to bring about desired consequences. Ritual texts contain prescribed utterances, such as incantations or prayers, together with complicated magical procedures often described in detail to ward off presaged evil. Such texts are known in great numbers from the Late period.[6] Rituals and their accompanying prayers and incantations were concerned largely with matters of health and well-being, including physical illness that could be treated pharmacologically or by exorcism, as well as mental illness: depression, feelings of inadequacy, persecution, neurosis, psychosis, abnormal behavior.[7] Sympathetic magic played an

---

1. R. Labat, *Traité akkadien de diagnostics et prognostics médicaux* (Leiden, 1951); P. Herrero, *Thérapeutique mésopotamienne*, ed. M. Sigrist (Paris, 1984); Maul, RLA 7, 64–66.

2. B. Böck, *Die Babylonisch-Assyrische Morphoskopie*, AfO Beiheft 27 (2000); Maul, RLA 7, 66–68.

3. F. Rochberg-Halton, "New Evidence for the History of Astrology," JNES 43 (1984), 115–140; E. Reiner, *Astral Magic in Babylonia, Transactions of the American Philosophical Society* 85/4 (1995); U. Koch-Westenholz, *Mesopotamian Astrology, An Introduction to Babylonian and Assyrian Celestial Divination* (Copenhagen, 1995); for publication information on the astrological series Enuma Anu Enlil, see Maul, RLA 7, 51–57.

4. S. M. Freedman, *If a City Is Set on a Height, The Akkadian Omen Series Šumma Alu ina Mēlê Šakin*, OPSNKF 17 (1998); Maul, RLA 7, 58–62.

5. D. J. Wiseman, "Assyrian Writing Boards," *Iraq* 17 (1955), 3–13.

6. Maul, *Zukunftsbewältigung*; in summary in "How the Babylonians Protected Themselves against Calamities Announced by Omens," in Abusch, ed., *Magic*, 123–129.

7. J. V. Kinnier Wilson, "An Introduction to Babylonian Psychiatry," AS 16 (1968), 289–298; Edith K. Ritter and J.V. Kinnier Wilson, "Prescription for an Anxiety State: A Study of BAM 234," AnSt 30 (1980), 23–30; J. V. Kinnier Wilson, "Mental Diseases of Ancient Mesopotamia," in D. Brothwell *et al.*, eds., *Diseases in Antiquity* (Springfield, Ill., 1967), 723–733; M. Stol, "Psychosomatic Suffering in Ancient Mesopotamia," in Abusch, ed., *Magic*, 57–68.

important part in medical rituals, which often prescribed symbolic washing off of the evil or interment, submersion, or burning of the sorcerer in the form of figurines created for the purpose.[1] Apotropaic rituals could ward off potential evils, while healing rituals dealt with evil already encountered.[2] Charms sought to bring about a personal consequence such as sexual contact, love, marriage, or successful childbirth.[3] Texts focusing on magic figurines, or on monsters and demons and their appearances, underlie the imagery of IV.5.[4] Rituals having to do with statues and images are referred to as "Cleansing the Mouth."[5]

The ritual series "House of the Ritual Bath" incorporated Sumerian and Akkadian prayers, the purpose of which was to cleanse the speaker, presumed to be the king, from contamination brought upon him by sorcery or other causes.[6] These prayers, sometimes called incantation prayers, often resort to legal phraseology, as if the god is judging the speaker's case or petition against an adversary in court (for example, II.28 and III.40c).

The exorcistic series called *Maqlû* "Burning" is primarily concerned with warding off the effects of black magic, especially through the burning or melting of figurines.[7] *Shurpu* "Incineration" is concerned primarily with evil from within the individual or of unknown origin, where fire purifies the affected person.[8] Various other series against sorcery, spells, and curses exist, some with long lists of possible evils in fixed sequences.[9]

1. See for example III.51h, lines 31–41, III.40b, lines 11–12.

2. See p. 774 note 6 and IV.51

3. IV.50, 53.

4. F. Wiggermann, *Babylonian Prophylactic Figures: The Ritual Texts* (Amsterdam, 1986); E. Reiner, "Magic Figurines, Amulets, and Talismans," in A. Farkas *et al.*, eds., *Monsters and Demons in the Ancient and Medieval Worlds: Papers Presented in Honor of Edith Porada* (Mainz, 1987), 27–36.

5. C. Walker, M. Dick, *The Induction of the Cult Image in Ancient Mesopotamia, The Mesopotamian Mis Pî Ritual*, SAACT 1 (2001). For extracts from this series, see III.37c and III.51l.

6. J. Laessøe, *Studies on the Assyrian Ritual Series bît rimki* (Copenhagen, 1955); A. Ungnad, "Bemerkungen zum bît-rimki-Ritual," OrNS 12 (1943), 196–198; C. J. Mullo-Weir, "The Prayer Cycle in the Assyrian Ritual bît rimki, Tablet IV," AfO 18 (1957/8), 371–372; C. Frank, "bît mēsiri," ZA 36 (1925), 215–217; G. Meier, "Die zweite Tafel der Serie bît mēseri," AfO 14 (1941/4), 139–152; R. Borger, "Die Beschwörungsserie Bît Mēseri und die Himmelfahrt Henochs," JNES 33 (1974), 183–196. For extracts from these series, see III.51h–k.

7. G. Meier, *Die Assyrische Beschwörungsserie Maqlû*, AfO Beiheft 2 (1937); "Studien zur Beschwörungssammlung Maqlû," AfO 21 (1966), 70–81; T. Abusch, "Mesopotamian Anti-Witchcraft Literature: Texts and Studies," JNES 33 (1974), 251–262; T. Abusch, *Babylonian Witchcraft Literature, Case Studies* (Atlanta, 1987); "Maqlû," RLA 7, 346–351. For extracts from this series, see III.40c, 41c, 48d, IV.49.

8. E. Reiner, *Šurpu, A Collection of Sumerian and Akkadian Incantations*, AfO Beiheft 11 (1958); W. G. Lambert, "Two Notes on Šurpu," AfO 19 (1959/60), 122; Borger, *Studies Lambert*, 15–90. For extracts from this series, see III.40d, IV.47.

9. F. Köcher, "Die Ritualtafel der magisch-medizinischen Tafelserie 'Einreibung'," AfO 21

Incantations or magic spells were sometimes grouped into series according to the classes of demons against which they were directed. Among these is Lamashtu, the female demon attacking children and women in childbirth, incantations against whom date from the Archaic (I.7), Classical (II.21), and Late (IV.42) periods.[1] There are also incantations in series, mostly in Sumerian, against sickness demons of various kinds. The longest of these series is called "Malignant Phantoms," portions of which are known from the Classical period, and whose Sumerian forerunners date even earlier.[2]

Menologies and hemerologies specify propitious times for activities such as the construction of buildings. They also arrange cultic activities in accordance with the calendar year.[3]

The social and historical background for late Assyro-Babylonian literary activity may be seen in the succession of empires—Assyrian, Babylonian, Achaemenid, Hellenistic, Parthian, spanning the first millennium B.C., insofar as much literature was written or studied in or near centers of political power.[4] Whereas Assyria reached its apogee during the late ninth through seventh centuries, Babylonia remained strong for most of the millennium and flourished under Persian and Hellenistic rule.[5] The grand side of empire is reflected

(1966), 13–20; E. Reiner, "'Lipšur-Litanies'," JNES 15 (1956), 126–149; E. Knudsen, "An Incantation Tablet from Nimrud," Iraq 21 (1959), 54–61; O. R. Gurney, "An Incantation of the Maqlû Type," AfO 11 (1936/7), 367–368; R. Caplice, The Akkadian Namburbi-Texts: An Introduction, SANE 1/1 (1974); E. Weidner, "Beschwörung gegen Böses aller Art," AfO 16 (1952/3), 56. For a study of the witch or sorcerer, see T. Abusch, "The Demonic Image of the Witch in Standard Babylonian Literature: The Reworking of Popular Conceptions by Learned Exorcists," in J. Neusner, et al., eds., Religion, Science, and Magic in Concert and in Conflict (Oxford, 1989), 27–58; Reiner, Astral Magic, 97–118.

1. D. Myhrman, "Die Labartu-Texte, babylonische Beschwörungsformeln gegen die Dämonin Labartu," ZA 16 (1902), 141–183; W. Farber, "Lamaštu," RLA 6, 439–446.

2. R. Campbell Thompson, The Devils and Evil Spirits of Babylonia (London, 1903); M. J. Geller, Forerunners to UDUG-HUL, Sumerian Exorcistic Incantations, FAOS 12 (1985). For extracts from this series, see III.36a, IV.36.

3. R. Labat, Un calendrier babylonien des travaux, des signes et des mois (series iqur ipuš) Bibliothèque de l'École Pratique des Hautes Études 321 (Paris, 1965). For a survey of the genre of hemerologies and almanacs, see R. Labat, "Hemerologien," RLA 4, 317–323; A. Livingstone, "The Case of Hemerologies: Official Cult, Learned Formulation and Popular Practice," in A. Matsushima, ed., Official Cult and Popular Religion in the Ancient Near East (Heidelberg, 1993), 97–113.

4. For surveys of Mesopotamian history in the first millennium B.C., see A. Kuhrt, The Ancient Near East c. 3000–300 B.C. (New York, 1997); J. Brinkman, Prelude to Empire, Babylonian Society and Politics, 747–626 B.C., OPSNKF 7 (1984); CAH³ 3/2 (with extensive bibliographies); M. Van De Mieroop, A History of the Ancient Near East ca. 3000–323 B.C. (London, 2004).

5. For considerations of scholarly conditions in the first millennium B.C., see Parpola, LAS 2 (1971), 6–25; A. L. Oppenheim, "The Position of the Intellectual in Mesopotamian Society," Daedalus Spring 1975, 37–46; "Divination and Celestial Observation in the Late Assyrian Empire," Centaurus 14 (1969), 97–135; M. A. Dandamayev, Vavilonskij Pisci (Moscow, 1983), with extensive

in texts like IV.1 and 57, with fulsome praises of the king and his prowess. The dark side is seen in Sargon's Eighth Campaign (IV.2c) and Erra and Ishum (IV.17). In the latter, indiscriminate cruelty and wanton destruction are lamented, and the question is raised of how, in a world supposedly controlled by gods, violence and destruction, even of sanctuaries, could take place. The old theme of divine justice and its relationship to human affairs is debated in IV.19 (compare III.14 and II.13).[1] The rights, duties, responsibilities, pretensions, and limitations of kings are dealt with prescriptively in IV.13 and elsewhere by implication (Gilgamesh), even satirically (IV.58).

Literary developments specific to the Late period include tendencies toward henotheism (III.44g, 47c) and perhaps an increase in religious skepticism (Gilgamesh Epic). Such traditional Mesopotamian literary concerns as divine hegemony (IV.17) and death (IV.5) continue to be explored in the Late period. Certain gods, especially Nabu, achieve greater prominence in the Late period than they had in the Mature period (see III.45). Marduk seems to age from a youthful warrior in the Epic of Creation (III.17) to a remote, sage-like figure in Erra and Ishum (IV.17). Ishtar tends to shed her militarism, as seen in II.4, to reveal her qualities as princess, lover, even prostitute (III.43e, IV.28; Gilgamesh Epic). Texts such as III.43e, IV.28, and IV.17 provide glimpses into aspects of her persona that may have seemed horrifying and perverted to some Babylonians (compare also IV.2b, lines 10–11).

The personalities of Late period rulers can be reflected in the literature of their times: the vainglory of Sargon II,[2] the anxieties and suspicions of Esarhaddon,[3] the scholarly interests of Assurbanipal,[4] the idiosyncratic theology of Nabonidus.[5]

bibliography; J. Pečirková, "Divination and Politics in the Late Assyrian Empire," ArOr 53 (1985), 155–168. For Babylonia under Persian rule, see Oppenheim, *Cambridge History of Iran* 2, 529–587 and P. Briant, *From Cyrus to Alexander, A History of the Persian Empire* (Winona Lake, Ind., 2002), 40–44, 70–76, 484–486, 543–545. For the Hellenistic period, see J. Oelsner, *Materialien zur babylonischen Gesellschaft und Kultur in hellenistischer Zeit* (Budapest, 1986); A. Kuhrt and S. Sherwin-White, eds., *Hellenism in the East, The Interaction of Greek and non-Greek Civilizations from Syria to Central Asia after Alexander* (Berkeley, 1987); S. Sherwin-White and A. Kuhrt, *From Samarkhand to Sardis. A New Approach to the Seleucid Empire* (Berkeley, 1993); H. Sommer, "Babylonien im Seleukidenreich: Indirekte Herrschaft und indigene Bevölkerung," *Klio* 82 (2000), 73–90.

   1. See General Introduction, p. 41 note 4.
   2. See IV.2 and Grayson, CAH[3] 3/2, 86–102.
   3. See W. von Soden, *Herrscher im alten Orient* (Berlin, 1956), 118–126; Parpola, LAS 2 (1971), 46–47; Grayson, CAH[3] 3/2, 122–141; F. M. Fales, "Esarhaddon e il potere della divinazione," in F. M. Fales, C. Grottanelli, ed., *Soprannaturale e potere nel mondo antico e nelle società tradizionali* (Milan, 1985), 95–118.
   4. See IV.4 and von Soden, *Herrscher*, 127–138; Grayson, CAH[3] 3/2, 142–161.
   5. Nabonidus is one of the most controversial figures of Mesopotamian antiquity; see IV.11 and

During the Late period, in addition to the Standard and Late Babylonian literary styles, some works were written down in a more vernacular style, such as IV.27 and 28, compare also IV.59, but the differences between higher and lower style in Akkadian literature in this period await further research.

Sometimes traces of resistance to foreign rule can be found. Perhaps anti-Persian sentiment lies behind redaction of the "Kedor-Laomer" texts (III.11). A group of late apocalypses or prophecies may well express Babylonian cultural resistance to the Achaemenids and Seleucids.[1]

Toward the end of the Late period, when Mesopotamia was under Greek rule, Akkadian was dying out as a spoken language. Some of the latest hymns show an awkwardness of expression that suggests that the authors were not native speakers of Akkadian (III.46b, IV.12). Acrostics and word games lend a precious, Alexandrian flavor to certain works of the Late period (III.45d, f; IV.4d, 8k, 19). The substrate influence of Sumerian, so prominent in works of the Classical period, was replaced by that of Aramaic.[2] Sumerian ossified into an academic and cultic argot known only to the most scholarly.[3]

Knowledge and wisdom, as seen in the literature of the Mature period, continued to be important in literature of the Late period, with increasing emphasis on specialized learning and scholarship. Slavish imitation of ancient styles or selected classics was not the norm; Akkadian literature was spared the sterility brought about by imitation and anthologizing. Above all, what is most impressive about Akkadian literature of the Late period is that it remained vital and productive even in the face of two thousand years of literary tradition.

the bibliography in P.-A. Beaulieu, *The Reign of Nabonidus King of Babylon 556–539 B.C.*, YNER 10 (1989).

1.   The theme of resistance is taken up in A. Finet, ed., *La Voix de l'opposition en mésopotamie* (Brussels, 1973); A. K. Grayson, BHLT, 24–27.

2.   J. C. Greenfield, "Babylonian-Aramaic Relationship," CRRAI 25 (1978), 471–482. For a survey of the role of Arameans in Assyria, see N. Postgate, "Ancient Assyria — A Multi-Racial State," *Aram* 1 (1989), 1–10. See also General Introduction, p. 2 note 2.

3.   G. Goosens, "Au déclin de la civilisation babylonienne: Uruk sous les Séleucides," *Bulletin de la Classe des Lettres et des Sciences morales et politiques*, series 5, vol. 27 (1941), 223–244; M. E. Cohen, *The Canonical Lamentations of Ancient Mesopotamia* (Potomac, Md., 1988), 1:24–27. For a detailed survey of cuneiform documents from Mesopotamia of the Hellenistic period, see J. Oelsner, *Materialien*, 137–246. See also p. 2 note 3.

A. Kings of Assyria and Their Times

IV.1 SHALMANESER III

Shalmaneser III (858–824 B.C.) was an Assyrian warrior king who made extensive conquests in Syria, Palestine, Anatolia, and the mountain lands of present-day Kurdistan. He was also drawn into Babylonian affairs and fought the Chaldeans threatening Babylonian cities. For a historical survey of his reign, see Grayson, CAH³ 3/1, 259–269.

(a) SHALMANESER IN ARARAT

This text is a poetic account of a campaign by an Assyrian king, Shalmaneser III, probably against Urartu, the region centering around Lake Van in eastern Anatolia. W. G. Lambert has suggested that it was produced by a specific Assyrian poetic school; see above, III.4. The historicity and geographical setting of the text are uncertain in many points; much of the narrative in the unique manuscript is fragmentary, poorly written, or obscure. Even the sequence of speeches in the text is difficult to discern. I propose the following interpretation:

1–9: Opening invocation of the gods, referring to Shalmaneser's conquests in north Syria.

10–24: Shalmaneser orders his general, Assur-bel-ka'in, to secure his new domains while the king marches against Urartu. The king exhorts his officers.

25–30: The Assyrians encourage Shalmaneser.

31–60: Shalmaneser narrates his own campaign in the style of Assyrian royal inscriptions.

61–64: The text concludes with a narrative of a festival for Ishtar of Arbela and a triumphant return to Assur.

[O Assur, great lord, lord] of the world, shepherd of all rulers, (1)
[   ] the lofty one, the lady of Nineveh,
[   ] justice,
[admın]isters everything,
[un]sparing, (5)
The Lord and Anu have [en]trusted you(?) ... [dis]tant [   ]!

[Having   ] ... the stubborn Bit-Adinian slave,[1]
Having t[orched] Til-barsip,[2] the mighty stonghold,
Having laid waste the dwellings of the Hittite kings,[3]
He spoke <to> Assur-bel-ka'in the general ... as follows,   (10)

"Let the fortresses be entrusted to you,
          let your security be strong,
"Let your preparedness be high, take their tribute.
"I have forced the rulers of the Hittites to submit,
"I will go see how the Urartians fight,
"I will go down and wash my weapons(?),
          be it a land of water or no water.   (15)
"From the yoke of Assurnasirpal[4]
          the land of Nairi[5] [   ] has arisen."

He inspects his officers that they keep discipline high,
"My fierce warriors! ...
"I go to plunder on a campaign of Assur ...
"I go to plunder on a campaign of Assur.[6]
"Let the iron swords be sharpened(?) ...   (20)
"The sharp darts [...] in [   ],
"[   ] coats of iron mail for the horses.
"Do not [   ] your powerful force,
"[   ] the warfare of the Urartian slave(s)!
"Assur has given me confidence and s[howed me   ]."   (25)

The people of Assyria heard(?)* ... [   ]
The best of good fortune to the lord,
"Go, O lord of kings, ... [   ],
"May Nergal go before you, Girra [behind you],

1. An Aramean state in North Syria and south-central Asia Minor in the ninth century B.C. "Slave" may be a poetic word for troops, and need not be derogatory; compare III.1 v 32'.
2. Modern Tell Ahmar, a city in North Syria, where the remains of a palace of this period have been excavated, capital of Bit-Adini.
3. The so-called "Neo-Hittite states," various small kingdoms in North Syria in the first part of the first millennium B.C.; see Hawkins, CAH³ 3/1, 372–441.
4. See III.4.
5. Corresponds roughly to Kurdistan, see M. Salvini, *Nairi e Ur(u)aṭri* (Rome, 1967).
6. Lambert suggests emending to "Assurnasirpal," but this is not adopted here.

"[   ] at your command, we will be full [   ]."   (30)

They set out on the march ... [   ]
[   ] of his battle like ... [   ]:

"[   ] picks of iron, arrows of [   ]
"Difficult [   ] mountains, [   ] ravines,
"[   ] ... we ... [   ]   (35)
"[The city Ubum]u together with the land of Shubri
        [I   ] like [   ],
"[   ] crossing the vast [   ] toward [   ],
"[I] rapidly [... the whole?] of the land of the Urartians,
"I conquered [st]rong [cities] and la[id waste] fortifications,
"I reminded(?) them of [fi]erce Assurnasirpal.   (40)
"On the first of September, [I] drew near [his] royal capital,
"The king(s) ...
"Terror of the lord of the world regions [fell] upon them.
"They forsook their cities,
        they went into [mountains] and forests,
"Everyone went into forbidding mountains
        to save their lives,   (45)
"Hard upon their heels,
        I chased them <into> arduous mountain terrain.
"I felled 18,000 of the enemy with my battle weapons,
"I cast their teams(?) in the open country like ...,
"I seized as booty innumerable mules, horses, and donkeys.
"I pillaged his palace for nine days,   (50)
"I burned down his numerous residences.
"I paraded the women(?) of his land before my troops,
"I set fire to the trees, the attraction of his royal capital,
"I set up images of my power by mountains and seas.
"I went down as far as the ... of the Nairi-lands,
        to the land of Gilzanu.   (55)
"I received horses as tribute
        from the cities Tikki and Hubushkia,
"I received the rest(?) of the tribute
        from the city(?) Turushpa.
"I ... [   ] to Assur, my god.

"I entered the temple of Ega[shankalamma] with a blithe heart,
"I [   ] the festival of the lady of Arbela."   (60)

The king, ... a lion, [   ] in Assur with joy,
He ..., with all his tribute he [entered] before Ishtar.
He hailed ...
He donated ... [   ].
"[   ] your land."   (65)

Text: Gurney, STT 43.

Edition: W. G. Lambert, AnSt 11 (1961), 143–158; Livingstone, *Court Poetry*, 44–47; Grayson, RIMA 3, 84–87 (with readings adopted here).

Literature: Schramm, EAK 2, 82 (from which several restorations are taken); Kinnier Wilson, *Iraq* 26 (1964), 107–108. For historical background on this campaign, in addition to Lambert's study, see B. B. Piotrovsky, *Il Regno di Van: Urartu*, trans. M. Salvini (Rome, 1966), 71–82. For a review of the chronological and geographical problems raised by this text, see J. Reade, "Shalmaneser or Ashurnasirpal in Ararat," SAAB 3 (1989), 93–97.

★*Notes to Text*: (1) Grayson, RIMA 3, 85. (15) Cf. Grayson, RIMA 3, 86. (26) AHw, 1212a; Grayson, "shouted."

(b) TO MULLISSU

This text is an address by Shalmaneser III(?)[1] to the goddess Mullissu(?)[2] commemorating his repairs to her cultic harp and asking for her blessing.

(large gap)

The priest who [   ],
Pious prince, favorite of Ishtar, ...
Reliable general of the gods, beloved of Ishtar,   (5')
Who leads you in procession,★
        who proclaims your divinity,
(When) you beheld him, O my lady,
        you desired that he be lord.
May they(?) hail his kingship above all other kings.
The diademed kings, whom you commit to his power,

1. Borger, HKL 1, 99; Schramm, EAK 2, 95.
2. M.-J. Seux, *Épithètes royales akkadiennes et sumériennes* (Paris, 1967), 165 note 57.

are assembled, kneeling, and doing homage to him.   (10')
The faithful shepherd, the provider for san[ctuaries],
Son of Assurnasirpal, priest of ... A[ssur],
Descendant of Tukulti-[Ninurta, ...]
Who guarantees your offerings,
     who maintains [your] food offerings,
The faithful shepherd who watches over(?) ... [   ]   (15')
The most great one, first in rank, who performs [your] rites:
The great harp that played(?) your songs of praise(?)
     having deteriorated,
He made [the ... of that] harp,
The harp ... [   ]
He made once again splendid
     and greater than it was [before].   (20')
He placed on your head a brilliant gem, shining like a star.
He who kneels and glorifies you, proclaiming your dominion,
O Mullissu, of your own free will bestow (long) life upon him!
As for the harp and drum beloved to [your] divinity,

Which are agreeable to you
     and which your loftiest feelings delight in,   (25')
He restored(?) the ... and ornamented its inside,
He decorated it(?) with a gazelle and onager(?),
     creatures of the high mountain.
They put earrings of finest gold on her ears,
[   ] joy ...

     (four more fragmentary lines, then breaks off)

Text: Ebeling, KAR 98.
Edition: None.
Literature: See Schramm, EAK 2, 95.
Notes to Text: (6') Reading *qa-at!-ka*.

IV.2 SARGON II

Sargon II (721–705 B.C.) proved to be a valorous warrior who undertook an extensive series of campaigns, on one of which he died in battle. Sargon's throne name, "The-King-is-Legitimate," was, of course, programmatically reminiscent of Sargon of Akkad (see I.3). For a historical survey of his reign, see Grayson, CAH³ 3/2, 86–102.

(a) PRAYERS FROM DUR-SHARRUKIN

Sargon II constructed a new capital city for himself at Dur-Sharrukin, modern Khorsabad, not far from Nineveh. Its grandiose plan included numerous temples and a royal palace. The prayers translated here were composed for the new temples at Dur-Sharrukin. Each appeals to a specific aspect of the deity's powers: rainfall (Adad), protection (Assur, Nabu), wisdom and spring water (Ea), progeny (Ningal), strength and prowess (Ninurta), and truth (Sin).

(a 1) TO ADAD

This prayer was inscribed on the threshold of the entrance to the Adad-temple at Dur-Sharrukin.

> O Adad, irrigator of heaven and earth, who brightens daises, for Sargon, king of the world, king of Assyria, governor of Babylon, king of the land of Sumer and Akkad, builder of your cella, bring the rains from heaven and the floods from underground in good season. Garner grain and oil in his leas, make his subjects lie down in safe pastures amidst plenty and abundance. Make firm the foundations of his throne, let his reign endure.

Text: Jacobsen *apud* G. Loud *et al.*, *Khorsabad* I, OIP 38 (1936), 130 no. 4.
Edition: Jacobsen, *Khorsabad* I, 130–131; Meissner, ZDMG 98 (1944), 32–33; Fuchs, *Inschriften*, 3.2.6.
Translation: von Soden, SAHG, 280 no. 24d; Seux, *Hymnes*, 529.

(a 2) TO ASSUR

This prayer concluded an inscription on the pavement of a palace gate at Dur-Sharrukin.

> May Assur, father of the gods, look steadfastly with the radiance of his holy features upon this palace. May its renewal always be ordered, until distant days. Let it be established from his holy utterance that protective spirit and safeguarding god be on the watch day and night within it and never leave its sides.
>
> At his command may the sovereign who built it live to a ripe old age. From his holy lips may (these words) fall, "May he who made it grow old, far into the future." May he who dwells therein rejoice within, in good health, happiness, and blithe spirits. May he enjoy well-being in full measure.

Text: H. Winckler, *Die Keilschrifttexte Sargons II.* (Leipzig, 1889), pl. 39–40, 131–150.
Edition: Borger, BAL 2, 58 131–150; Fuchs, *Inschriften*, 2.4, see 246–248.
Translation: von Soden, SAHG, 281–282 no. 24g.

(a 3) TO EA

This prayer was inscribed on the entrance to the Ea-temple at Dur-Sharrukin. It addresses Ea using his byname Ninshiku, which may mean "leader" or the like.

> O Ninshiku, lord of wisdom, creator of all and everything, for Sargon, king of the universe, king of Assyria, governor of Babylon, king of the lands of Sumer and Akkad, builder of your cella, make your underground depth open up, send him its spring waters, provide his leas with plentiful, abundant water. Ordain for his destiny great wisdom and profound understanding, make his project(s) succeed, may he enjoy well-being in full measure.

Text: Jacobsen *apud* G. Loud *et al.*, *Khorsabad* I, OIP 38 (1936), 132 no. 6; H. Winckler, *Die Keilschrifttexte Sargons II.* (Leipzig, 1889), pl. 49, no. 3B.
Edition: Jacobsen, *Khorsabad* I, 132–133; Meissner, ZDMG 98 (1944), 35; Fuchs, *Inschriften*, 3.2.1.
Translation: von Soden, SAHG, 279 no. 24a; Seux, *Hymnes*, 527–528.

(a 4) TO NABU

This prayer was inscribed on the threshold and around the steps in the sanctuary area of the Nabu-temple at Dur-Sharrukin.

> O Nabu, universal scribe, who checks on all, look steadfastly, in the fidelity of your heart, upon Sargon, king of the universe, king of Assyria, governor of Babylon, king of the lands of Sumer and Akkad, builder of your cella, and direct your just countenance upon him. Grant him days of good health till furthest time, ordain for his destiny years of happiness. Make his reign last as long as heaven and earth, let him continue to exercise shepherdship of all lands. May his support endure as (this) structure and its platform.

Text: Jacobsen *apud* G. Loud *et al.*, *Khorsabad* II, OIP 40 (1938), 103–104 no. 1.
Edition: Jacobsen, *Khorsabad* II, 103–104; Meissner, ZDMG 98 (1944), 36; Fuchs, *Inschriften*, 3.2.5.
Translation: von Soden, SAHG 281, no. 24f.; Seux, *Hymnes*, 529–530.

(a 5) TO NINGAL

This prayer was inscribed on the threshold of the entrance to the Ningal-temple at Dur-Sharrukin.

> O preeminent lady, exalted Ningal, [inter]cede for Sargon, king of the universe, king of Assyria, governor of Babylon, king of the land of Sumer and Akkad, builder of your cella, with Sin, your beloved spouse, speak a word favorable of him that his reign be [sta]ble. Let him ordain his destiny to live a life long of days. May his offspring hold dominion over all inhabited regions till the end of time.

Text: Jacobsen *apud* G. Loud *et al.*, *Khorsabad* I, OIP 38 (1936), 133 no. 7.
Edition: Jacobsen, *Khorsabad* I, 133; Meissner, ZDMG 98 (1944), 33; Fuchs, *Inschriften*, 3.2.3.
Translation: von Soden, SAHG, 280 no. 24c; Seux, *Hymnes*, 528.

(a 6) TO NINURTA

This prayer was inscribed on the threshold of the entrance to the Ninurta-temple at Dur-Sharrukin.

> O Ninurta, athlete of surpassing strength, bestow old age upon Sargon, king of the universe, king of Assyria, governor of Babylon, king of the land of Sumer and Akkad, builder of your cella. May he enjoy well-being in full measure. Make firm his reign in Esagila and Esharra. Guide straight his steeds, safeguard his teams, grant him [un]rivalled strength and manly might, make his weapon at the ready that he kill his foes.

Text: Jacobsen *apud* G. Loud *et al.*, *Khorsabad* I, OIP 38 (1940), 131 no. 5; H. Winckler, *Die Keilschrifttexte Sargons II.* (Leipzig, 1889), pl. 49 no. 3A.
Edition: Jacobsen, *Khorsabad* I, 131–132; Meissner, ZDMG 98 (1944), 34; Fuchs, *Inschriften*, 3.2.7.
Translation: von Soden, SAHG, 281 no. 24e; Seux, *Hymnes*, 529.

(a 7) TO SIN

This prayer was inscribed on the threshold of the entrance to the Sin-temple at Dur-Sharrukin.

> O Sin, pure god who renders verdicts and discloses decisions,[1] look steadfastly in the fidelity of your heart upon Sargon, king of the universe, king of Assyria, governor of Babylon, king of Sumer and Akkad, builder of your cella, and direct your just countenance upon him. Grant him days of good health till furthest time, ordain for his destiny years of happiness, make his reign last as long as heaven and earth, make firm his throne over the four world regions.

Text: Jacobsen *apud* G. Loud *et al.*, *Khorsabad* I, OIP 38 (1936), 130 no. 3.
Edition: Jacobsen, *Khorsabad* I, 130; Meissner, ZDMG 98 (1944), 34–35; Fuchs, *Inschriften*, 3.2.2.
Translation: von Soden, SAHG, 280 no. 24b; Seux, *Hymnes*, 528.

1. Reference to divination.

(b) TO NANAY

This fragmentary hymn includes a description of musicians and performers in col. i, a blessing on Sargon II, and a prayer against crop pests. The fighting alluded to in the first preserved lines may be war games that formed part of a ceremony in honor of this goddess.

i

(gap)

The naked sword [   ],
The pointed axe, symbols of [her?] divinity,
Battle is drawn up to her right and left.
She is first-ranked of the gods, whose amusement is combat,   (5)
Vanguard to those with (even) seven companions.
Skilled singers kneel before her,
Performers on the lyre, the small harp, and clappers,
Flute, shawm, and pipes,
Impersonators (who carry) spindle, lash(?), whip,   (10)
Relax her mood with "sweet reeds."[1]

(fragmentary lines, then gap)

ii

Daughter-in-law of Esagila,[2] princess [   ],
Spouse of Muati, beloved of the Lord [his] father,
Whom Belet-ili cherishes among all goddesses,
Be up and on the way,[3] most valiant of goddesses!   (5)
O Capable Lady, who acquits well a warrior's duty,
[   ] of heart, who spares no combatant,
[   ] till the end of time

(fragmentary lines, then large gap)

---

1. Possibly a reference to incense (so CAD K, 558a), but more likely a reference to music.
2. That is, bride to Nabu = Muati, Marduk's son.
3. To battle?

iv

(fragmentary lines)

The knowledgeable physician
    whom she does not [guide],
His hand is fal[tering] before his clients.[1]
Without her, who can do anything?
Hasten forth, learn her (song of) praise!   (10)
Cherish the merciful one, each month forever,
She who enriches the impoverished, prospers the poor.
Hear, O regions of the world, the praise of queen Nanay,
Glorify the beautiful one, extol her of voice resounding,
Exalt the splendid one, hail the mighty one,   (15)
Make continuous prayer and entreaty to her.

Calm yourself, O daughter of Sin, take up your abode.
Bless Sargon who grasps your hem in entreaty,[2]
The shepherd of Assur, who walks behind you,
Ordain for his destiny a life long of days,   (20)
Make firm his throne, make his reign endure,
Safeguard the steeds hitched to [his] yoke,
Keep affliction and loss afar off from him:
The fell locust plague that destroys the grain,
The vile cicada-pest that denudes the orchards,   (25)
That cut off the food offerings of god and goddess.
Enlil is heeding you, Tutu[3] awaits you,
At your command may they vanish into thin air!
[May] the protection and good fortune
    standing before you [   ],
[   ] steppe, mountains, and [   ]   (30)

(breaks off)

---

1. This line is apparently the end of a list of professionals whose duties are the goddess's special concern (for the reading, Livingstone, *Court Poetry*, 14).
2. See p. 576 note 1.
3. Marduk, see Epic of Creation (III.17) Tablet VII lines 9, 15, 19, 25, 33.

Text: K 3600 + DT 75 = Craig, ABRT 1, 54–55 = Macmillan, BA 5 (1905), 626–629 (collated).
    The parallel K 9898 and duplicate K 13773 have not been used here.
Edition: Livingstone, *Court Poetry*, 13–16; in Hallo, ed., *Context*, 1:472–473.
Translation: Seux, *Hymnes*, 107–109.
Literature: Lambert, AnSt 11 (1961), 143–144.

(c) THE EIGHTH CAMPAIGN

This narrative of a military campaign of Sargon to the east and north of Assyria in 718 B.C. is the most impressive surviving monument of Assyrian prose. It opens in the form of a letter or report to the god Assur and the other gods of his temple (Ehursagkurkurra), as well as to the city Assur and its population and to the royal administration. The author has gone to great lengths to compose a work in an elegant style with long periodic sentences. It abounds in literary references, poetic language, plays on words, and elaborate figures of speech. It is noteworthy not only for its narrative skill in the Assyrian historical tradition, in which the perfect and invincible king of Assyria, with divine support, triumphs over his enemies, but also for its portrayal of the enemy and incidental observations on the peoples and lands, civilized and uncivilized, that the Assyrian army traversed, including such matters as the training of horses and designation of the Urartian crown prince.[1] The climax of the story is Sargon's decision to invade the land of Urartu, the only Western Asiatic state comparable to Assyria in size and strength, centered in present-day Armenia, and finally to loot and destroy Musasir, its major cult center. Sargon blames this decision on the treachery of the Urartian king, Rusa, and on the disloyalty of Urzana, king of Musasir. He portrays with relish the Urartian king's distress on learning the terrible fate of one of his most important temples and its gods. Nearly a quarter of the composition is taken up with an inventory of the treasures looted at Musasir and wall reliefs at Sargon's palace showed the campaign in progress.

---

1. On these topics, see, for example, F. Fales, "Narrative and Ideological Variation in the Account of Sargon's Eighth Campaign," *Studies Tadmor*, 129–147 and F. Fales, ed., *Assyrian Royal Inscriptions: New Horizons in Literary, Ideological, and Historical Analysis*, OAIC 17 (Rome, 1981); C. Zaccagnini, "The Enemy in the Neo-Assyrian Royal Inscriptions: The 'Ethnographic Description'," CRRAI 25 (1978), 409–424; F. Fales, "The Enemy in Assyrian Royal Inscriptions: 'The Moral Judgement'," ibid., 425–436; B. Oded, *War, Peace, and Empire. Justifications for War in Assyrian Royal Inscriptions* (Wiesbaden, 1992); S. Maul, "Der assyrische König — Hüter der Weltordnung," in J. Assmann, *et al.*, eds., *Gerechtigkeit* (Munich, 1998), 65–77. For a general study of the literary form and style of Assyrian royal inscriptions, see A. K. Grayson, "Assyria and Babylonia," OrNS 49 (1980), 140–194.

The author made generous and original use of the standard poetic repertory of his time, especially in the first part of the story. Note, for example, the increasing upward velocity of Sargon's march to the mountains (lines 8-10, 26): he leaves Calah, jumps over rivers, then flies over mountains, or the heaping-up of similes when describing the actions and emotions of the enemy king: he is a criminal in flight, a woman in labor, a frightened bird, fleeing game. This is the product of a proud, learned mind, sure of itself and of its audience. There are touches of humor (see p. 793 note 3) but the dominant tone is Assyrian moral and military superiority.

(salutation)

(1) To Assur, father of the gods, great lord who dwells in Ehursag-galkurkurra, his great abode, hail, all hail! To the gods of destinies and the goddesses who dwell in Ehursagkurkurra, their great abode, hail, all hail! Hail to the city and its people, to the palace and the dweller therein! (5) Sargon, the sacrosanct priest, the servant who reveres your great divinity, and his army, hail you in well-being!

(Sargon, with favorable omens, departs from the military base at Calah, approaches the frontier.)

In the month of July, which determines the plans of the human denizens of this world, that month belonging to the valorous, first-ranked son of Enlil, the almighty of the gods, Ninurta, which Ninshiku, lord of wisdom, inscribed on a hoary tablet as that for mustering forces and preparing encampments, I set forth from Calah, my royal city, and I crossed apace the Upper Zab when it was cresting. On the third day, I prostrated myself reverently before Enlil and Ninlil that I muzzle the mouth of the insolent, fetter the feet of the rascal. I made the armies of Shamash and Marduk leap over the Lower Zab, the crossing of which is difficult, as if it were a ditch. (10) I entered the passes of Mount Kullar and the mountain ranges of the lands of the Lullubaeans, which they themselves call Zamua. I held an inspection of my troops in the district of Sumbi, I made a reckoning of the number of horses and chariots. With the great support of Assur, Shamash, Nabu, and Marduk, for the third time did I form up the march against the mountainous interior.

(The campaign in the mountains begins.)

I prepared the yoke of Nergal and Adad, whose standards march ahead of me, for the lands of Zikirtu and Andini. I passed between Mounts Nikippa and Upa, lofty peaks overgrown with every sort of tree, among which it is easy to lose one's way, whose very entry is fearsome,[1] over the entire fastness of which shadow glooms, as in that forest of cedars,[2] the traverser of which could not behold the glory of the sun.[3] I crossed the Puia, a torrent between those peaks, twenty-six times, nor did my troops, in their own rising flood, fear its high waters.

As for Mount Simirriu, a lofty peak that thrusts up sharp as a spear point and whose summit, the dwelling of Belet-ili, rises over the mountains, whose topmost summits, indeed, reach to the very sky, whose roots below thrust down to the depths of the netherworld,[4] (20) and which, like the back of a fish, offers no way to pass on either flank, and the ascent of which, from front to back, is exceedingly difficult,[5] on the sides of which yawn chasms and mountain ravines, a fearsome spectacle to behold, discouraging to the ascent of chariotry and to the high spirits of steeds, the worst possible going for the ascent of infantry, with that profound understanding and extensive resourcefulness with which Ea and Belet-ili endowed me and who, moreover, made broad my stride to knock prostrate the lands of the enemy,[6] I provided my engineers with heavy copper mattocks, so they broke up the sharp peak of the mountain into fragments as if it was limestone, and made good the going.(25) I took the lead position before my army, I made the chariotry, cavalry, and my combat

---

1. Wordplay on "overgrown" (*ḫitlupu*) and "fearsome" (*pitluḫu*).

2. Perhaps a reference to Sargon of Akkad, who marched through a tangled forest on his way to Burushhanda (see III.7a line 5'). For Sargon of Akkad's passage through darkness, see II.6a (p. 110 note 2). The hero Gilgamesh also passed through a forest of cedar (Tablet V line 5, Foster, *Gilgamesh*, 38), but in the epic the forest is described as easy to walk through.

3. Wordplay on "behold" (*amāru*) and "district" (*tamirtu*), here "fastness."

4. This image combines traditional language praising Mesopotamian temples with descriptions of cosmic mountains; thereby mountain is compared to a temple for the birth-goddess (Sumerian Ninhursag "Lady of the Mountain"). Similar imagery appears in the Epic of Gilgamesh, Tablet IX, lines 35–36, referring to the twin mountains blocking Gilgamesh's advance.

5. As understood here, the figure compares going over the peaks to ascending the spines of a fish because the sides offered no foothold (see further Hirsch, OrNS 35 [1966], 413–416).

6. This compares Sargon to the first (and presumably perfect) human being created by Ea and the birth-goddess (see II.36 Tablet I lines 189–203) and then formulates an original conceit on breadth of wisdom and breadth of stride. It may not be a coincidence that the hero Gilgamesh is described in the same manner: Foster, *Gilgamesh*, 5: Tablet I, lines 53–60.

troops[1] fly over it like valiant eagles, I brought after them the support troops and scouts. The camels and pack mules gamboled over its peak, one after another, like mountain goats bred in the hills. I brought the surging flood of Assyrian troops easily over its arduous crest and made camp right on top of that mountain. I traversed, amidst many hardships, the seven mountains of Sinahulzi and Biruatti, remote[2] ranges whose vegetation is pleasant-smelling wild leek and aromatic, and Mounts Turtani, Sinabir, Ahshuru, and Shuia, (30) I crossed the Rappa and Aratta rivers at the high point of their rapids as if they were irrigation channels. Down I went towards the land of Surikash, a frontier district of the lands of Karalli and Allabria.

(Sargon approaches the land of his Mannaean vassal, Ullusunu, which had been attacked by Urartu.)

Ullusunu the Mannaean, whose cause I had never failed, year in, year out, to uphold, heard of my advance and he, together with his most important dignitaries, elders, advisors, his royal family, officers and subordinates who govern his land, came out in haste to me from his land, with elation[3] of heart and happiness of visage, without even taking hostages. (35) He came to me from Izirti, his royal capital, to the city Sinihini, a frontier fortress of his land. He brought me his tribute of trained horses, along with their equipment, and cattle, sheep, and goats, and did homage to me.

I arrived at the city Latashe, a fort which is on the river of the land of Larueshe, a frontier district of Allapria. I received from Bel-apaliddina the Allabrian his tribute of horses, cattle, sheep, and goats. I went down to the land of Parsuash. The chieftains of the lands of Namri, Sangibute, Bit-Abdadani, and the lands of the mighty Medes heard of the advance of my expedition, (40) the destruction of their lands in my previous year of reign was still in their minds, so terror spread among them. They brought me from their lands their massive tribute and presented it to me in the land of Parsuash. I received from *(a list of twenty-three men and their cities follows)* (50) swift horses, high-spirited mules, camels native to their land, cattle, sheep, and goats.

---

1. Literally: "The battle troops that go at my side."
2. Wordplay on "remote" (*bērūti*) and the name of the mountain. Traversing seven mountain ranges was a well-known literary motif.
3. Wordplay on the name, Ullusunu, and "elated" (*ulluṣu*).

I set forth from the land of Parsuash, drawing near the land of
Missi, a district of the land of the Mannaeans. Ullusunu, together
with the people of his land, wholehearted in his desire to render service, awaited my army in the city Sirdakka, his fortress. As if he had
been one of my own officials or governors of the land of Assyria, he
had stocked provisions, products of mill and vine, to feed my troops.
He tendered me his eldest son, with presents and audience gifts, and
entrusted to me his stela, so as to guarantee his kingship.[1] (55) I received from him his tribute of huge trained horses, cattle, sheep, and
goats, and he beseeched me to uphold his cause. He, along with his
most important dignitaries and administrators of his land, prayed to
me, groveling on all fours like dogs, that I cut off the land of the Kak-
maeans, a malicious enemy, from his land, to rout Rusa in combat,
to resettle the scattered Mannaean where he had been, to triumph
over his enemy, and to realize his fondest hopes. I took pity on
them, acceded to their entreaties, heeded their discourse of supplication. I said of them "What a pity!" (60)

With the overwhelming strength that Assur and Marduk bestowed
upon me by making my weaponry superior to that of any other sovereign in the universe, I promised them to defeat the land of Urartu
and to bring relief to the troubled peoples of the land of the Mannaeans, so they took heart. I prepared a magnificent banquet for
Ullusunu the king,* their lord, and placed his chair higher than that
of Iranzi, his father who begot him, I had them take their places at a
joyful repast with people of the land of Assyria. They blessed my
reign before Assur and the gods of their land.

Zizi, of the city Appatar, Zalaia of the city of the Kitpataeans,
chieftains of the district of Gizilbundi, (65) which lies in a remote
place in the distant mountains, blocking the way into the lands of the
Mannaeans and the Medes like a barricade—for the inhabitants of
those cities trust in their own strength and acknowledge no master—
whose dwellings none of the kings, my predecessors, had seen nor
their names heard, nor received their tribute, according to the great
command of Assur, who bestowed upon me as a gift the submission
of the mountain kings and the receipt of their gifts, even these men

1. This probably means that Sargon was to guarantee the son's eventual accession and that
Ullusunu drew up a formal document that this son would succeed him (Luckenbill, *Ancient Records
of Assyria and Babylonia* [Chicago, 1927], 2:77).

heard of the [pas]sing of my expedition! Awe at my terrifying splendor overcame them, panic fell upon them in their own land. (70) They bore to me from the cities Appatar and Kitpat their tribute of countless trained horses, cattle, sheep, and goats, and brought it before me in the city Zirdiakka of the land of the Mannaeans. They pled with me to spare their lives and did homage to me lest I demolish their fortifications. And so I appointed over them, for the benefit of their land, an administrator, I assigned them to the authority of my own officers and the governor of Parsuash.

I set out from Zirdiakka, a fortress of the land of the Mannaeans, (75) I proceeded apace thirty double leagues of territory between the land of the Mannaeans, Bit-Kabsi, and the land of the mighty Medes, arriving at Panzish, its great fortress, which sits as a watch point over the lands of Zikirte and Andia, constructed against both these districts lest anyone come out and to hold back the enemy. I reinforced the construction of that fortress and brought into it food, o[ils, beverages and] battle equipment.

(Metatti, ruler of Zikirte, hides his people and goes over to the Urartian king.)

I set forth from Panzish, crossing the river Ishtarua and arrived at the land of A'ukane, a frontier district of the land of Zikirte. (80) Metatti the Zikirtaean, who had cast off his allegiance, who had held Ullusunu the king, his lord, in contempt and forgotten his duty to him, and who had put his trust in Rusa the Urartian, who, like him, had no common sense, an ally who could not save his life, ascended in terror Mount U'ashdirikka, an arduous mountain, and, when he saw from a distance the progress of my expedition, his flesh quaked. He gathered together all the people of his land and took them to a remote mountain amidst hardships, lest their location be detected. As for him, the city Parda, his royal capital, seemed of no value to him, as he abandoned the goods of his palace and went out into the open country. (85) He made ready his horses and battle troops and brought them to the assistance of Rusa as allies. I killed his fierce forces[1] who were posted as pickets at the pass of U'ashdirikka. I conquered in all twelve of their fortified cities and strongholds (*list follows*), along with eighty-four settlements in their environs. (90) I destroyed their fortifications, I set fire to the houses therein, I decimated them like a del-

1. Wordplay on "fierce" (*eqdūti*) and "battle" (*tidūki*).

uge, dumping them like heaps of debris.

I set forth from the land of A'ukane and arrived at Uishdish, a district of the land of the Mannaeans which Rusa had taken away from it. Before my arrival, Rusa, who did not observe the command of Assur and Marduk, who honored no oath to the lord of lords, a mountain man, spawn of a murderous lineage, without common sense, whose lips babbled foolishness and vicious talk, who did not observe the all-important command of Shamash, great justice of the gods; who, year in, year out, never failed to overstep his bounds, (95) he finally, after all his previous crimes, made the colossal blunder of smashing (Ullusunu's) land and slaying his people!

(Rusa prepares for battle with Sargon.)

It was in U'aush, a great mountain covered with clouds, the peak of which reaches to the sky, which no living creature had traversed since time immemorial, nor any wayfarer seen its hidden fastnesses, nor even a bird of heaven in flight passed over, nor built a nest to teach its little ones to spread their wings, a peak sharp-tipped as a dagger point, where chasms and mountain ravines [ ], and where, (100) during the hot season and the harshness of winter, when the Bow Star and the Arrow Star [ ] their glow at morn and evening,[1] perpetual snow is banked up upon it, and the whole of it [is locked]* in [frost] and ice, where the limbs of anyone who traverses it are buffeted by adverse winds and their flesh is frostbitten, there it was he had mobilized his large army, along with his support troops. To uphold the cause of [Metatti the Ziki]rtaean he had assembled his warriors, redoubtable in battle, the elite of his forces, [ ] he readied them [ ] (105) their swift riding horses [ ] provided them with weapons. Metatti the Zikirtaean who, from [ ] had been his ally like a [ ], who had turned to [ ] all the kings of the mountain regions and received their help for the bulk of his army and auxiliaries, he held the [the army of Assyria?] in contempt. [Savoring] praises of his own victories, and [imagining that his own strength] rivaled mine, (110) he felt himself eager to contest with me on the battlefield, and, preparing

---

1. The "Bow Star" is the area of Canis Major, the "Arrow Star" Sirius. The heliacal or morning rising of Sirius stands for the hot season; the acronychal or evening rising of Sirius stands for the cold season, so the mountain had snow on it the year round. For the figure, compare III.1 iv (A rev.) 23' and III.47a. I thank Izabela Zbikowska for assisting me with this passage.

remorselessly a strategy for the destruction of the army of Enlil and Assur, he drew up ranks in a defile of that mountain and sent me a messenger urging me to advance and engage him in battle.

I, Sargon, king of the four corners of the earth, shepherd of the land of Assyria, who observes the solemn oath of Enlil and Marduk, who heeds the judgment of Shamash, of Assyrian lineage, that city of wisdom and broad understanding, who attends reverently the commands of the great gods and does not transgress the bounds they have set, that legitimate king who speaks only propitious words, to whom treachery is abhorrent, whose mouth utters nothing wicked or destructive, (115) the wisest ruler in the universe, who was born with good sense and reason, who sustains with his own hands anyone who reveres divinities, to Assur, king of all the gods, lord of the world, begetter of the Mighty One,[1] king of all the great gods, who disciplines the four corners of the earth, almighty lord of Assyria who grinds up the sovereigns of the entire world in the prodigious fury of his wrath and pulverizes their bodies, that sublime warrior from whose battle snare the evil-doer has no escape, who demolishes anyone who has not revered an oath to him, (120) who charges furiously, in the clash of battle, against anyone who has not revered his name, or anyone who has trusted in his own strength alone, or anyone who has forgotten the greatness of his divinity, or anyone who boasts vaingloriously, shattering his weapons and evaporating his formations into thin air, but who places his terrible battle axe at the service of that ruler who observes the justice of the gods and trusts in the favorable judgment of Shamash[2] and who abides in reverence to Assur, Enlil of the gods, because, indeed, I had never transgressed the boundaries of Rusa the Urartian that demark his extensive country, nor had I shed the blood of his warriors, to Assur I prayed that he bring about Rusa's downfall in battle, that I cast his insolence in his teeth and make him bear his punishment!

(Sargon is victorious over Rusa and his allies.)

---

1. If correctly read, perhaps a reference to Ninurta, whose name was "Mighty One" (see III.23 Tablet I line 103 etc.), thereby another equation of Assur with Enlil (the father of Ninurta). The epithet may occur again in line 314 but a word has been omitted there. It may be preferable to emend the text here to read "begetter of all," as supplied in line 314.
2. Divination with a favorable reply.

(125) Assur, my lord, heard my just discourse, it pleased him. To
my honest plaidoyer gave he heed, he accepted my plea.[1] He dispatched to my side his furious weapons which, when they appear,
crush the disobedient from where the sun rises to where it sets. To
the tired troops of Assur who, having come such a long way, were
exhausted and weary, who had crossed over, one after another,
countless distant mountains, extremely arduous to ascend and descend, so that their faces had fallen, I gave no respite to their fatigue,
I gave them no water to slake their thirst, I made no bivouac nor did
I set up a redoubt. (130) I did not send forward my (advance) warriors
nor assemble my forces, I did not bring up my right and left wings, I
had no care for my rear. I had no fear of his entire army, I disdained
his cavalry, nor did I glance at the vast numbers of his armored warriors! With only my single chariot and the horsemen who ride with
me, who never leave me in hostile or friendly territory, the elite
squadron of Sin-ah-usur, I fell upon him like a furious arrow, I defeated him and forced him into retreat. I made a huge carnage of him,
spreading out the corpses of his warriors like malt and choking the
mountain slope with them. (135) I made the blood flow like river
water in chasms and gullies, I stained red the lowlands, foothills, and
ridges, as if with anemone-flowers. I beheaded and slaughtered at his
feet his allies, the security of his army, like lambs, and the bowmen
and lancers under his command. I broke in the course of the battle
the weapons of his dignitaries, counsellors, and courtiers, and took
them prisoners along with their steeds. I captured 260 members of his
royal family, his officials, governors, and riders, I broke up their battle
formation.

As for him, I surrounded him in his own encampment, I shot his
team of horses from under him with spears and arrows. (140) To save
his life, he abandoned his chariot, mounted a mare, and fled in full
view of his troops. I slew Metatti the Zikirtaean, together with his
neighboring kings, and cut their forces to pieces. I drove the troops
of Urartu, the wicked enemy, along with its auxiliaries, into retreat,
at Mount U'aush they turned tail. Their horses choked the chasms
and mountain gullies while they, like ants in distress, took whatever

1. Internal rhyme on two words for prayer (*taspītu, taslītu*) in a symmetrical construction,
object:verb:verb:object, with a small original touch: the rarer synonym is placed first, contrary to
practice.

difficult paths were open to them. I went up after them with the fury of my mighty weapons, I choked the ascents and descents with the corpses of combatants. (145) I followed him at arrow point for six stages of march, from U'aush to Zimur, the mountain of jasper. The remaining personnel, who had fled to save their lives, whom I had let go to proclaim the triumph of Assur, my lord, Adad, the mighty one, the valiant son of Anu, raised his great battle cry against them,[1] with a cloudburst and hail he finished off the rest.

Rusa, their sovereign, who had transgressed the bounds of Shamash and Marduk, and who did not honor his oath to Assur, king of the gods, became afraid at the clamor of my mighty weapons, his heart quaked in terror, like a rock partridge's trying to escape from an eagle. He absconded from Turushpa, his royal city, like a common murderer. Like game fleeing before the hunter he scuttled into hiding. He hurled himself on his bed, like a woman in labor, he banned food and water from his mouth, he inflicted upon himself irremediable pain.

(Sargon returns to his camp in triumph.)

I established the triumph of Assur, my lord, for the future over the land of Urartu, I instilled unforgettable terror of him for all time. In the furious battle I gave the land of Urartu a bitter taste of the might of my superior strength and of the assault of my overwhelming weapons, which have no equal in the four corners of the earth, and which never retreat. I spattered the peoples of Zikirte and Andia with the venom of death. (155) I blocked the wicked enemy from the land of the Mannaeans, I made their lord Ullusunu's heart rejoice and light to shine forth on his distressed people.

I, Sargon, the guardian of truth, who does not transgress the bounds of Assur and Shamash, who, humbly and without flagging, reveres Nabu and Marduk, achieved my objectives with their firm assent. I stood in triumph over my proud opponents, I spread terror throughout all the mountains, I laid consternation and lamentation upon the enemy peoples. I entered my encampment in joy and celebration, with players on lyres and flutes. (160) To Nergal, Adad, and Ishtar, lords of combat, to the gods who dwell in heaven and the netherworld, and to the gods who dwell in Assyria, I made splendid,

---

1. Thunder is meant.

holy libations. I stood before them in prayer and supplication and extolled their divinity.

(Sargon decides to invade Urartu.)

I broke off my campaign to the lands of Andia and Zikirte, where I had intended to go, and turned towards the land of Urartu. I conquered all of Uishdish, a district of the land of the Mannaeans which Rusa had taken away and turned to his own use, its settlements as numerous as the infinite stars of heaven. (165) I hacked down their mighty fortifications like pottery, down to their foundations, and turned them into flat ground. I opened their innumerable granaries and fed my troops on grain rations beyond measure.

I set forth from Uishdish and arrived at Ushqaia, a great fortress which is the frontier post of Urartu, which bars entry into the lands of Zaranda like a gate and holds back messengers, and which, on Mount Malla'u, a mountain of evergreens, sticks up sharp as a needle over the flatland of Subi, lending it an uncanny glamor. (170) The people who live in that district, of all the peoples in Urartu, have no equal in the training of riding horses. Every year, they take the promising young foals born in their extensive land, which they raise for the royal military. Until they are taken to Subi, the district that the people of Urartu call the land of the Mannaeans, and their potential can be observed, no one rides them, nor are they taught how to advance, turn, and retreat, in training for battle, and harness is withheld from them.[1] When these people, meaning those of that district, saw the rout of Rusa their lord, their legs tottered like roots on a riverbank, (175) and when their advance patrols, veterans of combat, reached them, fleeing before my weaponry and bespattered with the venom of death, telling them of the glory of Assur my lord, who, of all the combatants, let not one escape, they were as good as dead. They turned the city Ushqaia, the security of their land, along with the settlements around it, into ruins, abandoned their goods and took a road of no return. I mounted that fortress with the assault of my mighty arms, I plundered its vast goods and brought them into my encampment. (180) The massive wall, the base of which was founded

---

1. As understood here, no one broke the best horses of the realm but the Subians (differently Luckenbill, *Ancient Records* [above, p. 794 note 1] 2:84, who understands that the horses kept formation; Fales, *Studies Tadmor*, 133, who understands that the riders rode bareback).

on bedrock and was eight cubits thick, beginning at its parapet and going all the way down to its deepest foundations, I demolished completely and left it at ground level. I set fire to the houses inside, their lengthy timbers I turned into ashes. I burned 115 settlements in its environs like brushwood, I covered the face of the sky with the smoke of them, like a stormcloud. I made its territory as if a deluge had laid it waste. I left its inhabited settlements in heaps like dumps. I wrecked and turned into flat ground the city Aniashtaniu, his stock center, built on the border of Sangibute between Ushqaia and Tarmakisa, (185) along with seventeen settlements in its environs, I set their lengthy roof timbers on fire, I torched their crops and their fodder. I opened the storage granaries and fed my troops on grain rations beyond measure. I let loose my army's livestock on his pasturelands like a swarm of locusts, they tore up the pasturage he depended upon and laid waste his fields.

I set forth from Ushqaia and reached Bari, the source of his livestock, which they call the land of Sangibutu. The cities Tarui and Tarmakisa, mighty fortresses, were built in the land of the Dalaeans, as the center for his numerous grain stores. (190) Their fortifications are particularly strong, their outer wall solid, their moats surrounding their perimeters extra deep, within them were stabled the horses, the reserve of his royal army, which they fed on grain the year round. The people who dwelt in that district saw my lordly treatment that I had meted out, one after another, upon the settlements around them; they were overcome with terror. They forsook their settlements and fled for their lives into a dry wasteland, an arid place, like a desert. I covered that region like a closing trap, I flushed battle among its fortified cities. (195) I demolished their mighty fortresses, [beginning at their parapets], all the way down to their deepest foundations, leaving them at ground level. I set fire to the houses inside, their lengthy timbers I turned to ashes. I torched their rich crops, [I opened the storage granaries] and fed my troops on grain rations beyond measure.

(Sargon describes Rusa's resort town, Ulhu.)

I set forth towards Tarmakisa and reached [   ] (200) Ulhu, a stronghold at the foot of [Mount Kishpal], and its people [ ] like fish, but without enough to drink, Ursa the king and sovereign, with his own ingenuity, [   ] discovered a source of water.[1] He dug a canal to bring running water, he channeled water abundant as the Euphrates. He opened out from the main channel innumerable subsidiary channels [ ], [with the water he brought] he irrigated the fields. (205) His fields, which had hitherto been dry, [thereafter] would shower down fruit and grapes like a downpour. With plane trees and walnut(?) trees, worthy of a palace, [ ] he shaded his district, as if with a forest. And so in its hitherto uncultivated fields [ ] he caused his people to sing sweet songs of harvest. He made 300 measures of cultivated land produce the finest grain from [its] fur[rows]* and increased the surplus available for commerce. He made the waste areas of his agricultural land into fertile meadows [ ] very much in the spring, and grain and pasturage were perpetual, both winter and summer. (210) He turned them into a paddock for horses and herds of cattle and taught his entire inaccessible land the use of camels, so they could (use them) to build water works.

He built a palace, a royal pleasure resort on the bank of the watercourse, roofing it with timbers of evergreen trees of agreeable scent. [He built] the city Sardurhurda, a fortress to guard him, on Mount Kishter and brought in [ ] people to secure his land. When the people of that district heard of the painful rebuke I had cast into Rusa's teeth, they cried "Woe!" and slapped their thighs in grief. They forsook the city Ulhu, their stronghold, as well as the city Sardurihurda, the fortress for [their] security, and fled to difficult mountains by night. (215) In the wrath of my heart, [I covered] the extremities of that district like a fog, I locked it in on every side as with ice. I entered in state the city Ulhu, Ursa's pleasure resort, I went haughtily [into] his own royal palace. I hacked down with iron axes its strong wall made from stones of a tall mountain, as if it were pottery, and turned it into flat ground. I [tore out] the lengthy evergreen timbers that roofed his palace, smoothed them [with ad]zes(?), and took them to Assyria. I opened his storage granaries and fed my troops on grain rations numerous beyond measure. (220) I entered his private wine stores and the numerous troops of Assyria drank sweet wine like wa-

1. For a proposal that this passage describes the underground irrigation technique known as *qanat*, see J. Laessøe, "The Irrigation System at Ulhu, 8th Century B.C.," JCS 5 (1951), 21–28; for a discussion of the whole passage, proposing that it was based on an Urartian original, see C. Zaccagnini, "An Urartean Royal Inscription in the Report of Sargon's Eighth Campaign," OAIC 17 (1981), 259–295.

ter from a river, from waterskins and leather buckets. I dammed up
the outlets for the canal, the watercourse that he depended on, and
turned the abundant waters into a mudflat. I blocked the gurgling
outtakes branching off from its main channel, I exposed the deepest
pebbles on their bottoms to the sunlight.[1] I let my fierce troops into
his splendid garden, one of the attractions of his city, which was ornamented with fruit trees and vines, dripping (with fruit) like rain-
drops, and they made their iron axes roar like thunder. (225) They
picked his countless fruit and left no pleasure for the weary of heart*
for many years to come. I spread out, flat as malt, the great trees that
were the special feature of his palace, I defiled his famous city and
made its region a disgrace. I gathered into a heap all those trees I had
cut down and set them on fire. I uprooted their vast crops, countless
as reeds in a marsh, leaving not one ear to show what had been destroyed. His splendid fields, which looked like red faience, and cultivated plots well planted with spring growth and rising shoots, (230)
I passed over like a cyclone with chariotry, cavalry, and the tramping
of my foot soldiers, and turned the pasturage, which his horses depended on, into wasteland. I completely destroyed the city Sardurihurda, that great stronghold, as well as fifty-seven settlements around
it of the district Sangibuti, and turned it into flat ground. I set fire to
their roof timbers and burned them to ashes.

From the city Ulhu I set forth and arrived at the rural hamlets and
major fortified cities of that district land of Sangibute, a well-popu-
lated district, a possession of his land which kings who preceded him
annexed from of old to enlarge their land. (235) (*list follows*), twenty-
one strong cities which thrust up like mountain timber on the peaks
of Mount Arzabia, (240) mighty fortresses [ ] surrounded by walls,
the height of the parapets of which was 120 brick courses, [ ] for the
stationing of troops [ ], presenting an awe-inspiring aspect to the
combatant, extra deep moats [and] their portals ringed by towers.
Watercourses would bring plentiful water into [ ], which never
ceased in their region [ ]. Their people, in abundance and prosperity, [ ] … and vast wealth, (245) enormous palaces, like [in which]

---

1. This line could well be drawn from a now missing passage in the Gilgamesh Epic, Tablet VIII,
in which Gilgamesh dammed the Euphrates to construct a tomb for Enkidu (see Foster, *Gilgamesh*,
152); it occurs as well in a series of omens concerning the appearance of rivers. In any case, it is a
literary allusion.

were spread out furnishings fit for a king, fragrant timbers from evergreen trees [ ], which waft into the senses of anyone who enters like cedar. When the people of the district Sangibute, those who dw[elt in the hamlets] and those who dwelt in those cities, [saw] the cloud of dust raised by my army a double league away, panic befell the whole land of Urartu. For them to watch out for enemies(?) in the district, towers had been built on mountain peaks and provided with [stores of firewood for signals]. When they saw the (250) bonfires lit, signaling the approach of an enemy, [for which] torches [were kept ready(?)] day and night, announcing [ ], they feared my furious attack, which has no like, terror spread among them, and they were too af[raid to fight]. Without so much as a glance at their numerous possessions, they forsook their mighty fortresses and disappeared. I blanketed that district like a cloud at nightfall, [I overran] all their strong cities like a swirling flood. I advanced a distance of twelve double leagues between Mounts Arzabia and Irtia and made my encampment. (255) I had my furious troops pass through the mountain's remotest recesses, like mountain sheep, I spared not a single scout to hear their commands. I had the vast armies of Assur swarm over their cities like locusts and I let my swift, plundering troops enter their innermost chambers. The good, chattels and treasures [ ] they brought me, I laid hands on their accumulated wealth. I sent up auxiliaries and foot soldiers bearing [ ] onto their walls, I assigned demolition teams to the battlements and ravelins(?). I tore out the timbers of evergreen wood that roofed the palaces and the people of the land of the Mannaeans and the land of Nairi [ ]. (260) I [demolished] their high citadels, strongly built on the mountains, all the way to their foundations, like sand castles. I set fire to their artfully built houses and caused the smoke of them to rise up to cover the sky like a fog. My whole army loaded up horses, mules, camels, and donkeys with the great stores of barley and wheat which they had garnered, over a long time, to sustain their land and people, and piled them up like hillocks in my encampment. I fed my people on abundant and satisfying food, they joyfully laid up enormous supplies for the return march to the land of Assyria. (265) I chopped down his delightful orchards, I chopped down his numerous vineyards, so cut off his source of drink. I cut down his immense forests, the trees of which were as dense and impenetrable as a canebrake, and turned his region into a wasteland. I gathered all his cut-down trees and set them on fire. I torched 146 settlements in the environs like brushwood, the smoke of them blotted the sky like a storm cloud.

I set forth from the strong cities of Sangibute, I arrived at the district of Aramarili. (270) I destroyed completely the city Bubuzi, the fortress city Hundur, which was surrounded by two walls, the entry to its tower connected with a drawbridge(?)⋆ of rope,[1] (*list follows*), seven strong cities, as well as thirty settlements in their environs, which lie at the foot of Mount Ubianda, and I turned them into flat ground. I set fire to their roof timbers and burned them to ashes. I opened their storage granaries and fed my troops on their grain rations beyond measure. (275) I set fire to their crops, the support of his people, and the hay, the life of his livestock, like brushwood, and I turned his agricultural area into a wasteland. I cut down their orchards and I chopped down their forests, I gathered all their trees into a heap and set them on fire. As I passed, I went to Arbu, Rusa's ancestral city, and to Riar, the city of Sarduri.[2] I destroyed seven settlements in their environs, the favorite residences of his brothers, his royal family, and which were strongly guarded, I turned them into flat ground. I set fire to the temple of Haldia, his god, like brushwood, and I desecrated its inner sanctum.

(280) I set forth from Armariali, crossed Mount Uizuku, a mountain covered with evergreens and formed of breccia-stone, and arrived at Mount Aaidi. His thirty strong cities (*list follows, 285*), arranged regularly along the shore of the surfing sea,[3] on the outcroppings of the great mountains, Argishtiuna and Qallania, his mighty fortresses, were constructed among them. They rose like stars above Mounts Arsidu and Mahunnia, and looked down 240 cubits below. His best, veteran soldiers were stationed inside them with shields and spears, the security of his land. (290) When they saw the conquest of Armariali, the district next to theirs, their legs trembled, they forsook their cities along with their possessions, and flew away like birds to those fortresses. I sent up many troops to their cities and they looted their property, in vast quantities, for themselves. I demolished their mighty walls, as well as eighty-seven settlements in their environs,

---

1. Obscure, translation uncertain.
2. Probably Rusa's father and predecessor on the throne.
3. Presumably Lake Van is meant.

and rendered them flat ground. I set fire to the houses inside and burned their roof timbers to ashes. I opened their storage granaries and fed my troops on grain rations beyond measure. I cut down their orchards and chopped down their forests, I gathered all their trees and set them on fire.

I set forth from the land of Ayadi, crossed the rivers Alluria, Qallaria, and Innaya. I arrived at the city U'ayish, one of his key districts on the lower frontier of the land of Urartu, bordering on the Nairi-lands. U'ayish was his strongest city and greatest fortress, more strongly fortified than all his other fortresses, and artfully constructed, (300) his fiercest combat troops and scouts who gathered information on all the lands in the area were stationed there, and he had brought his governors with their forces inside it and manned its mighty ramparts with fighting men. I conquered that fortress from the rear, I slaughtered his warriors in front of its main gate like sacrificial sheep. I cut down his orchards and chopped down his forests, I gathered all of his cut-down trees and set them on fire. (305) I set fire to five mighty fortresses (*list follows*), as well as forty settlements in the environs.

I set forth from the city U'ayish, I arrived at the territory of Yanzu, king of the Nairi-lands. Yanzu, king of the Nairi-lands, came to my presence a distance of four double leagues from his royal capital, Hubushkia, and did homage to me. I received from him his tribute of trained horses, oxen, and sheep in Hubushkia, his city.

During my return march, Urzana of Musasir,[1] that criminal and malefactor who transgressed an oath to the gods, who did not acknowledge my lordship, (310) a vicious mountain man who, breaking a loyalty oath to Assur, Shamash, Nabu, and Marduk, rebelled against me, interrupted the progress of my return march by not doing homage to me with a massive greeting gift from him. He withheld his tribute payment and gift, nor did he send a single courier to greet me. In my fury of heart, I sent on all my chariotry, numerous cavalry, and my entire main army, along the road to Assyria. With the great support of Assur, father of the gods, lord of all lands, king of heaven

---

1. For the location of this place, perhaps northeast of modern Rowanduz in Iraq, see M. Salvini, M. Boehmer, "Muṣaṣir," RLA 8, 444–450. For the position of Urzana as king of a small state between Urartu and Assyria, see Deller in P. Pecorella, M. Salvini, eds., *Tra lo Zagros e l'Urmia* (Rome, 1984), 97–122; a new edition of these letters is G. Lanfranchi, S. Parpola, SAA 5 (1990), see pp. xiii–xx.

and earth, begetter of <all>(?), lord of lords, to whom (315) from of old the Enlil of the gods, Marduk, bestowed the gods of heaven and netherworld and the four corners of the earth, that they ever, without ceasing, honor him above all others, and that he (Assur) bring them into (his temple) Ehursaggalkurkurra with their accumulated treasures,[1] and at the sublime command of Nabu and Marduk, who had taken the course in the constellations favorable to my attack,[2] and, furthermore, at a favorable sign for conquest: the moon, lord of the tiara, prolonged (an eclipse?) for (more than one?)* watch, auguring the fall of Gutium,[3] and at the precious assent of Shamash the warrior, who caused an unambiguous omen to be inscribed for me on the liver (of a sacrificed animal), portending that he would go at my side, (320) I prepared just my own, single chariot and a thousand eager soldiers, troops with bow, shield, and spear, my fiercest warriors, veterans of combat, and I took the difficult road to Musasir. I took my army over Mount Arsi'u, a mighty mountain whose heights are unscalable ridges. I crossed the Upper Zab, which the people of the Nairi-lands and of the land of Habhi call Elamunia, past Mounts Sheiak, Ardikshi, Ulayu, and Alluri, high mountains, (325) lofty mountains, narrow mountain ledges which defy description(?)*, among which there is no pathway for the passage of infantry, through which mighty cascades have cut their way, the din of their falls roaring like thunder a double league off, and every kind of useful tree, shrub, and vine grows in a tangle like a canebrake, intimidating to anyone who thinks of entering them, which no king whatsoever had traversed nor any prince who preceded me had seen the pathways whereof. I cut through their dense growth and broke up their narrow ridges with bronze axes. (330) I made good going for my army among them with a narrow passage, a strait pathway, which the foot soldiers could get through only sideways. I laid my riding chariot on shoulders and proceeded on horseback at the head of my troops. I had my mounted warriors at my sides narrow down to single file and got them through their narrow places. I gave orders to my staff and

---

1.   That is, Marduk had ceded rule of heaven and earth to Assur (see Tallqvist, StOr 4/III, 60).

2.   This refers to a favorable astrological interpretation of the positions of the planets Mercury and Jupiter in the night sky.

3.   Gutium here is an obsolete literary term for mountain enemies; compare III.7b(3) and IV.30b.

officers, as well as to their forces, that he must not escape, and sent rapidly [   ].

(Succession and coronation of Urartian crown prince takes place in Musasir)[1]

When he saw the [   ] of my army, [Urzana ...(335)] the city [Musasir], his royal dwelling and the dwelling of Haldi [his god, the deity that is highest in] the entire extent of the land of Urartu, they know no higher god than he in heaven and earth [   ], without whom neither scepter nor crown is taken up, the symbols of govern[ment]. The sovereign who governs the people of Urartu [   ], they would bring him, and they would present whichever of his sons was to take the throne (340) before Haldi in Musasir with gold and silver and every sort of precious treasure from his palace and would give him gifts, they would offer huge [cat]tle, fatted sheep beyond number, and prepare a feast for his whole city. [In the presence of] Haldi his god they would place on him the crown of lordship and have him take up the scepter of kingship of Urartu, and the people would hail his name. Against that city I let my troops' battle cry roar like thunder and the inhabitants [   ], the old men and women of its people went up on the roofs of their houses to weep bitterly [   ] they groveled on all fours to save their lives.

(Sargon deports the residents of the city.)

Because Urzana their sovereign did not fear the name of Assur, had cast off his allegiance to me and forgotten his duty, I resolved to deport the people of that city and I commanded the removal of Haldi, the mainstay of the land of Urartu. I haughtily sat him down before his own gate[2] (to watch me) deport his wife, his son and daughters, and his entire royal family, I included them with 6110 people, 12 mules, 380 donkeys, 525 cattle, and 1235 sheep, and brought them into the enclosure of my encampment. (350) I haughtily entered the

1. M. Salvini, "Bemerkungen über die Thronfolge in Urartu," in H. Klengel, ed., *Gesellschaft und Kultur im alten Vorderasien, Schriften zur Geschichte und Kultur des Alten Orients* 15 (1982), 219–227, especially 226–227.

2. Some scholars consider that this refers to Haldi (see Kravitz, JNES 62 [2003], 87), but this seems unlikely because Sargon makes special mention of his efforts to prevent Urzana's flight (line 333) and this would presumably not have been the case if Urzana had escaped. On the other hand, there is no mention of Urzana's fate, though some letters from him to the Assyrian court may postdate the destruction of Musasir (see p. 806 note 1).

[city] Musasir, dwelling of the god Haldi, and took up residence in state in the palace, Urzana's dwelling.

(Sargon lists the plundered furnishings of the palace.)[1]

[ ] I opened all the seals of the treasures of the storerooms, replete with heaped-up precious objects: [34 talents 18] minas of gold, 167 talents, 2½ minas of silver, gleaming copper, tin, carnelian, lapis, agates, a choice assemblage of stones in great number, [chairs] of ivory, ebony, and boxwood, as well as wooden caskets set with gold and silver, [ ] huge tables of ivory, ebony, and boxwood, fit for a king, set with gold and silver; 8 items: heavy carving platters and vegetable baskets of ivory, ebony, and boxwood, with gold and silver decorations and mountings; 6 items: potstands, racks, screens, stools, and serving stands of ebony and boxwood with gold and silver decorations; 6 items: gold knives with pine cone-shaped handles, a smaller gold knife, a gold fly whisk, an alabaster bowl inlaid with gems and gold; 11 items: a silver bowl belonging to Rusa himself with its lid, bowls from the land of Tabal with gold handles, silver helmets, silver arrows with gold inlay; 34 items: silver bowls with deep, shallow, and [nar]row fluting, and smaller bowls and cups of silver; (360) 54 items: massive silver bowls with their covers and cups, (decorated with?) bosses, crescents, and rings of silver; 5 items: incense stands from the land of Tabal with silver holders(?),[2] covers, and fire platforms, and censers of silver; 13 items: copper kettles and cauldrons, wash basins, water pails, pots, and pans; 24 items: copper stands, kettles, dishes, vessels, rings, hooks, and lamps; 120 items: copper utensils, heavy and light, workmanship of their land, the words for which are impossible to spell, (365) [items]: an iron stove with fire rake, poker, shovel, and lamps of iron, 130 items: garments with multi-colored trim, made of linen, purple wool, and plain wool, and garments of red wool from the lands of Urartu and Habhi, together with the (other) possessions of his palace, (all this) I looted and I heaped up his property.

(Sargon plunders the temple of Haldi.)

---

1. For an illustrated study of the objects listed hereafter, see W. Mayer, "Die Finanzierung einer Kampagne," UF 11 (1979), 571–579; some may also appear in P. R. S. Moorey, "Metal Wine-Sets in the Ancient Near East," *Iranica Antiqua* 15 (1980), 181–197.
2. Literally: quivers.

I sent my officers and soldiers to the temple of Haldi. [x+] 3 talents. 3? minas of gold, 162 talents 20 minas 6 shekels of silver, 3600 talents of bronze in pieces: (370) [6 items]: shields of gold which hung to the right and left in his cella and shone brilliantly, with heads of snarling lions thrusting out from their centers, weighing 5 talents 12 minas of red gold, [1 item]: a horned [   ], the holding bar of his door, of poured, refined gold weighing 2 talents; 1 item: a latch of gold in the shape of a human hand, that secured the double doors, with a winged deluge monster crouching on top of it; 1 item: a lock pin of gold, that held the bar securing the temple lock and guarded the possessions and property stored there; (375) 2 items: gold keys in the shape of crowned female protective geniuses, holding rods and rings and trampling snarling lions underfoot, these four being the door closure decorating the inner chamber, having a weight of 2 talents 12 minas of gold, being what held the door in place; 1 item: a great sword, the weapon at his side, weighing 26 minas 3 shekels of gold; 96 items: silver spears, helmets, bows, and arrows, with gold mountings and decoration; 12 items: massive silver shields, the outer bands of which were decorated with flood monsters, lions, and wild bulls; 67 items: silver kettles, stands, pot racks,* and vegetable baskets, with gold decorations and mountings; 62 items: libation vessels, silver pomegranates, and miscellaneous silver implements with gold mountings and decoration; 33 items: silver chariots, bows, quivers, rods, staffs, ..., shields, cone(-shaped guards?), throw spears(?), and standards of silver; 393 items: silver plates, heavy and light, handiwork of the lands of Assyria, Urartu, and Habhi; 2 items: wild bull horns with decorations and platings of <silver>, with gold rivets surrounding their mountings; (385) 1 item: a gold harp for carrying out the rites of the goddess Bagamashtu,[1] the spouse of Haldi, covered with choice gems; 9 items: garments of the gods with gold disks and rosettes, their seams held with lattice(?) work; 7 each: pairs of boots covered with gold stars, with a crop of silver and stitching and mounting of gold; 1 item: a bed of ivory(?) and silver, the god's place of repose, inlaid with gems and gold; 139 items: staves, trays, vegetable baskets, knives, and smaller knives of ivory with gold decorations; (390) 10

---

1.   While an Iranian etymology for Haldi's spouse has been proposed (Biagov, *Oikumene* 2 [1978], 49–52, reference courtesy P. Zimansky), the reading of the name may be either Bagbartu or Bag(a)mashtu.

items: boxwood tables with frames of boxwood, legs of ebony and boxwood, and gold and silver mountings; 2 items: display boxes(?) with 14 assorted gems, being the divine adornments and jewelry of Haldi and his spouse, Bagamashtu.

25,212 items: copper shields, heavy and light, copper crests, helmets, and head armor; 1514 items: copper spears, heavy and light, and heavy copper spear points, throw spears(?), and lances, with their copper storage racks(?); 305,412 items: copper swords, heavy and light, copper bows, quivers, and arrows; (395) 607 items: copper kettles, heavy and light, copper wash basins, water pails, pots, and vases; 3 items: heavy copper cauldrons of fifty liquid measures capacity, together with their heavy copper stands; 1 item: a huge copper vessel of eighty liquid measures capacity, together with its huge copper stand, which the kings of Urartu would fill with wine libations to make offerings before Haldi; 4 items: statues of supernatural door attendants, to watch over his doors, four cubits high with their pedestals, cast in copper; (400) 1 item: a praying statue standing for the king, (dedicated) by Sarduri son of Ishpuini,[1] king of the land of Urartu, its pedestal cast in bronze; 1 item: a bull, a cow and her calf (dedicated) by Sarduri son of Ishpuini, metal objects dedicated to the temple, which he had inscribed; 1 item: a statue of Argishti,[2] king of the land of Urartu, wearing a starry crown like a god, his right hand raised in blessing, together with its housing, weighing 60 talents; 1 item: a statue of Rusa with his two horses and his charioteer, together with its base, cast in copper, (inscribed with) his self-glorification: "With my two horses and my one charioteer did I take over kingship of the land of Urartu" – these things did I plunder, (405) as well as countless other possessions of his, not to mention the innumerable utensils of gold, silver, tin, copper, lead, ivory, ebony, boxwood and every other sort of wood which the troops of Assur and Marduk plundered.

(The Urartian king learns of his loss.)

The property from the palace of Urzana and Haldi, as well as his

---

1. There was an Ishpuini who was a ninth-century king of Urartu, but no son of his named Sarduri is otherwise known, so this may be a local dynasty at Musasir using the same royal names (Mayer, UF 11 [1979], 572 note 2).
2. Presumably Argishti I (mid-eighth century), grandfather of Rusa.

extensive property which I plundered in the city Musasir, I loaded on my numerous troops in a body and had it transported to the land of Assyria. (410) I incorporated the people of the district of Musasir as people of the land of Assyria and imposed on them duties and labor service as if they were Assyrians.

When Rusa heard of this, he collapsed on the ground, tore his garments to shreds, and threw up his hands (in despair), He flung away his headgear, tore out his hair, pounded* his chest with both hands, then threw himself flat on his face. His heart stood still, his feelings burned within him, screams of grief rose from his lips. I caused cries of woe to resound throughout all of the land of Urartu and I caused perpetual mourning for the Nairi-lands.[1]

(Sargon returns to Assyria.)

With the sublime strength of Assur my lord, with the power and might of Marduk and Nabu, my divine allies, with the firm assent of Shamash, supreme judge of the gods, who opened the way and provided protection for my army, with the greatness of Nergal, mightiest of the gods, who marched beside me and guarded my camp, I came through the land of Sumbi, a district between Mounts Nikippa and Upa, difficult mountains, (420) having made a noble march that no one could resist through the lands of Urartu, Zikirte, the Mannaeans, Nairi-lands, and Musasir, like a terrifying, marauding lion! I defeated the great armies of Rusa the Urartian and Metatti the Zikirtaean, I conquered a total of 430 cities and settlements in seven districts belonging to Rusa the Urartian, and laid waste his land! I plundered Urzana the Musasirian, Haldi his god, and Bagamashti his goddess, as well as numerous goods of his palace, along with 6110 people, 12 mules, 380 donkeys, 525 cattle, 1285 sheep, and his wife, his sons, and his daughters! (425) I came out and returned safely to my land through the pass of Andurutta, a difficult mountain opposite the city Hipparna. (Herewith) one charioteer, two horsemen, and three scouts (of those who) were killed.[2]

---

1. In a later version of this episode, Sargon claimed that Rusa killed himself at this point (Kravitz, JNES 62 [20003], 94 note 59).

2. This does not mean the actual casualties but refers to a memorial ceremony in honor of all soldiers lost in the campaign (Luckenbill, *Ancient Records* [above, p. 794 note 1], 2:99 note 2).

I send herewith to Assur my lord the best orator, Tab-shar-Assur, chief steward.

(Tablet of Nabu-shallimshunu, chief royal scribe, amanuensis* and scholar to Sargon, king of the land of Assyria, son of Harmakku, royal scribe, a native of Assur, delivered in the eponymate of Ishtar-duri, governor of Arrapha.)

Text: Thureau-Dangin, TCL 3, pl. 1–30; Schroeder, KAH II 141; Weidner, AfO 12 (1937/8), 145–146 (pl. 11) (VAT 8696b, c).

Edition: F. Thureau-Dangin, *Une Relation de la huitième campagne de Sargon (714 av. J.-C.)* (Paris, 1912), 2–67; W. Mayer, "Sargons Feldzug gegen Urartu – 714 v. Chr., Text und Übersetzung," MDOG 115 (1983), 65–132.

Translation: D. D. Luckenbill, *Ancient Records of Assyria and Babylonia* (Chicago, 1927), 2:73–99, from which I have taken some felicitous wording.

Literature: Weidner, AfO 12 (1937/8), 144–148 (collations and improved readings); see also above, p. 809 note 1. The geography of the campaign has been studied several times, with different results: Lehmann-Haupt, MVAeG 21 [1916], 119–151; Rigg, JAOS 62 (1942), 130–138; Wright, JNES 2 (1943), 173–186; Levine in L. D. Levine, T. C. Young, Jr., ed., *Mountains and Lowlands: Essays in the Archaeology of Greater Mesopotamia*, Bibliotheca Mesopotamica 7 (1977), 135–151; Cilingiroglu, *Jahrbuch für Kleinasiatische Forschung* 4/5 (1976/7), 252–271; Kleiss, *Archäologische Mitteilungen aus Iran* 10 (1977), 137–141; Mayer, MDOG 112 (1980), 13–33; P. Zimansky, *Ecology and Empire: The Structure of the Urartian State*, SAOC 41 (1985), 40–47; Chamaza, *Archäologische Mitteilungen aus Iran* 27 (1994), 91–118; 28 (1995/6), 235–267; for a skeptical view, Burney in S. Mazzoni, ed., *Nuove fondazioni nel vicino oriente antico: realità e ideologica* (Pisa, 1994), 300: "speculations on inadequate data." For general studies, see above, p. 790 note 1; A. L. Oppenheim, "The City of Assur in 714 B. C.," JNES 19 (1960), 133–147; M. Kravitz, "A Last-Minute Revision to Sargon's Letter to the God," JNES 62 (2003), 81–95.

Notes to Text: (62) Borger, BiOr 21 (1964), 145. (101) Compare line 215. (208) Borger, BiOr 18 (1961), 154a. (225) Landsberger, ZA 42 (1934), 165. (270) Borger, BiOr 14 (1957), 121a = AHw, 1364b. (318) I follow CAD A/2, 104b. Mayer: "strengte die Beobachter sehr an." (325) Reading *ed-lu*!?, but obscure; Mayer: "mit nicht zählbaren Stufen." (380) Assuming a scribal error for *kankanne*. (412) Reading *u-rap-pi!-is*. (428) For *giburu*, see Reiner JNES 26 (1967), 200.

IV.3 ESARHADDON AND ISHTAR OF ARBELA

Esarhaddon (680–669 B.C.) ruled the Assyrian empire in one of its most power-ful and prosperous periods. This king is sometimes reputed to have been unusually superstitious and much under the influence of exorcists and diviners. These devised elaborate rituals for him to avoid evils, real or imagined (see p. 777 note 3). For a historical survey of his reign, see Grayson, CAH³ 3/2, 122–141.

Tablets from Nineveh preserve prayers of Esarhaddon and his son, Assurba-nipal, together with divine responses, or oracles. About fifty such oracles are known; for English translations of others, see Parpola, SAA 9.

(§1) I am Ishtar of [Arbela]. O Esarhaddon, king of the land of As[syria], I give long days and eternal years to Esarhaddon, my king in the City,[1] in Nine[veh], Calah, and Arbela. I am your great mid-wife, I your good wetnurse. I have made firm your throne for long days and eternal years under the great heavens. I watch over you in a golden abode in the midst of heaven. I will let a gemstone lamp glow before Esarhaddon, king of the land of Assyria, and I will watch over him like the very crown on my head.

(§2) Fear not, O King! I have spoken to you, I have not disappointed you. I will not let [you] come to shame. I will bring you over the river safely. O Esarhaddon, rightful heir of Mullissu, with a raging dagger in my hands I will finish off your enemies, O Esarhaddon, king of the land of Assyria, cupful of lye, an adze weighing (only) two shekels![2]

(§3) I will give you long days and eternal years in the City, O Es-arhaddon, in Arbela, I will be your good shield. O Esarhaddon, [rightful] heir of Mul[lissu], I am mindful of you. I have loved you so much. I hold you in heaven by your curly hair, I raise smoke at your right, I set fire at your left.

(gap)

Text: Pinches, IV R² 61, iii 7′–iv 19; photo Parpola, SAA 9 (1997), pl. I–III.
Edition: Parpola, SAA 9 (1997), 7–8.
Literature: S. Parpola, *Assyrian Prophecies*, SAA 9 (1997).

1. Assur.
2. This may mean that Esarhaddon is ineffective as a warrior without Ishtar's assistance.

IV.4 ASSURBANIPAL

The last great Assyrian king, Assurbanipal succeeded to the throne of the empire in 669 B.C. The events surrounding his accession are referred to in IV.4c below. Among his many military achievements was the conquest of Elam, the traditional enemy of Babylonia (see above, III.11 and III.12). This event is referred to in a prayer to Marduk[1] and other literary texts too fragmentary for translation here.[2]

At Assurbanipal's order was assembled a library at Nineveh, the largest known collection of Akkadian literary and scholarly texts (see General Introduction, B.2 and IV.4g). In his inscriptions Assurbanipal boasts of his scholarly attainments (IV.4d, g), so it is tempting to see in the turgid and verbose style of the compositions in his name some imprint of the royal personality. For another hymn in the name of Assurbanipal, see III.51g. For a historical survey of his reign, see Grayson, CAH[3] 3/2, 142–161.

(a) CORONATION PRAYER

This prayer was evidently composed for the coronation[3] of Assurbanipal. It alludes to the Middle Assyrian prayer translated above, III.5a and is closely related to Creation of the King (III.18c).

> (1) May Shamash, king of heaven and earth, elevate you to shepherdship of the four [world regions]. May Assur, who bestows [the scepter], prolong your days and your years. Enlarge the land at your feet, may my god(?) ascend to yours![4] (5) Just as grain and silver, oil, cattle, and the salt of Bariku[5] are desirable, so too may the name of Assurbanipal, king of Assyria, be desirable to the gods. May they grant him speaking and hearing, truth and justice.
> May the [resident] of Assur obtain 30 kor[6] of grain for 1 shekel of silver, may the [resi]dent of Assur obtain 30 quarts of oil for 1 shekel

---

1. S. Strong, *Journal Asiatique* 9 série 1893, 361–380.
2. Livingstone, *Court Poetry*, 48–51.
3. Ebeling, AfO 13 (1939/41), 324.
4. Obscure. The speaker may be the personage presiding at the ceremony; he may be saying that Assur is to become the king's personal god (differently Livingstone, *Court Poetry*, 26 note 4).
5. A place, the salt from which was used at the gods' repast; see p. 335 note 1.
6. Roughly 170 bushels. This and the following schematic figures are supposed to convey great prosperity.

of silver, (10) may the [resident] of Assur obtain 30 minas of wool for 1 shekel of silver. May the [great] listen when the lesser speak, may the [lesser] listen when the great speak, may harmony and peace be established [in Assur].

(15) Assign, may they protect [the life? of Assurba]nipal, king of Assyria.* May they give him a just scepter to enlarge [his] land and people. May his reign be ever renewed, may they establish his royal throne forever. May they bless him day, month, and year, may they [make] his reign [out]standing. (20) [During] his years, may the rain from heaven and the flood from the underground depths be un-fai[ling].

Grant to Assurbanipal, king of Assyria, our lord, long [days], m[any] years, a strong [wea]pon, a long reign, [year]s of abundance, a good name, and reputation, contentment, happiness, good rep[ute] and first rank among kings.[1]

(26) Anu has given [his] crown, Enlil has given his throne, Ninurta has given his weapon, Nergal has given his splendor, (30) Nusku has sent (wise) counselors to stand in attendance upon him.

He who shall speak insolence or falsehood to the king, be he important, he will die violently; be he rich, he will become poor. He who shall harbor ev[il] against the king in his heart, Erra will call him to account in a plague. He who thinks disrespectful thoughts of the king, his foundations will be a cyclone, his possessions will be empty air.*

Assemble, all ye gods of heaven and netherworld, bless Assurbanipal, king, counselor-man! Deliver the weapon of combat and battle into his hand. (40) Give him the people of this land, that he serve as their shepherd.

Text: Ebeling-Köcher-Rost, LKA 31.
Edition: Weidner, AfO 13 (1939/41), 210–213, 324–325; Livingstone, *Court Poetry*, 26–27.
Translation: Seux, *Hymnes*, 110–112; Livingstone in Hallo, ed., *Context*, 1:473–474.
Literature: Arneth, *Zeitschrift für Altorientalische und Biblische Rechtsgeschichte* 5 (1999), 28–53.
Notes to Text: (15) Seux, *Hymnes*, 111 note 10. (34f.) Mayer, OrNS 56 (1987), 66 and Seux, *Hymnes*, 112 note 21; Livingstone: "his foundation is (but) wind, the hem of his garment is (but) litter." Collation by Mayer, OrNS 66 (1997), 167–168.

1. A direction is inserted here for the officiant: "As soon as he has made the blessing, he turns around and makes a blessing toward the 'Censer Gate', that is, toward Shamash."

(b) TO ASSUR

This hymn glorifies Assur as Anshar, a primeval deity.[1] It concludes with a blessing upon the text and its royal speaker.

Most great one, noblest of the gods, omniscient,   (1)
Eminent, supreme Enlil[2] of the gods, ordainer of destinies,
Assur, most great lord, noblest of the gods, omniscient,
Eminent, supreme Enlil of the gods, ordainer of destinies,
[Let me ex]alt* Assur, the powerful, noblest of the gods,
    lord of the world,   (5)
[Let me pro]claim his greatness,
    let me ever make splendid his praise,
Let me proclaim the renown of [As]sur,
    let me exalt his name,
[He who] dwells in Ehursaggalkalamma,[3]
    let me ever make splendid his praise.
Let me ever invoke [the powerful one],*
    let me praise his valor,
[Him who] dwells in Esharra,[4] Assur,
    who ordains destinies,   (10)
Let me disclose* for all time, to [rev]eal to humankind,
[Let me bequeath] a reminder for later ones to hear,
[Let me exalt] the sovereignty of [Assur] forever.
[Cap]able one, profound of wisdom,
    sage of the gods, princely one,
[Father], creator of what is in the heavens and earth,
    who formed the mountains,   (15)
[Assur], creator of gods, begetter of goddess(es),
[Whose heart] is inscrutable, whose mind is ingenious,
Lofty [hero] whose name is feared,
His ow[n counselor], Assur, whose utterance is profound,

---

1. Assur is here written Anshar. According to the Epic of Creation (III.17) Tablet I line 14, Anshar was the father of Anu; here he is equated with Assur in order to give Assur a place among the primeval deities (ahead of Marduk). See also Livingstone, *Court Poetry*, xvii; Tadmor, JCS 12 (1958), 82.
2. That is, supreme god of the pantheon.
3. Part of the Assur temple in Assur.
4. The Assur temple in Assur.

The basis [of his word], like a mountain, cannot be moved,   (20)
[His command], like the graven signs of the starry sky,[1]
    cannot miss its appointed time.
[He whose] word cannot be [alter]ed,* whose command is sure,
[Assur, the basis of his word],
    like a mountain, cannot be moved,
[His command], like the graven signs of the starry sky,
    cannot miss its appointed time.
Your wo[rd] is [ ], spoken from of old!   (25)
No god, O Anshar, can comprehend [ ] of your [great]ness,
The reason for your [   ] cannot be perceived!
[w]hose battle is irresistible,
[   ], which splits open mountains,
[None can withstand him,
    who] relies upon his own strength   (30)

(fragmentary lines, then gap)

[A]nu, Enlil, Ea, Belet-ili, and [Ninl]il,
Who acknowledged the sovereignty of Assur
    in the Assembly Place of the Gods,[2]
Have said, "May Assurbanipal, vicegerent for Assur,
    alone be the provider!"[3]
Among descendants, in far-off days,
For future reigns, years without number,   (10′)
May th(is) praise of Assur be not forgotten,
    may it* keep one mindful of Esharra![4]
Let it be in (every) mouth,
    may it never cease to enlarge understanding,
So that, as to me, Assur will deliver into your[5] hands
    sovereignty of land and people.
Splendid is the name of Assur, most great his divinity.
The praise of Assur, lord of lords, the valiant one,
    is (doubly) sweet.*

1. The stars and planets, compared to writing, as if on the dome of the sky.
2. Ubshu-ukkenna, see Epic of Creation (III.17) Tablet II line 159, Tablet III line 119. This passage refers to an Assyrian version of the Epic in which Assur was substituted for Marduk.
3. Provider for temples, that is, the king.
4. Name of temple of Assur in the city Assur.
5. Future kings.

Text: K 3258 = Craig, ABRT 1 32–34 = Macmillan, BA 5 (1905), 652–653.

Edition: Livingstone, *Court Poetry*, 4–5.

Translation: von Soden, SAHG, 254–256 no. 8 (whence many of the restorations used here); Seux, *Hymnes*, 90–93.

Literature: Lawson, *Fate*, 64–68.

Notes to Text: (5) Seux, *Hymnes*, 90 note 4. (11) Seux, *Hymnes*, 91 note 8. (22) Seux, *Hymnes*, 92 note 22. (11′) Against Seux, *Hymnes*, 93 notes 38–40, and the literature cited there, I take this to refer to the text of this hymn (*tanittu*); see General Introduction, D.1. (15′) Text: TAB-*bat*, an artificed writing for *ṭābat*(?), perhaps in D-stem?

(c) TO ISHTAR OF NINEVEH AND ARBELA

At the beginning of his reign, Assurbanipal shared the empire with his brother, Shamash-shum-ukin, referred to diplomatically as the "twin." Assurbanipal, however, received larger territory. Since the inhabitants of the brother's domain were forced to swear allegiance to Assurbanipal, the division of power may have been more nominal than actual. The assertion of line 13 (see also IV.5) and the oblique allusion to the subsequent struggle with and disappearance of the brother (see line 36) refer to Assurbanipal's irregular succession, perhaps contrary to the will and preparations of his father, Esarhaddon.

> Extol, glorify the divine lady of Nineveh, (1)
> Exalt, praise the divine lady of Arbela,
> Those who have no rival among the great gods.
> Their names are precious to goddesses,
> Their holy places, all their sanctuaries, are unequalled. (5)
> The speech on their lips is a fire breaking out,
> Their utterance is cherished forever.
> I (am) Assurbanipal, their hearts' desire,
> Great seed of Baltil,[1] [bo]rn at Nineveh,
> Formed in the [Emashmash],[2] and the Egashankalamma,[3] (10)

---

1. Assur; see p. 316 note 2.
2. Temple of Ishtar of Nineveh. See also IV.4f.
3. Temple of Ishtar of Arbela (see Seux, *Hymnes*, 101 note 8).

Whose kingship they [sum]moned(?)
>   from the [crown prince's] palace.
They have [ordered] with their holy command that
>   my throne long endure.
I knew neither human father nor mother,*
>   I grew up on my goddesses' knees,
The great gods have guided me like an infant.
They have gone with me at my right and left,   (15)
They have set at my side
>   spirits of protection and good fortune,
They have confided my survival
>   to the guardians of well-being and life.
They made my physique splendid,
>   they made mighty my strength,
They exalted my name over any other ruler's.
[All] e[nemies] heard, trembling with fear,*   (20)
Rebellious [lands] which did not submit
>   to the kings my ancestors,
And that submitted neither [gifts]
>   nor presents before them,
[I], Assurbanipal, handiwork of the great gods,

(gap)

[   ] their command,
[   ] their words.
Neither [... by] my [might] nor by the might of my bow,
(But) by the st[rength and by the] might of my goddesses,
Did I cause the lands [disob]edient to me
>   to submit to the yoke of Assur.   (30)
[Numerous] gifts, unceasing, year by year they bring me,
They keep watch each day
>   at the great gate of Assur and Mullissu.[1]
They seek peace with me in supplication and plea,
With prayer and petition they do homage at my feet.
It was I, Assurbanipal, of the blood royal,   (35)

---

1.   This may refer in a general way to vassalage, but Assurbanipal is known to have put a defeated king to watch at a city gate in company with a bear and a dog (M. Streck, *Assurbanipal* [Leipzig, 1916], 66 viii 11); differently von Soden, WdO 22 (1991), 190.

Victor over rebels, who appeases the hearts of the gods,
Whom the great gods have given courage,
    whose weaponry they blessed!
The Lady-of-Nineveh, the mother who bore me,
Has given (me) an unrivalled kingship.   (40)
The Lady-of-Arbela, who created me,
    has ordered a long life for me.
They have ordained it my destiny to exercise sovereignty
    over all the inhabited world,
They have made all its kings submit at my feet.

O Lady-of-Nineveh, mistress of poetry, bless your king forever!

Text: Langdon, OECT 6, pl. XI; photo AfO 25 (1974/7), 46.
Edition: von Soden, AfO 25 (1974/7), 45–49 (with numerous improved readings adopted here);
   compare Livingstone, *Court Poetry*, 10–13; von Soden, WdO 22 (1991), 190.
Translation: Seux, *Hymnes*, 100–102.
★*Notes to Text*: (13, 20) Restoration von Soden, AfO 25 (1974/7), 46.

(d) ACROSTIC HYMN TO MARDUK

This hymn is divided into distiches and occasional tristiches, the first signs of
which form an acrostic reading "I am Assurbanipal, who has called upon you.
O Marduk, grant me life, let me sing your praises!" The lines of verse are
exceptionally long so as to give the impression of prose, the style known as
"*Kunstprosa.*" There are various allusions to the Epic of Creation (III.17).
Although this piece is of little aesthetic interest, it is included here as an example of late Assyrian style at its most ponderous.

I praise your name, O Marduk, mighty one among the gods,
    irrigator[1] of heaven and earth [   ],   (1)
Who were fair created, are alone on high [   ].

1. Epic of Creation (III.17) Tablet VII line 62.

You bear the responsibilities of Anu, Enlil, and Ea,
   lordship and kingship [   ],
You have gathered to yourself all wisdom,
   O perfect of strength [   ].

O cherished counsellor, sublime prince,
   omnipotent, most great [   ],   (5)
(Who) made splendid his lordship,
   (who) drew up for Anu's battle [   ].[1]

You are sublime in heaven, king in the netherworld,
   resourceful counsellor of the god[s   ],

Who establishes all habitations,
   who grasps the circumference
   of the starry sky and the [world   ].

You are the [gre]atest among the gods.
   Nudimmud[2] has formed your features fair [   ],
The great gods let you grasp the tablet of destinies
   in your hand, (the power) to raise
   and lower [is yours].*   (10)
[w]ho has made [the gods?] do homage at your feet,
   saying as they hailed (you), "He is [our king]!"[3]

[   ] of omens have exalted you, and Enl[il]
[gr]eatest of the gods, brilliant glow,
   lightning flash [   ],
[   ] who traverses innermost heaven [   ].

[   ] who struck the pate of Anzu,[4]
   overwhelmed [   ],   (15)

---

   1. This refers to the battle against Tiamat. Anu went out to her first, but returned unsuccessful; Epic of Creation (III.17) Tablet II lines 96–118.
   2. Ea.
   3. Epic of Creation Tablet IV line 28 (Seux, *Hymnes*, 116 note 11).
   4. For the Anzu story, see III.25. Here the exploit of Ninurta is assigned to Marduk. For discussion of this motif, see W. G. Lambert, CRRAI 32 (1985), 55–60.

[who defeated] the lion man, bison man, scorpion man,[1]
K[ing   ] who divided them [   ].[2]

Heir of N[udimmud ...] your eyes [   ]
Bow, arr[ow,   sw]ord, [battle] gear,
You defeated vast Tiamat [   ] Qingu [her] sp[ouse].[3]   (20)

May Babylon rejoice over you,
        may Esagila be joyful [over you   ],
        who judge [in truth] and justice,
Who render decisions and op[en wells],[4]
You rain down copious rainfall,
        you [   ] mas[sive] floods [   ].

Great is the greatness of the lord, irrigator of heaven,
        much mightier than [the gods, his fathers],[5]
He is surpassing in stature, lofty of form,
        splendid [   ] for his lordly garment.   (25)

He summoned the Igigi and Anunna-gods,
        they were kneeling before him,
        as the gods his forefathers
        sat in silent awe before [him   ],
For taking counsel,
        to deliberate in lordly(?) deliberation* are Marduk's,
They listen to Marduk alone.

Continuous are the offerings, the incense of the stand,
        the harp, the lyre, and the [   ],
They glorify the builder of Esagila,[6]
        Babylon rejoices and [   ] are joyful.

1. Monsters created by Tiamat in the Epic of Creation Tablet I lines 142f. See p. 444 note 2.
2. Epic of Creation (III.17) Tablet VI lines 39–40, 46, 145 (Seux, *Hymnes*, 120 note 45).
3. Epic of Creation (III.17) Tablet IV lines 95–104.
4. Epic of Creation (III.17) Tablet VII line 60 (if restoration is correct).
5. Epic of Creation (III.17) Tablet I line 19.
6. Marduk, see Epic of Creation (III.17) Tablet VI line 62.

There bow before you the Igigi and Anunna-gods, gods and
     goddesses of holy places, s[anctuaries], and daises,   (30)
Governors and rulers pray [to you].

[Fir]stborn(?) of Nudimmud, first-ranked, valiant, mighty,
     tempest unrelenting, raging fire, [   ] flame,
Who engulfs enemies, who, in battle, the clash of weapons,
     does not [fear   ].

Marduk is lofty of form, blazing sun, glowing torch,
     who, when he appears [   ],
(Who) purifies the impure and illumines [gloom   ],   (35)

May all gods and goddesses, Anu, [Enlil],
Constellations, depths, netherworld, Nudimmud,
     together with hairy hero-men, ... [   ],
Cancer, the Battle Goddess,[1] ...   [   ],
Behold the deeds of Marduk, lord of the gods,
     [may they] constantly [   ].

Give me for all time meal offerings,
     abundance of pure [   ],
(Which) the wrathful god established for living creatures,
     at [his] sublime command ... [   ].   (40)

Your [rad]iant name* is Sagmegar "noble, first-ranked god,[2]
     loftiest of the gods, [   ],
"Who, by his radiance, reveals a guidepost ... [   ]."

Splendid hero, Engishgalanna,[3] "g[reat] lord [who   ]
     the (celestial) positions of the Anunna-gods,"
Lustrations, rituals, offerings [   ].

Very great is your name, O furious Marduk [   ],   (45)
You are greatest among all the gods,

1. Pisces?
2. The planet Jupiter.
3. "Lord-in the-Heavenly-Station," a name for the planet Jupiter.

among the gods your divinity is [   ].

O circumspect prince, ... [   ] in your net,
    [is] at [your] right,
At your left is Erragal, mightiest of the gods,
    before you are the va[liant] Seven, [   ]
To your right and left fire scorches, where you ra[ged].

Most honored one, splendid one, how magnificent is the god
    who [   ] his divinity to the [rev]erent one who kneels, (50)
To all the gods who dwell on daises he grants food offerings,
    and portions rejoice [   ].
Marduk grasps firmly in hand the lead-rope of the Igigi and
    Anunna-gods, the bond of he[aven and netherworld],
At rising and setting he set up constellations,[1]
    he gave them a path and a way to go [   ].

Your weighty invocation is "Judge of the Four World Regions,"
    willful Enlil of the great gods,
Who implements the decrees of the depths,
    who grants portions and offerings to the gods.[2] (55)

Accept my entreaty, receive the prayers of suppliants,
    the petitions of the so[rrow-worn],
May one who pleases you always speak fair [to you].

May Anu, Enlil, and Ea rejoice your mood
    and make you cheerful,
May Damkina, your great mother, [say to you in] Esagila,
    which you love, "Calm yourself!"

She is eminent, important, queenly, mighty, head of the family,
    spouse, goddess, mistress, splendid, great, lofty, fair, [ ], (60)
O beloved of Tutu,[3] grant me (long) life,

1. Epic of Creation (III.17) Tablet V line 2 (Seux, *Hymnes*, 120 note 45).
2. Epic of Creation (III.17) Tablet VII line 85.
3. One of the names of Marduk in the Epic of Creation (III.17) Tablet VII lines 9, 15, 19, 25, 33. The passage refers to Sarpanitum, Marduk's wife.

I will si[ng] your praises.

I will glorify your valor, O sublime princess, queen of Esagila,
  supreme goddess, queen of que[ens],
Lofty ruler of all [   ], merciful goddess who loves prayers!

I implore you, magnificent lord, may your furious heart be calm,
  may [your] mood, which had turned to fury,
  relent and be appeased.
Let me live in your (favorable) breezes,
  O lofty sage of the gods, Mar[duk]!   (65)
The humble, imploring scholar[1]
  extols the greatness of Sarpanitu, great lady,
  spouse of Enbilulu,[2]
  daughter-in-law of Nud[immud],
He sings [her praises].

Text: Craig, ABRT 1, 29–31 + 2 x = Brünnow, ZA 4 (1889), 246–248 + ZA 5 (1890), 77–78; 1904-
  10-9,205 (unpub.); texts collated from photograph.
Edition: Livingstone, *Court Poetry*, 6–10.
Translation: von Soden, SAHG, 249–253 no. 6; Seux, *Hymnes*, 115–121; Hecker, TUAT II/5, 765–
  768.
★*Notes to Text:* (10) Differently AHw, 848 s.v. *pat(t)akkātu*. (27) Livingstone, *Court Poetry*, 8 note 27.
  (41) Seux, *Hymnes*, 119 note 36.

---

  1. Assurbanipal, who was proud of his literacy; see H. W. F. Saggs, *The Might that Was Assyria*
(London, 1984), 41; R. Labat, "Un prince éclairé: Ashurbanipal," *Comptes rendus de l'Académie des
Inscriptions et Belles-Lettres* (1972), 670–676; P. Villard, "L'éducation d'Assurbanipal," *Ktèma* 22
(1997), 135–149, and below, IV.4g.
  2. One of Marduk's names in the Epic of Creation (III.17) Tablet VII line 57.

(e) TO SHAMASH

This hymn glorifies Shamash, apparently in connection with work done on his temple by Assurbanipal, and prays for the king's long life. Like the hymn to Assur (IV.4b), it alludes to Assurbanipal's accession and ends with an epilogue addressed to future kings and performers of the song.

> [O lord, ra]diance of the great gods, light of the earth,
>> illuminator of the world regions,   (1)
> [O Shamash], lofty judge, creator of the above and below,
> You scan all lands in your light like a graven sign.
> [You w]ho never weary of divination,
>> you render daily verdicts for heaven and earth.
> Your [rising] is a fire blazing,
>> all the stars of heaven are covered.   (5)
> You alone are [mani]fest,
>> no one among the gods can rival you.
> You take counsel with Sin, your father,
>> and issue instructions,
> Nor do Anu and Enlil hold congress without you,
> Ea, who judges cases in the depths, looks into your face.
> All the gods are attentive to your brilliant rising,   (10)
> They [sm]ell incense, they receive pure food offerings.
> Exorcists [kneel] before you to avert evil portents,
> Diviners [pray?] to you to steady their hands,
>> to interpret the omens (aright).
> [I am] Assurbanipal, whose assumption of kingship
>> you commanded by oracle,
> [Who ...] the brilliant [ ] of your [divin]ity,
>> who makes splendid the symbol of your divinity,   (15)
> [Who ...] your [greatne]ss,
>> who proclaims your praises to the numerous peoples,
> [Look steadfastly upon him], judge his [ca]se,
>> render a favorable verdict for him,
> [Grant him long life?], let him proceed in well-being
>> in the dawn of your rising.

May he serve in justice as shepherd [for all time?]
    to the subjects you gave him.
[In the house] that he built,
    wherein he caused you to dwell in joy,   (20)
[May] his heart exult [   ], may his mood be joyful,
    may he enjoy life in full measure!
[The prince who?] performs this [song] of Shamash,
    who pronounces the name of Assurbanipal,
May he shepherd in prosperity and justice
    the subjects of Enlil [all] his days.
[The singer] who masters this text,
    who extols Shamash, judge of the gods,
May his [   ] place him in good esteem,
    may his performance be pleasing to people.   (25)
He who abandons this song to obscurity,
    who does not extol Shamash, light of the gods,
Or who makes substitution for the name of Assurbanipal,
    whose assumption of kingship
    Shamash commanded by oracle,
But names some other king,
May his string-playing be painful to people,
    may his joyful songs be the prick of a thorn!

Text: Ebeling, KAR 105, 361.
Edition: Ebeling, *Quellen* I, 25–27.
Translation: von Soden, SAHG, 247–249 no. 5; Stephens, ANET³, 386–387; Seux, *Hymnes*, 63–66;
    Livingstone in Hallo, ed., *Context*, 1:474.

(f) ASSURBANIPAL AND NABU

For these oracles, compare IV.3.

[I sin]g your praise, O Nabu, among the great gods. [Among?] my [ill-wisher]s, may my life not be continually sought.[1] I keep turning to you, O most valorous of the gods his brethren, [in the temple of the lady of] Nineveh. [You are the tru]st of Assurbanipal henceforth, for all time. [Since childhood]* I have cast myself at the feet of Nabu, [do not forsake me], O Nabu, among my ill-wishers!

Listen(?), O Assurbanipal, I am Nabu! Until the end of time, your feet shall not falter, your hands shall not tremble, nor shall these your lips weary of continual prayer to me, nor shall your tongue stumble at your lips, for I shall ever grant you fair speech. I shall raise your head and make you proud in Emashmash.[2]

(Nabu continues) That, your eloquent mouth, which always implores the lady of Uruk, and your own person, which I created, keep imploring me to remain(?) in Emashmash, your destiny, which I created, keeps imploring me as follows, "Bring good order(?)[3] to Egashankalamma."[4] Your spirit keeps imploring me as follows, "Prolong the life of Assurbanipal."

Assurbanipal, on bended knee, keeps praying to Nabu his lord, "Listen(?), O Nabu, do not forsake me! My life is inscribed[5] before you, my spirit is entrusted to the lap of Mullissu. Listen(?), do not forsake me among my ill-wishers!"

A dream-god answered from the presence of Nabu his lord, "Fear not, Assurbanipal, I will give you long life, I will entrust fair breezes with your spirit. This, my eloquent mouth, will ever bless you among the great gods."

---

1. Or, "May my ill-wishers not continually be seeking my life" (CAD K, 284a).
2. Temple of Ishtar at Nineveh.
3. Uncertain; the word translated here as "good order" may mean also a garment or headgear.
4. Temple of Ishtar at Arbela.
5. Reference to Tablet of Destinies, see p. 445 note 2.

Assurbanipal, spreading his hands, kept praying to Nabu his lord, "May he who seized the feet of the Queen of Nineveh not be disgraced among the great gods! May he who grasps the hem of the Lady of Uruk not be disgraced among his ill-wishers. Do not forsake me, O Nabu, do not forsake my life among my adversaries!"

"You were young, O Assurbanipal, when I left you to the Queen of Nineveh, you were a baby, O Assurbanipal, when you sat on the knee of the Queen of Nineveh. Her four teats were set in your mouth, with two you were suckled and with two you drew milk for yourself. Your ill-wishers, O Assurbanipal, will fly off like insects from the water's surface, they will be squashed at your feet like bugs in springtime. You will stand, O Assurbanipal, opposite the great gods, that you may praise Nabu."

Text: Craig, ABRT 1 5.
Edition: Livingstone, *Court Poetry*, 33–35; Ponchia, *Dialoghi*, 87–88, 113–114, 148–150.
Translation: von Soden, SAHG, 292–294 no. 39; Livingstone in Hallo, ed., *Context*, 1:475–476.
Notes to Text: (5) Restoration Livingstone, 33.

(g) PIOUS SCHOLAR

Among the colophons scribes appended to the manuscripts they copied for Assurbanipal's library are prayers for the king and his muse.

> I, Assurbanipal, king of the universe, king of Assyria, on whom Nabu and Tashmetu have bestowed vast intelligence, who acquired penetrating acumen for the most recondite details of scholarly erudition, no predecessors of whom among kings having any comprehension of such matters, I wrote down on tablets Nabu's wisdom, the impressing of each and every cuneiform sign, and I checked and collated them. I placed them for the future in the library of the temple of my lord Nabu, the great lord, at Nineveh, for my life and for the well-being of my soul, to avoid disease, and to sustain the foundations of my royal throne. O Nabu, look joyfully and bless my kingship forever! Help me whenever I call upon you! As I traverse your house, keep constant watch over my footsteps. When this work is deposited in your house and placed in your presence, look upon it and remember me with favor!

Text: See Hunger, AOAT 2 (1968), 105–106 no. 338.

Edition: Hunger, AOAT 2 (1968), 105–106 no. 338.

Literature: S. Lieberman, "Canonical Official Cuneiform Texts: Towards an Understanding of Assurbanipal's Personal Tablet Collection," *Studies Moran*, 305–336.

IV.5 THE NETHERWORLD VISION OF
AN ASSYRIAN CROWN PRINCE

Much of this bizarre narrative remains obscure, owing to the bad condition of the single manuscript that preserves it. The narrative was composed by a scribe who professed to set down the exact words of an Assyrian prince who had a vision of the netherworld.

The first fifteen lines of the text may deal with actions of the prince's father. There is reference to administrative acts, then the king may give himself over to gluttony and obsession with wealth. The mysterious scribe is introduced in line 17 in connection with some event that seems to cause the king considerable distress: he weeps, goes out alone in the streets, smashes things, ignores food—characteristic actions of a man undergoing personal misfortune.[1] He commits some final abomination that, one may surmise, was to name a different heir to the throne.

In line 27 Kumaya, who may be a son of the king and the same person as the "prince" referred to elsewhere in the narrative, incubates a dream, perhaps to find out when he is going to die. This might again suggest some situation of uncertainty with the succession. Ereshkigal, queen of the netherworld, appears to him and promises to reveal to him what he wants to know.

In line 37 Kumaya awakes and prays for the promised revelation. Kumaya's second dream is narrated directly in the first person, as overheard and set down by the scribe (line 73). Kumaya enters the netherworld, where he sees fifteen demonic figures, each one more ghastly than the preceding. The last two are so appalling that Kumaya cannot even name them. Next he sees a dark human figure wearing a red cloak, and finally Nergal himself, who grabs him by the hair to kill him.

The warrior-god Ishum intercedes, asking that the man be spared to sing Nergal's praises to the land. Nergal is pacified and asks the prince a question, perhaps why he prayed to Ereshkigal for the revelation. He then prophesies difficulties, rebellion, and anxieties for the prince. Nergal apparently shows the prince his own father, who, despite his innate excellence (67) has committed some evil act before his death (in connection with the succession?) that will be a cause of grief to the prince.

---

1. See, for example, III.1 Fragment C iii lines 7′–11′; III.14 Tablet II 86–89.

The prince awakens and declaims his misery in public, praising Nergal and Ereshkigal, who had vouchsafed him his revelation. The scribe remembers his words perfectly and out of loyalty reports them to the palace.

Following von Soden, it is tempting to associate this composition with Assurbanipal and his father, Esarhaddon. The delicacy of the matters referred to might explain the oblique diction. The scribe, who seems to have been in disgrace for some evil act of his own, calls to mind Urad-Gula, a scholar at the court of Esarhaddon who lost his post after the accession of Assurbanipal. He is sometimes compared with Ahiqar, the unfairly disgraced vizier of Aramaic tradition. All of this is speculation, however.

The prince's brush with death raises him, like Gilgamesh, to the company of those who know the "alpha and omega" of human wisdom, matters before the flood and after death.

[   ] responsibility for [   ]   (1)
[   ] of the house of examiners of ora[cles],
         he took coun[sel] with him [   ]
[   ] ... the wise administrators,
         who keep the [secre]ts of their lord,
[   ] the governors [and] great ones
         he commissioned together
         and reinforced the proper care of his possessions,
[   ] Dada, his cook, strong drink,
         whatever there was, wherever the sun illumined,   (5)
[   ] he delivered over to him [his] subjects, but he,
         disregarding his inner promptings,
         forgot what he (should have) held in awe,
[   ] ... he held in contempt what he (should have) feared,
         and thought evil, though his heart urged him to do good.
[   ] he reckoned [its acc]ounts(?), day and night
         he would shower his treasuries with jewels fit for a king,
         as if with a bucket from a well,
[   ] income, wealth, ... beloved by(?) the human race,
         (was) like pitch or tar coming up from the depths ...
[Like] potter's clay, he covered it (with) plaster, great [   ]
         he crammed it from foundation to parapet with silver,   (10)
[   ] and the walls [   ], within Nineveh, the royal city,
         the way of well-being and justice,

[   ] the good deeds(?) he had made it enjoy(?),
[   ] ... to enter Assur ..., made ready to speak
        and [addressed him] as if he were a man,
[   ] in his heart, nor did ill-omened words [   ]
[   ] of the god, lest [   ].   (15)
[At] that time, [   ] darkness ...
[   ] ... he went to a certain scribe ... [   ]
[   ] he took up his official post and [   ] the treasury,
[never] resting, nor did he hold back weeping,
[   ] ...   (20)
[   ] alone [   ] he went along its streets,
     [   ] a joyful song in the nuptial chamber [   ],
[   ] he ... of massive, ingenious workmanship
        with his sword ... [   ]
[   ] in the netherworld, which does not [   ] ...
        the royal repast, great banquets, all [   ] ...
[   ] his evil [   ], which were not rightfully his, [   ] ...
[   ] years of service and [   ] gold ... [   ] ...   (25)
[   ] an attack against [   ], they stood and ... [   ] ...
[   ] and the shepherd of ... people for good, eternally.
Then did Kumaya, son of [   ], enter the temple(?),
     [   ] to go down to the netherworld ...
     [   ] ... he desired.
He set up an incense burner with juniper [   ] ... and prayed,
        ... and made the god angry(?)
        while he uttered blessings,

     "O [   ], Allatu, Allatu, mistress of the netherworld,
          ... [   ] ...,   (30)
     "... of the lost orphan, let her disclose her face and [   ] ...
     "[On] lips that have spoken insolence,
          where there is no regret, as long as I live ...
     "[   ] on the day of my death [   ]
          to the (netherworld) Anunna-gods let me ... [   ]
     "[   ] mention of my name ..."

[E]reshkigal appeared in a dream
     in the middle of the night and said to him,

     "I have re[gard for] your (very) first offering,

"I will surely hear your [p]rayer, I will surely
reveal to you what you desire,   (35)
"[By com]mand of my great divine mouth,
you may interpret dreams,
(but) I (myself) will not answer you
the meaning of the sign,⋆
w[hy] did you [turn to me], and [   ] Shamash?"

Kumaya awoke and moaned like a dove, [saying],

"My earth, my earth …"

He wept and [   ] the dream.
[Again] he prayed, entreating Ereshkigal, before Nergal,
king of the netherworld, her spouse,
were his tears flowing down,

"[   ] your substitute the teeming peoples [   ]
whom they made to bow down,
"[   ] … [   ] I destroyed,
you opened to me a secret, … [   ]."   (40)

[Ku]maya lay down and was seeing a vision of the night.
In his dream, … [   ]

"I saw his terrifying splendor, [   ]
"I saw [Na]mtar, courier of the netherworld,
who issues decrees.
"A man stood before him,
he was holding his hair in his left hand,
he was [holding] a sword [in his right hand],
"[Na]mtartu, his female counterpart,
had the head of a protective spirit,
her hands and feet were human.
"Death had the head of a dragon,
his hands were human, his feet [   ],
"'Evil Spirit' had a human head and hands,
it was wearing a crown, its feet were those of an eagle,
with its left foot it trod upon a crocodile(?).
"Alluhappu had a lion's head, four human hands and feet.
"'Upholder-of-Evil' (had) the head of a bird,
his wings were opened as he flew to and fro,

(he had) human hands and feet.   (45)
"'Take-Away-Quickly', boatman of the netherworld,
        had the head of Anzu, four [ ] hands and feet.
"[ ] (had) an ox's head, four human hands and feet.
"'Malignant Phantom' (had) a lion's head,
        the hands and feet of Anzu.
"Shulak was a normal lion rea[ring] on his hind legs,
"[Ma]mitu had a goat's head, human hands and feet.
"Pituh, gatekeeper of the netherworld,
        (had) a lion's head, human hands, bird's feet.
"'Whatever-is-Evil' (had) two heads,
        one a lion's head, the other [   ].
"[Muh]ra (had) three feet,
        the two front ones were bird's feet,
        the rear was that of an ox, it had terrifying splendor.
"Two gods whose names I do not know:
        one (had) the head, hands, feet of Anzu,
        in its left hand [   ],
"The other had a human head and was wearing a crown.
        In its right hand was a mace, in its left ...
"Fifteen gods in all were in attendance.
"When I saw them I prayed [to them].
"A certain man, his body was black as pitch,
        his face was like that of Anzu,
        he was dressed in a red cloak,
        in his left hand he carried a bow,
        in his right he was ho[lding] a sword,
        he was treading on a serpent(?), ... with his left f[oot], (50)
"When I raised my eyes, there was valiant Nergal
        sitting on his royal throne wearing the royal crown,
        he held two terrible maces with both hands,
        each with two heads,
"[ ] were piled up ... lightning was flashing,
        the great (netherworld) Anunna-gods were knee[ling]
        to right and left [   ],
"The netherworld was full of terror,
        deep silence(?) reigned in the presence of the prince.
"He seized me by the forelock and dr[ew] me toward him.

"When [I] saw him my legs shook,
>   his wrathful splendor overwhelmed me,
>   I kissed the feet of his [great] divinity, I knelt.
"When I stood up, he was looking at me, shaking his head.
"He gave me a fierce [c]ry and shrieked at me wrathfully,
>   like a raging storm.
"He drew up his scepter, his divine symbol,
>   ghastly as a serpent, to kill me!   (55)
"Ishum, his counselor, intercessor, savior of life,
>   who loves truth and <justice>, said,

>   'Do not kill th(is) young man,
>>   O m[ight]y king of the v[as]t netherworld!
>   '... let the subjects of the land all
>>   and always hear your praises!'

"The heart of the formidable, mighty one,
>   who captures the wicked,
>   grew calm as pure well water,
> ... Nergal said(?) this,

>   'Why did you ... my beloved spouse,
>>   queen of the netherworld?'
>   '[By] her sublime command, which cannot be changed,
>>   may Bibbu, slaughterer of the netherworld,
>>   entrust you to Lugalsula the gatekeeper,
>>   that he may take [you] out of the gate
>>   of Ishtar and Aya.
>   'Do not forget me nor neglect me!
>>   I will not sentence you to death.
>   'By the command of Shamash
>>   there shall gust upon you
>>   want, violence, and revolts, all at once,   (60)
>   'You shall have no sleep because of their fierce clamor.
>   'This [corpse] that is interred in the netherworld
>>   belongs to that magnificent shepherd
>>   who fulfilled the heart's desire
>>   of my father [Assur], king of the gods.
>   '[Of the king] who treated all the lands he looked upon,
>>   from sunrise to sunset,

as plunder, who ruled over all,
'(To) whom Assur, at the beginning
      of his high priestly office [ordai]ned(?)
      construction of the sacred new year's festival house
      on the steppe, surrounded by a lush garden,
      the likeness of Lebanon, ... forever,
'And whose person Iabru and Humba-Napruhu[1]
      watch over,
      whose seed they preserved in well-being,
      whose army and camp they kept safe,
      lest a [chario]teer(?) approach him(?) in battle,   (65)
'He is your l[oft]y father, who understood matters,
      he of profound wisdom
      and penetrating understanding,
      who had in v[iew?] the designs of (how) the earth
      is linked (to heaven),
'Whoever ignored common sense when he spoke,
      who did what is forbidden,
      committed an abomination,
      the terrifying splendor of his kingship
      will overwhelm you all, until you are empty air!
'This saying shall lie like a thorn in your hearts,
'Do you go forth to the upper world
      until once again I call you to mind!'

   "As he spoke I awoke."

Like a young man who has shed blood,
      who wanders alone in a swamp,
      whom a pursuer has overtaken,
      and his heart is pounding,
Or, like a lusty young boar, mounting his mate
      with innards aswell,
      who lets out wind at his mouth and behind,   (70)
He cried out a lament, saying "Woe is me!"
He darted out into the street like an arrow
      and scooped up dirt from alley and square in his mouth,
      all the while setting up a frightful clamor,

---

1. An Elamite deity, see Hinz, JNES 24 (1965), 353–354.

"Woe! Alas! Why have you ordained this for me?"
He was shouting in front of the subjects of Assur,
        praising in his pain the valor of Nergal and Ereshkigal,
        who had stood forth to aid the prince.
As for him, the scribe who formerly had accepted a present,
        who assumed his father's post,
        with the astuteness that Ea bestowed upon him,
        he took th(ose) words of praise to heart, saying to himself,
        "Lest disloyalty bring me to harm,
        I shall always do what [   ] commanded."
So he went and reported it to the palace, saying,
        "This shall be my protection from evil."   (75)

Text: von Soden, ZA 43 (1936), Tafeln I–IV (photos only).

Edition: W. von Soden, "Die Unterweltsvision eines assyrischen Kronprinzen," ZA 43 (1936), 1–31 (most restorations and interpretations are taken from him); Livingstone, *Court Poetry*, 68–76 (with some improved readings and interpretations used here).

Translation: Speiser, ANET³, 109–110; Labat, *Religions*, 94–97.

Literature: Dalley, RA 74 (1980), 190 (to lines 44 and 48 rev.).

★*Notes to Text*: (36) von Soden, N.A.B.U. 1987/11.

IV.6 IN PRAISE OF ARBELA

Arbela, modern Irbil, was an important city in Assyria noted for its sanctuary of the goddess Ishtar.

> Arbela, Arbela!   (1)
> Heaven without rival, Arbela!
> City of joyful music, Arbela,
> City of festivals, Arbela,
> City of happy households, Arbela!   (5)
> O shrine of Arbela, sublime abode,
> Spacious sanctuary, delightful dais,
> The pride(?) of Arbela is [its] lofty holy place.
> City of splendor, Arbela,
> Abode of pleasure, Arbela,   (10)
> Arbela, home of reason and discretion.
> Bond of the world, Arbela,
> Sustainer of ancient rites, Arbela.
> Arbela is established like heaven,
> Her foundations are firm as the [netherworld].   (15)
> Arbela's head is held high, rivalling [heaven].
> Her image is Babylon, her double is [   ],
> Sublime holy place, dais of destinies, gateway to heaven.
>
> Tribute(?) from [all la]nds enters there,
> Ishtar dwells within it, Nanay, daughter of Sin [ ]   (20)
> Irnina, foremost of the gods, firstborn goddess.

(rest too fragmentary for translation)

Text: Ebeling-Köcher-Rost, LKA 32.
Edition: Ebeling, *Jahrbuch für Kleinasiatische Forschung* 2 (1952/3), 274–282; Livingstone, *Court Poetry*, 20–22.
Translation: Hecker, TUAT II/5, 768–770.

B. KINGS OF BABYLONIA AND THEIR TIMES

IV.7 NABOPOLASSAR

The Neo-Babylonian kings were heirs to the great conquests of Assyria. Under their rule, Babylon was destined to become the greatest city of its time. Numerous prayers in the names of the Neo-Babylonian kings are preserved in building inscriptions. Their language bespeaks great piety and reverence, but they give little hint of the personalities of the kings they name. Furthermore, except for certain prayers of Nabonidus, they generally lack the personal and political allusions often to be found in Assyrian prayers of the Late period.

Nabopolassar (625–605 B.C.) was the founder of this dynasty. He allied with the Medes against Assyria and, after the destruction of Assyria, set about to consolidate his substantial territorial gains. He bequeathed to his son, Nebuchadnezzar II, an empire stretching from southern Babylonia to the Mediterranean. For a historical survey of his reign, see D. J. Wiseman, CAH[3] 3/2, 229–230.

(a) TO MARDUK (1)

This prayer to Marduk concludes an inscription commemorating the reconstruction of the Etemenanki, temple of Marduk in Babylon.

> O lord Marduk, look joyfully upon my good works and, according to your sublime command, which cannot be altered, may my handiwork endure forever. Even as the brickwork of Etemenanki shall stand firm for all time, so sustain my throne till distant days.
>
> O Etemenanki, bless the king who renovated you. When, amidst jubilation, Marduk takes up his dwelling within you, do you, O house, speak favorably of me to Marduk, my lord.

Text: Hilprecht, BE 1 84, iii 38–59; Strassmaier, ZA 4 (1889), 134–136 lines 147–177.
Edition: Langdon, VAB 4, 64–65 no. 1, 31–61.
Translation: von Soden, SAHG, 283 no. 26; Seux, *Hymnes*, 505.
Literature: Berger, AOAT 4/1 (1973), Nabopolassar Zylinder III, 1.

(b) TO MARDUK (2)

This prayer concludes an inscription commemorating the reconstruction of the city fortification wall called Nemetti-Enlil in Babylon.

> O Marduk, Enlil of the gods, administrator of the four world regions, look joyfully upon my good works and, according to your sublime command, [grant] me [as my?] royal gift a just scepter, a firmly sustained throne, a reign till distant days, and that I proceed in the four world regions proudly, with head held high.

Text: Clay, BRM 4 51 = Stephens, YOS 9 84.
Edition: Clay, BRM 4, 48–50.
Translation: Seux, *Hymnes*, 505.
Literature: Berger, AOAT 4/1 (1973), Nabopolassar Zylinder II, 3.

IV.8 NEBUCHADNEZZAR II

The long reign of Nebuchadnezzar II (604–562 B.C.) saw expansion and consolidation of the empire founded by Nabopolassar. Babylon was extensively rebuilt, including new temples and a royal palace, the remains of which are still visible today. The prayers that follow come from texts commemorating building projects of this energetic and successful king. For a historical survey of his reign, see D. J. Wiseman, CAH³ 3/2, 230–240, *Nebuchadrezzar and Babylon* (Oxford, 1985); and R. H. Sack, *Images of Nebuchadnezzar: The Emergence of a Legend* (Selinsgrove, Pa., 1991).

(a) TO MARDUK (1)

This prayer to Marduk, which exists in two variant versions, concludes an inscription commemorating construction of the royal palace in Babylon.

O lord Marduk, wisest of the gods, proud prince, it was you who created me and entrusted to me the kingship of all peoples. I love your lofty form as (my own) precious life.[1] None of your holy places in the whole inhabited world did I render more renowned than your holy place, Babylon. Even as I love your divine splendor and have ever sought after your dominion, so accept my entreaty, hear my prayer! Let me be a royal provider who pleases you, let me be your faithful shepherd who keeps your people safe,[2] let me be a skilled governor who provides for all your holy places.

At your command, O merciful Marduk, may the house I built long endure and may I enjoy its delights in full measure. May I reach old age and enjoy venerable years therein. May I receive therein the massive tribute of the kings of the four world regions and of all humankind. From horizon to zenith, wherever the sun comes forth, may I have no opponents nor encounter those to affright me. Within it may my descendants hold dominion over the people of this land forever.

1. Variant omits.
2. Variant omits.

Text: Norris, I R 58 ix 47 - x 19; Ungnad, VAS I 38, iii 34–54; Ball, PSBA 11 (1889), 159–160 pl.
  VIII, iii 36–55; see also Stephens, YOS 9 143, 144.
Edition: Langdon, VAB 4, 120–121 no. 14, iii 36–55; 140–141 no. 15 ix 47 - x 19.
Literature: Berger, AOAT 4/1 (1973), Nebukadnezar Stein-Tafel X; Nebukadnezar Zylinder III, 5.
Translation: von Soden, SAHG, 283 no. 27a; Seux, *Hymnes*, 506–507; Hecker, TUAT II/5, 782–783.

(b) TO MARDUK (2)

This prayer concludes an inscription commemorating the reconstruction of
Etemenanki, temple of Marduk in Babylon.

O Marduk, fiercest of the gods, noble one, according to your
command the holy place of the gods is built, its brickwork
formed, the sanctuary restored, the temple completed. According
to your sublime word, which has no alteration, may my offering
be sound, may my handiwork be perfect, may whatsoever I
attempt be lasting and long endure, may I enjoy its delights. Even
as Etemenanki stands firm for all time, so sustain my throne forever.

O Etemenanki, bless me, Nebuchadnezzar, the king who
renovated you. When [I shall have completed your work],
according to the commands of Marduk, [do you, O house, speak
favorably of me to Marduk, my lord].*

Text: Hilprecht, BE 1 85, iv 5–28.
Edition: Langdon, VAB 4, 148–149 no. 17, iv 5–28.
Translation: von Soden, SAHG, 284 no. 27b; Seux, *Hymnes*, 507.
Literature: Berger, AOAT 4/1 (1973), Nebukadnezar Zylinder IV,1.
*Notes to Text: (28) von Soden, SAHG, 284; Seux, *Hymnes*, 507 note 2.

(c) TO MARDUK (3)

This prayer concludes an inscription commemorating construction of a fortification wall in Babylon.

> O Marduk, Enlil of the gods, my divine creator, may my works find your favor, may I live on forever. Grant me the gift of eternal life, venerable old age, a firm throne and an enduring reign. May you, Marduk, be my help and my trust. At your firm command, which cannot be altered, may my weapons be whetted and brandished, may they overwhelm the weapons of the enemy.

Text: Moldenke, JAOS 16 (1896), 76–77, lines 14–30; Ungnad, VAS 1 40, ii 13–32; Winckler, ZA 1 (1886), 341–342, lines 13–32.
Edition: Langdon, VAB 4, 82–83 no. 4, ii 13–32.
Translation: von Soden, SAHG, 284 no. 27c; Seux, *Hymnes*, 508.
Literature: Berger, AOAT 4/1 (1973), Nebukadnezar Zylinder II,8.

(d) TO MARDUK (4)

This prayer concludes an inscription commemorating construction of fortifications, including gates and a moat, at Babylon.

> O lord Marduk, look with favor upon my handiwork and grant me eternal life. Wherever are battle and warfare, may you, Marduk, be my help and my trust. May your raging weapons, which cannot be withstood, go beside me to slay my enemies.

Text: Winckler, ZA 2 (1887), 127, lines 17–29.
Edition: Langdon, VAB 4, 84–85 no. 5, ii 17–29.
Translation: von Soden, SAHG, 284 no. 27d; Seux, *Hymnes*, 508.
Literature: Berger, AOAT 4/1 (1973), Nebukadnezar Zylinder II,5.

(e) TO MARDUK (5)

This prayer concludes an inscription commemorating reconstruction of the old palace and construction of a new one at Babylon.

> What is there besides you, my lord? You have promoted the reputation and vouchsafed an honorable career to the king you love, whose name you pronounce, who is pleasing to you. I am the prince whom you preferred, your handiwork. It was you who created me and vouchsafed me kingship over all peoples. According to your favor, O Lord, which you are always ready to bestow upon all of them, make your sublime lordship merciful upon me, produce in my heart reverence for your divinity, grant me what you please that you sustain my life.

Text: Norris, I R 53, i 55–ii 1.
Edition: Langdon, VAB 4, 122–125 no. 15, i 55–ii 1.
Translation: Seux, *Hymnes*, 508–509.
Literature: Berger, AOAT 4/1 (1973), Nebukadnezar Stein-Tafel X.

(f) TO NABU

This prayer concludes an inscription commemorating the construction of a temple for Nabu at Borsippa.

> O Nabu, true heir, sublime courier, victorious one, beloved of Marduk, look joyfully upon my works for (my) favor. Grant me the gift of eternal life, venerable old age, a firm throne, an enduring reign, slaying of foes, conquest of the enemies' land. Proclaim from your steadfast tablet, which fixes the limits of heaven and netherworld, long days and a prolonged old age. Make my works acceptable to Marduk, king of heaven and netherworld, the father who begot you. Speak favorably of me, may this ever be on your lips, "Nebuchadnezzar is surely a provident king."

Text: Norris, I R 51 no. 1, ii 16–31.
Edition: Langdon, VAB 4, 98–101 no. 11, ii 16–31.
Translation: von Soden, SAHG, 286 no. 29; Seux, *Hymnes*, 511–512; Beaulieu in Hallo, ed., *Context*, 2:310.
Literature: Berger, AOAT 4/1 (1973), Nebukadnezar Zylinder II,12.

(g) TO NABU AND MARDUK.

This prayer, written on a brick, concludes an inscription commemorating construction of a processional street in Babylon.

> O Nabu and Marduk, as you go joyfully in procession through these streets, may words favorable of me be upon your lips. As I proceed before you within the(se streets), may I live a life enduring till distant days, in good health and [satisfac]tion forever.

Text: R. Koldewey, *Das Wiedererstandene Babylon*[4] (Leipzig, 1925), 54 figure 37.
Edition: Langdon, VAB 4, 196–197 no. 29, 5–7.
Translation: Seux, *Hymnes*, 513.
Literature: Berger, AOAT 4/1 (1973), Nebukadnezar Backstein BI,5.

(h) TO NINMAH

This prayer concludes an inscription commemorating reconstruction of the temple of the birth-goddess in Babylon.

> O Ninmah, merciful mother, look joyfully! May words in my favor be upon your lips. Multiply my descent, make numerous my posterity, administer in safety childbirth among my descendants.

Text: Ungnad, VAS 1 43, ii 5–19; Ball, PSBA 11 (1889), 249, ii 5–18; see also Bezold, ZA 1 (1886), 40–41, lines 23–30; Stephens, YOS 9 146.
Edition: Langdon, VAB 4, 84–85 no. 6, ii 5–19.
Translation: von Soden, SAHG, 287 no. 32; Seux, *Hymnes*, 514.
Literature: Berger, AOAT 4/1 (1973), Nebukadnezar Zylinder II,1; see also Backstein BI,12.

(i) TO SHAMASH (1)

This prayer concludes an inscription commemorating reconstruction of the temple of Shamash in Sippar.

O Shamash, great lord, as you enter joyfully Ebabbar, your radiant house, look steadfastly upon my precious handiwork, may words in my favor ever be upon your lips. At your steadfast command, may I enjoy venerable old age, the gift of life till distant days, and a firm throne. May my reign be long and prosperous forever. May a just scepter, good shepherdship, and a steadfast rod to safeguard the people be my royal portion forever.

O Shamash, be you the protection of my army amidst raging weaponry brandished for battle, answer me in oracle and divination. At your holy word, which cannot be transgressed, may my weapons be brandished and whetted, may they overwhelm the weapons of my foes.

Text: O'Connor, *Hebraica* 1 (1884/5), 207–208, lines 68–100.
Edition: Langdon, VAB 4, 102–103 no. 12, ii 41–iii 30.
Translation: Seux, *Hymnes*, 509–510.
Literature: Berger, AOAT 4/1 (1973), Nebukadnezar Zylinder III,1.

(j) TO SHAMASH (2)

This prayer concludes an inscription commemorating construction of the Shamash temple in Larsa.

O Shamash, great lord, as you enter Ebabbar, your lofty abode, in joy and jubilation, look happily upon the works of my good hands. Let a life till distant days, a firm throne, and an enduring reign be upon your lips. May doorsill, doorbolt, locks, and door leaves of Ebabbar ceaselessly voice words in my favor before you.

Text: Norris, I R 51 no. 2, ii 12–26, see also Stephens, YOS 9 140.
Edition: Langdon, VAB 4, 96–97 no. 10, ii 12–26.
Translation: von Soden, SAHG, 285 no. 28b; Seux, *Hymnes*, 510; Beaulieu in Hallo, ed., *Context*, 2:309.
Literature: Berger, AOAT 4/1 (1973), Nebukadnezar Zylinder II,4.

(k) ACROSTIC HYMN TO NABU

This acrostic hymn, the first sign of each stanza of which spells "God Nabu," glorifies him with many of the attributes normally ascribed to Marduk. It concludes with an account of the divine election of Nebuchadnezzar II to kingship.

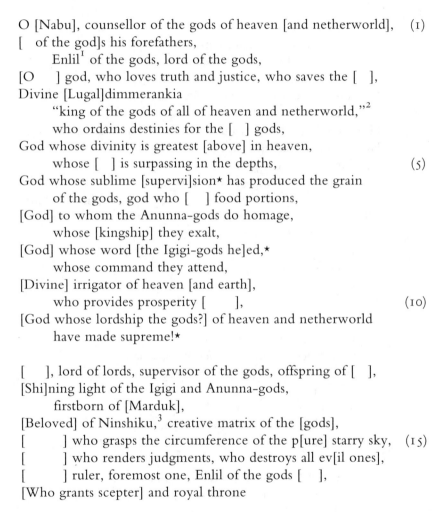

O [Nabu], counsellor of the gods of heaven [and netherworld],   (1)
[of the god]s his forefathers,
    Enlil[1] of the gods, lord of the gods,
[O   ] god, who loves truth and justice, who saves the [   ],
Divine [Lugal]dimmerankia
    "king of the gods of all of heaven and netherworld,"[2]
    who ordains destinies for the [   ] gods,
God whose divinity is greatest [above] in heaven,
    whose [   ] is surpassing in the depths,   (5)
God whose sublime [supervi]sion* has produced the grain
    of the gods, god who [   ] food portions,
[God] to whom the Anunna-gods do homage,
    whose [kingship] they exalt,
[God] whose word [the Igigi-gods he]ed,*
    whose command they attend,
[Divine] irrigator of heaven [and earth],
    who provides prosperity [   ],   (10)
[God whose lordship the gods?] of heaven and netherworld
    have made supreme!*

[   ], lord of lords, supervisor of the gods, offspring of [   ],
[Shi]ning light of the Igigi and Anunna-gods,
    firstborn of [Marduk],
[Beloved] of Ninshiku,[3] creative matrix of the [gods],
[   ] who grasps the circumference of the p[ure] starry sky,   (15)
[   ] who renders judgments, who destroys all ev[il ones],
[   ] ruler, foremost one, Enlil of the gods [   ],
[Who grants scepter] and royal throne

---

1. That is, supreme among the gods.
2. See Epic of Creation (III.17) Tablet VI line 139, where this is a name for Marduk.
3. Name for Ea; see IV.2a(3).

to the king who reveres [him],
[Who gives] truth and justice to those
    who seek after [his sanctuaries],
[who] gives his ordinances in the pure heavens,   (20)
[who] has established obed[ience]
    throughout the wide world,

The pure [starry sky], which he made as a cover,[1]
    [is entrusted]* to his hand,
An uncontested [deci]sion established the stations
    of the great gods within Ba[bylon],
His is to [ca]re for the sanctuaries
    and to restore the holy places,
He formed the shape of human [vi]sages, animate creatures,   (25)
He provided a shep[herd] for livestock and wildlife,
The lord of life, the god of [ ]
    grasps the living in his gentle hand.
Gods and m[en] are taught reverence for his sublime divinity,
All the gods of heaven and netherworld wait upon him,
    they stand and kn[eel] reverently [before him].
He has endowed the king's features with awesomeness
    beyond that of mortal men,   (30)
He has clad him in fearsomeness and [him]
    with divine splendor and radiance!

He has exalted his[2] lordship over all subject peoples,
He has subjected at his feet peoples and lands,
He has delivered the people of this land into his power,
    that he be their shepherd,
Finally, Marduk, who loves [his] kingship,   (35)
Resolved that Esagila and Ezida be provided for,
    and that Babylon, [his] beloved city, be restored:

He raised up for rulership Nebuchadnezzar,
    a prince who reveres him,
    who pleases him, [his] own handiwork,

---

1. See Epic of Creation (III.17) Tablet IV line 138, where this is said of Marduk.
2. Nebuchadnezzar's.

[And], having regard for his righteous [d]eeds,
    he nominated [him]
    to exercise kingship over all peoples,
[He caused] him to grasp in his hand
    the just scepter that enlarges the land,
[He placed] beside him mighty weaponry
    to vanquish his foes,   (40)
[He bes]towed upon him a merciless mace
    that conquers enemies and opponents!

Text: Strong, PSBA 20 (1898), 155–157.
Edition: Strong, PSBA 20 (1898), 154–162.
Translation: Seux, *Hymnes*, 124–128.
★*Notes to Text*: (6) Seux, *Hymnes*, 125 note 12. (9) Seux, *Hymnes*, 126 note 15. (11) So CAD B, 203a
  u-šá-t[i-ru], though the copy does not show enough room for this restoration. (22) Seux, *Hymnes*,
  127 note 37.

IV.9 THE LAMENT OF NABU-SHUMA-UKIN

This lament over undeserved imprisonment is the work of an erudite and pious man who had probably read and absorbed phraseology from such major works of Akkadian literature as the Gilgamesh Epic, the Shamash Hymn (III.32), the Literary Prayer to Marduk (III.29), the Epic of Creation (III.17), and the Advice to a Prince (IV.12). It has a litany-like, highly personal, even obsessive tone that seems, on the one hand, the work of an amateur author, on the other, deeply felt and genuine. The author, son of Nebuchadnezzar II, uses various forms of a word for "artfulness" twenty-three times in seventy-nine lines and repeats essentially the same ideas and expressions for most of the composition, dwelling on the trickery, slander, and deceit that have poisoned his father's mind against him. The work contains words known nowhere else, some of which could be learned coinings by the author himself or which may have belonged to the scholarly arcana of his time. It belongs to the small group of Akkadian literary texts that include the author's name and is perhaps the latest of those that deal with undeserved suffering.

Particularly noteworthy is its specific historical setting, as reconstructed by I. J. Finkel: "One might suggest the following: Nabu-shuma-ukin is the king's oldest son. He, at some time, falls victim to a court conspiracy, whereby a rival faction successfully poisons the king's mind against his own son. Nebuchadnezzar, convinced of his iniquity and deaf to his protestations, throws Nabu-shuma-ukin in the jail at Babylon...Nabu-shuma-ukin experiences the blackest despair in prison, since he has been imprisoned on a trumped-up charge, and he sees no prospect of escape. He makes a tryst with Marduk, that if Marduk rescues him from prison, he will undertake all manner of pious activities when he is king, and he will henceforth take the name of Amel-Marduk, 'Man of Marduk', in acknowledgment."[1] In fact, he was released and ruled briefly as king of Babylonia, 561–560 B.C.[2]

> Marduk thwarts actions of the evil among the gods.[3]   (1)
> The wind brings down the artful tricks of humankind.
> Marduk undoes the artful snare of the evil among [humankind],

---

1. Finkel in Renger, ed., *Babylon*, 328.
2. R. Sack, *Amel-Marduk 562–560 B.C.,* AOATS 4 (1972).
3. Perhaps a reference to Marduk's defeat of the enemy gods in the Epic of Creation (III.17 Tablet IV lines 65–122).

Marduk ties up the wicked,
>   seizes the mouth of the speaker [of wickedness].
Indeed he hears and understands talk bruited about artfully,
>   Marduk will turn it [back on the talker].   (5)
He undoes the snare of opponent and foe
>   so the wind can bring [them] down.
Marduk can undo the most artful snare
So the wind can bring down the one who
>   relied on his own artfulness.
Marduk glowers at the shifty eye,
He has Girra burn up lips that speak evil.   (10)
Marduk tends the unaware, the unseeing,
Who could make things as artful as he?[1]
Marduk tends the weak and helpless,
The (telltale) signs are obvious (to him),
>   he takes in everything artful.
He can undo the arts of the opponent,
>   the conspiracy of the enemy,   (15)
A whirlwind will overtake the man
>   who looks out only for himself.
The future of anyone who relies on
>   his own artfulness is empty air.
At the first glimmer of dawn,
When lying down for the afternoon nap,
In evening, at dusk,   (20)
All night, at the break of day,
(This) wretched, weary man was weeping,
(This) wretched, unaware man was shedding tears,
Because of the artfulness of humankind,
>   he was shedding tear upon tear,
He was weeping in his prison cell
>   because his case was so grievous,   (25)
[Because of un]speakable harm done him,
>   tear upon tear he shed.
[The conspiracy of opponent and foe was too artful for him,
[   ] the artfulness of humankind,
>   the conspiracy to harm him, were overwhelming.

---

1. Compare Epic of Creation (III.17) Tablet VI line 2.

(fragmentary lines)

(This) [hum]ble person was standing there,
    this weary man was weeping,
He was weeping in his prison cell, supplicating,
    calling upon Marduk:
"Restore me, that I may pray to you (always)!
"Let the snare [be undo]ne ... [   ]
"O Marduk ... [   ],   (35)
"O Marduk ... [   ],
"O [Mar]duk, [   ] the one who binds me,
"O Marduk, [   ] the woman(?) who does me harm,
"O Marduk, [   ] the man who does me harm,   (40)
"O Marduk, slay the worker of artful deeds against me,
"O Marduk, burn up the suborners of oaths against me,
"O M[arduk], destroy the ones
    who wag their heads against me,
"[O Marduk], smash in the heads of those who glower at me!   (45)
"You know full well the one whose arts seek to harm me,
    strike him down!
"With conciliatory words on his lips, his heart freigh[ted]
    with lies ... [   ]
"Probe the one who worked up this conspiracy to harm me,
    [send him] down to hell!
"Surround the malefactor with the same cruel web with
    which he artfully surroun[ded me]!
"May Nabu, beloved of Shazu, tend me,
    may he speak to [his father],   (50)
"He who in his own artfulness made ready
    a conspiracy to harm me,
    may he quickly [uproot(?)] him from [   ],
"He who manipulated me to benefit himself and to harm me,
    [impose upon him a heavy] punishment!
"O Marduk, be you the one to harm him!
"Single out for harm the one who stirred up harmful talk of me!
    O Marduk, the artful devices of humankind,
    who can thwart them but you?
"Be mindful, O Marduk, that he told tales about me
    to a gossip, to one who wanted to do me harm.   (55)

"Understand, O Marduk, that he who told tales [about me]
    did me harm,
    he had me speak to a scandal-monger supportive of him.
"Marduk has found out the criminal intent in the [words?]
    of the one who gossips about me, in the very presence
    of the ones who would do me harm.
"Understand, O Marduk, that I am no speaker of artful words,
    a gossip has me saying them.
"O Marduk, hear me! It was a turncoat who whipped up
    against me the baneful wind in my throat,
"O Marduk, turn away the baneful wind
    that he whipped up against me! (60)
"May the exiler of criminals turn back the harmful conspiracy
    against me.
"Let a whirlwind pass over his own artfulness,
    may his fondest hopes be empty air.
"O Marduk, single out for harm
    [the one who suborned] my mentor,
    whose favorite I was, [who ...] the one who taught me.
"He who prattled hypocrisy ... and tried to ...
"[   ] a clever trick [   ] prattling ...
"They made up a clever trick [   ] (65)
"They persuaded ..., their clever trick billowed over
    the father who begot me,
"... [ ] by a clever trick they made cruel my imprisonment.
"[   ] I learned of him lament, indeed the [   ] were cruel!
"His favorable ... [   ]
"[ ] in captivity until he himself makes right
    [my] oppres[sion]. (70)
"Understand, O Marduk, that what they prattled of me to
    the gossipers about me ... they made cruel report of me.
"Hear [   ] of the heart, the clever trick of my foe,
    dissolve his artfulness, [   ] the evil wind ...
"May a whirlwind [   ], his clever trick (be) empty air,
    his conspiracy unravel,
"May you take favorable thought of your [   ],
    take pity on this exhausted man who thinks of you!

"Triumph over the wor[ker of] clever trickery,
    who made a cruel conspiracy to harm me,   (75)
"Your weapon is the deluge, he who listened to the ...
    calumny against me,
    he who witnessed, time and again, the [wrong-doing?],
    were they mindful of your good name?
"May your heart be calmed, quickly let me triumph,
    release my bonds!
"May the Igigi-gods bless you, the Anunna-gods
    bless you time and again,
    may heaven and depths rejoice over you,
"May Ea, king of the depths, rejoice over you!"

(This is) the lament of the weary captive, whom a malefactor imprisoned. As he recites (it) to Marduk, through this lament to Marduk may he be released and may people and land behold his sublimity. (This is) the work of the weary, exhausted, Nabu-shuma-ukin, son of Nebuchadnezzar, [king of Babylon]. Let them bear witness to all these misfortunes!

Text: Finkel in Renger, ed., *Babylon*, 339–342.
Edition: I. Finkel, "The Lament of Nabû-šuma-ukin," in Renger, ed., *Babylon*, 323–342, on which this translation is based.

IV.10 NERIGLISSAR TO MARDUK

At the death of Nebuchadnezzar II began a period of political instability in Babylonia, wherein various kings reigned for short periods. Neriglissar (559–556 B.C.) was the most important of an undistinguished lot.

This prayer concludes an inscription commemorating reconstruction of the royal palace in Babylon.

> O Marduk, great lord, splendid Enlil of the gods, light of the gods his fathers, at your sublime command, which cannot be altered, may I enjoy the delights of the house I have built, may I grow old and attain a venerable old age within it. From horizon to zenith, wherever the sun comes forth, may I receive therein the massive tribute of the kings of the four world regions, of all peoples. May my offspring hold dominion therein over the people of this land forever.

Text: Norris, I R 67, ii 31–42.
Edition: Langdon, VAB 4, 214–215 no. 1 31–42.
Literature: Berger, AOAT 4/1 (1973), Ngl Zylinder II,3.
Translation: Seux, *Hymnes*, 575–576.

IV.11 NABONIDUS

Nabonidus (555–539 B.C.) came to the throne under obscure circumstances, ending a period of political instability. His reign was marked by religious controversy, for he promoted the cult of the moon-god to an extent some Babylonians found offensive. Part of his reign he spent at Teima, in northern Arabia, for reasons that are as yet unexplained, but which may have to do with the growing power of the Medes across the northern flanks of Mesopotamia. After his return to Babylon his policies seem to have met increased resistance, though his theological innovations are not fully understood. The invading armies of Cyrus the Persian entered Babylon without hindrance, and this ended native rule in Babylonia. For historical surveys of his reign, see P. Beaulieu, *The Reign of Nabonidus, King of Babylon 556–539 B.C.*, YNER 10 (New Haven, 1989); R. Sack, "Nabonidus of Babylon," *Studies Astour*, 455–473.

Some of the prayers translated below give elusive hints as to the personality and religious convictions of this complex and interesting man.

(a) TO ISHTAR OF AKKAD

This prayer concludes an inscription commemorating reconstruction of a temple of Ishtar in Babylon.

> Therefore, O Ishtar of Akkad, goddess of combat, look joyfully upon this house, your beloved dwelling, and command life (for me). Speak each day before Marduk, king of the gods, for the prolongation of my days and the increase of my years. Come to my side where there is battle and melee, may I kill my enemies and slay my foes.

Text: S. Smith, RA 22 (1925), 60 ii 16–31; see further Schaudig, AOAT 256 (2001), 353–354.
Edition: S. Smith, RA 22 (1925), 60–62 = Ehelolf, WVDOG 47 (1926), 136–137; Schaudig, AOAT 256 (2001), 356–358.
Translation: von Soden, SAHG, 290 no. 36; Seux, *Hymnes*, 523.
Literature: Berger, AOAT 4/1 (1973), Nabonid Zylinder II,3; Beaulieu, YNER 10 (1989), 39.

(b) TO MARDUK (1)

This prayer forms part of an inscription commemorating reconstruction of the Shamash temple in Larsa.

> O Lord, foremost of the gods, prince Marduk, without you no dwelling is founded nor is its design laid out. Were it not for you, who could do what? O Lord, at your sublime command, let me do what is pleasing to you.

Text: Bezold, PSBA 11 (1889), pl. iv (after p. 96), ii 35–40.
Edition: Langdon, VAB 4, 238–239 no. 3, ii 35–40; Schaudig, AOAT 256 (2001), 402, 408.
Translation: Seux, *Hymnes*, 516.
Literature: Berger, AOAT 4/1 (1973), Nabonid Zylinder III,1; Beaulieu, YNER 10 (1989), 27–28.

(c) TO MARDUK (2)

This prayer forms part of an inscription commemorating reconstruction of the Ehulhul, temple of the moon-god in Harran.

> Let me be king after your own heart, I who, in my ignorance, had no thought of kingship, whom you, lord of lords, have given more responsibility than others you have named and who held dominion from of old. Prolong my days, let my years endure, that I may be the provider (for your sanctuary).

Text: Messerschmidt, MVAeG 1896/1, 79 vii 45–56.
Edition: Langdon, VAB 4, 280–281 no. 8, vii 45–56; Schaudig, AOAT 256 (2001), 520, 526.
Translation: Seux, *Hymnes*, 516.
Literature: Berger, AOAT 4/1 (1973), Nabonidus Stelen-Fragment XI; Beaulieu, YNER 10 (1989), 20–21, 89.

(d) TO SHAMASH (1)

This prayer forms part of an inscription commemorating reconstruction of the Ebabbar, temple of Shamash in Sippar.

(15) O Shamash, sublime lord, as you enter Ebabbar, seat of your repose, may the gates, entrances, chapels, and courtyards rejoice before you like flowers(?).[1] As you take up your residence in your lordly cella, your judiciary seat, may the gods of your city and of your household put your feelings in repose, may the great gods please you. May Aya the great bride, (20) who dwells in the bedchamber, keep your features ever aglow and speak favorably of me every day.*

With your radiant features and joyful face look joyfully upon my precious handiwork, my good deeds, my inscription and my royal statue. May words in my favor be upon your lips, pronounce my name for all time. Let the house I built endure, may your dwelling be perpetual within it. (25) May the god(s) of the house, the design of the house, the crossbeams, lintel, doorframe, sill, bolt, threshold, anteroom, and door leaves guard my step and make straight your going, in your presence extol my deeds, and night and day may they invoke favor for me.

(30) At your sublime command, which cannot be altered, at the word of your great divinity, which cannot be transgressed, may truth, justice, and the divine judge of the gods who sits before you, set for my feet a way of well-being and wealth, a path of truth and justice. May your sublime courier* who stands before you, Bunene, whose counsel is good, who rides (your) chariot, who sits on the driver's seat, whose onslaught cannot be withstood, who hitches up the valorous steeds whose legs tire not (35) going or returning as he parades before you, make my repute favorable in street and way, and advise you that my kingship be lengthy of days, may he come to your aid in your precious mission.* Send beside me the divine splendor of your lightning bolt, symbol of dominion and the awesomeness of kingship, (40) to plunder the land of my enemy. May I overwhelm my foe's

---

1. Meaning uncertain, the simile may be that of a field full of spring flowers that seems to rejoice as the sunlight approaches. A similar expression occurs in IV.52b line 3.

land, may I kill my adversaries, may I partake of the booty of my enemy, may I garner to my land the possessions of all lands.

May I be a provident king who renews holy places, who completes sanctuaries for all time. At the invocation of my eminent name may all my enemies become timorous and weak, (45) may they bow down before me. May they bear my yoke till distant days and bring their massive tribute before me in my city Babylon. May my dwelling be eternal within Babylon, may I enjoy the thoroughfare of its byways in full measure, may my service endure in Esagila and Ezida, which I love. Before the Lord Nabu and Nergal, (50) my gods and the gods of the entire new year's festival house of the Enlil of the gods, Marduk,* may I always, for all time, proceed to offer libations and flour sacrifices, to care for Edadihegal,[1] and to entreat the lord of lords.

Text: Pinches, V R 65, ii 15–52 = Strassmeier, *Actes du sixième congrès international des orientalistes* (Leiden, 1885), II/1, pl. 106–110 (collated by Schaudig, AOAT 256 [2001], 754).
Edition: Langdon, VAB 4, 258–261, no. 6, 15–52; Schaudig, AOAT 256 (2001), 387–388, 393–394.
Translation: von Soden, SAHG, 288–290 no. 35b; Seux, *Hymnes*, 519–521.
Literature: Berger, AOAT 4/1 (1973), Nabonid Zylinder II,9; Beaulieu, YNER 10 (1989), 25.
Notes to Text: (20) Seux, *Hymnes*, 519 note 5. (32) Seux, *Hymnes*, 520 note 13. (38) Seux, *Hymnes*, 520 note 17. (50) Seux, *Hymnes*, 521 note 21.

1. Chapel in Esagila (George, *Topographical Texts*, 390).

(e) TO SHAMASH (2)

This prayer forms part of an inscription commemorating reconstruction of the Ebabbar, temple of Shamash in Sippar.

O Shamash, great lord of heaven and earth, light of the gods his ancestors, offspring of Sin and Ningal, as you enter the Ebabbar, your beloved house, as you take your place upon your eternal dais, look joyfully upon my good works, (15) mine, Nabonidus, king of Babylon, the prince who provides for you, who pleases you, builder of your sublime cella. Each day as you rise and set, make my signs favorable in sky and terrain. (20) Receive my entreaties and accept my prayers. May I hold dominion forever with the legitimate scepter and staff that you placed in my hand.

Text: Pinches, V R 64, iii 11–21; Ungnad, VAS 1 53, iii 11–22.

Edition: Langdon, VAB 4, 226–227 no. 1, iii 11–21; Schaudig, AOAT 256 (2001), 424, 439.

Translation: Seux, *Hymnes*, 518; Hecker, TUAT *Ergänzungslieferung*, 16–17; Beaulieu in Hallo, ed., *Context*, 2:313.

Literature: Berger, AOAT 4/1 (1973), Nabonid Zylinder III,2; Beaulieu, YNER 10 (1989), 34–35.

(f) TO SIN (1)

This prayer concludes an inscription commemorating reconstruction of the Ekishnugal, temple of Sin the moon-god at Ur. Here Nabonidus asserts that Esagila, temple of Marduk in Babylon, and Ezida, temple of Nabu in Borsippa, are also temples to the moon-god, Sin. Thereby this prayer gives evidence for his personal convictions. The reference to possible wrong-doing of his son, Belshazzar, suggests resistance to his religious program, even within his own family. This inscription may date to near the end of Nabonidus's reign, after his return from Arabia.

> O Sin, my lord god,* king of heaven and netherworld, (5) god of gods, who dwells in the great heavens, as you joyfully enter this temple, may there be upon your lips words favorable to Esagila, (10) Ezida, and Ekishnugal, the temples of your great divinity, and (15) instill reverence for your great divinity in the hearts of your[1] people, lest they do wrong against your great divinity. May its foundation last like heaven. Save me, Nabonidus, (20) from wrong-doing against your great divinity, grant me the gift of a life long of days. Instill as well in the heart of Belshazzar, (25) (my) firstborn son, my offspring, reverence for your great divinity. May he commit no (30) wrong-doing, may he enjoy the delights of living in full measure.

Text: Norris, I R 68, ii 3–31; see also As-Siwani, *Sumer* 20 (1964), 75–76.
Edition: Langdon, VAB 4, 252–253 no. 5, ii 3–31; Schaudig, AOAT 256 (2001), 352–353.
Translation: Seux, *Hymnes*, 521; Borger, TUAT 1/4, 406; Beaulieu in Hallo, ed., *Context*, 2:314.
Literature: Berger, AOAT 4/1 (1973), Nabonid Zylinder II.2; Beaulieu, YNER 10 (1989), 35–37, 61–62.
*Notes to Text: (ii 3) With Beaulieu in Hallo, ed., *Context*, 2:314 note 2.

1. Text: "his."

(g) TO SIN (2)

This prayer, from stelae set up by Nabonidus at Harran, commemorates his reconstruction of the Ehulhul, temple of Sin there. The language of the prayer shows Nabonidus's policy of promoting Sin over the other Mesopotamian gods. This aroused resistance in Babylon and elsewhere. The prayer is characterized by use of conventional phraseology in unconventional ways and by rambling, profuse diction.

> O Sin, lord of the gods, whose name on the first day of the month is (ii 15) "... of Anu,"[1] who can strike the heavens and shatter the earth, who appropriates the supremacy of Anu, (20) who controls the supremacy of Enlil, who takes over the supremacy of Ea, who grasps all and every heavenly responsibility in his hands, supreme god[2] of the gods, king of kings, lord of lords, whose command they do not contest and whose word is not spoken twice, the awesomeness of whose great divinity fills heaven (25) and earth, as his features overwhelm heaven and earth, without you, who can do anything?
>
> The land you have resolved to make your dwelling, you will establish therein (30) reverence for your great divinity for all time to come. The land you have resolved to shatter, you will remove reverence for you therefrom and you will overthrow it for all time to come.
>
> (You are the one) whom all gods and goddesses dwelling in heaven watch for, whose utterance they carry out, (that being) the command of (35) Nannaru,[3] the father who begot them, who controls the responsibilities of heaven and netherworld, without whose sublime command, which he speaks in heaven daily, no land can rest secure, nor will there be light in that land ... *(fragmentary lines, then gap)*

Text: Gadd, AnSt 8 (1958), 60–62.
Edition: Röllig, ZA 56 (1964), 221–223; Schaudig, AOAT 256 (2001), 491–493, 498.

---

1. "Crescent," "Weapon," and "Prince" have variously been suggested, but the word remains obscure.
2. Text: Enlil, perhaps etymologizing as *il-ili* "god of gods."
3. Name for Sin.

Translation: Oppenheim, ANET³, 562–563.

Literature: Berger, AOAT 4/1 (1973), Nabonid Stelen-Fragmente III.1; Moran, OrNS 28 (1959), 139; Beaulieu, YNER 10 (1989), 32–34, 60–62.

Notes to Text: (ii 23–25) With Schaudig, AOAT 256 (2001), 498 and note 718.

IV.12 ANTIOCHUS SOTER TO NABU

This stilted piece is primarily of interest because it is the latest datable Akkadian prayer. It concluded an inscription commemorating renovation of the Esagila and Ezida temples in the mid-third century B.C.

(§1) O Nabu, sublime son, wisest of the gods, stately one, worthy(?)* of praises, first-ranked son of Marduk, offspring of Arua,[1] queen who is fashioner of created things, look joyfully and, at your sublime command, (you) whose command cannot be changed, let overthrow of my enemy's land, attainment of my desire to stand in triumph over our foes, just kingship, prosperous reign, satisfaction, and venerable old age be the royal gift (to) Antiochus and Seleucus his son, forever.

(§2) O princely son Nabu, heir of Esagila, first-ranked son of Asaru,[2] offspring of Arua the queen, when amidst happiness and rejoicing you enter Ezida, the eternal house, the house of your divine supremacy, your pleasurable dwelling, by your eternal command, which cannot be set aside, may my days be long, may my years be many, may my throne be firmly founded, may my reign endure, through your sublime scepter, which fixes the limits of heaven and netherworld. May words favorable of me be always upon your pure lips. May I conquer the lands from the rising to the setting sun, may I behold their tribute and bring it for the perfection of Esagila and Ezida.

(§3) O Nabu, foremost son, when you enter Ezida, the eternal house, may there be on your lips a favorable word for Antiochus, king of the world, and favorable words for Seleucus the king, his son, and Stratonike his wife, the queen.

Text: Pinches, V R 66, i 16–ii 29.
Edition: Weissbach, VAB 3, 132–135.
Translation: von Soden, SAHG, 291–292 no. 38; Oppenheim, ANET[3], 317; Seux, *Hymnes*, 525–526.
Literature: A. Kuhrt, S. A. Sherwin-White, "Aspects of Seleucid Royal Ideology: The Cylinder of Antiochus I from Borsippa," *Journal of Hellenic Studies* 111 (1991), 71–86.
Notes to Text: (1) Text: "established."

1. Name for Sarpanitum, wife of Marduk.
2. Marduk.

IV.13 ADVICE TO A PRINCE

This warning, composed in the casuistic style of omens, lists misdeeds of an unnamed king and their consequences. Most of the misdeeds center around royal abuse of the privileges of the cities Sippar, Nippur, and Babylon. The detailed charges suggest that the writer had a specific king in mind, perhaps Merodach-Baladan, an eighth-century ruler of Babylonia.[1] Since this text was copied for Assurbanipal's library, was quoted from memory(?) by a scholar in a letter,[2] and has turned up in a late manuscript from Nippur, it was evidently studied as a literary work, whatever its original political purpose may have been.

(1) If the king has no regard for due process, his people will be thrown into chaos, his land will be devastated. If he has no regard for the due process of his land, Ea, king of destinies, will alter his destiny and misfortune will hound him.[3]

If he has no regard for his princes, his lifetime will be cut short. (5) If he has no regard for scholarly advisors, his land will rebel against him. If he has regard for a scoundrel, the mentality of his country will alter. If he has regard for a clever trick,[4] the great gods will hound him in right counsel and the cause of justice.

If he denies due process to a citizen of Sippar, but grants it to an alien, Shamash, judge of heaven and earth, (10) will establish an alien due process in his land and neither princes nor judges will have regard for due process. If citizens of Nippur are brought to him for due process (and) he accepts the (customary) remuneration, (but) denies them due process, Enlil, lord of the world, will

---

1. For a study of his reign, see J. Brinkman, "Merodach-Baladan II," *Studies Oppenheim*, 6–53; *Prelude to Empire* (Philadelphia, 1984), 47–54; R. van der Spek, JEOL 25 (1977/8), 56–66. The dating of the events referred to in the text to his reign was argued by Böhl, MAOG 11/3, 30–35 and afresh by Diakonoff, AS 16, 343–349, endorsed by Brinkman, *Studies Oppenheim*, 48. Labat, *Religions*, 316–317, suggests that this text refers to actions of Sennacherib.

2. Reiner, *Studies Diakonoff*, 320–323; Parpola, *Studies Reiner*, 273 note 12; Cole, SAAS 4 (1996), 76 with note 46.

3. Or: (Ea) "will hound him with misfortune," in contrast to line 8.

4. Literally: "a device of Ea." Some translators consider the "device of Ea" in a positive sense, but interpretation of the passage remains problematic (Hurowitz, SAAB 12 [1998], 42–43). One manuscript adds here: "(that means) defeat of the national army, among the great gods (some) will hound him..."

raise up against him a foreign enemy that will decimate his army,[1] the prince and his administrators will prowl about the streets like vagabonds.

(15) If he takes money of citizens of Babylon and appropriates (it) for (his own) property, (or) hears a case involving Babylonians but dismisses (it) for a triviality, Marduk, lord of heaven and earth, will establish his enemies over him and grant his possessions and property to his foe.

If (he) imposes a fine or imprisonment (20) upon a citizen of Nippur, Sippar, or Babylon, the city where that fine was imposed will be razed to its foundations and a foreign foe will enter the place of imprisonment.

If he calls up Sippar, Nippur, and Babylon collectively to impose forced labor on the peoples aforesaid, requiring of them (25) service at the recruiter's cry, Marduk, sage of the gods, deliberative prince, will turn his land over to his foe so that the troops of his land will do forced labor for his foe. Anu, Enlil, and Ea, the great gods (30) who dwell in heaven and earth, have confirmed in their assembly the exemption of these (people from such obligations)!

If he grants his steeds forage on the fodder of citizens of Sippar, Nippur, (or) Babylon, the steeds that consumed the fodder will be led off to an enemy's harness. (35) If the citizens aforesaid are conscripted into the king's troops in a time of national conscription, mighty Erra, [van]guard of his army, will shatter his front line and go at his [fo]e's side.

If he requisitions [their] oxen, alters [their] fields, (or) (40) grants (them) to an alien, Adad will come quickly. If he collects taxes★ on their sheep, Adad, irrigator of heaven and earth, will decimate his pasturing livestock with hunger and offer them up(?)[2] to the sun.

(45) If a scholarly advisor or administrator on the king's service denounces them[3] (the citizens aforesaid) and extorts bribes from them, by the command of Ea, king of the depths, that scholarly

---

1. Variant: "and will turn over his forces to the ruler of Elam"(?).
2. Meaning of the verb not clear. I take it to refer to the corpses of the starved beasts lying under the hot sun.
3. Variant: "the case of a 'lord'"; I adhere to the reading of BWL.

advisor or administrator will die violently, the place they were will be obliterated to a wasteland, (50) the wind will carry away their remains, their achievements will be reckoned as a puff of air.

If he nullifies their contracts, alters their steles, sends them out on service, or [forces] labor obligations upon them, Nabu, scribe of Esagila, who inspects the whole of heaven and earth, who directs everything, who appoints kingship, will nullify the bonds of his country and ordain misfortune (for it).

(55) If an officer or temple warden or royal administrator who holds wardenship of a temple in Sippar, Nippur, or Babylon, imposes forced labor upon them (the citizens aforesaid) for the temples of the great gods, the great gods will quit their sanctuaries in a fury, they will not enter their shrines.

Text: W. G. Lambert, BWL, pl. 31, 32; S. Cole, *The Early Neo-Babylonian Governor's Archive from Nippur*, OIP 114 (1996), 268, 271.

Edition: Lambert, BWL, 110–115; Cole, OIP 114 (1996), 268–274; Hurowitz, SAAB 12 (1998), 48–53.

Translation: Labat, *Religions*, 316–319; von Soden, TUAT III/1, 170–173.

Literature: I. M. Diakonoff, "A Babylonian Political Pamphlet from about 700 B.C.," AS 16 (1965), 343–349; E. Reiner, "The Babylonian Fürstenspiegel in Practice," *Studies Diakonoff*, 320–323; V. Hurowitz, "Advice to a Prince: A Message from Ea," SAAB 12 (1998), 39–53. For a critique of Diakonoff's interpretation of the text, see W. G. Lambert, JAOS 88 (1968), 124.

Notes to Text: (7) With respect to Hurowitz's proposal, SAAB 12 (1998), 44, that *šipir Ea* might, in some way, refer to this text (but only if the relevant manuscripts are emended!), compare, however, II.1, line 52 and p. 87 note 1. (40) With Cole, OIP 114 (1996), 274.

IV.14 THE KING OF JUSTICE

This text recounts certain signs and wonders of the reign of a Neo-Babylonian king that illustrate his concern for justice and the gods' favor for him. Of particular interest is the fullest description of a water ordeal to come down from antiquity. The narration suggests that such an ordeal had not been resorted to for a long time, so it may have been inspired by the provision for it in the laws of Hammurabi (see II.10a), which were studied in this period and which may be quoted here. Important parts of the text are missing, notably the beginning and end, that latter of which contained, among other things, a description of the king's domain (unfortunately too fragmentary to translate). The preserved text contains various errors and what seem to be anacolutha, but, with all these problems, the composition is singularly appealing and a notable contrast to the formalities of the royal inscriptions of the period. Whereas the king was originally indentified with Nebuchadnezzar II by Lambert, an attribution to Nabonidus seems more likely, even though the claims of conquest at the end seem more appropriate to Nebuchadnezzar II.

i

(At the beginning remains of about twenty-seven lines of text are preserved. These suggest that the composition opened with a third person preoration with numerous dependent clauses ["He who …"], with reference to the "Lord of Lords," climaxing in the mention of Babylon and the king's name [lines 10–11]. Thereupon the text may move into an account of his divinely directed birth and upbringing, and how he was chosen for dominion over the land.)

ii

    … (2) nor would he make a decision concerning them (the cripple or widow). They would eat each other like dogs. The strong would oppress the weak, while they had insufficient means to go to court for redress. The rich would take the belongings of the lowly. Neither governor nor prince would appear before the judge on behalf of the cripple or widow, they would come before the judges but they would not proceed with their case; a judge would accept a bribe or present and would not consider it (the case).[1]

---

    1. Not clear. The line may mean that judges were bribed not to hear cases, or that they accepted the usual fees to hear cases but then did not proceed.

They (the oppressors) would not receive his injunction (such as this):

(9) "The silver that you loaned at interest you have increased five-fold! You have forced households to be broken up, you have had fields and meadowland seized; people, servants, slaves, livestock, possessions, and property are sitting in front of and behind you. Even if you have used up the interest on the loans, (the principle) is still available to you."[1]

(14) A man who had nothing came before him, but he, the judge who had made the decision, drawn up a tablet, and sealed it, threw the tablet away and would not give (it) to him.* Were the man to pursue him (the judge), he risked his life.* Having no recourse, he would let out a cry and set up a sh[ou]t, invoking the lord of lords, "Abolish the (high) interest on loans being charged to the people!" [He (the judge) would not con]cern himself about them in any way, nor would they be given succor, nor would he even pay attention to them.

(22) For the sake of due process he (the king) did not neglect truth and justice, nor did he rest day or night! He was always drawing up, with reasoned deliberation, cases and decisions pleasing to the great lord Marduk (and) framed for the benefit of all the people and the stability of Babylonia. He drew up improved regulations for the city, he rebuilt the law court, he drew up regulations (for it). The im[age] of his kingship is eternal.* (*one line lost*).

iii

(2) The innocent man would take the ... [   ]. A man who returned to that law court (to reopen a case), such that, a tablet ag[ainst him] having been drawn up definitively, he was returning a second time for false and dishonest purposes, the king commanded the troops to cut off his head and paraded it through the land. In order that such a man's head be cut off in the future, he made a likeness of that man's head, and he had (the following) written upon that man's head and fastened forever after to the

---

1. Translation doubtful; the passage may mean that the creditor has waxed rich on interest alone.

outer gate of that law court for all the people to see, "A man whose case was judged, whose tablet of verdict has been written, but who afterward has changed the sealed document and come back for judgment, his head will be cut off like this one's." Base and wicked men would see it, abscond, and never be heard of again.

(14) He put a stop to bribes and presents among the people, he gave the people satisfaction, he caused the land to dwell in tranquility, allowing no one to alarm them.[1] He pleased his lords Sin, Shamash and Ishtar—they being Bel and Beltiya[2]—(and) Nabu, who dwells in Esagila and Ezida. On account of his legitimate rule and loving his kingship, they (the gods) became reconciled to (resumption of) regular offerings.[3]

(21) A man charged a man with murder but did not prove it. They were brought before him (the king) and he ordered them (to be taken) above Sippar, to the bank of the Euphrates, before Ea, king of the depths, for trial. The troops of the guard, keeping both under close surveillance all night, lit a fire. At daybreak the prince, governor, and troops assembled as the king commanded, and took their places around them. Both went down in order to [plunge into] the river. Ea, king of the depths, who loves his kingship, that truth be seen,* something never [seen] nor heard of from time immemorial: the innocent man, who had been made to plunge into the river, he (Ea) brought him safe to [the bank]! The one who had frivolously charged him sank in the water. From morning until noon no one saw him nor was aught heard of [him].* As for the troops of the guard, who had stood around them at the riverbank from evening until daybre[ak], their hearts sank and they set out to search [   ],* "What shall we report? How shall we answer the king?" When the king heard, he was furious at the troops. A courier was coming and going, "Did you not watch over the man? Has he gotten across the river and lain down in the open country?" Since none saw him at any time, they could

1. Compare II.10a, epilogue, to which this probably alludes.
2. For the understanding of this line, see Lambert, *Iraq* 27 (1965), 10 note to iii 17: "the line states quite clearly that Šamaš and Ištar are identified with Marduk and Sarpanitum ... "
3. This may refer to rebuilding of a temple of the moon-god in Harran during the reign of Nabonidus (Schaudig, AOAT 256 [2001], 587 note 990).

not answer. Boatman and soldiers went along the river, bank to bank, checking the edge. When high noon came his corpse rose up from the river. He had been struck on the head, blood was running from the mouth, ears, and nostrils. The top of his head was burned, as if with fire,[1] his body was covered with blisters. The people saw, and spoke (? of it) in reverence; all the world was borne down with awe. The evil-intentioned enemy and the foe betook themselves into hiding.

(iv 24) On another occasion, another man den[ounced]* another man (falsely). He swore an oath by Shamash and went into a magic circle,[2] [Sin?], the great lord who is Marduk, residing in Esagila (*one line lost*).

v

(1) He built anew [Ehulhul, the temple of Sin(?)]. He hitched up strong horses to wagons, the foremost of them decorated as an offering. He longed for the gods, they hurried to him and never left him.

(4) Every day, without ceasing, excellent bread, mighty oxen, fine fatted rams, [   ], geese, ducks, [wild fowl, pigeons], dormice, s[trings] of f[ish], cultivated [fr]uit in enormous [quantities], the [prid]e of orchards; [apples], figs, pomegranates, grapes, dates, imported dates, [dried figs?], [rai]sins, abundant vegetables, the [yield] of the garden, fine mixed beer, honey, ghee, refined oil, best-quality milk, sweet emmer beer, fine wine, the finest of grain and vine of all mountains and lands, the best of what was his, the fair products of mountains and seas he offered in abundance before the great gods. What no one had ever done to such an extent, they received, in perpetuity, from his pure hands, and blessed his kingship. [In] conquering from Egypt to Hume, Pirid-du, Lydia, [Mar]hashi,[3] king of [remote] regions [   ] (*breaks off*)

---

1. Guilty parties in the river ordeal were thought to be burned by subaquatic fire (Beaulieu, N.A.B.U. 1992/77).

2. In the Late period, oaths to Shamash could be sworn standing inside a magic circle; see G. Meier, "Beschwörung mittels eines Mehlkreises," AfO 11 (1936/7), 365–367.

3. Historical geographical term, perhaps referring to Iran.

Text: W. G. Lambert, CT 46 45.

Edition: W. G. Lambert, *Iraq* 27 (1965), 1–11; Schaudig, AOAT 256 (2001), 579–588, with collations and numerous improvements adopted here.

Literature: J. Bottéro, "L'Ordalie en Mésopotamie ancienne," *Annali della Scuola Normale Superiore di Pisa, Classe di Lettere e Filosofia*, Serie III vol. XI/4 (1981), 1005–1067 (cited below as "Bottéro, Ordalie"); von Soden, ZA 65 (1975), 283, where numerous new readings are proposed, many of which are adopted here. See also W. von Soden, "Kyros und Nabonid, Propaganda und Gegen-propaganda," *Archaeologische Mitteilungen aus Iran, Ergänzungsheft* 10 (1983), 61–68; Beaulieu, YNER 10 (1989), 4–5.

⋆Notes to Text: (ii 16) von Soden, ZA 65 (1974), 283. (ii 17–18) Schaudig, AOAT 256 (2001), 581–582 note 953, 585–586 note 983. (ii 27) With Schaudig, AOAT 256 (2001), 582 and note 957. (iv 2) See Bottéro, "Ordalie," 1049. (iv 6) von Soden, ZA 65 (1975), 283. (iv 9) Bottéro, "Ordalie," 1050 suggests: "calls upon his name were not heard." (iv 24) Schaudig, AOAT 256 (2001), 583 note 966.

IV.15 IN PRAISE OF EZIDA

The Ezida was the temple of Nabu in Borsippa, an important city and center of learning to the south of Babylon. For Nabu, see III.45.

How like heaven is the city Borsippa!	(1)
Lofty Ezida is the likeness of Esharra.[1]	
The whole(?)* is delightful to (its) god,	
The gardens enhance the city's pride.	
Its summit reaches the clouds,	(5)
Its well-founded roots thrust to the netherworld.	
Its brickwork is of soapstone(?),*	
Its parapet is of finest, choicest gold,	
Its retaining wall is of alabaster,	(10)
The apparel of Ezida is blue (glazed) pegs.	
He who dwells therein is scribe to the gods,	
Nabu, son of Esagila,	
He bears the tablet of destinies for all the gods,[2]	
He gives the decision(s).	(15)
He holds the stylus of truth,	
He scrutinizes the people of this land each day.	
Take up your abode in your dwelling, son of the Lord,	
May your house, Ezida, be replete with splendor!	

Text: Köcher, ZA 53 (1959), 237.
Edition: Köcher, ZA 53 (1959), 236–240.
Notes to Text: (3) See von Soden *apud* Köcher, 239. (7) So Köcher, 240; see CAD L, 65b.

1. See p. 462 note 3. This may refer to the heavenly abode of all the gods.
2. For tablet of destinies, see p. 445 note 2.

IV.16 IN PRAISE OF BABYLON

(a) SUBLIME HOLY PLACE

This text was composed in fifteen(?) five-line strophes, each line of a strophe beginning with the same sign. While the date of the composition is uncertain, it is generally ascribed to some pro-Babylonian Assyrian monarch, for example, Assurbanipal (Strong, PSBA 17 [1895], 131) or, as preferred here, Sargon II (Seux, *Hymnes,* 124 note 34). This latter attribution is based on the possibility that Sargon II is named in the last line of the text. As suggested originally by Strong, the acrostic probably read "[I will extol] its (Babylon's) name in the four [world regions]."

(gap)

iv

May months and years bless sublime Esagila,   (5)
May its brickwork give blessing to noble Marduk.*
At the month of life, (at?) the New Year's festival,
    let a celebration be held,
Let the four world regions gaze fixedly upon his features,
May he bestow a satisfying life upon the shepherd[1]
    who provides for him.

v

He who devised the plans of the sanctuaries,
    restored the daises,   (10)
Who completed his great holy place Babylon,
    city of universal dominion,
Who restored all its mighty sanctuaries,
He confirmed its suspended regular offerings
    as they were before,
His [   ] responded with an omen of well-being and a verdict.

---

1. The king.

vi

[In] Babylon, the sublime holy place that [   ]   (15)
[   ] a brilliant garment

(gap)

xiii(?)

(fragmentary lines)

May the sublime princess Sarpanitum bless his kingship,
May she make numerous his descent and multiply his progeny.   (5)

xiv(?)

May he attain his ambitions with none to oppose him,
May daily talk of him be favorable and submissive,
May he proceed through Shuanna[1]
        on a course of well-being and satisfaction,
May he go safely inside its temples and carry out its rites,
May he ever, in gladness, make rejoicing in sweet Babylon.   (10)

xv(?)

May its excellence be sung on the lyre and its hymn of praise ...
May he shower down finest oil in its famous holy places,
May he fill the coffers of its temples
        with precious goods beyond calculation,
May those deeds he performed be ... [   ],
May the name of Sar[gon   ].   (15)

Text: DT 83 = T. Pinches, *Texts in the Babylonian Wedge-writing* (London, 1882), 15 no. 4 (collated).
Edition: Strong, PSBA 17 (1895), 133–135.
Translation: Seux, *Hymnes*, 122–124.
★*Notes to Text*: (6) Or, according to Poebel, AS 9 (1939), 23, "May they (the months and years) bless
   its brickwork for the sake of prince Marduk." While this rendering better fits the parallelism, it
   requires an emendation of the text.

1. Babylon.

(b) THE BABYLONIANS

This composition is known from a tablet containing excerpts of various texts, presumably the work of a student. There appear to be numerous mistakes. The text may not be complete. For a fragment of a similar text, see George, *Topographical Texts*, 230–231.[1]

> They set out (offering) shares of beverage,
>> how reverently they bless the g[od]!   (1)
> They are heedful of divine judgment, observant of truth,
>> they [   ] boundary, truth, and design.
> Strength of Ningirsu, wealth of the sweet harvest song,
>> their ... cannot be compared with them.
> They have seemly ways(?), are well-advised and pleasing,
>> they brighten their mood and m[ake] merriment.
> Women who have gained understanding in their tasks,
>> high priestesses who are always faithful
>> to their (divine) husbands,   (5)
> Cloistered women who are skilled
>> in keeping the unborn child alive,
>> holy women who place [ ] in purifying water,
> Who observe interdicts and adhere to what is sacred,
>> they bless [ ] ...
> Reverent, circumspect, mindful of virtue,
>> the daughters of the gods always [   ] ...
> Well-tried in good works, they can (do) what is see[mly?],
>> the [   ] of all Babylon ...
> These are the ones whom Marduk freed of obligations,
>> [I have] extolled ..., nor did I impugn them!   (10)

Text: Ebeling, KAR 321, obv. 2–11.
Edition: None.

---

1. For the enigmatic composition edited by A. Kilmer, "An Oration on Babylon," AOF 18 (1991), 9–22, not included here, the closest parallel may be II.37, as it does not appear to be praises of the city Babylon.

(c) FULL OF JOY TO BEHOLD

A paean in Sumerian and Akkadian sounds praises to the city Babylon, comparing it to Nippur as the primary city of Mesopotamia; compare III.11a.

> [The citizens of Bab]ylon are freed from service by Enlil, (1′)
> Whoever shall put harm in their way,
> > he shall bear the onus for them.
> Nippur is the Lord's city, Babylon is his favorite,
> Nippur and Babylon have but one mind!
> Babylon is full of joy to behold. (5′)
> The resident of Babylon will live a long life.
> Babylon is sweet to the taste as a date from Dilmun![1]

> *(fragmentary lines, then breaks off)*

Text: Ebeling, KAR 8 obv.
Edition: Ebeling, OLZ 19 (1916), 132–133.

1. Today's Bahrein, famous in Mesopotamian antiquity for its superior dates.

C. Mythological and Historical Narratives

IV.17 ERRA AND ISHUM

Erra and Ishum is one of the most original and challenging compositions in Akkadian. The text is a portrayal of violence: its onset, course, and consequences—how it needs to be recognized and feared as potentially the most powerful of forces. Violence can eliminate even the order ordained by the gods and sweep away in its frenzy all the hopes and accomplishments of civilization. The author, Kabti-ilani-Marduk, who may have lived in the eighth century B.C., must have seen and suffered the consequences of violence and civil strife.[1] He gives witness to a society that had cast off restraints and so ceased to be in balance. If, the text tells, people understand the nature of violence, how it can rage out of control and overwhelm all, they can hope to avoid it. To the modern reader the most salient aspect of this text is its high level of feeling, the willingness of its author to experiment, and the complexity of its thought and structure.

Marduk, as chief Babylonian deity, plays a major role in this poem. He is portrayed as remote and all-wise; he knows Erra's plans even before Erra arrives at his temple. He speaks in sonorous, scholarly diction; there is never any doubt that he is king. Yet the poet is troubled that there could be disorder in his realm that could threaten even Marduk himself.

The form of the text is narrative poetry, most of it direct speech. Ishum, Erra's companion, is invoked near the beginning and plays a crucial role throughout the poem, though he is subordinate to Erra. The device, well known in Western literature, of telling the exploits of a hero from the standpoint of his closest companion, is attested here for the first time. While some narrative is in the third person, in one long passage (see Tablet II Pericope C2, lines 40ff.), Erra narrates his own actions. This represents, in modern critical terms, an attempt to fuse narrative and the narrated, discourse and event. Such an experiment builds on a tradition of self-narrative by a deity in Mesopotamian poetry (see II.4, III.25, 43f., IV.31). Perhaps the same tradition is refurbished in a self-praise by Marduk of his own cult statue (Tablet I lines 149ff.), not to mention a description by Marduk himself of destruction done to Babylon (Tablet IV lines 40ff.). Some of Erra's actions are narrated also in the second person by Ishum (see Tablet III Pericope C, lines 58ff.).

---

1. The precise date of the text is disputed; see, for example, Cagni, *Epopea*, 37–45; von Soden, UF 3 (1971), 253–263; AfO 34 (1987), 67–69.

The diction of this text seems strange, or at least idiosyncratic, to some modern readers. They regard this as indicative of an author untutored in the finer points of Akkadian poetics. One might equally consider it a determined effort to refurbish a rich inventory of inherited expressions to lend them greater force, to do such violence, so to speak, to traditional usage as to command attention.

Tablet I

(Narrator invokes Marduk, chief deity of Babylon, and Ishum, vanguard and companion of Erra. Erra is restless and breaks into a soliloquy. He is anxious to fight and campaign, but hesitates through natural inertia. Speaking of himself in the third person, Erra says that what he needs to stir him to action is Ishum's encouragement [i 9].)

> O king of all inhabited lands, creator of the wo[rld],   (1)
> O Hendursagga,[1] firstborn of Enlil [   ],
> Holder of the "sublime scepter,"[2]
>> herdsman of the people of this land,
>> shepherd [of humankind],
> O Ishum, "zealous slaughterer,"[3]
>> whose hands are suited to brandish fierce weapons,
> And to make his sharp spear flash, Erra, warrior of the gods,
>> was restless in his dwelling,   (5)
> His heart urged him to do battle!
> Says he to his weapons, "Smear yourselves with deadly venom!"
> To the Seven, warriors unrivalled,
>> "Let your weapons be girded!"
> He even says to you, "I will take to the field!"[4]
> "You are the torch, they will see your light,   (10)
> "You are the vanguard, the gods will [   ],

---

1. Another name for Ishum.
2. Translation of Hendursagga (Cagni, *Epopea*, 138–139; Edzard, RLA 4, 325).
3. A learned Sumerian etymologizing of Ishum's name (W. G. Lambert, AfO 18 [1957/58], 400).
4. It is not clear who speaks lines 9–20. Erra may be describing himself, or the narrator may be speaking of Erra. As interpreted here, the narrative statement is that Erra is restless (5–9), while Erra's speech to Ishum, showing both inclination and disinclination to stir, includes the entire passage 9–20. A different reading is offered by Machinist, JAOS 103 (1983), 222–223 (earlier by Hruška, BiOr 30 [1973], 5), whereby Ishum is the subject of I.6–14 and Erra is addressed in 9–14, thus the reverse of the reading adopted here. Although in some respects this is an attractive possibility, it seems excluded by 9a, for the "you" there, so far as I can see, must be Ishum (so also Edzard, Cagni, and others).

"You are the stanchion, [zealous] slaughterer!
"(So) up, Erra, from laying waste the land
"How cheerful your mood will be and joyful your heart.
"Erra's limbs are slug[gish],
     like those of a mortal lacking sleep,   (15)
"He says to himself, 'Shall I get up or go to sleep?'
"He says to his weapons, 'Stay in the corners!'
"To the Seven, warriors unrivalled,
     'Go back to your dwellings!'
"Until you rouse him, he will sleep in his bedroom,
"He will dally with Mami his mate."   (20)

(With a second invocation, now of Ishum, the narrator introduces the terrible
Seven, who stand ready to massacre the people of the land.)

O Engidudu "who patrols at night," "ever guiding the noble,"[1]
Who ever guides young men and women in safety,
     making light as day,
The Seven, warriors unrivalled, their divine nature is different,
Their origins are strange, they are terrifying,
Whoever sees them is numbed with fear.   (25)
Their breath is death,
People are too frightened to approach it!
Yet Ishum is the door, bolted before [them].[2]
When Anu, king of the gods, sowed his seed in the earth,
She bore him seven gods, he called them the "Seven."
They stood before him, that he ordain their destinies.   (30)
He summoned the first to give his instructions,
"Wherever you go and spread terror, have no equal."
He said to the second, "Burn like fire, scorch like flame."
He c[ommanded] the third, "Look like a lion,
     let him who sees you be paralyzed with fear."
He said to the fourth, "Let a mountain collapse
     when you present your fierce arms."   (35)

---

1. "Patrols at night" is a literal translation of the Sumerian epithet; "ever-guiding" is a learned wordplay on the same epithet (as shown by Tinney, N.A.B.U. 1989/3).
2. Variant: "it."

To the fifth he said, "Blast like the wind,
    scan the circumference of the earth."
The sixth he enjoined, "Go out everywhere (like the deluge)
    and spare no one."
The seventh he charged with viperous venom,
    "Slay whatever lives."
After Anu had ordained destinies for all of the Seven,
He gave those very ones to Erra, warrior of the gods,
    (saying), "Let them go beside you.   (40)
"When the clamor of human habitations
    becomes noisome to you,
"And you resolve to wreak destruction,
"To massacre the people of this land and fell the livestock,
"Let these be your fierce weaponry, let them go beside you."

(The Seven offer the encouragement that Erra needs. In a rousing call to arms, they extol the heroic excitement of the campaign, the honor, prestige, and gratification it brings. The Seven claim vaguely that they are not respected enough, that others are growing more important than they. They bring up the old charge [see II.36] that humans make too much noise for the gods to sleep, although this was not the cause Erra had given for his own lack of sleep. The Seven claim further that there are too many wild animals on the loose. Their final claim, no doubt the most important one, is that they are bored and out of training.)

These are the ones who are in a fury,
    holding their weapons aloft,   (45)
They are saying to Erra, "Up, do your duty!
"Why have you been sitting in the city like a feeble old man,
"Why sitting at home like a helpless child?
"Shall we eat woman food, like non-combatants?
"Have we turned timorous and trembling, as if we can't fight? (50)
"Going to the field for the young and vigorous
    is like to a very feast,
"(But) the noble who stays in the city can never eat enough.
"His people will hold him in low esteem,
    he will command no respect,
"How could he threaten a campaigner?
"However well developed is the strength of the city dweller, (55)
"How could he possibly best a campaigner?

"However toothsome city bread,
      it holds nothing to the campfire loaf,
"However sweet fine beer,
      it holds nothing to water from a skin,
"The terraced palace holds nothing
      to the [wayside] sleeping spot!
"Be off to the field, warrior Erra, make your weapons clatter,   (60)
"Make loud your battle cry that all around they quake,
"Let the Igigi-gods hear and extol your name,
"Let the Anunna-gods hear and flinch at the mention of you,
"Let (all) the gods hear and bend for your yoke,
"Let sovereigns hear and fall prostrate before you,   (65)
"Let countries hear and bring you their tribute,
"Let the lowly hear and [per]ish of their own accord,
"Let the mighty hear and his strength diminish,
"Let lofty mountains hear and their peaks crumble,
"Let the surfing sea hear and convulse,
      wiping out (her) in[crease]!   (70)
"Let the stalk be yanked from the tough thicket,
"Let reeds of the impenetrable morass be shorn off,
"Let men turn cowards and their clamor subside,
"Let beasts tremble and return to clay,
"Let the gods your ancestors see and praise your valor!   (75)
"Warrior Erra, why do you neglect the field for the city?
"The very beasts and creatures hold us in contempt!
"O warrior Erra, we will tell you,
      though what we say be offensive to you!
"Ere the whole land outgrows us,
"You must surely hear our words!   (80)
"Do a kindly deed for the gods of hell,
      who delight in deathly stillness,
"The Anunna-gods cannot fall asleep
      for the clamor of humankind.
"Beasts are overrunning the meadows, life of the land,
"The farmer sobs bitterly for his [field].
"Lion and wolf are felling the livestock,   (85)
"The shepherd, who cannot sleep day or night
      for the sake of his flocks, is calling upon you.

"We too, who know the mountain passes,
    we have [forgotten] how to go,
"Cobwebs are spun over our field gear,
"Our fine bow resists and is too strong for us,
"The tip of our sharp arrow is bent out of true,   (90)
"Our blade is corroded for want of a slaughter!"

(Erra brightens at this and asks Ishum why he does not proceed at once. Ishum remonstrates, saying that violence and destruction are evil. Erra, thoroughly aroused, launches into a self-praise. He is the bravest. If people do not respect the gods enough, and the others are too pusillanimous to do anything about it, he will remedy matters. Since the supposed lack of respect for him must be contrary to Marduk's wishes, Erra will cause Marduk to forsake his dwelling and thus bring about the punishment humankind deserves.)

The warrior Erra heard them,
What the Seven said pleased him like finest oil.
He made ready to speak and said to [Ish]um,
"Why, having heard, did you sit by silent?   (95)
"Lead the way, let me begin the campaign!
"[   ] the Seven, warriors without rival,
"Make my fierce weapons[1] march at my side,
"But you be the vanguard and rear guard."
When Ishum heard what he said,   (100)
He felt pity and said [to the war]rior Erra,[2]
"O lord Erra, why have you pl[otted evil] against the gods?
"You have remorselessly plotted evil,
        to lay waste the lands and decimate [the people]."
Erra [made ready to sp]eak and said,
To Ishum his vanguard he said [these words],   (105)
"Keep quiet, Ishum, listen to what I say.
"As concerns the people of the inhabited world,
        whom you would spare,
"O vanguard of the gods, wise Ishum,
        whose counsel is always for the best,
"I am the wild bull of heaven, I am the lion on earth,

1. That is, the Seven.
2. Variant: "He made ready to speak, [say]ing [to the warrior Erra]."

"I am king in the land, I am the fiercest among the gods,   (110)
"I am warrior among the Igigi-gods,
⠀⠀⠀⠀mighty one among the Anunna-gods!
"I am the smiter of beasts,
⠀⠀⠀⠀battering ram against the mountain,
"[I am] the blaze in the reed thicket,
⠀⠀⠀⠀the broad blade against the rushes,
"I am banner for the march,
"I blast like the wind, I thunder like the storm,   (115)
"Like the sun, I scan the circumference of the world.
"I am the wild ram striding forth in the steppe,
"I invade the range and take up my dwelling in the fold.
"All the gods are afraid of a fight,
"So the people of this land are contemptuous!   (120)
"As for me, since they do not fear my name,
"And have disregarded Marduk's command,
⠀⠀⠀⠀so he may act according to his wishes,[1]
"I will make Marduk angry, stir him from his dwelling,
⠀⠀⠀⠀and lay waste the people!"

(Erra repairs to Esagila and asks Marduk why his image is besmirched. In a sonorous speech [see General Introduction, p. 15 note 1] Marduk, having, in his omniscience, seen Erra's intent, recounts what transpired last time he forsook his dwelling: the universe went topsy-turvy, living creatures were nearly wiped out by the ensuing catastrophe. When Marduk found that his cult statue had been sullied, he caused it to be rebuilt by sublime craftsmen who were later dismissed, never to return. Marduk waxes lyrical in praise of his own cult statue and the wonderful tree from which it was fashioned. The present image of Marduk, divinely created, could never be duplicated.)

The warrior Erra set out for Shuanna,[2]
⠀⠀⠀⠀city of the king of the gods,
He entered Esagila, palace of heaven and earth,
⠀⠀⠀⠀and stood before him.   (125)
He made ready to speak, saying to the king of the gods,

---

1. Variant: "they act." As taken here, Erra will motivate Marduk to act as he really wanted to anyway, but had hesitated to for the reasons he gives in lines 132ff.
2. Babylon.

"Why has your precious image,[1] symbol of your lordship,
   which was full of splendor as the stars of heaven,
   lost its brilliance?"[2]
"Your lordly diadem, which made the inner sanctum shine
   like the outside tower,[3] (why is it) dimmed?"
The king of the gods made ready to speak, saying
To Erra, warrior of the gods, these words,   (130)
"O warrior Erra,
   concerning that deed you said you would do,[4]
"Once long ago indeed I grew angry,
   indeed I left my dwelling, and caused the deluge![5]
"When I left my dwelling,
   the regulation of heaven and earth disintegrated:
"The shaking of heaven meant:
   the positions of the heavenly bodies changed,
   nor did I restore them.
"The quaking of netherworld meant:
   the yield of the furrow diminished,
   being thereafter difficult to exploit.[6]   (135)
"The regulation of heaven and earth disintegrating meant:
   underground water diminished, high water receded.
   When I looked again, it was a struggle to get enough.
"Productivity of living offspring declined, nor did I renew it,
"Such that, were I a plowman,
   I (could) hold (all) seed in my hand.
"I built (another) house and settled therein.[7]

---

1. The Akkadian word here translated as "precious image" (Bottéro, *Annuaire* 1977/78, 152 note 35 = *Mythes*, 266; cf. W. G. Lambert, AfO 18 [1957/8], 399) can be understood also as "attire" or "fittings."
2. Translation uncertain; perhaps, with Cagni, *Epopea*, 183 "became dirty."
3. Literally, "which made Ehalanki shine like Etemenanki," meaning that the inner shrine shone as brightly as if in open daylight (differently Streck, AOAT 264 [1999], 85).
4. That is, line 123.
5. "Deluge" may be used here metaphorically for "catastrophe," as the consequence was low, not excessive, water (Tablet IV lines 46ff.) and no other Mesopotamian tradition associates Marduk with the deluge. However, a flood is implied in line 171 below.
6. Obscure. I take this to mean that the furrow could no longer be reliably "levied" for its "yield," that is, expected to give of its increase to the gatherer.
7. Perhaps a reference to (re)construction of Esagila after the deluge, or to a special building where his image was refurbished.

"As to my precious image,
    which had been struck by the deluge
    that its appearance was sullied,   (140)
"I commanded fire to make my features shine
    and cleanse my apparel.
"When it had shined my precious image
    and completed the task,
"I donned my lordly diadem and returned.
"Haughty* were my features, terrifying my glare!
"The survivors of the deluge saw what was done.   (145)
"Shall I raise my weapon and destroy the rest?[1]
"I sent those craftsmen[2] down to the depths,
    I ordered them not to come up.
"I removed the wood and gemstone[3]
    and showed no one where.
"Now then, warrior Erra,
    as concerns that deed you said you would do,
"Where is the wood, flesh of the gods,
    suitable for the lord of the uni[verse],   (150)
"The sacred tree, splendid stripling,[4] perfect for lordship,
"Whose roots thrust down a hundred leagues
    through the waters of the vast ocean to the depths of hell,
"Whose crown brushed [Anu's] heaven on high?
"Where is the clear gemstone that I reserved for [   ]?
"Where is Ninildum,
    great carpenter of my supreme divinity,   (155)
"Wielder of the glittering hatchet, who knows that tool,
"Who makes [it] shine like the day
    and puts it in subjection at my feet?
"Where is Kusigbanda, fashioner of god and man,
    whose hands are consecrated?

---

1. Variant: "Did you raise your weapon and destroy the re[st]?"
2. The divine craftsmen, or sages, who refurbished Marduk's image after it was damaged in the catastrophe.
3. The original depends upon a wordplay on *mēsu* (a tree) and *elmēšu* (a gemstone). The meaning is that the specific materials used to make the image are no longer to be had. The entire passage implies that the statue of Marduk dated to earliest time and could not be reproduced because it was not made by human hands.
4. A Sumero–Akkadian wordplay on *mēsu* (a tree) and Sumerian mes "young man."

"Where is Ninagal, wielder of the upper and lower millstone,¹
"Who grinds up hard copper like hide
    and who forges to[ols]?   (160)
"Where are the choice stones, created by the vast sea,
    to ornament my diadem?
"Where are the seven [sa]ges of the depths, those sacred fish,
    who, like Ea their lord, are perfect in sublime wisdom,
    the ones who cleansed my person?"

(Erra's reply is lost, but he may offer to produce suitable materials for refurbishing the statue. Marduk then asks who will ward off the forces of evil and chaos while he is being refurbished and is thereby non-combatant. Erra offers to reign in his stead. Marduk assents, forsakes his dwelling for repairs, and the universe is thrown into confusion.)

The warrior Erra [hea]rd him ... [ ],
He made ready to speak, saying to noble Marduk,
"[craftsmen],   (165)
"[tree   ],
"Clear gemstone [from] its [pl]ace shall I bring up."
When Marduk heard this,
He made ready to speak, saying to the [warrior] Erra:
"(When) I rise [from] my dwelling,
    the regulation [of heaven and earth] will disintegrate, (170)
"The [waters] will rise and sweep over the land,
"Bright [day will turn] to dar[k]ness,
"[Wh]irlwind will rise and the stars of heaven will be [ ],
"Ill winds will blow
    and the eyesight of living creatures [will be darkened?],
"Demons will rise up and seize [ ],   (175)
"[They will ...] the unarmed one who confronts them!
"The gods of hell will rise up and smite down living creatures.
"Who will keep them at bay
    till I gird on my weaponry (once more)?"
When Erra heard this,
He made ready to speak, saying to noble Marduk, (180)
"O noble Marduk, while you enter that house,²

1. Variant: "the perf[ect] ... tool."
2. The special building where the cult image is refurbished.

fire cleanses your apparel and you return to your place,
"For that time I will govern and keep strong
        the regulation of heaven and earth,
"I will go up to heaven and issue instructions to the Igigi-gods,
"I will go down to the depths
        and keep the Anunna-gods in order.
"I will dispatch the wild demons to the netherworld,   (185)
"I will brandish my fierce weaponry against them.
"I will truss the wings of the ill wind like a bird's.
"At that house you shall enter, O noble Marduk,
"I will station Anu and Enlil to the right and left, like bulls."[1]
Noble Marduk heard him,   (190)
The words that Erra spoke pleased him.

Tablet II

(Marduk leaves his palace, disaster ensues.)

Pericope A + B

He arose from his dwelling, an inaccessible place,   (1)
He set out for the dwelling of the Anunna-gods.
He entered that house and sto[od before them].
Shamash looked upon him
        and let his protective radiance fall ...,
The moon looked elsewhere,
        and did not [leave?] the netherworld.   (5)
Ill winds rose and the bright daylight was turned to gloom.
The clamor of the peoples throughout the land [was stilled].
The Igigi-gods were terrified and went up to h[eaven],
The Anunna-gods were [fright]ened
        and [went down] to the pit [of hell],
[   ] the entire circumference [   ]   (10)
[   ] in the dust.
[   ] let us see."
[   ] its doors.
[   ] like the stars of heaven,   (15)

---

1. The imagery seems to be of the great winged bulls, such as stood at the entrances to certain Assyrian palaces.

(gap)

(The gods convene to discuss the situation. Ea, intent upon restoring Marduk to his place, reasons that, even though the original sublime craftsmen cannot return, Marduk authorized reproductions of them to be made that are endowed with wondrous powers by Ea at Marduk's command. The repairs are proceeding well. Erra, while standing guard at the house where the work is being done lest harm approach, is taking the opportunity to usurp Marduk's power by keeping everyone away from him. So vainglorious is Erra's shouting that Ea resolves to see him humbled.)

"The diadem [   ]
"His heart [   ], let him make it happy.
"The governor's[1] [   ]
"The awe-inspiring radiance of [his] divine splendor [   ]
     his days [   ],
"[   ] like rain,   (20)
"[Let] Ea in the depths [   ] his springs,
"Let Shamash see … [   ] and let the people [   ],
"Let Sin behold, and at his sign let him [   ] to the land.
"Concerning that work, Ea [   ] is expert(?)."
"The warrior Erra became very angry,   (25)
"Why, because of foam on the w[aters],[2]
     the … of humankind,
"Which I myself created to bring offerings to the Anunna-gods,
"Did noble Marduk give up, not at the appointed time?
"He plotted to lay waste the lands and destroy their people!"
Ea the king considered and said these words,   (30)
"Even now that noble Marduk has arisen (from his dwelling),
     he did not command those craftsmen to c[ome up].
"How can images of them, which I made among humankind,
"Approach his sublime divinity, where no god has access?
"He himself gave those same (human) craftsmen
     great discretion and authority,
"He gave them wisdom and perfect dexterity.   (35)

---

1. Here possibly Erra, as temporary viceroy for Marduk, as opposed to the human governor who appears later in the poem.
2. In Tablet IV line 68, foam is used as a metaphor for the human race destroyed by the flood. Here it may refer to something transitory: why did Marduk sacrifice the human race for a passing whim (as it seemed to the speaker), and give the human beings over to Erra, when they were essential for feeding and maintaining the gods?

"They have made (his) precious image radiant,
>   even finer than before.
"Warrior Erra has stationed himself before him,
>   night and day without ceasing,
"Besetting the house for making radiant the precious image
>   for the sovereignty of the king, and saying,

>   'Don't come near the work!
>   '[He who dr]aws near it—
>>   I will cut short his life and prolong his death agony.'

"[   ] let him hasten at the work,   (40)
"[   ] has no equal.
"[   ] Erra was speaking like a mortal,
"[   ] trying to rival the noble one,
"[   ] may he be humbled."
[The images of the craftsmen] made his precious image radiant, (45)
[   ] ...
[They set the ...] at his door(?),
[   ] king Shamash girds it on,
[   ] he reoccupied his dwelling,
[   ] brilliance was reestablished.   (50)
[All the gods   ] were gathered,
Erra [nob]le Marduk,
"Noble Marduk, [   ]
"Godlike, you [   ]
"Small to great, [   ]   (55)
[   ] Erra ... [   ]
[   ] ... his uproar was terrifying,
"[   ] ... the image,
"[   ] of your [lord]ship are raised up and establi[shed]."   (60)

*(The repairs successfully completed, Marduk has returned to his dwelling [line 49]. In
a fragmentary passage, Marduk addresses the gods and orders them all to return to their
dwellings. The gods are alarmed by astral omens that presage Erra's dominance.)*

The king of the gods [made ready] to speak and said,
"[   ] and went up to heaven."
[   ] he commanded, "Return to your dwellings!"
[   ] ... his sign,

"[   ] upon your face,   (65)
"[   ] their peoples.
"[   ] you did not turn back."
[He heard him], ... said [to the k]ing of the gods,
"The word of Marduk [   ] of the day."
He said to him [   ]   (70)
"Come now, [   ]
"To destroy the lands [why did you plot?]."
Erra heard him [   ]
...

He entered [   ].
Anu heard in heaven [   ],   (75)
He bowed his lofty head [   ].
Antu, mother of the gods, was aghast [   ],
She entered [her] cham[ber].
Enlil's [   ]

(gap)

Pericope C1

[   ] father of the gods [   ]   (1′)
[   ] Enlil [   ]
Among the beasts, all of them [   ].
Erra among all the gods [   ].   (5′)
Among the stars of heaven the Fox Star[1] [   ]
Was shining bright and its radiance [   ] for him,
The stars of all the gods were dazzling [   ],
Because they were angry with each other
      and noble Marduk [   ] put [   ],
"The star of Erra is shining bright
      and is radiant: ... of warfare.   (10′)
"His awe-inspiring brilliance will ...
      and all people will perish(?).
"... the dazzling stars of heaven in his time are [dimmed?].
"... the ant, does it not rise [   ]?
"Among the beasts, their image of their star is the fox,
"Endowed with strength, a raging(?) lion [   ],   (15′)

1. Star associated with "the mighty one, Erra" (Al-Rawi and Black, *Iraq* 51 [1989], 112).

"Enlil is the father of [   ], he has [   ]."

(Even Ishtar, goddess of war, tries to calm Erra.)

Innina replied in the assembly of the gods [   ],
[   ] her words to Anu and Dagan [   ],
"Keep quiet, all of you, go into your chambers,
"Cover your lips, do not smell the in[cense],   (20')
"Do not debate noble Marduk's words, do not pl[ead   ]
"Until the days are drawn to a close,
        the [appointed time] passed,
"The word Marduk speaks is like a mountain where ...,
        he does not change (it) nor [   ]."

(gap)

Pericope C2

Ishtar went, they entered the ...,
She pled with Erra, but he would not agree.   (30')
Ishum made ready to speak, saying (these) words to Ishtar,
"I have ... that of heaven over what is not of heaven,
"Erra is angry and will heed no one,
"Let him come to rest in the mountains, and I(?) ...
        the seed of the people that you spoke about to [   ],
"The sublime son of Enlil will not go on campaign
        without Ishum the vanguard before [him?]."   (35')

(Erra is furious. All he has done is to perform guard duty, and now has been sent home, his services no longer required, without a campaign. This is because he is the most valiant god—no evil rises to oppose him. This he fails to perceive, but, in his blind rage, he resolves to fight his war anyway, to show Marduk and Ea that he is not to be taken so lightly. Erra's self-praise turns into a self-narrative. This passage is unusual in Akkadian and has been subjected to varying interpretations. In favor of that offered here, note that first-person narrative is nearly always past or future, hardly ever renderable as present and in progress. Since, as Cagni has shown [Epopea, 208–209], the passage cannot logically refer to the future, and since the past is difficult for grammatical reasons, we have here a present, first-person narrative, one of Kabti-ilani-Marduk's most interesting experiments.)

He was sitting in the Emeslam,[1] taking up his dwelling.
He thought to himself what had been done,[2]
His heart being stung, it could give him no answer,
But he asked it what it would have him do.[3]
"Lead the way, let me begin the campaign! (40′)
"The days are drawn to a close, the appointed time has passed.
"I give the command
    and despoil the sun of his protective radiance,
"By night I muffle the face of the moon.
"I say to the thunderstorm,

   'Hold back [your] young bulls!
   'Brush aside the clouds, cut off sn[ow and rain]!' (45′)

"I will make Marduk and Ea mindful!
"[He] who waxed great in days of plenty,
    they bury him on a day of drought,
"He who came by water, [they take him back] on a dusty road.
"I say to the king of the gods,

   'Take your place in E[sagila],
   'They must do what you commanded,
     they must carry out your or[der]. (50′)
   'The people of this land cry out to you,
     but do not accept their entreaties!'

"I obliterate [the land?] and reckon it for ruins,
"I lay waste cities and turn them into open spaces,
"I wreck mountains and fel[l] their wildlife,
"I convulse the sea and destroy its increase, (55′)
"I bring the stillness of death upon swamp and thicket,
    burning like fire,
"I fell humankind, I leave no living creatures,
"Not one do I retain, [nor any?] for seed to [   ] the land.
"I spare no livestock nor any living creatures,

1. Temple of Erra at Cutha.
2. That is, the successful completion of Marduk's repairs and his being packed off home again, needed no longer.
3. Obscure. As read here, Erra is furious at what he regards as high-handed treatment, and, consulting only his own wounded feelings, decides to go on a rampage. The lines imply that he debated with his "self," but took guidance from his heart (= emotions) alone. One may also understand (with Bottéro), "He (Ishum) asked him (Erra) his orders."

"I dispatch the soldier from one city against another,   (60')
"Neither son nor father has a care for the other's well-being,
"Mother p[lots ev]il against daughter with a leer.
"I let [yokels into] the abodes of gods,
     where harm must not approach,
"I settle the miscreant in the nobleman's dwelling.
"I let outlandish beasts into the shrines,   (65')
"I block access to any city where they appear,
"I send down beasts of the highlands,
"Wherever they set foot,
     they bring the stillness of death to the thoroughfares,
"I cause beasts of the steppe not to stay in the steppe,
     but to traverse the city street.
"I make omens unfavorable,
     I turn holy places into foraging grounds,   (70')
"I let the demon "Upholder-of-Evil"
     into the dwellings of the gods,
     where no evil should go,
"I devastate the king's palace [   ] and turn it into a ruin,
"I cu[t of]f the clamor of [humankind] in [dwellings]
     and rob them of happiness,
"As [I   ] orchards like fire ...
"I let evil enter [   ]   (75')

Tablet III

(Erra's speech continues, as he glories in the horrors of war, anarchy, and privation. There follows a gap in the text.)

Pericope A

"[   ] heeds no one,   (1)
"What he(?) reasoned [   ]
"Lions [   ]
"[   ]
"I make [   ] go toward [   ]   (5)
"I confiscate [... their] households and cut short their lives,
"I as[sassinate] the righteous man who intercedes,
"I set the wicked cutthroat in the highest rank.

"I estrange people's hearts so father listens not to son,
"And daughter cavils spitefully to mother.   (10)
"I make their utterances evil, they forget their gods,
"They speak gross blasphemy to their goddesses.
"I stir up the [rob]ber and so cut off travel absolutely,
"People rifle one another's belongings in the heart of the city.
"Lion and wolf fell the livestock.   (15)
"I aggravate [   ] and she cuts off birth-giving,
"I deprive the nurse of the wail of toddler and infant.
"I banish* the work song of harvest home from the fields,
"Shepherd and herdsman forget their field shelters.
"I cut the clothes from the bodies of men,
        the young man I parade naked through the city street,   (20)
"The young man without clothes I send down to hell.[1]
"The ordinary fellow has not so much as a sheep
        to offer up for his life,
"For the nobleman's divination lambs are few and precious.
"The patient yearns for a bit of roast to offer for his recovery,
"It does him no good, so he gets up and walks till he dies.   (25)
"I incapacitate the nobleman's mount like [   ],
"I cut [   ]

(fragmentary lines, then gap)

(Pericope B too fragmentary for translation)

(The deed spoken and done, Ishum is remonstrating that Enlil has forsaken his city. Erra, in a frenzy, cries for more, and, having done enough himself, lets loose the Seven. Ishum, distressed at Erra's "over-kill," demands the reason for it.)

Pericope C

(Ishum is speaking, restored from IV 33–39)

"The stro[ng   ]   (1)
"Like the blo[od   ]
"[You homed their weaponry upon] the people

---

1. Captives in war were sometimes paraded naked. Furthermore, the dead enter the netherworld naked; thus the people in the upper world are little better than dead.

under special protection, [sacred to Anu and Dagan],[1]
"You [made] their blood course
    like [ditchwater in the city streets],
"You [opened their] arteries
    [and let the watercourses bear (their) blood away].   (5)
"Enlil [cried], 'Woe!' [his heart was hardened],
"[He   ] from his dwelling,
"An irrever[sible curse rose to his lips],
"He swore that [he would not drink from the watercourses],
"He was revol[ted by] their blood
    [and] would not enter [Ekur]."   (10)
Erra said these words to Ishum his vanguard,
"The Seven, warrior[s unrivalled   ]
"For all of them [   ]
"Which no[ble   ]
"O [my] vanguard, [   ]   (15)
"Who can speak [   ]
"Who can [   ] like fire
"Who can [   ] before [   ]
"Who can [   ] like [   ]
"Who [   ]   (20)
"Who can [   ] Erra?
"The face of a r[avening] lion [   ]*
"In the rage of [ ] heart [   ]?
"Lead the way, [let me begin the campaign]!
"[Muster?] the Seven, warriors unrivalled,   (25)
"[Make] (them), fierce weaponry, [go at my side],
"And do [you] be [my] vanguard and [rear guard]."
When Ishum heard this [speech] of his,
He felt pity and sa[id to himself?],
"Alas for my people, victims of Erra's fury [ ],   (30)
"Whom the warrior Nergal [overwhelmed]
    like the storm of battle [against] the demons,
"As if to kill that conquered god, his arms lose no tension,

---

1. Certain Mesopotamian cities were exempt from military service, taxes, or other obligations to the crown, and Erra has violated their charters. While Cagni and others have interpreted this passage to mean that Erra armed the citizenry, it could also mean that they were exposed to the effects of weaponry. In favor of Cagni's view, however, see Tablet IV lines 6–10.

"As if to snare wicked Anzu, [his net] is spread!"[1]
Ishum made ready to speak,
Saying to warrior Erra these words,   (35)
"Why have you plotted evil against god and man?
"And why have you remorselessly plotted evil
    against the people of this land?"

(Erra replies exultantly that men are too stupid to understand the ways of the gods, so why take their part? Furthermore, Marduk did forsake his dwelling, so the world cannot be as it was before; that would be a denial of Marduk's centrality. Now Ishum narrates Erra's violent course in the second person, a literary experiment building upon the preceding. There follows a gap in the text.)

Erra made ready to speak,
Saying to Ishum his vanguard these words,
"You (who) know the reasoning of the Igigi-gods,
    the counsel of the Anunna-gods,   (40)
"Would you give guidance to the people of this land
    and try to make them understand?[2]
"Why are you, indeed, talking like a know-nothing?
"You are advising me as if you knew not Marduk's command!
"The king of the gods has risen from his dwelling!
"What of all lands has endured?   (45)
"He removed his lordly diadem:
"King and prince [   ] forget their duties.
"He has undone his girdle:
"The bond of god and man is undone,
    impossible to tighten it again.
"Fierce fire made his precious image glow like the day
    and heightened his protective splendor,   (50)
"His right hand grasped the mace, his enormous weapon.
"Noble Marduk's glare is terrifying!
"As for me, what you said to me [   ],

---

1.   That is, Erra is ready for even the most formidable encounter. Bottéro (*Annuaire* 1977/78, 126 note 16) suggests that the conquered god is Qingu (see Epic of Creation, III.17). For Anzu, see III.23.

2.   That is, why would one privy to the minds of the gods bother with any attempt to make humans understand them?

"O vanguard of the gods, wise [Ishum,
     whose counsels are sound],
"Why, just now, [did you   such a] speech?   (55)
"Marduk's command is not [satisfactory to you]?"
Ishum made ready to speak, saying to [the warrior Erra],
"O warrior Erra ... [   ]
"Humankind ... [   ]
"The livestock [   ]   (60)
"Swamps and reedbanks [   ]
"Now then, what you said, w[arrio]r Erra,
"One stood forth and you [   ] seven,
"You killed seven and did not let go a single one,
"Take away the livestock [   ] ...   (65)
"O Erra, when you strike with your weapons,
"Mountains to[tter], the sea [con]vulses,
"Such a flash of [your] stan[chion], they look east,
     [as if to] see the sun [rise]!
"The palace [   ]

(gap of unknown length)

(Ishum continues: Erra has taken over the universe, even Marduk's sanctuary.
     How can he now say that no one respects him?)

Pericope D

Ishum made ready to speak, saying to the warrior Erra,
"O [war]rior Erra, you hold the leadline of heaven,
"You are master of all the earth, lord in the land!
"You convulse the sea, obliterate mountains,   (5)
"You rule over humans and herd beasts.
"The primeval sanctuaries[1] are in your hands,
"You control Shuanna and command Esagila.
"You have gathered to yourself all authority,
     the gods revere you,
"The Igigi-gods stand in awe of you,
     the Anunna-gods are in dread of you.   (10)
"When you set forth counsel, even Anu heeds you,

---

1. Text: Esharra (Temple of Enlil at Nippur); Eengura (Temple of Ea at Eridu).

"Even Enlil agrees with you. Aside from you, is there opposition?

"Except for you, is there battle?

"The armor of strife is yours alone!

"But you have said to yourself, 'They hold me in contempt.'" (15)

Tablet IV

(Ishum's speech continues, one of the longest in Akkadian literature. He narrates the horrors and destruction of civil war, refers to atrocities committed in Babylon by an invading army, and, in lines 36ff. quotes Marduk's moving lament for his city. In 45–49 Ishum goes on to quote Marduk's own description of the appalling conditions there. Ishum then describes events at Sippar, where the city walls are destroyed, and at Uruk, overrun by the barbarous Sutaeans. This fierce nomadic people even went so far as to interfere with the cult devotees of Ishtar, whose practices may have been abhorrent to the poet. In 63–64 Dur-Kurigalzu is referred to, and in 65ff. Ishtaran of Der curses his city. It is not clear where Ishum's speech ends, but the poem continues with a passionate portrayal of indiscriminate violence. In 113ff. Ishum points out that even with decimation of the populace Erra is not satisfied; he must ruin the guidance of the land, its government and sanctuaries, even that of Marduk himself.)

"O warrior Erra, you are the one

    who feared not noble Marduk's name![1] (1)

"You have undone Dimkurkurra, "the bond of the world,"[2]

    the city of the king of the gods.

"You changed your divine nature

    and made yourself like a mortal,[3]

"You girded on your weaponry and entered Babylon.

"Inside Babylon you spoke like a rabble-rouser(?),

    as if to take over the city, (5)

"The citizenry of Babylon, like reeds in a thicket,

    had no one in charge, so they rallied around you:

"He who knew nothing of weapons—his sword was drawn,

"He who knew nothing of archery—his bow was taut,[4]

---

1. That is, granting that Erra is supreme, by virtue of Marduk's command, his continued fighting is tantamount to sin, since it would seem to admit of opposition, an apparent denial of Marduk's supremacy.

2. Babylon.

3. That is, by ravaging sanctuaries?

4. Literally: "He who knew nothing of the *tilpānu*-bow, his bow was nocked."

"He who knew nothing of fighting—set to the fray,

"He who knew nothing of wings—flew off like a bird.[1]   (10)

"The cripple could surpass the fleet of foot,
    the weakling could overpower the strong.

"They give voice to gross insolence against the governor
    who provides for their holy places,

"With their own hands they blockaded the gate of Babylon,
    their lifeline,

"They have torched the sanctuaries of Babylon
    like marauders of the land,

"You, the vanguard, took their lead!   (15)

"You aimed your shaft at the innermost wall,
    'Woe! My heart!' it exclaims,

"You flung the seat of Muhra, its gatekeeper,
    into the blood of young men and girls,

"The inhabitants of Babylon themselves—
    they the bird, you the decoy—

"You snared in a net, caught and killed them, warrior Erra![2]

"You quit the city and have gone out to the outskirts,   (20)

"You took on a lion's face and have entered the palace.

"When the troops saw you, they girded on their weapons,

"The heart of the governor, avenger of Babylon, turned to fury.

"He issued orders to his army to plunder,
    as if plundering enemies,

"He incited the commander to atrocities,   (25)

    'You, my man, for that city I am sending you to,
    'Fear no god, respect no man!
    'Do young and old alike to death!
    'Spare no one, not even the baby sucking milk!
    'You shall plunder the accumulated wealth of Babylon!'   (30)

"The royal troops drew up and have invaded the city,

"With flashing shafts and outstretched blades,

"You homed their weapons upon those under special protection,
    sacred to Anu and Dagan.

---

1. The reference seems to be to precipitous flight in the face of danger (Tsevat, RA 81 [1987], 184).

2. For a suggestion that this refers to a rebellion that Erra first instigated the Babylonians to foment, then cruelly suppressed himself in Marduk's name, see Vanstiphout, N.A.B.U. 1996/54, following Bottéro, *Mythologie*, 715.

"You made their blood course like ditchwater in the city streets,
"You opened their arteries
    and let the watercourses bear their blood away.   (35)
"When the great lord Marduk saw that,
    he cried 'Woe!' and his heart was hardened,
"An irreversible curse rose to his lips.
"He swore that he would not drink from the watercourses,
"He was revolted by their blood and would not enter Esagila,

    'Alas for Babylon,
        whose crown I fashioned luxuriant as a palm's,
        but which the wind has scorched!   (40)
    'Alas for Babylon,
        that I had laden with seed, like an evergreen,
        but of whose delights
        I could not have what I hoped for!
    'Alas for Babylon,
        that I tended like a thriving orchard,
        but whose fruit I could not taste!
    'Alas for Babylon,
        that I suspended like a gemstone seal
        on the neck of the sky!
    'Alas for Babylon,
        that I clasped in my hand like the tablet of destinies,
        not handing it over to anyone else!'

"[And this too has] noble Marduk said: (45)

    '[   ] from former days [   ]
    'Let one quit the wharf:
        he shall cross at two cubit's depth of water on foot,[1]*
    'Let one go down sixty fathoms in a well,
        not one man shall keep himself alive (on the water),
    'Let them (still have to) punt the fishing boat
        a hundred leagues out in the open sea!'

---

1. The sense may be that there will be so little water at the city docks that one can walk across the riverbed, starting at the pier, and the water will scarcely reach to one's waist (von Soden *apud* Cagni, *Epopea*, 229). Cutting off of water could also be a military maneuver; see B. Meissner, *Babylonien und Assyrien* (Heidelberg, 1920), 1: 108–109.

"As for Sippar, the primeval city,
>   through which the lord of the world
>   did not allow the deluge to pass,
>   because it was precious to him,   (50)

"You destroyed her ramparts against the will of Shamash,
>   and threw down her fortifications.

"As for Uruk, the dwelling of Anu and Ishtar,
>   the city of courtesans, harlots, and prostitutes (for the cult),

"Whom Ishtar deprived of husbands
>   and reckoned as her own(?),[1]

"There Sutaean nomads, men and women,
>   bandy war whoops![2]

"They turned out the actors and singers (of) Eanna,   (55)

"Whose manhood Ishtar changed to womanhood
>   to strike awe into the people,

"The wielders of daggers and razors,
>   vintner's shears and flint knives,

"Who take part in abominable acts
>   for the entertainment of Ishtar,[3]

"A haughty, remorseless governor you placed over them.

"He harassed them and interfered with their rites.   (60)

"Ishtar was angered, she flew into a rage against Uruk,

"She stirred up the enemy and swept clean the country,
>   like granules on the water's face.

"The dweller in Parsa had no respite from lamenting
>   the destroyed Eugal-sanctuary.[4]

"The enemy you roused has no desire to stop.

"Ishtaran responded thus: (65)

>   'You turned the city Der[5] into a wasteland,
>   'You fractured her populace like reeds,

---

1. With Bottéro; otherwise, "left to their own authority" (Diakonoff *apud* Cagni, *Poem*, 52–53).

2. The Sutaeans, from the point of view of the Mesopotamian city dweller, were marauding nomadic people; see M. Heltzer, *The Sutaeans* (Naples, 1981).

3. The cult of Ishtar was associated with prostitution, both male and female (lines 52, 56), and, perhaps, self-mutilation (57). See also IV.2b and p. 595 note 4.

4. Parsa (see Nashef, RA 77 [1983], 169–174) is to be identified with Dur-Kurigalzu, a large city northwest of Babylon; Eugal was the temple of Enlil there.

5. Important Mesopotamian city near present-day Badra, near the Iranian frontier.

'You extinguished their clamor
    like the (dying hiss of) foam on the water's face!
'And as for me, you did not spare me but gave me over
    to the Sutaean nomads!
'For the sake of my city Der,   (70)
'I will judge no disputed truth,
    nor make any ruling for the land,
'I will give no guidance nor aid in understanding.
'Men forsook truth and took up violence,
'They abandoned justice and were plotting wickedness.
'Against (but) one country I raised up seven winds.'   (75)

"He who did not die in battle will die in the epidemic,
"He who did not die in the epidemic,
    the enemy will plunder him,
"He whom the enemy has not pl[undered],
    the bandit will murder him,
"He whom the bandit did not murder,
    the king's weapon will vanquish him,
"He whom the king's weapon did not vanquish,
    the prince will slay him,   (80)
"He whom the prince did not slay,
    a thunderstorm will wash him away,
"He whom the thunderstorm did not wash away,
    the sun will parch him,⋆
"He who has gone out in the world,
    the wind will sweep him away,
"He who has gone into his home,[1] a demon will strike him,
"He who has gone up to a high place will perish of thirst,   (85)
"He who has gone down to a low place
    will perish in the waters!
"You have obliterated high and low place alike.
"The man in charge of the city says to his mother,[2]

    'If only I had stuck in your womb the day you bore me,
    'If only our lives had come to an end,   (90)

---

1. See p. 906 note 2.
2. As the text stands, it is difficult to decide who speaks what lines; the reading offered here is only a suggestion.

'If only we had died together,
'For you gave me a city whose walls are destroyed!
'Its people are the beasts,
     their god is he who hunts them down.
'He it is whose net is tight-meshed:
     they could not draw married men out of it
     but they died a violent death.'*

"He who begot a son, saying,

'This is my son,   (95)
'When I have reared him he will requite my pains,'

'I will put that son to death, his father must bury him,
'Afterward I will put that father to death,
     but he will have none to bury him.'[1]

"He who built a house, saying

'This is my home,[2]
'I built it for myself, I shall spend my leisure in it,   (100)
'On the day fate claims me, I shall fall asleep inside,"

'I will put him to death and wreck his home,
'Afterward, though it be wreckage(?),
     I will give it to another.'

"O warrior Erra, you have put the righteous person to death,
"You have put the unrighteous person to death,   (105)
"He who sinned against you, you put him to death,
"He who did not sin against you, you put him to death,
"The high priest, assiduous with divine offerings,
     you put to death,
"The functionary who served the king you put to death,
"The old men in the anterooms* you put to death,   (110)
"The young girls in their bedrooms you put to death,
"Even then you found no appeasement whatsoever!
"Even then you told yourself, 'They hold me in contempt!'
"Even then you said to yourself, O warrior Erra,

---

1. The first person here and in lines 102–103 quotes Erra.
2. The word translated here as "home" means "storehouse," but has also been interpreted as "tomb" (J. Westenholz, *Studies Cagni*, 1181–1201).

'I will strike down the mighty, I will terrorize the weak,   (115)
'I will kill the commander, I will scatter the troops,
'I will wreck the temple's sacred chamber,
        the rampart's battlement,
        the pride of the city I will destroy!
'I will tear out the mooring pole so the ship drifts away,
'I will smash the rudder so she cannot reach the shore,
'I will pluck out the mast, I will rip out the rigging.   (120)
'I will make breasts go dry so babies cannot thrive,
'I will block up springs so that even little channels
        can bring no life-sustaining water.
'I will make hell shake and heaven tremble,
'I will make the planets shed their splendor,
        I will wrench out the stars from the sky,
'I will hack the tree's roots
        so its branches cannot burgeon,   (125)
'I will wreck the wall's foundation so its top tumbles,
'I will approach the dwelling of the king of the gods,
        that no direction be forthcoming!'"

(Erra is gratified that the extent of his power is recognized; he has at last won his respect. He decrees that the rabble of the world should fight on; at length Babylon shall rule what is left. Erra then allows Ishum to campaign against a mountain that is apparently the homeland of the Sutaeans, the human arch-villains of the narrative. Erra has destroyed most of the world, but Ishum now puts violence to useful purpose.)

The warrior Erra heard him,
The speech that Ishum made pleased him like finest oil.
Thus spoke the warrior Erra,   (130)
"The Sealand the Sealand,[1] Subartu Subartu, Assyrian Assyrian,
"Elamite Elamite, Kassite Kassite,
"Sutaean Sutaean, Gutian Gutian,
"Lullubaean Lullubaean, land land, city city,
"House house, man man, brother brother
        must not spare (one another), let them kill each other!   (135)

1.   This and the following list the countries surrounding Babylonia to the south, north, east, and west, partly in contemporaneous, partly in archaizing terms. "Akkadian" in 136 refers to an unnamed Babylonian king whose victories are here "prophesied."

"Then, afterward, let the Akkadian arise to slay them all,
     to rule them,[1] every one."
The warrior Erra said these words to Ishum his vanguard,
"Go, Ishum, the matter you spoke of,[2] do as you wish."
Ishum set out for the mountain Sharshar,[3]
The Seven, warriors unrivalled, fell in behind him.   (140)
When the warriors reached the mountain Sharshar,
He raised his hand and destroyed the mountain,
He reckoned the mountain Sharshar as level ground.
He cut away the trunks of the cedar forest,
The thicket looked as if the deluge[4] had passed over,   (145)
He laid waste cities and turned them into open spaces,
He obliterated mountains and slew their wildlife,
He convulsed the sea and destroyed its increase,
He brought the stillness of death upon swamp and thicket,
     burning like fire,
He cursed the beasts and returned them to clay.   (150)

Tablet V

(Erra, in a last boast, addresses the gods. He praises Ishum and points out, not without pride, that in his rage and valor he, Erra, had made the blunder of attacking the leadership of the universe as well as its subjects. Were it not for Ishum's timely intervention, who knows where Erra's terrible strength might have led him? Ishum rejoins that this is all very well, but would Erra please calm himself now that his point has been made?)

After Erra was calmed and took up his own abode,   (1)
All the gods were gazing at his face,
All the Igigi-gods and Anunna-gods stood in awe.
Erra made ready to speak, saying to all the gods,
"Quiet, all of you, learn what I have to say.   (5)
"No doubt I intended evil in the bygone lapse,

---

1. Variant: "let him cast them."
2. If there was a referent for this speech, it is now missing in one of the gaps in the poem.
3. Perhaps Jebel Bishri, plausibly argued by Cagni, *Epopea*, 33–34 and 242–243 to be a reference to the homeland of the Sutaeans; see p. 562 notes 5 and 7.
4. Text: Hanish. (For the reading of the line I follow Cagni, *Epopea*, 244–245).

"I was angry and wanted to lay waste the people.
"Like a hireling, I took the lead ram from the flock,
"Like one who did not plant an orchard,
    I was quick to cut it down,
"Like a scorcher of the earth,
    I slew indiscriminately good and evil. (10)
"One would not snatch a carcass
    from the jaws of a ravening lion,
"So too no one can reason where one is in a frenzy.
"Were it not for Ishum my vanguard,
    what might have happened?
"Where would your provider be, where your high priest?
"Where your food offering? You would smell no incense." (15)
Ishum made ready to speak,
    saying to the warrior Erra these words,
"Quiet, warrior, hear what I have to say,
"No doubt this is true, now, calm down, let us serve you!
"At a time you are angry, where is he who can face you?"

(Erra returns to his home and pronounces a blessing upon Babylon, that she will at last prevail over her enemies and wax rich on the tribute of her foes throughout the world.)

When Erra heard this, his face beamed, (20)
Like radiant daylight his features glowed.
He entered Emeslam and took up his abode,
He called Ishum to tell him the sign,
To give him instructions
    concerning the scattered peoples of Akkad,
"Let the people of the country, who had dwindled,
    become numerous again, (25)
"Let short and tall alike traverse its paths,
"May weak Akkadian fell mighty Sutaean,
"May one drive off seven like sheep.
"You shall make his cities into ruins
    and his highlands into open ground,
"You shall take massive booty from them
    (and put it) in Shuanna, (30)
"You shall reconcile the angry gods with their own abodes,

"You shall make gods of livestock
and grain descend (once more) to the land,
"You shall make mountain deliver its yield, sea its produce,
"You shall make the ruined fields deliver produce.
"Let the governors of all cities haul their massive tribute
into Shuanna, (35)
"Let the tops of the [ru]ined temples come up
like the rising sun,
"Let Tigris and Euphrates bring abundant water,
"Let the governors of all cities make the provider
for Esagila and Babylon their lord."*

Erra's speech melds into that of the narrator. The poet introduces himself by name, and explains that the text, or "sign" of the god, was approved by Erra himself after it was revealed to the author in a half-waking state. Having become a sign, the text acquires prophylactic powers.)

Praise to the great lord Nergal[1] and warrior Ishum
for years without number!
How it came to pass that Erra grew angry and set out to lay
waste the lands and destroy their peoples, (40)
But Ishum his counsellor calmed him and left a remnant,
The composer of its text was Kabti-ilani-Marduk,
of the family Dabibi.
He revealed it at night, and, just as he (the god?)
had discoursed it while he (K.) was coming awake,*
he (K.) omitted nothing at all,
Nor one line did he add.
When Erra heard it he approved, (45)
What pertained to Ishum his vanguard satisfied him.
All the gods praised his sign.[2]
Then the warrior Erra spoke thus,
"In the sanctuary of the god who honors this poem,
may abundance accumulate,
"But let the one who neglects it never smell incense. (50)
"Let the king who extols my name rule the world,

1. Erra is here equated with the god Nergal (see III.20 and III.46).
2. This poem. See above, General Introduction, D.1.

"Let the prince who discourses the praise of my valor
  have no rival,
"Let the singer who chants (it) not die from pestilence,
"But his performance be pleasing to king and prince.
"The scribe who masters it
  shall be spared in the enemy country
  and honored in his own land,   (55)
"In the sanctum of the learned,
  where they shall constantly invoke my name,
  I shall grant them understanding.
"The house in which this tablet is placed,
  though Erra be angry and the Seven be murderous,
"The sword of pestilence shall not approach it,
  safety abides upon it.
"Let this poem stand forever, let it endure till eternity,
"Let all lands hear it and praise my valor,   (60)
"Let all inhabitants witness and extol my name."

Text: L. Cagni, *Das Erra-Epos, Keilschrifttext, Studia Pohl* 5 (Rome, 1970); W. G. Lambert, AfO 27 (1980), 76–81; Saggs, AfO 33 (1986), 29; Al-Rawi and Black, *Iraq* 51 (1989), 112–113, pl. XX.

Edition: L. Cagni, *L'Epopea di Erra, Studi Semitici* 34 (Naples, 1969). This contains a detailed commentary that is essential for close study of the text. Tablet II has been edited by Al-Rawi and Black, *Iraq* 51 (1989), 111–122.

Translation: L. Cagni, *The Poem of Erra*, SANE 1/3 (1977), with additions and modifications to his former commentary; J. Bottéro, *Annuaire* 1977–78, 107–164 = *Mythes*, 221–278; *Mythologie*, 680–727; Dalley, *Myths*, 282–315; G. G. W. Müller, TUAT III/4, 781–801.

Literature: In addition to the works cited in Cagni, 1977, and the essay by Bottéro, there is a discussion by Edzard, "Irra (Erra)-Epos," RLA 5, 166–170 with bibliography through 1977, and P. Machinist, "Rest and Violence in the Poem of Erra," JAOS 103 (1983), 221–226.

★Notes to Text: (I 144) I follow Cagni, *Poem*, 90 and others; see Lambert, JSS 27 (1982), 283 vs. AHw 1383a. (III A.17) Reading *našû* Š (with Bottéro). (III C.22) Schramm, OrNS 40 (1971), 271. (IV 47) For lines 47–49 see Vanstiphout, N.A.B.U. 1987/69. (IV 82) Text *ittabbal* "be carried off," though one expects a form of *'bl* "dry out." (IV 93–94) With Streck, AOAT 264 (1999), 137. (IV 110) Beaulieu, ZA 82 (1992), 102–103. (V 38) For discussion of this difficult line, see Cagni, *Epopea*, 253. The interpretation of *libilu* (variant: *šubēl*) as derived from *bēlu*, used here, was suggested by Brinkman, AnOr 43, 285 note 1852. (V 43) Deller-Meyer, OrNS 53 (1984), 121–122.

IV.18 THE BIRTH LEGEND OF SARGON OF AKKAD

This fragment of a pseudonymous text of uncertain character purports to tell the story of the birth and early life of Sargon of Akkad (see I.3), and how he became king of the Mesopotamians. Language and content point to a first-millennium date for this composition, which may have its origins in the court of Sargon II of Assyria, who named himself after Sargon (see IV.2). The point of this narrative may not be that Sargon was of humble origins but rather, as offspring of a high priestess, he was noble by birth, as confirmed by his subsequent success.

I am Sargon the great king, king of Agade.   (1)
My mother was a high priestess, I did not know my father.
My father's brother dwells in the uplands.
My city is Azupiranu, which lies on Euphrates bank.
My mother, the high priestess, conceived me,
    she bore me in secret.   (5)
She placed me in a reed basket,
    she sealed my hatch with pitch.
She left me to the river, whence I could not come up.
The river carried me off, it brought me to Aqqi,
    drawer of water.
Aqqi, drawer of water, brought me up as he dipped his bucket.
Aqqi, drawer of water, raised me as his adopted son.   (10)
Aqqi, drawer of water, set (me) to his orchard work.
During my orchard work, Ishtar loved me.
Fifty-four(?) years I ruled as king,
I became lord over and ruled the people of this land,
I c[ut through] hard mountains with picks of copper,   (15)
I ascended high mountains, one after another.
I crossed over low mountains, one after another.
The [la]nd of the sea I sieged three times,
    Dilmun k[nelt before me(?)].
I went against the greatest walls in the universe,   (20)
I destroyed [fortifications] and [   ].
Whatsoever king who shall arise after me,
[Let him rule as king fifty-four(?) years],
Let him become lo[rd over and rule] the people of this land.

Let him [cut through] hard mountains with picks [of copper], (25)
Let him ascend high mountains, one after another.
[Let him cross over low mountains, one after another].
Let him siege the [la]nd of the sea three times,
    [let Dilmun kneel before him].
Let him go against the greatest walls in the universe,
[Let him destroy fortifications and ...]
... from my city Agade (30)

(breaks off)

Text: King, CT 13 42, 43.

Edition: Brian Lewis, *The Sargon Legend: A Study of the Akkadian Text and the Tale of the Hero who Was Exposed at Birth*, *ASOR Dissertation Series* 4 (Cambridge, Mass., 1980); J. Westenholz, *Legends*, 36–49, whence some readings and proposals adopted here.

Translation: Speiser, ANET[3], 119; Labat, *Religions*, 307–308; Hecker, TUAT *Ergänzungslieferung*, 55–57.

Literature: J.-J. Glassner, "Le récit autobiographique de Sargon," RA 82 (1988), 1–11; H. Limet, "Aspect mythique de la royauté en Mesopotamie, Sargon l'Ancien et Cyrus le Grand," in F. Jouan and A. Motte, eds., *Mythe et Politique* (Paris, 1990), 167–169.

D. Dialogues and Debates

IV.19 THE BABYLONIAN THEODICY

The Theodicy takes the form of a debate between two friends on divine justice. The sufferer, a younger son without means, sees everywhere around him strength and wealth being equated with right and justice, while poverty is considered a crime. The gods take no notice of strict obedience to their rites and concede nothing to the serious seeker after understanding. Even injustice is of divine origin. As the debate proceeds, always with great courtesy and eloquence, the sufferer craves his friend's indulgence by acknowledging that his doubts about divine justice were merely fruits of his personal circumstances (compare Literary Prayer to Ishtar [III.28]), and were themselves faults of the kind he has normally tried to avoid. He concludes by voicing, in effect, a challenge to his gods to take better care of him in the future—at least, mercy and a greater sense of divine responsibility are his only hope. The reader is left to judge whether or not he concludes with a vote of no confidence.

The poem is a technical *tour-de-force*. Within a constrictive rhythmic scheme of four units to the line, the author begins each ten-line stanza with the same syllable. The beginnings of each stanza, read vertically, form an acrostic that reads, "I, Saggilkinamubbib, am adorant of god and king." The text contains numerous rare and dialectal words, partly because of its severe formal restrictions, and was the subject of an ancient philological commentary that is only partly preserved.

I. Sufferer

O sage, [ ], come, [let] me speak to you,	(1)
[ ], let me recount to you,	
[ ] ...	
[I ...], who have suffered greatly, let me always praise you,	
Where is one whose reflective capacity is as great as yours?	(5)
Who is he whose knowledge could rival yours?	
Wh[ere] is the counsellor to whom I can tell of woe?	
I am without recourse, heartache has come upon me.	
I was the youngest child when fate claimed (my) father,	
My mother who bore me departed to the land of no return,	(10)
My father and mother left me, and with no one my guardian!	

II. Friend

Considerate friend, what you tell is a sorrowful tale,
My dear friend, you have let your mind harbor ill.
You make your estimable discretion feeble-minded,
You alter your bright expression to a scowl.   (15)
Of course our fathers pay passage to go death's way,
I too will cross the river of the dead,[1]
      as is commanded from of old.
When you survey teeming humankind all together,
The poor man's son advanced, someone helped him get rich,*
Who did favors for the sleek and wealthy?   (20)
He who looks to his god has a protector,
The humble man who reveres his goddess will garner wealth.

III. Sufferer

My friend, your mind is a wellspring of depth unplumbed,
The upsurging swell of the ocean that brooks no inadequacy.
To you, then, let me pose a question, learn [what I would say].   (25)
Hearken to me but for a moment, hear my declaration.
My body is shrouded, craving wears me do[wn],*
My assets have vanished, my res[ources?] dwindled.
My energies have turned feeble, my prosperity is at a standstill,
Moaning and woe have clouded [my] features.   (30)
The grain of my mead is nowhere near satisfying [me],
Beer, the sustenance of humankind, is far from being enough.
Can a happy life be a certainty?
      I wish I knew how that might come about!

IV. Friend

My well-thought-out speech is the ulti[mate] in good advice,*
But you [make?] your well-ordered insight [sound] like babble.   (35)
You force [your ...] to be [sca]tter-brained, irrational,
You render your choicest offerings* without conviction.
As to your [ever]lasting, unremitting desire [   ],

---

1. Hubur, here the Mesopotamian equivalent of the Styx or the "River Jordan." The line may refer also to the forefathers rather than the speaker, "They say from of old 'I must cross the river of death'."

The [fore]most protection [lies] in prayer:
The reconciled goddess returns to [   ],   (40)
The re[conciled gods] will take pity on the fool(?),
    the wrong-doer.
Seek constantly after the [rites?] of justice.
Your mighty [   ] will surely show kindness,
[   ] ... will surely grant mercy.

V. Sufferer

I bow down before you, my [comrade],
    I apprehend your w[isdom],   (45)
[   ] what you say.
Come, let me [tell you],
The on[ager], the wild ass, that had its fill of [wild grass?],
Did it carefully ca[rry out?] a god's intentions?
The savage lion that devoured the choicest meat,   (50)
Did it bring its offerings to appease a goddess' anger?
The parvenu who multiplies his wealth,
Did he weigh out precious gold
    to the mother goddess for a family?*
[Have I] withheld my offerings? I prayed to my god,
[I] said the blessing over the regular sacrifice to
    my goddess, my speech [   ].   (55)

VI. Friend

O date palm, wealth-giving tree, my precious brother,
Perfect in all wisdom, O gem of wis[dom],
You are a mere child, the purpose of the gods is remote
    as the netherworld.
Consider that magnificent wild ass on the [plain],
The arrow will gash that headstrong trampler of the leas!   (60)
Come, look at that lion you called to mind,
    the enemy of livestock,
For the atrocity that lion committed, the pit yawns for him.
The well-heeled parvenu who treasured up possessions,
A king will put him to the flames before his time.
Would you wish to go the way these have gone?   (65)
Seek after the lasting reward of (your) god.

VII. Sufferer

Your reasoning is a cool breeze,
     a breath of fresh air for humankind,
Most particular friend, your advice is e[xcellent].
Let me [put] but one matter before you:
Those who seek not after a god can go the road of favor,   (70)
Those who pray to a goddess have grown poor and destitute.
Indeed, in my youth I tried to find out the will of (my) god,
With prayer and supplication I besought my goddess.
I bore a yoke of profitless servitude:
(My) god decreed (for me) poverty instead of wealth.   (75)
A cripple rises above me, a fool is ahead of me,
Rogues are in the ascendant, I am demoted.

VIII. Friend

O just, knowledgeable one, your logic is perverse,
You have cast off justice, you have scorned divine design.
In your emotional state you have an urge
     to disregard divine ordinances,   (80)
[   ] the sound rules of your goddess.
The strategy of a god is [as remote as] innermost heaven,
The command of a goddess cannot be dr[awn out].★
Teeming humanity well understands trouble,★

(fragmentary lines, then large gap)

XIII. Sufferer

I will forsake home [   ]
I will crave no property [   ]
I will ignore (my) god's regulations,
    [I will] trample on his rites.   (135)
I will slaughter a calf, I will [   ] the food,
I will go on the road,
    I will learn my way around distant places.
I will open a well, I will let loose a fl[ood?],
I will roam about the far outdoors like a bandit.
I will stave off hunger by forcing entry

into one house after another,   (140)
I will prowl the streets, casting about, ravenous.
Like a beggar I will [   ] inside [   ],
Good fortune lies afar off [   ].

XIV. Friend

My friend, [you have] resolved [upon   ]
The transactions of humankind,
        which you had no urge to [   ],   (145)
[   ] are in your mind,
Your discretion has forsaken [you   ]

(fragmentary lines)

XV. Sufferer

(four lines lost)

Daughter says [unjust words] to her mother,
The fowler who casts [his net] is fallen (into it),   (160)
All in all, which one [will find] profit?
Many are the wild creatures that [   ],
Which among them has gotten [   ]?
Shall I seek son and daughter [   ]?
Shall I not leave behind what I find [   ]?   (165)

XVI. Friend

O modest, submissive one, who [ ] all [   ],
Your mind is always receptive, most precious one [   ],

(fragmentary lines, then gap)

XVII. Sufferer

The son of a king is clad [in rags?],
The son of the destitute and naked is dressed in [fine raiment?].
The maltster [can pay in] finest gold,
While he who counted red gold shoulders a [debt?].

He who made do with vegetables [sates himself]
    at a princely banquet,   (185)
While the son of the eminent and wealthy
    (has only) carob to eat.
The man of substance is fallen, [his income] is removed.

(fragmentary lines, gap)

XX. Friend

You have let your subtle mind wander,
[   ] you have overthrown wisdom.
You have spurned propriety,
    you have besmirched (every) code.
Far will be the workman's basket from him who ...   (215)
[   ] is established as a person of importance,
[   ] he is called a scholar,
He is well served, he gets what he wants.
Follow in the way of a god, observe his rites,
[   ] be ready for good fortune!   (220)

(gap)

XXII. Friend

As for the rascal whose goodwill you wanted,   (235)
The ... of his feet will soon disappear.
The godless swindler who acquires wealth,
A deadly weapon is in pursuit of him.
Unless you serve the will of a god, what will be your profit?
He who bears a god's yoke will never want for food,
    though it may be meager.   (240)
Seek after the favorable breeze of the gods,
What you lost for a year you will recoup in a moment.

XXIII. Sufferer

I have looked around in society, indications are the contrary:
God does not block the progress of a demon.
A father hauls a boat up a channel,   (245)
While his firstborn sprawls in bed.
The eldest son makes his way like a lion,
The second son is content to drive a donkey.
The heir struts the street like a peddler,
The younger son makes provision for the destitute.[1]   (250)
What has it profited me that I knelt before my god?
It is I who must (now) bow before my inferior!
The riffraff despise me as much as the rich and proud.

XXIV. Friend

Adept scholar, master of erudition,
You blaspheme in the anguish of your thoughts.   (255)
Divine purpose is as remote as innermost heaven,
It is too difficult to understand, people cannot understand it.
Among all creatures the birth-goddess formed,
Why should offspring be completely unmatched(?)?
The cow's first calf is inferior,   (260)
Her subsequent offspring is twice as big.
The first child is born a weakling,
The second is called a capable warrior.
Even if one (tries to) apprehend divine intention,
        people cannot understand it.

XXV. Sufferer

Pay attention, my friend, learn my (next) parry,   (265)
Consider the well-chosen diction of my speech.
They extol the words of an important man
        who is accomplished in murder,
They denigrate the powerless who has committed no crime.
They esteem truthful the wicked
        to whom tr[uth] is abhorrent,

---

1. The meaning may be that the elder expects the world to provide him a living, while the younger provides for others as well as himself.

They reject the truthful man who he[eds] the will of god. (270)
They fill the oppressor's st[rongroom] with refined gold,
They empty the beggar's larder of [his] provisions.
They shore up the tyrant whose all is crime,
They ruin the weak, they oppress the powerless.
And as for me, without means, a parvenu harasses me. (275)

XXVI. Friend

Enlil,[1] king of the gods, who created teeming humankind,
Majestic Ea,[2] who pinched off their clay,
The queen who fashioned them, mistress Mami,
Gave twisted words to the human race,
They endowed them in perpetuity with lies and falsehood. (280)
Solemnly they speak well of a rich man,
"He's the king," they say, "he has much wealth."
They malign a poor man as a thief,
They lavish mischief upon him, they conspire to kill him.
They make him suffer every evil
 because he has no wherewithal(?). (285)
They bring him to a horrible end,
 they snuff him out like an ember.[3]

XXVII. Sufferer

You are sympathetic, my friend,
 be considerate of (my) misfortune.
Help me, see (my) distress, you should be cognizant of it.[4]
Though I am humble, learned, supplicant,
I have not seen help or succor for an instant. (290)
I would pass unobtrusively through the streets of my city,
My voice was not raised, I kept my speaking low.
I did not hold my head high, I would look at the ground.
I was not given to servile praise among my associates.

1. Text: Narru.
2. Text: Zulummar.
3. One would expect this speech from the sufferer rather than the friend. Is the text in disorder, or is he swayed by the sufferer?
4. That is, in judging his interlocutor's state of mind, the friend should weigh his dire circumstances and not condemn him too harshly. Compare III.28 lines 174–175.

May the god who has cast me off grant help,   (295)
May the goddess who has [forsaken me] take pity,
The shepherd Shamash will past[ure] people as a god should.¹

Text: W. G. Lambert, BWL, pl. 19–26.

Edition: W. G. Lambert, BWL, 63–89; Ponchia, *Dialoghi*, 73–82, 101–108, 131–142.

Translation: Biggs, ANET³, 601–604; Labat, *Religions*, 320–327; von Soden, TUAT III/1, 143–157, whence readings used here.

Literature: J. Bottéro, "La 'Théodicée'," *Annuaire* 1966/67, 100–116; G. Buccellati, "La Teodicea: Condanna dell'abulia politica," OrAn 11 (1972), 101–178; von Soden, MDOG 96 (1965), 51–55; Finkel, *Studies Sachs*, 144–145; Sitzler, *Vorwurf*, 99–109.

Notes to Text: (19) von Soden, TUAT III/1, 147. (27) So von Soden, AHw, 336b; the text, as read by Lambert, means something like "darkens me." The latter is the better parallel, though the former reading is here adopted. (34) von Soden, TUAT III/1, 148. (37) So dictionaries, but obscure. "Offering" may be intended, as taken here, as a metaphor for "proposal" or the like, though the expression would be unparalleled. (53) von Soden, TUAT III/1, 149. (83) von Soden, TUAT III/1, 151. (84) Unpublished ms. quoted by CAD A/2, 168b; S, 27a.

---

1. That is, a just god takes proper care of his subjects.

IV.20 THE DIALOGUE OF PESSIMISM

This satirical dialogue sets a master proposing various undertakings, for which his servant offers facile encouragements. When the master changes his mind and asserts the opposite, the servant is equally ready with facile discouragements. The master lapses into despair at the futility of life, and, when he finally asks what the best course for him to follow might be, the slave suggests suicide.

Whether one reads the mood of this text as somber or light-hearted, it has a clear, universal appeal and is an original and effective composition.

I

(1) "[Servant, listen to me]." "Yes, master, yes." "[Quickly, get me the chari]ot and hitch it up for me so I can drive to the palace." "[Drive, master, drive, it will bri]ng you where you want to go; the (others) will be outclassed, [the prince] will pay attention to you." (5) "[No, servant], I will certainly not drive to the palace." "[Do not drive, mas]ter, do not drive. [The pr]ince will send you off on a mission, he will send you on a journey that★ you do not know. He will expose you to discomfort [day and ni]ght."

II

(10) "Ser[vant, list]en to me." "Yes, master, yes." "Quic[kly br]ing me water (to wash) my hands, give it to me so I can dine." "Di[ne], master, dine. Regular dining expands the inner self, [he who eats well]★ is his own god. Shamash goes with him whose hands are washed." "No, [ser]vant, I will certainly not dine." (15) "Do not dine, master, do not dine. Hunger, (then) eating, thirst, (then) drinking—this is what agrees with a man."

III

"Servant, listen to me." "Yes, master, yes." "Quickly get me the chariot and hitch it up so I can drive to the open country." "Drive, master, drive. The roaming man has a full stomach, (20) the roving dog cracks open the bone, the roaming [bi]rd will find a nesting place, the wandering wild ram has all the [gra]ss he wants."★ "No, servant, I will certainly not d[rive to the open country]." "Do not drive, master, do n[ot dri]ve. (25) The roaming man loses his reason, the roving dog breaks his [te]eth(?), the roaming bird [puts] his home in the [   ] of a wall, and the wandering wild ass has to live in the open."

IVa

"Servant, listen to me." "Yes, master, yes." (30) "I am going to make a [household and have a so]n." "Do it, master, do it. [The man who makes] a household [   ] ...* "No, I will certainly <not> make a household." "Do not make a household. The one who follows such a course has broken up his father's household, [he has gone in] a door called 'the noose'.[1] [The man with a wife and child is ...] credulous(?), two thirds a fool."[2]

V

"Servant, listen to me." "Yes, master, yes." (40) "I will do something dishonest." "So, do it, master, do it. Unless you do something dishonest, what will [you] have to wear? Who will give you anything so you can fill [your] stomach?" "No, servant, I will certainly not do something dishonest." "<Do not do it, master, do not do it>. The man who does something dishonest is executed or skinned alive or (45) blinded or apprehended or jailed."

VI

"Servant, listen to me." "Yes, master, yes." "I will fall in love with a woman." "[So], fall in love, master, fall in love. The man who falls in love with a woman forgets sorrow and care." "No, servant, I will certainly not fall in love with a woman." "[Do not] fall in love, master, do not fall in love. A woman is a pitfall, a pitfall, a hole, a ditch, a woman is a sharp iron dagger that slashes a man's throat."

---

1. Obscure. The word normally refers to a proverbially strong rope, perhaps meaning that the door cannot be opened again.
2. Obscure and may not belong here.

VII

"Servant, listen to me." "Yes, master, yes." "Quickly bring me water (to wash) my hands, give it to me (55) so I can sacrifice to my god." "Sacrifice, master, sacrifice. The man who sacrifices to his god makes a satisfying transaction, he makes loan upon loan." "No, servant, I will certainly not sacrifice to my god." "Do not sacrifice, master, do not sacrifice. (60) You will train your god to follow you around like a dog. He will require of you rites or a magic figurine* or what have you."

VIII

"Servant, listen to me." "Yes, master, yes." "I will make loans." "So make them, master, [make them]. The man who makes loans, his grain is (still) his grain while his interest is profit." "No, servant, I will certainly not make loans." "Do not make them, master, do not make them. Loaning is [swee]t(?) as falling in love, getting back as pain[ful] as giving birth. They will consume your grain, be always abusing you, and finally they will swindle you out of the interest on your grain."

IX

(70) "Servant, listen to me." "Yes, master, yes." "I will do a good deed for my country." "So do it, master, do it. The man who does a good deed for his country, his good deed rests in Marduk's basket."[1] "No, servant, I will certainly not do a good deed for my country." (75) "Do not do it, master, do not do it. Go up on the ancient ruin heaps and walk around, look at the skulls of the lowly and great. Which was the doer of evil, and which was the doer of good deeds?"

X

"Servant, listen to me." "Yes, master, yes." "What, then, is good?" "To break my neck and your neck and throw (us) in the

---

1. The meaning of this expression is unclear. The idea may be that if one distributes largesse, the recipient is god himself, so good will thereby accrue to the giver.

river is good.[1] Who is so tall as to reach to heaven? Who is so broad as to encompass the netherworld?" "No, servant, I will kill you and let you go first." "Then my master will certainly not outlive me even three days!"[2]

Text: W. G. Lambert, BWL, pl. 37–38; Wiseman and Black, CTN 4 203 ii 6'.

Edition: W. G. Lambert, BWL, 139–149; Ponchia, *Dialoghi*, 83–85, 109–112, 142–148; C. Saporetti, *Arad mitanguranni, (Dialogo fra schiavo e padrone nell'antica Mesopotamia)* (Pisa, 1995).

Translation: Biggs, ANET³, 600–601; Bottéro, *Mesopotamia*, 253–257; Labat, *Religions*, 342–346; von Soden, TUAT III/1, 157–163 (dates to seventh century).

Literature: E. A. Speiser, "The Case of the Obliging Servant," JCS 8 (1954), 98–105; G. Buccellati, "Dialogo del Pessimismo: La scienza degli oppositi come idea sapienzale," OrAn 11 (1972), 81–100; F. M. Fales, "Un nuova sguardo al 'dialogo del pessimismo' accadico," *Annali Ca'Foscari* 20 (1981), 137–153; D'Agostino, *Studies Cagni*, 135–145; *Testi umoristici*, 78–108.

*Notes to Text: (8) CTN 4 ii 6' (ar-ni = ḫar-ra-ni?). (13) von Soden, TUAT III/1, 160. (24) CAD M/2, 308a; von Soden, TUAT III/1, 160. (31) Text corrupt here, and inserts part of a section dealing with litigation. The latter is too fragmentary to be intelligible. I insert lines 32–33 at the end of line 38; see BWL, 325. D'Agostino, *Studies Cagni*, 141, reconstructs this passage as lines 29–31 and 37–38. (61) von Soden, TUAT III/1, 162.

1. Possibly a wordplay on *ṭābu* "good" and *ṭebû* "sink in water" is intended; see Kinnier Wilson, *Etana*, 177.

2. Examples of this motif have been collected by Sir Walter Scott, *Quentin Durward*, Chapter xxix (Louis XI and his astrologer).

IV.21 THE TAMARISK AND THE PALM

Literary disputations were well known in Mesopotamia, especially in Sumerian. This Akkadian example begins with a cosmological introduction, then turns to a disputation between the date palm and the tamarisk over their merits, prestige, and usefulness to the human race. Several widely varying versions of this composition exist from the Classical, Mature, and Late periods. Of these, the most extensive is known from a group of fragments from Emar in Syria (thirteenth century B.C.), hence belonging to the Mature period but presented here for practical reasons. Translations of the other versions are in Lambert, BWL, 151–164 and Biggs, ANET[3], 592–593.

(1) In the bright days, the [da]rk n[ights], the long-ago years when the gods established the land, made cities for the long-ago peoples, when they had heaped up the mountains, had dug out the watercourses, life of the land, the gods of the land held an assembly. Anu, Enlil, and Ea took counsel together, Shamash sat among them, so also Mistress of the Great Gods.

(6) Before that, there was no kingship in the land and lordship was vested in the gods. The gods were feeling love for the people of this land, (so) g[ave them a king ... the people] of the land of Kish gathered around him to look at(?) [   ].

(8) The king planted a date palm in his palace, he filled the area around it with tamarisks. In the shade of the tamarisks meals were set out, in the shade of the date palm [songs?] were composed, drums were played, the people were merry, the palace rejoiced.

(10) The trees were unlike, they differed between them. Tamarisk and date palm disputed together, on and on. The tamarisk said, "I am the tallest!" The date palm said, "I spread out(?) farther than you!"

(15) "You, tamarisk, are a useless tree, what use are your fruitless twigs? My fruit [goes to the king's] table, the king eats, and the common folk say how good it is. I gain the orchardman a profit, he passes it on to the queen. As a mother raises her infant, the grown child partakes of the ... of my strength, my fruits are before royalty."

(21) The tamarisk made ready to speak, responded grandiloquently, full of pride, "My body is superior to yours. [   ] your

best features. Just as a slave girl brings her work to her mistress and hands (it) over, you bring the best and most precious to me."

(25) The date palm replied grandiloquently, [said] to his brother the tamarisk … *(gap)*

(32) [The tamarisk [made ready to speak], responded grandiloquently], full of pride, "Think of my furnishings in the king's palace, what is there in the king's palace that is not mine? The king eats from my table, the queen drinks from my goblet, the warrior eats from my spoon, the cook kneads dough in my trough. I am a loom, I weave threads, I clothe common folk and I make the king splendid. I am an exorcist, I renew the temple. [I am] indeed superb, if I may be so grandiloquent, I have no one to rival me."

(37) The date palm responded grandiloquently, said to his brother the tamarisk, "At the special (and) regular offering to the princely moon-god, the king makes no libation unless I stand by. My lustrations are made in all four directions, my core(?) is poured out onto the ground, and a festival is held. Meanwhile, the tamarisk is useful only for brewer's work,[1] so instead of a clump of dates you are a dump of wastes."

(43) [The tamarisk made ready to speak, responded grandiloquently], full of pride, "Come, let us go, you and I, to the district where the craftsmen work me, see if in fact there is not manna(?) round about me, nor aromatic scent.[2] The sacrosanct woman takes my sap and gives thanks, then a festival begins. Meanwhile, the date palm is in the hands of the slaughterer and he [slobbers] its core(?) with offal and gore."[3]

(50) [The date palm] responded grandiloquently, [said to his] brother [the tamarisk], "Come, let us go, you and I, to the district [of my festival], the place of merry-making. I seat your worker, tamarisk, the carpenter, on my (spread-out) fronds, he reveres me and praises me daily."

(53) The tamarisk made ready to speak, [responded grandiloquently], "I am for the workman whatever he has that is useful. For the cultivator, I am what he needs. The cultivator cuts my

---

1. Perhaps for firewood.

2. That is, in working the wood, essences are yielded quite different from the noxious dregs of the brewery.

3. Refers to a mallet used in slaughtering?

branches, ... he gets his pickax from my breast. With my spade he digs watercourse, ditch, opens canals, so the field can be watered. I have inspected the soil and I have [ ] the grain in the soil. I re[new] kingship and the grain-goddess is plenteous to renew the people."

(60) The [date] palm res[ponded grandiloquent]ly, said to his brother [the tamarisk], "[I] am more useful to workmen than you. For the cultivator, [I am] whatever he has that is useful, leadlines, whips, ropes for harness and girth, gear ... [ ], the wagon [cushion?], all utensils a cultivator has, I am greater [than] you!"

(rest fragmentary)

Text: Arnaud, *Emar* 783, 784.

Edition: C. Wilcke, "Die Emar-Version von 'Dattelpalme und Tamariske'—ein Rekonstruktions-versuch," ZA 79 (1989), 161–190, to which this translation is greatly indebted; Ponchia, *Dialoghi*, 67–69, 95–98, 121–128; Kämmerer, AOAT 251 (1998), 230–251.

IV.22 THE DOG'S BOAST

This excerpt is taken from a large but fragmentary composition dealing with a contest among a wolf, fox, and dog. In this passage, the dog praises his own prowess. See also IV.21.

> I am mighty in strength, the talon of Anzu,
>> the fury(?) of a lion,
> My legs run faster than birds on the wing,
> At my loud outcry mountains and rivers dry up(?).
> I take my onerous place before the sheep,
> Their lives are entrusted to me,
>> instead of to shepherds or herdsmen,   (20)
> I am sent off on my regular path in the open country
>> and the watering place, I go around the fold.
> At the clash of my fearsome weapons I flush out ...,
> At my baying, panther, tiger, lion, wildcat take to flight,
> The bird can[not] fly away or go on course.
> No rustler thieves [from] my pens!

Text: W. G. Lambert, BWL, pl. 50, 16–25.
Edition: Lambert, BWL, 192–193.
Literature: H. Vanstiphout, "The Importance of 'The Tale of the Fox'," ASJ 10 (1988), 191–227.

E. FOLKTALE, HUMOR

IV.23 THE POOR MAN OF NIPPUR

This is a unique example of a Babylonian folktale, in which a poor man takes revenge on a mayor who wronged him. There are numerous wordplays throughout the story, but these cannot be reflected in this translation.

There once was a man of Nippur, poor and needy,	(1)
His name was Gimil-Ninurta, a wretched man.	
He dwelt in his city Nippur in abject misery:	
He had no silver, as befits his people,	
He had no gold, as befits humankind,	(5)
His larder wanted for pure grain.	
His insides burned, craving for bread,	
His face was wretched, craving meat and good drink,	
Every day, for want of a meal, he went to sleep hungry.	
He wore a garment for which there was none to change.	(10)
He took counsel with his wretched heart,	
"I'll strip off my garment, for which there is none to change,	
"I'll buy a ram in the market of my city, Nippur."	
He stripped off his garment, for which	
there was none to change,	
He bought a three-year old[1] nanny goat in the market	
of his city Nippur.	(15)
He took counsel with his wretched heart,	
"What if I slaughter the nanny goat in my yard,	
"There won't be a meal, where will be the beer?	
"My friends in my neighborhood will hear of it and be angry,	
"My kith and kin will be furious with me.	(20)
"I'll take the nanny goat and bring it to the mayor's house,	
"I'll work up something good and fine for his pleasure."[2]	
Gimil-Ninurta took [his] nanny goat by the neck,	
[He went off] to the gate of the mayor of Nippur.	

---

1. Variant omits. Note the change of sex and species of the animal; for further discussion, see L. Milano, "Aspects of Meat Consumption in Mesopotamia and the Food Paradigm of the Poor Man of Nippur," SAAB 12 (1998), 111–127.
2. Wordplay on "his stomach" and "his mood" (*karšišu*).

To Tukulti-Enlil, who minded the gate,
      he sa[id] (these) words,   (25)
"Say that I wish to enter to see the ma[yor]."
The doorman said (these) words to his master,
"My lord, a citizen of Nippur is waiting at your gate,
"And as a greeting gift★ he has brought you a nanny goat."
The mayor was ang[ry with Tuk]ulti-Enlil,
"Why is a citizen of Nippur [(kept) waiting] at the gate?"   (30)
The doorman [   ] to [   ] ...,
Gimil-Ninurta [came] happily [be]fore the mayor.
When Gimil-Ninurta came before the mayor,
He held his nanny goat by the neck wi[th] his left hand,   (35)
With his right hand he greeted the mayor,
"May Enlil and Nippur bless the mayor,
"May Ninurta and Nusku make his (offering) flourish!"★
The mayor said (these) words to the citizen of Nippur,
"What is your trouble, that you bring me a gift?"   (40)
[Gimil]-Ninurta related his errand to the mayor of Nippur,
"Every [day], for want of a meal, I go to sleep hungry,
"[I stripped off] my garment,
      for which there is none to change,
"I bought a three-year-old nanny goat
      [in the market] of my city Nippur,
"I said to myself [on account] of my wretched heart,   (45)

   '[What if] I slaughter the nanny goat in my yard,
   '[There won't be] a meal, where will be the beer?
   'My friends in my neighborhood
      [will hear of it] and be angry,
   '[My kith and k]in will be furious with me.
   'I'll bring the nanny goat [to the may]or's [house],'   (50)

"[That's what I s]aid in the wretchedness(?) of my heart."

(fragmentary lines, then gap)

(The mayor has the goat slaughtered and the meal prepared.)

"Give him, the citizen of Nippur, a bone and gristle,
"Give him third-rate [beer] to drink from your flask,
"Expel him, throw him out the gate!"   (60)

He gave him, the citizen of Nippur, a [bone] and gristle,
He gave him [thi]rd-rate [beer] to drink from h[is] flask,
He expelled him, threw [him out] the gate.
As Gimil-Ninurta went out the gate,
He said to the doorman, who minded the gate, (these) words,   (65)
"Joy of the gods to your master! Tell him thus,

    'For the one disgrace you [laid] upon me,★
    'For that one I will requite you three!'"

When the mayor heard that, he laughed all day.
Gimil-Ninurta set out for the king's palace,   (70)
"By order of the king! Prince and governors give just verdicts."

Gimil-Ninurta came before the king,
He prostrated and did homage before him,
"O noble one, prince of the people,
    king whom a guardian spirit makes glorious,   (75)
"Let them give me, at your command, one chariot,
"That, for one day, I can do whatever I wish.
"For my one day my payment shall be a mina of red gold."
The king did not ask him, "What is your desire,
"That you [will parade about] all day in one chariot?"   (80)
They gave him a new chariot, f[it for] a nobleman,
They wrapped him in a sash, [ ] his [ ].
He mo[unted] the new chariot, fit for a nobleman,
He set out for [ ] Duranki.[1]
Gimil-Ninurta caught two birds,   (85)
He stuffed them in a box and sealed it with a seal,★
He we[nt off] to the gate of the mayor of Nippur.
The mayor came o[utside] to meet him,
"Who are you, my lord,
    who have traveled so la[te in the day]?"★
"The king, your lord, sent me, to [ ],   (90)
"I have brought gold for Ekur, temple of Enlil."
The mayor slaughtered a fine sheep
    to make a generous meal for him.
While in his presence the mayor said "Ho-hum, I'm tired!"

---

1. Nippur.

(But) Gimil-Ninurta sat up with the mayor
    one (whole) watch of the night.
From fatigue the mayor was overcome with sleep.   (95)
Gimil-Ninurta got up stealthily in the night,
He opened the box lid, the birds flew off into the sky.
"Wake up, mayor!
    The gold has been taken and the box opened!
"The box lid is open, the gold has been taken!"
Gimil-Ninurta rent his clothes in anguish(?),   (100)
He set upon the mayor, made him beg for mercy.
He thrashed him from head to toe,
He inflicted pain upon him.
The mayor at his feet cried out, ... pleading,★
"My lord, do not destroy a citizen of Nippur!   (105)
"The blood of a protected person, sacred to Enlil,
    must not stain your hands!"
They gave him for his present two minas of red gold,
For the clothes he had rent, he gave him others.
As Gimil-Ninurta went out the gate,
He said (these) words to Tukulti-Enlil,
    who minded the gate,   (110)
"Joy of the gods to your master! Say thus to him,

    'For the one disgrace you [laid upon me],
    'I've requited you one, [two remain].'"

When the mayor heard (that), he [   ] all day.
Gimil-Ninurta [went] to the b[arb]er,   (115)
He shaved off all his hair on the le[ft],[1]
He filled a fire-scorched pot [with water?].★
He [went off] to the gate of the mayor of Nippur,
He said to the doorman who minded the gate,
"Say that I want to come in to see [the mayor]."   (120)
"Who are you, that you should see [him]?"
"[I am] a physician, a native of Isin, who examines [ ],
"Where there are disease and emaciation [ ]
    in the body [   ]."
When Gimil-[Ninur]ta came before the mayor,

---

1. Reading doubtful; a shaved head was perhaps sign of being a physician.

He showed him his bruises
    where he had thrashed his body. (125)
The may[or] said [to] his servants, "This physician is skillful!"
"My lord, my remedies are carried out in the dark,
"In a private place, out of the way."
He brought him into an inaccessible chamber,
Where no friend or companion could take pity on him. (130)
He threw the pot into the fire,[1]
He drove five pegs into the hard-packed floor,
He tied his head, hands, and feet (to them),
Then he thrashed him from head to toe,
    he inflicted pain upon him.
Gimil-Ninurta, as he went out the gate, (135)
Said (these) words to Tukulti-Enlil, who minded the gate,
"Joy of the gods to your lord!" Say thus to him,

    'For one disgrace you laid upon me,
    'I have requited you two, one remains.'"

Gimil-Ninurta was careful, pricking up his ears like a dog,★ (140)
He looked carefully at the folk (around him),
    he scrutinized all the people.
He sent(?) a certain man, having recouped his losses(?),★
He gave him a nanny goat(?)★ for [his] present,
"Go to the gate of the mayor [of Nippur?], start shouting,
"So all the numerous [people]
    will crowd around at your shouting, (145)

    'I'm knocking(?) at the mayor's gate,
        I'm the man with the nanny goat!'"★

[Gimil-Ninurta] crouched [under] a bridge like a dog.
The mayor came out at the man's shouting,
He brought out the people of his household, male and female,
They rushed off, all of them, in pursuit of the man. (150)
While they, all of them, were in pursuit of the man,
[They left] the mayor outside alone.
Gimil-Ninurta s[prang] out from under the bridge
    and seized the [mayo]r,

---

1. To extinguish the fire and thus proceed in darkness?

He set upon the mayor, made him beg for mercy.
He thrashed him from head to toe,   (155)
He inflicted pain upon him.
"[For one disgrace you la]id upon me,
"I've requited you [three]!"
He [left him] and went out in the open country,
The mayor, crawling, went into the city.   (160)

Text: Gurney, STT 38, 39; K 3478 = Gurney, AnSt 6 (1956), 148; Ellis, JCS 26 (1974), 89.

Edition: Gurney, AnSt 6 (1956), 145–162; AnSt 7 (1957), 135–136; C. Saporetti, *La Storia del siciliano Peppe e del poveruomo babilonese* (Palermo, 1985), 57–80, 98–105.

Translation: von Soden, TUAT III/1, 174–180.

Literature: J. S. Cooper, "Structure, Humor, and Satire in the Poor Man of Nippur," JCS 27 (1975), 163–174; O. R. Gurney, "The Tale of the Poor Man of Nippur and Its Folktale Parallels," AnSt 22 (1972), 149–158; H. Jason, "The Poor Man of Nippur: An Ethnopoetic Analysis," JCS 31 (1979), 189–215; Leichty, *Studies Finkelstein*, 145–146; D'Agostino, *Testi umoristici*, 109–138. The study of J. S. Noegel, "Wordplay in the Tale of the Poor Man of Nippur," ASJ 18 (1996), 169–186 offers several convincing examples of puns on key words in the story.

*Notes to Text: (28, 38) George, *Iraq* 55 (1993), 75. (67) Moran, *Studies Tadmor*, 327–328. (86) Reiner, JNES 26 (1967), 183 note 7. (89) von Soden, TUAT III/1, 177. (104) Compare von Soden, TUAT III/1, 178. (117) For *nakmû*, Stol, BiOr 54 (1997), 409 proposes "cautery," but it is hard to see how "fill" could be used with a cauterizing implement, so this interpretation is not followed here; see further Saporetti, *Storia*, 72 note to line 117 (who reads, however, *naqmû*). (140) Leichty, *Studies Finkelstein*, 145. (142) von Soden, TUAT III/1, 179. (143) Leichty, *Studies Finkelstein*, 145. (146) Cooper, JCS 27 (1975), 174 note 36.

IV.24 WHY DO YOU CURSE ME?

This humorous scholastic tale involves a prominent physician from the city Isin, famed as a center for the healing arts, who goes to the city Nippur, a center of Sumerian learning, to collect a promised fee. As he asks directions, he is answered in elementary Sumerian, which, as a scholar, he is supposed to have mastered. Failing to recognize the academic language of the land, which even a vegetable seller in Nippur can speak, he assumes that his interlocutor is abusing him. The text ends with a plea that the school children should run such an ignoramus out of their city. One presumes the discomfited physician never got his fee.

(1) Ninurta-sagentarbi-zaemen, [brother of N]inurta-mizidesh-ki'aggani, [nephew] of Enlil-Nibru-kibigi, having been bitten by a dog, went to Isin, city of the Lady of Health, to be cured. (5) Amel-Ba'u, a citizen of Isin, priest to Gula, examined him, recited an incantation for him, and cured him.

"For this your cure of me, may Enlil, lord of Nippur, bless you! If you will come to Nippur, I will put a bib(?) on you, I will feast you on choice viands, and I will give you two massy(?) jugs of fine beer to drink."

"Where should I go in Nippur your city?"

"When you come (10) to Nippur my [city], you should enter by the Grand Gate and leave a street, a boulevard, a square, [Til]lazida Street, and the ways of Nusku and Nininema to your left. You should ask [Nin-lugal]-absu, daughter of Ki'agga-Enbilulu, [daughter-in-law] of Nishu(?)-ana-Ea-takla, (15) a gardening woman of the garden Henun-Enlil, sitting on the ground of Tillazida selling produce, and she will show you."

Amel-[Ba'u], citizen of Isin, priest of Gula, arriving at Nippur, entered by the Grand Gate and left a street, a boulevard, a square, Tillazida Street, [the way of Nusku and] Ninimena to his left. He s[aw (20) Nin-lu]gal-apsu, daughter of Ki'agga-Enbilulu, [daughter-in-law] of Nishu(?)-ana-Ea-takla, a gardening woman of the garden Henun-Enlil, [who was sitting on the gr]ound of Tillazida selling produce.

"Ni[n-lu]gal-apsu?"

"*anni lugalmu.*"

"Why do you curse me?"

"Why would I curse you? I said, 'Yes sir.'"

"May I ask you to show me the way to (25) the house of Nin[urta-sag]entarbi-zaemen, son of Mizidesh-ki'aggani, nephew of Enlil–Nibru–kibigi?"

"*ennutushmen.*"*

(30) "Why do you curse me?"

"Why would I curse you? I said, 'He is not at home.'"

"Where did he go?"

"*Edingirbi shuzianna sizkur gabari munbala.*"

"Why do you curse me?"

"Why would I curse you? I said,

> 'He is making an offering in the temple
> of his personal god Shuzianna.'"

What a [foo]l he is!

The students ought to get together and chase him out of the Grand Gate with their practice tablets!

Text: Cavigneaux, *Baghdader Mitteilungen* 10 (1979), 112–113.

Edition: George, *Iraq* 55 (1993), 63–72; Ponchia, *Dialoghi*, 71–72, 99–100, 128–131.

Translation: E. Reiner, "Why Do You Cuss Me?" PAPS 130/1 (1986), 1–6.

Literature: Michalowski in J. S. Cooper, G. M. Schwartz, eds., *The Study of the Near East in the Twenty-first Century, The William Foxwell Albright Centennial Conference* (Winona Lake, Ind., 1996), 186–187; F. D'Agostino, "Il medico come figura comica presso gli assiro-babilonesi," *Aula Orientalis* 19 (2001), 207–223; *Testi umoristici*, 61–78; Reiner, N.A.B.U. 2004/54.

*Notes to Text: (28) Finkel, N.A.B.U. 1994/41; for the proposed joke, see Foster, JANES 6 (1974), 84; compare also Alster, *Proverbs*, 5.1.

IV.25 THE JESTER

This text may record the routine of a buffoon or jester. The performer cracks a variety of jokes, some of them presumably of double-entendre. In a satire of professions, the jester acts the exorcist by burning down a house to rid it of its haunt. Next an unappetizing religious diet is set forth in prescriptive form. Other portions of the text dealt with a heroic quest and bizarre omens, but these are too fragmentary for connected translation.

(a)

(fragmentary lines)

The lion can terrify,	(1')
I can let out air too!	
The lion can swish his tail,	
I can wag my tail too!	
I'm as trustworthy as a sieve,	(5')
I hold onto my followers like a net.	
I sing like a she-ass.	
Theft is abhorrent to me:	
whatever I see doesn't stay where it was.	
I've gotten large from starvation, enormous from eating,	
I make myself throw up(?) ten quarts,	
I feast on thirty (more),	(10')
I don't leave off till I've filled the "bushel"[1] to the brim.	
Among the shortest of them, the tallest of them,	
there's none like me among women.	
My limbs are elephantine, my face a hyena's,	
I tower like a tortoise, I cannot be equalled.	
Even if I weren't alive,★	(15')
How much would my lover be loving me?	
He would keep turning around, forward and backward,	
like a trained crab!★	
He can't herd a ewe of his in the twenty-acre field	

---

1. His stomach?

by the city gate, on account of me and my rats,*[1]
I used up all the plants for my [   ]!

(fragmentary lines, then gap)

(b)

"Jester, what can you do?"
Rope [weaving] and singing laments,
Squeezing out fruit juice and brewing beer.

"Jester, what can you do?"
Snatching(?) on the run pod-weeds in turnips,
     groats in stink-wort, or anything else.[2]   (25′)

"Jester, what can you do?"
Of the whole exorcist's craft, nothing's beyond me.

"Jester, how do you exorcise?"
Here's how: I take over the haunted house,
    I set up the holy water,
I tie up the scapegoat,   (30′)
I skin a donkey and stuff it with straw.
I tie a bundle of reeds, set it on fire, and toss it inside.
I spared the boundaries of the house and its surroundings,
But the haunt of the house, the serpent,
    the scorpion, are not spared.[3]

(gap)

(c)

"In October what is your diet?"   (35′)
Thou shalt dine on spoiled oil in onions,
    and goose pluckings in porridge.
"In November what is your diet?"
Thou shalt dine on pod-weed in turnips,
    and "cleanser-plant" in crowfoot(?)"[4]

---

1. Obscure, possibly a play on words. Compare IV.28 (c).
2. The turnips and groats are presumably edible, the weeds not. Instead of "snatching," something like "rubbing on" may be intended (Römer, *Persica* 7 [1975/6], 61 note 85).
3. That is, he burns the house down to get rid of the pests in it.
4. Or: "asafoetida powder."

"In December what is your diet?"
Thou shalt dine on wild donkey dung in bitter garlic,   (40′)
And emmer chaff in sour milk.

"In January what is your diet?"
Thou shalt dine on goose eggs and dung(?) embedded in sand,
And cumin infused with Euphrates water in ghee.

"In February what is your diet?"   (45′)
Thou shalt dine on hot bread and donkey's anus,
Stuffed with dog turds and fly dirt.

(fragmentary lines, then gap)

Text: K 4334 = Norris, II R 60 no. 1; K 9886 = Pinches *apud* Weidner, AfO 16 (1952/3), pl. xiv;
   K 6392 = Virolleaud, *Revue Semitique* 9 (1901), 257 = Langdon, *Babyloniaca* 7 (1913/23), pl. xvi;
   K 9287 = Boissier, *Revue Semitique* 9 (1901), 159–160; K 8321 = Meissner, BA 3 (1898), 51; all
   mss. collated; van Dijk, VAS 24 118; Wiseman and Black, CTN 4 204–206.
Edition: Ebeling, TuL, 9–19.
Literature: B. R. Foster, "Humor and Cuneiform Literature," JANES 6 (1974), 74–79; W. Römer,
   "Der Spassmacher im alten Zweistromland, zum 'Sitz im Leben' altmesopotamischer Texte,"
   Persica 7 (1975/6), 43–68.
*Notes to Text: (15′–17′) von Schuler, ZA 53 (1959), 187. (18′) With Römer, *Persica* 7 (1975/6), 56
   note 49; differently CAD E, 367.

IV.26 THE BIRDS' PURCHASE

In this satirical legal document a bird-genie buys a tract of useless land near the entrance to Hell. Compare III.59.[1]

(§1) Harhanda, talon-footed genie of the household of [   ], has contracted to buy from Urburu son of Lipugu (as follows):

(§2) [Real estate consisting of x hectares of land in] the meadowland ..., adjoining the cemetery, where [there is no] wa[ter], where no barley is brou[ght] forth,

(§3) Real estate consisting of two hectares of land in the open country of ..., one cultivates this field with no profit, one [produces] no dried seed therefrom,[2]

(§4) Bounded by the River Ulaya at the Gate of Hell, all located in [   ], (as well as) a non-existent field in the duty-free zone[3] at the Gate of Hell, for [seven pounds] of mistletoe and five pounds of birdseed of ..., mother of talon-footed genies.

(§5) The money is [paid] in full, he has bought the profitless field, claim and contest shall be invalid.

(§6) Whosoever shall raise a claim at any time in the future, be it Urburu or his sons [or grandsons], who shall file [lawsuit] or contest against Harhanda and his sons, [he shall pay] ten talents of [   ], he shall [spend(?) a period of] four months of Augusts and Septembers at the wall of [   ], he shall render up four limestone slabs(?),[4] he shall pay five pounds of birdseed and seven po[unds of mistletoe], he shall contest his (own) lawsuit ....

Witness: Sa-sidqi, talon-footed genie of [   ]
Witness: Sasallu, deputy of [   ]
Witness: Tab-salame [   ]
Witness: Woo-woo the owl of [   ], the same
Witness: Caw-caw the crow of [   ], the same

---

1. For a Latin spoof of this type, see E. Champlin, "The Testament of the Piglet," *Phoenix* 41 (1987), 174–183.

2. That is, birdseed cannot be raised there.

3. Literally, "tax-exempt community."

4. Assyrian palaces were decorated with large limestone slabs, some of which were carved with bird-like representations of protective genies.

Witness: Longlegs the goose of [   ], the same
Witness: At-their-Hymens the wasp of ..., the same whose wife is
           in charge of the good-time girls(?) of Tur-Abdin
Witness: *(gap)*
Witness: [   ] the express mule [   ]
Witness: [   ], governor of the open country.

(The document is dated, with signatures of the witnesses in the form of
claw-shaped marks on the tablet.)

Text: C. W. Adams, *Assyrian Deeds and Documents* (Cambridge, U.K., 1898), no. 469.
Edition: Kwasman, Parpola, SAA 6 (1991), 232–233.
Translation: Scurlock, N.A.B.U. 1993/17.
Literature: Radner, N.A.B.U. 1995/62.

F. LOVE LYRICS

IV.27 LOVE LYRICS OF NABU AND TASHMETU

These lines are lovers' talk between Nabu and Tashmetu on the occasion of their marriage rite. The manuscript dates to the eighth century B.C. Indications of speakers are supplied by the translator; compare II.18.

(Singers)

Let whom will trust where he trusts,   (1)
As for us, our trust is in Nabu,
We give ourselves over to Tashmetu.
What is ours is ours: Nabu is our lord,
Tashmetu is the mountain we trust in.   (5)

(Singers, to Tashmetu)

Say to her, to her of the wall, to her of the wall, to Tashmetu,
..., take your place in the sanctuary,
May the scent of holy juniper fill the dais.

(Tashmetu?)

Shade of cedar, shade of cedar, shade of cedar
        (is) the king's shelter,
Shade of cypress is (for) his great ones,   (10)
The shade of a juniper branch is shelter for my Nabu,
        for my play.

(Singers)

Tashmetu dangles a gold ornament in my Nabu's lap,
'My lord, put an earring on me,
'Let me give you pleasure in the garden,

'Nabu, my darling,[1] put an earring on me,   (15)
'Let me make you happy in the [   ].'

(Nabu)

My [Tashmetu], I put on you bracelets of carnelian,
[   ] your bracelets of carnelian,
I will open [   ]

(gap)

(O Tashmetu), [whose] thighs are a gazelle in the steppe,   (1')
(O Tashmetu), [whose] ankles are a springtime apple,
(O Tashmetu), whose heels are obsidian stone,
(O Tashmetu), whose whole self is a tablet of lapis!

(Singers)

Tashmetu, looking voluptuous, entered the bedroom,   (5')
She locked her door, sending home the lapis bolt.
She washed herself, she climbed into bed.
From (one) lapis cup, from (the other) lapis cup,[2]
        her tears flow,
He wipes away her tears with a tuft of red wool,
There, ask (her), ask (her), find out, find out!   (10')

(Nabu)

'Why, why are you so adorned, [my] Tashmetu?'

(Tashmetu)

'So I can [go] to the garden with you, my Nabu.'
'Let me go to the garden, to the garden and [   ]
'Let me go alone to the exquisite garden,★
'They would not have me take my place
        among the wisefolk!'[3]   (15')

---

1. Literally: "my lord," a term of endearment; compare II.16 line 25.
2. Her eyes; for the metaphor, compare IV.37f.
3. Literally: "counsellors." This activity is to be private, not for the audience in her throne room.

(Singers)

I would see with my own eyes the plucking of your fruit,
I would hear with my own ears your birdsong.

(Nabu)

There, make and join a firm engagement,
Engage your days to the garden and to the lord,
Engage your nights to the exquisite garden,   (20')
Let my Tashmetu come with me to the garden,
(Though) among wise folk her place be foremost.

(gap)

May she see with her own eyes the plucking of my fruit,
May she hear with her own ears my birdsong,
May she see with her own eyes,
        may she hear with her own ears!   (25')

Text: van Dijk, TIM 9 54.

Edition: Matsushima, ASJ 9 (1987), 143–149, 164–175; Livingstone, *Court Poetry*, 35–37; Nissinen,
    AOAT 250 (1998), 587–592.

Literature: E. Matsushima, "Le rituel hiérogamique de Nabu," ASJ 9 (1987), 131–175; M. Nissinen,
    "Love Lyrics of Nabû and Tašmetu: An Assyrian Song of Songs?" AOAT 250 (1998), 585–634.

★Notes to Text: (rev. 14') von Soden, WdO 22 (1991), 191.

IV.28 LOVE LYRICS OF ISHTAR OF BABYLON

Fragmentary collections of enigmatic songs and rituals involving Ishtar of Babylon seem to a modern reader scurrilous, abusive, and bizarre. Scattered excerpts from this collection follow.

(a)

Into your vulva, where you put your trust, (1)
I'll bring in a dog and fasten the door,
Into your vulva, where you put your trust,
As if it were(?) your precious jewel in front of you.
O my girl friend's vulva, why do you keep acting like this? (5)
O my girl friend's vulva, Babylon-town is looking for a rag!
O vulva of two fingers, why do you keep making trouble?

★ ★ ★

(b)

By night there's no prudish housewife, (1)
By night there's no prudish housewife,
By night no man's wife makes objection!

★ ★ ★

(c)

Before her was a fieldmouse, (1)
Behind her was a rat.
He girded(?) his hems,
He's a shrew, son of a fieldmouse.
I sent [you?], my girl friend, to Kar-bel-matati,[1] (5)
Why did you break wind and feel mortified?
Why did you stink up her boyfriend's wagon like a wi[ld ox]?
At Kar-bel-matati's crossing point,
I saw my girl friend and was stunned:
You are chalky like a gecko, (10)

1. Name of a wharf at Babylon.

Your hide is swart like a cook[ing pot].
You are in full bloom, brought to [bliss].

★   ★   ★

(d)

O my girl friend's [genitals],
    Babylon-town is looking for a rag,   (1)
To swab your vulva, to swab your vagina.
[So] let him say to the women of Babylon,
"Won't they give her a rag,
"To swab her vulva, to swab her vagina?"   (5)

Into your vulva, where you put your trust,
I'll bring in a dog and fasten the door,
I'll bring in a watchbird so it can nest.
Whenever I go out or come in,
I'll instruct my little watchbirds,   (10)
"Please, my little watchbirds,
"Don't go near the fungus!
"Please, my little watchbird,
"Don't go near the stench of (her) armpits!"

You are mother, O Ishtar of Babylon,   (15)
You are mother, O queen of the Babylonians,
You are mother, O palm tree, O carnelian!
The beautiful one, oh so beautiful!
Whose figure is oh so lustrous, oh so beautiful!

Text: W. G. Lambert, in *Unity and Diversity* (Baltimore, 1975), 127–135.
Edition: W. G. Lambert, in *Unity and Diversity*, 98–126.
Literature: D. O. Edzard, "Zur Ritualtafel der sog. 'Love Lyrics'," *Studies Reiner*, 57–69; George, *Studies Lambert*, 270–280 and 260 note 6; Da-Riva and Frahm, AfO 46/47 (1999/2000), 175–182.

G. LAMENTS

IV.29 ELEGY FOR A WOMAN DEAD IN CHILDBIRTH

This poem tells the story of a woman's death in childbirth as if she were narrating it herself. Her pleas and those of her husband fail to move Belet-ili, goddess of birth.

Why are you cast adrift, like a boat in midstream,
Your planking stoven, your mooring rope cut?
With shrouded face, you cross the river of the City.[1]
How could I not be cast adrift,
      how could my mooring rope not be cut?
The day I carried the fruit, how happy I was,
Happy was I, happy my husband.
The day I went into labor, my face grew overcast,
The day I gave birth, my eyes grew cloudy.
I prayed to Belet-ili with my hands opened out,
'You are mother of those who give birth, save my life!'
Hearing this, Belet-ili shrouded her face,
'You [ ], why do you keep praying to me?'
[My husband, who lov]ed me, uttered a cry,
'[ ] me, the wife I adore!'

(gap)

[All ...] those days I was with my husband,
While I lived with him who was my lover,
Death was creeping stealthily into my bedroom,
It forced me from my house,
It cut me off from my lover,
It set my feet[2] toward the land from which I shall not return.

Text: Strong, BA 2 (1894), 634; photo in R. Albertz, *Persönliche Frommigkeit und offizielle Religion* (Stuttgart, 1978), plate after p. 54.
Edition: Reiner, *Poetry*, 86–89; Livingstone, *Court Poetry*, 37–39.
Translation: Hecker, TUAT II/5, 780–781.
Literature: Reiner, "An Assyrian Elegy," in *Poetry*, 85–93.

1. Assur and the Tigris are meant.
2. Or: "My feet are set ..."

IV.30 LAMENTS FOR DUMUZI

The god Dumuzi (also known as Tammuz) was a complex figure understood to be the lover or husband of Ishtar (see III.35). According to some accounts, he was killed and carried off to the netherworld (see III.19). He was sometimes understood as a god of shepherds (see II.19c, IV.61); he was also seen as the god of the spring vegetation which died in the heat of summer but which sprang to life again the following spring. In any case, his death was the occasion for mourning. For a study of Dumuzi, see T. Jacobsen, "Towards the Image of Tammuz," *History of Religions* 1 (1961), 189-213, reprinted in W. L. Moran, ed., *Towards the Image of Tammuz and Other Essays on Mesopotamian History and Culture, Harvard Semitic Studies* 21 (1970), 73-101.

(a) I STOOD TALL IN OUR ORCHARD

An Assyrian student tablet collects various short laments to Dumuzi's death.

(i)

[The agent], the Babylonian merchant,
    [who] gave his commission,
    has abandoned his donkeys,
The shepherd has been killed beside the sheep.
The agent, the Babylonian merchant,
    who gave his commission,
    has abandoned his donkeys!

(ii)

The shepherd has been killed among the sheep,
    the plowman at the plow,   (1)
The orchardman has been killed in the grove,
    the irrigator in the midst of his waterworks.
We weep bitterly, we weep for our orchardman,
For our orchardman, for our irrigator we weep,
Whose fruit we ate with gusto,
Whom we(?) praised amidst the grapes and the wine.   (5)

(fragmentary lines)

(iii)

I stood tall in our orchard [like a splendid tree],   (1)
I was tall as an almond, tall as a pine.
Like a splendid tree, I stood tall at the gate
    where folk passed by.
My father would look at me and rejoice for happiness,
Whenever you looked at me, you were happy as a [ ].   (5)
Now they have cut me down,
    they have done away with me forever.
When my father saw me, he burst into tears,
When my father saw me, he burst into tears!
Whenever you looked at me, (you said?)
    "Are you happy, dead man?"
You cut down this tree, what did you [gain]?   (10)
Do not abandon this splendid tree to hypocrite women!

Text: Gurney, STT 360.
Edition: Livingstone, *Court Poetry*, 39-41.

(b) THE HUSBAND IN WHOM I DELIGHTED

This lament, known from a tablet of the Hellenistic period, is cast in an antique Sumerian style, in the manner of a lament for Tammuz, lover of Ishtar, patron deity of Uruk. The text deals primarily with the devastation of war and the cries of women deprived of their husbands. Like Erra and Ishum (IV.17), it may refer to some specific warfare of the first millennium B.C. In its tone and content it may be compared to various passages in Erra and Ishum, for example Tablet IV lines 40ff.

> "O grieving (women) of Uruk,
> > O grieving (women) of Akkad, I am prostrate!"★   (1)
> The goddess of Uruk wept,
> > whose attendant was gone,
> The goddess of Uruk wept,
> > whose loincloth was snatched away.
> The daughter of Uruk wept,
> > the daughter of Akkad was crying aloud.
> The face of the daughter of Larak was shrouded
> > with the fringe of her garment.
> The goddess of Hursagkalamma wept,
> > who was deprived of her husband.   (5)
> The goddess of ... wept,
> > whose seven brothers were killed,
> > whose eight brothers-in-law were prostrate.
> The goddess of Akkad wept,
> > whose sandals were mangled,★
> > whose lord, in whom she delighted, was killed.
> The goddess of Kesh wept,
> > sitting in the alleyway,
> > the lord of her house slain by a lynx(?).★
> The goddess of Dunnu wept,
> > "For whom the couch, for whom the coverlet?
> > "For whom do I treasure the coverlet,
> > "(now) deathly still?"   (10)

The daughter of Nippur wept,
    "Finishing the task was for Gutians!"[1]
Her cheeks were sore (from weeping),
    she was deprived of her husband,
    in whom she delighted.
The goddess of Der \<wept\>,
    "Finishing the task was for Gutians!"
\<Her\> cheeks were sore (from weeping),
    she was deprived of her husband,
    in whom she delighted.
She whose city was wrecked, whose ancestral home
    was broken into and desecrated, (cried)   (15)
"(O women), weep for Uruk,
    (my) headband caught in thorns,
"As for me, I do not know where I stepped in the tempest.
"(O women), weep for Larak, [   ],*
    I am deprived of my cloak,
"My eyes cannot look upon ..., slashing of mothers' wombs,
"(O women), weep for Nippur,
    silence dwells upon me.   (20)
"The heavens have shrouded me,
"My chair that supported me has been overturned upon me.
"The lord has deprived me of my spouse,
    the husband in whom I delighted!"

Text: Pinches, PSBA 23 (1901), after p. 192.

Edition: W. G. Lambert, JAOS 103 (1983), 211–215 (with many improved readings and proposals adopted here).

Notes to Text: (1) As taken here, the goddess and women of Uruk are the referents of *marṣātu*. (7) With Lambert, JAOS 103 (1983), 213 note 8. (9) Doubtful, reading *a-za-ri*!?; differently Groneberg, JAOS 107 (1987), 323. (18) For proposed restorations, see CAD E, 66b; Lambert, *ad loc.*

---

1. The Gutians were a byword for hateful barbarian invaders; see I.5b, III.7b (3), IV.2c, line 318.

H. INCANTATIONS

IV.31 MARDUK AND THE DEMONS

This incantation-like composition is, in part at least, a first-person address by Marduk, setting forth his qualities that can counteract evil. The composition was once of considerable length (well over 200 lines?), and was evidently popular in learned circles, as numerous manuscripts have survived and a hermeneutic commentary was prepared on it in antiquity. The application of this text is unknown; W. G. Lambert has tentatively proposed that it was part of the Babylonian New Year's festival when the Marduk statue was taken in procession and hence was for a time more than usually vulnerable to attack. The last preserved line of the text seems intended for a human speaker. The repetitiveness and inclusiveness of this piece are typical of later Mesopotamian magical tradition.

Fragment A

[I am Asalluhi, by whose ri]tual [   ]
[I am Asalluhi, who in] combat and bat[tle]
[I am Asalluhi ...] furious [   ]   (5)
[I am Asalluhi, who] was formed in Eunir[1] and [   ],
[I am Asalluhi], radiant, furious, the princely sage of the gods,
[I am Asalluhi], who surveys the heights of the distant heavens,
[I am Asalluhi], who knows the bottom of
    the wide river of the dead,[2]
[I am Asalluhi], to whom ... call in the seas above,   (10)
[I am Asalluhi], whom Laguda glorifies in the seas below.[3]
[I am Asalluhi], indeed the bond of everything,
    firstborn of Mami,
[I am Asalluhi], who overthrows the one who harbors evil,
[I am Asalluhi], who ... the gods of distant heaven,
[I am Asalluhi ...], life to the numerous peoples,   (15)
[I am Asalluhi, w]ho overthrows the evil one,

---

1.   Ziggurat of Ea's temple in Eridu. This means that Marduk is the son of Ea.
2.   Text: Hubur. See p. 915 note 1.
3.   That is, in Babylonian cosmology, the waters above the sky and below the earth. Laguda is a little-known deity, cited here perhaps to associate Asalluhi=Marduk with primeval gods; compare Marduk Prophecy (III.13), opening lines.

Fragment B

[I am Asalluhi, com]mander of the Heavenly Abode,[1]   (5)
[I am Asalluhi], who is clad in fiery brilliance, full of terrors,
I am Asalluhi, wearing a tiara,
    whose divine splendor is laden with awe,
[I am Asalluhi, who feeds?] the hungry, who rescues the weak,
[I am Asalluhi, ...] watercourses,
    who sustains the life of the land,
I am Asalluhi, who perceives decisions (to be made),
    who decides ...,   (10)
I am Asalluhi, explainer of wedges,[2]
    destroyer of wicked and evil,
I am Asalluhi, who daily keeps watch on what people say,
I am Asalluhi, whose brilliance illumines the lands,
I am Asalluhi, whose effulgence destroys walls of stone,
I am Asalluhi, wise, experienced, who excels in understanding, (15)
I am Asalluhi, whose weapon is a raging deluge,
[I am Asalluhi, who bu]rns up foe and wicked,

Fragment C

I am Asalluhi, at whose words mountains [   ],
I am Asalluhi, who, like the sun, surveys the lands,   (5)
I am Asalluhi, who turns back calumnies, who helps the [   ],
I am Asalluhi, who purges good and evil in the river ordeal,
I am Asalluhi, powerful and fierce lord of the land,
I am Asalluhi, eminent, glorious, archetype of lordship,
I am Asalluhi, in the face of whose awesomeness
    every evil returns to its lair,   (10)
I am Asalluhi, who scans the hidden subterranean waters,
    who devises designs,

I am Asalluhi, who bestows pasture and drinking place,
    who showers down abundance,

1. Andurna, a cosmic locality; see Epic of Creation (III.17) Tablet I line 24.
2. Reference to cuneiform writing; compare Gula Hymn of Bullutsa-rabi (III.25) line 184.

I am Asalluhi, at whose command the assault of
    plague is driven back,
I am Asalluhi, whose divinity is supreme everywhere,
I am Asalluhi, who ever guides [his] peoples
    like father and mother,   (15)
[I] am Asalluhi, the response of whose heart
    the g[reat] gods do not know,
[I am Asallu]hi, who plucks out disease,
    who destroys demons [   ],
[I am Asalluhi], a fierce, onrush[ing] storm [ ],

Fragment D[1]

Or you (demons) [   ] who always glow,
Or you [ ] who are always in shadow,
Or you [ ] who always charge like a bull,   (5)
Or you [ ] who are always spying,
Or you who are ever intruding into houses,
Or you who loiter on thresholds,
Or you who pace about foundations,
Or you who are wont to squat in storage pits,   (10)
Or you who are always stalking attractive young men,
    attractive young women, in the street,
Or you who go peeking at naptime,
Or you who eavesdrop,
Or you who stand at the sufferer's head,
Or you who sit at the sufferer's head,   (15)
Or you who pace at the sufferer's head,
Or you who eat with him when he eats,
Or you who drink with him when he drinks,
Or you who haunt such-and-such a sufferer,
Or you who terrify such-and-such a sufferer,   (20)
Or you who startle such-and-such a sufferer,
Or you who scare such-and-such a sufferer,
Or you who sniff at such-and-such a sufferer,
Or you who bare your fangs at such-and-such a sufferer,

1. Variant manuscript has lines 14–16 followed by 26–33.

Or you who lie in wait for such-and-such a sufferer,   (25)
Or you who gnash your teeth at such-and-such a sufferer,
Or you who stick out your tongues at such-and-such a sufferer,
Or you who open your mouths at such-and-such a sufferer,
Or you who ... [   ] at such-and-such a sufferer,
Or you who charge like an ox [   ] at such-and-such a sufferer, (30)
Or you who [butt?] like a goat at such-and-such a sufferer,
Or you who [grunt?] like a pig at such-and-such a sufferer,
Or you who slither around like little snakes
    at such-and-such a sufferer,*   (a')
Or you who slither around like chameleon(s)
    at such-and-such a sufferer,
Or you who slither around like worms
    at such-and-such a sufferer,
Or you who slither around like geckoes
    at such-and-such a sufferer,

Fragment E

[Or you] who have no [father or mother],
Or you who h[ave no] brother [or sister],
Or you who h[ave no] kith [or kin],
Or you who h[ave no] son or [daughter],
Or you who h[ave no] be[loved?] heir,   (10)
Or you who [   ] in [   ]

[May   ] uproot you,
[May   ] uproot you,
[May   ] calm you,
[May   ] you   (15)

(two lines lost)

A[salluhi] has exorcised you [by   ],
Asalluhi has exorcised you by Nin[   ],
Asalluhi has exorcised you by Shamash, creator of [   ],   (20)
Asalluhi has exorcised you by Hendursagga, who traverses [   ],[1]

---

1. For Hendursagga as another name for Erra, see Erra and Ishum (IV.17), Tablet I line 2.

Asalluhi has exorcised you by Sharur and Shargaz,[1]
> [who   ] enemies!
May Meslamtaea give you over <to> the netherworld,
May he commit you to the seven doorkeepers [of] Ereshkigal,
May he commit you to Namtar, courier of the netherworld,
> who keeps the door of the p[risoners],   (25)
May he bring you through
> the ga[te of] the great [netherworld],
May he deliver you into the hands of the great devils,
May Bidu, chief doorkeeper of the netherworld,
> hold the door against you (inside),
May he give you over to Ningizzida,
> prefe[ct] of the vast [nether]world,
May the great gods of the netherworld burn you up!   (30)
I exorcise you by the great prefect of Allatu:[2]
May the netherworld river hold you back!
[You shall not] ... me, you shall not keep on hounding me,
> you shall not [   ] me, so-and-so, son of so-and-so!

(fragmentary lines, then breaks off)

Text: W. G. Lambert, AfO 17 (1954/6), pl. XIII–XVI; AfO 19 (1959/60), pl. XXIV–XXVII; various unpublished duplicates and joins noted by Borger, HKL 2, 156 could not be utilized here.
Edition: W. G. Lambert, AfO 17 (1954/6), 310–320; AfO 19 (1959/60), 114–119.
Literature: W. G. Lambert, "Marduk's Address to the Demons," in Abusch, ed., *Magic*, 291–296.
Notes to Text: (D 33) Lines a′–d′, placement not clear, are from an unpublished manuscript quoted CAD N/2, 56a (etc.).

1. Personified divine weapons, usually of Ninurta.
2. Netherworld deity, see IV.5 line 30.

IV.32 AGAINST AN ADVERSARY IN A LAWSUIT

To be said "when entering the palace." Blocking of the mouth and anus in connection with a lawsuit is referred to in an Assyrian curse formula, "He who talks too much in the Step Gate (= law court), the [demon] of ruins will seize his mouth and anus ..." (Grayson, ARI 1, 13). Compare also III.16d (6).

Listen, [ye] of heaven,	(1)
Hear my speech, ye of the netherworld!	
So-and-so, son of so-and-so, my adversary,	
Until I slap his cheek,	
Until I rip out his tongue,	(5)
Until I send his words back into his mouth,	
I will not allow his mouth to speak,	
I will not allow his bottom to break wind.★	

Text: Ebeling, KAR 71, rev. 1–8.
Edition: Ebeling, MAOG 5/3 (1931), 32–33.
★*Notes to Text*: (8) With CAD A/2, 305a against CAD N/1, 54b.

IV.33 AGAINST AN ANGRY MAN

(a) I WILL DISSOLVE YOUR ANGER

Why are you angry, seized (by rage),   (1)
Your eyes bloodshot,
Your gums spattered with gall,
The hair of your chest bristling?
Your (own) son,[1] taking my part, is angry at you
      and seized (by rage),   (5)
My eyes (too) are bloodshot,
My gums are spattered with gall,
The hairs of my chest bristle.
Be it a door, I will open your mouth,
Be it a bar, I will put a stop to your lips,   (10)
Be it bonding of a wall, I will dissolve your anger!

Text: Ebeling, KAR 43, rev. 7–17; KAR 63, rev. 4–15.
Edition: Ebeling, MAOG 5/3 (1931), 17, 19.

(b) ANGER

Spittle was considered to be endowed with magical properties; see Ebeling,
MAOG 5/3 (1931), 14–15.

I have escaped the spittle of your mouth,   (1)
I have given the word of your father,
      the word of your mother, the word of your sister,
(As if it were) the word of a trouper, a city whore,
To the covering earth,
That does not make ready to speak,   (5)
That does not wag its tongue.

Text: Ebeling, KAR 43, obv. 1–6; KAR 63, obv. 1–6.
Edition: Ebeling, MAOG 5/3 (1931), 16, 18.

1. Variant adds: "son of so-and-so."

IV.34 AGAINST BILE

Biliousness is here symbolized by a greenish goat browsing in a green world.

The she-goat is green, its offspring is green, (1)
Its shepherd is green, its herdsman is green,
It feeds on green grass in a green plot,
It drinks green water from a green canal.
He threw a stick at it, it did not turn around, (5)
He threw a clod at it, it did not raise its head,
He threw a wad(?) of thyme and salt at it:
The bile has begun to dispel like a mist.

(The spell is not mine, it is a spell of Ea, Asalluhi, Damu, and Gula.)

Text: Köcher, BAM 578, ii 45–49.
Edition: Böck, in Renger, ed., *Babylon*, 421–423.

IV.35 AGAINST THE EVIL EYE

For the evil eye, see II.22b.

    ... Eye, eye! It is hostile,[1]   (1)
    It is eye of a woman, it is eye of a m[an],
        it is [ey]e of an enemy, it is anyone's(?) eye,
    It is eye of a neighbor, it is eye of a neighbor (woman),[2]
        eye of a child minder(?), it is the eye!
    O eye, in evil purpose, you have called at the door,   (5)
    The threshold shook, the beams quaked.
    When you enter(ed)[3] a house, O eye, [   ].
    You smashed the potter's kiln, you scuttled the boatman's boat,
    You broke the yoke of the mighty ox,
    You broke the shin of the striding donkey,   (10)
    You broke the loom of the expert weaver,[4]
    You deprived the striding horse of its foal(?)
        and the ox of its food(?),[5]
    You have scattered the ... of the ignited stove,
    You have left the livestock(?) to the maw
        of the murderous storm,
    You have cast discord among harmonious brothers.   (15)
    Smash the eye! Send the eye away!
    Make the eye cross seven rivers,
    Make the eye cross seven canals,
    Make the eye cross seven mountains!
    Take the eye and tie its feet to an isolated r[ee]d stalk,   (20)
    Take the eye and smash it in its owner's face
        like a potter's vessel!

(fragmentary lines, then breaks off)

Text: Ebeling, ArOr 17/1 (1949), 203–204 VAT 10018 (transliteration only); VAT 14226 cited p. 204.
Edition: Ebeling, ArOr 17/1 (1949), 204–206; Thomsen, JNES 51 (1992), 24.

  1. Variant omits three lines.
  2. Text repeats "neighbor" without change of gender.
  3. Variant has third person here and following.
  4. Variant omits two lines.
  5. Or, perhaps, "companion."

IV.36 AGAINST EVIL SPIRITS

(a) THE SEVEN

They are seven, they the seven,   (1)
They are seven in the springs of the depths,
They are seven, adorned in heaven.
They grew up in the springs of the depths, in the cella.
They are not male, they are not female,   (5)
They are drifting phantoms,
They take no wife, they beget no son.
They know neither sparing of life nor mercy,
They heed neither prayers nor entreaties.
They are steeds that grew up in the mountains,   (10)
They are the evil ones of Ea,
They are the prefects of the gods.
They loiter in the side streets to make trouble on the highway.
They are evil, they are evil!
They are seven, they are seven, they are twice seven!   (15)
Be conjured by heaven, be conjured by the netherworld!

Text: Campbell Thompson, CT 16 15, v 29–59 (bilingual).
Edition: Campbell Thompson, *Devils* 1, 76–79.

(b) BLACK TRAGACANTH

Sumerian and Akkadian incantations changed their wording and meaning over centuries of use, sometimes evolving into altogether different texts. An example of this is a spell to be said while placing a piece of tragacanth (a thorny tree) near the head of a patient in connection with a healing ritual. This exists in an Archaic Sumerian version and Mature and Late bilingual versions, presented here separately for comparison. The various versions have been edited and compared by M. Geller, "A Middle Assyrian Tablet of Utukkū Lemnūtu, Tablet 12," *Iraq* 42 (1980), 23–51, on which this treatment is based. See also p. 55 note 6.

Archaic Sumerian Version (1)

[The king], like a black tragacanth, grew up in a pure place,   (1)
Enki, like a black tragacanth, grew up in a pure place.
His floods fill the land with abundance,
His place of walking is its shade that,
Like the appearance of pure lapis,   (5)
Stretches out in the midst of the sea ...

Mature Bilingual Version (2)

In Eridu a tragacanth was created in a pure place,   (1)
Its appearance was pure lapis, stretching out into the depths.
The way of Ea in Eridu is full of abundance,
His dwelling is at the netherworld.
In his bedchamber,   (5)
In the pure house in the forest,
The shade of which stretches where none may go forward,
Wherein are Shamash and Tammuz, between the two rivers,
The gods Kahegal, Igihegal, and Lahamu of Eridu
    cast the spell of Apsu,
They set it at the patient's head.   (10)
May Girra, guardian of the patient's well-being,
    walk at the patient's side.
The muzzler of his mouth, the seizer of his hand,
    who has not ... his face and heart,
Who sneaks around in the house, may he be blocked!

May Ningeshtina, sister of the king, go with him.
May the judge, wise and pure Ishtar, bar him from the house,   (15)
May the evil phantom, evil demon, evil wraith,
     evil sprite, evil god, evil lurker,
Be conjured by heaven, be conjured by the netherworld!
Th(is) man, son of his (personal) god, may the evil phantom
     who has seized him stay outside,
May the favorable protective spirit stand at his head,
May the favorable guardian spirit stand at his side,   (20)
May his (personal) god stand by his prayer,
May he praise Ea,
May that man praise Ea and Nammu,
May he make manifest the word of Ea,
May Damkina make it succeed!   (25)
O Asaralimnunna, foremost son of Apsu,
Yours is (to act) kindly and graciously.

Late Bilingual Version (3)

A black tragacanth grew up in Eridu,
     it was created in a pure place.   (1)
Its appearance was pure lapis, stretching out to the depths.
The way of Ea in Eridu is full of abundance,
His dwelling is at the netherworld,
His sanctuary is the bed of the watery deep.
In the pure house, the shade of which stretches like a forest's,
     where none may enter,   (5)
Therein are Shamash and Tammuz,
Between the mouths of the two rivers.
The gods Kahegal, Igihegal and [Lahama-absu] of Eridu
     [took] that tragacanth,*
They set it near the patient (to cure him).
Let a favorable spirit, a favorable genius
     always be at the side of (this) man,
     son of his (personal) god ...

(remainder of text too fragmentary for translation)

Text: (1) Legrain, MDP 14 91 (Sumerian only); (2) Geller, *Iraq* 42 (1980), 43 (bilingual); (3) Geller, *Iraq* 42 (1980), 43, 45, 46; Campbell Thompson, CT 16 46, 183–203 (bilingual).

Edition: Geller, *Iraq* 42 (1980), 28–29, 34–35; see also Langdon, JRAS 1928, 846–848; Heimpel, AOAT 253 (1998), 147–148 = note 41.

Literature: See Borger, HKL 2, 288.

★*Notes to Text*: (2 8) CAD K, 453b.

(c) MYSTERIOUS DEMONS

Evil phantom, evil demon, evil wraith,
　　evil sprite have come forth from the netherworld,　　　　　(1)
[They] have come forth from the infernal regions into the land.
They are not known in heaven,
They are not understood in the netherworld.
They do not know how to stand up,　　　　　(5)
They do not know how to sit down.
They eat no food,
They drink no water!

Text: Campbell Thompson, CT 17 41, K 2873, 1–10 (bilingual).

Edition: Campbell Thompson, *Devils* 2, 134–135.

IV.37 AGAINST EYE DISEASE

Eye disease was a common problem in Babylonia, so numerous incantations try to cure it. See J. C. Fincke, *Augenleiden nach Keilschriftlichen Quellen, Würzburger medezinhistorische Forschungen* 70 (2000).

(a) DAUGHTERS TO THE WIND

This incantation is known from a manuscript discovered at Ugarit on the Syrian coast.[1]

> Blurred eyes, troubled eyes! (1)
> Eyes, daughters to the wind,
> Eyes, porous blood vessels!
> You have brought upon me a rainfall [of blood?] and fire!*
> Let it be extinguished as if with water, (5)
> Let it cease (running) as if with algae.[2]
>
> (This incantation is not mine,
>   it is an incantation of Damu and Ninkarrak.
> O Ninkarrak, heal, that the specialist receive (his) fee.*
> Let it not go out above, let it go out below.)[3]

Text: Nougayrol, *Ugaritica* 5 19 (p. 379).
Edition: Nougayrol, *Ugaritica* 5, 64–65.
Notes to Text: (4) So Nougayrol, reading and translation doubtful. (8) So here, though in parallel texts reference is made to a gift for the goddess of healing.

1. For another Akkadian eye incantation from Syria, see Arnaud, *Emar* 737.
2. If correctly understood, may refer to clotting of blood or stanching a flow of fluid from the eye.
3. The disease is supposed to be excreted.

(b) BLOODSHOT EYES

Cloudy eyes, blurred eyes, bloodshot eyes!   (1)
Why do you cloud over, why do you blur?
Why do sand of river, pollen of date palm,
Pollen of fig tree, straw of winnower sting you?
If I called you, come,   (5)
If I did not call you, you must not come!
(Be off), before north, south, east, and west wind
      have risen against you!

Text: Köcher, BAM 514, iii 13′–18′.
Edition: Landsberger, JNES 17 (1958), 57 (partial).

(c) THEY ARE TWO

They are two, the daughters of Anu,   (1)
Between them bars a barrier,
Never goes sister to her sister!
Whom shall I send to the daughter(s) of Anu of heaven?
Let them bring their pots of chalcedony,
      their pots of pure bright lapis,   (5)
Let them draw water and quench the clouded eyes,
      the blurred and troubled eyes.

Text: Köcher, BAM 514, iii 22′–26′.
Edition: Landsberger-Jacobsen, JNES 14 (1955), 16.
Translation: Fincke, *Augenleiden* (see above, p. 967), 93.

(d) MOTE

In the beginning, before creation,
     the work song came down to the land, (1)
Seeder plow bore furrow, furrow bore sprout,
Sprout root, root node, node ear, ear mote.
Shamash reaped, Sin gleaned.
While Shamash was reaping and Sin was gleaning, (5)
Mote entered the young man's eye.
Shamash and Sin stand by, so the mote will come out!

Text: Köcher, BAM 510, iv 41–45.
Edition: Landsberger, JNES 17 (1958), 56.
Literature: See II.23d.

(e) WIND BLEW DOWN

Wind blew down from heaven
     and has set a sore in the man's eye, (1)
It has set a sore in the diseased eyes,
That man's eyes are distressed, his eyes are troubled,
This man is weeping bitterly for himself.
Enlil saw this man's disease, (5)
"Take crushed cassia,
"Cast the spell of the Deep,
"Bind the man's eye,
"When the Mother of the gods touches the man's eye
     with her pure hands,
"Let the wind that blew in the man's eye
     go out of his eye!" (10)

Text: Köcher, BAM 510, iv 5–21; 513, iv 11–31; 514, iv 10–26; Gurney, STT 279, 30–50.
Edition: Fincke, *Augenleiden* (see above, p. 967), 218.
Translation: Campbell Thompson, *Proceedings of the Royal Society of Medicine* 17 (1923/4), *Historical Section*, 32.

(f) VESSELS OF BLOOD

O eyes, porous vessels of blood!   (1)
Why do you carry away chaff, thorns,
      berries, riverweed?
Clods from the streets, litter from trash pits(?),*
      why do you carry them away?
Rain down like stars, soar down like sky-fire,
Before flint knives of Gula ..., get to you!*   (5)

(A spell of Asalluhi and Marduk,
A spell of Ningirimma, lord of spells, and Gula,
The lord of the physician's art cast it, I bore it up.)

Text: Köcher, BAM 510, iv 34–39.
Edition: Landsberger, JNES 17 (1958), 58.
*Notes to Text: (3) See Geller, ZA 74 (1984), 297. (5f.) Syntax of final lines not clear; compare II.23e.

IV.38 AGAINST FEVER

(a) FIRE, FIRE!

This incantation alludes to the spread of contagious disease.

Fire, fire!	(1)
Fire seized a lone man.	
It seized (his) insides, (his) temple,	
It spread (to others) the gnawing of (his) insides,	
The stock of the human race was diminished.	(5)
Belet-ili went before Ea the king,	
"O Ea, humankind was created by your spell,	
"Second, you pinched off their clay	
from the firmament of the depths.[1]	
"By your great command, you determined their capacities.	
"I cast a spell on the ...-disease, fever, boils,	(10)
"Leprosy(?), jaundice!	
"Rain down like dew,	
"Flow down like tears,	
"Go down to the netherworld!"*	

(This incantation is an incantation of Belet-ili, the great queen.)

Text: W. G. Lambert, AfO 23 (1970), pl. IV, V, IX.
Edition: W. G. Lambert, AfO 23 (1970), 42–43 lines 20–33.
Literature: Geller, *Studies Lambert*, 235.
Notes to Text: (14) Lambert, AfO 23 (1970), 43 note to III, 32.

1. That is, from the ground (Lambert, AfO 23 [1970], 43 note to III, 25–27).

(b) YOUR SMOKE HAS NO SMELL

Fire, fire!   (1)
Fire of storm, fire of battle,
Fire of death, fire of pestilence, consuming fire!
Your smoke has no smell.
Your fire has no warmth.   (5)
May Asalluhi drive you away
     and send you across the Tigris river.[1]
I conjure you by Anu your father,
I conjure you by Antu your mother,
Go out, like a snake from you(r hole in) the foundations,
Like a partridge(?) from your hiding place!   (10)
Do not go back toward your prey,*
Disperse like mist, rise like dew,
Go up, like smoke, to the heaven of Anu!

Text: W. G. Lambert, AfO 23 (1970), pl. I, III, VI, X.
Edition: W. G. Lambert, AfO 23 (1970), 40 lines 5–15.
Notes to Text: (11) Lambert, AfO 23 (1970), 40 note to II.13.

1. Variant: Tigris and Euph[rates].

IV.39 AGAINST FLATULENCE

This may be one of the few apotheoses of flatulence in world literature; see also II.23g.

> Wind, O wind!
> Wind, you are the fire of the gods.
> You are the wind between turd and urine.
> You have come out and taken your place
> Among the gods, your brethren.

Text: Köcher, BAM 574, iii 56–64.
Edition: Küchler, *Assyriologische Bibliothek* 18 (Berlin, 1909), no. 1.
Translation: Ritter, AS 16 (1965), 312; Farber, TUAT II/2, 272.

IV.40 AGAINST HEADACHE

(a) EPIDEMIC

[He]adache has come forth from the Ekur,   (1)
It has come forth [fr]om the house of Enlil.
A Lamashtu,[1] who wipes out (names),
It grants no rest, makes sleep unpleasant,
It is the sickness of night and day.   (5)
Its head is a demon, its body a deluge,
Its appearance is a darkened sky,
Its [fa]ce is the thick(?) shadow of a forest,
Its [ha]nd is a snare, its foot a noose(?),
… it makes the sinews smart …,   (10)
It makes the limbs smart,
It makes the [b]elly(?) tremble, it wastes the body,
It makes [the stomach] rumble like a porous pot,
It contorts the tendons, it twists the sinews,⋆
It twists the sinews like a heavy rope,
It contorts [the mus]cles,   (15)
It chokes the mouth and nostrils as with pitch,⋆
It crushes the armpit like malt,
It snaps off the [ha]nd like a thread in a tempest,
It destroys the shoulder like an embankment,
It slits open the breast like a (flimsy) basket,   (20)
It staves in the ribs like an old boat,
It gets a grip on the colon as if it were intestines,
It flattens the tall like a reed,
It slaughters the great one like an ox.
It struck the ox, it did not pity the ox,   (25)
It struck the wild ox, it did not relent to the wild ox,
It struck the ibex, it could not grow its horns full size,
It struck the wild ram, the mountain ram,
        it did not spare their young,
It struck the beasts of the steppe so they butted one another

---

1. A she-demon; see II.21, IV.42. For erasing of family names by killing offspring, see p. 253 note 1.

like an orchard whose branches are being torn away,[1]
It punctures everything like a ... throw-stick. (30)
Asalluhi saw it,

(Cure follows.)

Text: Campbell Thompson, CT 17 25, 1–48; cf. Ebeling, KAR 368 (bilingual).
Edition: Campbell Thompson, *Devils* 2, 86–87.
Literature: See Borger, HKL 2, 289.
Notes to Text: (14a) Landsberger, MSL 9, 23–24. (16) With CAD I/J, 310 etc., against Borger, BiOr 14 (1957), 194 note 7.

(b) AFFLICTION

Headache, applied[2] in heaven,
  removed in the netherworld, (1)
Which sapped the strength of the strong young man,
Which has not returned her energy
  to the beautiful young woman,
Which has set upon the sick man,
Ishtar, without whom no one has relaxation or delight,
  made (it) come down from the mountain. (5)
It drew near the limbs of the afflicted man,
The man stands (saying), "Alas!"
Who will remove it, who will cast it out?
Ishtar, daughter of Sin,
Enkum,[3] son of Enlil, (10)
Asalluhi, son of Enlil,
Let them cast it out from the body of the afflicted man!

(Cure follows.)

Text: Campbell Thompson, CT 17 19, 149–166; von Weiher, SBTU III 65 (bilingual).
Edition: Campbell Thompson, *Devils* 2, 76–79; von Weiher, SBTU III, 43–44.
Literature: Borger, HKL 2, 289.

1. The comparison may be between the thrashing of branches and the clashing of horns.
2. Literally: "bound on."
3. A servant god to Enki; see Geller, FAOS 12 (1985), 90; Borger, JCS 21 (1967), 11 (26+a).

(c) MISERY

Head disease charges about the steppe, blowing like the wind,   (1)
It flashes on and off like lightning, it is poured out,
    above and below.
It cut off, like a reed, the man who did not revere his god,
It slashed his sinews like a (flimsy) basket,
It wastes the flesh of him who has no protective goddess.   (5)
It flashes like stars of the sky, it runs like water at night,
It has confronted the afflicted man and paralyzed him,
    as if it were a storm.
It killed that man!
That man writhes like one with intestinal disease,
Like one disemboweled he tosses about.   (10)
He burns like one cast in a fire.
(He is) like an onager,[1] whose shrunken eyes are clouded,
He is fed up with his life, he is bound over for death.
Headache, whose course, like a thick fog's, no one knows,
Whose full sign, whose means of restraint no one knows!   (15)

(Cure follows.)

Text: Campbell Thompson, CT 17 19, 1–30; von Weiher, SBTU II 2, 1–27 (bilingual).
Edition: Campbell Thompson, *Devils* 2, 64–67; von Weiher, SBTU II, 22 lines 1–51.
Literature: See Borger, HKL 2, 289.

---

1. Sumerian adds: "fleet."

(d) DO NOT ENTER THE HOUSE I ENTER

Pazuzu son of Hanbu was one of the rare Mesopotamian demons with a personal name and patronymic. This demon appears only in first-millennium sources. In the following spell, which has many variant versions, Pazuzu is associated with headache. See also IV.59a.

> O mighty one, who comes over high mountains,
>> who withstands all winds, (1)
> Raging wind, whose rising is terrible, furious, raging,
>> who comes on furiously,
> Murderer of the world regions, wrecker of high mountains,
> Who parches the marshland, who parches its reeds.
>
> It beat on the forest, dropped its trees, (5)
> It passed into the garden, dropped down its fruit,
> It passed down the river, dropped down ice,
> It went up into the desert, dropped down frost,
> It peered down the well, dropped down ice,[1]
> It went up into the desert, dropped down frost! (10)
>
> O headache of humanity, head pain of humanity,
>> disease of humanity,
> Do not enter the house I enter,
> Do not come near the house I come near,
> Do not approach the house I approach!
>
> Be conjured by Anu and Antu, Enlil and Ninlil,
>> Ea and Damkina, heaven and netherworld! (15)

Text: See Borger, *Studies Reiner*, 16.
Edition: Borger, *Studies Reiner*, 19–22 lines 31–47.

---

1. Variant adds: "It struck the young man, hunched him over / It knocked against the young girl, deformed(?) her hips / When you blow, the world regions heave."

(e) I AM PAZUZU

Amulets and collections of spells preserve a short self-predication by Pazuzu, an evil demon. Although the original text is in Sumerian, it was probably composed at a late date, long after Sumerian was a dead language.[1] Several variant Akkadian translations are found. The mythological reference to climbing a mountain and overcoming a wind (see also IV.40d) is not known elsewhere in more detail.

> I am Pazuzu, son of Hanbu, king of the evil phantoms.
> I ascended the mighty mountain that quaked.
> The winds that I went against were headed toward the west.
> One by one I broke their wings.

Text: See Borger, *Studies Reiner*, 24–27.
Edition: W. G. Lambert, *Forschungen und Berichte* 12 (1970), 41–47.

---

1. W. G. Lambert, *Forschungen und Berichte* 12 (1970), 45.

IV.41 AGAINST INFERTILITY

A collection of rituals and spells against infertility of a woman contains the following two incantations. In the first of them, the woman embraces a potter's kiln, then recites the magic words. In the second, she embraces a date palm, then recites. As with the love charms (see IV.50) the symbolism of the two objects is obvious.

(a) THE KILN

O pure kiln, great daughter of Anu,	(1)
Within whom the fire flares into being,	
Within whom valiant Girra has taken up his dwelling,	
You are sound, your equipment is sound,	
Whether you be empty or full, you are [sound?].	(5)
But when I conceive,	
I cannot bring to term what is within me.	
Please give me your soundness,	
Take away my distress!¹	
Let no [imperfect vessel] come out from you,	
So too for me, may what is within me thrive,	(10)
May I see my baby,*	
May I find acceptance in the house wherein I dwell!	

Text: von Weiher, SBTU V 248, obv. 26–32.
Edition: von Weiher, SBTU V, 58–61.
Notes to Text: (11) Reading <*še*>-*er-ri*.

1. Wordplay on "equipment" of line 4.

(b) THE DATE PALM

O date palm, who receives whatever the wind bears,   (1)
Receive from me misdeed, offense, crime, sin
That I, who dwell in this house not die
From misery, sleeplessness, disease, anxiety, childbirth,
Or from any male or female slave whatsoever around me,   (5)
...
You make late grain come up where there was early grain,
You make early grain come up where there was late grain.
You let the [dama]ged tree produce fruit,[1]
You let the non-bearing tree produce fruit.   (10)
Receive from me in full whatever unsoundness of mind
          or body or litter[2]
          from my (personal) god or my (personal) goddess,
Which, unknowing, I may have seen or trod on,
          I don't know what it is,
That I may sing your praises.

Text: von Weiher, SBTU V 248, obv. 33-40.
Edition: von Weiher, SBTU V, 58-59, 61.

1. Text: "flies," presumably an error.
2. This strange expression normally refers to leaves and twigs dropped from a tree.

IV.42 AGAINST LAMASHTU

For the Lamashtu-demon, see above, I.7a and II.21. Here the magician outfits her for a long journey and gives her farewell presents to hasten her departure.

(a) "BRING ME YOUR SONS!"

She is furious, she is fierce, she is uncanny,
      she has an awful glamor, and she is a she-wolf,
      the daughter of Anu! (1)
Her feet are those of Anzu, her hands are unclean,
      the face of a ravening lion is her face.
She came up from the reed bed, her hair askew,
      her loincloth torn away.[1]
She stalks the cattle's tracks, she dogs the sheep's tracks,
      her hands are gory with flesh and blood.
She comes in the window, slithering like a serpent, (5)
She enters a house, she leaves a house (at will).
"Bring me your sons, that I may suckle (them),
      and your daughters, that I may nurse (them),
"Let me put my breast in your daughters' mouths!"
Ea his father heard her,
"O daughter of Anu, instead of trying to be
      the nursemaid of humankind, (10)
"Instead of your hands being gory with flesh and blood,
"Instead of entering a house, leaving a house (at will),
"Accept from the traveling merchant a cloak and provisions,
"Accept from the smith bracelets as befit your hands and feet,
"Accept from the jeweler an earring as befits your ears, (15)
"Accept from the gem cutter a carnelian as befits your neck,
"Accept from the woodworker a comb,
      a distaff, and your garment pin."
I conjure you by Anu your father, Antu your mother,
I conjure you by Ea, who created your name!

---

1. Compare I.7a line 8, a description of her wild state expanded here by having her come from a swamp.

Text: Thureau-Dangin, RA 18 (1921), 163; von Weiher, SBTU III 84, 63–78.
Edition: Thureau-Dangin, RA 18 (1921), 166–167, 170–171; von Weiher, SBTU III, 118, 121–122.

(b) SHE TORTURES BABIES

Great is the daughter of Anu, who tortures babies,   (1)
Her hand is a net, her embrace is dea[th].
She is cruel, raging, wrathful, rapacious,
A runner, an abductor is the daughter of Anu.
She touches the bellies of women in labor,   (5)
She yanks out the pregnant woman's baby.
She suckles it, she stands it up and it goes about.
Her breasts(?), her belly(?), her muscles are large.
The daughter of Anu is the one of the gods, her brethren,
    with no child of her own.
Her head is the head of a lion,   (10)
Her form is the form of a donkey,
Her lips are a rushing wind, they pour out [   ].
She came down from the peaks(?) of the mountains,
She roars like a lion,
She keeps up the howling of a demonic dog.   (15)

Text: Pinches, IV R² 58, iii 29–48; Lutz, PBS 1/2 113, iii 15–35.
Edition: Myhrman, ZA 16 (1902), 180–181.
Literature: See Borger, HKL 2, 230.

(c) "I AM THE DAUGHTER OF ANU"

"I am the daughter of Anu, the sky, (1)
"I am a Sutaean,[1] [I have] an awful glamor.
"I enter a house, I leave a house (at will),

    'Bring me your sons, that I may suckle (them),
    'Let me put my breast in your daughters' mouths!'" (5)

Anu heard and began to weep,
Aruru, mistress of the gods, shed her tears,
"Why shall we destroy what we have created?
"Shall she carry off what we brought to be?
"Take her and throw her into the ocean ..., (10)
"Tie her to a mountain tamarisk or a solitary reed stalk!
"Like a dead person who has no burial,
"Or a stillborn child who suckles not a mother's milk,
"May the daughter of Anu, like smoke,
        not return to (this) house!"

Text: Pinches, IV R² 58, iii 13–27; Lutz, PBS 1/2 113, ii 2–14.
Edition: Myhrman, ZA 16 (1902), 178–179.
Literature: See Borger, HKL 2, 230.

---

1. A bandit folk who were a byword for violence and marauding; see Erra and Ishum (IV.17) p. 904 note 2.

(d) SHE SEIZED

[She is furious, she is uncanny, she has an awful glamor],   (1)
[   ]
She crossed a watercourse and made its water muddy,
She leaned against a wall and smeared it with filth.
She seized an old man, they call her "wipe-out."   (5)
She seized a young man, they call her "sunstroke."
She seized a girl, they call her "Lamashtu."
She seized a boy, they call her "Lamashtu."
Because you have come,
      you seize the form of his features,
You seize the limbs, you destroy the members,   (10)
You consume(?) the sinews, you twist the muscles,
You make the face pale, you distort the countenance,
You cause depression, you burn the body like fire!
To remove you, to drive you out so you cannot return,
      so you cannot approach,   (15)
So you cannot come near the body of so-and-so,
      son of so-and-so,
I conjure you by Anu, father of the great gods,
I conjure you by Enlil, the great mountain,
I conjure you by Ea, king of the depths,
      creator of everything, lord of all,
I conjure you by Belet-ili, great queen,
      who formed created things,   (20)
I conjure you by Sin, lord of the tiara,
      who renders decisions, who discloses signs,
I conjure you by Shamash, light of above and below,
      creator of the universe,
I conjure you by Asalluhi, lord of exorcism,
I conjure you by Ninurta,
      foremost of the gods his brethren,
I conjure you by Ningirimma, mistress of incantations,   (25)
I conjure you by Ninkarrak, housekeeper of Ekur,
I conjure you by Ishtar, mistress of the lands!

Be conjured by Assembly Place of the Gods,[1]
    abode of counsel of the great gods in Ekur,
You will not return to so-and-so, son of so-and-so,
    nor draw near him.

(This incantation is not mine,
    it is an incantation of Ea and Asalluhi,
It is an incantation of Damu and Ninkarrak,   (30)
It is an incantation of Ningirimma, mistress of incantations.)

Text: Pinches, IV R² 56, [i 30]–ii 21; Lutz, PBS 1/2 113, i 23–41.
Edition: Myhrman, ZA 16 (1902), 156–160.
Literature: See Borger, HKL 2, 230.

1. Ubshu–ukkenna, a cosmic locality; see Epic of Creation (III.17) Tablet II line 159.

IV.43 AGAINST NURSES HARMFUL TO CHILDREN

O wetnurse!   (1)
Wetnurse, whose breast is (too) sweet,
Wetnurse, whose breast is (too) bitter,
Wetnurse, whose breast is infected,
Wetnurse, who died from an infected breast,   (5)
Nursemaid, whose armclasp is relaxed,
Nursemaid, whose armclasp is loose,
Nursemaid, whose armclasp is limp,
Nursemaid, whose armclasp is wrong,
Be conjured by heaven!   (10)
Be conjured by the netherworld!

Text: Haupt, ASKT 11, 35–44 (bilingual).
Edition: Borger, AOAT 1 (1969), 5 VII.

IV.44 AGAINST PHANTOMS

(a) LIFE PASSED THEM BY

Mesopotamian demonology recognized a wraith in the form of a young man or woman (Ardat-lili) that had never known a full or normal life. The excerpts translated below show the nature of this demon and the sometimes fervid descriptions lavished on it by the scribes.

(a, = Lackenbacher, Group 1 col. i)

[A young man who] sits stock still in the street, [all al]one,   (1)
A young man who groans bitterly in the grip of his fate,
A young man who, on account of his destiny, is aghast,
A young man whose mother, sobbing, bore him in the street,
A young man whose body is seared by woe,   (5)
A young man whose (personal) god bound him out of hostility,
A young man whose (personal) goddess forsook him,
A young man who took no wife, raised no child,
A young man who felt no pleasure in his wife's loins,
A young man who did not strip the garment
    from his wife's loins,   (10)
A young man expelled from his wedding ...

(b, = Lackenbacher, Group 1 col. ii, variant = Group 3 col. ii 1′–14′)

They (the demons) confront the man who has no god,   (1)
They s[et] their hands on his hand,[1]
[They set their] feet on his feet,
[They set their] neck with his neck,
They traded his self [for theirs].   (5)
"I am the son of a prince," he said to her,
"I will fill your lap with silver and gold,
"You be the wife,
"I will be your husband," he said to her,
He made himself as alluring to her as the fruit of an orchard.   (10)

---

1. Variant: "He (the demon) touched his hand and made it his own hand ..." (etc.).

(c, = SBTU II 6, 36–45, variant =Lackenbacher, Group 2 obv. i, rev. i 9′–26′)

Ardat-lili wafts through a man's window: (1)
The girl who has no (natural) destiny(?),
The girl who was never impregnated like a woman,
The girl who never lost her virginity like a woman,
The girl who felt no pleasure in her husband's loins,   (5)
The girl who never removed her garment
    at her husband's loins,
The girl whose garment pin no fine young man released,⋆
The girl who had no milk in her breasts,
    but only bitter fluid came out,
The girl who felt no pleasure in her husband's loins,
    whose desire was never fulfilled,
The girl without a bedroom, who did not call for her mother.   (10)

(d, continues directly in one version, = SBTU II 7, 4–13)

Who made her cheek ugly through unhappiness,   (1)
Who did not enjoy herself with (other) girls,[1]
Who never appeared at her city's festival,
Who never wanted anything,
Who was taken away from her husband in the bedchamber,   (5)
Who had no husband, bore no son,
Who had no husband, produced no son,
Whose husband was taken away, whose son was taken away,
Who was expelled from her wedding,
Ardat-lili, who was expelled from the window like air,   (10)
Ardat-lili, whose spirit was not in her breathing(?),
Ardat-lili, whose misery took her to the grave.

1. Variant: "go about the roads and streets."

(e, = Lackenbacher, Group I rev. ii 3′–17′, variant K 5443)

So long as you have not left (this) house,   (1)
So long as you have not left (this) city,
You shall eat no food, you shall drink no water,
You shall taste no sea water, fresh water, brackish water,
    Tigris water, Euphrates water, well water, canal water!   (5)
If you would fly toward heaven, you shall have no wings,
If you would stay on earth, you shall have no place to sit!

Text: Lackenbacher, RA 65 (1971), 123–154, figs. 1–14; von Weiher, SBTU II 6, 7; Geller, AfO 35
   (1988), 8, 10, 13, 16.
Edition: Lackenbacher, RA 65 (1971), 119–154; von Weiher, SBTU II, 22–30, 41–47; Geller, AfO
   35 (1988), 7–21.
Literature: Farber, ZA 79 (1989), 14–35; Geller, BSOAS 63 (2000), 331–332.
⋆*Notes to Texts*: (c 7) Malul, JEOL 32 (1991), 69–70.

(b) AGAINST A GHOST THAT HAS APPEARED

Mesopotamian magic included spells and rituals against ghosts and the dead. For a detailed study of this material, see J. Bottéro, "Les morts et l'au-delà dans rituels en accadien contre l'action des 'revenants'," ZA 73 (1983), 153–203; compare III.39.

> The ghost that has set upon me, keeps harassing me,
>> and [does not quit me] day or [nig]ht,   (1)
> Be it a stranger ghost,
> Be it a forgotten ghost,
> Be it a ghost without a name,
> Be it a ghost that has no one to provide for it,   (5)
> Be it a ghost of someone
>> who [has no one to invoke his name],
> Be it a ghost of someone killed by a weapon,
> Be it a ghost of someone who died for a sin against a god
>> or for a crime against a king,
> [Place] it [in the care of the ghosts of its family],
> May it accept this and let me go free!   (10)

Text: Campbell Thompson, CT 23 15, 6–9.
Edition: Castellino, OrNS 24 (1955), 244–245.
Literature: Borger, HKL 2 292; Bottéro, ZA 73 (1983), 157.

(c) WHY DO YOU KEEP APPEARING TO ME?

O dead people, why do you keep appearing to me,   (1)
People whose cities are ruin heaps,
Who themselves are just bones?
I don't go to Cutha,[1] where ghosts congregate,
Why do you keep coming after me?   (5)
Be conjured by Abatu[2] the queen and Ereshkigal,
By Ningeshtinanna, scribe of the gods,
Whose stylus is lapis and carnelian!

Text: Campbell Thompson, CT 23 15, 13–15.
Edition: Castellino, OrNS 24 (1955), 246–247.
Literature: Borger, HKL 2 292; Bottéro, ZA 73 (1983), 157.

1. Cult city of Nergal, king of the netherworld.
2. "Destruction"(?), otherwise unknown, perhaps a mistake for Allatu (see IV.5 line 30). Ereshkigal was queen of the netherworld (see III.20).

IV.45 AGAINST "REDNESS"

This spell may refer to a disease affecting the head and scalp.

> Worm, worm!   (1)
> Red worm arose, it covered red cloud,
> Red rain arose, flooded* red earth,
> Red flood arose, filled red watercourse!
> Let a red plowman bring a red [spa]de
>   and a red carrier,   (5)
> Let him dam up the red water.
> Red door, red bolt,
> Who is the plow that will open for you?
> *Irishmara, irishmara!*[1]

Text: Köcher, BAM 480, iii 65–68.
Edition: Finkel, *Studies Borger*, 81 note 10.
Translation: Campbell Thompson, AJSL 53 (1937), 235.
Literature: Nougayrol, ArOr 17/2 (1949), 225.

1. Abracadabra words, possibly from an unknown language (see p. 43 note 5; differently Finkel, *Studies Borger*, 81); compare II.23h.

IV.46 AGAINST SCORPIONS

(a) IT IS GREEN

This brief spell, mid-second millennium or earlier in date, is accompanied by an abracadabra and brief instructions as to how to treat the affected flesh.

> It is green in the thornbush(?),
> It is silent in the sand,
> It is venomous in the brickmold!

Text: Nougayrol, RA 66 (1972), 141.
Edition: Nougayrol, RA 66 (1972), 142.

(b) WOLF OF THE STOREROOM

The god Enlil encounters a scorpion as he builds a house, and brushes it away with his little finger.

> Wolf of the storeroom, lion of the larder,   (1)
> Its pincers stick out like a wild bull's horns,
> Its tail is curved up like a mighty lion's.
> Enlil built the house.
> When he mortars the brick stack,   (5)
> When he turns over the lapis-blue brick,
> Let Enlil's little finger take (it) away!
> O waters, … let the libation bear (it) off!
> Let gentle sleep(?)[1] fall upon (this) man.

(Incantation to relieve a scorpion's sting)

Text: Gadd, CT 38 38, 59–66; Caplice, OrNS 34 (1965), pl. xvi K 5944; Maul, *Zukunftsbewältigung*, 543, RM 2, 566.
Edition: Caplice, OrNS 34 (1965), 121–122; Maul, *Zukunftsbewältigung*, 344–347.

1. Or: "hand."

IV.47 AGAINST SICKNESS AND PAIN

The magical work *Shurpu*, "Incineration," deals primarily with ways to avert the consequences of a wide range of evils, especially in cases where the source of the trouble is not known with certainty or comes from within the sufferer (see further Introduction to Chapter IV, pp. 774–775). This excerpt is from a group of short spells that use incineration of garlic, dates, matting, various wools, goat's hair, and flour as a means of symbolically burning the evil besetting a person. See also III.40.

> As this garlic is peeled off and thrown into the fire,   (1)
> (And) Girra burns it up with fire,
> Which will not be cultivated in a garden patch,
> Which will not be hard by a ditch or canal,
> Whose roots will not take hold in the ground,   (5)
> Whose sprout will not come forth nor see the sun,
> Which will not be used for the repast of god or king,
> (So) may the curse, something evil, revenge, interrogation,
> The sickness of my suffering, wrong-doing,
>   crime, misdeed, sin,
> The sickness that is in my body, flesh, and sinews   (10)
> Be peeled off like this garlic,
> May Girra burn it with fire this day,
> May the wicked thing go forth, that I may see light.

Text: Pinches, IV R² 7–8, i 51–ii 7.
Edition: Reiner, *Šurpu*, 31 lines 60–72.
Translation: Farber, TUAT II/2, 265–267.

IV.48 AGAINST TOOTHACHE

This incantation tells how toothache found its place in the world.

After Anu created heaven,	(1)
Heaven created earth,	
Earth created rivers,	
Rivers created watercourses,	
Watercourses created marshland,	(5)
Marshland created the worm.	
The worm came crying before Shamash,	
Before Ea his tears flowed down,	
"What will you give me, that I may eat?	
"What will you give me, that I may suck?"	(10)
"I will give you a ripe fig and an apple."	
"What are a ripe fig and an apple to me?	
"Set me to dwell between teeth and jaw,	
"That I may suck the blood of the jaw,	
"That I may chew on the bits (of food) stuck in the jaw."	(15)

(Insert the peg, take hold of the 'foot')[1]

Because you said this, worm,
May Ea strike you with the might of his hand!

Text: Campbell Thompson, CT 17 50; cf. AMT 25/1 1–7 = BAM 538 iv; 25/2 15–28.
Edition: Dietrich, *Studies Cagni*, 209–220.
Translation: Campbell Thompson, *Proceedings of the Royal Society of Medicine* 19 (1925/6), *Historical Section*, 59–60; Speiser, ANET[3], 100–101; Heidel, *Babylonian Genesis*[2], 72–73; Thureau-Dangin, RA 36 (1939), 3–4; Hecker, TUAT III/4, 603–604.
Literature: See Borger, HKL 1, 547.

---

1. Instructions to the dentist. It is not clear if the "foot" refers to the root of the tooth or a supposed 'foot' of the worm.

IV.49 AGAINST WITCHCRAFT

The magical work *Maqlû*, "Burning," consists of nine large tablets of incantations, prayers, and rituals, mostly to be used against witchcraft (see further Introduction to Chapter IV, pp. 774–775).

(a) MY MAGIC WORKS

The magician calls upon the netherworld to enforce its curse on the sorceresses, asking that no one allow them opportunity to work their black magic.

> Netherworld, Netherworld, O Netherworld!   (1)
> Gilgamesh[1] is master of your curse,
> Whatever you have worked, I know it,
> Whatever I shall work, you know it not,
> Whatever my sorceresses will work,   (5)
> Must have no (god) to disregard, loosen, or set it free!

Text: Pinches, IV R² 49, 37–40; Tallqvist, *Maqlû* I, 37–41; Finkelstein, STT 78, 37–42.

Edition: Meier, *Maqlû*, 8 lines 37–41.

Literature: Abusch in J. Collins, M. Fishbane, eds., *Death, Ecstasy, and Other Worldly Journeys* (New York, 1995), 19.

(b) BLOCKADING

The magician cuts off all alien magic to ensure the efficacy of his alone.

> I blocked the ford, I have blocked the quay,   (1)
> I blocked the machination of all lands.
> Anu and Antu send me,
> Whom shall I send to Belet-seri (saying),
> "Put muzzles on the mouth of my sorcerer and sorceress,   (5)
> "Place the sealing★ of Marduk, sage of the gods!"[2]
> Let them call to you—you, (Belet-seri), shall not answer them.
> Let them speak to you, you shall not listen to them.

1. Here a god of the netherworld.
2. See p. 418 note 2.

Let me call upon you, answer me!
Let me speak to you, listen to me!   (10)
(This is) according to the command spoken by Anu,
      Antu, and Belet-seri.

Text: Pinches, IV R² 49, 48–58 = Tallqvist, *Maqlû* I, 50–60; Finkelstein, STT 78, 50–60.
Edition: Meier, *Maqlû*, 9 lines 50–60.
Literature: Farber, JNES 49 (1990), 320–321; Abusch in J. Collins, M. Fishbane, eds., *Death, Ecstasy, and Other Worldly Journeys* (New York, 1995), 23.
Notes to Text: (6) with Abusch, *loc. cit.*

(c) THEY ARE WORKING AGAINST ME

They worked and keep on working against me,   (1)
To roll me up like a mat,
To clamp down on me like a bird trap,
To wreck me like an embankment,
To close over me like a net,
To cord me like cordage,   (5)
To climb over me like a rampart,
To fill a foundation ditch with me,
      as if (I were) ditchwater,
To pitch me out at the door like sweepings!
I, by command of Marduk, lord of the evening (rites),
And Asalluhi, lord of exorcism,   (10)
Roll up my sorcerer and my sorceress like a mat,
Clamp down on them like a bird trap,
Wreck them like an embankment,
Close over them like a net,
Cord them like cordage,   (15)
Climb over them like a rampart,
Fill a foundation ditch with them, as if (they were) ditch water,
Pitch them out at the door like sweepings.
[May] the figurines of my sorcerer and my sorceress
      tu[rn to ashes?]!

Text: Tallqvist, *Maqlû* II, 148–168.
Edition: Meier, *Maqlû*, 19 lines 160–180.

(d) THE FOOTPAD

The sorceress, she who walks about the streets,   (1)
Who intrudes in houses,
Who prowls in alleys,
Who lurks in the square,
She keeps turning around in front and behind,   (5)
She stands in the street and turns foot(ways) around,
She has blocked passage on the square.
She robbed the fine young man of his vigor,
She took away the attractiveness of the fine young woman,
With her malignant stare she took away her charms,   (10)
She looked at the young man and took away his vigor,
She looked at the young woman
        and took away her attractiveness!
The sorceress saw me, she came up behind me,
She has blocked passage with her poison,
She cut off progress with her spell.   (15)
She drove away my (personal) god
        and my (personal) goddess away from my person!
I have pinched off my sorceress's clay from potter's clay,
I have fashioned a figurine of the woman who bewitched me.
I put tallow in your insides, it harms you!
I implant an ashwood stick in the small of your back
        to burn you!   (20)
The ashwood that burns you, may it cut off your poison![1]
I have kindled a fire above the city,
I have thrown ashes below the city,
I have cast fire toward the house you enter!
(For) what you have done, may Fire[2] consume you,   (25)
(For) what you worked, may Fire overcome you,
(For) what you plotted, may Fire kill you,
(For) what you conspired, may Fire burn you up!
May Fire, who harms you, send you on the road of no return,
May furious Girra burn your body!   (30)

1. Variant: "speech."
2. Girra, the fire god; see III.40.

Text: Tallqvist, *Maqlû* III, 1–30; Finkelstein, STT 82, 15–30; von Weiher, SBTU III 74A, i 1–32; 74B, i 1–11.
Edition: Meier, *Maqlû*, 22–23, lines 1–30; von Weiher, SBTU III, 76.
Literature: Meier, AfO 21 (1966), 74.

IV.50 LOVE CHARMS

For other love charms, see I.4c and II.26. For discussion, see R. D. Biggs, "ŠÀ.ZI.GA and the Babylonian Sexual Potency Texts," CRRAI 47 (2001), 71–78.

(a) THE HARPSTRING

Wind blow, orchard shake,	(1)
Clouds gather, droplets fall!	
Let my potency be (steady as) running river water,	
Let my penis be a (taut) harpstring,	
Let it not slip out of her!	(5)

Text: Ebeling-Köcher-Rost, LKA 95, rev. 6–11; 101, rev.(!) 12–15; Gurney, STT 280, iv 37–41. *Edition*: Biggs, ŠÀ.ZI.GA, 35.

(b) GET UP!

The magician takes control of the woman. Her clothes are to turn into an impromptu bower, her bed a covered spot for a tryst, and, if she is asleep when the spell is wrought, her own couch will unceremoniously awaken her to send her off to the embrace of her admirer.

I have seized you, I have seized you, I will not let you free!	(1)
As pitch holds fast to boat,	
As Sin to Ur, as Shamash to Larsa,	
As Ishtar to Ekur hold fast,[1]	
I have seized you and I will not let you free!	(5)
May the clothes you are wearing be your bower(?),	
May the bed you sleep on be a tent(?),	
May the bed dump you on the ground!	
May the [grou]nd say to you "Get up!"	
[At the com]mand spoken by the Capable Lady, Ishtar.	(10)

1. Ur was the sacred city of Sin, the moon-god, and Larsa the sacred city of Shamash, the sun-god, but the connection of Ishtar with a temple called Ekur is unknown.

Text: Ebeling, KAR 69, rev. 10–22.
Edition: Biggs, *ŚÀ.ZI.GA*, 77–78.

(c) I HAVE MADE A BED

Potency, potency! A bed for potency,   (1)
Such as Ishtar made for Dumuzi,
Nanay made for her lover,
Ishara made for her mate(?),[1]
I have made for my lover![2]   (5)
Let the flesh of so-and-so, son of so-and-so, tingle,
Let his penis stand erect!
May his ardor[3] not flag, night or day!
By command of the Capable Lady, Ishtar, Nanay,
    Gazbaba, Ishara.[4]

Text: Gurney, STT 280, ii 10–17; von Weiher, SBTU IV 135, obv. ii 4–11.
Edition: Biggs, *ŚÀ.ZI.GA*, 44–45; von Weiher, SBTU IV, 46–47.

1. Variant: "Almanu" (name of a god?).
2. Variant omits; variant leaves spaces for the name of the lover.
3. Variant: "May his penis not relax."
4. Love goddesses. See II.1, 2, and p. 238 note 5. Variant adds: Kanishurra.

(d) MAY I NOT MISS MY PREY!

Wind come, mountains [quak]e,   (1)
Clouds gather, droplets fall!
Let the (penis of the) ass become stiff,
        let him mount the jenny,
Let the he-goat have an erection,
        let him mount the she-goat ... time after time.
At the head of my bed a he-goat is tied,[1]   (5)
At the foot of my bed a ram is tied.
You at the head of my bed, have an erection,
        make love to me!
You at the foot of my bed, have an erection, caress me!
My vagina is a bitch's vagina, his penis is a dog's penis.
As the bitch's vagina holds tight the dog's penis,   (10)
So may my vagina hold tight his penis!
May your penis grow long as a warclub!
I'm sitting in a web of seduction,
May I not miss my prey!

Text: Ebeling, KAR 70, rev. 10–21; 236, obv. 1–13; 243, obv.! 1–10.
Edition: Biggs, ŠÀ.ZI.GA, 32–35.
Translation: Farber, TUAT II/2, 273–274.

1. Variant has here and in following lines "I have tied ..."

IV.51 FOR ABSOLUTION

Disease and suffering were often treated as consequences of sin or wrong-doing. These spells belong to a collection that seeks release or absolution from illness or other affliction.

(a) THE BRAZIER

I am the master exorcist, I have lit a fire,   (1)
I have set up a brazier,
    I have burned the absolving materials.
I am washed and pure, the clean (agent) of Ea,
    messenger of Asalluhi.
May all the gods I invoked bring about absolution,
By command of Ea and Asalluhi,
    may neither god nor goddess be angry.   (5)

I have damped [the brazier] I lit,
    I have put out the fire I kindled,
I have smothered the grain I poured (into the fire).
May the grain-goddess, who absolves god and man,
    loose his (the patient's) bond.
Just as I damped the brazier I lit,
Just as I put out the fire I kindled,   (10)
Just as I smothered the grain I poured (into the fire),
May the grain-goddess, who absolves god and man,
    loose his bond,
May the disease, the curse of so-and-so,
    son of so-and-so, be released
    and absolution brought about!

Text: Norris, II R 51 no. 1 (+), improved copy by Jensen in *Zeitschrift für Keilschriftforschung* 2 (1885), 320–321.
Edition: Reiner, JNES 15 (1956), 138–139, lines 109–121.

(b) MAY MY SIN RISE UP TO THE SKY!

May my sin [rise up to the sky like smoke],   (1)
May my sin [run off from my body like water],
May my sin, l[ike a drifting cloud,
    make rain in another field],
May my sin [burn out like a flame],
May my sin [flicker out like a flickering flame],   (5)
May my sin [be peeled off like an onion(skin)],
[May my sin be stripped off like a date(skin)],
[May my sin be unraveled like a mat],
[May my sin, like a shattered potter's vessel,
    not return where it was],
May my sin [be shattered like a potsherd],   (10)
May my sin, like silver and gold brought from [its] mine,
    [not return where it was],
May my sin, like … iron,[1] [not return where it was],
May my sin, like sweet waters of a river,
    [not return where it was],
May my sin, like an uprooted tamarisk,
    [not return where it was],[2]
May a bird take my sin up to the sky,   (15)
[May] a fish [take] my sin [down] to the de[pths]!

Text: Reiner, JNES 15 (1956), 140 K 3059+ (transliteration only); Ebeling, KAR 295 "2.Seite" +408+409; Ebeling-Köcher-Rost, LKA 29, i "Rs.", 148 obv. (= "2.S."); 149 obv. (= "2.S.").
Edition: Reiner, JNES 15 (1956), 140–141, lines 7′–22′.

1. Reiner suggests "meteoric(?)"; J. Bjorkman, *Meteoritics* 1973/8 = Center for Meteoritic Studies, Arizona State University, *Publication* 12, 113 suggests "smelted iron."
2. See III.37d line 32.

IV.52 FOR A RULER'S FAVOR

(a) I AM PROUD

Various spells and rituals were compiled for the use of people about to go to the law court or government buildings. These call for strength, dignity, and protection. IV.33a, b also belong to this group. Others hope to make a person in authority glad to see the speaker.

> I rub on oil for dignity, (1)
> My hands are full of oil for control.*
> I am proud before god, king, lord, prince, great men,
> My lord's face will show (enough) favor for seven maidens!

Text: Ebeling, KAR 237, 13–15.
Edition: Ebeling, MAOG 5/3 (1931), 37, 40.
Notes to Text: (2) Variant unclear.

(b) I'VE PUT MY SHOES ON MY FEET

This spell is to be said three times over a person's shoes when he puts them on, so that, wherever he goes, people will be glad to see him.

> I've put my shoes on my feet. (1)
> I've taken my place before you.
> My laughter is the flowering of my features,
> The winsome charm of my eyes.
> I'm a treat,[1] whatever I say to you will be amusing.*

Text: von Weiher, SBTU II 24, 36–40.
Edition: von Weiher, SBTU II, 127f., lines 36–40.
Notes to Text: (5) Variant unclear.

---

1. Text: "I am a festival," meaning a delight for the person who encounters the speaker.

IV.53 FOR A WOMAN IN LABOR

Numerous Sumerian and Akkadian incantations and rituals were intended for help in pregnancy and delivery.[1] See also II.20.

(a) THE BABY IS STUCK!

The woman in labor is having a difficult labor,	(1)
Her labor is difficult, the baby is stuck,	
The baby is stuck!	
The doorbolt is locked, about to end life,	
The door is fastened against the suckling kid, ...	(5)
The woman giving birth is covered with death's dust,	
She is covered with the dust of battle, like a chariot,	
She is covered with the dust of tuffets, like a plow.	
She sprawls in her own blood, like a struggling warrior,	
Her eyesight is waning, she cannot see,	(10)
Her lips are coated, she cannot open them ...,	
Her eyesight is dim, ... she is alarmed, her ears cannot hear!	
Her breast is not held in, her headbands are askew,	
She is not veiled with ..., she has no shame:	
Stand by me and keep calling out(?), O merciful Marduk,	(15)
"Here is the confusion, I'm surrounded, get to me!"[2]	
Bring out the one sealed up, created by the gods,	
Created by humankind, let him come out and see the light!	

Text: W. G. Lambert, *Iraq* 31 (1969), pl. VI.
Edition: W. G. Lambert, *Iraq* 31 (1969), 31 lines 33–50.

---

1. See, for example, N. Veldhuis, "The New Assyrian Compendium for a Woman in Childbirth," ASJ 11 (1989), 239–260, and the study of Stol, *Birth in Babylonia*.
2. This line is evidently spoken by the baby; see W. G. Lambert, *Iraq* 31 (1969), 36; Finkel, AfO 27 (1980), 45. Line 15 is evidently spoken by the midwife.

(b) SIN AND THE COW

The story of Sin, the moon-god, and the cow, exists in several widely varying versions from the mid-second millennium on. Only the most important variants have been noted here; for a full study, see Röllig's edition listed below and N. Veldhuis, *A Cow of Sin* (Groningen, 1991). Compare also II.20a.

There was once a moon-cow named Geme-Sin, (1)
Perfect in form, beautiful in limb.
When Sin saw her he fell in love with her,
He set the glory of moonlight ... upon her,[1]
He set her at the front of the herd, (5)
The cattle came after her.
He pastured her in moist grass,
He would let her drink in a meadow
      wherein was a watering place.
Out of sight of the cowherd, the herdsman not seeing,
A fierce young bull mounted her, raised her tail(?),* (10)
When her days were ended, her months fulfilled,
The cow knelt down, the cow went into labor.
Her cowherd's face was downcast,
All the herdboys with him felt distress for her.
The herdboys comforted her. (15)
At her shrieks of anguish, her cries in labor,
The radiant one was desperate,
The moon in heaven heard her cries, he raised his hand.
Two daughters of Anu[2] came down from heaven.
One brought a jar of oil,
The other brought water of labor. (20)
She rubbed oil from the jar on her brow,
She sprinkled her whole body with water of labor.
A second time she rubbed oil from the jar on her brow,
She sprinkled her whole body with water of labor.
A third time, as she rubbed oil from the jar on her brow, (25)
As she sprinkled the front of her body,
The calf fell like a (running) gazelle to the ground.

---

1. Line corrupt.
2. Variant: "Two protective spirits."

She called the calf's name "Suckling Calf."
Just as Geme-Sin, the moon-cow, gave birth successfully,
(So) let th(is) young woman who is having difficult labor
    give birth,   (30)
Let th(is) woman with child give birth successfully.[1]

Text: Köcher, BAM 248, iii 10–35; Campbell Thompson, AMT 67/1, iii 1–25; W. G. Lambert, AS
    16 (1965), 287–288 obv. 20–36; *Iraq* 31 (1969), pl. VI, 51–62.
Edition: Röllig, OrNS 54 (1985), 260–273.
Translation: Farber, TUAT II/2, 274–276 (whence readings used here).
★*Notes to Text*: (10) Farber, TUAT II/2, 275.

(c) RUN HITHER TO ME!

This little spell addresses the baby about to be born.

Run hither to me like a gazelle,
Slip out to me like a little snake!
I, Asalluhi, am the midwife,
I will receive you!

Text: Köcher, BAM 248, iv 2–3.
Edition: Ebeling, *Archiv für Geschichte der Medizin* 14 (1923), 72–73.

1. Variant adds: "Let her midwife not be hindered."

(d) THE BOAT

The mother having a difficult birth tosses like a ship in a storm.

(beginning fragmentary)

May her taut mooring rope be slackened,	(1′)
And her battened hatch be opened,	
The mooring rope of the boat for the quay of well-being,	
The mooring rope of the barge for the quay of health.	
May the limbs be relaxed, the sinews loosen,	(5′)
May sealed wombs relax, may the creature come forth,	
The separate framework, the human form,	
May it come forth soon and see the sunlight!	
Like rainfall, may it not turn back,	
Like one fallen from a wall, may it not return,	(10′)
Like an overflowing trough, may its waters not stay behind.	

(Asalluhi carries out the spell.)

Text: Köcher, BAM 248, ii 49–59.
Edition: Ebeling, *Archiv für Geschichte der Medizin* 14 (1923), 68–69.

IV.54 TO CALM A BABY

Those plagued by the crying of babies had various magic speeches to deal with the problem; compare also above, II.20c and the study by W. Farber, "Magic and the Cradle, Babylonian and Assyrian Lullabies," *Anthropos* 8 (1990), 139–148.

(a) BE PLACID AS A POND

For the simile, compare III.27, line 96.

> [Baby, who has aggravated his father], (1)
> [Who has brought tears to his mother's eyes],
> [At whose uproar, at the clamor of whose crying],
> The hairy hero-men were frightened,
> Ishtar got no sleep in her bedchamber,
> May sweet sleep bring you to rest!
> May sleep, life, and release (from care) befall you! (5)
> Burp like a drunkard, wheeze(?) like a barmaid's boy![1]
> Till your mother comes, touches you, and takes you up,
> Be placid as a pond,
> Be still as a pool!
> May sleep befall you, like an oxherd in repose. (10)
> Listen to me, child, you infant,
> You should be asleep, he who sleeps is released (from care).
>
> (The spell is not mine,
>   it is a spell of Ningir[imma, mistress of spells],
> A spell of Gula, mistress of healing,
> A spell of Ea and Asalluhi, may it work for you!)

Text: Craig, ABRT 2, 8 rev. 1–13 = Farber, *Baby-Beschwörungen*, pl. 7; Campbell Thompson, CT 51 193.
Edition: Farber, *Baby-Beschwörungen*, 84–89.

1. See II.320c, p. 172 note 3.

(b) BE STILL AS SWAMP WATER

Dwel[ler] in darkness, who had not seen the sunrise,
You've come out, [you've seen the sunlight].
Be still as swamp [water],
Sleep like a ba[by gazelle].[1]
Like a boundary stone (protected by) the gods,
May there be no one to disturb you!

Text: Hussey-van Dijk, YOS 11 96, 19–22.
Edition: Farber, *Baby-Beschwörungen*, 96 section 30.

---

1. Perhaps proverbial, like Italian *come un ghiro*, or perhaps a misunderstanding of *sabītu* "barmaid" (see II.20c). Babies coming speedily from the womb are also compared to gazelles; see IV.53c.

(c) LET MOTHER GET HER CHORES DONE

This spell was to be recited three times with a piece of bread set by the baby's head. Then the child was to be rubbed all over with the bread and the bread thrown to a dog. After this, the child was supposed to fall silent.

The one who dwelt in darkness, where no light shone,   (1)
He has come out and has seen sunlight.
Why does he scream till his mother sobs,
Till, in heaven, Antu herself's in tears?

"Who is this, that makes such a racket on earth?   (5)
"If it's a dog, someone give it some food!
"If it's a bird, someone fling a clod at it!
"If it's a human child that's angry,
"Someone cast the spell of Anu and Antu over him!
"Let his father lie down to get the rest of his sleep,   (10)
"Let his mother, who has her chores to do,
        get her chores done."

(The spell is not mine, it is a spell of Ea and Asalluhi,
A spell of Damu and Gula, a spell of Ningirimma, master [of spells].
They said it to me, I repeated it.)

Text: Ebeling, KAR 114, 1–15; Ebeling-Köcher-Rost, LKA 143, 1–15 = Farber, *Baby-Beschwörun-gen*, pl. 11.
Edition: Farber, *Baby-Beschwörungen*, 98–100.

IV.55 TO RECAPTURE A RUNAWAY SLAVE

O door of the bedroom, you who are so firm,
I have firmed up your support with oil and wine.
Just as you swing out from your position,
But tu[rn back] the other way to where you were,
(So) may so-and-so, a runaway slave, swing out
But turn back the other way to his master's house,
By command of Ea, Shamash, and Marduk.

Text: Ebeling-Köcher-Rost, LKA 135, obv. 11–17.
Edition: Ebeling, OrNS 23 (1954), 52–56.
Literature: Hurowitz, *Proceedings of the American Academy for Jewish Research* 58 (1992), 68–74.

IV.56 TO SECURE BRISK TRADE AT A TAVERN

Taverns, besides providing strong drink, could evidently serve as brothels as well. This incantation is part of a ritual designed to enliven traffic in such an establishment. For Ishtar and strong drink, compare III.26 iv 66. For taverns, especially in earlier periods, see H. Neumann in L. Milano, ed., *Drinking in Ancient Societies, History and Culture of Drinks in the Ancient Near East* (Padua, 1994), 326 note 46.

> O Ishtar of the lands, most valorous of goddesses,
> > this is your bower, rejoice and be glad! (1)
> Come, enter our house!
> Let your sweet bedmate enter with you,
> May your lover and boyfriend [enter] with you.
> May my lips be white honey, may my hands be charm,
> May the lips, my labia(?), be lips of honey! (5)
> As birds flutter around a serpent coming out of his hole,
> > so may these people fight over me!
> Seize him, bring him here, make him feel at home,
> > in the bower of Ishtar, the chamber of Ninlil,
> > the herds(?) of Ningizzida.
> May the far-off come around, may the angry come back,
> > may his heart come back to me as if (to) gold.[1]
> Just as when rain has fecundated the earth,
> > plants become plentiful,
> So too may there be many a basket
> > of (sprouting) malt[2] for me! (10)

Text: Ebeling, KAR 144, rev. 1–8; F. Lenormant, *Choix de Textes Cunéiformes ...* (Paris, 1873), no. 99 = Boissier, PSBA 23 (1901), 120–121 obv. 16 – rev. 12.
Edition: Zimmern, ZA 32 (1918), 174–175; Ebeling, RA 49 (1955), 182–183.
Translation: Caplice, SANE 1/1 (1974), 23–24; Farber, TUAT II/2, 280.
Literature: W. Farber, "Associative Magic: Some Rituals, Word Plays, and Philology," JAOS 106 (1986), 447–449.

1. Caplice (SANE 1/1, 24 note 6) suggests "like smoke."
2. This may refer to a "bumper crop" of excited customers; differently Farber (JAOS 106 [1986], 449), who proposes that a double entendre suggesting "proposition" is meant.

I. LETTERS AND MISCELLANEOUS

IV.57 WHEN OLD MEN DANCE

Adad-shuma-usur was a prominent scholar of the time of Esarhaddon and Assurbanipal. His letters to his royal patrons are remarkable for their elaborate rhetoric. In this letter, addressed to Assurbanipal, he pleads that a post be given to his son, Urad-Gula. This petition was unsuccessful, for Urad-Gula had offended Assurbanipal as crown prince. No plea could move him, so Urad-Gula languished in poverty and unemployment after Assurbanipal's accession. For the possibility that this family had some connection with the compostion of the "Netherworld Vision," see IV.5. For the life of Urad-Gula, see the study by Parpola cited IV.5.

(§1) To the king [my] lord, (from) your servant Adad-shuma-[usur]: May it be well with the king [my lord], may Nabu and Marduk bestow ever so many blessings upon the king [my lord]. Assu[r, king of the gods], nominated the [king] my lord for the kingship of the land of Assyria, Adad and Shamash have confirmed to the king my lord, through their truthful extispicy, the kingship of all lands.

(§2) The reign is propitious, truthful the days, the years are of justice. Rainfall is plentiful, spring floods surging, the economy is excellent. The gods are well disposed, there is much reverence for the divine, temples are prosperous, the great gods of heaven and netherworld have been prayed to in the time of the king my lord. Old men dance, young men sing, women and girls are happy and joyful, women are being married and rings set upon them, they bear boys and girls, the newborn thrive.

(§3) The king my lord has given a new life to the malefactor (and) the man condemned to death, you have released the man imprisoned [for year]s, the man sick for many days has revived. The hungry are filled, the parched anointed, the naked clothed in a garment.

(§4) Why should I and Urad-Gula, in the midst of them, be glum and downcast? Now the king my lord has displayed his love for Nineveh to the people, (saying) to the principal citizens, "Bring me your sons, let them be in my service." Urad-Gula is my son, he too should be with them in the service of the king my lord. We too should be joyful and dance along with the people (and) bless the king my lord.

(§5) My eyes dwell upon the king my lord. Of all those who serve in the palace, no one cares about me, there is no one of goodwill to me to whom I could give a present, (who) would accept it (and) take my part.

(§6) May the king my lord take pity upon his servant! Among all (those) people, may I not per[ish]. May my ill-wishers not have what they wish for!

Text: Harper, ABL 2.

Edition: Parpola, LAS 121; SAA 10 226.

Literature: K. Deller, "Die Briefe des Adad-šuma-uṣur," AOAT 1 (1969), 45–64; F. M. Fales, "L''Ideologico' Adad-šuma-uṣur," *Rendiconti della Classe di Scienze morali, storiche e filologiche, Accademia Nazionale dei Lincei*, ser. viii vol. xxix, 453–490.

IV.58 THE GILGAMESH LETTER

Assyrian school exercises from Sultantepe preserve three copies of a fictional letter from Gilgamesh to a foreign king, in which he makes gargantuan demands for goods and services. While there are obvious allusions to the epic of Gilgamesh here, one may wonder if a parody on the Assyrian royal style is intended (compare, for example, the penultimate paragraph to the Hunter [III.6]).

Whereas the "Sargon Letter" (II.6b) is the closest literary parallel, other texts with presumably fantastic figures and commodities may be compared to this one; see Foster, ArOr 50 (1982), 238–241; Wiseman, BSOAS 30 (1967), 495–504.

Say to Ti[ ], king of [ ]ranunna, thus says [Gilgamesh,   k]ing of Ur, the Kullabian, created by Anu, [Enlil], and Ea, favorite of Shamash, beloved of Marduk, who rules all lands from the horizon to the zenith like a cord [ ], (5) whose feet daised monarchs kiss, the king who has put all lands, from sunrise to sunset, under control,* as with a cord, this [according to the com]mand* of Enlil-of-Victory:

[I have formed up] and sent you 600 work-troops. I wrote to you concerning the great [blocks] of obsidian and lapis, overlaid with finest gold, to attach to (10) the [stat]ue* of my friend, Enkidu, but you said, "There are none."

Now I write once again! As soon as you see this letter, [make re]ady* and go to the land of Erish, take with you a caravan* of horses, send ahead of you(?) [ ] vicious dogs that attack like lions, [ ] white horses with black stripes, (15) 70,000 black horses with white stripes, 100,000 mares whose bodies have markings like wild tree roots, 40,000 continually gambolling miniature calves, 50,000 teams of dappled mules, 50,000 fine calves with well-turned hooves and horns intact, (20) 20,000 jars of pitch(?), 30,000 jars of ghee, 80,000 jugs of wine, 80,000 bundles of crocuses, 90,000 great tabletops of dark rosewood, 100,000 donkeys laden with cedar* and juniper, and then come yourself.

I want to fasten* one nugget of red gold, it should weigh 30 minas, to the chest of my friend Enkidu. I want to fashion [ ] thousand ...-stones, jasper(?)-stones, lapis, every sort of exotic stone into a necklace for him.

40,000 (ingots) of unalloyed(?)★ white tin for the treasury★ of the great lord Marduk, (25) 90,000 talents of iron: pure, excellent, choice, select, scrutinized, precious, first-rate, beaten, flawless, so the smith can make stags.

120,000 talents of pure, good [copper?], with all the goods required,★ the smith will do work for the temple.

A new chest,¹ unique, something precious, exotic, such as I have never seen. Look for myriad troops [to bri]ng them,★ ready or not(?),²★ and gather them together. (30) Fill big new barges(?)★ with silver and gold and float them down to the Euphrates with the silver and gold. You should send(?) them to the port of Babylon so I can see for myself and be struck dumb with awe.

If I don't meet you in the gate of my city Ur on the fifteenth day of the month Tashritu, then I swear by the great gods, whose oath cannot be done away with, and I swear by my gods Lugalbanda, Sin, Shamash, Palil, Lugalgirra, Meslamtaea, (35) Zababa, and (my personal?) god that I will send my lord "Attacker-in-My-Vanguard"(?), whose fame you always hear about, and he will wreck your cities, loot your palaces, uproot your orchards, and put wickets(?) in your canal mouths. I(?) will enter the ... of your fortified cities, who ... and speak of its ..., and I, Gilgamesh, will occupy them. None of this will be my fault.

[I will   ] your servants, your gener[al], your craftsmen(?), your children, your belongings, and your offspring (40) [   ] in the gate of Ur. I will bring you and your family(?) into the smithy to ... talents of copper for twelve ... I will write an inscription. I will set you up with the (statues of) protective spirits in the thoroughfare,★ [the citizens] of Ur will lord it over (you) as they go by.³

Quickly send me an an[swer to my letter]★ and come, you will not have to bear anything from me.

Letter of Gilgamesh, the mighty king, who has no rival.

---

1. Perhaps a coffin for Enkidu.
2. Unknown expression: "full or empty," here taken to refer to the preparedness of the addressee (having eaten or not).
3. It is not clear if this passage describes a reward for cooperation, in which case these are commemorative statues (compare II.6a line 37), or a punishment (compare IV.14 iii).

Text: Gurney, STT 40–42.

Edition: Gurney, AnSt 7 (1957), 127–135; AnSt 8 (1958), 245.

Translation: R. J. Tournay, A. Shaffer, *L'Épopée de Gilgamesh* (Paris, 1994), 276–281.

Literature: F. R. Kraus, "Der Brief des Gilgameš," AnSt 30 (1980), 109–121; B. R. Foster, "A Post-script to the Gilgamesh Letter," AnSt 32 (1982), 43–44; D'Agostino, *Testi umoristici*, 50–58.

★*Notes to Text*: (6) Tournay-Shaffer, 276 note 2. (7) Kraus, "Brief," 110 note 10. (10) Tournay-Shaffer, 276 note 5. (12) Kraus, "Brief," 110 notes 15, 16. (22–27) Kraus, "Brief," 111 note 30; Tournay-Shaffer, 278 *ad loc.* (28) Kraus, "Brief," 112 note 33. (29) Kraus, "Brief," 112 note 35. (30) Kraus, "Brief," 112 note 36. (42) Kraus, "Brief," 113 note 48. (44) Kraus, "Brief," 113 note 50.

IV.59 THE MAN WHO WOULD BE KING

Two Assyrian compositions preserve scurrilous invective against a certain Bel-etir. The first is cast as a fictitious stela on the model of the Cuthaean Legend of Naram-Sin (III.7b), which it quotes or alludes to in several passages (lines 1–3, 21–22. Unfortunately what remains of the main narrative is too broken for translation, but the beginning and end are clearly a parody of the Legend. The second is a parody of an incantation (see II.25g) abusing the same man, whose identity and crimes are unclear, but who apparently set himself up as a king somewhere and thereby incurred Assyrian wrath.

(a) OPEN THE TABLET BOX

Open the tablet box and re[ad] well the stela (1)
[That] Bel-etir,[1] son of Iba, [left behind him], like a dog!
When Salla had not yet passed away, he, an underling,
    whom the king knew naught of,
He, a lackey in attendance upon Shamash-ibni,
    son of a vile fisherman, [unwor]thy of kingship,
That shit bucket Zeru-kinu, that windbag,
    that catamite sidekick of Nummuraya, (5)
[Damned if he] didn't inscribe these words:
"In the land of Assyria and Babylonia I have none to rival me!"
This too: "Ms. Kissed has praised me,
    where is my equal in all the world?"

(fragmentary lines)

[   ] she talked frivolities to him, saying:
"Who has taken away baby Bibi,[2] who has clouded over
    your radiant countenance?"
Later, to make him cleaner than he had been,
    she called his name "Raging Pazuzu, son of Hanbu."[3] (20)
In the face of this, humanity bowed prayerfully, saying,
"This is right conduct and reverence!"

---

1. Written EN.KAR, perhaps a joke on the name Enmerkar (see III.7b).
2. Bibi may be an affectionate form of the name Bel-etir (see IV.59b line 5) or for Iba.
3. This means that he was particularly hideous and malignant; see IV.40e.

"This is the stela which the whore set up for the son
    of Iba, the fart factory,
(blank space ...) she left for the future."[1]   (25)
In the whole of it, in the essence of it,
    there is [.] for the future:
He praised himself, like a nitwit, a bungler,
[Bawling] countless obscenities about himself
    from his own imagination.
He made his own declaration, he did his own praising,
    he did his own talking, he [did his own bo]asting,
He made himself a byword and an insult in common speech,   (30)
Yet this man hadn't even enough sense to think straight!

(Though no abbreviated list, this that I have written,
it is (only) a trifle [compared to the whole].)

Text: K 1351 in Livingstone, *Court Poetry*, pl. XI.
Edition: Livingstone, *Court Poetry*, 64–65.

(b) LACKEY OF A DEAD GOD

O Bel-etir, you kidnapped catamite, doubly so,
    with runny eyes, doubly so,
    with shifty eyes, doubly so,   (1)
Son of Iba, that missed period, that shit bucket of a fart factory,
Of a vile family, lackey of a dead god,
    of a house whose star has vanished from the heavens,
(And of) a slave girl, a chattel, he,
    the slave of a Syrian country girl, the (only) bearded one
    among a passle of over-fornicated women!
My little Bibi, whose obscenities are beyond count,
    A[mmanap]pu provided your whitewash, saying,   (5)
"Mr. Weakling's house is in eclipse,
    starting at the head!(?)"[2]

---

1. The blank space was presumably meant to indicate that she had left nothing for the future.
2. Obscure. I take it to mean that his household, starting with him, is in a bad way.

He swore by the Lord:
    "I won't leave until I have fornicated with him!"
Get away from anything to do with Ammanappu,
    don't chase after Tamru!
Run away from Amman-open-pants,[1]
    hold back your groin from Haimbua!
Now that I have bespoken you,
    about face(?) and come to me!"
                                         (10)

Text: Livingstone, *Court Poetry*, pl. XII 82-5-22,88.
Edition: Livingstone, *Court Poetry*, 66.

1.   Text: Ammanipte, either another person or a play on the name of Ammanappu. The identity of all these people is unknown.

IV.60 IN PRAISE OF THE SCRIBAL ART

Babylonian and Assyrian scholars of Sumerian of the Mature and Late periods
studied this bilingual praise of their chosen profession. The Sumerian text may
be an academic concoction, for it is full of obscurities and unusual wording.

The scribal art is the mother of the eloquent,
    father of the erudite, (1)
The scribal art is enjoyable,
    one can never have enough of its charms.
The scribal art is not easy to learn, but he who masters it
    will no longer be intimidated by it.
Strive after the scribal art and it will surely enrich you, (5)
Work hard at the scribal art and it will bring you wealth.
Do not be careless in the scribal art, do not neglect it,
The scribal art is the abode of beauty,
    of the secret lore of Amanki,[1]
Work ceaselessly at it and it will reveal its secret lore to you,
Do not neglect it, lest you be ill spoken of. (10)
The scribal art is a good lot, one of wealth and plenty.
When you are a youngster, you suffer,
    when you are mature, you [prosper].
The scribal art is the nexus of all [wisdom(?)],
Pour yourself into it(?) [then draw from(?)] its excellence.
To learn Sumerian is the highest learning,
    the standard(?) (form),[2] the dialect form, (15)
To write a stela, to measure a field, to balance accounts, ...,
[   ] the palace [   ],
The scribe shall be its servitor,
    he shall call others for forced labor!

1. Name for Enki in the Sumerian dialect used for cultic laments sung during the Mature and
Late periods, the performance of which was a learned and specialized accomplishment, sustained in
Babylonian temples even after the Macedonian conquest, presumably chosen here because of its
association with a recondite specialty.
2. Obscure word, perhaps referring to the form of Sumerian used in legal documents, lexical
lists, or myths, epics, and wisdom literature.

Text: de Genouillac, TCL 16 96; Gadd, BSOAS 20 (1957), 263; Gurney, JCS 24 (1972), 130–131; Poebel, PBS 5 132 (+).

Edition: Sjöberg, JCS 24 (1972), 126–131.

Translation: Römer, TUAT III/1, 46–48.

Literature: V. Hurowitz, "Literary Observations on 'In Praise of the Scribal Art'," JANES 27 (2000), 49–56.

IV.61 SEEKING OUT DUMUZI

In this lyric about Ishtar and Dumuzi, Ishtar seeks her lover in the pastureland.

Ishtar keeps seeking out Dumuzi, my shepherd,
    she seeks my shepherd! (1)
He leads his cattle, one after another,
He seeks a pasture where the grass conceals the moistest areas,
Where anemone-flowers blossom at the edge of the wood.
His eyes scan pasture and meadow,
    they seek out springs in the open country
    and the forests of the mountains. (5)
When Ishtar saw her beloved, she sought him out,
    she went out(?) to the shepherds' hut,
    she said to him,
"You there, come here, shepherd,
    let me lead our children(?) to you,
    my shepherd, herd your livestock!
"May the Assyrian(?) go up(?) to our pasture,
    for it is splendid,
"You are the one to shepherd our pastureland,
    you shall shepherd our meadowland, for it is splendid!

(rest fragmentary)

Text: Ebeling-Köcher-Rost, LKA 15 obv.
Edition: Parpola *apud* Nissinen in *Melammu Symposia* 2 (1999), 118–119.

IV.62 A LITERARY PROPHECY

Toward the end of the Late period, a style of writing variously referred to as "prophetic" or "apocalyptic" appeared, in which events of the past were narrated as if they were to take place in the future, and past or present sovereigns were predicted in vague terms. The passage chosen here "predicts" the reign of Nabonidus (see IV.11), his defeat by Cyrus of Persia, here referred to as a "king of Elam," and the wars of Alexander and his successors, here referred to as "Hanaeans" (see p. 361 note 3). It is not clear who the last king in the prophecy may have been; perhaps the prediction refers to Seleucus or Antiochus triumphing over an enemy, such as Antigonus, in which case, the era of prosperity and happiness referred to here was inaugurated by the Seleucid dynasty (compare IV. 12).

For this group of compositions, see in general W. W. Hallo, "Akkadian Apocalypses," *Israel Exploration Journal* 16 (1966), 231–242; W. G. Lambert, *The Background of Jewish Apocalyptic* (London, 1978); A. K. Grayson, "The Babylonian Origin of Apocalyptic Literature," *Atti dell'Isituto Veneto di Scienze, Lettere et Arti* 148 (1989–90), Classe di Scienze Morali, Lettere ed Arti, 203–221, and compare III.13 iii 9 and p. 24 note 1.

(fragmentary lines)

(ii 11′) A rebellious prince will arise. [He will establish(?)] a dynasty from Harran.[1] [He will rule as king] for seventeen years. He will oppress the land and [he will cancel] the festival of Esagila. [He will build] a fortress in Babylon. He will plot evil against the land of Akkad.

(ii 17′) A king of Elam will arise. [   ] the scepter. He will remove him from his throne [   ] He will seize the throne, and that king who was removed from the throne [   ]. The king of Elam will change his place of [   ] He will make him dwell in another land and [   ]. All lands [will bring him] tribute. During his reign Akkad [will not] dwell in peace.

(iii 1) [   ] kings [   ] of his father [he will reign as king] two years. A courtier [will kill(?)] that king. A certain prince [will arise]. He will attack and [will seize the thron]e. He will [reign as king] for five years. [   ] army of the Hanaeans [   ] will attack

1. City in south central Anatolia with a sanctuary to the moon-god; see IV.11g.

[   ]. His army [   ] will plunder and ro[b]. Afterward, he will regroup [his ar]my and brandish his weapons. Enlil, Shamash, and [   ] will march at the side of his ar[my]. He will cause the over-throw of the Hanaean army. He will [carry] off its massive booty [and bring] it to his palace. The people who had ex[perienced] misfortune [will enjoy] well-being. The morale of the land [   ] exemption from service [   ].

Text: Grayson, BHLT, 28–29.
Edition: Grayson, BHLT, 24–37.
Translation: Longman, *Autobiography*, 149–152, 239–240; in Hallo, ed., *Context*, 2: 481–482.

INDEX OF TEXTS
TRANSLATED

This index is keyed to Borger, HKL where possible; therefore some texts will be cited here differently from how they are cited in the translations. For abbreviations used here and not found in the List of Abbreviations, see Borger, HKL 2, xiff. and the annual abbreviation list of *Orientalia* (Rome).

AbB 5 140 II.30; AbB 13 164 II.32; ABL 2 IV.57; 37, rev. 3–6 III.16d (9); 403, obv. 4–7, 13–15 III.16d (3); 555, rev. 3–6 III.16d (4); 652, rev. 9–13 III.16d (5); 1285, rev. 11–13 III.16d (8); ABRT 1 5 IV.4f; 29–31 IV.4d; 32–34 IV.4b; 54–55 IV.2b; 60–62, obv. 12–22 III.52d; rev. 10–17 III.52e; ABRT 2 3–5 III.51f; 8, rev. 1–13 IV.54a; 13, 1–16 III.57; ACH Sin I pl. 1 III.18e; ADD 469 IV.26; AEM I/1 192 II.12a (7) 194 II.12a (8); Al-Fouadi, *Sumer* 32, plate after p. 76 I.3d; Al-Rawi, *Iraq* 56, 136 II.39; Al-Rawi, *Iraq* 60, 202f. III.32; Al-Rawi, Black, *Iraq* 51, 111ff. IV.17; Al-Rawi, Black, JCS 46, 136ff. III.17; Al-Rawi, George, *Iraq* 52, 150ff. III.17; Al-Rawi, George, *Iraq* 57, 226f. III.37c; Al-Rawi, George, *Iraq* 60, 188ff. III.14; Alster, Jeyes ASJ 8, 10f. III.60; AMT 25/1, 1–7 IV.48; 25/2, 15–28 IV.48; 67/1, iii 1–25 IV.53b; 71–72/1, obv. 27 – rev. 24 III.510; AOAT 2 no. 338 IV.4g; AOAT 34 1 III.54b; 3–7 III.47b; 14 III.43b; 18, 19 III.42b; 23 III.51l; 26–30 III.44c; 33, 34 III.36b; 35–39 III.44a; 40–46 III.44b; 54–57 III.45a; 73 III.45b; AOAT 258, pl. 3, 4 K 3333+ III.51p; pl. 3 K 3333+ obv. III.48c; pl. 11 79–7–8.77 rev. III.48c; pl. 17 K 7664+ i 40'–48' III.48a; pl. 18 K 9000 14'–16' III.48a; pl. 20 K 11706+ obv 1'–3' III.48a; AOAT 267, 192f. II.19a, b; ARET 5 1 I.2; 6 I.1; ARMT I 5, 11–13 III.16d (1); ARMT X 7 II.12a (3); 8 II.12a (4); 80 II.12a (5); 150, 9–11 II.16d (2); ARMT XIII 23 II.12a (6); Arnaud, *Emar* 767 III.60; 778 III.16b (1); 783, 784 IV.21; ASKT 7 III.50i; 9, rev. 6–29 III.40d; 11, 35–44 IV.43; As-Siwani, *Sumer* 20, 75–76 IV.11f.

Ball, PSBA 11, 159f. IV.8a; 248f. IV.8h; BAM 248, ii 49–59 IV.53d; iii 10–35 IV.53b; iv 2–3 IV.53c; 323, obv. 19–35 III.51e; 339, 33'–44' III.35; 480, iii 65–68 IV.45; 510, iv 5–21 IV.37e; iv 34–39 IV.37f; iv 41–45 IV.37d; 513, iv 11–31 IV.37e; 514, iii 13'–18' IV.37b; iii 22'–26' IV.37c; iv 10–26 IV.37e; 538 iv IV.48; 574, iii 56–64 IV.49; 578, ii 45–49 IV.34; BBR, pl. LXII no. 75, 5–10 IV.52a; pl. LXIII no. 75, 56–61 III.52b; rev. 69–74 III.52c; BE 1 84 IV.7a; 85 IV.8b; BE 5 1 IV.36b (1); Beckman, Foster, ASJ 18, 21 II.24; Bertin, RA 1, 157ff. III.51q; Bezold, PSBA 10, pl. after p. 418 III.18c; PSBA 11, pl. IV, ii 35–40 IV.11b; ZA 1, 39ff. IV.8h; For El-Amarna, see Knudtzon; BHLT, 28–29 IV.62; Biggs, ŠÀ.ZI.GA, 28 III.43c; 32ff. IV.45d; 35 IV.45a; 44f. IV.45c; 77f. IV.45b; BIN 2 33 III.10a; 72 II.21a; BIN 4 126 I.7; Black, JAOS 103, 26f. II.19c; BMS 1, 1–27 III.54b; 1, 29–35 III.43b; 2, 11–41 III.47b; 3, 10–16 III.47b; 5, 11–19 III.43b; 6, 1–16 III.34; 6, 71–94 III.42b; 6, 97–130 III.51l; 7, 9'–33' III.42b; 8, 1–19 III.43b; 9, obv. III.44c; 10, 1–5 III.36b; 10, 7–25 III.51l;

ABBREVIATIONS

AASH	*Acta Antiqua Academiae Scientiarum Hungaricae* (Budapest)
AbB	F. R. Kraus, ed., *Altbabylonische Briefe in Umschrift und Übersetzung* (Leiden, 1964–)
ABL	R. F. Harper, *Assyrian and Babylonian Letters belonging to the Kouyunjik Collection of the British Museum* (London & Chicago, 1892–1914)
ABRT	J. A. Craig, *Assyrian and Babylonian Religious Texts*, 1 (Leipzig, 1895), 2 (Leipzig, 1897)
Adapa	S. Izre'el, *Adapa and the South Wind, Language Has the Power of Life and Death, Mesopotamian Civilizations* 10 (Winona Lake, Ind., 2001)
AEM	*Archives Épistolaires de Mari* (Paris)
AfO	*Archiv für Orientforschung* (Graz, Vienna)
AGH	E. Ebeling, *Die akkadische Gebetsserie "Handerhebung" von neuem gesammelt und herausgegeben* (Berlin, 1953)
AHw	W. von Soden, *Akkadisches Handwörterbuch* (Wiesbaden, 1959–1981)
AJSL	*American Journal of Semitic Languages and Literatures* (Chicago)
Amarna	S. Izre'el, *The Amarna Scholarly Tablets*, CM 9 (1997)
AMT	R. Campbell Thompson, *Assyrian Medical Texts* (London, 1923)
AnBi	*Analecta Biblica* (Rome)
Ancient Mesopotamia	A. L. Oppenheim, *Ancient Mesopotamia, Portrait of a Dead Civilization*[2] (Chicago, 1977)
ANET[3]	J. B. Pritchard, ed., *Ancient Near Eastern Texts Relating to the Old Testament*[3] (Princeton, 1969)
Annuaire	*Annuaire*, École Pratique des Hautes Etudes, IVe Section: sciences historiques et philologiques (Paris)
AnOr	*Analecta Orientalia* (Rome)
AnSt	*Anatolian Studies* (London)
AOAT	*Alter Orient und Altes Testament* (Neukirchen-Vluyn)
AOATS	*Alter Orient und Altes Testament, Sonderreihe* (Neukirchen-Vluyn)
AOF	*Altorientalische Forschungen* (Berlin)
ARI	A. K. Grayson, *Assyrian Royal Inscriptions* (Wiesbaden, 1972–)
ARM	*Archives Royales de Mari* (Paris)
ARMT	*Archives Royales de Mari, Textes* (Paris)

ArOr	*Archiv Orientálni* (Prague)
AS	*Assyriological Studies* (Chicago)
ASJ	*Acta Sumerologica* (Hiroshima)
ASKT	P. Haupt, *Akkadische und Sumerische Keilschrifttexte...* (Leipzig, 1882)
Atrahasis	W. G. Lambert, A. R. Millard, *Atra-ḫasīs, The Babylonian Story of the Flood* (Oxford, 1969)
Autobiography	T. Longman III, *Fictional Akkadian Autobiography, A Generic and Comparative Study* (Winona Lake, Ind., 1991)
BA	*Beiträge zur Assyriologie und semitische Sprachwissenschaft* (Leipzig)
Baby-Beschwörungen	W. Farber, *Schlaf Kindchen, Schlaf! Mesopotamische Baby-Beschwörungen und -Rituale* (Winona Lake, Ind., 1989)
Babylon	J. Renger, ed., *Babylon: Focus Mesopotamischer Geschichte, Wiege früher Gelehrsamkeit, Mythos in der Moderne, 2. Internationales Colloquium der Deutschen Orient-Gesellschaft 24.–26. März 1998 in Berlin* (Saarbrücken, 1999),
Babylonian Genesis	A. Heidel, *The Babylonian Genesis*² (Chicago, 1951)
BAL	R. Borger, *Babylonisch-assyrische Lesestücke* (Rome, 1963)
BAM	F. Köcher, *Die babylonische-assyrische Medizin in Texten und Untersuchungen* (Berlin, 1963–)
BASOR	*Bulletin of the American Schools of Oriental Research* (New Haven, etc.)
BBR	H. Zimmern, *Beiträge zur Kenntnis der babylonischen Religion* I (Leipzig, 1896), II (Leipzig, 1901)
BBST	L. W. King, *Babylonian Boundary-Stones in the British Museum* (London, 1912)
BE	*The Babylonian Expedition of the University of Pennsylvania* (Philadelphia)
BHLT	A. K. Grayson, *Babylonian Historical-Literary Texts* (Toronto, 1975)
BIN	*Babylonian Inscriptions in the Collection of J. B. Nies* (New Haven)
BiOr	*Bibliotheca Orientalis* (Leiden)
Birth in Babylonia	M. Stol, *Birth in Babylonia and the Bible, Its Mediterranean Setting, With a Chapter by F.A.M. Wiggermann*, CM 14 (Groningen, 2000)
Bit Rimki	J. Laessøe, *Studies in the Assyrian Ritual and Series bît rimki* (Copenhagen, 1955)
BL	S. Langdon, *Babylonian Liturgies* (Paris, 1913)
BM	*Bibliotheca Mesopotamica* (Malibu)
BMS	L. W. King, *Babylonian Magic and Sorcery, being "the Prayers of the Lifting of the Hand"* (London, 1896)
BRM	*Babylonian Records in the Library of J. Pierpont Morgan* (New Haven)
BSD	M. Vogelzang, *Bin šar dadmē, Edition and Analysis of the Akkadian Anzu Poem* (Groningen, 1988)

BSOAS	*Bulletin of the School of Oriental and African Studies* (London)
BWL	W. G. Lambert, *Babylonian Wisdom Literature* (Oxford, 1960)
CAD	*The Assyrian Dictionary of the University of Chicago* (Chicago, 1956–)
CAH³	*The Cambridge Ancient History³* (Cambridge, 1970–)
CANES	J. M. Sasson, J. Baines, G. Beckman, K. S. Rubinson, eds., *Civilizations of the Ancient Near East* (New York 1995)
CM	*Cuneiform Monographs* (Groningen, Leiden)
Clergé	D. Charpin, *Le Clergé d'Ur au siècle d'Hammurabi (xixe– xviiie siècle av. J.-C.)* (Paris and Geneva, 1986)
Context	W. W. Hallo, K. L. Younger, eds., *The Context of Scripture, Canonical Compositions from the Biblical World* (Leiden, 1997–2002)
Cosmic Geography	W. Horowitz, *Mesopotamian Cosmic Geography*, Mesopotamian Civilizations 8 (Winona Lake, Ind., 1998)
Court Poetry	A. Livingstone, *Court Poetry and Literary Miscellanea*, SAA 3 (Helsinki, 1989)
CRRAI 14	*La Divination en Mésopotamie et dans les regions voisines, XIVe Rencontre Assyriologique Internationale (Strasbourg, 2-6 juillet 1965), Bibliothèque des Centres d'Études Supérieures specialisé d'Histoire des Religions de Strasbourg* (Paris, 1966)
CRRAI 19	P. Garelli, ed., *Le Palais et la royauté, xixe rencontre assyriologique internationale (1971)* (Paris, 1974)
CRRAI 25	H.-J. Nissen, J. Renger, eds., *Mesopotamien und seine Nachbarn, Politische und kulturelle Wechselbeziehungen im Alten Vorderasien vom 4. bis 1. Jahrtausend v. Chr., xxv. rencontre assyriologique internationale (1978)*, Berliner Beiträge zum Vorderen Orient 1 (Berlin, 1982)
CRRAI 26	B. Alster, ed., *Death in Mesopotamia, xxvi^e rencontre assyriologique internationale (1979)* (Copenhagen, 1980)
CRRAI 28	*Vorträge gehalten auf der 28. Rencontre Assyriologique Internationale in Wien (1981)*, AfO Beiheft 19 (1982)
CRRAI 30	K. R. Veenhof, ed., *Cuneiform Archives and Libraries, Papers read at the 30^e rencontre assyriologique internationale (1983)* (Leiden, 1986)
CRRAI 32	K. Hecker, W. Sommerfeld, eds., *Keilschriftliche L.iteraturen, xxxii. rencontre assyriologique internationale (1985)*, Berliner Beiträge zum Vorderen Orient 6 (Berlin, 1986)
CRRAI 33	J.-M. Durand, ed., *La Femme dans le proche-orient antique, xxxiiie rencontre assyriologique internationale (1986)* (Paris, 1987)
CRRAI 34	*XXXIVème Rencontre Assyriologique Internationale, 6–10/VII/1987 - Istanbul, Türk Tarih Kurumu Yayınları XXVI. Dizi – Sa. 3* (Ankara, 1998)
CRRAI 36	L. De Meyer, et al., eds., *Mésopotamie et Elam, actes de la xxxvième rencontre assyriologique internationale (1985)*, Mesopotamian History and Environment, Occasional Publications 1 (Ghent, 1991)

CRRAI 39	H. Waetzoldt, H. Hauptmann, eds., *Assyrien im Wandel der Zeiten, XXXIXe Rencontre Assyriologique Internationale Heidelberg 6.–10. Juli 1992, Heidelberger Studien zum Alten Orient* 6 (Heidelberg, 1997)
CRRAI 42	K. Van Lerberghe, G. Voet, eds., *Languages and Cultures in Contact. At the Crossroads of Civilizations in the Syro-Mesopotamian Realm. Proceedings of the 42nd Rencontre Assyriologique Internationale, Orientalia Lovaniensia Analecta* 96 (Leuven, 1999)
CRRAI 43	J. Prosecky, ed., *Intellectual Life of the Ancient Near East, Papers Presented at the 43rd Rencontre Assyriologique Internationale Prague, July 1–5, 1996* (Prague, 1998)
CRRAI 44	L. Milano, S. de Martino, F. M. Fales, G. Lanfranchi, eds., *Landscapes, Territories, Frontiers and Horizons in the Ancient Near East, History of the Ancient Near East, Monographs* III/1 (Padua, 1999, 2000)
CRRAI 45	T. Abusch, P. Beaulieu, J. Huehnergard, P. Machinist, P. Steinkeller, eds., *Historiography in the Cuneiform World*, Part I, Harvard University; W. W. Hallo, I. Winter, eds., *Seals and Seal Impressions*, Part II, Yale University, *Proceedings of the XLVe Rencontre Assyriologique Internationale* (Bethesda, 2001)
CRRAI 47	S. Parpola, R. Whiting, eds., *Sex and Gender in the Ancient Near East, Proceedings of the 47th Rencontre Assyriologique Internationale, Helsinki, July 2-6, 2001* (Helsinki, 2002)
CT	*Cuneiform Texts from Tablets in the British Museum* (London)
CTN	*Cuneiform Texts from Nimrud* (London)
'Deliver Me from Evil'	G. Cunningham, *'Deliver Me from Evil', Mesopotamian Incantations 2500–1500 BC, Studia Pohl, Series Maior* 17 (Rome, 1997)
DEPM	J.-M. Durand, *Documents Épistolaires du Palais de Mari* (Paris, 1997–2000)
Devils	K. Campbell Thompson, *The Devils and Evil Spirits of Babylonia* I (London, 1903), II (London, 1904)
Dialoghi	S. Ponchia, *La palma e il tamarisco e altri dialoghi mesopotamici* (Venice, 1996)
Dreams	A. L. Oppenheim, *The Interpretation of Dreams in the Ancient Near East, with a Translation of an Assyrian Dream-book, Transactions of the American Philosophical Society New Series* 46/III (pp. 177–373) (Philadelphia, 1956)
EAK	*Einleitung in die assyrischen Königsinschriften* I = R. Borger, *Erster Teil* (Leiden, 1961), II = W. Schramm, *Zweiter Teil* (Leiden, 1973)
Emar	D. Arnaud, *Recherches au Pays d'Aštata, Emar* VI/1–4 (Paris, 1985–1987)
Epik	K. Hecker, *Untersuchungen zur akkadischen Epik*, AOATS 8 (1974)
Etana-Epos	M. Haul, *Das Etana-Epos, Ein Mythos von der Himmelfahrt des Königs von Kiš*, GAAL 1 (Göttingen, 2000)

Explanatory Works	A. Livingstone, *Mystical and Mythological Explanatory Works of Assyrian and Babylonian Scholars* (Oxford, 1986)
FAOS	*Freiburger Altorientalische Studien* (Stuttgart)
Fate	J. N. Lawson, *The Concept of Fate in Ancient Mesopotamia of the First Millennium, Towards an Understanding of Šīmtu, Orientalia Biblica et Christiana* 7 (Wiesbaden, 1994)
GAAL	*Göttinger Arbeitshefte zur Altorientalischen Literatur* (Göttingen)
GAG	W. von Soden, *Grundriss der akkadischen Grammatik*, AnOr 33 (Rome, 1952)
GETh	R. Campbell Thompson, *The Epic of Gilgamish* (Oxford, 1930)
Gilgamesh	B. R. Foster, *The Epic of Gilgamesh* (New York, 2001)
HBKI	S. Maul, *'Herzberuhigungsklagen,' Die sumerisch-akkadischen Eršahunga-Gebete* (Wiesbaden, 1988)
HKL	R. Borger, *Handbuch der Keilschriftliteratur* (Berlin, 1967–1975)
House Most High	A. R. George, *House Most High, The Temples of Ancient Mesopotamia* (Winona Lake, Ind., 1993)
HSAO	*Heidelberger Studien zum Alten Orient* (Wiesbaden)
HSS	*Harvard Semitic Studies* (Cambridge, Mass.)
Hymnes	M.-J. Seux, *Hymnes et prières aux dieux de babylonie et d'assyrie* (Paris, 1976)
IEJ	*Israel Exploration Journal* (Jerusalem)
I R	(E. Norris, H. Rawlinson), *The Cuneiform Inscriptions of Western Asia* I (London, 1861)
II R	(E. Norris, H. Rawlinson), *The Cuneiform Inscriptions of Western Asia* II (London, 1866)
III R	(G. Smith, H. Rawlinson), *The Cuneiform Inscriptions of Western Asia* III (London, 1870)
IV R²	(T. Pinches, H. Rawlinson, G. Smith) *The Cuneiform Inscriptions of Western Asia* IV (London, 1891)
Inschriften	A. Fuchs, *Die Inschriften Sargons II. aus Khorsabad* (Göttingen, 1994)
IRSA	E. Sollberger, J.-R. Kupper, *Inscriptions royales sumériennes et akkadiennes* (Paris, 1971)
Ištar und Dumuzi	W. Farber, *Beschörungsrituale an Ištar und Dumuzi* (Wiesbaden, 1977)
JANES	*Journal of the Ancient Near Eastern Society of Columbia University* (New York)
JAOS	*Journal of the American Oriental Society* (New Haven)
JCS	*Journal of Cuneiform Studies* (New Haven, Philadelphia)
JEOL	*Jaarbericht ... van het Vooraziatisch-Egyptisch Genootschap "Ex Oriente Lux"* (Leiden)
JESHO	*Journal of the Economic and Social History of the Orient* (Leiden)
JNES	*Journal of Near Eastern Studies* (Chicago)
JRAS	*Journal of the Royal Asiatic Society* (London)
JSS	*Journal of Semitic Studies* (Manchester)

JTVI	*Journal of the Transactions of the Victoria Institute* (London)
KAH	O. Schroeder, *Keilschrifttexte aus Assur historischen Inhalts, Zweites Heft* (Leipzig, 1922) = WVDOG 37
KAR	E. Ebeling, *Keilschrifttexte aus Assur religiösen Inhalts* (Leipzig, 1915–1923) = WVDOG 28 (=I), 34 (=II)
KAV	O. Schroeder, *Keilschrifttexte aus Assur verschiedenen Inhalts* (Leipzig, 1920) = WVDOG 35
KB	E. Schrader, ed., *Keilschriftliche Bibliothek, Sammlung von assyrischen und babylonischen Texten in Umschrift und Übersetzung* (Berlin)
KBo	*Keilschrifttexte aus Boghazköy* (Berlin)
Königsinschriften	S. Franke, *Königsinschriften und Königsideologie, Die Könige von Akkade zwischen Tradition und Neuerung, Altorientalistik* 1 (Hamburg, 1995)
KUB	*Keilschrifturkunden aus Boghazköy* (Berlin)
LAS	A. Parpola, *Letters from Assyrian Scholars*, 1 = AOAT 5/1 (1970), 2 (Helsinki, 1971)
Legends	J. G. Westenholz, *Legends of the Kings of Akkade, The Texts, Mesopotamian Civilizations* 7 (Winona Lake, Ind., 1997)
Literatur	E. Reiner, *"Die Akkadische Literatur"* in W. Röllig, ed., *Neues Handbuch der Literaturwissenschaft, Altorientalische Literaturen* (Wiesbaden, 1978) 151–210
LKA	E. Ebeling, F. Köcher, L. Jacob-Rost, *Literarische Keilschrifttexte aus Assur* (Berlin, 1953)
Lob der Ištar	B. Groneberg, *Lob der Ištar, Gebet und Ritual an die altbabylonische Venusgöttin*, CM 8 (Groningen, 1997)
LSS (NF)	*Leipziger Semitische Studien (Neue Folge)* (Leipzig)
MAD	I. J. Gelb, ed., *Materials for the Assyrian Dictionary* (Chicago)
Magic	T. Abusch, K. van der Toorn, eds., *Mesopotamian Magic, Textual, Historical, and Interpretive Perspectives, Ancient Magic and Divination* 1 (Groningen, 1999)
MAOG	*Mitteilungen der Altorientalischen Gesellschaft* (Leipzig)
Maqlû	K. Tallqvist, *Die assyrische Beschwörungsserie Maqlû* (Leipzig, 1895)
MARI	*Mari, Annales de Recherches Interdisciplinaires* (Paris)
MDOG	*Mitteilungen der Deutschen Orient-Gesellschaft* (Berlin)
MDP	*Mémoires de la Délégation en Perse* (Paris)
Mensch	F. R. Kraus, *Vom mesopotamischen Menschen der altbabyloni-schen Zeit und seiner Welt*, MKNAW NR 36/6 (1973)
Mesopotamia	J. Bottéro, *Mesopotamia, Writing, Reasoning, and the Gods*, trans. Z. Bahrani and M. Van De Mieroop (Chicago, 1992)
MIO	*Mitteilungen des Instituts für Orientforschung* (Berlin)
MKNAW (NR)	*Mededelingen der Koninklijke Nederlandse Akademie van Wetenschappen, afd letterkunde* (Amsterdam) (Nieuwe Reeks)

MSL	*Materialien zum Sumerischen Lexikon* (Rome)
MVAeG	*Mitteilungen der Vorderasiatisch-Aegyptischen Gesellschaft* (Leipzig)
Mythes	J. Bottéro, *Mythes et rites de babylone* (Paris, 1985)
Mythologie	J. Bottéro, S. N. Kramer, *Lorsque les dieux faisaient l'homme, Mythologie mésopotamienne* (Paris, 1989)
Myths	S. Dalley, *Myths from Mesopotamia* (Oxford, 1989)
N.A.B.U.	*Notes Assyriologiques Brèves et Utilitaires* (Paris)
Nergal	J. Böllenrücher, *Gebete und Hymnen an Nergal*, LSS 1/VI (Leipzig, 1904)
Nergal ed Ereškigal	G. Pettinato, *Nergal ed Ereškigal, Il Poema Assiro-babilonese degli Inferi, Atti della Accademia Nazionale dei Lincei, Classe di Scienze Morali, Storiche e Filologiche, Memorie* serie IX Volume XIII Fascicolo 1 (Rome, 2000)
OAC	*Orientis Antiqvi Collectio* (Rome)
OECT	*Oxford Edition of Cuneiform Texts* (Oxford)
OLA	*Orientalia Lovaniensia Analecta* (Leuven)
OLP	*Orientalia Lovaniensia Periodica* (Leuven)
OLZ	*Orientalistische Literaturzeitung* (Leipzig, Berlin)
OPSNKF	*Occasional Publications of the Samuel Noah Kramer Fund* (Philadelphia)
OrAn	*Oriens Antiqvvs* (Rome)
OrNS	*Orientalia Nova Series* (Rome)
PAPS	*Proceedings of the American Philosophical Society* (Philadelphia)
PBS	*Publications of the Babylonian Section, University Museum, University of Pennsylvania* (Philadelphia)
PHPKB	J. Brinkman, *A Political History of Post-Kassite Babylonia 1158–722 B.C.*, AnOr 43 (1968)
Poetic Language	M. Vogelzang, H. Vanstiphout, eds., *Mesopotamian Poetic Language*, CM 2 (Groningen, 1996)
Poemetto	S. Picchioni, *Il Poemetto di Adapa, Az Eötvös Loránd Tudományegytem Okori Történéti tanszékeinek kladványai* 27 (Budapest, 1981)
Poetry	E. Reiner, *Your Thwarts in Pieces, Your Mooring Rope Cut, Poetry from Babylonia and Assyria* (Ann Arbor, Mich., 1985)
PRAK	H. de Genouillac, *Premières recherches archéologiques à Kich* I (Paris, 1924), II (Paris, 1925)
Proverbs	B. Alster, *Proverbs of Ancient Sumer* (Bethesda, Md., 1997)
PSBA	*Proceedings of the Society of Biblical Archaeology* (London)
QuadSem	*Quaderni di Semitistica* (Florence)
Religions	R. Labat, *Les religions du Proche-Orient asiatique* (Paris, 1970)
RGTC	*Répertoire géographique des textes cunéiformes* (Wiesbaden)
RIMA	*Royal Inscriptions of Mesopotamia, Assyria* (Toronto)
RIMB	*Royal Inscriptions of Mesopotamia, Babylonia* (Toronto)
RIME 2	D. Frayne, *The Royal Inscriptions of Mesopotamia, Early Periods 2.*

	Sargonic and Gutian Periods (Toronto, 1993)
RLA	*Reallexikon der Assyriologie* (Berlin, 1932–)
RO	*Rocznik Orientalitsyczny* (Warsaw)
RSO	*Rivista degli Studi Orientali*
SAA	*State Archives of Assyria* (Helsinki)
SAAB	*State Archives of Assyria, Bulletin* (Helsinki)
SAACT	*State Archives of Assyria, Cuneiform Texts* (Helsinki)
SAAS	*State Archives of Assyria, Studies* (Helsinki)
SAHG	A. Falkenstein, W. von Soden, *Sumerische und Akkadische Hymnen und Gebete* (Zurich and Stuttgart, 1953)
Šamaš	A. Schollmeyer, *Sumerisch-babylonische Hymnen und Gebete an Šamaš* (Paderborn, 1912)
SANE	*Sources and Monographs from the Ancient Near East* (Malibu, Calif.)
ŠÀ.ZI.GA	R. D. Biggs, *ŠÀ.ZI.GA Ancient Mesopotamian Potency Incantations,* TCS 2 (1967)
SBTU	*Spätbabylonische Texte aus Uruk,* Teil I H. Hunger (Berlin, 1976), Teil II E. von Weiher (Berlin, 1983), Tell III E. von Weiher (Berlin, 1988), Teil IV E. von Weiher (Mainz, 1993), Teil V E. von Weiher (Mainz, 1998)
SED	*Studia et Documenta ad Iura Orientis Antiqvi Pertinentia* (Leiden)
SFS	V. Scheil, *Une Saison de fouilles à Sippar* (Cairo, 1902)
Sin	G. Perry, *Hymnen und Gebete an Sin,* LSS 2/IV (Leipzig, 1907)
SRT	C. D. Gray, *The Šamaš Religious Texts* (Chicago, 1901)
STC	L. W. King, *The Seven Tablets of Creation* (London, 1902)
StOr	*Studia Orientalia* (Helsinki)
STT	*The Sultantepe Tablets,* I O. R. Gurney and J. J. Finkelstein (London, 1957), II O. R. Gurney and P. Hulin (London, 1964)
Studies Astour	G. Young, M. Chavalas, R. Averbeck, eds., *Crossing Boundaries and Linking Horizons, Studies in Honor of Michael C. Astour on His 80th Birthday* (Bethesda, Md., 1997)
Studies Birot	J.-M. Durand, J.-R. Jupper, eds., *Miscellanea Babylonica, Mélanges offerts à Maurice Birot* (Paris, 1985)
Studies Böhl	M. A. Beek et al., eds., *Symbolae Biblicae et Mesopotamicae Francisco Mario Theodoro de Liagre Böhl Dedicatae* (Leiden, 1973)
Studies Borger	S. Maul, *Festschrift für Rykle Borger zu seinem 65. Geburtstag am 24. Mai 1994, tikip santakki mala bašmu…,* CM 10 (Groningen, 1998)
Studies De Meyer	*Cinquante-deux Réflexions sur le Proche-Orient Ancien offertes en hommage à Leon De Meyer, Mesopotamian History and Environment, Occasional Publications* 2 (Ghent, 1994)
Studies Diakonoff	*Societies and Languages of the Ancient Near East, Studies in Honour of I. M. Diakonoff* (Warminster, 1982)
Studies Finet	M. Lebeau, P. Talon, eds., *Reflets des deux Fleuves, Volume de Mélanges offerts à André Finet, Akkadica Supplementum* VI

(Leuven, 1989)

Studies Finkelstein	M. deJ. Ellis, ed., *Essays on the Ancient Near East in Memory of Jacob Joel Finkelstein, Memoirs of the Connecticut Academy of Arts and Sciences 19* (1977)
Studies Garelli	D. Charpin, F. Joannès, eds., *Marchands, Diplomates et Empereurs, Études sur la civilisation mésopotamienne offertes à Paul Garelli* (Paris, 1991)
Studies Hallo	M. E. Cohen, D. C. Snell, D. B. Weisberg, eds., *The Tablet and the Scroll, Near Eastern Studies in Honor of William W. Hallo* (Bethesda, Md., 1993)
Studies Kraus	G. Van Driel et al., eds., *Zikir Šumim, Assyriological Studies Presented to F. R. Kraus on the Occasion of His Seventieth Birthday* (Leiden, 1982)
Studies Lambert	A. George, I. Finkel, ed., *Wisdom, Gods and Literature, Studies in Assyriology in Honour of W. G. Lambert* (Winona Lake, Ind., 2000)
Studies Limet	Ö. Tunca, D. Deheselle, eds., *Tablettes et Images aux Pays de Sumer et Akkad, Mélanges offerts à Monsieur H. Limet*, Association pour la Promotion de l'Histoire et de l'Archéologie Orientales, *Mémoires* 1 (Liège, 1996).
Studies Moran	I. T. Abusch et al., eds., *Lingering over Words: Studies in Ancient Near Eastern Literature in Honor of William L. Moran* (Atlanta, 1990)
Studies Oppenheim	*From the Workshop of the Chicago Assyrian Dictionary, Studies Presented to A. Leo Oppenheim* (Chicago, 1964)
Studies Pope	J. H. Marks, R. M. Good, eds., *Love & Death in the Ancient Near East, Essays in Honor of Marvin H. Pope* (Guilford, Conn., 1987)
Studies Reiner	F. Rochberg-Halton, ed., *Language, Literature, and History, Philological and Historical Studies Presented to Erica Reiner, American Oriental Series 67* (New Haven, 1987)
Studies Sachs	E. Leichty et al., eds., *A Scientific Humanist, Studies in Memory of Abraham Sachs*, OPSNKF 9 (Philadelphia, 1988)
Studies Sjöberg	H. Behrens et al., eds., *Dumu e₂-dub-ba-a, Studies in Honor of Åke W. Sjöberg*, OPSNKF 11 (Philadelphia, 1989)
Studies Tadmor	M. Cogan, I. Eph'al, eds., *Ah Assyria ... Studies in Assyrian History and Ancient Near Eastern Historiography Presented to Hayim Tadmor, Scripta Hierosolymitana 33* (1991)
Studies Wilcke	W. Sallaberger, K. Volk, A. Zgoll, eds., *Literatur, Politik und Recht in Mesopotamien, Festschrift für Claus Wilcke, Orientalia Biblica et Christiana 14* (Wiesbaden, 2003)
Style	N. Wasserman, *Style and Form in Old-Babylonian Literary Texts*, CM 27 (Leiden, 2003)
Šurpu	E. Reiner, *Šurpu, A Collection of Sumerian and Akkadian Incantations, AfO Beiheft 11* (1958)

TCL	*Textes Cunéiformes du Louvre* (Paris)
TCS	*Texts from Cuneiform Sources* (Locust Valley, N.Y.)
Testi umoristici	F. D'Agostino, *Testi umoristici babilonesi e assiri, Testi del Vicino Oriente Antico* 2/4 (Brescia, 2000)
TIM	*Texts from the Iraq Museum* (Baghdad and Leiden)
Topographical Texts	A. R. George, *Babylonian Topographical Texts*, OLA 40 (Leuven, 1992)
TUAT	O. Kaiser, ed., *Texte aus der Umwelt des Alten Testaments* (Gütersloh, 1982–)
TuL	E. Ebeling, *Tod und Leben nach den Vorstellungen des Babylonier* (Berlin and Leipzig, 1931)
UET	*Ur Excavations, Texts* (London)
UF	*Ugarit Forschungen* (Neukirchen-Vluyn)
UFBG	W. Mayer, *Untersuchungen zur Formensprache der babylonischen "Gebetsbeschwörungen," Studia Pohl: Series Maior* 5 (Rome, 1976)
Ugaritica	C. F. M. Schaeffer, ed., *Ugaritica* (Paris)
VAB	*Vorderasiatische Bibliothek* (Leipzig)
VAS	*Vorderasiatische Schriftdenkmäler* (Berlin)
VO	*Vicino Oriente* (Rome)
Vorwurf	D. Sitzler, *"Vorwurf gegen Gott" : ein religiöses Motiv im alten Orient (Aegypten und Mesopotamien)* (Wiesbaden, 1995)
V R	(T. Pinches, H. Rawlinson) *The Cuneiform Inscriptions of Western Asia* V (London, 1909)
WdM	H. Haussig, ed., *Götter und Mythen im Vorderen Orient* (Stuttgart, 1965)
WGL	private communication, W. G. Lambert
Witchcraft	I. T. Abusch, *Babylonian Witchcraft Literature, Case Studies* (Atlanta, 1987)
WLM	private communication, W. L. Moran
WO	*Welt des Orients* (Göttingen)
WVDOG	*Wissenschaftliche Veröffentlichungen des Deutschen Orient-Gesellschaft* (Leipzig)
WZKM	*Wiener Zeitschrift für die Kunde des Morgenlandes* (Vienna)
YNER	*Yale Near Eastern Researches* (New Haven)
YOS	*Yale Oriental Series* (New Haven)
ZA	*Zeitschrift für Assyriologie und Verwandte Gebiete* (Berlin)
ZATW	*Zeitschrift für die alttestamentliche Wissenschaft* (Berlin)
ZDMG	*Zeitschrift der Deutschen Morgenländischen Gesellschaft* (Leipzig)
Zukunftsbewältigung	S. Maul, *Zukunftsbewältigung, Eine Untersuchung altorientalischen Denkens anhand der babylonisch-assyrischen Löserituale (Namburbi), Baghdader Forschungen* 18 (Mainz, 1994)